What's New in this Edition

With Visual FoxPro 3, Microsoft has significantly changed the focus of its key databa... ...object-oriented programming into the robust Xbase database product. This and other key changes make Visual ... ...best DBMS systems available today.

Visual FoxPro brings object-oriented development to FoxPro for the first time. This new development paradigm enables a developer to create applications based on objects modeled on real-world entities in the business being automated. Object orientation is not only a new way of organizing and writing code, it is a new way of thinking about software design and development. Here are some of its other new features:

- The Form Designer was totally redesigned to enable developers to create visually pleasing, easy-to-use Graphical User Interfaces (GUI) with pinpoint control over the controls on the forms.
- Redesigned into a tabbed screen, the all-new Project Manager provides easy access to all the files you'll use in an application.
- Views—one of the most exciting additions to Visual FoxPro—are like queries that are updatable and can be treated like tables.
- Connections between Visual FoxPro and a back-end (such as SQL Server) can be given names and stored in a database using the Connection Designer. Once defined, names connections can be used to access the data in the back-end with Remote Views.
- Visual FoxPro is fully compliant with OLE 2 standards, enabling you to use other OLE-enabled applications as if they were Visual FoxPro objects.
- Visual FoxPro now supports *persistent relationships* in a DBC.
- Referential integrity of databases can now be maintained with the *Referential Integrity Builder*, which enables you to easily define what should happen when a customer record is deleted.

To enable you to fully exploit Visual FoxPro 3, many new chapters have been added to this edition, and all existing chapters have been expanded considerably.

Here are a few of the highlights.

Chapter 16

"Leveraging FoxPro Power Using Wizards" examines the PivotTable, Import, Documenting, and Setup Wizards. Wizards are covered throughout the book, but a full explanation of the Wizards used in Visual FoxPro is provided here.

Chapter 8

"Creating and Updating Data with Views" details how you can create live views of your data by means of the View Wizards, which are new to the FoxPro environment in Visual FoxPro 3. *Views* are dynamic sets of data, sorted and filtered according to the design of the view.

Chapter 19

"Working with OLE for Non-OLE Applications" details the concepts of OLE (Object Linking and Embedding), and shows how you can put these capabilities—inherent in Visual FoxPro and recent versions of Windows—to work in your applications.

Chapter 38

"Client/Server Features" discusses the development of large-scale applications for the enterprise. Most large business today are either downsizing mainframe and midrange systems or upsizing PC-based applications to this popular medium. This chapter helps you learn the potential of client/server technologies.

Part V

"Object-Oriented Programming" discusses Object-Oriented programming with Visual FoxPro in detail in Chapters 27–31. Object orientation is one of the major new additions to Visual FoxPro 3. OOP revolutionizes nearly every aspect of developing applications with Visual FoxPro from the analysis and design phases to the coding and testing of applications and application components.

Chapter 37

"ODBC Integration" covers how Visual FoxPro uses Microsoft's standard Open Database Connectivity (ODBC). ODBC enables a system to establish a connection with a remote database. ODBC also enables applications to access data using Structured Query Language (SQL).

Chapter 39

"Microsoft Mail-Enabled Applications" shows how to use the Microsoft MAPI OLE 2 controls to create your own Visual FoxPro application that supports e-mail, called a *mail-enabled application*, that accesses e-mail from the Windows 95 Microsoft Exchange.

Visual FoxPro™ 3

UNLEASHED

Menachem Bazian, Jim Booth, Jeb Long, Doug Norman, et al.

201 West 103rd Street
Indianapolis, IN 46290

Publisher and President	*Richard K. Swadley*
Acquisitions Manager	*Greg Weigand*
Development Manager	*Dean Miller*
Managing Editor	*Cindy Morrow*
Marketing Manager	*Gregg Bushyeager*

Acquisitions Editor
Rosemarie Graham

Development Editor
Kelly Murdock

Software Development Specialist
Steve Straiger

Production Editors
Kristi Hart, Tonya Simpson

Copy Editors
Lisa Lord, Anne Owen, Bart Reed

Technical Reviewers
Ricardo Birmele, Chris Capossela, Jim Haentzchel, Doug Norman

Editorial Coordinator
Bill Whitmer

Technical Edit Coordinator
Lynette Quinn

Formatter
Frank Sinclair

Editorial Assistants
Sharon Cox, Andi Richter, Rhonda Tinch-Mize

Cover Designer
Jason Grisham

Book Designer
Alyssa Yesh

Production Team Supervisor
Brad Chinn

Production
Mary Ann Abramson, Angela Bannan, Carol Bowers, Georgiana Briggs, Michael Brumitt, Terrie Deemer, Michael Dietsch, Jason Hand, Michael Henry, Louisa Klucznik, Kevin Laseau, Brian-Kent Proffitt, Nancy Price, Erich J. Richter, Bobbi Satterfield, SA Springer, Andrew Stone, Susan Van Ness, Mark Walchle, Colleen Williams, Paul Wilson

Indexer
Bront Davis

Dedications

My work in this book is dedicated with love to my wife, Anna. "Her mouth opens with wisdom and the teachings of kindness are on her tongue." (Proverbs 31:26)—Menachem Bazian

I dedicate my work on this book to Violet and Jonathan, two children frolicking in heaven. —Jim Booth

To Mimi, my greatest source of inspiration and influence. To my wife, Renee, for believing in me. To my brothers, Rick and Tim, for being there. To Pepe, for your companionship. and to my unborn child, for giving me a new purpose.—Chris Buelow

To Nikki and Jarel Jones, the highlights of my life. Siempre tratar a ser lo maximo que tu puedes! —Ed Jones

I dedicate this book to my wife, Elizabeth Long.—Jeb Long

To my loving wife, Debra.—Ted Long

To my family.—Doug Norman

A todas las personas, grande y pequeno. Gracias! —Derek Sutton

Overview

Part IV   Programming in Visual FoxPro

Part V   Object-Oriented Programming

Acknowledgments

From Menachem Bazian

Writing a book, even a portion of one, is a harrowing experience not only for the author but also for those around him. Writing the section on object orientation for *Visual FoxPro 3 Unleashed* was a never-ending source of challenges. As is so often true with projects like this, without the key assistance and support of many people, this work would never have seen the light of day.

First of all, I would like to thank all my colleagues at Flash Creative Management. Thank you to my partners, David Blumenthal, Yair Alan Griver (and his cat, Chushie—this makes four) and Lior Hod; to my compadres in Visual FoxPro crime, Paul Bienick, Leslie Koorhan, and Ken Levy; to Annie Ahn, Bryan Caplovitz, Dan (a true prince among men) Freeman, Drew Georgeopolous, Pablo Geralnick, David Gerson, Robert Godbey, Avi Greengart, Noam Kaminetzky, David Lederer, Ari Neugroschl, Susan Vrona, Miriam Weinstein, Debra Wolff, Ed Ziv, and Elise Ziv. Together, you all comprise, in my humble opinion, the greatest collection of talent ever assembled under one roof, and I consider it an honor and a privilege not only to have worked with you but also to call each and every one of you a friend.

To my editor, Rosemarie Graham and her incomparable compatriots, Kelly Murdock, Kristi Hart, and Tonya Simpson. Thank you for your patience and assistance.

To the brilliant, dedicated, and hard-working people on the Visual FoxPro team: Susan Graham, Chris Pudlicki, Eric Burgess, and everyone on the beta team—too numerous to mention. Thank you for all your support. To the many talented developers who created this wonderful product: you made a winner!

To the people in the Fox community I have had the pleasure of knowing and working with. To Pat Adams, Steven Black, Jim Booth, Chaim Caron, Sue Cunningham, Doug Dodge, Mike Feltman, Tamar Granor, Nancy Jacobsen, Patrick Logan, Paul Maskens, Andy Neil, Alan Schwartz, Drew Speedie, Toni Taylor-Feltman, and so many more. There are so many of you that I cannot mention you all, but you all have had a special place in helping make my work possible and fun.

To my friend and mentor, Martin Star, possibly the best consultant it has ever been my pleasure to work with. Thanks for still being there when I need you.

To my friend Mordecai Glicksman, his wife Charlotte, and their new twins, Chana Tova and Elisheva. Welcome to the wonderful world of parenthood: may you only know of joy and happiness.

To Meryl and Mark Berow. If zaniness were an art, you two would rank with Picasso. You have made me smile when I most needed it, and for this precious gift I thank you.

I leave those most important for last. A special thank you for my father, Murray Bazian, and my brothers, Ben and Sol. Dad, you taught me the meaning of the words "dedication" and "professional." That I have been able to undertake and complete something like this is a testimony to the lessons you taught me and the examples you set. Ben and Sol, not only have you been there with the advice of big brothers but also with that of experienced professionals who have been around a few more blocks than I have. I may still be your little brother in your eyes, a mark I know I will never be able to shed, but you are valued confidants and advisors. I may not always take your advice, but I will always listen and cherish it. Finally, although I may not say it enough, I love you both and always will.

Finally, to those who mean the most to me. To my beloved wife Anna and my incredible twins, Barry and Sam. This book came out of the time I would have spent with you. You put up with my short temper as the deadlines approached, my constant long hours of writing after work, lost Sundays and days off, and much more. You have paid for this book as much as I have. I treasure your love and support. Without it, this would never have been possible.

Menachem Bazian
Passaic, NJ
October, 1995

From Jim Booth

I thank all of my colleagues on the Fox Fora of CompuServe for the free sharing of their wisdom and knowledge without which I could not have completed this work. I also would thank the Visual FoxPro development team at Microsoft for providing us with the exciting and challenging product that Visual FoxPro is.

From Chris Buelow

Special thanks to Todd Haehn for your assistance and encouragement. Thanks to Dave Schneider, Kearn Kelley, Steve Miske, Eric Sorensen, and Ron Schmidt for your efforts and support. Thanks to everyone at Sams Publishing for making this endeavor an enriching experience. Thanks to Harvey Johnson, the FoxPro Users group of Minnesota, FoxForum participants, and to all the betazoids for being the finest example of a developer community in the business.

From Jim Booth

I wish to acknowledge everyone at Sams Publishing and the developers of Visual FoxPro at Microsoft.

From Doug Norman

I owe a large debt to my family. My wife, Jan, and my two sons, Mike and Joey, work hard to provide balance in what would otherwise be a rather unbalanced ("… mom, he's working on the computer again!…") life.

About the Authors

Menachem Bazian is a shareholder and senior consultant with Flash Creative Management, Inc., a leading provider of business technology solutions. Flash builds long-term relationships with its clients in the spirit of partnership, creating intelligent organizations that can compete with grace and agility in a business environment characterized by change.

Menachem, a certified public accountant, is an expert on object-oriented, client/server applications development and business process reengineering. He has written and lectured extensively on these subjects. He is also a well-known software developer and author in the FoxPro community. He authored Volume #5 of *The Pros Talk Fox* series. His years of experience in accounting and in systems analysis and design have earned him a reputation as a leading authority on FoxPro programming and business software.

Mr. Bazian is the former chairperson of the New York State Society of Certified Public Accountants Committee on Managing a Consulting Practice. He also has designed curricula for SBT, a leading accounting software vendor.

He has written for many publications including *Data Based Advisor, FoxPro Advisor, FoxTalk, The FoxPro Developer's Journal,* and *New Accountant.* Menachem has also been a featured speaker at the FoxPro Developer's Conferences (1990–1995), DBExpo, The Foundation Accounting Education's CPA and Computer's Show (which he also co-chaired in November 1994), the New York State Society of CPAs (NYSSCPA) Evening Technical Sessions, and several FoxPro televideo conferences. He chaired the New York State Society of CPA's first-ever conference on Business Process Reengineering.

Menachem authored Chapters 1, 12, 27, 28, 29, 30, and 31, and co-authored Chapter 25. He can be reached on Compuserve at 76366,42 or via the Internet at 76366.42@compuserve.com.

Jim Booth is an independent developer/consultant specializing in database applications in FoxPro. He has been professionally doing this work since the early 1980s. Jim also teaches FoxPro for Application Developer Training Company in the United States. Jim's articles have been published in all the major FoxPro journals, and he has spoken to numerous users groups and at conferences in the United States and Canada. He also has received the Most Valuable Professional award from Microsoft three years' running for his work on CompuServe forums supporting FoxPro users.

Jim authored Chapters 3, 4, 16, 18, and 34, and co-authored Chapter 11. He can be reached at 72130,2570 on Compu-Serve or at 72130.2570@compuserve.com on the Internet.

Chris Buelow is the founder and president of Vision Software, Inc., a progressive, Minneapolis-based company specializing in client/server and multimedia development. Formerly a consultant with Coopers & Lybrand, LLP, he has developed a variety of applications for several Fortune 500 companies.

Although he uses a variety of development tools, such as PowerBuilder, Chris has been a dedicated user and advocate of FoxPro since its inception. He has published articles for several national newsletters and has been an instructor for a variety of FoxPro training programs.

Chris authored Chapter 38. He can be reached via CompuServe at 74204,1314 or via the Internet at 74204.1314@compuserve.com.

Ed Jones is a best-selling author of more than 30 computer books. He provides consulting, planning, software development, and training for federal government agencies, law firms, and corporate clients. He has designed and provided personnel management software to an installed base of approximately 100 companies nationwide through Computer Support Group of Annandale, Virginia. Jones has published articles in *Lotus*, *Database Advisor*, and *DBMS* magazines.

Ed co-authored Chapters 2, 5–15, 17, 19–23, 25, 32, and Appendix A.

Jeb Long has 30 years experience in software design and engineering at some of the most prestigious technical organizations in the country and has worked as an independent consultant and author. Long developed JPLDIS, the precursor to dBASE. He is the author of numerous articles for technical magazines and has written several books, including *Visual FoxPro 3 Developer's Guide*, Third Edition, *Do It Yourself Quick C for Windows*, *Do It Yourself Microsoft C/C++7*, and *dBASE IV 1.5 Programming Language* (co-authored with Alastair Dallas), all from Sams Publishing.

Jeb authored Chapters 24, 26, 33, 35, 36, and 39, and co-authored Chapters 10, 13, 15, and 17.

Ted Long is founder and president of Documation, Inc., a microcomputer consulting firm in Orlando, Flordia, specializing in software application development and training, as well as systems- and product-integration services.

Ted has over 20 years of accounting and administration experience in the construction, engineering, and food-service industries. With more than 10 years of database programming experience, Ted has been developing applications in MS FoxPro, Fox BASE, MS-Access, MS-Visual Basic, CS-Clipper, CS-dBFast, dBASE IV, and C programming languages using MS-DOS and Windows platforms. He also has trained programmers and end users in database-development products. He is a Certified Microsoft Product Specialist.

Ted authored Chapter 37.

Doug Norman is a software engineer who has developed small, medium, and large systems using FoxPro as the main programming language. He was the team leader for Hawkeye Software System's FIRMware, a large client/server-based case-management system for the legal vertical market. As a Principal Software Engineer with the Mitre Corporation, he develops (and evangelizes the development of) prototypes and applications using Visual FoxPro tools and scalable architectures.

Doug has been writing software since cutting his teeth on a Digital Equipment Corporation PDP-8e while studying for a Ph.D. (Neurobiology) in the 1970s. Discovering he enjoyed building software more than pursuing science, he completed a Masters in Computer Science (Artificial Intelligence) and was a principal doing exploratory research in the government's "Pilot Associate" program that attempted to introduce artificial intelligence into the fighter cockpit to aid the pilot's situation awareness and decision making. In this role, he did some of the early work on automatic problem recognition and decomposition for multiprocessing of intelligent algorithms.

Subsequent to this research, he was a faculty member in the Computer and Information Systems Graduate Program of St. Mary's University, where he taught Software Engineering, Operating System Theory, and Database Theory and Design. It was here that he discovered Xbase programming systems, including Foxbase and dBXL.

He has been a systems programmer, an application programmer for real-time laboratory systems, and an early adopter of client/server architectures and technology.

Doug co-authored Chapter 2, assisted on Chapters 5, 6, 8, 9, 20, 21, and 32, and ensured the accuracy and consistency of the sample files on the CD-ROM.

Derek Sutton is a contributing Sams author who provides consulting services in database management.

Derek co-authored Chapters 2, 5–15, 17, 19–23, 25, 32, and Appendix A.

Introduction

Welcome to *Visual FoxPro 3 Unleashed*, and congratulations on picking up one of the first and most comprehensive books on Visual FoxPro. Visual FoxPro represents a quantum leap technologically from its predecessor. The product has been almost totally revamped bringing with it a new set of tools, terminology, and an entirely new paradigm for developing mission-critical, enterprise-wide, object-oriented, client/server applications (Whew! That's a mouthful).

If you're a FoxPro 2.*x* developer (DOS, Windows, Macintosh, or UNIX), you'll be amazed at the tons of new features in Visual FoxPro. Here are just a few:

■ The best implementation of object orientation in the Xbase world

■ Seamless client/server integration, including

  • Remote, updatable views

  • Background row fetching

  • Deferred memo download

■ Access to the FoxPro Event Model (Bye, bye foundation read!)

■ Browse (on steroids) as an object in a read

■ Data dictionary supporting validation rules (both field and record level) and triggers (insert, update, and delete).

When designing Visual FoxPro, Microsoft spent hundreds, if not thousands, of person hours reviewing the requests of users. The resulting product shows the results of these requests plus the incredible drive of the FoxPro team at Microsoft to develop a database product that would compete not only in the Xbase world but also as the premier object-oriented tool for writing database and client/server applications. To quote Microsoft's Morris Simm when he demonstrated the product at the 1995 FoxPro Developer's Conference, "You asked for a glass of water, and we gave you a fire hose." How right he is.

Visual FoxPro and Its Role in the World of Business

What is the role of Visual FoxPro in business applications? When you think about it, Visual FoxPro represents a key weapon in the battle to reengineer business processes with object-oriented and client/server technology. Let's face it; information technology has moved well beyond the role of tool in business; it has acquired a role so central to doing business that it has become practically irreplaceable in the businesses they operate. As more businesses fight to compete in today's global economy, the pressure is on to become more efficient in delivering services to their customers. More and more, they are reengineering their business processes and enabling them with information technology.

Visual FoxPro represents the most significant advance in software-development technology to enter this arena to date. It is easy enough to use by many power users yet has the most powerful development platform and database engine of any PC development package in its class. This includes, but is not limited to, Visual Basic, PowerBuilder, Access, and Delphi. Borland's Visual dBASE, as of this writing, is still floating in a sea of vapor, and so there is no way to assess it.

Come on! How Different Can It Really Be?

Take my word for it when I say *very different.*

With object orientation in the mix, the whole development focus changes (see Part V, "Object-Oriented Programming," for a better discussion of this).

With the new Database Container and client/server in the mix, you need to be more careful where you put code. Does it go in the GUI (Graphical User Interface) or in the Database?

The Form Designer is totally new. The old screen designer has gone the way of the dinosaur (and good riddance, if you ask me) and has been replaced by a more visual design surface with radically improved design capabilities and access to more properties, events, and methods (called PEMs by the insiders; so use the term and impress your friends!) than you can shake a stick at. This provides you with finer control over your forms than you ever could have dreamed possible!

The Visual Class Designer is an entirely new tool (don't worry, it is based on the Form Designer).

Data sessions add a host of new power to your forms, reports, and processing programs.

The list goes on and on.

The bottom line is that developing applications in Visual FoxPro can be very different from the way they were developed in FoxPro 2.*x.*

Toto, I Don't Think We're in Kansas Anymore

If you're coming to the conclusion that the world has changed, you're right. But, don't let that throw you. It's very easy to let this kind of change scare you. Don't let it. It will take some time but, in the end result, you will be developing better, more bug-free applications faster than you ever did. You need to give the paradigm a chance. Learn it, work with it, try to *think* like it. The payback on your investment will be worth it.

So, how do I get there?

The first step is to get the product (okay, you probably have done that already). Once you've got it, make yourself a little project. Design a few forms, create a couple of classes, design a small database. You'll learn a ton of things that way.

Here's where *Visual FoxPro 3 Unleashed* can really help. The authors discuss the ins and outs of developing applications in Visual FoxPro. The hows, whys, wheres, and whos are all here. Keep this book at your computer and refer to it as you work. You'll be glad you did.

Some of you won't have a choice but to learn while doing the real thing: a full-blown project. Don't get scared, take your time at the beginning to get comfortable with Visual FoxPro. Read *Visual FoxPro 3 Unleashed* along with the manuals. You'll get through it just fine.

The moral here is simple. Visual FoxPro may be radically different, but different does not equate to *hard*. If others can do it, so can you.

What About My Legacy Code?

Your old applications should run unmodified under Visual FoxPro. Of course, you'll need to test this out, but that's the party line. In terms of upgrading it to Visual FoxPro, you have three options:

- **Continue coding the old way.** You can do this, to be sure, although once you modify a screen, Visual FoxPro will automatically convert it to a form. But, if you do this, why would you upgrade to Visual FoxPro? You may as well stick with 2.5/6.

- **Upgrade piece by piece.** I think this will be a popular method. As pieces of old systems need modification, you have an opportunity to upgrade that new piece to the new technology of Visual FoxPro even if that just means redoing the forms. This method has the benefit of having the least one time cost (i.e., the cost is spread out over multiple modification passes). The downside is that you will not gain as great a benefit from the Object Orientation and you will have a hybrid system for a while (part 2.5/6 and part Visual FoxPro).

- **Rewrite the sucker.** Not a bad idea, if you can afford it. In fact, taking an existing system and rewriting it in Visual FoxPro is a wonderful learning opportunity. Presumably, you'll have most of the requirements worked out already. You can just start with the object-oriented analysis and design and work it through to development. When you're finished, you'll have worked out many of the bugs in your development process, developed a host of reusable objects, and have a definite measure of success to work with. You'll be ready to take on the world with Visual FoxPro.

The downside to this approach, of course, is that it is the costliest. A great deal of time is spent doing what has already been done.

Who Should Read This Book?

So, now that you know where Visual FoxPro fits in, what you can do to bring yourself up the learning curve, and what you can do about upgrading your existing systems to Visual FoxPro (if you've a mind to).

The question is, will *Visual FoxPro 3 Unleashed* help you in this process? The answer is *yes* (did you expect any other answer from the introduction to the book?).

Seriously, *Visual FoxPro 3 Unleashed* is the book for you if you are:

- A power user
- An intermediate Xbase developer

Because this book is geared towards the intermediate to advanced level, a lot of the introductory stuff has been glossed over. However, this book does go into some introductory detail regarding the parts of the product that are radically new (for example, object orientation). This makes this book perfect for you if you are trying to get into Visual FoxPro from a prior version of FoxPro.

The book is also chock-full of practical routines and tips and tricks on using Visual FoxPro to its fullest as a development tool for mission-critical, object-oriented, client/server applications.

Are you ready to start the journey into the exciting new world of Visual FoxPro? Then sit back, strap yourself in, and read on. Prepare for the incredible power of *Visual FoxPro 3 Unleashed.*

IN THIS PART

Visual FoxPro Basics

PART

I

An Overview of
Visual FoxPro

1

Welcome to *Visual FoxPro 3 Unleashed!* This book discusses Microsoft's most significant contribution to the PC database market to date: Visual FoxPro. This chapter will introduce you to this incredibly exciting product, as well as put it in the necessary context for solving business problems.

Visual FoxPro Defined

The first thing to understand about Visual FoxPro is what it really is. Visual FoxPro is usually defined as a Relational Database Management System (RDBMS). This is only part of the story, however. In addition to being the most powerful PC/Windows database product on the planet, Visual FoxPro is also a flexible, powerful object-oriented visual development language. Put together, these two distinctive purposes make Visual FoxPro the supreme solution for developing applications that solve real-world, business problems.

Visual FoxPro as an RDBMS

When most people think of FoxPro, in any version, they think of a database management system (DBMS) that they can use to store, query, retrieve, and report on data in tables. Beyond that, its database capabilities have been almost ignored. FoxPro has taken it on the chin for many deficiencies in the past. Chief among them include

- Lack of a data dictionary
- No built-in referential integrity support
- Inability to build database-level business rule support
- Poor support for access to back-end data

The truth is, FoxPro has traditionally been thought of as almost a "toy" by corporate America. In many corporations, FoxPro made it into the company through the "back door"; it was brought in by a particular business unit to fill a need that could not be met by other products or the corporate Informarion Systems (IS) department.

Visual FoxPro changes the story radically. Virtually all of the concerns that you could bring to the table have been addressed in Visual FoxPro. The new database additions have propelled Visual FoxPro to a level of functionality and power that practically put it in a class by itself.

Visual FoxPro's New Database Features

Visual FoxPro is, first and foremost, a relational database management system (RDBMS). As such, it is not surprising that a great deal of the enhancements to Visual FoxPro have come in this arena.

Database

Visual FoxPro now supports a database in the more traditional sense of the word. A *database*, in Visual FoxPro terms, refers to a collection of tables, relations, views, and connections. Each of these *objects*, as they are termed in the Visual FoxPro documentation and help files, also have properties that are stored in the database. There properties include information such as field validation rules, record-level validation rules, triggers, and much more.

A database is also called a DBC file (or just DBC) because the extension of a Visual FoxPro database file is .DBC. Databases are created and maintained using the Database Designer, as shown in Figure 1.1.

FIGURE 1.1.

A database in the Database Designer.

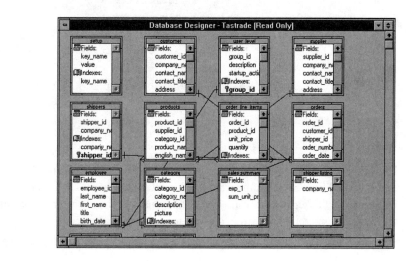

Tables

A table is a DBF file. If you used the term *database* in FoxPro 2.6 or earlier, you were probably discussing a table in Visual FoxPro terms. Tables can exist outside a database, in which case they are called *free tables*. Tables that have been added to a DBC are known as *attached tables*.

When a table is added to DBC, you can specify a great deal more information about the table and the fields in the Table Designer. As Figure 1.2 shows, you can specify validation rules at the table level both at the field and record level. The Validation Rule field in the Field Properties section of the dialog box is where you would specify the validation expression for a field. Placing validations in the table definition ensures that these rules are enforced regardless of where the data is accessed from— whether it is accessed from your application, from a user using Visual FoxPro itself, or even from another application accessing the information via the Visual FoxPro ODBC driver.

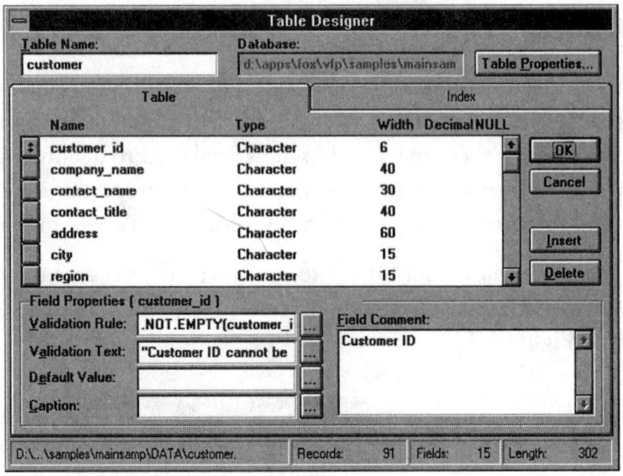

FIGURE 1.2.

The Table Designer for an attached table.

The Table Designer is discussed in more detail in Chapter 3, "Creating and Working with Tables."

Relations

In the past, relations were always set between tables manually using the SET RELATION command. Visual FoxPro now supports *persistent relationships* in a DBC. A persistent relationship, in Visual FoxPro terms, is a relationship that is used as the default relationship between tables whenever those tables are used in a form, report, view, or query.

Figure 1.1, shown earlier, illustrates how the Database Designer shows relationships. When tables are added to the data environments of forms and reports, as well as when they are referenced in queries and views, the relationships set in the Database Designer are automatically set in the Form, Report, Query, and View Designer, respectively.

The persistent relationships also serve another critical function in Visual FoxPro development: they are the basis for defining rules for maintaining referential integrity in your data. *Referential integrity* ensures that relationships in your data are properly maintained. A good example would be rules for deleting a customer in a customer table that is related to an invoice table. Using the Referential Integrity Builder, you can easily define what should happen when a customer record is deleted. You can choose to restrict the delete function (which means that a customer cannot be deleted if there are related invoices for that customer in the invoice table), cascade deletes throughout the relation (that is, deleting a customer will automatically delete related invoice records in the invoice table), or you can ignore the delete, in which case nothing happens to the invoice table when a customer is deleted.

This powerful feature corrects one of the most significant faults in earlier versions of FoxPro and now gives you an easy way to keep all your tables properly synchronized.

Figure 1.3 shows the Referential Integrity Builder, which is disucssed in more detail in Chapter 3.

FIGURE 1.3.

The Referential Integrity Builder.

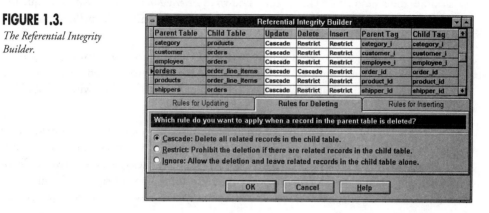

SQL Views

Views are one of the most exciting additions to Visual FoxPro. Basically, a *view* is a query that can be updated and, for the most part, can be treated like a table (that is, it can be used like any other table).

Bear in mind that SQL views, which are created and stored in the Database Designer, are not the same as view (.VUE) files that existed in earlier versions of FoxPro. The old views were simply "pictures" of a data environment (open tables, relations, and certain SET commands). SQL views are infinitely more powerful and useful than the old views (.VUE files).

Views are exciting for a number of reasons:

- Views, unlike queries, are updatable. This means that you can construct a query that relates many tables and, when data is updated, the underlying tables are automatically updated.

- Views can be either *local* or *remote*. A local view is a view that works with local data (such as Visual FoxPro tables). A remote view is a view that works with data coming from a source other than Visual FoxPro (such as Access, SQL Server, or Oracle). Working with remove views means that working with Client/Server data can be as simple as constructing some views and then using the views as if they were Visual FoxPro tables. This greatly eases the creation of Client/Server applications in Visual FoxPro.

- Remote views can be configured to download only a portion of the records from the back end before returning control to your programs. The rest of the records from the back end (for example, Oracle) are downloaded in the background. This feature, known as *background fetching*, optimizes client/server performance by limiting network traffic.

- Remote views can also be configured to defer the download of memo fields. Although the memo field is represented in the structure of the view, it is empty until the user accesses the memo field. This feature, known as *deferred memo download,* is unique to Visual FoxPro and also is a useful weapon in creating optimized Client/Server applications.

- If a system is designed to work with data in local views, the upgrade path to Client/Server is made significantly easier. By re-creating the local views as remote views of the same name, your application will practically run right out of the box with no modifications.

Views are also incredibly easy to create. As Figure 1.4 shows, the View Designer is made to be very user-friendly. All the necessary portions of the SQL view are neatly segregated into a neat, tabbed dialog box. There is also an added benefit. The Query Designer, discussed in Chapter 6, "Querying Data," uses virtually the same interface as the View Designer. The similarity of the Query and View Designer interfaces tremendously cuts down on your learning curve.

Views are discussed in Chapter 8, "Updating Data with Views."

FIGURE 1.4.

The View Designer.

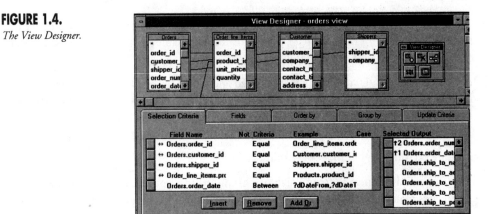

Connections

A *connection* is a defined "channel" between Visual FoxPro and a back end (such as SQL Server). You can give connections names and store them in a database. Once defined, you can use named connections to access the data in the back end with remote views.

Figure 1.5 shows the Connection Designer. Chapter 8 provides more information about the Connection Designer.

FIGURE 1.5.

The Connection Designer.

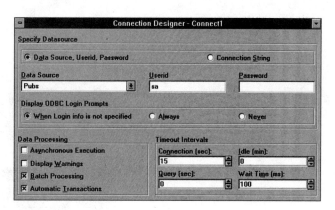

What the Changes Mean

What do all these changes mean? They mean that Visual FoxPro's new database features put it in a class by itself as a PC-based RDBMS. Visual FoxPro has a combination of features that no other PC-based RDBMS can boast for creating and managing mission-critical databases. However, the tremendous power of Visual FoxPro's database features tell only part of the story. Visual FoxPro is also a premier Windows development environment for creating event-driven applications better, faster, and more "Windowsy" than ever before.

Visual FoxPro as a Visual Development Language

As the name implies, Visual FoxPro is a true member of Microsoft's "visual" family of languages. Based on an extraordinarily powerful set of tools, Visual FoxPro enables you to use easy-to-use tools to develop applications with fine-tuned control.

Visual FoxPro is also fully compliant with OLE 2 standards, enabling you to use other OLE-enabled applications as if they were Visual FoxPro objects. As if adding OLE compliance weren't enough, Visual FoxPro raises the bar even further by adding object orientation to the mix.

Visual FoxPro's New Tools

The first step is to look at the "Visual" portion of Visual FoxPro. The new visual tools, called *designers*, give Visual FoxPro the "visual" in its name.

The Form Designer

Visual FoxPro's new Form Designer looks nothing like the old screen designer from FoxPro for Windows. Totally redesigned, the Form Designer was designed to enable developers to create visually pleasing, easy-to-use Graphical User Interfaces (GUI) with pinpoint control over the controls on the forms.

Figure 1.6 shows a form in the Form Designer.

FIGURE 1.6.

A form in the Form Designer.

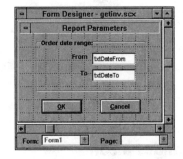

Microsoft has added support for a host of properties, events, and methods that are used to define and fine-tune objects on a form like never before. As shown in Figure 1.7, these properties, events, and methods can be accessed through the Property Sheet.

FIGURE 1.7.

The Property Sheet.

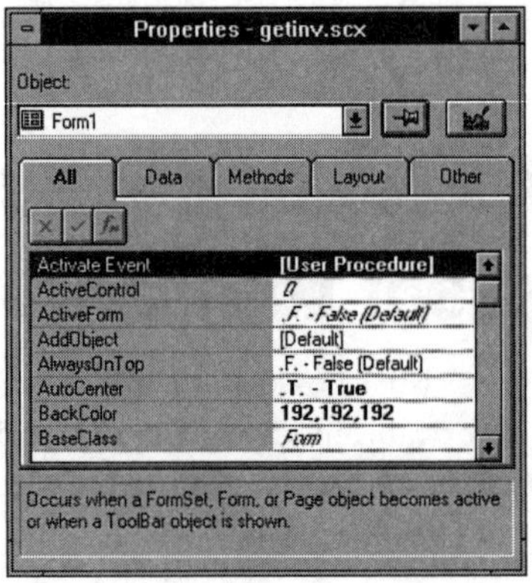

Once a difficult prospect, laying controls in a form and aligning them properly is now a breeze with the new Layout toolbar. This toolbar contains functions that enable you to automatically align controls to have the same left edge, right edge, center, and more. You can even make objects the same size or equalize the amount of space between controls with one option on this new toolbar. Figure 1.8 shows the Layout toolbar.

Forms no longer operate with the antiquated READ command and code generation is now a thing of the past. A form in design mode can be tested with one click of the mouse on the Run button (it's the button with the exclamation point icon) on the standard toolbar.

FIGURE 1.8.

The Layout toolbar.

You can also run forms more than once. This feature, coupled with the powerful new "Private Data Session" feature of Visual FoxPro forms means that you can have multiple "copies" (known as *instances*) of the same form running with the same table showing in each, with each table handled independently. Moving record pointers in one instance of a form will not affect the record pointers in other, independent instances. Figure 1.9 shows a single form running multiple times.

FIGURE 1.9.

Multiple-form instances.

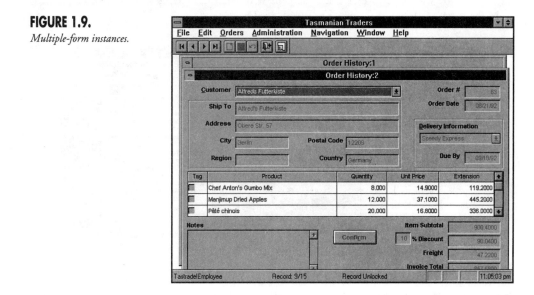

This certainly is not the old screens of FoxPro for Windows days! Interested in more? See Chapter 12, "Designing and Customizing Forms," for more fascinating information on the Form Designer.

The controls available in the Form Designer via the Form Controls toolbar, shown in Figure 1.10, include powerful new capabilities for application developers. Among these are the new Timer control, which enables you to create objects with code that executes at specific time intervals, a PageFrame control that enables you to make forms with multiple pages in it, the incredible new Grid control that provides the functionalty of a browse in a form (and then some), and OLE controls used to add the power of Object Linking and Embedding to your forms.

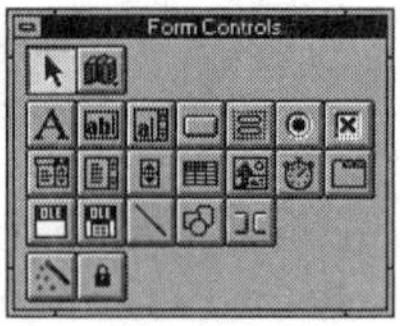

FIGURE 1.10.

*The Form Controls
toolbar.*

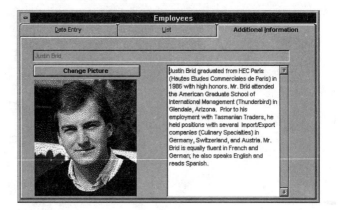

Pageframes

A pageframe is a control that enables you to create multiple "pages" in one form. Typically, pageframes are used to create "tabbed" screens with each tab having a separate "set" of controls. Figure 1.11 shows a running form with a tabbed interface.

FIGURE 1.11.

*A sample tabbed dialog
box.*

The Grid Control

For a long time, developers have been requesting the ability to have a browse work within a form. Microsoft's response is the grid control, which can be thought of as a browse on heavy-duty steroids.

With the grid control, you can control each column separately. You can have almost any type of object in the individual cells of the grid. You can control the color of the individual cells. You can even make the color conditional depending on the value of the cell (for example, showing negative numbers in red). Figure 1.12 shows a form with a grid control on it.

OLE Controls

Visual FoxPro supports OLE 2, which means that you can add new OCX controls (OLE 2 controls) to your form. OLE 2 controls give you the opportunity to expand the list of controls supplied by Microsoft even further with the myriad of OLE controls available on the market.

The Professional Edition of Visual FoxPro ships with five OLE controls. Figure 1.13 shows a form with one of those controls: the Outline control.

FIGURE 1.12.
A sample grid.

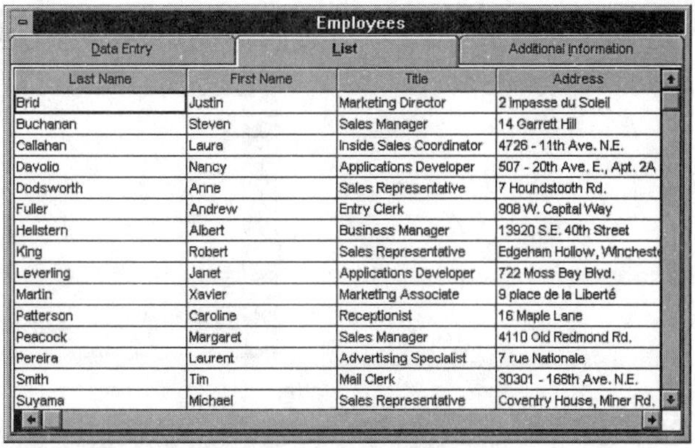

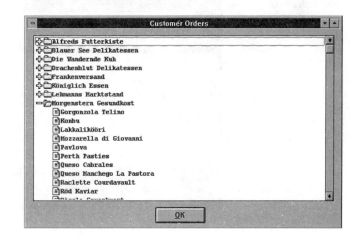

FIGURE 1.13.
*A form with the
Outline control.*

Other controls that ship with the Professional Edition include the communications control and two controls for enabling your applications to work with the Microsoft Mail API (MAPI).

In addition to OCX controls, Visual FoxPro also enables you to add objects from other OLE-enabled applications (such as Microsoft Word for Windows and Microsoft Excel). These objects can be manipulated much like other Visual FoxPro objects. With OLE 2 automation, users can get the power of these applications from within Visual FoxPro forms. Figure 1.14 shows a form with a Microsoft Excel object.

The Project Manager

The Project Manager is all new. Redesigned into a tabbed screen, the new Project Manager provides easy access to all the files you will use in an application.

Each tab in the dialog box shows files in the application segregated by type. Figure 1.15 shows the sample application, TasTrade, in the Project Manager.

FIGURE 1.14.

A form with an
Excel object.

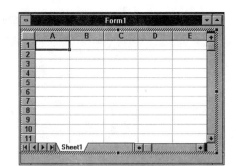

FIGURE 1.15.

The Project Manager.

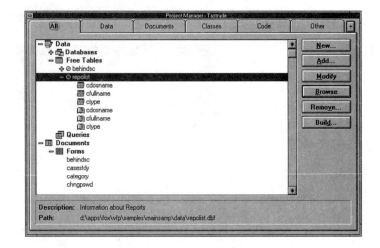

In addition to a new interface, the Project Manager also supports new functionality. Drag and drop is fully enabled between the Project Manager and the power tools such as the Form Designer. For example, grabbing a table from the Project Manager and dropping it on a form will automatically add a Grid control to the form and the table to the form's data environment. (By the way, drag-and-drop is supported throughout the product.)

Files created by other applications, such as bitmaps, documents, and spreadsheets, can be added to the Other section (available from the All tab and the Other tab) of the Project Manager. Modifying these objects causes the application associated with them to be launched to edit the object. For example, modifying a bitmap (by double-clicking on the name of the file) in the Project Manager launches Paintbrush to edit the file.

The Project Manager is discussed in Chapter 2, "Maximizing the Visual FoxPro User Interface."

FIGURE 1.16.

Paintbrush editing an object.

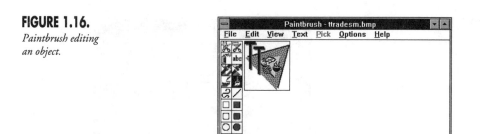

FIGURE 1.16.

Paintbrush editing an object.

The Report Designer

The Report Designer is largely unchanged from FoxPro 2.6. The interface is basically the same too, as you can see from Figure 1.17. The major changes to the Report Designer are the addition of a data environment to reports, which enables you to define the tables, views, and relations used in the report and the new Private Data Session option, which gives a report its own set of work areas to work with. This prevents a report from changing any settings and record pointers being used by other portions of the application.

Figure 1.18 shows the new Data Environment section of a report.

FIGURE 1.17.

The Report Designer.

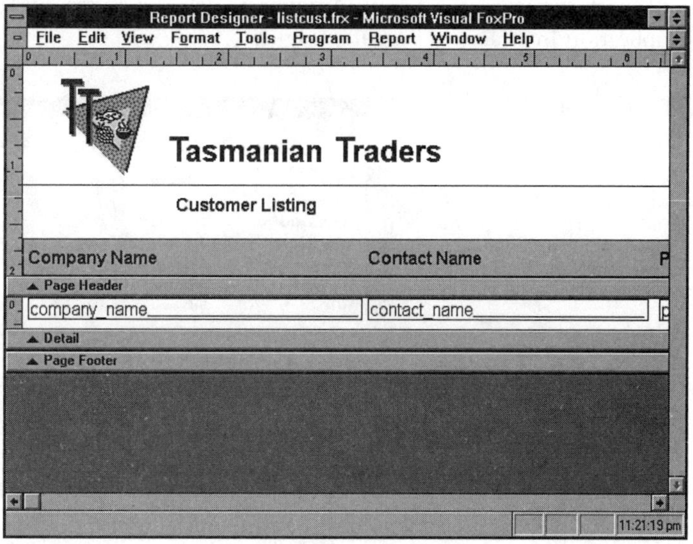

FIGURE 1.18.

*The Report Designer
Data Environment.*

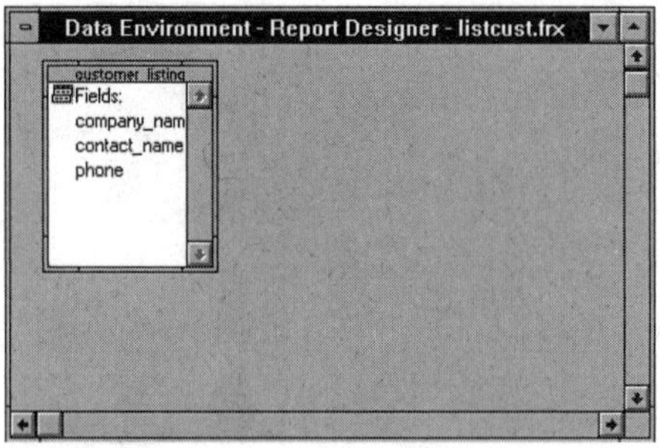

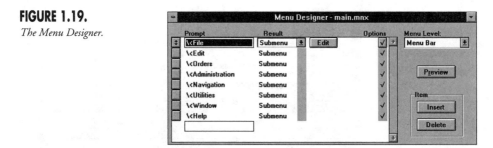

The Report Designer also now supports a much improved Preview mode that has a flexible ZOOM control (meaning you can zoom in and out of the report preview). Finally, you can specify expressions to execute on the way into and out of bands in the report.

The Report Designer is discussed in Chapter 13, "Designing and Customizing Reports."

Menu Designer

You use the Menu Designer in Visual FoxPro to create menus. The Menu Designer was a tool from FoxPro 2.*x* that remains the only power tool that generates code. The tool is also essentially unchanged from earlier versions of FoxPro.

The work surface of the Menu Designer, which is discussed in Chapter 24, "Designing the Application Interface," is shown in Figure 1.19.

FIGURE 1.19.

The Menu Designer.

Object-Oriented Extensions

Visual FoxPro brings object-oriented development to FoxPro for the first time. This new development paradigm enables a developer to create applications based on objects modeled on the real-world entities in the business being automated. Object orientation is not only a new way of organizing and writing code, it is a whole new way of thinking about software design and development.

Visual FoxPro's implementation of object orientation is among the most powerful in languages in its class. It supports not only the creation of visual classes but also non-visual and business classes. Visual FoxPro's robust object model adds a new degree of elegance and reusability to developing database applications.

Object orientation is discussed in Part V of this book, "Object-Oriented Programming."

In order to support object-oriented development, Visual FoxPro supports a new Visual Class Designer, which enables you to visually develop classes (in effect, you develop classes in a very similar way to developing forms). Figure 1.20 shows a class in the Visual Class Designer. The Visual Class Designer is discussed in Chapter 28, "OOP with Visual FoxPro."

FIGURE 1.20.

The Visual Class Designer.

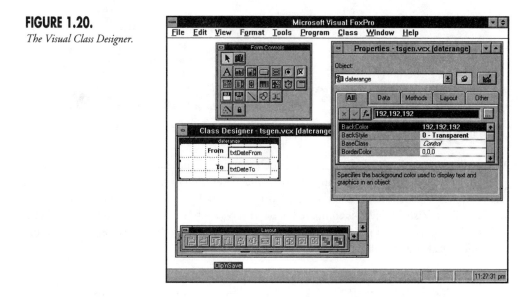

In order to support managing Visual FoxPro classes, Visual FoxPro's Professional Edition sports an exciting new tool, the Class Browser. The Class Browser, which is written in Visual FoxPro, is not only easy to use, it also has an open-ended architecture that enables developers to easily hook their own tools into the utility. Figure 1.21 shows the Class Browser. Chapter 30, "Managing Classes with Visual FoxPro," discusses the Class Browser in detail.

FIGURE 1.21.

The Class Browser.

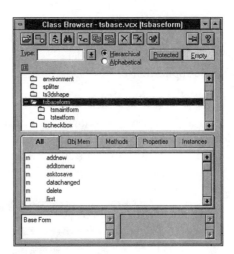

Visual FoxPro's Place in Business Software Development

When all of Visual FoxPro's features are taken as a unit, Visual FoxPro is clearly a powerful platform for developing business applications. The Client/Server capabilities of the product, the visual development tools, and the object-oriented paradigm rival all its competitors in the market. When Visual FoxPro is compared to other tools for business application development, either using local data or in the Client/Server arena, Visual FoxPro holds the key to developing mission-critical applications.

Visual FoxPro's principle competitors in database and Client/Server development are Visual Basic, Powerbuilder, Visual dBASE, and Delphi. All these products have been presented as the tool for developing applications to work with corporate data. However, a critical analysis of Visual FoxPro versus these products brings forward some interesting points.

■ Some of the products do not have a local data store. For example, Visual Basic does not have a local data store (it uses the JET engine and Access databases to store data). Neither do PowerBuilder and Delphi, each of which have to go to an outside database engine for all their data storage needs.

Visual FoxPro has a local data store and one of the most powerful data manipulation languages (DML) in the business. A local data store is important to Client/Server development, even when data is always accessed from the back end, because it enables you to download less often modified data into local tables for access. This increases the efficiency of the application because these more static tables (that is, tables that are not typically modified as much) can be downloaded to local tables and used without having to constantly go against the back end for that information.

A local data store is also very important for developing applications that will run both against a Client/Server database and against local information. Take, for example, the case of a traveling salesperson. When the salesperson is on the road he or she will want to have a subset of the corporate data on his or her notebook to look up customer credit history, book new orders, and more. When the salesperson gets back to the office, or dials in, he or she wants to update the back end with the new information.

A native, local data store makes developing a system that works on both local and remote data a much easier task.

■ Visual FoxPro's implementation of object orientation is the most complete of any of the packages mentioned here. Visual Basic is not object oriented. Powerbuilder only enables the creation of visual classes, whereas Visual FoxPro enables the creation of both visual and non-visual classes. Visual and non-visual classes and their respective benefits are discussed in detail in Chapter 29, "Creating Classes with Visual FoxPro."

Visual dBASE and Delphi have limitations on subclassing user-defined form classes that Visual FoxPro does not have.

■ Visual FoxPro's *deferred memo download* feature is unique in the industry. This feature, mentioned earlier in the section, "SQL Views," limits the amount of data coming down the network wire and downloads memo field data only when accessed (for example, when the memo field is edited by the user).

An analysis of the respective features of the most popular Client/Server market and Visual FoxPro clearly put Visual FoxPro in the forefront of Client/Server application development features.

Visual FoxPro and Business Process Re-engineering

Increasingly, in computer literature published in trade magazines and books, object orientation and Client/Server are linked with a process known as *Business Process Re-engineering*. Business Process Re-engineering (BPR) is the process in which a business organization is reviewed and its operations are reorganized to work in accordance with its processes. The intent behind BPR is to radically redesign how a company does business to achieve monumental increases in efficiency.

For example, one company processes its sales orders in the following manner:

■ A customer calls in with an order that is manually recorded on an order entry form.

■ The order is then manually checked against price lists to fill in the current pricing for each item on the order.

■ The completed order form is passed on to the credit department, which checks the customer credit status. Credit status information (such as credit OK, on credit hold) is recorded manually in an index file.

- If the customer is on credit hold, the customer is called back and told that his or her order will have to be prepaid in order to be shipped.
- Once the credit status has been checked, the form moves on to another desk where the freight charges on the order are calculated and added to the order.
- The order is then sent to the billing department, where it is entered into the company accounting system.
- Once a day, the shipping department prints out the list of orders to be filled, packs the orders, and then ships the order.

The entire process, in terms of elapsed time, could take more than an entire day to complete. If the order was processed too late in the day, the order would have to wait an entire day.

When this process was analyzed, by the company and its consultants, a few things quickly became apparent. Because the order form went through so many different departments and individuals, there was a high probability for error. Customers on credit hold were sometimes passed for credit (that is, they were allowed to purchase on credit) because a customer with a similar name might be in the Rolodex that was their manual credit index. The order also spent a significant amount of time sitting in "in-boxes" throughout the company.

The goal in re-engineering this process was to place in the hands of one individual the tools and the responsibility for completing all phases of processing the sales order. This individual would take the order from the customer, check the credit history, calculate freight, and enter the order into the accounting system.

Individual jobs in the process were reconfigured and each individual became sales professionals. They were equipped with a more powerful accounting system bolstered by a contact management program that front ended the accounting system. When a customer calls in now, the sales professional immediately calls the customer's record up in the contact management program. Salespeople have full access to all notes written about this customer by other sales professionals so they know all of the history the company has with that customer at the touch of a button. The customer record also clearly states whether the customer is on credit hold or not so this issue can be dealt with up front and immediately without having to deal with the ire of a customer who, several hours after placing an order, is then told that the order cannot be processed.

While the sales professional is on the phone, he or she immediately gets the order from the customer and places it in the computer as he or she gets it. The most current pricing is automatically filled in by the system. Freight calculation also takes place right away as the customer is on the phone.

The net result is that once the customer is done with his order it has already been placed in the system and is ready for shipping.

An added benefit to this approach is the notes kept in the contact management portion of the system. When a sales professional is finished with the sales call, he or she types in notes about it. Typical notes might include statements by the customer as to their preferences ("I prefer Red ones, you know"), problems, special requests, and so on. Sometimes personal information is also recorded ("By the way, please pardon the noise in the background but today's my birthday and the office is in the middle of throwing me a party"). Imagine how a customer feels when she calls and the sales professional knows a lot about her. In addition, by knowing a customer's preferences, a sales professional can know how a company special might interest the customer on the phone.

There is one last note to make about this example. In the course of the analysis of the company, care was also taken to define what management required in terms of sales and analysis reports. Although this is technically not part of the individual process under discussion, knowing this information up front allowed for mapping how the sales process intersected with other corporate processes.

This example illustrates several concepts. First of all, BPR relies on properly modeling the enterprise being re-engineered. Without knowing the client's business, it is very difficult to assist them in properly re-engineering themselves. Interestingly enough, object-oriented analysis and design (which is mentioned in Chapter 27, "Introduction to Object-Oriented Programming") starts with a similar concept (that is, modeling the entire problem domain before developing).

Second, this example illustrates one of the key goals of re-engineering. By redefining the order entry process to a *sales* process, the original process that was fragmented over several departments is now handled by a single individual doing more than the entire process did before. Thinking "outside the box" in this manner enabled the client to go from a reactive sales process (just taking orders) to a *proactive* one where suggestions can be made to customers and the sales professional does not merely take an order but also *services* the customer to take care of his or her needs. It's a win-win situation for the company and its customers.

The interesting part here is the role that technology takes in this undertaking. Technology is not merely the tool of the process; it is literally an integral part of it. Without the technology, this process could not happen. The role of technology in a re-engineered process is frequently so central that it becomes the *enabler* of the process.

Visual FoxPro, as an object-oriented development environment and tool for Client/Server development, holds a mighty answer to implementing custom solutions to re-engineer business processes. The structure of object-oriented analysis, design and development, is keyed around three central components: the business, the business and, finally, the business. The reusability of objects, both visual and non-visual, created in object-oriented programming is key to maintaining consistency throughout the company, as well as limiting the amount of programming required to implement process after process.

Another central tenet to BPR is sharing information. Without sharing information business processes cannot be enabled. Interestingly enough, sharing information is also a central tenet of Client/Server.

As companies look to compete in the customer-centric environment of the 1990s, Visual FoxPro takes its place as a key tool in their arsenal to make them more responsive and efficient in their business than ever before.

Summary

Now that you have a general overview of what Visual FoxPro is all about, you're ready to step into this exciting new world of working with data in Visual FoxPro and developing applications with it. The rest of the chapters in Part I of this book tell you how you can quickly put Visual FoxPro to work by using the Project Manager, the menu options, and the available FoxPro commands.

Maximizing the Visual FoxPro User Interface

IN THIS CHAPTER

This chapter details the user interface used by Visual FoxPro for Windows. Topics in this chapter include the use of the Project Manager, mouse and window techniques, and the effective use of menus, windows, and dialog boxes. Much of this chapter serves as a reference for those who are unfamiliar with the Visual FoxPro interface. When you can't recall where a specific menu option is located, you can refer to this chapter to find it.

Version 3.0 of Visual FoxPro is a flexible database manager in that it provides three distinct, yet interrelated, methods of accessing the program functionality: the Project Manager, a menu system, and a Command window. These different methods of working with Visual FoxPro appeal to different types of users, or to the same user at different times. You will find you develop your own style as you work with Visual FoxPro.

The Project Manager feature of Visual FoxPro is improved in Version 3.0. By borrowing heavily from other Windows user interfaces, the Project Manager enables you to work in Visual FoxPro without having a deep knowledge of the FoxPro language commands, or the menu options that invoke the commands.

The Project Manager enables you to manage complete projects or collections of data as well as documents (such as forms, reports, and views). With its easy user interface and the extensive use of drag-and-drop, the Project Manager insulates all users from unneeded details. Its design appeals to novice and expert users alike. The menu system gives you added flexibility; at the same time, you do not need an intricate knowledge of FoxPro commands. And finally, the Command window lets experienced users address the full power of Visual FoxPro through interactive commands. Most users find they use a mixture of all the methods.

> **TIP**
>
> Those who are upgrading to Visual FoxPro from older versions of Xbase products will likely be most comfortable with using the Command window. In the Command window, you can type FoxPro commands (many of which are shared with other Xbase products).

Starting Visual FoxPro

When you first start Visual FoxPro (by double-clicking the Visual FoxPro icon in the Visual FoxPro for Windows program group or by choosing Visual FoxPro from the Programs menu of the Windows 95 Start menu), the FoxPro main program window appears. (See Figure 2.1.)

When Visual FoxPro is opened, you see the Command window in Visual FoxPro. The Command window is the active window. Here you can enter FoxPro commands.

FIGURE 2.1.

The FoxPro program window.

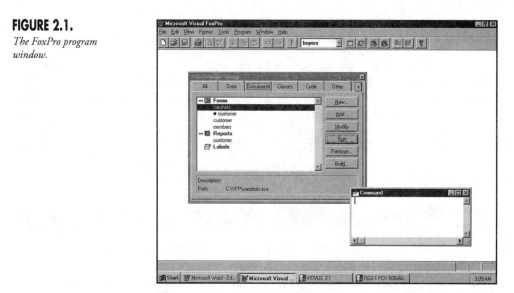

To open a file, choose Open from the File menu and select the name of the file you wish to open. You can also use the wizards to create new tables by opening the Tools menu, choosing the Wizards option, and selecting the desired wizard from the submenu that appears. (Visual FoxPro provides wizards for creating all basic objects, including tables, queries, forms, reports, and labels.)

> **TIP**
>
> When using menu selections that have FoxPro command equivalents, FoxPro writes the equivalent command in the Command window. Because you can select and copy any text from the Command window, you can use menu selections to achieve some desired action, and then copy the commands from the Command window and paste them into a program file for later use. This technique also helps you learn the FoxPro commands.

> **TIP**
>
> You can freely intermix the Project Manager, Command window, and menu selections to accomplish tasks in Visual FoxPro. Like all other Windows applications, click the desired item to have Windows grant it the focus. If you are in the Project Manager and want to switch to the menus and the Command window, click the Command window to make it active. The material that follows discusses both the Project Manager and the use of Visual FoxPro menu options in greater detail.

Using the Project Manager

The Project Manager is your single point for managing the development, integration, and building of your Visual FoxPro applications. The Project Manager is a user-friendly graphical interface that enables you to organize your database work using the popular tabbed file folder metaphor. For those who are upgrading, you might think of it as a Catalog Manager on steroids. A *project* is a named collection of files, data, documents, and objects used in Visual FoxPro. A project is saved as a file with a .PJX extension. The Project Manager gives you an excellent way to manage and organize your tables, databases, reports, forms, and queries during application development.

> **NOTE**
>
> In FoxPro 2.6 for Windows, the Catalog Manager consists of a tabbed dialog window that collects related items (tables, screens, programs, and so on) under each tab. Those who use FoxPro 2.6 interactively (as opposed to those who use FoxPro as a development platform) tend to use the Catalog Manager to collect and manage related FoxPro items. If you want to build an application (an .APP or a stand-alone .EXE) from your various FoxPro items, you would use the Project Manager, not the Catalog Manager.
>
> The FoxPro 2.6 Project Manager provides a tool for collecting and building applications (.APP or .EXE files). Unlike the independent FoxPro items that you would access using the Catalog, a FoxPro application is a unified, single whole. All the various items are combined into a single file. The Project tool is only available, however, when you use FoxPro 2.6 in the Command Window mode (not the Catalog mode).
>
> Visual FoxPro's Project Manager combines the functionality of both FoxPro 2.6's Catalog and Project tools and presents it using the now-familiar collapsible hierarchical list control (like that found in Windows 3.1 File Manager or in Windows 95 Explorer).

The Project Manager contains six sections, each identified by a corresponding tab. When you click any tab, that tab becomes active, and all the items related to that tab appear.

Characteristics of the Project Manager GUI

The user interface to the Project Manager has some interesting characteristics that should be explained. It has some characteristics which are its own, some of a dialog box, and some of a toolbar.

First, the dialog box can be collapsed so that only the tabs show. You do this by pressing the small button with the arrow on it in the upper-right corner of the Project Manager dialog box. When the Project Manager is collapsed, press the same button to expand it back to its full size. Pressing one of the tabs while the Project Manager is collapsed causes that tab to expand and show its contents.

Second, when the Project Manager is collapsed, you can tear off its tabs. That is, place your cursor over a tab and drag the tab to pull that section from the Project Manager and place that section (expanded) on the main screen. These "torn" sections have a push-pin icon on the top. By pressing the push-pin icon, you cause it to cycle between appearing pushed in and lying on its side pulled out. When pushed in, the torn tab always appears on top of other windows. Return the torn tab to the Project Manager by dragging the torn tab over to the Project Manager and placing the tab back in its correct position, or by closing the tab.

Third, the Project Manager can be docked, just like a toolbar. Whether expanded or collapsed, if the Project Manager is dragged up to the top toolbar area, it will dock itself as a toolbar would. Once docked, it is in its collapsed state and you must tear off tab sections to view or operate on the contents. Also like other toolbars, you can move the Project Manager from its toolbar location back to its position on-screen by grabbing a non-button section of the toolbar and dragging it back onto the screen.

Creating a New Project

To create a new project, choose the New option from the File menu. The New dialog box appears, as shown in Figure 2.2. From the New dialog box, choose Project, and then click New File. Next, you will see the Create dialog box, as show in Figure 2.3. Name the project and choose the Save button. Now you can begin building the project by creating the various Visual FoxPro objects (databases, tables, queries, forms, and reports) and adding them to the project.

FIGURE 2.2.

The New dialog box.

FIGURE 2.3.

The Create dialog box.

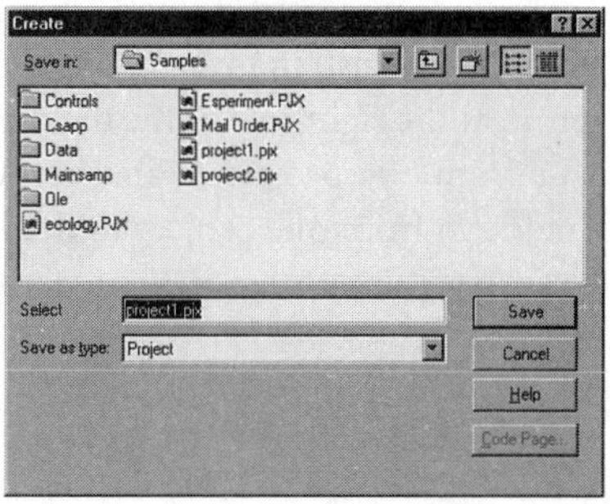

To create a new database from the All tab of the Project Manager, double-click the symbol to the left of the Data icon. This brings the Database icon into view with a list of the current databases in the Project Manager. Next, click the New button to open the Create menu, like the dialog box shown in Figure 2.3, but showing database types (.DBC), not project types (.PJX). Here you are prompted to enter a name for the database. After you have done so, the name of the database appears on the screen in the Project Manager. Building databases is discussed in more detail in Chapter 3, "Creating and Working with Tables." This example shows you how to add a database to a project.

NOTE

You can perform the same operation from the Data tab of the Project Manager. The single difference from the directions you just learned is the absence of the Data icon (after all, you're in the Data tab!). Just begin by double-clicking the Database icon and continue from there.

Clicking the Documents tab of the Project Manager reveals the documents stored in the project. From FoxPro's point of view, this includes all related forms, reports, and labels. Move the highlight to the Forms, Reports, or Labels icons and click the Add button to enable you to add any one of these items to your project. If you have reports, forms, or labels created and wish to modify them, move the highlight to the name of the item to be modified and choose the Modify button. The Run button is used to run any of the items you have in your project. A double click is assumed to be a request to modify the item. Double-clicking any item invokes the appropriate editor or designer.

The Build button is more involved than the rest. This button is used to perform tasks related to rebuilding projects, as well as building applications and executables (Professional Edition only).

The Data tab of the Project Manager contains all the data for a project. This includes free tables, views, and queries. Again, you can add, remove, browse, or modify any of the items in the project by selecting the item in the Project Manager and clicking the corresponding button.

The Document tab of the Project Manager contains all the documents you use when you work with data. This includes forms, reports, and labels. To see the contents of an item, click the plus sign of the item. If you wish to make changes to an item, highlight the item and click the corresponding button at the right side of the dialog box to add, modify, run, or remove it. You can also move a file from one project to another. (You do this by opening two projects and dragging the desired item from one project to the other.)

The Classes tab of the Project Manager is used to manage classes from within the Project Manager. When you click the Classes tab, any existing classes included in this project appear in the window.

NOTE

In Visual FoxPro, as in other object-oriented programming languages, classes are the blueprints for objects. Unlike classic procedural programming, which distinguishes between data and functions, *classes* contain both the definitions for data used by the class and the functions (or "methods") used by the class when operating on its data. An "object" is an instance of its "class." Classes do not exist at runtime; objects do. Classes, objects, and object-oriented programming are covered in Part V of this book, "Object-Oriented Programming."

The Code tab of the Project Manager is used to perform tasks related to creating or modifying programs. Tasks can also be performed related to API libraries and applications. These are all explained in more detail in various chapters of the Programming section of the book.

The Other tab of the Project Manager is used to perform tasks related to menus, text files, and other files such as icons and bitmaps. The Menu icon enables you to create, modify, or remove menu program files. Remember that you must highlight the item and then press the corresponding button on the right of the Project Manager.

As described earlier, the Project Manager can also be collapsed. This is very useful when you wish to look at other tables or databases and need to move the Project Manager. The collapsed Project Manager can be added to the toolbar as shown in Figure 2.4. When the Project Manager is docked in the toolbar, you can look at each of the tabs by clicking it. If you wish to move the tab, you can do that also simply by dragging the tab from the toolbar to the screen. This shows you the contents of the tab and enables you to look at the items if you wish. To return the tab to the collapsed Project Manager, click the Close button located on the upper-right corner of the tab.

FIGURE 2.4.

The collapsed Project Manager.

This gives you an overview of the Project Manager (see Figure 2.5) and the functionality it provides. Later in the book, each of the Project Manager aspects discussed will be covered in more detail.

FIGURE 2.5.

The Visual FoxPro Project Manager.

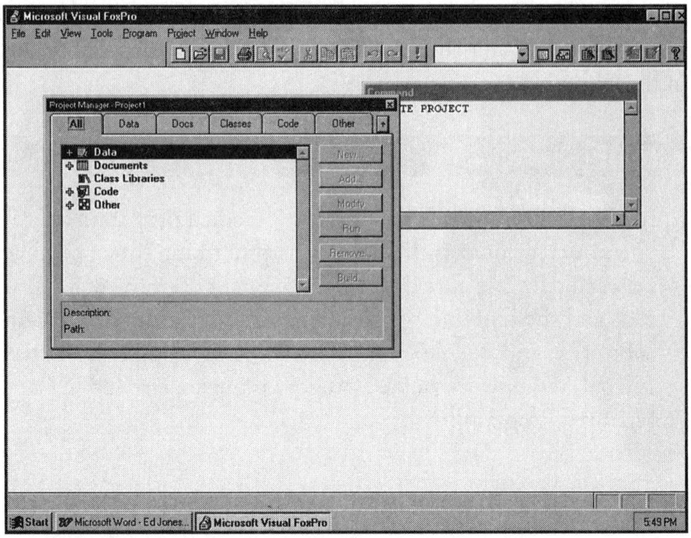

Organizing Data and Documents

This section discusses how the Project Manager organizes your documents and information. As explained earlier, each of the Project Manager tabs contains information related to the project. The Data tab lists all the databases, free tables, and queries. The Documents tab contains all your forms, reports, and labels in the project. The Classes tab contains all classes, and the Code tab contains all Visual FoxPro programs. The Other tab contains other files (such as text files and files related to menu creation). When you first create a project, it is empty. You build and manage each project by adding and removing files, as discussed in the next section.

Adding and Removing Files

As you've already learned, the Project Manager helps you collect and manage all the files that comprise your project. While modifying an existing project or creating a new one, you often add files to the Project Manager. You can add existing files or you can create new files of all the supported types directly within Project Manager. As an example, you add existing DBF tables to a project by performing the following steps:

1. Select the icon for the item you want to add (in this case, a DBF type).

2. Click the Add button.

3. From the Open dialog box, choose the name of the file you want to use.

Removing a file from a project is just as simple. Simply select the item you want to remove and click the Remove button.

> **NOTE**
>
> If your Project Manager is in the collapsed state, the buttons (New, Add, Modify, Open, Remove, and Build) are not visible and can't be clicked. In this case, you can still use the button accelerators to invoke the desired action. These are Alt+N for New, Alt+A for Add, Alt+M for Modify, Alt+O for Open, Alt+V for Remove, and Alt+D for Build.
>
> Also available are the equivalent menu picks under the Project menu. These are Project | New File, Project | Add File, Project | Modify File, Project | Open File, Project | Remove File, and Project | Build.
>
> Finally, you can expand the Project Manager and press the buttons directly.

Introducing Visual FoxPro's Visual Design Tools

Visual FoxPro's visual design tools are easily accessed from the Project Manager. These tools facilitate the creation of tables, forms, queries, databases, and reports for data management. Various chapters in this book cover the use of these tools. The items created by the design tools can be assembled into an application using the Project Manager.

Note, however, that the design tools can be used independently of the Project Manager. To launch a design tool, choose File | New from the main menu, choose the desired file type in the New dialog box that appears, and then click the New File button. The appropriate design tool is launched and is ready to create a new file. Later, the item created outside of a project can be included in a project. You will often do this when you create classes that will be shared among many projects. Table 2.1 shows the design tools and their functions.

Table 2.1. The FoxPro design tools and their functions.

Design Tool	Function
Database Designer	Used to define table membership in a database, create relationships among the tables, and design views that include the tables
Table Designer	Creates tables and sets indexes on tables
Query Designer	Runs queries on local tables
Connection Designer	Creates a connection for you when using views of a remote data source

continues

Table 2.1. continued

Design Tool	Function
View Designer	Runs queries on remote data sources and creates updatable queries
Form Designer	Creates a form for viewing and editing data in tables
Report Designer	Designs reports and labels
Menu Designer	Designs menus you create

These are the different design tools available in Visual FoxPro. Each of the tools is discussed in more detail in later chapters.

Using Wizards

Wizards are programs that help you quickly perform common tasks, such as creating forms, formatting reports, and setting up queries.

The wizards present a series of screens with questions that help you determine how you want to lay out a query, report, form, label, view, or menu using the wizards. Based on your responses, a report (for example) is created.

Follow these steps to start a wizard:

1. Choose the New option from the File menu.
2. Choose the item you wish to create.
3. If a wizard is available, the Wizard icon is activated, as shown in Figure 2.6.
4. Follow the steps presented by the wizard.

FIGURE 2.6.
*The active Wizard button
in the New dialog box.*

About Builders

In addition to the designers and wizards that Visual FoxPro provides to lighten the load of creating applications, when you create forms, FoxPro provides tools called *builders* for many of the controls that one can place on a form. In a manner similar to wizards, builders assist the developer by walking the developer through the control creation process step-by-step using a series of screens and questions. From the answers provided, the builder sets the control's properties for you, ensuring that nothing has been missed.

There are builders supplied for edit boxes, text boxes, option groups, list boxes, grid controls, and groups of command buttons. Choosing builders and using them is discussed in Chapter 9, "Creating and Using Simple Forms."

About the Visual FoxPro Menu System

When you start Visual FoxPro you see the Visual FoxPro desktop. (See Figure 2.7.) The menu system appears as part of the desktop, at the top of the screen.

FIGURE 2.7.

The Visual FoxPro desktop.

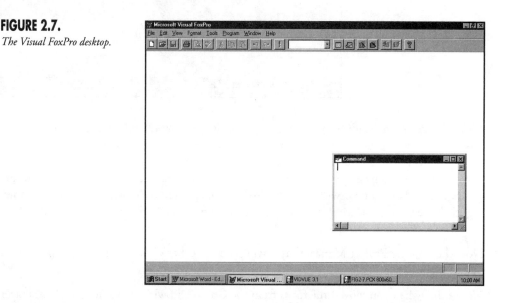

The Visual FoxPro menu system has four parts: a menu bar; menu pads, which reside along the menu bar; pull-down menus, which open from the menu pads; and menu options. When you open a menu by clicking the desired menu pad or by pressing Alt+ the underlined letter in the menu pad, the pull-down menu drops from the menu pad, and you can choose a desired option.

The Menu Bar

The menu bar appears at the top of the Visual FoxPro window and shows the names of the individual pull-down menus. Not only is this menu bar a standard way of working with Visual FoxPro, it also is representative of the interface design for most Visual FoxPro applications. Figure 2.8 shows the choices available on the File menu.

FIGURE 2.8.

The File menu in Visual FoxPro.

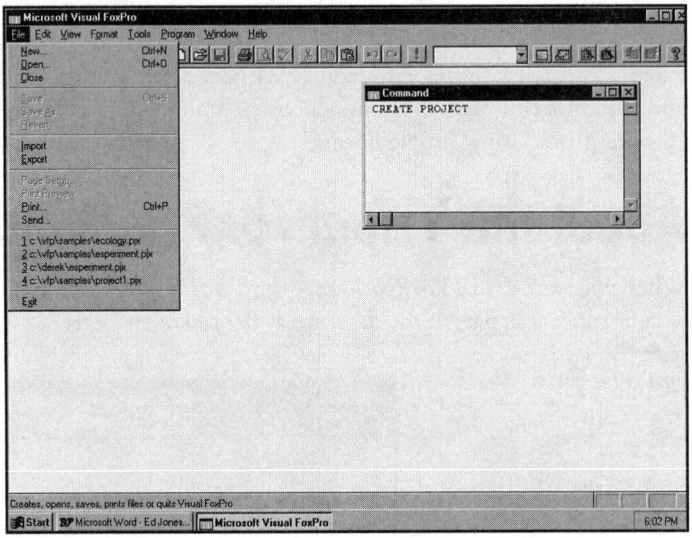

Visual FoxPro is an example of a Windows MDI interface. MDI, which stands for Multiple Document Interface, defines the behavior for an application that has a parent screen and multiple child windows. In the MDI application the main menu appears only at the top of the parent screen. As each child receives focus, the menu can change according to the needs of the child window. For example, with both the Project Manager and the Command windows showing, click the Command window and note the menu pads. You will see File, Edit, View, Format, Tools, Program, Window, and Help.

Now click on the Project Manager. You will see File, Edit, View, Tools, Program, Project, Window, and Help.

Notice that when you moved the focus from the Command window to the Project Manager window, the Format pad was removed from between the View and Tools pads, and a pad named Project was inserted between the Program and Window pads. This is typical for MDI and MDI-like applications, and it will characterize the menu systems for most of the applications you create in FoxPro.

Menu Pads

The menu pads are placed horizontally along the menu bar, and each pad is the name of a corresponding pull-down menu. If a menu pad's text is dimmed, the option is disabled and doesn't apply to the current operation. In Figure 2.8, for example, the Print Preview menu pad is dimmed because no table is open. Depending on the operation being performed, specific menu pads can be added to the menu bar by Visual FoxPro, or existing pads removed.

Pull-Down Menus

Pull-down menus are rectangular boxes that pull down from the menu pads when the pad is selected.

Menu Options

Each pull-down menu contains menu options relevant to the area in which you are working. If an option is dimmed, it is not available. For example, in Figure 2.8, the Save, Save As, Revert, Page Setup, and Print Preview options are unavailable because no file is currently open. The options that are followed by an ellipsis (...) cause dialog boxes to appear when selected. Some menu options also contain Ctrl+key combinations, which can be used as shortcut keys for those menu selections. For example, the Window menu contains a Cycle option with a Ctrl+F1 designation and a Command option with a Ctrl+F2 designation. Therefore, pressing Ctrl+F1 from anywhere in Visual FoxPro is equivalent to opening the Window menu and choosing Cycle.

Making Menu Selections

You can make menu selections using either the keyboard or the mouse, and there are advantages to each method. Mouse usage tends to be intuitive and easy to understand, whereas the keyboard appeals to users who find mouse navigation difficult. To use the mouse to select a desired menu option, click the menu by name on the menu pad with the left mouse button, and then click the desired option from the pull-down menu that opens. To use the keyboard to choose a desired menu option, press Alt+ the underlined letter of the desired menu pad to open the pull-down menu, and then press the underlined letter that corresponds to the desired menu option. For example, to open a file, press Alt+F (to open the File menu), followed by the letter O (for the Open option).

If you open a menu and then decide that you would rather do something else, you can cancel the menu selection. From the keyboard, press the Esc key. Or, with the mouse, you can click anywhere outside of the opened menu.

Visual FoxPro Toolbars

Visual FoxPro now offers toolbars as part of its user interface. Various ones are used throughout FoxPro; and for the developer, there is a toolbar class to permit the insertion of toolbars into the user interface created for—and distributed in—custom applications.

Toolbars offer a quick way to activate desired behavior once the icons have been mastered. They've become part of the expected look for modern Windows programs. To this end, Microsoft has included a standard toolbar that shares many common icons with its other Windows applications.

Also like other Windows programs, you can dock the toolbars along the side of any screen by dragging the toolbar to that side. The toolbar can also float stand-alone on the screen; you can alter its shape by pulling on the sides of the toolbar.

NOTE

To drag a toolbar, you must grab a portion of the toolbar real estate that is not occupied by an icon on the toolbar.

If tooltips is activated (see the View | Toolbars menu entry), when you move the cursor over a toolbar icon and hesitate for a few seconds, a text description of the icon will display (by the way, you can use tooltips in your Visual FoxPro programs, too).

Right Mouse Clicks

Following the new user interface standard for Windows 95 programs, Visual FoxPro uses the right mouse button to bring up pop-up menus that present actions or options appropriate for the item on which you right-clicked.

The pop-up menus appear near the point of clicking to further associate the actions with the item on which you right-clicked.

As mentioned earlier, this is part of the general user interface and an exhaustive description of all pop-ups would be beyond the scope of this book (and the patience of you, the reader). As an introduction to these, however, we will present the pop-up menus shown in a couple of typical situations.

On the Project Manager

A right-mouse click on the Project Manager brings up the following pop-up menu:

Expand All   Expands all the lists found under the tabs. Equivalent to double-clicking wherever a plus sign (+) is displayed.

Include	Exclude	Toggles between a file being included in the application when built, or excluded from the build and referenced only for project completeness.
Set Main	Marks a file as containing the starting point for the application.
Rename	Brings up a dialog box that enables you to rename the file that was highlighted when you right-mouse clicked.
Edit Description	Brings up the description dialog box, which is used for putting developer comments in.
Project Info	Brings up the Project Information dialog box, making it available for editing project information and setting project options.
Code Page	Enables you to set or change the code page. The code page is used to provide presentation information for the display and sorting of characters.
Help	Brings up context-sensitive help.

On Any Toolbar

A right-mouse click on any toolbar brings up the following pop-up menu:

Color Palette	Toggles the display of the Color Palette toolbar.
Database Designer	Toggles the display of the Database Designer toolbar.
Form Controls	Toggles the display of the Form Controls toolbar.
Form Designer	Toggles the display of the Form Designer toolbar.
Layout	Toggles the display of the Layout toolbar.
Print Preview	Toggles the display of the Print Preview toolbar.
Query Designer	Toggles the display of the Query Designer toolbar.
Report Controls	Toggles the display of the Report Controls toolbar.
Report Designer	Toggles the display of the Report Designer toolbar.
Standard	Toggles the display of the Standard toolbar.
View Designer	Toggles the display of the View Designer toolbar.
Toolbars	Brings up the Toolbars dialog box, which is used to set which toolbars are initially displayed at startup, and the characteristics of the toolbars such as color, use of tooltips, and so on.
Customize	Brings up a dialog box used to customize the contents of each of the toolbars. You can add or remove specific icons from the toolbars.

On the Form Designer

When in the Form Designer, a right-click with the mouse results in a pop-up menu whose choices vary depending on where the cursor is in the Form Designer when you click the mouse.

Common Pop-Up Menu Items

When the mouse cursor is in Form Designer, the following pop-up menus are brought up:

Properties	Displays the Properties dialog box if it's not up, and then brings it to the front and shifts focus to it.
Builders	Brings up the builder appropriate for the item (the form, or a control) with the focus at the time of right clicking.
Code	Brings up the code snippet for the control with the focus.
Help	Brings up context-sensitive help.

Additional Menu Entries When Not On a Control

When the mouse cursor is in Form Designer but the area it is over does not have a control, a right mouse click brings up the following pop-up menu items in addition to the common ones just listed:

Run	Runs the current form.
Paste	Pastes the control that is on the Clipboard onto the form (see Cut and Copy in the following section).
Data Environment	Brings up the Data Environment dialog box.

Additional Menu Entries When Right-Clicking On a Control

When the mouse cursor is in Form Designer, and it's over a control, a right mouse click brings up the following pop-up menu items in addition to the common ones listed earlier:

Cut	Cuts the control from the form and places it on the Clipboard (see Paste in preceding section).
Copy	Copies the control placing it on the Clipboard (see Paste in preceding section).

Menu Entries When Right-Clicking a Property On the Properties Page

When the mouse cursor is on the Properties Page of the Form Designer, a right mouse click brings up the following pop-up menu:

Reset to default	Resets the property to its default condition.
Help	Brings up context-sensitive help.

These listings were intended only to illustrate the characteristics of the right mouse click additions to the user interface. You've been paying for that right mouse button all these years; now it's used for something!

Drag-and-Drop Support

Visual FoxPro is dripping with drag and drop (excuse the alliteration, I couldn't resist). The combination of the Project Manager, Form Designer, and the drag-and-drop functionality make creating forms almost effortless. Again, this is a capability so pervasive and so powerful there is no way it can be appreciated except to experiment.

To illustrate the potential, bring up a project (any project) with data tables contained in it. The Ecology project you received with this book will work fine. Now bring up the Form Designer and arrange the Project Manager and Form Designer side by side. To add a field from the data tables to your form, grab the field from the Project Manager and drag it to your form, dropping it where you want it located. Easy, right? Try this one now: Instead of a field, grab the table name and drag it to your form. You've just created a grid (a well-behaved, and more powerful type of browse) and you've integrated it with your form.

FoxPro 2.6 coders spent literally weeks writing code to coordinate browse windows and read windows. Presenting them to the user in (what appeared to be) a single window required a resident FoxPro guru. I can't count the pages of text written about achieving this browse/read coordination. Those days are gone. And good riddance.

About Dialog Boxes

Dialog boxes are the common way Windows programs lead the user through the program. They are a nice way to collect context-specific information and actions in a visually cohesive way. The user can switch back and forth among many dialog boxes and instantly understand where he is in the program. Often, menu selections lead to dialog boxes.

When selected, a menu option that is followed by an ellipsis (...) displays a dialog box that asks for additional information. Dialog boxes contain the specific settings related to the chosen command, along with the assumptions that Visual FoxPro makes for that command. Figure 2.9 shows the dialog box that appears when you choose File | Print Setup. You can select OK (by clicking the OK button or pressing Enter) to accept the settings shown in the dialog box, or you can change any of them. Dialog boxes vary as to the available options within them, but they all contain some or all of the elements described in the following paragraphs.

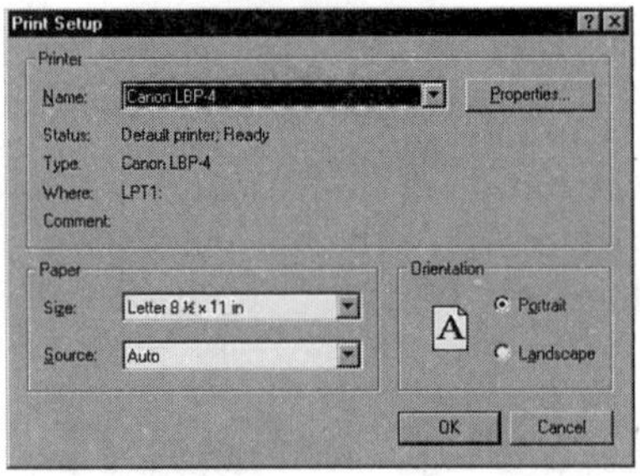

FIGURE 2.9.

The Print Setup dialog box.

Command Buttons

Command buttons (such as OK and Cancel buttons in Figure 2.9) are rectangular buttons that implement commands or other actions or display an additional dialog box. Most dialog boxes contain OK, Cancel, or Close command buttons, which are used to confirm or cancel an action. When the term in a command button is followed by an ellipsis, choosing that button causes another dialog box to appear. A command button labeled Options indicates that more options are available if you select the button.

Option Groups

Option groups (sometimes referred to as radio buttons), such as the Portrait and Landscape buttons in Figure 2.9, are controls that enable the selection of one option out of a group of mutually exclusive options. The chosen option is filled in while the other unchosen options are empty.

Text Boxes

Text boxes are rectangles that accept text you enter in response to a prompt, such as a filename or a numeric value for a margin setting. Text boxes that accept numeric values might also have double arrows at the right edge of the box (also known as *spinners*). Mouse users can click the arrows to increase or decrease the value entered. Text boxes are sometimes combined with list boxes (described in the next section) to form *combo boxes*. In a combo box, you can either type your selection in the text box or choose a selection from the list box.

List Boxes

List boxes (such as the Name, Size, and Source boxes in Figure 2.9) contain lists of available choices, such as filenames or font styles. Some list boxes display all possible choices, along with a scrollbar that enables you to view the choices. Other list boxes are called drop-down boxes, which initially show just one choice. To see additional choices, you click the down arrow at the side of the list box or tab to the list box and press the down-arrow key.

Check Boxes

A check box is a small square with associated descriptive text. It indicates an active/inactive, on/off, yes/no, or true/false type of condition. The check box contains a small check mark to indicate when the condition listed beside it is active (on, yes, true). If the condition is inactive (off, no, false), the square is blank. If the check box is disabled, the text is dimmed.

Check boxes can also appear as picture buttons. Each condition—active, inactive, disabled— can have its own picture (.BMP or .DIB) associated with the condition. Pressing an inactive button changes the button to active; pressing an active button changes it to inactive.

Working with Dialog Boxes

With the keyboard, you can move within a dialog box by using the Tab key and the Shift+Tab keys, or by pressing Alt+ the underlined letter of an option name. You can choose the OK and Cancel buttons by pressing Enter (for OK) or Esc (for Cancel). You can open list boxes from the keyboard by using the Tab key to move to the desired list box, and then pressing the down-arrow key to open the list. Once the list is open, you can navigate within it with the up- and down-arrow keys. When the desired option is highlighted within the list, press Enter to select it.

Mouse users have less of a hassle—with the mouse, just click the desired option. To turn the option buttons or check boxes on or off, click the desired button or box. To open a list box, click the arrow anywhere within the box.

The Available Visual FoxPro Menu Options

The following sections provide a summary of the Visual FoxPro menu options. Keep in mind that where ellipses appear with the named commands, a dialog box appears with more options when the command is chosen.

The File Menu

The File menu (shown in Figure 2.8) enables you to create new files, open existing files, and save changes to files. Various options within the File menu also provide access to system hardware such as disk drives and printers. The following options are available from the File menu:

New	This option displays the New dialog box (see Figure 2.10) from which you can select a desired file type to create— Project, Database, Table, Query, Connection, View, Remote View, Form, Report, Label, Program, Class, Text File, or Menu. (The specifics about each file type are discussed throughout this book.)

FIGURE 2.10.

The New dialog box.

| Open | This option displays the Open dialog box (see Figure 2.11), which you can use to open an existing file. You can use the Drive and Directory list boxes that appear in the Open dialog box to browse among the different disk drives and directories. File types appear in the order of their extensions. You can click in the Files of type box to choose a different file type to open. When you do this, the extension changes correspondingly. |

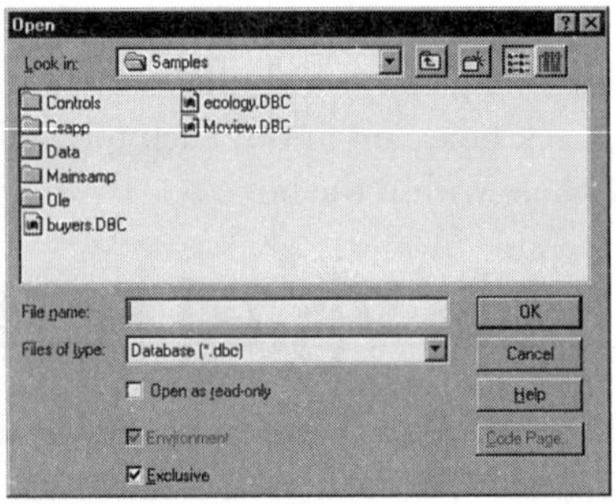

FIGURE 2.11.

The Open dialog box.

Close	This option closes the current window and removes it from the Visual FoxPro desktop.
Save	This option saves the active file and writes any changes to disk without closing the active file. If more than one file is open under Visual FoxPro, choosing the Save option saves only the file that's in the active window.
Save As	This option displays the Save As... dialog box, which you can use to copy the active file to disk under a new filename.
Save As Class	(Can be used only if the Form Designer is on the screen and has the focus.) This option displays the Save Class dialog box, which is used to save the characteristics of the selected controls, or the entire form, as a named class.

Revert	Use this option to abandon all modifications to the open file and to return to the last saved version of the file. Before this happens, Visual FoxPro asks if you want to discard the changes you've made to the file. In effect, this is an alternative to closing a file without saving the changes and then reopening the file.
Import	This option opens the Import dialog box and enables you to import information from other sources. (See Figure 2.12.)

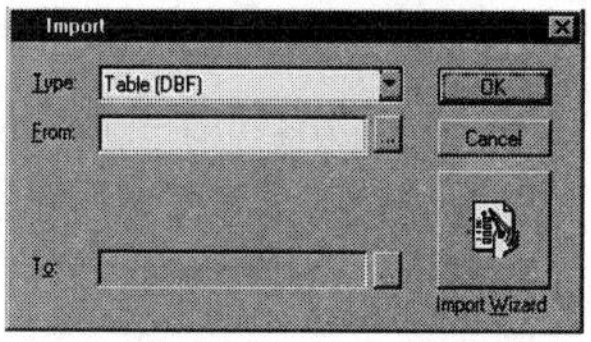

FIGURE 2.12.

The Import dialog box.

Export	This option opens the Export dialog box and enables you to export information from Visual FoxPro. (See Figure 2.13.)

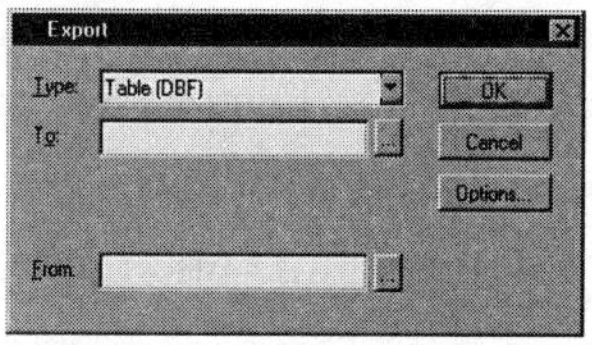

FIGURE 2.13.

The Export dialog box.

Page Setup	This menu pick is used to invoke the Page Setup dialog box. This is where print options such as margins, printable area, and number of columns in a report can be set. The Print Setup dialog box can be reached from this pick.
Print Preview	The Print Preview is used to show how a report will look when printed.
Print	This option displays the Print dialog box. (See Figure 2.14.) You can use the options in this dialog box to print the contents of the active window or to print the contents of a file that is not open (in which case you click the File button and choose the desired file from the dialog box that appears). You can also choose options such as whether line numbers appear with the printed file, and whether page ejects should be sent to the printer before or after printing starts. The Print Setup dialog box can be reached from this selection also.

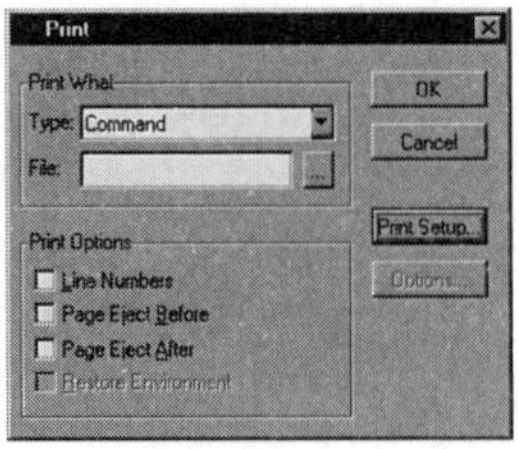

FIGURE 2.14.

The Print dialog box.

Send   This option is used to send information to another application
                    through Microsoft Mail, Microsoft Exchange, or other MAPI-
                    compliant mail system (if it is installed on your system).

Exit   This option closes Visual FoxPro and exits to Windows.

The Edit Menu

The various options of the Edit menu provide editing functions. Most Edit menu options relate to the editing of text, but the Insert Object, Change Link, and Convert To Static options
are specifically used with object linking and embedding (OLE) objects. The Edit menu OLE
options are available only for a general field of an opened table. General fields can be used to
store different types of Windows data, such as pictures or sound. (General fields are discussed
in more detail in Chapter 3.) The Edit menu contains the following options when you are editing
a table:

Undo   This option reverses your most recent editing action.

Redo   This option reverses your most recent undo.

Cut   This option removes selected text and places it in the Clip-
                    board.

Copy   This option duplicates the selected text and places an image of
                    it in the Clipboard.

Paste   This option places cut or copied text (the contents of the
                    Clipboard) at the cursor location.

Paste Special   This option displays a Paste Special dialog box. You can use
                    the options in this dialog box to move OLE objects to general
                    fields.

Clear   This option removes the selected text without placing it in the
                    Clipboard.

Select All   This option selects all controls or text in the active window
                    (except for browse windows, where only the current field's
                    data is selected), or all the controls on a report.

Find   This option displays the Find dialog box, which can be used to
                    search for text.

Replace	This option is used to replace an entry which you've searched for using the Find option.
GoTo Line	(Can be used only if a text window is on the screen and has the focus.) This option displays the GoTo Line dialog box, which can be used to move the cursor to a specified line number of a text file. This option is typically used when you are editing program files.
Insert Object	This option displays the Insert Object dialog box, which can be used to insert an OLE object into a general field.
Object	This option activates an OLE object.
Links	This option enables you to modify the links created in Visual FoxPro.

The View Menu

The View menu enables you to see the available options used to control the views in Visual FoxPro. The list that follows explains the purpose of the various options of the View menu. Also, note that many of these menu options are not available (they will appear dimmed) until a database is active. Also note that, as was discussed earlier when the FoxPro menu bars were introduced, menu options can change based on what activities are underway and the type of the active window. For example, when Visual FoxPro is first started, the only pick found under the View menu pad is Toolbars....

Because the View menu is a common menu pad across almost all Windows products, and because it is always present as a pad on the FoxPro menus, I have collected a representative listing of changes to the View menu I would expect you to see given the active window with the focus.

View Menu Options at Startup

Toolbars	This option enables you to turn toolbars on and off and set options such as icon size (large or small), color or shades of gray, and Tooltips (on or off).

Additional View Menu Options with Open and Selected Table

Browse	This option opens a browse window for the active data table.
Edit	This option changes the presentation of the table from browse mode into edit mode (note that "edit mode" used to be called "change mode" in FoxPro 2.6).
Append Mode	This option enables you to add records to a table.

Database Designer	This option is used to invoke the Database Designer to modify the current table.
Table Designer	This option is used to invoke the Table Designer to modify the current table.
Grid Lines	This option enables you to turn the grid lines on or off in the browse window.

Additional View Menu Options with Report Designer Active

Design	Presents the report in design mode, which enables you to modify the report definition.
Preview	Presents the current report in the Print Preview window.
Data Environment	Displays the Data Environment Designer for the current report.
Report Controls Toolbar	Displays the Report Controls toolbar when the option is turned on (a check mark appears). You can add the controls found on this toolbar to a report.
Layout Toolbar	Displays the Layout toolbar when the option is turned on.
Color Palette Toolbar	Displays the Color Palette toolbar when the option is turned on.
Report Preview Toolbar	Displays the Report Preview toolbar when in the Preview window the option is turned on.
Grid Lines	When turned on, displays reference grid lines on the report when in design mode.
Show Position	When turned on, displays current positions of the cursor or a selected control on the report when in design mode.

The Tools Menu

The Tools menu is used to activate wizards, to create macros, and to perform different editing and debugging tasks. The following list explains the purpose of the various options of the Tools menu.

Wizards	This option enables you to choose one of the different wizards to quickly create a table, query, or any other item listed on the Wizards menu. Note that this menu pick cascades to a submenu that lists the various wizards. You know that it is a cascading menu by the appearance of a right-facing dark triangle on the left side of the menu option.

Spelling	Where available, this menu option launches a spelling checker, which is used to check the spelling of text.
Macros	This option opens the Macro dialog box, which enables you to create or run a macro.
Class Browser	(Only available in the Professional Edition.) This option launches the class browser, which is used to examine class members found in visual classes.
Trace Window	This option opens the Trace window, which is used to find bugs when writing programs.
Debug Window	This option opens the Debug window.
Options	This option opens the Options dialog box, which enables you to set and change different options for Visual FoxPro.

The Program Menu

The Program menu contains options you'll find useful when running or writing programs in Visual FoxPro. The options include the following:

Do	This option displays the Do dialog box, which is used to run a program or application.
Cancel	This option ends program execution and returns control to Visual FoxPro.
Resume	This option continues the operation of a suspended program.
Suspend	This option is used to pause program execution and to return to interactive Visual FoxPro.
Compile	This option displays the Compile dialog box, which is used to convert a program's source code to object code.

The Window Menu

You can use the various Window menu options to work with the windows on the Visual FoxPro desktop. The menu provides the following options:

Arrange All	This option rearranges all windows, placing them as non-overlapped tiles inside the main window.
Hide	This option hides the current active window (makes the window invisible without closing it).
Clear	This option clears text from the current window.
Cycle	This option changes the focus from the current active window to the next open window in the windows list making it the active window.

Command Window	This option brings the Command window to the front.
View Window	This option displays the View window. You can use the View window to establish relationships between tables and to change various settings within Visual FoxPro.
window list	This portion of the menu contains a list of all windows currently open on the Visual FoxPro desktop. You can choose any window by name to bring it to the front and grant it the focus.

The Help Menu

The Help menu contains information about Visual FoxPro features, support, and special topics under the following options:

Contents	This option displays a table of contents containing the Help topics.
Search For Help On	This option displays the Help Search dialog box, which you can use to find help on a specific topic.
Technical Support	This option displays help regarding technical support as well as common questions about Visual FoxPro.
Office Compatible	This option displays information about Microsoft Office compatibility.
About Microsoft FoxPro	This option displays the version number of FoxPro.

Summary

This chapter provides an overview of the user interface that comes with Visual FoxPro for Windows. Probably the most important point to realize is that with Visual FoxPro, you are not locked into a single style of doing things. Depending on your comfort level and your familiarity with the program, you can use commands, menu options, or the Project Manager to work in Visual FoxPro; however, a familiarity with all three methods gives you the most flexibility.

As is common with computer programs in general, and graphical user interfaces in particular, we encourage you to play around in the FoxPro environment to get a better feel for the lay of the land.

We hope that what has become apparent from this overview of the Visual FoxPro user interface is the depth of the changes which have been wrought by Microsoft. FoxPro is now a full member of the Windows family of applications. And even more exciting for developers is the prospect of now being able to produce real Windows applications; applications with all the modern Windows "bells and whistles" using an old friend.

Creating and Working with Tables

IN THIS CHAPTER

Visual FoxPro is a development environment with special tools and a programming language that is specialized for dealing with large amounts of data. This data has to exist someplace within the computer, and that place is in data tables. Because the major functionality of applications developed with Visual FoxPro is managing data, the attention paid to the design and creation of these tables is paramount to the success of the development effort.

Relational Database Concepts

You have probably heard the phrase Relational Database Management System (RDBMS) before. What exactly does this phrase mean? The concept of relational databases was born in the mind of Dr. E.F. Codd in the 1970s. Dr. Codd is a mathematician who used mathematical set theory to define a structure for handling data that would enable consistent data storage and flexible data retrieval.

You can realize all the power of relational databases by carefully designing your tables. There are some concepts and rules that you need to know in order to effectively design these tables for your data needs.

Examine some terminology that will make it easier to discuss tables and databases later in this chapter. Table 3.1 defines some of the words that are used to describe relational database components. The two columns titled Relational Term and VFP Term show you the comparable terminology in relational theory and Visual FoxPro common usage.

Table 3.1. Relational term definitions.

Relational Term	VFP Term	Definition
Entity	Table	Person, place, thing, or concept about which you need to record information.
Attribute	Field	A piece of information that is descriptive of an entity.
Relationship	Relationship	An association between two entities.
Primary Key	Primary Key	An attribute or set of attributes that identifies a specific occurrence of an entity. The primary key identifies a specific row or record in the table. The primary key is absolutely unique within the table and is never NULL. Ideally, primary keys do not change value during the life of the record.
Candidate Key	Candidate Key	Attribute or set of attributes that meet the requirements for being the primary key, but that are not being used in the role of the primary key.

Relational Term	VFP Term	Definition
Foreign Key	Foreign Key	Attribute or set of attributes that identifies the entity with which another entity is associated. For example, in an Invoice table the Customer Number field is a foreign key because it identifies the customer that a particular invoice is associated with.
Key Business Rules	Triggers	Conditions under which primary and foreign keys can be inserted, updated, or deleted.
Domain	None	The definition of a column or attribute. Describes the data type, length, format (or mask), uniqueness, allowability of NULL, legal values, default value, and meaning of an attribute.

The following eight sections cover each of these terms and expand on each definition in Table 3.1. These sections examine the concepts and the rest of this chapter explains how to implement these concepts in Visual FoxPro.

Entity

When you meet with users to analyze their database needs, you would collect a lot of information from them regarding how their business works. You would probably record this information in notes that you took during interviews with the users. In these notes you would be able to identify a number of nouns such as customer, employee, invoice, purchase order, and so on. These nouns are your entities and these entities, can be represented in your database design by tables or DBF files.

Attribute

In your notes you would also likely see descriptive items about the nouns. For example, customers have names, addresses, and credit limits. These descriptive items are the fields in your tables, or the attributes of your entities.

Relationship

There would also be references in the notes to issues such as, invoices are for one customer only, or purchase orders specify the vendor for the items ordered. These phrases define the relationships in your design; invoices are related to customers and purchase orders are related to vendors.

Primary Key

The primary key is often misunderstood. The primary key has only one purpose, which is to uniquely identify a specific record in a table. There are no other required jobs for this key. Primary keys can be divided into two groups, those that occur naturally and those that are system-generated.

Naturally occurring primary keys are attributes or fields that are part of the record even if they aren't the primary key; for example, the Social Security number for an employee or the customer number for a customer. Either of these fields would be part of the record even if they weren't being used as the primary key.

System-generated primary keys are fields whose only reason for being in the table is to be unique and act as the primary key. These fields have no meaning outside of their role as the primary key. You create the values for these fields in your program code and the user probably doesn't even know they exist.

> **TIP**
>
> If the primary key has meaning to the users, at some time they might want to change its value. Changing the value of a primary key can cause all sorts of relational problems. The simplest way to avoid these problems is to use system-generated primary keys exclusively. These keys have no meaning to the user and therefore the user has no reason to change them.

Candidate Key

If you think about the possible structure of an employee table you will realize that there are a number of important fields that could be the primary key, such as Social Security Number, Clock Number, and the system-generated key if you made one. You need to select one of these to be the primary key. Those that you don't choose are candidate keys. Later in this chapter you will see that Visual FoxPro gives you tools to handle these candidate keys.

Foreign Key

In order to manage relationships between tables you need to be able to use the value of a field in one table to point to a record in another table. For example, you need to have a field in an invoice table that enables you to find the customer for a particular invoice. In this example, that field would be storing the primary key value for your customer table. This field, in the invoice table, is called a foreign key.

Key Business Rules

In the realm of relational database management there are some integrity issues that can arise. Earlier in this section you learned the idea of primary keys, foreign keys, and relationships based on these keys. Consider the relationship between an invoice table and a customer table. You have a field in the invoice table that holds the primary key value for a particular customer record in the customer table. What would happen if the customer to which an invoice points is deleted from the customer table? You would have an orphaned invoice that does not relate to any existing customer. Orphaned child records can pose serious problems to the integrity of your overall database.

As a database designer, you can handle this problem in one of two ways: either don't allow the customer to be deleted when there are invoices (a *restricted delete*) or delete all of the invoices for a customer being deleted (a *cascading delete*). Either of these approaches meets your relational concerns, but the business folks might have something to say about deleting all of a customer's invoices.

When you face this type of issue, you need to go to the business people involved in the project to get a ruling from them as to how to approach the situation. The rules that the business people give you are called the *key business rules*, because they are rules of the business regarding how to handle actions that affect the keys (primary and foreign) in the tables.

These key business rules affect how new records (new primary keys) are inserted, how records are deleted (the removal of primary keys), and how existing records (primary or foreign keys) are updated. Visual FoxPro contains triggers in the database container to handle these key business rules. Triggers are examined in detail later in this chapter in the "Referential Integrity" section.

Domain

Domain really refers to the universe of valid values that a column (field) can take on legally within your design. Imagine that there is a great big bucket containing pieces of paper and that each piece of paper has on it one of the valid values that a particular column (field) can have. This bucket has one piece of paper for every conceivable valid value for the column (field). This bucket contains the *domain* for that field.

The definition in Table 3.1 lists the aspects of a domain definition for a field. All of these items are necessary to understand and use the field in your application, but the phrase "the meaning of the attribute" is more important than the others.

The meaning of your fields is the item that is most often forgotten when documenting your design. This meaning can be documented with a simple sentence or two describing what the field contains. An example of field meanings is shown in Table 3.2.

Table 3.2. An example of column meanings for a customer table.

Column	Meaning
Cust_ID	The primary key for this table. System-generated and not seen or used by the users.
Cust_no	The customer number, a candidate key, which is used by the users to access the customer records.
Company	The company name for this customer.
Address	The street address where this customer is located.
City	The city where this customer is located.
State	The state where this customer is located.
Contact1	The name of a contact person at this customer.
Contact2	The name of a contact person at this customer.
CredLim	The credit limit for this customer.
Terms	A code, which references the Terms table, representing the sales terms for this customer.

You can see that the meaning doesn't have to be pages of text, but just a sentence or two describing the contents of the field.

Documenting and Checking Your Design

Now that you know the definitions of the major areas of relational design, you can review the information you have about the application you are going to build and design your database. You can lay out the tables and their fields, identify the keys (primary and foreign), and define the relationships between the tables. In order to complete your design, you'll need a mechanism for diagramming the design and a process for checking the design for accuracy.

Diagramming Your Design

You have met with the users and accumulated many pages of notes. You have analyzed those notes and identified the tables and fields, the primary and foreign keys, the key business rules, and the domains for your database. This analysis is probably held on many pages of notes, as well as partly in your head.

To understand your design, it is very helpful to have a method of drawing a picture that shows you the tables, the relationships between tables, the primary and foreign keys, and the fields in the tables. One methodology used to draw this type of diagram is called Entity-Relationship (E-R) diagramming. Let's examine a subset of E-R diagramming that will meet your needs.

E-R diagrams use boxes, lines, arrowheads, and text to draw a picture of a design. Figure 3.1 shows the components of E-R diagrams.

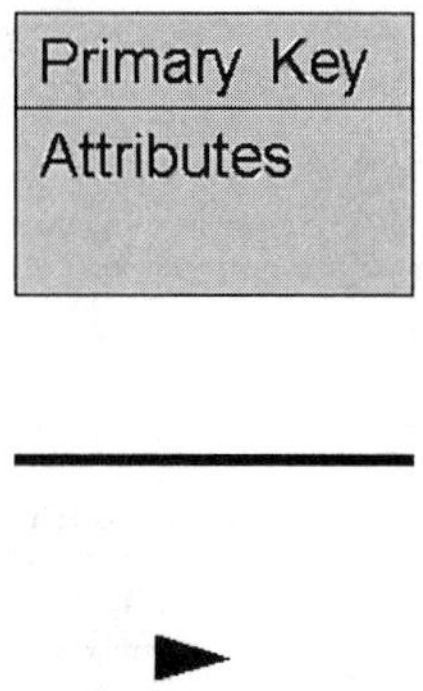

FIGURE 3.1.

The components of Entity-Relationship diagrams.

Figure 3.1 shows that you use boxes to represent your entities or tables. These boxes have a horizontal line in them, above which you write the names of the fields that comprise the primary key for the table. Below the line you write in the names of the other fields in the table.

You draw a line connecting the two boxes to represent relationships between tables. These relationships can be one of three possible types: one-to-one, one-to-many, or many-to-many. These types of relationships describe the number of records from each table that can be related to records in the other table. In the E-R diagrams you designate the nature of the relationship by putting an arrowhead on the many side of the lines connecting the related tables.

The following lists examples of the different types of relationships:

- One-to-one. An Inventory table can be related to a Location table one-to-one. In this relationship, an inventory item is located in one location and a location holds only one inventory item.

- One-to-many. A Customer table is related to an Invoice table one-to-many. In this relationship, one customer can have many invoices, but one invoice is related to only one customer.

- Many-to-many. An Invoice table is related to an Inventory table many-to-many. In this relationship, one Invoice can sell many inventory items and one inventory item can be sold on many invoices. This particular type of relationship causes problems when it is implemented because most database products can't handle the many-to-many relationship well. Later in this section you will see how to resolve this problem by using an intersection table.

You can further clarify your diagram by placing labels on the elements of the diagram, as shown in Figure 3.2.

Labels placed outside the boxes can be used to name the tables, and labels placed on the lines can identify the basis for the relationship. Figure 3.3 shows a real, descriptive E-R diagram.

FIGURE 3.2.

Adding labels to your diagram can further clarify the meaning.

FIGURE 3.3.

A real, descriptive E-R diagram.

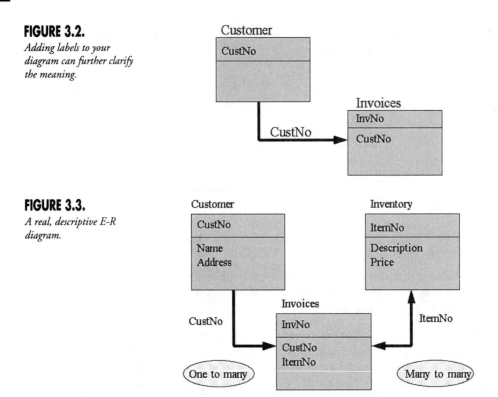

The diagram in Figure 3.3 gives you a lot of information. You can see that it is a diagram of an invoicing system that has tables for customers, invoices, and inventory. The Customer table has CustNo as its primary key, and the Invoice and Inventory tables have InvNo and ItemNo for primary keys, respectively. Each table also has a number of non-key fields.

The relationships are clearly diagrammed to show you that customers are related to invoices on a one-to-many basis, and that invoices are related to inventory on a many-to-many basis. The labels tell you that the Customer-Invoice relationship is based on CustNo and the Invoice-Inventory relationship uses ItemNo.

The Invoice-Inventory relationship is a many-to-many relationship. Earlier in this section it was stated that these types of relationships can cause implementation problems and that those problems could be avoided by using an intersecting table. An insertsecting table has one record in it for each "intersection" between the two many-to-many related tables. Let's see what these intersecting tables are all about.

Figure 3.4 shows the Invoice-Inventory section of the diagram in Figure 3.3 after an intersecting table has been added.

FIGURE 3.4.

The Invoice-Inventory relationship with an intersecting table added, which reduces the many-to-many relationship.

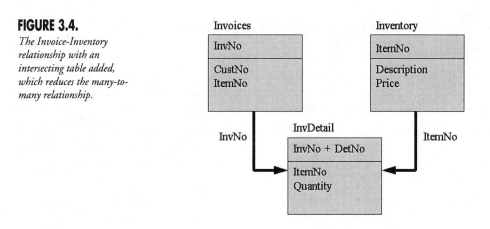

The intersecting table in Figure 3.4 is the InvDetail table. This table will hold one record for each intersection between the Invoice and Inventory tables. Adding this table to the diagram reduces the many-to-many relationship between Invoices and Inventory to two one-to-many relationships: Invoices-InvDetail and Inventory-InvDetail. This example is fairly easy to visualize because the idea of detail lines on an invoice, as represented by the intersecting table, is common; however, in your actual work you might encounter situations in which the intersecting table doesn't have any real-world counterpart and exists only to resolve the many-to-many relationship.

If you take the time to do this diagramming your application development project will be much more efficient. You can show these diagrams to, and discuss them with, the users. By reviewing the diagrams with the people who will actually use the system, you can find out very early in the project any misunderstandings and missing items, making it easier, and less costly, to fix the design.

Normalizing Your Design

After you have identified and designed the tables you will need you must validate those table designs. You use the process of normalization to evaluate your design and identify any potential problems.

Normalization is a process in which you successively examine each table and its fields to find any data redundancies or inconsistencies that might lie in the design. This process also prescribes the design changes to be made to eliminate these problems.

Before looking at the steps involved in normalizing your design in detail, let's answer the question of "why normalize at all"? There are four major reasons to go through the normalization process. These reasons are listed in Table 3.3.

Table 3.3. The reasons to normalize your table designs.

Reason	Explanation
Disk Space	Minimize the disk space required to store your data. Normalizing your design will eliminate the storage of redundant data as well as reduce wasted space by fields that are often empty.
Data Integrity	Minimize the possibility of data inconsistencies being introduced to the system. By ensuring that every piece of data can be stored in only one place, you eliminate the possibility of disagreement between values in different places.
Anomalies	Reduce the chance that insert, update, or delete anomalies can get into the system. To avoid anomolies when you manage data, make sure that all the fields in a table are dependent on that table's primary key, and make sure there are no fields in a table that really belong in some other table.
Stability	Maximize the stability of the design. This does not refer to stability issues such as disk file damage; rather, it means you should make sure that the system can have functional components added to it later without requiring modifications in the structures of existing tables.

The process of normalization is divided into six steps called the Normal Forms. These Normal Forms are progressive; you cannot apply the Second Normal Form until the table complies with the First Normal Form.

First Normal Form (1NF)

The First Normal Form (1NF) rule says "Reduce tables to first normal by removing repeating or multivalued fields to another, child, table." Figure 3.5 shows a diagram for a customer table.

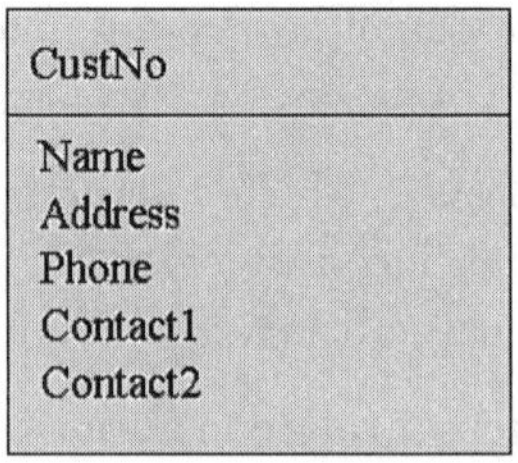

FIGURE 3.5.

A customer table.

To see the problem with the table in Figure 3.5 you need to review the domains for the fields, shown in Table 3.4.

Table 3.4. The domains for the customer table fields.

Field	Meaning
CustNo	The primary key for this table. System-generated and not seen or used by the users.
Name	The company name for this customer.
Address	The street address where this customer is located.
Phone	The phone number for this customer.
Contact1	The name of a contact person at this customer.
Contact2	The name of a contact person at this customer.

In review of these domains you can see that the fields Contact1 and Contact2 have the same domain. If two fields have the same domain, even though they may be two physically different fields in the table structure they are, in fact, the same field logically. They represent a multivalued field: one field that needs to store multiple values for the same record. You can eliminate this problem by creating another table in which to store the contact names and relating that table back to the customer table. Figure 3.6 shows this new design.

FIGURE 3.6.

The customer table with its related contacts table. The multivalued field is removed.

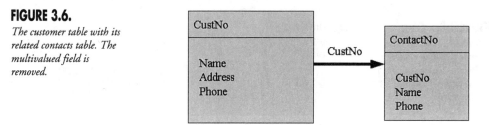

This new design reduces the disk space requirement because you no longer need to allow space for two contact names for every customer even if a customer has no contacts or only one contact. It also increases the stability of the design by enabling a virtually unlimited number of contact names to be recorded for any customer. The CustNo field in the Contacts table is a foreign key referring back to the Customer table.

Second Normal Form (2NF)

The Second Normal Form (2NF) rule says, "Tables that are in 1NF can be reduced to 2NF by removing fields that are not dependent on the whole primary key."

Figure 3.7 shows an invoice line-item file that has a primary key comprised of the combination of two fields, InvNo and LineNo.

FIGURE 3.7.

An invoice line-item table.

InvNo + LineNo
CustNo ItemNo

In the invoice line-item table, there are two other fields listed, ItemNo and CustNo. These fields must be dependent on the entire primary key (both parts) in order for this table to be in 2NF.

The ItemNo field is dependent on both the InvNo and LineNo fields because you need to know both the invoice number and the line number in order to know what item you are referring to.

The CustNo field is dependent on the InvNo field because you need to know the invoice in order to know which customer this item belongs to. However, CustNo is not dependent on the LineNo field because every line on an invoice will have the same customer; therefore, it is not necessary to know the LineNo in order to know the customer.

You put this table design into 2NF by moving the CustNo field out of the Line Items table and into the Invoice table, where it is dependent on the entire primary key. Figure 3.8 shows this change.

FIGURE 3.8.

The CustNo field has been moved to the Invoice table to eliminate the non-dependent field from the Line Items table.

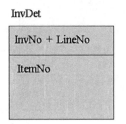
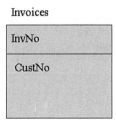

InvDet

InvNo + LineNo
ItemNo

Invoices

InvNo
CustNo

Third Normal Form (3NF)

The Third Normal Form (3NF) rule says "2NF tables can be reduced to 3NF by removing fields that are dependent on non-key fields other than candidate keys."

Figure 3.9 shows a purchase order table.

FIGURE 3.9.

A purchase order table.

PurchNo
VendNo VendCity

In the table diagrammed in Figure 3.9, you can see two non-key fields, VendNo and VendCity. VendNo is the primary key for the Vendor table. Both the VendNo and VendCity fields are dependent on the primary key for their value. You need to know what purchase order number you are concerned with to know either the vendor number or the vendor city. Are either of these fields dependent on a field other than the primary key for their value? VendCity is dependent on VendNo—if you change the VendNo then the VendCity will probably also change, therefore VendCity is dependent on a non-key field.

To put this table in 3NF, you need to get the VendCity field out of the purchase orders table. Figure 3.10 show the VendCity field being moved to the Vendor table, where it really belongs.

FIGURE 3.10.

The VendCity *field has been moved to the Vendor table.*

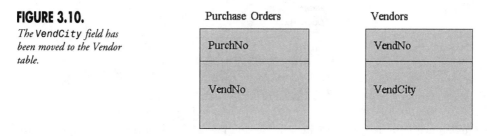

The last three normal forms apply only in very specific situations, so it is often said that you don't need to go further than Third Normal Form. This statement is true only if the situations in which the other normal forms apply don't exist.

Boyce-Codd Normal Form (BCNF)

The next normal form is called Boyce-Codd Normal Form (BCNF) and it applies only if a table has other candidate keys in addition to the primary key. If your table has only one candidate for the primary key then being in 3NF is the same as being in BCNF. The rule for BCNF is "3NF tables can be reduced to BCNF by ensuring that they are in 3NF for any choice of candidate key as the primary key."

For example, an employee table that has a social security number and a clock number field would have two candidate keys. If you choose to use the social security number as the primary key and you reach 3NF with this primary key, you would now go back to 1NF and work your way through the normal forms again to ensure that the table stays in 3NF if you use the clock number as the primary key.

Fourth Normal Form (4NF)

Fourth Normal Form (4NF) applies only if the primary key for a table is comprised of more than one field. If the primary key of your table is only one field, then being in BCNF is the same as being in 4NF. The rule for 4NF is "BCNF tables can be reduced to 4NF by removing any independently multivalued components of the primary key to new parent tables."

At first this rule might seem complex, but it is really quite simple. Figure 3.11 shows an example of a table for employee skills and objectives. Below the table structure is some sample data.

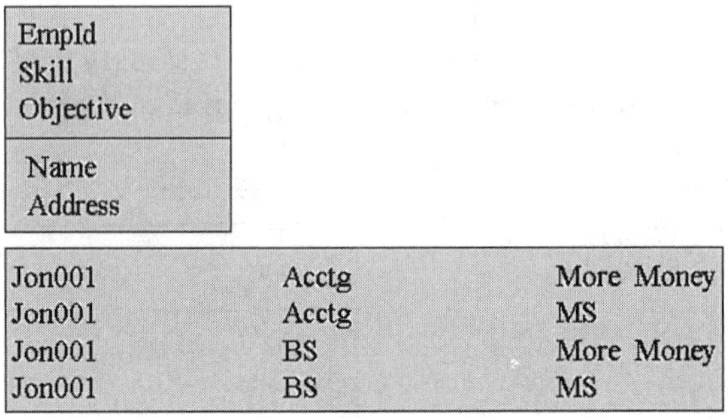

FIGURE 3.11.

The employee skill-objective table design with sample data.

EmpId		
Skill		
Objective		
Name		
Address		

Jon001	Acctg	More Money
Jon001	Acctg	MS
Jon001	BS	More Money
Jon001	BS	MS

The problem with this design lies in the primary key. Two of the three fields, `Skill` and `Objective`, can each have multiple values for a given `EmpID` and the value of `Skill` is not dependent on the value of `Objective`. Therefore, `Skill` and `Objective` are independently multivalued components of the primary key.

A look at the sample data shows where the trouble will lie. If Jon001 decides that he wants a masters degree, a new `Objective`, then you would need to add two records to the table, one for Jon001 and Acctg and one for Jon001 and BS. Just imagine what would happen later if Jon001 got his masters. Figure 3.12 shows the table design after this problem has been resolved.

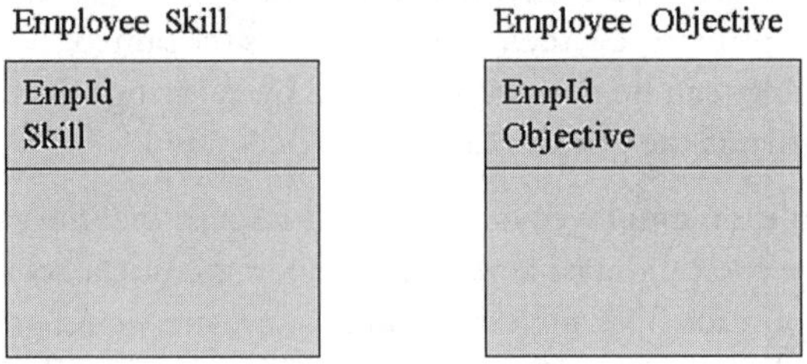

FIGURE 3.12.

The employee skill-objective design in 4NF.

Employee Skill

EmpId
Skill

Employee Objective

EmpId
Objective

Fifth Normal Form (5NF)

Fifth Normal Form (5NF) applies only if the primary key is comprised of three or more fields. If your table's primary key is two or less fields then being in 4NF is the same as being in 5NF. The 5NF rule is "4NF tables can be reduced to 5NF by removing pairwise cyclic dependencies (in primary keys comprised of three or more fields) to three or more new parent tables." This one is really a mouthful; looking at an example will make this more clear. Figure 3.13 shows a table that is used to keep track of retail store buyers, the vendors from which they buy, and the products that they buy.

FIGURE 3.13.

The buyer-vendor-product table design with sample data.

Buyer Vendor Product		

Sally	Jordache	Jeans
Sally	Jordache	Sneakers
Mary	Jordache	Jeans
Sally	Liz Claiborne	Blouses
Mary	Liz Claiborne	Blouses

You can see here the issue of "pairwise cyclic dependencies" by taking the three fields of the primary key—buyer, vendor, and product—and asking yourself what you need to know to determine the buyer. The answer is vendor and product. To determine the vendor you need to know the buyer and product. To determine the product you need to know the buyer and vendor. To know the value of any one component of the primary key you need to know the value of the other two, this is pairwise (you need to know two of the values to determine the third) cyclic (for any one value you need the other two) dependency.

A look at the sample data will show you the problem with this design. What if Liz Claiborne started to sell jeans? You would need to add two records to reflect this new vendor-product combination: one for Sally and one for Mary. Figure 13.14 shows how you can fix this design to remove the problem.

FIGURE 3.14.

Buyer-vendor-product design in 5NF.

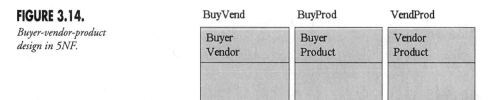

BuyVend	BuyProd	VendProd
Buyer Vendor	Buyer Product	Vendor Product

The normalization process has discovered and fixed misplaced fields, missing tables, poorly designed tables, and poorly designed primary keys. You now have a fully normalized design. You might have situations in which a fully normalized design raises some problems in other areas of the application. One common problem area is performance. Because of these possible situations, there is a concept called *denormalization*. Denormalization backs off from fully normalized design in order to deal with implementation issues.

The idea of denormalization does not indicate that the normalization process can be skipped. When you normalize your design you discover and fix a lot of problems in the design. If you skip the process you would miss these design changes and end up with some major problems later in the development of your application.

When I was in high school, I took a class in music theory and composition. This class spent two weeks studying the rules of classical harmony, making music pretty. I preferred dissonant music and asked why I had to spend this time learning the rules of classical harmony. The teacher gave me an answer that has applied to much more than music theory, "If you don't know the rules to make music pretty, how would you know what to do to make the music dissonant?"

This same idea applies to normalization; if you don't know what the fully normalized structure is, you wouldn't know what to do to denormalize it. Figure 13.15 shows an example of a situation in which you might want to denormalize the design. The top of the figure shows the 3NF design, and the bottom shows the denormalized design.

FIGURE 3.15.

A customer mailing system design.

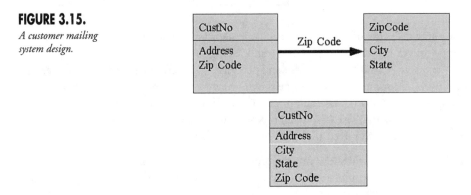

The 3NF design shows that the city and state information has been moved to a ZipCode table. This means that to produce a mailing label you need to access data in two files, Customer and ZipCode. If this design were meant for a mail-order house where they had to run 1,000,000 labels each Thursday and you discovered that it took longer to produce these labels from two tables rather than one table, you might choose to denormalized the design by moving the city and state data back into the Customer table.

Does this mean you should eliminate the ZipCode table? Not at all. Actually, the ZipCode table could be used to simplify data entry by enabling the users to type the ZIP code and having the program look up the city and state in the ZipCode table. This would eliminate data entry inconsistencies related to ZIP code, city, and state.

You now have a complete design of the data requirements for your application. It is time to investigate the tools that Visual FoxPro gives you to create the tables needed to implement this design.

Creating Tables

Visual FoxPro often provides more than one way to accomplish a particular task. In the case of creating a new table, you have two choices: the File | New menu item or the CREATE *<FileName>* command. The syntax of the CREATE *<FileName>* command is listed next.

```
CREATE [FileName ¦ ?]
```

You replace *FileName* with the name of the table that you want to create. You can use a question mark (?) instead of a filename to get Visual FoxPro to bring up its Create dialog box where you can name your table.

If you have a database open (databases are discussed in the "Creating a Database Container" section of this chapter) this new table will be added to the database.

> **NOTE**
>
> You cannot create a table with the name of an MS-DOS device. Names such as PRN, CON, COM1, COM2, LPT1, and LPT2 are all MS-DOS device names that cannot be used.

> **CAUTION**
>
> If you include hyphens in your table name the hyphens won't be displayed in the View window. This might also cause some confusion with the -> alias pointer used to refer to fields from a different work area.

Creating Tables with the Table Designer

First, use the File | New menu option to create a new table. Figure 3.16 shows the New dialog box you will see after you select File | New.

In the New dialog box select the Table option button and then click the New File command button (later in this section you will use the Table Wizard to create a new table). Figure 3.17 shows the Create dialog box.

This Create dialog box enables you to determine the name and directory that will be used to create your new table. The text box labeled Enter table name: is where you can type in the name for your table. The combo box labeled Drives: can be used to select the drive on which your file should be created, and the list box labeled Directories: is used to select the directory for your table.

FIGURE 3.16.

*The Visual FoxPro New
dialog box.*

FIGURE 3.17.

*The Visual FoxPro Create
dialog box.*

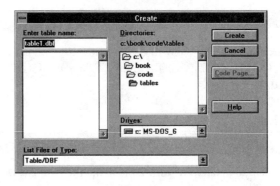

The command buttons on the right side of the Create dialog box enable you to Create your table, Cancel the creation of your table, and bring up the Visual FoxPro Help for the Create dialog box, respectively. The command button labeled Code Page is involved with international issues related to the display of the accented characters found in some languages.

You can click the Create command button to bring up the Table Designer as seen in Figure 3.18.

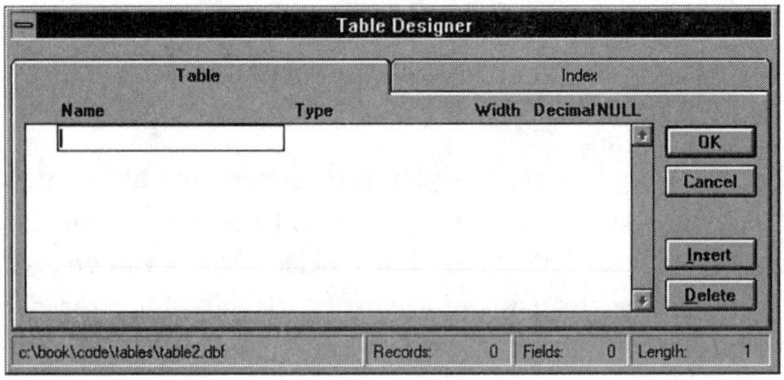

FIGURE 3.18.

*The Visual FoxPro Table
Designer.*

The Table Designer is a tabbed dialog box; it has file folder-type tabs displayed in it labeled Table and Index. These two tabs give you access to defining different aspects of your new table. Initially, you are on the Table tab, as seen in Figure 3.18.

The Table tab has a list with multiple columns labeled Name, Type, Width, Decimal, and NULL—let's call this the Fields list. To the right of this list are four command buttons labeled OK, Cancel, Insert, and Delete. Table 3.5 explains the columns in the Fields list.

Table 3.5. The Fields list in the Table Designer.

Label	Contents
Name	The name of the field. Field names can be up to 10 characters and can contain characters, digits, and underscores. Field names must begin with a character or an underscore.
Type	The data type for a field (data types are explained in Table 3.7 in this chapter).
Width	The total width of the field, including any decimal places, the decimal point, and any + or - sign for numbers. Some data types have a fixed width, which cannot be changed in this column (these are explained in Table 3.7).
Decimal	The number of decimal places for fields of type Numeric (explained in Table 3.7).
NULL	Whether or not the NULL value is allowed in a field. The NULL value is explained in "The .NULL. Value" section later in this chapter.

The command buttons in the Table Designer are explained in Table 3.6.

Table 3.6. The Table Designer command buttons.

Button Caption	Action
OK	Create the table from the entries in the Table Designer.
Cancel	Discard the Table Designer session and do not create the table.
Insert	Add a new field just before the highlighted field in the fields list.
Delete	Delete the highlighted field from the fields list.

Fill in the fields list to match the entries in Figure 3.19.

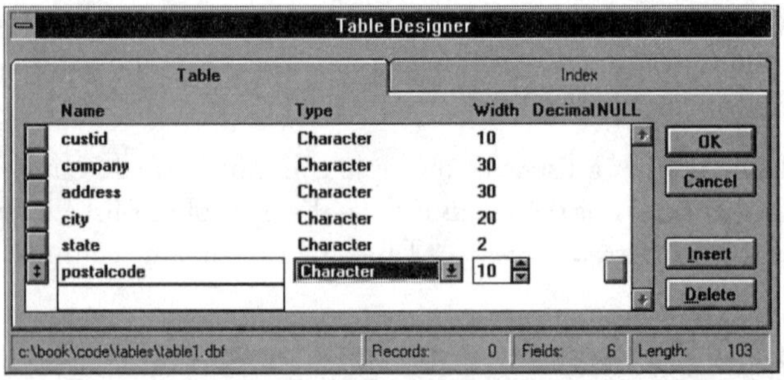

FIGURE 3.19.

The Visual FoxPro Table Designer with the Fields list filled in.

The field names are in lowercase; this will be true even if you try to type uppercase letters. The field names are case-insensitive in Visual FoxPro, so you can refer to these field names later with any case you choose regardless of the fact that they appear here in lowercase.

The Type column in the fields list is a combo box that lists all of the available data types in Visual FoxPro. You select the data type for a field from this combo box. The data types are described in Table 3.7.

Table 3.7. The Visual FoxPro data types.

Data Type	Size	Description
Character	1–254	Can contain any of the 254 ASCII characters (alpha, digits, symbols, or control characters). This is the most commonly used data type because it is able to store any character and it can be manipulated by any of the Visual FoxPro string functions.
Currency	8	Used to store currency amounts. This field type is fixed at 8 bytes. The decimal portion of the currency amount is fixed at 4 places. The range of values that this field type can store is −922337203685477.5808 to 922337203685477.5807. Yes, that is 922 trillion, 337 billion, 203 million, 685 thousand, 477 dollars, and 58.08 cents or approximately 230 times the U.S. national debt! Use this data type for currency amounts and your users will never have an amount that won't fit.

Data Type	Size	Description
Date	8	Used to store dates. These values are stored on disk in the ANSI standard date format of *yyyymmdd*. The range of dates is 01/01/100 to 12/31/9999.
DateTime	8	Month, year, date, and time to the second. The range of values is from 01/01/100 00:00:00am to 12/31/9999 11:59:59pm. Visual FoxPro has a set of functions that can extract the various parts out of the DateTime data type. SEC() gets the seconds, MINUTE() gets the minutes, HOUR() gets the hour, and TTOD() gets the date. After using TTOD() to get the date you can use DAY(), MONTH(), and YEAR() to extract those respective values from the date.
Logical	1	Boolean values of true or false. The range of values is .T. (true) or .F. (false).
Numeric	1–20	Stores integers or fractions in a range from –0.9999999999E+19 to 0.9999999999E+20. Even though the values that can be stored are very large the mathematical calculations are limited to a precision of 16 digits.
Double	8	Stores a double-precision floating-point number. The range of values is +/–4.94065645841247E-324 to +/–1.79769313486232E308. To put this range of values in perspective here's the highest number with all of the zeros: 49,406,564,584,124,700,000,000,000,000,000,000,000,000,000,000,000,000,000,000,000,000,000,000,000,000,000,000,000,000,000,000,000,000,000,000,000,000,000,000,000,000,000,000,000,000,000,000,000,000,000,000,000,000,000,000,000,000,000,000,000,000,000,000,000,000,000,000,000,000,000,000,000,000,000,000,000,000,000,000,000,000,000,000,000,000,000,000.
Float	1–20	The same as numeric. Contrary to its name, this data type does not store floating point numbers, but rather fixed decimal numbers.
General	4 (in DBF)	Stores a reference to an OLE object. When you add this data type, or a Memo or Memo Binary data type, your table will be comprised of two disk files, one

continues

Table 3.7. continued

Data Type	Size	Description
		with the .DBF extension and one with an .FPT extension. The contents of this data type is stored in the FPT file on disk.
Integer	4	Integer numbers. The range of values for integers is –2,147,483,647 to 2,147,483,646. Once a value exceeds 4 digits this data type can store that value in less disk space than the numeric data type would require.
Memo	4 (in DBF)	Reference to a block of data in the FPT file described for the General data type. Memo fields can literally contain anything that can be stored on a disk, including complete files. Most often these fields are used to store variable length textual data such as notes or comments.
Character (binary)	1-254	Used for character type data that you don't want changed across code pages; code pages are used for accented characters in some languages.
Memo (Binary)	4 (in DBF)	Used for memo fields that you don't want changed across code pages.

In the Table Designer click the OK button to save your new table. Figure 3.20 shows a message box asking if you want to input records now. Choose the No button and you will return to the Command window. You will put data in your new table later.

FIGURE 3.20.

The message box asking about inputting records now.

If you made a mistake in specifying your table structure in the Table Designer you can fix it using the MODIFY STRUCTURE command from the Command window. Before you can use the MODIFY STRUCTURE command you must open your table using either the File | Open dialog box or by using the USE command. In the Command window type the following command:

```
USE Table1
```

This command opens your table for you. Now you can type the MODIFY STRUCTURE command in the Command window.

MODIFY STRUCTURE

This command will bring you to the Table Designer with your table's structure displayed. In the Table Designer you can use the Delete and Insert buttons to remove or add fields to your design. You can also change any of the fields that are listed in the fields list.

Indexes

You will need to process the records in your table in a variety of different orders. For a customer table you might be able to see the records in alphabetical order on company name, alphabetically by state, numerical order by the balance they owe you, or even in date order by the last date you were in contact with them. The records can be in only one order physically in the table. Indexes enable you to see these records in orders other than the physical order in the table.

A Visual FoxPro index acts like the card catalog in a library. The books in the library are arranged on the shelves in a physical order based on the Dewey decimal system, yet in the card catalog you can find the books listed alphabetically by author or title. The records in your table are physically arranged in the order in which they were added to the table. An index enables you to provide an expression that is used to create a file separate from your table that provides a different order for the records. The order in the index is based on the expression that you provide when you create the index.

Indexes for a table will be dynamically maintained to reflect changes in the contents of the records as long as the indexes are open at the time of the change.

In the Table Designer select the Index tab by clicking that tab. Figure 3.21 shows the Table Designer with the index tab in front.

FIGURE 3.21.

The Index tab of the Table Designer.

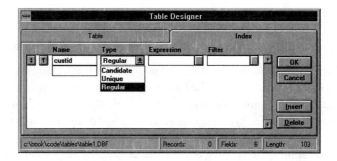

In Figure 3.21 there has already been an index name typed in and the index Type combo box has been dropped down to display the available types of indexes. These index types are described in Table 3.8.

Table 3.8. Visual FoxPro index types.

Index Type	Description
Candidate	Enforces only unique values in the field referred to in the expression and controls the order in which records are processed.
Regular	Controls the order in which records are processed. Allows duplicate values in the table for the expression.
Unique	This type of index is supported for backward compatibility with previous versions of FoxPro. Enables duplicate values to be entered in the expression field but only references one of the records in the index.

CAUTION

Using unique indexes can be hazardous to your application. These indexes do not prevent duplicate values from being entered, but they can cause those duplicate records to be difficult to locate and fix. If you have a table of customers with a unique index on the state field, this index would show you the unduplicated list of states in which you have customers. However, if you had 100 customers in New York and you edited the one customer referred to in the unique index, changing its state to New Jersey, the unique index would no longer reflect the fact that you have customers in New York until you rebuild the index.

Select Candidate as the index type for your custid index. The next column is labeled Expression and is used to enter the index expression.

The button with no caption on it to the right of the Expression column can be used to bring up the Visual FoxPro Expression Builder to assist in defining the index expression. You can type the name of the custid field in the text box in the Expression column.

The Filter column will be discussed in a while; for now, examine the two buttons to the left of the index Name column. The button on the extreme left, with the double-headed arrow on it, is an elevator button. When you have more than one index listed in the dialog box the elevator button can be dragged up or down to alter the order in which the indexes appear in the list. The button to the right of the elevator button, which has an upward-pointing arrow on it, is the Ascending/Descending button. The Ascending/Descending button is used to determine if the index will be in ascending or descending order based on the expression.

Now add another index to your table design. Figure 3.22 shows the Table Designer with this second index defined.

FIGURE 3.22.

The Index Tab of the Table Designer with the second index defined.

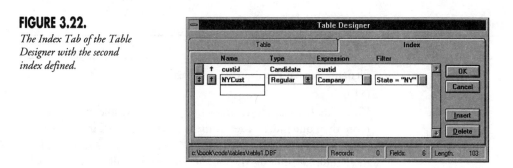

A filter condition has been added in the Filter column for the second index. This filter expression, State="NY", will restrict the records that are included in the index. If the NYCust index is controlling the order of the records you will see only the customers that have "NY" in the State field.

Click the OK button to save these changes to your table design. You will see a message box asking if you want to make the changes permanent. Click the Yes button to finish saving your changes.

You now have a table named Table1 that has two indexes named Custid and NYCust.

Now look at how you can create indexes by using commands. The command that will create, or rebuild, an index for you is *INDEX*. The following code shows this command's syntax:

```
INDEX ON exp TO FileName(IDX) | TAG TagName [OF FileName(CDX)]
        [FOR expL]
        [COMPACT]
        [ASCENDING | DESCENDING]
        [UNIQUE | CANDIDATE]
        [ADDITIVE]
```

Table 3.9 describes the options available on this command.

Table 3.9. The options for the INDEX command.

Option	Description
ON exp	The index key expression that can contain the name of a field or fields from the current table. Fields from other tables or memory variables can be referenced in the index expression, but this is not recommended. If there is a reference to a field in another table or a memory variable, and that table or variable is not available when you use this index, Visual FoxPro will generate an error.
TO FileName(IDX)	Specifying a filename here will create an index file with the default extension of IDX, unless you include the file extension in the

continues

Table 3.9. continued

Option	Description
	filename. Visual FoxPro IDX indexes contain a single index order per file.
TAG *TagName*	Visual FoxPro can create index files that are capable of storing more than one index order in them (these are CDX indexes described later in this table in the OF FileName *(CDX)* section). In these multikey indexes the individual keys are called *tags* and each tag has a unique name within the CDX file. This option is used to specify the tag name you are creating. Tag names can be up to 10 characters long and can contain letters, underscores, and digits. The tag name must begin with either an underscore or a letter.
OF *FileName(CDX)*	Used to specify the filename for the CDX index. This file will have the default extension of CDX unless you specify the extension as part of the filename. Visual FoxPro has two types of CDX index files: structural and non-structural. The *structural CDX file* has the same name as the table it belongs to, and the extension of CDX. The *non-structural CDX file* has a name that is different from the table's name. Structural CDX files are opened automatically whenever you use the table. The number of tags that can be contained in a CDX file is limited only by memory and disk space.
FOR *expL*	The logical expression for the filter condition on the index. This filter expression will restrict which records in the table are reflected in the index.
COMPACT	The IDX type of index files can be made compact or not. The uncompact type of IDX file will occupy more space on the disk drive than the compact IDX file. The only reason to create an uncompact IDX file is for backward compatibility with FoxPro versions prior to 2.0, which did not support the compact index. CDX indexes are all compact.
ASCENDING	Makes the indexing order of exp ascending. This is the default ordering that you will get if you omit both the ASCENDING and DESCENDING options.
DESCENDING	Makes the indexing order of exp descending. You can alter the ascending or descending order of the index at the time you make the index the master index.
UNIQUE	Creates a unique index (see the caution earlier in this chapter about these indexes).

Option	Description
CANDIDATE	Creates a candidate index tag in a structural CDX file. You can only use the CANDIDATE option when you are creating a tag in a structural CDX file, otherwise Visual FoxPro will generate an error. A candidate tag prevents duplicate values of the exp from getting into the table. If you try to create a candidate tag for an expression that already has duplicate values in the table, Visual FoxPro will generate an error.
ADDITIVE	Keeps open any indexes that were already open when this one was created. If you omit the ADDITIVE option when you create a new index file, any previously opened index files (excluding the structural CDX file) will be closed.

Work with the INDEX command a little. To prepare for this you need to make a copy of one of the tables that comes as part of Visual FoxPro. Into a working directory of your choice copy the files Objsamp.DBF, Objsamp.FPT, and Objsamp.CDX from the directory \SAMPLES\Controls below your main Visual FoxPro directory.

After you make the copy type the following commands in the Command window:

```
CD\<your working directory>
USE Objsamp
DELETE TAG ALL
BROWSE
```

The CD\<your working directory> will change the current directory to your working directory (replace <your working directory> with the full path to the directory where you copied the Objsamp files). The USE Objsamp opens the Objsamp table. DELETE TAG ALL deletes all of the index tags in the CDX index for this table. BROWSE displays the browse window shown in Figure 3.23.

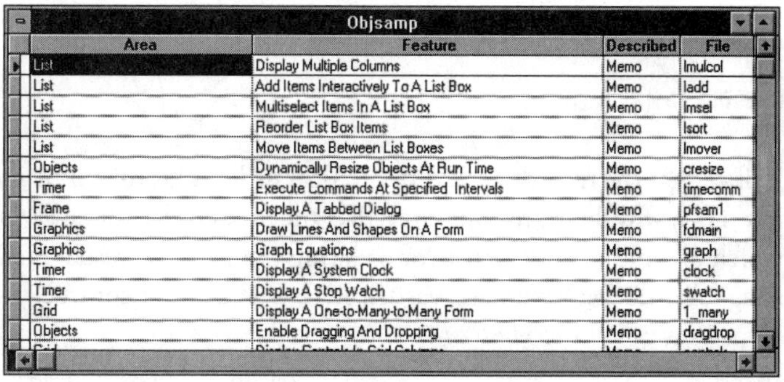

FIGURE 3.23.

The browse window of the Objsamp table.

Notice the order in which the records appear in the browse window. This is the physical order of the records in the table. Now create an index tag for this table. Click in the Command window and then type the following line in the Command window:

```
INDEX ON Area TAG Area
```

Click in the browse window again and notice the order of the records. They are now in alphabetical order on the Area field. This ordering of the records is logical rather than physical. The order is being controlled by the index you just created; the actual physical order of the records in the table has not been changed. Because you did not specify a CDX filename with the OF option on the INDEX command, Visual FoxPro created a structural CDX file that has the same name as the tables and the extension of CDX (Objsamp.CDX). Now add another index tag to this structural CDX file. Type the following command in the Command window:

```
INDEX ON File TAG File
```

Once again, click back into the browse window and notice the order of the records. They are now in order on the File field.

> **NOTE**
>
> The INDEX command not only creates a new index, it also makes that index the master, or controlling, index for the table.

Now close the Objsamp table by typing the following command in the Command window:

```
USE
```

The USE command does two things. First, it closes the current open table, and second, it opens the table named in the command line. If you don't provide a table name to be opened, then USE simply closes the current table. There are other options for the USE command, which will be explained later in this chapter.

Next, open the Objsamp table and browse it again by typing the following in the Command window:

```
USE Objsamp
BROWSE
```

Notice that the records appear in physical order. Has the CDX index file been opened? Yes, it has. Then why do the records not reflect the index order? Because you haven't told Visual FoxPro which tag in the index to use for ordering the records. Visual FoxPro will not randomly select a tag for ordering, so no tag was selected. The tag that controls the order in which the records are seen is called the *master tag*.

You can set the master tag by using the SET ORDER command. Type the following in the Command window and then click on the browse window:

```
SET ORDER TO Area
```

This command has made the tag named Area the master tag and the order of the records is now being controlled by that tag. You can also add ASCENDING or DESCENDING to the end of the SET ORDER TO command to control the ascending or descending nature of the record order.

You can open a table without any master tag, as you have seen, and the tags in the structural CDX file will still be dynamically maintained as you edit and add data to the table. There is a way to set the order when you open the table. The USE command has an ORDER option you can use to specify the tag name to be used as the master tag. Type the following commands in the Command window:

```
USE
USE Objsamp ORDER Area
BROWSE
```

These commands closed the Objsamp table, opened it again with the Area tag set as the master tag, and opened the browse window. Notice that the records in the browse window are ordered on the Area field.

The complete syntax of the USE command is shown next:

```
USE [TableName ¦ SQLViewName ¦ ?]
    [IN WorkArea ¦ AreaAlias]
    [AGAIN]
    [NOREQUERY [DataSessionNumber]]
    [NODATA]
    [INDEX IndexFileList ¦ ?
    [ORDER [IndexNumber ¦ IDXIndexFileName
    ¦ [TAG] TagName [OF CDXIndexFileName]
    [ASCENDING ¦ DESCENDING]]]]
    [ALIAS AreaAlias]
    [EXCLUSIVE]
    [SHARED]
    [NOUPDATE]
```

Table 3.10 thoroughly examines the options of the Visual FoxPro USE command.

Table 3.10. The Visual FoxPro USE command.

Option/Value	Description
TableName	The name of the table to open. In Windows 95 and Windows NT, spaces are significant in filenames, so avoid spaces when you specify TableName.
SQLViewName	The name of the SQL view in the current database to open. Databases are described in the "Creating a Database Container" section of this chapter.
?	Using ? instead of TableName or SQLViewName will display the Use dialog box, in which you can select a table to be opened.

continues

Table 3.10. continued

Option/Value	Description
IN *WorkArea*	Used to specify the work area in which a table will be opened. Visual FoxPro enables you to have more than one table opened simultaneously. Each of these tables is open in a work area, and any one work area can have only one table open in it. In Visual FoxPro there are 32,767 work areas available per data session (forms can have private data sessions that enable 32,767 work areas for each private data session in addition to the default data session). The work areas are numbered from 1 to 32,767. The work area number 0 is supported in the IN option. Using 0 for the work area causes the table to be open in the lowest numbered available work area. A *work area* is a location in the computer's memory where Visual FoxPro keeps track of an open data table. The opening of a table in a specific work area will close any table open previously in that work area.
IN *AreaAlias*	When a table is opened in a work area, the work area is assigned an alias name. The default alias name is the table's name unless that conflicts with another work area's name, then Visual FoxPro will generate a unique alias for the work area. The work area's alias name can be used to refer to the work area.
AGAIN	One table can be opened in more than one work area at the same time by using the AGAIN option. If you attempt to USE a table in a work area when it is already open in another work area without the AGAIN option, Visual FoxPro will generate an error. When you open a table again, the table in the new work area will take on the attribute set for the table in the original work area (such as read-only or exclusive access).
NOREQUERY [*DataSessionNumber*]	Specifies that the data for a remote view is not downloaded again when the view is being opened AGAIN. *DataSessionNumber* can be used to specify the data session that should not be downloaded again. If *DataSessionNumber* is omitted, the current data session is affected.

Option/Value	Description
NODATA	The structure of a SQL view, but no data, is downloaded. This is the fastest method for finding out the structure for a SQL view.
INDEX *IndexFileList*	Used to specify a list of index files to be opened with the table. If the table has a structural CDX file it will be opened in addition to this file list. This list of index files is separated by commas and can contain any combination of IDX and CDX indexes. The file extensions don't need to be specified unless they are something other than the default (IDX or CDX) or an IDX and CDX file included in the list have the same name. The first index in the list will be the master index and will control the order of the records. If the first file is a CDX index file then the records will be in physical order and there will be no master index. The number of index files that can be open for a table is limited only by memory and the availability of operating system file handles. CDX index files use one file handle.
INDEX ?	Using ? instead of a file list will display the Open dialog box with a list of available index files to choose from.
ORDER [*IndexNumber*]	Used to determine the IDX file that will be the master index. The first IDX file in the list is the master index. This option can be used to set the order to another file in the list. The number 0 can be used to set the physical order as the record order.
ORDER [*IDXFileName*]	You can use the index file's name instead of the numbered position in the list to set a particular file as the master index.
ORDER [TAG] *TagName*	Used to set the master index to a tag in a CDX file. The structural CDX file will be used unless the OF option specifies some other CDX file.
OF [*CDXFileName*]	Used to specify the CDX filename for the *TagName* used in the ORDER option.
ASCENDING	Access and display the records in ascending order.
DESCENDING	Access and display the records in descending order. Using the ASCENDING or DESCENDING options doesn't

continues

Table 3.10. continued

Option/Value	Description
	change the index, it only alters the order until the table is closed or the SET ORDER command is used to alter the order again.
ALIAS *AreaAlias*	Specifies the work area's alias name. When a table is opened in a work area the work area is given an alias name that can be used to refer to the table in that work area. The alias is automatically assigned by Visual FoxPro. You can override the automatic alias name by using this option to specify the alias name to be used. Alias names in Visual FoxPro can be up to 254 letters, digits, and underscores and must begin with a letter or underscore.
EXCLUSIVE	The table is opened for exclusive use. See Chapter 32, "Multiuser Programming and Techniques," for a thorough discussion of exclusive use.
SHARED	The table is opened for shared use. See Chapter 32 for a thorough discussion of shared use.
NOUPDATE	Opens the table read-only preventing changes to the data or structure of the table.

TIP

Because the ascending and descending order of an index can be set when you use it, you can create all of your indexes as ascending. This will enable you to specify the order at the time the index is used, thus preventing the accidental re-creation of an index in the wrong order, which would break any code that depends on the ascending or descending order of the index. This will also make your programs more self-documenting because the order of the index is specified right in the code instead of in the index.

The *.NULL.* Value

Visual FoxPro supports the value of NULL, specified in Visual FoxPro as .NULL., for all data types. This .NULL. value is worthy of some discussion because it can be both a godsend and a nightmare. The .NULL. value means missing data or a value of "I don't know." It is very different from an empty character string, the number 0, a logical false, or a blank date.

The result of comparing the `.NULL.` value to any other value is `.NULL.`. Even comparing `.NULL.` to `.NULL.` results in `.NULL.`—you can compare this to asking, "Is 'I don't know' equal to 'I don't know', answer 'I don't know'."

Using `.NULL.` to reflect missing data can be instrumental in providing accurate results in certain systems. For example, in calculating the mean of a series of numbers you are supposed to omit missing values from the calculation. The `.NULL.` value will enable you to recognize those missing values as different from valid values of 0. However, the following command would not leave out the `.NULL.` values:

```
AVERAGE Amount TO AvgAmnt FOR NOT (Amount = .NULL.)
```

This command would fail to get the correct results because `.NULL.` is not equal to `.NULL.`, so the `.NULL.` values would be included. Instead, you need to use the following command:

```
AVERAGE Amount TO AvgAmount FOR NOT ISNULL(Amount)
```

The `ISNULL()` function returns `True` if the expression is `.NULL.` and `False` if the expression is not `.NULL.`.

NOTE

`.NULL.` can be very valuable when it is needed, but it can wreak havoc when it isn't needed. Be careful to allow `NULL` values only when you need that functionality.

Creating a Table with the Table Wizard

Merlin was a wizard who, it was said, could turn lead into gold. The Visual FoxPro Wizards come close to that. Chapter 16, "Leveraging FoxPro Power Using Wizards," discusses a number of the available wizards in Visual FoxPro and Chapter 6, "Querying Data," describes the Query Wizard. Chapters 9, "Creating and Using Simple Forms," and 12, "Designing and Customizing Forms," deal with the Form Wizard. Chapters 10, "Creating and Using Simple Reports," and 13, "Designing and Customizing Reports," talk about the Report Wizard. In Chapter 15, "Producing Mailings," both the Label and Mail Merge Wizards are presented. Finally, Chapter 38, "Client/Server Features," presents the Upsizing Wizard. Here you will be introduced to the Table Wizard.

All of the wizards help you accomplish a task by presenting you with a series of steps on a screen. You complete each step by filling in that step's screen with your choices.

The Table Wizard gives you an easy way to create a table based on one of the sample tables provided. The steps in the process of creating a table with the Table Wizard are accomplished by filling in information on a number of screens that the Wizard presents to you.

There are a number of ways to launch the Table Wizard. If you select File | New from the system menu and then select Table in the New dialog box, you can click the Wizard button to get to the Table Wizard. You will see later in this chapter in the "Creating a Database Container" section, that the Table Wizard can be launched from there as well.

For this example use the third method of starting the Table Wizard. Select Tools | Wizards | Table from the system menu. Figure 3.24 shows the open Wizards menu.

FIGURE 3.24.

The Visual FoxPro Wizards menu.

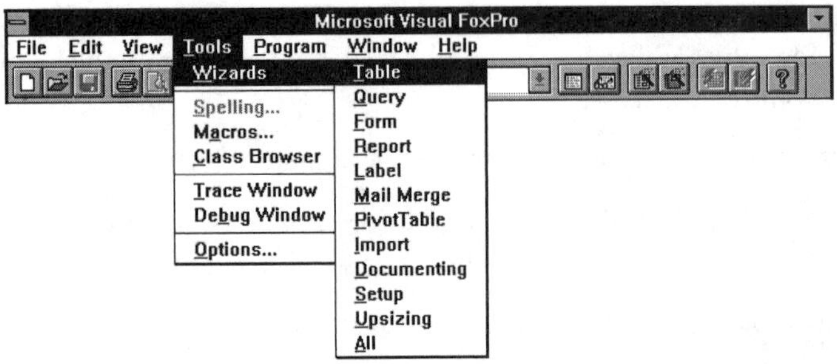

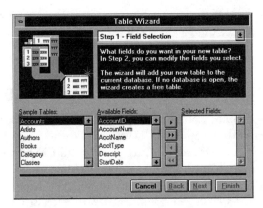

You now see the first screen in the Table Wizard as shown in Figure 3.25. Because this is the first visit you have made to a Visual FoxPro Wizard, take a moment to become familiar with the layout of the Wizard screens.

FIGURE 3.25.

The Table Wizard's first screen.

The picture you see in the upper-left area of the screen is used to give you a visual clue of what this step in the wizard will do. On the upper-right area of the screen is a combo box that currently says Step 1 - Field Selection. If you drop down this combo box by clicking on it you can see all of the steps involved in this Wizard. Figure 3.26 shows the Table Wizard's combo box dropped down.

In the combo box's list you can see that the Table Wizard has four steps. These are named Field Selection, Field Settings, Indexing, and Finish. These steps are referred to in this section by these names. You will also notice that all but the Field Selection step are disabled. That is because you cannot move to the other steps until you complete the Field Selection step.

In Figure 3.25 you can see some text just below the combo box. This text describes the purpose of the current step and tells you what the Wizard will do based on your selections.

FIGURE 3.26.

The Table Wizard's combo box is dropped down.

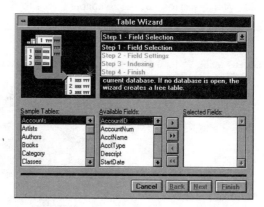

The lower half of the Wizard screen contains the controls that you will use to complete the selections related to the current step. These controls will vary according to the particular step you are on.

Step 1 - Field Selection of the Table Wizard has three lists at the bottom. The first, labeled Sample Tables, is used to select the sample table that most closely resembles the table you are creating. The Sample Tables list is scrollable, and contains more samples than you can immediately see. There are actually more than 40 sample tables in Visual FoxPro's Table Wizard. As long as you are creating a fairly common type of table, there is a good chance you will find among the sample tables one that is close to what you want.

The second list, in the middle, is labeled Available Fields and is updated when you select a different sample from the Sample Tables list to reflect the fields in the selected sample table.

The third list, on the right, is labeled Selected Fields. This list contains the fields that you have selected from the Available Fields list.

There are a number of methods you can use to select fields from the Available Fields list. Before you learn about these selection methods, choose the Friends sample table in the sample tables list. Click the Accounts table name in the Sample Tables list, and then type `Friend` on your keyboard. Notice that the highlight in the Sample Table list followed you while you were typing by highlighting the sample table name that matched what you had typed. This is called *Incremental Searching* and is available in all Visual FoxPro lists.

Once the highlight in the Sample Tables list is on the Friends sample table you are ready to start selecting fields from the Available Fields list. Click the `FriendID` field in the Available Fields list to highlight it. Your screen should look similar to Figure 3.27.

The set of command buttons between the Available Fields list and the Selected Fields list can be used to move fields from the Available Fields list to the Selected Fields list. From top to bottom these buttons are

SELECT	Move the highlighted field in the Available Fields list to the Selected Fields list
SELECT ALL	Move all the Available Fields to the Selected Fields list
UNSELECT	Move the highlighted field in the Selected Fields list back to the Available Fields list
UNSELECT ALL	Move all of the Selected Fields back to the Available Fields list

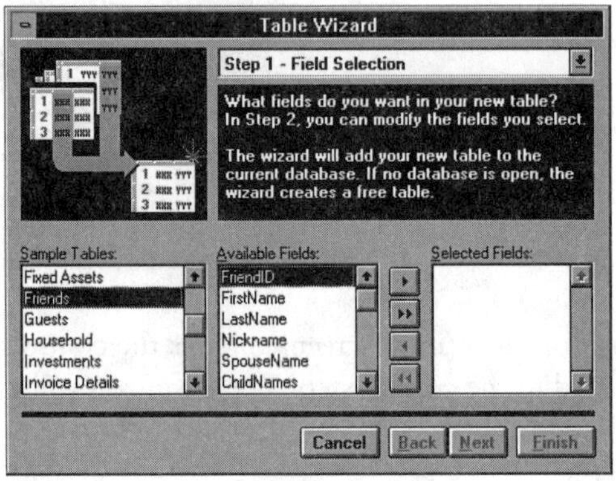

FIGURE 3.27.

The FriendID *field is highlighted in the Available Fields list.*

Click the SELECT button now to select the FriendID field. You will see the FriendID field disappear from the Available Fields list and appear in the Selected Fields list. Now try a different way to select the FirstName field; double-click FirstName in the Available Fields list. When you double-click a field you will move that field between the Available Fields list and the Selected Fields list.

Select the following fields from the Available Fields list:

```
FriendID
FirstName
LastName
Address
City
State
PostalCode
HomePhone
```

Next, click the Next command button at the bottom of the Wizard screen. Figure 3.28 shows the screen for Step 2 - Field Settings.

Before you learn the Field Settings step in the process, click the combo box of steps at the top of the screen. Notice that all of the steps are now enabled. You can use this combo box to move between the steps in the wizard. For example, you could now choose to return to the Field Selection step to add more fields to your table.

FIGURE 3.28.

*Step 2 - Field Settings in
the Table Wizard.*

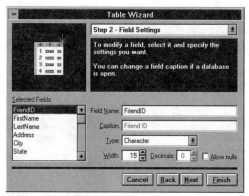

The bottom half of the Field Settings screen is divided into two parts, left and right. The left has a list labeled Selected Fields. The Selected Fields list shows you all of the fields you have selected for your table. You use the Selected Fields list to choose the field for which you want to establish settings.

The controls on the right side are used to change the settings for the field that is highlighted in the Selected Fields list. These controls are described in Table 3.11.

Table 3.11. The field setting controls in the Table Wizard.

Control Label	Control Type	Control Purpose
Field Name	Text Box	Used to change a field's name.
Caption	Text Box	Used to change the field's caption property in the database container. Databases are described later in this chapter. If a database is open when you use the Table Wizard, the table created will be added to that database. When a database is open the Caption control will be enabled; if there is no database open then the Caption control is disabled.
Type	Combo box	Used to change the data type for a field.
Width	Spinner	Used to change the width of a field. The width control will be enabled and disabled according to the data type for the field being changed.
Decimals	Spinner	Used to set the decimal places for a Numeric or Float type field. The decimal control is disabled unless the current field is a Numeric or Float type.
Allow nulls	Check Box	Determines whether the NULL value will be allowed in this field. Checked will enable NULLs and unchecked will not enable NULLs.

The command buttons at the very bottom of the wizard screen, Cancel, Back, Next, and Finish are used to cancel the creation process, move back one step, move forward to the next step, and finish the process creating the table as it is currently defined, respectively.

For the example leave the field setting unchanged and click the Next button. Figure 3.29 shows the Step 3 - Indexing wizard screen.

FIGURE 3.29.

The Step 3 - Indexing Table Wizard screen.

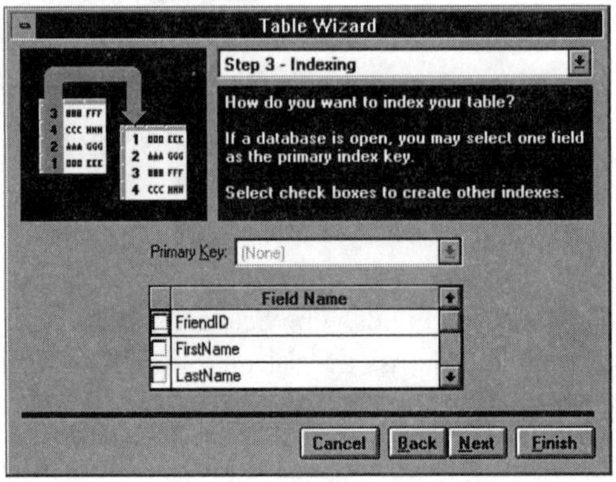

This step uses two controls in the lower part of the screen, the combo box for setting the Primary Key index if a database is open, and a grid that lists each field with a check box to the left of the field's name. The check boxes in the grid can be used to select fields to be indexed. Each field selected will become a tag in the structural CDX file for the table. The tag name for each index will be the same as the field name. Check the boxes for the FriendID and LastName fields and then click Next.

Figure 3.30 shows the Step 4 - Finish screen of the Table Wizard. On this screen you have a set of option buttons that enable you to choose the action to be taken. The three options are Save table for later use, Save table and browse it, and Save table and modify it in the Table Designer. The Save table for later use option will end the wizard and create your table, which you use at a later time. The Save table and browse it option will save your table and then open it and browse it so that you can start adding records right away. The Save table and modify it in the Table Designer option will save your table and immediately open it in the Table Designer so you can modify its structure.

Select Save table for later and then click the Finish button. The Save As dialog box will be displayed, as seen in Figure 3.31.

In this dialog box enter MyTable.dbf as the name for your table and click the Save button.

Your table has been created and has been saved with the name you gave it in the Save As dialog box.

The Table Wizard greatly simplifies the table creation process. This can be a real asset if the table you want to create closely matches one of the sample tables in the wizard. If you need to create a table that is drastically different from the samples, then you will probably find it faster to use the Table Designer directly to create your table.

FIGURE 3.30.

The Step 4 - Finish Table Wizard screen.

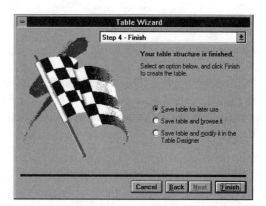

FIGURE 3.31.

The Save As dialog box.

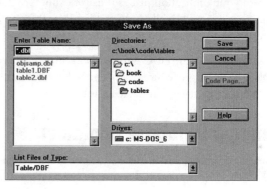

Database Versus Table

So far in this chapter you have spent a good deal of time learning about tables. You've seen how to design your tables and how to create them. You've seen how to control the order of the records in your tables using indexes. Now you encounter the term *database*. What is the difference between a table and a database?

A *database* is simply a collection of tables. For example, the Accounts Receivable database for a business might include Customer, Invoice, Invoice Detail, Inventory, Vendor, Cash Receipts, Accounts Receivable Journal, General Ledger Update, Shipping Address, and Shippers tables. All of these tables together make up the Accounts Receivable database.

In past versions of FoxPro, you had no place to store information about the database and the tables and fields that were included in it. In Visual FoxPro you have the Database Container (DBC). The DBC is a place in which you store information about the fields, tables, and indexes that comprise a database. The DBC can also contain rules about what constitutes valid data and what are the allowable actions taken on that data. All of this information about the data is called *metadata*, which means data about the data.

Visual FoxPro's DBC also gives you the ability to do some things that cannot be done without it, like use longer names for your tables and fields or designate a primary key index.

The real advantage of the DBC is found in the fact that once a table has been put in a DBC and rules have been established, there is no way to add or edit the records in that table without the DBC rules being applied. This means that the business rules for your data can be written once, in the DBC, and those rules will be applied consistently throughout your application. You don't need to repeat the code to enforce the rules in every screen or program that might alter the data.

The DBC can also keep track of SQL Queries, which are discussed in Chapter 6, Chapter 7, Chapter 11, "Working with Visual FoxPro's Relational Powers," and Chapter 38. In the DBC you can create the definition of a query, called a *view* in the DBC, and then have that view available to your application just as if it were another table. The views in the DBC can reference data that is stored locally in Visual FoxPro tables or data that is stored remotely on a database server like Microsoft SQL Server, Oracle, or any of a number of other database servers.

The last advantage of the DBC is found in its Stored Procedures. These Stored Procedures give you a place to write procedures that are needed for handling your data and have those procedures available whenever that database is open.

Creating a Database Container

Like creating a table, there is more than one way to create a database container. You can use the File | New menu option and then specify Database in the New dialog box, or you can type the `CREATE DATABASE <DatabaseName>` command in the Command window. Type the following command in the Command window to create a new database named MyDbc:

```
CREATE DATABASE MyDbc
```

At first glance, it seems that nothing has happened. Figure 3.32 shows the Visual FoxPro screen after you type the preceding command.

Look carefully in the toolbar just below the system menu. A little more than half-way to the right is a combo box. You can see the name of your new database container in that combo box. That combo box is a list of all of the database containers that are currently open. When you issued your `CREATE DATABASE` command Visual FoxPro created a DBC with the name MyDbc.DBC and opened it as the current database container.

The MyDbc database container is comprised of three files, MyDbc.DBC, MyDbc.DCT, and MyDbc.DCX. These files are actually the pieces of a Visual FoxPro table. MyDbc.DBC is the same as a DBF data table, except for the extension. MyDbc.DCT is the file that holds the contents of the memo fields in MyDbc.DBC. Finally, MyDbc.DCX is the structural index to

MyDbc.DBC. Because the data table that holds the database definition has the extension of .DBC, the database container is called a DBC.

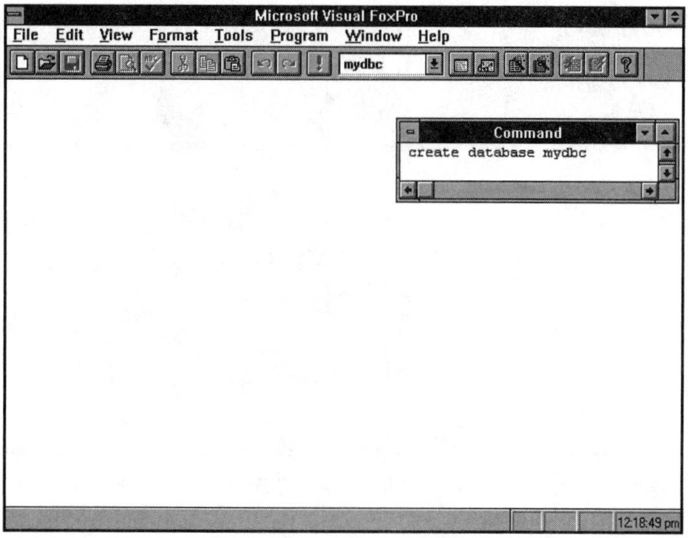

FIGURE 3.32.

The Visual FoxPro screen after your CREATE DATABASE command has been executed.

All of the information that you record about your database in the database container will be stored in MyDbc.DBC.

To begin adding tables to MyDbc.DBC you need to type the following command in the Command window:

```
MODIFY DATABASE
```

This command will open Visual FoxPro's Database Designer. At first the Database Designer is a large empty window on your screen. Look at the system menu and you will see that there is a new menu option there called Database. You might also see the Database Designer toolbar on your screen. If you don't have the Database Designer toolbar on your screen, choose View | Toolbars and check the box to the left of the Database Designer item in the Toolbars list of the Toolbars dialog box, and then click OK. Your screen should look similar to the one in Figure 3.33.

The tool buttons, from left to right, in the Database Designer toolbar are used to

- Create a new table and add it to the DBC
- Add an existing table to the DBC
- Remove a table from the DBC or completely delete the table
- Create a remote view
- Create a local view
- Modify a table in the DBC

■ Browse a table in the DBC

■ Edit the Stored Procedures in the DBC

FIGURE 3.33.

*The Database Designer
with the Database Designer
toolbar.*

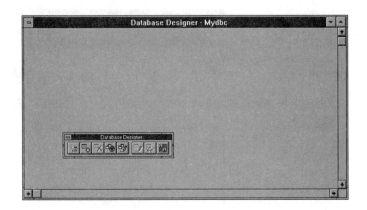

If you don't remember the purpose of these tools, you can use Visual Foxpro's tooltips feature to get a reminder. Simply place your mouse cursor over the tool button you want to know about and wait a second or two. A little box will appear telling you the purpose of the button under the mouse cursor as seen in Figure 3.34.

FIGURE 3.34.

*Tooltips can help you recall
the purpose of a tool
button.*

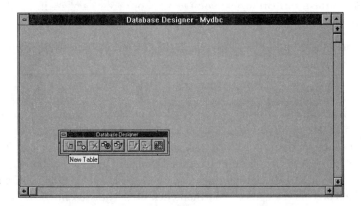

You can "dock" the Database Designer toolbar on any edge of the Visual FoxPro screen by clicking the title bar of the toolbar and dragging it to the edge of the screen you want it docked to. Figure 3.35 shows the toolbar docked at the bottom of the screen with the empty MyDbc Database Designer.

You can "undock" the toolbar by clicking your mouse within the box surrounding the toolbar and dragging it back onto the screen. When the toolbar is undocked you can click the dash in its upper-left corner to close the toolbar. If you double-click on the toolbar while it is floating, it will be docked at the top of the screen. Double-clicking on the docked toolbar will return it to floating.

The Database menu option in the system menu contains all of the options that are available on the Database Designer toolbar. Figure 3.36 shows the Database menu dropped down to see the options on it.

FIGURE 3.35.

The Database designer toolbar has been docked at the bottom of the screen.

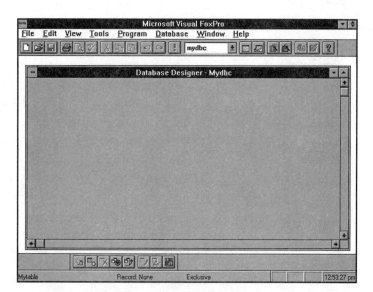

FIGURE 3.36.

The Database menu.

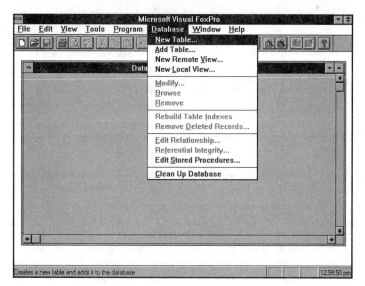

Table 3.12 describes each of the options on the Database menu.

Table 3.12. The options on the Database menu.

Option	Description
New Table	Used to create a new table and add it to the current DBC.
Add Table	Adds an existing table to the current DBC.
New Remote View	Creates a new remote view and adds it to the current DBC.
New Local View	Creates a new local view and adds it to the current DBC.
Modify	Brings up the Table Designer for the highlighted table in the Database Designer.
Browse	Opens a browse window for the table that is highlighted in the Database Designer.
Remove	Removes the highlighted table from the DBC. Optionally, can erase the table from the disk as well.
Rebuild Table Indexes	Re-create the indexes for the highlighted table.
Remove Deleted Records	When a record is deleted in a table it is marked as deleted but is not actually removed from the table. This option will run the PACK command on the highlighted table. The PACK command removes the deleted records from the table permanently.
Edit Relationship	Edit the relationship that is highlighted in the Database Designer.
Referential Integrity	Run the Referential Integrity Builder to edit the referential integrity rules.
Edit Stored Procedures	Open an edit window for editing the Stored Procedures.
Clean Up Database	Run a PACK command on the DBC file itself to permanently remove deleted records from the DBC file.

Some of the items in Table 3.12 that might be unfamiliar to you, like Relationships and the Referential Integrity Builder, are explained later in this chapter in the "Persistent Relationships" and "Referential Integrity" sections, respectively. Deleted records and the PACK command are explained in Chapter 4, "Adding and Changing Data."

There is one other way to get at the functions of the Database Designer; if you click your right mouse button anywhere inside the Database Designer window, you will see a menu of choices like the one in Figure 3.37.

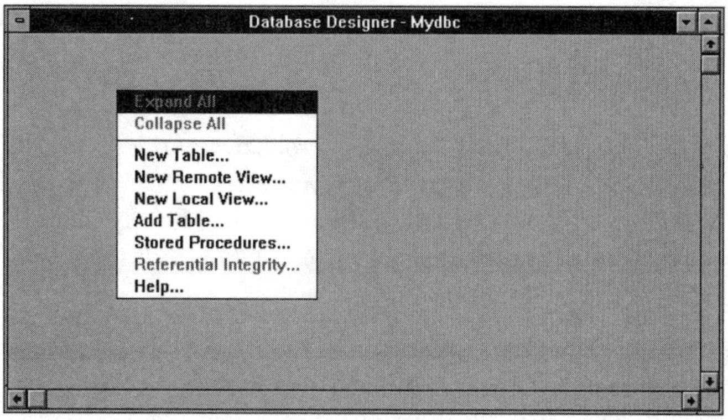

FIGURE 3.37.

A right-mouse click on the Database designer will bring up a context-sensitive menu called a Short Cut Menu.

The menu brought up by your right mouse click contains options relative to where you clicked. The right click in the Database Designer window brought up the Short Cut Menu for the Database Designer. The options on this menu are the same as their counterparts, with the same prompts, in the Database menu. There are three new options in this Short Cut Menu: Expand All, Collapse All, and Help. The Help option will bring up the Visual FoxPro Help screen for the Database Designer. The other two options, Expand All and Collapse All, are explained later in this section.

Choose Add Table from the Short Cut Menu. Then select MyTable.DBF, the table you created with the Table Wizard in the "Creating a Table with the Table Wizard" section of this chapter, from the Open dialog box.

Your Database Designer screen will now look similar to Figure 3.38.

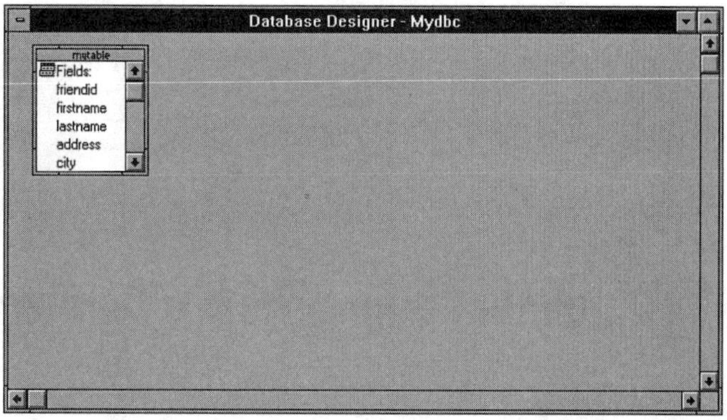

FIGURE 3.38.

The Database Designer with MyTable.DBF added to it.

MyTable has been added to the database MyDbc. Now right-click the Database Designer window's background and choose Collapse All. You see that MyTable has been reduced to just a title. Bring up the Database Designer Short Cut Menu again, choose Expand All, and MyTable is once again opened up so you can see the fields listed in it.

Click on MyTable in the Database designer to select it as the current table. MyTable's title bar has a different background color indicating that it is the selected, or highlighted, table in the Database Designer. Notice, also, that the first field in MyTable has been highlighted.

On the right side of MyTable is a scrollbar; use this to scroll down in the list of MyTable's fields. If you scroll down far enough you will see an entry in MyTable that says Indexes. Below the Indexes entry are listed the indexes that exist for MyTable. Visual FoxPro knew about these indexes because you created a structural CDX with the Table Wizard. The structural CDX goes with the table automatically.

Click your right mouse button on MyTable. A Short Cut Menu is displayed with five options on it. Browse will display MyTable in a browse window. Delete will remove MyTable from the DBC and optionally erase it from your disk. Collapse will reduce MyTable to just a title. If MyTable was already reduced to a title, then this option would be Expand and would expand MyTable. Modify will bring up the Table Designer for MyTable. Finally, Help will display the Database Designer help screen. Choose Modify from MyTable's Short Cut Menu. The Table Designer is opened with MyTable ready to be modified. Figure 3.39 shows how your screen will look now.

FIGURE 3.39.

The Database Designer's version of the Table Designer.

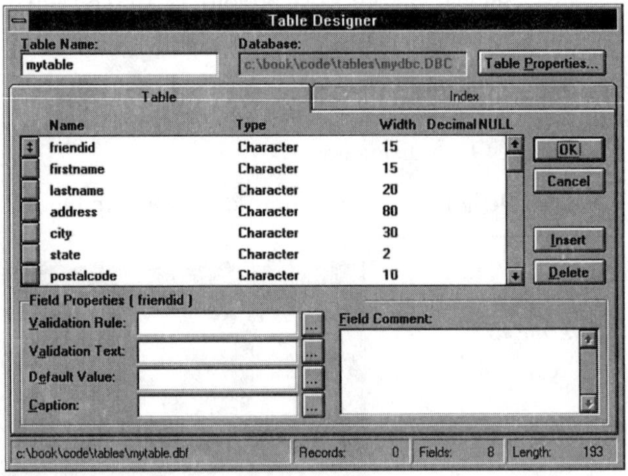

The Database Designer from a Database Container

The Table Designer looks different from inside the Database Designer, and it is different. There are more options for controlling the additional things that you can do to your table design. You have these additional options because your table is now part of a database. Additional information about your table and its fields can be stored in the DBC. The Table Designer seen in Figure 3.39 is like the Table Designer in Figure 3.18 on steroids.

The first thing that is new here is the Table Name: text box in the upper-left corner of the Table Designer. In this text box you can enter a name for your table that is not the same as the DBF file's name. As a matter of fact, this table name can be up to 128 characters long. In the Name column of the Fields list you can enter field names that are also up to 128 characters long. These long table and field names will be lost if you remove this table from the DBC later because the long names are stored in the DBC.

The field list in this version of the Table Designer is functionally the same as the field list described in the "Creating Tables with the Table Designer" section of this chapter.

Field-Level Options

Below the fields list is a set of controls for setting the field properties of the currently selected field in the field list. You can identify the currently selected field in the fields list by looking at the elevator button to the left of each field. The elevator button with the arrow on it is the currently selected field. The currently selected field is also named alongside the Field Properties label inside a set of parentheses.

The field properties options are explained in Table 3.13.

Table 3.13. The field properties options.

Option	Description
Validation Rule	Used to specify the field level validation rule. This rule is a logical expression. The value of the expression is true then the field "passes" validation, if the value is false the field "fails" validation and the Validation Text will be displayed as an error message.
Validation Text	A character expression that is displayed if the field fails the Validation Rule.
Default Value	Specifies the default value for this field on a newly appended record. This option can be used to help the user in data entry by making the default value the most likely value.
Caption	A descriptive name for the field. The caption will be used as a column header when browsing the table, and will be used for the column header when creating a grid for the table in a Visual FoxPro Form, unless the caption is overridden in creating the grid. Captions can be up to 128 characters long.
Field Comment	Stores a descriptive comment about the field. You can store anything you want here. One idea would be to type the domain definition for the field in the Field Comment.

To the right of each text box for entering the first four options is a command button with an ellipsis (…) for the prompt. Clicking any one of those buttons will bring up the Visual FoxPro Expression Builder to assist you in entering the respective option.

Now create a default value for the State field. Click the State field in the fields list, and then click the Default Value text box in the Field Properties section of the Table Designer. Type your state abbreviation in the text box surrounded by quotes, as in "CT". Now, whenever you add a new record to MyTable, the State field will start out with your state's abbreviation in it until you change the value by typing in something else.

Now add a Validation Rule and Validation text to another field. Click the City field in the fields list to select it as the current field. Now click in the text box for Validation Rule and type in the following expression:

```
NOT EMPTY( City )
```

This expression will be true if the City field is not empty, and false if the field is empty. Now click in the Validation Text text box and type this expression:

```
"City cannot be left blank"
```

This text will display whenever the City field's Validation Rule fails. Click the OK button, and answer Yes to the message box that asks if you want to make the changes permanent.

Click your right mouse button on MyTable and choose Browse from the Short Cut Menu. When the browse window is visible, type Ctrl+Y to add a new record to the table. Your screen will look like the one in Figure 3.40.

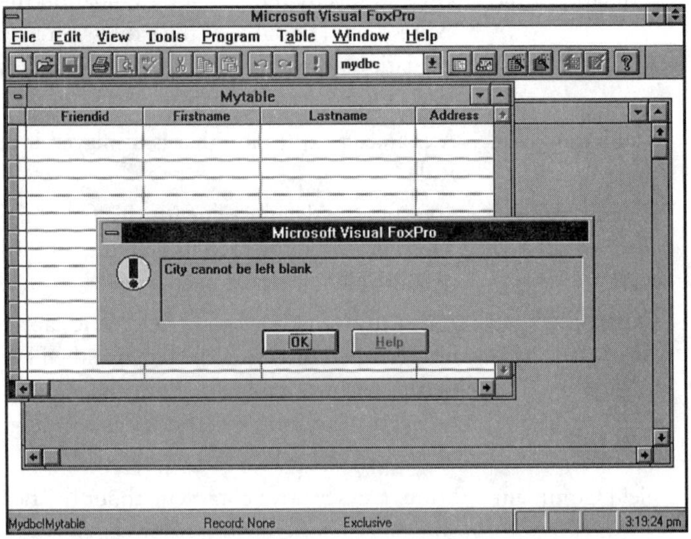

FIGURE 3.40.

The Validation Text is displayed for the City field because that field is empty and its Validation Rule does not allow empty City fields.

The Validation Text for the City field is displayed in a message box because your new record has an empty City field and the validation rule disallows this. Presently, you have no way of adding a new record to this table because the `City` field's validation will fail every time you try. Click the OK button in the message box and then press Esc to close the browse window.

Right-click on MyTable and choose Modify to return to the Table Designer. Click the `City` field in the fields list and then click the text box for Default Value. In the Default Value text box, type the name of your city surrounded in quotes, as in `"Prospect"`. Click the OK button and browse MyTable again, the same as you did previously.

Type Ctrl+Y again. This time your record got added. This is because you have provided a default value for the `City` field that is not blank. Use the horizontal scrollbar at the bottom of the browse window to scroll the display to the right until you can see the `City` field displayed.

The city for your new record should be the name you typed in as the Default value. Click in the `City` field for your new record and then type Ctrl+A to select the entire field. Press the Del key to delete the contents of the `City` field and then press Tab to move to the `State` field. A message box will come up with your Validation text for the `City` field because the `City` field failed its Validation Rule when you tried to leave it to go to the `State` field. Click the OK button in the message box and then click the dash at the upper-left corner of the browse window. Choose Close from the menu that comes up, which is called the Control Menu. You will again see the message box with your Validation text in it because you have attempted to leave the browse window when the `City` field fails its Validation Rule. You cannot save a record to the table that fails one of the validation rules.

Choose the OK button in the message box and type your city name back into the `City` field. Now choose Close from the browse window's control menu. Your browse window closes normally and your new record was saved in the MyTable table.

> **TIP**
>
> Make sure that a new record will pass the Validation Rules you have established in the database container by using the Default Value setting for the fields.

In the Table Designer, select the Index tab. Figure 3.41 shows the Index tab of the Table Designer with the index type combo box dropped down for the FRIENDID index.

Notice that there is one more type of index available here than there was in the Table Designer before. This Primary index type is used to designate the primary key index for the table. You can have only one Primary index for any table. The Primary index, like the Candidate index described earlier in this chapter, enforces uniqueness on the value of the key expression. It also prevents .NULL. values from the key expression or any part of the key expression. Make the FRIENDID index the Primary index for the table.

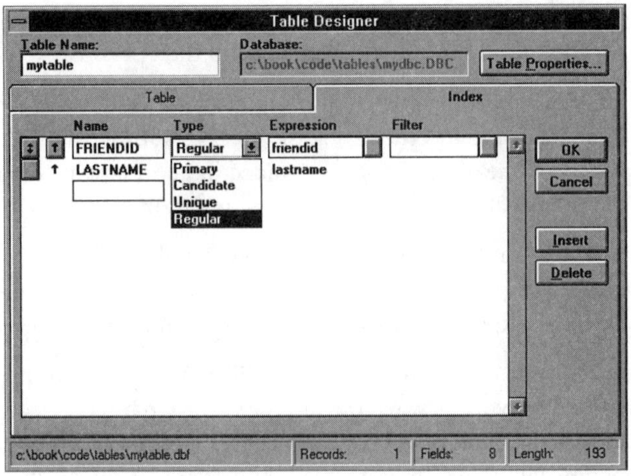

FIGURE 3.41.

The Index tab of the Table Designer.

Table Level Options

Use MyTable's Short Cut Menu to open the Table Designer again. Click the button labeled Table Properties. Figure 3.42 shows the dialog box that you will see.

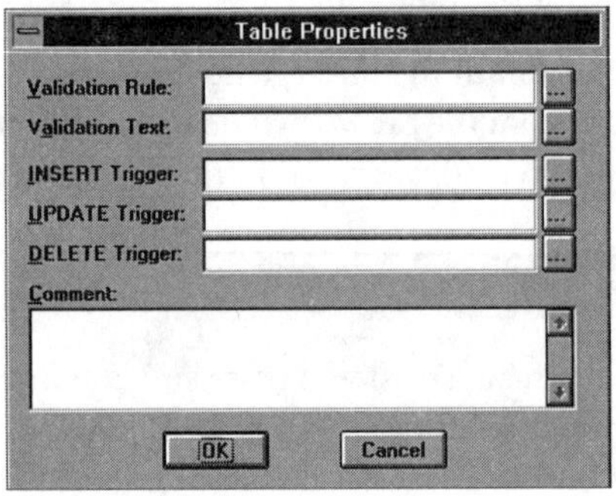

FIGURE 3.42.

The Table Properties dialog box.

The options in this dialog box are described in Table 3.14.

Table 3.14. The Table Properties dialog box options.

Option	Description
Validation Rule	Used to specify the row, or record, level Validation Rule. It is a logical expression—True indicates that the record "passes" validation and False indicates that the record "fails" validation.
Validation Text	Used to specify the error message text to be displayed if a record fails the Validation Rule.

Option	Description
INSERT Trigger	Used to specify a rule to be triggered whenever a record is inserted or added to the table. This "rule" is a Visual FoxPro expression that has a value of True (.T.) or False (.F.).
UPDATE Trigger	Specifies a rule to be triggered whenever a record in the table is updated.
DELETE Trigger	Used to specify a rule to be run whenever a record is deleted from the table.
Comment	A place where you can type a comment about the table. You can use this to type in a description of the meaning or purpose of the table as well as how it relates to other tables in the database.

The Validation Rule and Text in the Table Properties dialog box are similar to the Validation Rule and Text for fields except that the former apply to the entire record instead of just one field. The table's Validation Rule might be used to check on the values of fields whose acceptable values depend on the value of other fields. For example, on an Employee table you might have a field for marital status and another field for spouse. The rule might state that the Spouse field must be blank unless the marital status field indicates Married. This rule could not be properly stated at the field level because two fields are involved in the rule, and the user might not enter the fields in the order your rule requires. By specifying this rule at the Table level, you can postpone its evaluation until the user completes the record and then check the rule.

Persistent Relationships

The Database Container can store information about the relationships between your tables. When you record a relationship in the Database Container that relationship is called a *persistent relationship*. If you later use the tables involved in a persistent relationship in a form's data environment the persistent relationship will be respected (the data environment is described in Chapter 12, "Designing and Customizing Forms").

Before you can create a persistent relationship in the Database Designer you need to have at least two tables in the database. From the Database menu select New Table. Name your table Gotcard.DBF and add to it the fields in Table 3.15.

Table 3.15. The fields for the Gotcard.DBF table.

Name	Type	Width
FRIENDID	Character	15
DATERCVD	Date	8
HOLIDAY	Character	20

Also, create the indexes shown in Table 3.16.

Table 3.16. The indexes for the Gotcard.DBF table.

Name	Type	Expression
Card	Primary	FriendId + DTOS(DateRcvd)
FriendId	Regular	FriendId

Then click the OK button and answer No to the message box asking about inputting data records now.

Use the scrollbars on the right side of each of the tables to scroll down until the indexes for each table are shown. Figure 3.43 shows how your Database Designer should look now.

FIGURE 3.43.

The two tables have their indexes visible.

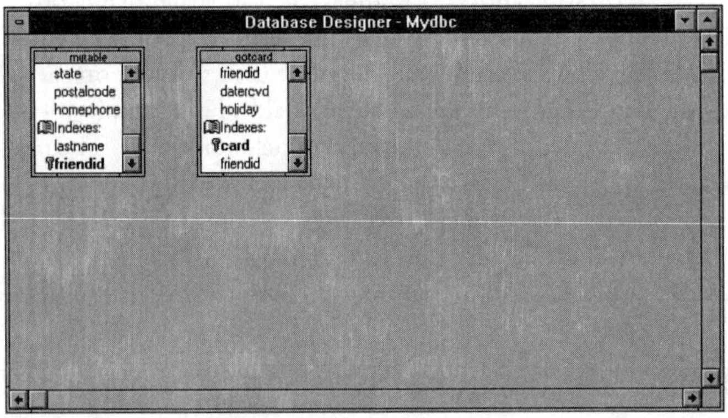

You created two indexes for the GotCard table. The first one, named Card, has the expression FriendId + DTOS(DateRcvd). This is the primary key to the GotCard table. You needed to include both of the fields, FriendId and DateRcvd, because neither of them alone would provide a unique value in the table. You might receive many cards from a particular friend and you might receive many cards of a particular date. The two together provide a unique value because you might never receive more than one card from a particular friend on the same date.

The DTOS() function converts a Date data type to a character data type in the form of *YYYYMMDD,* where *YYYY* is the year, *MM* is the month, and *DD* is the day. Using this function does two things for you. It converts the date to a character string so it can be concatenated to the FriendId field, and it retains the chronological sorting sequence for the dates.

The second index you created, named FriendId, is keyed on the FriendId field alone. This index is on the foreign key of FriendId in the GotCard table and will provide the capability to create the persistent relationship between the two tables.

Persistent relationships are created between the indexes of two tables. The Primary index of one table is related to an index in the second table. Now create a persistent relationship between MyTable and GotCard. A persistent relationship does not preclude you from setting your own relationships or altering the relationships in an application or program.

Click the `FriendId` index in the MyTable table and drag your mouse to the `FriendId` index in the GotCard table. When you let go of the mouse button, you will see the Edit Relationship dialog box, as seen in Figure 3.44.

FIGURE 3.44.

The Edit Relationship dialog box.

The Edit Relationship dialog box is showing you that MyTable is related to GotCard and that that relationship is based on the `FriendId` index in MyTable and the `FriendId` index in GotCard. The Edit Relationship dialog box also says that the Relationship Type: for this is One To Many. This relationship is one-to-many because you have used the Primary index of MyTable and related it to a Regular index in GotCard. Because a Regular index can have multiple entries for a given value, it is the many side of the relationship.

Click the OK button in the Edit Relationship dialog box. The Database Designer will look like Figure 3.45.

FIGURE 3.45.

The Database Designer showing a relationship between MyTable and GotCard.

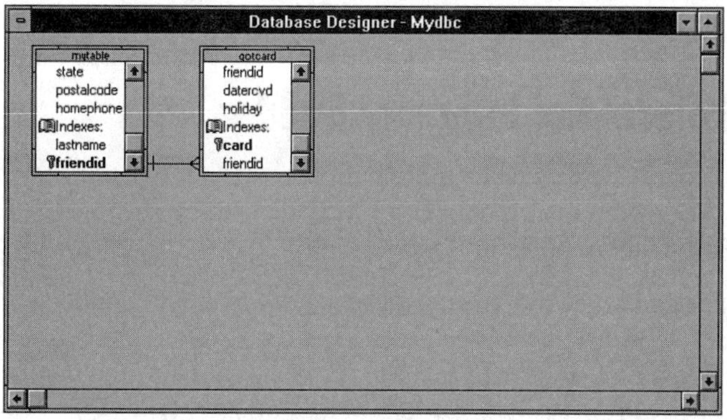

Notice the line connecting MyTable and GotCard. This is the visual representation of your persistent relationship between these two tables; note that the "crow's foot" points to the many side of the relationship. Double-click the line connecting the two tables to bring up the Edit Relationship dialog box for this relationship. Figure 3.46 shows the Edit Relationship dialog box as you will see it.

FIGURE 3.46.

The Edit Relationship dialog box for an existing persistent relationship.

Notice the new button to the right of the Relationship Type labeled Referential Integrity.

Referential Integrity

When you have tables related to each other there is an interdependence that exists between these two tables. The data in one table is, in a way, dependent on the data in the other table. In the example database you are creating, if you have a GotCard record that has a FriendId for which there is no FriendId that matches in MyTable there is a problem. The problem is that the reference in GotCard to records in MyTable is broken; you have a reference to a nonexistent record. When you have no problems with the references between tables the database is said to have Referential Integrity (RI).

Visual FoxPro's Database Container provides a mechanism for you to protect the RI of your database. You can use the Triggers listed in Table 3.14 to enforce RI. These three triggers—Insert, Update, and Delete—fire whenever an action is taken that could cause a breakdown in the RI.

You could use the Table Properties dialog box and enter program code into the triggers for each table involved in the relationship to make sure that the integrity of the relationship is not violated. There is, however, an easier way.

Referential Integrity Builder

Click the Referential Integrity button in the Edit Relationship dialog box seen in Figure 3.46. Clicking this button brings up Visual FoxPro's Referential Integrity Builder (RI Builder). The RI Builder is shown in Figure 3.47.

The grid at the top, the relationship grid, of the RI Builder shows a list of the persistent relationships that are defined in the Database Designer. In Figure 3.47 you see only one because there is only one relationship in the database. Click the mytable cell of the grid. Notice that there is an arrow on the left side of the grid next to mytable. This arrow indicates the currently selected relationship, the relationship that will be affected by what you do in the RI Builder.

The relationship grid has seven columns, the first two show what tables are involved and the last two show the indexes involved in the relationship. The middle three columns—Update,

Delete, and Insert—refer to the three triggers that the database container provides. Click in the Update column for the MyTable - GotCard relationship.

FIGURE 3.47.

The Referential Integrity Builder.

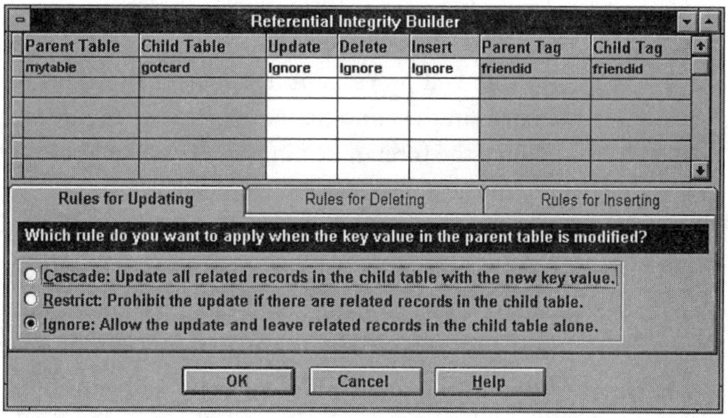

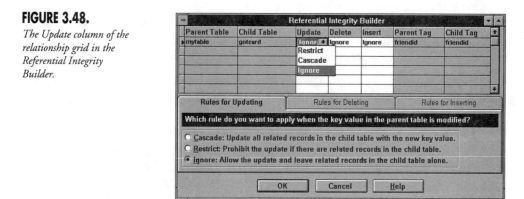

Notice that this column has a combo box in it with the options of Restrict, Cascade, and Ignore, as seen in Figure 3.48.

FIGURE 3.48.

The Update column of the relationship grid in the Referential Integrity Builder.

The Delete column has the same three options as the Update column. Finally, the Insert column has only two options, Restrict and Ignore. The three columns in the relationship grid are duplicated at the bottom of the RI Builder with tabbed pages. There are three tabbed pages, one for Rules for Updating, Rules for Deleting, and Rules for Inserting. You can set your RI rules in either the columns of the relationship grid or on the tabbed pages, whichever you find easiest.

The tabbed pages at the bottom each have a set of option buttons on them which explain the meaning of each option. Each rule is described in Table 3.17.

Table 3.17. The Referential Integrity rules.

Rule	Purpose
Updating	This rule governs the updating or changing of the primary key in the parent table. Ignore will apply no rule and enable free updating of the primary key. Restrict will prevent, or disallow, changing of the primary key if there are any records in the child tables referring to the record being updated. Cascade will change the foreign key in the related child table records when the primary key in the parent table is changed.
Deleting	Governs the deletion of parent table records. Ignore will enable any parent table record to be deleted. Restrict will disallow the deletion of a parent table record if there are any child table records related to it. Cascade will delete all of the child table records related to a parent table record that is being deleted.
Inserting	Governs the insertion of new child table records. Ignore enables the insertion of child records without any rule. Restrict disallows the insertion of a child record unless there is an existing parent table record to which the child record is related. There is no Cascade option for the insert rule.

Use either the relationship grid columns or the pages at the bottom of the RI Builder to set the three rules as Update=Restrict, Delete=Cascade, and Insert=Restrict. Notice that while you are setting these rules in one place, the other location is being updated to reflect your actions.

Click the OK button in the RI Builder and answer Yes to the message box about saving your changes. Figure 3.49 shows the next message box you will see.

FIGURE 3.49.

The Referential Integrity Builder message box.

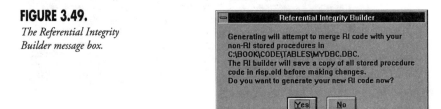

The message box in Figure 3.49 is informing you that the code that the RI Builder will create will be written in the stored procedures of your DBC. If you have written your own code in the stored procedures, the RI Builder will attempt to merge its code with yours. This is usually not a problem unless the code you wrote in some way conflicts with the code that the RI Builder will generate.

Click the OK button in the message box seen in Figure 3.49. You will, briefly, see a thermometer bar while the RI Builder writes the code into the stored procedures of the Database Container. Then the Edit Relationship dialog box will be redisplayed. Click the OK button to close the dialog box.

Bring up the Database Designer's Short Cut Menu with your right mouse button and choose Stored Procedures. You will get an Edit window with the stored procedures displayed in it. The program code you see here was written by the RI Builder. Notice the first line in the code:

```
**__RI_HEADER!@ Do NOT REMOVE or MODIFY this line!!!! @!__RI_HEADER**
```

This is a marker put there by the RI Builder so that if you ever changed your rules in the RI Builder it will be able to find its codes in the stored procedures and make the changes. There is another line at the end of the RI Builder code:

```
**__RI_FOOTER!@ Do NOT REMOVE or MODIFY this line!!!! @!__RI_FOOTER**
```

which marks the end of the RI Builder's code. *Do not remove or edit these lines.* If you do remove them, the RI Builder will not be able to properly identify its code in the stored procedures, and you will not be able to change the rules in the future using the RI Builder.

Summary

This chapter started out by defining the concepts involved in designing your database. Then you were introduced to the Rules of Normalization that are used to validate your design and ensure that there are no anomalies or redundancies in the design.

You used the various tools in Visual FoxPro to create a table and a database. Visual FoxPro can use tables that are in a database container and tables that are free standing (free tables). Which is the better way? The database container is the better way!

With the database container you can maintain all of the tables involved in a particular application together. You can specify the persistent relationships and the referential integrity rules for those tables and their relationships. You can specify the validation rules for fields and records. The rules you specify in the database container cannot be violated by the users or yourself.

To use the database container you must do careful and thorough analysis and design of your tables, the relationships, and the rules before you begin to create the database. This may sound like a pain, but it is really the only way to work. The major cause of failed application development projects is a poor database design.

Adding and Changing Data

4

IN THIS CHAPTER

Adding and changing data is a major part of any database management application. Visual FoxPro has some very powerful features for managing the addition and changing of data. There are both interactive methods and programmatic approaches available for managing your data.

This chapter uses one of the sample databases that comes with Visual FoxPro to demonstrate the concepts and commands presented. The database you will use is located in the directory \SAMPLES\DATA\ under your Visual FoxPro main directory and is named TestData.DBC.

Opening Databases

Before Visual FoxPro can use a table contained in a database container, that database container must be open. In the DBF file for a table contained in a database container, Visual FoxPro keeps track of the database to which the table belongs. This is called a *back link*. If you issue a USE `<filename>` command for a table that is in a database, Visual FoxPro automatically opens the respective database container. You can also open the database container before you USE any tables in the database.

Type the following command in the Command window to open the Testdata database container:

```
OPEN DATABASE C:\VFP\SAMPLES\DATA\TESTDATA.DBC
```

Replace C:\VFP with the drive and directory names for your Visual FoxPro directory. The database combo box in the standard toolbar should display `testdata`, indicating that the TestData.DBC database container has been opened.

The syntax for the OPEN DATABASE command follows and the command is described in Table 4.1.

```
OPEN DATABASE
    [DatabaseName | ?]
    [EXCLUSIVE | SHARED]
    [NOUPDATE]
    [VALIDATE]
```

Table 4.1. The OPEN DATABASE command options.

Option	Description
DatabaseName	The name of the database container to be opened. `DatabaseName` can include the path to the database container. You only need to specify the file extension if it is not .DBC. If you omit `DatabaseName`, Visual FoxPro will display the Open dialog box.
?	Displays the Visual FoxPro Open dialog box from which you can choose the database to open.
EXCLUSIVE	Using this option causes the database container to be opened in exclusive mode. The exclusive mode prevents other users from using the database

Option	Description
	container in a multiuser environment. If another user tries to open the database while it is open in exclusive mode, that user will receive an error. If you omit EXCLUSIVE and SHARED, the current setting of the SET EXCLUSIVE command is honored.
SHARED	Opens the database container in shared mode. Shared mode enables other users to open the database container from their machines in a multiuser environment.
NOUPDATE	Opens the database container in read-only mode, meaning that no changes can be made to the database definition. If you omit the NOUPDATE option, the database is opened in read-write mode and changes can be made. The NOUPDATE option on the OPEN DATABASE command has no effect on the tables in the database. You need to use the NOUPDATE option on the USE command for each table to enforce read-only mode on tables.
VALIDATE	Tells Visual FoxPro to ensure that the references in the database container are valid. The items checked are: tables and indexes referenced are available on the disk, referenced fields and index tags exist in the tables and indexes.

Opening a database container does not open the tables in that database. You need to USE any tables you want explicitly. The USE command is explained in Chapter 3, "Creating and Working with Tables." When you USE a table, Visual FoxPro first looks in the current database container for that table. If the table is not found there, Visual FoxPro looks for a free table. This search order for the named table means that if an open database has a table with the same name as a free table, the USE command finds and opens the table in the database.

TIP

To use a free table that has the same name as a table in the current database, first issue the command SET DATABASE TO. This command makes none of the open databases current, and you can USE the free table. Once you have the free table open, you can SET DATABASE back to your database container.

You can have more than one database container open at the same time. Each database you open will be opened in its own area (do not confuse this with the work areas that are used when opening tables; databases are automatically placed in separate areas, whereas you must specifically make sure that tables don't get opened on top of each other through the SELECT command or the IN option of the USE command). You use the SET DATABASE TO *<DatabaseName>* command to set the current database container from among the open database containers.

It is possible to USE a table that is contained in a database other than the current database. The ! symbol is used in the filename for the USE command to separate the database name from the table name. For example, the following command opens the Customer table in the TestData database even if TestData is not the current database.

```
USE TestData!Customer
```

Opening Tables

Chapter 3 introduced and documented the Visual FoxPro USE command. Like database containers, you can have more than one table open at the same time. It is necessary to have multiple tables open simultaneously in order to exploit the relational powers of Visual FoxPro. Chapter 11, "Working with Visual FoxPro's Relational Powers," covers these capabilities in detail.

Visual FoxPro provides the capability to have multiple tables open simultaneously through *work areas*. A work area is an area of memory that Visual FoxPro handles as an open table. There are 32,767 work areas available per *data session* in Visual FoxPro. Data sessions are explained in Chapter 12, "Designing and Customizing Forms." In this chapter, you will only use the default data session.

Whenever you USE a table, that table is opened in a work area. If the USE command that opens the table does not specify the work area with the IN option, the table is opened in the current work area. There is always a current work area selected. You can use the SELECT <WorkAreaNumber¦AliasName> command to choose a different work area to become the current work area. When you start Visual FoxPro work area, number 1 of the default data session is the current work area.

When you USE a table in a work area, that work area is assigned an alias name. The alias name is the name of the table you opened in the work area (unless you specify the alias name with the ALIAS option of the USE command). You can SELECT a work area by using either its number or its alias name.

> **TIP**
>
> It is a good idea to use a work area's alias name when selecting or otherwise referring to it. It is much easier to read and understand SELECT Customer than SELECT 23.

The following code opens the OrdItems table from the TestData database in work area 1 and the Customer table from the same database in work area 2:

```
SELECT 1
USE TestData!OrdItems
```

```
SELECT 2
USE TestData!Customer
```

In actual applications you may find yourself not knowing which work area is available (having no table open in it) to open a table. You can use the work area number 0 to handle this situation. When you SELECT 0 Visual FoxPro makes the lowest numbered work area without a table open the current work area. You can also specify IN 0 on the USE command to get the table open in the next available work area. The difference in these two approaches is that with SELECT 0 you are actually changing the current work area to a new one; however, with the IN 0 option of the USE command, the current work area is unchanged after the table has been opened in the next available work area.

Wait a minute here. If Visual FoxPro uses some unknown work area to open the table, how do you know which work area was used? You don't! And you don't need to know.

You can refer to the work area by its alias name. Always using the alias name to refer to the work area eliminates your need to know the actual work area number. The following code opens the OrdItem and Customer tables from the TestData database in two different work areas and then selects the work area with the Customer table.

```
USE TestData!Customer IN 0
SELECT 0
USE TestData!OrdItems
SELECT Customer
```

Referring to Fields in a Particular Table

When you have multiple tables open simultaneously, it is possible that two or more of those tables might have fields with the same name. How can you be specific about which field you want when more than one table has a field with the same name?

For example, if you had Customer and Vendor tables in different work areas, and both of those tables had a field named Company, what would be displayed on-screen when you issued the following command?

```
? Company
```

The answer is the field named Company in the current work area, if there were such a field in the current work area. If the current work area did not have a table open, or if the table open in the current work area did not have a field named Company, you would get a Variable Not Found error. You can specify that you want to display the field named Company in the work area with an alias name of Customer in the following way:

```
? Customer.Company
```

You use the work area's alias name and the field name separated by a period.

> **NOTE**
>
> Visual FoxPro has a reserved alias name for referring to memory variables. If there is
> both a field and a memory variable with the same name, Visual FoxPro will always use
> the field in the table unless you include the reserved alias M in the reference. Specifying
> ? m.Company displays the memory variable named Company; using ? Company displays
> the field in the table. Also, avoid using a single letter as an alias because these are
> reserved by Visual FoxPro.

Using the *BROWSE* Command to See Your Data

Visual FoxPro's BROWSE command can be used to display a table's records in a column per field,
row per record format. Type the following commands in the Command window after you have
the TestData database open:

```
USE Customer
BROWSE
```

You should see a window on your screen similar to the one in Figure 4.1.

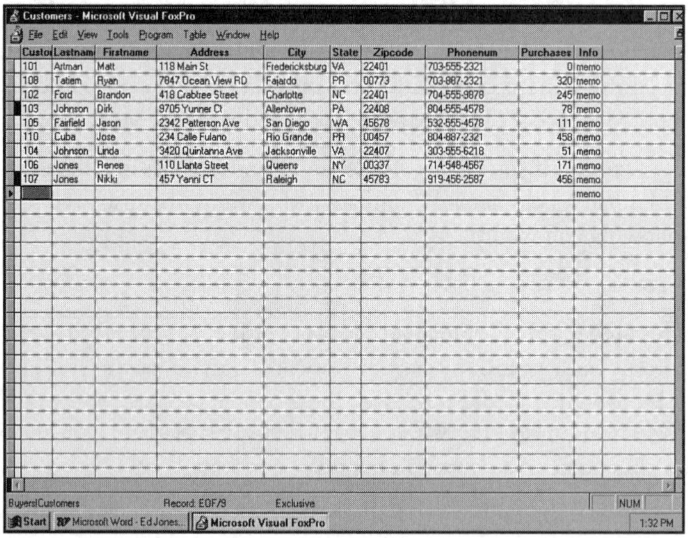

FIGURE 4.1.

*The Customer table
in a Browse window.*

In the browse window, each row is a record from the Customer table and each column is a
field from the Customer table. The scrollbars on the right and bottom of the browse window

can be used to scroll the records and fields, respectively. In the browse window, the row that has the arrow head in the farthest left column is the "current" record.

Visual FoxPro maintains a pointer in memory that indicates the current record. The current record is the one that will be affected by the commands you issue. For example, if the status bar at the bottom of the screen shows a message that says `Record: 1/91`, the current record is record number 1 and there are 91 records in the table.

Take some time now to scroll around in the Customer table. Notice that the browse window has more fields and records in it than you can see immediately. `BROWSE` is a very helpful command for perusing your tables interactively. `BROWSE` can also be used programmatically in your applications to present the records of a table to users who are working with the data.

This chapter describes some of the power of the `BROWSE` command in the "Using `BROWSE`" section. Chapter 12, "Designing and Customizing Forms," expands on displaying multiple records for editing in the form of grids in your Visual FoxPro forms.

In the browse window, you can edit the fields in your table. Simply typing the data you want in a field changes the values stored in the table. Of course, what you type must pass the validation rules and triggers stored in the database container. See Chapter 3 for information on the validation rules and triggers.

The browse windows can show you your data in either of two displays; the one in Figure 4.1 is called Browse, and the other view is called Edit. Select the View | Edit menu option. Your browse window should now look like Figure 4.2.

FIGURE 4.2.

The Customer table seen in the Edit view.

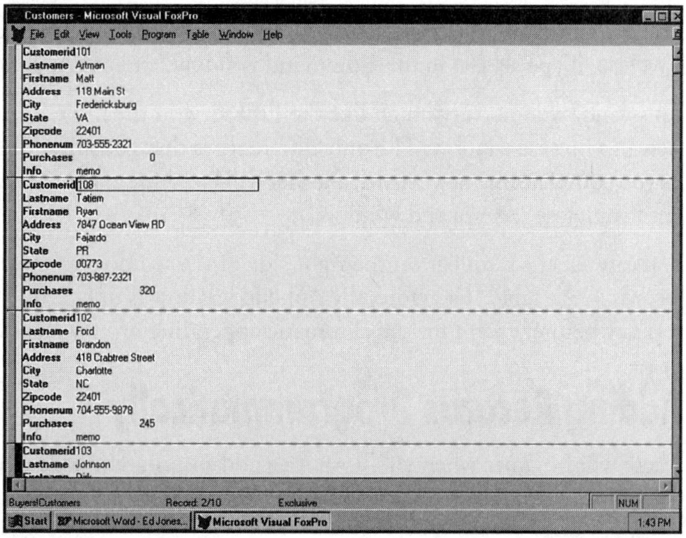

In Edit view, you can see more of the fields for each record in the browse window, but you can see fewer records at one time. This style of browse window can be achieved directly from the Command window by typing EDIT instead of BROWSE.

Adding Records to Your Table

One of the processes all database management systems must provide is adding records to tables. Visual FoxPro gives you both interactive methods and programming methods for adding records.

Using *BROWSE*

You can add new records to a table through the browse window. The Table menu gives you options for managing your table, and among those is Append New Record. The Table | Append New Record menu option shortcut keystroke is Ctrl+Y. You can press Ctrl+Y to execute the Table | Append New Record menu option without navigating the menu. If your browse window is in Edit view change to the Browse view and press Ctrl+Y.

You will see that a new record has been added to the Customer table and the cust_id field is selected in the browse window. You can now type the values for the fields in this new record. Fill the new record with any information you choose. Be sure to provide a unique cust_id value because that field is set up as the primary key index for this table.

Using *APPEND*

Another command that you can use from the Command window to add new records to a table is APPEND. Type APPEND in the Command window, and the Append window will appear.

This window looks very much like the Edit view in the browse window. In fact, it is the Edit view in a browse window. The only difference is that you are adding a new record to the table. As you complete one new record, another will be added and you will advance to that new record until you close the Append window.

You can use the scrollbar on the right side of the window to move back through the existing records in the table. Therefore, the Append window is in fact an edit window just like the one you saw before, except for the automatic appending of new records.

Adding Records Programmatically

There will be times when you'll want to add in program code a new record to a table rather than adding it interactively. Visual FoxPro provides two ways to get a new record into your table.

APPEND BLANK

The APPEND command has some options available, and among them is the BLANK option. The BLANK option of the APPEND command adds a new blank record to a table without bringing up the Append window. The APPEND command syntax follows and is described in Table 4.2.

```
APPEND
    [BLANK]
    [IN WorkAreaNumber ¦ AliasName]
    [NOMENU]
```

Table 4.2. The APPEND command.

Option	Description
BLANK	Appends one blank record to the current table. The record is added to the end of the table. When the BLANK option is included an edit window is *not* opened. You can use BROWSE, CHANGE, EDIT, or a form to edit the new record.
IN *WorkAreaNumber*	Specifies the work area number in which the new record will be appended.
IN *AliasName*	Used to specify the alias name of the work area in which the new record is to be appended. If you omit the *WorkAreaNumber* and the *AliasName,* the new record will be appended in the current work area. If you issue an APPEND command and there is no table open, the Open dialog box is displayed. If you specify either *WorkAreaNumber* or *AliasName* in the APPEND command, that work area becomes the current work area. If you include the BLANK option, a blank record is added in that work area, but the work area does not become the current work area.
NOMENU	Specifies that the Table menu should not be displayed in the system menu during the APPEND process, preventing changes to the format of the Append window.

After you add a blank record to your table with APPEND BLANK you will probably want to update the contents of that record. As Table 4.2 indicates, you can use any of the editing commands in Visual FoxPro to edit the new record. You can also update the contents of the new record, or any record for that matter, using either the REPLACE, GATHER, or UPDATE commands described later in this chapter in the "Using REPLACE," "Using SCATTER/GATHER," and "Using SQL UPDATE" sections.

SQL *INSERT INTO*

The fastest performer for adding a new record and updating the values in the fields of the new record is the SQL INSERT INTO command. This is the quickest method because in one command, it adds the new record and populates that record with data. The speed difference between the APPEND BLANK and then GATHER combination and the INSERT INTO command is most important in a mulituser environment where network communications become involved.

The syntax of the INSERT INTO command follows and is described in Table 4.3.

```
INSERT INTO TableName [(FName1, FName2, ...)]
      VALUES (Exp1, Exp2, ...)
- Or -
INSERT INTO TableName FROM ARRAY ArrayName ¦ FROM MEMVAR
```

Table 4.3. The SQL INSERT INTO command.

Option	Description
TableName	The name of the table that the new record is added to. *TableName* can include a path and can be a name expression. If the named table is not open, it will be opened exclusively in a new work area and the record will be added (if the table is contained in a database container, that database will be open but will not become the current database). The new work area will not be selected. If the table is open, the new record is added to that table. If the table is open in a work area other than the current work area, that work area is not selected.
(FName1, FName2, ...)	A list of the field names to be updated, separated by commas and enclosed in a set of parentheses.
VALUES *(Exp1, Exp2, ...)*	The values to be used in updating the fields in the fields list. These values will be placed in the respective fields of the fields list. If the fields list is omitted, the values will be placed in the fields of the table according to the order in which the fields were defined when the table was created.
FROM ARRAY *ArrayName*	Specifies the name of an array that will be used to update the values of the fields in the new record. The contents of the first array element are used to update the first field, the second element of the array updates the second field, and so on.
FROM MEMVAR	The fields of the new record are updated from the values in memory variables that share the same names as the fields.

> **CAUTION**
>
> The *TableName* used in the INSERT INTO command must be the table's actual filename and not the work area alias name. You can use the long table name stored in the database container if that database is the current database when INSERT INTO is issued.

Deleting Records in Your Table

One or more records in a table might have to be deleted for a variety of reasons. Deleting records in Visual FoxPro is a two-step process. The first step is to mark the record to be deleted, and the second step is to remove the marked records from the table. There is a third alternative, which never actually removes the deleted records, called recycling deleted records. In the recycling scenario, you would mark records to be deleted as usual, but instead of removing those marked records from the table, you reuse one of the marked records when a new record needs to be added to the table. This recycling technique will be explained in more detail in the "Permanently Removing Deleted Records from Your Table" section later in this chapter.

There are two commands in Visual FoxPro that can be used to mark records for deletion: the DELETE command and the DELETE FROM command.

Both of these commands mark a record or a number of records for deletion. These marked records are said to be deleted because they are marked, even though the marked records are still in the table.

Visual FoxPro has the SET DELETED ON¦OFF command to control whether or not these records get processed when using other commands. If SET DELETED ON is issued, the records marked for deletion are not processed by Visual FoxPro commands. These deleted records are not shown in a browse window, included in a report, or included in any other Visual FoxPro command. One notable exception to this is the RECCOUNT() function, which always returns the physical count of records in the table regardless of their deleted status.

If SET DELETED OFF is issued, the deleted records appear just like any other records.

The DELETE command is used to mark one or more records in a table to be deleted. This command is said to be a *scoped* command because it affects a scope of records. The default scope for the DELETE command is NEXT 1, indicating that the command will affect the NEXT 1 record.

The syntax for the DELETE command follows and is explained in Table 4.4.

```
DELETE
    [Scope]
    [FOR ExpL1]
    [WHILE ExpL2]
    [IN WorkAreaNumber ¦ AliasName]
    [NOOPTIMIZE]
```

Table 4.4. The options for the DELETE command.

Option	Description
Scope	The range of records to be considered for marking. Acceptable scopes are ALL, NEXT ##, RECORD ##, and REST. ALL considers all records in the table, NEXT ## considers the next ## records, RECORD ## considers only record number ##, and REST considers the rest of the records in the table starting with the current record. The default scope for DELETE is NEXT 1. Notice that Scope controls the records to be considered for deletion. The FOR and WHILE options determine whether a particular record is deleted. If both FOR and WHILE are omitted, all of the records within the scope are marked for deletion.
FOR *ExpL1*	Only the records within the scope that meet the FOR *ExpL1* expression are marked for deletion. The FOR option on the DELETE command can be optimized by Visual FoxPro's Rushmore optimization (see Chapter 11, "Working with Visual FoxPro's Relational Powers," and Chapter 21, "Power Techniques for Power Users," for more information about Rushmore optimization).
WHILE *ExpL2*	*ExpL2* specifies a logical condition, which, as soon as that condition becomes false, the DELETE command terminates. The FOR and WHILE options can be used together in the same DELETE command.
IN *WorkAreaNumber*¦*AliasName*	You can use either the *WorkAreaNumber* or the *AliasName* of a work area to cause the DELETE command to process records in a specific work area. If the IN option is not used, the deletions occur in the current work area.
NOOPTIMIZE	Disables Rushmore optimization for this DELETE command.

An example using the DELETE command to delete all the records that have a state of NY and a maximum order amount less than $100.00 within the next 500 records follow:

```
USE Customer ORDER TAG State
SEEK "NY"
DELETE NEXT 500 WHILE State = "NY" FOR MaxOrdAmt < 100
```

The other command you have for deleting records is the DELETE FROM command. The syntax of the DELETE FROM command follows and is explained in Table 4.5.

```
DELETE FROM [DatabaseName!]TableName
   [WHERE FilterCondition]
```

Table 4.5. The DELETE FROM command.

Option	Description
FROM [*DatabaseName!*]*TableName*	Specifies the name of the table in which records are to be deleted. You can refer to a table that is in a database other than the current database by including the *DatabaseName!*. The ! is the delimiter between the *DatabaseName* and the *TableName*.
WHERE *FilterCondition*	Establishes a condition or set of conditions that a record must be in if it is to be deleted. The *FilterCondition* is a logical expression for which a true value causes a record to be deleted and a false value causes that record to not be deleted. You can use AND and OR to connect multiple conditions into the *FilterCondition*.

The difference between the two delete commands is that one of them, DELETE, uses the standard Xbase syntax of FOR and/or WHILE clauses to selected the records to be deleted. The DELETE FROM command uses a SQL-like syntax of FROM and WHERE clauses.

The example used to illustrate the DELETE command is used with the DELETE FROM command in the following:

```
DELETE FROM TestData!Customer WHERE State = "NY" AND MaxOrdAmt < 100
```

Telling Whether a Record Is Deleted

Now you know how to mark the records in your tables for deletion. You also know that these deleted records are not removed from the table until you execute another step in the removal process. Then how can you tell if a particular record has been marked for deletion?

Visual FoxPro has the DELETED() function to do this for you. The DELETED() function will return a logical value of .T. (true) if the current record is deleted and .F. (false) if the record is not deleted. You can check the status of the current record in another work area by including inside the parentheses of the DELETED() function either the work area number or the alias name.

Recalling Records That Have Been Deleted

Because deleted records are not removed from the table, you can undelete, or recall, them. The RECALL command is used for this purpose.

RECALL is a scoped command that accepts a FOR and WHILE clause just like DELETE. The default scope for RECALL is NEXT 1. RECALL, with no options specified, will remove the deletion mark from the current record.

Permanently Removing Deleted Records from Your Table

If you want the deleted record permanently removed from a table, you can use the PACK command. PACK will copy to a temporary file all the records in a table that are not marked for deletion. When this copying is complete, PACK erases the original table and renames the temporary file to the name of the original table. Finally, PACK re-creates any indexes that were open when the PACK command was issued. If the Escape key is pressed during the PACK command, the original file is restored. The PACK command requires exclusive use of the table being packed. (See Chapter 32, "Multiuser Programming and Techniques," for more information regarding exclusive use of tables.)

PACK also reorganizes the contents of a memo file to recover lost space due to edits that might have occurred. Remember in Chapter 3 you found out that the memo field data is stored in a separate file from the table.

The PACK command has two options you can use: DBF and MEMO. Issuing the PACK DBF command only removes the deleted records and re-creates any open indexes; it does not reorganize the memo file. PACK MEMO only reorganizes the memo file and does not remove the deleted records or re-create the open indexes.

There is an alternative to packing your tables: recycling the deleted records. In record recycling, you leave the deleted record in the table. You make sure SET DELETED is ON in your application so that the deleted records won't influence the results of calculations or reports. Then, whenever a user wants to add a record to the table, your program first looks for a deleted record. If a deleted record is found, that record is recalled and used for the new data; otherwise, a new record is added to the table.

The advantages of the recycling approach are manyfold and are as follows:

- None of the commands used in the recycling requires exclusive use of the table.

- There is no copying of the entire table going on, so the performance is better.

- After a while, most of the additions to the table will find a deleted record to reuse, so the table is not being expanded and contracted often, which causes disk-file fragmentation and its associated performance degradation.

Commands That Change the Data in Your Table

There are three commands you can use to change the values contained in the fields of an existing record programmatically. These commands are introduced and described in the next three sections of this chapter.

Using *REPLACE*

The REPLACE command is one that is familiar to Xbase developers. REPLACE will update the contents of a field with the value of an expression. The syntax of the REPLACE command is shown below and described in Table 4.6.

```
REPLACE Field1 WITH Exp1 [ADDITIVE][, Field2 WITH Exp2 [ADDITIVE]]
   [Scope]
   [FOR ExpL1]
   [WHILE ExpL2]
   [IN WorkAreaNumber ¦ AliasName]
   [NOOPTIMIZE]
```

Table 4.6. The REPLACE command.

Option	Description
Field1 WITH Exp1	Specifies that the field named Field1 be updated with the value of Exp1. Multiple fields can be updated in one REPLACE command by including additional Field WITH Exp options separated by commas. When a numeric field is being updated and the value of the expression is larger, in some way, than the field being updated, the following rules are used to determine what value the field will get. - Decimals will be rounded to fit.

continues

Table 4.6. continued

Option	Description
	■ If the value still doesn't fit, scientific notation will be used to store the number.
	■ If the value still doesn't fit, the field will be filled with asterisks (*).
ADDITIVE	On each *Field1* WITH *Exp1* that is updating a memo field you can specify the ADDITIVE option. Using ADDITIVE will add the value of *Exp1* to the end of the existing value of the memo field. If the ADDITIVE option is omitted then the memo's contents will be overwritten by the value of *Exp1*.
Scope	The range of records to be updated. Acceptable scopes are ALL, NEXT ##, RECORD ##, and REST. ALL will consider all records in the table, NEXT ## will consider the next ## records, RECORD ## will only consider record number ##, and REST will consider the rest of the records in the table starting with the current record. The default scope for REPLACE is NEXT 1. Notice that the scope controls the records to be considered for update; the FOR and WHILE options will determine if a particular record is updated or not. If both FOR and WHILE are omitted, then all of the records within the scope will be updated.
FOR *ExpL1*	Only the records, within the scope, that meet the *ExpL1* FOR expression will be updated. The FOR option on the REPLACE command can be optimized by Visual FoxPro's Rushmore optimization (see Chapter 11 and Chapter 21 for more information about Rushmore optimization).
WHILE *ExpL2*	*ExpL2* specifies a logical condition which as soon as that condition becomes false the REPLACE command will terminate. The FOR and WHILE options can be used together in the same REPLACE command.
IN *WorkAreaNumber*|*AliasName*	You can use either the *WorkAreaNumber* or the *AliasName* of a work area to cause the REPLACE command to process records in a specific work area. If the IN option is not used the updates occur in the current work area.
NOOPTIMIZE	Disables Rushmore optimization for this REPLACE command.

In a REPLACE command, you can update fields in a work area other than the current work area by prefacing the field names with the alias for the work area, as in

```
REPLACE OtherAlias.Field WITH Exp
```

CAUTION

Although you can replace fields in another work area, the scope for the REPLACE command is controlled by the current work area. If you attempt to replace the fields in another work area while the current work area is at end of file, or has no table open, no updates take place. The reason for this is that the scope for REPLACE is, by default, NEXT 1, and there is no NEXT 1 record in the current work area, so no REPLACE occurs.

TIP

Replacing multiple fields with one REPLACE command executes faster than using multiple REPLACE commands to update each field separately.

Using *SCATTER/GATHER*

Sometimes it is helpful to move the values in a record into memory as memory variables, an array, or even an object (see Chapter 27, "Introduction to Object-Oriented Programming," for an explanation of object orientation) in order to facilitate working with the data. Visual FoxPro's SCATTER command is exactly what you need to accomplish this.

The SCATTER command syntax follows and is described in Table 4.7.

```
SCATTER
   [FIELDS [FieldList ¦
   LIKE Skeleton ¦
   EXCEPT Skeleton]]
   [MEMO]
   [TO ArrayName ¦ MEMVAR ¦ NAME ObjName]
   [BLANK]
```

Table 4.7. The SCATTER command.

Option	Description
FIELDS *FieldList*	Lists the fields to be scattered to memory variables or to the array. If you omit the FIELDS option, all fields in the record are scattered. Memo fields can be included in the *FieldList* if you follow the *FieldList* with the option MEMO. General fields

continues

Table 4.7. continued

Option	Description
	are always ignored by the SCATTER command regardless of the inclusion or omission of the MEMO option.
FIELDS LIKE *Skeleton* FIELDS EXCEPT *Skeleton*	You also can select the fields to be scattered by using the LIKE or EXCEPT *Skeletons* on the FIELDS option. LIKE scatters the fields that match the *Skeleton,* and EXCEPT scatters all fields except those that match the *Skeleton*. The *Skeleton* can include wildcard characters: * for any characters and ? for a single character. To scatter all fields with names that begin with P, use SCATTER FIELDS LIKE P* TO MEMVAR You can combine both LIKE and EXCEPT skeletons in the same SCATTER command, as in SCATTER FIELDS LIKE P* EXCEPT POSTAL* TO MEMVAR
MEMO	Specifies that memo fields should also be scattered. If the MEMO option is omitted, memo fields are *not* scattered. Memo fields can take up a lot of memory when they are scattered. If there is not enough memory, Visual FoxPro will generate an error message. If a memo field is too big to fit in memory, neither it nor any other memo fields included in the fields list are scattered to memory. The memory variables or array elements for these memo fields are given the value of .F..
TO *ArrayName*	Specify the name of an array to receive the values of the fields in the fields list. The array elements will correspond to the order of the fields in the fields list. If no fields list was provided, the elements of the array will match the order of the fields in the table's structure. If the array doesn't exist, it is created and dimensioned to the correct size to handle the fields being scattered. If the array exists and has too few elements for the fields list, the array is redimensioned to the correct size. If the array exists and is too large, the additional elements of the array are unchanged.
MEMVAR	Creates, or updates, memory variables that have the same names as the fields being scattered. You need to use the alias named to reference these memory variables because they will have the same names as the fields in the table. Visual FoxPro always uses the field when there is a conflict between a memory variable and field name. Important: do not include

Option	Description
	the word TO with MEMVAR; if you do, Visual FoxPro scatters the fields to an array named MEMVAR.
NAME *ObjName*	Creates an object that has properties with the same name as the fields in the fields list. The value of each of the object's properties are the values from the table's fields. Properties are not created for memo or general fields.
BLANK	The option BLANK will cause the SCATTER command to create a blank value for each field in the array or memvars being created.

Now you need to be able to perform the reverse of the SCATTER command. Visual FoxPro provides the GATHER command to perform this function. The syntax for the GATHER command is similar to the SCATTER command, so there is no table describing the options. The syntax for the GATHER command is as follows:

```
GATHER
    FROM ArrayName ¦ MEMVAR ¦ NAME ObjName
    [FIELDS FieldList ¦
    FIELDS LIKE Skeleton ¦
    FIELDS EXCEPT Skeleton]
    [MEMO]
```

Refer to Table 4.7 for the use and meaning of the various options in the GATHER command.

In the "Permanently Removing Deleted Records from Your Table" section earlier in this chapter, you were told about recycling deleted records. One of the things that needs to be done when recycling deleted records is to remove the data in that record before reusing it for new data. The SCATTER and GATHER commands can be used to blank out a record. The following code is one way of finding and blanking out a deleted record to prepare it for reuse.

```
* NewRec
*
* Purpose: Find a deleted record an drsuse it or if no deleted record
*          is available, append a new record in the current table.
*
PRIVATE lcDeleted, laTemp
* Save the current setting of deleted
lcDeleted = SET ( "DELETED" )
* Allow deleted records to be seen
SET DELETED OFF
* Find a deleted record
LOCATE FOR DELETED() = .T.
IF FOUND()
   * If we found a deleted record blank it
   SCATTER TO laTemp MEMO BLANK
   GATHER FROM laTemp MEMO
ELSE
```

```
    APPEND BLANK
ENDIF
IF lcDeleted = "ON"
    SET DELETED ON
ENDIF
RETURN
```

Using SQL *UPDATE*

As with INSERT INTO for adding new records, when you are updating existing records, Visual FoxPro has a SQL command that can perform the required work. The SQL command for updating records is UPDATE. The UPDATE command's syntax follows and is described in Table 4.8.

```
UPDATE [DatabaseName!]TableName
    SET Field1 = Exp1 [, Field2 = Exp2 ...]
    WHERE FilterCondition
```

Table 4.8. The SQL UPDATE command.

Option	Description
[DatabaseName!]TableName	Specifies the name of the table to be updated. DatabaseName! can be included to refer to a table in a noncurrent database.
SET Field1 = Exp1	Specifies the field to be updated and the value to use in updating the field. You can update more than one field by including a list of Field = Exp expressions separated by commas after the SET option.
WHERE FilterCondition	The FilterCondition is used to filter the records in the table that is being updated. You can specify filter conditions that are complex by using AND and OR to connect expressions in the filter condition. If the WHERE option is omitted, every record in the table is updated.

TIP

You can use the UPDATE command to update a single record by using a filter condition in the WHERE clause that refers to the desired record's primary key value. For example,

```
m.Cust_num = TestData!Customer.Cust_num
UPDATE TestData!Customer SET MaxOrdAmt = 0 ;
    WHERE TestData!Customer.Cust_num == m.Cust_num
```

Summary

Adding and changing data is an important operation within a database application. Visual FoxPro, as a database application development environment, provides a number of different methods of managing the addition and revision of data. The capabilities of the various commands provide a wealth of possibilities for designing your database application so that adding and changing data is convenient and robust.

Visual FoxPro also has powerful features for handling the multiuser issues in adding and changing data. Chapter 32, "Multiuser Programming and Techniques," covers these multiuser features. Visual FoxPro also provides for managing Client/Server data that resides on a database server. Chapter 38, "Client/Server Features," explains what is available in the Client/Server arena.

Data entry forms are a major aspect of designing your application. These data entry forms must deal with adding and changing data in your tables. Chapter 9, "Creating and Using Simple Forms," and Chapter 12, "Designing and Customizing Forms," cover the issues of binding your data tables to your data entry forms.

Arranging Data

Imagine a phone book in which the names were listed in arbitrary order instead of alphabetical order. I think you'd agree it wouldn't be too useful. Looking up someone's phone number would be rather daunting. You'd need to examine every name in the book before you could say the person's number was present or not, which would be unacceptable—we expect order in our data. In FoxPro, you can impose order on data in two ways: you can set the order in data tables temporarily by using an index, or you can rearrange the data permanently using a sort.

This chapter provides tips and techniques for ordering your data. In Visual FoxPro, as in any Xbase system, data is kept in a desired order using one of two methods: indexing or sorting.

Although indexing is by far the more common of the two, there are times when sorting makes sense. With *indexing*, a separate file is used to provide the order in which the records are accessed. With *sorting*, the data is physically copied in the desired order to a new table that permanently changes the order of the records. The first part of this chapter deals with indexing, the more commonly used and more complex technique. The second portion of the chapter covers sorting and provides examples of when sorting is the correct choice.

Indexing Defined

As stated previously, when you add an index to a Visual FoxPro table, you establish an order in which your records appear to be arranged, but the original table is not physically modified. When you index a Visual FoxPro table, FoxPro creates an index that contains record numbers and a minimum of one field (or an expression based on fields) from the corresponding table.

The index contains pointers to the physical records in the indexed table where the corresponding index value is found. Although the records within the associated table might not be sorted in any fashion physically, the table appears to be sorted in the manner of the index. An excellent analogy for understanding how Visual FoxPro indexes work is to compare the Visual FoxPro index to the index in the back of a book. Just as a book index is a separate section that provides a reference to where data is physically located elsewhere in the book, a Visual FoxPro index provides a reference for Visual FoxPro as to where records are physically located. Visual FoxPro then uses this reference to display or print the data in the desired order. In Visual FoxPro, you can create indexes with the Table Designer or in the command window using the appropriate commands.

The Benefits of Indexing

Why index a data table? Partly because Visual FoxPro offers so many variations on indexing, PC users new to Visual FoxPro sometimes wonder when indexing is necessary, if ever. An example may help. Remember the phone book. Generally, you know a person's name and are looking up the phone number. The order in which you expect to see the listings is alphabetical by name.

Suppose you had a phone number and wanted to know the name of the person who had this phone number (for example, a 911 call). You now expect a different order: by phone number.

By defining indexes on the phone book data table for both the name and phone number, you can make the order appear in either of the two orders; and, because an index is only a temporary ordering, you can switch back and forth at will by setting the index to use. Also implied in this discussion is the lookup speed advantage which indexes provide. FoxPro doesn't have to examine all the records in the data table to find a record you're interested in—it uses the index.

To summarize, indexing serves two purposes readily apparent to the FoxPro user: it keeps your data in a certain order and it speeds up searches on fields or expressions contained in the index.

The presence of indexes can also speed up Visual FoxPro's processing of Structured Query Language (SQL) queries. SQL queries tell FoxPro *what* data is desired but not *how* to get it. This is in contrast to procedural programming where each step required to perform the data-gathering task (that is, the *how)* must be described in complete detail. Visual FoxPro builds any needed indexes behind the scenes while processing the SQL query, but if the needed indexes already exist and are open, Visual FoxPro uses them to save time.

Along with the benefits comes a disadvantage: indexing can adversely affect overall performance. As you make changes to records in a table, Visual FoxPro updates all indexes that are open to reflect the changes to the table. If you have a large number of indexes open, this can have a degrading effect on performance. Each time you add a new record, for example, all of the open indexes must be updated to reflect the addition. You'll want to strike a balance between flexibility and performance by opening indexes that are truly needed while avoiding adding unnecessary indexes.

Types of Indexes

In the early days of Xbase, only one type of index was possible: separate index files were created, with the index data stored outside of the database (DBF) file. Everything was done from the command level, and each time you wanted to use an index file it had to be explicitly opened with a separate command along with opening the database file that contained the table. This led to a confusing directory structure for applications of any complexity—a single table could easily have a half-dozen different index files to help keep things in order in different ways. If your application used five or six different tables, the tables and corresponding index files alone could add 50 or more files to a single subdirectory.

When dBASE IV was introduced, it offered a technique that solved the problem of multiple index files cluttering a directory. With dBASE IV, *index tags* could be added to the database file containing the table. Different index tags could be added to a single database file, called a *compound index file.*

Visual FoxPro adopted this strategy to maintain compatibility with dBASE IV. Thus, you have two options for indexing information in Visual FoxPro: using a compound index file containing one or more index tags or creating single index files (in line with the indexing technique from the early days of Xbase).

Compound index files in Visual FoxPro have a .CDX extension, whereas single index files are assigned an .IDX extension. FoxPro provides commands and methods for creating either type of index.

From the command window, you can use different commands to create index tags or to create separate index files. The only area in which you do not have a choice is when you create indexes through the Table Designer. An index added through the Table Designer is stored in a special compound index file known as a *structural index file*. This .CDX has the same name as the data table that it indexes. It is opened automatically when you open the data table.

In general, it is advantageous to stick with the use of compound index files. One reason to use the older style of separate index files is when you need to maintain compatibility with early versions of FoxPro (1.*x* versions) or with other Xbase products (for example, dBASE III Plus).

Indexing from the Table Designer

When you're using the Table Designer, you can add or change indexes by choosing the table in the Project Manager and clicking Modify. The Table Designer dialog box is then opened with the Index tab displayed. You can create an index with the following steps:

1. Place the desired table in use, if it isn't already. (In the Project Manager, click the Table object and choose the Browse button.)

2. After the table is active, choose Modify from the Project Manager. The Table Designer is then opened.

3. On the Index tab of the Table Designer, choose the fields you wish to use in the index. By default, the index type is set as Regular, that is, a non-unique index on the table. There are three other index types available:

   Primary Index—This index type never permits duplicate values on specified fields or expressions. A primary index uniquely identifies a record in the table in which it is the primary index. Often, it is called the *primary key*. A primary index is presented as an option only for tables that are associated with a database container (in a .DBC), not free tables (stand-alone .DBFs). You can have only one primary index per table. Primary indexes, as well as candidate indexes, are used to maintain referential integrity among data tables in a database.

INTRODUCING REFERENTIAL INTEGRITY

Referential integrity is an area where FoxPro has stepped away from its Xbase roots and has grown into a complete relational-database management system. This growth introduces new SQL RDBMS database concepts, which need some explanation. An example may help to clarify referential integrity and show how some of new index types are used.

Suppose you define a personnel database that has a table called People. In this table, you've defined a field to hold a Social Security Number (SSAN). Because SSAN uniquely identifies each person in the People data table, it is a *candidate key* in this table. For the purposes of this example, that field is defined as the *primary key* and indexed as a *primary index*.

A primary key is a candidate key that is used for updates/additions to a table. There is only one primary key allowed per table even though there can be multiple candidate keys.

Suppose also that there are other tables in the Personnel database that need to refer to specific information found in the People table. By including a field for SSAN in those tables, the tables can refer to specific people in the People data table. Because this field refers to a primary key in another data table (the People table), it is called a *foreign key* in the referencing table.

For this example, let's invent a Jobs data table that lists details of jobs and positions in a company. In the Jobs table, you include a field called `incumbent_SSAN` and use a SSAN value here. You now can get any details on the incumbent from the People table without repeating any information other than the SSAN (that is, you've eliminated data redundancy, which is one of the goals of good database design). The `incumbent_SSAN` field *refers* to a record in the People table.

If Jim Smith with SSAN 011-010-0101 is a person in the People data table, and Jim holds the position of Lead Engineer, the `incumbent_SSAN` field in the Jobs data table would contain the value `011-010-0101`.

If Jim Smith were to leave the company, he would most likely be deleted from the People data table. This would remove the record that was keyed by the SSAN value `011-010-0101`. What about the entry in the Jobs table? The value found in the foreign key `incumbent_SSAN` certainly isn't correct; it points to a non-existent entry!

Maintaining the correctness of foreign-key references is known as *referential integrity*. FoxPro provides help establishing and maintaining persistent relationships and referential integrity among your tables.

Candidate Index—This index type does not permit the duplication of values on specified fields or expressions. *Candidate* refers to the status of the index. A candidate index can be used as the primary index on a table, and multiple candidate indexes can be created for a table. A candidate index can be used as the referencing or referenced index in a persistent relationship to establish referential integrity.

Unique Index—This index type does not prevent the creation of duplicate values of the index, but only the first record with this specific index value is referenced by the index. Unique indexes are provided primarily for backward compatibility.

Regular Index—This index is a non-unique index and is used for ordering and seeking records. This type of index makes it easy to gather collections of like items. For example, if State is a field indexed with a regular index, you might set the order to State to view the data in alphabetic state order.

4. After selecting the type of index you want to use, click the Expression button to open the Expression Builder dialog box, as shown in Figure 5.1. This is where you'll define what information will be used to compose the index. In the Functions section of the Expression Builder dialog box, you can choose the function types to use to build your expression. Also in the Expression Builder dialog box, you can see all of the available fields in the Fields list box and all of the available variables in the Variables list box that can be used in the construction of your expression.

   If needed, you can also add a filter to the index. Click the Filter button to activate the Expression Builder dialog box, where you can set up your filter.

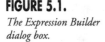

FIGURE 5.1.

*The Expression Builder
dialog box.*

5. After building your expressions and setting your filters, FoxPro provides a Verify button which examines your expression to be sure it is syntactically correct.

6. When you are finished choosing the fields or building the expressions that create the desired tags, click OK in the Expression Builder dialog box to return to the Index tab of the Table Designer dialog box.

7. Click OK to create the index.

Putting the Index to Use

Although you can create as many indexes as you want (within the limits of your hard disk), only one index can be *active* (controlling the order of the records) at one time. From the Project Manager, you decide which index should be the active index by clicking the *index object*, which is located at the end the list of fields for that table. If you want to change the structure of the index, double-click the index or click the Modify button. To activate the index, enter SET ORDER TO CITY in the command window or click the Browse button in the Project Manager. Next, enter BROWSE. Figure 5.2 shows the results.

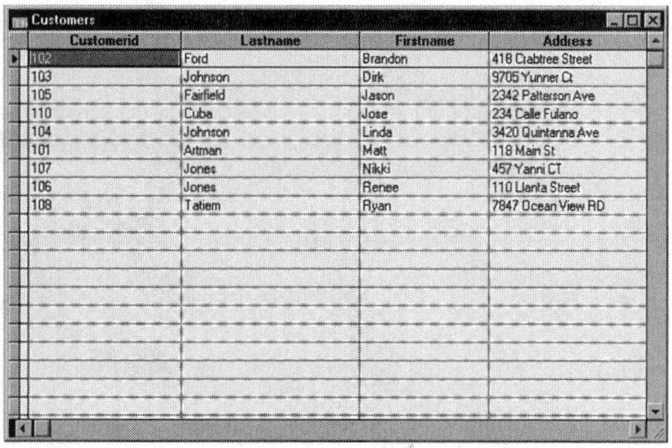

FIGURE 5.2.

A record displayed in browse mode using an active index.

Customerid	Lastname	Firstname	Address
102	Ford	Brandon	418 Crabtree Street
103	Johnson	Dirk	9705 Yunner Ct.
105	Fairfield	Jason	2342 Patterson Ave
110	Cuba	Jose	234 Calle Fulano
104	Johnson	Linda	3420 Quintanna Ave
101	Artman	Matt	118 Main St
107	Jones	Nikki	457 Yanni CT
106	Jones	Renee	110 Llanfa Street
108	Tatiem	Ryan	7847 Ocean View RD

Indexing on Multiple Fields from the Table Designer

It's common to need to index on more than one field. For example, you might want to see the records for a mailing list arranged in order of states, and where states are the same, in order of city names. You can do so by using the Expression Builder to build an expression that combines more than one field. In this example, you'll create an index that is the concatenation of two character strings.

TIP

Ensure that the items you wish to combine are of the same data type; otherwise, FoxPro will generate an error. You can cast them into the same data type by using the various functions FoxPro provides for this purpose.

To create an index on multiple fields, use these steps:

1. Place the desired table in use, if it isn't already. (From the Project Manager, choose the table's name in the Tables list and click the Modify button, then go directly to step 3.)

2. Next, double-click the index object to activate the Table Designer dialog box, or you can click the Modify button.

3. Choose the Index tab if it is not already selected. You now can see the tags that have been defined already in the list presented. The list consists of four columns: Name, Type, Expression, and Filter.

4. Choose the expression you wish to modify by clicking in the Expression column of the desired tag. When you click there, an unlabeled button appears in the column. Click this button to activate the Expression Builder.

5. In the Expression portion of the dialog box, enter the expression you want to use. The Expression Builder appears in Figure 5.3.

FIGURE 5.3.

The Expression Builder.

6. In the Fields list box, double-click the first field name that you want to use.

7. In the Functions portion of the Expression Builder, click the arrow beside the String drop-down list box, and then find and choose the plus symbol (+) that appears in the list. Recall that the plus symbol (+), when used between two strings, returns the concatenation of the two strings.

8. Double-click the next field you want to use as the basis for the index.

9. Repeat steps 7 and 8 for any more fields on which you want to base the index. Be sure to use the functions needed to render each field into a character string.

10. Click OK. The expression used to build your index appears in the Create Expression dialog box. (See Figure 5.4.)

FIGURE 5.4.

A completed expression in the Expression Builder dialog box.

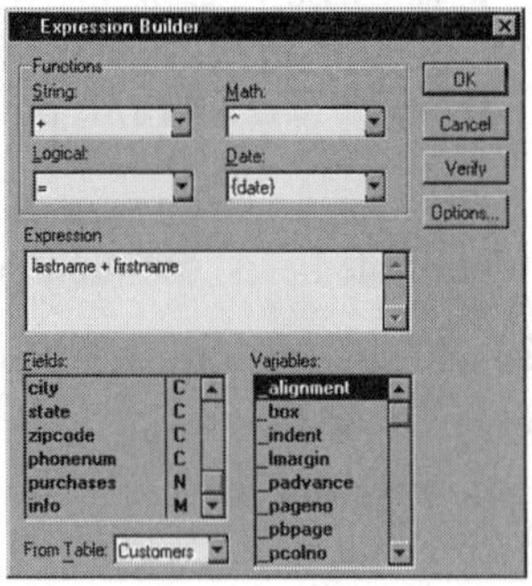

An Example of Creating and Using Indexes with the Table Designer

This example uses the sample data in the CUSTOMERS.DBF table provided on the CD-ROM that accompanies this book to demonstrate how to work with indexes from within the Project

Manager. The following steps build an index based on State and Lastname and then show you the results:

1. If you are not already at the Project Manager, return to the project that contains CUSTOMERS.DBF.
2. Click the Data tab, select Customers, and then click Browse.
3. Return to the Project Manager, highlight the Customers table, and then click the Modify button.
4. Choose the Index tab from the Table Designer dialog box.
5. For the first field, enter State.
6. Next, move to the Expression box and double-click on the Expression button.
7. When the Expression Builder opens, double-click State in the Fields list box, enter a plus sign, and then double-click Lastname.
8. Click OK.

The index you just created will index on State; when the state is the same, it will look at the last names.

The index is added, but you need to put it in use to see the effects. To do so, perform the following steps:

1. From the Project Manager, choose the index at the end of the field below the Customers table Object.
2. Next, Click the Browse button. The index is activated and the records are shown in the Browse window (see Figure 5.5).

FIGURE 5.5.

Data arranged in order of the State *and* Lastname *fields.*

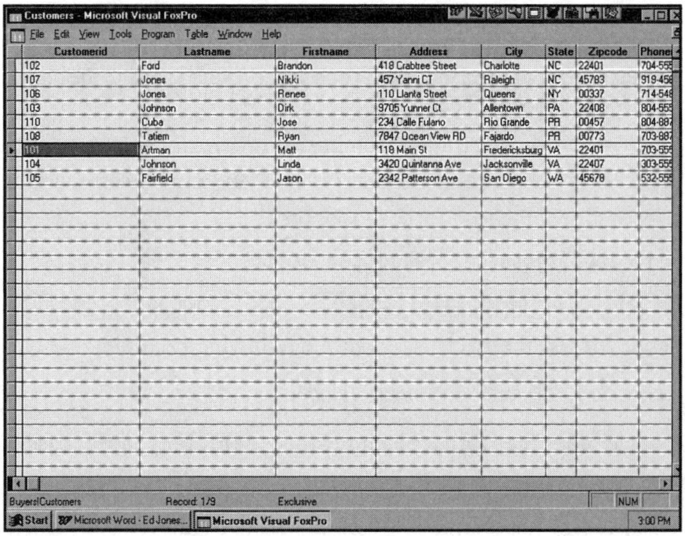

Placing Indexes in Use

With many indexes in existence at any one time, you must choose which index you want to be active. From the menu bar, you can do this by choosing the Open option from the File menu, choosing CDX files from the File Type box, and then choosing an index from the list of CDX files (see Figure 5.6).

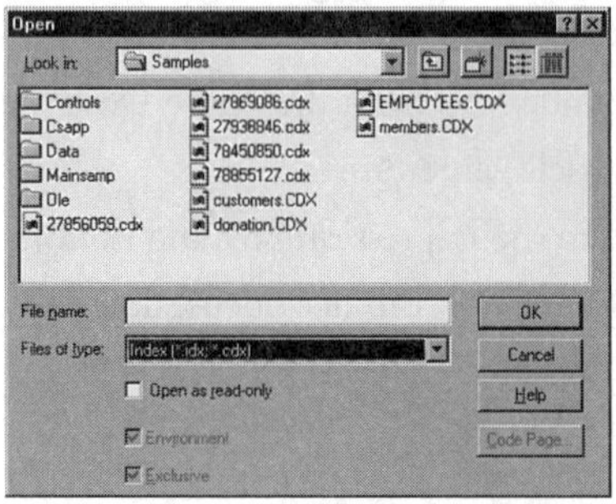

FIGURE 5.6.

The Open dialog box with CDX files displayed.

You can scroll within the list box if there are too many indexes to be viewed at one time. Click the name of the index you want to use to select it. Finally, click OK to close the dialog box. The SET INDEX TO command is automatically entered in the command box.

Indexing with Commands

From the command level, the creation of indexes is done with the INDEX command, a command familiar to any user of Xbase products. Here is the syntax for the index command in Visual FoxPro:

```
INDEX ON expression TO idx file ¦ TAG tagname [OF cdx file] ;
   [FOR logical expression] [COMPACT] [ASCENDING ¦ DESCENDING]
   [UNIQUE] [ADDITIVE]
```

The basic syntax determines whether the command you enter adds an index tag to a compound index file or creates a single index file. If you enter a command with the TAG clause, as in the following example,

```
INDEX ON LASTNAME+FIRSTNAME TAG NAMES
```

an index tag (called NAMES in this example) is added to a compound index file. If, on the other hand, you use the TO clause, as in the following example,

```
INDEX ON LASTNAME+FIRSTNAME TO NAMES
```

a single index file (with a filename of NAMES.IDX in this case) is created by Visual FoxPro.

If you use the TAG clause, but you do not specify a CDX filename, the index tag created is added automatically to the structural compound index file. (If no structural compound index file exists,

Visual FoxPro creates one.) For example, the following commands create an index tag called ZIPS that is added to BUYERS.CDX, the structural compound index file for the BUYERS table.

```
USE BUYERS
INDEX ON ZIPCODE TAG ZIPS
```

On the other hand, the following commands create an index tag called ZIPS that is added to a compound index file called MAILING.CDX. (If MAILING.CDX did not exist, Visual FoxPro would create it.)

```
USE BUYERS
INDEX ON ZIPCODE TAG ZIPS OF MAILING
```

From the command level, you can put indexes into use at the same time you open tables by including the index names as a part of the USE command. Here is the complete syntax for the USE command:

```
USE filename [INDEX index file list ¦ ;
   [ORDER [index tag ¦ idx index file ¦ [TAG] tagname [OF cdx file]
   [ASCENDING ¦ DESCENDING]]]]
```

Hence, you can name index tags (or a single index file) that should be opened and maintained as part of the USE command. For example, the following command opens the table named BUYERS.DBF and sets the index tag to the tag named ZIPCODE in the structural compound index file. (Because no OF *cdx filename* clause is specified, Visual FoxPro assumes the tag can be found in the structural compound index file.)

```
USE BUYERS ORDER TAG ZIPCODE
```

An index file, whether it is a compound index or a single index file, can be opened independently of the USE command with the SET INDEX TO command. As an example, to specify an index file named USERS as the active index file, you could enter the following command:

```
SET INDEX TO USERS
```

After the index is opened, it is updated automatically as records are added or edited.

When using multiple tags in a compound index file, you can change the tag that is currently active with the SET ORDER command. For example, if you create three index tags based on last name, city, and state with the following commands, STATES would be the active index tag, because it was the tag most recently created.

```
USE MAILER
INDEX ON LASTNAME TAG NAMES
INDEX ON CITY TAG CITIES
INDEX ON STATE TAG STATES
```

You can change the active index to the City field with the following command:

```
SET ORDER TO CITIES
```

The other tags remain open and are updated as changes are made to the table, but the records appear in the order of the contents of the City field.

> **TIP**
>
> Using the DESCENDING clause along with the SET ORDER TO command causes the data to be arranged in descending order, regardless of how the tag was ordered when it was created.

Indexing on Different Field Types

One limitation of indexing (which can be annoying at times) is that when you index on multiple fields, the fields must all be of the same data type. If you try to mix data types as part of the same INDEX command, Visual FoxPro generates an error message. For example, if you enter the following command

```
INDEX ON STATE + CRLIMIT TAG PEOPLE
```

a dialog box appears warning you of a type mismatch in the expression, and Visual FoxPro does not create the index. Because State is a character field and Crlimit is a numeric field, a type mismatch occurs and the index cannot be created. All is not lost, however. When you need to index in this manner, you can use Visual FoxPro *functions* to convert the field types so that they are compatible. Use the STR() function to convert the contents of a numeric field to characters, and use the DTOS() function to convert a date field to a string of characters. The overall syntax for the INDEX command, used in this manner, is the following:

```
INDEX ON character field + STR(numeric field) + DTOS(date field)
   TAG index tagname
```

Here is the syntax when used with individual index files:

```
INDEX ON character field + STR(numeric field) + DTOS(date field)
   TO .CDX index filename
```

For example, you can accomplish the task of indexing the Buyers table on a combination of the State and Crlimit fields with the following command:

```
INDEX ON STATE + STR(CRLIMIT) TAG PEOPLE
```

Here are the results:

```
LIST
<...show results...>
```

The index tag places the data in order of states, and when the states are the same, by credit limits.

Selective Indexing

One lesser-known technique that proves useful in certain situations is *selective indexing*— purposely creating an index that contains only those records that meet certain criteria. This is particularly useful for defining subsets of large data tables that are accessed over a network. Why? Because only those records that meet the criteria appear in the index. The size of the index file sent across the network to the FoxPro program that evaluates the index values is smaller.

To do this from the menu bar, click the Index Filter button in the Index dialog box that appears when you choose File | New | Index. To do this from the command level, include a FOR clause along with the INDEX command.

For example, if you open the CUSTOMERS.DBF table, choose Modify from the Project Manager. Select the Index tab and click the Filter button, and the Expression Builder appears. (See Figure 5.7.)

FIGURE 5.7.

The Expression Builder.

In the text box, you can manually type an expression that limits the records to be included in the index. Or, you can build the expression using the list boxes in the Expression Builder. For example, building an expression such as the following:

```
STATE = "MD"
```

limits the index to only those records containing the abbreviation for Maryland in the state field.

From the command level, you accomplish selective indexing by combining the INDEX command with the following syntax:

```
INDEX ON expression TAG tagname [OF .cdx filename] FOR condition
```

Or, if you want to create a single index file, use this syntax:

```
INDEX ON expression TO .idx filename FOR condition
```

condition is any expression that evaluates to a logical True or False. Only expressions that evaluate to True are included in the index. Continuing with the example of records that contain the abbreviation for Maryland, you could use the following command:

```
INDEX ON LASTNAME+FIRSTNAME TAG NAMES FOR STATE = "MD"
```

The resultant index causes the records to be arranged in order of the Lastname and Firstname fields, but only the records for the Maryland residents are included in the index. Hence, whenever the index is made active, the table appears containing only those records with MD in the State field.

Seasoned Xbase users who have always done things from a command level might be tempted to accomplish this sort of selective data retrieval by setting an ordinary index followed by a SET FILTER command, but there is a speed advantage to this kind of selective indexing. Using an INDEX ON...FOR variation of the INDEX command, as described here, is generally faster than using an INDEX command followed by a SET FILTER command. This is particularly true when retrieving data from large tables.

Using the *REINDEX* Command

If you open and modify a table without activating an accompanying index file, the index will not reflect the actual contents of the table. (This is one good reason to keep all of your index tags in the structural compound index file, because it is automatically opened along with the table—you don't have to remember to activate it.) To solve this problem, activate the desired index and then enter REINDEX in the command window. The REINDEX command tells Visual FoxPro to update all currently open indexes.

Sorting

Indexing is a commonly used technique, but it is not the only method for imposing an order on your data in Visual FoxPro. A lesser-used technique is *sorting*. With sorting, the records in the table are copied in a specified order to a new table, and the order is the physical ordering of the records in the data table. For example, if you sort a table based on a customer ID field in ascending order, the records are copied to the new table in ascending order of the customer ID numbers. When Visual FoxPro sorts a table, the results are always copied to a new file. It's not possible to sort a table into itself. (This drawback highlights one of the primary disadvantages of sorting: Significant disk space can be consumed because another table is always created as a result of the sorting process.)

Sorting is somewhat of a holdover from the days of dBASE II, which did not support indexing. Because sorting has fallen out of favor over the years, the Project Manager doesn't provide a way to do it. For novice users, this really isn't a drawback, as you should only consider sorting if it offers clear advantages over indexing. You can enhance table-access performance by periodically sorting the data table in the order in which it is normally accessed.

Sorting from the Command Level

You can perform sorts at the command level by entering a SORT command. The basic form of the SORT command has the following syntax:

```
SORT TO new filename ON fieldname1[/A/C/D], fieldname2[/A/C/D], ...
      fieldnameX[/A/C/D] [ASCENDING/DESCENDING] ;
```

As indicated by the syntax, you can sort on one or more fields. The ASCENDING/DESCENDING option is used to indicate whether the sorted file is arranged in ascending or descending order for all sort fields that don't have an explicit /A or /D. (The default value of Visual FoxPro is ascending order.) The /A and /D options enable you to sort in ascending or descending order on a single field. Character fields, when sorted in alphabetical order, display one trait of Xbase that can be annoying—uppercase letters have a higher value than their lowercase counterparts. As a result, records containing character fields are sorted to list fields in order of A through Z, then a through z. You can solve this problem by including the /C option, which tells Visual FoxPro to ignore the case of the letters during the sort.

If more than one field is named within the SORT command, the table is sorted in priority order according to the named fields. If date fields are chosen as a sort field, the sorted table is in chronological order. (You cannot sort on memo or general fields.) For example, to sort a table alphabetically by City and store the sorted output in a table called CITYFILE.DBF, you can use the following commands:

```
USE BUYERS
SORT ON CITY TO CITYFILE
```

Before the sort, the set of records might look like this:

```
Record# CUSTID LASTNAME      FIRSTNAME      CITY           STATE
1  101    Roberts       Jamie          Reston         VA
2  102    Sanderson     Lucy           Herndon        VA
3  103    Smith         Larry          Kensington     MD
4  104    Jones         Nikki          Washington     DC
5  105    Hernandez     Maria          Towson         MD
6  106    Jones         Jarel          McLean         VA
7  107    Zeibermann    Daniel         Arlington      VA
8  108    O'Neill       John           Merrifield     VA
9  109    Bannerton     Alicia         Falls Church   VA
10 110    Anderson      Harry          Santa Monica   CA
```

After the sort, the records look like this:

```
Record# CUSTID LASTNAME      FIRSTNAME      CITY           STATE
1  107    Zeibermann    Daniel         Arlington      VA
2  109    Bannerton     Alicia         Falls Church   VA
3  102    Sanderson     Lucy           Herndon        VA
4  103    Smith         Larry          Kensington     MD
5  106    Jones         Jarel          McLean         VA
6  108    O'Neill       John           Merrifield     VA
7  101    Roberts       Jamie          Reston         VA
8  110    Anderson      Harry          Santa Monica   CA
9  105    Hernandez     Maria          Towson         MD
10 104    Jones         Nikki          Washington     DC
```

To sort on a combination of the `Lastname` and `Firstname` fields, with the `Firstname` fields arranged in descending order and the `Lastname` field having priority over the `Firstname` field, you can use the following commands:

```
USE BUYERS
SORT ON LASTNAME, FIRSTNAME /D TO CITYFILE
```

Following the sort, the records appear like this:

```
Record#  CUSTID LASTNAME        FIRSTNAME       CITY            STATE
1  110    Anderson        Harry           Santa Monica    CA
2  109    Bannerton       Alicia          Falls Church    VA
3  105    Hernandez       Maria           Towson          MD
4  104    Jones           Nikki           Washington      DC
5  106    Jones           Jarel           McLean          VA
6  108    O'Neill         John            Merrifield      VA
7  101    Roberts         Jamie           Reston          VA
8  102    Sanderson       Lucy            Herndon         VA
9  103    Smith           Larry           Kensington      MD
10 107    Zeibermann      Daniel          Arlington       VA
```

Sorting Selected Records and Fields

By default, when you perform a sort operation, all of the records in the source table are rearranged and written to the new destination table. All fields from the source table also appear in the destination table. Visual FoxPro provides the flexibility of changing this default behavior. You can execute a sort that copies only selected records that meet a certain condition to the destination table. You can also execute a sort that copies specific fields from the source table to the destination table.

To produce a sorted file containing selected records, use the FOR clause along with the SORT command. The syntax for the SORT command, used in this manner, is as follows:

```
SORT ON fieldname1, fieldname2, ... fieldnameX TO newfile FOR condition
```

The expression you include as *condition* defines which records appear in the new table. For example, using the Buyers table as the original table, you can produce a table containing only records of buyers residing in Virginia with the following command:

```
SORT TO JUSTVA ON LASTNAME, FIRSTNAME FOR STATE = "VA"
```

If you were to use the following commands to open the new table and list some of the fields, you would see the following results:

```
USE JUSTVA
LIST LASTNAME, FIRSTNAME, CITY, STATE
```

```
Record#  LASTNAME        FIRSTNAME       CITY            STATE
1  Bannerton       Alicia          Falls Church    VA
2  Jones           Jarel           McLean          VA
3  O'Neill         John            Merrifield      VA
4  Roberts         Jamie           Reston          VA
5  Sanderson       Lucy            Herndon         VA
6  Zeibermann      Daniel          Arlington       VA
```

If you want to include specific fields in the new table, add the FIELDS *fieldlist* clause to the SORT command. Include the keyword FIELDS followed by a list of the specific fields you want to see in the new table. For example, you can create a sorted table, based on the Buyers table, that contains only the Lastname, Firstname, Address, City, State, and Zipcode fields by using the following SORT statement:

```
SORT ON ZIPCODE TO MAILER FIELDS LASTNAME, FIRSTNAME, ADDRESS, CITY,
                        STATE, ZIPCODE
```

As with all optional clauses used in a SORT command, these clauses can be combined to create a sorted table that contains selected records and selected fields from the original table.

If you prefer working from the menu bar, you can use the For Clause and Fields check boxes in the Sort dialog box to accomplish the same results. Click the For Clause check box to bring up the Expression Builder, which you can use to build an expression that defines which records are selected as a part of the sort. Click the Fields check box to display the Fields dialog box, which you can use to limit the available fields included in the results of the sort.

This type of selective sorting can be quite useful when you want a fast way to create data files that can be used with other software. For example, with a personnel file, you might need to copy just the names and salaries from a table to a file that the accounting department can import into a spreadsheet. The selective use of the SORT command is ideal for this task, because most spreadsheets can easily import a file in dBASE file format.

Why Not Sort?

Although sorting does the job as far as rearranging the order of a table, it is usually not the best method for doing so. There are three main disadvantages to sorting a table. First, unless a selective sort is done with a FOR or WHILE clause, a new table as large as the original table is created as a consequence of the sort. This not only wastes disk space; it can make sorting large tables impossible on a system with limited disk space. Second, sorting is a slow process compared to indexing—a faster alternative. Finally, if you add records to the sorted table, the table must be sorted all over again to keep the records in order. For all of these reasons, indexing is recommended over sorting.

One area where sorting can be useful is on local area networks when a specific subset of data is needed in a specific order to produce a report. You might prefer to perform a sort to create a separate table. The new table can then be used for the reporting needs and deleted when the report is completed. This keeps the main table available for the use of others on the network.

Summary

This chapter details indexing and sorting, the methods you use to keep tables in order. Although indexing is by far the most common technique, both methods have their places in different situations. Note that records can also be placed in a specific order as part of a query that retrieves the specific data you need. This is discussed in Chapter 6, "Querying Data."

Querying Data

6

In Visual FoxPro, a significant part of your work involves *queries*. With queries, you ask questions about the data stored in tables; Visual FoxPro provides an answer in the form of a subset of records that meet the conditions specified by the query. The most common reason for designing queries is to select desired fields and records.

Relational databases tend to have information spread among a number of tables. Because queries provide a simple method for combining the data from multiple tables into a single set of useful information, building queries is a useful and desirable skill to perfect. To reduce the learning curve, Visual FoxPro provides a Query Wizard to assist you in defining queries. (Another method of querying for specific data is to use Visual FoxPro commands; this approach is detailed in Chapter 7, "Queries with Commands.")

In Visual FoxPro, you create queries by using the Query Designer facility. When you create Visual FoxPro queries through the Query Designer, Visual FoxPro translates the specifications of the query into SQL SELECT commands. *SQL (Structured Query Language)* is a data-retrieval and -manipulation language originally developed by IBM scientists in the 1970s. A major part of the SQL language is the SELECT command, which can be used to obtain a subset of data meeting a specific condition.

As part of the overall query process, Visual FoxPro also utilizes a patented query optimization process called *Rushmore* to perform the query and to retrieve the results more quickly. When you create your queries by using the Query Designer facility, Visual FoxPro utilizes Rushmore automatically to obtain the fastest results.

Figure 6.1 shows an example of a query's design. Figure 6.2 shows the data produced as a result of the query. You can select specific fields for inclusion in the query and, by means of criteria, include certain records in the result. For example, in the members table shown in Figure 6.1, you see just the name, address, and member-since date for all members living in a certain city.

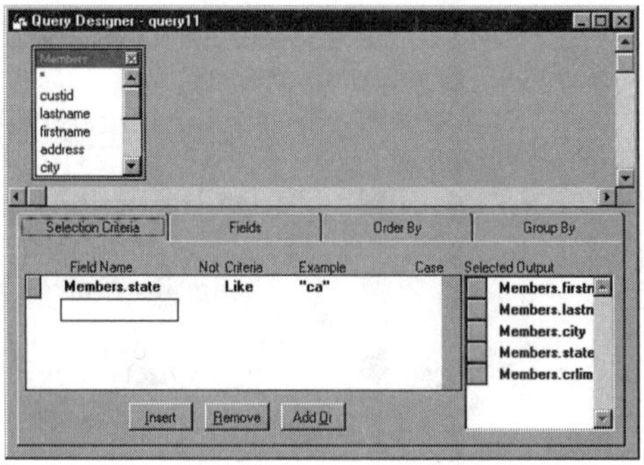

FIGURE 6.1.

A query's design.

FIGURE 6.2.

The SQL statement resulting from a Query Designer session.

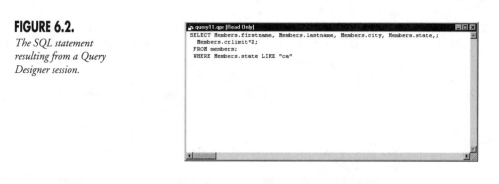

```
query11.qpr [Read Only]
SELECT Members.firstname, Members.lastname, Members.city, Members.state,;
    Members.crlimit*2;
  FROM members;
  WHERE Members.state LIKE "ca"
```

Visual FoxPro queries replace record-by-record procedural programming with a result-set oriented SQL facility. The results from executing a query are placed in one of the following:

- A new memory-resident table called a *cursor*
- A new disk-resident table
- An array

In any case, the result set contains only the requested data, not all the data from the tables.

In other database managers (such as dBASE), selected data was routinely provided with a series of commands, often stored within programs. Xbase developers are universally familiar with DO...ENDDO loops, in which multiple lines of program code perform repetitive operations that process certain records. In Visual FoxPro, a single query using the Query Designer can replace dozens of lines of programming code in Xbase. The SQL statements that make up the heart of any query can be used within any Visual FoxPro program to obtain specific data.

Because Visual FoxPro is backward compatible with its Xbase language heritage, you still can use the record-by-record approach if you're comfortable with it, but this is not required.

You can perform all of the following tasks with the aid of queries:

- **Selecting desired fields.** By clicking the Fields check box of a query window and by adding or removing fields in another dialog box that appears, you specify which fields should be included in the result set. In tables with large numbers of fields, you can choose just the fields you need for a particular task and ignore the rest. For example, in a personnel table, you could retrieve just the employee names and salary information and not retrieve addresses, phone numbers, and other unwanted personal data, even though these fields were also in the same table.

- **Selecting desired records.** By entering conditions in a Criteria row of the query window, you can limit the records returned by the query. As an example, you might be interested in seeing only your customers located in Miami. By entering City = "Miami" in the Selection Criteria area of the query window, you tell the query to retrieve only those records where Miami appears in the City field.

■ **Ordering records.** You can specify a sort order within queries to control the order in which the records appear in the result set from a query. The order may be ascending or descending based on the contents of one or more fields in the base tables. When you sort on multiple fields, you can establish a sorting priority by moving the fields around in the Ordering Criteria list box found on the Order By tab of the Query Designer. For example, in a query that retrieves selected records from a national mailing list, you might set the order by State, and where the States are equal, by City.

■ **Grouping Data.** You can specify queries that combine data into groups based on the contents of a field or fields.

Creating Queries

In Visual FoxPro, you can start a new query either by entering CREATE QUERY in the command window or choosing File | New | Query from the main menu bar. If you are at the Project Manager, you can click the Data tab, then click New, and then click Query Wizard or New Query in the next dialog box. If you click the New Query button the Add table or View dialog box appears, from which you choose the table on which you want to perform the query. Next you proceed to the Query Designer (see Figure 6.3).

FIGURE 6.3.

The Query Designer.

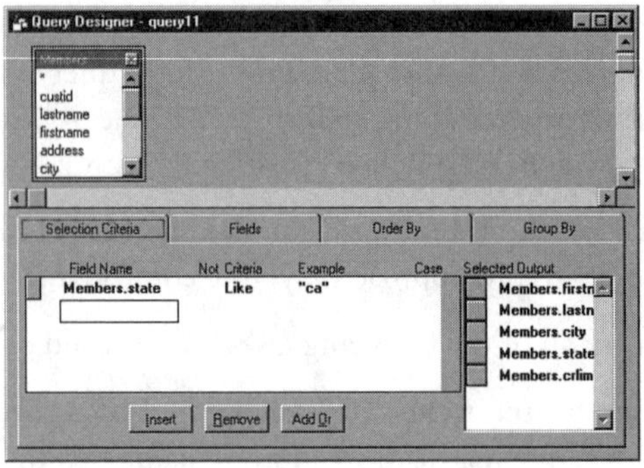

The general steps you follow after the Query Designer window has been opened are as follows:

■ In the Selection Criteria tab, click on the Field Name box and select the fields that determine which records from the base table are included in the result set. Next, for each of the fields, set the criteria in the Criteria list box; the default setting is Equal. In the Example box, you can specify Comparison value. Finally, press the Case button to specify the query as case-sensitive. Continue until you've specified all the selection criteria. Figure 6.4 shows a query being constructed that will select records which have VA in the state field.

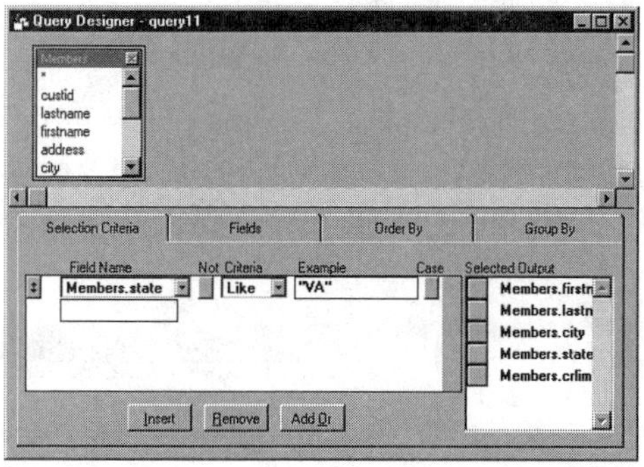

FIGURE 6.4.

*Criteria to retrieve records
with VA in the State field.*

- Now you will move on to the Fields tab. Here you specify the fields appearing in the result set table. You can specify fields from the base table, aggregate functions, and other expressions as output fields. This table lists all the available fields in the base table for easier picking. The Functions/Expressions box provides an easy way for you to enter a function or expression, or you can select a function or expression from the list box and select the field upon which you want it to act.

- The Order By tab specifies fields, aggregate functions such as SUM or COUNT, or other expressions used to set the order of records retrieved in the query.

- The Ordering Criteria tab is used to specify the fields and expressions used in the sort order of the query. The arrow that appears to the left of each field specifies an ascending (up) or descending (down) sort. The Mover box that appears at the left of the arrow is used to change the order of the fields.

- The Group By tab is used to group rows of query or view results. The List Field box lists the fields, aggregate functions, and other expressions for determining the grouping of the query results. The fields are grouped by the order they appear in the list. The field order and grouping hierarchy can be changed by dragging the double-headed arrow to the left of each field. Clicking the Having button specifies conditions for selecting which groups of records to include in query output.

- After you have created the query, close the Query Designer. You then are returned to the Project Manager. Now click the Run button to run the query you have created.

In addition to these basic steps, there's much more that can be done with queries in Visual FoxPro. You can perform math operations as part of the queries and provide averages or sum totals of numeric fields. The criteria can range from simple to quite complex. You can structure your criteria to provide a range of data based on AND and OR conditions, and you can save queries for later use.

SQL Behind the Scenes

As you fill in the desired options in the Query Designer window, Visual FoxPro generates a corresponding statement using SQL. You can see the corresponding SQL statement as you construct a query by choosing View SQL from the Query menu. A sample of the SQL statement for the query appears in Figure 6.5.

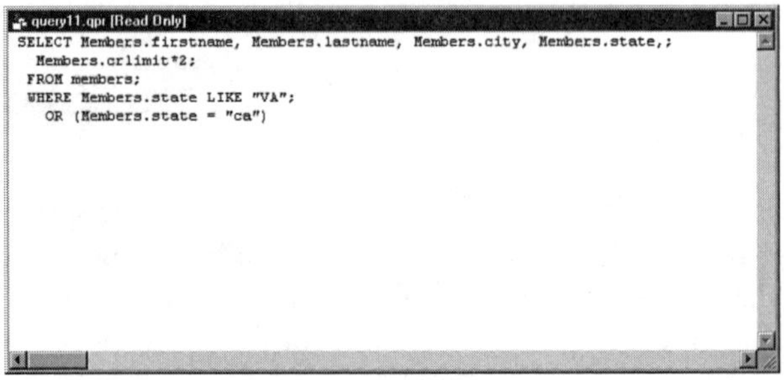

FIGURE 6.5.

The sample SQL statement.

```
query11.qpr [Read Only]
SELECT Members.firstname, Members.lastname, Members.city, Members.state,;
   Members.crlimit*2;
  FROM members;
 WHERE Members.state LIKE "VA";
   OR (Members.state = "ca")
```

If you are familiar with the SQL language, you might prefer to enter the SQL statements generated by queries into the command window to obtain the same results. You can also use the SQL statements within your Visual FoxPro programs.

An Example: Creating a Simple Query

This chapter makes extensive use of examples because the best way to learn the complete use of Visual FoxPro queries is to work with them. To provide realistic examples without typing in dozens of records, this chapter uses the example data in the Members table of the Ecology database provided on the disk that accompanies this book. Copy all the files from the disk into your Visual FoxPro working directory. Then choose File | Open and select MEMBERS.DBF in the Open dialog box to open the table.

To provide realistic examples without typing in dozens of records, this chapter uses the example data in the Members table provided on the disk that accompanies this book. Copy the files from the disk into your Visual FoxPro working directory. Then choose File¦Open and select MEMBERS.DBF in the Open dialog box to open the table.

To create a query that retrieves selected fields (the company name, contact name, and address) from those records where the company is based in California, follow these steps:

1. Choose File | New.
2. In the New dialog box, click Query and then click New file. This causes the Query Designer to appear. Note that because the Members table (the table used in this

example) is open, it appears in the Add table or View dialog box. Choose Members from the list presented by double-clicking on it. The Add Table or View dialog box will disappear, and the Members data table will appear in the top half of the Query Designer. Scroll through this list box and notice that Visual FoxPro presents all the fields in the table to you.

Notice that the first choice in the Members table's list of fields is an asterisk (*). This represents all fields. Double-click on the * and notice that all fields from the table now appear in the Selected Output list in the lower-right corner of the Query Designer.

3. Click under Field Name in the Selection Criteria tab of the dialog box and choose Members.state from the list box that opens. When you do so, the Equal operator automatically appears in the drop-down list in the center of the Selection Criteria portion of the dialog box. Choose the Like operator from the drop-down list.

4. Click in the Example box and type VA (the two-letter abbreviation for Virginia).

5. From the query menu, choose Run to run the query. The result will be all records that have VA as the state.

Changing the Query Specifications

The Add Table or View dialog box displays the tables that are available for use by the query. (This is seen when you activate the Query Designer.) The name of the table that was open in the current work area when you opened the Query Designer window appears in the Tables list box. You can add tables to the list box by clicking the Other button to the right of the list and selecting the additional tables desired. This technique is used when building relational queries, a topic covered in Chapter 10, "Working with Visual FoxPro's Relational Powers."

To the right in the Selection Criteria tab, you see the Selected Output box. This list box displays all fields that appear in the results of your query. This list box appears on both the Selection Criteria tab and the Fields tab. You can choose fields for inclusion in the result set of the query by double-clicking on the desired fields in the table list box located in the upper half of the Query Designer in either tab. In the Fields tab, you can click the Add button to move the complete list of fields from the Available Fields list to the Selected Output list.

Removing fields can be performed only in the Fields tab. To remove a field from the list, click the unwanted field and then click the Remove button. Repeat this step for any fields you don't want in the query. With tables that have a large number of fields, you may find it faster to click the Remove All button to remove all the fields from the query. Then click each desired field followed by the Add button (or double-click the desired field) to add it to the Selected Output portion of the dialog box.

Eliminating Duplicates from the Query Results

When you click the Fields on the Fields tab, you might also notice the No Duplicates check box within this dialog box. Turning on this option tells Visual FoxPro to remove all duplicate records from the query's results. (*Duplicate records* are those records in which all of the fields match.)

Determining the Order of the Query Results

Next is the Order By tab. This tab is used to specify a sort order for the results of the query.

To select the fields that determine the order of the data in the query results, follow these steps:

1. Click a field that you want to sort on in the Selected Output list box to select it.
2. Click Move to move the selected field into the Ordering Criteria portion of the dialog box.
3. Choose Ascending or Descending, as desired.

If you want to base the sort on more than one field, you can select multiple fields, in order of the desired priority. The first field you choose represents the first level of sorting, the second field represents the second level of sorting, and so on. When you are finished with the options in the dialog box, click OK.

Adding Grouping to the Query Results

Visual FoxPro also provides the option of grouping the results of your query based on a specific field. (For example, you might want to see the results of a query on the customer field divided into groups of states.) You can establish grouping by clicking the Group By tab. (See Figure 6.6.) You can select the field or fields that control how the results of the query will be grouped. When you're done selecting the desired fields, click OK.

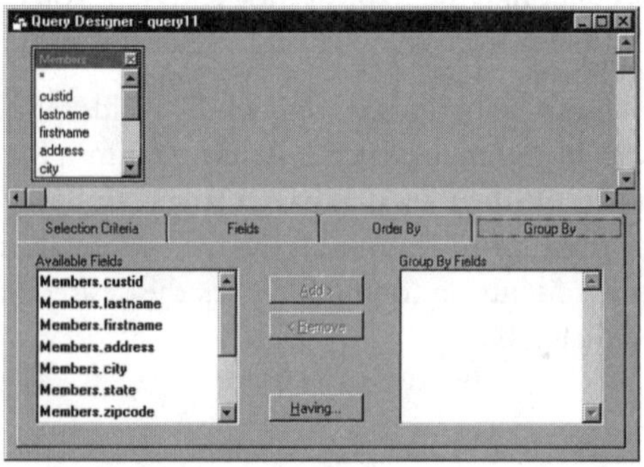

FIGURE 6.6.

The Group By tab of the Query Designer box.

To run the query, choose Run Query from the Query menu; or, if you want to see the equivalent SQL statement, choose View SQL. You can also specify where the result of a query will go by choosing Query Destination from the Query menu to bring up the Query Destination dialog box as shown in Figure 6.7. Directing a query's output is discussed more in the next section.

FIGURE 6.7.

The Query Destination dialog box.

Directing a Query's Output to a Report

By default, Visual FoxPro sends the output of a query you design into a browse window. Although you often want to see the results of a query in this fashion, you often might want a printed copy of the data. You have a wide range of options from which to choose if you select Query | Query. When you do this, the Query Destination dialog box appears (see Figure 6.8). By choosing each of the buttons, you can set options for each of the destinations.

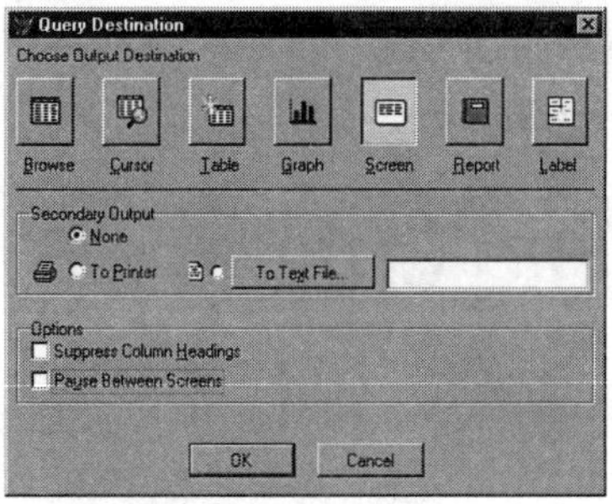

FIGURE 6.8.

The Query Destination dialog box with Screen chosen as the destination.

Saving and Running Queries

Queries can be saved for reuse at a later time, an important benefit if you perform the same query repeatedly. To save a query, choose File | Save while the query is open in the active window. If the query is being saved for the first time, Visual FoxPro displays the Save As dialog box, and you can enter a desired filename and click OK to save the query. (If the query has been saved previously, you won't see the Save As dialog box; Visual FoxPro just saves the latest changes to the query.) You can also close a query by double-clicking the window's Close box, or by pressing Ctrl+F4. If the query has not been saved, Visual FoxPro asks if you want to save the changes to the untitled query. Answer Yes, and the Save As dialog box appears, where you can enter a name for the query. If you choose not to save a query, you must re-create it if you want to rerun it.

To run an existing query, choose Query | Run Query, and the active query is run. If you want to run another query, choose the query from the Project Manager and click Run. The query opens and runs, with the output directed to whatever device was specified in the saved query. You can also run a query from the command level by entering the following command where *queryname* is the name under which you saved the query:

```
DO queryname.QPR
```

Modifying Existing Queries

To modify a previously saved query, select the name of the query from the Data tab under Queries and choose the Modify button. Query Designer is then opened, and you can make the needed changes.

You can also open a query for modifications from the command level by entering the following command, where *queryname* is the name under which you saved the query earlier:

```
MODIFY QUERY queryname
```

Specifying Criteria

To provide the specific data you want in the query, specify the criteria in one or more rows in the Selection Criteria portion of the Query Designer. Effective criteria design is a major part of working with queries. For that reason, most of the second half of this chapter deals with entering criteria. The criteria constitute an *expression* that tells Visual FoxPro how to limit the data retrieved. For example, for a City field, you might use City like New York as a criterion, to retrieve all records that have New York in the City field. For a Salary field, you might use a criterion of Ytdsales between 2000 and 5000 to retrieve all records with year-to-date sales amounts between the two values shown. If you were using an On Hand field of an Inventory table, you might use Onhand Less Than 5 to show all records with an inventory of less than five items.

Visual FoxPro divides the expression into three parts: the *field name*, the *comparison operator*, and the *example*. Visual FoxPro makes entering the expression easier by providing pull-down boxes for the field name and comparison operator selections, leaving you with the task of entering the proper examples to achieve your desired results. This is all done from the Selection Criteria tab. To enter your selection criteria, first click the Selection Criteria tab. Then click the field name from the list box (see Figure 6.9).

FIGURE 6.9.

The Selection Criteria tab with the Field Name list open.

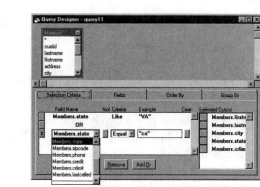

Note that although field names are what you want in nearly all cases, Visual FoxPro doesn't limit you to only field names. You can also use the Field Name list box to build an expression of your own devising; choose <Expression...> at the bottom of the list box and use the Expression Builder that appears.

After you choose a field, the default comparison operator, Like, appears in the center of the Selection Criteria area. If you click the arrow beside the Like entry, the list box of comparison operators opens, showing your available choices: Like, Exactly Like, More Than, Less Than, Between, and In. The comparison operators can be used to perform the following types of comparisons between data:

Equal	(Default option) Specifies that the field must be equal to the example. This can be used for any data type.
Like	Specifies that the field must match the example text for the record to be included in the query's output. For example, MEMBERS.STATE Like N would match records from North Carolina, North Dakota, and Nebraska.
Exactly Like	Specifies that the field must exactly match the example text, character for character, for the record to be included in the query's output.
More Than	Specifies that the field must be greater than the value in the example text for the record to be included in the query's output.
Less Than	Specifies that the field must be less than the value in the example text for the record to be included in the query's output.
Is NULL	Specifies that the field contains a NULL value.
Between	Specifies that the field must be greater than or equal to the lower value and less than or equal to the higher value provided in the example for the record to be included in the query's output. For example, MEMBERS.DATECALLED Between 06/01/93,06/30/93 would match records for the month of June 1993.

In   Specifies that the field must match one of several comma-delineated examples in the example text for the record to be included in the query's output.

You can check the Up/Lo check box, at the right edge of the Selection Criteria area, to tell Visual FoxPro to ignore capitalization of character data when the query runs.

The real power of queries lies in effectively formulating the different criteria that obtain the needed data. Visual FoxPro doesn't limit you to the simple kind of criteria entered in the sample query shown earlier in this chapter. You can use the operators described previously to build complex expressions. These operators, and how they can be used in criteria, are detailed in the examples throughout the rest of this chapter.

Using Text-Based Criteria

Literal text is a common entry in the Selection Criteria tab of the Query Designer window. With literal text, you use text entries to find a given name, such as that of a particular department, city, or country. For example, you might want to see the records of all members living in the city of San Francisco. Perform the following steps to do so:

1. Choose File | New. Click Query in the dialog box that appears, and then click New File.

2. Under the Selection Criteria tab of the Query Designer, click in the Field Name list box and choose Members.City.

3. Choose Like as the desired comparison operator.

4. Click in the Example text box and type `San Francisco` in the box. Next, click the Fields tab and choose City, Lastname, and Custid as the fields you want to include.

5. Choose Run Query from the Query menu. The result, shown in Figure 6.10, shows all records that contain the desired text in the City field. When done examining the data, press Ctrl+F4 to close the browse window. Because this query will not be reused, press Ctrl+F4 again to close the query dialog box and answer No to the Save Changes? prompt to avoid saving the example.

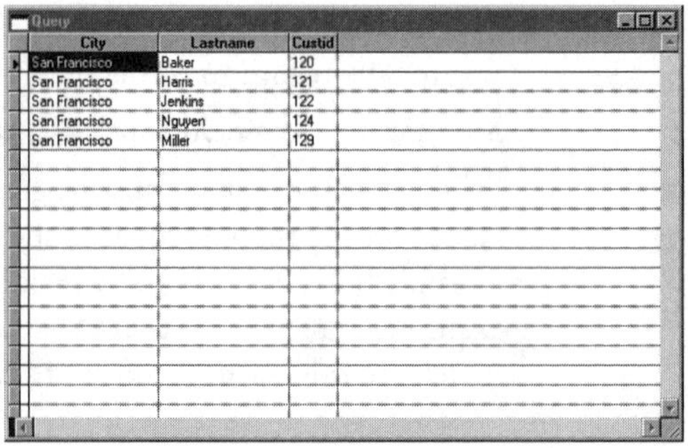

FIGURE 6.10.

The results of a simple query using text.

City	Lastname	Custid
San Francisco	Baker	120
San Francisco	Harris	121
San Francisco	Jenkins	122
San Francisco	Nguyen	124
San Francisco	Miller	129

Using Numeric Criteria

You can use the More Than, Less Than, and Between operators, as well as the Like operator, to obtain the desired matching data. These are commonly used with numeric values, but can be used with text as well. Perform the following steps as an example of using numeric data to find all members with credit limits greater than $700:

1. Choose File | New. Click Query in the dialog box that appears, and then click New File. Choose Customers from the Add table or View box.

2. Under the Selection Criteria tab, click in the Field Name list box and choose Members.crlimit.

3. Choose More Than as the desired comparison operator.

4. Click in the Example text box and type 200 in the box. Then, from the Fields tab, choose Custid, Lastname, Crlimit, and Phone number as the fields you want to include.

5. Choose Query | Run Query. The result is all the records containing purchases that are greater than 20. When done examining the data, press Ctrl+F4 to close the browse window. Press Ctrl+F4 again to close the Query Designer window and answer No to the Save Changes prompt.

When working with numeric values, keep in mind that the Like and Exactly Like operators have the same mathematical effect as an equal symbol. Therefore, if you were constructing a query and wanted to find all members with a credit limit of precisely $800, you could structure the selection criteria as either `Members.crlimit Like 800` or as `Members.crlimit Exactly Like 800` to obtain the desired data. Generally, for clarity, use the default Equal for numeric values.

Using Date-Based Criteria

In addition to working with text values, you can select records based on a date value or on a range of dates. The More Than, Less Than, and Between operators can be used to perform date-based logic. You could, for example, select all records with a hire date later than June 1, 1992, by entering `more than 6/1/92` as the criterion. As an example of date logic, you might want to find all members who were contacted in 1993. Perform the following steps to do so:

1. Choose File | New and click Query in the dialog box that appears. Then click New file. In the Add table or View box, choose the name of the table you want to use.

2. Under Selection Criteria, click in the Field Names list box and choose the date field you want to use.

3. Choose Between as the desired comparison operator.

4. In the Example text box, enter `1/1/93,12/31/93`.

5. Now choose Query | Run Query. The result will be all of the records with the dates that fall within the specified dates.

Searching for Dates Based on the Current Date

You can include the Date() function to structure queries that retrieve data based on the current date, according to the PC's clock. For example, after selecting a date field and choosing Between as a comparison operator, in the Example text box you could enter an expression like the following:

```
1/1/93, date()
```

This would translate to any dates between January 1, 1993, and the current date according to the PC's clock. An expression such as

```
date()-30, date()
```

would translate to all dates within the last 30 days.

Searching for Logical Values

When constructing queries to retrieve values based on a logical (True/False) field, note that you must use .T. to indicate True and .F. to indicate False (the letters must be surrounded by periods). For example, because the Credit field in the Members table is a logical field, a query with a selection criterion of Members.credit Like .T. would retrieve all records with a value of True in the Credit field.

Including Wildcard Characters

When entering expressions, you might find the use of *wildcard* characters to be helpful. You can use valid wildcards to find groups of records where the entries match a specific pattern. Note that the wildcard character in Visual FoxPro's query-by-example is *not* the usual asterisk-and/or-question mark combination that's common to DOS commands; instead, Visual FoxPro uses the percent symbol (%) to indicate any sequence of zero or more characters. For example, you might use the selection criterion

```
Members.lastname Like J%n
```

to find names such as Johnson, Jarlan, and James-Harrison. If you wanted to locate part of a string within a string of text, you would use a pattern with the search text surrounded by percent symbols. For example, %der% would find any records with the letters der located within the search text.

You can try an example of a wildcard in a query to find certain records in the Members table with a Lastname parameter that begins with the letter H and ends with n by performing these steps:

1. Choose File | New and click Query in the dialog box that appears. Then click New File. Choose the Customers table from the Add table or View box.

2. Under the Selection Criteria tab, click in the Field Name list box and choose Members.Lastname.

3. Choose Like as the desired comparison operator.

4. Click in the Example text box and type **H%z** in the box.

5. Choose Query | Run Query. The result (see Figure 6.11) shows all records that contain last names beginning with H and ending with z. When you're done examining the data, press Ctrl+F4 to close the browse window. Press Ctrl+F4 again to close the query dialog box and answer No to the Save Changes? prompt.

FIGURE 6.11.

The results of a query using the Like operator and a wildcard.

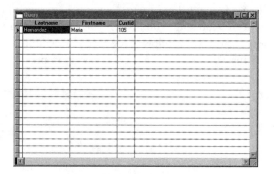

Using a Range of Values

One of the most common uses of queries is to select records that fall inside a certain range of values. For example, you might want to see all sales that occurred between January 1 and June 31 of a particular year, or all products that sell for between $20 and $50. With ranges, you use the Between comparison operator to structure your expressions. Examples of valid criteria for selecting ranges of data appear in Table 6.1.

Table 6.1. Valid criteria for selecting ranges of data.

Selection Criterion	Meaning
Crlimit Between 500, 1000	All values between 500 and 1000, inclusive, from a field called CRLIMIT
Lastcalled Between 1/1/94, 6/30/94	All dates from January 1 through June 30, 1994, in a field called LASTCALLED
Age Less Than 21	All values under 21 in a field called AGE
Quantity More Than 200	All values greater than 200 in a field called QUANTITY
More Than "M"	All text values starting with M through the end of the alphabet

For example, to see all members with credit limits between $500 and $700, perform the following steps:

1. Choose File | New, and click Query in the dialog box that appears. Then click New File.

2. Under the Selection Criteria tab, click in the Field Name list box and choose Members.crlimit.

3. Choose Between as the desired comparison operator.

4. Click in the Example text box and type **500, 700** in the box.

5. Choose Query | Run Query. Figure 6.12 shows all records that contain credit limits between $500 and $700. When you're done examining the data, press Ctrl+F4 to close the browse window. Press Ctrl+F4 again to close the Query Designer window and answer No to the Save Changes? prompt.

FIGURE 6.12.

The results of a range-based query using numeric amounts.

Crlimit	Phone	Lastname	Firstname	Custid
500.00	301-555-2815	Smith	Larry	103
500.00	703-555-1200	Bannerton	Alicia	109
500.00	415-555-5555	Anderson	Harry	110
500.00	703-555-6723	Johnson	Larry	112
500.00	213-555-4506	Roberts	Clarissa	115
500.00	415-555-2535	Askew	Charles	118
700.00	510-555-7614	Flores	Alicia	125
700.00	716-555-2301	Hayes	Rosario	128
500.00	415-555-7912	Miller	Ernest	129
700.00	703-555-2525	Sutton	Derek	131

Using the In Operator

Until now, the practice queries have demonstrated the use of the Like and Between comparison operators. Another operator that Visual FoxPro provides is the In operator, which can be used to find records that contain a group of individual values. As an example, to find those members whose last names are Jenkins, Baker, and Sutton, you could specify a selection criterion such as the following to accomplish this task:

```
Members.Lastname In Jenkins,Baker,Sutton
```

Using AND-Based Criteria

Whenever you need to retrieve selected data based on more than one condition, and each of the conditions must be true, you have a query that is using *AND-based logic*. For example, you might want to see all members who have credit limits over $700 *and* were contacted in 1993. Because one named criterion *and* another named criterion must be true for the record to be selected, this type of criterion is known as AND-based logic. You create such expressions by filling in as many rows in the Selection Criteria portion of the dialog box as are needed to accomplish the selection. To see how this works, you can duplicate the example described previously (all members who have credit limits over $700 and were contacted in 1993) by performing these steps:

1. Choose File | New, and click Query in the dialog box that appears. Then click New.
2. Under the Selection Criteria tab, click in the Field Name list box and choose Members.Crlimit.
3. Choose More Than as the desired comparison operator.
4. Click in the Example text box and type **700** in the box.
5. Click in the second row of the Selection Criteria area under Field Name and choose Members.state.
6. Choose Like as the desired comparison operator.
7. Click in the Example text box and type **CA** in the box.
8. Choose Query | Run Query. The result, shown in Figure 6.13, shows all records for members with credit limits greater than $700 and who live in California. When done examining the data, press Ctrl+F4 to close the browse window. Press Ctrl+F4 again to close the Query Designer window and answer No to the Save Changes? prompt.

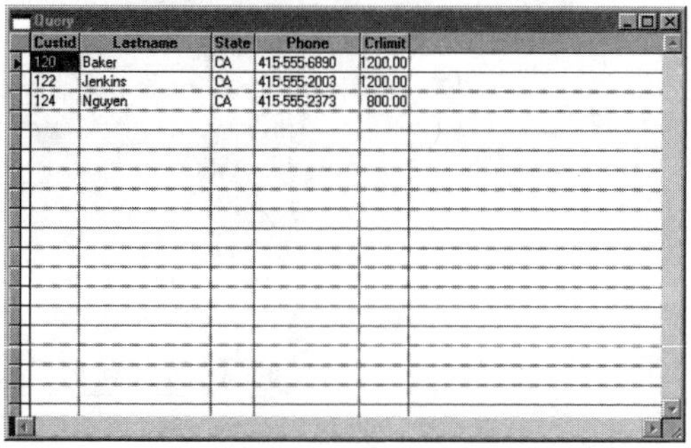

FIGURE 6.13.

The results of a query using AND-based logic.

Using OR-Based Criteria

When you need to retrieve selected data based on any of a number of conditions and only one of the conditions must be true, you have a query that is using *OR-based logic*. For example, you might want to see all members who reside in California *or* Texas. Because any one of the two named criteria can be true for the record to be selected, this type of criterion is known as OR-based logic. One way to create OR-based logic in a query is to fill in the different criteria, one underneath the other. You click the Or button after each row of selection criteria, and you can continue to fill in as many rows with criteria as are necessary. To see how this works, you can duplicate the example described previously (all customers who are based in California *or* Texas) by performing these steps:

1. Choose File | New, and click Query in the dialog box that appears. Then click New File.

2. Under the Selection Criteria tab, click in the Field Name list box and choose Members.State.

3. Select Like as the desired comparison operator.

4. Click in the Example text box and type **CA** in the box.

5. Click the Or button in the dialog box.

6. Click in the next row of the Selection Criteria tab under Field Name and again choose Members.State.

7. Leave Like selected as the desired comparison operator.

8. Click in the Example text box and type **TX** in the box.

9. Click the Or button in the dialog box.

10. Choose Query | Run Query. The result, shown in Figure 6.14, shows all records for members living in any one of the three states named. When done examining the data, press Ctrl+F4 to close the browse window. Press Ctrl+F4 again to close the query design box and answer No to the Save Changes? prompt.

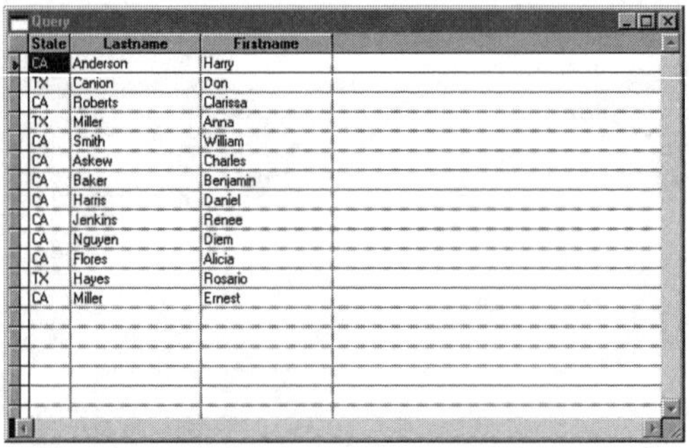

FIGURE 6.14.

The results of a query using OR logic.

Complex Queries

You can combine AND and OR conditions as necessary to obtain any subset of data you need. Suppose, for example, that you needed to see all customers residing in either California or in Texas, who were last contacted in 1995. This combination of AND and OR logic can be duplicated with the following steps:

1. Choose File | New, and click Query in the dialog box that appears. Then click New File. Choose the Members table. The Query Designer is now showing.

2. Under the Selection Criteria tab, click in the Field Name list box and choose the field you want to use, such as Members.State.

3. Choose Like as the desired comparison operator.

4. Click in the Example text box and type **CA** in the box.

5. Click in the second row of the Selection Criteria tab under Field Name and choose Members.Lastcalled.

6. Choose Between as the desired comparison operator.

7. Click in the Example text box and type **1/1/95,12/31/95** in the box.

8. Click the Add Or button in the dialog box.

9. Next, under the Selection Criteria tab, click in the Field Name list box and again choose Members.State.

10. Leave Like selected as the desired comparison operator.

11. Click in the Example text box and this time type **TX** in the box.

12. Click in the next row of the Selection Criteria tab under Field Name and again choose Members.Lastcalled.

13. Choose Between as the desired comparison operator.

14. Click in the Example text box and type **1/1/95,12/31/95** in the box.

15. Choose Query | Run Query. The result, shown in Figure 6.15, shows all records for members living in any one of the two states named, who were last contacted in 1995. When done examining the data, press Ctrl+F4 to close the browse window. Press Ctrl+F4 again to close the Query Designer window and answer No to the Save Changes? prompt.

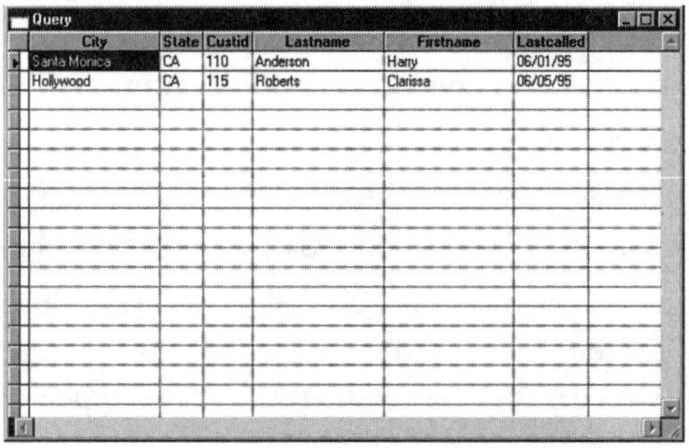

FIGURE 6.15.

The results of a query using a combination of AND and OR logic.

Searching for Records That Don't Match a Value

You can use the Not check box in the Query Designer to select records that do not meet a specified condition. For example, you could enter an expression such as Members.State Like CA in the Selection Criteria portion of a query and then check the Not button to retrieve records with any entry in the State field except the abbreviation CA.

Using Calculations in Queries

Visual FoxPro enables you to add *calculated fields* to a query, in addition to those fields that are part of a table's design. Calculated fields are used to display the results of calculations. These calculations are usually based on numeric fields in the tables. Calculated fields don't exist in any permanent location in the underlying tables; however, they exist only in the query where they are created.

You create a calculated field within a query by entering the expression that performs the calculation as an extra output field. You do this by clicking the Fields check box in the Query Designer and adding the expression in the Functions/Expressions portion of the Field Criteria list box that appears.

For example, if a query contained fields for Saleprice and Quantity, you could create a calculated field containing the total cost by entering an expression such as the following as an extra output field:

```
Saleprice*Quantity
```

When the query runs, Visual FoxPro multiplies each of the values in the `Saleprice` field by the corresponding values in the `Quantity` field to produce the new value, which is displayed in a calculated field within the query's results.

For example, you could use the following steps to add a calculated field to a query that shows the value in the `Crlimit` field of the Members table, multiplied by two:

1. Choose File | New, and click Query in the dialog box that appears. Then click New File. Then choose Members from the Add Table or View dialog box.

2. Under the Selection Criteria tab, click in the Field Name list box and choose Members.State.

3. Leave Like selected as the desired comparison operator.

4. Click in the Example text box and type **CA** in the box.

5. Click the Fields tab and add all of the available fields to the query by clicking the Add All button. Then, in the Functions/Expression portion of the dialog box (in the lower-left corner), click inside the text box and type the following expression:

   ```
   Members.crlimit*2
   ```

6. Next, click Add.

7. Choose Query | Run Query. Figure 6.13 shows the calculated field added as the last field in the browse window. When done examining the data, press Ctrl+F4 to close the browse window. Press Ctrl+F4 again to close the Query Designer window and answer No to the Save Changes? prompt.

Creating Summary Queries

Visual FoxPro offers the capability of building *summary queries*, which can summarize data in your tables. As an example, you might have a table of employee salaries and you might want to know the average, minimum, and maximum salaries for a specific group of employees. These kinds of calculations can be performed by using column functions, such as SUM(), AVG(), MIN(), and MAX(), and by including these functions as expressions within the Query Designer. Table 6.2 shows the available functions and their meanings.

Table 6.2. Available column functions.

Table Function	Meaning
COUNT()	Counts the occurrences of values in a column
SUM()	Sums (totals) the values in a column
AVG()	Calculates the average of the values in a column
MIN()	Determines the minimum value in a column
MAX()	Determines the maximum value in a column

Perform the following steps to see an example of how the column functions can be used to construct summary queries:

1. Choose File | New, and click Query in the dialog box that appears. Then click New File. Choose Members from the Add Table or View dialog box. The Query Designer is now showing.
2. From the Fields tab in the Query Designer, click the arrow to open the list box of the Functions/Expressions portion of the dialog box (in the lower-left corner).
3. Click SUM(). Then choose the Add button.
4. In the list box of fields that appears, click Members.Crlimit to select it.
5. Click Add in the dialog box to add the field to the Selected Output list box.
6. In the Functions/Expressions portion of the dialog box, again click the Functions arrow to open the list box.
7. Click AVG(). Then choose Add.
8. In the list box of fields that appears, click Members.Crlimit to select it.
9. Click Add in the dialog box to add the field to the Selected Output list box.
10. In the Functions/Expressions portion of the Fields tab, again click the Functions arrow to open the list box.

11. Click MAX(). Then choose Add.

12. In the list box of fields that appears, click Members.Crlimit to select it.

13. Click Add in the dialog box to add the field to the Selected Output list box.

14. Choose Query | Do Query. If you wanted to obtain these figures for a specific subset of records, you could do so by including appropriate selection criteria within the query. When done examining the data, press Ctrl+F4 to close the browse window. Press Ctrl+F4 again to close the Query Designer window and answer No to the Save Changes? prompt.

Using a Query's SQL Code Elsewhere

An important point to remember when working with queries is that underneath the flash and glitz of the Query Designer window lies a SQL statement that tells Visual FoxPro how to retrieve the desired data. A knowledge of the SQL statements used by Visual FoxPro can be quite useful because you can enter the statements directly as commands (which can be a time saver if you are familiar with the syntax of SQL). More importantly, you can use the SQL statements within Visual FoxPro programs that you write. (Programming in Visual FoxPro is covered beginning with Chapter 22, "Visual FoxPro Language Basics.") With the Query Designer window for any query open on the screen, choose View SQL from the Query menu, and a window containing the resulting query statement opens. Refer back to Figure 6.5 for an example of the query statement used to generate the query shown earlier.

You can use standard Windows cut-and-paste techniques to copy the text of the SQL statement for use in your programs. For example, you could click and drag to select the text of the entire SQL statement in the window and choose Edit | Copy to copy the text into the Windows Clipboard. You could then switch to editing a program in the Visual FoxPro Editor (or in another Windows editor) and choose Edit | Paste from the main menu to paste the SQL statement into the editor as a part of your program. Also keep in mind that any SQL statement can be typed directly into the Command window, and the results will be identical to opening and running the query.

Summary

This chapter provided a detailed examination of what is arguably the most powerful feature of Visual FoxPro, its query-by-example capability. The ultimate goal of most database management systems is to obtain the specific data that you need, and query-by-example is a fast, powerful, and easy way to accomplish this goal in Visual FoxPro. Chapter 10, "Creating and Using Simple Reports," provides additional details on how you can use query-by-example in a relational fashion, to link tables and to obtain needed relational data.

Queries with Commands

7

IN THIS CHAPTER

The ability to find information quickly in a database is invaluable when you make decisions. For example, you might want to find all the customers with a certain balance on their account in order to send notices to them. In Visual FoxPro, one of the ways you can accomplish this is through the use of a query. A *query* finds information in a database that fits the criteria set out in an expression, and it is used with a command such as LOCATE, SEEK, FIND, or SET FILTER.

SAMPLE TABLE

This chapter uses the Customer table in the Buyers database to illustrate the use of Xbase query techniques available in Visual FoxPro. The sample file is located in the VFU\SAMPLES\ directory:

File	Purpose
Customer.DBF	Source of dataused to illustrate the Xbase query techniques presented in the chapter.

The Makeup of an Expression

A logical expression (an expression that evaluates as either true or false) must be included in any query you compose using FoxPro commands. In Chapter 5, "Arranging Data," logical expressions are used to build indexes and perform sorts.

Expressions can contain one or more *functions* and *operators*. The logical functions are normally used in programming but can also be found in everyday FoxPro use. One example of this is the EOF() function, which stands for *end-of-file*. When you place the pointer on the last record and enter SKIP, EOF() becomes true. EOF() also becomes true if a query is executed and Visual FoxPro does not find what you are looking for. The EOF() function is discussed in more detail in the programming section of this book (Parts IV, V, and VI).

Operators indicate the relationship between a field's name and its contents. For example, in the following command, the = operator signifies equivalency:

```
State = "TX" .OR. State = "CA"
```

There are four types of operators: relational, logical, arithmetical, and string.

Relational Operators

Relational operators are used to compare numbers, strings, or dates; for example,

```
Purchases = 12, Firstname = "Aaron", or Since = {11/12/93}
```

There are many different relational operators you can use in Visual FoxPro. The following is a list of the different relational operators in Visual FoxPro and what they mean:

Operator	Meaning
=	Equal to
<>, !=, or #	Not equal to
<	Left operand is less than right operand
<=	Left operand is less than or equal to the right operand
>	Left operand is larger than the right operand
>=	Left operand is larger than or equal to the right operand
$	Substring comparison
==	Identical character string comparison

The double-equal operator (==) forces an identical comparison, which at times is what you need. For example, if you use the equal operator (=), as in the following command, the command returns all the last names starting with the characters Will:

```
Lastname = "Will"
```

Here is a list of records that could be returned by this command:

Record#	Lastname
1	Will
7	Williamson
9	Willston

On the other hand, if you use the == operator, Visual FoxPro matches last names containing only the specified characters. In this case, only record number 1 would be displayed, Will.

Logical Operators

Logical operators are used to create complex expressions involving true or false conditions. Sometimes it's necessary to find records that have two or more conditions. In those cases, you can use the following logical operators:

Operator	Meaning
( )	Used to group expressions.
.NOT. or !	The expression following the operator must be false in order for the entire expression to be evaluated as true.
.AND.	Both expressions are true.
.OR.	Either expression is true.

Arithmetical Operators

Arithmetical operators are used to construct numerical expressions. The following are some examples:

```
Weight = 3 * 75
Weekly = (30 * 160) /4
Total = ((50+90)/3) * 5
```

The following list shows the arithmetical operators and their meanings.

Operator	Meaning
( )	Used for grouping
** or ^	Exponentiation
*	Multiplication
/	Division
%	Modulus (remainder)
+	Addition
-	Subtraction

String Operators

Both of the string operators in Visual FoxPro are used for string concatenations. The + operator joins two strings. For example, the following expression:

```
"Alberta " + "Sutton"
```

evaluates to this concatenated string:

```
Alberta Sutton
```

The - operator is used to concatenate strings. Replacing the plus sign with a minus sign in the previous example causes the string to appear as AlbertaSutton.

Functions Defined

Visual FoxPro's built-in functions perform many common operations, including converting data and performing math operations. In Chapter 5 you used functions to convert numbers in a numeric field to character strings. Functions can also be used to return system information; for example, you can enter the following in the command window to make the current system time appear:

```
? Time ()
```

Performing Queries with Visual FoxPro Commands

Querying a database is usually done in order to find one record or to isolate a subgroup. To retrieve one record, the LOCATE and SEEK commands can be used. Using the sample CUSTOMER table provided on the accompanying CD, enter **USE CUSTOMER** in the command window to activate the CUSTOMER file. You will practice the SEEK and LOCATE commands in the next two sections of this chapter using this table.

The *CONTINUE* Command

The CONTINUE command finds the next occurrence of a search term and helps in cases where the first record located is not the one desired. If no other record is found to meet the specifications, the End of Locate Scope message is displayed.

The *LOCATE* Command

From the command level, you can use the LOCATE command to perform a search. This command finds the first occurrence of a record. The syntax is

```
Locate (scope) For condition
```

condition evaluates to a logical expression, such as firstname = "Maria". The scope is optional—it can be used to limit the search in the database. Any one of four scopes can be used: Next*n*, All, Rest, and Record *n*. Next*n* and Rest begin the search at the current record number. All sets the scope to the entire table, and Record *n* sets the search to a specific record number.

If you choose All or Rest for the scope and the first record found is not the one you're looking for, you can use the CONTINUE command to find the next record that fits the criteria.

For example, suppose you entered the following LOCATE command in the command window:

```
LOCATE FOR CITY = "Herndon"
DISPLAY
```

and you received the following result:

```
Record#   Custid  ...  Address                    City        State
2         102          931 Thames Ct., Apt. 2C    Herndon     VA
```

You could enter CONTINUE to find the next occurrence of the same city name. If no additional records met the specified scope, the End of Locate Scope message would be displayed in the status bar, showing that there were no other records that fit the search criteria.

The *SEEK* Command

Using the SEEK command can be faster than wading through menus and dialog boxes (which was the case in earlier versions of FoxPro) because you only have to enter the search value. The format for the SEEK command is

```
Seek expression
```

Expression can be a number, a character string surrounded by quotation marks, a variable (variables are covered in the programming sections of this book, Parts IV, V, and VI), or a combination of constants, variables, and operators. The SEEK command moves the record pointer to the specified record. For example, assuming that an index based on ZIP codes is active, you can use the following commands to search for the first entry of that value in the ZIPCODE field:

```
SET ORDER TO TAG ZipCode
SEEK "22046"
Display
```

You should receive the following in the result:

```
Record#   Custid  ...  Address          City           State
9         109          107 Embassy Row   Falls Church  VA
```

Subsequent SEEK commands move the record pointer to succeeding records containing the same value.

The *FIND* Command

The FIND command also performs an index search; therefore, an index must first be active. The format for the FIND command is

```
FIND character string
```

Character string is a group of characters that do not need to be surrounded by quotation marks. You can try using the FIND command by entering the following statement in the command window:

```
FIND Sanderson
```

After you enter this code, you can enter DISPLAY in the command window. Here is the result:

```
Record#      Custid    Lastname
2            102       Sanderson
```

Using the *SET FILTER* Command to Select Subsets of Data

For some applications, you may want to select a group of records, such as if you want to send invoices to a particular group of people. There are a number of ways you can do this. The query-by-example techniques presented in Chapter 6, "Querying Data," outline one way to select subgroups of records. Another way to do this is to use the SET FILTER command. When you set a filter, only specified records—those meeting the conditions—are affected by the commands. The format is

```
SET FILTER TO condition
```

Condition is a logical expression, such as LASTNAME = "Sanderson", that defines a search. Once you enter the command any subsequent commands, which normally affect the entire database, affect only those records that meet the conditions set by the filter. For example, the following command is limited to the records that meet the criteria set out in the filter—records for people who live in Virginia:

```
SET FILTER TO STATE = "VA"
```

The SET FILTER command is the equivalent of the filter option found on the Database/Setup menu. You can also isolate record groups by using the SET FILTER command followed by a LIST or BROWSE command.

You can also do complex searches with SET FILTER. Here is an example:

```
SET FILTER TO State = "VA" AND YEAR (Since) >= 1992 AND Purchases > 10
BROWSE
```

This filter limits the record available to those Virginia customers who have made 10 or more purchases since 1992. The browse displays the results.

This filter limits the records available to those with a value in the HIREDAY field of 1994 and with a value of "TX" in the STATE field.

To find out whether a filter is in effect, type DISPLAY STATUS or LIST STATUS in the command window. The result includes any filter currently in effect. You can also enter ? SET("FILTER") in the command window to display any filter in effect. To remove a filter, enter SET FILTER TO without any expression.

Summary

This chapter showed you the various commands and menu options you can use to find the data you need in Visual FoxPro. At times, the number of ways you can use to find your data might seem confusing—there is not just one correct way to do things in Visual FoxPro. The flexibility to be able to use different methods gives you many effective ways to accomplish tasks in various circumstances.

Creating and Updating Data with Views

8

IN THIS CHAPTER

This chapter details how you can create live views of your data by means of the View Wizards, which are new to the FoxPro environment in Visual FoxPro 3.0.

Views are dynamic sets of data, sorted and filtered according to the design of the view. The key to the power of views lies in the word *dynamic*. When you work with data in a view, you are working with the actual or "live" data that resides in the underlying FoxPro tables. Views are designed to select particular fields and records from one or more tables, just like a query. Unlike a query, however, which is a snapshot of the data in the underlying tables, when you update the data in a view, the base tables are updated also. This is a particularly powerful tool for relational databases because views provide you with the best method for retrieving selected data that you can then edit.

In addition to proving useful for interactive work in FoxPro, views are also an important tool to add to a FoxPro developer's bag of tricks. In the early days of dBASE, selected data was routinely provided with a series of commands, often stored within programs. dBASE developers are intimately familiar with DO...ENDDO loops, where multiple lines of program code perform repetitious operations that post certain records. In Visual FoxPro, there's no need to resort to such techniques to get at the desired data; a single view can do the same thing as dozens of lines of programming code.

In Visual FoxPro, you can create two overall types of views: local and remote. *Local views* provide you with views of the data stored in FoxPro tables on your system. *Remote views* provide you with views of data stored remotely on servers that use client/server architecture. You can easily create views by using the View Wizards that Visual FoxPro provides.

TIP

It's important not to confuse the live views that you can create by using the View Designer with the kinds of views provided by means of the view window, discussed in Chapter 11, "Working with Visual FoxPro's Relational Powers." The view window detailed in that chapter is very much a holdover from the days of dBASE for DOS; Visual FoxPro provides it to offer compatibility from a user standpoint with earlier versions of FoxPro. Compared with the use of the View Wizards detailed in this chapter, the view window is cumbersome and best left to the old Xbase world. If you are an experienced user of earlier versions of FoxPro and you really want the benefits of live views, forget about the old view window and use the View Wizards detailed in this chapter to create your views.

Creating Local Views

To create a view of data that's stored locally (as compared to remotely on a server), you can use the View Wizard. Understand that used in this context, the term *local* refers also to FoxPro tables available over a network on a shared network drive. The term is not restricted to FoxPro tables that reside physically on hardware attached to your computer. You can create the view by performing the following steps:

1. Open the project that contains the data to be included in your new view. (Note that existing views can be seen in the Project Manager under the All tab and under the Data tab.)

2. Click the Data tab in the Project Manager and click Local Views to select it. Then click New.

3. In the dialog box that appears, click View Wizard. In a moment, the first of the View Wizard dialog boxes appears (see Figure 8.1).

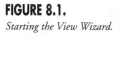

FIGURE 8.1.

Starting the View Wizard.

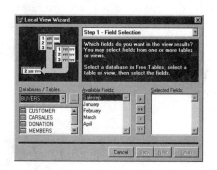

4. At the left side of the dialog box, under Databases/Tables, choose the desired database and then choose the first table you want to use fields from in the list of available tables. When you do this, you will see a list of the fields from that table in the Available Fields list shown at the center of the dialog box.

5. Using the buttons between the Available Fields and the Selected Fields list boxes, add the desired fields to the Selected Fields list box. You can click any one field in the Available Fields list box and then click the right-arrow button to add the field, or you can click the double right-arrow button to add all fields from the table to the Selected Fields list.

6. At the left side of the dialog box, choose the next table that you want to use to provide fields for the view and repeat step 5 for any more fields from tables that you want to add. When you are done adding all of the needed fields to the view, click Next.

7. The next dialog box that appears (see Figure 8.2) asks how you want to establish relationships between the tables. (If you chose fields from only one table, you won't see this dialog box.) From the list boxes showing the fields at the left and right sides of this dialog box, choose the matching fields that will serve as the basis of the relationship. (In most cases, FoxPro guesses correctly at the fields needed to draw the relationship.) Then click Add.

8. Repeat step 7 for any other relationships you need to establish, and then click Next.

FIGURE 8.2.

The View Wizard dialog box used to establish relationships.

9. The next dialog box presented by the wizard asks for a sort order (see Figure 8.3). You can add up to three fields as a sort order by clicking each desired field in the Available Fields list to select it, then clicking the right-arrow button to add the field to the Selected Fields list. In the center of the dialog box, you can choose Ascending or Descending for the sort, as desired. (Note that if you add more than one field, the sorting priority is highest for the first field added and lowest for the last field added.) When you are finished with the options in this dialog box, click Next.

FIGURE 8.3.

The View Wizard dialog box used to establish a sort order.

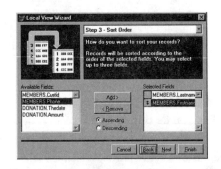

TIP

If you don't want any sort order to the records, you can bypass the Sort Order dialog box by clicking Next.

---

10. The next dialog box to appear (see Figure 8.4) asks you to enter any desired criteria, by means of which the desired records will be selected for inclusion in the view. (If you want to see all records in the view, click Next to bypass this dialog box.) You can specify a desired criterion by choosing a desired field, an operator, and a criteria value in the dialog boxes. You can specify multiple criteria by clicking the And or Or buttons and by entering additional criteria at the bottom of the dialog box. For more specifics on entering criteria, see Chapter 6, "Querying Data." You use criteria in the boxes of the View Wizard in the same manner as you use them in the boxes of the Query Wizard.

FIGURE 8.4.

The View Wizard dialog box used to establish criteria for selecting records.

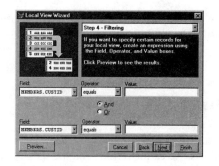

11. The last dialog box to appear (see Figure 8.5) provides you with a choice of saving the view, saving the view and browsing in the data provided by the view, or saving the view and opening it in the View Designer, where you can perform further modifications to the view. Choose your desired option and then click Finish.

FIGURE 8.5.

The final View Wizard dialog box.

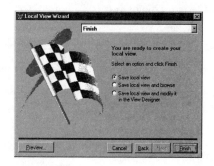

12. A View Name dialog box then appears, asking for a name for the view. Enter the desired name and then click OK to save the view.

Using Views

After you have created a view, you can use the view by finding it in the Data tab or the All tab of the Project Manager, and then clicking the view to select it. Finally, click the Browse button in the Project Manager. When you do this, the data appears in a browse window that looks just like a browse window based on a table. You can edit the data as desired through the browse window.

You also can base your forms and reports on your views. (For specifics on creating forms, see Chapter 9, "Creating and Using Simple Forms," and Chapter 12, "Designing and Customizing Forms"; for specifics on creating reports, see Chapter 10, "Creating and Using Simple Reports," and Chapter 13, "Designing and Customizing Reports.") When you begin the process of designing a form or a report (either by means of the wizards or through the Form Designer or the Report Designer), you must specify a data source for the data used in the form or report. You can select views as data sources in forms and reports, just as you select tables.

To modify an existing view, select the desired view in the Project Manager and then click the Modify button. The view appears in the View Designer, where you can make the needed changes to the view. (For specifics on the use of the View Designer, see "Creating Views Manually" later in this chapter.)

Creating Connections

Visual FoxPro lets you create views of remote (server-based) data as well as local data; the section that follows, "Creating Remote Views," details how you can do this. However, before you can create a remote view, you must first create and save a *connection* to the remote data source. (The connection will then be used by the remote views you create, to establish a link to the remote data.)

To create a connection, open the Project Manager (if it's not already open) and click the Data tab, and then click Connections to select it. Then click New. In a moment, you'll see the Connection Designer dialog box (see Figure 8.6).

FIGURE 8.6.

*The Connection Designer
dialog box.*

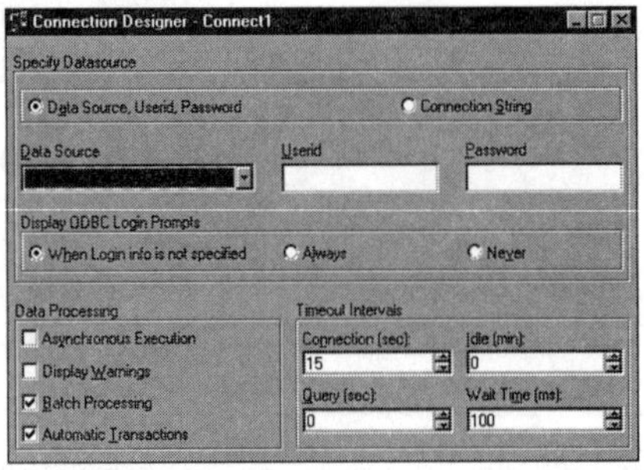

You will need to fill in the options in this dialog box according to the specifics that apply to your server setup. (You might need to get help from your network administrator in entering the correct options in this dialog box.) At the very least, you will need to supply a data source, a user ID, and a password in the respective boxes for these items. When you're finshed, double-click the icon in the upper-left corner of the dialog box to close it. You will be asked for a name for the connection; enter the desired name in the dialog box that appears and click OK to store the connection. After the connection is saved, it appears under the Connections entry in the Data tab of the Project Manager.

Creating Remote Views

You create remote views in much the same manner as you create local views, with one important new step at the beginning of the process. Before you can create the view (with either the View Wizard or with the View Designer), you must first establish a connection with the data source, using the connection that you created earlier. You can use the following steps to create a remote view:

1. In the Project Manager, click the Data tab and then click Remote Views. Then click New.

2. In the dialog box that appears, choose View Wizard. When you do this, the first Remote View Wizard dialog box appears, as shown in Figure 8.7.

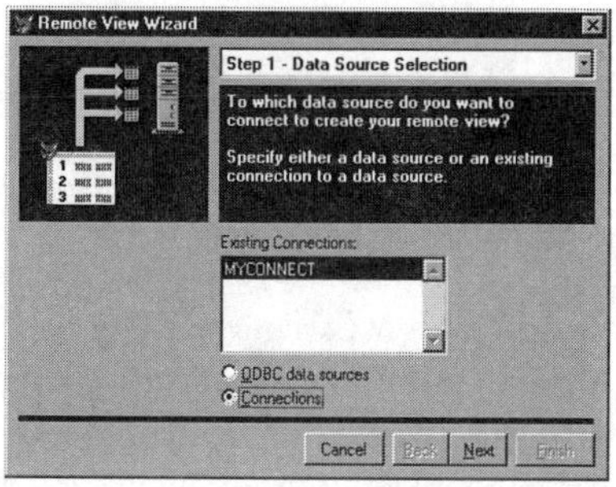

FIGURE 8.7.

The first Remote View Wizard dialog box.

3. Under the Existing Data Sources portion of the dialog box, choose ODBC data sources or Connections, as is appropriate. With either choice, the available data sources will appear in the list box.

4. Select the desired data source and click OK.

5. Depending on your data source, you might now see a login dialog box. If one appears, you will need to enter your login ID and password so that Visual FoxPro can establish the connection to the remote data. You might see an SQL Source dialog box; if you do, you will need to use its options to identify the source of the SQL data.

When the connection has been established, follow the directions that appear in the Remote View Wizard dialog boxes to finish creating the view. From this point on, the creation of the view will involve the same steps as creating a view locally (described earlier in the chapter).

Creating Views Manually

Besides creating views with the aid of the View Wizards, you can also create views manually by using Visual FoxPro's View Designer. When you click Local Views in the Data tab of the Project Manager and click New, the dialog box that appears gives you a choice of creating the view with the View Wizard or creating a new view. (You can also choose File | New from the menu, click View in the dialog box that appears, and then click New View.) With either method, if you choose New View as opposed to selecting the View Wizard, you next see the View Designer appear, and the Add Table or View dialog box appears over it, as shown in Figure 8.8.

FIGURE 8.8.

The View Designer with the Add Table or View dialog box.

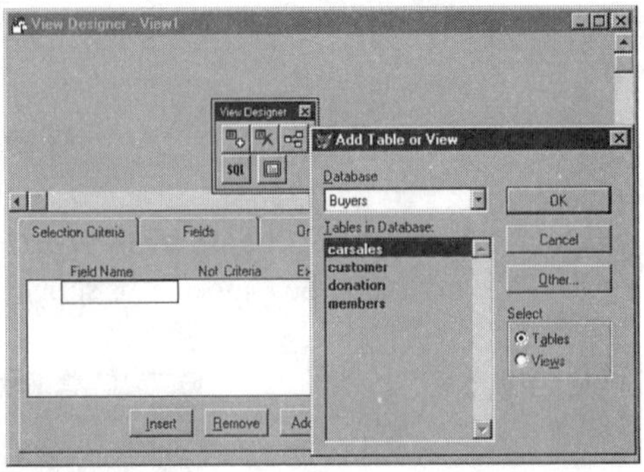

The mechanics of manually designing a view are virtually identical to those of designing a query. If you've worked with Visual FoxPro's Query Designer (detailed in Chapter 6), you should be quite familiar with the View Designer. Using the Add Table or View dialog box, you add the desired tables or views by selecting them and clicking OK; if you add more than one table, you specify the basis for the relationship in the Join Condition dialog box that appears. After you've added the underlying tables or views, you can use the Selection Criteria tab to identify criteria to select the records. The Fields tab can be used to choose which fields should be included in the view, and the Order By tab can be used to specify a sort order for the view. The Group By tab can be used to specify a level of grouping for the view. When done specifying the various options, you can close the window by choosing File | Close or by double-clicking the window's Close icon in the upper-left corner and answering Yes to the prompt that asks if you want to save the changes.

This chapter won't delve into any details about using the first four tabs of the View Designer because the options work the same as they do in the Query Designer. (You can refer to Chapter 6 for a detailed discussion of the Query Designer.) The View Designer does contain one tab that's not found in the Query Designer: the Update Criteria tab, shown in Figure 8.9.

FIGURE 8.9.

The Update Criteria tab of the View Designer.

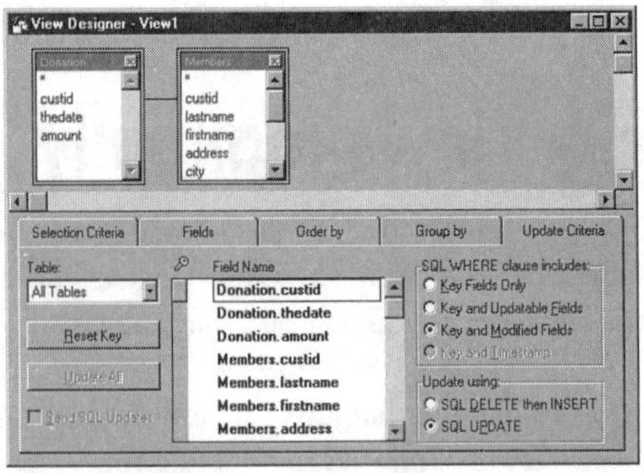

You use the various options of this tab to specify the conditions under which the view will be updated. Table 8.1 shows the purpose of the options in this tab.

Table 8.1. Options for the Update Criteria tab of the View Designer.

Item	*Purpose*
Table list box	Names the table that is affected by the remainder of the settings within this dialog box.
Reset Key button	Resets settings in the Key Field column, causing only primary key fields to be checked.
Update All button	Sets the settings in the Updatable column, causing all fields except key fields to be checked.
Send SQL Updates	Specifies whether data will be updated on disk. (The option is enabled when views are remote views to SQL data.)
Field Name pane	Lists the fields that are part of the view's output.
Key Field symbol (a key)	Identifies a key field.
Updatable symbol (a pencil)	Specifies whether a field is updatable.
Field Name list box	Displays the field names.
Key Fields Only button	When on, indicates that the WHERE clause used to update remote tables is made up of primary fields only.
Key and Updatable Fields button	When on, indicates that the WHERE clause used to update remote tables is made up of primary fields and any updatable fields.
Key and Modified Fields button	When on, indicates that the WHERE clause used to update remote tables is made up of primary fields and any fields that are modified.
Key and Timestamp button	When on, indicates that the WHERE clause used to update remote tables is made up of primary fields and a comparison of timestamps.
SQL DELETE then INSERT	When on, indicates that record modifications cause the original table record to be deleted and a new record added.
SQL UPDATE	When on, indicates that record modifications are performed by writing changes to the actual record.

You can fill in the desired options and then choose File | Close to close the view. (When prompted if you want to save the view, click Yes and provide a name for the view.) After the view has been saved, you can make use of it as you would any other view, using the techniques covered earlier in this chapter.

Summary

This chapter detailed the use of views and how you can put them to work with Visual FoxPro. Views are a very useful tool, particularly when you need to edit information that amounts to a "virtual table" made up of multiple tables. Keep in mind the usefulness of views as sources of data for your forms and reports as you work with the other aspects of interactive FoxPro.

Creating and Using Simple Forms

Forms provide another way to present and work with data in Visual FoxPro. Whereas the browse window displays your data in the familiar row-and-column format, forms enable you to view a record at a time, using any layout you prefer. Forms in FoxPro can be quickly created with the AutoForm Wizard button on the toolbar, or by means of the Form Wizards. Forms can also be designed manually through the Form Design window, which lets you drag objects (such as fields and text) to any desired location. Figure 9.1 shows a form for editing that table's data. In this example, the form was created in a single step, using the AutoForm Wizard button in the toolbar.

FIGURE 9.1.

A form for editing data.

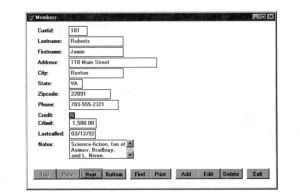

Forms can be based on queries or on views, providing a painless way to view and edit information. For example, you might design a view to show all sales records for a given month. A form could then be designed to view or edit the data for only those records. By basing the form on the view (rather than on the entire table), the correct records are automatically made available to the form whenever the form is opened.

FoxPro forms go beyond providing data and text labels. With forms, you can display graphics such as drawings, photos, or corporate logos. You can include calculated fields to provide totals or other summations of specific numeric information. Another important benefit of forms is that they provide the precise type of data needed. With a database, you could have several different form designs with the same set of fields, to provide different ways to present the relevant data to the user.

Why Use Forms Instead of the Browse Window?

Forms offer a number of advantages over the browse window when it comes to data entry and editing. With the browse window, you don't have a great deal of control over how your data is displayed. Although it is true that you can move columns around, change row heights and column widths, and modify font sizes, these are pretty much the limits of what you can do with the appearance of a browse window. With forms, you can move the fields to any location you like, not just to an area of a specific column. Forms can display data in a row-oriented or column-oriented fashion, or a combination of both. Whereas the browse windows must follow a row-and-column format, forms essentially use a free-form design. Forms also enable you to utilize color and shading within the controls, something that is not possible with the browse windows. You can add lines, boxes, or drawings in the form of bitmaps to enhance the form's appearance.

Some types of data are better suited for display in forms than in browse windows. Memo fields are difficult to view in the browse window, and general fields that contain pictures or other OLE data cannot be viewed in a browse window. Finally, forms can contain options such as list boxes or combination boxes to group various options that you specify. List boxes and combination boxes are not possible in the browse windows.

On What Should I Base My Forms?

Because FoxPro enables you to base forms on tables, queries, or views, some advance planning might be wise to help make the most effective use of forms. If you intend to use the form to examine any or all of the records in a single table, base the form on the table. If you need to examine data from multiple tables—or if you need to examine a selected subset of data—base the form on a query. If you need to update data stored in multiple tables, or in tables that are stored remotely on a server, base the form on a view. Note that when you base a form on a query, FoxPro must run the query as it opens the form. For this reason, forms that are based on large tables and/or complex queries might be slow to open.

Creating Simple Forms

This chapter details how you can create simple to moderately complex forms exclusively with the use of the AutoForm Wizard button and with the aid of the Form Wizards. Note that Chapter 12, "Designing and Customizing Forms," details how you can add more features to forms you design or enhance manually.

Creating a Form with the AutoForm Wizard Button

The simplest way to create a form is to use the AutoForm Wizard button on the toolbar. The AutoForm Wizard button builds a default single-column form for whatever table is selected in the Project Manager at the time you click the button. In the Project Manager, click the Data tab; then find and select the desired table, query, or view that is to serve as the source of the data for the form. Next, click the AutoForm Wizard button. When you do so, FoxPro builds a default form for the table, query, or view. An example of such a form was shown previously in Figure 9.1.

Creating a Form with the Form Wizards

FoxPro provides an automated way to create a wide variety of common forms with the aid of the Form Wizards. Like other FoxPro wizards, the Form Wizards step you through the process of form creation by asking a series of questions about the desired form. The overall steps, which are described in more detail in the following paragraphs, are these:

1. With the Project Manager open, click the Documents tab, click Forms, and then click New. When you do so, a dialog box appears asking if you want to use the Form Wizard or start with a blank form.

2. Click the Form Wizards button. Another dialog box appears asking if you want to create a form based on a single table, or a one-to-many form based on a parent table and a child table. Make the desired selection and then click OK.

3. Follow the directions in the Wizard dialog boxes. In the last dialog box that appears, click the Save and Run Form option and then click Finish to begin entering or viewing data, or click the Modify Form option and then click Finish to see the structure of the form in design view.

When you click the Documents tab in the Project Manager, click Forms and then click New. The New Form dialog box appears. Click Form Wizard and the dialog box shown in Figure 9.2 appears.

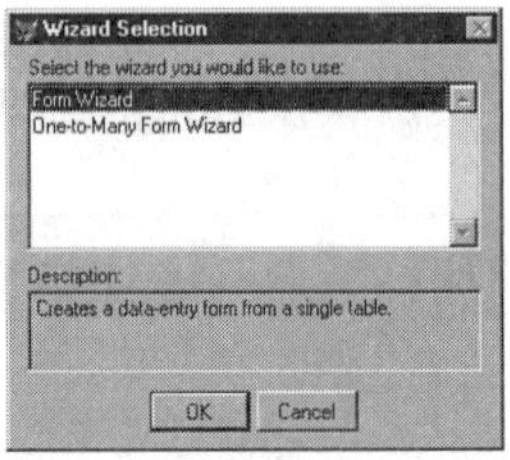

FIGURE 9.2.

The Wizard Selection dialog box.

Assuming you want a form that is based on a single table, query, or view, choose Form Wizard in the dialog box and click OK. In a moment, you will see the first dialog box of the Form Wizard, as shown in Figure 9.3.

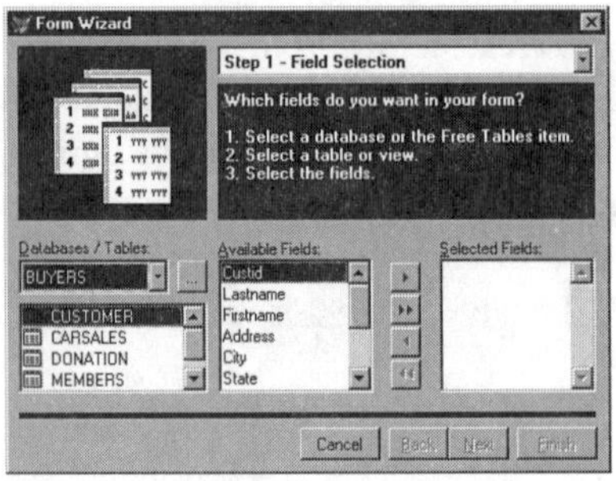

FIGURE 9.3.

A dialog box for choosing fields.

Choosing the Desired Fields

The first dialog box presented by the Form Wizard enables you to choose the desired fields that are included in the form.

At the left side of the dialog box, under Databases/Tables, choose the desired database and then choose the first table you want to use fields from in the list of available tables. When you do this, you will see a list of the fields from that table in the Available Fields list shown at the center of the dialog box.

Next, using the buttons between the Available Fields and the Selected Fields list boxes, add the desired fields to the Selected Fields list box. You can click any one field in the Available Fields list box and then click the right-arrow button to add the field, or you can click the double right-arrow button to add all fields from the table to the Selected Fields list. If you make a mistake and add an unwanted field, use the left-arrow button to remove a single field you've already added from the Field Order on Form list box, or the double left-arrow button to remove all of the fields. After adding the desired fields, click Next to proceed to the next dialog box.

TIP

You can add the fields in any order you like. The wizard doesn't force you to add fields in the order that they appear in the Available Fields list box. For example, if the Available Fields list box contains a Last Name field and directly beneath it a First Name field, you could choose to add the First Name field to the Field Order on Form list box, followed by the Last Name field. In the resulting form, cursor movement would be into the First Name field and then into the Last Name field.

Choosing a Style for the Form

The next dialog box presented by the Form Wizards asks which style you want for the form (see Figure 9.4). Your choices here are Standard, Chiseled, Shadowed, Boxed, or Embossed.

FIGURE 9.4.

A dialog box for choosing a style for the form.

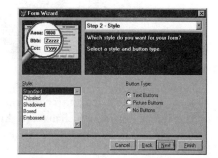

The standard form (see Figure 9.5) provides a simple combination of white fields containing gray text (when displayed) or black text (when edited) on a white background. If you plan to change a form's design manually, this style of design can be easier to modify than the others. (The other forms use fancy tricks with shadowed highlighting that can make modifications difficult.)

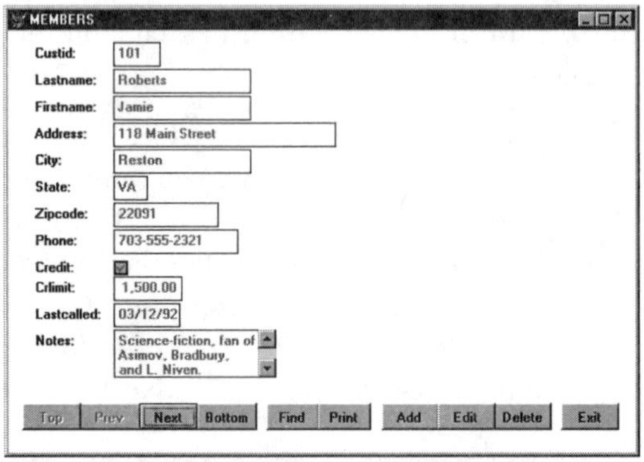

FIGURE 9.5.

The standard look for a form.

The chiseled form (see Figure 9.6) takes on an appearance similar to that of the standard form, but all fields and the form's title are underlined with a chiseled effect, and the form has a gray background and a black title bar.

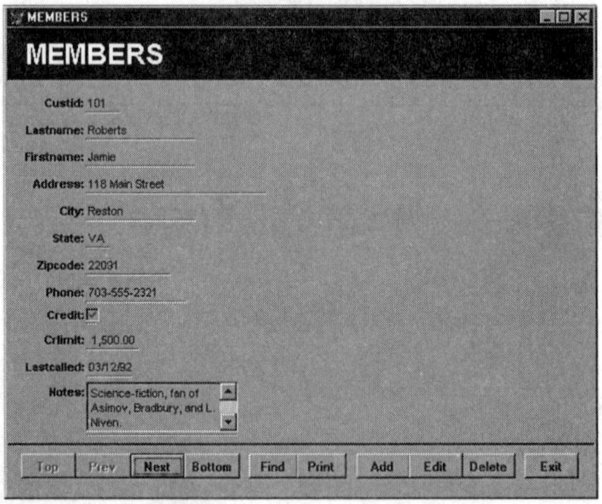

FIGURE 9.6.

The chiseled look for a form.

The shadowed look (see Figure 9.7) uses the same text, color, and background design as the chiseled look, but the fields are given a three-dimensional "drop shadow" effect. Note that it can be difficult to make manual design changes to this form because in design view it is often difficult to place the fields and the corresponding shadows in the same relative positions after moving them.

FIGURE 9.7.

The shadowed look for a form.

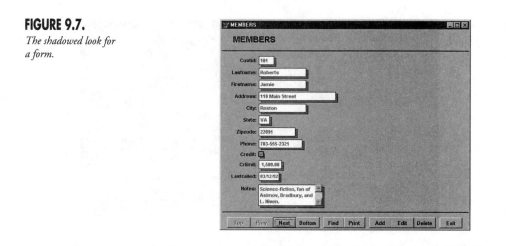

The boxed look (see Figure 9.8) provides a form with field labels in blue, field data in black on a white background, and the overall form background in gray. Each combination of field label and field is enclosed in a white box, with the labels placed at the upper left. As with the shadowed look, the boxed look can present difficulties if you want to make manual changes because it can be hard to keep the labels and fields in their respective positions as you move them.

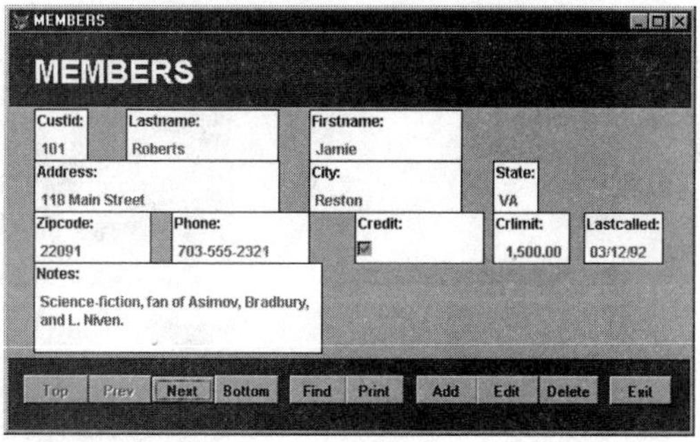

FIGURE 9.8.

The boxed look for a form.

Finally, the embossed look provides black text for field labels and white text boxes for the fields, but the fields are given a sunken effect (see Figure 9.9). The form's title is given an attractive serif font.

You can also click the Text or Picture button as desired to choose whether you want the form's navigation buttons to display text or pictures. The text on the buttons uses terms such as "Next," "First," "Last," and "Prev," whereas the pictures use VCR-style buttons with arrow pictures on them to represent these functions for moving around within a table. When you finish choosing an appearance for the form and selecting the options for the buttons, you can click Next to proceed with the Form Wizard.

FIGURE 9.9.
*The embossed look for
a form.*

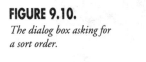

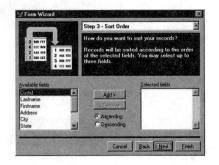

The next dialog box presented by the wizard asks for sort fields and the sort order (see Figure 9.10). You can add up to three fields on which to sort by clicking each desired field in the Available Fields list to select it, and then clicking the right-arrow button to add the field to the Selected Fields list. In the center of the dialog box, you can choose Ascending or Descending for each sort field, as desired. (Note that if you add more than one field, the sorting priority is highest for the first field added and lowest for the last field added.) When you're finished with the options in this dialog box, click Next.

FIGURE 9.10.
*The dialog box asking for
a sort order.*

Completing the Design Process

The last Form Wizard dialog box (see Figure 9.11) provides a box for entering a title for the form, along with choices to save the form for later use, to save and run the form, or to save the form and open it for modification in the Form Designer. The default title assigned to the form is the same as the underlying table or query, but you can change this as desired. (This title is not used as a filename that the form is saved under; instead, it appears as a title in the upper-left corner of the form when the form opens.) After entering a title, click the "Save and run form" option, and then click Finish to use the new form with your data. You can also click "Save form and modify it in the form designer," and then click Finish to open the form in FoxPro's Form Design window and make further modifications.

FIGURE 9.11.

*The final dialog box
for Form Wizard.*

You can also click "Save form for later use" if you want to save the form as is but don't plan to use it at the present time. Whichever choice you make, when you click Finish, FoxPro presents the Save As dialog box (see Figure 9.12). You must enter a filename under which the form is to be saved.

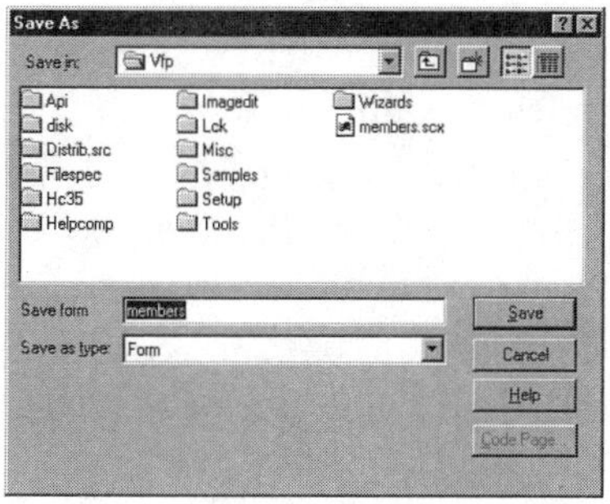

FIGURE 9.12.

The Save As dialog box.

Even if you prefer to design your own forms, the Form Wizards can often save time and effort by providing a form that is close to what you want. Use the wizards to create a form, and then switch to design view to make your desired changes. You'll find more on design techniques for forms in Chapter 12.

Opening a Form

Forms can be opened from the Project Manager by clicking on the form name in the Project Manager window and then clicking the Run button. (If the Documents tab is not visible, you must first click the Documents tab in the Project Manager so that all of the stored documents appear.) You can then open the desired form by clicking the symbol to the left of Forms to see all the forms, selecting the desired form, and then clicking the Run button in the Project Manager. Doing so causes the form to appear, with the first available record shown. (If an index is active, the first record that you see in the form is the first record according to the index.) A list of buttons for navigating among the records appears at the bottom of the form.

Navigating Within a Form and Editing

Navigation within a form is done by using the four navigation buttons at the bottom of the form. From left to right, the buttons are

Top   Displays the first record on the form with all of its fields (shown previously in Figure 9.1).

Prev   Displays the previous record on the form. If you are at the beginning of the file, this button is dimmed.

Next   Displays the next record in the file. If you are at the end of the file, the button is dimmed.

Bottom   Displays the last record in the file.

Six other command buttons are also present:

Find   Opens a search window used to find a record and display it on the form.

Add   Adds a blank record at the end of the table and opens that record for data entry within the form.

Edit   Enables editing on the current record. Click the Edit button, and you can change the entries to the fields. You can use either the mouse, Tab key, or the right- and left-arrow keys to move around the fields.

Delete   Deletes the current record shown.

Print   Accesses the Open dialog box listing all your stored reports. You can select a report and click OK to print the data based on that report. (For details on creating reports, see Chapter 10, "Creating and Using Simple Reports," and Chapter 13, "Designing and Customizing Reports.")

Exit   Closes the form and returns you to the Project Manager.

An Example: Creating a Form for the Buyer's Table

You can perform the following steps to demonstrate how you can create a data entry form for the Buyer's table created in Chapter 3, "Creating and Working with Tables." Perform the following steps:

1. Open the Ecology project.
2. Click the Documents tab in the Project Manager.
3. Click Forms and then click New.
4. In the New Form dialog box that appears, click Form Wizard.

5. In the Wizard Selection dialog box that appears, click Form Wizard and then click OK.

6. At the left side of the first Form Wizard dialog box that appears, click Customer as the desired table.

7. Click the double-arrow button to add all of the fields in the table to the form. Then click Next.

8. The next dialog box to appear asks for a sort order. Click the Zipcode field under Available Fields, and then click the Add button to add it to the Selected Fields list box. Then click Next.

9. The Final dialog box enables you to enter a title for your form. For this example, call it Customers. Then click Finish.

10. Next, the Save As dialog box appears so that a filename can be given to your form. Save the form as Customer and click Save. The form is now created. When the form is opened (by selecting it in the Documents tab of the Project Manager and clicking Run), the form bears the title Customers, as it was named in the Wizard dialog box.

Summary

This chapter detailed the creation of forms with the automated features added to Visual FoxPro. These features make it possible for you to work with custom forms with no knowledge of programming. You can, however, use manual form design and programming techniques to go beyond what is possible with the Form Wizards. Such techniques are covered beginning in Chapter 12.

Creating and Using Simple Reports

10

Reports are the end result of much of your work in Visual FoxPro, or in any database for that matter. They provide a way to organize, format, display, or print desired information. Visual FoxPro reports provide significant flexibility, especially if you are accustomed to the DOS-based database managers that were commonly used before Windows became popular. Visual FoxPro reports let you combine elements, such as data, text (in a variety of formats), graphs, and graphic elements (lines, rectangles, and so on) to provide the precise report you need. You can quickly create reports with the AutoReport button, or you can use the Report Wizards to guide you through the report design process while maintaining some control over the report's type and appearance. You can also design your reports manually using Visual FoxPro's Report Designer to place the needed objects in a blank report. Figure 10.1 shows a report for a table of customers. In this example, the report was created in a single step with the AutoReport button on the toolbar.

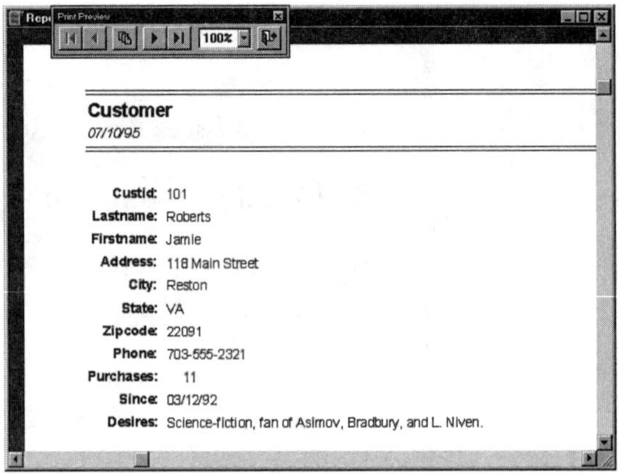

FIGURE 10.1.

An example of a report.

Although reports can be based on tables, another viable option is to base reports on queries. When a report is based on a table, the report includes every record in the table, but this is rarely needed. Most often, what's needed is a report that contains specific data: all sales during the first quarter, all vacation destinations in the Caribbean, or all surgical records for a specific patient. When a report is based on a query, the SQL statement behind the query runs whenever the report is opened, and the desired subset of data automatically appears in the report. Reports can include graphics, which are stored in general fields of a table or pasted into blank areas as design elements.

Reports share many design elements with forms, but there are some differences between the two. Reports use a *band-oriented* approach, where the design of the report can be divided into different bands containing separate elements, such as headers, footers, and group titles. Forms, by comparison, have no bands. Reports also provide specialized options that let you group the data produced by the report.

Design Issues Behind Reports

Proper planning can help you save wasted time and avoid reports that don't give users the needed information. When you design reports, your job is to take the raw data provided by a table or a query and to transform that data into a printed report that provides needed information in a way that makes sense to the user. An effective methodology for producing a report might consist of these steps:

1. Define the report's layout on paper.

    Before you begin work with the Report Wizards or with the manual design surfaces of FoxPro's Report Writer, you should have a concrete idea of what the report will look like—either on paper or mentally. A hand-drawn sketch passed around the ranks of those who use the system helps refine a report before anything is attempted on-screen. If you are using an existing manual system or are reimplementing an older computer-based application in FoxPro, you likely have the existing forms to compare with your new designs. One point of warning: just because a report already exists in an older computer-based system does not mean it is the right model to use for designing an equivalent report in FoxPro. The existing report might have design shortfalls, or you may be able to design a better report by taking advantage of FoxPro capabilities that the older system lacked. Again, getting the users of the report involved in the design process helps you produce a report that accomplishes the needed task.

2. Design and implement the underlying table or query.

    Unless you want a completely nonrelational report, which contains every iota of data in a table, you need a query to serve as the basis for the report. If the report is to be a relational one, you'll need to design a relational query (as outlined in Chapter 11, "Working with Visual FoxPro's Relational Powers") to provide the desired fields from the different tables. Queries can provide the selected records, the desired fields, and the needed sort order for the data before it is processed in the report.

    For example, consider a database used by a video rental store that has tables for customers, videos in stock, and rental records. You might need a report that shows all customer tape rentals for a specific month. The query would need to retrieve the customer names from the Customers table, the video titles from the Videos table, and the rental dates from the Rentals table. The query would also need to select records for a specific month and produce the results before a report based on the query could provide the needed data.

3. Design the report in Visual FoxPro.

    Once the query exists, you can design the report using either the Report Wizards or the manual method of report design.

4. Preview or print the report.

    You can print or preview the report when you are finished with the design stage. From the Project Manager, click a report to select it and then click the Print button. Choose

Run | Report, select the desired report in the Open dialog box, and then click Run. From the Command window, you can use the REPORT FORM command. All these methods are covered in this chapter.

Creating Reports

This chapter shows how you can create simple to moderately complex reports. The primary methods are the use of the AutoReport button and the use of the Report Wizards. Chapter 13, "Designing and Customizing Reports," contains additional information on how you can apply the more complex features of custom report design.

Creating a Report with the AutoReport Button

You can use the AutoReport button on the Standard toolbar to quickly create a default single-column report. The AutoReport button builds a simple columnar report for any table or query selected or active when you click the button. To produce such a report, first switch to the Project Manager. Click the desired table or query to select it, and then click the AutoReport button. (It's the button with the icon that resembles a notebook cover with a lightning bolt across it.) When you do this, Visual FoxPro builds a default report for the table or query and then displays the Report Designer. (See Figure 10.2.) You can choose the Preview button from the Document tab of the Project Manager to display an on-screen preview of the report. An example of such a report is shown in Figure 10.1.

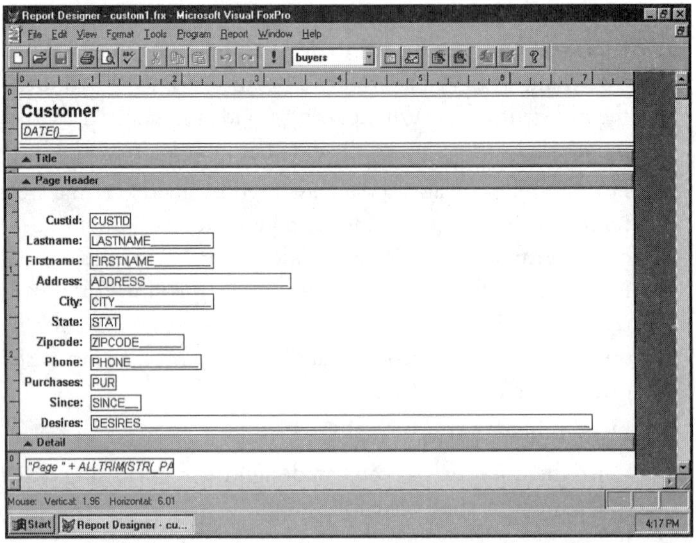

FIGURE 10.2.

The Report Designer.

The type of report you get with this technique is a simple columnar report. The field names appear at the top of each page as column headings. The disadvantage of using the AutoReport button is that the resultant report only contains as many fields as will fit across a single page, and any additional fields in the table or query are omitted from the report. You can get around this by designing a selective query that provides just the fields you need (assuming they will fit) or by customizing the report's design using the techniques outlined in Chapter 13.

Creating a Report with the Report Wizards

The built-in Report Wizards provide an automated way to create a number of commonly used reports by stepping you through the process of report design and asking you a number of questions about the desired report. Here are the overall steps, which are covered in detail in the paragraphs that follow:

1. From the Project Manager, click the Data Tab and select the table you wish to use.
2. Next, choose Tools | Wizards | Report to activate the Report Wizard.
3. The Wizard selection dialog box appears. Choose the Report Wizard option and click OK.
4. Follow the directions that appear in the dialog boxes. In the last dialog box, you can choose to display the report in Print Preview or Design view.

In the Documents tab, when you choose the report object and then click New, the New Report dialog box appears as shown in Figure 10.3.

FIGURE 10.3.

The New Report dialog box.

You can manually design a report using the Report Designer, which can help you fine tune the creation of your report. Techniques for using the Report Designer are described in Chapter 13.

When you click the Report Wizard button in the Project Manager, the Wizard selection dialog box appears. Choose the wizard you wish to use to create your report. You have the choice of a One-to-Many Report Wizard, a Group/Total Report Wizard, or a regular Report Wizard.

With group/totals reports, the data is organized with the selected fields placed in columns and each record occupying a row. The records are optionally sorted and grouped according to a value based on a field. Numeric totals can be included for numeric fields. If totals are included in the design, Visual FoxPro adds a grand total at the end of the report. Figure 10.4 shows an example of a group/totals report.

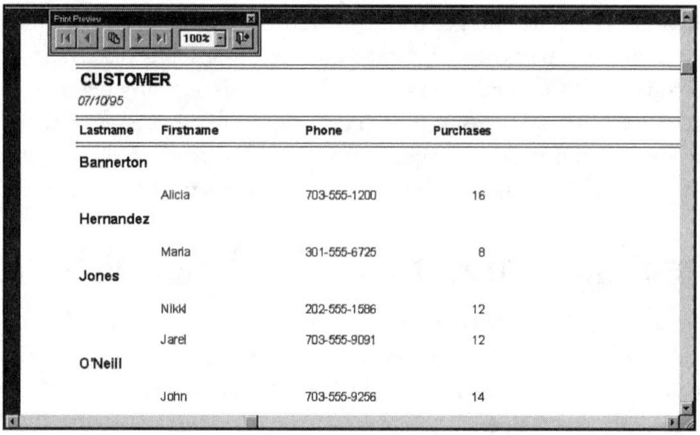

FIGURE 10.4.

A group/totals report.

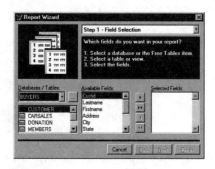

One-to-many reports are used to create relational reports. They show one record from the primary or parent table and a record from all associated records, in the secondary or child table.

The Report Wizard choice creates a report which has an appearance that varies depending on the style and layout you select in the dialog boxes.

Click the OK button after you choose the report you want to create, and the first dialog box of the Report Wizard appears, as shown in Figure 10.5.

FIGURE 10.5.

The first Report Wizard dialog box.

Choosing Fields for the Report

You use the first frame of the Report Wizard dialog box to choose fields that you want to include in your report. Select the fields in the order you want them to appear in the report.

When you select a field in the Available Fields list box and then click the Add button, the field is added to the Selected Fields list box. You can also double-click a field in the Available Fields list box to add the field to the Selected Fields list box. (As an alternative, you can click the Add All button to add all the fields in the Available Fields list to the Selected Fields list box.) If you make a mistake and add an unwanted field, use the Remove button to remove any field you've already added from the Field Order On Form list box. The Remove All button removes all the fields. After adding the desired fields, click Next to proceed to the next frame of the Report Wizard dialog box.

> **TIP**
>
> You can add the fields in any order you like. The wizard doesn't force you to add fields in the order they appear in the Available Fields list box. For example, if the Available Fields list box contains a Lastname field and directly beneath it a Firstname field, you could choose to add the Firstname field to the Selected Fields list box followed by the Lastname field. In the report, the Firstname field would appear to the left of the Lastname field.

Choosing a Look for the Report

The next frame of the Report Wizard dialog box asks you to choose a style for the report: Executive, Presentation, or Ledger. The Executive report (see Figure 10.6) adds thin, double lines in the header and uses a default 14-point font for the header and a default 10-point font for the remaining text.

FIGURE 10.6.

The Executive look for a report.

CARSALES 07/10/95				
Salesrep	**January**	**February**	**March**	**April**
John Smith	23,490.30	27,800.50	31,560.00	29,900.00
Jayne Williamson	31,500.00	26,450.50	29,900.00	34,500.00
Al Smithers	35,200.00	23,250.00	28,890.50	30,250.50

The Presentation report (see Figure 10.7) adds thick, single lines in the header and uses a default 14-point font for the header and a 10-point font for the remaining text.

FIGURE 10.7.

*The Presentation look
for a report.*

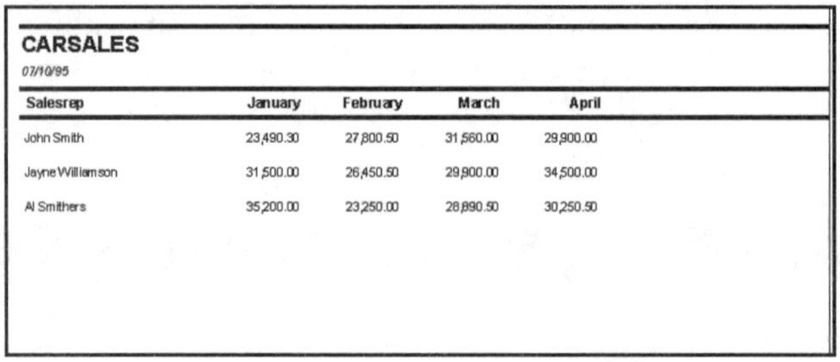

The Ledger report (see Figure 10.8) uses lines and fonts similar to those used by the Executive style, but the data is enclosed in a spreadsheet-like grid formed by horizontal and vertical lines.

FIGURE 10.8.

*The Ledger look
for a report.*

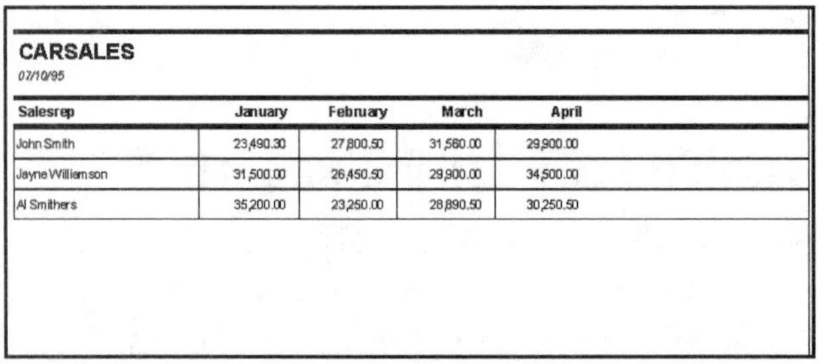

TIP

Of the three styles of reports provided, the Ledger look accommodates more data in a single page of printable space than the other styles. (Of course, you can always modify the other styles to suit your needs.)

As you click each option button in the dialog box, a representative sample of the report's appearance is displayed at the left side of the box. When you have chosen an appearance for the report, click Next to proceed.

Report Layout

The third frame of the Report Wizard dialog box enables you to choose a layout for the report. You can choose whether you want a row or column style report layout. If you choose the Columns options, fields are placed in columns, and the column headers are placed horizontally across the top of a report. If you choose the Rows option, field titles are placed along the report's left margin, and the field values are placed to the right of the field titles. You can also select the number of columns and the paper size. You can specify whether you want the report to be printed in portrait or landscape orientation. When you select a layout, a pictorial representation of the specified report layout is shown in the upper-left panel of the frame.

Setting Sort Order

In the fourth frame of the Report dialog box, you can choose the field sort order for the report. The sort order sorts the records according to the chosen fields in a descending or ascending order, depending on which you choose. This gives an order to the records in your report.

Completing the Design Process

The last frame of the Report Wizard dialog box (see Figure 10.9) provides a box for you to enter a title for the report. It also gives you three options: Save report for later use; Save report and modify it in the Report Designer; or Save and print report. After you enter a title (which appears at the top of the first page of the report), click Finish to use the new report with your data. You can also use the Wrap fields that do not fit option to make room for fields that do not fit. And finally, you can use the Preview button to see what your report will look like before it is printed.

FIGURE 10.9.

The final dialog box for the Report Wizard.

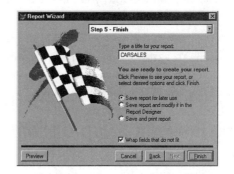

You can click Save report for later use if you want to save the report but don't need to use it at the present time. Whichever choice you make, when you click Finish, FoxPro presents the Save As dialog box. (See Figure 10.10.) You must enter a filename under which the form will be saved. By default, reports are saved with a filename extension of .FRX.

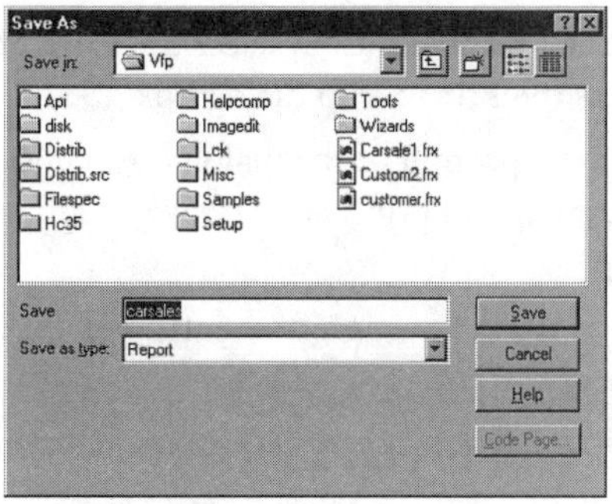

FIGURE 10.10.

The Save As dialog box.

Even if you prefer to design your own reports, the Report Wizards can often provide you with a report that is close to what you want and can save you time and effort as well. Use the wizards to create a report, then choose the Save reports and modify it in the Report Designer option to make any changes. You'll find more on design techniques for reports in Chapter 13.

How to Print the Report

In a nutshell, you can print a completed report using any of the following methods:

■ From the Project Manager, click the Document Tab, choose a report, and then click the Add button to add a report, or, from the Open dialog box, choose the report that you wish to add and click OK. The report is then added to the Project Manager. Next, click the Print button from the standard toolbar after highlighting the name of the report. If you want to print the report that is already in the Project Manager, just select the report and click the Print button on the toolbar.

■ From the Command window, you can use the REPORT FORM command using the following basic syntax:

```
REPORT FORM report filename [TO PRINT] ¦ [PREVIEW] ¦ [TO filename]
```

If you use the TO PRINT option, the report is printed; otherwise, it appears on-screen in the main window of the Visual FoxPro desktop. If you specify the PREVIEW keyword, the report displays in the Preview window.

Changing the Print Setup Options

Visual FoxPro stores a number of print setup and page orientation settings with the report. You can change these settings once, and they remain in effect for that particular report until you change them again. To set the page orientation and other print setup options for a report, perform these steps:

1. Open the existing report by choosing File | Open. In the Open dialog box that appears, change the List Files Of Type option to Report, and then select the desired report and click OK to open it.

2. Choose File | Print and then select the Print Setup button from the Print dialog box. This opens the Print Setup dialog box. (See Figure 10.11.)

3. In the Printer portion of the dialog box, choose the desired printer. (The drop-down list box contains all printers that have been installed for use with Windows on your system.)

4. In the Orientation portion of the dialog box, choose the desired orientation (Portrait or Landscape).

5. In the Paper portion of the dialog box, choose a paper size and then click OK.

FIGURE 10.11.

The Print Setup dialog box.

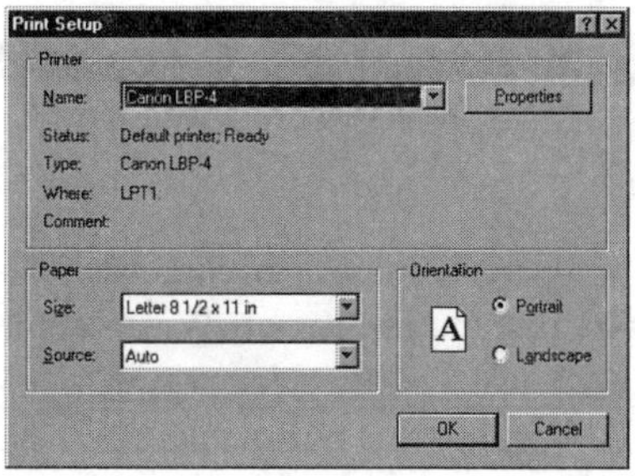

Click the Properties button in the dialog box to reveal additional options that apply to your specific printer. The dialog box you see when you click the Options button varies depending on your printer. Figure 10.12 shows the Printer Properties dialog box that appears for the Canon LBP-4 laser printer.

FIGURE 10.12.

The Printer Properties dialog box for a Canon printer.

Because there are hundreds of printers on the market, it is impossible to explain all of the possible settings. Each printer's dialog box contains options applicable to that particular printer. In addition, most laser printers contain list boxes for choosing from various installed fonts or font cartridges (or both). Your printer's documentation may be helpful in determining what fonts and other options can be used with your particular printer.

NOTE

When you click the Options button to display the printer's dialog box, the options you see are the default Windows settings for that printer. Changing these options is likely to affect printing in other Windows applications.

A Sample Report Created with the Report Wizards

For an example of a report design, you can use the following steps to create a report using both the AutoReport button and the Report Wizards. First, to create a default report with no additional steps involved, use the AutoReport button (located next to the AutoForm button on the standard toolbar). Clicking this button causes Visual FoxPro to build a default report with no questions asked. You can preview this report from the dialog box that appears after it is created. This is Visual FoxPro's quick and easy way to create a report.

You may, of course, have times when a more detailed report is needed. In these cases, you can use the Report Wizards. From the Project Manager, perform the following steps:

1. Click the Document tab in the Project Manager and then choose New for a new report.

2. The New Report window appears. Choose Report Wizard to help you make the report.

3. The Report Wizard asks you to choose one of the three wizards: Group/Total Report Wizard, One-to-Many Report Wizard, or Report Wizard. (The order of the successive frames of the Wizard dialog box and what appears in each frame is different depending on the options you choose.) For this example, follow the Report Wizard choice.

4. You are now asked which fields you want to include in your report. For this example, include only the Firstname, Lastname, Custid, and State fields by clicking each field and then clicking the Add button. (This frame is also used if you choose Group/Total report as the report type.)

5. Next, a window appears that enables you to choose between the different styles for the report. Choose Presentation for this example. (Note that as you choose the different styles, a representation of each layout displays in the dialog box. This enables you to see the styles for the different types of layouts before you implement them.)

6. The next frame of the Report Wizard dialog box asks you to choose the orientation of the report: Horizontal or Vertical. For this example, choose Vertical. You can also choose the field layout and the number of columns. (If you are creating a Group/Total report, you are asked which field should be used as the basis for the grouping.)

7. The next frame asks which field should serve as the basis for the sort. This frame enables you to sort the report's output by specified fields. For this example, sort according to Custid by selecting the Custid field and then clicking the right-arrow button. Leave the default Ascending Order setting selected and then click Next.

8. The next frame is the last one you see as part of the report's design process. By default, the report has the same title as the underlying table. You can change this by backspacing and typing a new name. (Note that this name is not the filename under which the

report is saved—it simply serves as a title, which appears on the first page of the report.) Enter Customers Report as the title for the report. Also in this dialog box, you have the option to either Save the report for later use; Save the report and then modify it in the Report Designer; or Save the report and print it. For this example, click the Save report for later use option.

9. When prompted for a filename under which to save the report, save the report as CUSTOMERS.

Keep in mind that when you create a report with the Report Wizard, the Group/Total reports differs from the sample report shown previously in step 5. With Group/Total reports, this step sets different grouping options. Fields can be grouped according to the entire contents of each field, by first character, or by the first two or three characters.

For example, if you grouped the names Sutton, Sanders, and Swanson, each of the names would appear in their own group. On the other hand, if grouped by first letter, these names would appear in the same group. Numeric fields, by default, constitute a separate group for each number. However, if you choose to group by 20s, then 1–19 would appear as one group.

Producing Simple Reports from the Command Window

Another common way to produce reports in Visual FoxPro is by entering commands. You can use the LIST and DISPLAY commands to generate simple listings of data. You can also use the REPORT FORM command to produce a report based on a previously saved report.

The *LIST* Command

The LIST command is one way of producing a simple report. The LIST TO PRINTER command produces a simple columnar listing. The output is sent to the active window and to the default installed printer. Here is the format of this command:

```
LIST [field1,field2...fieldn] TO PRINTER
```

As an example, enter the following command in the command window:

```
LIST CUSTID, LASTNAME, CITY, STATE TO PRINTER
```

This command prints all the customer ID numbers, last names, cities, and states. If you use a laser printer you might need to enter the eject command to make the paper feed out of the printer.

You can also be more specific and add a FOR condition to the list to produce a more exact report. As an example, consider the following command:

```
LIST LASTNAME, FIRSTNAME, CUSTID FOR LASTNAME = "Artman" TO PRINTER
```

This prints the last name, first name, and customer ID number of the buyer named Artman. If there is more than one Artman, that name would be printed also. As another example, you can also produce a report of only the customers with more than eight purchases. Use the following command:

```
LIST CUSTID, LASTNAME, PURCHASES FOR PURCHASES > 100  TO PRINTER
```

Here are the results:

Record#	CUSTID	LASTNAME	PURCHASES
2	106	Tatiem	320
3	102	Ford	245
5	105	Fairfield	111
6	110	Jose	112
8	106	Jones	171
9	107	Jones	456

> **NOTE**
>
> You can include the OFF keyword along with the command, as in
>
> ```
> LIST OFF CUSTID, LASTNAME, PURCHASES FOR PURCHASES > 100
> ```
>
> Doing so omits the record numbers. For example, specify the OFF keyword with the previous example:
>
> ```
> LIST CUSTID, LASTNAME, PURCHASES FOR PURCHASES > 100  TO PRINTER  OFF
> ```
>
> And the results appear as follows without the record number:
>
> | CUSTID | LASTNAME | PURCHASES |
> |--------|----------|-----------|
> | 106 | Tatiem | 320 |
> | 102 | Ford | 245 |
> | 105 | Fairfield | 111 |
> | 110 | Jose | 112 |
> | 106 | Jones | 171 |
> | 107 | Jones | 456 |
>
> You can also suppress the field heading display with the SET HEADINGS OFF command.

At times, you might need to print a report using a condition based on a date field. To do this, place curly braces around the date. For example, the following command:

```
LIST CUSTID, LASTNAME, SINCE FOR SINCE<= {08/15/92} TO PRINTER
```

produces a list of the following records:

Record#	Custid	Lastname	Since
1	101	Roberts	03/12/92
2	102	Sanderson	06/17/89
4	104	Jones	11/22/89
7	107	Zeibermann	08/15/92
8	108	O'Neill	10/02/91
9	109	Bannerton	04/15/90

In this example, all the dates in the SINCE field are prior or equal to 08/15/92.

You can add other conditions to make the report even more specific. Here is an example:

```
LIST CUSTID, LASTNAME, SINCE FOR SINCE <= {08/15/92} . And. STATE = "VA" TO PRINTER
```

This command prints all the records with a date in the SINCE field before 08/15/92 for customers who are residents of Virginia.

The *REPORT FORM* Command

You can use the REPORT FORM command to produce stored reports. Here is the syntax for the command:

```
REPORT FORM cFileName  [scope] [FOR expression] [WHILE expression]
  [TO PRINTER [PROMPT] ¦ TO FileName [ASCII]] ¦ [PREVIEW [NOWAIT]]
  [PLAIN] [SUMMARY] [NOEJECT] [NOOPTIMIZE] [NOCONSOLE] [HEADING cHeadingText]
  [ENVIRONMENT] NAME ObjectName
```

The FOR and WHILE options let you specify conditions that control which reports are printed. Adding the TO PRINTER option routes the output to the printer. If you specify the optional PROMPT keyword, the Printer Settings dialog box displays before printing begins. The TO FILE option directs the report to a text file. (The TO PRINT and the TO FILE clauses cannot be used at the same time.) The ASCII keyword instructs Visual FoxPro to create an ASCII text file from the report definition. The number of columns and rows in the resulting text file are determined by the _ASCIICOLS and _ASCIIROWS system memory variables, respectively. The default values for these two system memory variables are 80 and 63, respectively. If you do not specify ASCII, the output file will contain all the printer codes for the report.

If you specify the PREVIEW keyword instead of the TO PRINTER or TO FILE clauses, the report displays in the Preview window. You can specify the NOWAIT keyword with the PREVIEW to instruct Visual FoxPro to display the Preview window and continue executing.

You can specify an object variable name for the report's data environment with the NAME clause. You can use this name to access the methods and properties of the data environment object.

The PLAIN option prints a report with no standard heading. The SUMMARY option is used to print reports with summary fields only. The NOEJECT option suppresses the form feed codes that are normally sent to the printer at the end of each page. You can add custom headings using the HEADING option followed by a character expression. (The character expressions must be placed in quotation marks.)

The ENVIRONMENT keyword is included for compatibility with FoxPro 2.*x* reports. This keyword instructs Visual FoxPro to reestablish any environment that was saved when the FoxPro 2.*x* report was saved. The environment information includes any filter in effect, which fields are available through the use of the SET FIELDS command, and any relationships with other files. When you save a file, the environment is saved to a view file under the same name as the report (assuming you answer Yes to the Save Environment? option that appears when you save the FoxPro 2.*x* report). This option saves you the trouble of opening a database and corresponding index files before you print the report.

For Visual FoxPro, the data environment is established when you design a report with the Report Designer. You can request Visual FoxPro to automatically open the data environment by setting the data environment `AutoOpenTables` property to true (.T.) Likewise, you can set the `AutoCloseTables` property to true to instruct Visual FoxPro to close the report data environment when the report is finished printing. The default value for both of these data environment properties is true (.T.).

If you do not want the report to echo on the screen when the report prints, specify the `NOCONSOLE` keyword. Otherwise, the report displays on the screen while it prints.

Problems with Reports

As with any area of complex computer software, problems can arise when you print reports. Two of the most common problems and their possible solutions are described in the following sections.

Why Do I Get Extra Blank Pages Between Each Page?

This common printing problem occurs when the report's design surface is so large that it extends beyond the size of the printed page. The default settings for a report (visible in the dialog box when you choose File | Page Setup) are Portrait orientation and one-inch margins on all four sides. Subtract the margins from a standard 8 1/2-inch by 11-inch sheet of paper, and you are left with a *printable area* of 6 1/2 inches across and 9 inches from top to bottom. (Users of international paper sizes must make the same type of calculations—subtracting the number of centimeters for the margins from the paper size to come up with a printable area.) If the length or width of your report exceeds this printable area, Visual FoxPro prints whatever portion of the report it could not fit on the original page on an additional page. This is true even when the excess area contains no objects. Visual FoxPro prints as many pages as are needed to display the full length and width of the report. When the excess area contains no objects, what you get is a blank page on every other page of the report.

To remedy this situation, open the report in design mode and pull in the right and bottom edges of the design surface as much as possible. If the design surface is as small as possible and you still have the problem when you print the report, choose File | Page Setup and make sure that the margins are correct for your paper size. With most laser printers, you can reduce the margins from the one-inch default to one-half inch on all sides and still contain the data in the printer's printable area.

TIP

You can save paper by performing a print preview to check for this problem before you print a newly designed report for the first time. Preview the report and click the Next Record button in the Navigation area at the bottom of the Print Preview window. If every other page is blank, you can go back into design mode and reduce the size of the report as needed to solve this problem.

Why Is My Printer Printing Garbage or Nothing at All?

If what prints bears absolutely no resemblance to what you see on-screen, chances are that the problem lies outside of Visual FoxPro. If the printer name that appears near the top of the Print dialog box doesn't match the printer connected to your computer, choose File | Print and click on the Print Setup button, and the Print Setup dialog appears as shown in Figure 10.11. Click the Specific Printer button, and make sure the correct printer is selected in the list box. Choose OK and try the File | Print command again. If the correct printer is selected and you still can't print (or the printing is garbage), the problem is probably in Windows itself or in how it is installed on your system. Visual FoxPro uses the Windows software (specifically, the Windows Print Manager) to manage all printing. If you can't print from another Windows application (the Notepad, for example), you won't be able to print from Visual FoxPro. If you can't print from any application in Windows, check the obvious—make sure the printer is properly connected, turned on, and online. Also, verify that you can print from the operating system itself (if you are running Windows on top of a version of MS-DOS).

Summary

This chapter introduced you to reports with an emphasis on the report tools (such as the AutoReport button and the Report Wizards) you can use to quickly create a variety of reports. Chapter 13 gives much more detail on reports, as well as additional coverage of more advanced reporting topics.

PART

Advanced Visual FoxPro

Working with Visual FoxPro's Relational Powers

11

IN THIS CHAPTER

Some of the relational powers of Visual Foxpro have been introduced already. In Chapter 3, "Creating and Working with Tables," the concepts involved in relational data management, primary and foreign keys, and the rules of normalization are covered in detail. The various types of relationships, one to one, one to many, and many to many are all discussed in Chapter 3.

Chapter 6, "Querying Data," introduces the Query Designer interface and the process of building queries in Visual FoxPro. Chapter 3 shows how to create persistent relationships in a database and how to use the Referential Integrity builder to protect the integrity of those relationships at the database level.

This chapter will show you how to maximize the benefits of Visual FoxPro's relational powers. You will learn how to create SQL views as a part of your database. The concept and use of parameterized views will be discussed. You will learn about the new updatable views that are available and how these can increase the usefulness of SQL in Visual FoxPro. You will also see how to use Visual FoxPro's SQL SELECT command to produce results that are not directly available from the Query Designer.

SAMPLE FILES ON THE CD-ROM

Sample forms are provided on the CD-ROM as adjuncts to this chapter facilitate your experimentation and familiarization with views, tables, and their construction. The files are located in VFU\Chap11\ and VFP\SAMPLES\DATA\.

File	Purpose
PastDue.SCX	A form that displays the results of views which are created during the chapter exercises. Attempting to run this form before defining the views will result in an error.
TestData.DBC	Located in the Visual FoxPro distribution directory VFP\SAMPLES\DATA\. Provides the data used in this chapter's examples.

Using Views

First, you might ask the question: "What is a view?" A view is a virtual table definition that may refer to one or more actual tables or other views. A view can be stored in a database container. Views can be parameterized, which allows them to be dynamically altered at runtime. Views can also be updatable, meaning that you can edit the view's contents, and those edits will be automatically transmitted back to the actual tables that comprise the view. In the following sections of this chapter you will create views and then use them.

Adding Views to the Database Designer

In Chapter 4, "Adding and Changing Data," you used the Testdata database that is included with Visual FoxPro. You will be using that database again in this chapter. First, open the Testdata database using the File | Open menu. This opens the Database Designer for you, as shown in Figure 11.1.

FIGURE 11.1.

The Database Designer for the Testdata database.

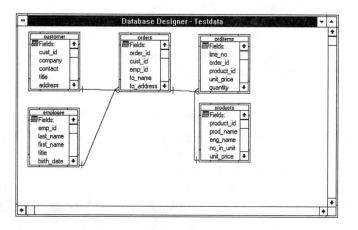

Right-click on the Database Designer background and select New Local View from the Short Cut Menu. Select Orders and click OK in the Add Table or View dialog. Your screen should now look like the one in Figure 11.2.

FIGURE 11.2.

The View Designer with the Orders table selected.

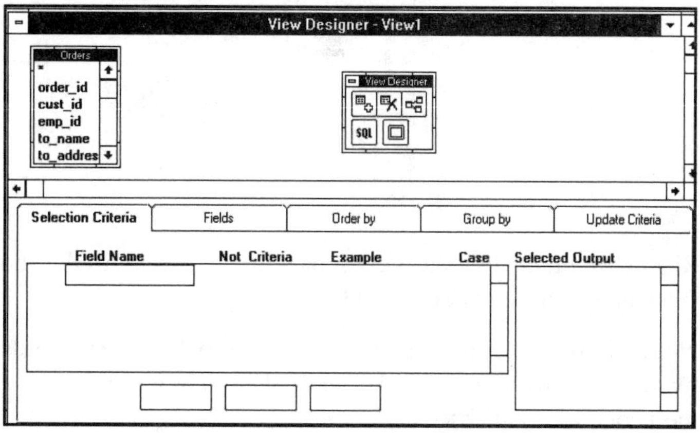

In the Selection criteria page, for Field Name, select Orders.require_by; for Criteria, select Less Than; and for Example, put the expression DATE() - 10. This criteria will cause the view to include all orders that were required 10 or more days before today. Now select a second Field Name of `Orders.shipped_on`, a Criteria of `Equals`, and an Example of `{  /  /  }`. This will further limit the records to only those that have a blank `shipped_on` date, meaning they haven't been shipped yet.

Switch to the Fields page and select the following fields:

```
Orders.Cust_id
Orders.order_id
Orders.order_date
Orders.require_by
Orders.order_dsc
Orders.order_amt
```

Finally, select the Order by page option and select `Orders.require_by`.

Now use the Control menu to close the View Designer, answer Yes to save the changes, and in the Save dialog box, name the view PastDue, and click OK. Figure 11.3 shows what the Database Designer should look like now.

FIGURE 11.3.

Your PastDue view has been added to the database.

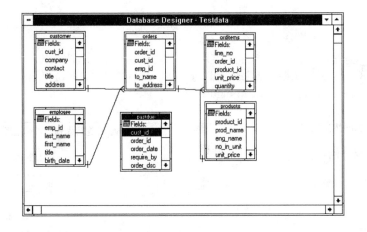

Right-click on the PastDue view and choose Browse from the Short Cut Menu. Your browse will look like the one in Figure 11.4.

Notice, in the status bar, that the PastDue view has fewer records in it than the Orders table (which has 1,078 records in it). The PastDue view is limiting the records for you to those that meet your selection criteria.

Scroll around the PastDue browse to see the records and fields that are displayed. Notice that you can see the Customer's ID, but this doesn't help in identifying who the customer is. It would be more helpful if the customer's name were displayed in the PastDue browse.

FIGURE 11.4.

Browse of the PastDue view.

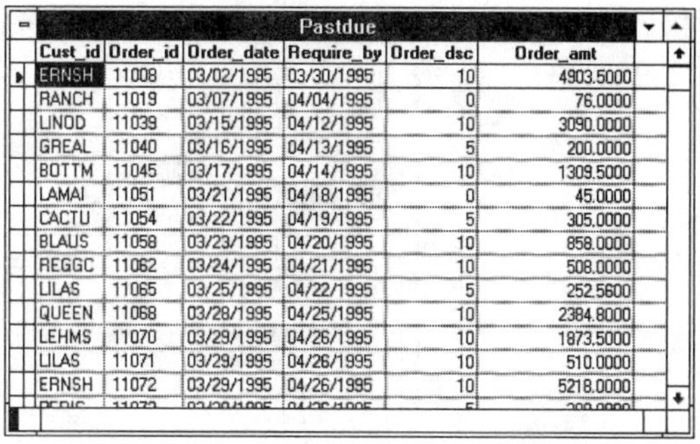

Cust_id	Order_id	Order_date	Require_by	Order_dsc	Order_amt
ERNSH	11008	03/02/1995	03/30/1995	10	4903.5000
RANCH	11019	03/07/1995	04/04/1995	0	76.0000
LINOD	11039	03/15/1995	04/12/1995	10	3090.0000
GREAL	11040	03/16/1995	04/13/1995	5	200.0000
BOTTM	11045	03/17/1995	04/14/1995	10	1309.5000
LAMAI	11051	03/21/1995	04/18/1995	0	45.0000
CACTU	11054	03/22/1995	04/19/1995	5	305.0000
BLAUS	11058	03/23/1995	04/20/1995	10	858.0000
REGGC	11062	03/24/1995	04/21/1995	10	508.0000
LILAS	11065	03/25/1995	04/22/1995	5	252.5600
QUEEN	11068	03/28/1995	04/25/1995	10	2384.8000
LEHMS	11070	03/29/1995	04/26/1995	10	1873.5000
LILAS	11071	03/29/1995	04/26/1995	10	510.0000
ERNSH	11072	03/29/1995	04/26/1995	10	5218.0000

What Is a Join?

In order to include the Customer's name in the PastDue view, we need to combine the fields from the Orders and Customer tables somehow. The process of making a view that is the result of combining information from two or more tables is called a *join.*

By definition, a join of two tables will provide as a result that set of records that appear in both of the two tables being joined. For example, assume you have two sets of marbles of various colors. You want to make a set of marbles from these two comprised of only blue marbles. You state "I want Set_1 Blues joined with Set_2 Blues." This new set of marbles is the join of the other two sets of marbles.

Using the View Designer to Create a Join

To add the Customer's name to your PastDue view, you need to modify the view. Close the Browse window and then right-click on the PastDue view and choose Modify from the Short Cut Menu. The View Designer will be displayed with the PastDue view loaded for modification.

Click on the Add a Table button in the View Designer toolbar, select Customer, and click OK in the Add Table or View dialog. Figure 11.5 shows the View Designer as it now appears.

You can see the Customer table in the upper half of the View Designer, but also notice that a new option in the Selection Criteria has been added to the beginning of the list. This criterion is the join condition that defines the relationship between the Orders and Customer tables. Notice the double-headed arrow to the left of this criterion; the arrow indicates that this is a join condition.

The join condition displayed here says that each Orders record should be joined with all of the Customer records that have the same value for the Cust_id field that the Orders record has. The Cust_id field is the primary key for the Customer table, and the Cust_id field in the Orders table is a foreign key.

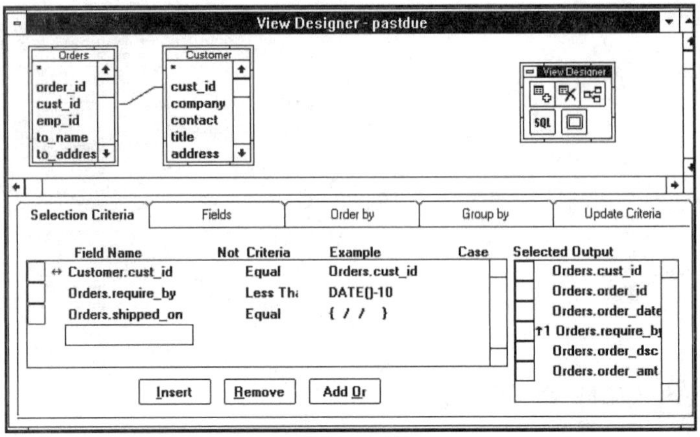

FIGURE 11.5.

The PastDue view with the Customer table added.

Click on the Field page and scroll the Available fields list down until you can see the `Customer.Company` field; highlight that field and add it to the selected fields list. Use the elevator button (also called a "mover") to the left of the field to drag it to the top of the Selected Output list.

Close the View Designer and answer Yes to save the changes. Next, right-click on the PastDue view and choose browse from the Short Cut Menu. Figure 11.6 shows what your new browse should look like.

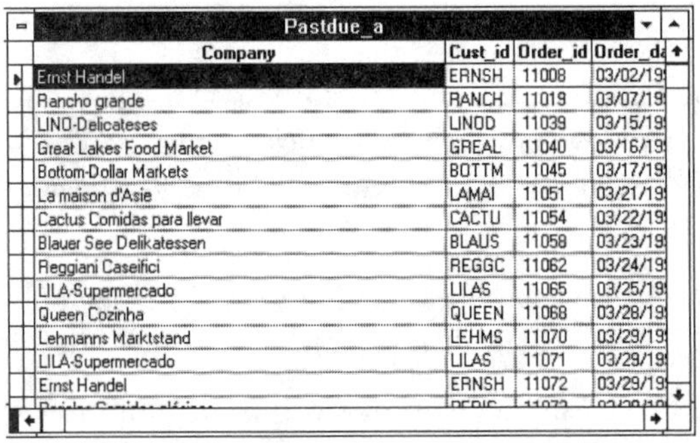

FIGURE 11.6.

Browsing the PastDue view when the Customer table is included.

You can now see the Customer's company name in the browse window. Click on the first record in the browse window to select it as the current record. Scroll to the right in the browse window until you see the `require_by` field column. Click in the `require_by` field for the record with ERNSH in the `cust_id` field. Change this date to a date in the future, perhaps `05/30/1997`. It seems that this change was accepted. Scroll back to the left and note the `order_id` for which you have changed the `require_by` date, then close the browse for the PastDue view.

Now right-click on the Orders table and choose Browse from the shortcut menu. Locate the record with the same Order_id as the one you changed in the PastDue view, and scroll to the right to see the `require_by` field. The date hasn't changed in the Orders table, though. Maybe you first need to close the view. Select the Command Window from the Window menu and type

```
SELECT PastDue
USE
```

Now click on the Orders browse window; the date still has not changed. It seems that your edit in the PastDue view has been lost.

Creating an Updatable View

In order to get your edits in a view written back to the actual tables that the data came from, you need to create an updatable view. The updatable view requires that you tell the View Designer what the primary key fields in the original tables are and to Send SQL Updates.

Close the Orders browse window and choose to modify the PastDue view by right-clicking on the view and then choosing Modify from the Short Cut Menu.

Click on the Update Criteria page. Figure 11.7 shows this page.

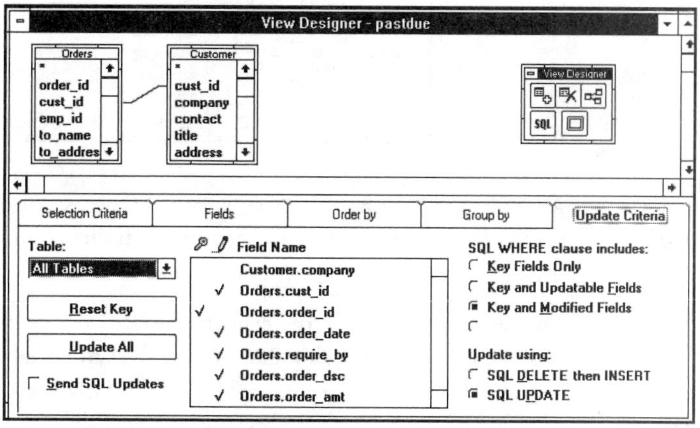

FIGURE 11.7.

The Update Criteria page for the PastDue view.

In this page, you can select which files and fields can be updated. You need to tell the View Designer which field is the primary key for each table you want to allow updates to.

The combo box labeled Table is used to designate which of the tables included in the view can be updated. Use this combo box to select the Orders table. (Because you have not included the primary key for the Customer table in the fields of the view, you cannot update its fields even if you did select All Tables). Notice that the Field Name list has been updated to show only the fields from the Orders table.

Now click on the Send SQL Updates check box. This tells the View Designer to issue a SQL UPDATE command when the view is closed that updates the Orders table with any changes made to the view's data.

Notice that in the Field name list, the two columns on the left—one of which is headed by a key and the other by a pencil. The column with the key is used to designate the key field on which the updates should be based and should be the primary key for the table being updated. The pencil column is used to designate which fields are allowed to be updated. You only want to allow updates to the require_by field, so click on each of the others to take the check mark off of (deselect) them. Figure 11.8 shows how the View Designer should look now.

FIGURE 11.8.

The View Designer with the Update Criteria set up for your PastDue view.

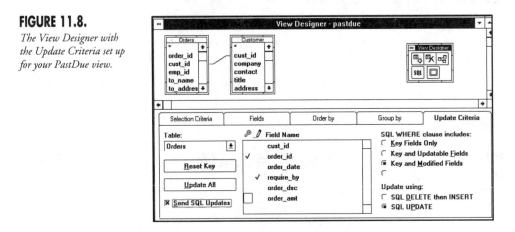

The SQL WHERE clause includes: and the Update using: sections of this page are involved with remote views of database server data and will be discussed in Chapter 38, "Client/Server Features." Now close the View Designer and browse the PastDue view again.

In the browse window, scroll over to the require_by field and change it to 05/30/1997. Close the browse window of the PastDue view and browse the Orders table. Locate the record for the Order_id you changed in the PastDue view, and scroll to the require_by field. Notice that the data has not yet changed. From the Window menu, select the Command window and type the following code:

```
SELECT PastDue
USE
```

Look at the require_by field for the current record in the Orders browse window—the date has been changed to the date you typed into the PastDue view. The SQL UPDATE command was issued when you closed the view.

You have just created an updatable view that is a join between two tables. You have done this without typing any code at all. The only code you typed was the code to close the view after you edited it.

Creating a Parameterized View

How do you create a view that allows you to choose some of the selection criteria at the time you use the view instead of when you create the view? For example, how can you change your PastDue view so you can get it to show you the PastDue orders for a particular customer, allowing you to decide which customer you want to see when you open the view. You need to create a parameterized view to do this.

Right click on the PastDue view and choose Modify. From the Query menu, choose View Parameters and type cCust_id into Name column of the View Parameters list. Select Character as the Type and click OK. You have just added a parameter to your view. Now you need to do something with the parameter.

On the Selection Criteria page, add a new Field name to the bottom of the Field name list for Orders.Cust_id. Make the Criteria Equal and type ?cCust_id into the Example column. The question mark indicates that this is a parameter that should be asked for at runtime if it doesn't exist in memory. cCust_id is a memory variable that will be used in the criteria for your view.

In the Command window, type the following code to close the PastDue view:

```
SELECT PastDue
USE
```

Now, right click on the PastDue view in the Database Designer and choose Browse. You should see the dialog shown in Figure 11.9.

FIGURE 11.9.

The View Parameter dialog.

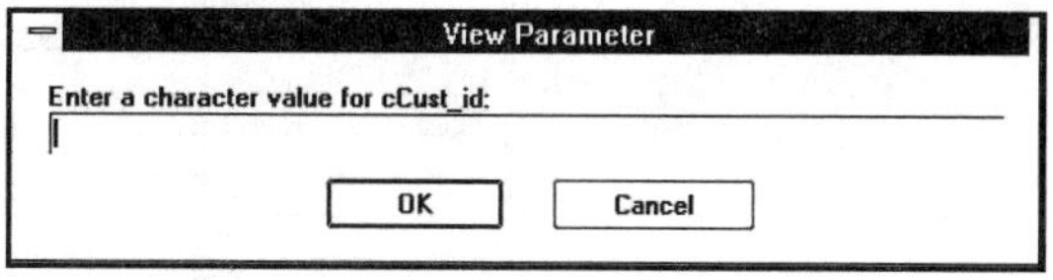

This View Parameter dialog is asking you for the cCust_id for the customer that you want PastDue orders for. Type in ERNSH and click OK. You get a browse of the PastDue query for the customer ERNSH.

Now let's see how you can control the query in program code, you will use the Command window to simulate a program. In the Command window type the following code to clean up memory for the next example:

```
RELEASE cCust_id
SELECT PastDue
USE
```

Now let's give cCust_id a value. In the Command window type

```
cCust_id = "RATTC"
USE PastDue
BROWSE
```

You have a browse window of the PastDue orders for the customer whose Cust_id is RATTC. You control which customer will be displayed when you created the memory variable cCust_id and assigned it the value of "RATTC". What if you now want to see another customer?

In the Command window type

```
cCust_id = "LILAS"
=REQUERY()
```

Look at the PastDue browse. You now see the past due orders for the Customer whose Cust_id is "LILAS". The REQUERY() function tells Visual FoxPro to rerun your query, and the new value of cCust_id is used in that rerun of the query.

Using a Parameterized View in a Form

As an example of how to put a parameterized view to work for you, let's build a form that uses the PastDue view. The details of building the form are discussed in Chapter 9, "Creating and Using Simple Forms," and Chapter 12, "Designing and Customizing Forms." Here, you will only be given the instructions that are critical to getting the parameterized view to work.

Figure 11.10 shows the finished form.

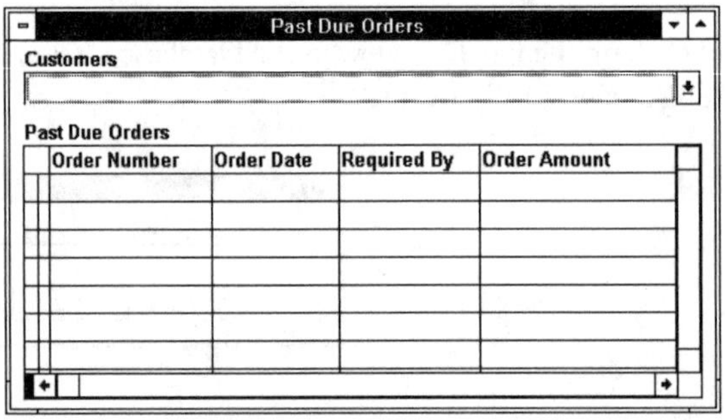

FIGURE 11.10.

The Past Due Orders form.

This form is on the disc that accompanies this book. To get the form started you need to open the Testdata database and drag the Customer table and PastDue view to the data environment of the form. Now, right-click on the PastDue view in the data environment and set the NoDataOnLoad property to .T.. This will stop the PastDue view from trying to load data before the form is initialized.

Then create a combo box and run the ComboboxCombobox builder. Select the Cust_id and Company fields from the Customer table for the ComboboxCombobox.

Next add a grid to the form and run the grid builder. Populate the grid with the Order_id, Order_date, Require_by, and Order_amt fields from the PastDue view.

Now the fun part—in the Grid's Refresh method, type this code:

```
cCust_id = THISFORM.cCust_id
=REQUERY()
```

In the combo box's InteractiveChange method, type this code:

```
THISFORM.cCust_id = THIS.Value
THISFORM.Grid1.Refresh()
```

Finally, while in the Form Designer, select the Form menu. Choose New Property and type cCust_id into the New Property dialog's combo box. Click OK. In the Properties sheet for the Form, at the bottom of the properties list, type " " (a space between quotes) as the value for the cCust_id property. Put the following code in the form's Init method:

```
THISFORM.cCust_id = Customer.Cust_id
THISFORM.Grid1.Refresh()
```

This Init code for the form loads the form's cCust_id property with the value of the Cust_id field in the Customer table, and then calls the grid's Refresh method.

The way this form works is that the combo box shows all of the Customers. Selecting a customer from the combo box fires the combo box's InteractiveChange method. In that method, you set the value of the selected item, the selected customer's cust_id, to the property cCust_id of the form and then tell the grid to refresh itself. When the grid gets the message to Refresh itself, the grid runs its Refresh method. The grid's Refresh method then creates a variable, cCust_id, and gives it the value of the Form's property cCust_id. Then the grid's Refresh executes the REQUERY() function, which causes the parameterized view to be rebuilt with the new value of the cCust_id variable, reflecting the selected customer in the combo box. The parameterized view uses the variable cCust_id because that is how you set up the view in the View Designer.

You now have a form that enables you to select a customer from the combo box and see the past due orders in the grid. If you were to edit the require_by field in the grid, then a SQL UPDATE would be sent to update the Orders table in the Testdata database because that's how you set up the view in the database.

What Is an Outer Join?

In Chapter 3, "Querying Data" you learned how to join two or more tables in a query. The join that you used is called a join or a simple join. Relational theory is based on mathematical set theory and the concept of a join of two sets is defined as being comprised of those members common to both of the sets. For example, assume you have two tables representing customers and contacts at those customers. The sample data shown in Tables 11.1 and 11.2.

Table 11.1. The Customer table's records.

CustNo	Company
0001	ACME Corp
0002	Jeremy Laundry
0003	Mitchell's Haberdashery
0004	Kare Oki

Table 11.2. The Contact table's records.

Custno	ContNo	Name
0001	01	John Miller
0001	02	Mary Mitchel
0003	01	Henry Hicks
0004	01	Willard Millard

Now if you join these two tables, the result would be as shown in Table 11.3.

Table 11.3. The join between Customer and Contact.

CustNo	ContNo	Company	Name
0001	01	ACME Corp	John Miller
0001	02	ACME Corp	Mary Mitchel
0003	01	Mitchell's Haberdashery	Henry Hicks
0004	01	Kare Oki	Willard Millard

The SELECT command to produce this join is shown in the following code:

```
SELECT Customer.CustNo, Contact.ContNo, Customer.Company, Contact.Name ;
  FROM Customer, Contact ;
 WHERE Customer.CustNo = Contact.CustNo ;
  INTO CURSOR MyJoin
```

Notice that Customer 0002, Jeremy's Laundry, is missing from this list. That is because Customer 0002 has no contacts related to it and therefore does not belong to both sets.

What if you want a list of all customers and, for those who had them, the contact names? Well, this is called an Outer Join. Visual FoxPro's SQL SELECT command's syntax does not directly support outer joins.

In order to produce an outer join, you must combine the results of two independent queries, the first being the join of the two tables and the second being the list from the first table, which do not have entries in the second table.

Using *UNION* Clause of SQL *SELECT*

Visual FoxPro's SELECT command syntax gives you the option to combine the results of two queries in the form of the UNION keyword.

The UNION keyword combines the results of one SELECT command with the results of another SELECT command, by default UNION will eliminate duplicate rows from the final result. There is an optional ALL keyword that prevents UNION from eliminating duplicate rows.

There are four rules that the UNION must follow:

- UNION cannot be used to combine subqueries (see the "Using Subselects" section)
- Both SELECT commands must have the same number of columns in their output.
- Each column in the two queries must match the corresponding column in the other query on data type and width.
- Only the final query can have an ORDER BY option specified. That ORDER BY must refer to output columns by number. The ORDER BY will affect the entire result.

Because the UNION keyword allows you to combine the results of two separate queries, and you need to combine two queries to produce an outer join, the UNION keyword is instrumental in allowing you to produce an outer join.

A pseudocode rendering of your outer join is shown here:

```
SELECT <The join of the two tables> ;
 UNION ;
 SELECT <Records from first table not reflected in second table>
```

You saw in the "What Is an Outer Join" section of this chapter how to write the SELECT command that would produce the join of the two tables. Now you need to see how to produce the list of Customers who don't have any contacts.

Using Subselects

You can start this SELECT with the following code:

```
SELECT Customer.Cust_no, Customer.Company ;
FROM Customer ;
WHERE ...
```

This brings you to the question of "How do you identify those Customers who have no Contacts?" A first thought might be to use something like Customer.CustNo <> Contact.CustNo, but this won't work. Look at the data in Tables 11.1 and 11.2 again. Take Customer number

0001; how many Contacts are there that are not equal to CustNo 0001? There are two, and you would get two entries for Customer 0001 in your result, which is not what you want.

To rephrase the question, you want a list of Customers whose CustNo does not show up anywhere in the Contacts table. This question says you need to produce a list of all of the CustNo values that are in the Contacts table and check each Customer CustNo against that list.

How do you produce a list of the CustNo values? Well, the SQL SELECT is a good command for doing that. You need to nest a SQL SELECT inside of another SQL SELECT; this is called a Nested SELECT.

To construct the finish of your WHERE clause in the above code, you would need to add the following code:

```
WHERE Customer.CustNo NOT IN(SELECT CustNo FROM Contact)
```

The following code is the completed SELECT command to produce the outer join of Customers and Contacts:

```
SELECT Customer.CustNo, Contact.ContNo, Customer.Company, Contact.Name ;
  FROM Customer, Contact ;
 WHERE Customer.CustNo = Contact.CustNo ;
 UNION ALL;
  SELECT Customer.Cust_no, SPACE(3), Customer.Company, SPACE(20) ;
    FROM Customer ;
   WHERE Customer.CustNo NOT IN(SELECT CustNo FROM Contact) ;
    INTO CURSOR OuterJn
```

Notice the SPACE() functions in the fields list of the second SELECT. These are there in order to meet the second and third rules for a UNION. The two SELECT commands must have the same number of fields, and those fields must be the same data type and width. These SPACE() functions are acting as place holders for the fields in the first SELECT that are not included in the second SELECT.

TIP

Unless you require the elimination of duplicate rows from the result, you can greatly improve the speed of the UNION by using the UNION ALL option to prevent the step of eliminating the duplicate rows from the processing of the query.

Summary

In this chapter, you added a view to your database and then made that view updatable. You increased the flexibility of the view by making it into a parameterized view, and then used that view to create a form that displayed the contents of the view in a grid. You were able to use another control in the form to select the parameter for the parameterized view. You also learned about the REQUERY() function and what it does.

In the end of the chapter, you used the SQL SELECT command to produce an outer join, something which is not directly supported by Visual FoxPro's SQL syntax.

So what's next? In Part VII, "Interactivity and Interconnectivity," a number of chapters will investigate using the relational powers of Visual FoxPro to get at data that is stored outside of Visual FoxPro. Chapter 37, "ODBC Integration," discusses Open Database Connectivity (ODBC) and how to use it from Visual FoxPro. Chapter 38, "Client/Server Features," shows you the new features of Visual FoxPro that make working with client/server data simple and powerful.

Designing and Customizing Forms

Chapter 9, "Creating and Using Simple Forms," introduced forms and discussed creating forms for manipulating data with the powerful Form Wizards. This chapter will discuss creating forms for applications and will cover what you need to know about forms and controls and their properties, events, and methods.

> **NOTE**
>
> Forms are provided on the CD-ROM as adjuncts to this chapter to facilitate your experimentation and familiarization with forms and their construction. This chapter's examples use files located in VFU\Chap12\ and VFP\SAMPLES\DATA\.
>
> | File | Purpose |
> |------|---------|
> | CustForm.SCX | A sample form that illustrates various form building principles. |
> | GridForm.SCX | A sample form that is used to illustrate building a grid object. |
> | Login.DBF | A data table used by the login form. |
> | Login.SCX | A sample form demonstrating form-building principles. |
> | TestData.DBC | Found in VFP\SAMPLES\DATA\. The database that contains the customer data displayed by the CustForm form. |

The Power of the GUI in an Application

Arguably, the graphical user interface (GUI) of an application is the most important piece of the system. This is not meant to say that processing and database design are not important (they are critical) but the GUI is the portion of the system that users see the most. Users interact with the GUI on a regular basis. Everything else is "programmer's magic" and typically of less interest to users. Many systems have failed, despite their wealth of features and processing power, because of a poor GUI. Other systems might be selected not because of their power but because they have a prettier interface.

The principle tool in designing and implementing a GUI in any system is a form. A *form*, which used to be called a screen in prior versions of FoxPro, is the primary vehicle used by developers to create interfaces for their applications.

Prior versions of FoxPro had limited GUI capabilities. With the advent of Visual FoxPro, however, FoxPro now has the capability to create application GUIs that rival any other development environment. Now you can create forms with all kinds of different controls that do everything from accept free form information (edit box) to others that will execute a command or series of commands at predetermined intervals (timer).

Anatomy of a Form

Figure 12.1 shows a sample form. The form consists of two basic components:

- The form itself
- Controls on the form

FIGURE 12.1.

The sample form.

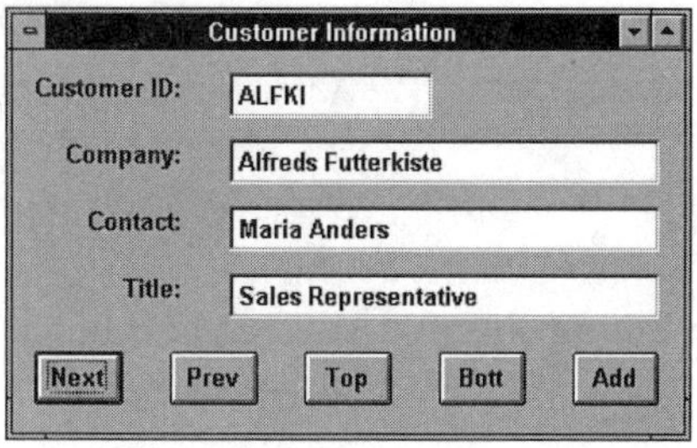

The "form" itself is the "background" on which the contents of the form sit. As you can see from the sample form shown in Figure 12.1, the form itself has characteristics. For example, the background color of the form is gray, the caption says "Customer Information," it has a single-line border, and so on.

Controls are elements on a form. Back in FoxPro 2.6 (for Windows), the controls available for designing screens were SAY, GET, EDIT, radio buttons, push buttons, popup lists, list boxes, spinners, check boxes, and pictures. Visual FoxPro supports the following controls on a form. Some of these controls are analogous to controls in FoxPro 2.6, in which case the analogous control is listed in Table 12.1. Please note, however, that the analogous control is presented as an aid to picturing the use of the control in your mind: Visual FoxPro controls do much more than their 2.6 counterparts could ever hope to do. For example, a text box control (which is analogous to the old GET) can also respond to double clicks of the mouse.

Table 12.1. Controls in Visual FoxPro.

Control Name	Description	FoxPro 2.6 Counterpart
Check Box	A control that shows an ON/OFF state.	Check Box
Combo Box	A control that presents a list. Only the Selected choice is shown but the rest of the list can be expanded at will. The control supports two different styles: It can operate as a	Popup

continues

Table 12.1. continued

Control Name	Description	FoxPro 2.6 Counterpart
	combo box (and text entry area with an expandable list) or as a drop-down list (in which case no text can be entered, only selections made from the list).	
Command Button	A button for the user to push and make something happen (for example, close the current form).	Push Button
Command Button Group	A group of command buttons that work together.	Push Buttons
Edit Box	Edit long strings of information.	EDIT
Grid	Browses a table on a form.	
Image	Shows a picture (.BMP file) on a form.	Picture
Label	Displays text.	SAY
Line	A line drawn on a form.	
List Box	A box that shows a list of items on the form.	Scrolling List
OLE Bound Control	An OLE Control that is "connected" to a general field in a table.	None
OLE Container Control	A control for OLE objects (such as WinWord, Excel) and controls (such as the Outline OCX control).	None
Option Group	A series of options presented as a group. Only one of the options can be selected at any one time.	Radio Buttons
Page Frame	A control that supports placing controls on multiple pages, one of which is visible at a time.	None
Separator	A special control for creating spaces in a toolbar.	None
Shape	A shape such as a square or oval.	None

Control Name	Description	FoxPro 2.6 Counterpart
Spinner	A combination of a text box and up and down arrow buttons. Used for numeric data, a spinner control enables the user to increment/decrement the number in the text portion of the control by clicking on the spinner's up or down arrows, respectively.	Spinner
Text Box	Enter information in free form fashion.	GET
Timer	Runs a command or series of commands at a predetermined interval.	None

Understanding Properties, Events, and Methods

Before discussing forms and controls and how they work together, it is important to understand properties, events, and methods (PEMs) and what they mean in designing and implementing a form in Visual FoxPro. What follows is a brief discussion of objects, properties, events, and methods. For a more complete discussion of these topics, please refer to Chapter 27, "Introduction to Object-Oriented Programming."

A *form* is made up of objects. A form is an object as are all the controls contained in a form. An *object* is a distinct unit with attributes and behaviors. The *attributes* of an object, such as a form, include what its color is, what its caption is, and so on. *Behaviors* refer to procedures that are attached to the object. Some procedures are executed in response to an *event* (such as clicking on the form or one of its controls), others are units of code that are placed in a procedure that are designed to be called by the developer from a program or another procedure within the object.

The attributes of an object are called its *properties*. Procedures that are attached to an object are called *methods*.

The key to designing and implementing a functional form is to understand the PEMs associated with each object used in the form.

Different objects have different properties, events, and methods. For example, a label has a property called Caption that refers to the text shown in the control. A form also has a Caption property, except that property refers to the caption at the top of the window. A text box, on the other hand, does not have a Caption property.

On the other hand, many objects do support similar properties, events, and methods. For example, most objects have a BackColor property, which specifies the background color of the object. Most controls also have a Click method, which executes when the mouse is clicked on the object.

Microsoft has compiled a list of events that are common to most objects. Table 12.2 presents the events that Microsoft considers to be the "core events" in Visual FoxPro.

Table 12.2. The core events in Visual FoxPro.

Name of Event	*Executes When...*
Init	An object is created.
Destroy	An object is released from memory.
Click	The user clicks the object using the primary mouse button.
DblClick	The user double-clicks the object using the primary mouse button.
RightClick	The user clicks the object using the secondary mouse button.
GotFocus	The object receives the focus, either by user action such as tabbing or clicking, or by changing the focus in code using the SetFocus method.
LostFocus	The object loses the focus, either by user action such as tabbing to or clicking on another object, or by changing the focus in code using the SetFocus method.
KeyPress	The user presses and releases a key.
MouseDown	The user presses a mouse button while the mouse pointer is over the object.
MouseMove	The user moves the mouse over the object.
MouseUp	The user releases a mouse button while the mouse pointer is over the object.
InteractiveChange	The value of the object is changed by the user.
ProgrammaticChange	The value of the object is changed in a program.

In addition to the core event set listed in Table 12.2, there are also properties that are common to many Visual FoxPro objects. Table 12.3 lists these common properties and what they mean.

Table 12.3. Common properties.

Property Name	Description	Supported Values	Default
Alignment	Specifies how text is aligned in a control.	0 = Left 1 = Right 2 = Center 3 = Automatic	Different controls have different default values for this control. For example, the default for a check box control is 0 (Left). For a text box, the default is 3 (Automatic).
AutoSize	Specifies whether the control is automatically sized to fit its caption.	.T. = Automatically size .F. = Do not automatically size	.F. = Do not automatically size.
BackColor	The background color of the object.	Any valid color number. Usually specified with the RGB() function.	Different controls have different defaults. For example, the Text Box control defaults to white (RGB(255,255, 255)). A page on a PageFrame defaults to gray (RGB(192,192, 192)).
BackStyle	Specifies whether the background of the object is opaque or transparent. If the background is transparent, the BackColor property of the object is ignored.	0 = Opaque 1 = Transparent	0 (Opaque)
BorderColor	The color of the border around the object.	Any valid color number. Usually specified with the RGB() function.	Black (RGB(0,0,0)).

continues

Table 12.3. continued

Property Name	Description	Supported Values	Default
Caption	Specifies the text displayed with an object. For example, the caption property of a form specifies the window title. For a check box, it specifies the text displayed next to the check box.	Any valid character expression.	The default name of the object (for example, Form1, Command1).
ColorScheme	Included for backward compatibility.		
Comment	A comment about the object. This property can be used to store anything you want; Visual FoxPro does not use it for processing.	Any string.	""
ControlSource	The source for the control's value. Placing the name of a field or memory variable in this property "binds" it to that field or memory variable. Any changes made to the control's value will be reflected in the Control Source.	Any valid field or memory variable.	""
DisabledBackColor	The background color of the control	Any valid color number. Usually	Depends on the control.

Property Name	Description	Supported Values	Default
	when it is disabled. The color specified here is automatically dithered in gray.	specified with the `RGB()` function.	
DisabledForeColor	The foreground color of the control when it is disabled. The color specified here is automatically dithered in gray.	Any valid color number. Usually specified with the `RGB()` function.	Depends on the control.
DragIcon	The icon to show when the control is being dragged.	Name of a CUR file.	""
DragMode	Defines whether clicking on a control automatically starts dragging the control. When set to Automatic, clicking the control automatically starts drag mode. When set to Manual, drag mode can be initiated with the `Drag` method.	0 = Manual 1 = Automatic	0 (Manual)
Enabled	Determines whether a control is enabled or disabled.	`.T.` = Control enabled. `.F.` = Control disabled.	`.T.` (Enabled)
FontBold	Determines whether the font for the control is in bold type.	`.T.` = Font is bold. `.F.` = Font is not bold.	`.F.` (Not bold)

continues

Table 12.3. continued

Property Name	Description	Supported Values	Default
FontItalic	Determines whether the font for the control is in italic type.	.T. = Font is italic. .F. = Font is not italic.	.F. (Not italic)
FontName	Name of the control's font.	Name of any valid, installed font.	Arial
FontOutline	Included for cross-platform compatibility with FoxPro for Macintosh.		
FontShadow	Included for cross-platform compatibility with FoxPro for Macintosh.		
FontSize	Size of the font (in points).	Number from 1–127 points.	10
FontStrikethru	Specifies whether the text in the control is shown with a line through it (as you might do to show a correction or deletion).	.T. = Strikethrough the text. .F. = Do not strikethrough the text.	.F. (No strikethrough)
FontUnderline	Specifies whether text is underlined.	.T. = Underlined. .F. = Not underlined.	.F. (No underline)
ForeColor	The color of the text in the control.	Any valid color number. Usually specified with the RGB() function.	Black (RGB(0,0,0))
Height	Height of the object.	Positive integer.	N/A
HelpContextId	A number identifying the proper help topic for the object.	A positive number.	0

Property Name	Description	Supported Values	Default
Left	The left-most co-ordinate of the object.	A number (can be positive or negative).	N/A
MousePointer	The shape of the mouse pointer when on the object.	0 = Shape is de-termined by the object. 1 = Arrow. 2 = Cross-hair pointer. 3 = I-beam. 4 = Icon. A small white square with-in a black square. 5 = Size. A four-pointed arrow pointing north, south, east, west. 6 = Size NE SW. A double arrow pointing northeast and southwest. 7 = Size NS. A double arrow pointing north and south. 8 = Size NW SE. A double arrow pointing north-west and southeast. 9 = Size WE. A double arrow pointing west and east. 10 = Up Arrow. 11 = Hourglass. 12 = No Drop. A circle with a line through it.	0 (Shape is determined by the object.)

continues

Table 12.3. continued

Property Name	Description	Supported Values	Default
Name	The name of the object. This property affects how the object is referenced in code, the command window, the debug window, and so on.	Any valid object name.	Depends on the control. Usually an abbreviated form of the control name with a number appended to it.
StatusBarText	The text that will show on the status bar when the object is selected or the mouse hovers over it.	Any character string.	""
Tag	This property has no processing value. It is a property that exists on objects for developers to place information that they can access in their programs.	Any text value.	""
ToolTipText	This property holds the text that will show as a tooltip when the mouse hovers over an object. Tooltips on objects in a form will display only if the form's ShowTips property has been set to .T.	Any text string.	""
Top	The top coordinate of the object. The coordinate is relative to the top of the form.	Any integer (negatives are allowed).	N/A

Property Name	Description	Supported Values	Default
Value	The value of a control. For example, the displayed contents of a text box.		
Visible	Determines whether the object is visible or hidden.	.T. = Visible .F. = Invisible	When added at design time, the property defaults to .T. When an object is added at run-time with AddObject(), the property defaults to .F.
Width	The width of an object.	A positive number.	N/A

Now that you have seen the basics about forms, controls, properties, events, and methods, the next step is to look at how forms are created.

Creating Forms

Forms are created with the command

```
CREATE FORM filename
```

where *filename* is the name of the form to create.

There are three other ways to create a new form:

- From the menu: Select File | New and then select Form from the resulting dialog box. You will be prompted for a filename when you save the form for the first time.
- From the toolbar: Select the New button and then select Form from the resulting dialog box. You will be prompted for a filename when you save the form for the first time.
- From the Project Manager: Select the Documents tab, click on Forms and then select New. You will be prompted for a filename when you save the form for the first time.

However you go about it, you should see Figure 12.2, the Form Designer with a blank form.

FIGURE 12.2.

The Form Designer with a new form.

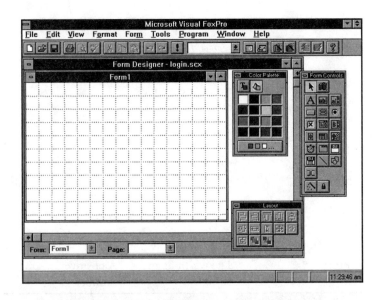

The examples presented in this chapter are drawn from the examples delivered with Visual FoxPro and from the CD-ROM accompanying *Visual FoxPro 3 Unleashed.* Follow the directions given on the Installation Page facing the inside back cover of this book to load the examples onto your hard disk from the CD.

The Login form (LOGIN.SCX) is provided to facilitate your experimentation. It is not complete; and it is not intended to be. It is a jump start. Complete it the way you want. Try the various techniques that are presented in this chapter to "get your feet wet." Above all: have fun!

Form Designer Components

The Form Designer consists of the following elements:

■ The form canvas. This is the "form" portion of the designer where controls are placed. It is also called the *container* because all the controls on a form are "inside" the form, much like the contents of a box are inside the box.

■ The Form Controls toolbar. This toolbar shows the controls available for use in a form (more about this in the section titled "Adding Controls to a Form").

You can use this toolbar to show controls you create as well. For more information on this, please see Chapter 34, "Programming OLE Links."

- The Layout toolbar. This toolbar provides the tools for properly aligning and sizing controls on the form (more about this in the section titled "Aligning Controls on a Form").

- The Form Designer toolbar. This toolbar operates like a "command center" for showing and hiding the other Form Designer toolbars.

- The Color Palette toolbar. This toolbar makes setting the colors of a form and its controls a snap.

Showing and Hiding Toolbars

When you bring up the Form Designer, some of its toolbars might not be visible. If they're not, you can show the toolbars by selecting the appropriate item from the View menu. For example, to show the Form Controls toolbar, select View | Form Controls.

You might want to close a toolbar if you are done with it and want to save the desktop real estate. To do this, just click on the close box of the toolbar, and it will be released.

Another way to manage toolbars in the Form Designer is to use the Form Designer toolbar. The Form Designer toolbar has buttons on it for showing and releasing the various toolbars and windows associated with the Form Designer.

TIP

Working with the Form Designer can get a little hairy on standard size monitors in 640×480 resolution. If you can increase the resolution to a higher resolution (for example, 800×600 or 1024×768), you will have more space to work with and will be thankful for every extra bit of it. Your ability to do this will depend on what your hardware will support.

If you have a larger monitor (for example, 17 inches), you'll be thankful for it. If you don't, you might want to consider getting one.

If you're worried about the size of the forms you're working on not working in 640×480 (which is what your users will most likely have), don't. You can define what resolution you are designing your forms for on the Tools | Options dialog box. It's on the Forms tab as shown in Figure 12.3.

TIP

If you try to turn on a toolbar from the View menu (or from the View | Toolbars menu item) and the toolbar does not display, double-check the menu. If there is a check next to the item on the View menu (or the box next to that toolbar's name is shown in the View | Toolbars dialog box) but the toolbar does not display anywhere, you probably have a problem with your resource file. Do the following:

1. Turn the toolbar off from the View menu.
2. Turn the resource file off by issuing SET RESOURCE OFF in the Command window.
3. Turn the toolbar back on.

The toolbar will display properly.

FIGURE 12.2.

The Forms tab of the Tools | Options dialog box.

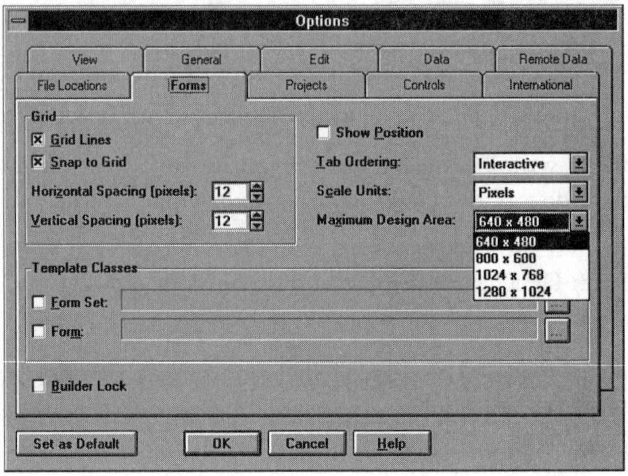

A Form Task

To provide this discussion with focus, the initial coverage of creating forms in Visual FoxPro focuses on creating a rudimentary login form for an application. The form will have the following characteristics:

- A logo for the application
- A place for the user to enter his or her user ID and password
- Appropriate prompts for the entry objects
- OK and Cancel buttons

To keep the form simple, it will only deal with the entry and validation of the user ID and password with appropriate error messages.

The form will validate the entries based on LOGIN.DBF that has the following structure and records:

```
Structure for table:    VFU\Chapt12\LOGIN.DBF
Number of data records: 0
Date of last update:    08/18/95
Code Page:              1252
Field  Field Name     Type            Width   Dec   Index   Collate Nulls
    1  CUSERID        Character          6                            No
    2  CPASSWORD      Character         10                            No
** Total **                            17

Record#  CUSERID CPASSWORD
    1    MB      BAZIAN
    2    JB      BOOTH
    3    JL      LONG
    4    DN      NORMAN
```

Changing the Colors of a Form

The first thing to set on the form here is its color. Windows 95 uses a gray background on the form as the standard color for a form.

There are two ways to change the background color of a form (or any object for that matter).

■ You can set the BackGroundColor property of the object using the Properties window (see the section "Setting the Properties of the Form and Its Objects" in this chapter for a discussion of the Properties window).

■ You can use the Color Palette toolbar.

Using the Color Palette Toolbar

The Color Palette toolbar, shown in Figure 12.4, provides a simple way to set the color of a form and its objects.

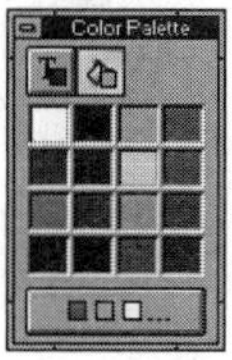

FIGURE 12.4.

The Color Palette toolbar.

The toolbar has three sections:

1. The two buttons on the top of the toolbar indicate which color setting (background and/or fore) is being applied. The left button, if pressed, will cause the color you select to be applied to the foreground; the right button refers to the background. Both can be pressed at the same time if you like, although if you do your object will become a single blob of the same color on your form.

2. The middle section is a series of the more common colors used in development. Clicking one of these color boxes will cause that color to be applied to the object.

3. If you want to be more creative with your colors, the button on the bottom will bring up a larger list of colors: it will even enable you to define your own colors if you like.

   Figure 12.5 shows the Color dialog box that displays when this button is pressed.

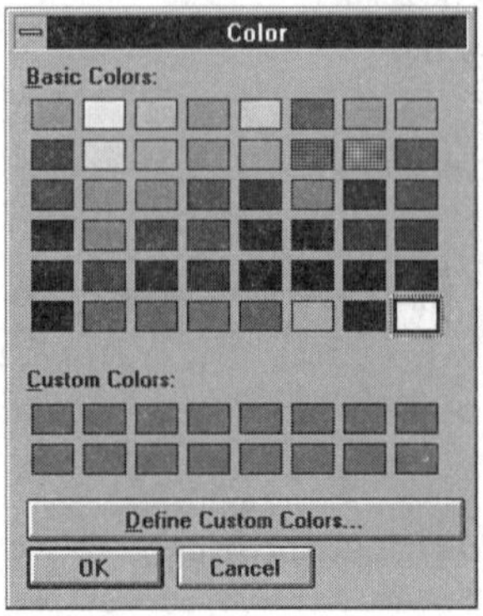

FIGURE 12.5.

The Color dialog box.

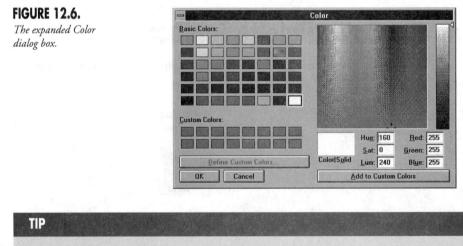

Selecting Define Custom Colors expands the Color dialog box to enable the creation of custom colors, as shown in Figure 12.6.

FIGURE 12.6.

*The expanded Color
dialog box.*

TIP

If you are color blind (as this author is), the Color Palette toolbar is still for you. Each color in the toolbar (not the Color dialog box), has a ToolTip that tells you the name of the color.

Once the color of the form is set, the form now looks like Figure 12.7.

FIGURE 12.7.
The gray form.

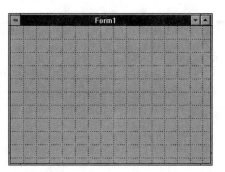

Adding Controls to a Form

You add controls to a form by first clicking on the appropriate control icon in the Form Controls toolbar. This action tells Form Designer that you want to drop that control on the form. To drop the control on the form, click and drag the mouse on the form until the object is the size you want. If you just click on the form (and don't drag the mouse at all), the object will be given a default size by Visual FoxPro. Figure 12.8 shows the Form Controls toolbar.

FIGURE 12.8.
The Form Controls toolbar.

All the buttons on this toolbar, with the exception of the first two and the last two buttons, represent different controls available in the Form Designer. These controls are, in order, as follows:

Label	Grid
Text Box	Image
Edit Box	Timer
Command Button	Page Frame
Command Group	OLE Container Control
Option Group	OLE Bound Control
Check Box	Line
Combo Box	Shape
List Box	Separator
Spinner	

Adding a Label to a Form

The label control is very useful for displaying text on a form. It is analogous to old @...SAY in FoxPro 2.*x*. Labels are not only useful for showing the "prompts" for field information in a data-entry form but can also be used to create logo-type strings on your forms. This example will show how to create a nice logo on your forms.

The first step is to add a label to the form using the steps described in the section titled "Adding Controls to a Form." Figure 12.9 shows a form with a new label on it.

FIGURE 12.9.

A form with a label.

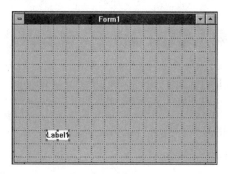

Of interest here is the default caption given to this label. Label1 was automatically chosen by Form Designer because it is the first label type control dropped on the form. Additional label controls added to the form would receive default captions of Label2, Label3, and so on.

> **NOTE**
>
> Please note that the caption and the name of an object are not the same. When referring to an object in a form, you always refer to the object by its name, not its caption.

This is a standard in Form Designer. Other controls, such as command buttons and check boxes, have default captions that follow the same rules (for example, Command1, Command2, Check1, Check2, and so on).

Now that the label has been dropped on the form, the next step is to set its caption to the text you want to show in the control. Caption is the name of one of the Label control's properties. In order to set the text, the next step is to set the Caption property.

Setting the Properties of the Form and Its Objects

The properties of a form and all of its objects can be accessed via the *Properties window*, which is shown in Figure 12.10. The Properties window can be brought down in the following ways:

- Select View | Properties from the system menu.
- Click the right mouse button anywhere on the form. This will display a shortcut menu of options. Select Properties from this menu and the Properties window will display.

FIGURE 12.10.

The Properties window.

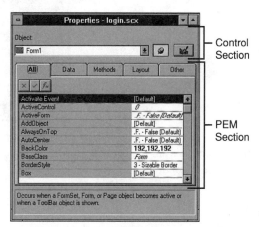

Control Section

PEM Section

The Properties Window

The Properties window can be thought of in two separate sections.

- The Control section
- The PEM section

The Control Section

The top section, termed here as the Control section, lies above the tabbed dialog box and consists of three separate objects: a drop-down showing objects on the form in hierarchical form, a push pin, and a button that accesses an object builder.

Object Drop-Down

The Object drop-down shows the form and all its objects in a hierarchical type list. Note how the label is listed in Figure 12.11. The label is indented in relation to Form1. This is because the label is *contained* in the form.

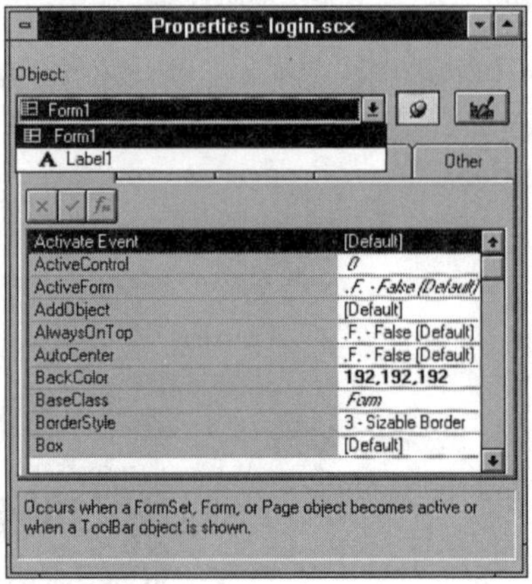

FIGURE 12.11.

The Properties window with expanded Object drop-down.

Selecting an object from the list will cause that object's PEMs to be listed in the PEM section of the Properties window.

Push Pin

The push pin is a means of "pinning" the Properties window to the desktop. When the Properties window is pinned to the desktop, it is kept "on top." Even the Command window, as shown in Figure 12.12, cannot be brought forward of the Properties window, but that does not mean that you cannot use the Command window when the Properties window is pinned to the desktop. As Figure 12.12 shows, you can type commands in. You just can't place the Command window on top of the Properties window.

This can be useful in managing your design surfaces. If you have a lot of windows and toolbars on the desktop, it can be easy to accidentally "lose" a window. Using the push pin ensures that you won't accidentally lose the Properties window amidst all the other windows on the desktop.

Builder Button

The Builder button activates the Builder for the selected object. Builders will be discussed later in the section "Using Builders to Develop Forms."

FIGURE 12.12.

The pinned Properties window and Command window.

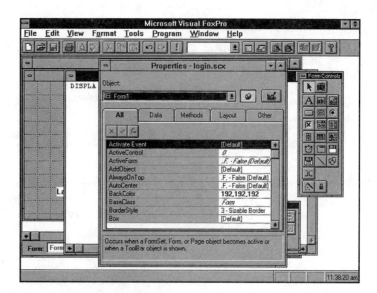

The PEM Section

The PEM section lists the properties, events, and methods available for the object and has five tabs: All, Data, Methods, Layout, and Other.

The left side of the list in each tab (shown in gray) shows the name of the property, event, or method. The white section shown on the right will show either a value if it is a property or [*method*] for an event or method.

Some properties, events, and methods are not available to be edited when you are designing a form. These are represented in the Properties window in *italic* text. For properties, as shown in Figure 12.13, the text box on top of the tab shows in gray.

FIGURE 12.13.

The Properties window showing Read Only property.

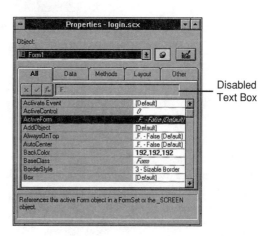

Disabled
Text Box

Changing a Property

To change a property, click the property, and then type the value in the text box above the list. Figure 12.14 shows the Properties window with a property selected.

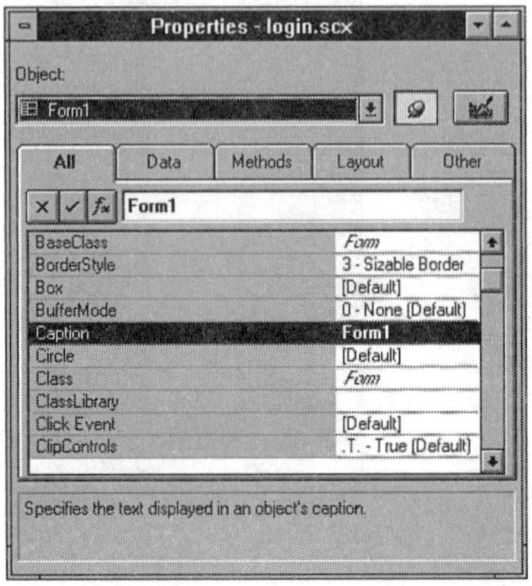

FIGURE 12.14.

The Properties window showing a property.

If you want to specify an expression for the property (as opposed to a literal value), click the right-most button next to the text box (the one with a caption of fx). This will bring up the Expression Builder and enable you to create the expression. The Expression Builder is shown in Figure 12.15.

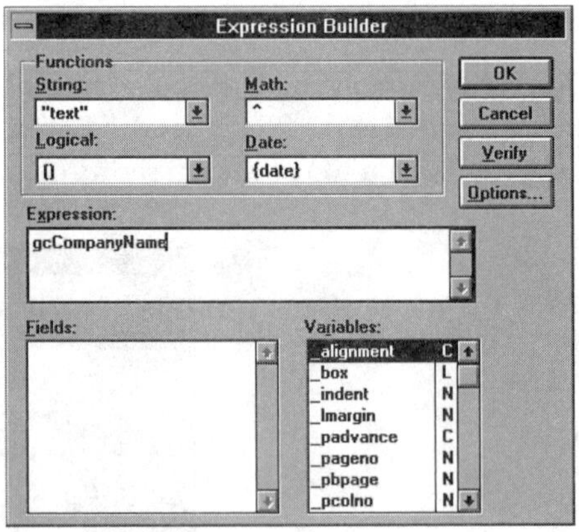

FIGURE 12.15.

The Expression Builder.

To specify an expression as the value of a property without using the Expression Builder, type an equal sign before the expression in the text box. For example, to set the Caption property of a form to be the contents of a global character variable called gcCompanyName, type in the following expression as the value of the property:

```
=gcCompanyName
```

Editing a Method

To edit the code behind a method, double-click the method name in the Properties window. The Code window appears for you to type in the instructions for that method, as shown in Figure 12.16.

FIGURE 12.16.

The Code window.

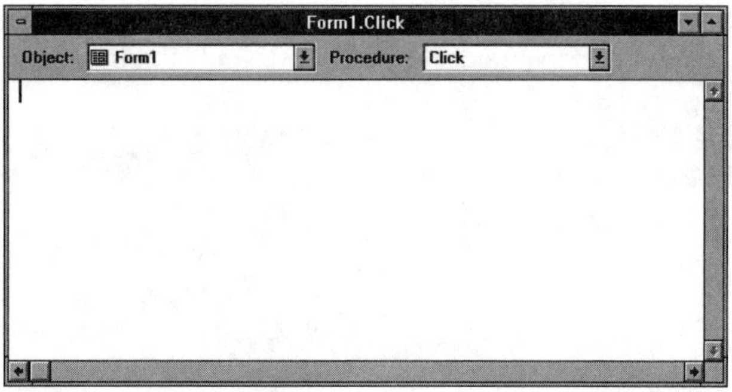

Note that when the selected item in the Properties window is a method, the text box on top of the list disappears. When you think about it, this makes sense: methods, after all, do not have values (they contain code). Figure 12.17 shows the Properties window with a method selected.

FIGURE 12.17.

The Properties window showing a method.

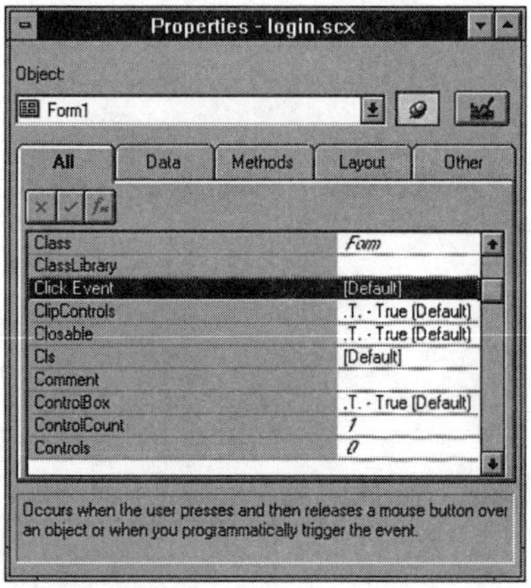

If a method responds to an event, the word event is appended to the name of the method. For example, Click event refers to the Click method that responds to a click of the mouse on the object.

All Tab

The All tab shows all the properties, events, and methods for the object in the list.

Data Tab

The Data tab shows only those properties related to the data of a control. Data properties include such properties that define where the contents of a control come from (such as where the items of a list are taken from) and where the value of the control is stored (such as the ControlSource property). Figure 12.18 shows the Data tab for a Form object. Note the properties shown. They deal with how the form handles data. BufferMode, for example, determines the default buffering mode for the form (None, Pessimistic, or Optimistic).

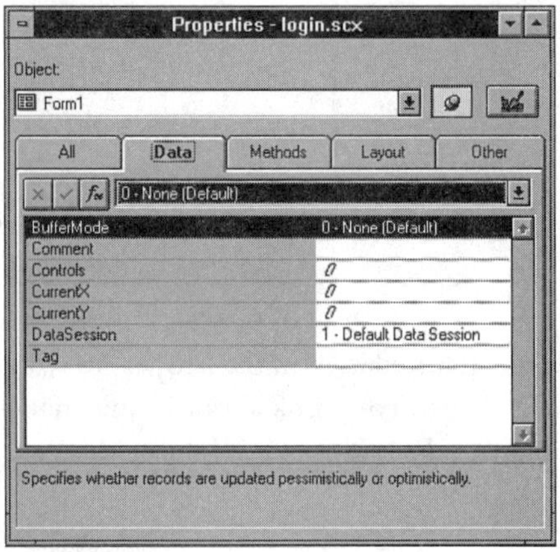

FIGURE 12.18.

The Data tab.

Methods Tab

The Methods tab only shows the events and methods for the object. Figure 12.19 shows the Methods tab for a Form object.

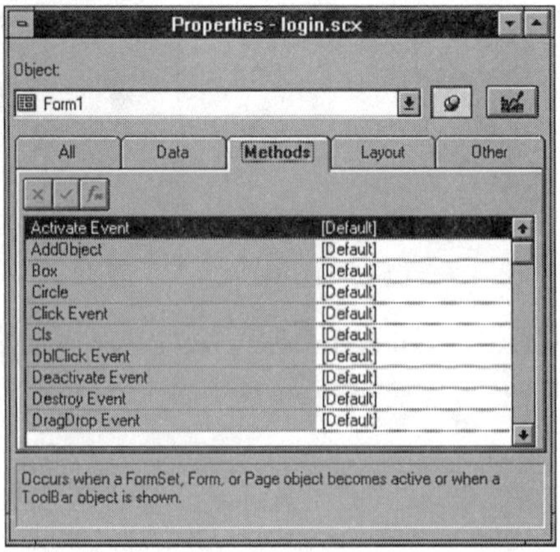

FIGURE 12.19.

The Methods tab.

Layout Tab

The Layout tab shows properties related to the physical appearance of the object. Figure 12.20 shows the Layout tab for a Form object.

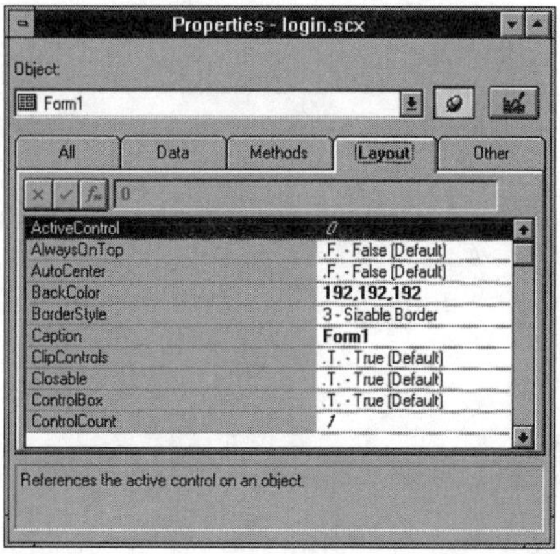

FIGURE 12.20.

The Layout tab.

Other Tab

The Other tab shows properties that do not fit logically into the Data and Layout categories. Figure 12.21 shows the Other tab for a Form Object.

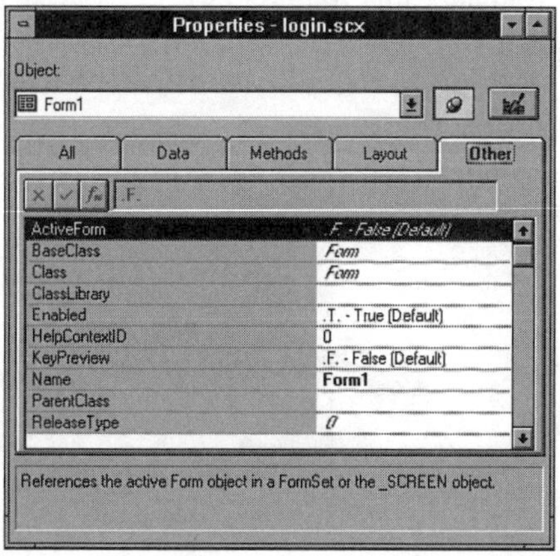

FIGURE 12.21.

The Other tab.

Working with Properties, Events, and Methods—A Final Word

The sheer number of properties, events, and methods available in Visual FoxPro can seem daunting. Just trying to find a property, event, or method in the lists can sometimes be overwhelming. Don't let it get to you. As you work with controls in Visual FoxPro, you will get used to the most commonly used properties, events, and methods after only a short while.

> **TIP**
>
> To find a property, event, or method in a Properties window list, you don't have to scroll through the entire list. If you know the name of the property you are looking for (or have an idea of the name), you can press Ctrl+Alt and the first letter of the name while the list has focus. The list will automatically reposition itself to the first property, event, or method starting with that letter. For example, to find the `ControlSource` property, press Ctrl+Alt+C when in either the All or Data tab and the list will position to the first entry in the list starting with the letter C.

Back to the Label Properties

When you add a label to a form, you will almost always reset the `Caption` property to something other than the default given it by Visual FoxPro. The caption property is on the Layout tab. The caption for this label will be `Visual FoxPro Unleashed!`. Figure 12.22 shows the form and the Properties window after the `Caption` property has been set. Note that the image of the label on the form automatically changes when the property is changed in the Properties window. This is a key feature of the Form Designer: it is truly WYSIWYG (What You See Is What You Get). It is much easier to design forms this way because you see what the form will look like at runtime.

FIGURE 12.22.

The Form and Properties windows with new caption.

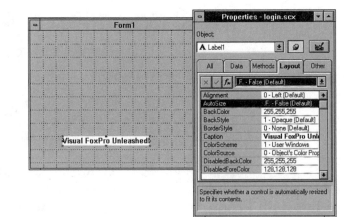

Working with Fonts

Visual FoxPro supports setting the font characteristics of each object. The FontName and FontSize properties are the most commonly used. These properties are on the Layout tab of the Properties window. Figure 12.23 shows the label with the FontSize property set to 20 points.

FIGURE 12.23.

A 20-point label.

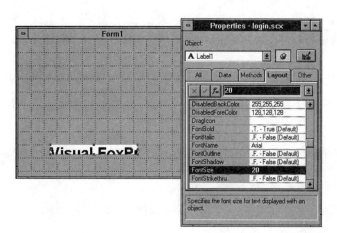

Note that the label is "cut off." When you adjust the font size of the label, it does not automatically make itself larger. You either have to do that yourself or tell the label to do it for you.

Sizing an Object

You can change the size of an object in several ways:

- Changing the values of the Height and Width properties (both found on the Layout tab) will automatically change an object's size.

- You can grab the "handles" of the object with the mouse (after clicking the object once to select it) by clicking on the "dots" that line the object and then dragging the mouse.

  Note that there are typically eight handles on an object. The handles on the sides enable you to make the object wider or narrower, taller or shorter. Clicking a corner of the object enables you to size both the height and width of the object at the same time.

- With the object selected, you can size the object with the keyboard by pressing the arrow keys (up, down, right, or left) with the Shift key pressed.

> **TIP**
>
> You can select an object either by clicking it with the mouse or by selecting that object in the Properties window's Object drop-down.

Telling the Object to Size Itself

You can set the AutoSize property (located on the Layout tab) to .T.. This tells the object to size itself based on the contents of the Caption property and the object's font properties.

The drawback to this property is that you cannot change the size manually when AutoSize is set to .T..

> **TIP**
>
> To resize an object to its optimal size without losing the ability to resize the object manually, set the AutoSize property to .T. (this resizes the object to its optimal size), and then set it back to .F..

> **TIP**
>
> Another way to show a label properly without having all the text on one line is to set the WordWrap property to .T. and make the label tall enough to wrap to multiple lines.

Dealing with the Object's Background

When a label is placed on a form, as can be seen from Figure 12.23, the background of the label is *opaque*. When the background of an object is opaque, the background color of the object shows behind the object. That's why the label is in a white background on the gray form.

The BackStyle property of the object governs whether the object is opaque or transparent. The property is on the Layout tab of the Properties window. When set to transparent, the background of the object disappears, and the background color of the form takes precedence as shown in Figure 12.24.

FIGURE 12.24.

The form with a transparent label.

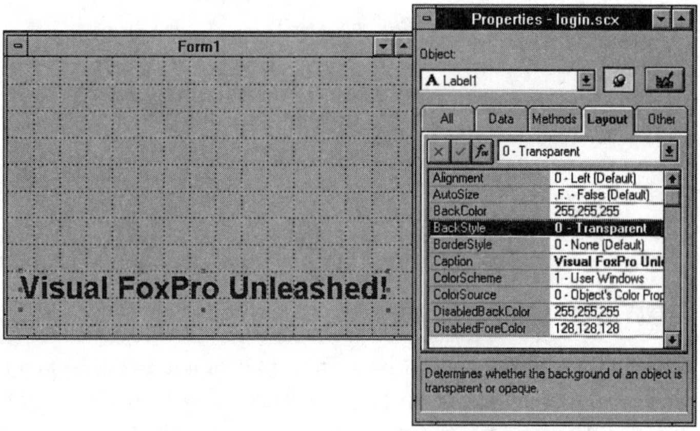

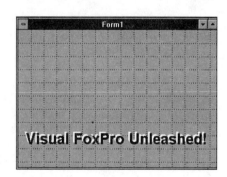

TIP

You can create a shadowed logo out of a label with ease. All you have to do is copy the label and position it three pixels beneath and to the right of the original label. Set the ForeColor of the second label to white.

If you prefer, you can set the label on the bottom to white and the top one to black.

What you get is a shadowed label as shown in Figure 12.25.

FIGURE 12.25.

Two shadowed labels.

Adding a Text Box to the Form

At this point, the login form has the logo called for in the requirements. The next step is to add a text box to the form for the user to enter and validate the user ID.

Naming Objects

When adding a text box to a form, Visual FoxPro automatically assigns it a sequential name beginning with the word Text (that is, Text1, Text2, and so on). It's usually a good idea to change the name of the object to something more descriptive such as txtUserId. In fact, it's not only a good idea for text boxes but also for just about any Visual FoxPro control that you will use in a form.

Naming Conventions

Naming conventions are an important part of good coding practices. Using naming conventions for variables, fields, and objects make source code easier to read and understand. Code that is well-written, documented, and uses naming conventions is much easier to enhance and support in the long run.

When naming objects, they are typically given a two-part name. The first three letters of an object's name indicate the type of control it is. For example, a text box's name starts with txt as you saw in the preceding paragraph. The second portion of the name is a descriptive word.

The combination of the two parts gives you both the type of control you are dealing with and the purpose of the control.

All of Visual FoxPro's controls have naming conventions suggested by Microsoft. Table 12.4 shows the naming conventions listed in the Developer's Guide and the help file.

Table 12.4. Object naming conventions.

Object Name Prefix	Object	Example
chk	CheckBox	chkReadOnly
cbo	ComboBox	cboEnglish
cmd	CommandButton	cmdCancel
cmg	CommandGroup	cmgChoices
cnt	Container	cntMoverList
ctl	Control	ctlFileList
<user-defined>	Custom	user-defined
edt	EditBox	edtTextArea
frm	Form	frmFileOpen
frs	FormSet	frsDataEntry
grd	Grid	grdPrices
grc	Column	grcCurrentPrice

Object Name Prefix	Object	Example
grh	Header	grhTotalInventory
img	Image	imgIcon
lbl	Label	lblHelpMessage
lin	Line	linVertical
lst	ListBox	lstPolicyCodes
olb	OLEBoundControl	olbObject1
ole	OLE	oleObject1
opt	OptionButton	optFrench
opg	OptionGroup	opgType
pag	Page	pagDataUpdate
pgf	PageFrame	pgfLeft
sep	Separator	sepToolSection1
shp	Shape	shpCircle
spn	Spinner	spnValues
txt	TextBox	txtGetText
tmr	Timer	tmrAlarm
tbr	ToolBar	tbrEditReport

Adding the Descriptive Label

A text box is fine for entering text, but it does not have a descriptive element (that is, a caption). It's nice to tell the users what information is expected in the text box. This is another opportunity for a label. In this case, the label has a caption of User ID: as shown in Figure 12.26.

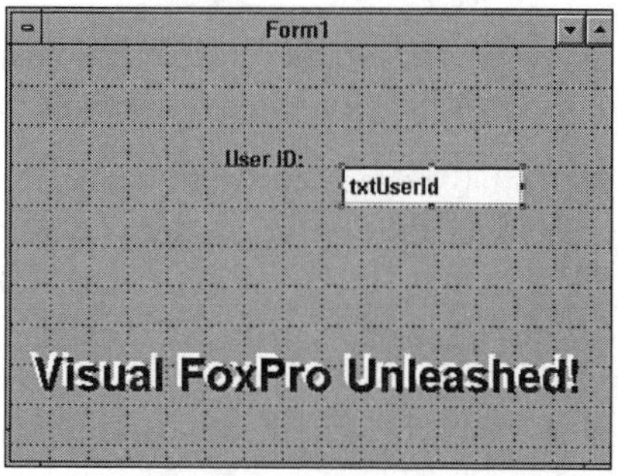

FIGURE 12.26.

A form with text box and descriptive label.

> **TIP**
>
> If you find yourself always adding a label control to the screen in addition to your text control, try defining a visual class that combines the two (see Chapter 29, "Creating Classes in Visual FoxPro"). This can save you time and effort in addition to standardizing your forms. By changing the class definition, you change all the class members with no additional work.

Validating Information in a Text Box

The text box just added to the form is designed for entering the user ID. The user ID has to be validated against the Login table.

Validation of the data entered in a text box is accomplished by placing the valid code in the `Valid` method (available on the Methods tab of the Properties window). The method can be edited by double-clicking on the method entry in the Properties window, which brings up the Code window. Figure 12.27 shows the valid code for `txtUserId`.

FIGURE 12.27.

The `Valid` *method.*

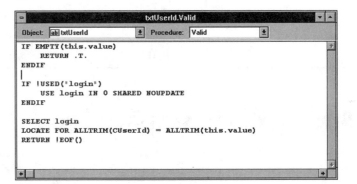

```
IF EMPTY(this.value)
    RETURN .T.
ENDIF

IF !USED("login")
    USE login IN 0 SHARED NOUPDATE
ENDIF

SELECT login
LOCATE FOR ALLTRIM(CUserId) = ALLTRIM(this.value)
RETURN !EOF()
```

Referencing Data in a Control

Obviously, in order to validate the data in a text box, or in any control that a user can modify, you need to know what the user entered into the control in order to validate it.

The data in user-editable controls is always placed in a property of the control called `Value`. The format for looking at the `Value` property of an object is always in the following format:

`ObjectName.Value`

`ObjectName` is the name of the object you are referencing. For example, if the object being referenced was called `txtTextField`, the `Value` would be referenced with this command:

`? txtTextField.Value`

Note that modifying the contents of the `Value` property automatically changes not only the contents of the control but also the value it displays. For example, if `txtTextField.Value` has a value of `Joe McCarthy`, changing the value to `Edgar Bergen` would automatically show `Edgar Bergen` in the display of the text box.

One issue you have to deal with is where an object is contained. For example, `txtUserId` is an object on the form. In order to reference an object that is *contained* in some other object, you need to specify the name of the container before the name of the object. For example, the following command references the `Value` property of the `txtUserId` object that is contained in a form called `frmLogin`:

```
frmLogin.txtUserId.Value
```

You might note from the `Valid` code shown in Figure 12.27 that the value of `txtUserId` is referenced as `this.Value` instead of `txtUserId`. `this` is a generic way of referencing an object within its own methods. Basically, `this` means that the object is talking to itself. Therefore, `this.Value` means that you are referencing the `Value` property of the current object.

Another generic name used often in method code is `ThisForm`, which refers to the *form* in which an object is contained.

For a more complete discussion of referencing objects, refer to Chapter 27 and Chapter 29.

Displaying an Error Message

You might notice that there is no code for displaying an error message in the `Valid` method. That goes in the `ErrorMessage` method, which is triggered automatically if `Valid` returns `.F.`. The code for `ErrorMessage` is shown in Figure 12.28.

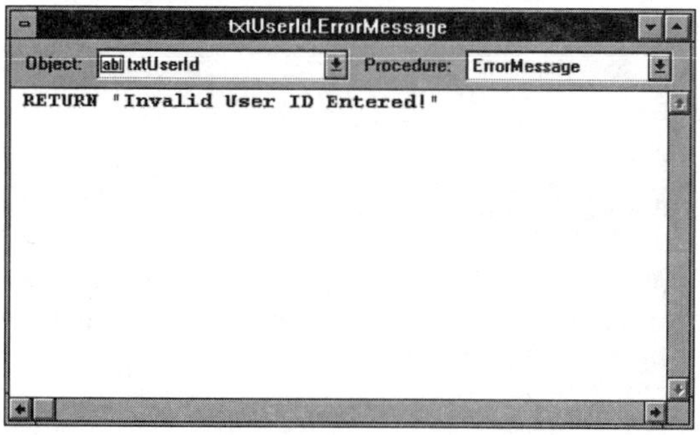

FIGURE 12.28.

The `ErrorMessage` *method.*

By the way, if you do not place code in the `ErrorMessage` method, a default error message of `Invalid Input` will display (assuming `SET NOTIFY` is `ON`).

The Code Window

This is a good opportunity to discuss the mechanics of the Code window. The Code window has two sections to it: The top section has two drop-down lists. The first, called the Object drop-down, enables you to select the object on the form whose code you want to work on. The second, called the Procedure drop-down, shows all the methods available for the object selected in the Object drop-down. When the Procedure drop-down is expanded, methods that have code in them are shown in bold type. Empty methods are shown in regular type.

Figure 12.29 shows the Code window with the Procedure drop-down expanded to show procedures. Note that the Valid method is listed in bold.

FIGURE 12.29.

The Code window with expanded Procedure drop-down.

TIP

You can also bring up the Code window by double-clicking the object whose code you want to edit. For example, if you double-click the txtUserid text box, the Code window opens.

Working with Formats and Input Masks

When implementing a text box you frequently want to set rules for the presentation and editing of information in the object. For example, you might want to show all characters in uppercase.

The Format and Input Mask properties of the text box are for this express purpose. The Format property sets display and edit characteristics for the entire object. In effect, the Format property is equivalent to the old Function keyword used in FoxPro 2.*x*-style GET objects.

The Input Mask property sets the picture clause for the object. Each character in Input Mask represents a template character for the object. For example, in order to enter numbers with commas in the appropriate positions, you can set the Input Mask to 999,999.

In the case of `txtUserId`, the user ID will be entered in uppercase only. In order to accomplish this, the `Format` property must be set to `!`.

You can find the list of format and input mask codes in the help file under "InputMask Property" and "Format Property."

Finishing the Input Section of the Form

The final portions of the form call for another text box for the password and a label to describe the text box. The caption of the label is set to Password:. The name of the text box is `txtPassword`.

Hiding Text Box Input

One thing that needs to be dealt with on `txtPassword` is hiding the input so someone looking over a user's shoulder won't see the password they are typing in the text box.

The text box control has a special property called `PasswordChar` that is specially designed for this. Setting `PasswordChar` to a single character (usually *) tells the text box to display that character in place of the characters in the `Value` property of the text box. Note, however, that the value stored is not encrypted. If security is a concern, you might want to encrypt the data yourself with an encryption routine.

Aligning Controls on a Form

You might have noticed that the controls in the form so far designed are not properly aligned. One way to align controls is to select each control and move it individually. This can be tedious. To move a block of controls you can select multiple controls at once and move them as if they were one control (they will all move in tandem).

To move a control or block of controls once they are selected, simply drag them with the mouse or use the appropriate arrow key.

Selecting Multiple Controls

There are two ways to select multiple controls on a form. The first is to hold the Shift key down and click the controls you want to select one at a time. The other way is to click on the form, hold the mouse button down, and drag the mouse. A box will be drawn while you drag the mouse. This box, known as the *Selection Marquee*, defines a boundary inside which all controls are automatically selected.

Controls that are selected show their handles as seen in Figure 12.30.

By the way, if the alignment of the controls looks a little strange to you, don't worry. You will learn to align them in the following sections.

FIGURE 12.30.

A form with multiple controls selected.

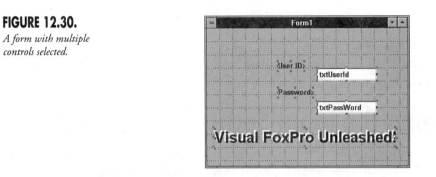

To select all controls on a form, press Ctrl+A.

You might want to select a group of controls that you can grab with the Selection Marquee along with others that are outside the region you want to grab. You can grab the controls with the Selection Marquee and, holding down the Shift key, select some more by either clicking on individual controls or using another Selection Marquee.

Using the Layout Toolbar

Aligning controls on a form is a breeze with the new Layout toolbar, shown in Figure 12.31. Typically, when aligning controls, you are attempting to align controls to start at the same top, right, left, or bottom coordinate. Other typical activities include making controls the same height, width, or size (both height and width). The Layout toolbar has all these functions.

FIGURE 12.31.

The Layout toolbar.

The buttons on the Layout toolbar do the following (taken in the order shown in Figure 12.31).

Align Left Sides

This option is available when multiple controls are selected in a form and automatically moves all controls to have the same left coordinate. Clicking this option will align all selected controls to the left coordinate of the *farthest left* object. If you hold the Ctrl key down, and then click on the button, the controls are moved to be left-aligned with the *farthest right* object.

Align Right Sides

This option is the same as the Align Left Sides button except that it aligns all controls so their right edges are aligned. Clicking on the button aligns the selected control to the farthest right edge of the selected controls. If you hold the Ctrl key down, and then click on the button, the right edges are aligned to the left-most right edge.

Align Top Edges

This option aligns all selected controls to share the same top coordinate. Clicking this button aligns controls to the top-most object. Ctrl+click on this button to align controls to the top of the *lowest* object.

Align Bottom Edges

This option aligns all selected controls to share the same bottom coordinate. Clicking on this button aligns controls to the bottom-most object. Ctrl+click on this button to align controls to the bottom of the *highest* object.

Align Vertical Centers

This option aligns all selected controls to be vertically aligned at the middle.

Align Horizontal Centers

This option aligns all selected controls to be vertically aligned at the center.

Same Width

This option makes all the selected controls the same width. Clicking on this button sizes the object based on the widest object. Holding the Ctrl key plus clicking sizes the objects to the narrowest selected object.

Same Height

This option makes all the selected controls the same height. Clicking on this button sizes the object based on the tallest object. Ctrl+click sizes the objects to the shortest selected object.

Same Size

This option makes all the selected controls the same size by adjusting both their heights and widths. Clicking on this button sizes all the controls to the widest selected dimension (that is, the widest width and the highest height are used to size the controls). Ctrl+click uses the smallest dimensions.

Center Horizontally

This option centers an object horizontally on the form.

Center Vertically

This option centers an object vertically on the form.

Bring to Front

Objects placed on a form exist in layers. Each control placed on a form is placed on a layer "higher" than the previous controls. This option brings the selected object to the "front" and makes the object the foremost object on the form. It also moves the object to the bottom of the tab order. This means that the object is the last one the user will get to by moving from control to control with the Tab key.

Send to Back

This option moves the selected object to the "back." This makes the object the object farthest back on the form. It also moves the object to the top of the tab order. This means that the object is the first object the user gains access to on the form.

Aligning the Controls on the Login Form

The controls on the Login form will be aligned as follows:

- All the description labels will be right-aligned.
- All the text boxes will be left-aligned.
- Each description label will be vertically center-aligned with its accompanying text box control.

Figure 12.32 shows the form after the alignments are done.

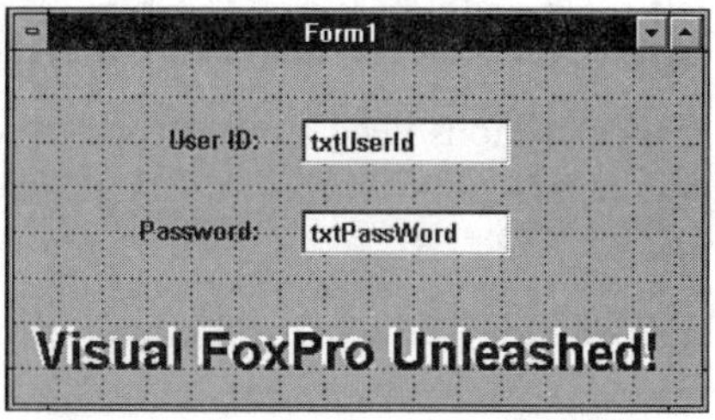

FIGURE 12.32.
*The Login form with
proper control alignment.*

Adding the OK and Cancel Buttons

The final GUI step is to add buttons to the form for the user to press. OK indicates that the form was properly completed, and Cancel indicates that login was being aborted. The OK button should be the default button (that is, pressing Enter is the same as clicking this button), and Cancel should be the cancel button (that is, pressing Escape is the same as clicking this button).

Properties for the OK and Cancel Buttons

Tables 12.5 and 12.6 show the properties for the OK and Cancel buttons, respectively.

Table 12.5. OK button properties.

Property Name	Property Window Tab	Setting
Name	Other	cmdOK
Caption	Layout	\<Ok
Default	Other	.T.

Table 12.6. Cancel button properties.

Property Name	Property Window Tab	Setting
Name	Other	cmdCancel
Caption	Layout	\<Cancel
Cancel	Other	.T.

The \< at the beginning the captions make the preceding letter a hot key—when the user presses Alt+*hot key*, they are selecting that object. The hot key is also underlined automatically.

Code for the OK and Cancel Buttons

The OK and Cancel buttons need a bit of code to release the form. Don't be fooled by the TerminateRead property: it only works for READ-based forms (that is, forms created in the old FoxPro 2.*x* way).

Basically, one line of code in the Click methods of each button will do the trick. Here's the line of code:

```
thisform.Release()
```

Alternatively, you could also use the RELEASE command as follows:

```
RELEASE thisform
```

The two methods are equivalent.

Finishing the Form

The Login form is almost finished. Only a few details remain to be taken care of.

First, the caption of the form should be set to something other than Form1. In this case, the caption will be set to Login to Visual FoxPro Unleashed!.

Second, the form should be made modal. A *modal* form is a form that you cannot leave until the actions required in the form have been completed. A form is made modal by setting the WindowType property (found on the Other tab in the Properties window) to 1 - Modal.

Third, when the form is run, it should automatically be positioned in the center of the desktop. You can tell the form to do this by setting the AutoCenter property (on the Layout tab) to .T..

Finally, a form such as this login form should not be sizable by the user (that is, the user should not be able to make the form larger or smaller). A nice way to do this is to set the BorderStyle property (on the Layout tab) to 2 - Double Wide.

Figure 12.33 shows the completed form in the Form Designer.

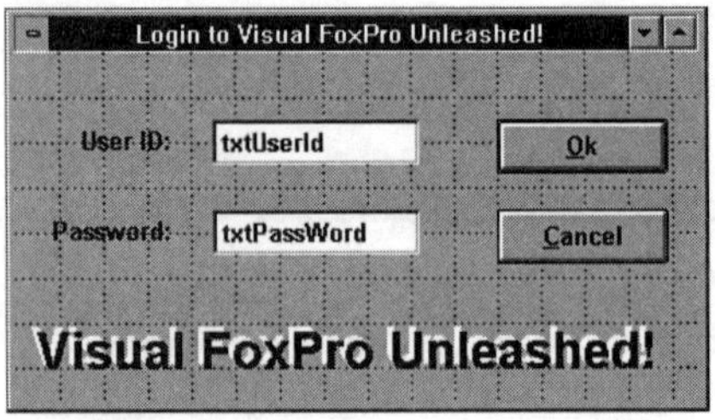

FIGURE 12.33.

The completed login form in design mode.

Running a Form

Now that the form is complete, the next step is to run it. There are two ways to accomplish this. The first is to click the Run button on the Visual FoxPro Standard toolbar. The Run button is the button with the exclamation mark (!) as its picture.

From the Command window you can run the form with the DO FORM command:

```
DO FORM login
```

Figure 12.34 shows the Login form with the information filled in.

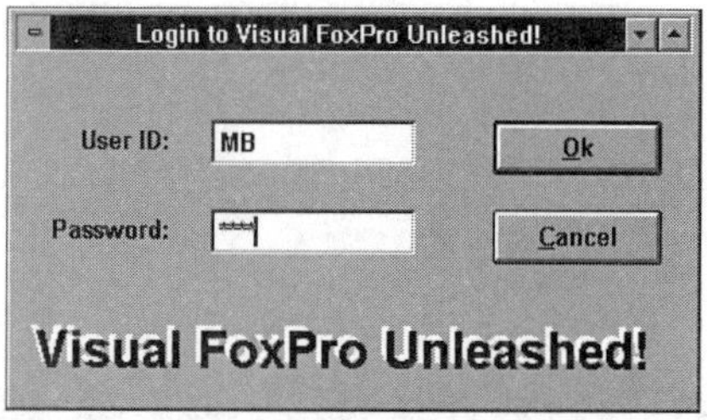

FIGURE 12.34.

The Login form.

Returning a Value from a Form

The one thing still missing from the Login form is a means of determining whether the user properly logged in or not. The basic idea here is to tell the form to return a value (a logical value in this case) specifying the results of the login attempt.

The mechanics of this is quite simple in theory. There is a special version of the DO FORM command. It looks like this:

```
DO FORM frmname TO varname
```

The value returned from a form run with this command is placed in the variable specified in *varname*.

The RETURN statement to return the value is placed in the form's Unload method.

There is one gotcha here: this special version of the DO FORM command will work only with modal forms. You cannot return a value from a modeless form.

In the case of the Login form, we have a special consideration. How can you keep track of whether the user logged in properly or not when the Unload event executes? Basically, what you need to accomplish this is a variable that is scoped to the form (any variable created in a method will be released when that method is completed).

As a rule of thumb, when you think of a variable that you need to be scoped to the form, you should think of a property of the form. The question then becomes, which property should you use? The answer is, you have a choice. You could use the Tag property, which is not used by Visual FoxPro, or you could create your own.

The Tag property has one limitation, though: you can use only character values.

Here's how you could use the Tag property to solve the return value issue:

In the cmdOK's Click method, before releasing the form, set the Tag property as follows:

```
thisform.Tag = "OK"
```

The Cancel button would have the following line added to its Click method:

```
thisform.Tag = "CANCEL"
```

Finally, in the form's Unload method, you would state:

```
RETURN thisform.Tag
```

Adding Properties to a Form

The other way to accomplish the task of keeping track of whether login was successful is to add a property to the form. You can do this with the Form | New Property menu option. Selecting this menu item will display the New Property dialog box as shown in Figure 12.35. Note the name of the property added to this form (lSuccess) and the description given the property.

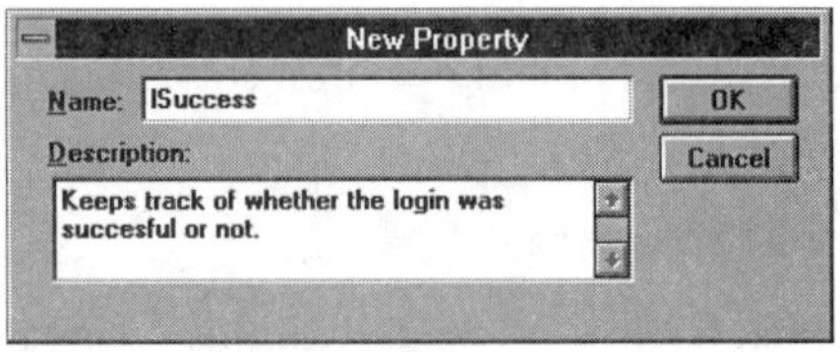

FIGURE 12.35.

The New Property
dialog box.

You should always give descriptions to your custom properties: it will help you remember why you created them.

New properties you add are shown in the Properties window at the bottom of the Other tab as shown in Figure 12.36. Note how the description entered in the New Property dialog box automatically shows in the description portion of the Properties window. Note also how a default value of .F. is automatically entered into the property by Visual FoxPro. If the default value for the property is different from .F., you should modify it in the Properties window.

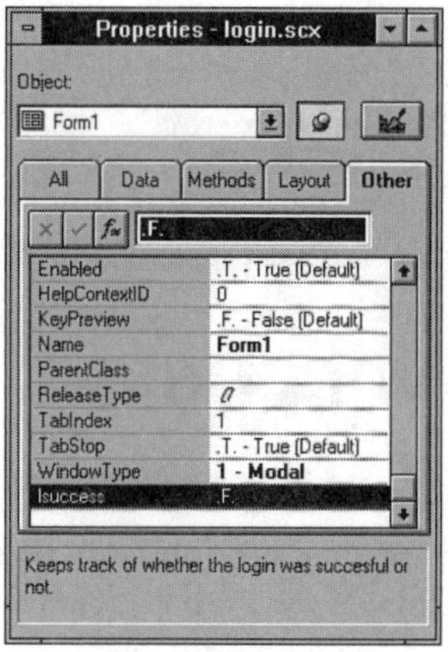

FIGURE 12.36.

The new property in the Properties window.

Naming Conventions for Properties

It's a good idea to use some naming conventions in your programs and forms. You saw earlier some naming conventions for objects placed on forms. Properties also have a simple naming convention that you can use: the first character of the property would correspond to the type of data (Logical, Character, Numeric, and so on) that will be stored in the property.

Using *lSuccess* to Return the Value

With this new property defined, you can access it in the form and its objects as if the property were a "standard" property of the form. In this case, lSuccess would be set to .T. if the user clicked OK and .F. if the user clicked Cancel. The command to do this in the appropriate Click method would be:

```
thisform.lSuccess = logical value or expression
```

The form's Unload method would return thisform.lSuccess.

Additional Issues for the Login Form

Some additional issues to consider for a login form deal with making sure that the user cannot select OK unless the login data is properly entered. You can accomplish this as follows:

1. Set the Enabled property of cmdOK to .F. when designing the form.

2. In the Valid method of both txtUserId and txtPassword, check to make sure that the user has properly specified a user ID and password. If they have, issue the following command:

   ```
   thisform.cmdOK.Enabled = .T.
   ```

   If they have not, set the enabled property of cmdOK to .F. in the same manner.

Alternatively, you can allow the user to click OK and check the user ID and password in the Click method. If the ID and password are valid, release the form. Otherwise, display an error message with the MessageBox function.

Of the two methods, the first is a little more work but it is the preferred method because it gives the user a visual clue that they have not yet completed the requirements of the form.

Working with Data

Now that you have seen a simple login-type form, the next step is to create a data-entry form.

When working with a data-entry form, you will be dealing with information from a table or tables or even a modifiable view. You can tell a form what tables or views it is dealing with by setting up the form's Data Environment.

Before going further, it should be noted that the tables used in this portion of this chapter are the sample tables that ship with Visual FoxPro. They are located in the SAMPLES\DATA directory and are contained in the TESTDATA database. The forms you'll be creating and modifying are available in the VFU\Chap12 directory if you need a jump start.

If you haven't opened the TESTDATA database, do so now to make it available. Then, either bring up the Form Designer with a new, blank form (for those brave few); or bring it up with CUSTFORM.SCX (located in VFU\Chap12).

For more information about databases, tables, and views, see Chapters 3, 4, and 11.

The Data Environment

Establishing the form's Data Environment is a simple matter. You can open a form's Data Environment by selecting View | Data Environment from the menu or right-clicking on the form and selecting Data Environment from the shortcut menu.

Figure 12.37 shows the Data Environment designer.

FIGURE 12.37.

The Data Environment designer.

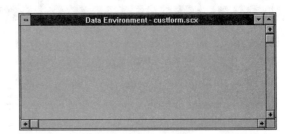

Adding Tables to the Data Environment

The Data Environment designer has a shortcut menu available by right-clicking the mouse on the Data Environment designer background. You can add tables to the Data Environment by bringing down the shortcut menu and selecting Add. Alternatively, you can select DataEnvironment | Add from the menu. Figure 12.38 shows the Add Table or View dialog box. Note that the Testdata database is opened: I opened it before calling for the dialog box.

FIGURE 12.38.

The Add Table or View dialog box.

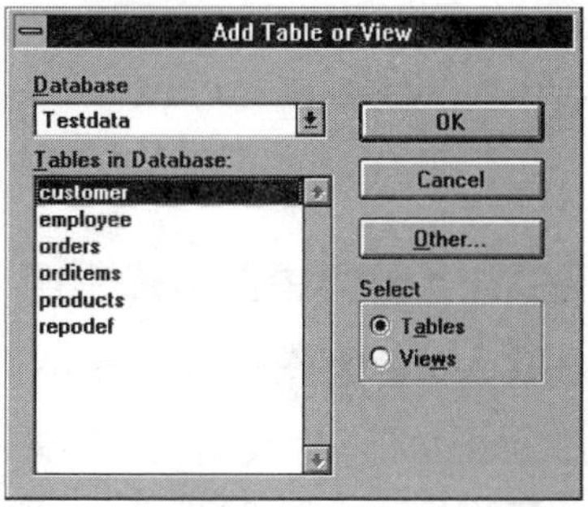

The form being designed will enable entry of customer information, so the Customer table is the correct table to select. You can select the table by highlighting it in the list called Tables in Database and selecting OK.

If the table you need is not part of a database, or the database is not open, you can select Other, and a `GetFile()` dialog box will appear asking you to find the table to add. If you select a table that is part of a database that is not yet open, Visual FoxPro backlinks the table to the database and opens the database automatically.

If you want to work with a view instead of a table, select the View option button, and the list of tables will be replaced by a list of views in the database.

When you select OK, the customer table is added to the Data Environment, as shown in Figure 12.39.

FIGURE 12.39.

The Data Environment with the Customer table.

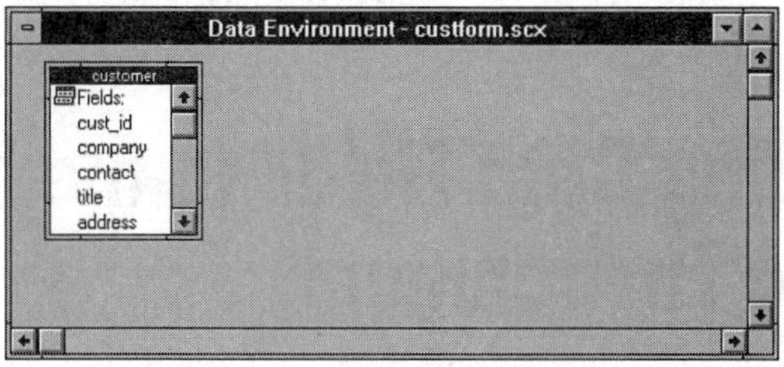

Once the table or view is in the Data Environment, you can browse it by right-clicking on the table/view and selecting Browse from the shortcut menu, selecting DataEnvironment | Browse from the system menu, or by double-clicking on the table in the Data Environment. Note that for the system menu method to work you will have to have the view or table you want to browse selected (you select it by clicking it).

TIP

You can also drag a table or view from the Project Manager into the Data Environment window to add it to the Data Environment.

Working with Relationships in the Data Environment Designer

Normally, you should not have to worry much about relationships between tables in the Data Environment designer. If you have defined persistent relationships between tables in the Database Designer, those relationships are automatically carried forward to the Data Environment designer when the related tables are added.

For example, if the Orders table is added in precisely the same manner as the Customer table was added, the relationship between Customers and Orders would automatically be established in the Data Environment designer.

TIP

If you need to create a relationship between tables in the Data Environment designer that have not been defined in the database, the procedure is simple. Just grab the field in the parent table that will control the relationship and drag it over the index tag in the child table to which it is related. The relationship is automatically created for you (for example 1:M). See Chapter 11, "Working with Visual FoxPro's Relational Powers," for more information about relationships.

Adding Data Fields to the Form from the Data Environment

Once the Data Environment has been established, the next step is to add fields from the table(s) in the Data Environment to the form. This is a simple task. All you need to do is click the field in the cursor object in the Data Environment that you want to add to the form, drag it onto the form, and then drop it. You will automatically have a control placed on the form that will work with that field.

Visual FoxPro tries to determine the best type of control to work with that field based on the data type of the field being dropped on the form. In most cases, Visual FoxPro will place a text box on the form. If the field is a memo field, Visual FoxPro will add an edit box to the form. For logical fields, Visual FoxPro adds a check box.

In many cases, the control selected by Visual FoxPro will not be the one you want. For example, if the field is a numeric field, Visual FoxPro adds a text box. However, the data in the field might be more suited to a spinner than a text box. In this case, you will have to add the control to the form on your own.

See Chapter 24, "Designing the Application Interface," for more information on selecting the right controls to do the job.

TIP

You can add all the fields in a table to a form in one step by selecting the Fields: item in the cursor object displayed in the Data Environment and dragging it on to the form and dropping it. Controls for all the fields are automatically added by Visual FoxPro.

TIP

You can also add fields to a form by dragging a field from a table in the Project Manager and dropping it on the form. If the field's table is not in the Data Environment of the form, Visual FoxPro automatically adds it to the Data Environment for you.

Binding Controls to Data

What makes a control talk to a data field? Back in the login form that was created earlier in this chapter, the controls on the form did not place their information in any fields; the information was placed in the Value property, and that's as far as it went.

The process of telling a control to work with the data in a field or memory variable is called *binding the control to data*. The term "bound control" refers to a control that is bound to a data source such as a field or memory variable.

When a control is bound to data, any changes that occur to its Value property are automatically placed in the control's source of data. If the source is changed, the control has to be refreshed (by calling its Refresh method) for the new information to be placed in its Value property.

You bind a control to data by entering the source of its data in the ControlSource property (located on the Data tab in the Properties window). When controls are dropped on a form from the Data Environment, the ControlSource property is automatically populated with the name of the field dropped on the form. Figure 12.40 shows ControlSource in the Properties window.

FIGURE 12.40.

ControlSource in the Properties window.

When a control is dropped on a form with an established Data Environment, the ControlSource can be populated by expanding the list at the top of the Properties window; otherwise, the name of the memory variable or field has to be typed in manually.

Enter Data to Fields or Memory Variables

Once again, the issue of whether to accept data entry values to memory variables read from the fields or directly to fields themselves rears its ugly head.

Conventional wisdom, in prior versions of FoxPro, called for a record to be read into memory variables that were read back in to the record when the user finished editing the information. The major reasons behind the strategy dealt with multiuser issues (preventing a user from locking a record for an unduly long period of time), to ease in reverting data to its prior state, to being able to easily determine what data has been changed by the user.

Visual FoxPro's data buffering features (discussed in Chapter 32, "Multiuser Programming and Techniques") change the whole equation. If you are buffering data, you can now easily revert data to its prior form, handle update conflicts, prevent "lunch lock" (that is, a user locks a record and then goes out to lunch), and so on. Because of data buffering, it makes sense now to edit data directly to fields in a buffered data source.

Setting the Form's Buffering Mode

You can set the form's default buffering mode using the BufferMode property (in the Data tab). For more information on data buffering and the various methods of buffering data in Visual FoxPro, see Chapter 32.

Note that you can override the form's buffering mode at the individual cursor object. The BufferModeOverride property on the Cursor object in the Data Environment (you have to open the Data Environment designer, display the Properties window and look at the Data tab for the cursor object) enables you to set a buffering mode for the cursor object that differs from the default buffering mode set for the form.

Completing the Data-Entry Form

For the most part, a data-entry form consists of data-entry controls (text boxes, edit boxes, spinners, check boxes, and so on) and labels to identify the controls. Once the controls for the fields are dropped on the form, the next steps to complete the form are

- Give all the controls names that will make it easier to work with those controls. A good naming convention to use is as follows:

  First three characters—Control abbreviation

  Rest of control name—The name of the ControlSource (for example, txtUserId)

- Add labels and set their captions.

- Add validations and other behaviors where necessary (bear in mind that a great deal of your data validations might not occur at the control level but rather in the database. See Chapter 4, "Adding and Changing Data," for more information.)

At this point, you have a basic data-entry form. Depending on the requirements of your form, you might have more options on it—you can determine that on a case-by-case basis.

TIP

If you create a label with a hot-key definition in the caption, pressing that hot key will move the cursor into the first selectable object after the label in the tab order.

For example, if you have a label with a caption of \<Description, the letter D will become a hot key. When the user presses Alt+D, the cursor will automatically move to the first object *after* that label in the tab order.

Figure 12.41 shows the Customer data-entry form after these steps have been completed.

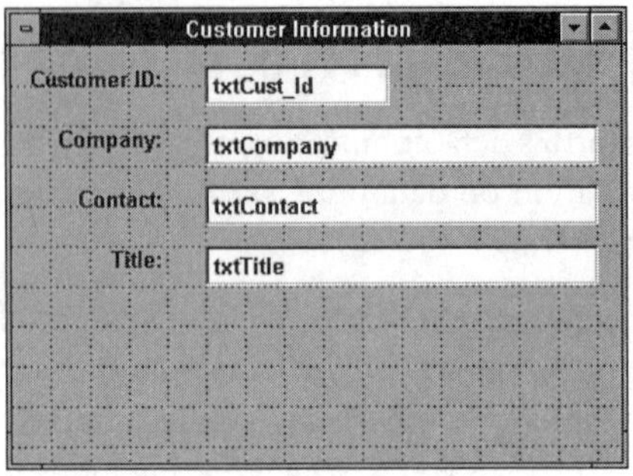

FIGURE 12.41.

The Customer data-entry form.

Adding Navigation Buttons

At this point, the form has the capability to show one record. No provision has yet been made to navigate within the data file.

To provide navigation, all you need is a set of command buttons with the appropriate navigation buttons. A typical set of navigation buttons will add the capability to move within the file (top, bottom, next, and previous) as well as add a record.

The basic strategy is simple. Each button moves the record pointer as appropriate with a SKIP or GO command. For example, the Next button will have the following code to move the record pointer:

```
Skip 1
IF EOF()
    GO BOTTOM
ENDIF
thisform.Refresh()
```

The call to the form's Refresh method calls the Refresh method for all the controls in the form, which, in turn, refreshes the Value property and refreshes the display of each control.

The Add button has the following code:

```
APPEND BLANK
thisform.Refresh()
```

What about a button for delete? Well, you could certainly add a button for deleting a record but it might be a better idea to leave that on a menu. Delete is a destructive function, so it makes sense not to make that too accessible for the user. If the users want to delete a record, make sure that they do so knowingly.

Figure 12.42 shows the Customer form with the navigation buttons added.

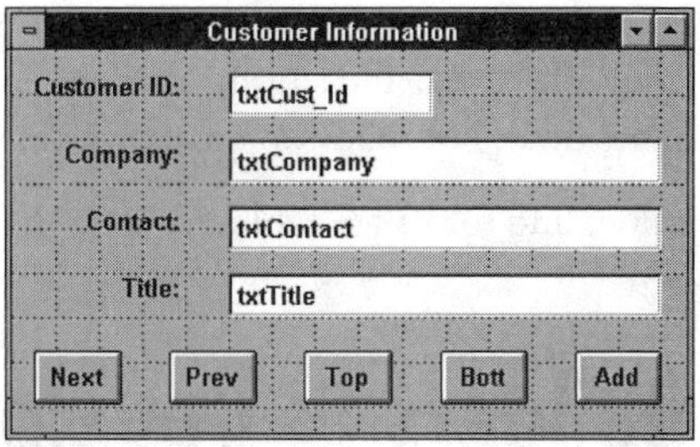

FIGURE 12.42.

The Customer form with navigation buttons.

Reusing Common Objects

The obvious question in the approach just mentioned regarding the navigation buttons is two-fold. First, the navigation button functionality would be common to almost all the data-entry forms in a system. You certainly would not want to create these buttons each time you create a data-entry form.

The second question relates to the approach of placing the buttons on the form itself as op-posed to creating a generic toolbar and reusing them for all your data-entry forms.

The answer to both these questions can be found in the section on object orientation. Strate-gies and methods for creating navigation controls can be found in Chapter 29, "Creating Classes with Visual FoxPro."

Understanding Private Data Sessions

One of the issues to deal with when working with forms that modify data is the issue of data sessions. A *data session* is an environment of work areas and data settings. Each data session has 32,767 work areas. If a form is set to work within a private data session, the form gets its own 32,767 work areas. You can think of this as if the form is running in its own data area. Changes made by the form to record pointers, relationships, index orders, and so on within its own data session do not affect other data sessions.

Private data sessions are a very powerful feature. Basically, private data sessions mean that a form's data environment is encapsulated within itself. A developer can create forms and do whatever needs to be done to the data environment without disturbing other forms in use.

You can assign a form its own data session by setting the DataSession property of the form (located on the Data tab of the Properties window) to 2 - Private Data Session.

A good way to view this is to run a form with the DataSession property set to 2 and then access the View window by selecting Windows | View. Expand the Current Session drop-down list. Note that there are now two data sessions that are independent of each other. Opening or clos-ing tables in one data session will have no effect on any other data session.

One of the nicer things about using private data sessions is that it enables you to have the same form running multiple times. This means that a user can work on multiple customers (for example) at the same time. For many applications, this gives a user wonderful flexibility.

Private data sessions and forms are explored again in Chapter 31, "Advanced Object-Oriented Programming."

Using Builders to Develop Forms

Builders are a wonderful new addition to the world of visual development. Put simply, a builder is kind of like a wizard. A builder is a dialog box that enables you to easily define the behavior of a form and its controls. Like a wizard, a builder takes a potentially complex task and makes it very easy. There is one critical difference between a builder and a wizard: a wizard works once, a builder is reentrant. When you run a wizard, the wizard performs its task and then is finished. You cannot run the wizard again to change something you have done previously. Builders can be run on the same object again and again and again (you get the idea).

In short, a builder is a user interface to setting the properties of many Visual FoxPro objects.

Visual FoxPro ships with the following builders:

- AutoFormat Builder
- Combo Box Builder
- Command Group Builder
- Edit Box Builder
- Form Builder
- Grid Builder
- List Box Builder
- Option Group Builder
- Referential Integrity Builder
- Text Box Builder

As you can see, each builder (with the exception of the AutoFormat Builder and the Referential Integrity Builder) are designed to work with different Visual FoxPro objects.

When you design forms, you can use builders to make defining the attributes of a form and its objects a simple matter. Running a builder can be accomplished in one of the following ways:

- Select the object you want to build and click the Builder button on the Properties window.
- Right-click the object you want to build and select Builder from the shortcut menu.

Builders range in complexity and functionality based upon the object being built. The Form Builder, for example, is a full wizard that enables you to select fields in a table to show on the form and the style you want the form to have. Figure 12.43 shows the Form Builder dialog box showing fields selected for an embossed style form (style is selected on the Style tab of the Form Builder). Figure 12.44 shows the resulting form (shown in the Form Designer).

> **NOTE**
>
> The forms shown in Figures 12.43 through 12.46 are not included in the CD-ROM–supplied data.

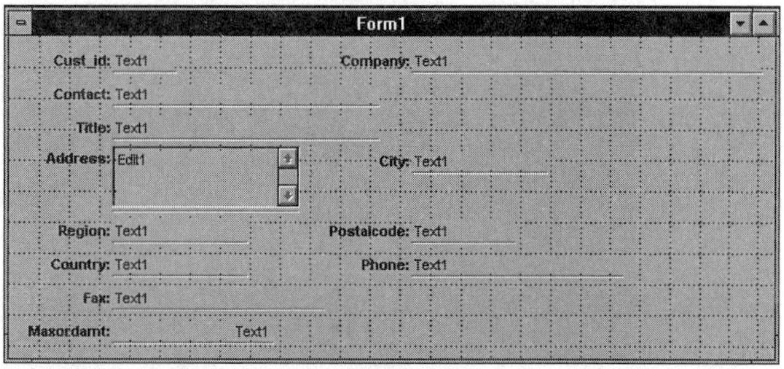

FIGURE 12.43.

The Form Builder dialog box.

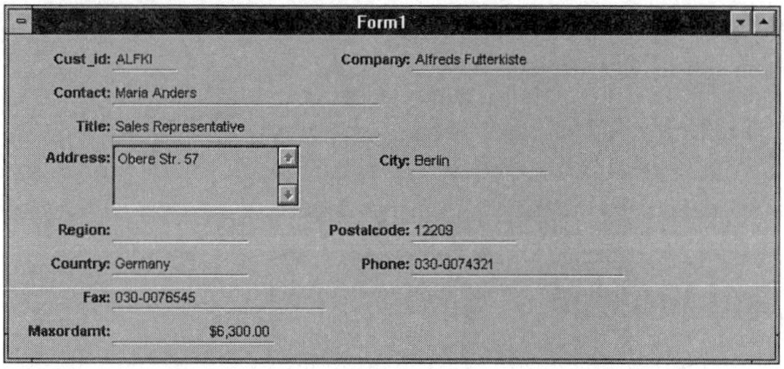

FIGURE 12.44.

A form created with Form Builder.

Other builders deal with the characteristics of an individual object on the form. For example, the Text Box Builder, shown in Figure 12.45, has three tabs of information enabling you to define how the text box should behave, including how it should look and what field in a table the text box should be bound to.

Sometimes you might want to set some display characteristics for many controls at once. You can accomplish this with the AutoFormat Builder. If you select multiple controls and then bring up the builder, the AutoFormat Builder runs. You can select a type of style that you want the controls to be displayed in and then format them automatically, as shown in Figure 12.46. You can even choose which formatting options to apply by selecting or deselecting the check boxes at the bottom of the dialog box. For example, deselecting Fonts tells the AutoFormat Builder not to change the font settings of the selected controls.

FIGURE 12.45.

The Text Box Builder.

FIGURE 12.46.

The AutoFormat Builder.

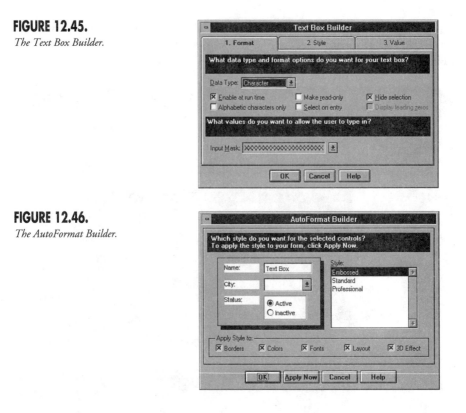

In addition to the control builders that come with Visual FoxPro, there is a Referential Integrity Builder that is used to define the nature of the relationships between tables in a database. The Referential Integrity Builder is discussed in Chapter 3, "Creating and Working with Tables."

Grid Builder

A builder can make some of the complex tasks dealing with creating objects much easier. A prime example of this is the Grid Builder. The Grid control is a browse-type control. The Grid control and its member objects have literally dozens of properties, events, and methods.

NOTE

This form is located in VFU\Chap12\GRIDFORM.SCX.

The Grid Builder makes the process of defining the basics of a grid a snap. Figure 12.47 shows the Grid Builder, with the Grid Items tab showing. This tab enables you to select the fields to show in the grid.

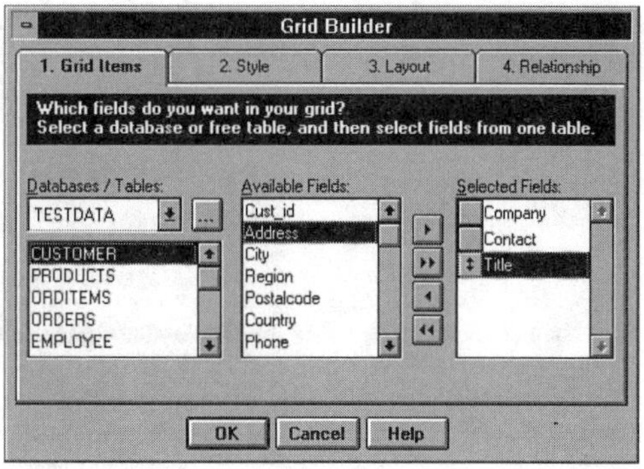

FIGURE 12.47.

The Grid Builder.

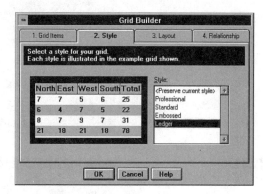

The Style tab, shown in Figure 12.48, offers a variety of "looks" for the grid. Note that you can even select a "Ledger" look, which alternately colors the rows gray and white.

FIGURE 12.48.

The Grid Builder Style tab.

The Layout tab, shown in Figure 12.49, enables you to determine what caption should be at the top of a column and even what type of control most properly represents the data in the field bound to the column. For example, if the column were bound to a logical field, a check box would most likely be more effective than a text box. You could select this with the Control Type drop-down. Even more important, the Control Type drop-down, as shown in Figure 12.50, enables you to select only controls that are appropriate for the data type of the bound column. In the case shown in Figure 12.50, the field is a character field. Thus, controls such as a spinner are inappropriate and are, therefore, dimmed.

The Relationship tab, shown in Figure 12.51, enables you to define the relationship the table shown in the grid has with a parent table. This is useful when creating one-to-many forms.

When the OK button is selected on the Grid Builder, the grid is automatically formatted based on the builder options selected and you are returned to the Form Designer. The grid is now ready to run and looks like Figure 12.52.

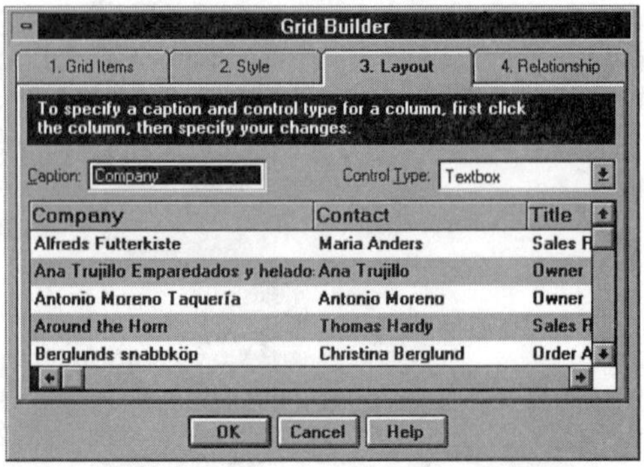

FIGURE 12.49

The Grid Builder Layout tab.

FIGURE 12.50.

The Grid Builder control types.

FIGURE 12.51.

The Grid Builder Relationship tab.

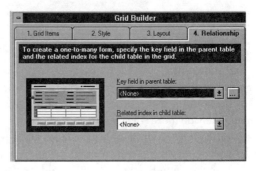

FIGURE 12.52.

The running grid.

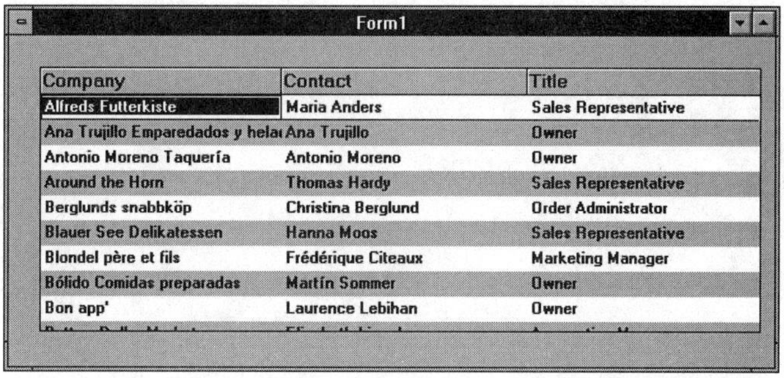

Summary

Of all the design features in Visual FoxPro, it can be argued that the most changes have occurred in the Form Designer. (Databases probably vie with forms for this honor.) Not only has the flexibility of the designer been radically increased, the very way in which forms are designed and implemented has been changed. You need to think about forms differently. With each control an object, and therefore an independent entity, development of forms now calls for a more encapsulated approach. The behavior of each control is now placed within that control. Time must be taken to determine which control has what responsibilities.

Form design and development goes well with object-oriented programming concepts, discussed in Part V, "Object-Oriented Programming." Issues of creating controls once and reusing them over and over again are discussed in Part V. Communicating between objects is discussed there, too.

Designing and Customizing Reports

13

IN THIS CHAPTER

Chapter 10, "Creating and Using Simple Reports," introduced the topic of reports. That chapter showed how the Report Wizards can be used to create reports and focused on manually creating and using reports.

To create reports manually with Visual FoxPro, you use the Report Designer, a visually oriented interface used for manually designing reports and mailing labels. You create the report by placing different objects, such as fields, text, graphics, and expressions, into the report wherever you want. A Quick Report menu option can help you with some design tasks by providing a default layout for the report. After you finish the report's design, save the report. The file that is saved to disk can later be used to produce the report on-screen or with the default printer.

Types of Reports

Reports in Visual FoxPro can be column-oriented or form-oriented reports. With column-oriented reports, the data for each field appears in a single column—the title of each column is at the top of the page. (See Figure 13.1.) Column-oriented reports easily support *grouping*, where groups of records meeting a certain condition are arranged together within the report. The report in Figure 13.1 shows data grouped by state. Most reports that contain numeric data, along with totals, are column-oriented reports.

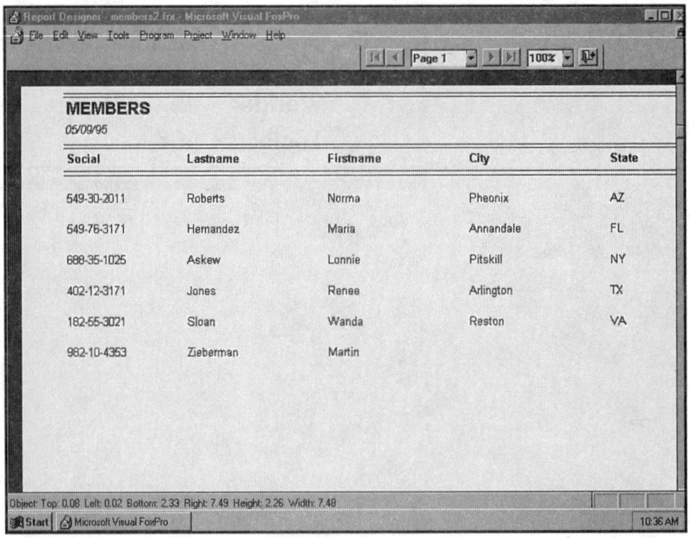

FIGURE 13.1.

A column-oriented report.

However, it is hard to fit a lot of fields on a single page unless they are extremely narrow. One way around this drawback is to print the report "sideways," or in landscape mode, but the type of report you want may not lend itself to this format.

In form-oriented reports, the data for each record is displayed or printed in a separate section or page of the report. Fields are usually routinely placed sequentially along the left side of the report. (See Figure 13.2.) You can place many fields on each page with form-oriented reports, but you usually can't fit a lot of records on each page. Also, grouping is not as effective a technique with form-oriented reports as with column-oriented reports.

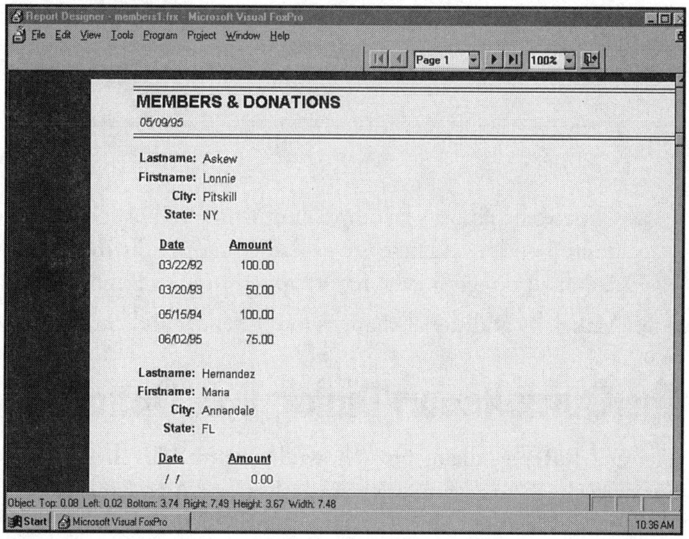

FIGURE 13.2.

A form-oriented report.

Creating Reports the Easy Way with Quick Report

When you want to save time and let Visual FoxPro make most design decisions, you can open a new report in the Report Designer and use the Quick Report option of the Report menu to create a report with a default layout. Using this option, you have the flexibility of producing column-oriented reports (where the data appears in columns) or form-oriented reports (where the data is arranged with one field beneath another). Use the following steps to produce a quick report:

1. Open the table on which the report is based (choose File | Open and select the table by name in the dialog box or enter USE *filename*, where *filename* is the name of the table).

2. From the system menu bar, choose File | New, then click Report, and then click New File. In the Command window you can also enter CREATE REPORT.

3. When the Report Designer window appears, open the Report menu with the mouse or with Alt+R.

4. Choose Quick Report from the menu. If prompted to choose a table, select the table in the dialog box, and click OK. When you do so, the Quick Report dialog box appears. (See Figure 13.3.)

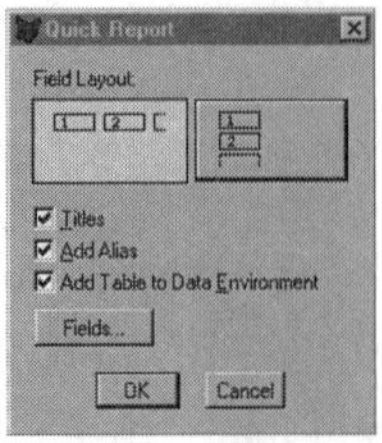

FIGURE 13.3.

The Quick Report dialog box.

5. Choose the report's layout (column-oriented or form-oriented) and check any other desired options. (These are explained more fully in the following section.) Click OK. A default design for the report appears in the Report Designer window.

6. Make any additional changes to the report and choose File | Save to save the report.

The Quick Report Dialog Box Options

The Quick Report dialog box (shown in Figure 13.3) has buttons that let you choose the layout type; check boxes for Titles, Add Alias, and Add Table to Data Environment; and a Fields button for selecting fields. Clicking the Field Layout button on the left chooses a column-oriented layout, with the fields arranged in columns across the top of the page. Clicking the Field Layout button on the right selects a form-oriented layout, with the fields arranged along the left margin of the report.

Checking the Titles option will include a title *beside* every field, in form-oriented reports, or *above* every field, in column-oriented reports. If you don't want the field names included in the report, turn off the Titles check box.

The Add Alias check box determines whether alias names are automatically added to the expressions that fields appearing in the report are based on. Turning on this option is recommended if you plan to use the reports in a relational environment, where you have multiple tables open in different work areas, and you plan to design a report that takes its data from more than one table.

The Add Table to Data Environment option, when checked, adds the table to the Data Environment window. (For specifics on using the Data Environment window, see Chapter 12, "Designing and Customizing Forms.")

The Fields button can be used to select specific fields from the active table that should be included in the report. By default, Visual FoxPro includes all fields in a quick report. If you click the Fields button, the Field Picker appears, and you can click each field, and then click the Move button in the dialog box to choose the fields you want in the report. Click OK when you're done.

TIP

If you plan to use the same report with different tables that have the same table structure, turn off the Add Alias option. When you save the report, answer No to the prompt that asks if you want to save the environmental information.

Producing a Quick Report That's Based on a Query

Designing a quick report based on a query is a useful technique for quickly getting the precise data you need. You can do this as part of the query design process by changing the query's destination to Report/Label, clicking the Options check box, and choosing Quick Report in the next dialog box that opens. (For details on designing queries, refer to Chapter 6, "Querying Data.") Use the following steps to produce a quick report as a part of the query design process:

1. Open the Query Designer window using the techniques outlined in Chapter 6 and design the query that retrieves the desired records.

2. Choose Query | Query Destination, click the Report or Label button, then click OK. When you do so, the dialog box expands to show the options for directing the query's output. (See Figure 13.4.)

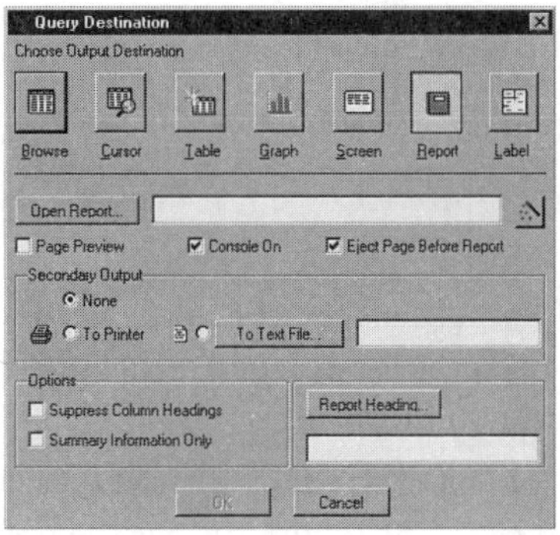

FIGURE 13.4.

An expanded Query Destination dialog box.

3. Click the Open Report button. In the dialog box that opens, select the desired report, and then click OK.

4. Set any of the remaining options you want in the Query Destination dialog box. You can choose whether the report should appear in Page Preview mode, whether the Console option should be turned on (which shows the report's output on the screen and sends it to the printer), and whether a page eject code should be sent to the printer at the start of the report. You can also choose a secondary output to a text file in the Secondary Output area, and in the Options area, you can choose to suppress column headings and to include summary information only. When you're done with the dialog box options, click OK.

After you complete these steps, you can save the query (by choosing File | Save) and the query will refer to the quick report by name when you run it. Running the query selects the specific data based on the query specifications and produces the report.

Working with a Report's Layout

If you prefer to design your report without using the Quick Report option, you use the Report Designer as a working surface and add the desired fields, text, graphics, and other objects where you want them in the report. You can open a new report using any of the following three techniques:

■ Choose File | New. Click Report in the dialog box that opens and click the New button.

■ From the Project Manager, click the Documents tab, select the Report icon in the Document list, and click on the New button. The New Report dialog box appears. Click the New Report button in the New Report dialog box.

■ From the Command window, enter CREATE REPORT.

Any of these methods opens a window with a blank report in Visual FoxPro's Report Designer.

To open an existing report, use any of these techniques:

■ Choose File | Open. Change List Files of Type in the dialog box to Report, click the desired report by name, and click OK.

■ From the Project Manager, click the Documents tab, click the plus symbol beside Reports to open the list of reports, click the report's name to select it, and click the Modify button in the dialog box.

■ From the Command window, enter MODIFY REPORT *filename*, where *filename* is the name that the existing report was saved under.

With any of these methods, the existing report appears in the Report Designer window.

When you open a report in the Report Designer using any of these methods, you see a view similar to the one in Figure 13.5. In report design, Visual FoxPro uses the popular band-oriented approach. You need to understand what each band, or section, of the report is for to effectively design your reports. Where you place an object (such as text, an expression, or a field's contents) in a report determines exactly where, and how often, the data prints.

FIGURE 13.5.

An existing report in the Report Designer window.

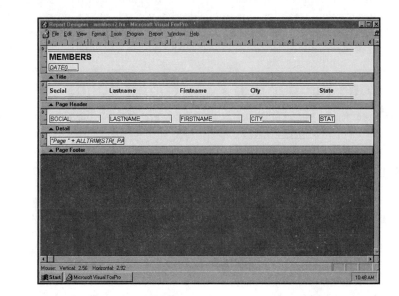

If you did not assign a filename to a new report when you created it, Visual FoxPro names it Report1 in the title bar and adds an extension of .FRX. By default, Visual FoxPro saves reports with this extension. When you save the report later, Visual FoxPro asks for a filename and replaces Report1 with the name you assign. If you create another new report and the report named Report1.FRX already exists, Visual FoxPro names the next report Report2.FRX. If you keep creating new reports and let Visual FoxPro name them, the integer following the word "Report" will increment for each new report. This naming convention does not suggest the function of the report. It is best if you name each report with a name that suggests its use. You can do this once you open a new report with File | Save As and specify your own filename.

Reports normally have a detail band, which contains the data that prints in the main portion of the report. Objects are placed in the report to determine what data is provided. The difference between designing reports and designing forms is that the objects placed in reports cannot by nature be interactive. Form objects can be used for interactive tasks such as editing, but report objects serve a one-way purpose—producing the data in on-screen or printed form. Reports also can have title bands, summary bands, and page header and page footer bands. When designing a report, you will also see horizontal and vertical rulers and a grid (unless it has been turned off with the Grid Lines option of the View menu).

Title and Summary Bands

The title band of a report contains any data that appears once at the start of the report, and the summary band shows data that appears once at the end of the report. Title bands are commonly used for titles and the current date. The reports created by the Report Wizards place the title of the report in the title band. Summary bands are often used for summary information, such as grand totals for numeric fields, that you want to show at the end of the report only. If you want an object to appear once at the start of a report, add it to the title band. If you want an object to appear once at the end of the report, add it to the report's summary band.

Page Header and Page Footer Bands

Page header bands and page footer bands are also common in report designs. If you look at actual printed pages from any hard copy of a report, there will normally be information that you see once on each page. That page-repetitive data is what goes in the page header and page footer bands of a report. Any data inserted in the page header band shows once at the top of each page, and any data inserted in the page footer band shows once at the bottom of each page. In the column-oriented reports designed by the Report Wizards, field names appear in the page header bands so that each page has the field names at the top of the columns. If you want an object (such as text or a field) to appear once at the start of every page, add it to the page header. If you want an object to appear once at the end of every page (such as a page number), place it in the page footer.

Group Header and Group Footer Bands

Reports can also contain optional group header bands and group footer bands. Group header bands and group footer bands let you arrange a report by groups. For example, you might want to see a mailing list printed by groups of each country's residents and, inside the country groupings, in groups by ZIP or postal codes. You would add group bands to the report to accomplish this task. (Adding group bands to a report is covered in the section "Adding Groups to a Report.") Figure 13.6 shows a report with group bands in page preview mode. Figure 13.7 shows the same report in design mode. In the report's design, the State header and footer are the group bands that group the data alphabetically, by name of State.

FIGURE 13.6.

A report with group bands in page preview mode.

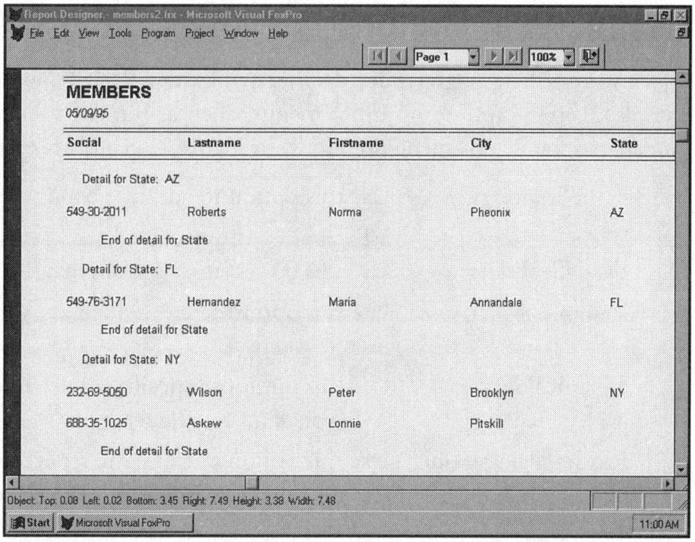

FIGURE 13.7.

A report with group bands in design mode.

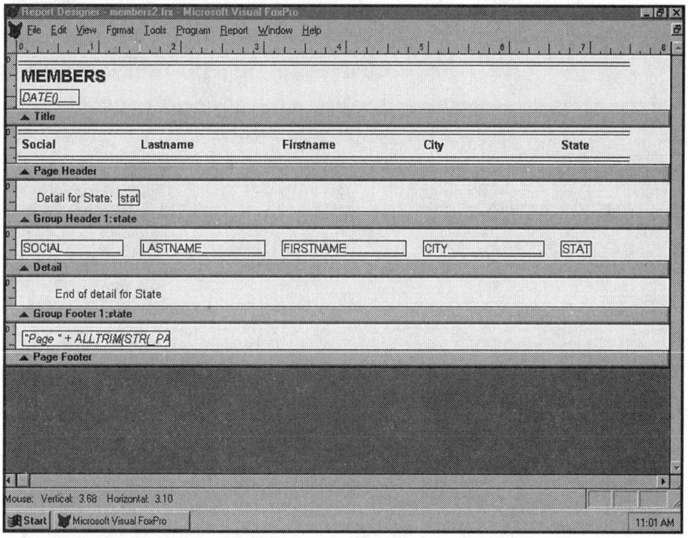

Column Headers and Column Footers

Reports in Visual FoxPro can have multiple columns, which you add by choosing File | Page Setup and entering the number of columns in the dialog box. Once you change this setting to any value greater than 1, the column headers are added to the report's design. When you have more than one column in a report, the data you place in the Column Header appears at the top of each column, and data you place in the Column Footer appears at the bottom of each column.

Useful Menu Options

When you are designing a report, another menu titled Report appears on Visual FoxPro's menu bar; also, certain options on other menus (such as the File menu) are enabled. The choices available in the Report menu are shown in Figure 13.8 and are explained in the following list:

Title/Summary	Use this option to add title bands or summary bands to a report.
Data Grouping	Use this option to add group bands to a report.
Variables	Use this option to create memory variables, which can then be used in a report.
Default Font	Use this option to specify the default font, font size, and font style you want for the report.
Private Data Session	Use this option to cause the report to run in a private data session, which doesn't change if you open other tables or queries elsewhere in Visual FoxPro.
Quick Report	Use this option to create a default design for a report.
Run Report	Use this option to run the report. If you have made any changes to the report since the last save, you will be asked to save the changes before the report runs.

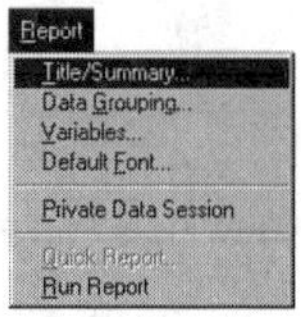

FIGURE 13.8.

The Report menu options.

When you open the File menu while designing a report, you can use the Page Setup command. Choosing File | Page Setup opens the Page Setup dialog box. (See Figure 13.9.) You can use the options in this dialog box to specify dimensions for the report, the number of columns and the order they print in, and whether the print area encompasses the printable page or the whole page. You can also access printer setup settings by clicking the Print Setup button in the dialog box. (This option is explained in the section, "The Page Setup Dialog Box.")

When you open the Format menu while designing a report, you can use two commands that will prove useful: the Snap to Grid command and the Set Grid Scale command.

Snap to Grid	This option causes objects that you place in a report to snap to alignment with the grid (the objects are automatically aligned to the closest grid lines).
Set Grid Scale	This option brings up a Ruler/Grid dialog box. (See Figure 13.10.) You can use this dialog box to specify grid spacing and measuring

the ruler scale by pixels or the Windows default (inches or centimeters, depending on the Control Panel setting).

FIGURE 13.9.

The Page Setup dialog box.

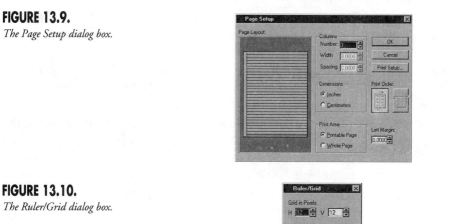

FIGURE 13.10.

The Ruler/Grid dialog box.

When you open the View menu while designing a report, you can use the Show Position command. You can use this option to turn on and off the display of the mouse pointer's position or a selected object. When this option is on, the position of the mouse pointer or a selected object shows in the status bar. Other View menu options are available for use in designing a report and are discussed later in this chapter.

The Page Setup Dialog Box

You can specify values that affect the overall page layout with options in the Page Setup dialog box. To get to the Page Setup dialog box, choose File | Page Setup. (Refer to Figure 13.9.) These values include column specifications, the print area, and the left margin. Each of the controls in the Page Setup dialog box is explained in Table 13.1.

Table 13.1. Page Setup dialog box controls.

Control	Description
Number spinner	Use this spinner to increase or decrease the number of columns in your report. You can change the value by clicking the spinner's up and down arrows or by typing the number in the text box.

continues

Table 13.1. continued

Control	Description
Width spinner	Use this spinner to set the width of the columns. You can change the value by clicking the spinner's up and down arrows or by typing the value in the text box.
Spacing spinner	Use this spinner to set the width of the space between columns. You can change the value by clicking the spinner's up and down arrows or by typing the value in the text box.
Print Area	Use the options in this area to determine how printer margins are handled in the report. If you select the Printable Page button, the printed area of the page is determined according to the default printer specifications and is shown in the Page Layout area of the dialog box. If you select the Whole Page button, your report fills the entire page.
Print Setup button	Use this button to open the Windows Print Setup dialog box, where you can change the default printer setup for the printer installed under Windows.
Print Order buttons	Use these buttons to determine whether vertical columns are filled from top to bottom beginning at the left side of the page or whether horizontal rows are filled from left to right starting at the top of the page.
Left Margin spinner	Use this spinner to set the width of the left margin. You can change the value by clicking the spinner's up and down arrows or by typing the value in the text box.

The Object Menu Options

When an object within a report is selected, some Format menu options are available. (See Figure 13.11.) The functions of these options are described in Table 13.2.

FIGURE 13.11.

The Format menu options.

Table 13.2. Format Menu options used to design reports.

Option	Description
Bring to Front	This option brings selected objects to the front, which means they show up over overlapping objects.
Send to Back	This option sends selected objects to the back, which means they show up under overlapping objects.
Group	This option joins selected objects. Once joined, you can move, cut, and paste them as if they were a single object.
Ungroup	This option separates previously grouped objects so you can manipulate them individually.
Snap to Grid	This option moves selected objects to align flush with the grid setting. If you have a group of fields, you can ensure that they line up perfectly by selecting the fields, then choosing Align to Grid.
Font	This option opens the Font dialog box, which you use to select a font, font style, and font size for the characters in the selected object.
Text Alignment	This option displays another menu that lets you adjust the alignment and spacing of text within fields or text objects in the report. (Text objects must be on multiple lines before these options have any effect on them.) The menu contains these options:
	Left — Left-justifies selected text.
	Center — Centers selected text.
	Right — Right-justifies selected text.
	Single Space — Displays selected text single-spaced, with no blank lines appearing between lines of text.
	$1\frac{1}{2}$ Space — Displays selected text with $1\frac{1}{2}$ blank lines appearing between lines of text.
	Double — Displays selected text double-spaced with one blank line appearing between lines of text.
Fill	This option displays another menu that lets you fill selected objects with one of seven hatched and crosshatched patterns. (The default pattern is None.)
Pen	This option displays another menu that lets you set the point size and design pattern for lines and borders of rectangles and rounded rectangles in the report. The menu contains these options:
	Hairline — One-pixel width outline for the selected object.
	1 Point — One-point width outline for the selected object.

continues

Table 13.2. continued

Option	Description	
	2 Point	Two-point width outline for the selected object.
	4 Point	Four-point width outline for the selected object.
	6 Point	Six-point width outline for the selected object.
	None	No outline for the selected object.
	Dotted	Dotted-line outline for the selected object.
	Dashed	Dashed-line outline for the selected object.
	Dash-dot	Alternating dashes and dots for the outline.
	Dash-dot-dot	Alternating dashes and two dots for the outline of the selected object.
Mode		This option displays another menu that lets you determine whether the selected object is opaque or transparent. Mode only affects text objects, rectangles, and rounded rectangles that have been assigned fill patterns.

Working with the Report Designer Toolbars

As you work with designing reports, you'll find the Report Designer toolbars to be useful aids. They provide fast access to often-used commands and ways to modify the layout, alignment, and colors of controls. Four toolbars are particularly helpful when designing reports: the Report Design toolbar, the Report Controls toolbar, the Color Palette toolbar, and the Layout toolbar. (See Figure 13.12.)

When you design a report, the toolbars can be switched on and off with the appropriate option of the View menu. Choose View | Report Controls Toolbar; View | Report Design Toolbar; View | Layout Toolbar; or View | Color Palette Toolbar to display the toolbar you want. You'll probably make the most use of the Report Controls toolbar because it has different control types (such as text boxes, list and combo boxes, and graphic frames) that you can add to your reports. The Layout toolbar is useful for aligning and sizing groups of controls in relation to each other, and the Color Palette toolbar lets you set the colors of controls and the report background. You'll use the Report Design toolbar to set design modes and to control the display of the various windows and the toolbars.

FIGURE 13.12.

The four toolbars in the Report Designer.

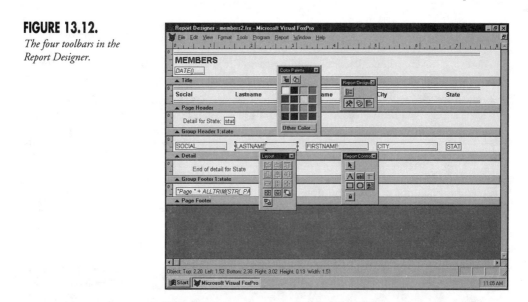

You can get an explanation of any control in a toolbar by holding the mouse pointer over the control for more than one second. When you do this, a small help window shows the control's name, and the status bar explains the control's use in the lower-left corner of the report's window.

Working with Objects

You work with three different types of objects as you design reports: *text objects, field objects,* and *graphics objects.* Text objects contain text that you type directly into the report's design. Field objects are used to display data stored in fields or data that's supplied by expressions or user-defined functions. Graphics objects are pictures, lines, or rectangles. (Pictures in Visual FoxPro reports must be stored either in a table's general fields or as Windows Paintbrush files with an extension of .BMP.)

As you add objects to the report's design, you need to manipulate them in different ways. Use the following steps to select, move, duplicate, and delete them when necessary.

■ To select an object, make sure the Select Objects button (the upward-pointing arrow) is selected in the Report Controls toolbar. Then point to and click the desired object. When an object is selected, small rectangles, called *handles,* surround it.

TIP

You can select multiple objects by holding the Shift key while clicking each object. You can also select all the objects in a band by double-clicking the band marker (directly beneath the band). You can also select multiple objects by clicking on the report layout and dragging the pointer. As you drag the pointer, Visual FoxPro draws a box between the initial pointer position and the current pointer position. You drag this box around the controls you want to select.

- To move an object, click and drag the desired object to the new location. Unlike the report designers in some database managers, Visual FoxPro lets you drag objects between bands. For example, you could drag selected text from the Page Header band to the Page Footer band.

TIP

The easiest way to move an object is to use the arrow keys. Each time you press a key, the field moves 1/100 inch in the direction of the arrow key.

- To duplicate an object, first click the object to select it. Next, choose Edit | Copy, and then choose Edit | Paste. When you do so, a copy of the object appears near its original location. You can then move the copy of the object to the location you want.
- To delete an object, select the object by clicking it, then press the Delete key or choose Edit | Cut.

Adding and Resizing Fields

When you're designing a report, your most common task will probably be adding fields to the report. To add fields, use the field control in the toolbox. First, click the field control in the Report Controls toolbar, then click in the report where you want the upper-left corner of the field to appear and drag the field to the desired size. When you do so, the Report Expression dialog box opens. Click the Build button to the right of the Expression text box to reveal Visual FoxPro's Expression Builder. In the Expression Builder, double-click the field name you want, then click OK to add it to the Expression text box of the Report Expression dialog box.

TIP

If you don't see any fields in the Expression Builder's Fields list, choose View | Data Environment to open the Data Environment window. Then choose Data Environment | Add to open a dialog box where you can add the table to the data environment.

To resize an existing field, click the field to select it so that you can see its handles. Then click on any of the handles and drag it in the desired direction to resize the field.

TIP

The easiest way to resize a field or any other object is to hold down the Shift key and press an arrow key. Each time you press a key, the object expands or contracts by one pixel or scale unit at a time.

TIP

In the Expression Builder, you can *concatenate* (combine on a textual basis) text fields with a space separating them by double-clicking the name of the first field, typing a comma, and double-clicking the name of the next field. The comma tells Visual FoxPro to separate the data with a space and remove trailing spaces. For example, assuming you have a table with field names FIRSTNAME and LASTNAME, you could double-click the FIRSTNAME field in the Expression Builder, type a comma, and double-click the LASTNAME field, then click OK twice to insert the expression in the report. If the table were printed, the expression would display the contents of the FIRSTNAME field, followed by a space, followed by the contents of the LASTNAME field.

Using Variables

Occasionally, you might have a calculation that does not correspond to any field. For these cases, you might consider using a *report variable*. A report variable is similar to a memory variable, except it is present only during report processing. You can use a report variable to display results in a field control in a report or to perform certain calculations. You can use a report variable in a calculation, or you can display its value in a field control.

You define a report variable by choosing Report | Variables, which displays the Report Variables dialog box. In the Report Variables dialog box, select the Variables box and type a name of the variable. In the Value to Store box, type a field name or any other expression. In the Initial Value box, type an initial value. You can click on the Builder button to display the Expression Builder to build an expression for the Value to Store or the Initial Value boxes.

In addition, you can choose a calculation option. You can designate that calculations are performed as records are processed. Before the calculation is performed, the value from the Initial Value box is stored in the variable. Calculations are then performed until it is reset to this initial value. A calculation is reset to the initial value at a group, page, column, or end-of-report breakpoint. The types of calculation options supported by Visual FoxPro are presented in Table 13.3.

Table 13.3. Calculation options for report variables.

Option	Description
Nothing	Designates that no calculations will be performed on this variable.
Count	Counts the number of detail records processed for a group, page, column, or report.
Sum	Computes the additive sum of the variable's values for a group, page, column, or report.
Average	Computes the arithmetic mean (average) of the variable values within a group, page, column, or report.
Lowest	Computes the lowest value for the report variable that occurred in that variable for a group, page, column, or report.
Highest	Computes the highest value that occurred of the report variable for a group, page, column, or report.
Std. Deviation	Computes the square root of the variance for the variable values within a group, page, column, or report.
Variance	Computes the degree to which individual computed report variable values vary from the average of all the values in the group, page, column, or report.

Adding Text

To add text, typically used for titles or captions in a report, you use the text control in the Report Controls toolbar. Click the text control, then click in the report to place a flashing insertion pointer where you want to begin the text. As you type the text, it appears in the report.

When you are done typing the text, you can click anywhere outside the text to complete the process. You can change the text's font and appearance by clicking the text to select it. (When selected, the text is surrounded by four handles.) With the text selected, choose Format | Font to open the Font dialog box. (See Figure 13.13.)

You can use the options in the Font dialog box to choose a desired font, font size, and font style. After you have selected the options you want, click OK to apply them.

FIGURE 13.13.
The Font dialog box.

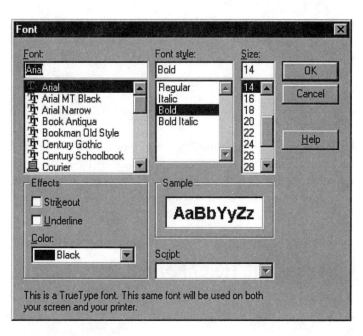

Drawing Lines and Rectangles

The toolbox has tools for drawing lines and two types of rectangles: ones with squared corners and ones with rounded corners.) You can add visual emphasis to your reports by adding these design elements in appropriate locations.

To draw a line in a report, click the Line control, place the cursor where you want one end of the line and drag until the line is the desired length. To draw a rectangle with squared corners, click the rectangle control, place the cursor where you want a corner of the rectangle to be, and drag until the rectangle is the right size. To draw a rectangle with rounded corners, click the rounded-rectangle control, place the cursor where you want a corner of the rounded rectangle to be, and drag until the rounded rectangle is the size you want. You can specify how rounded the rectangle is by double-clicking on the rounded-rectangle object to open the Round Rectangle dialog box. Then you can choose the shape of the rounded rectangle, from completely oval to slightly rounded. Incidentally, you can stretch a rectangle across band boundaries.

Adding Title and Summary Bands

A new report that you create contains a Detail band, a Page Header band, and a Page Footer band by default. Title bands and summary bands can be added by choosing Report | Title/ Summary, which opens the Title/Summary dialog box. (See Figure 13.14.)

FIGURE 13.14.

The Title/Summary dialog box.

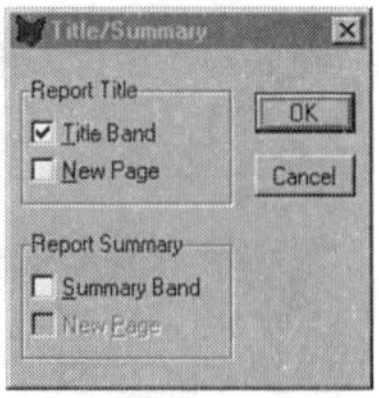

Under Report Title, click the Title Band option to add a title band. Under Report Summary, click the Summary Band option to add a summary band. With either option on, you can click the corresponding New Page option if you want the chosen band to always print its contents on a separate page. Click OK when you're done with the options. Once you've added a title or summary band to a report, add the desired objects to that band using the techniques outlined at the beginning of this section.

Changing the Height of Bands

By default, Visual FoxPro sets the size of any bands in a report to the minimum amount needed to enclose any fields. You can change the height of the bands using two methods. You can move the cursor to the left edge of the band's title line (where the cursor changes to the shape of a double-headed arrow), click, and drag the band upward or downward. You can also double-click the left edge of the band's title line to open a dialog box for the band's height. (See Figure 13.15.) Enter the desired value for the height and click OK. You can turn on the Constant Band Height check box in this dialog box if you don't want the band to adjust its height to accommodate lengthy data (such as memo fields) that has been allowed to expand during printing.

FIGURE 13.15.

The dialog box for adjusting band height.

> **TIP**
>
> If you don't want the page header or page footer bands that Visual FoxPro adds to a new report by default, you can eliminate them by changing their heights to zero using either of the techniques discussed previously.

Modifying an Object's Properties

In Visual FoxPro's Report Designer, you can easily change the properties of an object, (such as a field, text box, line, or graphic). Double-click the object and a dialog box opens. The options in the dialog box let you change the properties of the selected object. Which dialog box appears depends on what type of object you double-click.

Modifying a Field's Properties

Double-click a field in a report, and the Report Expression dialog box opens. (See Figure 13.16.) As mentioned previously under "Adding and Resizing Fields," you use this dialog box to enter a field name or an expression in the field. Clicking the Expression button displays the Expression Builder, which you can use to build a desired expression. Clicking the Format button opens the Format dialog box, which you can use to specify different formatting options. (For more on these options, see the section, "Format Dialog Box Options," later in this chapter.)

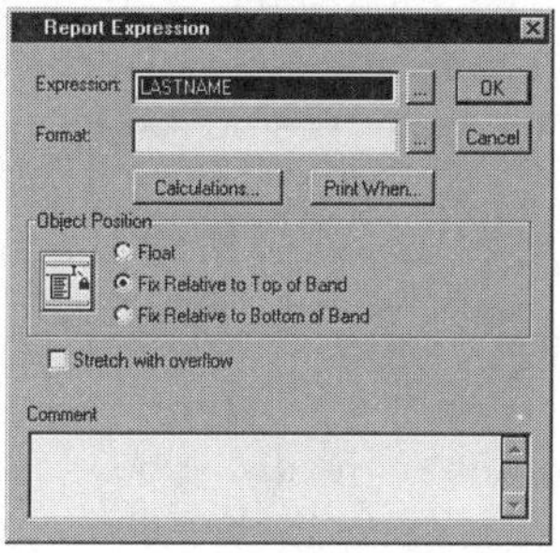

FIGURE 13.16.

The Report Expression dialog box.

Clicking the Calculations button opens the Subtotal or Calculate Field dialog box. (See Figure 13.17.) You can use it to establish a calculation for the expression. For example, if the expression is a field with a numeric value, you could click Sum to get the sum of the values. The Reset list box in the Subtotal or Calculate Field dialog box lets you define whether the calculation occurs at the end of the report, the end of each page, or the end of each column. The available Calculation options are the same as for report variables, which were described earlier in Table 13.3.

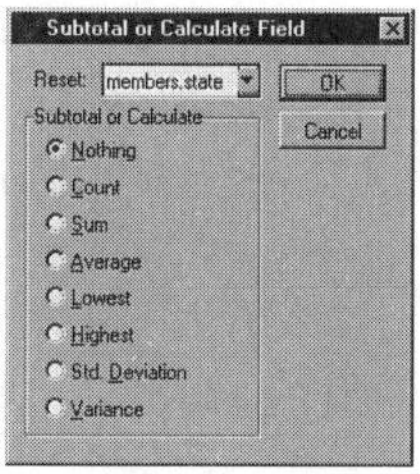

FIGURE 13.17.

The Subtotal or Calculate Field dialog box.

Clicking the Print When button opens the Print When dialog box. (See Figure 13.18.) You can use it to determine when the object is printed. By default, an object is printed whenever the contents of its band are printed, but you can change that default. For example, you can choose not to print values that repeat, or in reports with grouping, you can choose to print when the basis for the group changes. The Print Only When Expression is True text box lets you define another expression that determines whether the field prints.

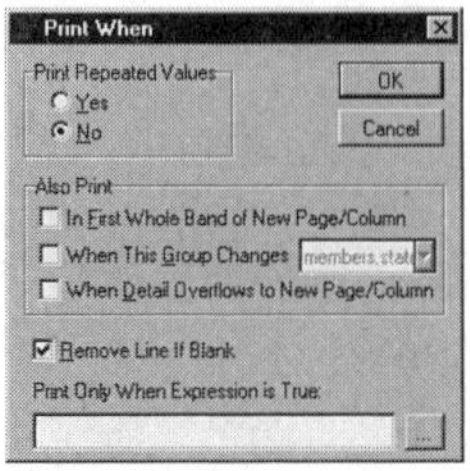

FIGURE 13.18.

The Print When dialog box.

The Object Position portion of the Report Expression dialog box has three options: Float, Fix Relative to Top of Band, and Fix Relative to Bottom of Band. The Fix Relative to Top of Band option maintains the field's position in relation to the top of the band and does not enable field "stretching" to accommodate lengthy data. However, the Fix Relative to Bottom of Band option will enable field stretching to accommodate lengthy data, as well as maintain the field's position in relation to the bottom of the band. If you select the Float option, the field will float in relation to the bands' position.

The Comment portion of the dialog box can be used to enter comments for your reference; they do not appear anywhere in the report.

Modifying Text, Line, and Rectangle Properties

Double-click a text object in a report, and the Text dialog box appears. (See Figure 13.19.)

Clicking the Print When box opens the Print When dialog box. (See Figure 13.18.) Use the options in this dialog box to determine when the text prints, as described in the preceding paragraphs. The Object Position portion of the Text dialog box has three options: Float, Fix Relative to Top of Band, and Fix Relative to Bottom of Band. The Fix Relative to Top of Band option maintains the text's position in relation to the top of the band and does not enable field stretching to accommodate lengthy data. The Fix Relative to Bottom of Band option maintains the text's position in relation to the bottom of the band and enables field stretching to accommodate lengthy data. The Float option enables the text to float in relation to the bands' position.

FIGURE 13.19.

The Text dialog box.

The Comment portion of the Text dialog box can be used to enter comments for your reference; the comments do not appear anywhere in the report.

If you double-click a line in a report, the dialog box looks the same as the Text dialog box, except that it has a vertical line or rectangle and additional check boxes titled No Stretch, Stretch Relative to Tallest Object in Group, and Stretch Relative to Height of Band. The No Stretch option restricts vertical lines or rectangles from stretching. The Stretch Relative to Tallest Object in Group option enables a vertical line or rectangle to stretch to the height of the tallest object in the group, while the Stretch Relative to Height of Band option enables the vertical line or rectangle to stretch in relation to the height of its band.

If you double-click a rounded rectangle, a similar dialog box appears, but it also contains five different style buttons for rounded rectangles. (See Figure 13.20.) In addition to specifying any of the options just described, you can click the desired style of rounded rectangle.

FIGURE 13.20.

The Round Rectangle dialog box.

Modifying a Picture's Properties

If you double-click a picture in a report, a Report Picture dialog box appears. You can use the options in this dialog box to control where pictures in reports come from, when they should print, and how the size and scaling of the picture should be handled. For more specifics on the dialog box and the use of these options, see the section "Adding Graphics to a Report," later in this chapter.

Format Dialog Box Options

When you double-click a field to bring up the Report Expression dialog box and then click the Build button to the right of the Format text box, the Format dialog box appears. (See Figure 13.21.) You can use the options in this dialog box to control the formatting applied to the selected field.

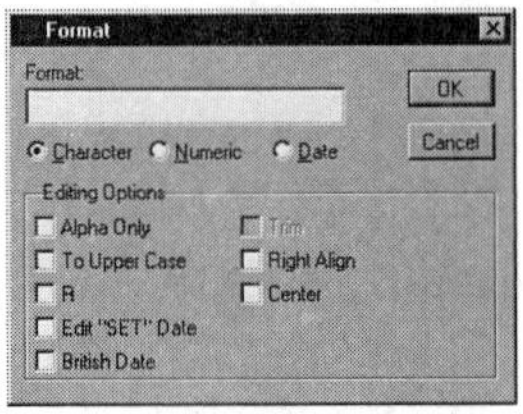

FIGURE 13.21.

The Format dialog box.

The editing options you see in this dialog box vary, depending on whether you select the Character, Numeric, or Date button. Table 13.4 shows the results of using options in the Format dialog box when the Character button is selected.

Table 13.4. The results of using Format dialog box options with the Character button selected.

Option	Result
Alpha Only	Allows only alphabetic characters
To Upper Case	Converts characters to uppercase
R	Displays characters, but does not store them
Edit "SET" Date	Prints data as a date using the SET DATE format that is in effect
British Date	Prints data as a date using the British (or European) date format
Trim	Strips leading and trailing blanks
Right Align	Prints data flush right
Center	Prints data centered

Table 13.5 shows the results of using options in the Format dialog box when the Numeric button is selected.

Table 13.5. The results of using Format dialog box options with the Numeric button selected.

Option	Result
Left Justify	Numeric data is aligned flush left
Blank if Zero	Field is blank if it contains a zero value
(Negative)	Negative numbers are enclosed in parentheses
Edit SET Date	Prints data as a date using the SET DATE format that is in effect
British Date	Prints data as a date using the British (or European) date format
CR if Positive	Positive numbers are followed with the letters CR
DB if Negative	Negative numbers are followed with the letters DB
Leading Zero	Leading zeroes are printed
Currency	Values are printed using currency format
Scientific	Values are printed using scientific notation

Table 13.6 shows the results of using options in the Format dialog box when the Character button is selected.

Table 13.6. The results of using Format dialog box options with the Date button selected.

Option	Result
Edit SET Date	Prints data as a date using the SET DATE format that is in effect
British Date	Prints data as a date using the British (or European) date format

If you are familiar with the formatting codes used in the Xbase language to format data, you can type those codes directly into the Format text box in the dialog box. However, most users find it much easier to select options by clicking the appropriate check boxes.

Adding Groups to a Report

With most column-oriented reports (and many form-oriented ones), you'll want to subdivide the data into groups. For instance, if you were printing a report of employee phone numbers for a multinational corporation, you might need the report grouped by country, then by office or plant location in each country, then by department in each office or plant. Each category would form a separate group. Visual FoxPro's Report Designer overcomes the limitations of earlier Xbase programs by supporting up to 20 levels of grouping within a single report.

To add a group band, choose Report | Data Grouping to open the Data Grouping dialog box. (See Figure 13.22.)

FIGURE 13.22.

The Data Grouping dialog box.

In the Group Expressions list box, you see the names of any existing groups you've added to the report. The Insert and Delete buttons can be used to add a group or delete an existing group.

To add the group, click the Insert button. Click in the Group text box and type the expression or click the Build button to the right of the Group text box to bring up Visual FoxPro's Expression Builder, where you can build the expression. When groups are used, the report begins a new group (or *breakpoint*) each time the basis of the group expression changes. Remember that when you use groups, you must index or sort the table on the field or expression used as the basis for the group. For example, if a report is grouped on the basis of a ZIP code field within a table, the report has a breakpoint, with any included subtotals of numeric fields or expressions, each time the contents of the ZIP code field change. Although many reports require entering a single field name as the expression, you can use any valid Visual FoxPro expression. For example, if you wanted the group to be based on a single field, such as the ZIP code field, you would enter the field's name (in this example, Zipcode) as the expression in the Group text box. On the other hand, if a table was indexed on a combination of fields called Office and Department, and you wanted to base the grouping on that combination of fields, you could enter the expression Office + Department in the text box.

The Start Group on New Column box, when checked, starts a new column each time the group expression changes. (This option has an effect only if your report has more than one column. You can add columns to a report by choosing Report | Page Setup and specifying the number of columns in the dialog box.) The Start Each Group on a New Page box, when checked, inserts a page break each time the group expression changes. The Reset Page Number to 1 for Each Group box, when checked, sets the page number to 1 each time the group expression changes. The Reprint Group Header on Each Page box, when checked, tells Visual FoxPro to reprint the header on each page spanned by the group.

The Start Group on New Page when less than spinner control lets you avoid having a group header print near the bottom of the page while most of its detail lines are printed on the next page. Use the spinner to choose the *minimum* distance from the bottom of the page that a group header should print.

When you're done with the options in this dialog box, click OK to close it. The new bands you added appear in the report. However, by default, they occupy no space. You need to increase the width of the new bands to the amount you want, using the techniques covered previously in this chapter.

Adding Graphics to a Report

By using Visual FoxPro in the Windows environment, you can add graphics to reports. These graphics can be from pictures stored in a general field of a Visual FoxPro table or they can be design elements created in a drawing or paint program elsewhere in Windows. (Pictures that are used as design elements must be saved in Windows Paintbrush [.BMP] file format.) For example, Figure 13.23 shows a report with a picture that has been copied into the report's title band as a design element. This picture appears at the top of the first page for every report printed.

FIGURE 13.23.

A report containing a picture.

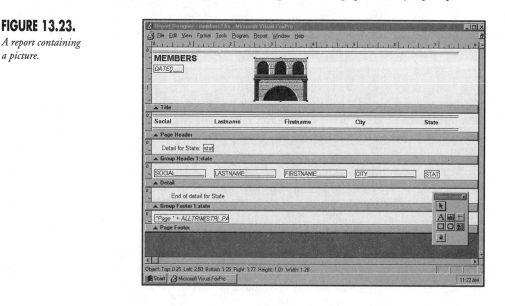

To add a picture to a report, perform the following steps:

1. Design the report using the steps outlined in this chapter.

2. In the Report Controls toolbox, click the Picture/OLE Bound Control control.

3. Click at the starting point for the graphic and drag until the frame reaches the desired size for the picture. When you release the mouse, the Report Picture dialog box appears. (See Figure 13.24.)

4. Use the options in this dialog box (discussed in the following paragraphs) to tell Visual FoxPro where to find the picture and how to handle pictures that are not the same size as the frame they are in.

5. When you're done selecting options, click OK. The picture then appears in the report's design. (See Figure 13.23.)

The Report Picture dialog box, which is shown in Figure 13.24, has options that let you exercise control over where the picture comes from and how it is handled within the report.

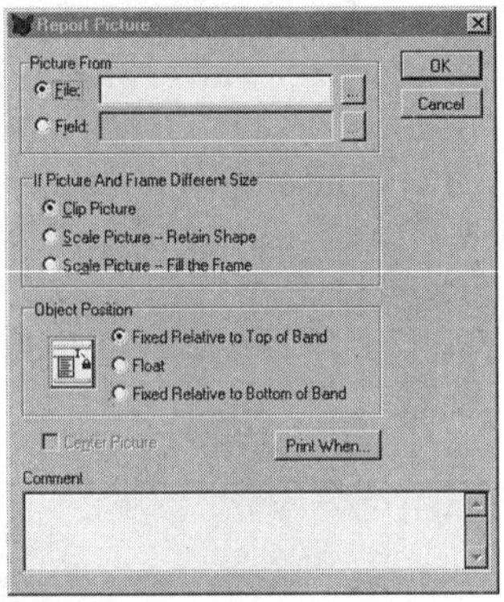

FIGURE 13.24.

The Report Picture dialog box.

The Picture From area of the dialog box has File and Field buttons and corresponding rectangular buttons and text boxes, where you can type in the filename or field name. You use the options in this area to tell Visual FoxPro where to find the picture that's placed in the report. To include a single bitmap picture in your report, click the File radio button. Then, click the rectangular File button to open a Picture dialog box that you can use to select the .BMP file. You can also type the name (including the path) of the .BMP file in the text box to the right of the File button. To base the picture on the contents of a table's general field, click the Field radio button. Then, click the rectangular Field button to open a Choose Field/Variable dialog box, which you can use to select the field. Or you can type the field name in the text box to the right of the Field button. Note that when a table's general fields have a document other than a picture or a chart (such as Word for Windows documents or Excel spreadsheets), an icon representing the object appears in the field that's printed in the report.

The If Picture And Frame Different Size area of the dialog box has three options: Clip Picture; Scale Picture—Retain Shape; and Scale Picture—Fill the Frame. When the picture is larger than the frame you added to the report, the Clip Picture option tells Visual FoxPro to clip the picture at the right and the bottom as needed to fit in the frame. The Scale Picture—Retain Shape option tells Visual FoxPro to show the entire picture, filling as much of the frame as possible while keeping the relative proportions of the bitmap picture. (This method of scaling helps avoid vertical or horizontal distortion.) The Scale Picture—Fill the Frame option shows the entire picture, filling the frame completely. Depending on the dimensions of the frame, this may cause horizontal or vertical distortion as Visual FoxPro scales the picture to fit the frame.

The Center Picture check box is used with pictures stored in a table's general fields. (Pictures in .BMP files placed in reports as design elements are not affected by this option.) Because bitmaps stored in a table's general fields can come in a variety of shapes and sizes, this option enables you to tell Visual FoxPro whether to center the pictures shown in the report. When the bitmap stored in a general field is smaller than the frame, it appears in the upper-left corner of the frame unless you check Center Picture. This option ensures that pictures stored in general fields that are smaller than the frame are centered in the frame within the report.

The Print When button opens a Print When dialog box. You can use the options in this dialog box to tell Visual FoxPro how often the picture should print (in relation to its band) and under what conditions it should be printed. (If you don't use any options in this dialog box, by default Visual FoxPro always prints the picture.) The Print Once Per Band option in this dialog box can be set to Yes or No. If you choose No, you can use options under Also Print to tell Visual FoxPro to print the picture in the first whole band of a new page or column, when a group changes, or when the detail band overflows to a new page or column. You can use the Remove Line If Blank option to tell Visual FoxPro not to include a line around the picture if the graphic is blank, and you can use the Print Only When Expression is True text box to specify an expression that controls whether or not the picture prints.

The Object Position area of the dialog box has three options: Fix Relative to Top of Band, Fix Relative to Bottom of Band, and Float. The Fix Relative to Top of Band option maintains the text's position in relation to the top of the band and does not enable field stretching to accommodate lengthy data. The Fix Relative to Bottom of Band option *will* enable field stretching to accommodate lengthy data, but maintains the text's position in relation to the *bottom* of the band. The Float option enables the text to float in relation to the bands' position.

The Comment portion of the dialog box can be used to add comments about the picture. (Comments are for your reference only; they do not appear in the printed report.)

Previewing the Report

Once the report's design is complete, you can see it with actual data by choosing File | Print Preview. You can also click on the Preview button on the Standard toolbar. A preview of the report appears in a Page Preview window. (See Figure 13.25.)

TIP

You can use the preview feature at any time during the report's design to get an idea of how it is shaping up.

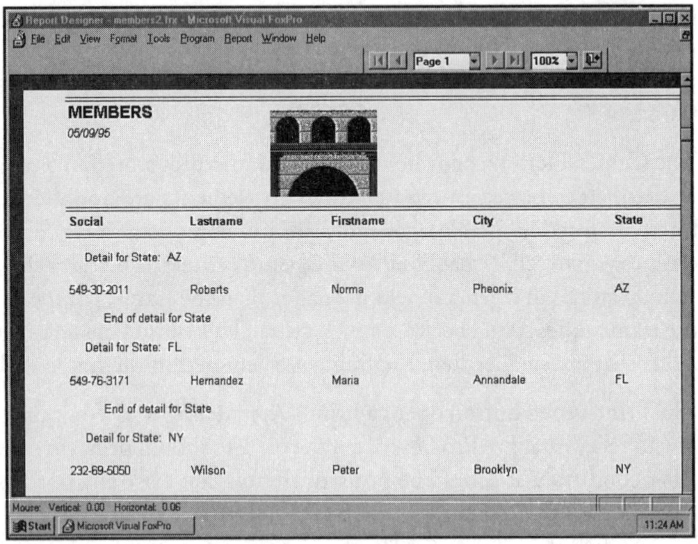

FIGURE 13.25.
The Page Preview window containing a report.

The preview mode of a report enables you to see what the report looks like before it is printed, complete with all fonts and design elements included in the report's design. The preview mode initially shows the page at 100% magnification, and a Print Preview toolbar appears, as shown in the figure. By moving to any area of the report and clicking, you can switch back and forth between a full-page view and a "zoomed" or enlarged view of the area. The Print Preview toolbar has buttons you can use for navigating between pages of the report. Click the Next Page and Previous Page buttons to move to the next and previous pages of a report. You can also click the GoTo Page button, and the GoTo Page dialog box appears. Use the spinner to select the desired page of the report to display in the Preview window. Then choose a page using the spinner. You can also click in the text box beside the spinner, type a page number, and click OK to move to that page number. When you are finished previewing a report, click the Close button in the toolbar to return to the report's design.

Saving, Printing, and Displaying Reports

Chapter 10 provides details on saving and printing reports, both from the menu bar and from the Command window. General techniques are reviewed here as a reference; see Chapter 10 for details.

To save the completed report, choose File | Save. If you did not name the report when you started the report creation process, Visual FoxPro displays the Save As dialog box. Enter a name for the file (if you are running Windows 3.*x* on top of DOS, filenames must be eight or fewer characters, with no spaces), then click Save. Visual FoxPro saves the reports with a default extension .FRX.

To print a report click on the Print button on the Standard toolbar or choose File | Print and the Print dialog box appears. Choose Report in the Type list box, then select the report in the File dialog box and click OK. In the Print Setup dialog box that appears next, click OK to send the report's output to the printer. Click Run to produce the report. From the Command window, you can print a report with the REPORT FORM command, with the following basic syntax:

```
REPORT FORM report filename [TO PRINTER]
```

If the TO PRINTER option is used, the report is printed; otherwise, it appears on-screen in the main window of the Visual FoxPro desktop.

You can also print reports by selecting the report in the Project Manager and choosing File | Print (or clicking on the Standard toolbar's Print icon). You will see the same Print dialog box shown earlier; click OK to print the report.

An Exercise Creating a Custom Report

You can follow the steps shown here to practice using the techniques described in this chapter. This exercise creates a custom report that uses multiple columns to display a phone directory. The report is grouped on the basis of the State field in the underlying table. The report uses the MEMBERS.DBF table that's stored on the accompanying disc. If you have not already copied MEMBERS.DBF from the disk into your working directory, you need to do so before you can follow this exercise. Use the following steps to create the report:

1. In the Command window, enter OPEN DATABASE ECOLOGY to open the database, then enter USE MEMBERS to open the table.

2. In the Command window, enter INDEX ON STATE TAG STATES to build and put into effect an index that supports the grouping added to the report.

3. Choose File | New, click Report, and then click New File to open a new report.

4. Choose View | Data Environment, then choose Data Environment ¦ Add. In the dialog box that appears, select Members as the table, then click OK. Press Ctrl+F4 to close the Data Environment window.

5. Click the label control. Then click in the Page Header band, about one inch to the right of the left edge and 1/2 inch down from the top, and type Membership Listing.

6. Click anywhere outside the text, then click the text to select it. Choose Format | Font to open the Font dialog box and choose a larger font of your choice, with a bold style.

7. Click the Button Lock control, then click the Field control to select it and lock in the selection.

8. In the Detail band, click roughly ¹/₂ inch to the right of the left edge and ¹/₂ inch down from the top of the band. The Report Expression dialog box appears. (See Figure 13.26.)

FIGURE 13.26.

The Report Expression dialog box.

9. Click the Build button to the right of the Expression text box to bring up the Expression Builder. In the Expression Builder, double-click the Lastname field, then type a comma, then double-click the Firstname field. Click OK to close the Expression Builder, click OK again to close the Report Expression dialog box.

10. In the Detail band, click roughly ¹/₄ inch to the right of the field that you just placed to display the Report Expression dialog box again.

11. Click the Build button to the right of the Expression text box to bring up the Expression Builder. In the Expression Builder, double-click the City field. Click OK to put away the Expression Builder, and click OK again to close the Report Expression dialog box. Repeat this step for the State field.

12. Open the Format menu, and if the Snap to Grid option is on, turn it off. (You can tell when the option is on by the presence of a check mark beside its name in the menu.)

13. Click the rounded rectangle control in the toolbox. Then click at a point just above and to the left of the title and drag down and to the right until the rectangle fully encloses the text. If necessary, select the rectangle and move it so the text is evenly centered within the rectangle.

14. Click the field control in the toolbox, then click in the Page Footer band at a point roughly three inches to the right of the left edge and ¹/₂ inch down from the top of the band, and drag to place a field roughly ¹/₈ by ¹/₂ inch in size.

15. In the Report Expression dialog box, click the Build button to the right of the Expression text box to bring up the Expression Builder.

16. In the Expression Builder, click the arrow to the right of the Date functions list box to open the list box. In the list box, double-click DATE().

17. Click OK to close the Expression Builder, and click OK again to close the Report Expression dialog box beneath it.

18. Choose File | Page Setup to open the Page Setup dialog box.

19. Change the number of columns from one to two. Increase the distance between columns (the lowest spinner in the dialog box) to 0.2 inches, then click OK in the dialog box to close it.

20. Click the line control in the toolbox. Then click at a point just to the right of the right edge of the Phone field, at the top of the Detail band, and drag straight down to the bottom of the Detail band. Doing so places a line to the right of each State field, which helps divide the names in the left column from those in the right column. When you are done with this step, your report should resemble the one shown in Figure 13.27.

21. Choose File | Save. When prompted for a name, enter PHONELST as the desired name. Answer Yes to the prompt that asks if you want to save the environment information, and choose File | Close to close the report.

FIGURE 13.27.

The completed report in design mode.

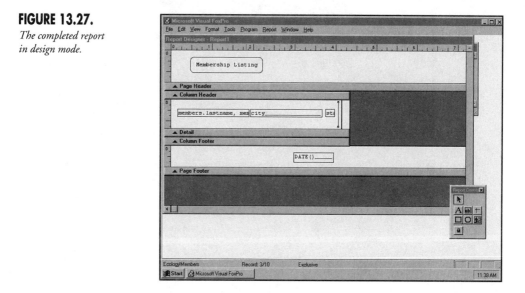

To produce the report, choose File | Print, and in the Print dialog box that opens, change the Type list box to Report, then click the File button, select PHONELST.FRX in the Open dialog box that appears, and click OK. Finally, click OK in the Print dialog box to produce the report.

Summary

This chapter explained the techniques you use in designing and producing reports. In Visual FoxPro, the secret to meeting your reporting needs is a complete familiarity with the Report Designer because its capabilities make it possible to produce almost any type of report imaginable. If you plan to call stored reports that you create in Visual FoxPro programs, be sure to study the material in Chapter 25, "Programming for Reporting Needs," which shows how you can produce reports while under the control of a program.

Using Expressions and Functions

IN THIS CHAPTER

Expressions and functions come into regular use throughout FoxPro. As previously noted, you use them in queries—both when constructing queries through commands and when using the query-by-example facility. Expressions and functions are also particularly useful in forms and reports, where you can use them to calculate the values that appear in calculated fields. You can use expressions for any of the following tasks:

- Constructing queries within the Query Designer
- Building queries with commands entered in the command window
- Adding a calculation to a form or a report
- Adding a system variable, such as the current date or time, to a form or report
- Providing totals or averages for an entire report or for a group of records in a report

This chapter explores how expressions are constructed and explains how you can use different types of expressions and functions to get results like those described in the preceding list.

Expressions, Defined

An *expression* is a calculation made up of any combination of functions, operators, constants, and field names, which FoxPro evaluates to equal some kind of value. Typically, you use an expression because you need a value of some sort that cannot be directly obtained from a table's field. For example, if a table of video sales contained a Quantity field and a Price field, you might use an expression like this one to get a value that is the result of the Quantity field multiplied by the Price field:

```
Quantity * Price
```

Parts of an Expression

An expression can include any needed combination of operators, field names, functions, constants, and literal values. Figure 14.1 shows an expression and its parts.

FIGURE 14.1.

The parts of an expression.

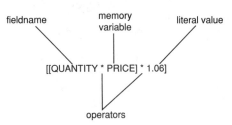

Operators

Most expressions use specific *operators*, which act on data to produce values. FoxPro provides *math operators* (for performing addition, subtraction, multiplication, and division), *relational operators* (such as equals, greater than, and less than) to assign and compare values, *logical operators* to deal with true and false values, and *concatenation operators* to combine character strings. Table 14.1 shows operators you'll commonly use in expressions.

Table 14.1. Operators used in expressions.

Operator	Description
	Math Operators
*	Multiplication
+	Addition
-	Subtraction
/	Division
^	Exponentiation (raises one number to the power of another)
	Assignment and Comparison Operators
<	Less than
<=	Less than or equal to
>	Greater than
>=	Greater than or equal to
=	Equal to
<> or # or !	Not equal to
$	Contained within (used only with text strings)
==	Exactly equals (used only with text strings)
	Logical Operators
.AND.	Both comparisons are true
.OR.	Either comparison is true
.NOT.	Entire comparison is true, or expression named by .NOT. is false
	Concatenation Operators
+	String concatenation (combines two text strings)
, (comma)	String concatenation with trailing blanks trimmed and a space added between the two strings

Math Operators

You use math operators in FoxPro to produce numeric results; the usual operators are addition (+), subtraction (-), multiplication (*), and division (/). In addition, FoxPro provides *unary minus* (the minus sign changes a value into its negative equivalent) and *exponentiation* (raising a number to the power of another number). Unary operators take single operands—hence their name—and binary operators take two operands. Also, note that in Visual FoxPro, only the minus sign and the NOT operator are unary operators.

Assignment and Comparison Operators

The equal symbol may be common to math formulas, but in FoxPro it isn't considered a math operation. In FoxPro, the equal sign is both an assignment operator and a comparison operator, used alone to assign values or used in combination with other operators to compare values. You use the equal sign alone to assign a value to an object or variable (for example, the statement Salary = 12 assigns a value of 12 to the variable named Salary). The less-than and greater-than symbols can be used alone or with the equal symbol as comparison operators. Used in this manner, the operators return a true or false value depending on the result of the expression. For example, a simple comparison of 5 < 9 would result in a logical true, while the result of 5 < NUMBER would depend on the value of the variable called NUMBER.

Logical Operators

You use the logical operators—.AND., .OR., and .NOT.—to compare values and produce a logical true or false.

Concatenation Operators

Use the concatenation operator (+) to combine text strings. For example, if a table has fields named Lastname and Firstname, you could produce a text string with the full name separated by a space with this expression:

```
trim(Firstname) + " " + LastName
```

You can also use the comma symbol as a concatenation operator to perform a similar function. When used between two expressions that evaluate as text, the comma concatenates (combines) the text strings and inserts a space between them. Therefore, the expression

```
trim(Firstname),Lastname
```

would produce the same result as the expression

```
trim(Firstname) + " " + LastName
```

Operator Precedence

Note that there's a specific order, or *precedence*, in which math operations are performed. FoxPro performs exponentiation first, then negation (making a number a negative number), then multiplication and division, then addition and subtraction, then concatenation, then logical operations. In cases where operators maintain equal precedence (such as multiplication and division), the order of precedence is from left to right. You can use parentheses in your expressions to force a different order of precedence. When parentheses are used, FoxPro calculates from the innermost pair of parentheses and works outward.

Functions

Functions can be thought of as special-purpose programs, built into FoxPro, that perform tasks that would otherwise require large amounts of program code. Functions accept data, perform an internal calculation of some sort, and return data. You can use functions to convert data from one type to another, to perform specialized math operations, to test for various conditions, and to manipulate data in various ways. FoxPro contains dozens of functions for specialized purposes, such as finding the average of a group of values, looking up a field value within a specified set of records, converting characters of a string to uppercase, and returning a value representing the day of the week. You can see a complete list of all available functions by choosing Help | Contents from the menus and clicking Commands and Functions under the Language Reference subheading.

Literals

Literals are actual values, such as text, numbers, or dates. `Jayne Smith`, `36`, and `3/10/94` are examples of literals. String literals must be enclosed in quotation marks, and dates must be enclosed in curly braces, as in {03/10/94}.

Entering Expressions in Screens and Reports

Expressions can be added to screens and reports with the field tool, which is also used to add table fields to screen and report designs. With screens, you open the screen in design mode, then you add an expression as a field using the following steps:

1. Click the Text Box tool in the Forms Control toolbar, then click and drag to place the field.
2. Right-click the desired field, and choose Builder from the shortcut menu that appears.
3. When the Text Box Builder dialog box opens, click the Value tab.
4. Type the desired expression into the text box.

With reports, you open the report in design mode, then you add an expression as a field using the following steps:

1. Click the field tool in the toolbox, then click where you want the upper-left corner of the field to appear.

2. In the Report Expression dialog box that appears, click the Build button to the right of the Expression text box to open the Expression Builder.

3. Type the expression or use the Expression Builder to build it.

In FoxPro, the Expression Builder can be a big help in adding expressions. Besides providing a way to construct expressions while minimizing possible syntax errors, the Expression Builder also contains several standard expressions for values, such as the current date and time and the current page number of a report. (See Figure 14.2.)

FIGURE 14.2.

The Expression Builder.

With the Expression Builder, you construct the expression by double-clicking your choices in the Functions list boxes or the Fields and Variables list boxes to insert them where needed. As you double-click the items, they show in the middle window of the Expression Builder. As you build the expression, you can also type characters directly into the window at any time. When you are done constructing the expression, click OK to close the Expression Builder. The Verify button can be used to verify that a particular expression is valid to FoxPro. If the expression is valid, you will see a message in the status bar when you click the button.

Using Concatenation

You can use the concatenation operator (+) to combine text strings within a field. This technique is commonly used in reports to combine fields such as last name, first name, and middle initial into a single field containing the full name, or to combine city, state, and postal code fields into a single field. For example, in a table with fields named Lastname, Firstname, and Midinit used as the underlying table for a report, you could use an expression like the following within a text box control:

```
trim(Firstname) + " " + Midinit + ". " + Lastname
```

This might yield a text string like `"Steve A. Hairston"`. In this example, if there were no entry in the `Middle Initial` field, you would get an unwanted space and a period. But you can avoid this by using the `IIF` (immediate `IF`) function, which is covered later in this chapter.

When working with text, keep in mind that you can use the FoxPro string functions, including `Left()` and `Right()`, to print a portion of text. For example, if the underlying table or query contains a field called `Midname` and you want to display only the first character of whatever entry is in that field, you could use an expression like `Left(Midname,1)` to display the first character of that field's contents.

Working with Dates, Times, and Page Numbers

A common use for expressions in forms and reports is to show the current date or time, and in reports, the current page number or the total number of pages. If you want to display the current date, time, or both, add a field using the field tool and enter any of the following expressions into the Expression Builder:

`DATE()`	Display the current date.
`TIME()`	Display the current time.
`DTOC(DATE())+" "+TIME()`	Display the current date and time.
`_PAGENO`	Display the current page number in a report.

Including Percentages in a Report

A report might include a numeric column of data, such as a sale price for each item sold, and you might want to display another column beside the numeric column that shows each sales value as a percentage of the total sales. You can do this by first creating a memory variable that calculates the total for the field. You could use a command like

```
SUM SALES TO TOTSALES
```

to accomplish this. Then, you would add a calculated field to the report's Detail band. The field would contain the expression

```
(SALES/TOTSALES)*100
```

and the column that appears as a result of the field contains the calculated value. A disadvantage to this technique, when working with FoxPro interactively, is that you must remember to use the `SUM` command to create the memory variable before running the report. You can solve this problem by storing the commands to create the memory variable and then printing the report in a program file; you can then run the program each time you want to produce the report. In the code, you might want to also include formatting, such as a percent symbol, by using concatenation operators, as discussed earlier in this chapter.

Including Running Totals in Reports

You can also use memory variables as part of expressions to display running totals in a report. To add a variable to a report that can be used to display a running total, open the report in design mode and choose Report | Variables from the menus. A Report Variables dialog box appears. (See Figure 14.3.)

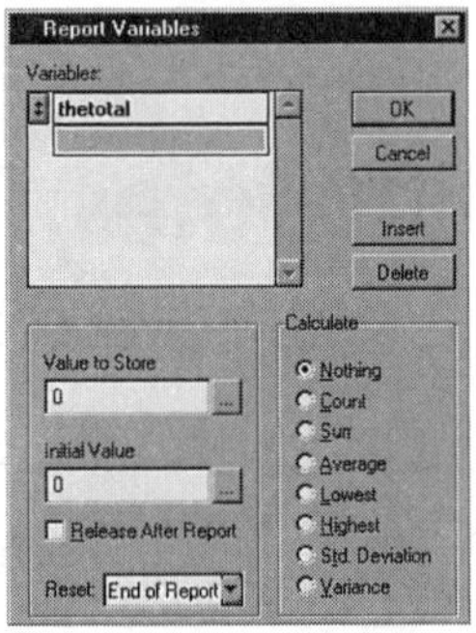

FIGURE 14.3.

A Report Variables dialog box.

Enter a name for the variable in the Variables list box, and then click the button to the right of the Value to Store text box. In the next dialog box, select the field to be used as the basis for the running total and click OK. In the Calculate portion of the Variable Definition dialog box, click Sum, and then OK. Finally, click OK to close the Variable Definition dialog box. You can then use the field tool and the Report Expression dialog box (explained in Chapter 13, "Designing and Customizing Reports") to add the expression that calculates the running total to the report.

Using the *IIF* Function

The immediate IF function, or IIF(), can also be useful as part of an expression in forms and reports when you need to display one set of data if a condition is true and another set of data if the condition is false. For instance, a field called Credit might contain values of 1 indicating yes and 0 indicating no. In a form or a report, you could indicate the value in the field with words rather than numeric amounts with an expression like this one:

```
=IIF(CREDIT=1, "Yes", "No")
```

Or you might want to indicate in a personnel report how many weeks of vacation an employee receives; the company permits two weeks of vacation once an employee has one or more years with the company. Assuming the table or query has a field named Dayhired, you could display the amount of vacation in a form or report with an expression like the following:

```
IIF(DATE() - (DATE(DAYHIRED)) < 365, "none","two weeks")
```

You could place the entire expression within a field on a form or report, which would display the appropriate amount of vacation for each employee.

Summary

This chapter explains how to use expressions in FoxPro for queries, forms, and reports. Using expressions provides yet another way to extend the power of FoxPro. Keep in mind that FoxPro's Expression Builder can be a significant aid in constructing expressions that run without errors from the start.

Producing Mailings

15

IN THIS CHAPTER

This chapter shows you techniques you can use when dealing with mailings, which are a major business task handled by database software. Topics in this chapter include how you can produce mailing labels with the Label Wizard or by designing them manually, how you can generate form letters from within Visual FoxPro, and how you can generate form letters by exporting files for use with Word for Windows and other word processors.

Creating Mailing Labels with the Label Wizard

Mailing labels are among the most common report types produced from database managers, and Visual FoxPro is no slouch in this area. If you work through the Project Manager, Visual FoxPro makes the mailing label creation process easy through the addition of a wizard designed specifically for mailing labels. (You may want to first design a query that selects the desired records for the mailing labels before starting the wizard. With the query designed and saved, you can base the labels you create on that query.) From the Project Manager, use the following steps to create mailing labels:

1. Start the Project Manager which contains the table that you wish to use if it is not already open.

2. Click the Documents tab, highlight the Labels icon, and then click the New button. The New Label dialog box appears as shown in Figure 15.1. Then click on the Label Wizard button, and the Label Wizard dialog box appears.

FIGURE 15.1.
The New Label dialog box.

3. The first frame of the Label Wizard, shown in Figure 15.2, enables you to choose which table or view to use to generate mailing labels. Choose a table and click the Next Button to proceed to the next frame.

4. The second frame of the Label Wizard, shown in Figure 15.3, enables you to select a label size. Once you have selected a label size, click the Next button to proceed to the next frame.

5. The third frame of the Label Wizard dialog box (see Figure 15.4) gives you a list of fields from the underlying table or query. You can add any of these fields to the Selected Fields box by double-clicking on a field name or by selecting a field and clicking on the right-arrow button. Also provided in the dialog box are punctuation buttons, which you use to add punctuation such as spaces, commas, and line breaks (or returns), and a text box where you can type in text that appears in the label.

FIGURE 15.2.

Step 1 frame of the Label Wizard dialog box used to select a table.

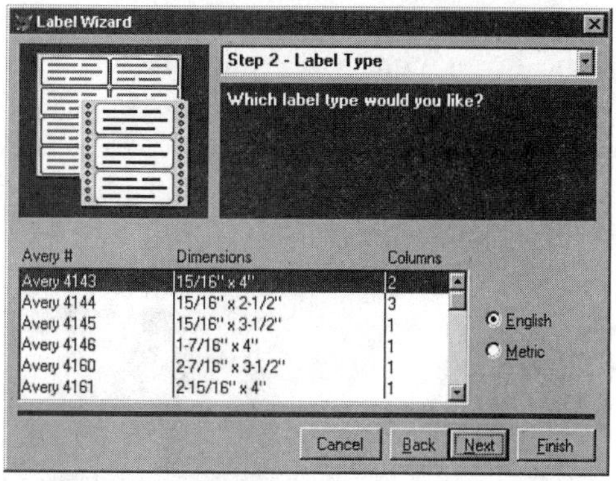

FIGURE 15.3.

Step 2 frame of the Label Wizard dialog box used to select a label size.

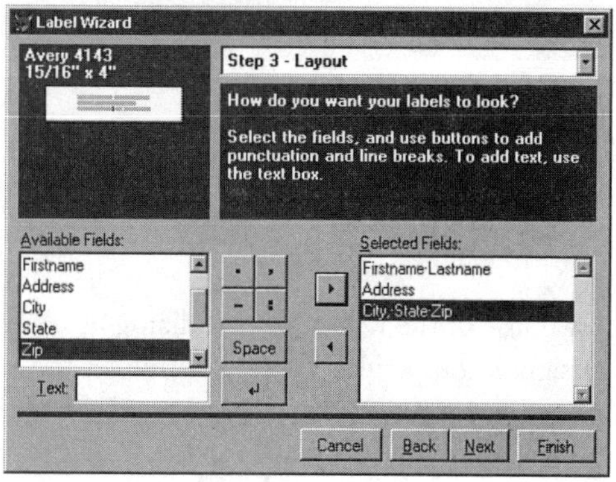

FIGURE 15.4.

Step 3 frame of the Label Wizard dialog box used to select fields for the label.

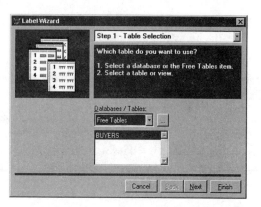

6. Add the desired fields to the label by clicking the field name in the list of fields to select it and by clicking the right-arrow button. (You can also just double-click the field.) To add a space or to add other punctuation, click the Space or the desired punctuation button. To move to a new line on the label, click the Return/Enter button. To add text in the label, type the desired text in the text box, and then click

the right-arrow button to add the text to the label. As you add fields, punctuation, and text, the items you add appear in the Selected Fields box at the right side of the dialog box.

TIP

As you build the label, a representation of where the data will appear within the label appears in the upper-left corner of the dialog box, along with the chosen label's dimensions. This can be helpful for making sure that you don't add data that is too large for a particular label size.

---

7. When the label's design is complete, click the Next button. The next frame of the Label Wizard dialog box (see Figure 15.5) asks you to choose a sort order. Click the field or fields you want to determine the sort order followed by the Add button, and click either Ascending or Descending option. Click Next when you are finished choosing a sort order. (Note that you can also click Next without specifying any sort order, in which case the labels are printed based on the order they occur in the underlying table or query.)

FIGURE 15.5.

Step 4 frame of the Label Wizard dialog box for choosing a sort order.

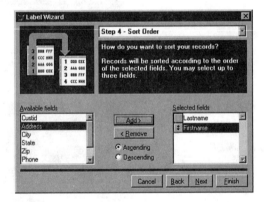

8. The last frame of the Label Wizard dialog box (see Figure 15.6) informs you that the label design is completed. This box provides three buttons to save the label for later use, to save and print the label, or to open the label using Visual FoxPro's Label Designer, so that you can make further modifications to the label's design.

You can also click the Preview button in the dialog box to see the labels in page preview mode before you save them. If you click the Preview button, the labels appear in a page preview window (see Figure 15.7). In the last Label Wizard dialog box, click the desired option, and then click Finish to save the mailing labels or make changes to the design.

FIGURE 15.6.

The last frame of the Label Wizard dialog box.

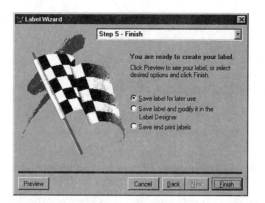

FIGURE 15.7.

A completed label design in Print Preview.

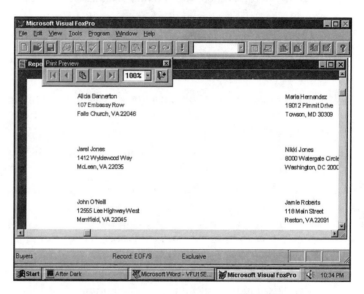

You can get to the Label Wizard from the menus as well as from the Project Manager. From the system menu bar, choose the Tools menu, Wizards option, and from the next cascading menu that appears, choose Label. The first Label Wizard dialog box appears, and you can proceed to choose the desired options in the wizard dialog boxes to design the label.

Sample Project: Creating Mailing Labels

You can see how quickly you can use the Label Wizard to create mailing labels by designing labels for the members in the Buyers table. To try this, perform the following steps:

1. Start the Project Manager that contains the table you wish to use if it is not already open.

2. Click the Documents tab, select the Label icon, and then click the New Label Wizard button (shown previously in Figure 15.1).

3. In the Select a Database/Table list box, choose Members.DBF and press the Next button. (See Figure 15.2.)

4. The next frame of the Label Wizard dialog box (as shown in Figure 15.3) asks which label size you want to use. Click the English option, select the Avery 4143 label in the list box, and then click the Next button.

5. The next frame of the Label Wizard dialog box (shown previously in Figure 15.4) is used to lay out the design of the label. Double-click the First Name field, click the Space button, and then double-click the Last Name field.

6. Click the Return/Enter button to begin another line in the label.

7. Double-click the Address button, and then click the Return/Enter button.

8. Scroll down in the list box and double-click the City field.

9. Click the Comma button, then click the Space button, and then double-click the State field.

10. Click the Space button, and then double-click the Zip field. The layout window should resemble Figure 15.4. Finally, click the Next button.

11. The next frame of the Label Wizard dialog box (shown previously in Figure 15.5) asks which field you want to sort by. Double-click the Zip field in the list box and then click the Next button.

12. The last frame of the Label Wizard dialog box appears and asks whether you want to save the report for later use, save and print the report, or make further changes to the design. If you want to see the labels but not print them, click the Preview button. When you've finished examining the labels, click OK in the Page Preview window, click the Save label for later use option in the Label Wizard dialog box, and then click Finish. If you want to print the labels, click the Save and print label option in the dialog box, and then click Finish. When prompted for a name for the report, type MEMBERS and click Save. If you choose to preview the labels, they should resemble the example shown previously in Figure 15.7.

Printing Existing Mailing Labels

Once a mailing label exists, you can print the labels using any of the following methods:

■ From the Project Manager, click the Document tab, and then click the desired label to select it. Then choose Print from the File menu, or click the Print button on the standard toolbar. The Print dialog box appears, as shown in Figure 15.8.

Click the OK button in this dialog box to print the labels.

FIGURE 15.8.

The Print dialog box.

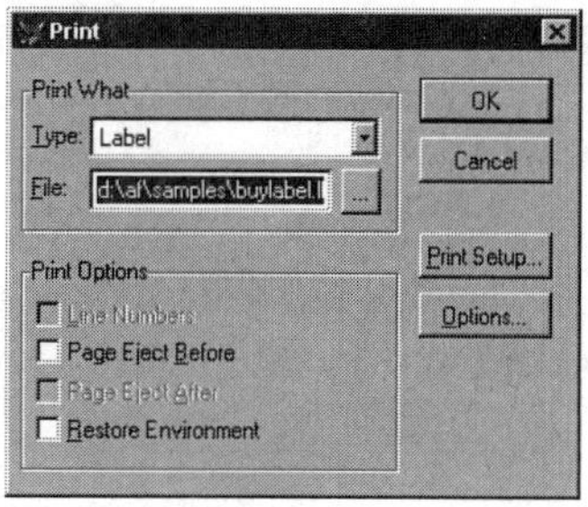

- From the File menu, choose the Print option, and the Print dialog box appears. Select the Label item from the Type list and select a Label file to print. Click the OK button in this dialog box to print the labels.

- From the command window, use the LABEL FORM command with the following basic syntax:

```
LABEL FORM label_filename [SCOPE] [FOR condition] [WHILE condition]
          [TO PRINTER [PROMPT] ¦ TO FILE filename] ¦ [PREVIEW [NOWAIT]]
          [NOCONSOLE] [NOOPTIMIZE] [SAMPLE]  [NAME ObjectName]
```

If the TO PRINTER option is used, the label is printed; otherwise, it appears on-screen in the main window of the Visual FoxPro desktop. If you specify the optional PROMPT keyword, the Printer Settings dialog box displays before printing begins. The NOCONSOLE keyword suppresses printing of labels to the screen while printing. If you specify the TO FILE clause, output is directed to the specified file instead of the printer. If you specify the PREVIEW keyword instead of the TO PRINTER or TO FILE clauses, the report displays in the Preview window. You can specify the NOWAIT keyword with the PREVIEW keyword to instruct Visual FoxPro to display the Preview window and continue executing.

You can specify an object variable name for the report's data environment with the NAME clause. You can use this name to access the methods and properties of the data environment object.

All of the clauses within the brackets, as with all commands, are optional. The SCOPE, FOR, and WHILE clauses are added to limit the records included in the mailing labels. (For a complete discussion of SCOPE, FOR, and WHILE, refer to Chapter 7, "Queries with Commands.")

You probably will want to print the labels in a certain order. To do this, you must index or sort the file before the labels are printed, so they are printed in the sorted or indexed order.

Preview Existing Mailing Labels

If you want to preview existing labels from the Project Manager, click the Documents tab and then click the desired label filename to select it. Click the Preview button, and the Preview window displays. (See Figure 15.7.)

Use Label Wizards to Speed the Manual Label Design Process

Even when you prefer to design your own labels, the Label wizards can often save time and effort by providing a label that is close to what you want. Use the wizards to create a label, and then open the label in Visual FoxPro's Label Designer tool and make any desired changes to the existing label.

Creating Mailing Labels Manually

Mailing labels can also be created manually from the command window or by using the menus. From the system menu bar, Choose File | New. In the New dialog box, click the Label option, and then click New File. From the command window, enter CREATE LABEL *filename*, where *filename* is the name under which the label will be saved. With either of these methods, the New Label dialog box appears next. (See Figure 15.9). This dialog box offers the different sizes for the labels, with heights, widths, and Avery office label numbers shown for each size.

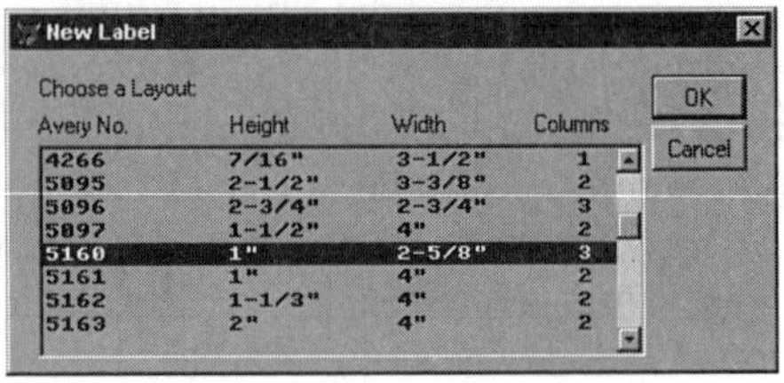

FIGURE 15.9.

The New Label dialog box.

After you choose the label size, click OK. The Label Designer then opens. Figure 15.10 shows the report layout that appears as a result of choosing Avery 5160 as a label size.

You can add fields to the design area by choosing two important toolbars: the system menu bar View menu | Layout Toolbar option to activate the Layout toolbar, and the View menu | Report Controls toolbar option to activate the Report Controls toolbar. Between these two toolbars, shown in Figure 15.10, you can design the labels the way you like using the available tools.

Because a label is just a specialized type of report with its dimensions and column layout suited for the label's size, the process of designing (adding fields, text, graphics, lines, and so on) is no different for labels than for reports. For specifics on designing reports, see Chapter 13, "Designing and Customizing Reports."

FIGURE 15.10.

The report format for Avery 5160 labels.

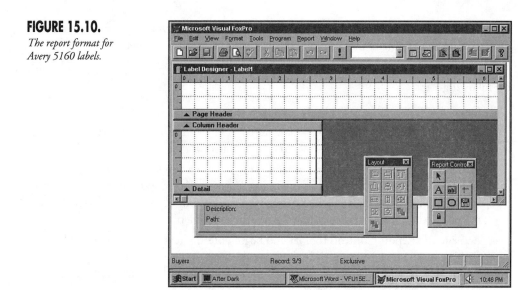

Saving Label Designs

When you have finished designing the label, save the design. To do this, choose the Save option from the File menu, and if prompted for a name, enter the desired filename. (If you named the label as part of a CREATE LABEL command when you started the process, Visual FoxPro does not ask for a label name.)

Modifying Labels

To modify an existing label, you have two options: use the command MODIFY LABEL *filename* or from the Project Manager, choose the name of the label and double-click it to activate it and open the Label Designer. Then make the needed changes. Either method causes the report design window to appear, containing the label's layout. Double-click the desired field to display the Expression Builder, which enables you to make the desired changes to the fields in the label. You can use the techniques detailed in Chapter 12, "Designing and Customizing Forms," to move fields or add lines and graphics. When you have made the desired changes, choose File | Save to save your changes.

Designing Form Letters

In many cases when you create form letters, it is necessary to export a file for use with a word processor. Visual FoxPro has an advantage here because it enables you to create form letters without leaving Visual FoxPro. You can do this by designing reports that serve as form letters. First, increase the size of the Detail band in the Report Writer Window. Then enter the text of the letter and the necessary fields within the band. You can add fields as needed within the letter. A Summary band should be added at the bottom, and the New Page option should be turned on for the Summary band so each record prints on a different page.

To have a better understanding of how this works, you can create an example form letter with the following steps:

1. Open the Buyers table to begin the example.

2. Create a new report by entering CREATE REPORT LETTER1 in the command window. (You need to maximize the window to see the entire work area.)

3. At the left edge of the Page Header band is the sizing rectangle. Click the rectangle and drag it upward to the top of the window. Also, at the left edge of the Detail band is another sizing rectangle; click and drag it to the bottom of the window to increase the size of the Detail band to accommodate the text of letter.

4. Activate the Report Controls toolbar and begin entering text in the Detail area by clicking on the text tool to activate it. Click the Text tool to begin entering text. About an inch and a half from the top of the window and a half-inch from the left margin enter the date, and then click outside the date to deselect it.

5. Click the Field tool and just below the date, click and drag to form a box roughly $^1/_4$-inch high and 1-inch long. When you release the mouse, the Report Expression dialog box appears.

6. Click the button next to the Expression entry box and open the Expression Builder. Enter the following in the Expression for Field on Report text box:

   TRIM(FIRSTNAME)+"," + LASTNAME

   The previous expression causes the contents of the Firstname field to appear trimmed of blank spaces and the contents of the Lastname field to appear with a leading space.

7. Click OK twice to close the two dialog boxes. Align the new field with the text. (You may want to turn off the Report|Snap to Grid menu option to make aligning the field easier.)

8. Click the Field tool again and click and drag a rectangle $^1/_4$-inch high and $2 ^1/_2$-inches long. Again when the mouse is released, the Report Expression dialog box appears.

9. Click the button next to the Expression Entry box to open the Expression Builder, and double-click the Address field in the Fields list box to place it in the Expression for Field text box.

10. Click OK twice to close the two dialog boxes, and then align the new field with the Name field.

    To add the City, State, and Zip fields to the report, you need to create another field using the Field tool from the toolbar. Make the field roughly $^1/_4$-inch high and 2-inches long. In the Expression for Field on Report text box, enter

    TRIM(CITY) + ", " + STATE + " " + ZIP

This command causes the information to appear in the standard city-state-zip code format.

Now, the remainder of the job is to enter the text portion of the form letter. Click the Text tool, then click below the field you just placed and enter the following:

```
Valued Member:
We thank you for your recent order and prompt payment. At
this time we would like to encourage you to renew your
membership. As the year comes to a close, just for your
renewal you will receive free, the book of your choice.
```

Click outside the text, and then click the Text tool again to select it. Click just below the paragraph you just typed to start another paragraph, and type the rest of the text shown here:

```
A friend may also be encouraged to join and receive the
selection of the month absolutely free. And for encouraging
a friend to join, you will receive the next two monthly
selections free. So act today to take advantage of this offer.
```

In this example, the two paragraphs are entered separately because Visual FoxPro imposes a limit of 255 characters in any single text object.

Finally, from the system menu bar, choose Report | Data Grouping, and in the dialog box that appears add the Custid field and turn on the New Page option to print each record on an separate page. At this point, you can save the report and print the form letters at any time by running the report. This technique for generating form letters works well if the letters are short and if being able to easily edit the form letters is not of prime importance; this is also useful if no rich text formatting is needed. With long letters, or with letters that must be repeatedly edited, you are better off creating merge files that can be used with your favorite word processor, as described in the sections that follow.

Exporting Data for Use in Word Processing

One of the common tasks that requires an exchange of data is the creation of form letters or other documents in word processing, based on data stored in Visual FoxPro. This part of the chapter examines how users of word processing can use Visual FoxPro data to create print merge documents (also known as "form letters"). You can export data from a Visual FoxPro table or query in a variety of formats.

Creating a Print Merge in Word for Windows

The following steps required to set up a merge for word processing are general. However, because users of Visual FoxPro often have a preference for other Microsoft products, the exercise that follows it is designed for Word for Windows.

1. Check the word processor's manual. Almost all word processing programs will merge data from other programs, but the preferred format varies not only with the product you have, but with the *version* of the word processor you intend to use.

2. Use the system menu bar File | Export option in Visual FoxPro to export data for word processing. In the dialog box that appears when you choose this option, change the data type to the one required by your word processing program.

3. If your word processing program (like WordPerfect for DOS) has a conversion program to change data to merge input, run the conversion program.

4. In your word processing program, follow the instructions for setting up the rest of the merge job.

An Example of a Print Merge Operation

Microsoft Word for Windows (versions 2.0, 6.0, and 7.0) will link directly to a Visual FoxPro file and pull all the variable information directly from the file. If your Visual FoxPro file is a large one and you want to select only some records or some fields, you can use the COPY TO command to copy only the data you need.

To demonstrate how you can use Visual FoxPro data along with the Print Merge facility in Word for Windows, the following exercise helps you combine a Visual FoxPro file (created by exporting the data in the Buyers table) with a main document (created within Word for Windows) to generate form letters. Open the Members table if it is not already open and perform these steps:

1. Choose the File menu Export option. The Export dialog box appears (see Figure 15.11).

FIGURE 15.11.

The Export, Export Options, and Field Picker dialog boxes.

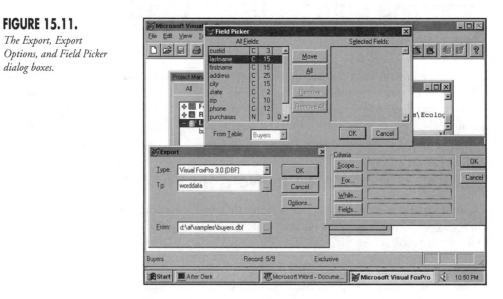

2. In the From box, enter the filename from which you want to export. Next click the Options button, and the Export Options dialog box appears. (See Figure 15.11.) Enter the criteria for your export operation. Click the Fields button, and the Field Picker dialog box appears, which is also shown in Figure 15.11. You can choose the fields you wish to export. Double-click the following fields: Lastname, Firstname, Address, City, State, and Zip. Click OK.

3. Enter the directory and filename of the target file in the To text box. Name the target file WORDDATA.DBF. You can click the browser button (...) at the right of the box to help you locate the target file's directory.

4. Click the OK button in the Export dialog box to perform the export operation and create the new file.

With the data exported, you can now proceed to the following steps, where you will attach the Visual FoxPro file and create the main document containing the form letter itself. Use standard Windows techniques to switch to Word for Windows 6.0 and perform the following steps.

1. Choose the Mail Merge option from the Tools menu. The version 6.0 Mail Merge screen appears as shown in Figure 15.12.

FIGURE 15.12.

The Mail Merge Helper dialog box.

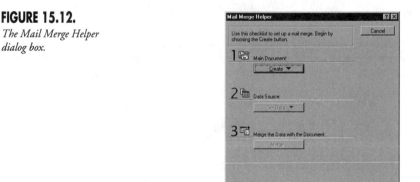

2. Click the Create button and a list of options appears. Click the Mailing Labels option from the list, and then next click the Active document button from the dialog box that appears. Next, click the Get data button and Choose Open Data Source. A dialog box appears showing all document files in the current directory.

3. Type worddata.dbf, the file you created earlier in Visual FoxPro, to select it. Then click OK.

4. Press Enter twice, and then click the Insert Merge Field button in the toolbar. In the list box of fields that appears, double-click Firstname.

5. Add a space, and then click the Insert Merge Field button again. In the list box, double-click Lastname, and then press Enter.

352

6. Click the Insert Merge Field button. In the list box, double-click Address, and then press Enter.

7. Click the Insert Merge Field button. In the list box, double-click City, and then add a comma and a space.

8. Click the Insert Merge Field button. In the list box, double-click State, and then add a space.

9. Click the Insert Merge Field button. In the list box, double-click Zip, and then press Enter.

10. Press Enter twice. Type the following text, using the Insert Merge Field button on the toolbar to add the named fields in the locations indicated:

```
You may have won $12 billion dollars! Surely you can only dream
of what you and the <<Lastname>> family would do with $12 billion
dollars! That trip to Spain... A new car... an entire car
dealership... the space shuttle Atlantis... your very own savings
and loan... all this and more can belong to the <<Lastname>> family
of <<City>>, <<State>>.
```

11. With the letter completed, choose the Tools | Mail Merge option and click the Merge button, or choose the Merge to Printer button on the Mailmerge toolbar. In the Print Merge Setup dialog box, click Merge. This causes the Print Merge dialog box to appear.

12. Click the Merge to Printer option to select it and to print the form letters. You can also click the Merge to New Document option to select it if you want to see the form letters in a separate document. (You could then save this document and print it later, using the usual techniques under Word for Windows.)

Using the Mail Merge Wizard

If you are using Word for Windows, Word for DOS, or another word processor, you can create exported files that can be used with your word processor to perform a mail merge, using the Mail Merge Wizard provided by Visual FoxPro. The Mail Merge Wizard takes a Visual FoxPro table and uses it to create a data file that can be used by your particular word processor. You can then follow the steps that are appropriate for your word processor to merge this data file with a main document such as a form letter, labels, or a series of envelopes. You can use the following steps to generate a data file with the Mail Merge Wizard:

1. Open the desired table that will supply the data for the mail merge (enter USE *filename* in the command window or choose Wizard | Mail Merge from the Tools menu). (See Figure 15.13.) The next box asks you to choose the table and fields you wish to use.

FIGURE 15.13.

The first frame of the Mail Merge Wizard dialog box.

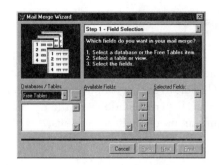

2. After choosing which table and fields you want to use, you will see the box that prompts you to enter a word processor that you want to use. Enter Word 6.0 or use a comma-delimited file. The next screen lets you create a new main document or select a main document that was created earlier. (If you need to create a main document, click the Create New Document option, then click Next to continue.) If you created a main document previously, click the Use Existing Document option and enter a filename, or click the File button to open the document, and then click Next. At this point, the wizard will skip to step 5.

3. If you are using Word for Windows 6.0 and you choose to create a new main document, you are next asked to specify the type and name of the main document you will be using in the following box. Choose the type of Word 6.0 main document you want to create: form letter, label, envelope, or catalog. (See your Word documentation for more details about these options.)

4. Click Finish. If you are using Word for Windows 2.0 or 6.0, choosing the Finish button starts Microsoft Word, and you can continue with the mail merge process. (Note: If your computer does not have enough memory to run Visual FoxPro and Word at the same time, you will not be able to use this wizard.) If you are using another word processor, choosing the Finish button displays Visual FoxPro's Save As dialog box. You can enter a name and click Save to save the source document as a data file. Next, switch to your word processor and use the document you created as a data source for the mail merge.

Regardless of which method you use to generate the form letters, keep in mind that the data file exported from Visual FoxPro is a snapshot of the data that existed at the time you exported the data. If you are generating form letters on a regular basis, you need to export the source of the data each time you want to generate form letters to be sure that you have the most accurate data as the basis for your form letters.

Summary

This chapter has detailed how features of Visual FoxPro can be used to implement mail-merge operations quickly. One point to keep in mind is that if you use other Windows word processors, you may be able to use the techniques outlined in this chapter that apply to your particular word processor. Experimentation with these techniques, in conjunction with your preferred word processor, can produce effective results.

PART

Extending Visual FoxPro

Leveraging FoxPro Power Using Wizards

16

You have already been introduced to the idea of wizards in earlier chapters. In Chapter 3 you worked with the Table Wizard to create DBF tables; in Chapter 6 the Query Wizard was described. Chapters 9 and 12 dealt with the Form Wizard, and Chapters 10 and 13 talked about the Report Wizard. In Chapter 15 both the Label and Mail Merge Wizards were used.

This chapter examines the PivotTable, Import, Documenting, and Setup Wizards. The Documenting and Setup Wizards are available in the Professional Edition of Visual FoxPro only; therefore, if you don't have the Professional version, you won't be able to use those two wizards. A brief description of each of these wizards is given in the following discussion, and a full explanation of the wizards and their uses is discussed in each of the following sections.

The PivotTable Wizard works in conjunction with Microsoft Excel to produce a spreadsheet that summarizes your data. You must have Microsoft Excel and Microsoft Query, which comes with Microsoft Excel, installed on your machine in order to use the PivotTable Wizard.

You can use the Import Wizard to bring data from other applications into Visual FoxPro tables. Various file formats are supported for applications that have data files that Visual FoxPro cannot directly read. This Wizard can also import ASCII text files of various formats.

You can use the Documenting Wizard to produce technical documentation for your Visual FoxPro applications.

Finally, the Setup Wizard can be used to produce distribution disks for installing your application.

Let's look at each of these wizards in more detail.

PivotTable Wizard

Visual FoxPro's PivotTable Wizard works with Microsoft Excel and Microsoft Query to produce a crosstab type of spreadsheet. A crosstab table is similar to the mileage charts you have seen with some road maps. With those mileage charts, you locate your city of origin on the top row and then find the city of destination on the first column; the cell where the column and row intersect tells you the mileage between those two cities. With a crosstab you have one variable across the top (X), another down the left side (Y), and one variable for the intersecting cells (Z). You locate the values for X and Y and then find the Z value in the intersecting cell in the table.

Any three fields in Visual FoxPro can be used to produce a crosstab table making one field the top row, one field the first column, and the last field the intersection data. *PivotTables* take this process a step further. Excel enables you to have multiple sheets in a book (see the Microsoft Excel documentation for more information on this). The PivotTable in Excel can use four fields of data and can use the extra field to represent which sheet the intersection lies on, producing a three-dimensional crosstab.

Once the Excel PivotTable is created, you can drag and drop the fields to rearrange the view of the data. The actual use of the PivotTable is controlled by Microsoft Excel; therefore, this section only covers the use of the Visual FoxPro PivotTable Wizard to create a PivotTable and does not cover the subsequent use of that PivotTable. You should refer to the Microsoft Excel documentation to learn more about how to tap the power of a PivotTable.

The DBF File

To create a PivotTable, you need to use a Visual FoxPro table. The structure for the demo table is shown in Figure 16.1.

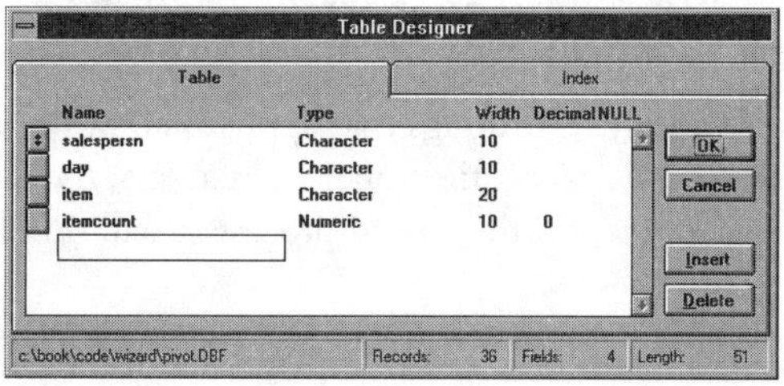

FIGURE 16.1.

The structure for the demo table.

You will use the demo table in Figure 16.1 to create a PivotTable in Excel that has each salesperson on a different sheet, each item on a row, and each day of the week as a column. The item count will be in the intersection cells.

Your example table has two sales counts for each item for each salesperson on each day. Now, let's run the PivotTable Wizard and see how it works.

Field Selection

From the Visual FoxPro system menu, select Tools | Wizards | PivotTable (see Figure 16.2).

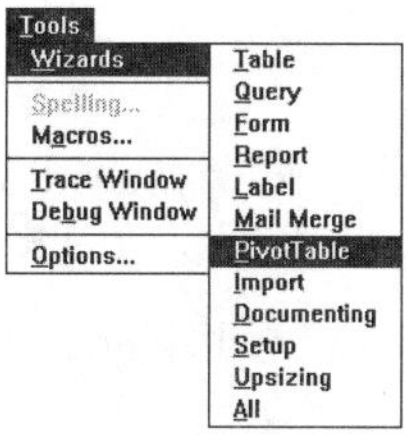

FIGURE 16.2.

The PivotTable Wizard is available from the Visual FoxPro Tools menu.

The first dialog box you see is the Field Selection step of the PivotTable Wizard, as shown in Figure 16.3.

FIGURE 16.3.

The Field Selection dialog box of the PivotTable Wizard.

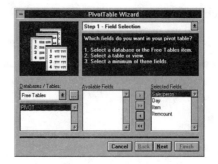

The Field Selection dialog box enables you to select which table or view you want to build your PivotTable from, as well as which fields you want included in the PivotTable.

There are some general things that apply to all of the wizards in Visual FoxPro. First among these is the combo box at the upper-right area of the dialog box. This combo box enables you to jump to any step in the wizard process at will simply by selecting the step from the drop-down list.

Just below this combo box is an explanation of the current step in the wizard; all of the wizards' dialog boxes will give you this information in the same location.

Finally, at the bottom right of the dialog box are a set of command buttons to Cancel, go Back one dialog box in the wizard, go to the Next dialog, or Finish the wizard. These buttons will be enabled and disabled according to the context of the wizard. You won't be able to select to Finish the wizard until you have completed all of the required steps.

In the dialog box in Figure 16.3, the example table, named Pivot, and all of the fields in that table have been selected (they are in the third list of selected fields). You must select at least three fields to produce a PivotTable, but you can choose four to get the three-dimensional PivotTable that was described earlier. For this example, you will produce a three-dimensional PivotTable.

Layout

After you click the Next button, you will see the dialog in Figure 16.4. In this dialog box, you have already assigned your fields to the respective layout positions you want.

You make the assignments by clicking on the field you want and then dragging the field to the layout option desired.

FIGURE 16.4.
You have assigned the fields to the layout positions you want.

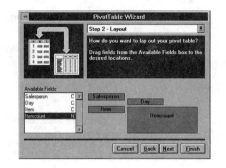

Finish

Next, you need to choose the options you want on the Finish dialog, which is shown in Figure 16.5.

FIGURE 16.5.
Selecting the options for your finished PivotTable.

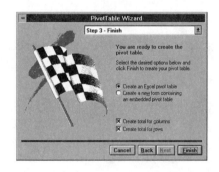

In this dialog, you can decide to create an Excel file with your PivotTable or you can create a Visual FoxPro form that contains your PivotTable as an OLE object. For this example, select to create the Excel sheet. Also, you can choose to total the rows, columns, both, or neither with the check boxes toward the bottom of the dialog. You will total both the rows and columns.

Finally, you can click the Finish button and then see your Excel sheet. When you click the Finish button, you will see the Save As dialog box. Use this dialog box to give the form a name (choose the default, which is the same name as the table from which you built the PivotTable).

This chapter was written during the beta of Visual FoxPro, and at that time the ODBC drivers for the Visual FoxPro 3.0 table were not yet available. If you don't have those drivers, you will see the message box in Figure 16.6 after you have selected a name for your form.

If you choose not to let the data be copied, you will not be able to complete your PivotTable. Select Yes from this message box to complete the PivotTable.

The Save As dialog box will be displayed to enable you to name the FoxPro 2.*x* DBF file. Visual FoxPro will next launch Microsoft Excel to produce the PivotTable. In Figure 16.7, the result of your PivotTable creation is displayed.

FIGURE 16.6.

Visual FoxPro will offer to copy your data to a FoxPro 2.x DBF format if the Visual FoxPro 3.0 ODBC drivers are not available.

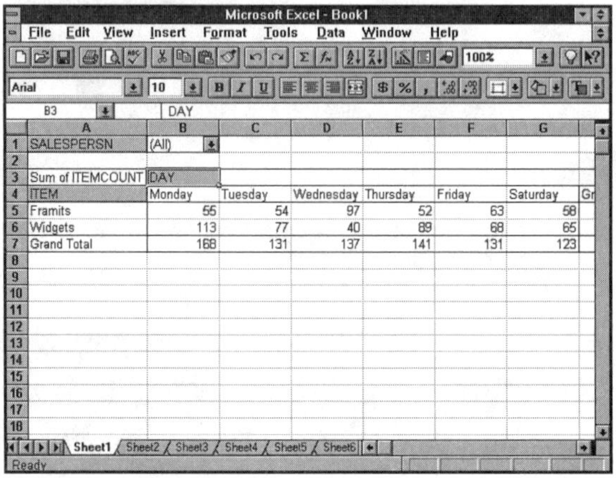

FIGURE 16.7.

The finished Excel PivotTable for your data.

You can use the combo box at the top left to see the various salespersons. The rows and columns are set up as you specified in your wizard dialogs. The real power of PivotTables is that you can now change the information layout by dragging and dropping. Try this; drag the button for DAY to the position of ITEM, and then drag ITEM to where DAY was before. You should see a sheet similar to the one in Figure 16.8. You have pivoted your table. You can drag SALESPERSON as well to change the table again.

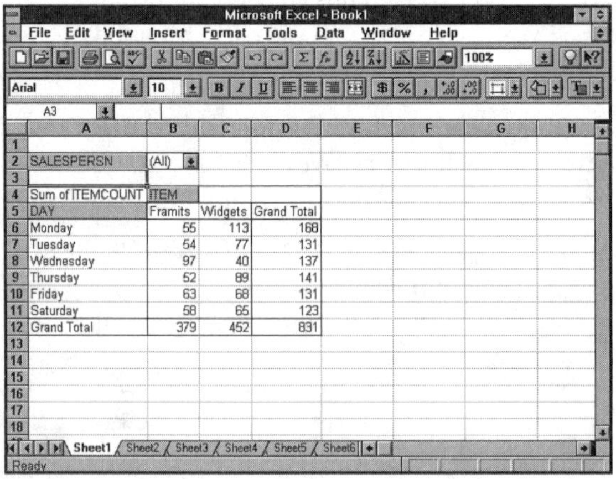

FIGURE 16.8.

Your PivotTable has been pivoted by simply dragging and dropping.

Import Wizard

The capability to get data into Visual FoxPro tables from other file types is greatly simplified through the Import Wizard. This wizard enables you to import data from a variety of different file types including

Text Files
Microsoft Excel 5.0 (XLS)
Microsoft Excel 2.0, 3.0, 4.0 (XLS)
Lotus 1-2-3 3.*x* (WK3)
Lotus 1-2-3 2.*x* (WK1)
Lotus 1-2-3 1.*x* (WKS)
Paradox 3.5, 4.0 (DB)
Lotus Symphony 1.10 (WR1)
Lotus Symphony 1.01 (WRK)
Multiplan (MOD)
Rapid File (RPD)

Now, you will import a text file that is comma-delimited.

Source and Destination Files

Start the Import Wizard by selecting Tools | Wizards | Import Wizard. The first dialog is shown in Figure 16.9.

FIGURE 16.9.

The first dialog of the Visual FoxPro Import Wizard.

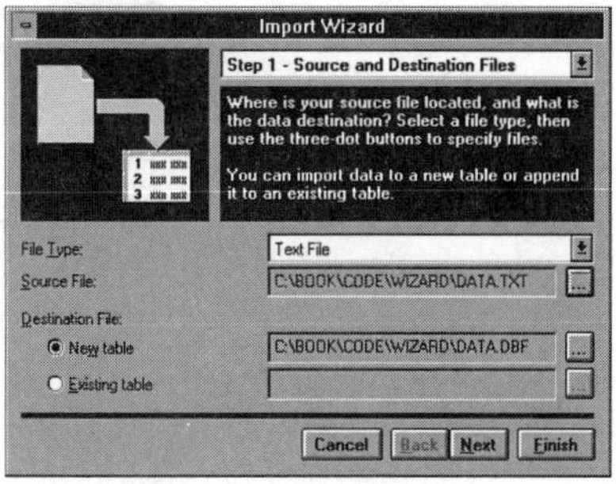

The combo box at the top right of this dialog, like all the wizard dialogs, enables you to jump to a specific step in the process. This wizard has four steps numbered 1, 1a, 2, and 3.

You also see the description of this step below the combo box. The lower portion of this dialog box is where you designate the source file, the type of source file, and the destination file for the import process. You have set the source file type to Text and then identified the file named Data.TXT as the one you want to import. The destination is set to create a new DBF table named Data.DBF.

NOTE

The Visual FoxPro wizard will default the name of a new destination file to be the same as the source file with a DBF extension added in place of the original extension. You can override this by typing the name you want into the text box.

TIP

To select both the source and destination files, you can use the ellipsis button (...) to the right of the respective text box. This will get you to the Visual FoxPro File Open dialog box. The file you select in that dialog box will become the file for the source or destination.

Options

The next step in the process is to set the options for your import process. Figure 16.10 shows you the Step 1a - Options dialog of the Import Wizard.

FIGURE 16.10.

Step 1a - Options of the Import Wizard.

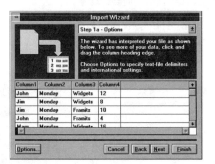

This dialog shows you how Visual FoxPro is seeing the data in your source file. The records are in rows, and the fields are in columns. The command button labeled Options is where you can do your magic in this dialog. Clicking the Options button brings up the Import Wizard Options dialog box seen in Figure 16.11.

In this dialog box, you can specify how the text file you want to import is structured. The two general structures are represented by the radio buttons in the upper-left corner of the dialog box; these are fixed-field length or delimited. Fixed-field-length text files are sometimes called SDF files because that is the file extension most often used for them. (The SDF stands for Standard Data Format.) In these SDF files, the fields are all the same length down a column, and the records are separated by a carriage return and line feed pair of characters (CRLF).

Leveraging FoxPro Power Using Wizards

Chapter 16

365

FIGURE 16.11

The Import Wizard Options diolog box from the Step 1a–Options dialog.

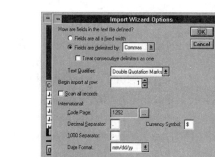

The delimited text file has fields that vary in length, but every field is delimited (or separated) from the next by the delimiter character. In the Import Wizard Options dialog box, you can specify the delimiter character as either commas, tabs, or semicolons. For your example, leave the defaults for a delimited file because that is the structure of your text data.

The Text Qualifier is referring to the character that surrounds the character type data in the file, as in the default double quotes. This is the structure of your data source. The choices you have here are Double Quotation Marks, Single Quotation Marks, or None. An example of two text file records with your formatting is shown here:

```
"John","Monday","Widgets",12
"Mary","Tuesday","Framits",15
```

Notice the quotes around the character strings and the commas separating each field of data. Also, the records each end with a carriage return and line feed pair.

For contrast, see the following example of the same two records in a fixed field length text file:

```
John       Monday     Widgets      12
Mary       Tuesday    Framits      15
```

In this format, notice that each field lines up with the same field in the rows below or above it.

The spinner next to the label "Begin import at row" enables you to make a record other than the first one become the first record in your DBF table. When you import a spreadsheet file, you can use this to eliminate the headings row from your data.

You can use the "Scan all records" check box to tell the Import Wizard to scan all of the records in the source file before the Wizard determines the size to make the fields in the destination file. This can be a time-consuming process on very large files. If this check box is not checked, the Import Wizard will scan only the first 50 records to make its determination.

TIP

If you are using the delimited type of text file, it is wise to check "Scan all records" to be sure the fields in your destination table are set up wide enough to hold all the data in the text file.

The rest of the options in this dialog box are explained in the following list:

Code Page	Use this option to specify the code page with which the source file was created. See Chapter 21, "Power Techniques for Power Users," for a discussion of code pages and their meanings.
Decimal Separator	Specify the decimal point character used in the source file. Some countries use characters other than the U.S.'s period (.).
1000 Separator	Specify the thousands separated in numbers in the source file. Again, some countries use a period rather than the U.S.'s comma.
Date Format	Specify the format for the dates in the source file.
Currency Symbol	Specify the currency symbol used in the source file.

NOTE

The previously listed decimal separator, 1000 separator, date format, and currency symbol can affect the data you are importing if the source file was created in a country other than yours. These settings affect the Numeric, Currency, Date, DateTime, and Integer data types. You will be setting the data types in the next step. Make sure that you specify the proper settings for these options or your data may surprise you.

Columns

If you are importing a fixed-length text file, Step 1a will be titled Columns, as shown in Figure 16.12.

FIGURE 16.12.

The Step 1a - Columns dialog for handling fixed-length text files.

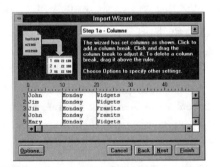

The vertical lines in the grid on this dialog mark the separation of the fields in your resulting DBF table after the import. You can add a separator by clicking the mouse in the grid where you want the separator to appear. You can move a separator by dragging it from where it is to where you want it to be. Finally, you can remove a line by dragging it to above the ruler at the top of the grid.

Field Settings

Returning to the comma-delimited text file, you can see the Step 2 - Field Settings dialog in Figure 16.13.

FIGURE 16.13.

The Step 2 - Field Settings dialog of the Import Wizard.

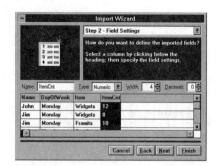

The grid shows you the data in the delimited file. You use controls above the grid to set your options for each field. To select a field, click the data in the grid. Then you can set up the field name, data type, width, and decimals as appropriate for the selected data type. Do this for each field in the grid. Then choose the Next button to get to the Finish dialog.

Field Mappings

If in Step 1 - Source and Destination Files you had selected to use an existing DBF file to import into, Step 2 would be Field Mappings instead of Field Settings. Figure 16.14 shows this dialog.

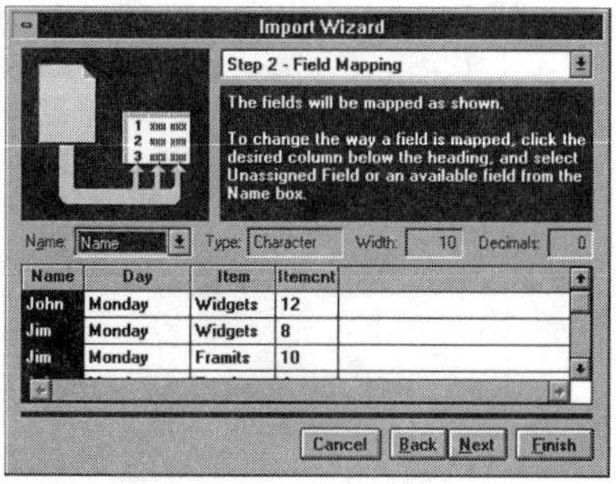

FIGURE 16.14.

The Step 2 dialog is slightly different if you are importing to an existing DBF table.

The only difference here is that your only option in the controls above the grid is to set the field name into which you want a column's data to be placed.

Finish

At last, you reach the finish line. This dialog is the last thing in your wizard process, and it has only one choice for you to make: finish the import, go back to the previous step, or cancel the import. Figure 16.15 shows this dialog.

FIGURE 16.15.

The Finish dialog of the Import Wizard.

Documenting Wizard

The Documenting Wizard is used to produce technical documentation for an application or program file. This wizard is very flexible regarding what documentation you want to produce and how you want that information formatted. For your example documentation, you will be using the Controls.PJX project, which can be found in the \SAMPLES\CONTROLS directory under your main Visual FoxPro directory.

You will examine this wizard in three parts: first, you will learn the uses and outputs of the wizard; second, you will run the wizard on the Controls.PJX file and examine the documentation produced; and third, you will learn advanced customization through the use of document directives and modifying the FdKeyword.DBF file.

Uses and Outputs of the Documenting Wizard

The Documenting Wizard can be used to perform a number of different analyses on your projects or programs. It can produce reports, in the form of text files, that show you the structure of your application in different ways. It can also apply formatting to your program code based on options that you designate in the wizard's dialogs.

The reports that can be produced with this wizard are the following:

Action Diagram — Filename: *<ProjectName>*.ACT. A hierarchical diagram showing the calling tree for the programs and procedures within your project.

Cross Reference — Filename: XREF.LST. Lists all of the user-defined symbols (see following listing of meanings for FDXREF.DBF).

File Listing — Filename: FILES.LST. A listing of all of the files in the project.

Source Code — Filename: *<ProjectName>*.LST. All of your source code in a single file.

Tree Diagram — Filename: TREE.LST. The procedure calling tree diagram.

All of the reports listed in the preceding list can be optionally turned off for any given run of the wizard.

The wizard also produces the following additional files that can be very helpful in analyzing your application:

FILES.DBF   A Visual FoxPro DBF table that contains one record for each file in your project.

FDXREF.DBF   A Visual FoxPro DBF table that contains one record for each instance of a user symbol in your project.

FILES.DBF has the structure shown in Table 16.1. Each of the fields is explained in the Comment column of the table.

Table 16.1. The structure of FILES.DBF as produced by the Documenting Wizard.

Field Name	Type	Width	Comment
FILETYPE	C	1	A code used by the wizard.
FLAGS	C	1	A code used by the wizard.
FILE	C	161	The name of the file.
DONE	C	1	A code used by the wizard.

The FDXREF.DBF table is shown in Table 16.2.

Table 16.2. The structure of FDXREF.DBF as produced by the Documenting Wizard.

Field Name	Type	Width	Comment
SYMBOL	C	65	The symbol to which this record refers.
PROCNAME	C	40	The procedure in which this symbol is found.
FLAG	C	1	A code identifying the type of symbol this is (explained in Table 16.3).
LINENO	N	5	The line number on which this symbol is located.
SNIPRECNO	N	5	The record number in FILENAME where this reference is found.
SNIPFLD	C	10	The field name in FILENAME where this reference is found.

continues

Table 16.2. continued

Field Name	Type	Width	Comment
SNIPLINENO	N	5	The line number for this reference within SNIPFLD.
ADJUST	N	5	A field that is used by the wizard.
FILENAME	C	161	The name of the file within which this reference is found.

The codes used in the Flag field of FDXREF.DBF are explained in Table 16.3. The C and N in the Type column mean Character and Numeric, respectively.

Table 16.3. The codes used in the Flag field of FDXREF.DBF.

Flag	Description
B	A base class definition
C	A class name
D	A user-defined procedure or function (does not include methods)
F	A function call, as in `MyProc()` or `DO MyProc`
K	A keyword
M	A method definition (does include `PROCEDURE`s or `FUNCTION`s)
N	The name of a file
O	An object reference
P	Reference to a property of an object
R	A user symbol reference
V	A user symbol (or variable) definition (`PARAMETERS`, `PRIVATE`, `PUBLIC`, `DIMENSION`)

Finally, you can have the wizard write out a set of program files for you that have been formatted according to your selections. These formatted program files can be placed in a single directory of your choice, or you can tell the wizard to create a new directory for them. If you are adventurous, you can even tell the wizard to overwrite your existing program files with the new formatted ones.

CAUTION

It is not a good idea to let any program automatically overwrite the only copy of your code. Before you ever let the Documenting Wizard overwrite your program code, be sure you have made a backup copy first.

Running the Documenting Wizard

You start the Documenting Wizard the same way you start the other wizards. Select Tools | Wizards | Documenting.

Source File

In the first dialog (Figure 16.16), you designate the name of the project or program that you want to document. You can either type the path and name in the text box or click the ellipsis (…), which will bring you to the Visual FoxPro Open File dialog box that you can use to find the file you want.

FIGURE 16.16.

The source file selection dialog of the Documenting Wizard.

Capitalization

Once you have set up the file you want, click the Next button to open the Capitalization dialog, shown in Figure 16.17.

FIGURE 16.17.

The Capitalization dialog of the Documenting Wizard.

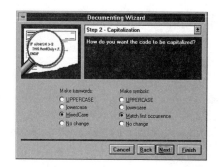

In this dialog, you tell the wizard how you want your source code to be capitalized. You can control the capitalization of *keywords* and *symbols* in the code. The keywords are the Visual FoxPro reserved words, and the symbols are the names and variables that you define.

For keywords, you can choose between UPPERCASE (shift all keywords to all uppercase), lowercase (shift all keywords to lowercase), MixedCase (make all keywords mixed case), or No change (leave the keywords alone).

For symbols, you can choose the same options except for the mixed-case option. Instead of this option, you have a Match first occurrence option, which will change all occurrences of the symbol to match the capitalization of the first occurrence of that symbol.

Indentation

Choose the Next button to move to the Indentation dialog in Figure 16.18. In this dialog, you set up the method you want the wizard to use for indenting your source code programs. You can affect certain aspects of the code in terms of the indentation by using the options Comments, Control structures, and Lines continued by a semi-colon.

FIGURE 16.18.

The Indentation dialog of the Documenting Wizard.

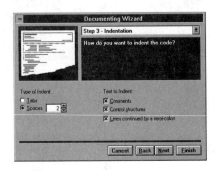

You also designate whether you want tabs or spaces as the indentation character. If you click the Spaces option, you can set the number of spaces to be used. In the example, the indenting has been changed from the default of Tabs to Spaces, and the number of spaces has been set to 2.

> **TIP**
>
> Using spaces rather than tabs for indenting your code can be very helpful if there are other people who will need to work with your code. Tab settings can vary from one editor to another, and using spaces will cause your code to look the same in all editors.

Headings

When you click the Next button, you go to the Headings dialog, as shown in Figure 16.19.

FIGURE 16.19.

The Headings dialog of the Documenting Wizard.

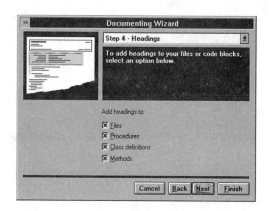

The Documenting Wizard will add headings to your source code for you. The code you can add headings to are program files, procedure and function declarations, class definitions, and method code.

These headings will include such information as the name of the item, where it is called from, what items it calls, what parameters and variables it uses, and so on. These headings can be very useful when you revisit your program code later to try to repair or enhance it.

Reports

Click the Next button to bring you to the Reports dialog, as shown in Figure 16.20. This section first tells you how to use this dialog and then it tells you the reports it sets up for you.

FIGURE 16.20.

The Reports dialog of the Documenting Wizard.

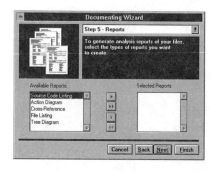

The two lists you see are used to select the reports you want to produce. It is not necessary to choose any of them if all you want is the formatted source code. The Available Reports list, on the left, shows you the reports that are available. The buttons between the two lists are used to move reports from one list to the other. The Selected Reports list, on the right, shows you the reports you have selected.

The reports that the wizard produces are actually text files. These reports are described in the "Uses and Outputs of the Documenting Wizard" section, earlier in this chapter.

Figures 16.21, 16.22, 16.23, and 16.24 show you samples of the Action Diagram, Cross Reference, File Listing, and Tree Diagram, respectively.

FIGURE 16.21.

The Action Diagram from the Documenting Wizard.

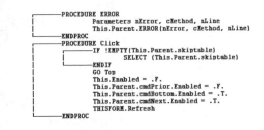

```
        ┌─PROCEDURE ERROR
        │        Parameters nError, cMethod, nLine
        │        This.Parent.ERROR(nError, cMethod, nLine)
        └─ENDPROC
        ┌─PROCEDURE Click
        │   ┌──IF !EMPTY(This.Parent.skiptable)
        │   │        SELECT (This.Parent.skiptable)
        │   └──ENDIF
        │        GO Top
        │        This.Enabled = .F.
        │        This.Parent.cmdPrior.Enabled = .F.
        │        This.Parent.cmdBottom.Enabled = .T.
        │        This.Parent.cmdNext.Enabled = .T.
        │        THISFORM.Refresh
        └─ENDPROC
```

This diagram shows you your source code with the control construct logic graphically displayed. Be sure to set your font to one of the fonts in Windows that has the line and box drawing characters, or you will see some strange characters where the lines and boxes should be. You can use FoxFont, FoxPrint, or MS Line Draw fonts to see the diagram correctly.

FIGURE 16.22.

The Cross Reference from the Documenting Wizard.

```
cmdQuit

            C       13      GRAPH.SCX
            C       31      LAUNCH.SCX
            C        5      OBJECTS.SCX
            R       51      DRAGDROP.PRG
            R       97      DRAGDROP.PRG
            R       97      DRAGDROP.PRG
            R      135      DRAGDROP.PRG
cmdRed

            R       86      FDPROC.PRG
            R      233      FDPROC.PRG
cmdRun

            C       16      MAIN.SCX
            R        2      MAIN.SCX
```

The Cross Reference shows you all of the symbols and keywords (if you selected them in the Finish dialog), the name of the program in which the symbol or keyword appears, and the code, as described earlier in Table 16.3.

FIGURE 16.23.

The File Listing from the Documenting Wizard.

```
GRAPHICS\ARWO8UP.BMP

GRAPHICS\CGRAPH.PRG

GRAPHICS\FDMAIN.SCX

GRAPHICS\FDPROC.PRG

GRAPHICS\FOXDRAW.VCX

GRAPHICS\GRAPH.SCX

GRAPHICS\PGRAPH.PRG

GRID\1_MANY.SCX

GRID\CONTROLS.SCX

GRID\GRD_PRP.SCX

HELP.BMP

HELP.MSK
```

The File Listing shows you each file that is included in your application with the path to it relative to the location of your project file.

FIGURE 16.24.

The Tree Diagram from the Documenting Wizard.

```
Class Hierarchy
checkbox
   |------Check1                      EVENTS.SCX
   |------chkAddCoords                GRAPH.SCX
   |------chkaddnums                  GRAPH.SCX
   |------chkPriceSparse              CONTROLS.SCX
   |------chkStockedSparse            CONTROLS.SCX
   |------chkDroppedSparse            CONTROLS.SCX
   |------chkItalic                   OBJECTS.SCX
   |------chkBold                     OBJECTS.SCX

container
   |------vcr                         BUTTONS.VCX
   |   |------Vcr1                     1 MANY.SCX
   |   |------Vcr1                     MULTI.SCX
   |------stopwatch                   SAMPLES.VCX
   |   |------stopwatch1               SWATCH.SCX
   |------clock                       SAMPLES.VCX
   |   |------Clock1                   CLOCK.SCX
   |------shaper                      SAMPLES.VCX
   |   |------Shaper1                  EVENTS.SCX
   |------moverlists                  SAMPLES.VCX
          |------MoverLists1           LMOVER.SCX
```

This diagram shows you the calling pattern of your code. The graphics show which procedures are called from which other procedures. Also, you get a class hierarchy showing you which subclasses inherit from which parent classes.

Finish

Figure 16.25 shows the Finish dialog of the Documenting Wizard. In this dialog, you designate where you want the formatted program code to go and whether or not you want the Visual FoxPro keywords to be included in the Cross Reference report.

FIGURE 16.25.

The Finish dialog of the Documenting Wizard.

The three choices you have for the destination of your formatted program code are Overwrite existing files (see the earlier caution), Place files in a single directory, or Place files in a new directory tree. These choices are represented by the three buttons in the option button set on the dialog, respectively.

If you choose the Place files in a single directory option, clicking the Finish button will bring you to Visual FoxPro's Open File dialog box, where you can choose the directory to be used. Choosing the Place files in a new directory tree option gets you to the Create File dialog box after you click the Finish button.

Finally, the check box at the bottom of the dialog enables you to determine if the Visual FoxPro keywords will be included in the Cross Reference report or not.

> **CAUTION**
>
> Selecting to include the Visual FoxPro keywords in your Cross Reference report can produce a very large report and can be quite time consuming.

Advanced Customization of the Documenting Wizard

You can customize certain aspects of the Documenting Wizard's behavior by using Documenting Wizard directives. You can also control the way DO CASE..ENDCASE constructs are indented by changing a record in the FDKEYWORD.DBF table.

Customizing *DO CASE..ENDCASE* Indentation

Some programmers like the CASE lines indented under the DO CASE, and others do not. By default, the Documenting Wizard will not indent the CASE lines in your code. If you prefer that these lines be indented, you can make the wizard do this for you by opening the FDKEYWORD.DBF table found in the WIZARDS directory under your main Visual FoxPro directory and by changing one field of one record.

Open the FDKEYWORD.DBF table with the USE command and then issue the BROWSE command in the Command Window. Find the record for ENDCASE in the Token field and change the code from U to UU. That will cause the Documenting Wizard to indent your CASE lines within the DO CASE..ENDCASE construct.

Using Documenting Wizard Directives

You can place commands for the Documenting Wizard in your program code to control various behaviors of the wizard. These commands are called *documenting directives*, and they can really enhance the value of your documentation.

These directives are described in detail in the following paragraphs. Each paragraph is preceded by an example of the directive described in the text.

**# document ACTIONCHARS "abcdef"*

When the Documenting Wizard creates an action diagram or a tree diagram, it uses the line and box drawing characters of the ASCII IBM-US character set (ASCII code page 1250, ANSI code page 1252) to draw the lines and boxes. These character codes are mapped to different characters when the ASCII code page is not 1250 or the ANSI code page is not 1252 (if you are using ANSI).

The codes used by the Documenting Wizard are listed in Table 16.4.

Table 16.4. The codes used in the **# document* ACTIONCHARS **directive.**

Code	Default chr() Value Used
a	32
b	196
c	179
d	218
e	192
f	195

TIP

If you are using code pages other than ASCII 1250 or ANSI 1252, be sure to use the following directive to get tree diagrams and action diagrams that have lines that look like lines:

```
*# document ACTIONCHARS " -¦+++"
```

**# document* XREF ON/OFF/SUSPENDED

This line turns a cross referencing of variables on or off. The default setting is ON. ON enables cross referencing, OFF disables cross referencing, and SUSPENDED disables the cross referencing only for the file that the directive appears in.

**# document* EXPANDKEYWORDS ON/OFF/SUSPENDED

This code controls the expansion of abbreviated keywords. Visual FoxPro keywords can be abbreviated to the first four characters of their name; for example, MODIFY can be used as MODI. The Documenting Wizard can expand these abbreviations to their full word. Set this directive ON to expand keywords, OFF to disable the expansion, and SUSPENDED to disable expansion only for the file the directive appears in. The default is OFF.

CAUTION

Although all keywords in Visual FoxPro can be abbreviated to their first four letters, not all keywords have a unique four-letter abbreviation. For example, REPLACE and REPLICATE both abbreviate to REPL. Be careful if you choose to enable keyword expansion that you do not choose to overwrite your files.

*# document XREFKEYWORDS ON/OFF/SUSPENDED

This directive does the same thing that the check box on the Finish dialog does. It enables you to include or exclude the Visual FoxPro keywords from the cross reference report. ON, OFF, and SUSPENDED work just like the previous directives. The default is OFF.

*# document ARRAYBRACKETS ON/OFF

Arrays can use square brackets or parentheses in their syntax. This is sometimes confusing because it makes arrays look like function calls, so many programmers choose to use only the square brackets for arrays. With this directive, you can tell the Documenting Wizard that you only use square brackets or that you use parens (parentheses) for array references.

A setting of ON indicates that arrays always use square brackets; OFF indicates that either the square brackets or the parens may be used on arrays. The default is OFF.

*# document ACTIONINDENTLENGTH <NumberOfSpaces>

This line controls how many spaces the indenting will use. The minimum number of spaces allowed is 2. This functions the same as the spinner shown previously in Figure 16.18, the Indentation dialog for the wizard.

Setup Wizard

The Setup Wizard is used to create a set of disk image directories on your hard disk to aid in the production of disks to distribute your Visual FoxPro applications. This wizard is included only in the Professional Edition of Visual FoxPro.

After you have used the Visual FoxPro Project Manager to create the executable version of an application, you can use this wizard to compress the files required by your application and organize them into a set of directories that can then be used to produce disks. A setup program will also be created to make it easier for your users to install your application.

This process is divided into a series of eight steps, which are listed in Table 16.5. These steps are described in more detail in the following sections of this chapter.

Table 16.5. The steps in the Setup Wizard process.

Step	Description
Distribution Tree	The directory that the Setup Wizard will use to determine the directory tree for your distributed application. This directory should contain all of the files that your application needs.
Optional Components	Enables you to designate which support files your application needs and which operating systems your application supports.

Step	Description
Disk Images	Specify where the disk image directories should be created.
Setup Options	The Dialog Caption entry enables you to specify the title for the Setup dialog box your users will see and the Setup Copyright entry enables you to enter the copyright notice that will be displayed when your user selects the About option during setup of the application. These options must be filled in to move on to the next step.
Default Destination	The directory that you want as the default when your users install from your distribution disks.
File Summary	You are given a grid of your files and are allowed to modify certain settings for them.
Finish	The wizard will produce the disk image directories.
Reports	The Setup Wizard can print reports about your setup disks.

Before you use the Setup Wizard, you should analyze your application to identify all of the files that are required in addition to the executable and the system files. Make a list of all of these files. Also, be sure they are in your distribution tree so that the wizard can find them. Don't forget files like data tables, indexes, reports, icons, bitmaps, .WAV files, text files, and any others needed by your application. The wizard will find the Visual FoxPro runtime library and system files.

The example you are using in this chapter is the Controls.PJX project located in the SAMPLES\CONTROLS\ directory under your Visual FoxPro directory. You will have this project and the directory if you choose to install the sample files during the Visual FoxPro installation. You have already used the Project Manager to create your executable and have placed it in a directory named C:\COPY.

Distribution Tree

Now select Tools | Wizards | Setup from the system menu and you are greeted by the dialog box shown in Figure 16.26. This is where you will tell the Setup Wizard how to find your distribution directory tree. In Figure 16.26, the directory C:\COPY is selected. Select the directory for your application.

The directory you specify here must contain all of the subdirectories and files that your application will need at runtime. The wizard will use this tree in setting up the user's machine during installation.

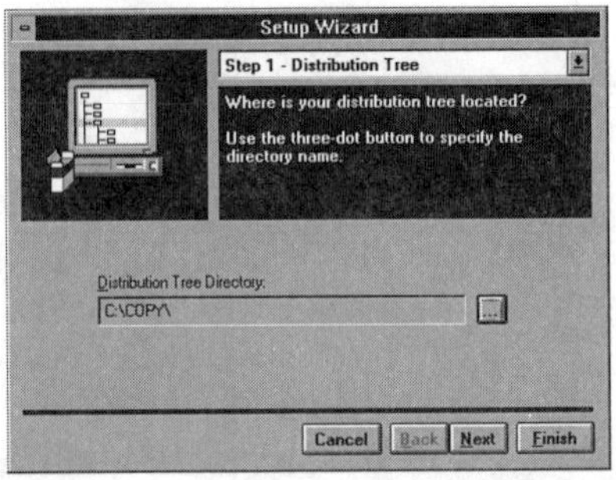

FIGURE 16.26.

The Distribution Tree dialog for the Setup Wizard.

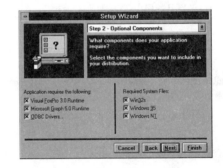

> **NOTE**
>
> It is a good idea to keep your distribution tree outside of the Visual FoxPro directory structure. This will keep your Visual FoxPro directory separate from your application directories, which makes disk management much easier in the long run.

Optional Components

Selecting the Next button brings you to the Optional Components dialog, as shown in Figure 16.27.

FIGURE 16.27.

The Optional Components dialog for the Setup Wizard.

In this dialog box, you tell the wizard which support system files are needed by your application. The two check box groups at the bottom of the dialog box each enable you to set up the support files and the operating systems that your application will use.

With the check box set on the left, you can choose to include the Visual FoxPro 3.0 Runtime library file, Microsoft Graph 5.0 Runtime file, and/or the ODBC Drivers. The check boxes on the right are used to establish the operating systems on which your application will be able to run. The choices are Win32s (for 16-bit versions of Windows), Windows 95, and/or Windows NT.

Table 16.6 lists the options, the sizes of the files included, and the times that you would want to include this option.

Table 16.6. The optional components available in the Setup Wizard.

Option	File Size	When to Use
Visual FoxPro 3.0 Runtime	3.5MB	If you want the Visual FoxPro Runtime file (VFP300.ESL) included on your distribution disks. You might not want this option if your target users already have the runtime file.
MS Graph 5.0 Runtime	2.2MB	If any of your forms include OLE containers for Microsoft Graph graphs.
ODBC Drivers	4.3MB Maximum	If your application accesses data stored in files other than Visual FoxPro DBF tables. When you choose this option, will get the ODBC driver dialog box so you can select which drivers you want to include.
Win32s	4.0MB	If your users will be running your application on Windows 3.11, this option is required. Visual FoxPro is a 32-bit application and requires Win32s in order to run on the 16-bit version of Windows.
Windows 95	0.5MB	These drivers are needed for running on Windows 95. The drivers for Windows 95 that are included with Visual FoxPro are preliminary because Windows 95 was not released at the time Visual FoxPro 3.0 was released. Final drivers for Windows 95 were released with Windows 95.
Windows NT	0.5MB	If your application will be running on Windows NT.

> **NOTE**
>
> You might want to produce different installation disk sets for different operating systems. You can use the Setup Wizard once for each operating system and identify different Disk Image directories for each. Then you can make a set of master disks for each operating system.

Disk Images

After setting the options you want in the Optional Components dialog, select the Next button to go to the Disk Images dialog in Figure 16.28.

FIGURE 16.28.

The Disk Images dialog for the Setup Wizard.

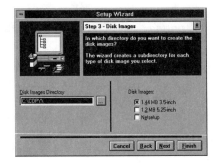

You control two aspects of the Setup Wizard's operation here: the directory in which the disk image directories will be created and the types of disk images to be created.

On the left, you establish the directory to hold your disk images. The command button with the ellipsis (...) can be used to bring up Visual FoxPro's Open File dialog box to help in selecting the directory.

On the right, the check boxes are used to determine what types of disk images you want to create. You can create disk image directories for 1.44MB $3^1/_2$-inch disks or 1.2MB $5^1/_4$-inch disks. The third option, Netsetup, will create a single directory with the entire set of compressed files for installation from a network file server.

Setup Options

Once you have selected your choices for directory and disk sizes, select the Next button to get to the Setup Options dialog, as seen in Figure 16.29.

This is a fairly simple dialog; here you can specify the title for the Setup dialog when your users are installing the application. Also, you can enter the copyright notice that the users will see when they select About from your setup program.

FIGURE 16.29.

The Setup Options dialog for the Setup Wizard.

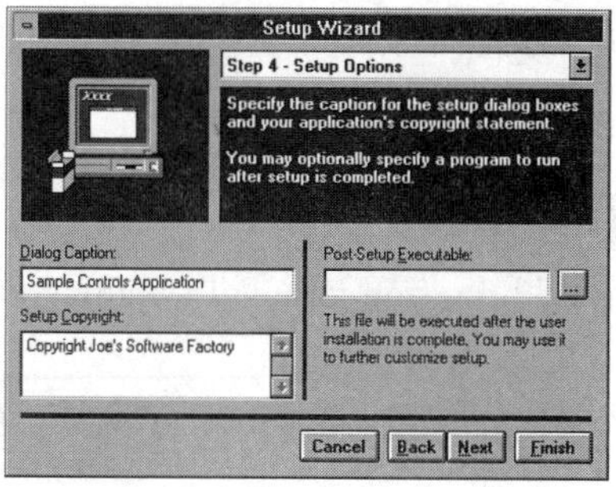

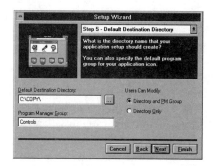

You can also provide the name of a program to be run when the setup installation completes. This could be a program that would extend the setup process, or it could be used to run your application after the setup has completed.

This step requires that you provide a title and copyright notice in order to move to the next step. The post setup program is optional.

> **NOTE**
>
> You must move the insertion point out of the Setup Copyright edit box and the Dialog Caption text box in order to move on to the next step. You can press Tab to do this.

Default Destination Directory

Selecting the Next button brings you to the Default Destination Directory dialog shown in Figure 16.30.

FIGURE 16.30.

The Default Destination Directory dialog for the Setup Wizard.

This dialog box is used to specify the directory that your setup will create during installation of the application. You can also tell setup the name of the Program Manager group in which to place the icon for your application.

The option button group enables you to determine what the user can override during installation.

File Summary

Selecting Next will bring you to the File Summary dialog shown in Figure 16.31.

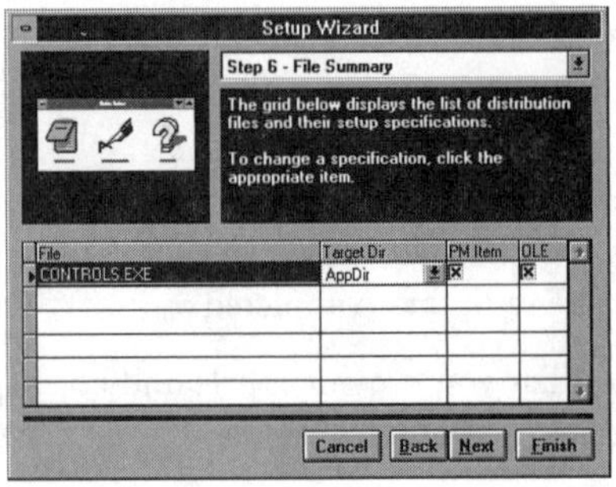

FIGURE 16.31.

The File Summary dialog for the Setup Wizard.

The grid in Figure 16.31 is a list of your files that are included in the setup disk set. You can modify various settings for these files by using the columns in the grid. The grid columns are described in Table 16.7.

Table 16.7. The options in the File Summary dialog of the Setup Wizard.

Column Heading	Description
File	The filename for each of your files.
Target Dir	The directory to which this file should be installed. Your options are the AppDir (the application's directory), the WinDir (the Windows directory), and the WinSysDir (the Windows System directory).
PM Item	Make this file have a Program Manager item created. Selecting this option will bring you to a dialog box where you can specify the description, command line, and icon for the Program Manager item.
OLE	Use this option for any OLE controls that are in the files list. When you select this option, the setup program will register the OLE control during installation. It is a very good idea to select this option for any OLE controls you include in your application because it will ensure that even if the user already has the control on his or her machine, your application will use the correct version of the control.

Figure 16.32 shows the program item dialog box that you get when you select the PM Item option for a file.

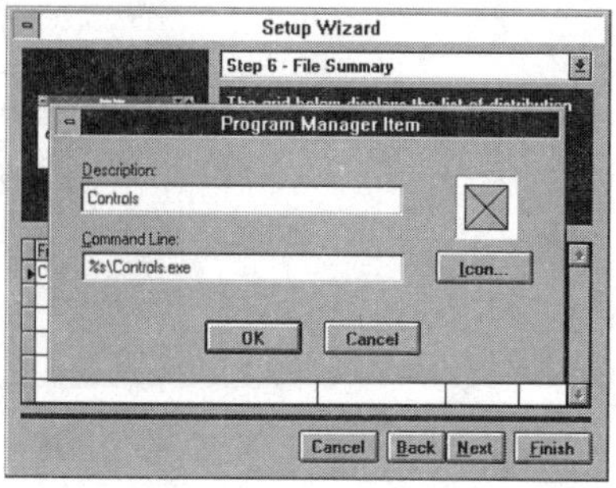

FIGURE 16.32.

The Program Manager Item dialog box for the Setup Wizard.

In the text box labeled Description in this dialog box, you can specify the text to appear under the icon in the Program Group. The command line can be entered in the Command Line text box. You can use the Icon button to select the icon file for your application from an Open File dialog box.

TIP

When you are providing the command line for a Program Manager item, you can use the %s macro to refer to the application's directory. The "s" must be lowercase in this macro. Using this macro will enable the user to change the application directory name during installation and have the application still run properly from the Program Manager item.

NOTE

If the icon file you select is not located in the distribution tree you specified, then that icon file will be installed in the application directory.

Select OK from the Open File dialog box to return to the File Summary dialog.

Finish

When you have finished setting the options for all of your files, select the Next button to go to the Finish dialog, as shown in Figure 16.33.

There are no settings to establish in this dialog, so you can immediately select the Finish button to produce your disk images. The process can take a considerable period of time to complete, so always allow enough time for the task.

During the processing, you will see the progress in the dialog box shown in Figure 16.34.

FIGURE 16.33.

The Finish dialog for the Setup Wizard.

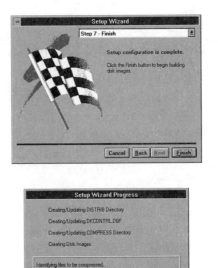

FIGURE 16.34.

The Progress dialog box for the Setup Wizard.

Each item in the list will be checked off as it is completed.

Setup Wizard Disk Statistics

Figure 16.35 shows you the Disk Statistics dialog box that you see after the disk images are complete.

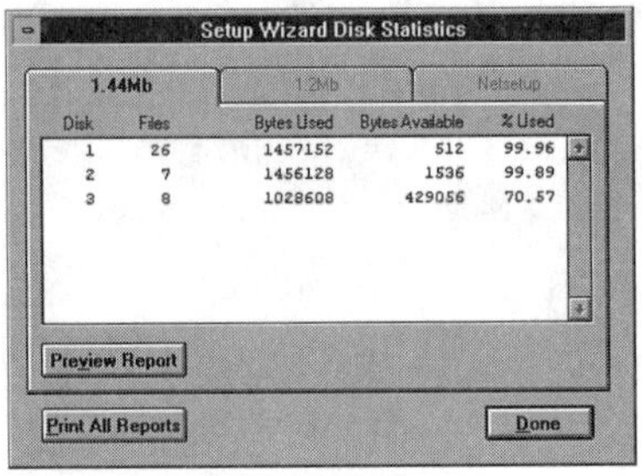

FIGURE 16.35.

The Disk Statistics dialog box for the Setup Wizard.

This dialog box shows you how many disks are required for each size of disk. You also see the Bytes Used, Bytes Available, and the percent of each disk used.

If you click the Preview Report button, you get a preview of the detailed listing for each disk in the set showing you every file on that disk.

The Print All Reports button will print the disk reports for each disk size for which you produced images.

If you had produced images for more than one size of disk, you could click on the page tabs to switch between the three reports.

You can now copy your disk image directories to a set of master disks to be used in producing the installation disks. Once you have made your master disks, you can delete the disk image directories from your hard disk.

> **TIP**
>
> During the processing of your setup, the wizard compresses a number of files into a COMPRESS directory. These compressed files are used in producing your disk image directories. When you have finished making your master disk and you erase the disk image directories from the hard disk, be sure not to erase the COMPRESS directory. This directory will be used in future running of the Setup Wizard. Leaving it on your hard disk will enable the wizard to compress only those files that have changed since the last run, thus speeding up the process considerably.

Summary

You have looked at four of the wizards in this chapter: the Import Wizard, the PivotTable Wizard, the Documenting Wizard, and the Setup Wizard. Each of these wizards accomplishes a relatively complex task with a high degree of ease. The wizards help you by guiding you through each step of a process and by providing easy-to-use dialog boxes for inputting your requirements.

There are other wizards available in Visual FoxPro besides the four discussed in this chapter. Each of these is described in the chapters for their respective operations.

Sharing Data with Other Software

17

Because no PC in today's world is an island, existing data can come into Visual FoxPro from a wide variety of sources, and Visual FoxPro can export data in many formats for use in other programs. The capability of sharing data is particularly important in a world where mission-critical data can be found anywhere from older dBASE or Paradox for DOS files to SQL Servers stored on local area networks.

> **NOTE**
>
> One common use of exported data is to create form letters in word processors based on the exported data. With many word processors, you can export the data as fixed text, delimited text, or as dBASE files. You can then use the data in your word processor to produce the form letters (see your word processor's documentation for details). Using exported data to create form letters in Microsoft Word for Windows is not detailed in this chapter because that task is detailed in Chapter 15, "Producing Mailings." If you need to create form letters in Word for Windows based on FoxPro data, see Chapter 15.

Many users come to a full-fledged database manager like Visual FoxPro carrying established data-management needs that have outgrown a spreadsheet or a word processor. For example, a user might have dozens or even hundreds of expense records stored in an Excel worksheet. The office mailing list might have hundreds of names stored in Word for Windows. Re-entry of this kind of data is not only incredibly time-consuming, it is also nearly always unnecessary. You can use the capabilities that Visual FoxPro offers to move the existing data into a FoxPro table. When other departments within your organization need to get at your data, you can use those same capabilities to produce data in a file format that virtually any modern software package can work with.

> **TIP**
>
> If you regularly import or export data, you can combine the techniques learned in this chapter with those detailed in Chapter 22, "Visual FoxPro Language Basics," to create programs that import or export data. For more details on programming in Visual FoxPro, see Chapter 22.

Using Data from dBASE

Many Visual FoxPro users come to Visual FoxPro from dBASE IV, dBASE III Plus, or dBASE III. dBASE III Plus and dBASE IV tables can be used unchanged in Visual FoxPro. You can also run your dBASE III Plus programs unchanged in Visual FoxPro because the Visual FoxPro language is a superset of the dBASE III Plus language. dBASE IV programs will, for the most part, also run unchanged. Of the hundreds of commands and functions present in the Xbase language, only a few used by dBASE IV are not compatible with Visual FoxPro. They include the SQL statements used in dBASE IV SQL programs (which aren't commonly used by most dBASE developers) and the following commands and functions:

ACCESS()	DGEN()	SET DESIGN
CALL()	ISMARKED()	SET IBLOCK
CERROR()	LKSYS()	SET INSTRUCT
CHANGE()	PROTECT	SET LDCHECK
COMPLETED()	RESET	SET PRECISION
CONVERT	RUN	SET TRAP
DEBUG	SET CATALOG	USER()
DEXPORT	SET DBTRAP	

There are significant differences in the support of SQL in dBASE IV and Visual FoxPro. Some dBASE IV SQL commands are not supported in Visual FoxPro. The SQL commands in dBASE IV are quite different from the SQL commands in Visual FoxPro. Before you can use SQL commands in dBASE IV, you must first create a SQL database. Furthermore, you can run dBASE SQL commands only in a special mode (SET SQL ON). Any SQL programs must be separate and distinct from other dBASE programs. SQL programs are stored in PRS files, whereas programs containing standard dBASE IV langauage are in PRG files.

The Visual FoxPro SQL commands are completely integrated in Visual FoxPro. You can use SQL commands exactly as you would use any other Visual FoxPro commands. You can inter-mix Visual FoxPro and SQL commands any way you like. Visual FoxPro supports the following SQL commands:

```
ALTER TABLE
CREATE CURSOR
CREATE TABLE
DELETE
INSERT
SELECT
UPDATE
```

Because there is a significant difference between the implementation of SQL in dBASE IV and in Visual FoxPro, complex dBASE IV SQL programs most likely will not function properly in Visual FoxPro. You will have to rewrite them.

The transaction processing commands operate differently in Visual FoxPro than in dBASE. The BEGIN TRANSACTION, END TRANSACTION, and ROLLBACK commands in Visual FoxPro are only supported for tables in a database.

If your dBASE program uses any of the preceding commands you need to remove them from the program before running the program in Visual FoxPro. These commands were not available in dBASE III or dBASE III Plus, so any dBASE III/III Plus program can be run in Visual FoxPro with no modifications.

Enhancing Compatibility with dBASE IV Programs

You can maximize compatibility with existing dBASE IV programs by issuing the command

```
SET COMPATIBLE DB4
```

in the Command window. (As an alternative syntax, you can use SET COMPATIBLE ON.) Doing so changes the way Visual FoxPro executes certain commands and functions to more closely match the way dBASE IV behaves. In many cases, this is all that's needed to get a program written in dBASE IV up and running in Visual FoxPro. As you work with the dBASE application, you might want to make changes to the program code to take advantage of Visual FoxPro's features (such as its use of windows and pull-down menus).

Can I Maintain Files Shared Between dBASE and Visual FoxPro?

In many network environments, users are faced with a situation in which different users might need to work with the same data files, but they are doing so with different software packages. You might be using Visual FoxPro, but other users might be using dBASE to work on the same data; hence, the question arises, "Can I maintain files shared between dBASE and Visual FoxPro?" In a nutshell, the answer is yes, but it's not a wise idea. The network file-locking mechanisms used by Visual FoxPro and dBASE are incompatible with each other, and this can lead to conflicts on a network. Also, because the indexing schemes and the memo-field storage methods used by Visual FoxPro and dBASE also differ, properly maintaining indexes and memo files for shared tables can become a logistical nightmare.

What About dBASE for Windows?

The area in which Visual FoxPro and dBASE part company in a significant manner is with dBASE for Windows. You can read and write tables using the COPY TO command with the FOXPLUS keyword specified, as discussed later in this chapter, but don't expect any programs written using the full capabilities of dBASE for Windows to run under Visual FoxPro. Like Visual FoxPro, dBASE for Windows provides an object-oriented superset of the original dBASE language. Unlike Visual FoxPro, dBASE for Windows uses its own extensions to the language, and they are very much incompatible with those of Visual FoxPro. Because Visual FoxPro and dBASE for Windows are basically aimed at the same marketplace, you'll have to decide on which product to use as your development platform, and stick with it. (You must have a preference for Visual FoxPro; otherwise, you would be reading a dBASE book.) Basically, it's not possible to move applications back and forth between the two platforms unless you write your applications with dBASE III Plus-compatible code (and if that's the case, why go to Windows in the first place?).

Importing Data from Other Software

Visual FoxPro stores its files in the DBF file format made popular by dBASE. However, other applications often store their information in files formatted differently. For example, Microsoft Excel worksheet files store their information in the .XLS extension, whereas Lotus 1-2-3 Version 3 files are stored in the .WK3 file extension.

Sometimes you might want to bring in information from one of the other applications to use in Visual FoxPro. For example, you might want to import information from Excel to use in a Visual FoxPro table, or you might want to export information to Excel to do advanced calculations.

Visual FoxPro is at no loss in providing a way to work with information from other applications. In Visual FoxPro, there are several commands available for this. For *importing*, or bringing in information from other applications, two commands are provided. There are also two commands available for *exporting*, which is the conversion of Visual FoxPro information for use in other applications. (*Object Linking and Embedding*, or *OLE*, is also supported by Visual FoxPro. OLE enables you to embed or link other Windows data to a general field in a FoxPro table. Techniques for using OLE are detailed in Chapter 19.)

Because most other applications save their files in different formats than Visual FoxPro, they need to be converted in order to be used in Visual FoxPro. Visual FoxPro has the conversion routines built-in to make the conversions. This feature makes the sharing of information with Visual FoxPro easy.

> **TIP**
>
> Before spending time exporting data to another file format, check to see if the other software package can directly read dBASE IV data files. Due to the popularity of the dBASE data format, many software packages can work directly with data stored in dBASE IV format, and exporting from FoxPro to the dBASE IV format will preserve the data types of the various fields to the highest degree possible.

File Formats

Visual FoxPro can transfer information stored in a number of file formats. They include Delimited, SDF, DIF, SYLK, FW2, RPD, WKS, WR1, WRK, XLS, and XL5 file formats. The following is a description of the different file formats Visual FoxPro can use.

Delimited Format

Files that use the Delimited option contain data with fields separated by a specific character or characters (usually a comma). Each record occupies an individual line, and the line always ends with a carriage return and line feed. Within the record, each field is separated from the next field by a comma. Each character field is normally enclosed in quotation marks, and trailing blanks are stripped. The default separator of quotation marks can change by adding a WITH *delimiter* option to the TYPE specification. For example, consider the Buyers table used in various parts of this text. The command

```
USE BUYERS
COPY TO FILEA.TXT FIELDS LASTNAME, FIRSTNAME, ADDRESS, CITY, STATE,
    ZIPCODE TYPE DELIMITED
```

copies the Visual FoxPro data to a new file with data stored in the following format:

```
"Roberts","Jamie","118 Main Street","Reston","VA","22091"
"Sanderson","Lucy","931 Thames Ct., Apt. 2C","Herndon","VA","22070"
"Smith","Larry","142 Haven Way","Kensington","MD","31025"
"Jones","Nikki","8000 Watergate Circle","Washington","DC","20005"
"Hernandez","Maria","19012 Pimmit Drive","Towson","MD","30309"
"Jones","Jarel","1412 Wyldewood Way","McLean","VA","22035"
"Zeibermann","Danial","235 White Oak Way","Arlington","VA","22032"
"O'Neill","John","12555 Lee Highway West","Merrifield","VA","22045"
"Bannerton","Alicia","107 Embassy Row","Falls Church","VA","22046"
"Johnson","Ivan","","","",""
"Bannerton","Alicia","107 Embassy Row","Falls Church","VA","22046"
"Hernandez","Maria","19012 Pimmit Drive","Towson","MD","30309"
"Hernandez","Maria","19012 Pimmit Drive","Towson","MD","30309"
"Bannerton","Alicia","107 Embassy Row","Falls Church","VA","22046"
"Bannerton","Alicia","107 Embassy Row","Falls Church","VA","22046"
```

Date values in a table that is exported to a delimited format are represented by an eight-digit number. The first four digits indicate the year, the fifth and sixth digits indicate the month, and the seventh and eighth digits indicate the day. Memo fields are not copied out to a delimited file. If there are any memo fields in the table they will be dropped during the copying process and will not exist in the newly created file. A number of other software packages, including most PC-based database managers, can import files in delimited format.

SDF Files

SDF files store data in columnar fields, with an equal number of spaces between the start of each successive field. Each record represented by a line in an SDF file is of equal length, and each line always ends with a carriage return and line feed. Spaces are used to pad the field contents, when necessary, so that the length of each record is identical. SDF files are useful for transferring data to spreadsheets that don't accept the DIF, WKS, or SYLK file formats. The following commands create the SDF file that follows:

```
USE DONATIONS
COPY TO FILEC SDF FIELDS CUSTID, DATE, AMOUNT
7 records copied
```

```
TYPE FILEC.TXT
10119930302 100.00
10119920301 100.00
10219900720  75.00
10219910803  50.00
10219921202  50.00
10219931112  75.00
10319910904 200.00
10319921101 200.00
10319940205 250.00
104199402051000.00
```

As with delimited files, SDF files do not contain the contents of a memo field. Date fields are represented by an eight-digit number; the first four digits is the year, the next two are the month, and the last two are the day.

DIF, SYLK, FW2, MOD, RPD, WKS, WR1, WRK, and XLS Files

Files with the extensions .DIF, SYLK, .FW2, .MOD, .RPD, .WKS, .WR1, .WRK, and .XLS contain data within a proprietary format that can be read by many other programs. The DIF file internally resembles delimited files. DIF was developed as an aid in transferring data from first-generation PC spreadsheet software packages. SYLK is used by Microsoft for a number of Microsoft application packages, including Multiplan, Chart, and File. Older Ashton-Tate products use the RPD and FW2 file formats. RPD is Rapidfile file-manager format, and FW2 files are used by Framework II. .MOD files are used by some versions of Microsoft's Multiplan. The WKS, WR1, and WRK formats are used by various versions of Lotus 1-2-3 and by Symphony. Due to the popularity of Lotus 1-2-3, a number of other software packages can also work with files in WKS format. The XLS and XL5 file types are used to create files with an .XLS extension, which are used by various versions of Excel, the popular Microsoft spreadsheet.

Files with the extensions .DIF, SYLK, .RPD, and .WKS will not contain the contents of a memo field. Date fields are represented by an eight-digit number: the first four digits is the year, the next two are the month, and the last two are the day.

FOX2X Format

The FOX2X file format is used for writing files that are compatible with FoxPro 2.0 and FoxPro 2.6 for DOS and Windows, and with FoxPro for the Macintosh. In making the jump to a true object-oriented database platform, Microsoft had to make some changes to the FoxPro file format used by earlier versions of FoxPro. Files created in earlier versions of FoxPro can be opened transparently in Visual FoxPro. However, files created by Visual FoxPro can't be directly read by any earlier version of FoxPro. If you want to use your tables in versions 2.0 or 2.6 of FoxPro for DOS, Windows, or the Macintosh, you should use the COPY TO command along with the FOX2X keyword specified to write those files in the older FoxPro file format. (For FoxPro versions 1.*x*, use the FOXPLUS keyword with the COPY TO command.)

FoxBase+ Format

Files are created in dBASE III/III Plus and FoxBase Plus file formats by specifying the FOXPLUS keyword with the COPY TO command. These format options help in importing and exporting files that contain memo fields.

Visual FoxPro stores memo fields in a more efficient manner than most other dBASE-language products, but is not compatible with them. For this reason, an error message is received when you try to open a Visual FoxPro table file with a memo field in products that accept dBASE files (Lotus 1-2-3, dBASE III Plus, dBASE IV, and FoxBase+).

You get around problems with other packages that can't deal with native FoxPro files by specifying the FOXPLUS keyword with the COPY TO command. This option creates a file in the FoxBase/dBASE III Plus format, which enables the file to be read by any product that has the capacity to read dBASE files. Because Visual FoxPro and dBASE III Plus use different methods of data storage, you need to use the FoxBASE+ format when you are transferring data to dBASE III Plus.

> **NOTE**
>
> Visual FoxPro also appends files from RapidFile and Framework file formats. However, due to the age of these products, they are not discussed in detail in this chapter.

Excel Formats

Visual FoxPro can work with Excel files in version 2.0 or 5.0 formats. In Visual FoxPro, you can read and write Excel version 2.0 files to be used with Excel versions 2, 3, and 4. You can also read and write Excel version 5.0 files to be used with Excel version 5.0 and Excel 95.

Using the Import Wizard

To import files, FoxPro offers an Import Wizard that turns the process of importing data into a simple matter. Like all wizards, the Import Wizard presents a series of dialog boxes to step you through the process. To use the Import Wizard, perform these steps:

1. From the system menu bar, choose File | Import option and the Import dialog box appears. Click the Import Wizard dialog box, and in a moment, you'll see the first frame of the Import Wizard dialog box, as shown in Figure 17.1. You can also execute the Import Wizard using the systems menu bar Tools | Wizards option.

FIGURE 17.1.

The first frame of the Import Wizard dialog box.

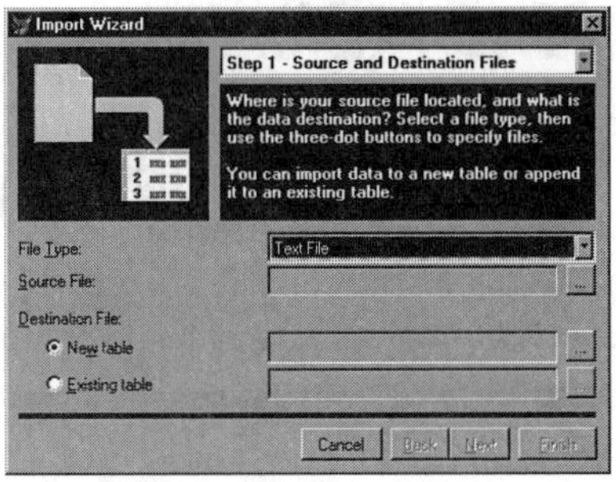

2. Click in the File Type box and choose the desired type of file you want to import.

3. Under Destination File, click New table if the file is to be stored as a new table, or click Existing table if the records are to be added to an existing table. (If you choose Existing table the wizard will also ask you for the name of the table in which the records should be stored.)

4. Click the button to the right of the Source File text box to display an Open dialog box (see Figure 17.2).

FIGURE 17.2.

The Open dialog box.

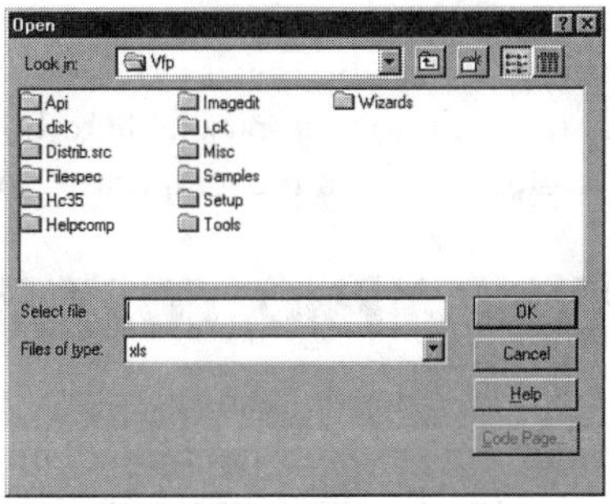

5. Select the desired file to import in the dialog box, and then click Next.

The remainder of the steps that you will perform will vary, depending on what type of file you are importing. But in all cases, the dialog boxes presented by the Import Wizard will direct you through the process. When you are finished answering the questions presented by the wizard, you can click Finish in the last dialog box presented to import the file.

Importing Data with Commands

Visual FoxPro has two commands available for importing data. The first, the IMPORT command, creates a new table in which to place the imported information. The other command, the AP-PEND FROM command, adds information to an existing FoxPro table as opposed to creating a new file for the imported data. The APPEND FROM command also supports ASCII delimited and SDF file formats, whereas the IMPORT command does not.

Using *APPEND FROM*

Visual FoxPro also provides a method to import files of the 16 named file formats: DELIM-ITED, SDF, DIF, MOD (Excel 4.01), SYLK (Multiplan file format), WKS, WK1, WK3, WR1, WRK (Lotus 1-2-3 and Symphony format), RPD (RapidFile file format), FW2 (Framework II file format), .XLS (Excel file format), and DB (Paradox file format). The APPEND FROM command can use the same Type option as is specified with the COPY TO command. The syntax for the command is

```
APPEND FROM  filename [FOR condition]
_[[TYPE] DELIMITED [WITH delimiter¦ WITH BLANK ¦ WITH TAB]
 ¦ SDF ¦ DIF ¦ MOD ¦ SYLK  ¦ RPD ¦
   FW2 ¦ PDOX ¦ WK1 ¦ WK3 ¦ WKS ¦ WR1 ¦ WRK ¦ XLS ¦ XL5]
```

If you are using the Delimited or SDF Type options and no extension is specified as a part of the filename, Visual FoxPro assumes that the filename has an extension of .TXT. You therefore might need to specify the filename when using the SDF or Delimited option of APPEND FROM. As an example of APPEND FROM, the command

```
APPEND FROM LOTUSFL1 TYPE WK1
```

would read in a file created by Lotus 1-2-3, Release 2 and append the contents of the file to the table currently in use. Note that when you use APPEND FROM to read foreign files, the data structure must match that of the table that is to receive the data. With some applications, you might find it necessary to create a temporary table to hold the data imported from the foreign file. You can later transfer data from the temporary table into other tables on a selective basis.

Using *APPEND MEMO, COPY MEMO,* and *SET ALTERNATE*

Visual FoxPro offers specific commands, APPEND MEMO and COPY MEMO, that can be used to import and export the contents of memo fields. The APPEND MEMO command writes the contents of a memo field out to a text file, and the COPY MEMO command reads a text file into a memo field. The syntax for the APPEND MEMO command is

```
APPEND MEMO memo field name FROM filename [OVERWRITE] [AS nCodePage]
```

where *memo field name* contains the name of the memo field, and *filename* is the name of the file containing the text to be added to the memo field. An extension of .TXT is assumed for the text file; if the extension is different, it must be included with the filename. Text from the file is normally added to the memo field after any existing data in the memo field. If the Overwrite option is used, the text read in for the file will overwrite any existing text in the memo field. The AS clause specifies the code page number of the text copied to the memo field.

The syntax for the COPY MEMO command, which is used to copy the contents of the memo field to a file, is

```
COPY MEMO memo field name  TO filename [ADDITIVE] [AS nCodePage]
```

where *memo field name* is the name of the memo field, and *filename* is the name of the text file to be written. An extension of .TXT is assigned to the text file. If a different extension is desired, it must be included with the filename. If a file by the name specified already exists, it is normally overwritten by the COPY MEMO command. The Additive option can be specified, in which case the memo field text is added to the end of any existing file. The AS clause specifies the code page number of the text in the resulting text file.

Because the APPEND MEMO and the COPY MEMO commands work with the current record in the active table, it is up to your program to position the record pointer at the desired record. If you are exporting the memo field contents from a group of records, you can use the COPY MEMO command within a DO WHILE or a SCAN...ENDSCAN loop. Include the Additive option so that the exported file gets each successive memo field's contents added to the end of the file. An example of a program that copies the contents of a memo field to a text file follows:

```
CLEAR
SET MEMOWIDTH TO 65    && Width that memo field display line
SET ALTERNATE TO WPFILE.TXT
SET ALTERNATE ON
*names the alternate file and turns on data capture to the file.
? "Memo fields from litigation file. Date 06/04/95
? "==================================================="
?
CLOSE ALTERNATE
*stops data capture and closes the alternate file.
USE LITIGATE
DO WHILE .NOT. EOF()
COPY MEMO COMMENTS TO WPFILE.TXT ADDITIVE
SKIP
ENDDO
```

The SET ALTERNATE commands are used to initially create the file as well as add a header. When the Additive option is used with COPY MEMO, the named file must exist prior to the use of the COPY MEMO command, or Visual FoxPro displays an error message. The results of the preceding program appear in the form of ASCII text, as shown here:

```
Memo fields from litigation file. 03/04/94
===================================================
This may be the smoking gun we need. Phillips said that Jones
 promised him that he would pay Phillips $300,000 to keep his
mouth shut about the impending takeover. Conversation took place
in a bar on Wisconsin Avenue.
At this point the entire transaction began to unravel. First
time that Phillips said that he was considering retaining counsel
and filling suit to block the takeover. This is beginning to sound
like a plot from a soap opera. Smith said if Phillips didn't stay
away from his spouse, he (Smith) would resort to draconian measures.
To further complicate matters, Jones claims to have hard evidence
the president's daughter has been laundering profits from her
illegal exotic bird business through the company.
```

The text file produced can then be imported into most word processors using the READ ASCII FILE commands. (See your word processor manual for details.)

Exporting Data

The COPY TO command can also be used to copy the contents of a table into foreign files, which you intend to export from Visual FoxPro for use with other software. When you use the COPY command, the TYPE clause instructs Visual FoxPro which file format to use in writing the foreign file. The Type options include

```
DELIMITED
SDF (System Data format)
DIF (VisiCalc DIF format)
MOD (Mutiplan 4.01)
SYLK (Multiplan file format)
WKS (Lotus 1-2-3 revision 1-A format)
WK1(Lotus 1-2-3 format)
WR1 (Lotus  Symphony version 1.01 format)
WRK (Lotus Symphony version 1.10 format)
XLS (Excel spreadsheet  format)
XL5 (Excel 5.0 format)
RPD (RapidFile file format)
FW2 (Framework II file format)
FOXPLUS (FoxBase+ or,dBASE III and dBASE III Plus with memo fields)
FOX2X (FoxPro 2.0, FoxPro 2.6, or FoxPro for the Macintosh)
```

As an example of the use of the Type option, the following command creates a spreadsheet file that can be used by Lotus 1-2-3:

```
COPY TO OUTFILE FIELDS L_NAME, F_NAME_M_I, AGE, SALARY, TAXRATE TYPE WKS
```

There are two commands available in Visual FoxPro for exporting data: the EXPORT and COPY TO commands. The EXPORT command enables you to export information in Visual FoxPro to other applications. The COPY TO command enables you to copy part of a table to a file. For the most part, the two commands function equally, but the COPY TO command must be used to export data in the ASCII format. This is useful because many applications support ASCII and SDF formats.

The *EXPORT* Command

Unlike previous versions of FoxPro, the EXPORT command in Visual FoxPro performs a function very similar to that of the COPY TO command: it creates a new file in a different file format based on the currently active table. (In previous versions of FoxPro the EXPORT command was used to build tables and corresponding screen forms for PFS:File, dBASE II, RapidFile, and Framework. Because all of these products are obsolete, Visual FoxPro uses the EXPORT command for a function like that of the COPY TO command. The only major difference between the two is that the COPY TO command can write files in ASCII text format and the EXPORT command cannot. The syntax for this command is

```
EXPORT TO  filename [scope] [FIELDS field list]
   [WHILE condition] [FOR condition]
   TYPE DIF ¦ MOD ¦ SYLK ¦ WK1 ¦ WKS ¦ WR1 ¦ WRK ¦ XLS ¦ XL5
```

COPY TO

The COPY TO command copies part or all of a table to a specified file. A field list can be used to specify a list of fields included in the file being created. The *scope*, FOR, and WHILE *condition* options can be used to specify conditions that must apply before records are copied. The AS clause specifies the code page number of the text in the resulting text file. The various TYPE options specify the file type that Visual FoxPro should export the data to. The syntax for the COPY TO command is

```
COPY TO filename [scope] [FIELDS field list] [WHILE condition] [AS nCodePage]
   [FOR condition] [TYPE FOXPLUS ¦ FOX2X ¦ DIF ¦ MOD ¦ SDF ¦
   SYLK ¦ WK1 ¦ WKS ¦ WR1 ¦ WRK ¦ XLS ¦ XL5]
```

Exercises in Transferring Data

The next section of this chapter deals with the transfer of files to different applications. Different packages are used in the examples; you might not have some of the packages in the examples. Because of this, you might not be able to follow all of the examples in this section. If you do not have the software in the example, try transferring data with some of your software.

Transferring Data to Lotus 1-2-3

Visual FoxPro can read and write in most Lotus formats. Only the earliest versions of Lotus are not able to read and write Visual FoxPro files that have been written out using the FOXPLUS file format.

Use the COPY TO command to transfer files from Visual FoxPro to Lotus with a Lotus file Type option. If memo fields are included in the table, use the FOXPLUS option to create the FoxBASE+ file type. To bring files in from Lotus 1-2-3 to Visual FoxPro, open the existing FoxPro table and use the correct Type option of the APPEND command.

If you have Lotus 1-2-3 or Quattro Pro, which is 1-2-3 compatible, try the following example of transferring data. Enter the following commands at the Command window:

```
USE BUYERS
COPY TO 123DATA TYPE WKS
```

Switch to the Windows Task List window and open Lotus. Use the File ¦ Open command (or with older versions of 1-2-3, File ¦ Load) to load the spreadsheet. The Set Column-Width command in Lotus can be used to fully display the information in the fields.

TIP

When you transfer data from a spreadsheet to FoxPro, a worksheet file should be saved with only the data range for the worksheet. This does not include titles, explanatory text, or macro references.

Transferring Data to a Word Processor

In virtually all cases, word processors can deal with data stored in the ASCII format. For example, you might want to use your word processor to create a document that would contain a listing of the persons in the Buyers table. You could accomplish this with the following steps:

1. Open the Ecology project (it's stored on the sample disk, along with all the associated files).

2. From the system menu bar, choose File ¦ Export. The Export dialog box appears (see Figure 17.3).

FIGURE 17.3.

The Export dialog box.

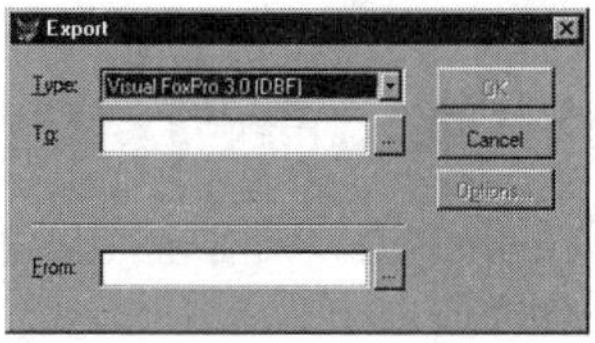

3. Click in the Type list box and choose System Data Format (SDF) from the list.

4. Click the button at the right of the To text box to open the Save As dialog box (see Figure 17.4).

FIGURE 17.4.

The Save As dialog box.

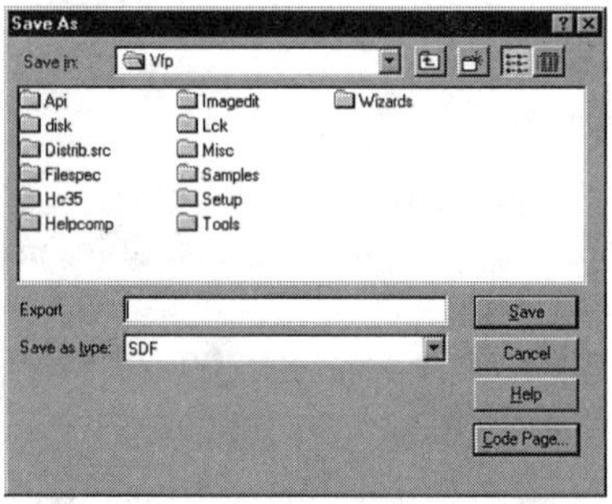

5. If desired, you can use the Save As dialog box to select a directory in which to save the text file. You can also specify the name of the text file to create at this point.

6. In the Export text box, enter PEOPLE.DOC as a name for the file to create if you have not already specified the name of the file using the Save As dialog box.

7. Click the button to the right of the From text box to open the Open dialog box (see Figure 17.5).

8. In the Open dialog box, select the Members.DBF table as the desired table to export, and then click OK.

FIGURE 17.5.

The Open dialog box.

Open

Look in: Samples

Controls	Assets	Details	Expenses
Csapp	Authors	Donation	Friends
Data	Bkdetail	Empl	Gusts
Graphics	Bksales	Employ~1	Househ~1
Mainsamp	Customers	Event	Invest~1
Ole	customers2	Exercise	Invoices

Export

Files of type: Table/DBF

OK

Cancel

Help

Code Page...

9. Click OK in the Export dialog box to carry out the operation.

10. Use the usual Windows techniques to switch to your word processor, and then open the file in the directory in which you saved it. If you are using Word for Windows, you might see the Convert File box. Click OK for text only, and the file appears in a format similar to that shown here. The information can then be edited in the way you desire.

```
182-55-3021Sloan       Wanda    199210152723 Hunters W             Reston      VA22091
402-12-3171Jones       Renee    199205152508 Columbia Pike        Arlington   TX75780
549-30-2011Roberts     Norma    199103016120 Brandon Ave          Pheonix     AZ80555
549-76-3171Hernandez   Maria    199407217105 Little River Lane    Annandale   FL30508
688-35-1025Askew       Lonnie   19890308103 Maple Ave West        Pitskill    NY12512
982-10-4353Zieberman   Martin   19900622153 South Lakes Drive     Reston      VA22090
121-55-2030Williamson  Lydia    199402121205 Hunter Hill Lane     Herndon     VA22075
304-59-02010'Rielly    Sharon   199403171400 Sugar Hill Way       Sterling    VA22082
232-69-5050Wilson      Peter    199503192705 Archer Ave           Brooklyn    NY10235
190-44-8038Rodgers     Carl     1995032147 Pine Bluff Way         Dallas      TX75252
```

Summary

This chapter detailed the techniques you'll find useful when exchanging Visual FoxPro data with other software and when importing data from other software formats into Visual FoxPro. Windows users have an advantage in that other Windows programs support additional features (such as the use of DDE and OLE, which are detailed in Chapter 18, "Programming with DDE," and Chapter 19, "Working with OLE for Non-OLE 2 Applications") which make sharing data with Visual FoxPro a less complex matter.

Programming
with DDE

18

Dynamic data exchange (DDE) is a mechanism of interapplication communication that is supported under Windows. Two Windows applications can carry on a conversation by sending messages back and forth, as you can in a telephone conversation.

One of the two programs will "call" the other one. The application placing the telephone call is a DDE client; the application receiving the call is a DDE server. The telephone company supplying the phone lines for this activity is Windows.

When a DDE client places a call, it sends a message to Windows stating whom it wants to talk with and what it wants to talk about. Windows checks to see if the requested server is available. If it is, the message is sent on to the server; if the server is not available, an error message is returned to the client.

When the server receives this initial message, it checks to see if it understands the subject the client says it wishes to discuss. If it does, it enables the conversation to begin; otherwise, it tells Windows it doesn't want to talk and Windows returns an error message to the client.

Once the conversation has begun, the client can request services from the server. These services can be anything from asking for a piece of data the server knows about to telling the server to execute some process it is capable of handling.

Visual FoxPro gives you the ability to program a DDE client application or a DDE server application. Visual FoxPro can't be a DDE server by itself, so you need to write a program that acts as a DDE server.

DDE requests are specific to the server application because they take the form of commands in the server's programming or macro language, so you must understand the server's language. Microsoft Word and Microsoft Excel are two examples of DDE servers' languages. This chapter will show you how to program a DDE client and server in Visual FoxPro.

SAMPLE PROGRAM AND FORMS ON THE CD-ROM

Examples of a DDE client and server program, and associated forms, can be found in the data from the accompanying CD-ROM.

If you have performed the data setup, look in the directory VFU\Chap18\ for the material appropriate for this chapter.

File	Purpose
DDEServ.PRG	An example of FoxPro as a DDE server to other DDE client programs.
ExcelDDE.PRG	Used to define a DDE session between FoxPro and Excel. Launches ExcelDDE.SCX.
ExcelDDE.SCX	The GUI for the DDE demonstration.

DDE Versus OLE

Object linking and embedding (OLE) is another Windows service that enables two applications to interact with each other. DDE and OLE both deal with two applications interacting, but they use different technology to accomplish this and perform different functions.

It has been said that OLE is the technology of tomorrow and DDE is the technology of yesterday. This statement might make you think you shouldn't use DDE; however, some OLE servers are missing important capabilities that are available when these applications are called through DDE. OLE is now in version 2.0, and there are many applications out there that support only OLE 1.0. Also, many applications can act as DDE servers but aren't capable being OLE servers. For more information about OLE, see Chapter 19, "Working with OLE for Non-OLE 2 Applications," Chapter 28, "OOP with Visual FoxPro," and Chapter 34, "Programming OLE Links."

The Basics of DDE

In Visual FoxPro, DDE activities are handled by the DDE functions, which will be explained in detail later in this chapter. For now, an overview will help you understand the big picture of DDE.

First, the client must place the call to start a DDE conversation. In Visual FoxPro, you use the DDEInitiate() function to do this. It takes two arguments—the name of the server you are calling and the topic you want to talk about.

The DDEInitiate() function actually calls Windows to request a DDE channel to conduct the conversation. Once Windows ensures there is a channel and the server is available and willing to talk, it sends back a channel number. Visual FoxPro's DDEInitiate() function returns this channel number, and you can assign it to a variable for future use. Most of the other DDE functions will require providing the DDE channel number as an argument.

Once you have successfully established a DDE channel, you can talk with the DDE server by using other Visual FoxPro functions, such as DDEREquest(), DDEExecute(), and DDEAdvise(), which are explained later in this chapter.

When you are finished with the conversation, use the DDETerminate() function to hang up the phone.

Visual FoxPro's DDE Functions

Before DDE functions can be discussed in depth, you need to understand three terms:

- *Service name*—the name the server responds to when a client tries to establish a DDE link. A particular DDE server application may have many different service names.

- *Topic name*—the name of a subject that the server understands, often a filename. It may also be a topic specific to the server. To establish a DDE link, you must specify a valid topic for the server you are linking to.
- *Item name*—the name of the piece of data you are asking for. Again, this may be a filename or an item specific to the server you are connected to.

The following sections introduce DDE functions in alphabetical order. Later in this chapter, you will have the chance to see how they work together to provide both DDE client activities and DDE server processes.

DDEAbortTrans()

`DDEAbortTrans()` is used to end a DDE transaction that is asynchronous. DDE transactions can be *synchronous* or *asynchronous*. In a synchronous transaction, the client waits for a response from the server after placing a request. These requests can time out if the server takes too long to answer. When a client places an asynchronous request, it does not wait for the answer but tells Windows to send the answer whenever it gets one from the server.

When you use `DDERequest()`, `DDEExecute()`, or `DDEPoke()` you can specify a user-defined function (UDF) to be called when the server responds. If you do specify a UDF, then the request is asynchronous.

This is the syntax of the `DDEAbortTrans()` function:

```
DDEAbortTrans(nTransactionNumber)
```

`nTransactionNumber` is the value returned by the function that established the request. (See this chapter's sections on `DDEExecute()`, `DDERequest()`, and `DDEPoke()`.)

This function returns a logical value indicating whether the abort transaction was successful. If the value returned is .F., then you can use `DDELastError()` to find out what went wrong.

DDEAdvise()

It is possible to tell the DDE server that you are interested in a certain item name. You can set up the server to tell you if that item has been changed and its new value. This is called a DDE *link*.

The syntax of this function is

```
DDEAdvise(nChannelNumber, cItemName, cUDFName, nLinkType)
```

`nChannelNumber`	This is the channel number for the DDE server you are calling. It was established with the `DDEInitiate()` call.
`cItemName`	The name of the item in which you are interested; it may be a filename, a variable, or a range name, depending on the particular server you are linked to.

cUDFName	The name of the user-defined function you want to run when a message comes in from the server about this link.
nLinkType	The type of link you want: 0=manual (Cold), 1=notify (Warm), or 2=automatic (Hot).

DDEAdvise() returns a logical value of .T. if the call was successful or .F. if the call failed. We can use DDELastError() to find out why it failed.

Manual, or Cold, Links

In cold links you tell the server about your interest in the item, but you don't ask the server to do anything for you. You probably will rarely, if ever, use this type of link because you can use the DDERequest() (explained later in this chapter) to access data any time you want to.

Notify, or Warm, Links

In warm links you ask the server to notify you if the value of the item changes, but you tell the server not to send the new value unless you ask for it. This type of link enables you to decide whether or not you actually want the data when a message comes in telling you that the data has changed.

Automatic, or Hot, Links

The most automatic of all the DDE links, hot links ask the server to notify you of any change in the item's value and send you the new value with the notification. Hot links enable you to get both the notice of a change and the data simultaneously, enabling you to update a screen display in what looks like real time to the user.

With the two automatic links, warm and hot, you must tell Windows the name of a UDF to be called whenever a message comes in from the server. This UDF has some required parameters that it must get from Windows when it is called. The following list explains the parameters:

Channel Number	The channel number of the server sending the response.
Action	Is the server sending you a notice or the data, or is the server terminating the link? The action parameter will be either ADVISE or TERMINATE.
Item	The name of the data item that the message is about.
Data	In a hot link the new data will be in this parameter. In a warm link this parameter will be an empty string.
Format	The type of data being sent, such as CF_TEXT.

Advise Status   The type of link the message originated from (`0`=manual, `1`=notify, `2`=automatic).

A UDF for handling messages from the server is discussed later in the chapter.

DDEEnabled()

Besides finding out whether DDE is enabled for a particular channel, this function is invaluable when you are writing a DDE server application or the UDF that the `DDEAdvise()` message will call. When either of these processes is running, you don't want them interrupted by another DDE message, so you can use `DDEEnable()` to shut off DDE services on that channel while you process the message. Then when you are finished, you can turn DDE back on again.

This is the syntax for this function:

```
DDEEnabled([lExpression1 ¦ nChannelNumber [, lExpression2]])
```

The following list explains the arguments in `DDEEnabled()`:

lExpression1	The first logical expression can be `.T.` or `.F.`; `.T.` turns DDE on, and `.F.` turns DDE off.
nChannelNumber	You can use a channel number to ask if DDE is enabled or disabled on that channel. A return of `.T.` means DDE is enabled on the channel and `.F.` means DDE is disabled.
lExpression2	If you want to turn DDE on or off for a particular channel, you can pass the first logical expression to tell Visual FoxPro to turn DDE on or off, and then pass the channel number as the second argument to specify which channel should be affected.

`DDEEnabled()` returns a logical value; if you are asking what the status of DDE is, a logical true means on and false means off. If you are attempting to turn DDE on or off, then true means you succeeded and false means you failed. If you fail, you can use `DDELastError()` to find out what went wrong.

DDEExecute()

`DDEExecute()` is used to tell the DDE server to execute a command.

This is the syntax of the `DDEExecute()` function:

```
DDEExecute(nChannelNumber, cCommand [, cUDFName])
```

The following list explains the arguments this function accepts:

nChannelNumber	Used to specify the DDE channel number you are sending a command to.

cCommand	This is the command you are sending to the DDE server. The format and syntax of the command are determined by the server application you are talking to. This command must be in a syntax that the server can understand. Using DDE requires a thorough knowledge of the server application and its programming or macro language.
cUDFName	By naming a user-defined function to be called when the server finishes, you can establish asynchronous communication. If you omit the UDF name, then the client (the Visual FoxPro application) will wait for the time period set with DDESetOption() for a response from the server. If there is no response in that time period, then a DDE time-out error will be generated.
	By specifying the UDF to be called when the server finishes with the execute command, your Visual FoxPro application will continue executing immediately after the DDEExecute() is sent. When the server finishes with the execute command, a message will be sent to the UDF you named. Six parameters are passed to this UDF.

The parameters passed are described in the following list:

Parameter	*Contents*
Channel Number	The channel number for this conversation.
Action	XACTCOMPLETE means the command was successful; XACTFAIL means the command failed.
Item	The name of the item the command was affecting.
Data	Any data the execute needs to pass back to you.
Format	The format of the data, such as CF_TEXT.
Transaction Number	The transaction number identifying the transaction.

DDEExecute() returns a logical true if it succeeded or false if it failed. If you include the UDF name and set up asynchronous DDE, then the return is a number representing the transaction number for this execute or -1 to indicate failure.

You can use DDELastError() to find out why DDEExecute() failed. DDEAbortTrans() can be used to cancel a transaction before it finishes.

DDEInitiate()

DDEInitiate() starts a DDE conversation with another Windows application. This is its syntax:

```
DDEInitiate(cServiceName, cTopicName)
```

The following list explains the arguments for `DDEInitiate()`:

cServiceName	The DDE service name for the server application with which you want to initiate a DDE conversation. This is often the name of the executable file for the server without its extension. However, this is not true for all applications. For example, Microsoft Excel's service name is Excel, and Microsoft Word is WinWord. The Windows Program Manager's service name is Progman.
cTopicName	The name of the topic you want to talk to the server about. This topic is server specific and must be a topic that the server understands. One topic that most servers understand is System. You must check the documentation for each server to find out which topics it understands. One example of an exception to the System topic is the Windows Program Manager—it doesn't understand the System topic, but it does understand the topic of Progman.

`DDEInitiate()` returns a number representing the channel number for the conversation. It will return -1 to indicate failure. You can use `DDELastError()` to discover why `DDEInitiate()` failed.

DDELastError()

`DDELastError()` returns a number representing the cause of the error for the last DDE function executed. It will return 0 if the last DDE function succeeded.

`DDELastError()` takes no arguments. The following list explains the meaning of each return number:

Error Number	Description
1	Service busy
2	Topic busy
3	Channel busy
4	No such service
5	No such topic
6	Bad channel
7	Insufficient memory
8	Acknowledge time-out
9	Request time-out
10	No `DDEInitiate()`
11	Client attempted server transaction
12	Execute time-out
13	Bad parameter
14	Low memory
15	Memory error

16	Connect failure
17	Request failure
18	Poke time-out
19	Could not display message
20	Multiple synchronous transactions
21	Server died
22	Internal DDE error
23	Advise time-out
24	Invalid transaction identifier
25	Unknown

DDEPoke()

DDEPoke() is used to send data to a server application. This is the syntax for this function:

```
DDEPoke(nChannelNumber, cItemName, cDataSent;
     [, cDataFormat [, cUDFName]])
```

The following list explains the arguments DDEPoke() takes:

nChannelNumber	The DDE channel to which you are sending data.
cItemName	The item name in which the server should put this data.
cDataSent	The data you are sending.
cDataFormat	The type of data you are sending. The default data type is character (CF_TEXT). The CF_TEXT type has fields separated by tabs and records by carriage return and line feed.
cUDFName	This argument has the same use as the one described for DDEExecute(). It has the same effect of setting up asynchronous communications as well.

DDEPoke() has the same return types as DDEExecute(). If no UDF is specified, the return type is logical; true means success and false means failure. If a UDF *is* specified, the function returns a number indicating the transaction number for this request or -1 to indicate failure. DDELastError() can be used to find why a DDEPoke() call failed.

DDERequest()

DDERequest() is the inverse of DDEPoke()—it requests a piece of data from the server. This is the syntax for this function:

```
DDERequest(nChannelNumber, cItemName [, cDataFormat [, cUDFName]])
```

The following list explains the arguments `DDERequest()` takes:

`nChannelNumber`	The channel number for the DDE conversation.
`cItemName`	The item name for the data you are requesting.
`cDataFormat`	The format for the data you are requesting. The default format is `CF_TEXT`.
`cUDFName`	This argument has the same effect here as it does for `DDEExecute()` and `DDEPoke()`. The UDF must accept the same parameters described for `DDEExecute()`.

The return types for this function are the same as for `DDEExecute()` and `DDEPoke()`.

DDESetOption()

`DDESetOption()` can be used to change various DDE options or to find out what the current settings are. This is the syntax:

`DDESetOption(cOption [, nTimeoutValue ¦ lExpression])`

The following list describes the arguments for this function:

`cOption`	The option you are setting or checking.
`nTimeoutValue`	The number of milliseconds before a DDE function will time-out with a DDE Timeout error.
`lExpression`	Used to control whether the Safety dialogs will display.

The following list describes the two options that can be affected by `DDESetOption`—TIMEOUT and SAFETY:

TIMEOUT	The number of milliseconds before a DDE transaction will time-out while the client is waiting for a response from the server. The default setting is 2,000 milliseconds. If you omit the `nTimeOutValue` this function will return the current time-out setting.
SAFETY	If you attempt to do a `DDEInitiate()` and the server doesn't respond, Windows can display a dialog box asking if you would like to launch the server application. The Safety option controls whether this dialog will be displayed. If you pass `lExpression` as `.T.`, the dialog will be displayed; pass `.F.` and it won't. Omit `lExpression` and `DDESetOption()` will return the current setting for Safety.

`DDESetOption()` can return logical or numeric values depending on the arguments you pass to it.

DDESetService()

You can use Visual FoxPro to write a DDE server application that other Microsoft Windows applications can call on for services. You use DDESetService() to establish these services and register them with the Windows DDE system. This function can be used to create, modify, or release service names or their settings. DDESetTopic() is used to create the topic names. This is the syntax for DDESetService():

DDESetService(*cServiceName, cOption* [, *cDataFormat* ¦ *lExpression*])

The following list explains the arguments it takes:

cServiceName	The name of the service to be created, released, or modified or the service you want information on.
cOption	The option specifies what you want DDESetService() to do. The available options are described in the following list:

DEFINE	Used to define a new service.
RELEASE	Used to release an existing service name. To release the default Visual FoxPro service you use the service name Visual FoxPro.
ADVISE	Default value is .F., meaning that the client will not be notified of changes to the item names. See the section on DDEAdvise() to understand what item names you might be advising the client about. Passing lExpression as .T. will enable ADVISE and .F. will disable it. Omit lExpression to have DDESetService() return the current setting.
EXECUTE	Default value is .F., which will enable you to enable or disable EXECUTE for the named service. Pass .T. as lExpression to turn this option on and .F. to turn it off. Omitting the lExpression will cause DDESetService() to return the current setting for EXECUTE.
POKE	Default value is .F.. You can enable or disable the acceptance of POKE requests from DDE clients for a particular service. Pass .T. as lExpression to accept POKE requests and .F. to disable them. Omitting lExpression will cause DDESetService() to return the current POKE setting for the named service.
REQUEST	Default value is .T.. Like POKE, this option enables you to turn on or off the acceptance for DDE REQUEST. You use lExpression to affect the setting: .T. turns the feature on and .F. turns it off. Omitting lExpression will cause DDESetService() to return the current setting.

FORMATS   Default setting is CF_TEXT. It is used to specify the data formats that the service will accept. DDE requests for data formats not established with the FORMATS option will be rejected by the service. To accept multiple data formats, list them in *cDataFormat* separated by commas.

cDataFormat   Used to specify the data formats the service will support. Requests for data in an unlisted format will be rejected. If you omit *cDataFormat*, only the CF_TEXT format will be accepted. *cDataFormat* must be a standard or registered Clipboard format. The standard Clipboard formats are CF_BITMAP, CF_DIB, CF_DIF, CF_ENHMETAFILE, CF_METAFILEPICT, CF_OEMTEXT, CF_PALETTE, CF_PENDATA, CF_RIFF, CF_SYLK, CF_TEXT, CF_TIFF, CF_WAVE, and CF_UNICODETEXT. The most common format used is CF_TEXT.

lExpression   Used to set the state of the REQUEST, EXECUTE, POKE, or ADVISE options. True (.T.) will enable the option; false (.F.) will disable it.

The return value from DDESetService() depends on the specifics of the arguments passed.

DDESetTopic()

DDESetTopic() is used to create or release a topic name from a DDE service. The syntax for this function is

DDESetTopic(*cServiceName, cTopicName* [, *cUDFName*])

The following list describes the arguments it takes:

cServiceName   The name of the service for which you are creating or releasing a topic.

cTopicName   The name of the topic to be created or released. If you supply a UDF name in the *cUDFName* parameter, you will create the topic; if you omit the *cUDFName* parameter, you will release the named topic. If you pass the empty string " " as *cTopicName*, then the UDF named in *cUDFName* will be executed for any topic that isn't explicitly declared.

cUDFName   The name of the UDF to be executed when a client application makes a request to the topic named in *cTopicName*. This UDF must meet the same requirements as the one described for DDEAdvise().

The return value from DDESetTopic() is logical and indicates whether the topic was successfully created or released; true means success and false means failure. If the function fails, you can use DDELastError() to find out why it failed.

DDETerminate()

`DDETerminate()` is used to terminate a DDE conversation. The syntax for this function is

`DDETerminate(nChannelNumber ¦ cServiceName)`

It takes the following arguments:

`nChannelNumber`	The DDE channel number to be terminated.
`cServiceName`	The service name whose channel is to be terminated.

The function returns a logical value indicating whether the channel or service was terminated; true means success and false means failure. You can use `DDELastError()` to find out why a `DDETerminate()` failed.

The Steps in a DDE Conversation

Starting a DDE client conversation with a DDE server from Visual FoxPro requires a series of steps that must follow a specific order.

1. Initialize the connection to the server.
2. Execute the necessary DDE requests to accomplish the desired task.
3. Terminate the DDE connection.

Starting the Conversation

Follow the preceding steps in a DDE session with Visual FoxPro as the client and Microsoft Excel as the server. You can use Figure 18.1 as a reference as you follow the steps.

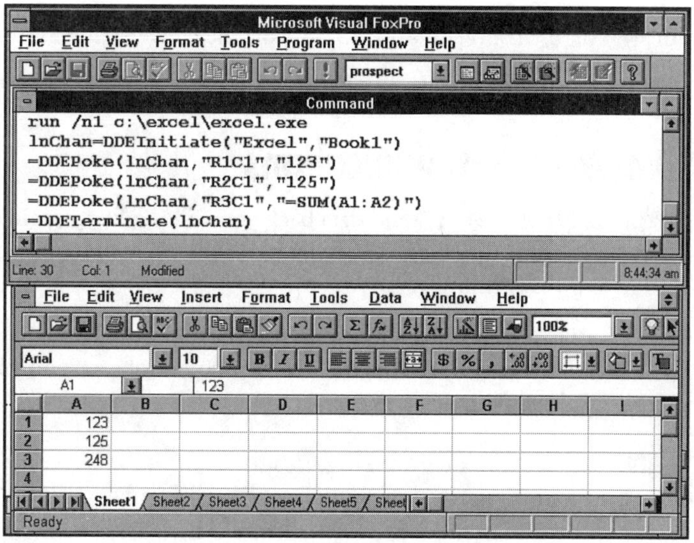

FIGURE 18.1.

A Visual FoxPro DDE session with Microsoft Excel.

```
run /n1 c:\excel\excel.exe
lnChan=DDEInitiate("Excel","Book1")
=DDEPoke(lnChan,"R1C1","123")
=DDEPoke(lnChan,"R2C1","125")
=DDEPoke(lnChan,"R3C1","=SUM(A1:A2)")
=DDETerminate(lnChan)
```

As stated, all DDE conversations begin by establishing a link to the server program. Enter the following line in the Visual FoxPro command window to establish a DDE link with Excel:

```
lnChan=DDEInitiate("Excel","Book1")
```

You have saved the return value of the DDEInitiate() function to the variable lnChan. This variable will be used in your subsequent DDE functions to refer to the channel for your Excel conversation. Now that you have your DDE session started, send some data to Excel.

If variable lnChan equals -1, it indicates that the DDEInitiate() call failed. The most likely reason for a failure here is that Excel is not running. You need to get Microsoft Excel running. Use Visual FoxPro's RUN command to do this:

```
RUN /N1 C:\Excel\Excel.exe
```

Once Excel is up, you can connect to it by repeating the DDEInitiate() function call. You will use the Book1 sheet as the topic because you want to send data to that sheet.

Talking with the Server

Use DDEPoke() to send two numbers and a formula to be placed in Rows 1, 2, and 3, respectively, of Column A:

```
=DDEPoke(lnChan,"R1C1","123")
=DDEPoke(lnChan,"R2C1","125")
=DDEPoke(lnChan,"R3C1","=SUM(A1:A2)")
```

Note in Figure 18.1 that the Excel Book1 sheet has your values in Rows 1 and 2 of Column A and that your *formula,* the sum of the two values, has been placed in Row 3.

Terminating the Conversation

Finally, you use DDETerminate() to close off the conversation and terminate the channel:

```
=DDETerminate(lnChan)
```

Two-Way Communications

To get the DDE server to send data back you will use Excel again and set up a hot link using DDEAdvise() from Visual FoxPro. Refer to Figure 18.2 to arrange your screen with both Visual FoxPro and Excel running.

On the Visual FoxPro side, you will be using a PRG program that calls your form so that your DDE handler user-defined function will not go out of scope on you. The source code for the program is listed here:

NOTE

The source code for the following program (ExcelDDE.PRG) and the form ExcelDDE.SCX are located in VFU\Chap18\.

```
gnChan = -1
DO FORM ExcelDDE NAME ExcelDDE
READ EVENTS

PROCEDURE HandleDDE
* This is the DDE call back function for receiving messages
* back from the server after the DDEAdvise() is set up

PARAMETERS pnChannel, pcAction, pcItem, pcData, pcFormat, pcStatus

* Turn off DDE so you won't be interrupted
=DDEEnabled(.F.)

* Take the value passed from the server (Excel)
* and update the text box on the form
_SCREEN.ActiveForm.Text1.Value = TRANSFORM( VAL(pcData), "999,999,999.99")
_SCREEN.ActiveForm.Text1.Refresh()

* Turn DDE back on
=DDEEnabled(.T.)
RETURN
```

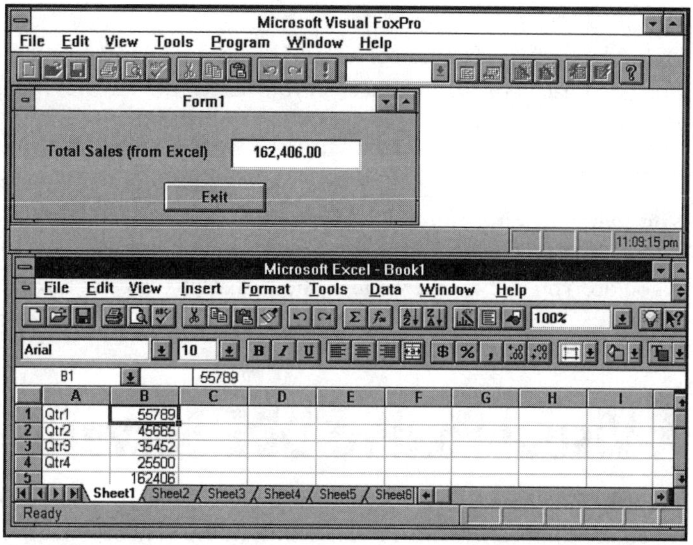

FIGURE 18.2.
A DDE hot link example using Visual FoxPro and Microsoft Excel.

The beginning of this program sets up a global variable, `gnChan`, to hold the DDE channel number for your communications with Excel. Then your form ExcelDDE is launched. A `READ EVENTS` is issued to keep the program running until you exit your form (a `CLEAR EVENTS` is issued in the form's `Release` method).

The procedure `HandleDDE` is your callback function for the `DDEAdvise()` hot link established in the form's `Load` method. Take a look at the methods in the form that are involved with the DDE; they are the form's `Load` and `Release`. Here is the code in the form's `Load` method:

```
* Initiate the DDE conversation with Excel
gnChan = DDEInitiate("Excel","Sheet1")

IF gnChan = -1
   * If the DDEInitiate failed launch Excel
   RUN /N1 Excel
   * Try again
   gnChan = DDEInitiate("Excel","Sheet1")
   IF gnChan = -1
      * If you fail the second time abort the form
      WAIT WINDOW "Unable to connect to Excel"
      RELEASE THISFORM
      CLEAR EVENTS
   ENDIF
ENDIF

* If you succeeded in initiating the conversation set up
* the hot link
=DDEAdvise( gnChan, "R5C2", "HandleDDE", 2 )
```

The form's `Release` method is used to terminate the DDE conversation:

```
IF gnChan >= 0
   * If you had succeeded in setting up the DDE conversation
   * You now need to terminate it
   =DDETerminate( gnChan )
ENDIF
```

To finish this demonstration of hot links, you need to prepare the Excel sheet. Once you have arranged Visual FoxPro and Excel on your screen the way it is in Figure 18.2, put this formula in Cell B-5 of Sheet1:

```
=SUM(B1:B4)
```

Now switch to Visual FoxPro and run the form. When the form has finished loading, switch to Excel and type some numbers in Cells B1 through B4 and watch the text box in Visual FoxPro as you do. You will see the value in the Visual FoxPro text box changing as you enter data in Excel because, with the hot link you have set up, Excel is sending a message to Visual FoxPro every time the value of Cell B-5 changes.

A Visual FoxPro DDE Server

The following code is for a Visual FoxPro DDE server program. It is based on DDEData.PRG, which was shipped with FoxPro for Windows 2.6. The sections following the code will explore the various parts of the program:

```
* DDEServ.prg
*
* A simple DDE server program for Visual FoxPro 3.0
* Based on DDEData.prg that shipped with FoxPro 2.6

#DEFINE    kNAME  "VFPServ"

PUBLIC ARRAY laChan(100)

= DDESetService(kName, "define")
= DDESetService(kName, "request", .T.)
= DDESetService(kName, "execute", .T.)
= DDESetService(kName, "poke", .T.)
= DDESetService(kName, "advise", .F.)

= DDESetTopic(kName, "", "Responder")

RETURN


* Responder - call back for Table, Query or SQL topics
*
* Valid Topics:
*     <database>;TABLE <table name>
*
* Any other topic will cause the INITIATE to fail
*
* Valid Items:
*     All - all data, including field names
*     Data - all data, without field names
*     FieldNames - a list of field names
*     NextRow - the next row of data
*     PrevRow - the previous row
*     FirstRow - the first row of data
*     Last row - the last row of data
*     FieldCount - the number of fields in the table
*
* A Poke request expects the field name as the Item, and
* the new data for that field.
*

PROCEDURE Responder

PARAMETERS pnChannel, pcAction, pcItem, pcData, pcFormat, pcStatus
PRIVATE llResult, pcDatabase, lcRowType, lcRowSrc, lnTemp,
PRIVATE lcUpItem, lcUpData, lcResult, lnTemp2, llEnabStat
PRIVATE lcTagTable, lcTagSql, lcCRLF, lcTAB

* Avoid interruptions
= DDEEnabled(.F.)
```

```
* must be uppercase
lcTagTable  = ";TABLE"

llResult = .T.

DO CASE

CASE pcAction = "INITIATE"
  * Shift to upper case
  lcUpData = UPPER(pcData)

  * Check for ";TABLE" in the data passed
  IF ! lcTagTable $ lcUpData
    * ";TABLE" is not there, so FAIL
    llResult = .F.
  ELSE
    * Get the path
    lnTemp = AT(lcTagTable, lcUpData)
    pcDatabase = LTRIM(SUBSTR(lcUpData, 1, lnTemp-1))
    SET DEFAULT TO (pcDatabase)

    * Get the table name
    lcRowSrc = ALLTRIM(SUBSTR(pcData, lnTemp + LEN(lcTagTable)))

    * Check for the existence of the table
    IF NOT (FILE(lcRowSrc) OR FILE(lcRowSrc+".dbf"))
      * Table does not exist, so FAIL
      llResult = .F.
    ELSE
      * Keep track of work areas used by separate DDE channels.
      lnTemp = ASCAN(laChan, .F.)

      IF lnTemp = 0
        * No empty rows in the array, so FAIL
        llResult = .F.
      ELSE
        * Post this channel number in the appropriate
        * row of the array and open the table
        laChan[lnTemp] = pnChannel
        USE (lcRowSrc) IN (lnTemp) AGAIN
      ENDIF
    ENDIF
  ENDIF

CASE pcAction = "REQUEST"
  * Select work area for this DDE channel.
  lnTemp = ASCAN(laChan, pnChannel)
  IF lnTemp <> 0
    SELECT (lnTemp)
  ENDIF

  lcUpItem = UPPER(pcItem)
  DO CASE
  CASE lcUpItem = "FIELDNAMES"
    lcResult = FldNames()

  CASE lcUpItem = "FIELDCOUNT"
```

```
       lcResult = FldCount()

   CASE lcUpItem = "FIRSTROW"
     GOTO TOP
     lcResult = RowData()

   CASE lcUpItem = "LASTROW"
     GOTO BOTTOM
     lcResult = RowData()

   CASE lcUpItem = "NEXTROW"
     IF EOF()
       llResult = .F.
     ELSE
       SKIP
       lcResult = RowData()
     ENDIF

   CASE lcUpItem = "PREVROW"
     IF BOF()
       llResult = .F.
     ELSE
       SKIP -1
       lcResult = RowData()
     ENDIF

   CASE lcUpItem = "ALL"
     lcResult = FldNames() + AllData()

   CASE lcUpItem = "DATA"
     lcResult = AllData()

   OTHERWISE
     llResult = .F.
   ENDCASE

   * Send the requested data to the other application.

   IF llResult
     = DDEPoke(pnChannel, pcItem, lcResult)
   ENDIF

CASE pcAction = "POKE"
  FOR lnTemp = 1 TO FCOUNT()
    IF FIELD(lnTemp) = UPPER(pcItem)
      lnTemp = 0
      REPLACE &pcItem WITH CharToFld(TYPE('&pcItem'), pcData)
      EXIT
    ENDIF
  ENDFOR
  IF lnTemp <> 0
    llResult = .F.
  ENDIF

CASE pcAction = "TERMINATE"
  lnTemp = ASCAN(laChan, pnChannel)
  IF lnTemp <> 0
    SELECT (lnTemp)
```

```
   USE
   laChan[lnTemp] = .F.
 ENDIF

OTHERWISE
  llResult = .F.
ENDCASE

= DDEEnabled(.T.)

RETURN llResult


*  Utility functions

#DEFINE    kCRLF  CHR(13) + CHR(10)
#DEFINE    kTAB   CHR(9)


FUNCTION FldNames
PRIVATE lcResult, lnTemp

lcResult = ""
FOR lnTemp = 1 TO FCOUNT()
  lcResult = lcResult + FIELD(lnTemp) + kTAB
ENDFOR
lcResult = SUBSTR(lcResult, 1, LEN(lcResult)-1) + kCRLF

RETURN lcResult


FUNCTION FldCount
PRIVATE lcResult

lcResult = STR(FCOUNT())+kCRLF

RETURN lcResult


FUNCTION RowData
PRIVATE lcResult, lnTemp, laData

SCATTER MEMO TO laData

lcResult = ""
FOR lnTemp = 1 TO FCOUNT()
  lcResult = lcResult + ;
             FldToChar(TYPE('laData[lnTemp]'), laData[lnTemp]) + kTAB
ENDFOR
lcResult = SUBSTR(lcResult, 1, LEN(lcResult)-1) + kCRLF

RETURN lcResult


FUNCTION AllData
PRIVATE lcResult

lcResult = ""
```

```
   SCAN
     lcResult = lcResult + RowData()
   ENDSCAN

   RETURN lcResult


   FUNCTION FldToChar
   * Converts field data to character data
   PARAMETERS pcType, pxValue
   PRIVATE  lcTemp

   DO CASE
   CASE INLIST(pcType, 'C', 'M')
     lcTemp = pxValue
   CASE INLIST(pcType, 'N', 'F')
     lcTemp = ALLTRIM(STR(pxValue,15))
   CASE pcType = 'D'
     lcTemp = DTOC(pxValue)
   CASE pcType = 'L'
     lcTemp = IIF(pxValue, 'YES', 'NO')
   ENDCASE

   RETURN lcTemp


   FUNCTION CharToFld
   * Converts character data to field data
   PARAMETERS pcType, pcValue
   PRIVATE lxTemp

   DO CASE
   CASE INLIST(pcType, 'C', 'M')
     lxTemp = pcValue
   CASE INLIST(pcType, 'N', 'F')
     lxTemp = VAL(pcValue)
   CASE pcType = 'D'
     lxTemp = CTOD(pcValue)
   CASE pcType = 'L'
     lxTemp = IIF(UPPER(ALLTRIM(pcValue)) $ 'YES~TRUE', .T., .F.)
   ENDCASE
   RETURN lxTemp
```

Registering the Server

The first thing this program does is register the DDE server in Windows. You can use the following code to do this:

```
#DEFINE    kNAME   "VFPServ"

PUBLIC ARRAY laChan(100)

= DDESetService(kName, "define")
= DDESetService(kName, "request", .T.)
= DDESetService(kName, "execute", .T.)
= DDESetService(kName, "poke", .T.)
= DDESetService(kName, "advise", .F.)
```

```
= DDESetTopic(kName, "", "Respond")

RETURN
```

`DDESetService()` is used to register the server's name and the services it provides. `DDESetTopic()` is used to name the user-defined function that will be called as requests come in for this server. This is the code you use to set up this server under Visual FoxPro:

```
SET PROCEDURE TO DDEServ.prg
DO DDEServ
```

The first line will make the UDF visible to Visual FoxPro; the second will run the server's set code. Once this server is set up, other Windows applications can call the server through DDE to request services.

Responding to Requests

The UDF named Respond processes all the requests coming into this DDE server. Most of the code is straightforward FoxPro programming; however, note that the list of parameters accepted by Respond matches those described previously in the section "Automatic, or Hot, Links." These same parameters are passed by Windows when sending a request to a DDE server.

This server is generic and fairly simple in its functionality. Most of the DDE servers that are actually used in FoxPro applications are more specific to the application's work. For example, you might use a DDE server to enable a word processing application to request data for a mail merge operation from your Visual FoxPro database.

Summary

With DDE you can communicate with other DDE-enabled Windows applications. Although this DDE technology is being replaced by OLE, (described in Chapter 19, "Working with OLE for Non-OLE 2 Applications," Chapter 28, "OOP with Visual FoxPro," and Chapter 34, "Programming OLE Links") there are still many Windows-based applications in use that don't support all the features of OLE. With these applications you will need to use DDE to communicate between applications.

As you can see in the DDE client examples of this chapter, you need a thorough knowledge of the DDE server application when you are writing the Visual FoxPro side of a DDE session. Also, in the Visual FoxPro DDE server example, you can see that the syntax of requests coming from the DDE client must be properly phrased and formatted for the communication to succeed.

Working with OLE for Non-OLE Applications

This chapter explains the concepts of object linking and embedding (OLE) and shows how you can put these capabilities—part of Visual FoxPro and recent versions of Windows—to work in your applications. Chapter 3, "Creating and Working with Tables," introduces the concept of the *general field,* which can be used to store OLE data from other Windows applications. Such data could include pictures, spreadsheets, part or all of word processing documents, and even sound or video. OLE lets you merge much of the capabilities of other Windows software into Visual FoxPro, and Visual FoxPro provides full support for OLE 2.

SAMPLE TABLE AND FILES ON THE CD-ROM

A sample table and sample files are provided on the CD-ROM as an adjunct to this chapter to demonstrate various data linking/embedding techniques using General fields in a Visual FoxPro data table. Five images are included in the table Clipart.DBF. Each of the images is embedded into the database in one record and linked to the original file in another record.

This chapter's example uses files located in the VFU\Chap19\ directory on the CD-ROM.

CarLogo. Bmp	A Paintbrush file that is linked to Clipart.DBF. (The same image is also embedded in Clipart.DBF for comparison purposes.)
Clipart.DBF	A table that contains linked and embedded Paintbrush images.
Clipart.FRX	A report that demonstrates the use of images that are found in general fields of a data table in a printed report.
LglLogo.BMP	A Paintbrush file that is linked to Clipart.DBF. (The same image is also embedded in Clipart.DBF for comparison purposes.)
Music.BMP	A Paintbrush file that is linked to Clipart.DBF. (The same image is also embedded in Clipart.DBF for comparison purposes.)
Sftware.BMP	A Paintbrush file that is linked to Clipart.DBF. (The same image is also embedded in Clipart.DBF for comparison purposes.)
Tape.BMP	A Paintbrush file that is linked to Clipart.DBF. (The same image is also embedded in Clipart.DBF for comparison purposes.)

About OLE

If you've worked with Windows quite a bit, you've probably already used OLE. Copying pictures from recent versions of Windows Paintbrush or other Windows graphics programs into a word processing document uses OLE capabilities. OLE objects can be created using any Windows application that supports OLE. An OLE object can be a complete file (such as a Word for Windows document) or a portion of a file (such as a single paragraph from that same document). You can add OLE objects to a Visual FoxPro table either by linking them or by embedding them.

Simply defined, object linking and embedding is a Windows *protocol,* or set of communication rules, that permits objects stored in one Windows application to be linked or embedded in the documents of another Windows application. The one common requirement is that the Windows package you are trying to use with Visual FoxPro must support OLE. Different Windows packages support OLE in different ways. Some Windows packages (including MS Graph and Windows Paintbrush) are OLE *servers* only, meaning they can supply data to other Windows packages but they can't accept OLE data. Some Windows packages are OLE *clients*, meaning they can accept OLE data but can't supply OLE data to other software. Visual FoxPro is an OLE client, but not an OLE server. Some packages like Word and Excel can act as both clients and servers of data using OLE.

Before working with OLE, you must understand the difference between *linking* and *embedding*, as both have their advantages and disadvantages. When you link to an OLE object, the object is stored elsewhere and Visual FoxPro maintains a link to the object. As an example, if a series of pictures in CorelDRAW! are linked to a general field for different records in a table, the drawings exist only in the CorelDRAW! subdirectory in which they were originally stored. Use linking when you want the data shown in Visual FoxPro to be updated whenever the data in the original Windows application changes. With linking, when data in the pictures changes, the data shown in the corresponding Visual FoxPro table changes as well.

By comparison, when you embed an object in a FoxPro table, the object becomes part of the FoxPro table. (It still exists in the original source directory, but the object in Visual FoxPro is a copy of the original source object.) Once the object is embedded, there is no longer any connection between it and the original object, and any changes made to the original object are not reflected in the embedded object. For example, if you embed a series of CorelDRAW! images in a FoxPro table, you can change them by double-clicking the images (which launches CorelDRAW! to make the desired changes). However, the images are stored as part of the FoxPro table, and the original application is used only to make changes to the object. The original CorelDRAW! image files would remain unchanged, regardless of changes made to the images while in Visual FoxPro.

An advantage to embedding is that it keeps your application portable: you can copy the table to a disk that might be on another computer. As long as that computer has the same Windows applications used to create the objects, you can still work with the data. (With linked objects, moving tables between PCs could create problems because the drive and directory structures would probably not be identical between machines.) A serious disadvantage to embedding is the additional disk space consumed. Since the embedded objects are copies of the original data, a lot of disk space is used, particularly if the objects consume much space to begin with (as do spreadsheets, sound, and video).

Editing OLE Objects in Visual FoxPro

Once you have inserted an OLE object in a FoxPro table, you can edit that object by double-clicking it whether the object is linked or embedded. When you double-click the object, the original application used to create the object opens. You can make changes to the object and then choose File | Exit from the application's menus to return to Visual FoxPro. Figure 19.1 shows a Paintbrush picture embedded in a general field of a FoxPro table.

FIGURE 19.1.

A Paintbrush picture stored in a table's general field.

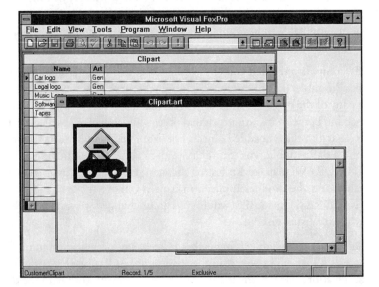

Figure 19.2 shows the results when the picture in Figure 19.1 is double-clicked. Windows Paintbrush opens and displays the embedded image. Note that the image is titled Paintbrush Picture in Visual FoxPro, which reflects the name of the OLE container for the embedded object—in this case, a FoxPro table. Also, when Paintbrush opens, its File menu gets an additional choice titled Exit and Return to Visual FoxPro. This menu option lets you exit from

Paintbrush, at which point any changes made to the image while in Paintbrush appear in the embedded image in Visual FoxPro.

FIGURE 19.2.

Windows Paintbrush with an embedded image.

Inserting an OLE Object in a Field

Once you've created the tables and any forms you will use with the OLE data, you can embed or link OLE data to a field using the following steps.

Embedding an OLE Object in a Field

When you want to embed an OLE object in a field of a table, you can do this by performing the following steps:

1. Open the table and begin editing data using your preferred method (such as the BROWSE or CHANGE commands or their menu equivalents).

2. Move to the record where the OLE data should be embedded.

3. Double-click the general field where the OLE object should be added to open a window in the field.

4. From the menus choose Edit | Insert Object to open the Insert Object dialog box. (See Figure 19.3.)

5. Under Object Type, click the type of object you want to embed, leave the Create New check box turned on, and then click OK. When you do so, Visual FoxPro launches the source application for the chosen object.

6. Use the source application to create the object.

7. In the source application, choose File | Exit and Return To FoxPro from its main menu. (If the source application has no such command, choose File | Update. If neither command exists, check the source application's documentation for the proper

sequence of steps to update the embedded object and exit.) If you are asked whether you want to update the document before exiting, click Yes.

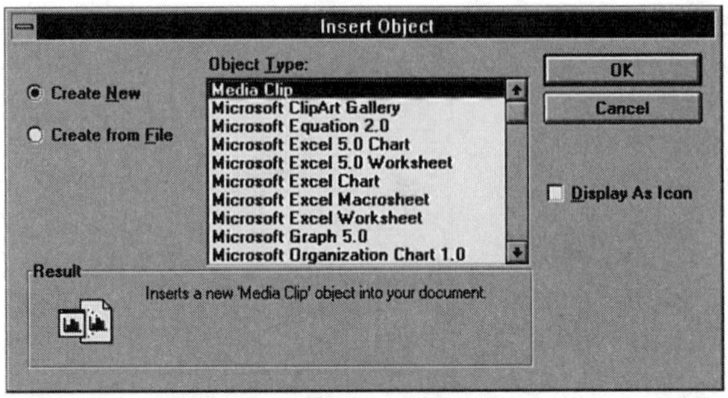

FIGURE 19.3.

The Insert Object dialog box.

> **NOTE**
>
> In the Insert Object dialog box shown in Figure 19.3, the Create From File option can be turned on when you want to base the OLE object on an existing file. When you choose this option, you must also enter a filename and path in the File text box (or choose one from a File dialog box by clicking the Browse button).

> **TIP**
>
> If the object you want to embed does not appear in the Object Type list box as part of step 5, this is a hint that the Windows application you have in mind may not support OLE, or its name may not be in the Windows registration database. In such cases, you can often achieve satisfactory results by using Windows cut-and-paste techniques. Try switching to the application, selecting the desired data, and choosing Edit | Copy. Switch back to Visual FoxPro, click in the general field, and choose Edit | Paste Special, then use the OLE Object option in the dialog box that appears.

Linking an Object to a Field

You can also link data in another application (such as a Windows Paintbrush picture or cells of an Excel spreadsheet) to a field in a FoxPro table or form. To link the data, use these steps:

1. In the server application (the application that will provide the data), open the file that contains the information you want to link to Visual FoxPro.

2. Use the selection techniques for that program to select the information.

3. From the menus choose Edit | Copy.

4. Switch to Visual FoxPro (in Windows 95, you can click the Taskbar icon for FoxPro. In Windows 3.*x*, you can press Ctrl+Esc and choose Visual FoxPro from the Task

List), then open a form in Form view (or open the datasheet for a form, table, or query).

5. Move to the record where you want to link the data from the other application.

6. Double-click the field where you want to place the link to the data to open a window in the field.

7. From the menus choose Edit | Paste Special, which opens the Paste Special dialog box. (See Figure 19.4.)

FIGURE 19.4.

The Paste Special dialog box.

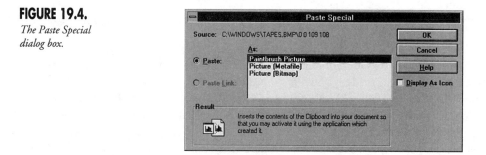

8. Choose the desired data type in the As list box, turn on the Paste Link option in the dialog box, then click OK. When you do this, Visual FoxPro creates the link and displays the object in the general field when you double-click it to open a window in the field. If you are linking a spreadsheet or word processing document, you will see an icon representing the document in the field.

Embedding an Existing OLE Object in a Field

When you have already created data in another Windows program that supports OLE, you can use the following steps to copy and paste all or part of the data as an OLE object into a field of a form, table, or query:

1. Open the other application, then open the document or file with the data you want to place in Visual FoxPro.

2. Use the other program's selection techniques to select the data you want.

3. From the application's menus choose Edit | Copy to paste the data into the Windows Clipboard.

4. Switch to Visual FoxPro (you can press Ctrl+Esc and choose Visual FoxPro from the Task List), then move to the record where you want to link the data from the other application.

5. Double-click in the general field where you want to place the link to the data to open a window in the field.

6. From the menus choose Edit | Paste to display the data in the field.

Playing Sound and Video

If you store sound or video in a general field of a table, you can play the sound or video using the following steps:

1. Open the table with the data.
2. Find the record and click in the field that has the sound or video you want to play.
3. Open the Edit command and choose the appropriate Object command from the Edit menu.
4. From the submenu that appears, choose Play, or Run if the submenu has no Play option, to play the sound or video.

For example, if you paste sound objects using the Edit | Copy menu option of the Windows Media Player into general fields of a FoxPro table, FoxPro's Edit menu will have a Sound Object menu option whenever you click in a field with sound data. You could click Sound Object, then click Play from the submenu to play the sound. You could also click Edit from the submenu to open the Media Player and edit the sound. (Using Media Player requires sound drivers and compatible sound hardware. Refer to your Windows documentation for details on Windows Media Player.)

Displaying the Contents of General Fields

As you work with your FoxPro data, you'll likely want to view and edit the contents of your general fields. One easy way to do this is to open a browse window in the table, move to the general field, and double-click it. You can then move and size both the browse window and the window in the general field so you can see both windows simultaneously. Make the browse window the active window by clicking it or choosing it by name from the Window menu. You can then move around among the records in the browse window. As you do so, you will see the corresponding data for the general field in the other window. (See Figure 19.5.)

FIGURE 19.5.

A browse window and general field data.

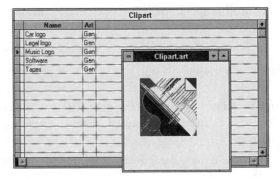

Inserting General Fields in Forms

You can use the OLE bound container control of the Form Controls toolbar to add OLE objects that are bound to a table's fields or a form's query. Use the following steps to add an OLE object (which is bound to a field) to a form:

1. Click the OLE bound container control on the Form Controls toolbar.

2. Click at the starting location on the form and drag until the frame reaches the desired size.

3. Right-click the frame and choose Properties from the shortcut menu that appears to open the properties window for the frame.

4. In the Data tab, set the frame's `ControlSource` property to the general field that contains the data.

Inserting General Fields in Reports

You can use the techniques in Chapter 13, "Designing and Customizing Reports," to add the contents of general fields to your reports. As that chapter notes, general fields can easily be added to a report's design by clicking the picture tool in the Report Controls toolbar, then clicking and dragging in the report to add a picture frame containing the general field. When you release the mouse button, the Report Picture dialog box appears. (See Figure 19.6.)

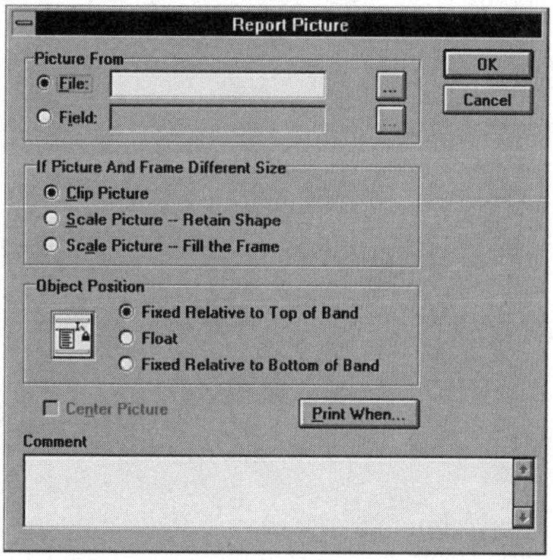

FIGURE 19.6.

The Report Picture dialog box.

Click the Field button, then click the Build button to the right of the Field text box to display a Choose Field/Variable dialog box. In this dialog box, double-click the name of the general field you want to place in the report, then click OK. Finally, click OK to close the Report Picture dialog box. You will then see a shaded rectangle representing the general field's contents. (See Figure 19.7.)

FIGURE 19.7.

An example of a report's design with a general field.

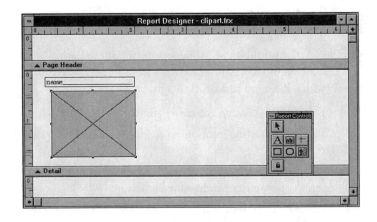

When you print the report, it displays the data stored in the general field as a graphic if a graphic is stored there, or as an icon representing the source application of a spreadsheet, word processing document, sound or video clip, or other type of OLE data stored there. Figure 19.8 shows a completed version of the report described here.

FIGURE 19.8.

The completed report with a general field.

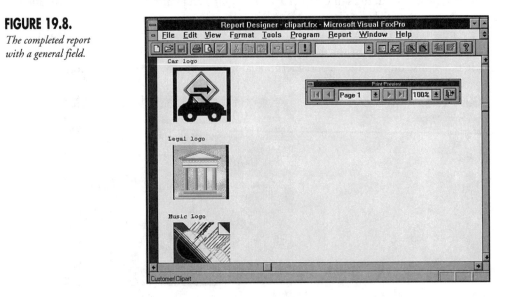

You can use the techniques in Chapter 12, "Designing and Customizing Forms," to enhance the report. Chapter 13 explains how you can add pictures stored in Windows Paintbrush format as design elements in your reports.

Summary

This chapter explains the techniques you'll find useful when sharing data with other programs by using object linking and embedding, or OLE. These techniques can help you take full advantage of the capability of other Windows software to work with your Visual FoxPro applications.

Working with Graphs

20

One feature of Visual FoxPro that isn't offered by many database-management packages is the capability to create business graphs. The graphs can be based on numeric data stored in a table. Visual FoxPro provides a Graph Wizard that asks the necessary questions to produce the graph almost automatically. After it's produced, a business graph can be printed or stored in a general field of a Visual FoxPro table, or it can be saved to a query that can be run to produce the graph. The graphs produced in Visual FoxPro are generated with MS Graph, a Windows mini-application provided with many Microsoft applications (including Visual FoxPro, Access, and Word for Windows). Because the latest version of MS Graph supports OLE 2 (as does Visual FoxPro), you can work with the graphs without leaving Visual FoxPro.

SAMPLE FILES

Sample files are provided as an adjunct to this chapter to demonstrate various charting techniques available using Visual FoxPro. The files are located in VFU\SAMPLES\.

File	Purpose
Buyers.DBC	The database that contains the data table CarSales.DBF.
CarSales.DBF	Provides the data used for the charting examples.
Ecology.PJX	Project that contains all the referenced files and data.

A Typical Graph

Figure 20.1 shows a typical graph produced within Visual FoxPro. (Graphs are also called *charts*; in fact, Microsoft uses the terms interchangeably.) Graphs are made up of *markers*, which represent the data produced by the query. The appearance of the markers changes depending on the type of graph you tell the Graph Wizard to create. In a bar graph or a column graph, the markers appear as horizontal or vertical bars. In a line graph, the markers appear as lines containing small symbols used for identification. In a pie chart, the markers are displayed as wedges of a pie. With the exception of pie charts, all graphs contain two axes: a horizontal axis known as the *category axis* and a vertical axis known as the *value axis*. (Three-dimensional graphs also contain a third axis, known as the *series axis*.) Graphs can also contain titles and legends that identify the markers. All of these items can be defined and changed by means of the MS Graph application after the graph has been created and stored in a table or a query.

FIGURE 20.1.

A typical graph.

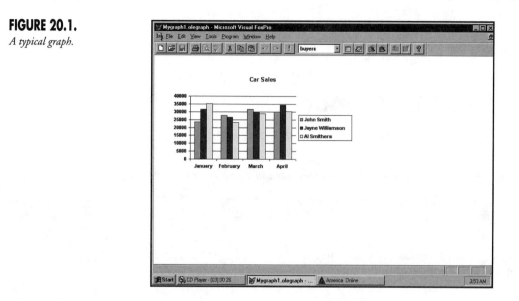

Preparing the Source of the Data

Before creating a graph, you need to prepare the source of the data on which the graph will be based. To do this, you might want to design a query that retrieves the appropriate data and use that query to create a new table containing just the data you want graphed. When the Graph Wizard runs, it will ask you to choose a table that provides the data to be graphed. If the table is not structured properly, the Graph Wizard will be unable to produce a graph with the proper results. It's all too easy to overlook this fact and jump right into the creation of the graph, but the results might be unexpected. By their very nature, most tables are likely to contain far more data than you want to graph at any time. Most likely you will want to base the data on some kind of summary, and that usually calls for refining the raw data into that summary. If the graph is based on a single table's data, you can use that table as the underlying data source within the query, design the query to select just the data you want to graph, and direct the query's output to a new table (which you can then use as the source of the data for the Graph Wizard). If the data comes from more than one table, you'll need to design and save a relational query that will provide the data source and direct that query's output to a new table. You'll want your table that contains the data to be graphed to contain the following:

- One or two fields that categorize the data. If the graph is to contain one horizontal axis, you'll use one field as a data category. If the graph is to contain two horizontal axes, you'll need two fields for this purpose. As an example, if you were tracking performance for a team of sales reps, you might use a field containing the names of the sales reps as a category. If you wanted to track those same sales reps by date, you might include two fields as categories in the graph: the name of the sales rep and the date the products were sold.

■ One or more numeric fields that are summarized or averaged in the graph. Each field you add results in an additional *data series*, or a set of markers used to plot a specific group of data on the graph.

Creating a Graph

The following steps outline the overall process of creating a graph. After these steps comes an exercise that you can follow to demonstrate this process.

1. Open the desired table that will serve as the source of data for the graph.

TIP

You might want to open the project that contains the table (either as part of a database or as a free table). With the project open already, you can easily save results and queries you construct with the appropriate project for later use.

2. From the menu, choose Tools | Wizards | Query to open the Wizard Selection dialog box for queries (see Figure 20.2).

FIGURE 20.2.

The Wizard Selection dialog box for queries.

3. Click Graph Wizard in the list box and then click OK. This causes the first Graph Wizard dialog box to appear, which asks which fields you want in your graph (see Figure 20.3).

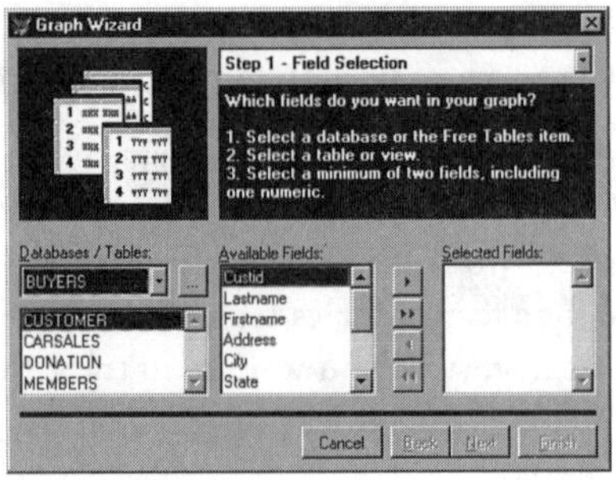

FIGURE 20.3.

The first Graph Wizard dialog box.

4. At the left side of the dialog box, you can select from any of the tables in the current database. After selecting the desired table, use the right-arrow buttons in the dialog box to add the desired fields to the Selected Fields list box. You can click each desired field and then click the single right-arrow button to add just that field, or you can click the double right-arrow button to add all of the fields. When you are finished, click Next to reveal the second Graph Wizard dialog box (see Figure 20.4).

FIGURE 20.4.

The Graph Wizard dialog box asking for a layout.

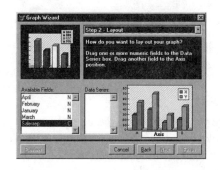

5. You use the second Graph Wizard dialog box to specify how the graph should be laid out. Drag the field that you'll use as a category axis from the Available Fields list box to the Axis position in the dialog box, and then drag one or more fields containing your values from the Available Fields list box to the Data Series list box. (Each field that you drag to the Data Series list box represents an additional data series, or set of markers, in the chart.) Then click Next.

6. The next dialog box to appear asks which style of graph you want (see Figure 20.5). Click the desired style of graph and then click Next. (For additional details on the available styles, see the section "About the Graph Styles," later in this chapter.)

FIGURE 20.5.

The dialog box asking for a desired style for the graph.

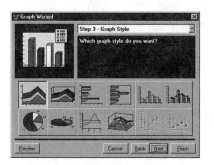

7. The last dialog box to appear (see Figure 20.6) asks for a title for the graph and gives you the option of saving the graph to a table or of saving and creating a query with the graph. You can also leave the Add a legend to the graph check box turned on if you want the graph to include a legend. Enter any desired title and choose the desired

options; then click Finish. You will see a Save As dialog box, asking for the name for the table or query where the graph is to be stored. Enter a name and click Save.

FIGURE 20.6.

The final Graph Wizard dialog box.

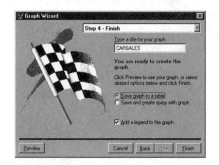

Visual FoxPro will add the data to the graph and in a moment, you'll see the graph displayed in a window like that shown earlier in Figure 20.1. You can print the graph by choosing File | Print. You can change various aspects of the graph's appearance by double-clicking it and using the techniques described in the section "Using MS Graph to Customize the Graph," later in this chapter.

Note that when you save a graph to a table, Visual FoxPro creates a new table and adds a single record to it. The graph is stored in the general field of that record. When you save a graph as a query, Visual FoxPro saves a query containing the information needed to build the graph when the query runs.

An Example: Creating a Graph

You can demonstrate how the Graph Wizard is used to create a graph by opening the CARSALES.DBF table. The CARSALES.DBF table is stored as part of the Buyers database in the Ecology project on the accompanying disk, and it contains the data shown here.

```
(CARSALES.DBF)
SALESREP            JANUARY     FEBRUARY     MARCH        APRIL
John Smith          23490.30    27800.50     31560.00     29900.00
Jayne Williamson    31500.00    26450.50     29900.00     34500.00
Al Smithers         35200.00    23250.00     28890.50     30250.50
```

You can perform these steps to create a column graph representing the car sales for each sales rep:

1. Open the Ecology project containing the Buyers database and the Carsales table; you'll use the Carsales table as the source of data for the graph.

2. From the menu, choose Tools | Wizards | Query to open the Wizard Selection dialog box for queries.

3. Click Graph Wizard in the list box and then click OK. This causes the first Graph Wizard dialog box to appear, which asks which fields you want in your graph.

4. Choose the Carsales table from the list of tables. Then click the double right-arrow button to add all of the fields to the Selected Fields list box. Then click Next to reveal the second Graph Wizard dialog box.

5. Drag the Salesrep field to the Axis position in the dialog box, then, one by one, drag all of the remaining fields (January, February, March, and April) to the Data Series list box. Then click Next.

6. The next dialog box to appear asks which style of graph is desired. Click the first Column style (it's the fifth from the left in the top row of styles) and then click Next.

7. The last dialog box to appear asks for a title for the graph and gives you the option of saving the graph to a table or saving and creating a query for the graph. Choose the Save Graph to a Table option and enter a title of Car Sales in the Title text box. Then click Finish. You will see a Save As dialog box asking for the name of the table where the graph is to be stored; enter Mygraph1 as a name and click Save. In a moment, the graph will appear in a window like the example shown earlier in Figure 20.1.

When you're done examining the graph, press Ctrl+F4 (or double-click the window's Close box) to close the graph window. If you want a printed copy, click the Print button in the toolbar or choose File | Print to print the graph.

About the Graph Styles

MS Graph provides nine different styles of graphs: area, bar, column, line, pie, hi-low, scatter, doughnut, and radar. (Note that you don't see doughnut and radar presented in the choices of styles offered by the Graph Wizard, but you can choose them by modifying the graph's design, as discussed in the next section of this chapter.) Each of the available types also provides numerous options, so you can choose from a wide variety of possible graph designs. The available types of graphs and their possible uses are described here:

- *Area graphs* indicate the importance of data over a period of time. Visually, such graphs are cumulative in nature, as they highlight the magnitude of change rather than the rate of change.

- *Bar graphs* show individual figures at a specific time, offering a visual emphasis of different values oriented horizontally.

- *Column graphs* are similar in design to bar graphs but are oriented vertically. Any passage of time is generally more apparent with a column graph.

- *Line graphs* are ideal for indicating trends in data that occur over a period of time. Line graphs are similar in design to area graphs, but line graphs highlight the rate of the change rather than the magnitude of the change.

- *Pie charts* identify the relationship between the pieces of a picture, or between a single part and the entire picture. Because each portion of the pie represents a part of the total series, a pie chart can represent only one data series at a time.

- *Hi-low graphs* are variations on line graphs. They show relationships among prices over a period of time and are commonly used to indicate fluctuations in stock and commodity prices.

- *Scatter graphs* show relationships between various points of data, or plot two groups of numbers as one set of X and Y coordinates. Scatter graphs are routinely used to plot scientific data.

- *Radar graphs* show relationships between a specific data series and the remainder of the data series. (They are commonly used in scientific applications, but unless you are used to viewing them, they can be difficult to interpret.)

- *Doughnut graphs* identify the relationship between the pieces of a picture, or between a single part and the entire picture. They serve the same purpose as pie charts. You can think of doughnut graphs as a type of multi-series pie chart.

Experimenting in MS Graph is an excellent way to discover the available graphs and their various formats. As you create graphs with the aid of the wizard, you can select different options in the dialog box to create graphs using the different available styles.

Customizing a Graph

Because graphs are actually OLE objects produced by MS Graph, you must double-click a graph to get into MS Graph to customize it. The OLE 2 in-place editing in Visual FoxPro provides a major improvement over the previous version of FoxPro for Windows in this area—when you get into MS Graph, your menu options and toolbar buttons change but you appear to remain in FoxPro. With OLE 1 the serving application took control and appeared on top of FoxPro. Only when you finished the editing and left the serving application did you return to FoxPro. Some users found this transition disturbing.

Using MS Graph to Customize the Graph

When you want to change a specific aspect of the graph itself, you can open the graph inside of MS Graph by performing the following steps:

1. If the graph is stored as a query, run the query to produce the graph. If the graph is stored in a table, open the table that contains the graph you want to modify. Find the record with the general field where the graph is stored and double-click in the general field to open a window into the field. (If the graph is visible because you've just completed the final step of the Graph Wizard, you can also double-click the graph.)

2. Double-click the graph.

When you double-click the graph, MS Graph takes partial control of the environment by means of OLE 2, and the FoxPro menus and toolbars change to reflect the options possible with MS Graph (see Figure 20.7).

FIGURE 20.7.

The Visual FoxPro main window under control of MS Graph.

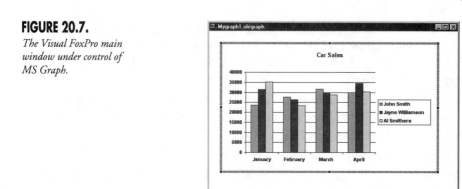

Because MS Graph is its own application independent of Visual FoxPro, the menus are different than any you've worked with in Visual FoxPro. A full discussion of all options presented by MS Graph is beyond the scope of this book, but you can refer to the MS Graph documentation packaged along with your Visual FoxPro documentation. The following paragraphs provide details on how you can perform the more common customizations of a graph.

■ To change the graph type (or style), open the Format menu and choose Chart Type. A Chart Type dialog box appears (see Figure 20.8). You can select area, bar, column, line, pie, scatter, or radar from among the possible graph types, as well as choose two-dimensional (2D) or three-dimensional (3D) graph types. Depending on the type of graph chosen, various other options can be selected. For example, by clicking the Options button in the dialog box, you can display an additional dialog box that enables you to change the overlap and gap width of bars and columns, the angle of the first slice in a pie chart, the depths used by 3D charts, and numerous other settings. When you're done choosing the desired options, click OK.

FIGURE 20.8.

The Chart Type dialog box.

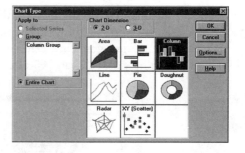

■ To change the font used by axis labels or by a title or a legend in the graph, first select the axis labels or title containing the text and then choose Format | Font from the main menu bar. In the dialog box that appears, select a desired font, font style, size, and color.

- To add a legend to an existing graph, choose Chart | Add Legend from the menus. To delete an existing legend, click the legend within the chart to select it and press the Delete key. To change the location of the legend, click and drag the legend to the desired location in the chart.

- You can change the colors and patterns used for any data series by double-clicking the data series and choosing a desired color or pattern in the Patterns dialog box that appears.

- To change the settings or line styles used by an axis, double-click the axis to open the Axis dialog box and choose the desired settings in the various tabs shown.

When you are done with the changes to the graph, click anywhere outside of the graph. The menus will revert back to FoxPro's normal menus, and the changes you made to the graph will appear.

Adding a Graph Using External Data

You can use Visual FoxPro to add a graph that contains data that is not stored in Visual FoxPro using the Datasheet window that is a part of MS Graph. When you want to do this, instead of using the Graph Wizard to base the graph on existing Visual FoxPro data, double-click in a general field of a table's record (where the graph will be stored) and choose Edit | Insert Object from the menus. When the Insert Object dialog box appears, choose Microsoft Graph 5.0 as the desired type of object and click OK. MS Graph starts automatically, and you can create the graph using the following steps. You can perform these steps to add a graph that is not based on any data in Visual FoxPro:

1. Open any table that has a general field and add a new record to that table.

2. Double-click in the general field of the record to open a window into the field.

3. From the menus, choose Edit | Insert Object. In the dialog box, click Microsoft Graph 5.0 to select it and then click OK. In a moment, an MS Graph window opens that contains sample data for a graph in a Datasheet window, and a resulting column graph based on that sample data appears beneath it (see Figure 20.9).

FIGURE 20.9.

MS Graph window containing sample data.

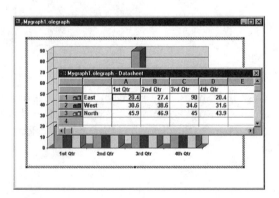

4. Type your data directly into the Datasheet window (see the following section, "Entering Data in the Datasheet Window," for details).

5. Choose Format | Chart Type to select the desired type of graph. Add any other objects (such as legends or titles) with the options of the Insert menu.

6. When the graph is complete, click anywhere outside of the graph. The graph is inserted into the general field of the Visual FoxPro table. If you later want to make changes to the graph, double-click the field to open the graph in a window. Double-click the graph again, and an MS Graph window containing the graph opens.

Entering Data in the Datasheet Window

To enter data in the Datasheet window, simply click in the desired cell and type the data directly into the cell. Enter a name for each data series, a label for each category, and a number for every value that is to be plotted in the graph. When you enter the data into the Datasheet window, MS Graph automatically creates a column chart. You can choose Format | Chart Type from the menus to change this to whatever type of chart you want. When you include text in the cells—labels to the left of the values, headings above the values, or both—MS Graph uses the text to add labels and a legend to the graph. In Figure 20.9, shown previously, the labels (East, West, and North) in the first column of the datasheet are used in the legend that appears in the graph. The headings (1st, 2nd, 3rd, and 4th Quarter) that appear above the values are used as labels in the graph.

You can move around in the datasheet with the cursor keys or by clicking in any cell with the mouse. If a column is too narrow to accommodate your data, you can widen it. Just click on a cell in the desired column (or move to the cell with the cursor keys), choose Format | Column Width from the menus, enter the desired width in the dialog box that appears, and click OK (or press Enter).

Formatting Data in the Datasheet Window

You can format the numbers you have entered in the datasheet. The format that you apply to the numbers is used by MS Graph to determine the type of tick marks that appear on the chart axes. For example, if you use a format that includes dollar signs for the numbers entered in the datasheet, MS Graph places dollar signs before the numbers that appear along the vertical axis.

If you do not choose a specific number format, MS Graph displays the numbers using a default format called the *General format*. The General format displays numbers with as much precision as possible. If a number is too wide to fit in a cell, General format causes the number to be displayed using scientific notation. To change the format of the numbers in the datasheet, select the cell or cells you want to format. Choose Format | Number from the menus. In the Number dialog box that appears, select the desired number format and then click OK.

About Pie Charts

Because pie charts show the relationship between parts and a whole, you can plot only a single data series in a pie chart. If you enter more than one row or column of data in the datasheet and choose Pie as the desired type of graph, MS Graph uses the data in the first row or column to build the graph. All additional data is ignored. (The commands available on the Data menu determine whether the chart is based on a row or a column.)

When working with pie charts, choose Data | Series in Rows or Data | Series in Columns menu commands (or the equivalent By Row and By Column buttons of the toolbar) to tell MS Graph whether the graph should be drawn based on a data series stored in rows or a data series stored in columns. Open the Data menu and choose Series in Rows if your data series is stored in the row; choose Series in Columns if your data series is stored in the column.

Exiting from MS Graph

To exit from MS Graph, click anywhere outside of the graph. The graph will be updated with its latest version, and the MS Graph window will close. The graph will be stored in the general field of the record, and you can print the graph by including the contents of the general field in your reports.

Summary

This chapter has detailed how you can effectively use graphs from within Visual FoxPro; no longer is it necessary (as it often is with older database managers) to export data to another program to create business graphs. If you often deal with numeric values, the use of graphs provides another way to highlight your information and emphasize trends. Additionally, if you use other Microsoft applications, you can use the techniques pertaining to MS Graph with many of those applications.

Power Techniques for Power Users

21

This chapter covers an assortment of topics that can be used to further extend Visual FoxPro and to get the most out of Visual FoxPro in combination with your specific applications. You learn how to work with dates and times, deal with memo fields, optimize performance, make use of various international settings, and deal with damaged database files. Note that some of the topics covered in this chapter require a familiarity with FoxPro programming. If you are unfamiliar with programming in Visual FoxPro, you can read about this topic beginning with Chapter 22, "Visual FoxPro Language Basics."

SAMPLE TABLE

A sample data table is provided as an adjunct to this chapter to demonstrate various techniques available using Visual FoxPro. The file is located in VFU\SAMPLES\.

File	Purpose
Customer.DBF	Used to supply the data for demonstrating actions with memo fields.

Handling Dates and Times

Like all variations of the Xbase language, Visual FoxPro has a date field type to handle the storage of dates. But just having the field type available doesn't solve all the potential problems involved in working with dates. You must perform calculations, deal with holidays, and you must often delete weekends from work time calculations. To make matters worse, dates are not dealt with in an equal manner worldwide. For example, 09/05/30 means September 5, 1930 to Americans; May 9, 1930 to most people in Europe; and May 30, 1909 to the Japanese. Visual FoxPro offers a wide variety of commands and functions to deal with dates, but you have to know how to use them to achieve the desired results.

As far as Visual FoxPro is concerned, dates are just a special kind of numeric value, and that is the key to using dates in calculations. Visual FoxPro stores dates internally in the format *YYYYMMDD*. For example, 19940322 equates to March 22, 1994. This means that you can (to a degree) perform math operations on date values. You can add a number of days to a date to produce another date, or you can subtract a date from another date and get the number of days between two dates. When you work with date values in calculations, remember to enclose the dates in curly braces so that Visual FoxPro knows the value is a date. For example, the expression

12/5/93 - 30

when evaluated by Visual FoxPro returns 29.97 because Visual FoxPro takes 12 and divides it by 5, takes the result and divides it by 93, and then subtracts 30 from the result. Obviously, this isn't what you want in an expression. On the other hand, the expression

```
{12/5/93} - 30
```

when evaluated by Visual FoxPro returns a date value of 11/5/93, or 30 days earlier than 12/5/93. You can add a number to a day to come up with a day in the future. For example, {1/30/94} + 30 yields 3/1/94, which is 30 days after 1/30/94. Expressions based on date calculations can often be useful in the design of your forms and reports. For example, assuming there is a date field called DAYHIRED in a table, a report could contain a calculated field indicating the number of months on the job using the following expression:

```
Int((Date()-DAYHIRED)/12)
```

You can display dates in a number of formats, depending on the SET DATE command or its equivalent Date setting within the view window. You can create a chronological index based on the contents of a date field by indexing on that field as you would on any other field. For example, the command

```
INDEX ON HIREDATE TAG DATES
```

creates an index tag based on the contents of the HIREDATE date field. To index in descending order, use the DESCENDING option of the INDEX command. (If you are indexing through the menus, you can also click the Descending button in the Index dialog box.) If you must create indexes that are compatible with FoxPro 1.x or FoxBase (which cannot create descending indexes), you can use a command like

```
INDEX ON CTOD("01/01/2199") - HIREDATE TO DATES
```

to build an index based on an expression that subtracts the date from some meaningless date in the future. Such an index has the characteristics of an index created in descending order, and the TO clause as part of the INDEX statement builds an index file that is compatible with FoxBase.

You can display dates in Visual FoxPro in several formats depending on the setting of the SET DATE command. The default value is American, which displays dates in a *mm/dd/yy* format (or in a *mm/dd/yyyy* format if SET CENTURY is On). Another useful choice for formats is ANSI (American National Standards Institute), which displays dates as *yy.mm.dd* (or *yyyy.mm.dd* if SET CENTURY is On). If you transfer the contents of tables containing date fields to older software packages or to mainframes, the other system will probably best deal with dates copied out in the ANSI format. The remaining options of the SET DATE command include British and French (both display as *dd/mm/yy*), Italian (displays as *dd/mm/yy*), German (displays as *dd.mm.yy*), Japanese (displays as *yy/mm/dd*), USA (*mm/dd/yy*), MDY (for month/day/year—*mm/dd/yy*), DMY (for day/month/year—*dd/mm/yy*), and YMD (for year/month/day—*yy/mm/dd*).

You set the date format using the SET DATE command. If you want to include all four characters of the year, turn on the Show Century check box. From the command window, you can put a desired setting for the date display in effect with the SET DATE command. Enter SET DATE *type*, where *type* is one of the 11 acceptable formats—American, ANSI, British, French, German, Italian, Japanese, USA, MDY, DMY, or YMD.

If you need to break a date into character strings, you can do so with one of the date conversion functions. For example, you might want to spell out the date at the top of a report. You could enter an expression into a field of the report and place that field in the report's header. The expression could contain the following:

```
CDOW(DATE()) + ", " + CMONTH(DATE()) + " " +
➥LTRIM(STR(DAY(DATE()))) + ", " + LTRIM(STR(YEAR(DATE())))
```

The expression causes a date (Friday, April 7, 1995, for example) to appear in the report.

Visual FoxPro offers a number of functions that convert dates to characters and character values to dates and that help you handle date data in other ways. Table 21.1 summarizes Visual FoxPro's commonly used date-related functions.

Table 21.1. Common date functions.

Function	Description
Between (d1,d2,d3)	Returns True if date d1 falls between dates d2 and d3.
CDOW(*date value* ¦ *DateTime Value*)	Returns the name of the day of the week that corresponds to the date value.
CMONTH(*date value* ¦ *DateTime Value*)	Returns the name of the month that corresponds to the date value.
CTOD(*char. string*)	Converts a character string to a date value. (The character string must be in a date format that matches the current settings of SET DATE and SET CENTURY.)
CTOT(char. string)	Returns a DateTime value from a character expression.
DATE()	Returns the system date.
DATETIME( )	Returns the current date and time in DateTime format.
DAY(*date value* ¦ *DateTime Value*)	Returns a number corresponding to the day of the date value.
DMY(*date value* ¦ *DateTime Value*)	Returns the date in *DDMMYY* format (or in *DDMMYY* format if SET CENTURY is On).
DOW(*date value* ¦ *DateTime Value*)	Returns a number corresponding to the day of the week for the date value.
DTOC(*date value*,[1])	Converts the date value to a character string. If the optional 1 parameter is included, the character string takes the *YYYYMMDD* format (same as the DTOS() function).

Function	Description
DTOS(*date value ¦ DateTime Value*)	Converts the date value to a character string with the *YYYYMMDD* format.
DTOT(date value)	Returns a DateTime value from a Date expression.
EMPTY(*date value¦ DateTime Value*)	Returns a logical True if the date value is empty.
GOMONTH(*date value¦ DateTime Value,n*)	Returns a date that is *n* months before or after the date value.
MDY(*date value¦ DateTime Value*)	Returns the date in *MM DD, YYYY* format (or in *MM DD, YYYY* format if SET CENTURY is On).
MONTH(*date value¦ DateTime Value*)	Returns a number representing the month of the date value.
SECONDS()	Returns the number of seconds since midnight.
TIME()	Returns the system time as a character string in the 24-hour format *HH:MM:SS*.
TTOC(DateTime value [,1])	Returns a character value from a DateTime expression. [,1] sets the option whereby a character string suitable for indexing is returned. The character string has a 14-character yyyy:mm:dd:hh:mm:ss format that is not affected by the settings of SET CENTURY or SET SECONDS.
YEAR(date value)	Returns a four-digit number representing the year of the date value.

One area that might cause problems in a date-intensive application is how to handle dates that stretch into the twenty-first century. This is a problem that is going to haunt programmers and developers worldwide as systems that were not designed to deal with anything but a twentieth-century date are maintained, for better or for worse, into and beyond the year 2000. For this reason, Visual FoxPro provides the SET CENTURY command (and the equivalent Show Century check box in the view window), which switches on the full four-digit display of dates. You must turn on the SET CENTURY setting if you want to enter, display, or edit dates other than twentieth-century dates.

DateTime Data Types

Visual FoxPro introduces a new data type called DateTime that is a combination of both date and time types. A DateTime value can store both a date and time, or only a date, or only a time. It is stored as a yyyymmddhhmmss character string. If you don't specify a date value, Visual FoxPro uses a default date value of December 30, 1899. If you don't specify a time value, Visual FoxPro uses a default time value of midnight (00:00:00).

DateTime values are useful for capturing and manipulating time intervals and can be directly added and subtracted from one another. As an example of a one-hour time interval crossing a day, type the following in the Command window:

```
dt1 = {1/1/95 11:50PM}
dt2 = {1/2/95 00:50AM}
```

then type

```
?(dt2 - dt1)
```

This makes the number 3600 appear. This is exactly the number of seconds one expects (note that the results are in seconds) for a one-hour interval, but it would require more coding without the DateTime data type.

The following rules apply to both Date and DateTime data types:

- {00:00:00AM} is the same as {12:00:00AM}, Midnight.
- {00:00:00PM} is the same as {12:00:00PM}, Noon.
- {00:00:00} to {11:59:59} is the same as {12:00:00AM} to {11:59:59AM}
- {12:00:00} to {23:59:59} is the same as {12:00:00PM} to {11:59:59PM}

Working with Memo Fields

Since their introduction in the earlier days of Xbase, memo fields and commands for dealing with the contents of memo fields have become an important part of the Xbase language. The obvious reason for the use of memo fields is to accommodate the storage of lengthy text, particularly where that length varies wildly between records. If you are working with a large amount of textual data you can store that data in memo fields and still maintain the ability to perform effective searches based on the contents of those fields.

Editing the Contents of Memo Fields

By default, a memo field in a change/edit or browse window appears as a small field containing the word *memo* (in all lowercase letters) if no data has been stored in the field or *Memo* (capitalized) if data has been stored in the field. Double-clicking the memo field opens a window in the field. However, there are better ways to display and edit a memo field. (If you use the Form Wizards to design a form, any memo fields are placed into edit regions automatically.) Techniques for adding edit regions are covered in detail in Chapter 12, "Designing and Customizing Forms." In a nutshell, you perform the following steps to add an edit region for editing memo fields to a form's design:

1. Open the form in design view, and in the Forms Control toolbar, click the Edit Box tool.
2. Click and drag in the form to size the box on the form.
3. After you size the box, right-click the box and choose Properties from the shortcut menu. You do this to choose a field with which to associate the edit box.
4. Now choose Control | Source from the Data tab of the Properties menu.
5. Double-click the choice until you see the name of the memo field appear. (Be sure that the Builder Lock button is depressed in the Form Controls toolbox.)
6. Next, close the Form Designer and run the form.

Figure 21.1 shows a completed screen containing an edit region added for the entry and editing of memo field data. By default, edit regions that you add contain scrollbars, which are useful for viewing memo field data that spans many paragraphs or pages.

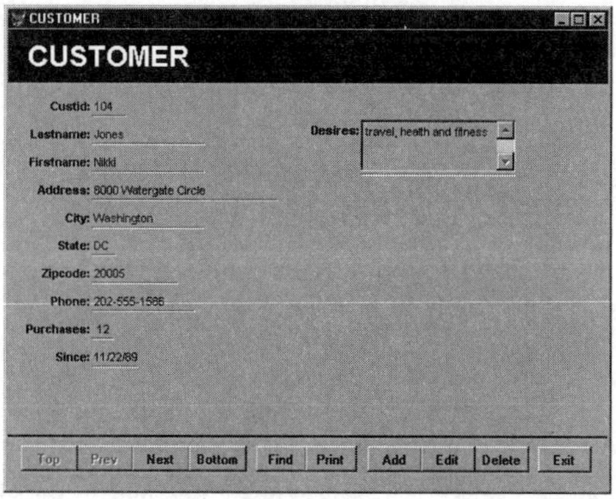

FIGURE 21.1.

A form with an edit region for adding and editing memo field data.

You can also use commands within a program to define and then open a window in a memo field. You can use Visual FoxPro's SET WINDOW OF MEMO TO *windowname* command to permit editing of a memo field within a window you previously defined with the DEFINE WINDOW command. For instance, the following statements within a program would cause the contents of a memo field (called "Notes" in this example) to appear in the defined window. (See Figure 21.2.)

```
DEFINE WINDOW ForNotes SYSTEM FROM 10,5 TO 18,60
MODIFY MEMO Notes WINDOW ForNotes
```

FIGURE 21.2.

The contents of a memo field displayed in a window.

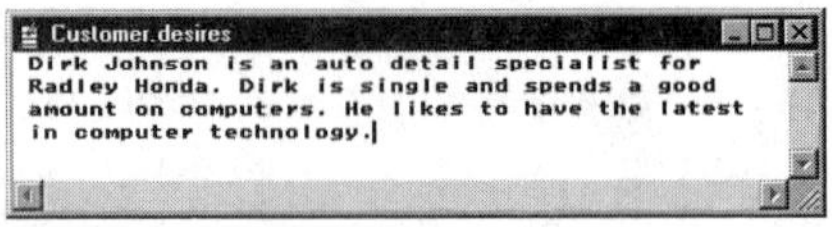

Displaying Memo Field Data

You can display memo field data with the LIST or DISPLAY command. Include the name of the memo field in a FIELDS clause as part of the LIST or DISPLAY command. If you do not do so, you get a column with just the word *memo* or *Memo* instead of the actual contents of the field. For example, if the following command is issued on the Customers table, here are the results:

```
USE Customer
SET FIELDS TO lastname, firstname, phone, desires
LIST OFF
```

LASTNAME	FIRSTNAME	PHONE	DESIRES
Roberts	Jamie	703-555-2321	Memo
Sanderson	Lucy	703-555-5681	Memo
Smith	Larry	301-555-2815	Memo
Jones	Nikki	202-555-1586	Memo
Hernandez	Maria	301-555-6725	Memo
Jones	Jarel	703-555-9091	Memo
Zeibermann	Daniel	703-555-2114	Memo
O'Neill	John	703-555-9256	Memo
Bannerton	Alicia	703-555-1200	Memo

On the other hand, when a FIELDS clause includes the memo field by name, the results are distinctly different, as shown here:

```
USE CUSTOMER
LIST OFF LASTNAME, FIRSTNAME, DESIRES
```

LASTNAME	FIRSTNAME	DESIRES
Roberts	Jamie	Science-fiction, fan of Asimov, Bradbury, and L. Niven.
Sanderson	Lucy	American and world history, computer programming texts
Smith	Larry	travel books and videos
Jones	Nikki	travel, health and fitness
Hernandez	Maria	books on aviation and pilot safety.
Jones	Jarel	graphic novels and out-of-print comic books
Zeibermann	Daniel	science and technology, computers
O'Neill	John	photography
Bannerton	Alicia	home improvement, landscaping techniques

Note that when you list memo field data this way, Visual FoxPro defaults to a width of 50 for the memo field data. This may or may not be ideal for your purposes. If you want, you can change this default width by entering SET MEMOWIDTH TO *numeric expression*, where *numeric expression* is the desired width. For example, consider the same data shown above after the SET MEMOWIDTH statement is used to change the default width. In the listing that follows, the maximum memo width of 25 characters forces the memo field data to occupy more lines in the listing.

```
LASTNAME        FIRSTNAME       DESIRES
Roberts         Jamie           Science-fiction, fan of
                                Asimov, Bradbury, and L.
                                Niven.
Sanderson       Lucy            American and world
                                history, computer
                                programming texts
Smith           Larry           travel books and videos
Jones           Nikki           travel, health and
                                fitness
Hernandez       Maria           books on aviation and
                                pilot safety.
Jones           Jarel           graphic novels and
                                out-of-print comic books
Zeibermann      Daniel          science and technology,
                                computers
O'Neill         John            photography
Bannerton       Alicia          home improvement,
                                landscaping techniques
```

Of course, you can also include memo fields in the stored reports you create using Visual FoxPro's Report Designer. An advantage of using stored reports is that Visual FoxPro handles all formatting automatically. When you place memo fields within a report, you might want to turn on the Field Can Stretch option in the Report Expression dialog box to enable the field to stretch to accommodate lengthy data.

Using Memo Fields for Binary Large Object (BLOB) Storage

Although memo field usage is usually associated with the storage and manipulation of text, it is really able to store any binary data. Your imagination is the only limit to how you choose to use memo fields.

Not all documents are produced by OLE-enabled applications. You can embed non-OLE documents in your database by placing them into a memo field rather than a general field. When it is time to edit these documents you can re-create the memo-embedded document again as a file, and then the serving application can be called to operate on it.

Because the document resides in your memo field you can use text-searching techniques on it from within FoxPro as well.

One caveat: Manipulating (writing into or altering) the memo field might break the internal structure of the stored document. FoxPro functions that operate on memo fields assume the fields are text; therefore, the results are unspecified when they are used to modify non-text data.

A Note About Memo Field Incompatibilities

Keep in mind that earlier Xbase products (including dBASE III Plus and FoxBase+) cannot read the contents of memo fields created with Visual FoxPro. Use the FOXPLUS type option of the COPY TO command, as detailed in Chapter 17, "Sharing Data with Other Software," to create tables with memo fields that are compatible with earlier Xbase products.

Optimizing Performance

Performance is obviously a sort of Holy Grail among database users—if magazine ads that pit one product's speed against another are any indication. Since its inception, FoxPro has had a reputation for speed above all else. One could argue that some Windows database managers are easier to use than Visual FoxPro, but if raw speed is what you're after, Visual FoxPro is the product for you. With the capability to retrieve subsets of data from tables of more than 500,000 records in a matter of seconds, Visual FoxPro is no slouch. However, those who must press toward the ultimate goal of accomplishing everything in zero time can speed up an already fast product.

Normally you want your indexes, files, and tags to be open so they can remain updated, but you must remember that this comes at a performance price. You can strike an effective balance between data retrieval speed and data entry speed and editing by building indexes that are used only as needed. For example, if a report that uses an unusual index key is printed only once a month, don't add a tag for that key to the structural compound index file. Instead, build the index as an individual (.IDX) index file before printing the report, and erase the index file when you are finished with the report.

Another performance tip is that you should occasionally rebuild your compound index (.CDX) files. This can reduce the .CDX file size and improve performance. When you are re-creating tags in a compound index file, you should first remove the tags using the DELETE TAG ALL command.

When SET DOHISTORY is left on, it noticeably reduces program execution; therefore, be sure it is not left on from any debugging activities. For the same reason, be sure that unneeded SET TALK ON commands are not left within your programs.

The use of macro substitution (the & character in programs) should be kept to a minimum. Occurrences of the macro character can often be replaced with something else, such as an indirect reference or the use of the EVALUATE() function.

Another performance tip is to pack your tables from time to time. Doing so reduces the size of the tables and improves performance. Use the PACK MEMO command to reduce the size of associated memo files, particularly with tables in which you often make changes to memo fields.

To improve the general performance of BROWSE commands, periodically sort tables to the order most frequently used by your indexes.

To optimize performance during updates to records, use the following tips:

- If you create applications with preset index tags, use as few tags as possible to accomplish the needed tasks within the application.

- Create tags to support specific relationships, commonly performed SEEK commands, BROWSE commands with Keys clauses, and all Rushmore-optimizable FOR clauses.

- Where possible, use the *masterbase-childbase* or *batch-update* system of data entry, particularly with large tables. With this design approach, new records are not added to the main table but instead are added to a temporary table with the same structure as the main table. After the data entry is completed, you can add the new records from the child table to the master table by using the APPEND FROM command. The module you use for the batch entry of records works at top speed and lets the master table contain the tags that are needed to support your queries without slowing performance during the data entry process.

Keep Windows in Mind...

When you are looking to get the most in performance from Visual FoxPro for Windows, remember that the overall Windows environment is also going to have an effect on how well Visual FoxPro works. Like all Windows applications, Visual FoxPro for Windows is dependent on a sufficient allocation of Windows system resources to accomplish operations with reasonable speed. The more Windows applications you have running, the less system resources Visual FoxPro can find; therefore, it makes sense to shut down any unneeded applications. On machines with only 4MB of RAM, it is a wise idea to run Visual FoxPro without any other Windows applications open. Also, on 4MB machines, avoid the use of wallpaper (in Windows, open the Main window, double-click Control Panel, double-click Desktop, and change Wallpaper to None). These tips apply whether you are using Windows 3.*x* or Windows 95.

Optimizing for Rushmore

A significant reason behind Visual FoxPro's claim to fame in the area of performance is *Rushmore*, a patent-pending technology that Visual FoxPro uses to speed searches and data retrievals—all versions of FoxPro since FoxPro 2.0 use it. Precisely how Rushmore works might be a closely guarded Microsoft secret, but what Rushmore does with FoxPro commands is open knowledge. If you understand what Rushmore does, you can structure your data operations so that Rushmore can accomplish the most. Rushmore does the following:

- Analyzes any commands that contain FOR *expression* clauses and uses any available indexes to speed response time. (How much of a speed improvement is gained depends on how closely the expression included in the FOR clause matches the index key.) Rushmore can use any available indexes, whether they are tags of compound index files or standard or compact index files in FoxPro's IDX format.

- Analyzes any SQL SELECT statements and looks for available indexes to help speed processing of these statements. If no indexes exist that will help in the processing of a SQL SELECT statement, Rushmore builds temporary indexes as needed to effectively perform the query.

■ Analyzes SET FILTER statements to see if the expression used as part of the statement can be optimized by Rushmore technology. If the expression is optimizable, Rushmore uses existing indexes to speed the execution of the SET FILTER statement.

In cases in which Rushmore cannot optimize or speed the execution of a command, the operation occurs at speeds equivalent to those in versions of FoxPro prior to Version 2.0. Also, note that in low-memory situations, Visual FoxPro might not be able to use Rushmore.

TIP

To take advantage of Rushmore when retrieving data from more than one table, you *must* use the SQL SELECT command (either by constructing a query through the RQBE window or by typing it directly into the Command window). Rushmore is the basic technology used to optimize all SQL queries.

One point to remember is that *available indexes* refers to indexes that are open, not just indexes that have been created at some point in time and might exist on the disk. If an index is not opened along with a table, Rushmore cannot use it. (This does not apply to SQL queries, because Rushmore automatically handles all indexing needs.) This is another argument in favor of storing all your indexes as tags in the structural compound index file, because these are opened automatically along with the table. Another point to remember is that for best performance you should not set the order of the table. You can use a SET ORDER TO statement without naming an index (see "The SET ORDER Trick" section later in this chapter).

In deciding how to structure your commands to get the most out of Rushmore, you need to determine whether an expression is *optimizable*. If an expression is optimizable, Rushmore can speed the execution of certain commands using that expression. Rushmore can optimize any of the following commands when a FOR clause is included and when the expression itself is optimizable (as discussed in the following paragraphs):

AVERAGE	INDEX
BROWSE	LABEL
CALCULATE	LIST
CHANGE	LOCATE
COPY TO	RECALL
COPY TO ARRAY	REPLACE
COUNT	REPORT
DELETE	SCAN
DISPLAY	SORT
EDIT	SUM
EXPORT	TOTAL

For Rushmore to do any good, the FOR clause included with the preceding commands must be optimizable. FOR clauses are optimizable when indexes are available to support the use of the FOR clause. For example, you might have active index tags for a table based on the following expressions:

```
LASTNAME + FIRSTNAME
CUSTID
ZIPCODE
HIREDATE
```

and in such a case, the following expressions are optimizable:

```
LASTNAME = "Miller"
LASTNAME = "Miller" .AND. FIRSTNAME = "Susan"
CUSTID = 1022
ZIPCODE >= "90210"
HIREDATE > {01/31/93}
```

Because the expression used by a FOR clause can be made up of more than one condition, the FOR clauses might be fully optimizable, partially optimizable, or not optimizable at all. Consider the following command:

```
LOCATE FOR LASTNAME = "Johnson"
```

In the past, serious Xbase users would avoid such a command like the plague because LOCATE was very slow compared to FIND or SEEK. But with Rushmore, if an index based on the LASTNAME field is created with the following statement and the index is active, the LOCATE command will find the desired data very quickly due to Rushmore's optimization.

```
INDEX ON LASTNAME TAG NAMES
```

In this example, the LOCATE command is *fully optimizable*. By comparison, if the LOCATE command uses the following statement and the index is constructed only on the basis of the LASTNAME field, the statement is *partially optimizable* by Rushmore:

```
LOCATE FOR LASTNAME = "Johnson" .AND. FIRSTNAME = "linda"
```

To be fully optimizable in this case, you would need an active index with a key based on a combination of the LASTNAME and FIRSTNAME fields.

When trying to determine to what degree FOR clauses are optimizable, keep the following guidelines in mind:

- When all expressions in a FOR clause are optimizable, the clause is fully optimizable.
- The clause FOR *expression A* .AND. *expression B* is partially optimizable when *expression A* is optimizable and *expression B* is not.
- The clause FOR *expression A* .OR. *expression B* is partially optimizable only when both *expression A* and *expression B* are at least partially optimizable.

- When no expressions in the FOR clause are optimizable, the clause is said to be *non-optimizable*.

When you build indexes, keep in mind that there are some restrictions on Rushmore. Rushmore cannot work with indexes created with the UNIQUE keyword or with the INDEX FOR variation of the INDEX command. Rushmore also cannot work with indexes that contain database alias names within the index expression or with indexes that use NOT operators as part of the index key. Finally, Rushmore cannot optimize any commands that contain WHILE clauses.

> **TIP**
>
> You can improve Rushmore's performance by setting DELETED to OFF, particularly with queries that return a large number of records.

Turning Rushmore Off

If for any reason you want to disable Rushmore, you can do so in one of two ways. You can add the keyword NOOPTIMIZE to any command that uses a FOR clause to disable Rushmore for that command. You can also enter SET OPTIMIZE OFF when you no longer want to use Rushmore for any reason, and Rushmore is disabled for all commands until you enter SET OPTIMIZE ON. One case in which you should disable Rushmore is when you use a command (which could be optimized) that will modify the very index key used as part of the command's FOR clause. In such cases, Rushmore's internal record set can become out of sync, resulting in improper retrieval of data. You should disable Rushmore by adding the NOOPTIMIZE clause to the statement to prevent this from happening.

The *SET ORDER* Trick

In many cases, Rushmore works best when tables are in their natural order (that is, when no index is controlling the order of the records). You can put an open table in its natural order after indexes have been activated by using a SET ORDER TO statement without naming any indexes after the statement.

A Note About Rushmore and Indexes

Because Rushmore does its work with FOR clauses and SET FILTER statements when supporting indexes are active, you might be tempted to add an index tag that corresponds to most or all fields of a table. In most cases this is not a good idea. Doing so can work wonders for the speed of searches and reporting, but the adding and editing of individual records can slow to a crawl. Each time a record is added or edited all of the index tags for that record must be updated. You'll have to strike a balance between a sufficient number of open indexes to support effective data retrieval with the aid of Rushmore while not slowing the data entry and editing processes to an unacceptable level.

International Issues

Visual FoxPro enables you to change a number of settings in the International section. Among these changes are the currency symbols used and the method of time display. This section deals with how to change the settings in the International section by using the view window.

The date is the first thing that can be changed in the International section. Open the Tools menu and choose Options, then click the International tab of the Options dialog box (see Figure 21.3). The current values are set for the American formats. Click the arrow beside Date Format, and you will see a list of countries from which you can select the desired date format. You can also show the century by clicking the Century option. The date delimiter enables you to change the delimiter that separates the months, dates, and years.

FIGURE 21.3.

The International tab of the Options dialog box.

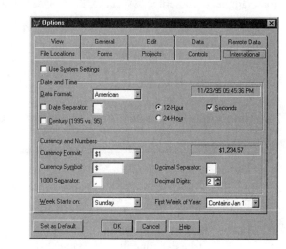

You can also change the currency symbol. The symbol can also be moved from the left to the right of the numbers. You can also change decimal places from zero decimal places to up to 18 places.

Some users prefer the 24-hour clock to the 12-hour clock. You can change the format by choosing the desired option (12-hour clock or 24-hour clock).

You can also use commands to change the international settings. The following is a list of the commands:

- For the date there is the SET DATE *country* command, where *country* is the name of the country, as in SET DATE AMERICAN or SET DATE JAPAN.
- To add the century, enter SET CENTURY ON.

- To change the delimiter, enter SET MARK TO *delimiter*, where *delimiter* is the character that you want to use as the delimiter.
- To move the currency symbol, use SET CURRENCY RIGHT or SET CURRENCY LEFT. The LEFT option positions the currency symbol to the left of the amount, and the RIGHT option positions the currency symbol to the right of the amount.
- To change the decimal setting, enter SET DECIMALS TO *number of decimal places desired*.
- To change the hours, enter SET HOURS TO 12 or SET HOURS TO 24.

Setting an International Sort Order

Visual FoxPro provides the SET COLLATE TO command, which lets you specify a sorting or *collating* order that is adapted to a specific language. SET COLLATE TO can be used to properly sort and index tables that contain accented characters for any of the languages supported by Visual FoxPro. For example, if you enter SET COLLATE TO SPANISH, a sort or index operation would consider *ch* and *ll* to be separate letters of the alphabet.

You specify the collation sequence with the command SET COLLATE TO *character expression*, where *character expression* is any of the following choices: DUTCH, GENERAL, ICELAND, MACHINE, NORDAN, SPANISH, and SWEFIN. These options are used for the languages shown in Table 21.2.

Table 21.2. Languages for the Set Collate command.

Option	Languages used
DUTCH	Dutch
GENERAL	English, French, German, modern Spanish, Portuguese, and other Western European languages
ICELAND	Icelandic
MACHINE	Machine (the default collation sequence for earlier versions of FoxPro)
NORDAN	Norwegian and Danish
SPANISH	Traditional Spanish
SWEFIN	Swedish and Finnish

Note that once you use SET COLLATE, the new collating order takes effect for indexes created from then on. SET COLLATE does not affect the order of records according to previously created indexes. This is advantageous because you can maintain different index orders for different languages by creating the indexes while SET COLLATE is set to different settings. The default for SET COLLATE is GENERAL, which matches the default collation order used by FoxPro.

> **TIP**
>
> If you regularly use the same collation order, you can specify that order when you start Visual FoxPro by choosing Tools | Options, clicking the Data tab in the dialog box that appears, and choosing the order you want in the Collating Sequence list box.
>
> ```
> COLLATE = character expression
> ```
>
> This is identical to issuing the command SET COLLATE TO *character expression* from the Command window.

When you use a different collation order, keep in mind that FoxPro's Rushmore technology can only take advantage of indexes that have a collation sequence that matches the current collation sequence. If you are building indexes to support several languages, make sure that the current collation sequence matches the collation sequences for the active indexes and index tags.

Repairing Damaged Database Files

A somber adage says that there are only two kinds of computer users in this world: those who have lost data, and those who will. Visual FoxPro is a complex database management system, and as with any complex system there is always a possibility that data will be damaged or lost. As a developer, you can minimize the chances of data loss with good housekeeping techniques (opening files only when necessary, closing files as soon as possible, and including good backup routines in your programs). However, it helps to understand a little more than the average Visual FoxPro user about how Visual FoxPro stores data in a table file. Such knowledge might come in handy if one of your application files gets inexplicably damaged and, contrary to dire warnings, the users haven't performed a backup in two months.

A FoxPro table (.DBF) file consists of a file header, the file data (in the form of individual records), and an end-of-file marker (ASCII Decimal 26 or Hex 1A). The contents of the memo fields are another matter entirely. They are stored in a separate file with a .DBT extension. The memo field in the database (.DBF) file contains a pointer used to find the text in the associated .DBT file. The file header contains the date of the last file update, the number of records present in the file, a rather cryptic description of the database structure, and other information needed by Visual FoxPro.

The contents of the fields are packed into records that are not delimited or separated with any special characters. Each record begins with one byte that contains a space (ASCII Decimal 32 or Hex 20) if the record is not deleted and an asterisk (ASCII Decimal 42 or Hex 2A) if the record is deleted. Visual FoxPro keeps a count of the number of records in a database by means of various hex codes stored in the file header. If the header is damaged or destroyed, you have run up against the more serious type of damage that can occur. Visual FoxPro will think that there are fewer records in the file than are actually present, or worse yet, will refuse to open the file and instead displays the following heart-stopping error message when your program attempts to use the file:

```
Not a Table/DBF
```

If the header has been damaged, any attempt to repair the damage requires a program that lets you edit the data contained in the header. If you are familiar with the DOS DEBUG utility, you can use it to change the contents of the header. (See your DOS manual for more instructions about DEBUG.) If the file is relatively small, you can use a good program editor (such as PC-Write, a shareware product available on bulletin boards) to edit the header in a word processing mode.

In either case, make a backup copy of the damaged file before you attempt to perform any repairs. Once you have made a backup copy, you can try to manually calculate the proper hex values and rebuild the header to the point where Visual FoxPro will recognize it as a valid database header. If Visual FoxPro manages to open a file with a damaged header, the record count within the file should be immediately suspect. Because the record count is the last part of a header that is updated just before the file is closed, any system crash that occurs while a file is open will probably leave the header with an incorrect record count. You should use the COPY command to immediately create a new file by copying the records out to the damaged file with the following commands:

```
USE Damaged
COPY TO GoodFile
```

When the COPY command has finished copying valid records to the new file, it updates the reccount count in the header of the new file with an accurate figure. The old file can then be deleted and the new file substituted in its place.

Good Header, Bad Data

More common among trashed table files is a file that contains a valid header but damaged data in the file. For example, the display for some of the records are garbled when your program performs an EDIT function. Or when you use LIST, you get something that looks like this:

```
LNAME       FNAME      ADDRESS            CITY        STATE ZIP
Hobbs       Kerie      1607 Valencia Way  Reston      VA    22090
Hoffman     Carol      1569 Trails Edge Ln Reston     VA    22091
Hoffman     Carol^!       1569 Trails Edge L[]ResHogan       Debra
982 Gr anby Court  Ste rling       VA22070     Hummer      Annette
1528 Sca ndia Circle Lee sburg     VA22075     Hunt        John W.
1604 Sto we Road    Her ndon       VA22070     Hutcheson   Charles
```

For reasons unknown, random extra data has been introduced to your data file and has corrupted the database: the contents of the fields appear to straddle the field limits, and it appears that a re-keying of the data is the only way to proceed. Before resorting to such a drastic solution, try restoring the file first. Copy the file to another temporary file, which you will use to attempt to repair the database.

First, using the temporary file, go to the first damaged record. Delete that record and the record prior to it (in many cases, the record prior to the first record that appears damaged is the one causing the problem). Then, pack the database. These simple steps might repair the damage.

If the problem still exists you must resort to a program other than Visual FoxPro that lets you directly edit the database file containing the table. Use DEBUG or a program editor to find the damaged record and insert or remove Hex 20 (blank spaces) as needed until the data aligns properly within the fields when in Visual FoxPro. You can probably manage to do this by deleting characters that don't appear to belong or by inserting spaces in the faulty record on a trial-and-error basis (or by using both methods). Go in and out of browse mode in Visual FoxPro to check your progress until the data appears to fill the fields properly.

Random End-Of-File Marker

Another type of damage that occasionally occurs is when an extra end-of-file marker (Hex 1A) gets placed somewhere in the table file. This is commonly caused by an abnormal exit; perhaps the system was rebooted before Visual FoxPro had a chance to properly close the file.

Extra end-of-file markers cause Visual FoxPro to behave in an interesting and baffling manner. Here are some sample telltale signs: you enter LIST STRUCTURE and Visual FoxPro tells you that there are 198 records in the database. You do a LIST and Visual FoxPro shows you everything up to Record 82 and then dumps you back at the command level. The BROWSE command gives you bizarre results, sometimes displaying some of the records and sometimes displaying all of the records in a normal fashion. Your report-generating and label-generating programs pretend that nothing exists above Record 82. If you enter GO 84 to move to Record 84 and then enter LIST NEXT 200, Visual FoxPro shows you the remaining records in the database.

What has happened is this: somehow an extra end-of-file character occupies a space at or near the end of Record 82. This problem can be corrected without leaving Visual FoxPro although, if you are fluent with DEBUG or with your program editor, you should by all means use that route. Use the COPY command to copy the records before the end-of-file character to a temporary file. Here is an example:

```
USE CLIENTS
COPY TO TEMP1
```

Then, go to the record following the false end-of-file marker and copy the remaining records to another table. Here is an example:

```
GO 84
COPY NEXT 9999 TO TEMP2
```

Then, use the first temporary file and copy the records from the second file into the first with the following command:

```
USE TEMP1
APPEND FROM TEMP2
```

Finally, delete your damaged file and then rename your temporary file to the name of the damaged file. At the most, you might lose one record with this approach.

Index Files

When a database has been damaged, all associated index files become immediately suspect. Any index files should be re-created from scratch before the application is used again. Don't use the REINDEX command because it is possible that the structure of the index file has also been damaged.

The best time to think about recovering from the effects of damaged files is before such damage occurs. Assume the worst will happen and take steps to provide recovery from system crashes. In case your users don't remember to back up files, a forceful reminder using the RUN command to run your chosen backup utility regularly is a wise addition to any application. If money is no object when it comes to data security, you should use good surge protection, a high-speed tape backup system, and an uninterruptible power supply. Don't wait until someone calls frantically pleading for help to decide how you'll go about the business of crash recovery.

Summary

Visual FoxPro provides a wealth of tools and techniques for accomplishing your programming tasks. Most professional FoxPro developers have a personal library of tricks and tips that they reach into with every programming job. This chapter just scratched the surface of what's possible, and perhaps hinted at what you might place in your "programmer's grab bag."

Internationalization is a hot topic for developers these days. The world is becoming a smaller place, and the code you write might find its way to non-English users. How to approach multiple languages and currencies begins with your development tools. This chapter has introduced these to you.

This chapter also discussed data damage and how to address the problem when you face it.

PART

Programming in Visual FoxPro

Visual FoxPro Language Basics

This chapter introduces the real power behind Visual FoxPro—programming. You'll learn how programs are created and executed under the FoxPro programming language and how expressions, functions, and memory variables can be used effectively in your Visual FoxPro programs.

No programming experience is assumed. Our approach will be to develop a notion of "programming" for a user who is conversant with Visual FoxPro commands and functions typed into the Command window. Once this level of sophistication is reached, the step from single command entry to lists of stored commands is relatively straightforward. As a minimal definition, a list of instructions or commands that directs a computer's operation is a *program.* Visual FoxPro programs can be no more than lists of commands written in the FoxPro programming language and saved in a file. Command files—files made up of Visual FoxPro commands—make it possible to program with Visual FoxPro.

The FoxPro programming language uses the same commands you enter manually in the Command window and supplements these with control structures. Any series of commands entered in the Command window can also be stored in a text file. (The text file can be created by the editor built into Visual FoxPro or by any editor that can create normal text files of ASCII characters.) Files with FoxPro commands are known as command files or as programs. The two terms are often used interchangeably.

Visual FoxPro programs can range from a simple list of a few commands to dozens of interrelated files with hundreds of commands. When multiple files of commands are used to perform specific tasks related to a specific business goal, the collection of files is often referred to as an *application.* For example, some command files may be designed to process transactions in an accounting system. Those command files are called an accounting application running under Visual FoxPro. Much of the work done behind the scenes in Visual FoxPro is done by FoxPro programs. The Project Manager, for instance, is a sophisticated FoxPro program.

For the new programmer, the ability to issue commands interactively in the Command window or by running a program makes Visual FoxPro programming possible. Most new programmers start by saving a series of commands they often use in a command file. This file (program) is then run by issuing a `DO` command with the file's name. This is the syntax for this command:

```
DO <filename>
```

where `filename` is a text file with the FoxPro commands to be executed. The underlying operation of Visual FoxPro is the same, whether in the interactive or program mode. The only difference is that Visual FoxPro reads commands from the keyboard in the interactive mode and from a disk file in the program mode. Each command in a command file occupies an individual line. Some programming languages allow more than one command on a single line, but Visual FoxPro does not.

A line in a FoxPro program normally begins with a command verb, which is a reserved FoxPro word such as `DO` or `INDEX`. The command verb is followed by a statement, made up of values or conditions that control the effect of the operation performed by the command. Lines of a program can start at the left margin or be indented for easier reading. Lines cannot be longer than a maximum of 256 characters, including spaces.

SAMPLE TABLE AND FILES

Sample files are provided as adjuncts to this chapter to illustrate the various programming techniques used in Visual FoxPro.

This chapter's example uses files located in VFU\SAMPLES\ and VFU\Chap22\.

File	Purpose
Buyers.DBF	Located in VFU\SAMPLES\. Used to supply the data for demonstrating simple programming techniques.
Exceeds.PRG	Located in VFU\Chap22\. A small program demonstrating simple decision structures.
Repairs.DBF	Located in VFU\Chap22\. Data table used to supply data to the Exceeds.PRG program.
Test.PRG	Located in VFU\Chap22\. A small program showing how a list of commands can be saved and later used.

A Simple Program

In a simple programming task, it might be necessary to enter a series of commands that would open the Buyers table, set the index to alphabetical order by last name, and show the contents of the last_name, first_name, city, and state fields. To do this, enter the following commands in the Command window:

```
USE BUYERS
SET ORDER TO TAG NAMES
LIST OFF LASTNAME, FIRSTNAME, CITY, STATE
```

Your results would look like this:

```
LASTNAME        FIRSTNAME       CITY            STATE
Bannerton       Alicia          Falls Church    VA
Hernandez       Maria           Towson          MD
Jones           Nikki           Washington      DC
Jones           Jarel           McLean          VA
O'Neill         John            Merrifield      VA
Roberts         Jamie           Reston          VA
Sanderson       Lucy            Herndon         VA
Smith           Larry           Kensington      MD
Zeibermann      Daniel          Arlington       VA
```

The same commands could be stored in a program named TEST.PRG, as shown in the following example:

```
NOTE**TEST.PRG
*This is an example of a command file.
USE BUYERS
SET ORDER TO  TAG NAMES
LIST OFF LASTNAME, FIRSTNAME, CITY, STATE
```

The lines in the program that begin with NOTE, or with an asterisk (*), are comment lines. Comment lines are ignored by Visual FoxPro when the program is executed. Comment lines are helpful (and highly recommended) for documenting the operation of a program.

Once the commands are stored in the file, they can be executed in sequential order by entering the single command

```
DO TEST
```

which produces the following result:

LASTNAME	FIRSTNAME	CITY	STATE
Bannerton	Alicia	Falls Church	VA
Hernandez	Maria	Towson	MD
Jones	Nikki	Washington	DC
Jones	Jarel	McLean	VA
O'Neill	John	Merrifield	VA
Roberts	Jamie	Reston	VA
Sanderson	Lucy	Herndon	VA
Smith	Larry	Kensington	MD
Zeibermann	Daniel	Arlington	VA

Creating a Program

You can create programs with the Visual FoxPro Editor or a text editor of your choice. If you use a text editor, it must have the capability to create ASCII text files without any control characters. Program files are normally assigned the extension .PRG. If you use a different extension, you must specify it as part of the filename when running the program with the DO command.

To create a program with the Visual FoxPro Editor, choose File | New. In the dialog box that opens, click Program, and then click New. You can also enter MODIFY COMMAND in the command window. This is the syntax for this command:

```
MODIFY COMMAND <filename>
```

where *filename* is the name of the program file to be created. The .PRG extension is assigned if you don't specify one. If no filename is supplied, the Editor opens a window called Untitled and you are asked for a filename when you close the window. For example, entering the command

```
MODIFY COMMAND TEST
```

creates a file called TEST.PRG and displays the Visual FoxPro Editor in a window. You can then type commands a line at a time, pressing Enter at the end of each line.

You can correct typing errors with the cursor keys and the Backspace and Delete keys. Pressing the Insert key switches back and forth between the insert and overwrite modes of the Visual FoxPro Editor. In the insert mode, characters are inserted at the cursor position as you type them. If any existing characters occupy the cursor position, they are pushed to the right to make room for the new characters. In the overwrite mode, new typed characters write over existing characters. Control key combinations can also be used with the Visual FoxPro Editor for scrolling the screen, moving the cursor, and deleting characters, words, and entire lines. Table 22.1 lists these key combinations. After you finish editing with the Visual FoxPro Editor, save your files to disk by choosing File | Save or using the Ctrl+End key combination. The Escape key can be used to abort an editing process without saving the text.

Table 22.1. The editing keys for Visual FoxPro Editor.

Key	Result
Up arrow	Moves cursor up one line
Down arrow	Moves cursor down one line
Left arrow	Moves cursor left one space
Right arrow	Moves cursor right one space
Insert	Switches between insert and overwrite modes
Delete	Deletes character at cursor
Backspace	Deletes character to left of cursor
Home	Moves cursor to beginning to line
End	Moves cursor to end of line
Page Up	Scrolls up one screen
Page Down	Scrolls down one screen
Ctrl+End	Saves file to disk
Esc	Aborts editing; doesn't save file

Operators

Each FoxPro data type (with the exception of memo and general fields) has specific operators that can be used with those data elements. *Operators* perform operations on data to produce a value. Mathematic, character string or alphanumeric, relational, and logical operators are available in the FoxPro language.

The following are the math operators (used to perform operations that yield numeric results):

Operator	Meaning
+ and -	Unary signs
^ and **	Exponentiation
*	Multiplication
/	Division
+	Addition
-	Subtraction
( )	Grouping

Note that the order, or *precedence,* among the math operators is unary, then exponentiation, then multiplication or division, then addition or subtraction. When operators have equal precedence (such as multiplication and division), the order of precedence is from left to right. Parentheses can be used in the expression to force a different order. When parentheses are used, Visual FoxPro calculates from the innermost pair of parentheses and works outward.

These are the character string operators:

Operator	Meaning
+	Concatenation
-	Concatenation (strips any trailing spaces)

When used with character strings, the plus sign *concatenates,* or combines, strings of characters. For example, "Mr. " + "Smith" equates to the character string "Mr. Smith".

These are the relational operators:

Operator	Meaning
=	Equal to
<> or #	Not equal to
<	Less than
>	Greater than
<=	Less than or equal to
>=	Greater than or equal to
$	Substring contained within a string

These are the logical operators:

Operator	Meaning
.NOT.	Negation or complement
.AND.	Logical AND
.OR.	Logical OR
( )	Grouping

The order of precedence for logical operators is .NOT., then .AND., then .OR.. If different types of operators are used in a single expression, the order of precedence is math and string operators, followed by relational operators, followed by logical operators.

> **NOTE**
>
> The periods surrounding the logical operators are optional.

Expressions

Expressions are combinations of fields, memory variables, constants, functions, and operators. The only rule governing what may be placed in expressions states that all elements of the expression must be the same type. You cannot, for example, combine numeric elements and character elements in the same expression. The following are examples of valid expressions:

```
(SALARY-(TAXES+2.78))
"Ms. " + LAST_NAME
"Robinson"
3.14159
```

Numeric expressions are the most commonly used expressions in FoxPro programs. They can be numeric memory variables, numeric fields, constants, or any combination of these, linked by any combination of math operators. For example, if a table's numeric fields are named SALARY and HOURS, the following would be numeric expressions:

```
48
SALARY + 500.50
SALARY * HOURS
 ((SALARY * HOURS)+2.75)
```

Character expressions are also found in FoxPro programs. Character expressions can be character variables, the contents of character fields, or literal character strings enclosed in quotation marks, usually joined by a plus sign. These are examples of character expressions:

```
"Bob Smith"
FIRST_NAME + LAST_NAME
"Client name is: " + LAST_NAME
```

Memory Variables

Visual FoxPro allocates an area of memory for storing memory variables. *Memory variables* are storage areas set aside to contain data, which can be characters, numbers, dates, or logical (true/false) expressions. Memory variables are designated by assigning a value to a name for the variable. Memory variable names may be up to 256 characters in length but must all be unique in the first 10 characters. The first character must be a letter or an underscore.

In the FoxPro programming language, memory variables must be created or initialized before they can be used in the program, but in a programming language like BASIC, memory variables can be created "on the fly." Memory variables can be initialized in one of two ways: with the STORE command or as part of an assignment statement. This is the syntax of the STORE command:

```
STORE <value> TO <memory variable>
```

This is the syntax of an assignment statement:

```
<memory variable> = <value>
```

The value stored to a memory variable can be a literal value, the contents of a table field, or the contents of another memory variable. For example, to store the word Robert to a memory variable called FNAME, either of the following commands could be used:

```
STORE "Robert" TO FNAME
FNAME = "Robert"
```

Visual FoxPro allows the following types of memory variables: character, currency, numeric, logical, date, and datetime.

Character variables will contain strings of characters, which can be a combination of letters, numbers, and punctuation symbols.

```
STORE "PC-486" TO SYSTYPE
```

Currency variables are used to hold fixed-point numbers used in monetary calculations. FoxPro will round to four decimal places when using this type.

```
MyMoney = $1.30
LotaPrecision = $123.456789
?LotaPrecision
123.4568
```

Numeric values contain numbers, recognized as numbers and not as characters by Visual FoxPro; you can do calculations on numeric variables. Numbers stored in numeric variables can be whole numbers or fractional (decimal) numbers.

```
STORE 2.72 TO e
```

Logical variables hold the special constants *True* or *False*, which are denoted by .T. and .F., respectively. The following example sets a flag called AnAdministrator (perhaps used to assess privilege levels) to false:

```
AnAdministrator = .F.
```

Date variables have dates that follow the Visual FoxPro date format. These are examples of commands for initializing all four types of memory variables:

```
STORE {12/21/94} TO PURCHDATE
```

`DateTime` variables offer a convenient way to collect and operate on both attributes in one variable. For example, try the following:

```
DayOfInfamy = {12/07/41 07:00 am}
RightNow = DATETIME()
SecondsSincePearl = (RightNow - DayOfInfamy)
```

In each case, the type of memory variable (character, numeric, date, or logical) is ascertained by Visual FoxPro from the way the data is supplied. For example, single or double quotation marks identify data as a character string. The letters *T* and *F* surrounded by two periods identify the data as a logical variable. Numbers are assumed to be numeric variables unless the numbers are enclosed in quotation marks. Dates are stored to a memory variable by surrounding them with curly braces. Use the proper syntax when declaring memory variables. You could get into trouble with a command like

```
STORE "$1344.85" TO SYSCOST
```

because the quotation marks tell Visual FoxPro that this is a character variable. If you tried to do math calculations directly on the variable, Visual FoxPro would respond with an error message.

Displaying Memory Variables

To display the contents of memory variables at any time, use the DISPLAY MEMORY and LIST MEMORY commands. The commands perform the same function with one difference: LIST MEMORY displays the contents of all memory variables without pausing, but DISPLAY MEMORY pauses when the window fills with data; you simply press any key to see the next window of data. Both commands show the name of the memory variable, its type, the contents, and whether the memory variable is public (available to all parts of the program) or private (available only to the part of the program in which you are working). If you enter DISPLAY MEMORY in the Command window, you see a display whose first few lines look like this:

```
INDEX      Pub   [] 45              (        45.00000000)
PDATE      Pub   D  02/28/94
2 variables defined,    0 bytes used
1022 variables available
```

You can use the ? command to display the contents of a single memory variable. This is the syntax of the command, when used in this manner:

```
? <memory variable name>
```

For example, the following commands produce the results shown:

```
? systype
PC-486

? purchdate
12/21/94
```

Functions

Visual FoxPro also has functions available for the programmer to perform various tasks. *Functions* are special-purpose programs that perform useful tasks. In Visual FoxPro, functions are used to convert data from one type to another, to perform specialized math operations, to test for various conditions, and to manipulate data. Functions always provide a value and are used either as an expression or in an expression. This is the common format for a function:

```
name of function(expression)
```

For example, the square root (SQRT()) function can be combined with an expression, such as a given number, to determine the square root of that number:

```
? SQRT(9)
3.00
```

Some functions are not used with an expression. These functions require only the name of the function to operate. An example is the Date() function, which returns the date maintained by the system clock:

```
? DATE()
04/18/95
```

Some commonly used functions are described in the following sections.

MIN() and MAX()

The MIN() and MAX() functions return the minimum and maximum values, respectively, of two numeric expressions. This is the syntax:

```
MIN (<numeric expression 1>,<numeric expression 2>)
MAX (<numeric expression 1>,<numeric expression 2>)
```

The MIN() function returns the lower of the two expressions, and the MAX() function returns the higher of the two expressions. In a program, one expression is usually the contents of a numeric field, and the other expression is a memory variable that contains some predefined high or low value.

For instance, the following code determines the higher of two expressions (one is a ceiling of repair costs, and the other is an actual figure for repair costs in a table):

```
*Exceeds.PRG lists ceilings exceeded for building repairs.
INPUT "Enter maximum value for repairs: " TO MAXVAL
USE REPAIRS
LIST COST, MAX(MAXVAL, COST)

do exceeds
Enter maximum value for repairs: 150.00

Record#    COST        MAX(MAXVAL, COST)
1          56.00       150.00
2          128.53      150.00
```

```
3          69.90       150.00
4         218.54       218.54
5          78.77       150.00
6         432.95       432.95
7          45.67       150.00
```

ROUND()

The ROUND() function rounds off numbers, keeping a specific number of decimal places; this is its syntax:

```
ROUND(<numeric expression>,<number of decimal places>)
```

The following lines of code demonstrate an example of the ROUND() function:

```
? ROUND(5.867,2)
5.870

? ROUND(5.867,0)
6.000
```

If the numeric expression used to specify the number of decimal places is a negative value, the result is a rounded whole number as opposed to a number followed by decimal places, as shown in the following examples:

```
? ROUND(5.867,-0)
6
? ROUND(5.867,-1)
10
```

LTRIM()

The LTRIM() function removes any leading blanks from a character string. This is its syntax:

```
LTRIM(<character expression>)
```

Here is an example:

```
STORE "   FoxPro" TO mystring
? mystring
    FoxPro
? LTRIM(mystring)
FoxPro
```

LOWER()

The LOWER() function is used to convert uppercase letters to lowercase. The LOWER() function has no effect on lowercase letters, numbers, spaces, or punctuation marks. This is the syntax for the LOWER() function:

```
LOWER(<character expression>)
```

Here is an example:

```
STORE "SMITH" TO TEST
? LOWER(TEST)
smith
```

UPPER()

The UPPER() function performs the reverse of the LOWER() function—it converts lowercase letters to uppercase. The UPPER() function has no effect on uppercase letters, numbers, spaces, or punctuation marks. This is the syntax for the UPPER() function:

```
UPPER(<character expression>)
```

Here is an example:

```
STORE "rotunda" TO TEST
? UPPER(TEST)
ROTUNDA
```

The LOWER() and UPPER() functions are useful to force consistency and to overcome problems caused by the case-sensitive nature of Visual FoxPro. For example, if a record contains the name JOHNSON in a lastname field, and the name is stored as shown (in all uppercase letters), a LOCATE statement using the following syntax would *not* find the record:

```
LOCATE FOR LASTNAME = "johnson"
```

But with a LOWER() function used as shown, the name is found whether it is stored in the table as lowercase letters, uppercase letters, or a combination of both:

```
LOCATE FOR LOWER(LASTNAME) = "johnson"
```

TRIM()

The TRIM() function strips trailing spaces from a character string. This is the syntax for the TRIM() function:

```
TRIM(<character expression>)
```

The TRIM() function is useful for removing undesired gaps of white space between the contents of character fields that are combined as part of an expression, such as the following:

```
USE MAILER
GO 5
? FIRSTNAME + LASTNAME
Maria        Hernandez
? TRIM(FIRSTNAME) + " " + LASTNAME
Maria Hernandez
```

SPACE()

The SPACE() function creates a character string containing a specified number of blank spaces. This is the syntax for the SPACE() function:

```
SPACE(<numeric expression>)
```

where *<numeric expression>* translates to a value between 1 and 254.

Here is an example:

```
STORE SPACE(15) TO GAP
? "System" + GAP + "Main" + GAP + "Menu"
System          Main          Menu
```

DATE() and TIME()

The DATE() and TIME() functions provide the current date and time. The value provided by the DATE() function will be a date variable; the value provided by the TIME() function will be a character variable. Visual FoxPro does not provide any function for setting the system clock date or time.

Here is an example:

```
? date()
03/01/95
? time()
22:09:29
store date() to today
03/01/95
store time() to rightnow
22:09:42
display memory
TODAY    pub  D 03/01/95
RIGHTNOW pub  C "22:09:42"
```

CTOD()

The CTOD() function is the character-to-date conversion function. CTOD() converts a character expression with a string of characters formatted as a date into a date variable. The default for the characters' format is MM/DD/YY, but this format can be changed with the SET DATE command. This is the syntax for the CTOD() function:

```
CTOD(<character expression>)
```

The character string supplied by the expression can vary from "1/1/100" to "12/31/9999".

Here is an example:

```
STORE CTOD("07/06/94") TO WEDDING
07/06/94
DISPLAY MEMORY
WEDDING   pub  D 07/06/94
```

DTOC()

The DTOC() function is the date-to-character conversion function. DTOC() converts a date expression into a string of characters. The format of the characters supplied by DTOC() follows the current settings for displaying dates, which can be altered with the SET DATE command. This is the syntax for the DTOC() function:

```
DTOC(<date expression>)
```

Here is an example:

```
STORE {07/06/94} TO WEDDING
STORE DTOC(WEDDING) TO TEST
07/06/94
? TEST
07/06/94
DISPLAY MEMORY
WEDDING    pub  D 07/06/94
TEST       pub  C "07/06/94"
2 variables defined,    19 bytes used
254 variables available,  5981 bytes available
```

BOF()

The BOF() function is the beginning-of-file function. BOF() provides a logical value of True if the record pointer is at the beginning of the table and a logical value of False if it is not. This is the syntax for the BOF() function:

```
BOF()
```

Here is an example:

```
USE MAILER
? BOF()
.T.
SKIP
? BOF()
.F.
```

EOF()

The EOF() function is the end-of-file function. EOF() provides a logical value of True if the record pointer is at the end of the table and a logical value of False if it is not. This is the syntax for the EOF() function:

```
EOF()
```

Here is an example:

```
USE CLIENTS
? EOF()
.F.
```

```
GO BOTTOM
? EOF()
.T.
```

FOUND()

The FOUND() function is used to test for successfully finding a record with a LOCATE, CONTINUE, SEEK, or FIND command. If the command used to search for the record is successful, the FOUND() function provides a logical value of True. Programs can use a statement containing the FOUND() function to test for a successful find, as shown in this program:

```
USE IFILES
SET ORDER TO STOCKNO
INPUT "Stock number? " TO SNUMB
SEEK SNUMB
IF .NOT. FOUND()
? "No such record!"
RETURN
ENDIF
```

You'll find these functions to be useful ones. Keep in mind that this is by no means a complete list; Visual FoxPro offers hundreds of different functions.

Control Structures

A well-known rule of programming states that any problem, no matter how large, can be easily solved if it is broken down into smaller, manageable pieces. Visual FoxPro lends itself to this philosophy by providing commands that enable control in a program to be passed back and forth between smaller parts, or *modules*. Until now, examples of FoxPro programs have been fairly simple, with most programs following a simple flow from beginning to end. In real life, applications are never simple enough to warrant a program flow that runs uninterrupted from start to finish without changing direction. Most programming languages offer three types of control structures that let you control a program's flow. Visual FoxPro's control structures are branching, conditional, and repetitive. Control structures are commonly used in a FoxPro program to give you flexibility. Using control structures, you can design a program to deal with any condition or to respond to varying user requests.

Branching Controls: *DO, RETURN,* and *RETURN TO MASTER*

In a branching control structure, one program calls, or *executes*, another program. A branching structure lets the program deviate from its normal (sequential) path. The following illustration compares a nonbranching program with a branching program:

```
Command A          Command A
|                  |
|                  |
```

```
Command B              Command B==========>Command AA

Command C              Command C<=======¦  Command BB

Command D              Command D            <==Command CC


No branching           Branching
```

Using *DO* and *RETURN*

The DO command is used to run a FoxPro command file or program. Because commands can be placed into command files, the DO command can also be used in a program to call (or branch to) another program. Once that program has finished its tasks, control can be passed back to the original (calling) program with the RETURN command, as though the commands in the other program file have become a part of the first program file. This type of program flow is illustrated here:

```
MAIN.PRG               NOFIND.PRG

IF MZIPCODE <> ZIPCODE
CONTINUE
IF EOF()
DO NOFIND              *NOFIND.PRG
RETURN                 *Prints a message if person isn't in database
LOOP                   CLEAR
ENDIF                      @7,10 SAY "This person not in database!"
@8,10 SAY "Return to menu to enter"
@9,10 SAY "new names, or to try different"
@10,10 SAY "name."
WAIT
RETURN
```

In this example of program code, NOFIND.PRG can be considered a subprogram, or module, of the main program. When used in a program, the DO command transfers program control to the first line of the command file named by the DO command. Program control remains in that command file until a RETURN command, or the end of the command file, is encountered. When the RETURN command is encountered, program control returns to the line immediately following the DO command that originally called the module.

The DO command is only one method for transferring program control to another program module in Visual FoxPro. Another way is by calling a program as a user-defined function (UDF) within an expression or by using the = operator. You also can reference an object's method in a line of code or add lines of code to an event handler that will then run upon the occurrence of the event (properties, events, and methods are discussed in Chapter 12, "Designing and Customizing Forms"). The FoxPro programming language encourages structured programming by default—there is no equivalent to the GOTO command in BASIC and similar languages.

You can't transfer program control to another part of the same program with the DO command— you can only branch to another module.

Branches to a module can be conditional (occurring only when a specified condition is met) or unconditional (always occurring at a given point in the program). The previous example of a branch is conditional; the program NOFIND.PRG is run only if the test for End-Of-File in the main program returns a value of True.

Visual FoxPro supports multiple nesting of subroutines, or submodules, in a program. Such nesting takes place when one program uses a DO statement to run another program, which uses a DO statement to run yet another program, and so on, as shown here:

```
MainMenu.PRG

DO PrinMenu =====>  PrinMenu.PRG

DO Label1.PRG =====>  Label1.PRG
```

Using *RETURN TO MASTER*

RETURN is usually enough to end the execution of the module; however, a useful option of the RETURN command is RETURN TO MASTER. It passes program control to the highest level module of a program. Complex applications often produce programs that are many levels deep. In such cases, a user's request to return to the main menu (if it is in the highest level program) can be done with a RETURN TO MASTER command. Using RETURN TO MASTER eliminates wading through an annoying number of menus in a large application just to get back to the first menu to choose an option to leave the application.

Conditional Controls: *IF...ENDIF* and *DO CASE*

Conditional controls are used to alter the flow of a program depending on the outcome of an evaluated condition. Conditional commands in a FoxPro program are most commonly used for constructing an application's menus. Visual FoxPro offers two commands for conditional controls: the IF...ELSE...ENDIF command and the DO CASE command.

Using *IF...ENDIF*

The IF...ENDIF command provides a true/false evaluation of a given condition, enabling Visual FoxPro to perform one operation if the condition is true and a different operation if the condition is false. The syntax for the statement resembles English, and in planning a program it helps to think of the statement in English as documenting the way that the program flows:

```
IF <condition>
   <commands>
ENDIF
```

or, as an alternative method,

```
IF <condition>
   <commands>
ELSE
   <commands>
ENDIF
```

The IF and ENDIF commands are a matched set. Each IF command sequence must be closed with an ENDIF command. The ELSE command is optional and can be used to denote an alternative path for program flow. If the ELSE command is omitted, then all statements in the IF and the ENDIF commands are carried out if the condition specified is true. If the condition is not true, program control passes to the first statement following the ENDIF command. In the following example, an IF...ENDIF set of commands is used to evaluate whether a printing program is executed:

```
IF CHOICE = 1
   DO PRINTER
ENDIF
```

In this example, no alternate path is provided; either the condition is true and the PRINTER program is run, or the condition is false and program control passes to the command immediately following the ENDIF command. When you want an alternate path, the ELSE statement can be used to specify commands that are executed if the evaluated condition is false, as shown in the following example:

```
IF CHOICE = 1
   DO PRINTER1
ELSE
   DO PRINTER2
ENDIF
```

In this case, if the condition is false (the memory variable CHOICE is not equal to 1), the command file named PRINTER2 is run. Simple conditions can be replaced with very complex conditions, when necessary, to form the basis for the desired condition.

Using *Immediate IF*

The IIF(), or Immediate IF function, lets you duplicate an IF...ENDIF conditional structure in a single command, enabling the use of IF conditionals both in a program and from the dot prompt. This is the syntax for the command:

```
IIF(<logical expression>,<expression 1>,<expression 2>)
```

It helps to think of the function as actually working something like this:

```
IF(<logical expression is true, then>,<expression 1>, OTHERWISE
<expression 2>)
```

The following code is an example of an IF...ENDIF construction:

```
IF AGE >= 21
   STORE "Legal drinking age" TO MSTRING
```

```
ELSE
   STORE "No alcohol to minors" TO MSTRING
ENDIF
```

Using the Immediate IF function, the entire construction could be done with one line of a program:

```
MSTRING = IIF(AGE >= 21,"Legal drinking age","No alcohol to minors")
```

Using the Immediate IF function gives you two benefits. First, it speeds program execution time. Second, it can be used in an expression inside a report or label form, enabling you to produce reports or labels with different data based on the logical expression of the IIF() function. The IIF() function is faster than the IF...ENDIF construction and can be used in reports and labels.

When you're using complex conditions as part of a program, make sure that the conditional statements are designed to get the proper results. The following code shows how complicated the program can get with complex conditions:

```
IF SALARY >= 22500
   IF EXEMPTION > 1
      DO TAXCALC1
   ELSE
      DO TAXCALC2
   ENDIF
ELSE
   IF EXEMPTION > 1
      DO TAXCALC3
   ELSE
      DO TAXCALC4
   ENDIF
ENDIF
```

The most common error when designing such conditionals is omitting a closing statement, which can give you compilation errors.

Using *DO CASE* and *ENDCASE*

The DO CASE and ENDCASE commands are used when you need to make decisions on any one of several conditions. This is the syntax for the DO CASE and ENDCASE commands:

```
DO CASE
   CASE <first condition>
      <commands>
   CASE <second condition>
      <commands>
   CASE <third condition>
      <commands>
   CASE <fourth condition>
      <commands>
   OTHERWISE
      <other commands>
ENDCASE
```

When Visual FoxPro encounters a DO CASE command, it begins evaluating the condition following each CASE statement, beginning with the first one, until it finds a CASE statement whose condition can be evaluated as true. Once it finds such a statement, it carries out the commands identified by that statement, then continues with the next command that follows the ENDCASE command. If no CASE statement in the series evaluates as true, then program control proceeds to the next command following the ENDCASE command, unless you have included the optional OTHERWISE statement. If you have, the OTHERWISE statement's commands are executed if no other CASE statements can be executed.

DO CASE commands are often used to design and implement menus in which one choice of several is usually appropriate, as shown in the following example:

```
STORE SPACE " " TO ANS
@ 17,33 SAY " select choice: "
@ 17,50 GET ANS
READ
DO CASE
   CASE selectnum = 0
      CLEAR ALL
      QUIT    CASE selectnum = 1
      SET FORMAT TO MYFORM
      APPEND
      STORE ' ' TO wait_subst
      @ 23,0 SAY 'Press any key to continue...' GET wait_subst
      READ

   CASE selectnum = 2
      SET FORMAT TO MYFORM
      DO MyEdit
      STORE ' ' TO wait_subst
      @ 23,0 SAY 'Press any key to continue...' GET wait_subst
      READ

   CASE selectnum = 3
      DO Eraser
      STORE ' ' TO wait_subst
      @ 23,0 SAY 'Press any key to continue...' GET wait_subst
      READ

   CASE selectnum = 4
      DO Reporter
      STORE ' ' TO wait_subst
      @ 23,0 SAY 'Press any key to continue...' GET wait_subst
      READ
   OTHERWISE
      CLEAR
      ? "Invalid entry!"
      WAIT "Press any key..."
ENDCASE
```

In the example, a number entered by the user is stored as a memory variable (selectnum). The CASE statements then compare the contents of selectnum to each of the alternatives listed between the DO CASE and ENDCASE commands. When a match is found, the statements following that CASE statement are carried out and the remaining CASE statements in the set are ignored.

Any choices made with a CASE command could also be carried out with multiple IF...ENDIF commands, so which approach is better? Generally, if more than two pairs of IF...ENDIF commands are needed, it is better to use CASE statements. The following example shows a simplified menu program using DO CASE and its equivalent using IF...ENDIF commands:

```
? "Enter selection of 1 to 4."        ? "Enter selection of 1 to 4."
INPUT TO CHOOSY                        INPUT TO CHOOSY
DO CASE                                IF CHOOSY = 1
    CASE CHOOSY = 1                        DO MAKEREC
        DO MAKEREC                     ENDIF
    CASE CHOOSY = 2                    IF CHOOSY = 2
        DO CHANGREC                        DO CHANGREC
    CASE CHOOSY = 3                    ENDIF
        DO REMOVE                      IF CHOOSY = 3
    CASE CHOOSY = 4                        DO REMOVE
        DO PRINTED                     ENDIF
    OTHERWISE                          IF CHOOSY = 4
        ? "Invalid entry!"                 DO PRINTED
ENDCASE                                ELSE
                                           ? "Invalid entry!"
                                       ENDIF
```

Not only are CASE statements easier to read, but they are executed by the FoxPro interpreter slightly faster than an equivalent number of IF...ENDIF commands.

Repetitive Controls: *DO WHILE* and *ENDDO*

Many sequential processes performed by programs require some kind of repetitive, or *looping*, process. Often, sequential processing of records in a database means that some sort of operation is repeated once for each record in the database. The DO WHILE and ENDDO commands give you looping capability in a FoxPro program. This is the syntax for the DO WHILE and ENDDO commands:

```
DO WHILE <condition>
    <commands>
ENDDO
```

All loops in a FoxPro program are performed by a DO WHILE...ENDDO structure. Most loops are conditional; the loop is terminated when a specified condition changes. Some loops, however, are unconditional; they never terminate on their own but by a branch in the loop that calls another submodule of the program.

The process specified by the commands between the DO WHILE and ENDDO commands is repeated until the condition specified as part of the DO WHILE command is no longer true. Usually, the commands in the DO WHILE and ENDDO commands include a statement that causes a change in the specified condition, resulting in the repetitive loop's termination. Without such a statement, the loop would repeat endlessly. Look at the following example:

```
DO WHILE .NOT. EOF()
    ? TRIM(FIRSTNAME) + " " + LASTNAME
    ? ADDRESS + CITY + STATE
```

```
    ? ZIP
    SKIP
ENDDO
```

The statements between the DO WHILE and ENDDO commands are repeated until the SKIP command takes the record pointer to the end of the database (EOF). Once this happens, the condition specified as part of the DO WHILE statement (.NOT. EOF()) is no longer true, so the loop terminates, and program control passes to the statement immediately following the ENDDO statement.

An unconditional, or *endless*, loop in a FoxPro program is commonly used when the popular DO WHILE TRUE construction is used to display a prompt or a menu until the user makes an appropriate choice. Because no condition is specified following the DO WHILE command, a DO WHILE TRUE loop is always true, and the commands in the loop are repeated until one of the commands causes an exit, usually by running another module in the program. This use of the DO WHILE command is illustrated in the following code lines:

```
DO WHILE .T.
    ? "Enter 1 for trial report, or 2 for summary report."
    INPUT TO CHOICE
    IF CHOICE = 1
        DO REPORT1
        RETURN
    ENDIF
    IF CHOICE = 2
        DO REPORT2
        RETURN
    ENDIF
    CLEAR
ENDDO
```

The user is asked to enter a choice for printed reports. If any response other than 1 or 2 is entered, the loop is repeated and the user is again asked to supply a valid choice.

Keep in mind that Visual FoxPro's DO WHILE...ENDDO loop is a leading test loop, meaning that the condition to be tested is evaluated at the start of the loop. If the condition is not true, the loop is never executed. If you want to execute a loop once and then test for a condition to check whether the loop should terminate or repeat, it may be better to use an endless DO WHILE TRUE loop and an IF...ENDIF conditional statement just before the end of the loop to determine whether the program should continue in the loop.

Using *LOOP* and *EXIT* to Terminate Loops

You can also use the LOOP and EXIT commands to terminate a repetitive loop. The LOOP command returns the program flow to the DO WHILE command that started the loop for another test of the condition. LOOP is used to skip any conditional tests that follow the LOOP command, possibly saving some program execution time by immediately returning program control to the start of the DO WHILE loop. The EXIT command, which is more abrupt in its action, causes the program flow to leave the DO WHILE loop and continue at the first command following the ENDDO command. Both LOOP and EXIT should be used sparingly because both commands interrupt the structured flow of a program, making the program logic more difficult to follow and debug. The following code lines show you how to terminate a repetitive loop:

```
(LOOP)                                    (EXIT)

(loop causes
another test of                              (exit causes
condition.)                                   branch to
DO WHILE AMOUNT > 50<***<***     DO WHILE AMOUNT > 50    first command
<commands...>            *       <commands...>        after ENDDO.)
IF ZIP <= 10000         *        IF ZIP <= 10000
LOOP ******>*****>                EXIT******>***********>
ENDIF                             ENDIF                         *
<more commands...>                <more commands...>            *
ENDDO                             ENDDO                             *
STORE 1 + COUNTER TO COUNTER      STORE 1 + COUNTER TO COUNTER<***
<more commands...>                <more commands...>
```

Using Single-Choice Versus Multiple-Choice Logic

The types of conditional commands you use depend on whether the programming task requires a single-choice decision or a multiple-choice decision. *Single-choice decisions* present a simple task to the programmer. Normally, a simple IF...ENDIF set of commands is enough to do the job, as shown here:

```
IF CURRSTOCK < 1
   STORE .T. TO OUTSTOCK
ENDIF
```

Single-choice decisions are common in FoxPro programs. *Multiple-choice decisions,* on the other hand, often require planning because the choices can affect the flow of a program in many different ways. When a multiple-choice decision is evaluated, a single action may result, several actions result, or one action may be taken as a result of several decisions. When a program has several possible choices—and only one choice will be executed—use the CASE...ENDCASE commands shown in the following code lines as part of the menu program:

```
DO CASE
   CASE UPPER(CHOICE) = "ADD"
      DO ADDER
   CASE UPPER(CHOICE) = "EDIT"
      DO EDITREC
   CASE UPPER(CHOICE) = "PRINT"
      DO PRINTREC
ENDCASE
```

In this example, only one action will result from the three possible choices. You need a different approach for programming situations where several processes must be performed when one condition is met. In such cases, a combination of IF...ENDIF commands is usually more effective for testing all required conditions. In the following example a value of 2 is entered in response to the user prompt:

```
? "Current inventory level?"
INPUT TO AMOUNT
IF AMOUNT < 10
   STORE AMOUNT TO REORDER
ENDIF
IF AMOUNT < 5
   STORE PARTNO TO XPRESSHIP
ENDIF
IF AMOUNT < 3
   DO NOTIFY
ENDIF
```

A value of 2 satisfies all three `IF...ENDIF` conditional tests. Each condition is tested independently of the others.

When a decision must be based on a combination of conditions, you can also nest `IF...ENDIF` commands within each other. The following example uses this approach to test for matching last names, first names, and ZIP codes in a mailing list program:

```
IF MLAST = LASTNAME
   IF MFIRST = FIRSTNAME
      IF MZIP = ZIPCODE
         EDIT
      ENDIF
   ENDIF
ENDIF
```

In this example, each condition is evaluated in sequential order. For the second condition to be evaluated, the first must be true, and for the third condition to be evaluated, the second must be true. If any of the conditions test as false, the `EDIT` command is not carried out. The same logic can be carried out with a single `IF...ENDIF` series of commands and logical functions, as demonstrated here:

```
IF MLAST = LASTNAME .AND. MFIRST = FIRSTNAME .AND. MZIP = ZIPCODE
   EDIT
ENDIF
```

You will end up with the same analysis in both examples. Neither approach is better than the other for a given application. Combining `IF...ENDIF` commands is easier to understand at a glance. When decisions get more complex (and they will), visually following the logic in a structure with `IF...ENDIF` commands nested within each other becomes difficult. When a program requires complex logic, try executing conditions from the dot prompt. This is an excellent way to discover what works before you write a complex condition as part of a program.

Each of the basic control structures can be nested in other control structures to any level required by the program, as shown in the following example. When you design programs like this, it often helps to draw lines between the matching statements to avoid leaving out any closing statements:

```
===DO WHILE
|    ===DO CASE
|    |       CASE 1
|    |          ===IF
```

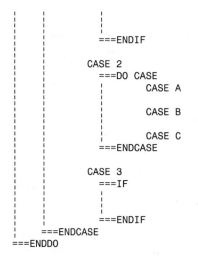

```
          ===ENDIF

     CASE 2
        ===DO CASE
                   CASE A

                   CASE B

                   CASE C
        ===ENDCASE

     CASE 3
        ===IF


        ===ENDIF
  ===ENDCASE
===ENDDO
```

Terminating Program Execution

Programs can be halted with the CANCEL and QUIT commands. The CANCEL command halts a program and returns program control to the Command window. The QUIT command halts the program and Visual FoxPro ends all operations and returns you to the Windows environment. CANCEL is commonly used in a FoxPro program during the development and testing phase. Before the program is turned over to users, any CANCEL command should be replaced with a QUIT command that is normally an option from the application's main menu. Users should not be given an unexplained FoxPro desktop and Command window, which could be confusing.

Programming for Data Entry and Editing

Because Visual FoxPro offers all the power of Xbase, which has been around for more than a decade, you can enter and edit data in a program in several ways. A common approach from the past that this book intentionally steers clear of is writing reams of program code using @...SAY statements to print forms used for data entry and editing. Using @...SAY statements can be handy for simple user-interface tasks, and their use is explained in the following section. However, when you need to include forms for adding and editing records, don't tie yourself to a programming technique as antiquated as executing dozens of @...SAY statements in code. Design the forms you need with the Form Wizards and run them from in your program when you need to give the user the ability to add and edit records.

Using @...SAY...GET Commands to Display and Retrieve Data

If you're working with basic data entry, you'll probably need the @...SAY and @...GET commands of the FoxPro language. They can be used to place data at a given screen location and to retrieve data (stored in fields or as memory variables) from the user. The @...SAY command can be used to place data at any screen location. The basic syntax for the command is @ *(row,col)* SAY expression. If the expression is a character expression, it must be enclosed in quotes. For instance, to display the contents of the field LASTNAME at the screen position of row 5, column 30, you'd use this command:

```
@ 5,30 SAY LASTNAME
```

The positions begin at 0,0 for the upper-left corner of the main Visual FoxPro window. In DOS predecessors for FoxPro/Windows (like FoxPro for DOS and other Xbase products), the numbers stood for a precisely defined location, based on rows down from the top of the screen and characters across from the left edge. In the DOS products, a screen location of 0,0 meant the upper-left corner, and a form location of 23,79 was at the lower-right corner. Because Windows is not a character-based environment, the actual numbers vary depending on your screen hardware, but they are still used to maintain compatibility with Xbase programs. The old maximum of 23,79 for DOS-based screens places data at the right edge and about two-thirds down in a maximized FoxPro desktop window under Visual FoxPro for Windows on a machine running in standard (600×480) VGA mode.

The expression used as a part of the @...SAY command can contain any combination of valid field names, character strings, or numeric data. Functions can also be used with the @...SAY command to provide formatting. For example, the command

```
@ 12,5 SAY "Employee " + NAME + " is " + STR(AGE) + " years old."
```

results in the text "Employee Bill Smith is 34 years old" displayed beginning at row 12, column 5.

The GET option displays a blank fill-in field that is highlighted in reverse video. The GET option can be used alone or in combination with SAY to display a prompt and allow you to enter data. After one or more @...GET or @...SAY commands are encountered, a READ command causes Visual FoxPro to read the values supplied by the user and store them to the memory variables or fields specified after the GET. If variables are used with GET, they must be initialized before using GET or an error message occurs. For example, you can initialize memory variables and then use a series of @...SAY...GET commands, followed by a READ command to prompt for user data, as shown:

```
CLEAR
STORE SPACE(30) TO NAME
STORE 0 TO AGE
STORE 0.00 TO SALARY
@ 5,10 SAY "Name?"
@ 5,20 GET NAME
@ 7,10 SAY "Age?"
@ 7,20 GET AGE
@ 9,10 SAY "Salary?"
@ 9,20 GET SALARY
READ
```

When the commands are encountered, the prompts and blanks for data entry appear on the form. (See Figure 22.1.)

FIGURE 22.1.

The prompts and fill-in fields from @...SAY *and* @...GET.

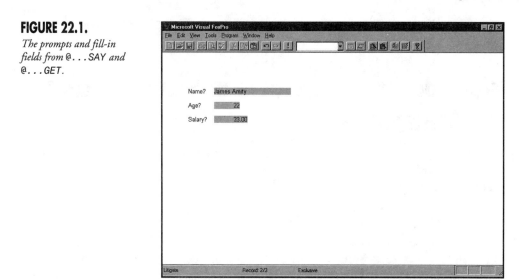

If field names are used instead of variables, the data entered in the highlighted fill-in fields is stored directly in the database. In the past, such use of @...SAY...GET commands often replaced the less-attractive EDIT and APPEND commands. However, using the Form Designer in Visual FoxPro makes this technique cumbersome by comparison. In general, coding your own statements using @...SAY...GET commands makes sense if you have few fields or data to display or to prompt the user for. But if you have a form full of fields, use the Form Designer or the Form Wizards to create forms that you call from inside the application.

Using *CLEAR*

The CLEAR command can be used to clear all or part of the form. This is its syntax:

```
CLEAR
@(row,column) CLEAR
@(row,column) TO (row,column) CLEAR
```

The first use of the CLEAR command, without any screen coordinates, clears the entire active window (which is the Visual FoxPro main window, unless you've defined and activated a window with the DEFINE WINDOW and ACTIVATE WINDOW commands). The second use of CLEAR clears the screen to the right of and below the specified cursor location. The final use clears a rectangular area extending from the first specified location to the second specified location. For instance, the command

```
@ 5,10 CLEAR
```

clears all areas of the active window to the right of column 10 and below row 5. The command

```
@ 15,40 TO 19,60 CLEAR
```

clears a rectangular area in the active window with the upper-left corner at row 15, column 40, and the lower-right corner at row 19, column 60.

Working with Windows in Visual FoxPro for Windows

You can place your prompts and your data entry fields (created with the @...SAY...GET commands) in separate windows that you define with the DEFINE WINDOW command. This is the basic syntax for the DEFINE WINDOW command:

```
DEFINE WINDOW window-name FROM row1,col1 TO row2,col2
➥[TITLE character-expression] [SYSTEM] [CLOSE/NOCLOSE] [GROW/NOGROW]
```

The *row1,col1* coordinates indicate the row and column location for the window's upper-left corner, and the *row2,col2* coordinates indicate the row and column location for the window's lower-right corner. The TITLE clause, followed by an optional character expression, puts that character expression in the window's title bar. Use the SYSTEM clause to define a window that resembles the standard Visual FoxPro windows. The CLOSE/NO CLOSE option specifies whether the window has a Close box in the upper-left corner that you can use to close the window, and the GROW/NOGROW option controls whether you can change the window's size (There are additional optional clauses that make the DEFINE WINDOW command compatible with its FoxPro for DOS counterpart, but these options are not discussed here.)

For example, the command

```
DEFINE WINDOW MyWind FROM 10,5 TO 18,50 SYSTEM CLOSE GROW
```

defines a window with the upper-left corner at row 10, column 5, and the lower-right corner at row 18, column 50. The window resembles the standard FoxPro windows and can be sized and closed with the mouse. After defining the window, activate it when you want to display data inside the window with the ACTIVATE WINDOW command. The following is the syntax for this command:

```
ACTIVATE WINDOW window-name / ALL
```

where *window-name* is the name of the window defined earlier with the DEFINE WINDOW command. Using the ALL option activates all windows previously defined.

Once you have activated the window, all screen operations work in relation to the window, which means that screen coordinates of 0,0 refer to the upper-left corner of the window you activated, not the entire FoxPro main window. If you've activated a series of windows with the ALL option of the ACTIVATE WINDOW command, the last window defined is the one that will be in current use. As you use the DEACTIVATE WINDOW command, multiple windows are closed in order until the first window you defined is closed. You can use this effect to present a "layered" or "tiled" look to data entry or help screens.

For simple editing of a large character field, you could define a window with the DEFINE WINDOW command, activate that window with the ACTIVATE WINDOW command, and display the field's data at desired locations in the window, using coordinates 0,0 as the window's upper-left corner as a reference point. The following code lines are an example of a simple program:

```
USE LITIGATE
INPUT "Enter record number to edit: " TO ANS
GOTO ANS
CLEAR
@ 5,5 SAY "Please enter names of the people involved."
DEFINE WINDOW MYWIND FROM 6,5 TO 18,60 SYSTEM CLOSE
ACTIVATE WINDOW MYWIND
@ 1,1 SAY "Document Number:" GET DOCNUMB
@ 3,1 GET PERSONS
@ 7,1 SAY "Date of the document: " GET DOCDATE
READ
DEACTIVATE WINDOW MyWind
RETURN
*end of program*
```

After positioning the record pointer to the desired record with the GOTO statement, the DEFINE WINDOW statement defines a window used for editing the fields. The ACTIVATE WINDOW statement activates the window. The @...SAY...GETs then display the data inside the window. If a field is too long for a single line in the window, it is automatically wrapped to the next line at the window borders. The results of the program are shown in Figure 22.2.

FIGURE 22.2.

The use of user-defined windows.

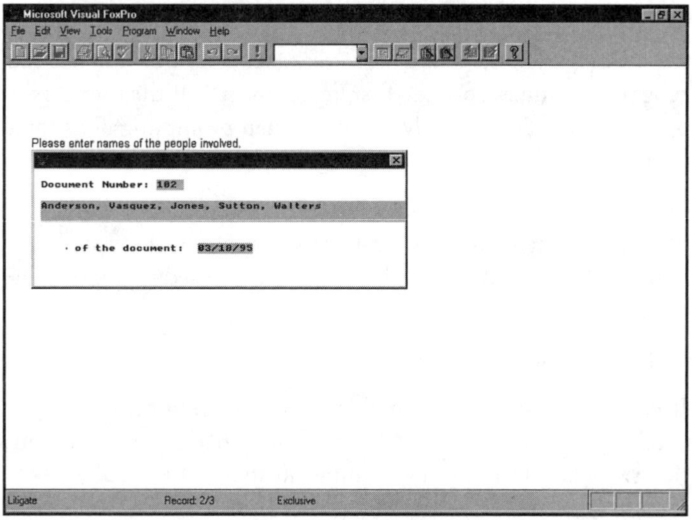

After entries or edits are made and Ctrl+End is pressed (or the cursor moves past the last field), the DEACTIVATE WINDOW statement clears the window from the form. When the window is deactivated, any form text that was underneath the window before it was activated reappears.

Using *WAIT, ACCEPT,* and *INPUT*

The WAIT, ACCEPT, and INPUT commands are also used to get input from users. These commands are most appropriate when a single-character or one-line response is all that's needed by the program.

The WAIT command pauses the program execution and waits for a single key to be pressed. Once a key is pressed, program execution continues. The key you pressed can be stored to a character variable for later use by the program. This is the syntax of the WAIT command:

```
WAIT <message> TO <variable>
```

The message is optional but must be enclosed in quotes if you use it. If no message is included, the default message Press any key to continue... appears. The following example uses WAIT to indicate when a program can proceed:

```
? "Make sure the printer is turned on, then-"
WAIT
SET PRINT ON
LIST L_Name, F_Name_M_I, SCHOOL, CITY, STATE
EJECT
SET PRINT OFF
```

If no message is desired, the default message can be shut off by using a null character variable ("").

Some programmers use WAIT as a way to get variables for a choice in menus. This is a matter of style. Contrary to its name, however, WAIT does not wait around for user confirmation; the program continues after the first key is pressed. If the user presses the wrong key, there is no opportunity to immediately recover. When prompting users for a response, ACCEPT, INPUT, or an @...SAY...GET command is often a better option.

The ACCEPT command requests input from the user and stores it as a character string. The user entry is terminated by pressing Return. An optional message can be included as a part of the ACCEPT command; if included, it must be enclosed in quotes. The following is the syntax for the command:

```
ACCEPT <message> TO <variable>
```

It is not necessary for the variable to be initialized before using ACCEPT. If no variable by the specified name exists, ACCEPT creates a new character variable and stores the entry supplied to that variable. The following example illustrates the use of ACCEPT:

```
ACCEPT "Enter name:" TO MNAME
Enter name: Douglas
ACCEPT "Enter amount:" TO MAMOUNT
Enter amount: 245

DISPLAY MEMORY

MNAME        Pub    C  "Douglas"
```

```
MAMOUNT      Pub    C   "245"
2 variables defined,    24 bytes used
1022 variables available
```

The INPUT command also requests input from the user and stores the data to a memory variable. However, INPUT is a more flexible command because it does not necessarily store the data as a character variable. INPUT accepts any type of value or expression—even field names or the names of other variables can be entered. If an expression is entered, INPUT first evaluates the expression and then stores the result as the named variable. If a character string is to be supplied to INPUT, it must be enclosed in quotes. An optional message can be included as part of the INPUT command; if included, it must be enclosed in quotes. This is the syntax for the command:

```
INPUT <message> TO <variable>
```

Note the following examples of INPUT:

```
INPUT "Enter name, in quotes: " TO VAR1
Enter name, in quotes: "Johnson"

INPUT "Enter age: " TO VAR2
Enter age: 22

INPUT "Enter a valid expression: " TO VAR3
Enter a valid expression: CTOD("02/24/52")

DISPLAY MEMORY
VAR1        pub    C   "Johnson"
VAR2        pub    N          22   (        22.00000000)
VAR3        pub    D   02/24/52
3 variables defined,        27 bytes used
253 variables available,    5973 bytes available
```

Validating Data

Programs can check for valid data using several techniques. One effective technique is using the PICTURE and RANGE options of the @...SAY...GET commands to restrict the values accepted by the GETs. This is the syntax for the @...SAY...GET command, when used with the PICTURE or RANGE option:

```
@(<row>,<column>)[SAY<expression>][PICTURE<clause>]
➥[GET<variable>] [PICTURE<clause>][RANGE<expression,expression>]
```

The clauses that follow PICTURE contain template symbols and/or functions. *Template symbols* restrict the display or entry of a single character, and one symbol is used to represent each position in the blank. *Template functions* affect the entire display for the entry field rather than single characters. Functions are preceded by an @ sign, and both the template functions and template symbols are enclosed in quotes. If functions and templates are combined in one clause, they must be separated with a space. Tables 22.2 and 22.3 list the functions and templates, respectively.

Table 22.2. Picture templates.

Template	Result
!	Forces letters to uppercase
$	Leading zeros are displayed as dollar signs
*	Leading zeros are displayed as asterisks
.	Identifies a decimal position
,	Identifies a comma if there are numbers to the left of the comma
#	Permits digits, blanks, and signs only
9	Permits digits for character data and digits and signs for numeric data
A	Permits letters only
L	Permits logical data (true/false)
N	Permits letters and digits only
X	Permits any characters
Y	Permits logical data as Y or N only

Table 22.3. Picture functions.

Function	Result
!	Forces letters to uppercase
(	Negative numbers will be surrounded by parentheses
^	Numbers displayed in scientific notation
A	Accepts alphabetic characters only
B	Numeric data will be left-justified
C	Letters *CR* (credit) displayed following positive numbers
D	American date format
E	European date format
I	Centers text
J	Right-justifies text
L	Shows leading zeros
M	Permits list of choices for GET
Sn	Limits display to *n* characters wide and scrolls text in field
T	Trims leading and trailing blanks
X	Letters *DB* (debit) are displayed following negative numbers
Z	Zeros displayed as blanks

To use PICTURE to restrict data entry, for example, the ! template can be used to convert all character data to uppercase, lessening the chance that searches might be confusing if some names were stored in uppercase and others in lowercase:

```
@ 5,6 SAY "Enter name: " GET L_Name PICTURE '@!'
```

For numbers, specific places for digits, decimal points, and asterisks in place of leading zeros can be displayed by using the following example:

```
@ 10,12 GET AMOUNT PICTURE '*****.99'
```

With this template, leading zeros in the amount appear as asterisks, and two decimal places are provided following the decimal point. Only digits are accepted during data entry. Any attempt to enter alphabetic characters causes a beep. If you are using logical fields, the Y template allows entering the letters Y or N only, and lowercase letters will be converted to uppercase. PICTURE functions and templates can't perform all needed validation for you, but they can help you prevent data entry errors.

Using *RANGE*

The RANGE option of the @...SAY...GET command can be used as part of a data validation process to limit entries to an acceptable range of data. RANGE works with numeric data and with dates if appropriate conversion functions are used. This is the syntax for the RANGE option:

```
@(row,column) GET variable/fieldname RANGE[lower limit],[upper limit]
```

For example, to restrict the entry of Zip codes to California, use the following example:

```
@ 12,2 GET ZIPCODE RANGE 90000,99999
```

To restrict a single end of the range, include the comma and specify the value for the desired end. For instance,

```
@ 15,9 GET HOURLYPAY RANGE 2.70,
```

sets a minimum of 2.70 for the salary, with no maximum. The command

```
@ 15,9 GET HOURLYPAY RANGE ,20.05
```

sets no minimum for the salary and a maximum of 20.05. To use RANGE with dates, enclose the dates in braces. For example, the following command

```
@15,5 GET HIREDATE RANGE {05/15/88}, {06/01/93}
```

restricts entries to valid dates that fall between 5/15/88 and 6/1/93. The command

```
@15,5 GET HIREDATE RANGE {05/15/88}, DATE()
```

restricts entries to valid dates that fall between 5/15/88 and the current date maintained in the system clock, which means the PC's clock must be correct. If it isn't, users could find it impossible to enter what would otherwise be an acceptable date.

Summary

This chapter examined Visual FoxPro programming to give you the familiarity needed to begin working with its language. This chapter focused on developing elementary procedural programming skills. Even when programming using Visual FoxPro's object-oriented extensions, basic procedural code is found underneath; therefore, it is not only reasonable to develop these skills, it's required. In the next four chapters, you'll see how application development techniques can be used to manage tasks in database management, such as user interface design, reporting, and building complete applications. The next chapter starts you on the road to understanding and using the event model that underlies Visual FoxPro applications.

Working with FoxPro's Event Model

23

By fully embracing the concepts of object-oriented programming, Visual FoxPro takes what you can accomplish using the event-driven model of applications development to a new level. The prior version of FoxPro for Windows (Version 2.6) introduced the concept of *event handlers*, and this chapter includes details on how to use those event handlers. However, Visual FoxPro gives you far more than just a handful of event handlers to track events. In Visual FoxPro, events take place in response to virtually everything a user does, even if it's just the movement of the mouse across a window in Visual FoxPro. You can cause your application to respond, in whatever way desired, to events in Visual FoxPro by writing code for those events. A good example is the addition of a command button to a form—a button that does nothing is a pretty useless item. If you added a command button to a form, you would want to attach code to the button's Click event so that when the button is clicked the code would tell your application what to do in response. Here, you're following the Windows event-driven model, by responding in some way to a given event.

In developing applications with Visual FoxPro for Windows, you're faced with a new set of design choices that didn't exist in the early days of Xbase. Because Visual FoxPro is an Xbase product, you can develop applications along the same lines that Xbase applications have been developing for years: with main menus and cascading menu choices that tightly control user access and let users accomplish one specific task at a time. You can also develop applications along the lines of Windows user-interface standards, which provides an *event-driven* approach to everything a user does. With the event-driven approach to applications design, the user isn't necessarily locked into a limited series of menu options or to doing a single task at a time. With an event-driven interface, the application must be prepared to respond to any one of a series of possible events that might occur.

With many applications written in the procedural style common to programs from the early days of Xbase programming, user possibilities were limited to a small number of menu options presented by the system, and each user's choice often led to additional menus, and eventually to the performing of a specific task (such as editing a record in a table or printing a report). In contrast to this way of thinking, consider the example shown in Figure 23.1. This example shows an application designed along the style of event-driven programming. This application has an interface that gives the user a number of possible options and waits to respond to any of the events triggered by the user's choices.

One important point to note is that the Windows "look" (meaning pull-down menus, dialog boxes, and mouse support) is not sufficient by itself to mark an application as being truly event-driven. With the various wizards and the design surfaces in Visual FoxPro, it would be a relatively simple matter to design and implement an interface that made full use of pull-down menus, dialog boxes, and full mouse support. However, if the application always restricted the user to doing one thing (and only one thing) at a time, the application would still be a classic "modal" application in the style of early dBASE, rather than being a "modeless" or event-driven application. To be event-driven, an application must be aware of any one of a number of actions that a user might take from a single point. A user might click in any one of a number of windows presented for browsing or editing, or the user might click a Print button within a Control Panel, or the user might choose an option from a menu bar at the top of the main FoxPro window. The application would need to respond appropriately to any of these events.

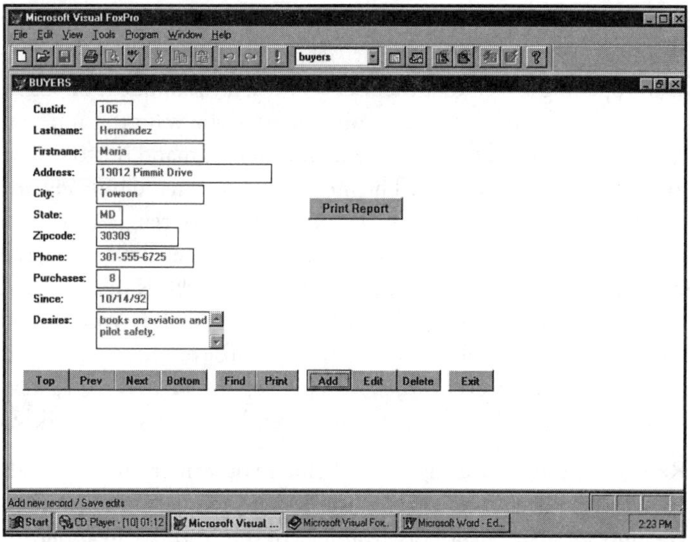

FIGURE 23.1.

A typical application using the event-driven style of programming.

Visual FoxPro's own interface is a classic example of an event-driven application. While you are working in Visual FoxPro, you might have three Browse windows open, a report shown in a page preview window, and a form's design visible in a Form Designer window. Under these circumstances, you could move at will between any of the windows, accomplishing different tasks. This kind of multifunctionality is what one strives for when designing event-driven applications.

SAMPLE TABLE AND FILES ON THE CD-ROM

Sample files are provided on the CD-ROM as adjuncts to this chapter to illustrate the various events and methods used in Visual FoxPro.

This chapter's example uses files located in the directories VFU\SAMPLES\ and VFU\Chap23\.

File	Purpose
Buyers.DBF	Used to supply the data for demonstrating simple programming techniques. Located in VFU\SAMPLES\.
Buyers.SCX	Contains the form that is used for the illustrations in this chapter. Located in VFU\Chap23\.

Understanding the Role of Forms as an Application Hub

If you're to take full advantage of what Visual FoxPro has to offer in terms of application programming, it makes sense to plan your applications around the use of *forms* as a principal user interface. With this kind of approach to applications design, a main form is usually presented as the opening screen that the user sees when the application loads. The form may or may not contain data from tables (depending on how you want the appearance of the application structured), but you will usually have menus or command buttons that give users a way to accomplish what they want to do. The menus and command buttons can have code attached to their events, and your application can respond appropriately to those events, using code to open other forms, to print reports, or to perform other desired tasks. When a user interacts with your application, events are generated. The methods that are attached to the objects in your form, whether built-in by Visual FoxPro or added by you in the form of attached code, will control how your application responds to those events. To a large degree, understanding when and how to use the events that are a part of Visual FoxPro is a key to accomplishing what you need to accomplish in a true event-driven Visual FoxPro application.

Recognize, too, that using forms (which you can create and modify by using the Form Wizards and the Form Designer) as the center of your application is one approach, and there are certainly others. A major disadvantage of the "form as an applications hub" approach is that it tends to emphasize one table as the basis of your application, and most work done has a natural tendency to center around that table as a result. Perhaps your application is one that uses a number of tables, and no one table is used more extensively than the others. In such a case, it might make more sense to build the application around a menu bar that would let the user choose the desired table to work with. Appropriate forms could then be presented, depending on which table was chosen. Finally, remember too that it's perfectly acceptable to bypass Visual FoxPro's own methods of applications design entirely and use a third-party code generator to build much or all of the application. Many FoxPro developers are comfortable with various third-party products, and these can provide solid applications in the hands of those developers who know them well.

Yeah, But Where Does My Code Go?

If you are used to writing code in a linear programming environment (and what veteran Xbase programmer isn't?), one of the major challenges you will face with object-oriented programming (OOP) is deciding exactly where you should put your program code. Unfortunately, there's no easy answer to this question; if there were, the transition to OOP would be simple. Where you should attach your code depends on when the code should be executed, what object the code will be attached to, and what methods come into play. Because your code will act in response to events in Visual FoxPro, the design of your application has to include planning for the events that you want to track.

For example: if you want to open a certain form when a user clicks a command button, you would need to add code that would open the form with the Click method for that command button. If something should happen as a user moves the focus into a certain text box on a form, you would need to attach code to the Arrive method for that text box. As you plan how you will implement the responses to the events that you want to track, keep in mind that code often changes the behavior of an object other than what it is attached to. Again, a command button is a good example; the code that you attach to command buttons never does anything with the button itself, but instead performs some desired action (like opening a form).

Understanding Events in Container and Class Hierarchies

Visual FoxPro offers two types of classes, *container* classes and *control* classes. (The types of classes aren't discussed in great detail here because they are explained in Part IV of this book, "Programming in Visual FoxPro"; but you need to know about classes just for the purpose of making sense of how Visual FoxPro tracks events.) Container classes can be thought of as objects that can contain other objects. Forms, for example, are containers because you can put objects—such as grids for displaying tables, text boxes, and command buttons—inside of forms. Control classes can be thought of as objects that can't contain other objects. A command button, for example, is a control. (You can't put anything inside of a command button.) When a user interacts with an object in some way—such as by moving the mouse over it, by clicking on it, or by moving the focus into the object—events occur, and you can respond to those events programmatically.

For example, if you add a command button to a form, right-click the button, and choose Properties from the shortcut menu, you will open the Properties window for the button. Click the Methods tab in the window to select it, and you'll see the various events for the button, as shown in Figure 23.2.

If the Click event (shown at the top of the list in Figure 23.2) has no code attached to it, Visual FoxPro does absolutely nothing when you click the button, other than show a button being depressed (which is a behavior designed into the button). You can have code associated with the Click event for the form that contains the button, but that code will not be affected by the fact that the button inside the form was clicked by the user. This discussion highlights two major points that you must keep in mind when you write code for the controls in your Visual FoxPro applications.

■ *Containers don't process events for the controls that are contained in them.* As illustrated in the preceding discussion, if a form has code attached to it and an object in the form receives an event, the code attached to the form is not triggered by the object in the form receiving an event. This differs from some other object-oriented database environments (notably Paradox for Windows, which does use a containership hierarchy in which events are passed from controls in forms to the forms themselves). If you are used to working in an environment like Paradox for Windows, it is important to understand that Visual FoxPro does not work like this.

■ *If no event code is attached to a control that receives an event, Visual FoxPro checks higher up the class hierarchy (not the container hierarchy) for the control to see if there is any code associated with the event.* When a control that's in a form is based on a custom class and there is no code attached to the appropriate event for that control, Visual FoxPro goes up the class hierarchy by one level, looking for code attached to the desired event. Hence, if a button that you add is based on another button in a base class and the button in the base class has code attached to it, Visual FoxPro will use that code when it can't find any code for the first button. If all this talk of classes and hierarchies makes no sense, hang on until Part VI of this book. It is mentioned in this chapter because the hierarchy structure used by Visual FoxPro does have a direct bearing on what code gets executed in response to certain events.

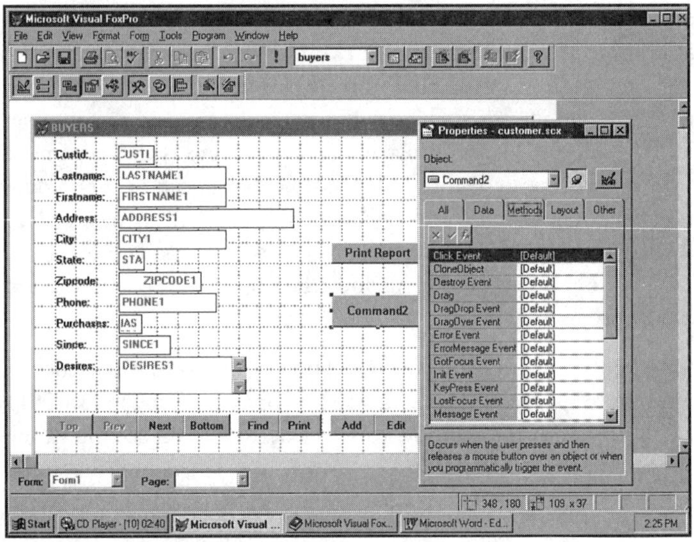

FIGURE 23.2.

Events for a command button.

Assigning Code to Events

As mentioned, you must associate or "attach" code to an event for that code to be processed when the event occurs. You add your desired code by using the Form Designer and by going into the Properties window for the object. Right-click the object and choose Properties from the shortcut menu that appears. Click the Method tab of the Properties window, and then double-click the desired event. A window opens where you can type your code. Figure 23.3 shows the code window for the Click event of a command button placed within a form.

In the window, you can type the appropriate Visual FoxPro program code. (For more specifics on the basics of the FoxPro language, refer to Chapter 22, "Visual FoxPro Language Basics.")

FIGURE 23.3.

Code window for the
`Click` *event of a*
command button.

Using Visual FoxPro's Event Handlers

If you must work with program code based on FoxPro 2.6 applications, you'll need to be familiar with the event handlers introduced to the language by that version of FoxPro. The event handlers introduced in FoxPro 2.6 are commands that begin with the word ON, and they include the commands and their uses, as shown in Table 23.1.

Table 23.1. Visual FoxPro event handlers.

Command	Purpose
ON BAR	Activates a menu when a specific bar of a popup is selected.
ON ERROR	Executes a command when an error occurs. In most cases the command runs an error-trapping routine.
ON ESCAPE	Executes a command when the Esc key is pressed. The command is often a DO command.
ON KEY	Traps for any key press during program execution and branches to a subroutine when any key is pressed.
ON KEY LABEL	Traps for a specific key during program execution and branches to a subroutine when the specific key is pressed.
ON PAD	Links a specific pad in a bar menu to a specific popup and displays that popup when the pad is selected.

continues

514

Table 23.1. continued

Command	Purpose
ON SELECTION BAR	Executes a command upon selection of a specific bar in a bar menu.
ON SELECTION MENU	Executes a command upon selection of any bar in a bar menu.
ON SELECTION PAD	Executes a command upon selection of a specific pad within a menu.
ON SELECTION POPUP	Executes a command upon selection of a specific bar within a popup.

What distinguishes the event handlers from other FoxPro commands is how they behave. With other FoxPro commands, as soon as the command is executed a corresponding action is carried out. Visual FoxPro's event handlers are different; they identify an action that will take place in the future when a corresponding event occurs. In effect, an event handler tells Visual FoxPro to watch for a specific occurrence of an event, and to take some action when that event occurs. For example, a specific bar of a menu popup could be used to launch the Windows clock by calling the program (CLOCK.EXE) from within Visual FoxPro with a RUN statement. Inside the program that constructs the main menu, you could have a statement like the following:

```
ON SELECTION BAR 2 of Windows RUN /N CLOCK.EXE
```

When the specified event takes place (in this example, the choosing of the second bar in a menu popup), the corresponding action occurs.

Summary

The overall point of this entire section is this: event-driven applications come easy in Visual FoxPro if you use forms as a major part of your applications and if you add the needed code to respond to the appropriate events of your choice throughout the objects of those forms. For veteran Xbase programmers, event-driven programming is a different way of thinking and may take some getting used to.

Since the early days of Xbase, programmers have always been accustomed to writing a main menu that leads to all available tasks and programming an entire application from the top down. Although applications development in Visual FoxPro still requires good top-down planning (as does any development language), programmers must resist any urge to code every part of an application. Instead, programmers should take full advantage of Visual FoxPro's event-driven, object-oriented behavior to achieve an application that is event driven and easier for end users to use. In the long run, helping users get the job done with the least amount of hassle is what it all comes down to.

Designing the Application Interface

24

The most important part of your application is the application interface because that is the first thing the users see. Your application's user interface can be centered around a menu system, a dialog box, or a toolbar. Regardless of the type of user interface your application has, the first thing that most users do when they run your application is to browse through all the options so that they can build a mental image of the structure and content of your application. It is like browsing the table of contents of a reference book. Your application can have the greatest algorithms devised by humans, but if your application's interface confuses users, the full potential and usefulness of your application might not be appreciated by the target audience. However, if you spend time and effort designing your user interface, users will praise your application and quickly learn how to use it to its full potential.

SAMPLE PROJECT, FORMS, AND MENUS ON THE CD-ROM

A sample project and sample forms and menus are provided in the data on the accompanying CD-ROM.

If you have performed the data setup, look in the VFU\Chap24\ for the material appropriate for this chapter.

File	Purpose
Assist.APP	This is an example of an application that demonstrates a form as an application hub.
Assist.PJT	This is the complete project. Review this to understand the details of creating the Assist application. This project contains all the files used to create Assist, including class definitions and bitmaps for the pictures on the buttons.
Controls.SCX	The form illustrates the control types available to you for building forms.
Friends.SCX	This is a form that appears in Assist. It is run as the "address book," and it uses the Friends.DBF data table.
MyHelper.MPX	This is a menu definition that, when generated, demonstrates using a menu as an application hub. It provides a menu pad whose entries launch the "Assistant" functionality.
MyHelper.SCX	This is a form that appears in Assist. It is the main user interface used to launch the "Assistant" functionality.
Shapes.SCX	This form illustrates the various shapes possible with the shape objects.

Using the Menu System as an Application Hub

For many applications, the menu system is the foundation of the application. A well-designed menu system gives the user easy access to the various features of an application. The Visual FoxPro menu system lets you quickly and easily build a new menu system or make modifications to the existing Visual FoxPro menu system. Before you jump in to create a menu system you should decide what menus the user needs and then design all of the menus and submenus that you are going to need.

Here are some tips for planning the user interface for your applications.

- Programmers sometimes tend to organize an interface based on the hierarchy of the programs in the application. Don't do that. Organize the user interface in the order that users will perform. Think like a user and not like a programmer when you design your menu system.

- If possible, organize menu options in the order they are most frequently used. If you do not know, then organize them in alphabetical order.

- Make sure the menu titles are as brief as possible but also meaningful. Avoid computer jargon, such as dump, flush, buffer, zip, and so forth.

- Use upper- and lowercase letters for menu items.

- Use separator lines between logical groups of commands.

- Limit the number of items in a menu. Too many items confuse people. If the menu gets too long, use submenus.

- Use access keys or keyboard shortcuts for frequently used commands. (For example, Ctrl+C.)

- Use hot keys with menu items (place \< in front of the hot key when defining options).

- Use words that clearly describe menu items. Try to use simple, active verbs.

The Visual FoxPro system menu is a good example of a menu that pretty much follows the tips in the preceding list.

The Visual FoxPro Form as an Application Hub

A form is not just a data entry screen anymore. In Visual FoxPro, you can add various types of controls that launch various features of your system. Furthermore, you do not always have to use a menu system as a hub for your application. You can create a Visual FoxPro form with buttons to control all of the functions of the system.

Because Visual FoxPro is a true event-driven system, you can launch any number of forms from a central form. All you have to do is add a push button to the form. Then you add code to the push button's Click event method to launch another task or other form. A method is like a procedure or function that contains Visual FoxPro program code. When the user clicks on the push button, Visual FoxPro executes the code in the Click event method. There are many events associated with forms, form sets, containers, and controls. Therefore, you can write code for event methods to make a form or control behave just about any way you like. The Visual FoxPro event model is quite versatile.

One example of a form that is the hub of an application is the Personal Assistant application shown in Figure 24.1. This has six push buttons, called *control buttons* in Visual FoxPro. Each button executes a different component of the application. The Assistant form also has a Timer control that updates the date and time displayed in a text box every time the timer event expires. The timer interval is specified by the Interval property and is set to 1000 (milliseconds). As a result, the Timer event fires (occurs) every second. The Timer event method code consists of the following statement:

```
THISFORM.Text1.Value = DATETIME()
```

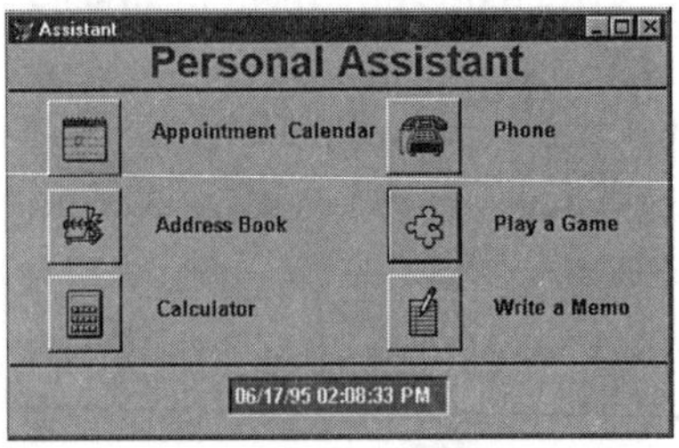

FIGURE 24.1.

Personal Assistant dialog box that illustrates how Forms can be used as the hub of an application.

The Click event method code for the six control buttons is also a very simple single line of code. The code for each control button is portrayed in the following table:

Control Button	*Code for* Click *Method*
Appointment Calendar	ACTIVATE WINDOW "Calendar"
Address Book	DO FORM Friends
Calculator	ACTIVATE WINDOW "Calculator"
Phone	DO FORM DIALER
Play a game	ACTIVATE WINDOW "Puzzle"
Write a memo	MODIFY FILE ?

The Assistant form (MYHELPER.SCX) shown in Figure 24.1 was easily generated by using the Visual FoxPro Form Designer. The Address book application (FRIENDS.SCX) launched by the Personal Assistant application, as shown in Figure 24.2, was also easily created using the Form Wizard, although I did use the Form Designer to move some fields around and change the field labels. The Calculator, Calendar, and Puzzle applications are built into Visual FoxPro. However, these three applications are not accessible through the Visual FoxPro menus. They are just kept around for the sake of old times.

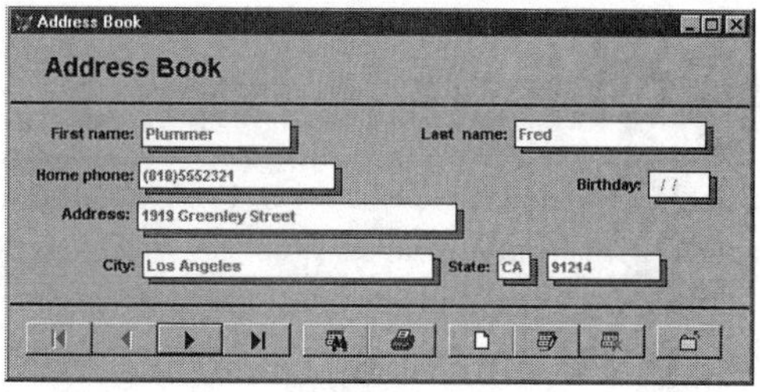

FIGURE 24.2.

Example Address Book dialog box launched by the Personal Assistant application.

A form created by the Form Wizard is another example of an application with its own built-in application interface. It contains buttons that launch database maintenance and positioning processes. It also contains a button that runs a report.

TIP

The Form Wizard creates a Container object and adds a Label, Text, and Shape control to the Container object for each field it adds to the form. If you want to change the Label control Caption property (or any other property), you are instructed to choose the proper Label control from the Properties window and Objects list. With lots of fields, it is sometimes hard to find the proper Label control.

However, the quickest and easiest way to select one of the Label controls is to right-click on the Container object (see Figure 24.3). Choose the Edit option from the shortcut menu. Then click on the Label control to select it. Change the Caption property in the Properties window. You can use the same technique (right-click) when you select a grid column or a Page control in a Page Frame container. Try it.

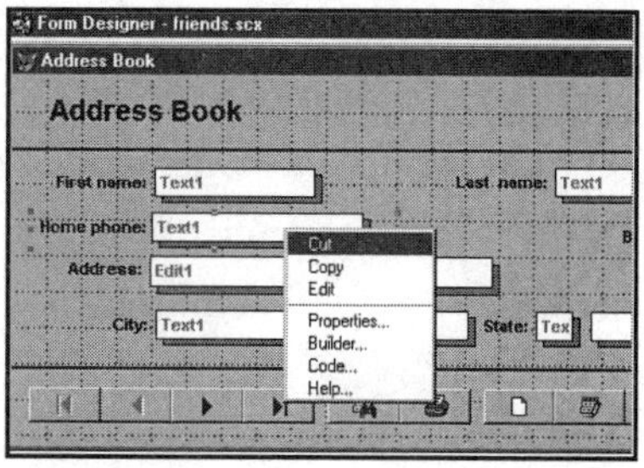

FIGURE 24.3.

Form Designer with the Address Book dialog box and open shortcut menu.

Many applications have both buttons on the application to execute other components and have corresponding menu options and toolbar buttons that execute the same components. The Project Manager is an example of such an application. This gives the user more flexible interface alternatives.

Adding Objects to Forms

As you have already learned, the Visual FoxPro Form Designer makes it easy for you to create a form or a set of forms that contain a plentiful group of controls, all of which can respond to numerous events. This empowers you to rapidly create and maintain advanced interfaces and data entry forms for the most complex database management. The process of creating a form involves adding the appropriate containers and control objects to the form, setting the properties for the form and the controls, and writing code that responds to events.

The types of objects that you can add to a form are controls, containers, user-defined classes, and OLE objects. You will learn about user-defined classes and OLE objects in Part V, "Object-Oriented Programming." You have already been introduced to the controls and learned how to place them on the form in Chapter 12, "Designing and Customizing Forms." Now it's time to discuss the controls and containers in more detail.

Objects in Visual FoxPro can be either a *container* or a *control*. A container can be a parent object for other objects. For example, a form is a container object. It is the parent object for control objects or other containers. A form can contain a *grid*, which is a container object that contains columns, headers, and other controls. On the other hand, a control cannot be a parent object for another object. In other words, it cannot contain, but it can be contained. Table 24.1 shows a list of containers that you can add to a form and describes what they can contain.

Table 24.1. Containers you can add to a form.

Container	What It Can Contain
Column	Headers
Command button group	Command buttons
Form set	Forms, toolbars
Form	Page frames, grids, any controls
Grid	Columns
Option button group	Option buttons
Page frame	Pages
Page	Grids, any controls

When you open the Form Designer to create a form, a pristine new form appears in the Form Designer. If you want a form set, you can add a form set and then add other forms from the Form menu. All of the rest of the containers appear on the Controls toolbar (see Figure 24.3). You can click on one of the containers and drag it to size in the form.

Adding Controls to Forms

To add a control to a form, all you have to do is click on the control and drag it to the form. An example of all of the available controls is shown in Figure 24.4. In this section, you will learn more about how to effectively use the following Visual FoxPro controls:

Check boxes	Labels
Combo boxes	List boxes
Command buttons	Option button groups
Command button groups	Shape and line controls
Edit boxes	Spinners
Grid controls	Text boxes
Image controls	Timer controls

FIGURE 24.4.

An example of Visual FoxPro controls and containers.

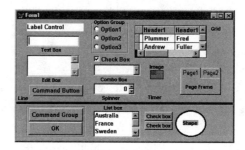

OLE bound and OLE controls are discussed in Chapter 31, "Advanced Object-Oriented Programming."

To add a control to a form, click on a button in the Controls toolbar and drag it to size in the form.

Visual FoxPro supports some visual techniques of placing controls to access table data on a form. You can add table data to a form visually by clicking on a field or table in the Project Manager or the Data Environment Designer and dragging it to the form. If you drag a field to a form, Visual FoxPro adds a text box object to the form. If you drag a table to the form, Visual FoxPro adds a grid to the form. In Figure 24.5 the FirstName field is placed on the form and a grid is placed on the form that will display fields from table FRIENDS.DBF.

FIGURE 24.5.

*Dragging field and grid
from Project Manager
to Form Designer.*

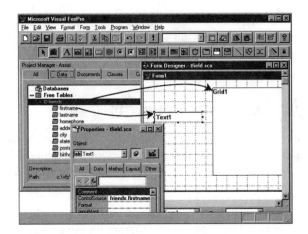

Adding User-Defined Objects to a Form

You can develop your own custom classes and store them in a visual class library (VCX) file using the Visual Class Designer (see Chapter 28, "OOP with Visual FoxPro"). Then you can add to your form or form set an object based on your custom class. Here is one way to add a custom object to your form:

1. Create your own custom class with the Visual Class Designer and save it as a visual class library (VCX) file.

2. Add the visual class library to your project by using the Project Manager Add button.

3. Drag the custom class from the Project Manager to your form or form set in the Form Designer.

You can add a visual class library to the Controls toolbar. This operation is called *registering* the visual class library. To register a class in the Form Designer, click the View Classes button in the Controls toolbar. When a menu appears, choose the Add option which displays an Open file dialog box. Select a visual class library (VCX) file and choose Open. The custom classes in the class library will be added to the Controls toolbar. Then you can add an object based on the custom class to a form or form set just as you add any other control. That is, you click on the button in the Controls toolbar and drag to size in the form.

Incidentally, you can register a visual class library (VCX) file from the Controls tab of the Options dialog box. (From the Tools menu, choose Options to display the Options dialog box.)

Choosing the Right Control for the Job

With Visual FoxPro control objects as building blocks, you have the materials you need to design an excellent advanced user interface that will satisfy your most discriminating clients. Figure 24.4 shows examples of all the available controls.

When you are considering which control to use to perform a particular task, think about it from the user's point of view. Think about how the user expects a control to react and which control the user expects to use for a certain task. For example, to perform an action, the user expects to click on a command button, not a label, option button, or text box control. It is important to choose the right control for a task and then it is just as important to effectively use that control.

Most of the tasks you might want to perform with a control are included in the following categories, along with a list of controls that you can use to provide the functionality:

- Present the user with a set of predetermined choices that ensure that the user specifies valid input by controlling the user's choice. This category includes the following controls:

  Check box

  Drop-down list box

  List box

  Option button group

- Accept general user input. You can use the following controls depending on the type of data:

  Combo Box

  Edit box

  Text box

- Accept user input within a predetermined range of values. You can use the Spinner control to specify a range of values.

- Let the user perform specific actions. You can use either the Command button or a Command button group.

- Perform designated actions at designated time intervals. You can use the Timer control.

- You can use the following controls to display information:

  Edit Box

  Label

  Line

  Grid

  Text

  Shape

  Image

In the following sections, you will learn the effective use of each type of control.

The Check Box Control

A check box is normally used to represent two-state Boolean logic: Yes or No, True or False. The ControlSource property for a check box can be a Logical or Numeric field in a table. The check box is selected if a logical field has a true (.T.) value or a numeric field contains a non-zero value. A check box is cleared if the logical field has a false (.F.) or .NULL. value, or a numeric field has a 0 or .NULL. value. When a condition is true, an X appears in the check box.

You use the Caption property to specify the text that appears next to a check box.

There is a third state you can represent with a check box—a disabled state. This state can represent an option for which it is not appropriate for the user to make a choice. You represent this third state by disabling the check box by setting the Enabled property to false (.F.).

The Combo Box and List Box Controls

A combo box can have two modes depending on the value of its Style property. If the Style property is set to 0, a drop-down combo box is created, in which case you can either type in a value or choose a value from a list. On the other hand, if the Style property is set to 2, a drop-down list box is created. A drop-down combo box is useful when you want a control that lets your user type a value if the appropriate value is not in the list.

Drop-down list box controls (combo box controls with their Style property set to 2) and list box controls provide a variety of types of scrollable lists from which the user can select an item. Multiple options are always visible for a list box control. However, only one option is always visible for a combo box control. When you open a combo box control by clicking the down button, all of the options display in a scrollable drop-down list box control. You normally use a list box control instead of a combo box control when you have sufficient space on the form to display a list box control and to accentuate the choices. In contrast, you use a combo box control if you want to conserve space and to accentuate the currently selected value.

The Command Button Control

A command button is the best control to use to launch an action. It is simple to implement. All you have to do is place a command button on the form, change its Caption property, and write click event code to perform some action.

The Command Group Control

The Command group control is a container that contains command button controls. The important properties of this container are the ButtonCount, ControlSource, and Caption properties. You set the ButtonCount properties to define the number of command button controls in the group. Because you need to change the captions for each individual button, you need to select the button from the Object drop-down combo box in the Properties window (or right-click on the control and choose the Edit option from the shortcut menu). Then change its properties. You can control the buttons from the command group Click event method. For example, if you have three buttons in the group, you can add the following example code to the group's Click event method:

```
DO CASE
    CASE THIS.VALUE = 1
        * Do some action for first button
    CASE THIS.VALUE = 2
        * Do some action for second button
    CASE THIS.VALUE = 3
        * Do some action for third button
ENDCASE
```

If you add Click event code to a button in a group and click on the button, the code for that button executes, and the code for its button group's Click event is not executed. However, if you place code in the Click event method for an individual command button, you might as well use individual command button controls.

You might want to use the command group control to give the user a multiple choice selection for a numeric field. To do this, you set the ControlSource property of the command group control to the name of the field. When the user clicks on a command button in the group, the number corresponding to the Value property of the field is stored in the field.

The Edit Box Control

The edit box control is a fully operational word processor with the capability to select, cut, paste, and copy text; to word wrap automatically; and to move through text with the arrow keys. You can edit long character strings and memo fields in an edit box control.

The Grid Container

The grid control is one of the most powerful controls in Visual FoxPro. It is similar to the BROWSE command because it displays data in tabular form. Remember that a Grid object is a container that contains column controls. Column controls contain a header control and any other type of control used to display columns of data. In fact, a column control can even contain another grid control.

You can easily create a simple grid. All you have to do is drag a table to the Form Designer Layout window from the Data Environment Designer, the Project Manager, or the Database Designer. You might have to add better column headings if you do not use a database table with long field names.

The Image Control

You can add a bitmap (BMP), icon (ICO), or general field graphics picture to a form using an image control. Image controls are not just for displaying pictures because Image controls support many of the same properties, events, and methods supported by other controls. For example, you can add code that responds to events, such as the Click and DblClick events, for an Image control when the user clicks on the image.

The Label Control

A label control displays static text on a form. It is Visual FoxPro's rendition of the FoxPro @...SAY command. There is no data source for a label control, and you cannot edit data. However, you can programmatically change the Caption property, which changes the Label control's displayed text.

You can disable a label control using the Enabled property. When a label control is disabled, the access key is inactive, the same as it is for the other controls.

You can also display text on a form using a text box or edit box control with the ReadOnly property set to True.

The Option Button Group Control

An option button group is a container group that contains option buttons. You use option buttons to give the user a predefined set of options so that the user cannot specify invalid information.

After you place an option group on the form, you need to designate how many option buttons you have by setting the ButtonCount property. Interface studies indicate that a group of options should not be more than seven. It is better to use a list box or drop-down combo box control if you have a large number of options.

You will need to set properties for the individual buttons. Use the Object box in the Properties window to select individual option buttons or right-click and choose the Edit option. At the very least, you need to set the Caption property of each option button. You can also set properties of individual option buttons by specifying the names at runtime. For example, to set the Caption properties at runtime for the option buttons in the option group opgParity, you can specify the following code:

```
THISFORM.opgParity.Option1.Caption = "Odd"
THISFORM.opgParity.Option2.Caption = "Even"
THISFORM.opgParity.Option3.Caption = "None"
```

You can accomplish the same thing using the Buttons property for the group option buttons control. Here is an example:

```
THISFORM.opgParity.Buttons(1).Caption = "Odd"
THISFORM.opgParity.Buttons(2).Caption = "Even"
THISFORM.opgParity.Buttons(3).Caption = "None"
```

You can use the SetAll method of the group option buttons control to set a property of all of the option buttons in the group. For example, suppose that you wanted to set the background color of all of the buttons for opgParity group to light gray. Use the following line of code:

```
THISFORM.opgParity.SetAll("BackColor", COLOR_GRAY, "OptionButton")
```

This example assumes that you used the Form menu Include File option to include the FOXPRO.H header file that contains the COLOR_GRAY definition.

You can determine which option button of a group of option buttons is selected by examining the Value property of the option button group. The Value property contains a numeric value that designates which button is selected. For example, if you have four buttons in a group and the third button is selected, then Value equals 3. If no buttons are selected, the Value property is 0. Suppose that you have a group (opgTwenty) of three option buttons with Animal, Vegetable, and Mineral captions. You can display the caption of the selected button when it changes by placing the following statements in the Click event method for the opgTwenty group:

```
WAIT WINDOW "You Selected button: "+THIS.Buttons(THIS.Value).Caption
```

The Value property of the option button group is initially set to 0 (no buttons selected); and as indicated previously, it returns the number of the selected button. If you set the Value property to the caption of a button, then that button will be initially selected. If you set the Value property to an empty string, no button will be initially selected. Also, when an option button is selected, a character string containing the caption of the option button is returned. In the preceding example, you can set Value = "" and use the following code to display the Caption property:

```
WAIT WINDOW "You Selected button: "+THIS.Value
```

This dual role of the Value property can be illustrated with the following sample Click event method for the OptionGroup1 control in the CONTROLS.SCX example shown in Figure 24.4:

```
IF  TYPE("THIS.Value")="C"   && Is Value property Character data type?
    WAIT WINDOW TIMEOUT 1 THIS.Value + ;
       " (Value is Character type)"
       THIS.Value = 0
ELSE
    IF  TYPE("THIS.Value")="N"   && Is Value property Numeric data type?
        WAIT WINDOW TIMEOUT 1 ;
           THIS.Buttons(THIS.VALUE).Caption +" (Value is Numeric)"
           THIS.Value = ""
    ENDIF
ENDIF
```

This silly example illustrates the different values the Value property can have depending on its data type.

The Spinner Control

The spinner control, as shown in Figure 24.4, is used to "spin" through numeric values. You set the range of allowed values with the KeyboardHighValue, SpinnerHighValue, KeyboardLowValue, and SpinnerLowValue properties.

A spinner control has a text box in which you can enter a number. It also has an up and down arrow. If you click on the up arrow, the value in the associated text box increases by the value of the `Interval` property. If you click on the down arrow, the value in the associated text box decreases by the value of the `Interval` property. The `Interval` property defaults to 1. However, it can have any non-zero positive or negative value.

The Text Box Control

You use the text box control to add or edit data in non-memo fields and memory variables. When you set a `ControlSource` property for a text box to a field of a table or cursor, the value of that field displays in the text box control, and the `Value` property is set to that value. You can programmatically assign a new value to the `Value` property, and the value displays in the text box control and is stored in the field. Table 24.2 lists properties commonly used with the text box control.

Table 24.2. Typical properties used with the text box control.

Property	Default	Description
ControlSource	" "	Specifies the non-memo field in a table, cursor, or memory variable to be edited.
InputMask	" "	A character string that designates the data entry rule each character entered must follow. It is similar to a FORMAT clause on an @...GET statement. The characters in the mask are defined as follows: 9—Digits and signs (+ and –). #—Digits, blanks, and signs. $—Displays currency symbol. *—Displays asterisks to the left of the value. .—(period) Specifies decimal point position. ,—(comma) Separates digits. Y—For Logical character type, this allows you to type T, F, Y, N, t, f, y, or n.
DisabledBackColor	255,255,255	Designates the background color displayed when a control is disabled.
DisabledForeColor	0,0,0	Designates the foreground color displayed when a control is disabled.
PasswordChar	" "	Designates whether characters entered by a user or place holder characters are displayed in a text box; if you specify a character, such as an

Property	Default	Description
		asterisk (*), the character becomes a placeholder and displays in the field as you type. This hides what you actually type.
TabStop	.T.	Designates whether or not (.T. or .F.) the user can tab to the control. A text box control can also be selected by the user clicking it.

The following code shows examples of how to use the InputMask property to control the values that can be typed into a text box:

```
InputMask="999,999.99"  Displays example:  3,456.32
InputMask="$999,999.99" Displays example: $3,456.32
InputMask="###-##-####" Displays example: 123-345-3333
InputMask="***,***.99"  Displays example: **3,456.32
InputMask="999,999.99"  Displays example: 123,456.32
```

The Timer Control

You can place a timer control on your form and then program the timer to perform a designated action at regular timed intervals. You might use it to schedule tasks to be run at a certain time, to time a process to make sure it is successfully completed, to animate controls, or simply to place a special clock on a form. You can place multiple timers on a form to schedule multiple processes.

There are really only two properties that are important to the timer control: the Interval and the Enabled properties. The Enabled property turns on (.T.) and off (.F.) the timer. The default setting for the Enabled property is .T.. If you do not want the timer to be on when the form loads, you set the Enabled property to .F. when you design the form. Then you can turn it on and off, as required, at runtime.

The Interval property specifies the approximate number of milliseconds between events. When the specified interval expires, the Timer event code executes. The Interval property does not specify how long—it specifies how often the Timer event code executes. The Timer event continues to trigger at each interval until you turn it off by setting the Enabled property to .F..

You should be aware of the limitations of the Interval property when you are programming a timer. Here are the limitations:

- The Interval property can be set between 0 and 2,147,483,647 ($2^{31}-1$) or about 24.9 days or 596.52 hours.
- There is no guarantee that the Timer event will fire precisely on time. To get an accurate time, you should retrieve the time from the system clock with the TIME() function.

- The computer system clock generates a systems timer interrupt 18 times a second; although the `Interval` property is measured in milliseconds, the actual precision is no better than $^1/_{18}$ of a second.

- If the computer performing intensive calculations or processing I/O interrupts, the interval between `Timer` events may vary even more than $^1/_{18}$ of a second.

The Personal Assistant form (MYHELPER.SCX), shown in Figure 24.1, illustrates how to use the timer control. To design this example, you add the timer control to the form the same way you would any other control. The timer control displays on the form in the Form Designer as a little clock. However, the timer control is invisible when you run the form. The timer's `Interval` property is set at 1,000 milliseconds. The `Timer` event method contains the following line of code to display the date and time in a text box, Text1, every second:

```
THISFORM.Text1.Value = DATETIME()
```

The Shape and Line Controls

You can use shape and line controls to group forms together and to divide the form into logical panels to enhance readability.

A *line control* is a simple line that displays horizontally, vertically, or diagonally. The line control property that you are most likely to change is the `BorderWidth` property. This property specifies the width of the line in pixels.

You can use the shape control to display a box, circle, or ellipse. The properties that are often set for the shape control are presented in Table 24.3.

Table 24.3. Typical properties used with the shape control.

Property	Default	Description
Curvature	0	Specifies the curvature of the shape with values between 0 and 99. Examples are shown in Figure 24.6.
FillStyle	1	Specifies whether a shape is solid, transparent, or has a fill pattern, as shown in Figure 24.6.
BorderStyle	1	Specifies the border style of an object. Styles are shown in Figure 24.6. Applies only if `BorderWidth` is greater than 1 pixel. Applies to lines and shapes.
BorderWidth	1	Specifies the width in pixels of the border for the shape. Applies to lines and shapes.
SpecialEffects	1	Specifies whether the shape control is plain or in 3D. This property applies only when the `Curvature` property equals 0.

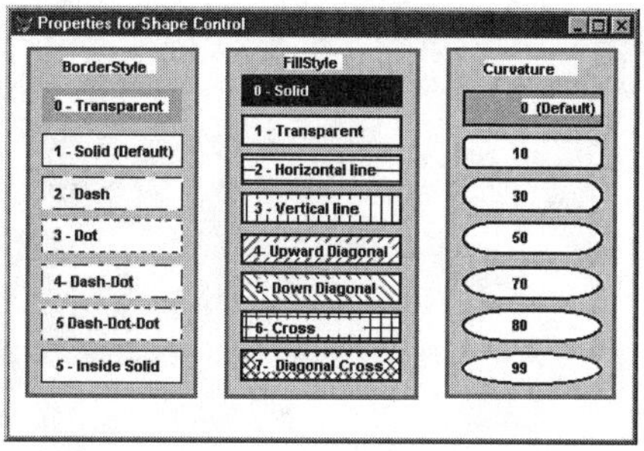

FIGURE 24.6.

An example that illustrates the FillStyle, BorderStyle, *and* Curvature *properties for the shape control.*

The line and shape controls normally are not changed directly at runtime. However, both controls possess many of the same properties, events, and methods other controls have. Both controls can respond to events such as Click, DblClick, and DragOver and can be changed at runtime.

There is another way to display graphics on a form. You can draw graphics objects on the form using the following form methods:

Method	Object Drawn on a Form
Circle	Circular figure or arc
Cls	Clears graphics and text
Line	Line
Pset	Sets a point on a form to a specific color
Print	Prints a character string on a form

Form properties, such as DrawWidth, DrawStyle, DrawMode, FillColor, FillStyle, and ForeColor, define properties of objects drawn on the form.

Adding Properties and Methods to Forms

Your application will need variables to store information. As you will learn in Part V, data is stored with the object in a variable called a *property*. Each control and container has built-in properties that define its behavior, such as the Height, Width, and BackColor properties. You can add your own user-defined properties using the Form Designer. These properties are stored with the highest-level object. For example, user-defined properties are stored with the Form object unless you have a form set object. Then, the user-defined properties are stored with the FormSet object.

Likewise, you can define your own user-defined methods. A *method* is an object-oriented form of a procedure or function. In other words, methods contain Visual FoxPro program code. You can add as many new user-defined properties and methods as you want to a form or form set.

To add a new user-defined property to a form or form set, choose the Form|New Property option and the New Property dialog box appears, as shown in Figure 24.7. Type the name of your user-defined property. You can also type a description of the property. The description displays at the bottom of the Properties window when the user-defined property is selected.

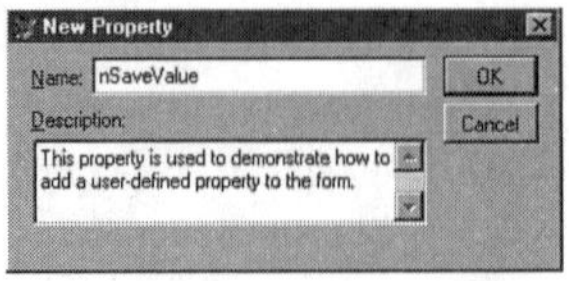

FIGURE 24.7.

The New Property dialog box.

You can reference a user-defined property the same way you would any other array. But remember, an array belongs to either a form or a form set. Suppose that you have two user-defined properties named nTweedleDee and nTweedleDum, and you have a single form (No form set); you can reference them in the following example:

```
IF THISFORM.nTweedleDee = 3
    THISFORM.nTweedleDum = 42
    THISFORM.cmdPanic.Enabled = .F.
ELSE
    THISFORM.nTweedleDum = 0
    THISFORM.cmdPanic.Enabled = .T.
ENDIF
```

You can specify an array property by typing the name of the array followed by its size and dimensions. For example, you could type ArrayProp[3,12] in the Name box of the New Property dialog box to create a two-dimensional array with 3 columns and 12 rows. You cannot initialize array values in the Properties window. You must assign values to the array in your method.

To add a new user-defined method to a form or form set, choose the Form|New Method option and the New Method dialog box appears. It looks exactly like the New Properties dialog box. Type the name of your user-defined method. You can also type a description of the method. The description displays at the bottom of the properties window when the user-defined method is selected.

You can edit the name or description or delete a user-defined property or method by choosing the Form menu, Edit Property/Method option. The Edit Property/Method dialog box appears, as shown in Figure 24.8.

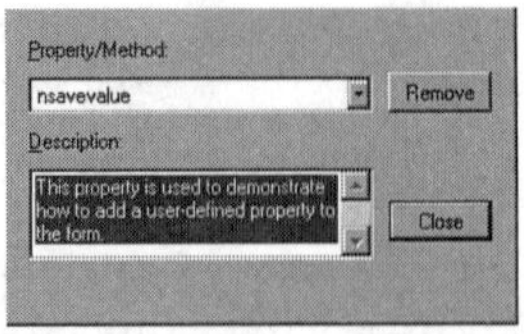

FIGURE 24.8.

Edit Property/Method dialog box.

Notice in Figure 24.8 that the user-defined property nsavename displays at the bottom of the list in the Properties window. Visual FoxPro sets its initial value to false (.F.). You can change its initial value in the Properties window.

When you are ready to add code to your user-defined method, double-click on the form, and the code window appears. Choose your user-defined method from the code window Procedure list. Now enter your code. Do not begin your code with a PROCEDURE or FUNCTION statement. You can call your user-defined methods from any other method in any object in the form the same way you call any other method. Here are some examples of the use of user-defined properties and methods for a single form (no form set):

```
THISFORM.MyProc1
IF  THISFORM.Animals("Elephant",3) = 3
   THISFORM.MyProc3
ELSE
   THISFORM.cMyData = 7
   THISFORM.nTweedleDum = THISFORM.MyProc7(THISFORM.nValue)
ENDIF
```

In the preceding example, cMyData and nTweedleDum are user-defined properties. MyProc1, Animals, MyProc3, and MyProc7 are user-defined methods. Notice that if the user-defined methods have parameters, the method call statement has a corresponding argument list.

Defining the Form's Behavior

There are about 76 properties for the form object that affect the appearance and behavior of the form. The object is derived from a Visual FoxPro Form base class. When a form object is initially created, all of the properties are set to some nominal default value. The default properties reflect the appearance and behavior of the form when it is created. Typically, you will want to alter the behavior of the form. The nice thing is that you need to modify only a few of the properties of the form to make the form look and act the way you want it to. Most of the properties are seldom used. There is a set of a dozen typically used form object properties. You will want to consider these properties when you are designing a form. These properties are presented in Table 24.4.

Table 24.4. Commonly used form properties.

Property	Default	Description
AlwaysOnTop	.F.	Specifies whether (.T.) or not (.F.) the form is always on top of the other forms when it is active.
AutoCenter	.F.	Specifies whether (.T.) or not (.F.) the form is centered in the Visual FoxPro main window when the form is initially displayed.
BackColor	255,255,255	Specifies the color of the form window in RGB format.
BorderStyle	3	Specifies whether the form has no border (0), a single line border (1), a double line border (3), or a system-style border (3).

continues

Table 24.4. continued

Property	Default	Description
Caption	Form1	Specifies the text displayed in the form's title bar.
Closable	.T.	Specifies whether (.T.) or not (.F.) the user can close the form by double-clicking on the Close box, or for Windows 95, clicking on the Close button.
MaxButton	.T.	Specifies whether (.T.) or not (.F.) the form has a maximize button.
MinButton	.T.	Specifies whether (.T.) or not (.F.) the form has a minimize button.
Movable	.T.	Specifies whether(.T.) or not (.F.) the form can be moved to a new location on the screen.
ScaleMode	3 - Pixels	Specifies the unit of measurement in the object size and position properties as foxels (0) or pixels (3). The 3 is the recommended default. However, you can set the default to either value from the Forms tab in the Options dialog box from the Tools menu.
ShowTips	.F.	Specifies whether (.T.) or not (.F.) ToolTipText property text displays. When you rest the mouse pointer over a control for a second or two, a little box describing the control appears. You define the text in the little box for any control using the ToolTipText property. The ToolTips text only displays if the ShowTips property for its form is .T..
WindowState	0 - Normal	Specifies whether the form is initialized in its minimized (1), maximized (2), or normal (0) state.
WindowType	0 - Modeless	Specifies whether a form is modal (1) or modeless (0). You must close a modal form before accessing any other elements of your interface for your application.

There are other properties that you set, such as Top, Height, and Width. However, you set them visually by clicking, dragging, and other operations, so you normally don't concern yourself with them. However, all of the properties display in the Properties window. If you want any more information about a particular property in the Properties list, just right-click on the property and choose the Help option in the shortcut menu.

The Visual FoxPro Form Designer is an active designer. That means that when you change a property the appearance and behavior changes immediately to reflect the new property setting. If you set the BackColor property to blue, the background color immediately changes to blue.

If you set the Movable property to false (.F.), a user will not be able to move the form at runtime, and you cannot move the form at design time, either. If you set the AutoCenter property to true (.T.), the form will immediately center itself in the Form Designer window. You will have to drag it to the upper-left corner of the Form Designer window so that you can work on it. It is recommended that you not make the changes that make the form hard to work with until you have made all of the other required changes.

Editing Events and Method Code

For many types of controls, you will need to add code to support events. For example, you usually need to provide code for the Click event for the command buttons. When the user clicks on a command button, the Click event method executes. For more details regarding the actual code that you write, see Part V.

You use the code window to add code for methods. The easiest way to activate the code window is to double-click on the control in the Form Designer layout. The code window appears, and you enter the event code. There are two combo box controls on the code window. One of the combo boxes contains the events and methods for the method code shown in the code window. The other combo box contains a hierarchical list of the names of the classes for the form set, form, and controls that correspond to the code in the code window. An example of a code window is shown in Figure 24.9. The code in the window is for the Click event for a command button.

FIGURE 24.9.

The code window.

There is more than one way to activate the code window, as described in the following list:

- Double-click on a control or form on the Form Designer Layout screen.
- Select a control and choose View | Code.
- Select a control and click on the Code Window button on the Form Designer toolbar.
- Double-click on the method in the Properties menu.
- Right-click on the control and choose the Code option from the shortcut menu.

When the code window appears, you can start writing the code you want to be executed when the event occurs or when the method is called.

Typically, an OK command button exits from the form and makes the form disappear from the screen. To make this happen, you add code to the `Click` event method that releases the form from memory with the following command:

```
THISFORM.Release
```

You can make the form disappear from the screen but retain it in memory by executing the following command instead of the RELEASE command:

```
THISFORM.Hide
```

You can move to another event or method procedure by selecting a different event or method from the Procedure box. You can also move between the procedures with the Page Up and Page Down keys. You can edit event or method code for another form or control by selecting another form or control from the Object box.

Running the Form

When you have finished designing your form, you can run it. This option saves the form, exits from the Form Designer, and executes the newly created or modified form. You can also use the Run (!) button on the Standard toolbar. You can also run the form from the Project Manager, Run command, or from the Program DO option.

You can execute a form from the command window or from within a program with the DO FORM command. The syntax of the DO FORM command is

```
DO FORM FormName | ? [NAME MemVarName]
    [WITH cParameterList][LINKED MemVarName]
    [TO MemVarName] [NOREAD]
```

The FORM FormName clause specifies the name of the form file to run. If you specify a ? instead of a filename, the DO dialog box appears, and you select a file to execute.

The NAME clause specifies the name of a memory variable with which you can reference the form object. If you do not specify the NAME clause, Visual FoxPro creates a memory variable with the same name as the form file without the extension. In the following example, two form object reference memory variables are created, Orange and Peach:

```
DO FORM Apple NAME Orange
DO FORM Peach
```

You can use the object name to reference the object. For example, you can change the background color of the two forms APPLE.SCX and PEACH.SCX to red in the preceding code with the following statements:

```
Orange.BackColor = RGB(255,0,0)
Peach.BackColor  = RGB(255,0,0)
```

The WITH cParameterList clause specifies a list of parameters passed to the Init method of the Form object. However, if the form file is a form set, the parameters are passed to the Init method of the form set's Init method.

The LINKED MemVarName clause specifies a memory variable associated with the form object in such a way that if the named memory variable goes out of scope (variable is released), the form can still be active. A form is still active if you omit the LINKED clause. However, there is no object variable associated with the form.

The TO MemVarName clause specifies a memory variable to hold a value returned by the Unload event method. If the Unload event does not return a value, a default value of true (.T.) value is returned. A value is only returned if you have a modal (WindowType property equals 1) form.

If you specify the NOREAD clause, the form set is created and displayed, but controls are not activated until a READ command executes.

Designing a Menu System

As we noted at the beginning of the chapter, the most important part of your application is the application interface because that is the first thing the user sees. In the previous sections, you saw how you can have a form as your application's user interface. In this section, you will learn how to center your application around a menu system.

After you have finished planning your menu system, you can now create it with the Visual FoxPro Menu Designer. You can build a menu system that corresponds to the style of the Visual FoxPro system menu. Specifically, the Menu Designer creates a horizontal system type menu bar with pop-up lists associated with each menu bar menu.

There are several ways to start the Menu Designer.

- Choose File | New, and the New dialog box appears. Click the Menu option.
- Execute the CREATE MENU command from the command window.
- From the Project Manager, select the Other tab, select Menus, and click on the New button.

Regardless of the way you launch the Menu Designer, an empty Menu Designer window appears, as shown in Figure 24.10.

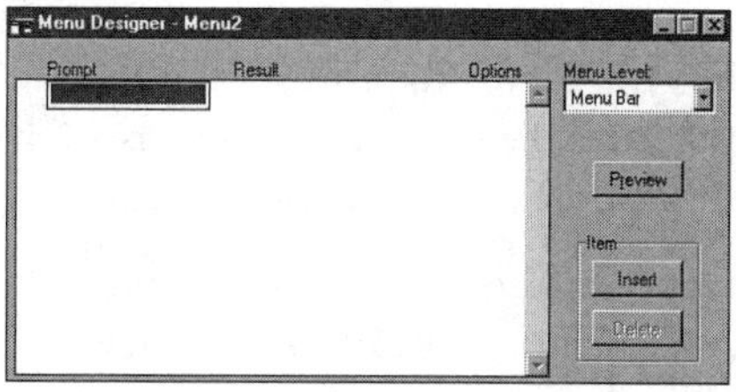

FIGURE 24.10.

The New Menu Designer window with the menu open.

The Menu Designer window is quite uncomplicated, especially if you compare it to the Form Designer or Report Designer. It contains a three-column list, three push buttons, and a combo box. In addition, when the Menu Designer executes, a Menu menu appears on the Visual FoxPro

System menu bar. Two additional options (General Options and Menu Options) appear on the View menu when the Menu Designer is active.

Menu Designer Layout Window

As Figure 24.10 illustrates, the menu structure table has three columns: Prompt, Result, and Options. Within this structure table, you can create either a menu bar or a pop-up menu. The initial table structure is the Visual FoxPro System (called SYSMENU) menu bar. All other menus are subordinate to SYSMENU. The rows in the table represent either menu pads or popup menu bars (options).

The Prompt Column

To create a new menu pad or popup option, type the prompt name for a pad or option in the Prompt column. You can specify a hot key by preceding one of the characters in the name with the \< two-character sequence. For popup menus, you can specify a separation bar by using the \- two-character sequence.

The Result Column

Next, you specify a result. Under the Result column, specify what happens if the user chooses the named prompt. You choose one of four options (Command, Pad Name or Bar #, Procedure, or Submenu) from the Result column.

Select the Command option to define a command for a pad or an option. Then a text box appears, and you type a command into the text box. For example: WAIT WINDOW "Menu was selected".

If you choose the Pad Name or Bar # option, a Pad Name appears when you are defining pads, and the Bar # appears when you are defining submenu options. In either case, a text box appears, and you enter the pad name or bar number in the text box.

If you choose the Procedure option, you can specify the name of a procedure that executes when the pad, option, or procedure is chosen. A Create button appears to the right of the word *Procedure*. When you choose the Create push button, the text editing window displays so that you can enter and edit the snippet. A *snippet* is a FoxPro procedure. The Create button label changes to Edit after the procedure is designed.

The Submenu option (default) creates a submenu for the current pad or option. When you choose the Submenu option, the Create pushbutton appears to the right of the word *Submenu*. When you choose the Create pushbutton, a new empty menu structure appears so that you can define the submenu. When you finish designing the new submenu, use the popup at the right of the Menu Designer window to return to the parent menu. The Create button label changes to Edit after the submenu is designed.

Reordering Menu Items

You can change the order of items in the structure by clicking on the button with the double-headed arrow at the left of the prompt name and dragging the item to the desired location in the list.

The Options Column

The Options column in the table contains a push button for each item in the table. When you choose a button for an item in the table, the Prompt Options dialog box appears. The Prompt Options dialog box contains options that you can establish for the current menu item. These options correspond to the DEFINE PAD or DEFINE BAR command clauses. You can specify a message that displays on the Windows-style status bar. You can specify a shortcut key, a comment for the generated code, a bar number or pad name, and a SKIP FOR condition. The SKIP FOR condition disables the menu item if the condition evaluates to a true (.T.) value.

The Expression Builder dialog box launches to let you input a message and SKIP FOR expressions.

The Negotiate option is new in Visual FoxPro. This option specifies the location of a menu item when editing an OLE object in your applicaton. This is part of the "in-place editing" provided by OLE 2.0. If you want one or more of your menu items to remain as part of the menu during an in-place editing session, select this option.

When you select Negotiate, a dialog box appears that offers the following options:

Option	Purpose
None	If selected, the menu title will not appear on the menu bar. This is the default behavior.
Left	If selected, the menu title be placed in the left group of menu titles on the menu bar.
Middle	If selected, the menu title be placed in the middle group of menu titles on the menu bar.
Right	If selected, the menu title be placed in the right group of menu titles on the menu bar.

The Menu Selection Combo Box

In the upper-right corner of the Menu Designer dialog box is a combo box. Its options contain the current and higher-level menus. If the structure of a submenu displays in the table, you can choose a higher-level menu or submenu from this popup. Then the structure of the higher-level menu displays in this table.

The Menu Design Dialog Box Pushbuttons

The Preview, Insert, and Delete pushbuttons let you preview a menu, insert a new menu item, and delete the selected menu item, respectively.

Creating a Menu System

This section describes various ways of using the Menu Designer to create menus.

The Quick Menu Option

One technique of creating a menu is to start with the Visual FoxPro menu system and add new menus and options or remove existing menus or options until you have created your own custom menu.

Initially, the Menu Designer window is empty. At that time, you can choose Menu | Quick Menu. The Menu Designer creates a complete menu structure based in the default FoxPro system menu and displays this structure in the Menu Designer window list, as shown in Figure 24.11.

FIGURE 24.11.

The Menu Designer Window with a menu created by the Quick Menu option.

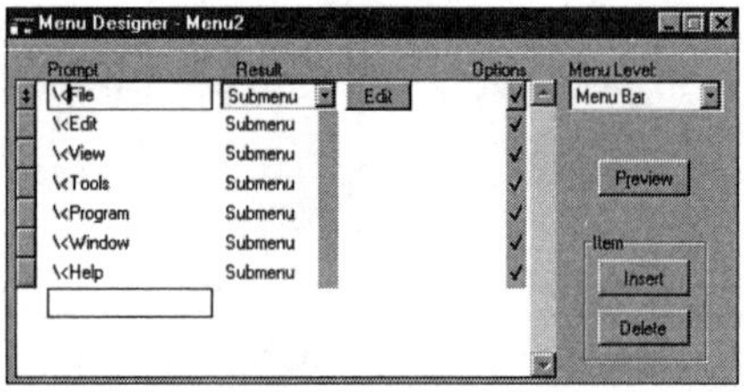

Creating Menus

Whether you start out with an empty Menu Designer or you create a quick menu, you still start out adding menus in the same manner. The following steps are used to add a new menu:

1. Type the prompt label in the text box at the bottom of the Prompt column (for example: \<Assistant).

2. Click on the mover bar (left column of buttons) and drag the mover bar to the new position, as shown in Figure 24.12.

FIGURE 24.12.

A Customized menu.

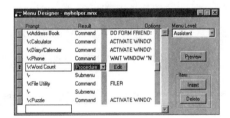

Creating Menu Items

Now that you have created the Assistant menu, you can start adding menu items. The following steps are used to add a menu item:

1. In the Prompt column, click the menu to which you want to add a menu item. (In Figure 24.12, Assistant is selected.)
2. In the Result column, select the Submenu item, and the Create button appears.
3. Click the Create button. A blank menu design window appears. Next, you will enter your menu item names.
4. In the Prompt column, type the names of the new menu items, as shown in Figure 24.13.

FIGURE 24.13.

Adding menu items to a submenu.

At the beginning of this chapter, you learned how to create a form that is the application interface of the Personal Assistant Application. Now you will learn how to create a submenu that is used for the same purpose. Figure 24.13 shows a submenu, Assistant, that is not just the application interface of the Personal Assistant, it lets the Personal Assistant become an add-in application for Visual FoxPro. The next step is to add functionality to the Assistant submenu.

Assigning Tasks to Menus and Menu Items

When your user chooses a menu or menu item, Visual FoxPro performs some operation, such as displaying another submenu, executing a command, or displaying a form. This is done by executing a single command or procedure.

Performing Menu Tasks with Commands

You can assign any valid Visual FoxPro command to a menu or menu item. The command can be a DO command that executes a procedure. However, if you assign a DO command to a menu or menu item, the procedure must be in the path, be a procedure, or be specified in the General Options dialog box. If the command calls a procedure in the menu's cleanup code, specify the IN clause with the DO command. The command must reference the menu program file that has an MPR extension. For example, if you call a procedure, DIALER, in the cleanup code (see the section "The View Menu, General Options Option" that appears later in this chapter) for this menu file (MYHELPER.MPR), specify the following command:

```
DO DIALER IN MYHELPER.MPR
```

To add a command to a menu or menu item, select the menu or menu item. Then, from the Results column, choose the Command item. A text box appears at the right of the Result column. Type the command in the box.

In the example shown in Figure 24.13, the menu items have been assigned by the following commands:

Menu Item	*Command*
Address Book...	DO FORM FRIENDS
Calculator...	ACTIVATE WINDOW Calculator
Diary/Calendar...	ACTIVATE WINDOW Calendar
File Utility...	FILER
Puzzle...	ACTIVATE WINDOW Puzzle

Performing Menu Tasks with Procedures

To add a call to a procedure to a menu item, select the menu item. Then, from the Results column, choose the Procedure item. A Create (or Edit) button appears at the right of the Result column. Click it, and a code window appears. Type the procedure code in the window. Do not include a PROCEDURE statement.

In the example shown in Figure 24.14, the Word Count menu item is associated with a procedure. The menu code window contains the code for the procedure.

If you want to associate a menu with a procedure, choose View, Menu Options, and the Menu Options dialog box appears. Type the procedure code in the Procedure edit box. You can also add setup code and cleanup code to the menu system. The process is described in the next section.

Figure 24.15 shows the completed MYHELPER.MPR menu system in action. The new Assistant menu is open.

FIGURE 24.14.

Assigning a procedure to a menu item submenu.

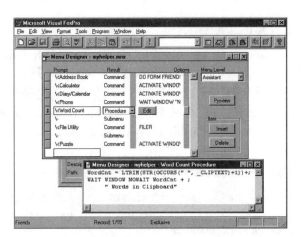

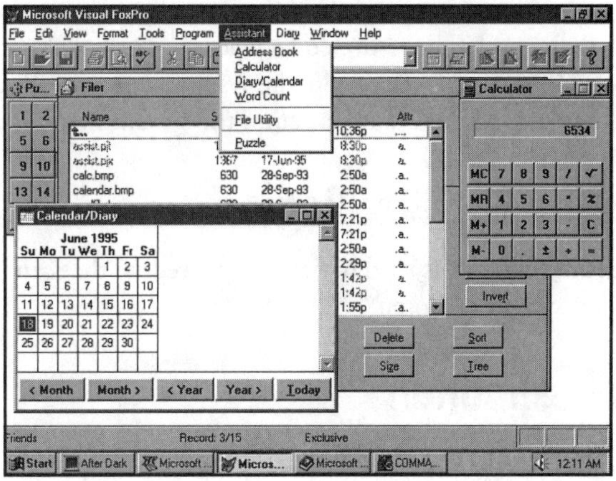

FIGURE 24.15.

Custom application interface with New Assistant menu open.

The View Menu's General Options Option

The General Options option on the View menu displays the General Options dialog box shown in Figure 24.16. This dialog box contains the options discussed in the following sections.

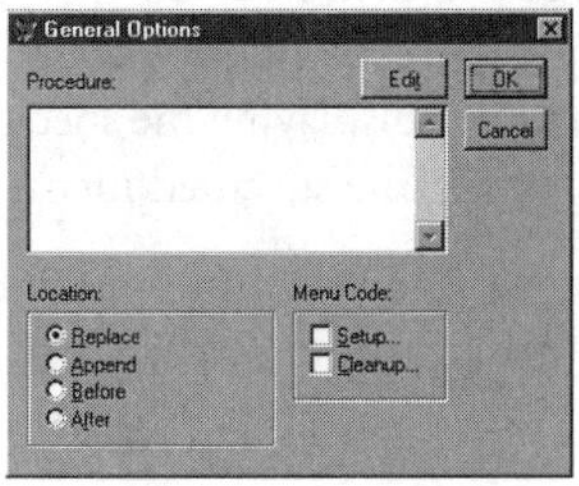

FIGURE 24.16.

The General Options dialog box.

Setup... Check Box

When you select the Setup... check box in the General Options dialog box, a program editing window appears in which you enter FoxPro setup code. The setup code executes before menu definition code executes. Once you add setup code, this check box remains checked.

You can add setup code to open files, to save and initialize the environment, to save the original menu system, and so forth.

Cleanup... Check Box

When you select the Cleanup... check box, a program editing window displays in which you enter cleanup code that executes after menu definition code executes. After you add cleanup code, this check box remains checked.

You can make your menu program the main program for your application. You can include a PUSH MENU command in the setup code, place the READ EVENTS command in your cleanup code, and place code (POP MENU) to restore the system menu after the READ EVENTS command. Then, when a CLEAR EVENTS command executes the system menu is restored.

Procedure Edit Box Region

The Procedure edit box is used to define a procedure that can be executed when any menu pad in the menu system is chosen.

Edit... Pushbutton

This pushbutton displays a program editing window. You enter code in this window for the selected procedure.

Location Option Button Group

The Location options (Replace, Append, Before, and After) designate where the new menu system is placed. You can choose one of the options. The Replace option button, which is the default, replaces the existing menu system with the new menu system. The Append button adds the new menu system to the right of the current menu system. The Before button displays the menu system before displaying the specified menu pad. The After button displays the menu system after displaying the specified menu pad.

Using the Menu Designer Quick Menu option is not always the best way to make a change to the Visual FoxPro system menu. Rather than replacing the entire system menu, you can insert the new menu into the Visual FoxPro system menu using a Location option other than Replace.

If you are doing something really simple, such as adding an option to a SYSMENU pop-up menu, you might not even use the Menu Designer at all. You just use procedural code. For example, if you would like to add the built-in file utility, FILER, to the Tools menu, you can use the following code:

```
DEFINE BAR 99 OF _MTOOLS AFTER _mtl_spell;
               PROMPT "\<File Utilities "
          ON SELECTION BAR 99 OF _MTOOLS  FILER
```

Code Generation

After you complete your menu design, you must choose the Menu menu Generate… option to generate the menu program (MPR file). When you choose the Generate… option, you are given the opportunity to save the current menu design. If you haven't provided a name for the menu design file yet, a Save As dialog box appears and you can choose a drive and directory and then specify the name of the design file. After the new or modified menu design file (MNX) is saved, the Generate Menu dialog box displays.

The Generate Menu dialog box contains two push buttons, a text box, and a browser (…) button. The text box contains the fully qualified path for the menu program MPR file. It has the same filename as the menu design file, but the filename extension is .MPR. You can change the name in the text box. You can also press the Browser push button, and the Save As dialog box appears to assist you in choosing a drive and directory. Finally, press the Generate button, and the menu program MPR file is generated.

You can execute the menu program (MPR) file using the DO option from the Program menu or the Run button from the Project Manager. You can also execute the menu program from within a program or by typing the DO command in the command window. For example:

```
DO MYHELPER.MPR
```

Summary

This chapter illustrates how to build a true event-driven applications interface taking advantage of the Visual FoxPro event model and the Visual FoxPro design tools. You were given guidelines to plan and design an application interface that is easy to learn and easy to use. This chapter also taught you the best control to use when designing a Visual FoxPro form. You also were shown that you can use either a form or a custom menu system as the foundation of your application.

Programming for Reporting Needs

25

Any database consultant knows that the job is half done, at best, when data is put into a database. Generating reports is the end result for most database users. It is also a major weakness of many custom applications (if the popularity of add-on report writers is any indication). Visual FoxPro applications need not be constrained when it comes to flexibility in reporting because the Report Designer can produce virtually any kind of report needed. If it is mailing labels you need, the Label Designer offers the same kind of flexibility in the design of mailing labels. Chapter 12, "Designing and Customizing Forms," and Chapter 15, "Producing Mailings," detail how you can design reports and labels using the Report Designer and Label Designer, respectively, in Visual FoxPro. This chapter shows how you can put the reports and labels you create to work within Visual FoxPro programs. You can call your reports or labels from within your programs by using the REPORT FORM or LABEL FORM commands, and you can use these commands in code that you attach to menu items and buttons in forms or on toolbars.

Using *REPORT FORM* and *LABEL FORM*

You can run reports from within your programs with the REPORT FORM command, which offers a number of flexible options. You can produce mailing labels with the similar LABEL FORM command. Here is the syntax for the REPORT FORM command:

```
REPORT FORM filename / ? ;
    [ENVIRONMENT] ;
    [scope] [WHILE condition] [FOR condition] ;
    [PLAIN] [HEADING character expression] ;
    [NOEJECT] [TO PRINT/TO FILE filename] [SUMMARY] [OFF] [ASCII]
```

As covered in Chapter 12, this command produces a report based on the report design saved as *filename* with Visual FoxPro's Report Designer. You can include the FOR clause to specify a condition that must be met in order for records to be included in the report. Use the WHILE condition along with an index to specify which records are to be included in the report while the specified condition is true. The ENVIRONMENT option, which is included for backward compatibility with reports converted from FoxPro 2.x, tells Visual FoxPro to use the same environmental settings that were in effect when the report was saved. An optional scope (All, Next *x*, or Rest) can be included. If the scope is omitted, Visual FoxPro assumes all records.

The PLAIN option drops the system clock date and page numbers, and the Heading option followed by a character expression causes the heading to appear at the top of each page. (This is in addition to any heading that you might have specified within the report's design.) The NOEJECT option cancels the form feed that normally occurs when the TO PRINT option (which routes output to the printer) is used. The TO FILE option can be used to store the output to a text file. The text file is assigned a .TXT extension unless a different extension is specified. The SUMMARY option cancels the normal display or printing of detail lines within a report. If SUMMARY is used, only totals and subtotals appear.

ASCII, which is new to Visual FoxPro, tells Visual FoxPro to ignore font styles and to generate a pure ASCII report. It is designed for use with the TO FILE option.

For example, the command

```
REPORT FORM MYFILE
```

causes the specified report with no conditions to be displayed on the screen. The command

```
REPORT FORM MYFILE NEXT 30 FOR LNAME = "Smith" PLAIN TO PRINT
```

causes only the next 30 records in the table to be included in the processing of the report. FOR LNAME = "Smith" further refines the report contents to specified records, where "Smith" appears in the LNAME field. The PLAIN option drops the page numbers and date normally printed in a report, and the TO PRINT option causes the report to be printed as well as displayed.

In the same manner, you can use the LABEL FORM command (detailed in Chapter 15) to generate mailing labels from within a program. The syntax, which is similar to the REPORT FORM command, is

```
LABEL FORM filename / ? ;
    [ENVIRONMENT] ;
    [scope] [WHILE condition] [FOR condition] ;
    [NOCONSOLE] [PREVIEW] [SAMPLE] [TO PRINT/TO FILE filename]
```

The SAMPLE option lets you print a sample label (that is, a label filled with Xs). This is usually done to test the label alignment on dot-matrix printers before you begin a print run. The NOCONSOLE option suppresses the display of data in the active window. The PREVIEW option causes the labels to be displayed in a preview window before printing. The other options work the same as they do with the REPORT FORM command, described previously in this chapter.

As with reports, if you want the labels printed in a particular order, you should create or open an index with the SET ORDER TO command before you use the LABEL FORM command. With the LABEL FORM command, you can limit the labels to a subset of records from within the table by using the WHILE or FOR clauses or by setting a filter with the SET FILTER command.

Strategies for Setting Up the Report's Data Environment

The basic strategy for generating reports in Visual FoxPro is relatively simple. The first step is to establish the data environment for the report. Establishing the data environment refers to setting up the data so that the report can properly output the information. This section discusses some of the options you can use.

Reporting on Related Tables

One strategy to setting up the required data for reporting is to establish relationships between tables. You would then place on the report field objects from the related tables. There are two ways to do this: you can use the report's data environment or you can establish the relationships in a program before you run the report.

Using the Data Environment

If you need to generate a report based on a relationship between multiple tables, the best way to do so in Visual FoxPro is to use the data environment capabilities of Visual FoxPro while you are designing the report. You can define a data environment, which tells the report where to find the needed tables and how to establish the relationship. How to use the Data Environment window is covered in more detail in Chapter 13, "Designing and Customizing Reports," but in a nutshell, here are the steps involved in creating a relational report using this technique:

1. Open the database with the related tables containing the information you want to display in the relational report.

2. Choose File | New | Report to launch the Report Designer with a new report.

3. From the View menu, choose Data Environment and then add the two tables that are related.

4. In the Data Environment window, click the common field in one table and drag it to the common field of the other table. When you do this, a line appears between the tables. The line indicates the presence of the link.

> **NOTE**
>
> In order to create the relationship, you will need an index tag on the relation field in the child table. If you attempt to create a relation and no index tag exists on the field in the child table to which you want to relate, Visual FoxPro will tell you that you are missing the index and will build it for you if you want.

5. In the Report Designer, add a data grouping to the report based on the master or *parent* side of your relationship. This step is useful if you have a one-to-many relationship and need to show summary information for each element on the "one" side. If you do not need to show summary information, you may skip this step.

6. Place the fields in the report. In most cases, you would probably want to add the fields from the master or parent table to the report's group header band and the fields for the child table to the report's detail band.

7. Save the report by choosing File | Save.

For more details on the data modeling process and report design, refer to Chapter 13; for more details on working with relationships in Visual FoxPro, see Chapter 11, "Working with Visual FoxPro's Relational Powers."

The advantage of using Visual FoxPro's data modeling capability is that once the report is saved, you do not need any special commands to establish an environment before running the report; just use the REPORT FORM command at the appropriate place in your application. When FoxPro opens the report, the needed relationships will be set automatically.

Establishing Relationships with Code

Another way to handle relationships is to write a program that opens the tables in separate work areas, sets the appropriate index orders, and issues SET RELATION commands to establish the relations. Using a program to set up the relations is code-compatible with earlier versions of FoxPro (which do not provide the data modeling capabilities of Visual FoxPro) but is clearly not the preferred way of doing things in Visual FoxPro.

If you have designed the report with alias names to open multiple tables in different work areas, you must set up the work areas and identify the relationships between the files before using the REPORT FORM command. If you use this approach to relational reports, remember that you must take this step each time you run the report. For example, the programming steps for a report designed to simultaneously use two tables, CUSTOMER and ORDERS, might resemble the following:

```
SELECT 1
USE CUSTOMER
SET ORDER TO ACCTNUMB
SELECT 2
USE SALES
SET ORDER TO ACCTNUMB
SET RELATION TO ACCTNUMB INTO CUSTOMER
REPORT FORM SALES TO PRINT
```

If these commands are unfamiliar to you, you can find details on using commands to establish relationships between multiple tables in Chapter 11.

If you have a report that uses the preceding approach, you can surely leave it alone. Still, when the time comes to modify the report, it is probably a good idea to set up the report with a data environment, especially if the tables have been moved into a database and persistent relationships have been defined. In many cases, the whole process of moving the tables and relationships into the report's data environment will take a few short minutes.

Limiting and Summarizing Data in a Report

Frequently, when reporting, you will not want to show all the information in the tables. For example, if you were printing a listing of customers, it is common to print the listing for a single state or range of states. If you were printing invoices, you might only want to print invoices that have not yet been printed.

Merely opening tables and establishing relationships won't do the trick here: You have to be able to limit the information that the report will process. The following subsections describe several strategies for accomplishing this.

Use a Scope on the Report Form Command

One way to accomplish this is to use a scope on the REPORT FORM command as shown earlier. For example, you could use the following command to print invoices that have not yet been printed (assuming that printed invoices have a logical field called lPrinted set to .T.):

```
REPORT FORM invoices TO PRINT FOR !lPrinted
```

Set a Filter on the Main Table

Setting a filter on the main table in a relationship will limit the records that show on the report. You can accomplish this with a SET FILTER command as follows:

```
SELECT invoices
SET FILTER TO !lPrinted
```

You can place this code in the program that calls the report (assuming that the tables are not opened in the report's data environment).

You can also place a filter expression in the Filter property of the cursor object for the main table of the report. The Filter property is on the Data tab for the cursor object in the Properties window. You have to have the Data Environment Designer open in order to access the data environment's properties.

If you are using a data environment, and you want to use the Filter method for limiting data, using the Filter property is preferred. It uses less code and appropriately uses the power of the data environment to accomplish the task.

Use a Query

The methods so far discussed do not address summarizing data: only limiting it. Any summarizing of the data would have to occur within the report using any combination of report variables, group summaries, and the report summary band.

A very popular approach to limiting data and summarizing it for reporting purposes is to use a query. Queries are covered in Chapter 6, "Querying Data."

The strategy here is simple. Running the query pulls in all the data from related tables and limits it based on the contents of the WHERE clause in the SQL SELECT. All of the data is placed in one alias (either a table or a cursor). Having to deal with one alias makes managing the report very easy. In addition, Visual FoxPro queries access the power of Rushmore ™. This makes processing the data extraordinarily fast.

Another benefit of SQL is the ability to summarize data with aggregate functions like SUM(). You can also specify the order in which information is presented with the ORDER BY clause.

In effect, a SQL query sets up the data for a report in one command.

> **NOTE**
>
> A typical strategy for running reports based on SQL queries is to run the query and then run the report, thereafter accessing the information in the resulting cursor or table.

The one disadvantage to working with a query in a report is that you do not get the visual benefits of the Data Environment Designer. Tables added to the Data Environment Designer are automatically available in the Report Designer. Dragging fields from objects in the Data Environment Designer to the report adds those fields to the report automatically. You do not get these advantages when you are working with code.

Fortunately, Visual FoxPro has an answer. You can still get the awesome power of Rushmore™, the benefits of the SQL approach, and still keep the visual design aspects of the Data Environment Designer—you can use a View.

Using a View

Creating views is discussed in Chapter 8, "Updating Data with Views." One of the great aspects of working with a view is the ability to reference the view as if it were a table. All you need to do is design the view in the Database Designer and add it to the report's data environment. When the report is run, it automatically opens the view (if it is not already open) and accesses it as if it were a table. In design mode, the fields of a view can be used in visual development in the same manner as a table.

Report Setup Code and the Data Environment

One of the primary benefits of using a data environment with a report is the ability to use a private data session with the report. A private data session, as discussed in Chapter 12, "Designing and Customizing Forms," gives a report a separate set of work areas all its own (you actually get 32,767 of them). The benefit of a private data session is that it protects other data sessions from changes in filter conditions, table index orders, record pointers, and so forth.

You can set a report to use a private data session by selecting Report | Private Data Session. If the Private Data Session option on the Report menu is checked, the report will use a private data session.

If you have code that you want to run to set up a report, the code can be added to the Init method. The code can be anything you need, from a query to manual code that opens tables and sets relationships.

Allowing User Input for Report Selections

It would be very nice if you could always predefine the report selection criteria. Truth be told, you can't always do that. Users will need the ability to make selections at runtime to affect what is shown on the report.

A typical example of this is the ability to select date ranges for an invoice report. Criteria, such as a range of dates to print, cannot be specified by the developer; the user must be able to specify them.

The strategy here is simple. All you have to do is present a form to users that enables them to enter the dates they want to see on the report. Then, reference the dates in your query, filter, or view.

Here's an example: Suppose you have a report that lists invoices by customer and totals their purchases within the given time frame. You could write a SQL Select that looks like the following code. (Note: the tables used here are in the TESTDATA database in the Visual FoxPro SAMPLES\DATA directory.)

```
SELECT Customer.company, Orders.order_date, Orders.order_amt;
  FROM testdata!customer, testdata!orders;
 WHERE Customer.cust_id = Orders.cust_id;
   AND Orders.order_date BETWEEN ldStart AND ldEnd;
 ORDER BY Customer.company, Orders.order_date ;
   INTO CURSOR OrdRpt
```

Note that `ldStart` and `ldEnd` are memory variables. In order for this SQL Select to run, you will need values for these variables. The way to get those values is to initialize the variables `ldStart` and `ldEnd` and then call a form like the one shown in Figure 25.1.

FIGURE 25.1.

SelDate.SCX.

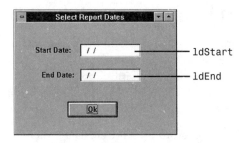

The text boxes on the form are bound to the memory variables, `ldStart` and `ldEnd`.

Here's what the code to set up the report looks like with the call to the form added:

```
m.ldStart = {}
m.ldEnd = {}

DO FORM SelDate

SELECT Customer.company, Orders.order_date, Orders.order_amt;
```

```
   FROM testdata!customer, testdata!orders;
 WHERE Customer.cust_id = Orders.cust_id;
   AND Orders.order_date BETWEEN ldStart AND ldEnd;
 ORDER BY Customer.company, Orders.order_date ;
   INTO CURSOR OrdRpt
```

Following is a representation of the form using code exported from the Class Browser (for more information on exported code and the Class Browser, see Chapter 30, "Managing Classes with Visual FoxPro").

```
*  Form...............: SELDATE.SCX
*  Author.............: Menachem Bazian, CPA
*  Project............: Visual FoxPro Unleashed!
*  Copyright..........: (c) Flash Creative Management, Inc. 1995
*  Notes..............: Exported code from Class Browser.

****************************************************
*-- Form:          frmseldate (d:\data\docs\books\vfu\code\seldate.scx)
*-- ParentClass:   form
*-- BaseClass:     form
*
DEFINE CLASS frmseldate AS form

    Height = 200
    Width = 296
    DoCreate = .T.
    AutoCenter = .T.
    BackColor = RGB(192,192,192)
    BorderStyle = 2
    Caption = "Select Report Dates"
    WindowType = 1
    Name = "frmSelDate"

    ADD OBJECT txtdstart AS textbox WITH ;
        ControlSource = "m.ldStart", ;
        Format = "D", ;
        Height = 24, ;
        Left = 120, ;
        Top = 39, ;
        Width = 113, ;
        Name = "txtDStart"

    ADD OBJECT tctdend AS textbox WITH ;
        ControlSource = "m.ldEnd", ;
        Format = "D", ;
        Height = 24, ;
        Left = 120, ;
        Top = 84, ;
        Width = 113, ;
        Name = "tctDEnd"

    ADD OBJECT label1 AS label WITH ;
        AutoSize = .T., ;
        BackStyle = 0, ;
        Caption = "Start Date:", ;
        Height = 18, ;
        Left = 36, ;
        Top = 42, ;
```

```
            Width = 67, ;
            Name = "Label1"

    ADD OBJECT label2 AS label WITH ;
        AutoSize = .T., ;
        BackStyle = 0, ;
        Caption = "End Date:", ;
        Height = 18, ;
        Left = 48, ;
        Top = 87, ;
        Width = 61, ;
        Name = "Label2"

    ADD OBJECT cmdok AS commandbutton WITH ;
        Top = 144, ;
        Left = 96, ;
        Height = 29, ;
        Width = 94, ;
        Cancel = .T., ;
        Caption = "\<Ok", ;
        Default = .T., ;
        Name = "cmdOK"

    PROCEDURE cmdok.Click
        thisform.release()
    ENDPROC

ENDDEFINE
*
*-- EndDefine: frmseldate
***************************************************
```

Note the ControlSource properties on the text box objects. They are set to reference the memory variables defined in the program.

For more information on creating forms, see Chapter 12, "Designing and Customizing Forms."

The really cool thing about this approach is that you can add all this code to the data environment code. In effect, this means that the SelDate form is now attached to the report: If a user runs a report outside of an application, the selection form will still be called.

Using Parameterized Views

Views can have parameters built into them. Unlike queries, which have to be modified as a program in order to reference memory variable parameters, views can have parameters defined within them. For more information on creating paramaterized views, see Chapter 11.

The issue with parameterized views is that the view is part of the data environment. This means that the report will automatically open the view when the report is run. If the variables defined as parameters in the view are not defined before the view is run, Visual FoxPro automatically will ask for the values, one at a time. Clearly, having Visual FoxPro ask for the information one variable at a time is not optimal.

Unlike coded data setups, such as opening tables manually or using queries, you do not open the tables yourself. Instead, you want to call the OpenTables event of the data environment to do the job (that's what the OpenTables event is there for, and it saves you from having to write the code). Here's how you can accomplish this. To make this example easier, the same parameters (ldStart and ldEnd) and form (SelDate.SCX) used in the query example will be used here.

The first step is to set the AutoOpenTables property of the data environment to .F.. This tells the data environment not to automatically open the tables; you will do that yourself by calling the OpenTables method. Then, place the following code in the data environment's Init:

```
m.ldStart = {}
m.ldEnd = {}

DO FORM seldate

this.OpenTables()
```

Setting Up the Data Environment—A Final Note

There is an additional benefit to setting up a report's data requirements using the report's data environment by placing code in the methods of the data environment or by adding objects to the data environment visually. When it comes time to run the report, all you have to do is a REPORT FORM and everything is handled when the report is run. Letting the report do the work makes strategies for running the reports much easier.

Strategies for Running Reports

You have already seen how the REPORT FORM and LABEL FORM commands work. The issue here is how to integrate running the reports into your application.

You have the following options:

1. Run the report from a menu item.
2. Run the report from a control in a form.
3. Run the report from a program.
4. Create a Reporting Subsystem.

In each case, the theory behind running the reports is the same. If the program has setup code that needs to be run, it is run before the REPORT FORM command is issued.

From a menu item, the code would be placed either in a command or a procedure attached to the menu item. From a control on a form, the code would be run from a method of the control. A typical example would be a command button on a form which, when clicked, would run the report. In this case, the code would be placed in the command button's Click method.

When working with programs, menus, and methods, the report to be run is usually specifically coded for that option. For example, a menu item to run an invoice report would have the code to run only the invoice report.

When working with specific programs that call each report, a program change is required every time a new report is added to an application. As a rule of thumb, it is better to avoid coding modifications when you can. After all, any time you make a change to a program you run the risk of breaking something.

One way to do this is by creating a data-driven reporting subsystem.

Creating a Reporting Subsystem

A reporting subsystem typically centers around a form that lists reports available in the application. The user selects a report to run, specifies the destination for the report, and off it goes.

Here's how you can create a reporting subsystem (the code for the subsystem presented here is on the disk that accompanies this book).

The Report Definition Table

The first step is to create a report definition table. Basically, this table has fields for the name of the report form (FRX) file and an English description for display.

Here's the structure for REPODEF.DBF:

```
Structure for table:      D:\DATA\DOCS\BOOKS\VFU\CODE\REPODEF.DBF
Number of data records: 1
Date of last update:      08/23/95
Code Page:                1252
Field   Field Name    Type                Width   Dec   Index   Collate Nulls
    1   CREPOFILE     Character              8                             No
    2   CREPODESC     Character             30                             No
** Total **                                 39
```

cRepoFile has the name of the FRX file to run for the report. cRepoDesc has the English description for the report that will display on the report selection form.

Here are some sample records for the table:

```
Record#   CREPOFILE CREPODESC
      1   TEST      This report is a test report
      2   CUSTORD   Customer Order Report
      3   CUSTINV   Customer Invoice Report
```

The Report Selection Form

The next step is to create a form that enables the user to select a report and run it. Figure 25.2 shows the Report Selection form.

FIGURE 25.2.

The Report Selection form.

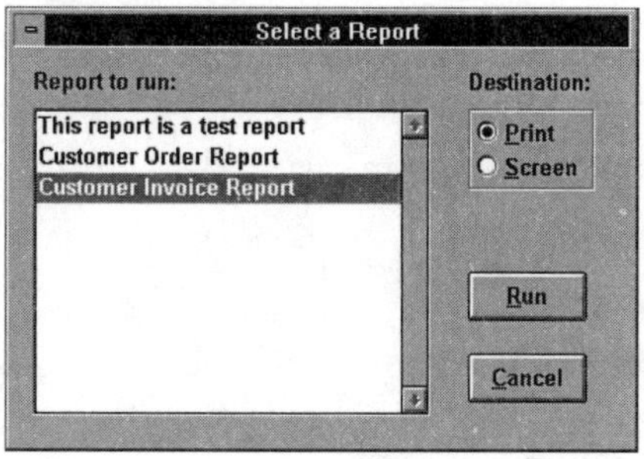

The list box on the form shows the records in REPODEF.DBF. The Option Group enables the user to select the destination for the report and the Run button executes the report with a single REPORT FORM command.

Here's a code representation of the form:

```
*  Form.............: RepoSel
*  Author...........: Menachem Bazian, CPA
*  Project..........: Visual FoxPro Unleashed!
*  Copyright........: (c) Flash Creative Management, Inc. 1995
*  Notes............: Exported code from Class Browser.


****************************************************
*-- Form:        form1 (d:\data\docs\books\vfu\code\reposel.scx)
*-- ParentClass:  form
*-- BaseClass:    form
*
DEFINE CLASS frmRepoSel AS form

    DataSession = 2
    Height = 233
    Width = 375
    DoCreate = .T.
    AutoCenter = .T.
    BackColor = RGB(192,192,192)
    BorderStyle = 2
    Caption = "Select a Report"
    MaxButton = .F.
    MinButton = .F.
    WindowType = 1
    LockScreen = .F.
    Name = "Form1"

    ADD OBJECT list1 AS listbox WITH ;
        ColumnCount = 0, ;
        ColumnWidths = "", ;
        RowSourceType = 6, ;
        RowSource = "Repodef.Crepodesc", ;
        FirstElement = 1, ;
        Height = 181, ;
        Left = 12, ;
        NumberOfElements = 0, ;
        Top = 36, ;
        Width = 241, ;
        Name = "List1"
```

```
ADD OBJECT label1 AS label WITH ;
    AutoSize = .T., ;
    BackStyle = 0, ;
    Caption = "Report to run:", ;
    Height = 18, ;
    Left = 12, ;
    Top = 12, ;
    Width = 87, ;
    Name = "Label1"

ADD OBJECT opgdestination AS optiongroup WITH ;
    ButtonCount = 2, ;
    BackStyle = 0, ;
    Value = 1, ;
    Height = 48, ;
    Left = 276, ;
    Top = 36, ;
    Width = 78, ;
    Name = "opgDestination", ;
    Option1.BackStyle = 0, ;
    Option1.Caption = "\<Print", ;
    Option1.Value = 1, ;
    Option1.Height = 18, ;
    Option1.Left = 5, ;
    Option1.Top = 5, ;
    Option1.Width = 68, ;
    Option1.Name = "optPrint", ;
    Option2.BackStyle = 0, ;
    Option2.Caption = "\<Screen", ;
    Option2.Value = 0, ;
    Option2.Height = 18, ;
    Option2.Left = 5, ;
    Option2.Top = 25, ;
    Option2.Width = 68, ;
    Option2.Name = "optScreen"

ADD OBJECT label2 AS label WITH ;
    AutoSize = .T., ;
    BackStyle = 0, ;
    Caption = "Destination:", ;
    Height = 18, ;
    Left = 276, ;
    Top = 12, ;
    Width = 75, ;
    Name = "Label2"

ADD OBJECT cmdrun AS commandbutton WITH ;
    Top = 132, ;
    Left = 276, ;
    Height = 29, ;
    Width = 73, ;
    Caption = "\<Run", ;
    Name = "cmdRun"

ADD OBJECT cmdcancel AS commandbutton WITH ;
    Top = 180, ;
    Left = 276, ;
```

```
            Height = 29, ;
            Width = 73, ;
            Cancel = .T., ;
            Caption = "\<Cancel", ;
            Name = "cmdCancel"

      PROCEDURE cmdrun.Click
          LOCAL lcReportFile
          lcReportFile = ALLTRIM(repodef.cRepoFile)

          IF thisform.opgDestination.Value = 1
              REPORT FORM (lcReportFile) TO PRINT OFF
          ELSE
              REPORT FORM (lcReportFile) PREVIEW
          ENDIF
          RETURN
      ENDPROC

      PROCEDURE cmdcancel.Click
          thisform.release()
      ENDPROC

ENDDEFINE
*
*-- EndDefine: form1
****************************************************
```

This reporting subsystem assumes that all code for setting up a report is done in the data environment of the report. If you are dealing with code that is outside the report, you could add a field to REPODEF that has the name of the program to run to set up the report and then reference the name of that program in the `Click` method of the Run button.

There are other modifications you might want to make to this simple reporting subsystem. You might decide to have different types of reports and segregate them. You can do this by adding a TYPE field to REPODEF and filtering the data in the list box based on the type of report the user wants to see. You could also add options to send the report to an ASCII file with `REPORT FORM ... TO filename ASCII`. The key here is that the modifications would be made once to the REPOSEL form, and you can reuse it from there from application to application.

Summary

This chapter provided coding techniques you can use to produce reports from within your Visual FoxPro applications. The biggest time-saving hint in this chapter is to make full use of the Visual FoxPro Report Designer, Label Designer, and Data Environment Designer as well as the stored reports created within the Report Designer in your programs. Doing this can save you an enormous amount of time in coding. In Chapter 26, "Putting It All Together," the techniques touched on in the last four chapters are combined with application design techniques to form the basis for a complete application.

Putting It All Together

As you have discovered during your journey through this book, each Visual FoxPro 3.0 rapid application development (RAD) tool enables you to create a component of an application easily. Each component is a functionally complete element of the application. You can verify that the component operates correctly as you create it. When you create a report form, you can determine whether it generates accurate output. You can verify that your forms function correctly and that queries generate the expected results. You can even perform user testing on the individual components. After you have verified that all of the components of your applications are functioning properly, you can put them all together and form your complete application.

The purpose of this chapter is to convey how to combine modular components to create a complete Visual FoxPro application.

SAMPLE PROJECT, FORMS, AND MENUS ON THE CD-ROM

Samples of a project, forms, and menus are available in the data on the accompanying CD-ROM.

If you've performed the data setup, look in the directory VFU\Chap26\ for the material appropriate for this chapter.

FilePurpose

SaveEnv.PRG The main program that demonstrates the use of an object to achieve the saving and restoring of environment variables.

SignON.SCX A form that demonstrates a splash screen. It uses a timer object to dismiss the form after a time interval.

Structuring the Application

Most database applications consist of roughly the same group of components; they have a menu system, data input forms, query forms, and reporting capabilities. When you design your application, you determine which components you need and what the relationship is between the components. To organize your modular components, you use the Visual FoxPro Project Manager, a centralized container for the files in an application. You use it when you add, modify, or execute any of the modular components of your applications. You use the Project Manager to combine all of the components into an application (.APP) or executable (.EXE) file. It is an indispensable organizational tool. Assume that you have created the following application components:

- The application's user interface (BOOKS.MPR)
- The form used as an application hub (MAIN.SCX)
- The data entry forms (ORDER.SCX, SHIPADDR.SCX, REVIEWER.SCX, and BOOKSX.SCX)
- Reports (ORDERS.FRX and BOOKORD.FRX)

Assume that all of these files have been independently created and tested; it is now time to tie them together into an application. One way to do this is to create a main program.

Creating a Main Program

Assuming that you have used the Project Manager to organize your application and create and maintain each component, you now have a group of independent components. You need to create a main program that kicks off the application and establishes the event loop. This main program can be very simple because all it needs to do is to establish the application's environment, launch the initial user interface, establish the event loop, and restore the environment when the application exits. For example, the simple main program could look like this:

```
**************************************************
* Program: BOOKS.PRG
* Purpose: Main Program for Book Store Application
DO Setup.PRG    && Set up the environment
DO Books.MPR    && Establish User environment
READ EVENTS     && Establish Event Loop
DO Cleanup.PRG  && Restore the environment
```

The Setup procedure saves environmental parameters, performs any program initialization, and establishes the data environment for the application. The Cleanup procedure restores all of the saved environmental parameters and performs any program cleanup operations.

This application is centralized around the menu system. The menu system executes the various components of the event loop. After the menu system is activated, the READ EVENTS command establishes the event loop. The event loop remains active until a CLEAR EVENT command is encountered. See the section, "Controlling the Event Loop," later in this chapter.

After you create the main program, you need to inform the Project Manager that the main program is the starting point for the application. To do this, you select the main program and choose the Project menu Set Main option. The main file is denoted in the Project Manager by a bullet symbol, as shown in Figure 26.1.

FIGURE 26.1.

Establishing a main program.

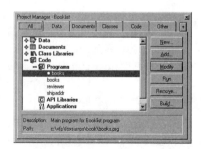

The main file does not have to be a program (.PRG) file. It can be a query, program, or form file included in the project. However, in most cases the program file containing a READ EVENTS command is usually the best choice.

Defining the Main Form

If you decide to have a form file as the hub of your application, you can make a form or form set file the starting point of an application. If that is the case, you can place the initialization code for the application in the method for the Load event of the form or form set. You can place the code to restore the original environment and any other cleanup operations in the method for the Unload event. In the example shown in Figure 26.2, the Main form is the starting point for the application. It is the central hub of the entire application. All of the actions that the user performs are done by choosing a button on this form.

FIGURE 26.2.

Establishing a main form.

There are limitations when using a form as the main file of an application. For example, if you want to create a stand-alone application (.EXE), you must make the form modal. (You set the WindowType property to 1 to make the form modal.) The problem is that if you have a modal form you cannot access the menu system.

Another limitation is that if a form or form set is the main file of an application the form does not exist as an object. That means that there exists no variable to reference the form. However, on the other hand, if you use a program as the main file you can use the DO FORM command or CreateObject() function to create an object variable for referencing a form.

Establishing the Application Environment

When you first start up Visual FoxPro, it contains default values for all of the environmental parameters (SET commands) and system memory variables, which define the Visual FoxPro development environment. The default development environment might not be the optimum environment for running your application. It probably isn't.

If you ever wonder what the status of the current development environment is, you can execute the DISPLAY STATUS command from the command window. You can also view the settings by activating the Options dialog box by choosing Tools | Options.

You can use the SET command to alter the settings of an environmental parameter. However, it is a good idea to save the current environmental setting when you initialize the environment and to restore the original value just before you exit the application.

One of the responsibilities of the Setup procedure, mentioned in the "Creating a Main Program" section of this chapter, is to save environmental settings for any environmental parameters changed by the application and to establish new values for the settings. The following is an example:

```
cSaveTalk = SET("TALK")  && Save SET TALK
SET TALK OFF
...
```

Other initialization tasks involve establishing a default path to the application's files. Again, you want to save the original default directory. Here is an example:

```
cSaveDirectory = SET("DIRECTORY") && default directory
SET DIRECTORY TO HOME()+"FOXSAMPS\BOOKLIST"
```

The HOME() function returns the name of the directory from which Visual FoxPro was started.

Also, you might want to establish any required external libraries and procedure files. For example, if you need to load the FOXTOOLS.FLL library, which resides in the same directory as the FoxPro executable, you can use the following command:

```
SET LIBRARY TO HOME()+"FOXTOOLS.FLL" ADDITIVE
```

Displaying the Initial Interface

After you have established the environment for your application, you display the initial interface. In the example presented in the "Creating a Main Program" section earlier in this chapter, the BOOKS.MPR menu was run. However, the initial interface can be activated with a DO FORM command to display and run a form or form set.

You can display a sign-on window after you establish the interface. The sign-on window, shown in Figure 26.3, contains a timer control with its Interval property set to 2000 (2 seconds) and the THISFORM.Release statement placed in the timer control's Timer event method. When the timer interval expires, the sign-on form is released and then disappears. The form's KeyPress event also contains a THISFORM.Release statement so that the form disappears if the user presses any key.

FIGURE 26.3.

A timer controlled sign-on form.

Controlling the Event Loop

After your main program displays the initial interface, it is ready to transfer program control to the Visual FoxPro event loop. The statement that performs this operation is the READ EVENTS command. The event loop then waits for user interaction. The event loop will remain in control of the execution until the CLEAR EVENTS command executes. The CLEAR EVENTS command exits from the event loop and returns program control to the statement in the main program following the READ EVENTS command.

You must provide a way to exit from the event loop. Typically, the menu system contains an Exit option that executes the CLEAR EVENTS command. If a form or form set is used as the hub of the system, the CLEAR EVENTS command can be added to the Destroy event code of the form or form set. Then, you can add a statement in the Click event code of an Exit button that calls the Release method of the form (THISFORM.Release) or form set (THISFORMSET.Release). Regardless of where the CLEAR EVENTS command executes, once it executes, Visual FoxPro returns program control to the command following the READ EVENTS command in the main program.

Exiting the Application Upon the Close of a Main Form

Just before the application exits, the original development environment should be restored (unless of course you plan to exit from Visual FoxPro). The purpose of the Cleanup procedure in the main program is to re-establish the original environment. One of its responsibilities is to restore the settings of the environmental parameters. For example, in the example presented in "Establishing the Application Environment" of this chapter, the settings of the SET TALK and SET DIRECTORY commands are stored in the cSaveTalk and cSaveDirectory variables, respectively. You can restore the settings using the following commands:

```
SET TALK &cSaveTalk
SET DIRECTORY TO (cSaveDirectory)
```

Also, you must restore the Visual FoxPro systems menu. You do this by executing the following command:

```
SET SYSMENU TO DEFAULT
```

An object-oriented technique for saving and restoring settings is portrayed in Listing 26.1, which is a main program for an application. To save a setting, you create a SaveEnv class object, which saves a reference to the object in a memory variable. The SaveEnv Init event saves the environmental parameter setting in a property. When the main program exits, its memory variables go out of scope and the Destroy event for each of the objects is called. The code in the Destroy event method restores the original setting for an environmental parameter.

Listing 26.1. A main program for an application that uses object-oriented techniques to save and restore the SET command value.

```
***********************************************************
* Application main program
***********************************************************
cSaveSet = CreateObject("SaveEnv","TALK")
cSaveDirectory = CreateObject("SaveEnv","DIRECTORY TO")
SET TALK OFF
SET DIRECTORY TO HOME() + "\FOXSAMPS\MYAPPS"
DO BOOKS.MPR
READ EVENTS
SET SYSMENU TO
***********************************************************
* Class SaveEnv Saves Enviornmental parameters when
*                object is created and restores 'em
*                when object reference variable goes
*                out of scope.
***********************************************************
* Limitation:   Only works when SET function returns
*                a character string
***********************************************************
DEFINE CLASS SaveEnv AS CUSTOM
    PROTECTED cSaveSet
    PROCEDURE INIT(cSave)
        THIS.cSaveSet = cSave + " " + SET(cSave)
    ENDPROC
    PROCEDURE DESTROY
        LOCAL temp
        temp = THIS.cSaveSet
        SET &temp
    ENDIF
    PROCEDURE SHOWVALUE
        WAIT WINDOW "SET " + THIS.cSaveSet
    ENDPROC
ENDDEFINE
```

Adding All the Files to a Project

If you use the Project Manager to build all of your files in the application, most of the files are already included. Any files that are referenced by your program are added automatically when you build the project. To build an application, click the Build button, and the Build dialog box appears, as shown in Figure 26.4. Choose the Rebuild Project option and press OK.

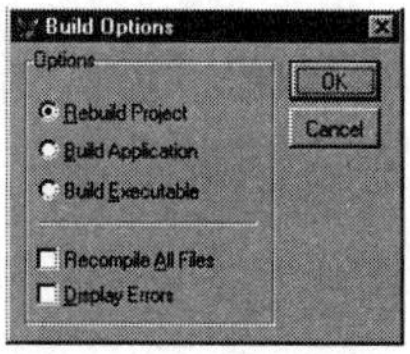

FIGURE 26.4.

The Build Options dialog box in the Project Manager.

When you build a project, the Project Manager reads each program file to determine which files are a part of the project. It searches for commands (such as DO, SET LIBRARY TO, and REPORT) to look for the names of files that are referenced.

When you refer to a filename in a program and specify a literal name, the Project Manager has no trouble interpreting it, as in the following example:

```
DO MYPROG
REPORT FORM TALLYHO
DO MYMENU.MPR
```

However, when you indirectly designate a filename with a filename expression or use a program macro substitution (&), the Project Manager has no way to know its name, as in the following example:

```
Prog="MYPROG"
DO &Prog
filter = "NOT 'GREEN'$UPPER(Descript)"
REPORT FORM Apple FOR &filter
DO (Prog)
```

The Project Manager does not process any command that contains a macro substitution. In the preceding example, the Project Manager does not process the REPORT command and cannot locate the Apple report file in the command.

It is a good idea to include all the required files in a project when you build the project. The Project Manager tracks arrays and must be informed if an array was created in another procedure. You can inform the Project Manager that a file was referenced in a program, even if it was referenced indirectly (as a filename expression or in macro substitution), by using the EXTERNAL command.

Only the Project Manager recognizes the EXTERNAL command. It is used to search for references to files and arrays. The command is ignored by the compiler. In fact, if you don't use the Project Manager to maintain your applications, you never need the EXTERNAL command. The following is the syntax of the EXTERNAL command:

```
EXTERNAL ARRAY ArrayName

EXTERNAL LABEL ¦ LIBRARY ¦ MENU ¦ PROCEDURE
   ¦ REPORT ¦ SCREEN  cFileName list
```

The EXTERNAL command specifies files and arrays that are referenced within a program so that the Project Manager can resolve undefined references in a project. Files specified by EXTERNAL are included in a project by Project Manager. You must include a keyword (such as LABEL, LIBRARY, MENU, PROCEDURE, REPORT, or SCREEN) before the filenames so that the Project Manager knows the type of files to include in the project.

You might need to add bitmap, icon, or other files manually. To add a file to the project, choose the Project Manager Add button. Then select the file to add from the Open File dialog box.

When you have a visual class referenced, you might have to add the visual class to the project. The problem is that Visual FoxPro maintains a relative path between a form and a visual class library. If the visual class library is not included, the Project Manager might store a relative path during the application building process. This would make it so that you cannot execute the application if you move it to a new location.

If the Project Manager does not locate one of the files in the project, it displays an error box. You can ignore the file, choose Locate to find the file in another directory, or cancel the build. Errors that occur are placed in the Build Error log. You can view them with the Project menu Errors option.

After you have located all of the files in the project and have added them to the project with no errors during the build, you are ready to build your application (.APP) file.

When you set up a project file in preparation for creating an application, be sure that only read-only files are included in the application. When you build a project, the Project Manager guesses which files are read-only and which files are editable. The Project Manager then includes read-only files and excludes the others. Obviously, database tables and indexes associated with the project are editable. However, the Project Manager considers all other files read-only; therefore, they are included. You can manually exclude files that you don't want to include in the application by using the Project menu Exclude option. If a circle with a diagonal line appears to the right of the filename for an item listed in the Project dialog box, the file is excluded and is not included in the application.

Building an Application File

After you have added all of the required files to the project and are able to build the project without receiving any errors, you are ready to build the application (.APP) file. The application build process compiles all of the files in the project and includes them in a single file with an .APP extension.

To build an application, click the Build button in the Project Manager and the Build Options dialog box appears, as shown previously in Figure 26.4. Then, choose the Build Application option and press the OK button. You have the option of recompiling all of the files or just recompiling those files that have changed since they were last compiled. If there are no errors during compilation and no missing files, Visual FoxPro combines the files and builds the application file.

You can select the Build Executable option, which enables you to build an .EXE file that you can execute from Windows (the same as for any other Windows application). However, this option is disabled unless you have installed the Visual FoxPro Professional Edition. This version contains the Visual FoxPro distribution kit, which enables you to distribute an application as a stand-alone executable—the customer does not need a copy of Visual FoxPro. Several other options are available when you build an application with the distribution kit.

The simplest option is the *runtime application*. You develop a runtime application by creating an application (.APP) file and distributing a runtime package. This package consists of your .APP file, any editable files (normally database tables and index files). For this option, the user must own Visual FoxPro, or the .APP must be called from a Visual FoxPro .EXE.

You can choose the Build Executable option in the Build Options dialog box to create an *executable* (.EXE) file. The size of the EXE file is slightly larger than its corresponding application (.APP) file (10–15KB). You can execute compact executable files from Windows, but you still need to distribute the runtime support library files (VFP300.ESL)to the customer along with the .EXE file and the editable files.

The principal advantage of compact executables and runtime applications is that your license gives you limitless distribution of your application to users in your organization. The Microsoft rules for runtime distribution do not require you to charge a fee for distribution.

Running the Application

Now that you have created an application (.APP) file, you can execute your application simply by choosing the Program menu Do option or by executing the program from the command window with the DO command.

You have traveled down a long path of developing individual components, testing them, and then combining them into a final application file. All that remains is to test the final assembly. This process is called *end-to-end testing*. The Hubble telescope failed to perform correctly because NASA failed to do end-to-end testing before they launched it into space. As you probably know, the repairs to the telescope were costly.

Summary

In this chapter you learned how to assemble all of the components of an application into a single application file. The Visual FoxPro Project Manager is a valuable organizational tool that helps you put all the components together, and it even creates an application for you.

V

PART

Object-Oriented Programming

Introduction to Object-Oriented Programming

Object orientation is one of the major new additions to FoxPro with the advent of Visual FoxPro 3.0. Object-oriented programming (OOP) revolutionizes nearly every aspect of application development with Visual FoxPro from the analysis and design phases to the coding and testing of applications and application components.

This and the next four chapters discuss object-oriented programming with Visual FoxPro in detail and include the following information:

- This chapter discusses the basic concepts of object-oriented programming with examples shown in Visual FoxPro.

- Chapter 28, "OOP with Visual FoxPro," covers how to create classes with Visual FoxPro using programs and the Visual Class Designer.

- Chapter 29, "Creating Classes with Visual FoxPro," covers the different kinds of classes typically created in Visual FoxPro with examples of each.

- Chapter 30, "Managing Classes with Visual FoxPro," delves into the critical issue of managing class libraries and reviews the commands related to managing class libraries. The Class Browser, a powerful new addition to the FoxPro suite of tools, is also covered.

- Chapter 31, "Advanced Object-Oriented Programming," discusses some advanced topics related to OOP with Visual FoxPro.

Chapter Introduction

In this chapter you will learn the fundamental concepts of object orientation in Visual FoxPro. The subsequent chapters cover object-oriented development with Visual FoxPro in more detail.

Visual FoxPro, like Visual C++, is a *hybrid* language. This means that the developers have the option of developing applications using OOP methods or modular programming. If you develop applications in other languages, such as SmallTalk, you must use OOP.

If Visual FoxPro does not require the use of OOP, why should you consider leaving the warm comfort of developing the old way to go to the radically new mind-set of OOP? To answer this question, it is first necessary to review the background of what is called the *software crisis*.

The Software Crisis

Businesses today are experiencing a software crisis that stems from the inability of today's programming methodologies to adapt to the rapidly changing world of business. Applications developed in modular form often require a long development cycle, are based on marginally reusable code bases, and are frequently outdated before they hit the user's desk. The premise of modular development is to create software based on *modules* that are typically, by their very nature, different from business to business and even from department to department within a single company.

Take the example of accounting applications. At the most basic level, they are the same— accounts receivable manages and tracks the money owed to the company, accounts payable manages the bills owed by the company, and so on. However, when you drill down to the operations of the individual business functions, differences typically arise from organization to organization. For example, the format of a bill for a service organization is different from the format of a bill for a merchandising firm.

When software is developed in modules, as it was in FoxPro 2.*x*, individual programs are combined to create an application. If an application is brought from one company to another, or even from one department to another, typically the software is copied and the source code is modified to fit the requirements of the new users. Imagine what happens when an upgrade is released for the original software. The new users do not get the benefits of the new upgrade unless a second effort is made to incorporate the changes into the copied version. If a bug is found in one version of the software, the software must be fixed in two places. Obviously, this is not the optimal way to do things.

OOP takes a radically different approach. Software is created not in modules but rather in terms of *entities* (or objects). For example, using OOP, you do not create an accounts receivable module per se but instead create customer objects, invoice objects, and so on, and then combine them into an application. In effect, *components* are developed that are put together into an application.

Using this new method of development, you focus on the entities being modeled in the *problem domain* (a fancy term meaning the business problem you are trying to solve with software). The design of a customer object is based on the simple concept of trying to determine what a customer does and what a customer knows within the context of a business. "Within the context" means that we will be coming up with a *theoretical* model for the customer based on what the "customer" is within the business environment. For example, a customer knows his or her name, address, telephone number, and credit balance. The customer would also know how to print itself, save itself and more. This does not mean that Joe Customer knows how to print his own record or save himself to the database. Rather, it means that a customer *object* would have these responsibilities.

If an application is taken from one business to another, the differences can be accommodated by basing new objects on existing ones (a process known as *subclassing*). The behaviors and attributes of the original object are automatically brought forward (*inherited*) and are changed as needed for the new software. This results in radically fewer code modifications. If changes are made to an original object, they are automatically brought forward to the new objects.

Why would you want to change to OOP from the familiar old world of modular programming? Because the old world is broken and OOP can fix it. Specifically, object orientation is designed to provide the following:

- Enhanced code reusability
- Enhanced code maintenance

Now that you know what to look for from OOP, the following is an overview of the concepts that make up object orientation.

Objects and Encapsulation

If you've ever read a book or article on object orientation, you might have noticed many terms thrown about as if they were self-explanatory. Terms such as *inheritance, encapsulation,* and *polymorphism* are used to express OOP concepts. Because of these odd and difficult terms, OOP is often thought to be complex. The truth could not be more different.

The first and most key concept in OOP is the object. An *object* is a package of information and actions. Like a package, an object is self-contained. An object has things on the inside that only it knows about, characteristics that everyone can see, and ways of doing things.

Use an elevator as an example. An elevator is an object in that it has properties (such as a maximum weight load), it performs actions (such as opening and closing the door), and it has a public interface (the control buttons) that enables it to interact with the environment around it. This is precisely what an object is.

The key to understanding objects is to view them like an elevator. When you think about an elevator, all you think about is the public interface—the buttons that tell the elevator where to go, the door that opens to let you in and out, and so on. However, there is a great deal more to the elevator that you never think about. For example, you probably don't know how the elevator interprets the buttons you press into a destination or how the elevator knows which floor it is on. And, for that matter, you probably don't care. These functions, while part of the elevator, do not concern you.

This introduces a few concepts. First of all, all the knowledge and behaviors of an object are contained within the object. This is known as *encapsulation.* An object knows what it needs to know and how to do what it needs to do without relying on the outside world. The data and behaviors are encapsulated within the object.

Properties

The data in an object is called a property. A *property* (in Visual FoxPro terms) is simply a memory variable that is attached and scoped to an object. You query the value and modify it by using the object name followed by a period (.) and then the name of the property. (For the record, properties are also called *member variables* in some texts.) Properties can have any data types that are valid for a plain old Visual FoxPro memory variable. A property exists as long as the object it is attached to exists.

For example, if you have a property called lIsNew that is attached to an object called oCust, you could query the value of the property by stating the following:

```
? oCust.lIsNew
```

Methods

In addition to having attached data, objects have actions to perform. These actions are coded in procedures that are attached to the object. These procedures are known as *methods*. There is little difference between a "regular" procedure and a method except in the way they are called. You call a method by stating the name of the object followed by a period (.) and then the name of the method. For example, here is how to call a method named Print that is attached to the oCust object:

```
oCust.Print()
```

Technically, the parentheses at the end of the method name are required only if you expect a return value or if you are passing parameters to the method. I suggest that you always use the parentheses for consistency. It also makes it clear that you're calling a method.

Note, by the way, the manner in which this method is called. Unlike for Visual FoxPro procedures and user-defined functions, you do not have to use a DO-type syntax or specify the function with an expression. To call a method that is a procedure (assuming you do not expect a return value), all you need to do is call the method as shown in the previous example. If you expect a return value, you can use the old UDF-type syntax. For example, if the Print method returns a logical stating whether the customer was properly printed, you could capture the value with this:

```
llReturnValue = oCust.Print()
```

Events

Events are things that happen. For example, clicking the mouse is an event. Events can be caused by a user's action (such as clicking a mouse) or by the system itself (such as when an error occurs). When you are creating a class (such as a pushbutton) in Visual FoxPro, you can attach code (such as methods) to events. When the event happens (for example, the user clicks the left mouse button while on the object), the associated method (that is, the click method) is automatically called.

Events are not new. Developers have been using them since the advent of FoxPro 2.0. Valid clauses, for example, are simply procedures that are attached to an event (such as attempting to exit a modified field or clicking a pushbutton). Part of the power of using objects comes from attaching methods to an object that automatically execute when something specific happens. In Visual FoxPro you can attach methods to all kinds of events: when the mouse is clicked, when the mouse is released, and so on. You can even attach code to events that execute automatically when the object is created (the `Init` event) and when the object is released (the `Destroy` event).

There is one major difference between events in an object-oriented development environment and the old `Valid` and `When` clauses. In FoxPro 2.6, there was no direct method for manually executing the code snippet attached to an event (well, there *was* a way, but it was a kludge). In other words, there was no single command that ran the procedure attached to a screen object's `Valid` event. In an object-oriented development environment you can do this easily by calling the event the same way you would call a method. For example, if you had a pushbutton called `cmdOK`, you could execute the code attached to the `Click` event (that is, the `Click()` method) at any time by issuing the following:

```
cmdOk.Click()
```

By attaching code to events, you greatly increase the control you have over the behavior of an object. In fact, with the myriad of events to which Visual FoxPro enables you to respond, you can have acute, pinpoint control over forms and objects—greater than ever before.

So far, you have seen that you can create objects as well as assign properties to them and create methods for them. If you had to write code to fine-tune an object every time you created it, you would be in for a lot of coding. Fortunately, OOP has the answer for this as well—classes.

Classes

To this point, all of the discussion in this chapter has centered around the object. But what is the basis for an object? How is an object coded?

Consider a candle for a moment. A candlemaker typically creates a candle from a mold rather than creating each one individually. If the design of a candle needed to change, where would it be changed? On every individual candle? Not likely. Instead, the mold would be changed. Once the mold is changed, all new candles get the change automatically.

In object-oriented programming, objects are never coded. Rather, object molds (called *classes*) are coded. All objects are then *instantiated* (that is, created) from that class. All coding is done at the class level. Once an object is instantiated from a class, all you do is interact with it. You do not add methods or change existing methods in an object, but rather you add and change methods in a class.

Here's an example of a class:

```
DEFINE CLASS myClass AS Custom
    cName = ""
    cType = ""
    lIsNew = .F.

    PROCEDURE ShowVals
        ? this.cName
```

```
        ? this.cType

        IF this.lIsNew
              ? "I'M NEW"
        ELSE
              ? "I'M OLD"
        ENDIF
   ENDPROC
ENDDEFINE
```

A brief dissection of this block of code follows; however, for a more definitive description of the syntax associated with coding classes, refer to Chapter 28, "OOP with Visual FoxPro."

```
Define Class myClass as Custom
```

This line of code tells Visual FoxPro that you are defining a new class called `MyClass` that is based on another class called `Custom`, which is discussed in more detail later in the chapter.

```
cName = ""
cType = ""
lIsNew = .F.
```

The preceding lines are known as *declaration code*. In this part of the class definition you list the member variables (properties) of the object and their initial values. If one of the member variables is an array, the `DECLARE` statement would be placed here.

```
PROCEDURE ShowVals
      ? this.cName
      ? this.cType

      IF this.lIsNew
            ? "I'M NEW"
      ELSE
            ? "I'M OLD"
      ENDIF
ENDPROC
```

This is a method definition. Calling a method executes all the code from the `PROCEDURE` line to the `ENDPROC` line. A method is very similar to a procedure in a FoxPro 2.*x* procedure file, except that the method is called through its object.

Instantiating Objects

An object is instantiated with the `CREATEOBJECT()` function. Here is the syntax for creating an instance of `MyClass`:

```
oMyClass = CREATEOBJECT("MyClass")
```

By the way, `oMyClass` is simply a memory variable of type "Object."

In order to access the members of `oMyClass`, you could use the following commands:

```
? oMyClass.cName    && Initially blank
oMyClass.cName = "Menachem Bazian"
```

```
? oMyClass.cName    && Now shows "Menachem Bazian"
oMyClass.ShowVals() && Runs the showvals method
```

Referencing a Method or Property in a Class

An issue that arises with this method of development is that it is difficult to know what the name of an object's instance variable is inside a class. When coding the class, the name of the variable that holds the instance should be, and is, irrelevant.

In order to refer to an object's properties or methods within itself, the identifier THIS, in place of the object name, is used. (You saw this previously in procedure SHOWVALS.)

```
IF this.lIsNew
        ? "I'M NEW"
    ELSE
        ? "I'M OLD"
    ENDIF
```

The keyword THIS means that you are accessing the method or member variable of the object itself. It's that simple.

Subclassing—Basing a Class on Another Class

So far you have learned just about all there is to know about objects, and you have also learned about properties, methods, and events. You have also seen how to create an object's blueprint with a class, which you then use to instantiate the object. However, one more important piece remains (the really exciting part as it turns out): creating classes based on prior classes.

Suppose you had a class called Light that models a light in a room. The class would need a method for turning the light on and off and a property for the current status of the light. It might look something like this:

```
DEFINE CLASS light AS custom
  status = "OFF"

  PROCEDURE Toggle
   IF this.status = "OFF"
     this.status = "ON"
   ELSE
     this.status = "OFF"
   ENDIF
  ENDPROC
ENDDEFINE
```

In the sample Light class, you create an object that basically has one property and one method. This works well for light switches that just turn on and off. But suppose you want to create a light switch that can dim as well? What do you do? Do you have to write a whole new class? The toggle is still applicable: the light can still be turned on and off. What you need is a modified version of the Light class that has all the same capabilities of the Light class plus the capability of dimming the light.

For the purposes of this illustration, I'll set the following rules: When you attempt to use the dimmer, it goes from full light to half light and then back again. In order to turn the light on or off, you still need to use the original light switch method.

Here's how you could accomplish this using an OOP model:

```
DEFINE CLASS dimmer AS light
  intensity = "FULL"

  PROCEDURE DimmIt
    IF this.status = "OFF"
      RETURN
    ENDIF

    this.intensity = IIF(this.intensity = "FULL", ;
             "HALF", "FULL")
    WAIT WINDOW "Lights are now "+this.intensity+" power."
  ENDPROC
ENDDEFINE
```

Note the original DEFINE of the class. In the original DEFINE (class Light), I used Custom as the base class. Custom is the simplest base class that is built into Visual FoxPro; you use it when you are creating objects of your own from scratch. (In Chapter 29 you learn what Custom is in more detail and how you would use it.) In the DEFINE used here the base class is Light. This means that class Dimmer automatically *inherits* everything that Light has. Thus, although no code exists in the Dimmer class to handle the LightSwitch method and the Status property, Dimmer gets the method and property automatically because it is a subclass of Light. This process is known as *inheritance*.

In effect, a subclass (Dimmer) is a more specialized version of the *superclass* (Light).

Overriding Inherited Behavior

One of the nice things about inheritance is that you can accept what you like from the superclass and override the rest. A method is overridden when it is "recoded" in the subclass. Here is an example:

```
DEFINE CLASS offdimmer AS dimmer
    intensity = "FULL"

    PROCEDURE DimmIt
        WAIT WINDOW "Dimmer is DIsabled"
    ENDPROC
ENDDEFINE
```

In this case, the `DimmIt` method has been overridden. The `DimmIt` method from the `Dimmer` class is not called.

Suppose you want to run the method from the `Dimmer` class's `DimmIt` method and then add additional code. Here's how you could do it:

```
DEFINE CLASS AnotherDimmer AS offdimmer
    intensity = "FULL"

    PROCEDURE DimmIt
        Dimmer::Dimmit()
        OffDimmer::Dimmit()
        WAIT WINDOW "Isn't this cool?"
    ENDPROC
ENDDEFINE
```

The double colon operator (::) is used to call methods from classes higher in the class hierarchy. Note that you can only call methods from classes that have been inherited from.

Protecting Methods and Properties

When you create an object, you should take great care to decide what the public interface of the class is going to be. A class will typically have properties and methods that are intended for use inside the class only. Other properties and methods, if accessed from the outside, can have a disastrous effect on the inner workings of a class.

Consider the sample `Light` class and suppose that the `Toggle` method has code in it that turns the light on and off based on the `Status` property. If you modify the `Status` property by accessing it outside of the class, the `Toggle` method will not work properly.

The solution to this problem is to protect the methods and properties that should not be accessible outside of the class. When you code the classes, you can protect the properties by adding `PROTECTED` *<propertyname>* definitions in the declaration section of the code. For methods, add the keyword `PROTECTED` to the `PROCEDURE` line. Here is an example:

```
DEFINE CLASS myClass AS Custom
    PROTECTED cName
    cName = ""
    cType = ""
    lIsNew = .F.

    PROTECTED PROCEDURE ShowVals
        ? this.cName
        ? this.cType

        IF this.lIsNew
            ? "I'M NEW"
        ELSE
            ? "I'M OLD"
        ENDIF
    ENDPROC
ENDDEFINE
```

In this example, both the cName property and the ShowVals method are protected. Attempts to access them from outside of the class will produce an error as if the property and method did not exist (and as far as the world outside of the class is concerned, they don't exist).

If a class has a property that has to be tightly controlled (such as the Status property, which can only be changed by the Toggle method), you should protect it. If the user needs to read the value of that property, provide a method that returns the value of the protected property. For example, in order to access the cName property in the sample class shown previously, you might create a method called ShowName as follows:

```
FUNCTION ShowName
     RETURN (this.cName)
ENDFUNC
```

Understanding Polymorphism

Polymorphism is the next term that needs to be covered in this discussion. *Polymorphism* is the ability to give methods and properties in different classes the same name even if they do and mean different things.

For example, consider the Light objects. They all have a method called Toggle, which turns the light on and off. Suppose now that you were to create an entirely different object—a telephone. The Telephone object might not have anything to do with a Light object, but there is a method attached to it also called Toggle. The Toggle method in the Telephone class might or might not do anything like the Toggle method in the Light classes.

Compare the following commands:

```
oLight = CREATEOBJECT("Light")
oPhone = CREATEOBJECT("Telephone")
oLight.Toggle()   &&Runs the Toggle method from
                  &&the Light object
oPhone.Toggle()   &&Runs the Toggle method from
                  &&the Phone object
```

Note how similar the code is between oLight and oPhone. You can call the Toggle method from either object in a similar fashion although they might do different things.

Polymorphism is an extremely useful way to develop classes. It enables you to put standards in place for naming methods that do similar things. For example, you can have a Show method for different objects that is designed to bring up the display portion of the object (for example, oCust.Show() might display the customer form, whereas oInv.Show() might display the invoice form). The beauty of this comes from a user perspective. It means that you can use the objects with much greater ease because you can develop a consistent interface when you work with your classes (imagine the difficulty you would have if the display method were called Show in one class and Display in another).

Messages, Messages, Messages

If you read any literature on OOP, the concept of *messages* can be found throughout. Everything you have learned so far that deals with working with OOP-based systems can be described as "sending a message." The following sections redefine previous examples of working with objects and discusses them in terms of messages.

Creating an Object

The following line of code sends a message to the `Invoice` class, telling it to create an object called `oInv` based on itself:

```
oInv = CREATEOBJECT("Invoice")
```

Getting the Value of a Property

The following line of code can be described as sending a message to the `oInv` object, telling it to get the value of the `nAmount` property and to return it to `lnAmount`:

```
lnAmount = oInv.nAmount
```

Calling a Method

The following line of code can be described as sending a message to the `oInv` object, telling it to execute its `Display` method:

```
oInv.Display && Show the Invoice
```

If you understand the concept of a message, a great deal of the gobbledygook you read in OOP literature becomes understandable. For example, polymorphism has been defined in OOP literature as "the ability to send the same message to different objects and have different actions take place." The practical definition of a message presented in this chapter earlier means the same thing, but it is easier to understand than the OOP literature definition.

The moral of this story is this: do not let the language throw you.

Encapsulation Revisited

Taking the concepts that you have seen so far in this chapter, the concept of *encapsulation* becomes clearer. Basically, encapsulation means that an object is a self-contained unit. The object contains data, in the form of properties (also called *member variables*), and methods that are associated with the object to perform whatever actions need to be done.

You can also create a Customer class if you want to. You can associate data and methods with it that encapsulate customer information and actions.

A Customer object's data could be items such as a name, address, phone number, credit limit, and so on. Methods associated with the object could be actions related to displaying customer data, enabling the user to edit or add customers, printing a customer, and so on. If you develop naming conventions for your object methods and properties, using the objects becomes a breeze.

Naming conventions means adopting standards for the names of the methods and properties. A good example would be a method that displays an object (for example, the form associated with a customer object). This method could be called Show(), Display(), ShowForm(), or even ShowTheFormForThisClassRightNow(). To a degree, what you call it really doesn't matter as long as you are consistent. The only area where you might have problems is with some of the more popular-type of actions such as Print(). If Microsoft has a method that does the type of action the method does (such as the Show() method that shows a form), it might make sense to adhere to that standard. I am not suggesting that you are bound to someone else's standard, but imagine the tower of Babel–type development that will occur if one class calls the method Show(), another calls it Display(), and yet a third uses the name ShowForm(). This is not a situation I would want to be in.

To illustrate polymorphism, take a look at the following example, which uses two sample classes: Customer and Invoice. Note how the code to work with the two classes, at this level, can be exceedingly similar. In fact, by using OOP, the developer who takes the objects and puts them together in the form of a system will have a much easier job.

```
oCust = CREATEOBJECT("Customer")
oCust.Show()        && Show the customer
oCust.Edit()        && Edit the Customer
oCust.Save()        && Save Customer
oCust.Print()       && Print the customer

oInv = CREATEOBJECT("Invoice")
oInv.Display()      && Show the Invoice
oInv.Edit()         && Edit the Invoice
oInv.Save()         && Save Invoice
oInv.Print()        && Print the Invoice
```

OOP and Its Effect on Development

Now that you have seen what objects are and what all the ten-dollar words mean, the next question is "Big deal. What does this do for me?"

OOP shifts the focus of development from coding procedures to the designing and defining of classes. Because objects are, in effect, complete and independent "modules," it is possible to have developers just working on classes of objects. The application developers can then use these classes, either directly or by subclassing them, and put them together to form a system.

Does this mean that once you have a library of classes you will never need to write code again? Not quite, but a class library will make your life a lot easier once it is developed, debugged, and ready to go.

Analysis and Design with OOP

Object-oriented programming does not start with code. Although the discussions in this chapter basically center around the implementation phase of writing objects, this step is the last step in creating object-oriented software.

The first step is to analyze the problem domain and to design the class hierarchies that make up the system. Sounds simple, right? In fact, object-oriented analysis and object-oriented design (OOA and OOD) are not difficult processes to perform—they just require discipline. Many different methodologies have been proposed and written about over the years. The more popular authors in this realm are Grady Booch, Ivar Jacobsen, and Rebecca Wirfs-Brock. Personally, I use the Wirfs-Brock method of CRC cards, but that is a whole different story. Her book, *Designing Object-Oriented Software*, should be required reading for all developers working on object-oriented analysis and design in my opinion. But don't go by just what I recommend because others feel strongly about other authors.

Analysts have stated that as much as 70 percent of the time allotted for an object-oriented project is spent on analysis and design. That's a lot of time. Therefore, you should take the time you need to do your research and to find a methodology with which you are comfortable.

Whichever methodology you choose, the end result of object-oriented analysis and design is a coherent, well-thought-out, logical class design that will clearly show the classes in the application as well as the public interface (that is, the unprotected properties and methods) and how they interact. Once you have all this, coding can begin.

Multideveloper Issues with Object-Oriented Software

The focus of object orientation, which is based on objects rather than modules, has another interesting effect on the development process: It makes multideveloper situations much easier to handle. If the analysis and design phases have been properly done, the system is broken down into discrete pieces. The design will call for a particular class hierarchy and will state what each class can expect from other classes in the system. Once you have accomplished this, coding each class tree can be done independently of others in the system.

Take the following example. The design document for a system calls for a `Customer` class and a `Statement` class. The `Customer` class calls the `Statement` class to create and print a statement that shows open invoices for customers. The design document states what methods and properties are available in the `Statement` class. For example, there might be a `Create()` method that creates the statement and accepts a customer number as a parameter, a `Print()` method that prints the statement, and a property called `cStatementNumber` for the statement number. The developer of the `Customer` class could write the following method:

```
PROCEDURE CustomerStatement
    LOCAL loStatement

    *— The next line creates the object
    loStatement = CREATEOBJECT("statement")

    *— Now create the statement's contents.
    loStatement.Create(this.CustomerNumber)

    *— Now print the statement
    loStatement.Print()

    *— Finally, tell the user that we are done
    WAIT WINDOW "Statement number " + ;
                loStatement.cStatementNumber + ;
                " has been created and printed!"
ENDPROC
```

You can write this method without ever seeing a line of the `Statement` object's code. In fact, this is part of the whole point. Just like you could not care less what makes an elevator work, you could not care less what makes the `Statement` object tick. As long as the developer who created the `Statement` class did the job properly, you can rely on the design document to know how you need to interact with the class. That's all you need.

You can test the method by trading files. You should never have to modify someone else's code—it's none of your business.

By segregating development in this theoretical manner, OOP creates a situation that minimizes the need to modify shared code and, therefore, makes multideveloper teams easier to manage.

Of course, there is another issue to be dealt with here—the issue of integrating classes created by developers into the application's class libraries. This is the job of the class librarian. For more information on the class librarian, refer to Chapter 30.

System Maintenance with OOP

Users like to change things, right? Using the light example, suppose that the user changes the base definition of the light switch. In this example, a light switch has only one property (`Status`) and one method (`Toggle`). Suppose that the company redefined the base light switch (the `Light` class) to add another feature. Now, when the user turns the light off or on, the system tells the user what has been done.

In order to accomplish this, all you need to do is to modify the Light class definition as follows:

```
DEFINE CLASS light AS custom
    status = "OFF"

    PROCEDURE LightSwitch
        IF this.status = "OFF"
            this.status = "ON"
        ELSE
            this.status = "OFF"
        ENDIF
        WAIT WINDOW "Light is now " + this.status
    ENDPROC
ENDDEFINE
```

From this point on, all objects instantiated from the Light class get the changed method. In effect, you have changed the behavior of every object based on this class by adding one line of code to the class definition.

But wait, there's more. Not only have you modified all the objects based on the Light class, but you have also modified every object based on subclasses of light (Dimmer, for example). This is a powerful way to develop reusable code.

The flip side of this is that if you break a class, you might also break all the subclasses based on it, regardless of the application in which the class is used. If you have used a class in a production application, you'll need to be very careful with this.

Summary

In this chapter, you learned object-oriented programming, the concepts behind this supposedly difficult method of creating software, and why you need to use OOP. Now that you know the secrets behind all the ten-dollar words, the next step is to move into the world of OOP with Visual FoxPro.

OOP with Visual FoxPro

28

In Chapter 27, "Introduction to Object-Oriented Programming," you learned the basics of object orientation. This chapter introduces object-oriented programming with Visual FoxPro. You will learn the syntax involved with creating and using visual classes with Visual FoxPro and also look at the Visual Class Designer, a superset of the Form Designer. Finally, you will learn the functions you need so that you can work with and manage class instances.

Creating and Using Classes with Visual FoxPro

In Chapter 27 you briefly learned some of the issues related to creating classes in Visual FoxPro. All the work was done in code, which is a good way to look at creating classes because it provides a clear view of what you can do when you create classes.

The following sections provide a definitive look at the syntax of creating and using classes in Visual FoxPro.

Defining Classes

You define classes using the DEFINE CLASS/ENDDEFINE construct. Here is an example:

```
DEFINE CLASS <classname> AS <baseclass>
    *-- Declaration Code Here
    PROTECTED <list of member variables>

    PROCEDURE <methodproc> (param1, param2 ....)
        LOCAL <list of local variables>
        *-- Procedure Code Here
    ENDPROC

    FUNCTION <methodfunc> (param1, param2 ....)
        LOCAL <list of local variables>
        *-- Function code here
        RETURN <returnval>
    ENDFUNC
ENDDEFINE
```

In the following sections you will read about each portion of the construct separately.

DEFINE CLASS <classname> AS <superclass>

This line of code tells Visual FoxPro that you are creating a class. All code between DEFINE and ENDDEFINE relates to this class. <classname> is the name of the class. <superclass> is the name of the class upon which the class is based. This can be a built-in class provided with Visual FoxPro 3.0 or a class that you create or purchase.

The term *superclass* used here is in line with terminology used in most texts that discuss object orientation. Unfortunately, Microsoft uses the term *parentclass* to mean the same thing. Don't let the terminology throw you.

By definition, every class created in Visual FoxPro is a subclass of another class. At the highest level, classes created in Visual FoxPro are subclasses of what Microsoft calls *base classes*, the classes that ship with Visual FoxPro. Visual FoxPro 3.0 comes with the base classes shown in Table 28.1.

Table 28.1. Visual FoxPro 3.0 base classes.

Class Name	Description	Visual	Form Controls Toolbar	Subclass Only
CheckBox	A standard check box control similar to the check box created in FoxPro 2.*x*.	√	√	
Column	A column on a grid control.	√	√	
ComboBox	A combo box similar to the pop-up control in FoxPro 2.*x*.	√	√	
CommandButton	Equivalent to a push button in FoxPro 2.*x*.	√	√	
CommandGroup	A group of command buttons that operate together. Equivalent to a group of push buttons in FoxPro 2.*x* controlled by one variable.	√	√	
Container	A generic object designed to hold other objects. This is useful when you are creating a class that has more than one object on it.	√		√
Control	The same as the container class with one major difference: In a container class, when the object is instantiated from the class, you can address all objects within the container. The Control class hides all internal objects and only allows communication with the control class.	√		√
Cursor	A cursor definition in a data environment.			

continues

Table 28.1. continued

Class Name	Description	Visual	Form Controls Toolbar	Subclass Only
Custom	Primarily used for objects that are not visual but may contain visual objects as members.			√
Data Environment	A collection of cursors and relations to open or close as a unit.			
EditBox	The equivalent of a FoxPro 2.6 edit region.	√	√	√
Form	A single "screen." This is a container object in that it may (and usually does) contain other objects. The equivalent of a FoxPro 2.x screen.	√	√	√
FormSet	A container-type object that has one or more forms as members. This is the equivalent to a FoxPro 2.x screen set.		√	√
Grid	A container-type object that allows display and editing of information in browse-type format.	√	√	√
Header	The header of a grid column.	√		
Image	A picture.	√	√	√
Label	The equivalent of placing text on a screen in FoxPro 2.x.	√	√	√
Line	A drawn line.	√	√	√
ListBox	The equivalent of the FoxPro 2.x scrolling list control.	√	√	√
OleControl	A control based on an OLE 2 object.	√	√	√
OptionButton	A single radio button–type object.	√		
OptionGroup	Multiple radio buttons that operate as a single control. This is the equivalent of a FoxPro 2.x radio button object.	√	√	√
Page	A single page within a page frame.	√		
PageFrame	A tabbed control. Each tab within a tab control is a separate page. The page frame control is a container-type control because it can (and usually does) contain many objects.	√	√	√

Class Name	Description	Visual	Form Controls Toolbar	Subclass Only
Relation	A definition of a relation between two cursors in a data environment.			
Shape	A shape (such as a circle or a box).	√	√	
Spinner	The equivalent of the FoxPro 2.*x* spinner control.	√	√	
TextBox	The equivalent of a FoxPro 2.*x* "plain" GET control.	√	√	
Timer	A visual object that does not display on a form. This control is designed to allow for actions at certain timed intervals.		√	
ToolBar	A toolbar, which is a group of objects that can be docked at the the top or bottom, or on the sides of the desktop. When not docked, a toolbar looks something like a form.	√		√

As Table 28.1 indicates, classes can be categorized in three ways. "Visual," "Form Control Toolbar," and "Visual Class Designer Only." Classes can be visual or nonvisual. A visual class "displays," whereas a nonvisual class does not have a display component attached to it. In addition, some classes are not available from the Form Controls toolbar. Finally, some classes are available only in the Visual Class Designer for subclassing, not for use as controls.

The Visual column specifies whether a base class is visual or nonvisual in nature. Form Controls Toolbar specifies whether the base class is available on that toolbar. Subclass Only specifies those base classes that are intended for subclassing and provide little functionality on their own (for example, the Container class).

Most classes are available in the Form Designer from the Form Controls toolbar, but others are not. Of those classes that are not available from the Form Controls toolbar, some (such as Page, Header, and OptionButton) are not available because they are members of other objects. For example, Page is a member of PageFrame, Header is a member of Grid, and OptionButton is a member of OptionGroup. FormSet is not a control per se but rather a container of forms; it is created by combining multiple forms together.

Finally, some classes are specifically designed for subclassing and are only available either in code or through the Visual Class Designer. You will learn about the Visual Class Designer in the section, "The Visual Class Designer."

The classes that are controls available within the Form Designer are discussed in Chapter 12, "Designing and Customizing Forms." In addition to the base classes included with Visual FoxPro 3.0, you can base classes on your own classes. Finally, the DEFINE CLASS/ENDCLASS structure must live on its own and cannot be nested within a loop or a decision structure (such as IF/ENDIF). Think of each class definition construct as its own "procedure" and you'll be fine.

*--Declaration Code Here/PROTECTED <list of member variables>

Declaration code is the code you use to declare your class member variables. Only the member variables listed here will be properties of objects instantiated from this class (with the exception of member objects, which are discussed later in this chapter in the section titled "Creating Composite Classes"). If a member variable is an array, you would declare the array in this section of code.

Another important piece in this section is the declaration of protected members. A *protected member* is a member variable that is not visible outside of the class. In other words, methods within the class can access and modify that variable, but the variable does not exist as far as the outside world (anything that is not a method of the class) is concerned.

You declare member variables protected by using the keyword PROTECTED and then listing the member variables that you want protected. For example,

```
PROTECTED cProtected
```

will create a protected member variable called cProtected. You must declare a property protected within the declaration section of the DEFINE CLASS construct.

An example of a member variable that would be declared PROTECTED is a member that saves the state of the environment when the object is instantiated. The variable can be used to reset the environment when the object is released, but it serves no purpose to programs instantiating the object and interacting with it. As a matter of fact, you would not want this member variable to be changed by the outside world. Hence, you would protect it in the declaration section of code.

PROCEDURE <methodproc> (param1, param2...)/ENDPROC
FUNCTION <methodfunc> (param1, param2...)/ENDFUNC

This line of code defines a method. *<methodproc>* and *<methodfunc>* refer to the name of the method. Note that you can call a method a PROCEDURE or a FUNCTION as you prefer—both syntaxes are equivalent. I like to use the FUNCTION syntax if the method is intended to return a value, otherwise I use PROCEDURE.

Parameters sent to a method can be accepted with a PARAMETERS statement (more typically LPARAMETERS), or the parameters can be accepted in parentheses after the name of the method. For example, if a method called ShowVals were to accept two parameters (Parm1 and Parm2), the code to accept these parameters would look like this:

```
PROCEDURE ShowVals
LPARAMETERS Parm1, Parm2
```

Or this:

```
PROCEDURE ShowVals(Parm1, Parm2)
```

Of the two, I prefer the second syntax because I think it reads better. But you can choose either one.

Be aware that parameters sent through to methods, whether the parameters are called as a procedure (such as loObject.Method(Parm1)) or a function (such as lcVar = loObject.Method(Parm1)), are treated like parameters sent through to a user-defined function: They are sent through by VALUE unless either SET UDFPARMS has been set to REFERENCE (I don't recommend changing the setting of SET UDFPARMS) or the name of the parameter is sent through with the @ sign.

For example, note the following test procedure. The return values quoted assume the default setting of SET UDFPARMS.

```
lcText = "Menachem"
loX = CREATEOBJECT("test")

*-- Call testfunc first as a procedure and then as a method
*-- without specificying by reference.

loX.testfunc(lcText)      && "Proc" Syntax
? lcText                  && Shows "Menachem"

=loX.testfunc(lcText)     && Func Syntax
? lcText                  && Shows "Menachem"

loX.testfunc(@lcText)     && "Proc" Syntax
? lcText                  && Shows 10
lcText = "Menachem"       && Reset for next test

=loX.testfunc(@lcText)    && Func Syntax
? lcText                  && Shows 10
lcText = "Menachem"       && Reset for next test

loX.testproc(lcText)      && "Proc" Syntax
? lcText                  && Shows "Menachem"

=loX.testproc(lcText)     && Func Syntax
? lcText                  && Shows "Menachem"

loX.testproc(@lcText)     && "Proc" Syntax
? lcText                  && Shows 10
lcText = "Menachem"       && Reset for next test

=loX.testproc(@lcText)    && Func Syntax
? lcText                  && Shows 10
lcText = "Menachem"       && Reset for next test

DEFINE CLASS test AS custom
    FUNCTION testfunc (Parm1)
        Parm1 = 10
```

```
    ENDFUNC

    PROCEDURE testproc (Parm1)
        Parm1 = 10
    ENDPROC
ENDDEFINE
```

Methods can be protected like member variables (that is, they can only be called from other methods in the class) by adding the keyword PROTECTED before PROCEDURE or FUNCTION (that is, PROTECTED PROCEDURE *<methodproc>*). Methods that are protected do not exist outside the class, and if an attempt is made to call them, an error is generated.

As a general rule, methods should be protected if they are not intended for the "outside world." This saves you a lot of trouble down the road. For example, a method that is intended only to be called by other methods in the class would be protected.

If a method has to return a value, a RETURN statement would precede the ENDPROC/ENDFUNC statement as shown in the following example:

```
PROCEDURE ShowDate
    RETURN date()
ENDPROC

FUNCTION FuncShowDate
    RETURN date()
ENDFUNC
```

Methods are closed with the ENDPROC or ENDFUNC command (which command you use depends on the command used to start the method definition).

Instantiating Objects

Objects are instantiated from their classes with the CREATEOBJECT function. Here's the syntax:

```
loObject = CREATEOBJECT(<classname> [, <Parameter list>])
```

The CREATEOBJECT function returns an object reference that is stored in loObject. *<className>* is a string indicating the class to be used for instantiation. Parameters follow in the CREATEOBJECT function (one at a time and separated by commas). Parameters are accepted in the object's Init method. (You will learn the Init method and sending parameters later in this chapter in the section "A Technical Tip—Sending Parameters to an Object.")

In order to instantiate an object with CREATEOBJECT, the class definition has to be available when the CREATEOBJECT function is used. If you have manually coded your classes as opposed to using the Visual Class Designer, as shown in Chapter 29, "Creating Classes with Visual FoxPro," the program that has the class definitions must be available. The program is made available with SET PROCEDURE or by placing the class definitions in a program that is higher in the calling chain.

If you use SET PROCEDURE you can release the procedure file once the object is instantiated. Visual FoxPro loads all the methods into memory when the object is instantiated.

Always remember that an instance is just a memory variable and follows almost all of the same rules as regular memory variables. Objects can be made local, public, or private and will lose or keep scope like any other memory variable.

There is one significant difference between an object (known as an *instance variable*) and other Visual FoxPro variables: Variables can be thought of as holding *values*, whereas instance variables do not hold values—they hold references to an object which in turn holds the values.

This has three implications. First, an instance variable is always passed to procedures and functions by reference. Second, if an instance variable is copied into another variable, all changes in the second variable affect the same object. Finally, an object is not released until all references to it have been released. Here is an example:

```
loInstance = CREATEOBJECT("Form")
loInstance.Show()                    && Show the form
loVar = loInstance                     && loVar points to the form too, now.
loInstance.Caption = "Hello"      && Caption changes
loVar.Caption = "There"              && Caption changes again
RELEASE loInstance                      && Form does not disappear
RELEASE loVar                              && Now it disappears
```

Calling Methods

You always call methods by specifying the name of the instance variable, then a period, and then the name of the method. Here is an example:

```
loClass.MyMethod
```

Parameters are sent through to a method by listing them in parentheses after the method name. Here is an example:

```
loClass.MyMethod(Parm1, "StringParm2")
```

There is no DO syntax for a method. To call a method and get a return value, the syntax is almost identical. You specify a variable to accept the value as follows:

```
lcRetVal = loClass.MyMethod(Parm1, "StringParm2")
```

If no parameters are sent through to the method, you can still use parentheses after the method name. Here is an example:

```
loClass.MyMethod
```

I use this syntax exclusively because it is much clearer that the member you are accessing is a method and not a property.

Base Events, Methods, and Properties

As you know from reading the Form Designer chapters, different controls have different events, methods, and properties. For example, the Label control has a `Caption` property, whereas the TextBox control has a `Value` property.

Each control shown in the default Form Controls toolbar is a base class in Visual FoxPro and can be used as the basis for your own classes.

In addition to the classes shown in the Form Controls toolbar, there are four classes specifically designed to be used as the basis for user-defined classes. They do not show up on the Form Controls toolbar nor are they part of other classes (such as an OptionButton, which is part of an OptionGroup control). These classes are `Container`, `Control`, `Custom`, and `ToolBar`.

Although each base class supports its own set of events, properties, and methods, there is a common set of events, methods, and properties that apply to all base classes in Visual FoxPro.

Base Properties

The following list shows the properties that are common to all of Visual FoxPro's base classes.

Property	Description
Class	The name of the object's class
BaseClass	The name of the object's base class
ClassLibrary	The full path of the class library where this class is defined
ParentClass	The name of the class this class is based on

Base Events and Methods

The following list shows the events and methods that are common to all of Visual FoxPro's base classes.

Event	Description
Init	Invoked when the object is created. Accepts parameters sent through to the object. Returning `.F.` aborts object instantiation.
Destroy	Invoked when the object is released.
Error	Invoked when an error occurs inside one of the object's methods.

In the next chapter you will learn the properties and methods of the four special base classes just mentioned.

The *Error* Method

The `Error` method is important and is worthy of special note. The `Error` method is called in the event an `ON ERROR`-type error occurs in a class. The `Error` method takes precedence over the setting of `ON ERROR`, which is important because this enables you to encapsulate error handling where it belongs—within the class itself. You will see examples of the `Error` method and its uses in the next chapter.

Creating Composite Classes

A *composite class* is a class that has members that are themselves instances of other classes. A perfect example of this is a class based on a container-type class, such as a form. When you think of it, a form in and of itself is a class; yet, the objects in it are classes, too. Therefore, you have one object that has other objects contained in it (hence the name container class).

When you work with code you can add object members in one of two ways. The first way uses the `ADD OBJECT` command and is called within the declaration section of code. Here is the syntax:

```
ADD OBJECT <ObjectName> AS <ClassName> ;
    [ WITH <membervar> = <value>, <membervar> = <value> ... ]
```

`<ObjectName>` is the name you want to give to the instance variable being added to the class. `<ClassName>` is the class upon which `<ObjectName>` is based. You can, optionally, specify special settings for member variables of the added object by setting them after a `WITH` clause. Here is an example:

```
DEFINE CLASS Foo AS FORM
    ADD OBJECT myCommandButton AS CommandButton ;
        WITH    caption = "Hello", ;
                height = 50
ENDDEFINE
```

When class `Foo` is instantiated, a member variable called `myCommandButton` is added to the form with a height of 50 pixels and a caption of "Hello." When the form is shown, the command button will be happily waiting for you to click it.

The second syntax is the `AddObject` method. This method can be called from either inside the class or outside the class. This means that you can add objects to container-type objects on the fly. Here is the syntax of the `AddObject` method:

```
<object>.AddObject(<Member Name>,<Class Name>[, Parameters])
```

To mimic the prior example (note that I will not even define a class for this one), I could do this:

```
loFoo = CREATEOBJECT("Form")
loFoo.AddObject("myCommandButton", "CommandButton")
```

```
loFoo.MyCommandButton.Caption = "Hello"
loFoo.MyCommandButton.Height = 50
loFoo.MyCommandButton.Visible = .T.
loFoo.Show
```

Accessing Child Member Variables and Methods

As far as Visual FoxPro is concerned, using the object names from the previous example, `loFoo` is a parent object and `MyCommandButton` is a child object. As you just saw, the properties of the child object, `MyCommandButton`, can only be accessed by going through its parent.

> **TIP**
>
> Composite objects can have members that are themselves composite objects. This can lead to a very long "path" to get to a member variable. If you want to cut through the keystrokes, copy a reference to the object to which you're trying to get to another memory variable and work with it that way. For example, if you have an object with the following hierarchy:
>
> `MyForm.MyPageFrame.myContainer.myTextBox`
>
> and you want to work with the text box for a little while, just do this:
>
> `loMyObj = MyForm.MyPageFrame.myContainer.myTextBox`
>
> From here on you can access all the properties and methods of `MyTextBox` through `loMyObj`. This can save you a lot of typing. Remember, though, that you will not be able to get rid of any parent objects of `myTextBox` without first releasing `loMyObj`.

Differences Between *ADD OBJECT* and *AddObject*

A review of the code examples for `ADD OBJECT` and `AddObject` show some differences. First of all, `ADD OBJECT` enables you to set properties on the calling line, whereas `AddObject` does not. You have to access the member variables individually. Secondly, when a visual object is added to a container with `AddObject`, the object is hidden by default (its `Visible` property is set to `.F.`) to enable you to set the display characteristics before showing the control. `AddObject` enables you to send parameters to the object's `Init` method, whereas `ADD OBJECT` does not. Finally, `ADD OBJECT` enables you to turn off the `Init` method when you instantiate the member object with the `NOINIT` clause; `AddObject` does not have this capability.

THIS Revisited

In the last chapter you learned a special keyword called THIS. The purpose of the THIS keyword is to enable a class to refer to itself. There are three additional keywords along this line that are applicable for composite classes only. Here is a list of these keywords:

THISFORM	This keyword is special for members of Form-based classes. It refers to the form on which an object lies.
THISFORMSET	This keyword is special for members of a form that is part of FormSet. It refers to the FormSet object of which the current object is a member.
PARENT	This keyword refers to the parent of the current object.

Note that you can move up the hierarchy with this.parent.parent.parent (you get the idea).

Adding Objects with *CreateObject*

Can you add an object to another object with CREATEOBJECT? In effect, can you do this:

```
DEFINE CLASS test AS custom
    oForm = .NULL.

    PROCEDURE INIT
        this.oForm = CREATEOBJECT("form")
    ENDPROC
ENDDEFINE
```

The short answer is yes and no. Sound confusing? Let me explain. The code snippet shown here does indeed create an object with a member called oForm that is an object. However, oForm is not a child of the object. oForm is a member variable that is an object. This might sound as if I'm splitting hairs, but there are some very important differences.

First of all, the PARENT keyword will not work with oForm. Second, because the member object is not a child object, you can do some interesting things. Take a look at this bit of code:

```
DEFINE CLASS foo AS form
    ADD OBJECT myForm AS Form ;
        WITH    caption = "Hello", ;
                height = 50
ENDDEFINE

DEFINE CLASS bar AS form
    PROCEDURE init
        this.addobject("myForm", "Form")
    ENDPROC
ENDDEFINE

DEFINE CLASS foobar AS Form
    oForm = .NULL.
```

```
    PROCEDURE init
        this.oForm = CREATEOBJECT("form")
    ENDPROC
ENDDEFINE
```

Neither class Foo nor Bar will work. If you try to instantiate them, you get an error because you cannot add an object based on any descendant of the Form class to a form-based object. The last iteration, class FooBar, works just fine. You'll see a more practical example of this capability in Chapter 31, "Advanced Object-Oriented Programming."

How Are Classes Created in Visual FoxPro?

So far, all the examples you have seen for creating classes in Visual FoxPro deal with code. In fact, as shown in Table 28.1 and further detailed in Chapter 29, there are some classes that can only be created using a coded program.

For the most part, however, creating classes is much more efficient using the Visual Class Designer—the tool provided with Visual FoxPro to make the job of creating classes easier.

Why a Visual Class Designer?

Why do you need a Visual Class Designer when you can easily create classes with code? There are three reasons why the Visual Class Designer is integral to class development. The first reason is that it insulates you from the intricacies of code. Although you have learned the syntax for creating classes, you should not have to remember and type in the constructs and keywords related to the structure of a defined class. The Visual Class Designer handles this for you.

The second reason is that some classes can get complex rather quickly. This is especially true of some visual classes, such as forms (where the placement of the objects within the container are critical). Creating complex classes can best be done visually.

Finally, only classes created with the Visual Class Designer can be managed with the Class Browser, a wonderful tool provided with the product. The Class Browser is discussed in Chapter 30, "Managing Classes with Visual FoxPro."

All three reasons are valid for using the Visual Class Designer. That's why I recommend that you use it whenever you can for developing classes.

The Visual Class Designer

The Visual Class Designer is a superset of the Form Designer. In fact, the Visual Class Designer is so much like a Form Designer that the metafile it uses to store the classes you create is a copy of the SCX/SCT file structure. The only difference here is that the extension given a class file is .VCX instead of .SCX, and a .VCX can hold many classes in one file as opposed to just one form (in an .SCX).

When you create classes visually, Visual FoxPro 3.0 gives you access to the Controls toolbar, the Properties window, and the visual canvas.

Figure 28.1 shows the Visual Class Designer when you are working on a command button–based class.

FIGURE 28.1.

The Visual Class Designer.

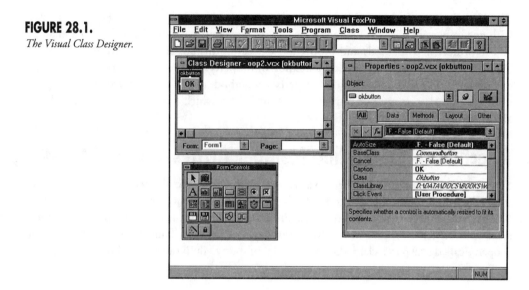

All the options on the menu operate in an almost identical manner to their counterparts on the Form Designer. Rather than cover the Visual Class Designer in detail, I only cover instances where it differs from the Form Designer.

Design Surface Differences

The first difference is the most apparent but technically is not really a difference at all. In the Form Designer, the object being modified is a form. A form is a container object and therefore can have many objects on it. Figure 28.1 only shows a command button. That's because the class being designed is a subclass of CommandButton, which does not support adding other objects to it. Therefore, all you see is the single object on which you are working. If you are working on a Form type class in the Visual Class Designer, the canvas looks the same as it does in the Form Designer.

Menu Differences

Menu options that are specific to forms, such as Create Form Set, Remove Form Set, and so on, are not on the Visual Class Designer's class menu. The Visual Class Designer does add one menu option, Class Info, and the operation of New Methods and New Properties is slightly changed. These changes are discussed first.

Adding Properties and Methods

The New Property and New Method menu options work as they do in the Form Designer, with one important change: There is a new check box control on the dialog box that enables you to protect new methods and properties. Checking this box means that the property or method is protected. To "unprotect" a method or property, you need to use the Edit Property or Edit Method option. Note that a property or method, once protected, cannot be unprotected in a subclass. It must be unprotected at the level at which it was added to the class hierarchy.

A Technical Tip—Adding Member Arrays to a VCX Class

Suppose you want to add a property to a class that is an array. In code, because you have access to the declaration section of the code, this is not a problem. However, with visually designed classes you do not have access to the declaration code. The trick is to specify the name of the array with its default length in the New Properties dialog box. Thus, for example, to add a property called aProp to a class, the name of the property you type in would be this:

```
aProp[1]
```

The array subscript tells Visual FoxPro that the property you are adding is an array. If you look at the new property in the Properties window, you'll notice that the new array is read-only. Don't worry about this; it just means that you have to work with the array in code. There is no provision for setting values in arrays in the Properties window.

Accessing Class Information

The Class Info menu option gives the developer access to information about the class being modified with the dialog box shown in Figure 28.2.

The Class tab on this page frame shows some basic information about the class. Here is a list of the options:

Toolbar Icon	This modifiable option specifies which icon will show in the Form Controls toolbar when the VCX file is loaded. Clicking the command button to the right of the text box displays a GETPICT dialog box that enables you to select a graphics file.

Container Icon	This is the same idea as the Toolbar Icon except that it deals with the icon shown for this class in the Class Browser. The Class Browser is discussed in Chapter 30.
Scale Units	This option determines whether the grid is measured in terms of pixels or foxels.
Description	This is an edit box in which the developer can enter a description of the class.
Class Name	This is the name of the class being modified.
Parent Class	This is the name of the class upon which this class is based (that is, the immediate superclass).
Class Library	This is the name of the VCX file in which the class is stored.

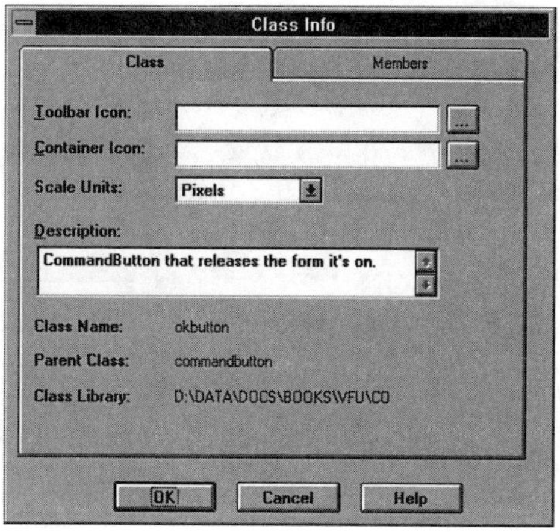

FIGURE 28.2.

The Class Info dialog box.

The next tab is the Members tab, and it shows the members of the current class. Members of the class can be properties, methods, events, or objects. Object members occur if the class is a composite (container-type) class.

This tab, which is shown in Figure 28.3, has a list of all the members of the class and enables the developer to protect any or all of them by checking the box in the Protected column. The No Init column is only applicable for object members and tells Visual FoxPro whether or not to run the Init event for this object when it is added at runtime. Checking the box means that the Init event is skipped.

Now that you have seen how to use the Visual Class Designer, the next step is to look at the syntax involved in getting into the Visual Class Designer. Obviously, there are two modes: CREATE and MODIFY.

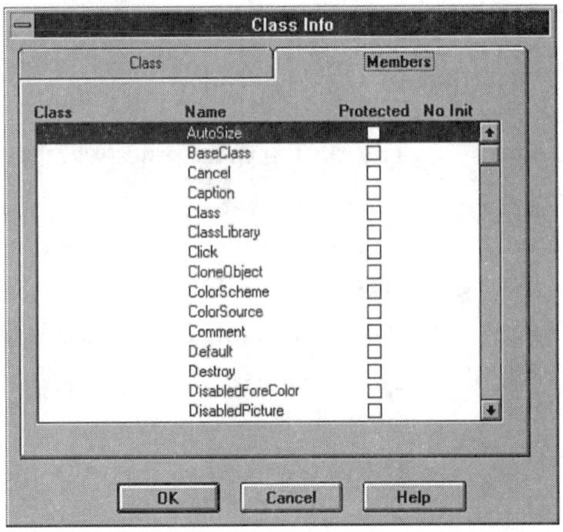

FIGURE 28.3.

The Members tab for the Class Info dialog box.

Creating a Class

A new class can be created with the CREATE CLASS command. Issuing CREATE CLASS with no additional information presents the dialog box shown in Figure 28.4.

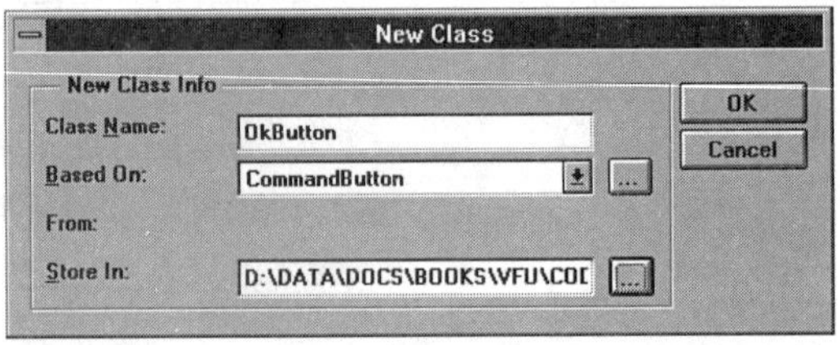

FIGURE 28.4.

The New Class dialog box.

Classes can be based on Visual FoxPro base classes (listed in the drop-down list box) or on any class you create. In order to base your new class on a class you have created (as opposed to one Visual FoxPro supplies for you), click the ellipsis (…) command button, and a dialog box will display enabling you to select the class you want to use (shown in Figure 28.5). The left portion of the dialog box is a GETFILE type display that enables you to select a VCX file. Once you select a VCX file, the classes it contains will show in the list to the right. You can then select a class to open and click the Open command button. The Visual Class Designer then comes up.

Note that you can only use a class stored in a VCX file as the base class for another VCX-stored class. Figure 28.6 shows the New Class dialog box once the parent class has been selected.

Another way to create a class and bypass the dialog box is to provide all the information needed to create the class on the command line. Here's the syntax for this:

```
CREATE CLASS <ClassName> OF <ClassLibraryName1>    ;
      AS cBaseClassName [FROM ClassLibraryName2]
```

FIGURE 28.5.

The dialog box in which you can select a class.

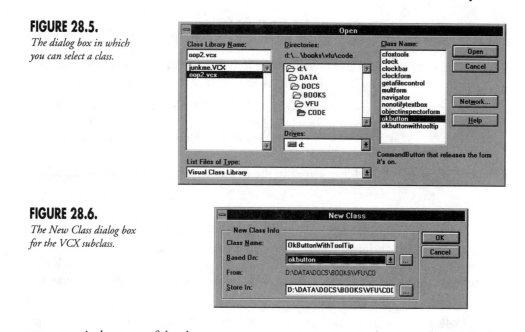

FIGURE 28.6.

The New Class dialog box for the VCX subclass.

ClassName is the name of the class to create. *ClassLibraryName1* is the name of the VCX file in which to store the class. If the VCX file does not exist, Visual FoxPro creates it for you (note that you can create a class library too with the CREATE CLASSLIB command). *cBaseClassName* is the name of the class on which to base the new class. This can be a Visual FoxPro base class or a class you create. If it's a class you have created, you must specify the VCX file it is stored in with *ClassLibraryName2*. You'll need to specify the class library name from where the super-class is coming even if it comes from the same VCX file where the new class is stored.

Modifying Classes in a VCX File

Classes are loaded for modification into the Visual Class Designer with the MODIFY CLASS command. Here's the basic syntax:

```
MODIFY CLASS <ClassName> OF <ClassLibraryName>
```

ClassName is the name of the class to modify, and *ClassLibraryName* is the name of the VCX file containing the class to be modified. If you prefer a more visual method of selecting a class to edit, you can issue this:

```
MODIFY CLASS
```

without any additional information, and Visual FoxPro will display the same dialog box shown in Figure 28.5.

Using Classes in a VCX File

Classes created with the Visual Class Designer are stored in a VCX file (also called a *class library*). The structure of the table is the same as the structure of the SCX file.

In order to instantiate an object from a class stored in a VCX file, the class library must be loaded with the SET CLASSLIB command. Here is the syntax:

```
SET CLASSLIB TO <vcxFileName> [ADDITIVE]
```

Once the class library is loaded, any classes in the class library can be used for instantiating objects.

Be careful of one thing. As you saw previously in this chapter, a class in a VCX file can be a subclass of a class stored in another class library. Make sure that all the VCX files you need are loaded with SET CLASSLIB before you instantiate objects. A good strategy is to load all the VCX files used in an application at the beginning. This way you will be sure not to miss a VCX file when you need it. Also, be sure to use the ADDITIVE keyword when adding additional class libraries or else the ones already loaded will be released.

In order to release a single class library, use the RELEASE CLASSLIB command. To release all the class libraries, issue a SET CLASSLIB TO command without specifying a class library file. By the way, if all of this syntax looks familiar, it should. This is one thing Microsoft did really well—they kept the syntax for similar commands, such as SET LIBRARY and SET PROCEDURE, virtually identical.

A Technical Tip—Sending Parameters to an Object

Sometimes, when you instantiate an object it may be necessary to send parameters through to the object. For example, if you were creating an object that displays a message (I know there is a MessageBox function, but please bear with me), you might want to send parameters through that indicate the message text, the form caption, and so on.

The syntax for sending parameters through when instantiating an object is simple—all you do is add the parameters (separated by commas) after the name of the class from which you are instantiating. Here is an example:

```
loForm = CREATEOBJECT("MyMsgForm", "Hello. This is a message.")
```

This line of code instantiates an object called loForm from the "MyMsgForm" class and passes through the string "Hello. This is a message." as a parameter.

The next question is where do you accept the parameters? The answer is in the Init method. But beware, unlike sending parameters through in FoxPro 2.6, parameters in Visual FoxPro that are accepted in the Init method will be released when the Init method completes. Don't forget that Init is a procedure and thus causes its parameters to lose scope when it returns from where it was called.

How do you keep the parameters around? If the parameters are intended to be sent through by value (which is usually the case) you can move the parameters' values into the custom properties of the object. You can't pass a parameter and have it stick around to be modified.

Managing Instances with *AInstance*

Visual FoxPro can give you a list of instances created for a particular class with the AInstance function. Here is the syntax of this function:

```
lnNumInstances = AInstance(<ArrayName>, <ClassName>)
```

The AInstance function returns a numeric value: the number of instances found.

For example, in order to determine how many instances have been created for class FORM, you would issue the following command:

```
lnNumInstances = AInstance(laInstances, "Form")
```

The variable lnNumInstances has the number of instances found, and the array laInstances has a list of the instance variables instantiated from class Form.

Note that this function only returns member variables created with CREATEOBJECT that are not themselves members of other objects. For example, if you had an instance of class Form that was a member of another object, this instance would not show up with AInstance.

AInstance can have many uses. A more common one is to use it to manage multiple instances of a class (a form, for example). The following example illustrates such a use. In the Init method of this form class, the AInstance function checks for the number of instances of this class. Each instance of the class has a custom property called nInstanceNumber that holds the instance number of the form. The Init method determines the instance number for this instance and then adds the instance number to the caption of the form. (Note that if this is the first instance of the form, the caption remains unmodified.) The Init method could do more. For instance, many developers adjust the Top and Left properties to cascade the form on the desktop. Here's the code:

```
*   Class.............: Multform
*   Author............: Menachem Bazian, CPA
*   Project...........: Visual FoxPro Unleashed!
*   Copyright.........: (c) Flash Creative Management, Inc. 1995
*   Notes.............: Exported code from Class Browser.

****************************************************
*-- Class:        multform (d:\data\docs\books\vfu\code\oop2.vcx)
*-- ParentClass:  form
*-- BaseClass:    form
*
```

```
DEFINE CLASS multform AS form

    DoCreate = .T.
    Caption = "Form"
    Name = "multform"

    *-- The Instance Number of this form
    ninstancenumber = .F.

    PROCEDURE Init
        *-- This code will determine what instance number
        *-- this form is and set the header accordingly.

        LOCAL lnNumInstances, lnThisInstance, lcInstance

        lnNumInstances = AInstance(laInstances, this.class)
        lnThisInstance = 1
        FOR lnCounter = 1 TO lnNumInstances
            lcInstance = laInstances[lnCounter]
            lnThisInstance = MAX(lnThisInstance,&lcInstance..nInstanceNumber + 1)
        ENDFOR

        this.nInstanceNumber = lnThisInstance

        IF lnThisInstance > 1
            this.caption = ALLTRIM(this.caption) + ": " + ALLT(STR(lnThisInstance))
        ENDIF
    ENDPROC

ENDDEFINE
*
*-- EndDefine: multform
****************************************************
```

ACLASS

If you have an involved class hierarchy, it can be difficult to remember what classes precede the instantiated class in the hierarchy. Take, for example, the following class hierarchy:

```
DEFINE CLASS myBaseForm AS FORM
ENDDEFINE

DEFINE CLASS myModalBaseForm AS MyBaseForm
ENDDEFINE

DEFINE CLASS ModalDialog AS myModalBaseForm
ENDDEFINE
```

When an object is instantiated from ModalDialog, you might wonder what the class hierarchy looks like. ACLASS answers that question. If you assume this:

```
loModalDialog = CREATEOBJECT("ModalDialog")
lnNumClasses = ACLASS(laClasses, loModalDialog)
```

then laClasses will have this:

```
LACLASSES  Pub                 A
   ( 1)  C        "MODALDIALOG"
   ( 2)  C        "MYMODALBASEFORM"
   ( 3)  C        "MYBASEFORM"
   ( 4)  C        "FORM"
```

AMembers

Another very useful function is the AMembers function. This function populates an array with the members of an instance. It comes in two flavors:

```
lnNumMembers = AMembers(<ArrayName>, <InstanceVar>)
```

and

```
lnNumMembers = AMembers(<ArrayName>, <InstanceVar>, 1)
```

The first version of this function creates an array with the properties of an instance. The array is unidimensional. For example, to see the properties of the _Screen object, you would state this:

```
lnNumMembers = AMembers(laMembers, _screen)
```

This function returns an array with the following information (for brevity, only the first few elements are shown here):

```
LAMEMBERS   Pub                    A
             (    1)  C        "ACTIVECONTROL"
             (    2)  C        "ACTIVEFORM"
             (    3)  C        "ALWAYSONTOP"
             (    4)  C        "AUTOCENTER"
             (    5)  C        "BACKCOLOR"
             (    6)  C        "BASECLASS"
             (    7)  C        "BORDERSTYLE"
             (    8)  C        "BUFFERMODE"
             (    9)  C        "CAPTION"
             (   10)  C        "CLASS"
```

The second version creates a two-dimensional array. The first column is the name of the member and the second column is the type of the member (event, method, object, or property). Here is an example that inspects _Screen and returns the following results:

```
lnNumMembers = AMembers(laMembers, _screen, 1)

LAMEMBERS   Pub        A
  (  1,  1)  C        "ACTIVATE"
  (  1,  2)  C        "Event"
  (  2,  1)  C        "ACTIVECONTROL"
  (  2,  2)  C        "Property"
  (  3,  1)  C        "ACTIVEFORM"
  (  3,  2)  C        "Property"
  (  4,  1)  C        "ADDOBJECT"
  (  4,  2)  C        "Method"
```

```
(  5, 1) C      "ALWAYSONTOP"
(  5, 2) C      "Property"
(  6, 1) C      "AUTOCENTER"
(  6, 2) C      "Property"
(  7, 1) C      "BACKCOLOR"
(  7, 2) C      "Property"
(  8, 1) C      "BASECLASS"
(  8, 2) C      "Property"
(  9, 1) C      "BORDERSTYLE"
(  9, 2) C      "Property"
( 10, 1) C      "BOX"
( 10, 2) C      "Method"
```

Note that the second version of AMembers returns a two-dimensional array and shows more members of the object than the first version. Without the additional ,1 parameter, only properties of the object are returned. The ,1 parameter adds methods, objects, and events to the list. Each version of this function has its uses. To look at an object when you are concerned only with its properties, you would use the first version of this function. To get more information, you would use the second version.

Inspecting Objects with *AMembers*

One of the more difficult aspects of working with object-oriented code is that a single memory variable can have a great deal of data and code attached to it. Take _Screen, for example. _Screen is a system memory variable that is an object based on the class Form. Changes made to _Screen are reflected in the main Visual FoxPro window. Thus, you could reset the title of the main Visual FoxPro window with this line of code:

```
_Screen.Caption = "Visual FoxPro UNLEASHED With Object Orientation!"
```

In order to properly use this nifty little object, it is necessary to learn what is attached to the memory variable. AMembers is a useful way to get this information, as you saw in the previous example. The basic problem with this approach, though, is that there is so much information returned by AMembers that it is very difficult to make sense of it all. Clearly it would be beneficial to have some manner of presenting the information in a more useful format.

There are several ways to accomplish this goal. One simple method is to create the array with AMembers and to read the resultant array into a cursor. Here's a procedure that accomplishes this for you:

```
*   Program...........: CURSMEMB.PRG
*   Author............: Menachem Bazian, CPA
*   Project...........: Visual FoxPro Unleashed!
*   Created...........: May 16, 1995 - 21:23:07
*   Copyright.........: (c) Flash Creative Management, Inc., 1995
*) Description.......: Creates a cursor of the members of an object
*   Calling Samples...: =CURSMEMB(oObject)
*   Parameter List....: toObject - The Object to View
```

```
*  Major change list.:

LPARAMETERS toObject

IF TYPE("toObject") # "O"
    =MessageBox("Parameter must be an object!", 16)
    RETURN
ENDIF

*-- If we get this far, we can read the object...

LOCAL laMembers[1]
=AMEMBERS(laMembers, toObject, 1)

CREATE CURSOR _members (cMembName C(25), ;
                        cMembtype C(25))

INSERT INTO _members FROM ARRAY laMembers

*-- And that's it
RETURN
```

This procedure is called with one parameter: the object to inspect. To see the members of the object, simply browse the _members cursor.

Taking the Inspector One Step Further

The CURSMEMB program provides a simple view of an object, but it still does not go far enough. CURSMEMB replaces an array view with the capability to browse and index a cursor. Although this is certainly an advance in how you can look at an object, it would be useful to see property values where possible and maybe even to get a prettier interface behind the information.

ObjectInspectorForm is a class that accomplishes this. The purpose of this form-based class is to give you a clean and easily readable form that you can use to view the contents of an object. The next section gives you a look at the interface. I will show you how to call the object as well as explain the code behind it.

The User Interface

The interface has three controls. The first is the Order option group object, which enables you to switch between two display orders in the list: alphabetical and grouped. The Alphabetical option button shows all the members of the object in alphabetical order without regard to the type of the members. The Grouped option button shows all the members of a particular type together in alphabetical order. Events show first, then methods, objects, and properties. Figures 28.7 and 28.8 show an example of each display order.

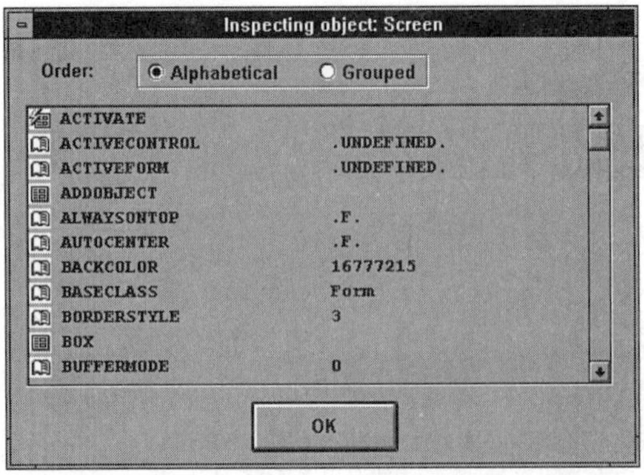

FIGURE 28.7.

*The Object Inspector
showing members in
alphabetical order.*

FIGURE 28.7.

*The Object Inspector
showing members in
alphabetical order.*

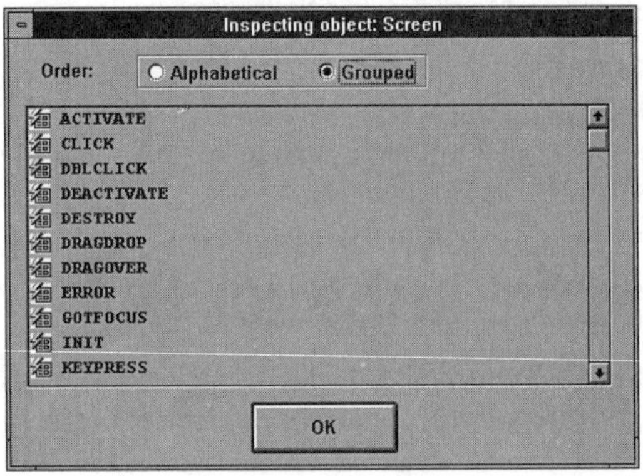

FIGURE 28.8.

*Object Inspector showing
members in grouped order.*

The second control is a list box that lists all the members of the object. The pictures in the following list indicate the type of the objects:

Picture	Description
	Event
	Method
	Object
	Property

Finally, the third control is the OK command button, which releases the form.

All the properties in the list are shown with their values, as best as they can be determined, within the screen. Here is how this is accomplished—first, the class's code:

```
*  Class.............: Objectinspectorform
*  Author............: Menachem Bazian, CPA
*  Project...........: Visual FoxPro Unleashed!
*  Copyright.........: (c) Flash Creative Management, Inc. 1995
*) Description.......:
*  Notes.............: Exported code from Class Browser.

**************************************************
*-- Class:         objectinspectorform (d:\data\docs\books\vfu\code\oop2.vcx)
*-- ParentClass:   form
*-- BaseClass:     form
*
DEFINE CLASS objectinspectorform AS form

    DataSession = 2
    Height = 309
    Width = 466
    DoCreate = .T.
    AutoCenter = .T.
    BackColor = RGB(192,192,192)
    BorderStyle = 3
    Caption = ""
    MaxButton = .F.
    MinButton = .F.
    ClipControls = .F.
    WindowType = 1
    PROTECTED cobjectbmpfile
    cobjectbmpfile = (home()+"SAMPLES\GRAPHICS\BMPS\FOX\APPS.BMP")
    PROTECTED cmethodbmpfile
    cmethodbmpfile = (home()+"SAMPLES\GRAPHICS\BMPS\FOX\CLASSES.BMP")
    PROTECTED cpropertybmpfile
    cpropertybmpfile = (home()+"SAMPLES\GRAPHICS\BMPS\FOX\INDEXES.BMP")
    PROTECTED ceventbmpfile
    ceventbmpfile = (home()+"SAMPLES\GRAPHICS\BMPS\FOX\AUTOFORM.BMP")
    Name = "objectinspectorform"

    ADD OBJECT lstmembers AS listbox WITH ;
        FontName = "Courier New", ;
        Height = 205, ;
        Left = 12, ;
        Top = 48, ;
        Width = 438, ;
        ItemBackColor = RGB(192,192,192), ;
        Name = "lstMembers"

    ADD OBJECT cmdok AS commandbutton WITH ;
        Top = 264, ;
        Left = 180, ;
        Height = 37, ;
        Width = 109, ;
        Cancel = .T., ;
        Caption = "OK", ;
        Default = .T., ;
        Name = "cmdOK"

    ADD OBJECT label1 AS label WITH ;
        AutoSize = .F., ;
        BackStyle = 0, ;
```

```
    Caption = "Order:", ;
    Height = 18, ;
    Left = 24, ;
    Top = 15, ;
    Width = 40, ;
    Name = "Label1"

ADD OBJECT opgorder AS optiongroup WITH ;
    ButtonCount = 2, ;
    BackStyle = 0, ;
    Value = 1, ;
    Height = 25, ;
    Left = 96, ;
    Top = 12, ;
    Width = 217, ;
    Name = "opgOrder", ;
    Option1.BackStyle = 0, ;
    Option1.Caption = "Alphabetical", ;
    Option1.Value = 1, ;
    Option1.Height = 18, ;
    Option1.Left = 0, ;
    Option1.Top = 4, ;
    Option1.Width = 109, ;
    Option1.Name = "optAlphabetical", ;
    Option2.BackStyle = 0, ;
    Option2.Caption = "Grouped", ;
    Option2.Value = 0, ;
    Option2.Height = 18, ;
    Option2.Left = 127, ;
    Option2.Top = 4, ;
    Option2.Width = 73, ;
    Option2.Name = "optGrouped"

PROCEDURE buildlist
    LPARAMETERS toObject

    #DEFINE COLUMNLENGTH 25

    WAIT WINDOW NOWAIT "Building members list. Please stand by..."

    this.lockscreen = .t.
    this.lstMembers.clear()

    SELECT _members

    IF this.opgOrder.value = 1
        SET ORDER TO TAG Alpha
    ELSE
        SET ORDER TO TAG Grouped
    ENDIF

    GO TOP

    lnCounter = 0

    SCAN
        lnCounter = lnCounter + 1
        lcText = PADR(_members.cMembName, COLUMNLENGTH)
```

```
        IF _members.cMembType = "Prop"
            *-- Now we need to get the value of the property
            lcText = lcText + ALLTRIM(_members.cMembVal)
        ENDIF

        thisform.lstMembers.additem(" " + lcText)

        lcBmpVar = "this.c" + alltrim(_members.cMembType)+"bmpfile"
        thisform.lstMembers.picture(lnCounter) = EVAL(lcBmpVar)
    ENDSCAN

    this.lockscreen = .f.
    thisform.refresh()

    WAIT CLEAR
ENDPROC

PROCEDURE Resize
    this.lockscreen = .t.

    this.lstMembers.width = this.width - 24
    this.cmdOk.left = (this.width-this.cmdOk.width)/2
    this.cmdOK.top = (this.height - 8 - this.cmdOK.height)
    this.lstMembers.height = this.cmdOK.top - this.lstMembers.top - 11

    this.lockscreen = .F.
ENDPROC

PROCEDURE Init
    * Class............: OBJECTINSPECTORFORM
    * Author...........: Menachem Bazian, CPA
    * Project..........: Visual FoxPro Unleashed
    * Created..........: May 16, 1995 - 07:44:03
    * Copyright........: (c) Flash Creative Management, Inc., 1995
    *) Description......: When passed an object, it builds a list of the
    *)                  : members and displays them nicely.
    * Calling Samples...: oForm = CREATEOBJECT("OBJECTINSPECTORFORM", oObject)
    * Parameter List....: toObject - Object to inspect
    * Major change list.:

    LPARAMETERS toObject

    this.caption = "Inspecting object: " + ALLT(toObject.Name)

    IF TYPE("toObject") # 'O'
        =MessagebOx("You can only pass OBJECT type parameters!", 16)
        RETURN .F.
    ENDIF

    *-- If we get this far, we can inspect the object
    *-- Let's define some memory variables and do the AMembers()

    LOCAL laMembers[1], lcText, lcName
    =AMembers(laMembers,toObject,1)

    *-- In order to create the list in proper order, it is useful to have
    *-- a table to work off of (so we can INDEX). Hence:
```

```
CREATE CURSOR _members (cMembName C(25), cMembtype C(25), cMembVal C(40))
INSERT INTO _members FROM ARRAY laMembers

INDEX ON cMembName TAG Alpha
INDEX ON cMembType + cMembName TAG Grouped

SCAN FOR _members.cMembType = "Prop"

    *-- Determine the value of the property and place it in the
    *-- cMembVal field

    lcName = "toObject."+ALLTRIM(_members.cMembName)
    DO CASE
        CASE TYPE(lcName) = 'U'
            lcText = ".UNDEFINED."
        CASE isnull(EVAL(lcName))
            lcText = ".NULL."
        CASE TYPE(lcName) = 'L'
            lcText = IIF(EVAL(lcName), ".T.", ".F.")
        OTHERWISE
            lcText = ALLTRIM(PADR(EVALUATE(lcName),50))
    ENDCASE
    REPLACE _members.cMembVal WITH lcText
ENDSCAN

    this.buildlist()
ENDPROC

PROCEDURE cmdok.Click
    release thisform
ENDPROC

PROCEDURE opgorder.Click
    thisform.buildlist()
ENDPROC

ENDDEFINE
*
*-- EndDefine: objectinspectorform
******************************************************
```

You can call the form as follows. (The example shows how you can call the InspectorForm to inspect the _Screen object.)

```
ox=crea("ObjectInspectorForm", _screen)
ox.show()
```

The key work in this class takes place in the form's Init method and in a custom method called BuildList.

The *Init* Method

The Init method has several responsibilities. First of all, it accepts the parameter toObject and makes sure that its data type is Object. If the parameter sent through is not an object, an error message is returned. Note that an error condition causes Init to return .F.. When .F. is returned from Init, the object is not instantiated.

The next step is to create a cursor, much like the one in the CURSMEMB program shown earlier in this chapter. The differences here are threefold. First of all, an additional field called cMembValue is added to the cursor. Second, cMembValue is populated with the actual value of the property. Third, the cursor is indexed. I will use the indexes in BuildList later in this chapter.

You fill in the cMembValue field by creating a text string beginning with "toObject." (remember that toObject is the object passed through on the parameter line) and then adding the name of the object as recorded in the cMembName field. This gives you the name of the property you are trying to evaluate in a format you can use to query the value.

The next step is a little tricky. Sometimes an object might have a property that does not have a value. For example, if _Screen.ActiveForm is queried with no form open, Visual FoxPro returns an error. Checking the type of the property with the TYPE function (? TYPE("_Screen.ActiveForm"), for example) will return "U" for undefined. Therefore, a check has to be made of the data type of the property so as to avoid an error.

A property can also be NULL. You trap for that with the ISNULL function. Finally, a logical value is checked for and converted to a string. All other value types can be converted to a string with the PADR function, as done in the OTHERWISE clause of the CASE statement.

The *BuildList* Method

BuildList is responsible for building the contents of the list box based on the cursor. The method is very simple. It begins by clearing the list with the Clear method. Then the value of the Order option group is queried and the index order is set accordingly. The next step is to loop through the cursor records and add the items from the cursor to the list. This is accomplished by using the AddItem method. Note that the value is added to the string passed through to AddItem for all the PROPERTY-type members. Finally, the picture property of each row is set, based on the type of member stored in the row. The four picture filenames and locations are stored in the custom form properties cEventBMPFile, cMethodBMPFile, cObjectBMPFile, and cPropertyBMPFile.

One interesting tip that comes out of the BuildList method is the use of the LockScreen property of the form. When LockScreen is set to .T., it prevents the display of the form from changing. This is very important in this case because every time AddItem is issued a list box automatically refreshes itself. This slows the process down considerably. By setting LockScreen to .T. for the duration of the list building, you ensure that you get maximum performance out of Visual FoxPro during this process. A final call to the Refresh method after LockScreen is reset redraws everything nicely.

The *Resize* Method

The default size of the form might not be large enough to display a property and its value if the value is a lengthy string. It would be nice to be able to resize the form and have the controls on the form automatically adjust to the new size of the form.

The `Resize` method responds to an event (when the user changes the size of the form, for example). Once the user is done resizing the form, the method is called. The `Resize` method in this case simply recalculates the height and width of the list box and makes sure that the command button is still situated at the bottom of the form. Setting `LockScreen` to `.T.` while the recalculation takes place prevents the controls from adjusting one at a time. It looks cleaner this way (and is more efficient, too).

Summary

In this chapter, you learned object orientation with Visual FoxPro and how to create classes by using code and by using Visual FoxPro's powerful Visual Class Designer. You also saw the tools Visual FoxPro provides to enable you to manage objects and to debug them.

You are now ready for the next step in your journey: a look at the kind of classes you can create in Visual FoxPro with examples for each type of class.

Creating Classes with Visual FoxPro

29

The previous two chapters covered the nuts and bolts of OOP in Visual FoxPro. You learned the applicable concepts behind object orientation in Visual FoxPro in Chapter 27, "Introduction to Object-Oriented Programming," and how classes are created in Chapter 28, "OOP with Visual FoxPro."

In this chapter you learn the typical types of classes you create with Visual FoxPro. Different categories of classes are investigated and explained, and examples of each type of class are presented as well.

Before I go further, I must say that there is no realistic limit to the types of classes you can create with Visual FoxPro (unless you think there are limits to your imagination). For the most part, the classifications presented in this chapter should be representative of what you can do. Don't let anyone tell you that a class you have dreamed up is invalid because it is not listed or does not fit into a category detailed in this or any book. You are the master of your system's destiny. Don't let anyone tell you otherwise.

The types of classes created in this chapter can be placed in two general categories: visual classes and nonvisual classes.

Visual Classes

A *visual class* is a class designed for display purposes. For example, a form is a visual class; so is a command button and a check box. The main purpose behind visual classes is for interface (usually called a Graphical User Interface or GUI) work.

Within this class category you can typically design classes in the following subcategories:

> Single controls
> Combination controls
> Containers
> Forms
> Toolbars

A TERMINOLOGY ISSUE

One of the base classes that comes built in to Visual FoxPro is a control class. In addition to this base class, all other classes used within a form (such as `TextBox`, `CommandButton`, and so on) are also given the generic name of *control.* Sound confusing? You're right, it is.

In order to bring some sense to this terminology, I have adopted the following conventions. When you learn how to create classes based on a form control, such as a

`CommandButton`, you will see the term *single control*. For controls created from the control class, you will see the term *combination control*. These naming conventions work because the purpose of the control class is to combine multiple controls together so that they work as one control.

SHOWING CLASSES IN PRINT

I want to take a moment to explain the code presented in this chapter. You develop classes in Visual FoxPro visually (using the Visual Class Designer). However, for the purpose of this chapter, code is the best way to present the contents of a class.

Fortunately, the Class Browser (which is discussed in Chapter 30, "Managing Classes with Visual FoxPro") includes a function that exports the code of a visual class. The code shown in this chapter (as well as in Chapters 30 and 31, "Advanced Object-Orientated Programming") is exported using the Class Browser.

If you prefer seeing the classes in their original form, they're on the CD-ROM in Chap29.VCX.

Single Control Classes

A *single control* is a class designed to be used as a control on a form. This type of class is based on any FoxPro form control class that does not support the capability to add additional objects to itself. These classes include `CommandButtons`, `TextBoxes`, `Labels`, and so on.

There are two kinds of single control classes you typically create. The first kind is a single control class designed to default to the display characteristics of the control for future use. For example, if you were to decide on a standard font for all your controls (Windows 95 uses 9-point Arial as its standard), you could create single control classes with the proper settings and then subclass them. This ensures a common look throughout your applications. It also provides functionality. The second type of single control classes are created once you are done with the standard look and feel. The classes you create from there on will in all likelihood be for functionality. I will illustrate this second type of class with a few examples.

The OK Command Button

A good example of a single control class is an OK button, which, when pressed, releases the form it is on. `OkButton` is a class that does this.

The following code shows a sample OK button:

```
*   Class.............: Okbutton
*   Author............: Menachem Bazian, CPA
*   Project...........: Visual FoxPro Unleashed!
*   Copyright.........: (c)Flash Creative Management, Inc. 1995
*   Notes.............: Exported code from Class Browser.


**************************************************
*-- Class:         okbutton
*-- ParentClass:   CommandButton
*-- BaseClass:     CommandButton
*-- CommandButton that releases the form it's on.
*
DEFINE CLASS okbutton AS CommandButton

    AutoSize = .F.
    Height = 29
    Width = 41
    Caption = "OK"
    Default = .T.
    Name = "okbutton"

    PROCEDURE Click
        RELEASE thisform
    ENDPROC

ENDDEFINE
*
*-- EndDefine: okbutton
**************************************************
```

This button can be dropped on any form. When it is clicked, it will release the form. Figure 29.1 shows what the OK button looks like when you drop it on a form.

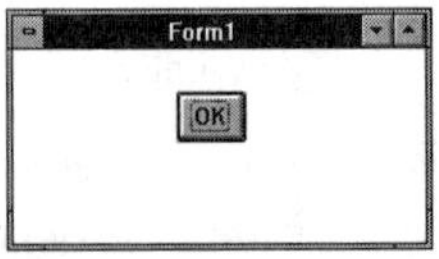

FIGURE 29.1.

*A form with an
OK button.*

Notice that the method for releasing the form is to use RELEASE THISFORM in the Click event. The THISFORM keyword is mentioned in Chapter 28. This command releases the form the OK button is on.

By setting the Default property to .T., the command button's Click event is made to fire automatically when the user presses the Enter key when the cursor is not in an EditBox control. Conversely, if you want the button's Click event to fire when the user presses Esc, you should set the Cancel property of the button to .T..

Subclassing a Single Control Class

Technically, every class created in Visual FoxPro is a subclass of another class. Even the Custom-based classes are subclasses (Custom is the name of a FoxPro base class).

After you create a class, you can subclass it. How this works is detailed in Chapter 28, but here's a little example of it. Suppose you want a special version of the OK button that has ToolTip text attached to it. (*ToolTip text* is the text that pops up when the mouse hovers over a control.) The following code, which creates a class called `OkButtonWithToolTip`, shows how to do this:

```
*  Class.............: Okbuttonwithtooltip
*  Author............: Menachem Bazian, CPA
*  Project...........: Visual FoxPro Unleashed!
*  Copyright.........: (c)Flash Creative Management, Inc. 1995
*  Notes.............: Exported code from Class Browser.


**************************************************
*-- Class:        okbuttonwithtooltip (d:\data\docs\books\vfu\code\oop2.vcx)
*-- ParentClass:  okbutton (d:\data\docs\books\vfu\code\oop2.vcx)
*-- BaseClass:    CommandButton
*-- Subclass of an OK button - adds a ToolTip.
*
DEFINE CLASS okbuttonwithtooltip AS okbutton

    Height = 29
    Width = 41
    ToolTipText = "Releases the form"
    Name = "okbuttonwithtooltip"

ENDDEFINE
*
*-- EndDefine: okbuttonwithtooltip
**************************************************
```

That's all there is to it. Note that there is very little code attached to this button. The `Click` event is not represented here at all. It is inherited from the parent class. In fact, the only relevant code in this class is the value in the `ToolTipText` property.

For the record, most controls have a `ToolTipText` property. You might notice that although the property has been filled, the ToolTip text does not show up when the mouse hovers over the control. If this happens, check out the `ShowTips` property on the form and make sure that it is set to `.T.`. Figure 29.2 shows an example of what you should expect to see.

FIGURE 29.2.

*A sample button
with ToolTip text.*

To make sure that your ToolTip shows up all the time, you should place code in the `MouseMove` event that checks the setting of the `ShowTips` property on the form and sets it to `.T.`. If you're wondering why the code does not go in the `Init` of the button, the answer has to do with the order in which controls are initialized with a container. You will learn about this in a little bit.

Why Subclass?

OkButtonWithToolTip seems to be a rather silly example of a subclass. After all, adding ToolTip text is very simple. Why subclass the button at all? Why not make the change to the OK button itself? It's a judgment call, certainly. However, it is vital to bear in mind that changing a class will change every instance of that class as well as all the descendant subclasses. If you modify the base class, you would be making the assumption that all instances of the OK button would have this ToolTip. This assumption might not be a valid one. Hence, you choose to subclass.

Another Single Control Example

Believe it or not, there is a series of published standards for Windows GUI interfaces. In fact, there is one standard for the Windows 3.1–based interface that applies to Window 3.1, Windows for Workgroups, and Windows NT (I am currently on Version 3.51). Windows 95 has its own set of guidelines.

One standard for Windows applications calls for error messages to be placed in a MessageBox()-type window. Visual FoxPro has the capability to automatically display an error message when the Valid method returns .F.. The error message is the character string returned from the ErrorMessage method. The problem is that the ErrorMessage method puts the error message in the form of a wait window instead of a dialog box.

The ErrorMessage event fires automatically when the Valid method returns .F.—that is, Valid fires when the control tries to lose focus. Therefore, the solution would seem to be to put a MessageBox()-type message in the ErrorMessage method and not return a value.

However, there is one little problem. If the ErrorMessage does not return a string, Visual FoxPro displays a default message of Invalid Input. The only way to turn this off is to set the SET NOTIFY command to OFF.

Not a big problem, right? Unfortunately, other classes may monkey with this setting or may rely on the setting to be ON. In effect, you cannot rely on the SET NOTIFY setting unless you set it yourself. To do so, use SET NOTIFY OFF when the control gains focus and then set it back the way it was on the way out (that is, when the control loses focus).

NoNotifyTextBox is a sample of this type of control. A protected property called cNotifySetting has been added to hold the setting of SET NOTIFY before the class changes it. Here's the code:

```
*   Class............: NonotifyTextBox
*   Author...........: Menachem Bazian, CPA
*   Project..........: Visual FoxPro Unleashed!
*   Copyright........: (c)Flash Creative Management, Inc. 1995
*   Notes............: Exported code from Class Browser.

****************************************************
*-- Class:      nonotifyTextBox
*-- ParentClass: TextBox
*-- BaseClass:   TextBox
```

```
*-- Text box that sets NOTIFY off for error messaging.
*
DEFINE CLASS nonotifyTextBox AS TextBox

    Height = 24
    Width = 113
    Name = "nonotifyTextBox"

    *-- The setting of SET NOTIFY when the control got focus.
    PROTECTED cnotifysetting

    PROCEDURE LostFocus
        LOCAL lcNotify
        lcNotify = this.cNotifySetting
        SET NOTIFY &lcNotify
    ENDPROC

    PROCEDURE GotFocus
        this.cNotifySetting = SET("notify")
        SET NOTIFY OFF
    ENDPROC

ENDDEFINE
*
*-- EndDefine: nonotifyTextBox
****************************************************
```

Note that the property `cNotifySetting` is protected. This follows the guidelines discussed in the last chapter for protecting properties. Because this property has no use to the outside world and, in fact, could harm the system if changed by the outside world, you just hide it and forget about it.

Once you have created classes like `NoNotifyTextBox` you can use them in forms or subclass them as you see fit and be sure that you will have the behavior for which you are looking.

Combination Controls

Sometimes you might want to combine several controls together to operate as one. For example, take the task of specifying the name of an existing file on a form. This requires two controls interacting as one: a text box that enables the user to enter a filename to validate a file's existence and a command button that displays a `GetFile()` box and places the results in the text box.

You could create each control separately and drop them individually on a form. However, both controls are coming together to do one task; it makes sense to make one control out of the two and drop them on the form as one control. This achieves several goals. First, you can encapsulate all the behavior and information in one place. Second, it makes it easier to add this functionality to a form. Third, you can duplicate the look and functionality on forms with ease. Fourth, it avoids any code at the form level (code necessary to get the two controls to interact).

The base class for this is the control class. The *control class* is a class designed to create composite classes where several controls come together to act as one. Conceptually, the control class is not much of anything except a *package* into which controls can be placed. You will learn the specifics of the control class "package" further in "The General Idea" section. First, here is a sample class called `GetaFile`, which illustrates what you try to accomplish with a combination control.

```
*  Class.............: Getafilecontrol
*  Author............: Menachem Bazian, CPA
*  Project...........: Visual FoxPro Unleashed!
*  Copyright.........: (c)Flash Creative Management, Inc. 1995
*  Notes.............: Exported code from Class Browser.

**************************************************
*-- Class:       getafilecontrol
*-- ParentClass: control
*-- BaseClass:   control
*-- A combination of controls that allow a user to select an existing file.
*
DEFINE CLASS getafilecontrol AS control

    Width = 358
    Height = 26
    BackStyle = 0
    BorderWidth = 0
    cvalue = ""
    *-- The caption to display on the GETFILE box.
    cdisplaycaption = "Please select a file."
    *-- Caption for the OPEN button. See GetFile() for more information on this.
    copenbuttoncaption = "Open"
    *-- File extensions to allow for. See GetFile()
    *-- for more information on this.
    cfileextensions = ""
    *-- The type of buttons on the GetFile() dialog.
    *-- See GetFile() for more information on this.
    nbuttontype = 0
    *-- Should the path shown be a minimum path or not?
    lminimumpath = .T.
    Name = "getafilecontrol"

    ADD OBJECT cmdgetfile AS CommandButton WITH ;
        Top = 0, ;
        Left = 330, ;
        Height = 24, ;
        Width = 24, ;
        Caption = "...", ;
        Name = "cmdGetFile"

    ADD OBJECT cfilenameTextBox AS nonotifyTextBox WITH ;
        Value = "", ;
        Format = "!", ;
        Height = 24, ;
        Left = 0, ;
        Top = 0, ;
        Width = 325, ;
        Name = "cFileNameTextBox"

    PROCEDURE Refresh
        this.cFileNameTextBox.Value = this.cValue
        this.cFileNameTextBox.SetFocus()
    ENDPROC
```

```
    *-- Accepts a string parameter and validates that it is an existing file.
    PROCEDURE validatefilename
        LPARAMETERS tcFileName
        LOCAL llRetVal

        llRetVal = EMPTY(tcFileName) OR FILE(ALLTRIM(tcFileName))

        IF !llRetVal
            =MessageBox("File does not exist: " + ALLTRIM(tcFileName))
        ENDIF

        tcFileName = ALLTRIM(tcFileName)

        IF llRetVal
            this.cValue = tcFileName
        ENDIF

        RETURN llRetVal
    ENDPROC

    *-- Display the files for the user to select from with a GetFile() dialog.
    PROCEDURE displayfiles
        LOCAL lcValue, lcDialogCaption, lcOpenButtonCaption, lnButtonType

        lcDialogCaption = this.cDisplayCaption
        lcOpenButtonCaption = this.cOpenButtonCaption
        lcFileExtensions = this.cFileExtensions
        lnButtonType = this.nButtonType

        lcValue =     GETFILE(lcFileExtensions, ;
                              lcDialogCaption, ;
                              lcOpenButtonCaption, ;
                              lnButtonType)

        IF !EMPTY(lcValue)
            IF this.lminimumpath
                lcValue = SYS(2014, lcValue)
            ENDIF
            this.cValue = lcValue
        ENDIF

        this.refresh()
    ENDPROC

    PROCEDURE cmdgetfile.Click
        this.parent.DisplayFiles()
    ENDPROC

    PROCEDURE cfilenameTextBox.Valid
        RETURN this.parent.validatefilename(this.value)
    ENDPROC

ENDDEFINE
*
*-- EndDefine: getafilecontrol
**************************************************
```

The General Idea

First, some general theory: The idea is for the text box and the command button to work together to enable the user to select a file. The text box provides for manual, type-it-in functionality. The command button brings up a `GetFile()` dialog box from which the user can select a file. If a file is selected, it is shown in the text box.

The job of the container around these controls (that's the *controls* referred to in the class names) is to give the interface to the controls. From the outside world, the two controls packaged together are one control. The fact that a text box and a command button are working together is something the developer of the class needs to know but not something the developer using the control in an application needs to know.

The job of the interface is to communicate with the outside world in terms of the options the user wants to set when selecting a file. An interface also holds the name of the file selected. This brings me to my next point.

The Control Package's Custom Properties

The package around the controls has the following custom properties added to it:

```
cvalue = ""
cdisplaycaption = "Please select a file."
copenbuttoncaption = "Open"
cfileextensions = ""
nbuttontype = 0
lminimumpath = .T.
```

The `cValue` property is the name of the file selected by the user. I used the name `cValue` because it is equivalent to the `Value` property of most data controls: It holds the value returned by the control. By the way, if you're wondering about the `c` in `cValue`, it's a common naming convention for all custom properties—the first character of the name indicates the data type of the property (which in this case is Character).

The `cDisplayCaption` property is the message that displays on the `GetFile()` box, which is displayed by the command button. The property name is based on the name of the corresponding parameter discussed in the `GetFile()` help topic.

The `cOpenButtonCaption` property is the caption for the Open button. By default, the name of the button on the `GetFile()` dialog box is OK; however, this class sets the default to Open instead. Again, the name is a naming convention version of the parameter name in the help file.

The `cFileExtensions` property is a list of file extensions to show in the `GetFile()` box (you can still select any file you like, by the way). The list of file extensions is separated by semicolons or vertical bars (¦). Visual FoxPro automatically parses out the file extensions in the `GetFile()` box. Again, the name is a naming convention version of the parameter name in the help file.

The nButtonType property is a numeric property that is also used for the GetFile() box. The number defaults to 0, which shows an OK button (which is really named Open by default) and Cancel button. A value of 1 shows OK, New, and Cancel buttons. A value of 2 shows OK, None, and Cancel buttons. Once again, the name is a naming convention version of the parameter name in the help file.

The lMinimumPath property specifies whether a minimum or absolute path is used. A filename specified with a path may be shown in one of two ways. The path can be an *absolute* path; in other words, the specified path is the path you want to store. The other way is to store a *relative* path, which adjusts the path to show the minimum path designation to get to the file from a directory. An absolute path, which is the type of value returned from GetFile(), can be converted to a relative path with SYS(2014). If lMinimumPath is set to .T. (as it is, by default), then the filename returned by the GetFile() dialog box is adjusted with SYS(2014) against the current directory.

The purpose of naming properties in this manner is to give the developer using the class a clue as to the values allowed. That is, it makes the class a little easier to use and understand.

Custom and Overridden Methods

The Refresh method is the conceptual equivalent to the old SHOW clause except that it refers to the control it is on. The Refresh method sets the text box's Value property to match the cValue property of the control package. The SetFocus call to the text box puts the cursor in the text box for editing.

ValidateFileName is a custom method that tests the validity of a filename entered in the text box and is called by the text box's Valid method.

DisplayFiles is the method that actually displays the GetFile() dialog box and uses the properties of the control package as part of the GetFile() call. After GetFile() is done and the user has made a selection, the selected value is placed in the control package's cValue property. A call to Refresh keeps everything in synch.

Object Members

The object members are CmdGetFile and cFileNameTextBox.

CmdGetFile

This is a command button. The Click method cmdGetFile calls DisplayFiles, which displays a GetFile() based on the settings in the control package. The returned value is then stored to the cValue property of the package, and the box's Refresh method is called. The Refresh method puts the text box in synch.

cFileNameTextBox

This control enables the user to enter the filename manually. It is based on the `NoNotifyTextBox` class created previously in this chapter. Basing `cFileNameTextBox` on `NoNotifyTextBox` is a good example of how classes are reused in other classes.

The `Valid` method in this control checks the entered filename to make sure it is valid. An empty filename is considered valid; if it weren't, the user would have no way of exiting the `TextBox` control to get to the command button. If the text box's `Valid` method returns `.F.`, the `ErrorMessage` event calls the `ErrorMessage` method, which in turn displays an error message telling the user that file was not found.

If the entered filename is valid, the filename is stored in the `cValue` property of the control package.

Using the Combination Control in a Form

As far as the outside world is concerned (the outside world is anything outside `GetaFileControl`), the operative property is the `cValue` property. In order to get the name of the file entered or selected by the user, the outside world would just query the `cValue` property. In order to set up the control the outside world would set the properties discussed previously. Figure 29.3 shows a form with `GetaFileControl` on it.

FIGURE 29.3.

A form with
GetaFileControl.

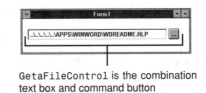

GetaFileControl is the combination
text box and command button

As far as the outside world is concerned, the only control that exists is `GetaFileControl`. The embedded text box and command button do not exist. In other words, if this combination control were dropped on a form with the name `GetaFileControl1`, then attempting to query `GetaFileControl1.cFileNameTextBox.Value` from the outside world would generate an error.

Why is this so? To understand why, you need to take a little closer look under the hood of the control class.

The Control Class

Now that you have seen an example of a combination control take a step backward and learn the technical issues related to working with this class.

First of all, although a control-based class is a composite class with additional member objects, the control class automatically makes all its member objects private. This means that anything using the class cannot see those member objects.

To illustrate this, take a look at Figure 29.4, which shows the property window of a form with GetaFileControl placed on it. I've expanded the list of objects to make the point. Note that only the control package is on the list. The individual objects inside the control package do not exist as far as the form is concerned. You access the individual objects within the combination control class.

FIGURE 29.4.

Objects shown for the GetaFileControl instance.

This behavior makes perfect sense. Because you're creating a *control*, as far as the outside world is concerned, all the components of the control are one object. This does introduce some interesting issues, which are discussed next one at a time.

Communicating with Combination Controls

By definition, the outside world can only communicate with a combination control through the package. This means that any information passing first goes to the package; the package must then transmit the information to the individual members.

A good example of this is the cValue property added to the GetaFileControl class. cValue can be set from the outside world but will be shown in the text box only when the Refresh method is called—it is the Refresh method's responsibility to transmit the value to the text box. Likewise, the text box and command button have the responsibility of telling the package about changes to cValue that happen as a result of actions taken within their control.

This also means that any methods to which the outside world needs access must be contained at the package level. For example, if the Click method of the command button were applicable to the outside world, then a method would have had to be added to the package that the command button would have called (as opposed to placing the code directly within the command button's Click method). Alternatively, the code could be placed in the command button's Click method but you would still have to add a method to the package for the outside world to run the command button's Click method. The method added to the package would just call the Click method of the command button.

Adding Objects at Runtime

Control classes do not have an `AddObject()` method; therefore, you cannot add controls to the package at runtime.

Subclassing Combination Controls

There are a few ramifications regarding subclassing combination controls.

Adding Controls to a Subclass

You cannot add controls to the package in a subclass (just as you cannot add a control to a subclass of the `CommandButton` class).

Accessing Package Contents in a Subclass

The objects contained in the combination control's package are not visible when you subclass it. This means that any methods or properties you might want to modify in a subclass must be hooked to the package as opposed to one of the member objects. This requires some care in designing the class hierarchy.

If you look at `GetaFileControl`, you'll notice that all the methods for the text box and the command button call methods on the package. In effect, this hedges your bets. You should do a little more work up front to preserve flexibility down the road.

A Final Word

As container type classes go, the control class does have limitations, but the limitations of the control class are its strength. It gives you the opportunity to create tightly controlled classes to use on your forms. However, many developers can find control classes limiting. The lack of ability to add controls at runtime, to add controls to a subclass, or to access the controls within the package can present a restrictive working environment.

The container class, on the other hand, gives you the ability to create composite classes with more flexibility. This is the next topic.

The Container Class

A container class is similar to the control class with one major exception: The controls in a container class's package are visible to the outside world (unless specifically protected in the class).

By the way, there are many classes that support containership. For example, a form is a type of container class (only more specialized). Page frames and grids are also examples of classes that support containership. This discussion focuses on the container class, but many of the discussions are applicable to the other container-type classes as well.

Container classes are wonderful for a whole host of different jobs. In fact, any time multiple objects need to be brought together, a container can do the job. (I usually prefer to combine controls in a container to accomplish a task.)

To illustrate the difference between a control class and a container class, I'll redefine the GetFileControl class to work off the container class instead of the control class. First, here's the exported code:

```
*   Class.............: Getafilecontainer
*   Author............: Menachem Bazian, CPA
*   Project...........: Visual FoxPro Unleashed!
*   Copyright.........: (c)Flash Creative Management, Inc. 1995
*   Notes.............: Exported code from Class Browser.


****************************************************
*-- Class:         getafilecontainer
*-- ParentClass:   container
*-- BaseClass:     container
*-- A combination of controls that allow a user to select an existing file.
*
DEFINE CLASS getafilecontainer AS container

    Width = 358
    Height = 26
    BackStyle = 0
    BorderWidth = 0
    cvalue = ""
    *-- The caption to display on the GETFILE box.
    cdisplaycaption = "Please select a file."
    *-- Caption for the OPEN button. See GetFile() for more information on this.
    copenbuttoncaption = "Open"
    *-- File extensions to allow for. See GetFile() for more information on this.
    cfileextensions = ""
    *-- The type of buttons on the GetFile() dialog. See GetFile() for more
information on this.
    nbuttontype = 0
    *-- Should the path shown be a minimum path or not?
    lminimumpath = .T.
    Name = "getafilecontainer"

    ADD OBJECT cmdgetfile AS CommandButton WITH ;
        Top = 0, ;
        Left = 330, ;
        Height = 24, ;
        Width = 24, ;
        Caption = "...", ;
        Name = "cmdGetFile"

    ADD OBJECT cfilenameTextBox AS nonotifyTextBox WITH ;
        Value = "", ;
        Format = "!", ;
        Height = 24, ;
        Left = 0, ;
```

```
        Top = 0, ;
        Width = 325, ;
        Name = "cFileNameTextBox"

*-- Accepts a string parameter and validates that it is an existing file.
PROCEDURE validatefilename
    LPARAMETERS tcFileName
    LOCAL llRetVal

    llRetVal = EMPTY(tcFileName) OR FILE(ALLTRIM(tcFileName))

    IF !llRetVal
        =MessageBox("File does not exist: " + ALLTRIM(tcFileName))
    ENDIF

    tcFileName = ALLTRIM(tcFileName)

    IF llRetVal
        this.cValue = tcFileName
    ENDIF

    RETURN llRetVal
ENDPROC

*-- Display the files for the user to select from with a GetFile() dialog.
PROCEDURE displayfiles
    LOCAL lcValue, lcDialogCaption, lcOpenButtonCaption, lnButtonType

    lcDialogCaption = this.cDisplayCaption
    lcOpenButtonCaption = this.cOpenButtonCaption
    lcFileExtensions = this.cFileExtensions
    lnButtonType = this.nButtonType

    lcValue =    GETFILE(lcFileExtensions, ;
                         lcDialogCaption, ;
                         lcOpenButtonCaption, ;
                         lnButtonType)

    IF !EMPTY(lcValue)
        IF this.lminimumpath
            lcValue = SYS(2014, lcValue)
        ENDIF
        this.cValue = lcValue
    ENDIF

    this.refresh()
ENDPROC

PROCEDURE Refresh
    this.cFileNameTextBox.Value = this.cValue
    this.cFileNameTextBox.SetFocus()
ENDPROC

PROCEDURE cmdgetfile.Click
    this.parent.DisplayFiles()
ENDPROC

PROCEDURE cfilenameTextBox.Valid
```

```
        RETURN this.parent.validatefilename(this.value)
    ENDPROC

ENDDEFINE
*
*— EndDefine: getafilecontainer
***************************************************
```

At first glance the code does not seem very different than the GetaFileControl class from the previous section. In fact, it isn't. What is very different is how the two classes (GetaFileControl and GetaFileContainer) operate within the form.

Figures 29.5 and 29.6 show a key difference between when you are working with control-based classes as opposed to container-based classes. Note the value of _screen.activeform.-activecontrol.name, which is tracked in the Debug window, and how it differs from the top control (an instance of GetaFileControl) and the lower container (an instance of GetaFileContainer).

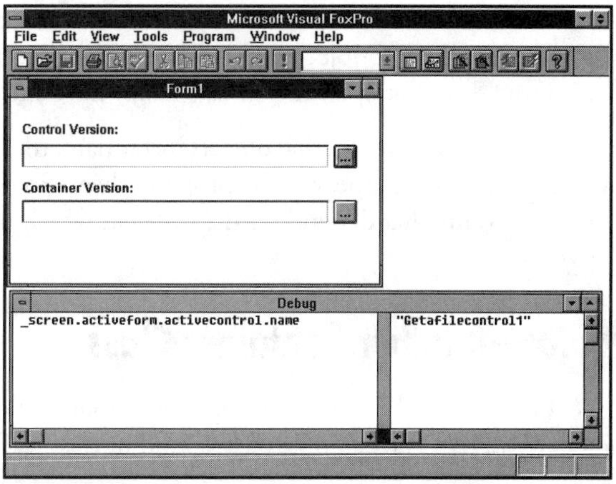

FIGURE 29.5.

A form with GetaFileControl active.

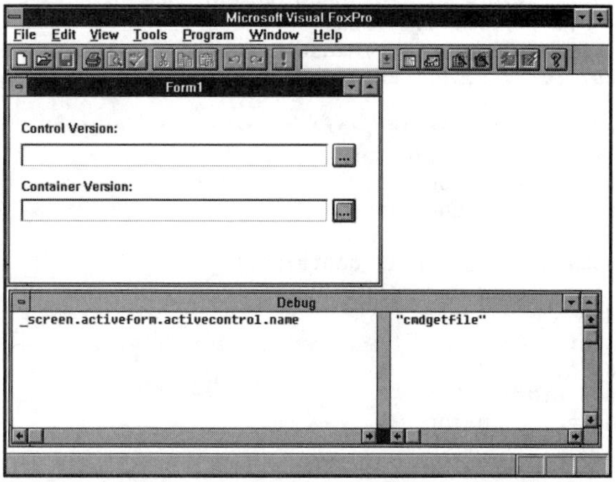

FIGURE 29.6.

A form with GetaFileContainer active.

To the next naked eye, the two controls seem the same. Behind the scenes, they are very different—the control version has the name GetaFileControl1 regardless of whether the text box has the focus or the command button has the focus. The container version, on the other hand, shows the name of the text box as the name of the active control.

By the way, this is a good example of the use of _screen to assist in debugging. You might not always know the name of the variable behind a form, but you can usually count on _screen.activeform to give you a reference to the active form. You will learn more about _screen.activeform in the section "The _screen.activeform Follies."

Order of *Inits*

Therefore, you have a package with multiple objects in it. You put code in one object's Init that references the container. However, when you try to instantiate the package you get an error message in the Init code and the package refuses to instantiate. What did you do wrong?

The answer to this puzzle lies in the order in which the objects are created. As it turns out, the container package is the last object to get created. The objects inside are created first, and the container is created only after all the objects inside have successfully been created.

As to the order in which the internal objects instantiate, the best way to know is to look at the order in which the objects appear in the property sheet. For best results, try not to put code in any of the Init events that depend on the order in which objects instantiate. You'll be a lot safer that way.

Navigator—Another Container Class

A container of command buttons for navigating through a table in a form is a good example of a container class. Here's an example of this kind of class, called Navigator:

```
*   Class............: Navigator
*   Author...........: Menachem Bazian, CPA
*   Project..........: Visual FoxPro Unleashed!
*   Copyright........: (c)Flash Creative Management, Inc. 1995
*   Notes............: Exported code from Class Browser.

**************************************************
*-- Class:       navigator
*-- ParentClass: container
*-- BaseClass:   container
*
DEFINE CLASS navigator AS container

    Width = 350
    Height = 32
    BackStyle = 0
    BorderWidth = 0
    Name = "navigator"
```

```
ADD OBJECT cmdnext AS CommandButton WITH ;
    Top = 0, ;
    Left = 0, ;
    Height = 31, ;
    Width = 60, ;
    Caption = "Next", ;
    Name = "cmdNext"

ADD OBJECT cmdprev AS CommandButton WITH ;
    Top = 0, ;
    Left = 72, ;
    Height = 31, ;
    Width = 60, ;
    Caption = "Prev", ;
    Name = "cmdPrev"

ADD OBJECT cmdtop AS CommandButton WITH ;
    Top = 0, ;
    Left = 144, ;
    Height = 31, ;
    Width = 60, ;
    Caption = "Top", ;
    Name = "cmdTop"

ADD OBJECT cmdbottom AS CommandButton WITH ;
    Top = 0, ;
    Left = 216, ;
    Height = 31, ;
    Width = 60, ;
    Caption = "Bottom", ;
    Name = "cmdBottom"

ADD OBJECT cmdok AS okbuttonwithtooltip WITH ;
    Top = 0, ;
    Left = 288, ;
    Height = 31, ;
    Width = 60, ;
    Name = "cmdOK"

PROCEDURE cmdnext.Click
    SKIP 1
    IF EOF()
        =Messagebox("At end of file!", 16)
        GO BOTTOM
    ENDIF

    thisform.refresh()
ENDPROC

PROCEDURE cmdprev.Click
    SKIP -1
    IF BOF()
        =Messagebox("At beginning of file!", 16)
        GO TOP
    ENDIF

    thisform.refresh()
ENDPROC
```

```
PROCEDURE cmdtop.Click
    GO TOP
    thisform.refresh()
ENDPROC

PROCEDURE cmdbottom.Click
    GO BOTTOM
    thisform.refresh()
ENDPROC

ENDDEFINE
*
*-- EndDefine: navigator
**************************************************
```

Each button on the container executes the necessary navigation instructions and then executes a call to the host form's Refresh method. It might seem strange to put code to work with a form on a class that is not yet physically part of a form, but that's OK. When you document the class, just make sure to specify how it is meant to be used.

In order to use the Navigator class, all you need to do is drop it on a data entry form, and you have the ability, without coding one line, to move within the file. Figure 29.7 shows a sample data entry form with this class dropped on it. By the way, this sample form is on the CD as WithBtns.SCX.

FIGURE 29.7.

A form with a Navigator container.

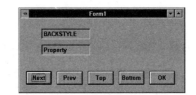

When this class is dropped on a form, as shown in Figure 29.8, a view of a form's property window, all the controls are available for editing and on-the-fly subclassing. You can even extend the container and add another control to it in the form. The additional control, of course, is not added to the class in the VCX file; it's a special version for that form only.

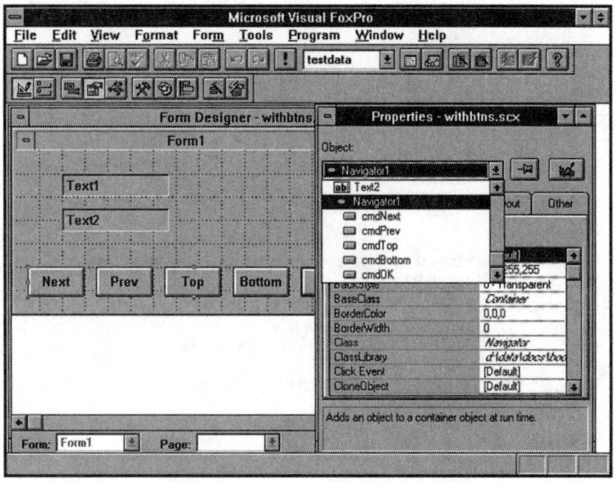

FIGURE 29.8.

The property window of a container.

The next bit of code is a representation of a form that adds a New button to the container (it's on the CD-ROM as MoreBtns.SCX).

```
*  Form.............: Form1
*  Author...........: Menachem Bazian, CPA
*  Project..........: Visual FoxPro Unleashed!
*  Copyright........: (c)Flash Creative Management, Inc. 1995
*  Notes............: Exported code from Class Browser.

**************************************************
*-- Form:         form1 (morebtns.scx)
*-- ParentClass:  form
*-- BaseClass:    form
*
DEFINE CLASS form1 AS form

    Top = 0
    Left = 0
    Height = 182
    Width = 463
    DoCreate = .T.
    BackColor = RGB(192,192,192)
    BorderStyle = 2
    Caption = "Form1"
    Name = "Form1"

    ADD OBJECT text1 AS textbox WITH ;
        BackColor = RGB(192,192,192), ;
        ControlSource = "test.cmembname", ;
        Height = 24, ;
        Left = 48, ;
        Top = 24, ;
        Width = 113, ;
        Name = "Text1"

    ADD OBJECT text2 AS textbox WITH ;
        BackColor = RGB(192,192,192), ;
        ControlSource = "test.cmembtype", ;
        Height = 24, ;
```

```
        Left = 48, ;
        Top = 60, ;
        Width = 113, ;
        Name = "Text2"

    ADD OBJECT navigator1 AS navigator WITH ;
        Top = 120, ;
        Left = 12, ;
        Width = 421, ;
        Height = 32, ;
        Name = "Navigator1", ;
        cmdNext.Name = "cmdNext", ;
        cmdPrev.Name = "cmdPrev", ;
        cmdTop.Name = "cmdTop", ;
        cmdBottom.Name = "cmdBottom", ;
        cmdOK.Top = 0, ;
        cmdOK.Left = 360, ;
        cmdOK.Height = 31, ;
        cmdOK.Width = 61, ;
        cmdOK.Name = "cmdOK"

    ADD OBJECT form1.navigator1.cmdnew AS commandbutton WITH ;
        Top = 0, ;
        Left = 288, ;
        Height = 31, ;
        Width = 61, ;
        Caption = "New", ;
        Name = "cmdNew"

    PROCEDURE cmdnew.Click
        APPEND BLANK
        thisform.refresh()
    ENDPROC

ENDDEFINE
*
*-- EndDefine: form1
***************************************************
```

Notice how the additional command button (cmdNew) is added within the code. An ADD OBJECT command adds the command button to the container. This is just one of the powerful capabilities of the container class: You can add objects to it on-the-fly.

Figure 29.9 shows what the form looks like. As you can see, there is no visible indication that the additional command button was not part of the original class.

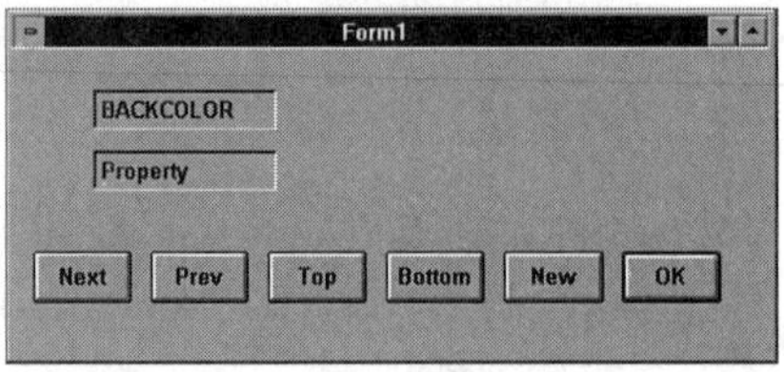

FIGURE 29.9.

A form with an additional CommandButton.

The Flexibility of the Container Class

The container class is a very versatile class. It has little display baggage and yet has the full capabilities one would expect from a container. You can add controls to it on-the-fly with ADD OBJECT and AddObject() and can combine virtually any control to create combinations that are limited only by your imagination.

Think about two simple controls: a TextBox and a Timer control. Individually, they each have specific duties. Combine them in a container and you can create something totally different—a clock.

A *Clock* Class

A clock, as a class, is a combination of a timer and a text box as follows:

```
*   Class.............: Clock
*   Author............: Menachem Bazian, CPA
*   Project...........: Visual FoxPro Unleashed!
*   Copyright.........: (c)Flash Creative Management, Inc. 1995
*   Notes.............: Exported code from Class Browser.


**************************************************
*-- Class:       clock
*-- ParentClass: container
*-- BaseClass:   container
*
DEFINE CLASS clock AS container

    Width = 367
    Height = 27
    BorderWidth = 0
    SpecialEffect = 2
    ntimeformat = 0
    Name = "clock"

    ADD OBJECT txtdate AS textbox WITH ;
        Alignment = 0, ;
        BackColor = RGB(255,255,0), ;
        BorderStyle = 0, ;
        Value = (CDOW(date())+" "+CMONTH(date())+" "+ ;
                ALLT(STR(DAY(date())))+", "+ALLT(STR(YEAR(date())))), ;
        Enabled = .F., ;
        Height = 22, ;
        Left = 5, ;
        Top = 3, ;
        Width = 250, ;
        DisabledForeColor = RGB(0,0,0), ;
        DisabledBackColor = RGB(255,255,255), ;
        Name = "txtDate"

    ADD OBJECT txttime AS textbox WITH ;
        Alignment = 0, ;
        BorderStyle = 0, ;
        Value = (IIF(THIS.PARENT.TimeFormat = 0, ;
```

```
                    IIF(VAL(SUBSTR(time(),1,2))>12,;
                    ALLT(STR((VAL(SUBSTR(time(),1,2))-12)))+SUBSTR(time(),3,6),;
                    time())),time())), ;
        Enabled = .F., ;
        Height = 22, ;
        Left = 268, ;
        Top = 3, ;
        Width = 77, ;
        DisabledForeColor = RGB(0,0,0), ;
        DisabledBackColor = RGB(255,255,255), ;
        Name = "txtTime"

    ADD OBJECT tmrtimer AS timer WITH ;
        Top = 0, ;
        Left = 120, ;
        Height = 24, ;
        Width = 25, ;
        Interval = 1000, ;
        Name = "tmrTimer"

    PROCEDURE tmrtimer.Timer
        this.Parent.txtDate.Value = CDOW(date()) + " " + ;
                            CMONTH(date())+" "+ ;
                            ALLT(STR(DAY(date()))) + ;
                            ", "+ALLT(STR(YEAR(date())))

        IF this.Parent.nTimeFormat = 0
            this.Parent.txtTime.Value = ;
                    IIF(VAL(SUBSTR(time(),1,2))>12, ;
                    ALLT(STR((VAL(SUBSTR(time(),1,2))-12))) + ;
                    SUBSTR(time(),3,6),time())
        ELSE
            this.Parent.txtTime.Value = time()
        ENDIF
    ENDPROC

ENDDEFINE
*
*-- EndDefine: clock
****************************************************
```

The timer control enables you to run a command or series of commands at timed intervals. When the Interval property is set to a value greater than zero it controls the amount of time between executions of the timer's Timer event (in 1/1000 of a second units). When you combine this capability with the display characteristics of the text box control to display the time calculated by the timer, you have a clock.

Attached to the container is a custom property, nTimeFormat, which governs whether the time is shown in 12- or 24-hour format. Setting the property to 0 shows the time in a.m./p.m. format, whereas setting the property to 1 shows the time in military form. Figure 29.10 shows what the clock looks like when you drop it on a form (it's on the CD as a class called ClockForm in CHAP29.VCX).

FIGURE 29.10.

The Clock *form.*

Once a second the Timer event fires and recalculates the time. The results of the calculation are placed in the Value property of the txtTime text box.

Providing a Consistent Interface

Notice the placement of the nTimeFormat property in the Clock class. It is placed on the container. Why put it there? You could have just as easily put the property on the timer or even the text box.

Whenever you work with a composite class, it is very important to provide a consistent interface for the user of the control. It is crucial not to force the users of your classes to drill down into the member controls in order to accomplish what they need to do, especially when you are working with a container that can have many controls.

You should use the container to communicate with the outside world. Controls within the container can communicate with each other, but users should not have to communicate with the controls inside the container in order to use your classes. Chapter 30 shows some more examples of container-based controls.

The Form

There is not much to talk about regarding form-based classes that you have not already come across in the discussions of the Form Designer or other classes. Rather than discuss how to create form classes, I will show you how form classes are different from SCX-based forms.

Bringing Up the Form

You are familiar with the DO FORM syntax; however, this syntax is no longer used to work with forms stored as classes in a VCX file. Instead, the familiar CreateObject() syntax, the means by which all objects are instantiated from their classes, is used. Note that once a form is instantiated with CreateObject() you must call the Show method to display it.

Making a Form Modal

There are two ways to make a form modal. One is to set the WindowType property to 1 (0 is modeless). The other is to call the Show method with a parameter of 1. Here is an example:

```
oForm = CreateObject("Form")
oForm.Show(1)
```

Modeless forms raise two issues when dealing with VCX-based forms. The first issue deals with reading systems events, and the second issue deals with variable scoping.

Reading System Events

Consider the following procedure:

```
*-- ShowForm.Prg

SET CLASS TO junkme
oFooForm = CreateObject("Form")
oFooForm.Show()
```

If you run this program from the Command window you will see the form flash and then disappear. This happens because of the scoping of oFooForm. Because oFooForm is a memory variable, the procedure ends and oFooForm loses scope once the Show method finishes and the form appears. Because the variable is released, the form it references is released too and disappears. The main problem is that the program never stops. There is no wait state to tell Visual FoxPro to stop and read system events. This is not an issue with the DO FORM command because it contains its own inherent wait state in which the form operates.

The answer to this problem is to issue a READ EVENTS command, which, in effect, is a replacement for the old foundation read. It tells Visual FoxPro to stop and read system events. Without it, the program does not stop and eventually terminates.

Variable Scoping Revisited

The READ EVENTS command does not completely eliminate the issue of variable scoping. The READ EVENTS command stops the program so that it can read system events. You can still instantiate a form in a procedure and have it flash if the variable loses focus.

You need to be careful with the scoping of your form instance variables. Just issuing a Show method does not stop processing. The Show method completes, and control is returned to the calling program. A typical example is a form called from the Click event of a command button. Unless something is done to keep the variable around, the variable loses scope and the form flashes. There are several strategies to deal with this problem, and all the strategies deal with the same issue: keeping the instance variable in scope.

Attaching the Variable to Another Object

One way to keep the variable in scope is to attach the instance variable to the object calling the form. For example, consider the following class:

```
*   Class............: Launchform
*   Author...........: Menachem Bazian, CPA
*   Project..........: Visual FoxPro Unleashed!
*   Copyright........: (c)Flash Creative Management, Inc. 1995
```

```
*  Notes............: Exported code from Class Browser.

***************************************************
*-- Class:        launchform
*-- ParentClass:  CommandButton
*-- BaseClass:    CommandButton
*
DEFINE CLASS launchform AS CommandButton

    Height = 29
    Width = 94
    Caption = "LaunchForm"
    *-- The form to Launch
    oform = .NULL.
    Name = "launchform"

    PROCEDURE Click
        this.oForm = CreateObject("Form")
        this.oForm.Show()
    ENDPROC

ENDDEFINE
*
*-- EndDefine: launchform
***************************************************
```

This command button maintains scope as long as the form it is attached to maintains scope; therefore, any properties of the command button retain scope, too. In this example, the form launched from within the Click event of the command button would stick around.

A similar strategy is to attach the form instance variable to a public object. For example, it could be added to _screen. There is an example of this in Chapter 31.

Making the Variable Global

Another way to keep the variable in scope is to make the variable holding the form reference global (or public). This is not the most elegant of solutions, but it does work. Perhaps a more elegant method is to declare a public array and to use the array as the repository for forms you want to keep around.

The problem with the global approach is managing the public variables. Having many public variables in a system that can be used and modified in many programs can be a little hairy at times. It's really the same issue with using public variables in a system in general. Conventional wisdom seems to shy away from this type of solution, but it will work if you need it.

The _screen.activeform Follies

You learned about the _screen.activeform property previously in this chapter. This property is a reference to the currently active form. In fact, the reference normally remains even if you click off the form onto the command window.

There is one situation in which _screen.activeform is not reliable: if a form is set to remain on top (AlwaysOnTop is set to .T.). Under these circumstances _screen.activeform does not retain the reference to the form because the form is, in effect, removed for the _screen.activeform stack.

Be careful with this one, it can bite you when you least expect it.

Data Environments

One of the more significant differences between forms in an SCX file and form classes is in the area of data environments. You use a *data environment* to specify what tables, views, and relations are used in the form. When a form class is created you cannot save a data environment with it. If you save a form as a class that had a data environment attached to it the data environment is lost.

This might look terribly negative, but it really isn't. Although you lose the graphically created data environment capabilities, you can still create data environment classes in code (this is discussed in Chapter 31). Also, there might be many cases in which the data environment for the form is not determined by the form but rather by another class on the form (for example, a business object, which is also discussed in Chapter 31).

If you don't want to get involved with data environment classes, you can still do what you want with relative ease. All you need to do is place code in the Load event to open the tables.

Take the following example, which opens the Customer table in the TESTDATA database and then presents some of the fields for editing (the form is shown in Figure 29.11):

```
*   Class.............: Customerdataform
*   Author............: Menachem Bazian, CPA
*   Project...........: Visual FoxPro Unleashed!
*   Copyright.........: (c)Flash Creative Management, Inc. 1995
*   Notes.............: Exported code from Class Browser.

**************************************************
*-- Class:        customerdataform
*-- ParentClass:  form
*-- BaseClass:    form

*
DEFINE CLASS customerdataform AS form

    DataSession = 2
    Height = 238
    Width = 356
    DoCreate = .T.
    AutoCenter = .T.
    BackColor = RGB(192,192,192)
    Caption = "Sample Customer Data"
    Name = "dataform"

    ADD OBJECT txtcust_id AS TextBox WITH ;
```

```
        ControlSource = "customer.cust_id", ;
        Enabled = .F., ;
        Height = 24, ;
        Left = 120, ;
        Top = 24, ;
        Width = 205, ;
        Name = "txtCust_Id"

ADD OBJECT txtcompany AS TextBox WITH ;
        ControlSource = "customer.company", ;
        Height = 24, ;
        Left = 120, ;
        Top = 72, ;
        Width = 205, ;
        Name = "txtCompany"

ADD OBJECT txtcontact AS TextBox WITH ;
        ControlSource = "customer.contact", ;
        Height = 24, ;
        Left = 120, ;
        Top = 120, ;
        Width = 205, ;
        Name = "txtContact"

ADD OBJECT txttitle AS TextBox WITH ;
        ControlSource = "customer.title", ;
        Height = 24, ;
        Left = 120, ;
        Top = 168, ;
        Width = 205, ;
        Name = "txtTitle"

ADD OBJECT label1 AS label WITH ;
        AutoSize = .T., ;
        BackStyle = 0, ;
        Caption = "Customer Id:", ;
        Height = 18, ;
        Left = 12, ;
        Top = 24, ;
        Width = 80, ;
        Name = "Label1"

ADD OBJECT label2 AS label WITH ;
        AutoSize = .T., ;
        BackStyle = 0, ;
        Caption = "Company:", ;
        Height = 18, ;
        Left = 12, ;
        Top = 72, ;
        Width = 64, ;
        Name = "Label2"

ADD OBJECT label3 AS label WITH ;
        AutoSize = .T., ;
        BackStyle = 0, ;
        Caption = "Contact:", ;
        Height = 18, ;
        Left = 12, ;
```

```
        Top = 120, ;
        Width = 52, ;
        Name = "Label3"

    ADD OBJECT label4 AS label WITH ;
        AutoSize = .T., ;
        BackStyle = 0, ;
        Caption = "Title:", ;
        Height = 18, ;
        Left = 12, ;
        Top = 168, ;
        Width = 32, ;
        Name = "Label4"

    PROCEDURE Load
        OPEN DATA home()+"samples\data\testdata.dbc"
        USE customer
    ENDPROC

ENDDEFINE
*
*-- EndDefine: customerdataform
**************************************************
```

FIGURE 29.11.

The Customer data form.

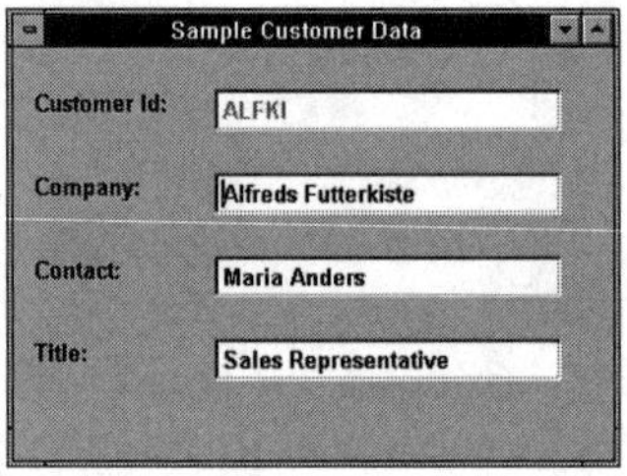

If you combine this form with the Navigator container you saw earlier you have a complete data entry package. Here's what it looks like, first in code and then a visual representation in Figure 29.12:

```
*    Class............: Custformwithnavcontainer
*    Author...........: Menachem Bazian, CPA
*    Project..........: Visual FoxPro Unleashed!
*    Copyright........: (c)Flash Creative Management, Inc. 1995
*    Notes............: Exported code from Class Browser.

**************************************************
*-- Class:       custformwithnavcontainer
*-- ParentClass: customerdataform (d:\data\docs\books\vfu\code\oop2.vcx)
*-- BaseClass:   form
*
DEFINE CLASS custformwithnavcontainer AS customerdataform

    Height = 283
    Width = 370
    DoCreate = .T.
    Name = "custformwithnavcontainer"
    txtCust_Id.Name = "txtCust_Id"
```

```
    txtCompany.Name = "txtCompany"
    txtContact.Name = "txtContact"
    txtTitle.Name = "txtTitle"
    Label1.Name = "Label1"
    Label2.Name = "Label2"
    Label3.Name = "Label3"
    Label4.Name = "Label4"

    ADD OBJECT navigator1 AS navigator WITH ;
        Top = 240, ;
        Left = 12, ;
        Width = 350, ;
        Height = 32, ;
        Name = "Navigator1", ;
        cmdNext.Name = "cmdNext", ;
        cmdPrev.Name = "cmdPrev", ;
        cmdTop.Name = "cmdTop", ;
        cmdBottom.Name = "cmdBottom", ;
        cmdOK.Name = "cmdOK"

ENDDEFINE
*
*-- EndDefine: custformwithnavcontainer
****************************************************
```

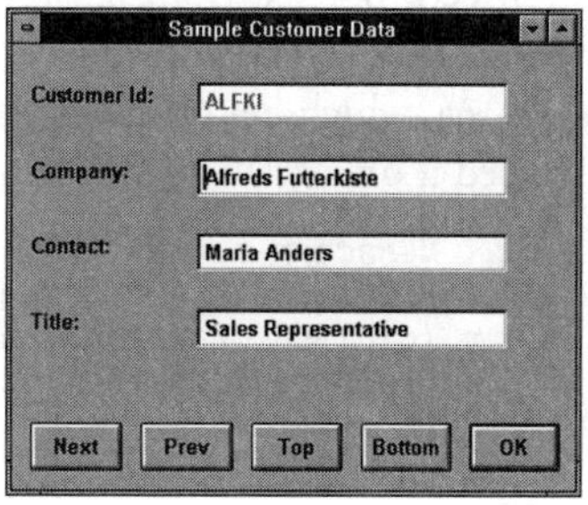

FIGURE 29.12.

*The Customer data form
with the Navigator
container.*

As it turns out, even without the native data environment capabilities creating forms as classes is a very viable way to create and display forms in Visual FoxPro.

CreateObject("form") Versus DO FORM

Why should you create a form as a class instead of using an SCX file and calling it with DO FORM? This question brings up a few issues you should bear in mind.

The first issue is subclassing. You can subclass forms only if they are stored as classes. Another benefit to using a VCX file is that many forms can be handled in one VCX file, whereas an SCX file can handle only one form.

Form classes are also more flexible to use than the DO FORM syntax. I like the ability to instantiate a form object with CreateObject() and then to monkey with it a little before issuing a call to the Show() method. Finally, the CreateObject() syntax does provide a uniformity among the components of an application. I like the simple elegance of having a similar syntax for all my objects as opposed to using CreateObject() most of the time and DO FORM some of the time.

Having said this, you can handle the situation in any way you feel comfortable. To a degree, it does come down to programmer preference.

Protecting Members on Forms

In earlier chapters you learned how to protect members from the outside world. If you recall, the rule of thumb for protecting members is to protect them if the outside world has no use for them.

With forms, the rules are changed on this issue. It is conceivable that you might want to protect something (a method, property, or even an object on the form) from the outside world but you want it accessible to objects within the form. Unfortunately, if you protect something within the form it is private throughout the form. In other words, if it is private it is considered private to everything.

In addition, beware of protected members on objects themselves. If you protect a member on an object, it may even be protected from itself. Sound strange? Then get a load of this. Remember the NoNotifyTextBox text box created earlier in this chapter? It had a protected member called cNotifySetting, which held the setting of SET NOTIFY when the control got focus. Now, suppose I dropped it on a form, as shown in the next bit of code.

```
*   Author..............: Menachem Bazian, CPA
*   Project.............: Visual FoxPro Unleashed!
*   Copyright...........: (c)Flash Creative Management, Inc. 1995
*   Notes...............: Exported code from Class Browser.

PUBLIC oform1

SET CLASSLIB TO chap29.vcx ADDITIVE

oform1=CREATEOBJECT("form1")
oform1.Show()
RETURN


******************************************************
*-- Form:        form1 (d:\data\docs\books\vfu\code\protect.scx)
*-- ParentClass: form
*-- BaseClass:   form
*
DEFINE CLASS form1 AS form

     Top = 0
     Left = 0
     Height = 57
     Width = 301
     DoCreate = .T.
     Caption = "Form1"
     Name = "Form1"
```

```
    ADD OBJECT nonotifytextbox1 AS nonotifytextbox WITH ;
        Left = 84, ;
        Top = 12, ;
        Name = "Nonotifytextbox1"

    PROCEDURE nonotifytextbox1.MouseMove
        LPARAMETERS nButton, nShift, nXCoord, nYCoord
        WAIT WINDOW this.cNotifySetting
    ENDPROC

ENDDEFINE
*
*-- EndDefine: form1
**************************************************
```

This is an SCX-type form with a `NoNotifyTextBox` text box in it. Note the `MouseMove` event for `NoNotifyTextBox`. The code has been entered into the property at the form level (that is, the control was not subclassed in a VCX file and the code added in the subclass).

If you run this form and move the mouse over the text box you will get an error stating that `cNotifySetting` does not exist (see Figure 29.13). This is because the code was not put in the class itself or in a subclass—it was entered at the form.

FIGURE 29.13.

A form with an error message.

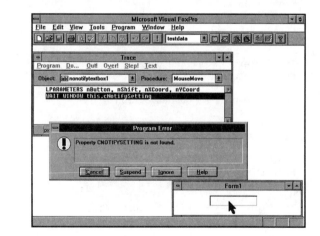

That's the way it works. Keep an eye out for this one.

Toolbars

The final type of visual class covered in this chapter is the `Toolbar`. You can think of toolbars as a special type of form. You create them by dropping objects on them (usually command buttons but other objects can be added as well). The object always stays on top, docks itself automatically (by default) when dragged to the top, bottom, right, or left borders of the FoxPro desktop, and resizes just like any other toolbar in Visual FoxPro or even in other applications, such as Word for Windows and Excel. I will illustrate this with a simple navigation toolbar.

```
*  Class.............: Simplenavbar
*  Author...........: Menachem Bazian, CPA
*  Project..........: Visual FoxPro Unleashed!
*  Copyright........: (c)Flash Creative Management, Inc. 1995
*  Notes............: Exported code from Class Browser.

****************************************************
*-- Class:       simplenavbar
*-- ParentClass: toolbar
*-- BaseClass:   toolbar
*
DEFINE CLASS simplenavbar AS toolbar

     Caption = "Navigator Buttons"
     Height = 31
     Left = 0
     Top = 0
     Width = 177
     Name = "simplenavbar"

     ADD OBJECT cmdnext AS CommandButton WITH ;
          Top = 4, ;
          Left = 6, ;
          Height = 25, ;
          Width = 33, ;
          FontBold = .F., ;
          FontSize = 8, ;
          Caption = "Next", ;
          Default = .F., ;
          ToolTipText = "Next record", ;
          Name = "cmdNext"

     ADD OBJECT cmdprev AS CommandButton WITH ;
          Top = 4, ;
          Left = 38, ;
          Height = 25, ;
          Width = 33, ;
          FontBold = .F., ;
          FontSize = 8, ;
          Caption = "Prev", ;
          Default = .F., ;
          ToolTipText = "Previous record", ;
          Name = "cmdPrev"

     ADD OBJECT cmdtop AS CommandButton WITH ;
          Top = 4, ;
          Left = 70, ;
          Height = 25, ;
          Width = 33, ;
          FontBold = .F., ;
          FontSize = 8, ;
          Caption = "Top", ;
          Default = .F., ;
          ToolTipText = "First record", ;
          Name = "cmdTop"

     ADD OBJECT cmdbottom AS CommandButton WITH ;
          Top = 4, ;
```

```
            Left = 102, ;
            Height = 25, ;
            Width = 33, ;
            FontBold = .F., ;
            FontSize = 8, ;
            Caption = "Bott", ;
            Default = .F., ;
            ToolTipText = "Last record", ;
            Name = "cmdBottom"

    ADD OBJECT separator1 AS separator WITH ;
            Top = 4, ;
            Left = 140, ;
            Height = 0, ;
            Width = 0, ;
            Name = "Separator1"

    ADD OBJECT cmdok AS okbuttonwithtooltip WITH ;
            Top = 4, ;
            Left = 140, ;
            Height = 25, ;
            Width = 33, ;
            FontBold = .F., ;
            FontSize = 8, ;
            Default = .F., ;
            Name = "cmdOK"

    PROCEDURE cmdnext.Click
        IF TYPE("_screen.activeform") # 'O' ;
           OR isNull(_screen.activeform)

            WAIT WINDOW "No form active!"
            RETURN
        ENDIF

        SET DATASESSION TO _screen.activeform.datasessionid

        SKIP 1
        IF EOF()
            =Messagebox("At end of file!", 16)
            GO BOTTOM
        ENDIF

        _screen.activeform.refresh()
    ENDPROC

    PROCEDURE cmdprev.Click
        IF TYPE("_screen.activeform") # 'O' ;
           OR isNull(_screen.activeform)

            WAIT WINDOW "No form active!"
            RETURN
        ENDIF

        SET DATASESSION TO _screen.activeform.datasessionid

        SKIP -1
        IF BOF()
```

```
                    =Messagebox("At beginning of file!", 16)
                    GO TOP
            ENDIF

            _screen.activeform.refresh()
        ENDPROC

        PROCEDURE cmdtop.Click
            IF TYPE("_screen.activeform") # 'O' ;
                OR isNull(_screen.activeform)

                WAIT WINDOW "No form active!"
                RETURN
            ENDIF

            SET DATASESSION TO _screen.activeform.datasessionid

            GO TOP
            _screen.activeform.refresh()
        ENDPROC

        PROCEDURE cmdbottom.Click
            IF TYPE("_screen.activeform") # 'O' ;
                OR isNull(_screen.activeform)

                WAIT WINDOW "No form active!"
                RETURN
            ENDIF

            SET DATASESSION TO _screen.activeform.datasessionid

            GO BOTTOM
            _screen.activeform.refresh()
        ENDPROC

        PROCEDURE cmdok.Click
            IF TYPE("_screen.activeform") # 'O' ;
                OR isNull(_screen.activeform)

                WAIT WINDOW "No form active!"
                RETURN
            ENDIF

            SET DATASESSION TO _screen.activeform.datasessionid

            _screen.activeform.release()
        ENDPROC

ENDDEFINE
*
*-- EndDefine: simplenavbar
**************************************************
```

Note the differences between this version of the Navigator buttons and the container version previously shown. In the container-based version each button had the code to move within the current table. The code was simple and straightforward. The code for the toolbar version is a bit more obtuse. Instead of working directly with the form, I use _screen.activeform, and there is a SET DATASESSION command thrown in. The OK button does not issue RELEASE thisform but rather calls the Release method. Why the additional work?

The container version is designed to work with a single form; each form that uses the container version has an instance of the container on it. The toolbar is designed to work generically with many forms.

Because the toolbar exists independently of any individual form, you have to deal with the issue of data sessions. A form might work in its own data session or in the default one. There is no way at design time to know the one with which you will be dealing (unless you set rules one way or the other).

The solution to this issue is to specifically set the current data session with the SET DATASESSION command to the current form's data session (which is stored in the form's DataSessionId property). One way to get to the current form is to use _screen.activeform. The problem is that _screen.activeform may be null even if a form is visible—hence the check on _screen.activeform in the command button's Click methods.

Furthermore, note how the form is released. The Release method (which is a built-in method in the form base class) takes care of this action quite nicely. The reason for not using something like RELEASE thisform is because the command button is not sitting on a form at all; in addition, it has no clue as to the name of the instance variable to release. _screen.activeform.Release handles these issues for you.

One final note. When objects are added to the toolbar they are placed flush against each other. Unlike other classes that support containership, you cannot dictate the placement of the objects in the toolbar—the class handles that for you. All you can dictate is the order in which they are placed.

In order to achieve a separation between objects you need to add a separator control. The control doesn't really do much of anything, it just adds a space between controls on the toolbar. Figure 29.14 shows an example of a data form with the toolbar. In this case, the data form is the simple Customer form with the SimpleNavBar class; both are instantiated separately.

FIGURE 29.14.

A form with
`SimpleNavBar.`

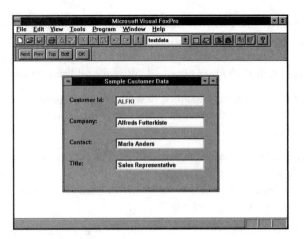

Internal Characteristics of a Toolbar

Toolbars to do not behave like other forms. They have some specific characteristics, including the following:

- Toolbars are always on top.
- Toolbars automatically dock when they are moved to any of the main Visual FoxPro window borders.
- When toolbars aren't docked they have a half-height title bar.
- When the size of a toolbar is changed, the controls are arranged to fit.
- You can move a toolbar by clicking and dragging in any area of the toolbar that isn't a control.
- Many controls placed on the toolbar do not receive the focus when they're chosen.
- Access keys in controls placed in a toolbar are disabled.
- Timer controls do not work on a toolbar.

In addition to these built-in behaviors, there are some additional characteristics that good toolbars should have. Here's a list of them:

- All objects on a toolbar should have ToolTips.
- Pictures are very effective on a toolbar.
- Buttons should all be the same size.
- Avoid large objects (such as a list box) on docked toolbars.

Large Objects on a Toolbar

If you need to put a lot of data on a toolbar, it is a good idea not to force a large object to exist on the toolbar when it is docked. For the most part, large objects (such as a list box) can be mimicked with other objects that take up less space (a drop-down list object, for example). The idea here is to create a toolbar with both the large versions and small versions of the objects on it and to show or hide the objects based on whether the toolbar is docked or not.

Consider the following scenario. You have a toolbar that displays a list of customers in the table. (The specific functionality isn't important, but only that you need to have a toolbar with a list.) You prefer using the list box because it is larger, but you cannot afford the space on the desktop when the toolbar is docked.

Here's how you could handle the situation:

```
*   Class.............: Morphbar
*   Author............: Menachem Bazian, CPA
*   Project...........: Visual FoxPro Unleashed!
*   Copyright.........: (c) Flash Creative Management, Inc. 1995
*   Notes.............: Exported code from Class Browser.


***************************************************
*-- Class:       morphbar
*-- ParentClass: toolbar
*-- BaseClass:   toolbar
*
DEFINE CLASS morphbar AS toolbar

    Caption = "Toolbar1"
    DataSession = 1
    Height = 121
    Left = 0
    Top = 0
    Width = 332
    Name = "morphbar"

    ADD OBJECT list1 AS listbox WITH ;
        RowSourceType = 6, ;
        RowSource = "customer.company", ;
        Height = 115, ;
        Left = 6, ;
        Top = 4, ;
        Width = 170, ;
        Name = "List1"

    ADD OBJECT combo1 AS combobox WITH ;
        RowSourceType = 6, ;
        RowSource = "customer.company", ;
        Height = 21, ;
        Left = 175, ;
        Style = 2, ;
        Top = 4, ;
        Width = 153, ;
        Name = "Combo1"

    PROCEDURE AfterDock
        IF this.DockPosition = 1 or this.DockPosition = 2
            *-- Note, you cannot use the Dock() method to undock
            *-- a toolbar... you have to use the Move() method.
            *-- Using the Dock() method with the -1 parameter results
```

```
            *-- in a totally bogus error message.

            this.move(1,1)
        ENDIF
    ENDPROC

    PROCEDURE Init
        IF this.docked
            this.list1.visible = .F.
            this.combo1.visible = .T.
        ELSE
            this.list1.visible = .T.
            this.combo1.visible = .F.
        ENDIF
    ENDPROC

    PROCEDURE BeforeDock
        *-- nLocation shows where the toolbar will be after
        *-- is complete. -1 means it will be undocked. 0,1,2,3
        *-- mean top, left, right and bottom respectively.

        LPARAMETERS nLocation

        DO CASE
            CASE nLocation = -1  && Not DOcked
                this.List1.Visible = .T.
                this.list1.Enabled = .T.
                this.Combo1.visible = .F.

            CASE nLocation = 0 OR nLocation = 3  && Top or bottom
                this.List1.Visible = .F.
                this.Combo1.visible = .T.
                this.Combo1.Enabled = .T.
        ENDCASE
    ENDPROC

ENDDEFINE
*
*-- EndDefine: morphbar
****************************************************
```

Note that there are two objects on this toolbar. The list box is kept visible whenever the toolbar is not docked. The combo box is made visible whenever the toolbar is not docked. The toolbar automatically adjusts its size based on the visible controls on it. Cool stuff, no?

Neither a combo box nor a list box work well when docked to the side because they just take up too much real estate on the desktop. The solution taken in this example is not to let the user dock the toolbar to the left or right sides. For more information on how to accomplish this, see the next tip (you gotta see this one).

Figure 29.15 shows the MorphBar toolbar docked, and Figure 29.16 shows MorphBar undocked.

FIGURE 29.15.

*MorphBar when
docked.*

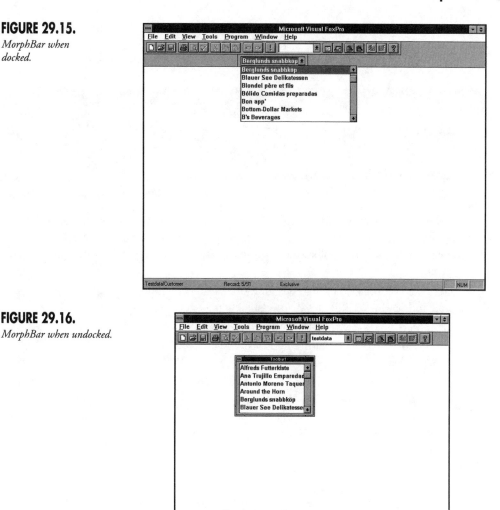

FIGURE 29.16.

MorphBar when undocked.

The BeforeDock event fires when an attempt is made to dock or undock the toolbar. The nLocation parameter tells the event where the toolbar is going. Based on where the toolbar is being docked, the visible properties of the lists are adjusted appropriately.

A few notes are in order here about the data behind the lists. In order to use this class, the TESTDATA database, located in the SAMPLES\DATA directory, has to be opened and the Customer table has to be in use. Here are the commands to do this:

```
OPEN DATABASE home()+"samples\data\testdata.dbc"
USE customer
```

You can't really open the data in this class. Unlike its cousin, the Form class, the ToolBar class does not have a LOAD method. The RecordSource properties of both lists look to the customer file. As a result, when Visual FoxPro tries to instantiate the class it looks at the properties of the contained objects and validates them. If the Customer table is not open the object does not instantiate. Even opening the table in the `Init` method of the lists won't work.

TIP

Undocking a toolbar is not always as simple as it sounds. According to the help file (and it should know, right?) you can issue a call to the `Dock` method with a parameter of -1 to undock a toolbar. Thus, if you have a toolbar called `oToolBar` you could undock it with the following command:

```
oToolBar.Dock(-1)
```

However, don't try to use this command within the `BeforeDock` or `AfterDock` methods. If you do, you will get a really bogus error message that really deals with filters and has nothing at all to do with toolbars (according to the help file, anyway). Sound confusing? You're right... it is.

The real way to undock a toolbar within the `AfterDock` method is to use the `Move` method and send it coordinates that lie outside the dock area (`Move(1,1)` works fine).

What about the `BeforeDock` method? Calling the `Move` method within the `BeforeDock` method doesn't help; you'll have to put it in the `AfterDock` method.

Coordinating Forms with Toolbars

Another issue to consider is that of coordinating forms with toolbars. You have already learned how to coordinate data sessions with a form; however, there are many other issues to consider. Here are just a few:

- Dealing with forms that do not "do" data
- Releasing the toolbar when the last data form is released
- Making sure the toolbar is up when a form that needs it is instantiated

Coordination is merely a matter of sending the appropriate messages back and forth. By placing a custom property on data forms, you can determine, by the existence of the property, whether a form is a data form. When a data form is instantiated it looks for a global variable (`goNavToolBar`). If the variable exists, then the toolbar is assumed to exist (you make the toolbar nonclosable). Each new instance of a data form also sends a message to `goNavToolBar` telling it that there is a new data form in town (in the following example the toolbar maintains a count variable and the new instances increase it by one). When an instantiated form is released, it tells the toolbar that there is one less data form. If this is the last data form visible on the desktop, the toolbar releases itself. Here is the code for the example, followed by Figure 29.17, which shows you what it looks like:

```
*   Class..............: Navigatortoolbar
*   Author.............: Menachem Bazian, CPA
*   Project............: Visual FoxPro Unleashed!
*   Copyright..........: (c)Flash Creative Management, Inc. 1995
*   Notes..............: Exported code from Class Browser.


**************************************************
*-- Class:          navigatortoolbar
*-- ParentClass:    simplenavbar
*-- BaseClass:      toolbar
*
DEFINE CLASS navigatortoolbar AS simplenavbar

    Height = 31
    Left = 0
    Top = 0
    Width = 171
    *-- The number of forms active that use this toolbar.
    *-- When this property reaches 0, the toolbar will release.
    PROTECTED nnumforms
    nnumforms = 0
    Name = "navigatortoolbar"
    cmdNext.Top = 4
    cmdNext.Left = 6
    cmdNext.Default = .F.
    cmdNext.Name = "cmdNext"
    cmdPrev.Top = 4
    cmdPrev.Left = 38
    cmdPrev.Default = .F.
    cmdPrev.Name = "cmdPrev"
    cmdTop.Top = 4
    cmdTop.Left = 70
    cmdTop.Default = .F.
    cmdTop.Name = "cmdTop"
    cmdBottom.Top = 4
    cmdBottom.Left = 102
    cmdBottom.Default = .F.
    cmdBottom.Name = "cmdBottom"
    cmdOK.Top = 4
    cmdOK.Left = 134
    cmdOK.Default = .F.
    cmdOK.Name = "cmdOK"

    *-- Add a form to the toolbar form count.
    PROCEDURE addform
        *-- This method should be called by form.init()

        this.nNumForms = this.nNumForms + 1
    ENDPROC

    *-- Remove a form from the toolbar form count.
    PROCEDURE removeform
        *-- This method should be called by form.destroy()

        this.nNumForms = this.nNumForms - 1

        IF this.nNumForms = 0
            this.release()
```

```
            ENDIF
        ENDPROC

        *-- Release the toolbar. Mimics a form's RELEASE method.
        PROCEDURE release
            RELEASE thisform
        ENDPROC

        PROCEDURE Refresh
            IF TYPE("_screen.activeform.lIsDataForm") = 'L'
                this.cmdNext.Enabled = .T.
                this.cmdPrev.Enabled = .T.
                this.cmdTop.Enabled = .T.
                this.cmdBottom.Enabled = .T.
            ELSE
                this.cmdNext.Enabled = .F.
                this.cmdPrev.Enabled = .F.
                this.cmdTop.Enabled = .F.
                this.cmdBottom.Enabled = .F.
            ENDIF
        ENDPROC

        PROCEDURE Destroy
            this.visible = .f.
        ENDPROC

ENDDEFINE
*
*-- EndDefine: navigatortoolbar
**************************************************

*   Class.............: Custformlinkedtotoolbar
*   Author............: Menachem Bazian, CPA
*   Project...........: Visual FoxPro Unleashed!
*   Copyright.........: (c)Flash Creative Management, Inc. 1995
*   Notes.............: Exported code from Class Browser.

**************************************************
*-- Class:        custformlinkedtotoolbar
*-- ParentClass:  customerdataform
*-- BaseClass:    form
*
DEFINE CLASS custformlinkedtotoolbar AS customerdataform

    DoCreate = .T.
    Name = "custformlinkedtotoolbar"
    txtCust_Id.Name = "txtCust_Id"
    txtCompany.Name = "txtCompany"
    txtContact.Name = "txtContact"
    txtTitle.Name = "txtTitle"
    Label1.Name = "Label1"
    Label2.Name = "Label2"
    Label3.Name = "Label3"
    Label4.Name = "Label4"
    lisdataform = .F.

    PROCEDURE Init
        IF TYPE ("goNavToolBar") # 'O' OR isnull(goNavToolBar)
```

```
            RELEASE goNavToolBar
            PUBLIC goNavToolBar
            goNavToolBar = CreateObject("NavigatorToolBar")
            goNavToolBar.Dock(0,1,0)
            goNavToolBar.Show()
        ENDIF

        goNavToolBar.AddForm()
        goNavToolBar.Refresh()
    ENDPROC

    PROCEDURE Activate
        goNavToolBar.Refresh()
    ENDPROC

    PROCEDURE Deactivate
        goNavToolBar.Refresh()
    ENDPROC

    PROCEDURE Destroy
        goNavToolBar.RemoveForm()
    ENDPROC

ENDDEFINE
*
*-- EndDefine: custformlinkedtotoolbar
****************************************************
```

FIGURE 29.17.

The Customer data form with NavigationToolBar.

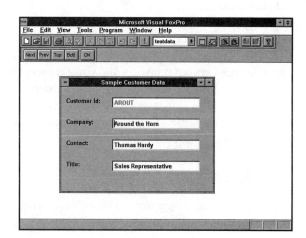

A Final Word on Visual Classes

When you create classes in Visual FoxPro it is not uncommon to think only in terms of visual classes. Visual classes certainly are fun to create—working with GUI elements has an element of art to it. Creating a form that is both functional and pleasing to the eye is something of an achievement.

However, OOP does not stop with visual classes. Unlike some languages that only support GUI classes, Visual FoxPro supports nonvisual classes. What you can do with nonvisual classes is no less remarkable.

Nonvisual Classes

A *nonvisual class* is any class that is not designed primarily to be displayed. For example, CommandButton is a class that is specifically designed to display on a form. The Timer class, on the other hand, does not show on a form at all.

Nonvisual classes in Visual FoxPro are typically descendants of the Custom or Timer class and often have no display component attached to them at all. However, nonvisual classes may have a visual component attached to it. And to make matters more confusing, classes typically thought of as *visual* classes can be the basis for nonvisual classes too.

Why Create Nonvisual Classes?

There are many reasons why you would create a nonvisual class. In fact, there are as many reasons to create nonvisual classes as there are to create visual ones. Here are the main reasons:

- Code maintenance
- Code reuse
- Functionality enhancement

What's the difference between nonvisual and visual classes? The basic difference lies in the type of classes you create. Visual classes typically center around the user interface, whereas nonvisual classes play key roles in management functions. Nonvisual classes also incorporate the type of class that is most often neglected when people discuss object orientation in systems development: business classes.

Types of Nonvisual Classes

Here are some of the more common types of nonvisual classes that you will typically create and use in your applications.

Wrapper Classes

When you create classes written for management roles you will want to consider the many different aspects of management for which you can create a class. One aspect is to manage the interface between one program and another. A good example of this would be the management of the interface between Visual FoxPro code and DLLs, FLLs, or other function libraries. These classes are created for several reasons:

- To make it easier to use these sources of functions
- To enhance their capabilities
- To encapsulate the definition, loading, and error trapping required when working with the function library

This process is known as *wrapping a class* around some existing functionality. Appropriately, these classes are called *wrapper classes.*

Manager Classes

Another typical nonvisual class is a class that manages other classes. A good example is a class that handles multiple instances of forms. Such a class enables you to create functions such as Tile All Windows. These classes are known as *manager classes.*

Business Classes

A *business class* is a class designed to model an entity in a business environment. A good example is the Customer class. These classes are a combination of information and actions designed to do what a business entity needs to do within the context of the problem domain (that is, the environment being modeled and automated).

The responsibilities of a business class are often determined after careful analysis and design. Business class responsibilities can be very abstract in nature and require careful modeling before implementation. Some common responsibilities might be the following:

- Can retrieve its information from the database
- Can print itself
- Can save itself to the database

Business classes are a little more difficult to classify as visual or nonvisual. Business classes can, and often do, have visual components. A business class can be based on a visual class (a form class, for example) with the appropriate properties and methods added to the form. In which category does a business class belong? It depends on how the object is created. In reality, it's all semantics anyway; you can call it what you want.

Wrapper Classes

The purpose of a wrapper class is to create a class that manages and perhaps even enhances the functionality of some other code. Any code can be wrapped into a class. If you have an old procedure library written in earlier versions of FoxPro, you could wrap a class around it if you like. The tough part is deciding when it is appropriate to wrap a class around something.

The best reasons to wrap a class around something is to make it easier and better to use. A perfect example of a candidate for a wrapper class is a DLL or FLL. These function libraries can be obscure, their parameters can be difficult to determine, and their error-handling requirements can be rather extensive. For example, if you are using an FLL library (for example, FOXTOOLS), what do you do if someone else's code unloads it accidentally with SET LIBRARY TO? Can you rely on the fact that the library is there all the time? Take the example of calling some of the Windows API functions (the functions to write and read from INI files, for example). These can be difficult to learn to use.

When a class is wrapped around some other piece of code, the class developer has the ability to control which portions of the DLL or FLL are available to the outside world, how they are called, and even what values are returned.

Wrapper classes carry a myriad of benefits with them. First of all, if a DLL or FLL is used with a wrapper class, the developers who use that class do not have to know anything about the DLL or FLL that serves as the basis for the class. They also do not have to be concerned with issues of loading the DLL or FLL or registering its functions. In effect, the result is a much reduced learning curve and coding time for all concerned.

The following is an example of a wrapper class. This class is a wrapper around a library of functions called FOXTOOLS.FLL that ships with Visual FoxPro. Here is the code:

```
*   Class.............: Foxtools
*   Author............: Menachem Bazian, CPA
*   Project...........: Visual FoxPro Unleashed!
*   Copyright.........: (c)Flash Creative Management, Inc. 1995
*   Notes.............: Exported code from Class Browser.


***************************************************
*-- Class:       foxtools
*-- ParentClass: custom
*-- BaseClass:   custom
*
*
DEFINE CLASS foxtools AS custom

    Name = "foxtools"
    PROTECTED lloaded

    PROCEDURE loadlib
        IF !"FOXTOOLS" $ SET("library")
            SET LIBRARY TO (SYS(2004)+"FOXTOOLS")
            this.lLoaded = .T.
        ENDIF
    ENDPROC

    PROCEDURE drivetype
        LPARAMETERS tcDrive
        LOCAL lnRetVal
        lnRetVal = (drivetype(tcDrive))
        RETURN lnRetVal
    ENDPROC

    PROCEDURE justfname
        LPARAMETERS tcString
```

```
        LOCAL lcRetVal
        lcRetVal = (justfname(tcString))
        RETURN lcRetVal
ENDPROC

PROCEDURE juststem
    LPARAMETERS tcString
    LOCAL lcRetVal
    lcRetVal = (juststem(tcString))
    RETURN lcRetVal
ENDPROC

PROCEDURE justpath
    LPARAMETERS tcString
    LOCAL lcRetVal
    lcRetVal = (this.addbs(justpath(tcString)))
    RETURN lcRetVal
ENDPROC

PROCEDURE justdrive
    LPARAMETERS tcString
    LOCAL lcRetVal
    lcRetVal = (this.addbs(justpath(tcString)))
    RETURN lcRetVal
ENDPROC

PROCEDURE justpathnodrive
    LPARAMETERS tcString
    LOCAL     lcRetval, ;
              lnAtPos

    lcRetVal = this.justpath(tcString)
    lnAtPos  = AT(':', lcRetVal)
    IF lnAtPos > 0
        IF lnAtPos < LEN(lcRetVal)
            lcRetVal = this.addbs(SUBST(lcRetVal,lnAtPos+1))
        ELSE
            lcRetVal = ""
        ENDIF
    ENDIF

    RETURN (lcRetVal)
ENDPROC

PROCEDURE addbs
    LPARAMETERS tcString
    LOCAL lcRetVal
    lcRetVal = (addbs(tcString))
    RETURN lcRetVal
ENDPROC

PROCEDURE isdir
    LPARAMETERS tcString
    LOCAL llRetVal, lcTestString, laFiles[1]

    lcTestString = ALLTRIM(this.addbs(tcString)) - "*.*"
    IF ADIR(laFiles, lcTestString, "DSH") > 0
        llRetVal = .t.
```

```
            ELSE
                llRetVal = .F.
            ENDIF

            RETURN (llRetVal)
        ENDPROC

        PROCEDURE cleandir
            LPARAMETERS tcString
            RETURN(UPPER(sys(2027, tcString)))
        ENDPROC

        PROCEDURE cut
            =_edcut(_wontop())
        ENDPROC

        PROCEDURE copy
            =_edcopy(_wontop())
        ENDPROC

        PROCEDURE paste
            =_edpaste(_wontop())
        ENDPROC

        PROCEDURE Error
            LPARAMETERS tnError, tcMethod, tnLine
            LOCAL lcMessage

            tcMethod = UPPER(tcMethod)

            DO CASE
                CASE tnError = 1  && File not found — Cause by the library not loaded
                    this.loadlib()
                    RETRY

                OTHERWISE
                    ?? CHR(7)
                    lcMessage = "An error has occurred:" + CHR(13) + ;
                                "Error Number: " + PADL(tnError,5) + CHR(13) + ;
                                "      Method: " + tcMethod + CHR(13) + ;
                                " Line Number: " + PADL(tnLine,5)

                    =MESSAGEBOX(lcMessage, 48, "Foxtools Error")
            ENDCASE
        ENDPROC

        PROCEDURE Destroy
            IF this.lLoaded
                RELEASE LIBRARY (SYS(2004)+"foxtools.fll")
            ENDIF
        ENDPROC

        PROCEDURE Init
            this.lLoaded = .F.
            this.loadlib()
        ENDPROC

ENDDEFINE
```

```
*
*-- EndDefine: foxtools
****************************************************
```

Before you go into the theory behind the class, learn all the methods and properties that make up this wrapper class. Table 29.1 presents the methods and properties for `Foxtools`.

Table 29.1. The methods and properties for `Foxtools`.

Property/Method	Description
lLoaded	The `lLoaded` property is a protected property that keeps track of whether the FOXTOOLS library was loaded by this class or from the outside world. If `Foxtools` loaded the library, it releases the library when the instance is cleared.
addbs([tcPath])	This function is the equivalent of the `AddBs()` function in FOXTOOLS. It accepts a path string as a parameter and adds a backslash to it if there isn't one already.
cleandir([tcPath])	This function really doesn't use FOXTOOLS.FLL at all but has related functionality. It accepts a filename with a path attached and cleans it up with `SYS(2027)`. *Cleaning up* means interpreting back steps in path strings and redrawing them. Here is an example: `oFtools.CleanDir("D:\APPS\FOX\VFP\..\") && Returns "D:\APPS\FOX\"`
copy()	This method copies selected text to the Clipboard. Uses the `_edCopy()` function.
cut()	This method copies selected text to the Clipboard and then deletes it. Uses the `_edCut()` function.
Destroy()	This method is called when the object is released. The method releases FOXTOOLS.FLL if the object loaded it.
drivetype([tcDriveLetter])	This method calls the `DriveType()` function to get the type of the drive specified.
Error()	This method is called when a program error occurs in the class. It takes precedence over ON ERROR. If the error is an error number 1 (that is, file not found), the method assumes it occurred because someone unloaded FOXTOOLS.FLL, in which case the `Error()` method

continues

Table 29.1. continued

Property/Method	Description
	just loads the library with `LoadLib()` and then retries the command. If the error is something other than a `File Not Found` error, an error dialog box is presented.
`Init()`	This method is called when the object is instantiated. It calls `LoadLib()` to load the library if needed.
`isdir([tcPath])`	This method accepts a path string as a parameter and tests it to make sure it's a directory. This method returns a logical value.
	`IsDir()` does not really use FOXTOOLS, but it is related to the functionality of the library and was therefore included.
`justdrive([tcPath])`	This method accepts a filename with path string and returns only the drive designation.
`justfname([tcPath])`	This method is the same as `JustDrive()` but it returns the filename.
`justpath([tcPath])`	This method is the same as `JustDrive()` except that it returns the path. The drive designator is included in the return value.
`justpathnodrive`	This method is the same as `JustPath` except that the drive designator is removed from the string.
`juststem([tcPath])`	This method is the same as `JustFName()` except that this returns the filename minus the extension.
`loadlib()`	This method loads FOXTOOLS if it is not already loaded. `lLoaded` is set to `.T.` if this method loads the library.
`paste()`	This method pastes the contents of the Clipboard at the insertion point.

This class shows the various purposes of a wrapper:

■ **Ease of use—encapsulating error trapping**

When a library is loaded within Visual FoxPro, it can be unloaded by other objects by issuing one command. The FOXTOOLS class automatically loads FOXTOOLS.FLL (if it is not already loaded) when the object is instantiated. If the library is released by another module or object and a FoxTools function is called, Visual FoxPro generates a `File Not Found` error message. In this case, the error method calls the `LoadLib()`

method to reload the library. This gives developers a simple way to use FOXTOOLS without having to worry about someone else's code unloading the library.

■ **Enhancing existing functionality**

The `JustPath()` function in FOXTOOLS calculates what portion of a filename string is the path designation and returns that path as a string. The string can have a backslash at the end. In order to promote consistency, the method that calls `JustPath()` also calls the `AddBs()` method to add a backslash at the end of the string if one does not already exist there. This is an example of enhancing functionality, which gives developers a simple, consistent return value.

■ **Adding functionality**

The `CleanDir()` method is designed to adjust a path string for back steps. For example, a path string of C:\WINAPPS\VFP\SAMPLES\DATA\..\GRAPHICS\ adjusts to C:\WINAPPS\VFP\SAMPLES\GRAPHICS\. This function does not call FOXTOOLS at all; however, its functionality is related to the other functions included in this class. By adding a method for this function you are giving developers access to related functionality in one place without requiring them to load multiple classes.

The ability to create and use wrapper classes is a major benefit to software development. Because the complexity of working with something can be hidden within a class without compromising the class's functionality, developers who use the wrapper will immediately notice an increase in their productivity—they can have the wrapper in their arsenals without the cost of learning its intricacies.

Manager Classes

A second type of nonvisual class that is often created is a manager class. This class typically manages instances of another class. A good example of this is the management of multiple instances of a form to ensure that subsequent instances are properly placed on the screen with an identifiable header (for example, `Document1`, `Document2`, and so on).

This next example deals with this issue. It shows a manager class that manages a simple form class. Here is the code:

```
*   Program..........: MANAGER.PRG
*   Author...........: Menachem Bazian, CPA
*   Created..........: 05/03/95
*)  Description.......: Sample Manager Class with Managed Form Class
*   Major change list.:

*-- This class is designed to manage a particular form class and make
*-- sure that when the forms are run they are "tiled" properly.

DEFINE CLASS FormManager AS Custom
    DECLARE aForms[1]
    nInstance = 0
```

```
        PROCEDURE RunForm
            *-- This method runs the form. The instance of the form class
            *-- is created in the aForms[] member array.

            LOCAL lnFormLeft, llnFormTop, lcFormCaption
            nInstance = ALEN(THIS.aForms)

            *-- Set the Top and Left Properties to Cascade the new Form
            IF nInstance > 1 AND TYPE('THIS.aForms[nInstance -1]') = 'O' ;
                    AND NOT ISNULL(THIS.aForms[nInstance -1])
                lnFormTop = THIS.aForms[nInstance -1].Top + 20
                lnFormLeft = THIS.aForms[nInstance -1].Left + 10
            ELSE
                lnFormTop = 1
                lnFormLeft = 1
            ENDIF

            *-- Set the caption to reflect the instance number
            lcFormCaption = "Instance " + ALLTRIM(STR(nInstance))

            *-- Instantiate the form and assign the object variable
            *-- to the array element

            THIS.aForms[nInstance] = CreateObject("TestForm")
            THIS.aForms[nInstance].top = lnFormTop
            THIS.aForms[nInstance].left = lnFormLeft
            THIS.aForms[nInstance].caption = lcFormCaption
            THIS.aForms[nInstance].Show()

            *-- Redimension the array so that more instances of
            *-- the form can be launched
            DIMENSION THIS.aforms[nInstance + 1]
        ENDPROC
ENDDEFINE

*-- This class is a form class that is designed to work with
*-- the manager class.

DEFINE CLASS TestForm AS form
        Top = 0
        Left = 0
        Height = 87
        Width = 294
        DoCreate = .T.
        BackColor = RGB(192,192,192)
        BorderStyle = 2
        Caption = "Form1"
        Name = "Form1"

        ADD OBJECT label1 AS label WITH ;
            FontName = "Courier New", ;
            FontSize = 30, ;
            BackStyle = 0, ;
            Caption = (time()), ;
            Height = 61, ;
            Left = 48, ;
            Top = 12, ;
            Width = 205, ;
```

```
        Name = "Label1"
ENDDEFINE
```

Note that forms are instantiated through the RUNFORM method rather than directly with a CreateObject() function. This enables the manager function to maintain control over the objects it instantiates.

By the way, this can be considered a downside to working with manager classes, too. If a developer is used to working with the familiar CreateObject() function to instantiate classes, working through a method like the RUNFORM method may be a bit confusing at first.

By the way, remember the discussion in this chapter about instance variable scoping (see "Reading System Events" and "Variable Scoping Revisited")? FormManager is an example of how to manage instance variable scoping. The aForm[] property is an array property. Each row in the array holds an instance of the form.

Figure 29.18 shows what the forms look like when they are instantiated. Note how they are properly tiled (with the exception of a few moved aside to show the contents of the form) and that each one has a different caption and time showing.

FIGURE 29.18.

Managed forms.

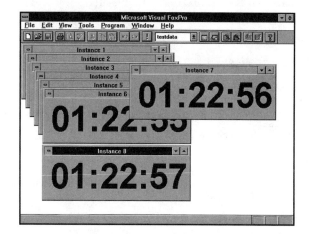

Manager functions are very useful. They provide a simple way to encapsulate code that would normally have to be duplicated every time an object is instantiated into one single place.

Business Classes

Business classes are object-oriented representations of business entities (for example, a customer). The responsibilities of these classes will vary depending on the behavior of a particular object within the problem domain.

The purpose of a business class is multifold. At an abstract level, it is possible to determine the basic functionality of a business object and then to create a class around it. For example, the basic responsibilities of a business object might be the following:

- To retrieve itself from the database
- To move within the database tables (First, Last, Prev, or Next)
- To display itself
- To print itself

These functions could be abstracted in a class. *Abstracting*, in this sense, means that the functionality can be placed in its own class rather than repeating it in multiple classes. The abstract class is created as a basis for other classes, not to be used in instantiating objects. Here is an example:

```
DEFINE CLASS BaseBusiness AS custom
    cAlias = ""
    oData = .NULL.

    PROCEDURE INIT
        IF !EMPTY(this.cAlias) AND !used(this.cAlias)
            =MessageBox("Alias is not open!", 16)
        ENDIF
    ENDPROC

    PROCEDURE next
        SELECT (this.cAlias)
        SKIP 1
        IF EOF()
            GO BOTTOM
        ELSE
            this.readrecord()
        ENDIF
    ENDPROC

    *-- Additional methods here for movement would mimic
    *-- procedure NEXT

    PROCEDURE readrecord
        *-- This procedure is initially empty
        SCATTER NAME this.oData
    ENDPROC

    *-- Additional methods for saving would follow mimicking
    *-- procedure readrecord.

ENDDEFINE
```

In order to create a `Customer` object, all you need to do is subclass it as follows:

```
DEFINE CLASS customer AS basebusiness
    cAlias = "Customer"
ENDDEFINE
```

The fields in the Customer alias are automatically added as members of oData. Thus, if an object called oCust were instantiated from the Customer class, the cName field would be held in oCust.oData.cName.

Of course, the beauty of this method of development is that there is little coding to do from one business class to another. In effect, all you do is code by exception.

This is one way to create business classes. You will learn more about business classes and a sample framework for working with business classes in Chapter 31.

Rounding Out the Story—Creating a Framework

The classes you create in Visual FoxPro, as in any object-oriented language, cover many different areas and serve many different purposes. Some classes will be created to serve a specific need in the software. For example, creating a Customer class might be an example of a class designed specifically to the needs of a software project. However, as you learned previously, classes can be created simply because the functionality represented in the class provides a good basis for further subclassing. For example, NoNotifyTextBox is a good example of a generic-type class you can create and reuse and from which you can subclass.

When you are starting out with an object-oriented language, the first step you probably take is to create a series of classes that will be the basis on which you create classes for your applications. These classes, taken together, are known as the *application framework*. Part of the framework will be generic; that is, they will be based on the FoxPro base classes to provide baseline functionality. For example, a subclass of the controls can be created with default font and size characteristics. A base form class can be created with a default background color, logo, and so on.

In addition, the framework may also call for a methodology for adding business classes to applications. Although working with a framework imposes some limitations, it is well worth it in terms of standardization among applications as well as speed in development. Chapter 31 shows a portion of a framework.

A good framework is the key to success in an object-oriented environment. It is as important as a good library of routines was in FoxPro 2.*x*. Creating a solid framework (or purchasing one) saves you hours in the long run. However, if the framework is shoddy your application can suffer greatly. Be careful.

Summary

This chapter taught you issues relating to the creation of classes in Visual FoxPro. It covered the typical types of classes you might want to create while working with Visual FoxPro. The list is not exhaustive because creating classes is limited only by your imagination. Experiment and see where it leads you—you might be very pleasantly surprised.

The next step in this section is to discuss another make or break issue: managing your Visual FoxPro class libraries. You can find this in Chapter 30, "Managing Classes with Visual FoxPro."

Managing Classes
with Visual FoxPro

30

IN THIS CHAPTER

In the last few chapters, you learned issues concerning the creation of classes in Visual FoxPro. How the class libraries are maintained and managed is the next issue for discussion. In this chapter, you learn about the issues relating to managing class libraries, who should do the management, and what tools and commands come with Visual FoxPro to assist in this all-important task.

What's the Big Deal?

What's the big deal about managing classes? You have VCX files with classes in them. What can be so difficult? Well, as it turns out, managing class libraries is not something to take lightly. Without proper management, disaster can easily strike not only one application but an entire department or even a company.

In Chapter 29, "Creating Classes with Visual FoxPro," you learned about application frameworks. An *application framework* can consist of hundreds of classes on which you can design other classes for your applications.

In order to properly keep track of the classes you will probably want to keep them grouped in a logical manner in different files. For example, the *base classes* (such as NoNotifyTextBox, discussed in Chapter 29) in the framework might be stored in a VCX file called CONTROLS.VCX. Another VCX file might have a more specialized version of these controls (such as the OKButton and OKButtonWithToolTip classes discussed in Chapter 29). Yet a third VCX file might have combination classes, such as the Navigator toolbar. There might be a UTILS.VCX file as well that has ObjectInspectorForm.

When you put all these disparate class libraries together, you have a basis for creating all your applications. Now, imagine what might happen if someone modified the TextBox base class and introduced a bug into it. Conceivably, every application in the company could up and die right there. Sound farfetched? Believe it.

Recently, I was speaking to a user group in New York, and we got into the issue of managing class libraries. One of the attendees, who programmed in a mainframe environment (and you know how tightly a mainframe environment is controlled), told me that an application he had just modified and tested began dying shortly after he updated the production software. Immediately, the company reverted the prior version of the software, but still the problems persisted. This set off two weeks of hectic work trying to track down the cause of the problem, but all efforts failed. Finally, as he was almost ready to give up he bumped into a friend in the company cafeteria. After his friend remarked that he had not seen him for several weeks, the attendee explained that he had been going nuts trying to track down this problem. His friend turned red. It seems he modified one line of code in a base routine and never told anyone—he had inadvertently introduced this bug.

The problem illustrated in this story can become even more acute in OOP. Objects, which are self-contained, are not meant to be reviewed and understood by everyone in depth; all a user needs to know is how to interact with them. If something high in the class hierarchy is accidentally broken, hundreds of classes can go south for the winter and no one will understand what happened. The key, therefore, is to ensure proper control over the class libraries.

Class Library Structure

Typically in an organization, you might see as many as three levels of class libraries. The first level is a corporate-wide set of standard libraries. For example, the corporate framework and standard utilities might be part of these libraries. As a second level, a specific department or business unit within a company might have a more specialized set of classes used across their applications. For example, a set of base business classes could be created for each business unit. Finally, as a third level, each application has class libraries specifically for its own use. Figure 30.1 shows what the hierarchy would look like in terms of an organization chart.

FIGURE 30.1.

The class library structure.

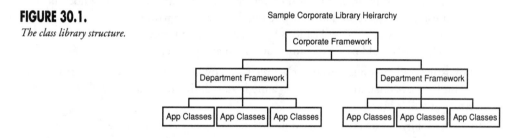

Each level of classes requires an individual responsible for managing the libraries. The generic term for such an individual is the *class librarian.*

The Class Librarian

The class librarian's job is to control what goes into the class libraries. At the corporate level, a class librarian is responsible for the content and integrity of the corporate framework. Each department has similar responsibilities. The leader of each application project, or someone he or she designates, does the same for the application libraries.

Criteria for Inclusion in Class Libraries

It would be unfair to assume that the class libraries at any level should be static and not subject to change. First of all, as time goes by enhancements can and should be introduced. Developers will work on applications and might have significant contributions to make to the frameworks in terms of new and enhanced classes. No one is suggesting that this should not take place, but rather that it should be controlled.

Classes that are created for inclusion in the class libraries at any of the three levels are created by the developers and stored in temporary VCX files. When the developer is done with the classes and is satisfied about their completion, the classes are submitted to the appropriate class librarian for consideration.

The class librarian should carefully review each class for the following items:

- Completeness—The class must accomplish the agreed-to responsibilities. It should also trap the appropriate errors, and so on.

- Standards—Many organizations have standards, such as naming conventions for variables, properties, and methods, commenting requirements, and so on. The class librarian, or someone designated by the class librarian, reviews the code to ensure that it meets the organization's standards. Without strict adherence to standards the class library will be almost impossible to maintain.

- Documentation—Any good class library is well-documented. The documentation should discuss the public interface (such as methods that are callable, what public properties do and mean and what their return values are, and so on). The documentation must be complete so that someone totally unfamiliar with the class can use it in the course of developing applications by either directly instantiating or subclassing the class. The rule should be no documentation, no acceptance.

- Robustness—The robustness of a class refers to how resistant the class is to errors. For example, if a bad parameter is sent to a method, will the method gracefully catch the errors or will it bomb?

- Compatibility—The class librarian must ascertain that the new class will not break any old code. It is probably a good idea to have a test case for every new class so that subsequent versions can be tested for compatibility. It should be taken as an axiom that any new or modified class must be properly and completely tested against existing code. This should be viewed as a primary responsibility for the class librarian.

Merging the New Classes

Once the submitted classes have been reviewed and approved, the next step is to merge the classes into the class libraries. Merging classes into the class libraries should take place at regular intervals—once a week or once a month. A rapidly changing class library is difficult on developers because it removes the important element of stability. In addition, once merging is complete the class librarian should inform all users of the class libraries of the changes and additions made to the libraries.

As a good rule of thumb, never make a change to the class libraries without telling everyone about it. That way, if something does accidentally break the developer will have a good idea where to look.

Technical Aspects of Managing Class Libraries

On the technical side, there are three basic actions a librarian normally has to take regarding the management of classes in VCX files.

- Moving or copying a class from one class library file to another
- Changing the name of a class
- Removing a class from a class library

Visual FoxPro has commands for each of these tasks.

Copying a Class

The ADD CLASS command is used to copy a class from one visual class library file to another. Here's the syntax:

```
ADD CLASS ClassName;
    [OF ClassLibrary1] ;
    TO ClassLibrary2 ;
    [OVERWRITE]
```

`ClassName` is the name of an existing class. The class can be a class already accessible in a VCX file loaded with SET CLASSLIB or it can be one you specifically reference from `ClassLibrary1` with the optional OF `ClassLibrary1` clause. The name of the VCX file in which to store the class is specified with the TO `ClassLibrary2` clause.

If the class already exists in `ClassLibrary2`, an error is generated by Visual FoxPro to prevent accidentally overwriting a class in a class library. The OVERWRITE keyword overrides this message and automatically overwrites the existing class.

Removing a Class

The REMOVE CLASS command removes a class from a class library. Here is the syntax:

```
REMOVE CLASS ClassName OF ClassLibrary
```

`ClassName` is the name of the class to remove, and `ClassLibrary` is the name of the VCX file from which the class is removed.

> **CAUTION**
>
> Removing a class is very dangerous because it can break the chain in a class hierarchy. For example, if you have a class hierarchy and remove one of the classes in the middle of the hierarchy, you will invalidate everything from the class you delete on down. You will not be able to even edit those classes. As far as native Visual FoxPro is concerned, the class is toast. Period.
>
> So, what do you do if you accidentally remove a class? The simple answer is to open the VCX file as a table and recall (using the RECALL command) the records you just deleted. Visual FoxPro does not have a command for deleting a level from a class hierarchy. You can do it with the Class Browser's Redefine feature, which is covered later in this chapter.

Moving a Class Between Class Libraries

There is no MOVE CLASS command. In order to move a class you need to copy it into the new class library and then remove it from the original one.

Renaming a Class

You can change a class in a visual class library file using the RENAME CLASS command. Here is the syntax:

```
RENAME CLASS OldClassName ;
    OF ClassLibrary ;
    TO NewClassName
```

OldClassName is the class name as it exists in the VCX file prior to the renaming. ClassLibrary is the name of the VCX file, and NewClassName is the new name for the class.

> **CAUTION**
>
> Be *very* careful with this command. If you rename a class, it only affects the one class; therefore, any classes subclassed from this class will no longer be able to find it.

> **TIP**
>
> How would you successfully rename a class that has subclasses? The easiest way is also the scariest. A VCX file is a table and can be opened with the USE command. Open the VCX file, look for instances of the old class name in the CLASS field, and manually change them to the new class name.

I know this sounds scary, but I have done this many times successfully. If you're worried, back up the old class library first. Actually, come to think of it, you should back up the old class library anyway. Paranoia is definitely your friend here.

If you missed a record in the VCX, don't worry. When you try to edit a class based on the renamed class that has not had the parent class name changed, FoxPro will return an error. You can cancel at that point, find the offending name in the class field, and fix it before moving on.

Finally, if you use the class in a form or container, that container will be affected as well and will not be editable until the appropriate change is made.

TIP

If you don't like the idea of opening the VCX file manually and doing batch updates, there is another alternative. Using the Class Browser's Redefine feature, you can manually redefine each class to work off the newly renamed class. You can do it only one class at a time, but it will work.

The other alternative is to create an add-in for the Class Browser so that it can go through the class tree and handle all the work for you. The Class Browser is covered in this chapter in the section "The Class Browser." Look for an add-in to take care of this issue for you.

Managing Classes Visually

Visual FoxPro gives you the commands to perform the rudimentary functions associated with managing class libraries. Add, Remove, and Rename basically cover the bulk of what you want to do.

On the other hand, they aren't very pretty. After you see the fancy Form Designer and Visual Class Designer, you would probably be disappointed if you had to manage class libraries by hand alone. Fortunately, you don't. That's where the Class Browser comes in.

The Class Browser

The Class Browser is a Visual FoxPro application (written entirely in Visual FoxPro) that ships with the Professional Edition of the product and is designed to provide a user-friendly, visual way to work with and manage class libraries. Loading a class library into the Class Browser provides all the functionality you have learned (and much more) at the touch of a mouse button.

There is one interesting note about the Class Browser to make up front. When I think of the Class Browser, I think of it for managing classes. However, because the file structures of SCX and VCX files are identical, the Class Browser also enables you to load SCX files. This is really nice because most (but not all) of the Class Browser's functionality works equally well with a SCX-based form as it does with a VCX file. Figure 30.2 shows you what the Class Browser looks like.

FIGURE 30.2.

The Class Browser.

The interface is very clean. The following sections explain the features presented in the Class Browser.

Form Caption

The title of the Class Browser form shows the name of the currently selected class and the name of the VCX or SCX file to which the selected class belongs.

Action Buttons

At the top of this modeless form is a series of command buttons that launch the bulk of the Class Browser's actions. Here is a list of them:

Button	Purpose
Open	Opens a class library. Any open class libraries are closed when the new one is opened.
View Additional File	Opens an additional class library and shows it with the current one. This is useful when the parent class of a class is stored in a different VCX file.

Button	Purpose
View Class Code	Exports the code for the currently selected class and shows it in a window. If the currently selected class is the VCX file itself, the entire class library is exported all at once.
Find	Finds text within a class in the open libraries.
New Class	Creates a new class based on the currently selected class. To create a new class in a VCX file based on a Visual FoxPro base class, position the list on the VCX file item and then click the New Class button.
Rename	Renames the currently selected class.
Redefine	Changes the parent class of the current class.
Remove	Deletes the currently highlighted class.
Clean Up Class Library	Packs the VCX file associated with the currently selected class.
Add-Ins	Runs an installed add-in.

As you can see, there is a lot here. The following sections explain the functions of the command buttons.

Open

This button opens a file; both VCX and SCX files can be opened. Visual FoxPro shows a GetFile() dialog box with the list of VCX files in the current directory (actually, the last directory GetFile() looked to, but that's another story). From this dialog box you select a file. To select an SCX file, change the file filter at the bottom of the dialog box. Figure 30.3 shows the dialog box with SCX files.

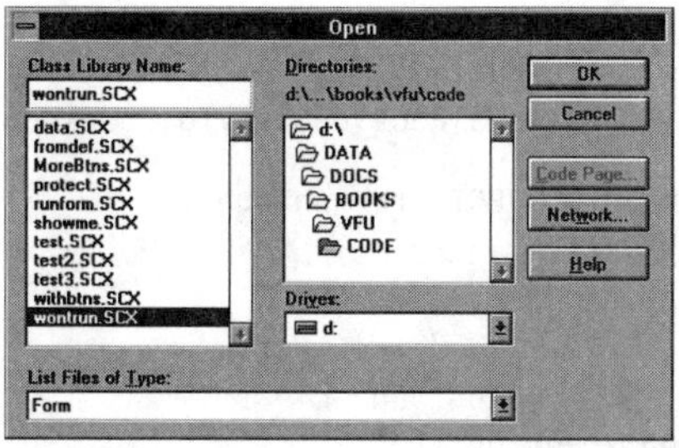

FIGURE 30.3.

The Class Browser GetFile() dialog box showing SCX files.

Selecting Cancel aborts the request to open a file. Also, when you open a new file, all files already opened in the Class Browser are closed.

View Additional File

This button enables you to show an additional file in the Class Browser. This is extremely useful when files are stored in more than one VCX file.

View Class Code

This button generates code for the currently selected class and shows the code in a window. If a file is selected in the class list, all classes in the file are generated and shown.

For the most part, the code generated will run if it is pasted into a PRG file, but there are limitations to this. For example, if you have a container on a form (such as a page frame) with objects added to the class, the code generated by the Class Browser will not run. Figure 30.4 shows what the form looks like in the designer. Here's a sample form that will not run.

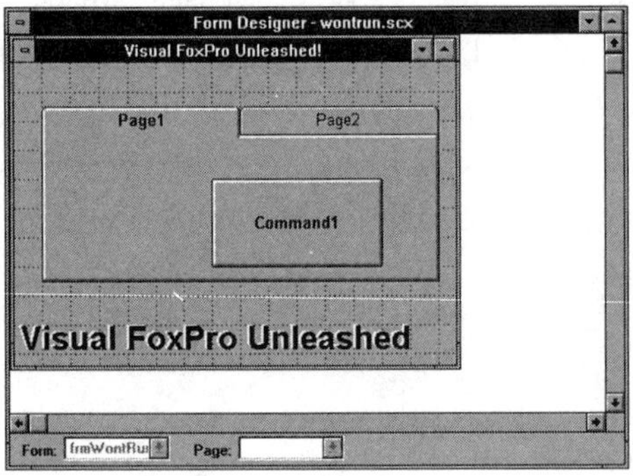

FIGURE 30.4.

The WontRun form.

```
*   Form.............: WontRun
*   Author...........: Menachem Bazian, CPA
*   Project..........: Visual FoxPro Unleashed!
*   Copyright........: (c)Flash Creative Management, Inc. 1995
*   Notes............: Exported code from Class Browser.

PUBLIC ofrmwontrun

SET CLASSLIB TO d:\data\docs\books\vfu\code\oop2.VCX ADDITIVE

ofrmwontrun=CREATEOBJECT("frmwontrun")
ofrmwontrun.Show()
RETURN


****************************************************
*-- Form:         frmwontrun
*-- ParentClass:  defaultform
*-- BaseClass:    form
*
DEFINE CLASS frmwontrun AS defaultform

    DoCreate = .T.
    Name = "frmWontRun"
```

```
        Label1.Name = "Label1"
        Label2.Name = "Label2"

    ADD OBJECT pageframe1 AS pageframe WITH ;
        ErasePage = .T., ;
        PageCount = 2, ;
        Top = 36, ;
        Left = 24, ;
        Width = 337, ;
        Height = 145, ;
        Name = "Pageframe1", ;
        Page1.Caption = "Page1", ;
        Page1.Name = "Page1", ;
        Page2.Caption = "Page2", ;
        Page2.Name = "Page2"

    ADD OBJECT frmwontrun.pageframe1.page1.command1 AS commandbutton WITH ;
        Top = 34, ;
        Left = 141, ;
        Height = 73, ;
        Width = 145, ;
        Caption = "Command1", ;
        Name = "Command1"

ENDDEFINE
*
*-- EndDefine: frmwontrun
******************************************************
```

Note that this form will run fine if it is run with a DO FORM command. Running it as a PRG file doesn't work—it will bomb when it attempts to add the command button to the page frame.

Find

This button presents a dialog box (see Figure 30.5) in which you enter the text you want to find. The text is first searched for in the names of the classes, then the class descriptions, and finally in the descriptions of the custom methods and properties.

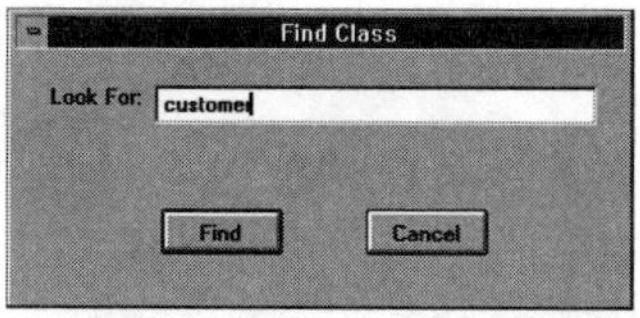

FIGURE 30.5.

The Find Class dialog box.

New Class

This button creates a new class. If the currently selected class is actually a filename, the Class Browser assumes that the parent class is a base class and displays the New Class dialog box accordingly (see Figure 30.6). Note how the name of the file in which to store the new class is automatically filled in. The Store In object on the dialog box defaults to the name of the VCX where the currently selected class is stored.

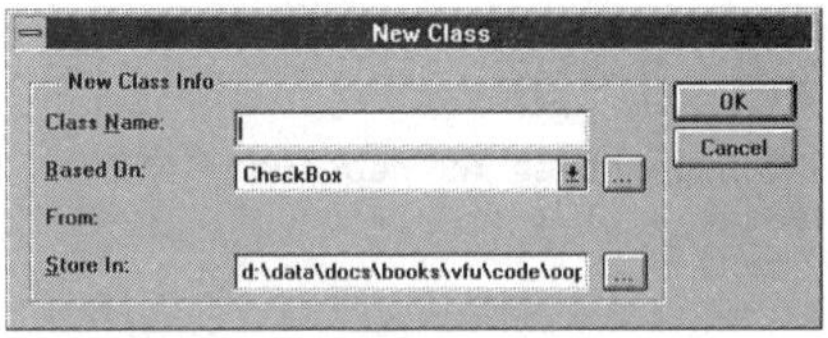

FIGURE 30.6.

The New Class dialog box based on a base class.

If a class is selected in the class list, the Class Browser assumes that the new class is a subclass of the currently selected class. Accordingly, all the fields in the dialog box are automatically filled in; all you have to supply is a class name (see Figure 30.7).

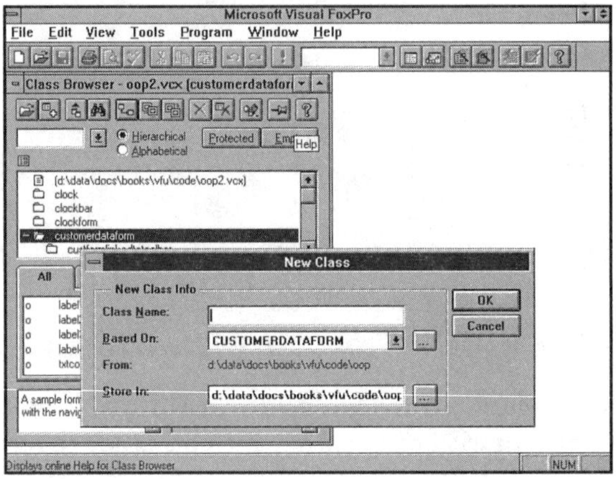

FIGURE 30.7.

A new subclass.

Rename

This button enables you to rename a class in the dialog box that displays (see Figure 30.8).

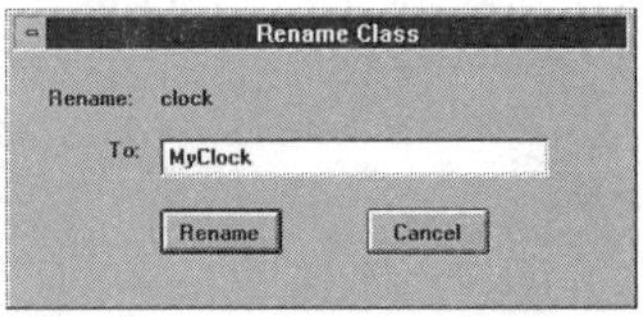

FIGURE 30.8.

The Rename Class dialog box.

> **CAUTION**
>
> Just a friendly reminder—the caution I gave you for the RENAME CLASS command in the section, "Renaming a Class," applies here, too.

Redefine

This button enables you to change the parent class of the currently selected class. This function, by the way, is available only in the Class Browser. Here's how it works.

The Redefine Class dialog box displays (see Figure 30.9). In order to redefine a class as a subclass of its Visual FoxPro base class, leave the fields blank and select Redefine. Otherwise, type in the name of the class to be the new parent class. Note that the dialog box automatically assumes that the new parent class is in the same class library as the class you are redefining. If it isn't, you will have to either type in the name of the class library or click the command button with the ellipses on it to get a GetFile() dialog box in order to select the VCX file.

FIGURE 30.9.

The Redefine Class dialog box.

There is one restriction on this function. The new parent class must have the same base class as the prior one (that is, you can't redefine a CommandButton-based class as a CheckBox-based class).

Remove

The Remove option deletes the currently selected class. You are given a warning by the Class Browser before it deletes the class.

> **CAUTION**
>
> The caution I gave about REMOVE CLASS in the section "Removing a Class" applies here, too.

Clean Up Class Library

This option packs the VCX file.

Add-Ins

This option displays a list of add-ins. See the section on add-ins ("Putting It All Together with Add-Ins") for more information.

The Push Pin and Help Button

In the far top-right corner is a push pin that defines whether or not the Class Browser stays on top all the time and a help button that launches the Visual FoxPro help for the Class Browser.

Type Filter

If you have multiple VCX files open or have a lot of classes in one file, it might be difficult to find classes in the list. The Type filter gives you the ability to set a filter on the type of class in the list. The drop-down list box shows the list of Visual FoxPro base classes (CommandButton, ToolBar, and so on). As an alternative, you can type in class names to filter the list. Figure 30.10 shows the Class Browser with a filter applied.

FIGURE 30.10.

The Class Browser with a filter applied.

The Type filter fully supports wildcards. For example, to find every class with Button in the name, you could specify %Button% (case doesn't matter). Button* shows all classes with names beginning with Button. The question mark (?) is a single-character wildcard.

If you type in your own filters they are automatically added to the filter list for that session.

Display Method

The Class Browser can show the classes in hierarchical order (the default order) or in alphabetical order. Hierarchical order shows the classes in tree form with subclasses beneath parent classes. Alphabetical order ignores the class hierarchy and just shows all the listed classes in alphabetical order. Figure 30.11 shows the Class Browser in alphabetical order.

FIGURE 30.11.

The class list in alphabetical order.

Protected Member

By default, the Class Browser will not list protected properties and methods when a class is displayed. If this button is pressed, the protected members display in the appropriate tabs at the bottom of the form. If a property or method is protected, it is shown in the Members tab and is preceded with an asterisk (*).

Empty Method

By default, custom methods (not methods inherited from prior classes) attached to a class will show only if there is code in them. This button, when shown pressed, causes the empty methods to show in the All and Methods tabs.

If an empty method is shown in the Members tab, the name of the method is preceded by a tilde (~).

Class Icon

The Class icon is the picture just above the left corner of the list of classes. It's a visual representation of the class currently selected in the list. You can set the icon in the Class Information screens. This is discussed in Chapter 28, "OOP with Visual FoxPro."

The icon is more than a picture, though. It is also the Drag/Drop button. Clicking and dragging this icon to a form in design mode will automatically add that class to the form. It is functionally equivalent to loading the class library into the Form Controls toolbar and dropping the class library on the form.

But there's more. By dropping the icon on the desktop, you attempt to instantiate and run the class right then and there. This can be a cool way to test your classes, especially for most form classes.

Finally, you can use drag and drop to copy classes from one VCX file to another. Here's how you do it. Open the Class Browser twice (once for each VCX file). Grab the class icon you want to copy and drag it to the other Class Browser instance. Be careful and watch the drag icon to make sure that it changes to the Copy drag icon (shown in Figure 30.12) before you drop the class. When you drop the class, it will be added to the second Class Browser instance.

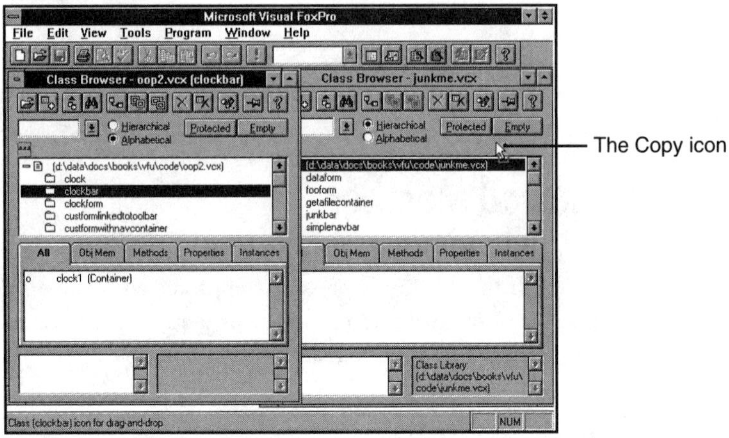

FIGURE 30.12.

The Class Browser with the Copy icon.

List of Classes

The list of classes is based on the outline control that ships with Visual FoxPro. When the class list is in hierarchical mode, you can expand or contract a branch of classes by clicking the + or - icons.

Double-clicking the class name loads the class into the Visual Class Designer for editing. Double-clicking the folder moves to the parent class for that class.

If a class is based on a class in another VCX file that is not shown, a chevron (<<) appears in between the folder and the class name. (See Figure 30.13.) Clicking the Folder icon for that class automatically loads the VCX file with the parent class, as shown in Figure 30.14, before moving to the parent class.

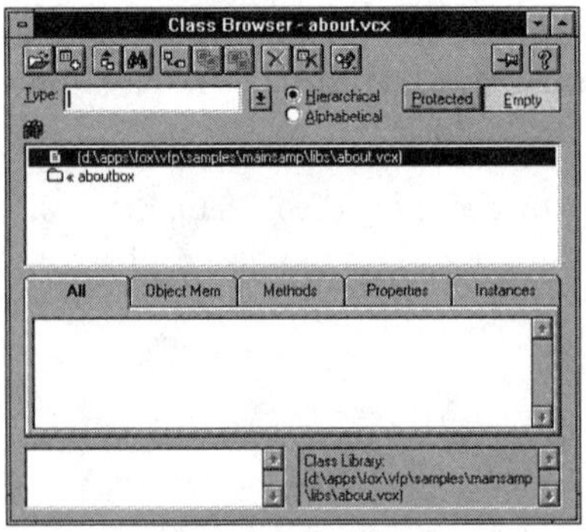

FIGURE 30.13.

A class based on another VCX class.

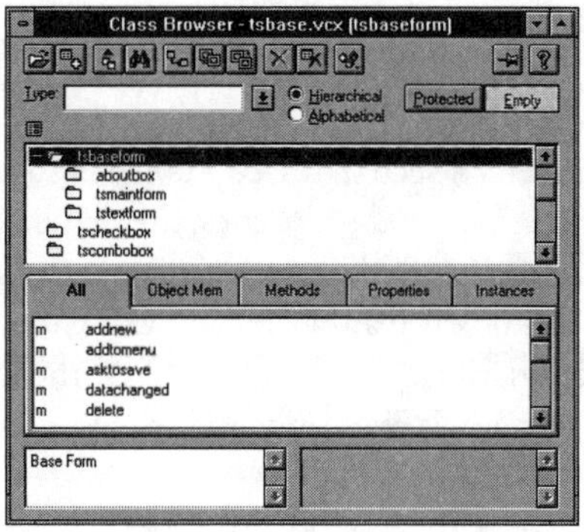

FIGURE 30.14.

The Class Browser with a parent VCX file loaded.

Members Tab

The tabbed portion of the form shows the members of the currently selected class. The All tab shows all the members and does not filter the list. The other tabs (Object Members, Methods, Properties, and Instances) filter the information to the type specified in the tab name.

The Instances tab is interesting and deserves a special mention. This tab shows the instances for a particular class. For example, if you have two instances for a class, called ox and oy, they would show up in the Instances tab, as shown in Figure 30.15.

FIGURE 30.15.

Object instances.

Class Description

This edit box enables you to view and edit the description for a class. The description entered in this box is automatically placed in the VCX file and shows in the Description box in the Class Info dialog box. This is particularly nice because it is not uncommon to add some descriptions at the end of the process, and this saves having to go into the Visual Class Designer to edit the description.

Member Description

This edit box is the description of a selected member in the Member tab lists. For example, if an object member is selected, the edit box will show the class and base class names of the object member. For methods and properties, the edit box is read-write and has the description for the property or method entered in the New Property/Method or Edit Property/Method dialog box. Because this edit box is read-write, you can enter or edit the description in the Class Browser and have the description carry forward to the VCX file. Finally, if an instance variable is selected, the edit box is read-only and shows information about the instance.

Starting the Class Browser

You can start the Class Browser in one of two ways. One way is to use the menu—Select Tools | Class Browser. A dialog box appears and prompts you for the name of the class library to load. If you type in the name of a class library that does not exist, the Class Browser creates it for you.

The second way to load the Class Browser is to use the _browser system variable. _browser is typically set to BROWSER.APP, which is located in the Visual FoxPro home directory. Issuing the command

```
DO (_browser)
```

is equivalent to using the menus. In addition, you can pass a parameter through with the name of the class library to load. The following example will load ABOUT.VCX for the TASTRADE sample application:

```
DO (_browser) WITH HOME()+"samples\mainsamp\libs\about"
```

Optionally, you can add a second parameter to the command that will automatically select a particular class in the list. The following example will load the About library and select the Aboutbox class:

```
DO (_browser) WITH HOME()+"samples\mainsamp\libs\about", ;
    "aboutbox"
```

The next example will start the Class Browser with the form Customer.SCX loaded:

```
DO (_browser) WITH HOME()+"samples\mainsamp\forms\customer.scx"
```

The Class Browser and SCX Files

TIP

A neat feature of the Class Browser shows an SCX file in the hierarchy with its parent class.

Visual FoxPro enables you to use the Tools | Options menu item on the Forms tab to specify what the form template class is (see Figure 30.16). The template form is the form used as the base class when a new form is created with CREATE FORM.

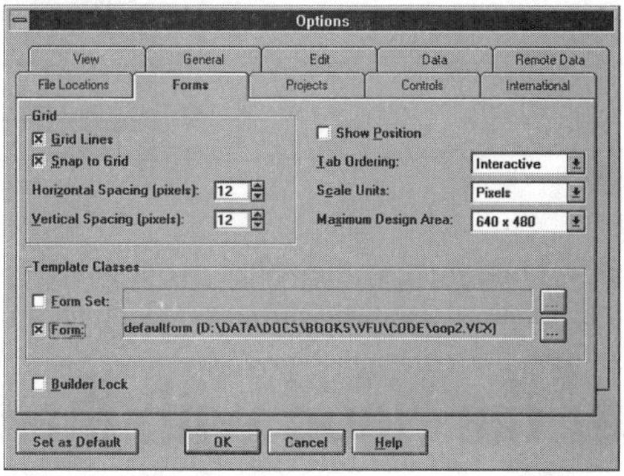

FIGURE 30.16.

Specifying DefaultForm.

Suppose you have a form class called DefaultForm and you create a form with CREATE FORM. The form I created to illustrate this is called FromDef. Figure 30.17 shows the form in the Form Designer.

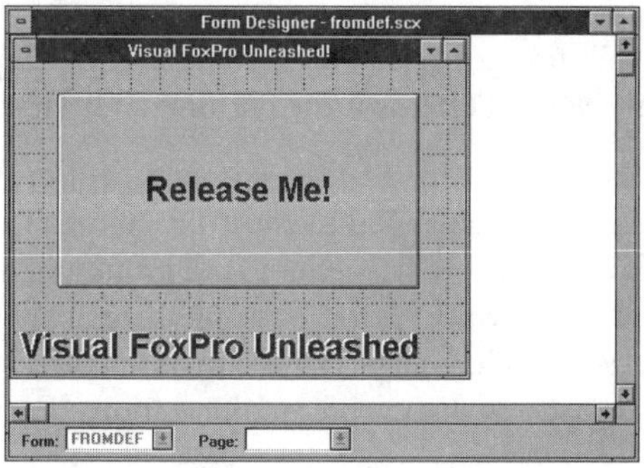

FIGURE 30.17.

FromDef.SCX in the Form Designer.

Now you can bring the form up in the Class Browser, as shown in Figure 30.18. For the record, I have also added the VCX file with the DefaultForm class in it. Although FromDef is a SCX-based form, it shows up in the proper place in the class hierarchy in the Class Browser class list.

FIGURE 30.18.

Class Browser with FormDef.SCX.

There's more. Once you get a view like this one going, you can even change your form's parent class (that is, its super class) with the Redefine function. Cool stuff.

Under the Hood with the Class Browser

The next step in working with the Class Browser is to understand the methods, properties, and object members that make up the class. Why, you ask? One of the nicest features about the Class Browser is that, as an object, it is totally open and extensible. You can manually call methods from outside the Class Browser. Here is an example:

```
_obrowser.cmdexport.click()
```

This example runs the Click() method behind the Export button and brings up the code for the currently selected class as if the button had been clicked.

Being able to access the methods and properties of the Class Browser is important for two reasons. First of all, it enables you to create programs that can interact with the Class Browser in all kinds of ways. The public methods and properties of the Class Browser and all its members are open for you to work with at your pleasure. The second reason is that the Class Browser supports add-ins, which can be hooked to objects and methods in the Class Browser. You learn about add-ins later in this chapter in the section, "Putting It All Together with Add-Ins."

The point here, however, is that in order to use these powerful capabilities you have to know what goes on under the hood of the Class Browser.

By the way, _obrowser is the name of a system memory variable that references the Class Browser when it is up (otherwise it is .NULL.). This is typically the way in which you would access the Class Browser's properties and methods (as opposed to using _screen.activeform). If you find the name lengthy, you can always assign it to another, shorter variable name.

The next step: the object members, methods, and properties of the Class Browser.

Object Members

The object members listed here are all named with standard naming conventions. For example, an object with a name starting with CMD is a command button.

Object Name	Class Browser Object
cmdOpen	Open command button
cmdAdd	Add command button
cmdExport	View Class Definition Code command button
cmdFind	Find command button
cmdSubclass	Add Subclass command button
cmdRename	Rename command button
cmdRedefine	Redefine command button
cmdRemove	Remove command button
cmdCleanup	Clean Up Library command button
opgDisplayMode	Display Mode option group
optHierarchical	Hierarchical option button
optAlphabetical	Alphabetical option button
chkProtected	Protected check box
chkEmpty	Empty check box
imgClassIcon	Class Icon image
cmdClassIcon	Class Icon command button
lblClassType	Type label for the Type combo box
cboClassType	Type combo box
txtClassList3D	Class List highlight text
oleClassList	Class List Outline OLE container
pgfMembers	Member Tabs page frame
fpgAll	All page
lstAll	All list box
fpgObjects	Object Member page
lstObjects	Object Member list box
fpgMethods	Methods page
lstMethods	Methods list box
fpgProperties	Properties page
lstProperties	Properties list box
fpgInstances	Instances page
lstInstances	Instances list box
txtClassDesc	Class Description text box
txtMemberDesc	Member Description text box

The properties and methods of these objects are available for your use. As you saw earlier, you can call the methods with ease. You can also change the properties of these objects. For example, you could change the ToolTipText property of the cmdExport button as follows:

```
_oBrowser.cmdExport.ToolTipText = "Export Code"
```

Once this line of code executes, the Export Code tooltip will show when the mouse button hovers over the View Class Code button (as shown in Figure 30.19).

FIGURE 30.19.

The Class Browser showing new tooltip text.

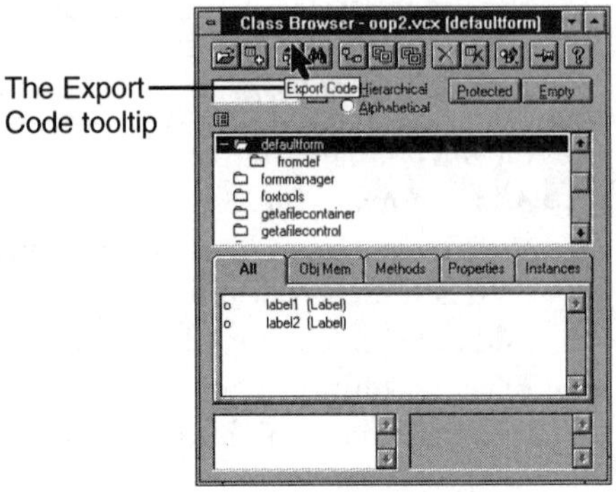

The Export — Code tooltip

You can also hide an object by setting its visible property to .F.. This is a way to temporarily "remove" an object from the Class Browser form. Keep this one in mind, I'll come back to it.

Methods

The Class Browser supports all the methods in the Form class (upon which it is based). In addition, the following methods are supported.

AddClass()

This method copies a class from one class library (VCX) file to another. AddClass() is used after a drag-and-drop operation between instances of the Class Browser. If the specified class does not exist, a class is created.

AddFile([<VCXFileName>])

This method adds a VCX file to the Class Browser class list. It is used by the cmdAdd button to add a file to the Class Browser. If no parameters are passed, an AddFile dialog box appears by using the Class Browser GetFile method.

VCXFileName is the name of the file to add. It can be a VCX file (which is the assumed extension) or a SCX file (if you specify .SCX in the filename).

AddIn()

This method registers or removes an add-in in the Class Browser. See the sections on add-ins beginning with "Putting It All Together with Add-Ins" for a discussion of add-ins in the Class Browser, what they mean and how they can help you, and what methods the Class Browser has to support them.

AddInMenu()

This method displays the menu of installed add-ins. See the section on add-ins.

AddInMethod()

This method runs a method associated with an add-in. See the section on add-ins.

AutoRefresh()

This method determines whether the current class needs to be refreshed and automatically refreshes the class if needed (that is, the list of members is automatically rebuilt).

CleanUpFile()

This method packs the VCX file associated with the currently selected class.

ClearBrowser()

This method is for internal use only.

DeactivateMenu()

This method closes the menu of installed add-ins. See the section on add-ins.

DoAddIn()

This method executes an add-in. See the section on add-ins.

ExportClass([*tlShow*])

This method generates the code for the currently selected class and then returns the text as a string. If the optional logical parameter is sent through as .T., a window will pop up with the code.

FindClass([*tcTextToFind*])

This method looks through the classes loaded in the Class Browser for the text passed. It first searches for the text as the name of a class in the list. If it does not find the text to match a name of a class, it then searches the class description. If it does not find the text in the class description, it then looks in the member names and descriptions for the text.

If the optional parameter *tcTextToFind* is not passed, a dialog box displays that enables you to type in the text to find.

FormAddObject(*Object Name* [, *X Coord*] [, *Y Coord*] [, *Activate Form?*] [, *Design Mode?*])

This method adds an instance of the selected class to an external form. Here is what the parameters mean:

Object Name	*Object Name* is the name of the form to which you want to add the class. The form can be running or a form in design mode.
X Coord	This parameter is the horizontal position. It defaults to the current mouse position.
Y Coord	This parameter is the vertical position. It defaults to the current mouse position used.
Activate Form?	This is a logical parameter. If the parameter is true (.T.), the destination form is activated when the object is added to it; if the parameter is false (.F.), the Class Browser remains active.
Design Mode?	This is a logical parameter. If true (.T.), the object reference is an object currently in the Form Designer or Class Designer.

FormAddObject is a useful method that enables you to do some interesting things. For example, consider the following form:

```
*   Form..............: RUNFORM.SCX
*   Author............: Menachem Bazian, CPA
*   Project...........: Visual FoxPro Unleashed!
*   Copyright.........: (c)Flash Creative Management, Inc. 1995
*   Notes.............: Exported code from Class Browser.

**************************************************
*-- Form:         form1 (runform.scx)
*-- ParentClass:  form
*-- BaseClass:    form
*
DEFINE CLASS form1 AS form

    DoCreate = .T.
    Caption = "Form1"
    Name = "Form1"

    PROCEDURE DragDrop
        LPARAMETERS oSource, nXCoord, nYCoord

        oSource.Parent.FormAddObject(this)
    ENDPROC

ENDDEFINE
*
*-- EndDefine: form1
**************************************************
```

The code in the DragDrop method accepts a parameter called oSource, which is the object dropped on the form.

With this code, run the form with the Class Browser running. Then take a class from the Class Browser and drag it over the running form and drop it. The DragDrop event for the form fires. In this case, oSource represents the oSource property of the Class Browser. Thus, oSource.Parent references the Class Browser itself. Calling FormAddObject and passing it the form as a parameter adds the currently selected class in the Class Browser (that is, the class you dropped onto the running form) to the form.

FormatMethods(*Method Text*)

This method formats the text of generated methods in the display of the class definition code. The text of the methods is passed in the one parameter to the method. This method is designed for internal use but could be useful if you want to create your own export utility.

FormatProperties(*Properties Text*, *lAddObject*)

This method formats the text of generated properties in the display of the class definition code (that is, lines with ADD OBJECT and a list of properties set on that command line). The text of the ADD OBJECT command is passed through in the one parameter to the method. This method is designed for internal use but could be useful if you want to create your own export utility.

GetFile(*File Extensions*)

This method opens the Class Browser GetFile dialog box and is intended for internal use. The difference between the GetFile method and the GetFile function is that the GetFile method will automatically read the cFileExt property of the Class Browser for the list of file extensions to list in the file filter on the GetFile dialog box.

IndentText(*Code*)

This method indents a block of text (passed in the Code parameter) one tab.

ModifyClass()

This method opens the Visual Class Designer for the currently highlighted class.

MsgBox(*Message* [, *Dialog box Type*] [, *Dialog box Title*])

Based on the MessageBox function, this method brings up a message dialog box. The differences between this method and the MessageBox function are that the icon defaults to the exclamation point, the title defaults to the caption of the Class Browser window, and the buttons are OK and Cancel by default.

NewClass()

This method creates a subclass of the selected class in the class list. To create a new class in a VCX file based on a Visual FoxPro base class, you position the list on the VCX file item and then run `NewClass()`.

NewFile(*FileName* [, *Open Automatically?*])

This method creates a new VCX file. If no parameters are passed, the Open File dialog box is displayed. If the `FileName` parameter is passed and is a new class library (VCX file), the VCX is automatically created (without the dialog box). Specifying `.T.` to the second parameter will automatically add the new VCX file to the class list in Class Browser.

OpenFile(*FileName*)

This method opens a file and is the equivalent of the Open button. Passing a filename will open the file. If no filename is passed, an Open dialog box displays.

ProperBaseClass(*Base Class Name*)

This method accepts a class name and makes a "proper" name out of it. For example, `commandbutton` becomes `CommandButton`. If the class name passed through is not the name of a FoxPro base class, the method capitalizes it (for example, `mycommandbutton` becomes `Mycommandbutton`).

RedefineClass(*New Parent Class* [, *VCX File*])

`RedefineClass` redefines the currently selected class to be a subclass of *New Parent Class*, which is contained in *VCX File*.

> **CAUTION**
>
> The same caution regarding the renaming classes discussed in the "Renaming a Class" section applies here.

RefreshButtons()

This method refreshes the Class Browser command buttons based on the file type. Different command buttons are enabled and disabled based on the type of file loaded (VCX or SCX file). This method checks the buttons against the file type.

RefreshClassList([*Class to Select*][, *Ignore the table?*])

This method refreshes the class list. The first parameter dictates which class should be selected when the refresh is done. The second rebuilds the list based on the internal arrays and ignores the underlying VCX file table.

RefreshClassListSubclass()

This method is for internal use only.

RefreshFileAttrib()

The Class Browser has a property called lReadOnly that signifies the read-only attribute of a Visual Class library. (A file can be flagged as read-only in FILER, for example.) This method checks the read-only attribute of the VCX file and updates lReadOnly based on what it determines.

RefreshCaption()

This method refreshes the caption of the Class Browser form.

RefreshMembers()

This method refreshes the Members tabs to display the members associated with the selected class in the class list.

RefreshPrefRecNo()

This method refreshes the BROWSER.DBF preference record pointer for the class library (VCX file) or form (SCX file) being edited.

RefreshRecNo()

This method refreshes the current record pointer of the class library (VCX file) or form table (SCX file) for the file of the selected class.

RemoveClass(*Confirm Before Removal?*)

This method removes the selected class in the class list from its associated class library (VCX) file. If .T. is passed, the Class Browser will present a warning before removing the class.

> **CAUTION**
>
> By default, this method removes the selected class without a warning. Beware of this. If you accidentally remove a class it will be deleted from the VCX file. To recover a class, you will have to open the VCX file and recall the records manually.

RenameClass(*New Class Name*)

This method changes the class name of the selected class in the class list to the name specified in the parameter. If a name is not passed, a dialog box is presented that enables you to enter the new class name.

SavePreferences()

This method saves current preference settings to the BROWSER.DBF registration table. BROWSER.DBF is a table similar to the FOXUSER file. It saves preferences for every VCX file opened. The preferences saved include items such as form size, left and top coordinates, and so on. Add-in registrations are also saved in BROWSER.DBF.

ScaleResize()

When the Class Browser form is resized, the controls on it automatically resize to fit the form. ScaleResize is the method that handles this process.

SeekClass(*Class* [, *VCX File*])

This method moves the list pointer to a specified class. The parameter can be either numeric (that is, the list pointer moves to the class *n* in the list, where *n* is the number passed through as the Class parameter) or the name of the class to find.

The *VCX File* parameter is useful if you have multiple class libraries open and the same class name is in several viewed VCX files. Specifying the VCX filename will limit the search to that VCX file.

The parameters are not case-sensitive. The class you search for must be visible in order for it to be found, and the method returns a logical value indicating whether SEEK() was successful.

SeekParentClass()

This method displays the parent class for the selected class. If the parent class is in a different VCX file not shown in the list, the associated VCX file is automatically loaded. This method returns a logical value indicating the success of the search.

SetBusyState(*BusyState*)

Sets the lBusyStatus property to true (.T.) or false (.F.) based on the logical parameter *BusyState*. If the Class Browser is set to busy (.T.), the mouse pointer shape is set to an hourglass; otherwise, it is set to an arrow. Other than this, SetBusyState does not really do much.

SetFont(*FontName,FontSize*)

This method sets the font and font size used by the Class Browser for its form, controls, and dialog boxes. Note that you do not have to pass the font name each time. You could use the following example:

```
_oBrowser.SetFont(,10)
```

to set the Class Browser to 10-point font size without changing the font itself. (See Figure 30.20.)

FIGURE 30.20.

The Class Browser with a 10-point font size setting.

ShowMenu(*Menu Array*[, *Command on Select*])

This method displays a menu based on an array. If a menu is a single-dimension array, this method displays a list of all items in the menu. When an item is selected, the command specified in *command on select* is executed. Here is an example:

```
DECLARE laMenu2[2]
laMenu2[1] = "Benjamin"
laMenu2[2] = "Jonathan"
_oBrowser.ShowMenu(@laMenu2, "Wait Window Prompt()")
```

`Wait Window Prompt()` is the *command on select* and will execute if any of the items on the menu are selected. As shown in Figure 30.21, the menu is brought up at the location of the mouse pointer.

FIGURE 30.21.

The Class Browser with a menu showing.

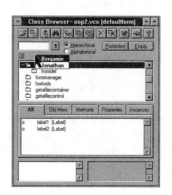

If the array is two-dimensional, the first column becomes the list of prompts on the array and the second column is assumed to be the command to execute when the associated menu item is selected. Here is an example:

```
declare laMenu[3,2]
laMenu[1,1] = "Menachem"
laMenu[2,1] = "Avi"
laMenu[3,1] = "David"
laMenu[1,2] = "WAIT WINDOW 'Bazian'"
laMenu[2,2] = "WAIT WINDOW 'Greengart'"
laMenu[3,2] = "WAIT WINDOW 'Blumenthal'"
_oBrowser.ShowMenu(@laMenu2)
```

If an item is selected, the command in the second column in that array is executed. For example, selecting Avi will execute the WAIT WINDOW 'Greengart' command.

TrimExt(*FileName*)

This method accepts a filename as a parameter and returns the name minus the extension. Here is an example:

```
? _oBrowser.TrimExt("BROWSE.DBF") && Returns "BROWSE"
```

TrimFile(*FileName with Path*)

This method accepts a filename as a parameter and returns the path only (that is, it trims off the filename).

TrimPath(*FileName with Path*)

This method accepts a filename as a parameter and returns the filename and extension only (the path is removed).

Here is an example:

```
? _oBrowser.TrimPath("D:\APPS\BROWSE.DBF")
* Returns "BROWSE.DBF"
```

VersionCheck(*Show Error Message?*)

This method validates the open class library (VCX file) or form (SCX file) and returns .T. if the file is valid, .F. if it is not. If a parameter of .T. is passed, an invalid file will cause an error message to show.

How does this method work? It checks the contents of the field Reserved1 for a proper version number. If you want to call this method on your own, make sure that the record pointer in the VCX file is set to the top of the file (setting the list selection won't work—that works off an array). The VCX file you are looking for is open in the Class Browser's data session with an alias of Metadata<*n*>, where *n* is the number of the VCX file (the first VCX file opened is given an alias of metadata1, the second metadata2, and so on).

You can find which metadata file to work with by checking the DBF file underlying the metadata<*n*> alias with the DBF function. When DBF matches the name of the current VCX file (you can get this from the Class Browser's cFileName property), simply issue GO TOP and then run the versioncheck method.

This method runs automatically when the VCX file is loaded into the Class Browser—you shouldn't have to use this method too often. Still, it's good to know.

WildcardMatch(*Wild Card Expression List, Expression to Search*)

This method compares strings for a wildcard match with the filters specified in the Type box. Here is an example:

```
? ox.Wildcardmatch("ox?", "OxyMoron")        && Returns .F.
? ox.Wildcardmatch("ox?, ox*", "OxyMoron")   && Returns .T.
```

Properties

Table 30.1 presents the properties of the Class Browser.

CAUTION

Note that some properties are marked as No in the "Can It Be Changed?" column. This does not mean that these properties cannot be changed if you issue the commands to do so. These properties are, in fact, not protected. However, if you do change the properties marked No in the "Can It Be Changed?" column, you could cause the Class Browser problems (it may abend, work improperly, and who knows what all).

Simple lesson: if the chart says No, it means that if you change the property on your own, you do so at your own risk.

Table 30.1. Properties of the Class Browser.

Property Name	Description	Can It Be Changed?
aClassList	An array with two dimensions that holds information about each class in the class list. Here's the structure of the array: [Row,1] The class name. [Row,2] The record number in the VCX file.	No

continues

Table 30.1. continued

Property Name	Description	Can It Be Changed?
	[Row,3] The number of levels indented in the list.	
	[Row,4] The VCX file with the parent class.	
	[Row,5] The parent class name.	
	[Row,6] The path of the parent class's VCX file.	
aFiles	An array listing the files open in the Class Browser.	No
aInstances	An array of instances for the selected class in the list.	No
BackColor	The background color of the form.	Yes
cAddInMethod	The name of the method that called the currently executing add-in. See the section on add-ins beginning with "Putting It All Together with Add-Ins."	No
cAlias	The alias of the VCX file for the current class (for example, METADATA).	
Caption	The caption of the window.	Yes
cBaseClass	The name of the base class of the currently selected class in the Class Browser.	No
cBrowserTable	The name and full path to the Class Browser registration table (BROWSER .DBF).	No
cClass	The name of the currently selected class.	No
cClassLibrary	The name of the VCX file where the parent of the current class is located. This is empty for classes based on a base class.	No
cClassType	The current Type filter.	No
cDefaultClass	The name of the initial class to select in the Class Browser (the third parameter on the DO (_browser) command line).	Yes
cDragIcon	The name of the icon file used as the picture for the drag icon.	Yes

Property Name	Description	Can It Be Changed?
cFileName	The VCX filename of the currently selected class.	No
cFilter	The filter set on the VCX file for the current class.	No
cGetFileExt	The extensions shown in the GETFILE() displayed by the Open button.	Yes
cLastSetComp	SET("compatible") before the Class Browser loaded.	No
cLastSetESC	SET("escape") before the Class Browser loaded.	No
cLastValue	For internal use only.	No
cParentClass	The parent class of the currently selected class.	No
cPlatform	The current platform (Windows, for example).	No
cProgramName	Full path to BROWSER.APP.	No
cStartName	The name of the Class Browser before it was incremented by additional instances. (Showing more Class Browsers will increment the name to Classbrowser1, Classbrowser2, and so on.)	No
cTimeStamp	The timestamp of the currently selected class. For internal use only.	No
DataSession	The data session setting for this form. (The Class Browser runs in a private data session.)	No
DoCreate	For internal use only.	No
FontName	Default form font.	Yes
FontSize	Default form font size.	Yes
Height	Form height.	Yes
HelpContextID	The Help ID for the Class Browser.	No
Icon	The icon file for the form when minimized.	Yes
lActive	Specifies whether the Class Browser has focus. For internal use only.	No

continues

Table 30.1. continued

Property Name	Description	Can It Be Changed?
lAddInMode	Is .T. when an add-in is running and .F. when it is complete.	No
lAddInTrace	If set to .T., the Class Browser lists each method to which an add-in can be hooked as it is executed. See the section on add-ins (beginning with "Putting It All Together with Add-Ins") for more information.	Yes
lAutoExpand	Determines whether class hierarchies are shown expanded or collapsed by default.	Yes
lBusyState	If .T., a refresh operation is in progress. For internal use only.	No
lFileMode	If .T., the currently selected class is really a file.	No
lInitialized	For internal use only.	No
lNoDefault	Determines whether default method behavior is executed after the add-ins are registered for that method.	Yes
lReadOnly	The status of the read-only attribute for the VCX file associated with the currently selected class.	No
lRelease	For internal use only.	No
lResizeMode	For internal use only.	No
lSCXMode	If .T., the currently selected class is actually an SCX file.	No
Left	The left coordinate of the Class Browser form.	Yes
MinHeight	The smallest height the form can have.	No
MinWidth	The narrowest width the form can have.	No
Name	The name of the Class Browser instance.	No
nAtPos	For internal use only.	No
nClassCount	The number of classes in the list.	No
nClassListIndex	The position of the selected class in the class list.	No
nDisplayMode	Display mode (hierarchical or alphabetical). 1 is hierarchical and 2 is alphabetical. The	No

Property Name	Description	Can It Be Changed?
	default value is 1. Note that changing this property will not change the display mode. In order to do that, you need to change the value of opgDisplayMode.	
nFileCount	The number of files open.	No
nInstances	The number of instances of the currently selected class.	No
nLastHeight	The height of the Class Browser form before it was last changed.	No
nLastRecno	For internal use only.	No
nLastWidth	The width of the form before the last resize.	No
nPixelOffset	For internal use only.	No
nRecCount	The total number of records in the VCX file.	No
nStrLen	For internal use only.	No
oSource	The reference for an object dropped on a form from the Class Browser.	No
ScaleMode	Specifies how numbers are translated into coordinates.	No
ShowTips	Specifies whether tooltips for the objects show or not.	Yes
tcDefaultClass	The name of the class sent through as the second parameter to the Class Browser.	No
tcFileName	The name of the file to open passed through on the commandline calling the Class Browser.	No
Top	The top coordinate of the form.	Yes
Width	The width of the form.	Yes

Working with the properties of the Class Browser provides a neat beginning to customizing it for your own use and tastes. For example, you could change the height of the form with this:

```
_obrowser.height = _obrowser.height + 10
```

If you try it, you'll also notice that the form controls will automatically resize. This happens because changing the height property automatically fires the Resize() method.

Putting It All Together with Add-Ins

Now you know all about the Class Browser internals. You know what the objects, properties, and methods are. What can you do with this knowledge?

The Class Browser has a wonderful little feature called add-ins. Basically, an *add-in* is a program you write that you can register with the Class Browser. Once registered, you can call the add-in to perform just about anything you like.

An Add-In Program

I will start with a simple example of an add-in. This add-in just displays a wait window with the name of the currently selected class. Although it's not very useful, it does give a good and simple starting place for understanding add-ins. Here's the code:

```
*   Program...........: CLSNAME.PRG
*   Author............: Menachem Bazian, CPA
*   Project...........: Visual FoxPro Unleashed!
*   Created...........: June 09, 1995 - 08:24:38
*   Copyright.........: (c)Flash Creative Management, Inc., 1995
*) Description.......: Simple add in for the Class Browser that
*)                   : displays the current class' name.
*   Calling Samples...:
*   Parameter List....:
*   Major change list.:

LPARAMETERS toSource

WAIT WINDOW toSource.ProperBaseClass(toSource.cClass)
RETURN
```

Note the parameter. When the Class Browser calls the add-in it passes itself as a parameter to the add-in. This enables you to do all kinds of neat things. Before I get into those, I will cover the nuts and bolts of registering and running add-ins.

Registering the Add-In

Next, register the add-in with the Class Browser. Note that the Class Browser has to be running in order to do this.

```
_oBrowser.AddIn("Class Name", "ClsName")
```

The AddIn method registers an add-in. The syntax shown here specifies a name for the add-in (Class Name) and the program to run (ClsName.PRG).

Running the Add-In

You can run the add-in in several ways. First of all, the add-in can be run with the DoAddIn method. Here's the syntax for this method:

```
_oBrowser.DoAddIn("Class Name")
```

Passing the name of a registered add-in to the DoAddIn method will run that add-in. Another way that it can be called is with the Add-In button. Clicking the Add-In button activates a menu with the installed add-ins. Figure 30.22 shows the Class Browser with the Add-In menu activated from the Add-In button.

FIGURE 30.22.

The Add-In button.

You can manually expand the same menu using the AddInMenu method as follows:

```
_oBrowser.AddInMenu
```

Running this method will expand the menu at the location of the mouse pointer. You can close the menu with _oBrowser.DeactivateMenu, although you shouldn't need to because the menu is automatically closed when a selection is made.

Unregistering an Add-In

You can remove an add-in from the Class Browser registration table with the AddIn method too. Here's how to do it:

```
_oBrowser.AddIn("Class Name",.NULL.)
```

If the program name is provided as a value of .NULL., the add-in record in the Class Browser registration table is marked for deletion.

TIP

The help file says that the add-in is deleted if the second parameter (the name of the add-in program) is "empty." Don't believe it. You have to pass through the parameter as a value of .NULL. for the add-in to be deleted.

Boosting Power with Add-Ins

Add-ins let you do all kinds of great things. The example you saw in the last section is a simple example. Basically, it displays the name of the currently selected class. It accomplishes this by accepting the object parameter (remember, the Class Browser is the parameter) and then accessing the cClass property in the WAIT WINDOW command.

Although this example is not particularly useful, it does illustrate a few key concepts. First, because the Class Browser sends itself as the parameter to the add-ins, every add-in has access to the full power of the Class Browser. That's why it is so important to take the time to learn about the properties and methods of the Class Browser. Another key point is that there is not much that an add-in cannot do for you. The remainder of this chapter talks about examples of this.

Here's another example of an add-in. You saw previously that all the class code shown in this chapter is exported with the Class Browser. If, for example, you wanted to add some additional information at the top of the exported code (author name, copyright, and so on), you could do it with the following add-in:

```
*   Program...........: DOCCLASS.PRG
*   Author............: Menachem Bazian, CPA
*   Project...........: Visual FoxPro Unleashed
*   Created...........: May 22, 1995 - 07:02:54
*   Copyright.........: (c)Flash Creative Management, Inc., 1995
*) Description.......: DocClass is an addin program for
*)                    : the Class Browser that exports
*)                    : the code for a class with a
*)                    : FlashStandard type heading at the top.
*   Calling Samples...:
*   Parameter List....:
*   Major change list.:

LPARAMETERS toObject
#DEFINE cr_lf chr(13)+chr(10)

_cliptext = toObject.ExportClass()

LOCAL laHdrLine[5], lcText, lnCounter

laHdrLine[1] = "*   Class.............: " + ;
        toObject.ProperBaseClass(toObject.cClass)
laHdrLine[2] = "*   Author............: " + ;
        "Menachem Bazian, CPA"
laHdrLine[3] = "*   Project...........: " + ;
        "Visual FoxPro Unleashed!"
laHdrLine[4] = "*   Copyright.........: " + ;
        "(c)Flash Creative Management, Inc. 1995"
laHdrLine[5] = "*   Notes.............: " + ;
        "Exported code from Class Browser."

lcText = ""
```

```
FOR lnCounter = 1 TO ALEN(laHdrLine,1)
    lcText = lcText + ;
                laHdrLine[lnCounter] + cr_lf
ENDFOR

lcText = lcText + cr_lf

_cliptext = lcText + _cliptext

=MessageBox("Code exported to clipboard!", 32)

RETURN
```

In theory, this add-in is very simple. The ExportClass method is used to dump the code for the class into the Clipboard (you modify the Clipboard by modifying _cliptext). The array holds the additional header lines, which are then added with carriage returns and linefeeds to the output text. Once the add-in is run, all you have to do is paste the code into the word processor. This is a fairly good example of an add-in—it automates a procedure you need to do and reduces it to a few, simple keystrokes.

Here's another add-in. This one attempts to provide a runtime preview of an object shown in the Class Browser by bringing up the ObjectInspectorForm shown in Chapter 29, "Creating Classes with Visual FoxPro." The idea is fairly simple. You make sure that the class library for the class is in the SET CLASS list, instantiate it, and then send it off to the ObjectInspectorForm class (same as in Chapter 29). Here's the code:

```
*   Program.........: OBJINSP.PRG
*   Author..........: Menachem Bazian, CPA
*   Project.........: Visual FoxPro Unleashed!
*   Created.........: June 09, 1995 - 17:09:48
*   Copyright.......: (c)Flash Creative Management, Inc., 1995
*)  Description.....: Add-in to Inspect the current selected class
*   Calling Samples.:
*   Parameter List..:
*   Major change list.:

LPARAMETERS toSource

*-- This Add-in instantiates an object based on
*-- the currently selected class and then passes
*-- it off to the ObjectInspectorForm
*-- class for display.

*-- First check to make sure we are not on the
*-- .VCX

IF '.' $ toSource.cClass
    =MessageBox("You must have a class currently selected!", 16)
    RETURN
ENDIF

*-- Step one, add the Class Library with the object
*-- we are instantiating to the SET CLASS list
```

```
LOCAL lcCLassLib
lcClassLibrary = toSource.cFileName
lcCurrentClassLibraries = SET("classlib")

IF !(UPPER(toSource.TrimPath(lcClassLibrary)) # SET("CLASSLIB"))
    SET CLASS TO (lcClassLibrary) ADDITIVE
ENDIF

IF !"CHAP29" $ SET("classlib")
    SET CLASSLIB TO chap29 ADDITIVE
ENDIF

*-- Instantiate the object

LOCAL loX, loObjInspect
loX = CREATEOBJECT(toSource.cClass)

*-- Send it off to the ObjectInspectorForm

loObjInspect = CREA("ObjectInspectorForm", loX)

*-- Show it as a modal form

loObjInspect.Show(1)

*-- Reset everything

SET CLASSLIB TO (lcCurrentClassLibraries)

*-- We're done

RETURN
```

Again, note how the Class Browser as a parameter is so useful. The Class Browser's properties give the necessary information to check that the current class is a class and not the VCX file itself, what the class library needed is, and so on.

Changing Class Browser Behavior with Add-Ins

By installing the sample add-in in the manner shown in the previous section, you can run it by selecting a class, clicking the Add-In command button, and selecting the appropriate menu item.

Go back to the ObjInsp add-in for a moment. This is a powerful add-in. However, when you think about it, it is a utility to see what a particular class is like. This seems to be analogous to the Export command button, which is designed to show the class code for a "quick view" of the class.

If a left mouse click on the View Class Code command button exports the code to a window, wouldn't it be nice to have a right mouse click on the command button run the `ObjInsp` add-in? In fact, you can do just that.

To show how this is accomplished, take a closer look at the syntax of the `AddIn()` method:

```
AddIn(AddInName, ;ProgramName, ;MethodName, ;ActiveForFiles, ;
    PlatForm, ;Comment)
```

This method installs or removes a Class Browser add-in.

The `AddInName` parameter is the name of the add-in. The name of the add-in can be one or more words and case is not important (except that it will display on the menu in the same manner as it is specified here). The add-in will display in the Add-In menu if the third parameter (`MethodName`) is not specified.

The `ProgramName` parameter is the name of a program to run. The program can be a PRG, APP, EXE, or FXP. In addition, you can specify an SCX file. The assumed extension is .PRG; you can specify other extensions as appropriate.

The `ProgramName` parameter can also be the name of an object. The syntax for this is `VCXFileName, ClassName`. Here is an example:

```
_oBrowser.AddIn("MyAddIn", "MyVcxVCX, MyClass")
```

When the add-in is run, the class `MyClass` of MyVcx.VCX file is instantiated. Remember that an object parameter is sent through to the class.

It's not a bad idea to specify a full path to the program in this parameter. This ensures that the add-in runs properly wherever you are in your hard disk. If the Class Browser cannot find the program or VCX file when it tries to call an add-in, an error is generated.

The `MethodName` parameter is the name of a method to automatically call the add-in. Any valid method, either a method of the Class Browser form or one of its objects, can be a hook for a method. For example, if you wanted to hook `MyAddIn` to the Export command button's `Click` method, you could state this:

```
_oBrowser.AddIn("MyAddIn", , "CmdExport.Click")
```

Note, by the way, that I did not specify the second parameter in this command. Because I did not need to modify the parameter, I left it out. The `AddIn()` method is smart enough to handle that.

This parameter is the key to the task that was just set out. By specifying the `cmdExport.RightClick` method in the third parameter, you can hook the add-in to the `RightClick()` event on the Export command button.

By the way, if you hook into a method that already has behavior (the `Click` method of `cmdExport` calls `ExportClass`, for example), the add-in runs first and then the original behavior runs. If you have multiple add-ins registered for a method, they will run in the order they were registered.

Finally, if you want to totally override the behavior of a method (you do not want `cmdExport` to call `ExportClass`, for example), the add-in must set the `lNoDefault` property on the Class Browser to `.T.`. If this property is set to `.T.`, the Class Browser method will detect this and ignore the rest of the method.

The *ActiveForFiles* parameter enables you to determine the files for which the add-in will work. By default, when an add-in is added to the Class Browser registration table it is available for all the VCX and SCX files with which you might work. This parameter enables you to specify a file or list of files (separated by commas) for which this add-in is available. For other files loaded into the Class Browser, the add-in simply does not exist.

The *Platform* parameter specifies the platform (for example, Windows) in which the add-in will work. By default, it is available for all platforms.

The *Comment* parameter is an optional comment you can store with the add-in.

If you take a close look at the `AddIn()` method, it gives a wealth of insight into the power and flexibility of the Class Browser. Add-ins can enable you to totally customize the Class Browser to run your code at almost any interval.

For example, assume you prefer to use Courier New as the font for the Class Browser. All you need to do is create an add-in like the following one (FONTSET.PRG) and register it for the Init method:

```
*   Program..........: FONTSET.PRG
*   Author...........: Menachem Bazian, CPA
*   Project..........: Visual FoxPro Unleashed!
*   Created..........: June 11, 1995 - 03:11:56
*   Copyright........: (c)Flash Creative Management, Inc., 1995
*)  Description......:
*   Calling Samples...:
*   Parameter List....:
*   Major change list.:

LPARAMETERS toSource

toSource.SetFont("Courier New")
```

Here is how to register the add-in:

```
_oBrowser.AddIn("FontSet", "FontSet", "Init")
```

Figure 30.23 shows the Class Browser form with this add-in installed.

FIGURE 30.23.

The Class Browser with FontSet *installed.*

Handling the Rename Crisis with an Add-In

Here's one final add-in. Previously in this chapter you were warned of the dangers in renaming a class. I also hinted that you could take care of the dangers (or at least minimize them) with an add-in.

Here's an add-in that takes care of this problem. This add-in, called RenmAll.PRG, is designed to handle the renaming of all classes and objects based on the current object. Thus, if you rename a class from MyOriginalClass to MyNewClass, all subclasses of MyOriginalClass will be changed to reference MyNewClass instead.

The key to understanding this add-in is knowing that the name of the class on which an object is based is stored in the Class field in the VCX file. The only limitation to this add-in is that it can only adjust classes and forms that are loaded in the Class Browser.

Here's the code:

```
*   Program..........: RENMALL.PRG
*   Author...........: Menachem Bazian, CPA
*   Project..........: Visual FoxPro Unleashed!
*   Created..........: June 19, 1995 - 12:02:01
*   Copyright.........: (c)Flash Creative Management, Inc., 1995
*) Description.......: Renames a class in the Class Browser
*)                   : and keeps the class heirarchy alive
*   Calling Samples...:
*   Parameter List....:
*   Major change list.:

LPARAMETERS toSource

LOCAL lcOldClassName, lcNewClassName, lnOldDataSession, lnOldArea, lnOldDisplayMode

*-- The idea here is very simple. So long as the classes are
*-- loaded in the Class Browser, we can get at the metadata
*-- tables (metadata1 - <n>)
*--
```

```
*-- All we need to do is get to all the records with the
*-- OLD class name in the CLASS field and change it to the new name.

*-- Note, by the way, that this will REPLACE the cmdRename button's
*-- Click Method entirely.

toSource.lNoDefault = .T.
toSource.lError = .F.
a;sldkfjsl;kj

*-- First, get and save the current class name.

lcOldClassName = ALLTRIM(LOWER(toSource.cClass))

*-- In order to prevent an error message, we need to
*-- set display mode to alphabetical. We'll set it back
*-- on the way out.

lnOldDisplayMode = toSource.opgDisplayMode.Value
toSource.opgDisplayMode.Value = 2

*-- Now, the name dialog box.

toSource.RenameClass()

*-- Get the new class name

lcNewClassName = ALLTRIM(LOWER(toSource.cClass))

*-- Now, go through all the classes in all open MetaData tables

lnOldDataSess = SET("datasession")

SET DATASESSION TO (toSource.DataSessionId)

*-- A quick note. You can have up to 255 tables open per
*-- data session (according to the help file, anyway).
*--
*-- There is a slim chance that the Class Browser will have
*-- that many files open. However, since the following loop
*-- will only run until it finds an empty work area, this is
*-- an easy way to run through all the work areas.

lnOldArea = SELECT()

FOR lnCounter = 1 TO 255
    SELECT (lnCounter)

    IF EMPTY(alias())
        EXIT
    ENDIF

    IF "METADATA" $ UPPER(ALIAS())
        =RenameClasses(lcOldClassName, lcNewClassName)
    ENDIF
ENDFOR
```

```
SELECT (lnOldArea)
SET DATASESSION TO (lnOldDataSess)

*toSource.RefreshClassList()
toSource.opgDisplayMode.Value = lnOldDisplayMode

RETURN

*    Procedure.........: RenameClasses
*    Author...........: Menachem Bazian, CPA
*    Project..........: Visual FoxPro Unleashed!
*    Created..........: June 19, 1995 - 12:23:43
*    Copyright........: (c)Flash Creative Management, Inc., 1995
*)   Description......: Loops through the metadata table and rename
*    Calling Samples...:
*    Parameter List....:
*    Major change list.:

************************************************************
PROCEDURE RenameClasses
************************************************************

LPARAMETERS tcOldClassName, tcNewClassName

GO TOP
SCAN
    IF LOWER(ALLTRIM(tcOldClassName)) == LOWER(ALLTRIM(Class))
        REPLACE Class WITH LOWER(ALLTRIM(tcNewClassName))
    ENDIF
ENDSCAN

RETURN
```

The idea is simple. Call the `RenameClass` method from here and trap the class name both before and after the class is renamed. Then, loop through all the records in all the open VCX and SCX files (that is, all files with an alias of METADATA*) and change all occurrences of the old class name to the new one.

Note that the add-in starts out by setting the display mode to Alphabetical before playing with the class names. If the display is in hierarchical mode, the Class Browser generates an error (after renaming a parent class) stating that it cannot rebuild the tree (because the chain has been broken). Once all the names have been modified, the `RefreshClassList` method is called to read in the classes again, and the display is reset to what it was before the add-in ran.

Note also that this method is designed to replace the functionality of `cmdRename.Click`. By setting `lNoDefault` to `.T.`, you are ensuring that the Rename button's original `Click` method does not run.

Here is how to register this add-in:

```
_oBrowser.AddIn("Full Rename", CURDIR()+"RenmAll", "cmdRename.Click")
```

Summary

The true test of a development environment lies not only in the features of the language but also in the tools it provides to get the job done.

Managing class libraries is not an easy task. The Class Browser represents, in its vanilla form, a powerful tool for managing class libraries. However, the hidden power of the Class Browser (in the form of the open architecture inherent in the class-driven design and in the add-in feature) increases the Class Browser's utility tremendously. Even at this early time (I am writing this at the very end of Visual FoxPro's beta cycle), add-ins are being created to perform a myriad of tasks. Keep an eye on CompuServe's FoxForum for more details as they become available.

The moral here is simple. The job of managing class libraries is tough enough without having to worry about the manual aspects. The Class Browser gives developers and class librarians alike a powerhouse to perform their already too-difficult jobs.

Advanced Object-Oriented Programming

31

In this chapter, the final chapter of Part V, "Object-Oriented Programming," I discuss some more advanced concepts in developing object-oriented applications with Visual FoxPro. I also present classes to illustrate these concepts.

Data Environment Classes

Back in Chapter 29, "Creating Classes with Visual FoxPro," I mentioned the concept of manually created data environment classes. You might already be familiar with data environments from working with forms. The following section is a quick review of data environments from that perspective.

Data Environments with Forms

When you create a form with Visual FoxPro's Form Designer, you can specify the tables that the form works with by creating a *data environment* for the form. As Figure 31.1 shows, a form's data environment is made up of cursors and relations. If you'd like, you can think of a data environment as a package (that is, a container) that holds the information necessary for setting up the data environment.

FIGURE 31.1.

The data environment of a form.

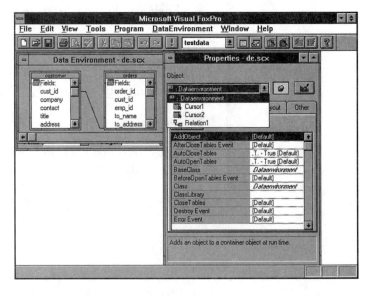

Data Environments and Form Classes

One of the limitations of a form class is that data environments cannot be saved with the class. However, as it turns out, data environments, cursors, and relations are classes in and of themselves. That means we can create data environment definitions by combining cursors and relations into one package.

There is one limitation on the DataEnvironment, cursor, and relation classes: they cannot be created visually. They can only be created in code.

The *cursor* Class

The first class to examine is the cursor class. A cursor *class* defines the contents of a work area. Following is a brief review of the properties, events, and methods of the cursor class.

Properties

Table 31.1 describes the properties of the cursor class. The cursor class also supports the base properties discussed in Chapter 28, "OOP with Visual FoxPro."

Table 31.1. The properties of the cursor class.

Property	Description
Alias	This property is the alias to give the work area when opened.
Buffermodeoverride	This property specifies the buffering mode for the cursor. Here are the values: 0 None (no buffering is done) 1 Use whatever is set at the form level 2 Pessimistic row buffering 3 Optimistic row buffering 4 Pessimistic table buffering 5 Optimistic table buffering If the data environment class is not used on a form, you should use a value other than 1.
CursorSource	This property is the source for the cursor's data. This could be a table from a database, a view (local or remote) from a database, or a free table. If CursorSource is a free table, you must specify the path to the DBF file.
Database	This property is the database that has the cursor source. If the cursor source comes from a database, this field must be completed with a fully valid path, including drive and directories.
Exclusive	This property specifies whether the cursor source is opened in exclusive mode. It accepts a logical value.

continues

Table 31.1. continued

Property	Description
Filter	This property is the Filter expression to place on the cursor source. The string placed here would be the string you would specify in a SET FILTER TO command.
NoDataOnLoad	This property, if set to .T., opens the cursor and creates a structure, but no data is downloaded for the cursor. Requery() will download the data.
Order	This property specifies the initial order in which to display the data. You must specify an index tag name.
ReadOnly	This property, if set to .T., opens the cursor as read-only; therefore, the data cannot be modified.

Events and Methods

The cursor class supports only the Init, Destroy, and Error events.

The *relation* Class

The *relation class* specifies the information needed to set up a relationship between two cursors in a data environment. Following are the properties, events, and methods.

Properties

In order to more easily explain the properties of the relation class, consider the following situation. You have two tables in a cursor, one called Customer and the other named Invoice. Customer has a field called CID that holds the customer ID. Invoice has a field called cCustId that also holds the customer ID. Here is how you would normally set the relation:

```
SELECT Invoice
SET ORDER to cCustId
SELECT Customer
SET RELATION TO cId INTO Invoice
```

Table 31.2 presents the properties and their descriptions.

Table 31.2. The properties of the relation class.

Property	Description
ChildAlias	This property is the alias of the child table. In this example, it would be Invoice.

Property	Description
ChildOrder	This property specifies the order of the child table. In this example, it would be cCustId.
OneToMany	This property specifies whether the relationship is a one-to-many relationship.
ParentAlias	This property is the alias of the controlling alias. In this example, it would be Customer.
RelationalExpr	This property is the expression of the relationship. In this example, it would be CID.

Events and Methods

The relation class supports only the Init, Destroy, and Error events.

The *DataEnvironment* Class

The *DataEnvironment class* is a container for cursors and relations, which, when taken together, make up an environment of data.

Properties

Table 31.3 presents the properties of the DataEnvironment class.

Table 31.3. The properties of the DataEnvironment class.

Property	Description
AutoCloseTables	This property specifies that tables should be closed automatically when the object is released. AutoCloseTables works in a form environment. In a coded DataEnvironment class, you would have to put code in the Destroy method for the tables to be closed. You would close the tables in the Destroy method by calling the DataEnvironment's OpenTables method.
AutoOpenTables	This property specifies that tables should be opened automatically when the object is instantiated. AutoOpenTables works in a form environment. In a coded DataEnvironment class, you would have to put code in the

continues

Table 31.3. continued

Property	Description
	Init method for the tables to be opened. You would open the tables in the Init method by calling the DataEnvironment's OpenTables method.
InitialSelectedAlias	This property specifies which alias should be selected initially.

Methods

Unlike the cursor and relation classes, the DataEnvironment class has two methods in addition to the base methods, as shown in Table 31.4.

Table 31.4. The additional methods of the DataEnvironment class.

Method	Description
CloseTables()	This method closes all of the tables and cursors in the DataEnvironment class.
OpenTables()	This method opens all of the tables and cursors in the DataEnvironment class.

Events

Table 31.5 presents the events supported by the DataEnvironment class.

Table 31.5. The events supported by the DataEnvironment class.

Event	Description
BeforeOpenTables()	This event runs before tables are opened.
AfterCloseTables()	This event runs after tables are closed.

Building a *DataEnvironment* Class

Now that you have seen all of the elements that go into creating a DataEnvironment class, the next step is to build one. The examples I use here are based on the TESTDATA database located in Visual FoxPro's SAMPLES\DATA directory.

```
*   Program...........: DE1.PRG
*   Author............: Menachem Bazian, CPA
*   Project...........: Visual FoxPro Unleashed!
*   Created...........: June 21, 1995 - 07:56:00
*   Copyright.........: (c) Flash Creative Management, Inc., 1995
*)  Description.......: A sample data environment class

DEFINE CLASS CUSTOMER AS cursor
    alias = "CUSTOMER"
    cursorsource = "CUSTOMER"
    database = HOME()+"SAMPLES\DATA\TESTDATA.DBC"
ENDDEFINE

DEFINE CLASS ORDERS AS cursor
    alias = "ORDERS"
    cursorsource = "ORDERS"
    database = HOME()+"SAMPLES\DATA\TESTDATA.DBC"
ENDDEFINE

DEFINE CLASS ORDITEMS AS cursor
    alias = "ORDITEMS"
    cursorsource = "ORDITEMS"
    database = HOME()+"SAMPLES\DATA\TESTDATA.DBC"
ENDDEFINE

DEFINE CLASS Cust_To_Orders AS relation
    childalias = "ORDERS"
    parentalias = "CUSTOMER"
    childorder = "CUST_ID"
    RelationalExpr = "CUST_ID"
ENDDEFINE

DEFINE CLASS Orders_To_OrdItems AS relation
    childalias = "ORDITEMS"
    parentalias = "ORDERS"
    childorder = "ORDER_ID"
    RelationalExpr = "ORDER_ID"
ENDDEFINE

DEFINE CLASS DE AS DataEnvironment
    ADD OBJECT oCUSTOMER              AS CUSTOMER
    ADD OBJECT oORDERS               AS ORDERS
    ADD OBJECT oORDITEMS             AS ORDITEMS
    ADD OBJECT oCust_To_Orders       AS CUST_TO_ORDERS
    ADD OBJECT oOrders_To_OrdItems   AS ORDERS_TO_ORDITEMS

    PROCEDURE Init
        this.OpenTables()
    ENDPROC

    PROCEDURE Destroy
        this.CloseTables()
    ENDPROC
ENDDEFINE
```

Notice how all of the first classes (that is, the cursor and relation classes) are manifestations based on the contents of the DBC file. The final class, DE, merely combines the cursor and relation classes under one roof. The Init method calls the OpenTables method so that all of the tables are automatically opened when the object is instantiated, and the `CloseTables()` method is called when the object is released.

Notice that the `DE` class shown in DE1.PRG uses all of the `cursor` and `relation` classes in the program. You don't have to do this. Typically, when you work with `DataEnvironment` classes, you have one `DataEnvironment` class that opens all of the tables (I call it a "default" data environment). You also have many other `DataEnvironment` classes that have only the cursor and relation objects that a particular function needs. For example, I could see the following `DataEnvironment` class added to `DE1`:

```
DEFINE CLASS SMALLDE AS DataEnvironment
    ADD OBJECT oCUSTOMER              AS CUSTOMER
    ADD OBJECT oORDERS                 AS ORDERS
    ADD OBJECT oCust_To_Orders       AS CUST_TO_ORDERS

    PROCEDURE Init
        this.OpenTables()
    ENDPROC

    PROCEDURE Destroy
        this.CloseTables()
    ENDPROC
ENDDEFINE
```

This `DataEnvironment` class uses only the `Customer` and `Orders` cursors and the relation between them. It might be used, for example, for a list of order numbers belonging to a customer. This is not to say you *couldn't* use the default `DataEnvironment` class for everything. As a matter of course, however, I prefer to have only those cursors and relations referenced that I need.

One other item of interest in DE1.PRG is the settings for the `Database` property in all of the classes. Using the `Home` function is perfectly reasonable: As long as the database name evaluates with a full path, the cursor will work fine.

Retrieving Definitions from a DBC File

There is one problem with retrieving definitions from a DBC file: It can be a major pain to type in all of the cursor and relation classes you have in your DBC file. Furthermore, you might make changes to your DBC file during development and will then have to update the program with the `DataEnvironment` classes each time. This is not a pretty prospect.

Fortunately, it is relatively easy to get information from the database and generate your own program directly from the DBC file. Using functions such as `ADBObjects`, which retrieve information from the database, you can build a program automatically from the DBC file itself, thus saving yourself a lot of work. `DumpDbc` is a class that retrieves the information from a database and creates a program with the `cursor` and `relation` classes representing the contents of the database.

Class: *DUMPDBC*

DumpDbc is a subclass of the Custom class. The following sections discuss its properties, events, and methods.

Properties

Table 31.6 presents DumpDbc's properties.

Table 31.6. The properties of the DumpDbc subclass.

Property	Description
PROTECTED aRelations	A list of relation objects in the DBC file.
PROTECTED aTables	A list of table objects in the DBC file.
PROTECTED aViews	A list of view objects in the DBC.
cDBCName	The name of the DBC file you are exporting.
cPRGName	The name of the PRG file to be created.
PROTECTED cPath	The directory path to the database.
PROTECTED nRelations	The number of relation objects in the DBC file.
PROTECTED nTables	The number of table objects in the DBC file.
PROTECTED nViews	The number of view objects in the DBC file.

NOTE

Note that all properties preceded by the keyword PROTECTED are protected members.

Events and Methods

Now that you have seen the properties of DumpDbc, the next step is to learn the events and methods.

doit

This method initiates the action of writing the program. It is the only public method in the class to ensure that the entire process is run properly from start to finish.

As part of getting the process going, this method checks to see if a DBC file to generate and a program to create have been specified in the cDBCName and cPRGName properties, respectively. If either of these has not been specified, a Getfile() or Putfile() dialog box is displayed. Failure to select a file will terminate the operation.

cursorclasses

This PROTECTED method runs through all of the tables and views in the DBC file (as listed in aTables and aViews) and generates cursor classes for them by calling the WriteCursorClass method.

readdbc

This PROTECTED method reads the relation, table, and view definitions from DBC using ADBObjects and places them in the aRelations, aTables, and aViews members' arrays.

relationclasses

This PROTECTED method generates all of the relation classes for the DBC file and writes them to the output program file.

Unlike cursor classes, which can be given names based on the name of the table or view with which they are associated, relation classes are more difficult to name objectively. This class names them in consecutive order (Relation1, Relation2, and so on).

writeclasses()

This PROTECTED method launches the process of writing all of the classes. It is called by Doit after ReadDbc is complete. Writeclasses calls CursorClasses and RelationClasses to write the individual classes to the output file.

> **NOTE**
>
> There are a few items to note. When developing applications, you might put the data in one place on the hard disk, but the data might live in a different place when installed at the user site. Because cursor classes require a full path to the database containing the cursor source, this could be a problem.

The solution I have allowed for here is to use a declared constant called DATABASEPATH when generating the program. DATABASEPATH will have the path to the database when the program is generated. If you need to change paths somewhere along the line, you can modify this one defined constant. Otherwise, you could change this method in Dumpdbc and have DATABASENAME refer to a table field, public variable, or property that has the data path. The advantage of this approach is that it does not require any code changes when moving the database.

The #DEFINE command is placed at the end of a header this method generates. The header enables you to keep track of how and when this generated program was created.

Finally, at the end of this method, WriteDefaultClass is called. This method writes a default data environment class that has all of the cursors and relations in it.

writecursorclass(tcClassName)

This PROTECTED method writes a single cursor class to the program. The name of the class is always the name as the name of the view or cursor (which is passed through as tcClassName).

writedefaultclass

This PROTECTED method writes a DataEnvironment class called Default_de, which has all of the cursor and relation classes from the DBC file.

The Code for the *Dumpdbc* Class

The following is the code for the class, which can be found on the CD as Chap31.VCX.

```
*   Class.............: Dumpdbc
*   Author............: Menachem Bazian, CPA
*   Project...........: Visual FoxPro Unleashed!
*   Copyright.........: (c) Flash Creative Management, Inc. 1995
*   Notes.............: Exported code from Class Browser.

***************************************************
*-- Class:        dumpdbc
*-- ParentClass:  custom
*-- BaseClass:    custom
*-- Create CURSOR and RELATION classes for a .DBC .
*
DEFINE CLASS dumpdbc AS custom

    *-- Number of relation objects in the .DBC
    PROTECTED nrelations
    nrelations = 0
    *-- Number of table objects in the .DBC
    PROTECTED ntables
    ntables = 0
    *-- Number of view objects in the .DBC
    PROTECTED nviews
    nviews = 0
    *-- Name of the .DBC to dump
    cdbcname = ""
    *-- Name of program file to create.
    cprgname = ""
    Name = "dumpdbc"

    *-- Path to the database
    PROTECTED cpath
```

```
*-- List of relation objects in the .DBC
PROTECTED arelations[1]

*-- List of view objects in the .DBC
PROTECTED aviews[1]

*-- List of table objects in the .DBC
PROTECTED atables[1]
PROTECTED init

*-- Reads the DBC into the arrays.
PROTECTED PROCEDURE readdbc
    IF !dbused(this.cDbcName)
        OPEN DATABASE (this.cDbcName)
    ENDIF

    *-- I need FoxTools for some work here

    LOCAL loFtools
    loFtools = CREATEOBJECT("foxtools")
    this.cPath       = loFtools.JustPath(DBC())

    *-- And, just to make sure that there is no
    *-- path in the .DBC name...

    this.cDbcName    = loFtools.JustfName(DBC())

    *-- Now read the .DBC

    this.nTables     = aDBObjects(this.aTables, "Table")
    this.nViews      = aDBObjects(this.aViews, "View")
    this.nRelations  = aDBObjects(this.aRelations, "Relation")
ENDPROC

*-- Writes all the classes.
PROTECTED PROCEDURE writeclasses
    SET TEXTMERGE TO (this.cPRGNAME) NOSHOW

    *-- Write the header first

    SET TEXTMERGE ON

    LOCAL lcOldCentury
    lcOldCentury = SET("century")
    SET CENTURY ON

    \*  Program...........: <<this.cPRGName>>
    \*  DBC...............: <<this.cDBCName>>
    \*  Generated.........: <<MDY(DATE()) + " - " + TIME()>>
    \
    \#DEFINE databasepath "<<this.cPath>>"

    SET TEXTMERGE OFF

    IF this.nTables > 0    OR this.nViews > 0
        this.CursorClasses()
    ENDIF
```

```
    IF this.nRelations > 0
        this.RelationClasses()
    ENDIF

    this.WriteDefaultClass()

    SET TEXTMERGE OFF
    SET TEXTMERGE TO
ENDPROC

*-- Processes all the cursor classes in the .DBC.
PROTECTED PROCEDURE cursorclasses
    LOCAL lnCounter
    SET TEXTMERGE ON
    FOR lnCounter = 1 TO this.nTables
        this.WriteCursorClass(this.aTables[lnCounter])
    ENDFOR

    FOR lnCounter = 1 TO this.nViews
        this.WriteCursorClass(this.aViews[lnCounter])
    ENDFOR
    SET TEXTMERGE OFF
ENDPROC

*-- Writes a cursor class to the output program file.
PROTECTED PROCEDURE writecursorclass
    LPARAMETERS tcClassName

    \DEFINE CLASS <<STRTRAN(tcClassName, chr(32), "_")>> AS cursor
    \    alias = "<<tcClassName>>"
    \    cursorsource = "<<tcClassName>>"
    \    database = DATABASEPATH + "<<this.cDbcName>>"
    \ENDDEFINE
    \
ENDPROC

*-- Processes and writes all the relation classes.
PROTECTED PROCEDURE relationclasses
    LOCAL    lnCounter, ;
             lcClassName, ;
             lcChildAlias, ;
             lcParentAlias, ;
             lcChildOrder, ;
             lcRelationalExpr

    SET TEXTMERGE ON

    FOR lnCounter = 1 TO this.nRelations
        lcClassName = "RELATION"-Alltrim(Str(lnCounter))
        lcChildAlias = this.aRelations[lnCounter,1]
        lcParentAlias = this.aRelations[lnCounter,2]
        lcChildOrder = this.aRelations[lnCounter,3]
        lcRelationalExpr = this.aRelations[lnCounter,4]

        \DEFINE CLASS <<lcClassName>> AS relation
        \    childalias = "<<lcChildAlias>>"
        \    parentalias = "<<lcParentAlias>>"
        \    childorder = "<<lcChildOrder>>"
```

```
        \      RelationalExpr = "<<lcRelationalExpr>>"
        \ENDDEFINE
        \
    ENDFOR

    SET TEXTMERGE OFF
ENDPROC

*-- Writes the default DE class to the program
PROTECTED PROCEDURE writedefaultclass
    LOCAL laClasses[this.nTables + this.nViews + this.nRelations]

    FOR lnCounter = 1 TO this.nTables
        laClasses[lnCounter] = this.aTables[lnCounter]
    ENDFOR

    FOR lnCounter = 1 TO this.nViews
        laClasses[lnCounter+this.nTables] = this.aViews[lnCounter]
    ENDFOR

    FOR lnCounter = 1 TO this.nRelations
        laClasses[lnCounter+this.nTables+this.nViews] = ;
            "Relation" + ALLTRIM(STR(lnCounter))
    ENDFOR

    SET TEXTMERGE ON

    \DEFINE CLASS default_de AS DataEnvironment

    FOR lnCounter = 1 TO ALEN(laClasses,1)
        lcObjectName = 'o'+laClasses[lnCounter]
        lcClassName = laClasses[lnCounter]
    \     ADD OBJECT <<lcObjectName>> AS <<lcClassName>>
    ENDFOR
    \ENDDEFINE
    \

    SET TEXTMERGE OFF
ENDPROC

PROCEDURE doit
    *-- If no dbc name is specified, ask for one.

    IF EMPTY(this.cDBCName)
        this.cDBCName = GETFILE("DBC", "Please select DBC to dump:")
        IF !FILE(this.cDBCName)
            =MESSAGEBOX("No DBC selected! Aborted!",16)
            RETURN .F.
        ENDIF
    ENDIF

    *-- Same deal with a .PRG

    IF EMPTY(this.cPRGName)
        this.cPRGName = PUTFILE("PRG to create:","","PRG")

        IF EMPTY(this.cPRGName)
            =Messagebox("Operation cancelled!", 16)
            RETURN
```

```
            ENDIF
        ENDIF

        *-- As for overwrite permission here. I prefer to do this manually
        *-- (rather than let VFP handle it automatically) because it gives
        *-- me control.
        *--
        *-- Note how the SAFETY setting is queries first.

        IF SET("safety") = "ON" AND ;
            FILE(this.cPRGName) AND ;
            MessageBox("Overwrite existing " + ;
                        ALLTRIM(this.cPRGName) + "?", 36) # 6

            =Messagebox("Operation cancelled!", 16)
            RETURN
        ENDIF

        *-- save the SAFETY setting

        LOCAL lcOldSafety
        lcOldSafety = SET("safety")
        SET SAFETY OFF

        this.readdbc()
        this.writeclasses()

        SET SAFETY &lcOldSafety
    ENDPROC

ENDDEFINE
*
*-- EndDefine: dumpdbc
****************************************************
```

NOTE

DumpDbc uses the FoxTools class created in Chapter 29, "Creating Classes with Visual FoxPro." It can be found on the CD in Chap29.VCX. You will need to load that class library with SET CLASSLIB TO before instantiating an object from the Dumpdbc class.

TESTDBC is a small test program that illustrates how this class can be used to generate a program for the TESTDATA database. Here is the code:

```
*   Program...........: TESTDBC.PRG
*   Author............: Menachem Bazian, CPA
*   Project...........: Visual FoxPro Unleashed!
*   Created...........: June 21, 1995 - 10:13:07
*   Copyright.........: (c) Flash Creative Management, Inc., 1995
*)  Description.......: Illustrates usage of the DumpDbc class
*   Calling Samples...:
*   Parameter List....:
*   Major change list.:

*-- Note, Chap31.VCX and Chap29.VCX must be in the same
*-- Directory for this program to work.
```

```
Set ClassLib to Chap31
Set ClassLib to Chap29 ADDI
oDbcGen = CREATEOBJECT("dumpdbc")
oDbcGen.cDBCName = HOME()+"samples\data\testdata"
oDbcGen.cPRGName = "\deleteme.prg"
oDbcGen.DoIt()
```

DELETEME.PRG is created by TESTDBC. Here's what was generated:

```
*   Program...........: \deleteme.prg
*   DBC...............: TESTDATA.DBC
*   Generated.........: June 21, 1995 - 10:16:23

#DEFINE databasepath "D:\APPS\FOX\VFP\SAMPLES\DATA\"
DEFINE CLASS CUSTOMER AS cursor
    alias = "CUSTOMER"
    cursorsource = "CUSTOMER"
    database = DATABASEPATH + "TESTDATA.DBC"
ENDDEFINE

DEFINE CLASS PRODUCTS AS cursor
    alias = "PRODUCTS"
    cursorsource = "PRODUCTS"
    database = DATABASEPATH + "TESTDATA.DBC"
ENDDEFINE

DEFINE CLASS ORDITEMS AS cursor
    alias = "ORDITEMS"
    cursorsource = "ORDITEMS"
    database = DATABASEPATH + "TESTDATA.DBC"
ENDDEFINE

DEFINE CLASS ORDERS AS cursor
    alias = "ORDERS"
    cursorsource = "ORDERS"
    database = DATABASEPATH + "TESTDATA.DBC"
ENDDEFINE

DEFINE CLASS EMPLOYEE AS cursor
    alias = "EMPLOYEE"
    cursorsource = "EMPLOYEE"
    database = DATABASEPATH + "TESTDATA.DBC"
ENDDEFINE

DEFINE CLASS RELATION1 AS relation
    childalias = "ORDERS"
    parentalias = "CUSTOMER"
    childorder = "CUST_ID"
    RelationalExpr = "CUST_ID"
ENDDEFINE

DEFINE CLASS RELATION2 AS relation
    childalias = "ORDERS"
    parentalias = "EMPLOYEE"
    childorder = "EMP_ID"
    RelationalExpr = "EMP_ID"
ENDDEFINE
```

```
DEFINE CLASS RELATION3 AS relation
    childalias = "ORDITEMS"
    parentalias = "ORDERS"
    childorder = "ORDER_ID"
    RelationalExpr = "ORDER_ID"
ENDDEFINE

DEFINE CLASS RELATION4 AS relation
    childalias = "ORDITEMS"
    parentalias = "PRODUCTS"
    childorder = "PRODUCT_ID"
    RelationalExpr = "PRODUCT_ID"
ENDDEFINE

DEFINE CLASS default_de AS DataEnvironment
    ADD OBJECT oCUSTOMER AS CUSTOMER
    ADD OBJECT oPRODUCTS AS PRODUCTS
    ADD OBJECT oORDITEMS AS ORDITEMS
    ADD OBJECT oORDERS AS ORDERS
    ADD OBJECT oEMPLOYEE AS EMPLOYEE
    ADD OBJECT oRelation1 AS Relation1
    ADD OBJECT oRelation2 AS Relation2
    ADD OBJECT oRelation3 AS Relation3
    ADD OBJECT oRelation4 AS Relation4
ENDDEFINE
```

Note than just instantiating Default_De, in this case, is not enough to get the tables opened. In order to open the tables, you have to call the OpenTables() method. Furthermore, in order to close the tables, you need to run the CloseTables() method.

If you prefer to have these actions happen by default, you could create a subclass of the DataEnvironment class as follows:

```
DEFINE CLASS MyDeBase AS DataEnvironment
    PROCEDURE Init
        this.OpenTables()
    ENDPROC

    PROCEDURE Destroy
        this.CloseTables()
    ENDPROC
ENDDEFINE
```

Then, when generating classes, you could use the subclass as the parent of the DataEnvironment classes you create.

Increasing the Power of Data Environments with *DataSession*

Data environments are powerful, no doubt about that. But wait a minute. Back in the old days of FoxPro 2.*x*, most developers opened all their tables and relations once at the beginning of their applications and left them open throughout the application session. If this were still the strategy in Visual FoxPro, data environments would seem to be a whole lot to do about nothing.

The truth is, however, that data environments are extraordinarily useful because the basic strategy of opening all tables and relations up front is no longer the way to do things. Why not open all the tables and relations at the beginning of an application? Because of multiple data sessions, which give you a tremendous amount of additional flexibility. With data sessions, you can segregate the data manipulation in one function from the data manipulation of another.

However, there's a catch here: only forms can create independent data sessions. This could be insurmountable except for one fact: no one ever said a form has to be able to display. In other words, just because a form is a visual class, there is no reason I can't use it as a nonvisual class.

Consider the following form class:

```
*   Class.............: Newdatasession
*   Author............: Menachem Bazian, CPA
*   Project...........: Visual FoxPro Unleashed!
*   Copyright.........: (c) Flash Creative Management, Inc. 1995
*   Notes.............: Exported code from Class Browser.


**************************************************
*-- Class:       newdatasession
*-- ParentClass: form
*-- BaseClass:   form
*
DEFINE CLASS newdatasession AS form

    DataSession = 2
    Top = 0
    Left = 0
    Height = 35
    Width = 162
    DoCreate = .T.
    Caption = "Form"
    Visible = .F.
    Name = "newdatasession"
    PROTECTED show
    PROTECTED visible

ENDDEFINE
*
*-- EndDefine: newdatasession
**************************************************
```

Notice that the Visible property has been set to .F. and has been protected. The SHOW method has been protected as well. In other words, I have just created a form that cannot be displayed.

This concept would be ludicrous except for the fact that the DataSession property has been set to 2, which indicates that this form has its own data session. When the object is instantiated, a new DataSession is created and can be referenced with the SET DATASESSION command (the ID of the form's data session is stored in its DataSessionId property).

This is a prime example of using a class that is normally thought of as a visual class as the basis for creating a nonvisual class.

> **CAUTION**
>
> In order to use the `NewDataSession` class, the instance must live as its own object and cannot be added to a container. If you want this object to be a property of another object, create the instance with `CREATEOBJECT()` and not with `ADD OBJECT` or `ADDOBJECT()`. If you use one of the two latter methods, you will not get a private data session because the data session is governed by the container package in a composite class. See Chapter 28, "OOP with Visual FoxPro," for more information.

Modeling Objects on the Real World

Objects are supposed to model the real world, right? Up until now, the classes I covered have focused on functionality rather than modeling the real world. Now it's time to look at classes designed to model real-world objects.

The first object I present is a familiar one that presents a good opportunity to look at modeling functionality in objects: a stopwatch.

Defining the Stopwatch

The first step in any attempt to create an object is to define what the object is all about. This usually happens, when developing object-oriented software, in the analysis and design phase of the project. I briefly discussed this phase in Chapter 27, "Introduction to Object-Oriented Programming." In this case, it's a relatively simple exercise.

Consider a stopwatch. If you happen to have one, take it out and look at it. Note that it has a display (usually showing the time elapsed in *HH:MM:SS.SS* format). The stopwatch has buttons that enable you to start it, stop it, pause it (lap time), and reset the display. Naturally, a stopwatch has the capability to track time from when it is started until it is stopped. This is a good list of the functionality for a stopwatch class. When you have the required behavior of the object, you can then work on designing the implementation of the class.

Implementing the Stopwatch

Many factors can affect how a class is implemented, ranging from how the class is intended to be used to the personal preferences of the developer.

In this case, when designing the implementation of the stopwatch class, the functionality is divided into two parts. The first part is the engine (the portion of the stopwatch that has the functionality for calculating the time as well as for starting, stopping, and pausing the stopwatch). The second class combines the engine with the display to create a full stopwatch.

Frequently when working on a single class's implementation, opportunities present themselves for creating additional functionality at little cost. In this case, breaking the functionality of the stopwatch into an engine and a display portion gives you the ability either to subclass the engine into something different or to use the engine on its own without being burdened by the display component.

It's always a good idea to look at the implementation design of a class and ask the following question: Is there a way I can increase the reusability of the classes I create by abstracting (separating) functionality? The more you can make your classes reusable, the easier your life will be down the road.

The *SwatchEngine* Class

This class may be thought of as the mechanism behind the stopwatch. Based on the Timer class, the SwatchEngine class basically counts time from when it is started to when it is stopped. It does not allow for any display of the data. (A stopwatch with a display is added in class SWATCH). This class is useful for when you want to track the time elapsed between events.

```
*   Class.............: Swatchengine
*   Author............: Menachem Bazian, CPA
*   Project...........: Visual FoxPro Unleashed!
*   Copyright.........: (c) Flash Creative Management, Inc. 1995
*   Notes.............: Exported code from Class Browser.


*****************************************************
*-- Class:       swatchengine
*-- ParentClass: timer
*-- BaseClass:   timer
*-- Engine behind the SWATCH class.
*
DEFINE CLASS swatchengine AS timer

    Height = 23
    Width = 26
    *-- Number of seconds on the clock
    nsecs = 0
    *-- Time the clock was last updated
    PROTECTED nlast
    nlast = 0
    *-- Time the clock was started
    nstart = 0
    Name = "swatchengine"

    *-- Start the clock
    PROCEDURE start
        this.nstart   = SECONDS()
        this.nLast    = this.nStart
        this.nSecs    = 0
        this.Interval = 200
```

```
    ENDPROC

    *-- Stop the clock
    PROCEDURE stop
        this.timer()

        this.Interval = 0
        this.nLast    = 0
    ENDPROC

    *-- Pause the clock.
    PROCEDURE pause
        this.timer()
        this.interval = 0
    ENDPROC

    *-- Resume the clock
    PROCEDURE resume
        If this.nLast = 0 && Clock was stopped
            this.nLast = SECONDS() && Pick up from now
            this.interval = 200
        ELSE
            this.interval = 200
        ENDIF
    ENDPROC

    PROCEDURE Init
        this.nstart = 0
        this.Interval = 0
        this.nSecs = 0
        this.nLast = 0
    ENDPROC

    PROCEDURE Timer
        LOCAL lnSeconds

        lnSeconds     = SECONDS()
        this.nSecs    = this.nSecs + (lnSeconds - this.nLast)
        this.nLast    = lnSeconds
    ENDPROC

ENDDEFINE
*
*-- EndDefine: swatchengine
**************************************************
```

Properties

Table 31.7 presents the properties for SwatchEngine.

Table 31.7. The properties for `SwatchEngine`.

Properties	Description
Interval	The Interval property is not a new property—it is standard to the Timer class. If Interval is set to zero, the clock does not run; if Interval is set to a value greater than zero, the clock runs.
	In SwatchEngine, the clock runs at a "standard" interval of 200 milliseconds.
nsecs	This property is the number of seconds counted. It is carried out to three decimal places and is what the SECONDS function returns.
PROTECTED nlast	This property is the last time the Timer event fired. This is a protected property.
nstart	This property is the time the watch was started, measured in seconds since midnight.

NOTE

For the record, the Timer's Interval property governs how often the Timer event fires. If set to 0, the Timer event does not run. A positive Interval determines how often the Timer event runs. The Interval is specified in milliseconds.

Events and Methods

The following methods have a common theme: there is very little action happening. For the most part, all of these methods accomplish their actions by setting properties in the timer. For example, the clock can be started and stopped by setting the Interval property (a value of zero stops the clock, and anything greater than zero starts the clock). Table 31.8 presents the methods for SwatchEngine.

Table 31.8. The methods for `SwatchEngine`.

Method	Description
Init	This method initializes the nstart, Interval, nSecs, and nLast properties to zero.
Pause	This method calls the Timer() method to update the time counter and then stops the clock by setting the Interval property to 0.
Resume	This method restarts the clock by setting the Interval property to 200 (1/5 of a second). If nLast is not set to 0, the Resume() method knows that

Method	Description
	the clock was paused and picks up the count as if the clock were never stopped. Otherwise, all the time since the clock was stopped is ignored and the clock begins from that point.
Start	This method starts the clock and records when the clock was started.
Stop	This method stops the clock and sets nLast to 0.
Timer	This method updates the number of seconds (nSecs) property.

The *Swatch* Class

Now that the engine is done, you can combine the engine with a display component to create a stopwatch. The Swatch class is a container-based class that combines a label object (which is used to display the amount of time on the stopwatch) with a swatch engine object to complete the functional stopwatch.

Design Strategy

The key to this class is SwatchEngine. The parent (that is, the container) has properties and methods to mirror SwatchEngine, such as nStart, Start(), Stop(), Pause(), and Resume(). This enables a form using the class to have a consistent interface to control the stopwatch. In other words, the form does not have to know there are separate objects within the container—all the form has to do is communicate with the container.

Figure 31.2 shows what the class looks like in the Visual Class Designer.

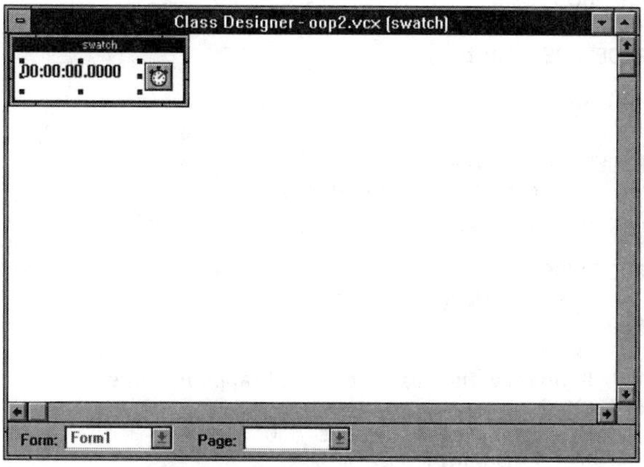

FIGURE 31.2.

The Swatch *class in the Visual Class Designer.*

Here's the code:

```
*   Class.............: Swatch
*   Author............: Menachem Bazian, CPA
*   Project...........: Visual FoxPro Unleashed!
*   Copyright.........: (c) Flash Creative Management, Inc. 1995
*   Notes.............: Exported code from Class Browser.


**************************************************
*-- Class:       swatch
*-- ParentClass: container
*-- BaseClass:   container
*
DEFINE CLASS swatch AS container

    Width = 141
    Height = 41
    nsecs = 0
    nstart = (seconds())
    Name = "swatch"

    ADD OBJECT lbltime AS label WITH ;
        Caption = "00:00:00.0000", ;
        Height = 25, ;
        Left = 7, ;
        Top = 8, ;
        Width = 97, ;
        Name = "lblTime"

    ADD OBJECT tmrswengine AS swatchengine WITH ;
        Top = 9, ;
        Left = 108, ;
        Height = 24, ;
        Width = 25, ;
        Name = "tmrSWEngine"

    PROCEDURE stop
        this.tmrSWEngine.Stop()
    ENDPROC

    PROCEDURE start
        this.tmrSWEngine.Start()
    ENDPROC

    PROCEDURE resume
        this.tmrSWEngine.Resume()
    ENDPROC

    PROCEDURE pause
        this.tmrSWEngine.Pause()
    ENDPROC

    *-- ,Property Description will appear here.
    PROCEDURE reset
        this.tmrSWEngine.nSecs = 0
        this.Refresh()
    ENDPROC
```

```
PROCEDURE Refresh
    LOCAL lcTime, ;
          lnSecs, ;
          lnHours, ;
          lnMins, ;
          lcSecs, ;
          lnLen

    this.nSecs  = this.tmrSWEngine.nSecs
    this.nStart = this.tmrSWEngine.nStart

    *-- Take the number of seconds on the clock (nSecs property)
    *-- and convert it to a string for display.

    lcTime     = ""
    lnSecs     = this.tmrSWEngine.nSecs

    lnHours     = INT(lnSecs/3600)

    lnSecs     = MOD(lnSecs,3600)
    lnMins     = INT(lnSecs/60)

    lnSecs     = MOD(lnSecs,60)

    lcSecs     = STR(lnSecs,6,3)
    lnLen      = LEN(ALLT(LEFT(lcSecs,AT('.', lcSecs)-1)))
    lcSecs     = REPL('0', 2-lnLen) + LTRIM(lcSecs)

    lnLen      = LEN(ALLT(SUBST(lcSecs,AT('.', lcSecs)+1)))
    lcSecs     = RTRIM(lcSecs) + REPL('0', 3-lnLen)

    lcTime     = PADL(lnHours,2,'0') + ":" + ;
                 PADL(lnMins,2,'0') + ":" + ;
                 lcSecs

    this.lblTime.Caption = lcTime
ENDPROC

PROCEDURE tmrswengine.Timer
    Swatchengine::Timer()
    this.Parent.refresh()
ENDPROC

ENDDEFINE
*
*-- EndDefine: swatch
**************************************************
```

Member Objects

The Swatch class has two member objects:

- lblTime (Label)
- tmrSWEngine (Swatch Engine)

Custom Properties

Note that the properties, shown in Table 31.9, are properties of the container itself.

Table 31.9. The custom properties.

Properties	Description
nStart	This property is the time the watch was started, measured in seconds since midnight.
nSecs	This property is the number of seconds counted. It is carried out to three decimal places and is what the SECONDS() function returns. The SwatchEngine properties in tmrSWEngine remain intact as inherited from the base class.

Events and Methods

Table 31.10 presents the events and methods in the Swatch class.

Table 31.10. The events and methods in the Swatch class.

Event/Method	Description
Swatch.Start	This method calls tmrSWEngine.Start.
Swatch.Stop	This method calls tmrSWEngine.Stop.
Swatch.Pause	This method calls tmrSWEngine.Pause.
Swatch.Resume	This method calls tmrSWEngine.Resume.
Swatch.Reset	This method resets the nSecs counter to 0 and then calls the Refresh method. This is designed to enable the display portion of the stopwatch to be reset to 00:00:00.000.
Swatch.Refresh()	This method updates the container properties nStart and nSecs from the timer and converts the number of seconds counted to *HH:MM:SS.SSS* format.
tmrSWEngine.Timer()	This method calls the SwatchEngine::Timer method, followed by the container's Refresh method.

Putting It Together on a Form

And now for the final step: putting all of this functionality together on a form. The form is shown in Figure 31.3.

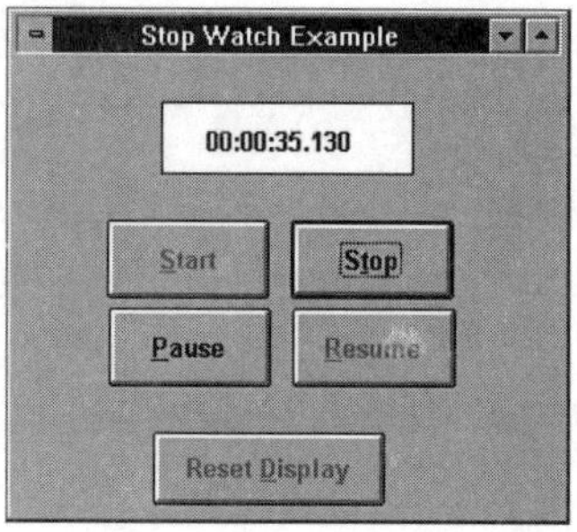

FIGURE 31.3.

The Stopwatch form.

```
*   Class.............: Swatchform
*   Author............: Menachem Bazian, CPA
*   Project...........: Visual FoxPro Unleashed!
*   Copyright.........: (c) Flash Creative Management, Inc. 1995
*   Notes.............: Exported code from Class Browser.

**************************************************
*-- Class:       swatchform
*-- ParentClass: form
*-- BaseClass:   form
*
DEFINE CLASS swatchform AS form

    ScaleMode = 3
    Top = 0
    Left = 0
    Height = 233
    Width = 285
    DoCreate = .T.
    BackColor = RGB(192,192,192)
    BorderStyle = 2
    Caption = "Stop Watch Example"
    Name = "swatchform"

    ADD OBJECT swatch1 AS swatch WITH ;
        Top = 24, ;
        Left = 76, ;
        Width = 132, ;
        Height = 37, ;
        Name = "Swatch1", ;
        lbltime.Caption = "00:00:00.0000", ;
        lbltime.Left = 24, ;
        lbltime.Top = 12, ;
        lbltime.Name = "lbltime", ;
        tmrswengine.Top = 9, ;
        tmrswengine.Left = 108, ;
        tmrswengine.Name = "tmrswengine"

    ADD OBJECT cmdstart AS commandbutton WITH ;
        Top = 84, ;
        Left = 48, ;
        Height = 40, ;
        Width = 85, ;
        Caption = "\<Start", ;
        Name = "cmdStart"
```

```
ADD OBJECT cmdstop AS commandbutton WITH ;
    Top = 84, ;
    Left = 144, ;
    Height = 40, ;
    Width = 85, ;
    Caption = "S\<top", ;
    Enabled = .F., ;
    Name = "cmdStop"

ADD OBJECT cmdpause AS commandbutton WITH ;
    Top = 129, ;
    Left = 49, ;
    Height = 40, ;
    Width = 85, ;
    Caption = "\<Pause", ;
    Enabled = .F., ;
    Name = "cmdPause"

ADD OBJECT cmdresume AS commandbutton WITH ;
    Top = 129, ;
    Left = 145, ;
    Height = 40, ;
    Width = 85, ;
    Caption = "\<Resume", ;
    Name = "cmdResume"

ADD OBJECT cmdreset AS commandbutton WITH ;
    Top = 192, ;
    Left = 72, ;
    Height = 37, ;
    Width = 121, ;
    Caption = "Reset \<Display", ;
    Name = "cmdReset"

PROCEDURE cmdstart.Click
    this.enabled = .F.
    thisform.cmdStop.enabled = .T.
    thisform.cmdPause.enabled = .T.
    thisform.cmdResume.enabled = .F.
    thisform.cmdReset.enabled = .F.
    thisform.Swatch1.Start()
ENDPROC

PROCEDURE cmdstop.Click
    this.enabled = .F.
    thisform.cmdStart.enabled = .T.
    thisform.cmdPause.enabled = .F.
    thisform.cmdResume.enabled = .T.
    thisform.cmdReset.enabled = .T.
    thisform.swatch1.stop()
ENDPROC

PROCEDURE cmdpause.Click
    this.enabled = .F.
    thisform.cmdStop.enabled = .T.
    thisform.cmdStart.enabled = .F.
    thisform.cmdResume.enabled = .T.
    thisform.cmdReset.enabled = .F.
    ThisForm.Swatch1.Pause()
ENDPROC
```

```
    PROCEDURE cmdresume.Click
        this.enabled = .F.
        thisform.cmdStart.enabled = .F.
        thisform.cmdPause.enabled = .T.
        thisform.cmdStop.enabled = .T.
        thisform.cmdResume.enabled = .F.
        thisform.cmdReset.enabled = .F.
        thisform.swatch1.resume()
    ENDPROC

    PROCEDURE cmdreset.Click
        thisform.swatch1.reset()
    ENDPROC

ENDDEFINE
*
*-- EndDefine: swatchform
***************************************************
```

The form, `SwatchForm`, is a form-based class with a `Swatch` object dropped on it. The command buttons on the form call the appropriate `Swatch` methods to manage the stopwatch (that is, start it, stop it, and so on).

There isn't much to this form, as the preceding code shows. All the real work has already been done in the `Swatch` class. The only thing the objects on the form do is call methods from the `Swatch` class.

Member Objects

Table 31.11 presents the member objects of the `Swatch` class.

Table 31.11. The member objects of the `Swatch` class.

Member Object	Description
Swatch1	(Swatch Class) This object is an instance of the `Swatch` class.
cmdStart	(Command Button) This object is the Start button, which starts the clock and appropriately enables or disables the other buttons.
cmdStop	(Command Button) This object is the Stop button, which stops the clock and appropriately enables or disables the other buttons.
cmdPause	(Command Button) This object is the Pause button, which pauses the clock and appropriately enables or disables the other buttons.
cmdResume	(Command Button) This object is the Resume button. It resumes the clock and appropriately enables or disables the other buttons.
cmdReset	(Command Button) This object is the Reset button, which resets the clock display.

The *Swatch* Class: A Final Word

One of the keys to achieving reuse is to look for it when designing functionality. There is no magic to this process, but there are methodologies designed to assist in the process. The intent behind showing the Swatch class is to illustrate how a single class, when created, can evolve into more classes than one in order to support greater reusability. When you think of your design, think about reusability.

Working with Frameworks

In Chapter 29 I introduced the concept of a framework. A *framework*, put simply, is the collection of classes that, when taken together, represent the foundation on which you will base your applications. A framework represents two things. First, it represents the parent classes for your subclasses. Second, it represents a structure for implementing functionality within your applications.

Take the issue of creating business classes. A properly designed framework can make creating business objects easy. In the next section I show you why.

The Nature of Business Objects

At the simplest level, a business object (a customer, for example) has the functionality that would normally be associated with data entry and editing. For example, the responsibilities could include the following:

- Display for editing
- Moving between records (top, bottom, next, and previous)

You can add as you see fit to this list of common responsibilities. Obviously, you would need functions for adding new records, for deleting records, and so on. The five functions presented in this section serve as an example and are modeled in the framework.

In terms of creating the framework, the goal is to create a series of classes that interact with each other to provide the functionality you need. In order to make the framework usable, you want to keep the number of modifications needed for combining the classes into a business class as minimal as possible.

The framework I present breaks down the functionality as follows:

- Navigation class—This is similar to the navigation classes I showed in Chapter 29. This class will be a series of command buttons for navigation within a form containing a business class.
- Form class—This is a combination of a form and the navigation class and is designed to work with business objects.

■ Data environment loader class—This is a class that handles loading the data environment for a business class.

■ Business class—This class has the data and methods for the business class being modeled and has a data environment loader class in it.

The nice thing about this framework, as it will work out in the end, is that the only work necessary for implementing a business class will occur in the business class. All the other classes are designed generically and refer to the business class for specific functionality. I go through the classes one at a time in the following sections.

The *Base_Navigation* Class

The Base_Navigation class is a set of navigation buttons designed to be used with forms that display a business class. Figure 31.4 shows the Base_Navigation class. The code listing follows Figure 31.4.

> **NOTE**
>
> The framework classes shown in this chapter can be found on the CD in FW.VCX.

FIGURE 31.4.

The Base_Navigation *class.*

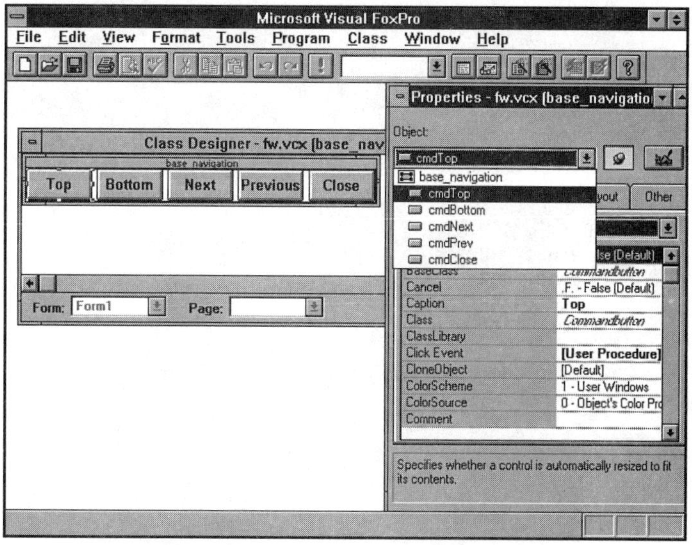

```
*  Class...........: Base_navigation
*  Author..........: Menachem Bazian, CPA
*  Project.........: Visual FoxPro Unleashed!
*  Copyright.......: (c) Flash Creative Management, Inc. 1995
*  Notes...........: Exported code from Class Browser.
```

```
****************************************************
*-- Class:        base_navigation
*-- ParentClass:  container
*-- BaseClass:    container
*-- Collection of nav buttons for business class forms.
*
DEFINE CLASS base_navigation AS container

    Width = 328
    Height = 30
    Name = "base_navigation"

    ADD OBJECT cmdtop AS commandbutton WITH ;
        Top = 0, ;
        Left = 0, ;
        Height = 29, ;
        Width = 62, ;
        Caption = "Top", ;
        Name = "cmdTop"

    ADD OBJECT cmdbottom AS commandbutton WITH ;
        Top = 0, ;
        Left = 66, ;
        Height = 29, ;
        Width = 62, ;
        Caption = "Bottom", ;
        Name = "cmdBottom"

    ADD OBJECT cmdnext AS commandbutton WITH ;
        Top = 0, ;
        Left = 132, ;
        Height = 29, ;
        Width = 62, ;
        Caption = "Next", ;
        Name = "cmdNext"

    ADD OBJECT cmdprev AS commandbutton WITH ;
        Top = 0, ;
        Left = 198, ;
        Height = 29, ;
        Width = 62, ;
        Caption = "Previous", ;
        Name = "cmdPrev"

    ADD OBJECT cmdclose AS commandbutton WITH ;
        Top = 0, ;
        Left = 265, ;
        Height = 29, ;
        Width = 62, ;
        Caption = "Close", ;
        Name = "cmdClose"

    PROCEDURE cmdtop.Click
        LOCAL lcClassName

        lcClassName = thisform.cClass
        ThisForm.&lcClassName..Topit()
    ENDPROC
```

```
    PROCEDURE cmdbottom.Click
        LOCAL lcClassName

        lcClassName = thisform.cClass
        ThisForm.&lcClassName..Bottomit()
    ENDPROC

    PROCEDURE cmdnext.Click
        LOCAL lcClassName

        lcClassName = thisform.cClass
        ThisForm.&lcClassName..Nextit()
    ENDPROC

    PROCEDURE cmdprev.Click
        LOCAL lcClassName

        lcClassName = thisform.cClass
        ThisForm.&lcClassName..Previt()
    ENDPROC

    PROCEDURE cmdclose.Click
        Release ThisForm
    ENDPROC

ENDDEFINE
*
*-- EndDefine: base_navigation
****************************************************
```

There is nothing too exciting here. The class is almost a yawner—it doesn't seem to present anything new. However, there is one very important difference between this class and all the other navigation functionality we have seen so far. The Base_Navigation class looks for the custom property cClass on the form. This property has the name of the business class residing on the form. With that name, the navigation buttons can call the appropriate movement methods *in the business object.* The navigation class, in other words, has no clue as to how to move to the next record, for example. It delegates that responsibility to the business class.

The *Base_Form*

The next step is to create a form that has the cClass property and has an instance of the Base_Navigation class on it. This form will be subclassed for all business object data entry forms (you'll see this in the section "Using the Framework").

The class Base_Form is shown in Figure 31.5 followed by the code for the class.

FIGURE 31.5.

The base Business form.

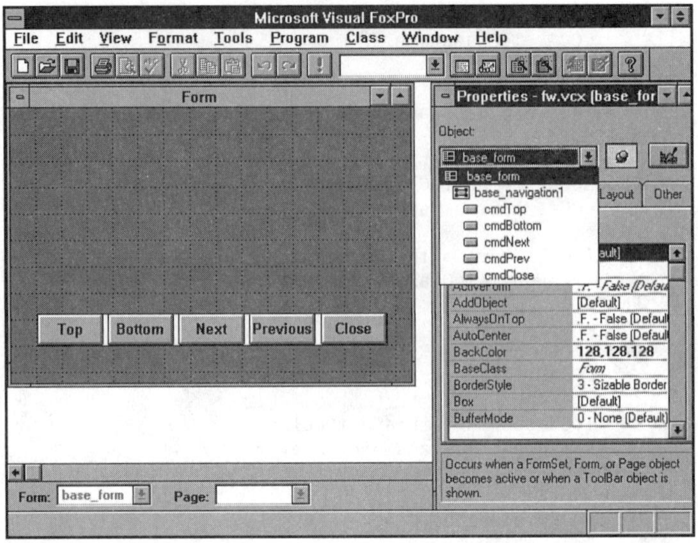

```
*    Class............: Base_form
*    Author...........: Menachem Bazian, CPA
*    Project..........: Visual FoxPro Unleashed!
*    Copyright........: (c) Flash Creative Management, Inc. 1995
*    Notes............: Exported code from Class Browser.

*****************************************************
*-- Class:        base_form
*-- ParentClass:  form
*-- BaseClass:    form
*-- Base form for business classes
*
DEFINE CLASS base_form AS form

    DataSession = 2
    DoCreate = .T.
    BackColor = RGB(128,128,128)
    Caption = "Form"
    Name = "base_form"

    *-- Name of business class on the form.
    cclass = .F.

    ADD OBJECT base_navigation1 AS base_navigation WITH ;
        Top = 187, ;
        Left = 25, ;
        Width = 328, ;
        Height = 30, ;
        Name = "base_navigation1", ;
        cmdTop.Name = "cmdTop", ;
        cmdBottom.Name = "cmdBottom", ;
        cmdNext.Name = "cmdNext", ;
        cmdPrev.Name = "cmdPrev", ;
        cmdClose.Name = "cmdClose"
```

```
ENDDEFINE
*
*-- EndDefine: base_form
***************************************************
```

There is nothing really exciting here either. This form has a custom property called cClass that is designed to tell the navigation class onto which class to delegate the navigation method responsibilities. It also has an instance of the navigation class on it.

The Base Data Environment Class

Business classes use tables. Using tables typically calls for a data environment. The framework class for this is the Base_De class shown in the following code listing:

```
*   Class.............: Base_de
*   Author............: Menachem Bazian, CPA
*   Project...........: Visual FoxPro Unleashed!
*   Copyright.........: (c) Flash Creative Management, Inc. 1995
*   Notes.............: Exported code from Class Browser.

***************************************************
*-- Class:       base_de
*-- ParentClass: custom
*-- BaseClass:   custom
*-- DataEnvironment Loader
*
DEFINE CLASS base_de AS custom

    Height = 36
    Width = 36
    Name = "base_de"

    *-- Name of the DE Class to load
    cdeclassname = .F.

    *-- The name of the program holding the DE class
    cdeprgname = .F.

    *-- Ensures that a dataenvironment class name has been specified
    PROTECTED PROCEDURE chk4de
        IF TYPE("this.cDeClassName") # 'C' OR EMPTY(this.cDeClassName)
            =MessageBox("No Data Environment was specified. " + ;
                          "Cannot instantiate object.", ;
                    16, ;
                    "Instantiation Error")
            RETURN .F.
        ENDIF
    ENDPROC

    *-- Opens the Data Environment
    PROCEDURE opende
        *-- Method OPENDE
        *-- This method will instantiate a DE class and run the
        *-- OpenTables() method.
        *--
        *-- Since the Container is not yet instantiated, I cannot do
        *--an AddObject() to it.
```

```
        *--
        *-- I'll do that in the container's Init.

        LOCAL loDe, lcClassName

        IF !EMPTY(this.cDEPrgName)
            SET PROCEDURE TO (this.cDEPrgName) ADDITIVE
        ENDIF

        lcClassName = this.cDeClassName
        loDe = CREATEOBJECT(lcClassName)

        IF TYPE("loDe") # "O"
            IF !EMPTY(this.cDEPrgName)
                RELEASE PROCEDURE (this.cDEPrgName)
            ENDIF
            RETURN .F.
        ENDIF

        *-- If we get this far, we can run the opentables method.

        loDe.OpenTables()

        IF !EMPTY(this.cDEPrgName)
            RELEASE PROCEDURE (this.cDEPrgName)
        ENDIF
    ENDPROC

    PROCEDURE Init
        IF !this.Chk4dE()
            RETURN .f.
        ENDIF

        *-- Add code here to add the DE object at runtime and run the OPENTABLES
        *-- event. I will leave that out for now....

        RETURN this.openDE()
    ENDPROC

ENDDEFINE
*
*-- EndDefine: base_de
**************************************************
```

Finally, here is something interesting to discuss. This class, based on Custom, is designed to load a data environment for the business class. It has two properties: the name of the data environment class to load and the name of the PRG file where the data environment class resides. Because data environment classes cannot be created visually, this class acts as a wrapper.

Why separate this class out? To be sure, the functionality for this class could have been rolled into the business class; however, when creating this framework, I could see the use of having this type of Loader class on many different kinds of forms and classes. By abstracting the functionality out into a different class, I can now use this class whenever and wherever I please.

Events and Methods

Table 31.12 presents the `Base_De` class's events and methods.

Table 31.12. The `Base_De` class's events and methods.

Event/Method	Description
Init	The `Init` method first calls the `Chk4De` method to make sure that a data environment class name has been specified. If not, the object's instantiation is aborted. It then calls `OpenDe` to open the tables and relations.
Chk4De	This method checks that a data environment was specified.
OpenDe	This method instantiates the data environment class and runs the `OpenTables` method.
	What about closing the tables? Well, the base form is set to run in its own data session. When the form instance is released, the data session is closed along with all of the tables in it. Don't you love it when a plan comes together?

The *Base_Business* Class

The next class is the framework class for creating business classes. Figure 31.6 shows the `Base_Business` class and is followed by the code listing.

FIGURE 31.6.

The `Base_Business` *class.*

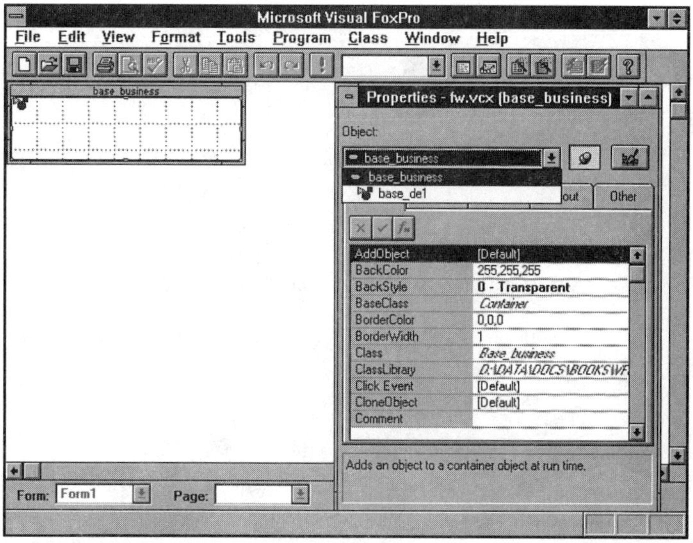

```
*  Class.............: Base_business
*  Author............: Menachem Bazian, CPA
*  Project...........: Visual FoxPro Unleashed!
*  Copyright.........: (c) Flash Creative Management, Inc. 1995
*  Notes.............: Exported code from Class Browser.

***************************************************
*-- Class:        base_business
*-- ParentClass:  container
*-- BaseClass:    container
*-- Abstract business class.
*
DEFINE CLASS base_business AS container

    Width = 215
    Height = 58
    BackStyle = 0
    TabIndex = 1
    Name = "base_business"

    *-- Name of the table controlling the class
    PROTECTED ctablename

    ADD OBJECT base_de1 AS base_de WITH ;
        Top = 0, ;
        Left = 0, ;
        Height = 61, ;
        Width = 217, ;
        cdeclassname = "", ;
        Name = "base_de1"

    *-- Add a record
    PROCEDURE addit
        SELECT (this.cTableName)
        APPEND BLANK

        IF TYPE("thisform") = "O"
            Thisform.refresh()
        ENDIF
    ENDPROC

    *-- Go to the next record
    PROCEDURE nextit
        SELECT (this.cTableName)

        SKIP 1
        IF EOF()
            ?? CHR(7)
            WAIT WINDOW NOWAIT "At end of file"
            GO BOTTOM
        ENDIF

        IF TYPE("thisform") = "O"
            Thisform.refresh()
        ENDIF
    ENDPROC

    *-- Move to prior record
    PROCEDURE previt
```

```
            SELECT (this.cTableName)

            SKIP -1
            IF BOF()
                ?? CHR(7)
                WAIT WINDOW NOWAIT "At beginning of file"
                GO top
            ENDIF

            IF TYPE("thisform") = "O"
                Thisform.refresh()
            ENDIF
        ENDPROC

    *-- Move to the first record
    PROCEDURE topit
        SELECT (this.cTableName)

        GO TOP
        IF TYPE("thisform") = "O"
            Thisform.refresh()
        ENDIF
    ENDPROC

    *-- Move to the last record
    PROCEDURE bottomit
        SELECT (this.cTableName)

        GO BOTTOM

        IF TYPE("thisform") = "O"
            Thisform.refresh()
        ENDIF
    ENDPROC

    PROCEDURE Init
        SELECT (this.cTableName)

        IF TYPE("thisform.cClass") # 'U'
            thisform.cClass = this.Name
        ENDIF
    ENDPROC


    PROCEDURE editit
    ENDPROC

    PROCEDURE getit
    ENDPROC

ENDDEFINE
*
*-- EndDefine: base_business
*****************************************************
```

This class is based on a *container* class. In Chapter 29 I discuss the flexibility of the container class, and here is a perfect example. The Base_Business class is a container with methods attached to it that handle the functionality of the business class. The container also serves as a receptacle for a base data environment loader class. When subclassing the `Base_Business` class, you would add the GUI elements that make up the data for the business class. Because the data environment loader class is added as the first object on the container, it instantiates *first.* Thus, if you have controls in a business class that reference a table as the control source, the business class will work because the data environment loader will open the tables before those other objects get around to instantiating.

The `Base_Business` class has one custom property, `cTableName`, which holds the alias of the table that controls navigation. For example, for an order business class, `cTableName` would most likely be the Orders table even though the Order Items table is used as well. The following sections discusses the events and methods.

Events and Methods

Table 31.13 presents the events and methods for `Base_Business`.

Table 31.13. The events and methods for `Base_Business`.

Event/Method	Description
Init	The `Init` method selects the controlling table. Remember, because the container will initialize *last,* by the time this method runs the data environment should already be set up.
	The next bit of code is interesting. The `Init` method checks to make sure that the `cClass` property exists on the form (it should—the check is a result of just a bit of paranoia at work) and then sets it to be the name of the business class. In other words, *you do not have to play with the form when dropping a business class on it.* The framework is designed to enable you to just drop a business class on the form and let it go from there.
Addit	This method adds a record to the controlling table. If the class resides on a form, the form's `Refresh` method is called.
Bottomit	This method moves to the last record of the controlling table. If the class resides on a form, the form's `Refresh` method is called.
Nextit	This method moves to the next record of the controlling table. If the class resides on a form, the form's `Refresh` method is called.
Previt	This method moves back one record in the controlling table. If the class resides on a form, the form's `Refresh` method is called.
Topit	This method moves to the top record of the controlling table. If the class resides on a form, the form's `Refresh` method is called.

Enhancing the Framework

Now that the framework is set up, the next step is to put it to use. In this case, a customer class is created to handle customer information in the TESTDATA database.

The first step in working with a corporate framework might be to customize it slightly for the use of a department or an application. In this case, I created a subclass of the Base_Business class for the business class I will show here. The subclass specifies the name of the data environment class to load as default_de (remember, default_de is automatically generated by Dumpdbc). You'll probably want to use different data environment classes for different business classes. In this case, to show how you might want to customize a framework (and to keep the business classes simple), I decided that I would always load the whole shebang. This being the case, it made sense to set it up once and subclass from there.

The subclass, called Base_TestData, also sets the name of the program to TD_DE.PRG, which is the name of a program I created with Dumpdbc. Again, the point here is that you can enhance the framework for your use. In fact, you probably will to some degree. These modifications make up the department or application framework. In this case, Base_TestData would probably be part of the application framework.

```
*  Class.............: Base_testdata
*  Author............: Menachem Bazian, CPA
*  Project...........: Visual FoxPro Unleashed!
*  Copyright.........: (c) Flash Creative Management, Inc. 1995
*  Notes.............: Exported code from Class Browser.

**************************************************
*-- Class:        base_testdata
*-- ParentClass:  base_business
*-- BaseClass:    container
*
DEFINE CLASS base_testdata AS base_business

    Width = 215
    Height = 58
    Name = "base_tastrade"
    base_de1.cdeprgname = "td_de.prg"
    base_de1.cdeclassname = "default_de"
    base_de1.Name = "base_de1"

ENDDEFINE
*
*-- EndDefine: base_testdata
**************************************************
```

Using the Framework

Now that I have the framework just where I want it, I'll use it to create a business class for the customer table and build a form for it. Just to illustrate how easy it is to use a framework (or at least how easy it should be), I will review the steps it takes to go from start to finish.

1. Subclass the base business class (see Figure 31.7).

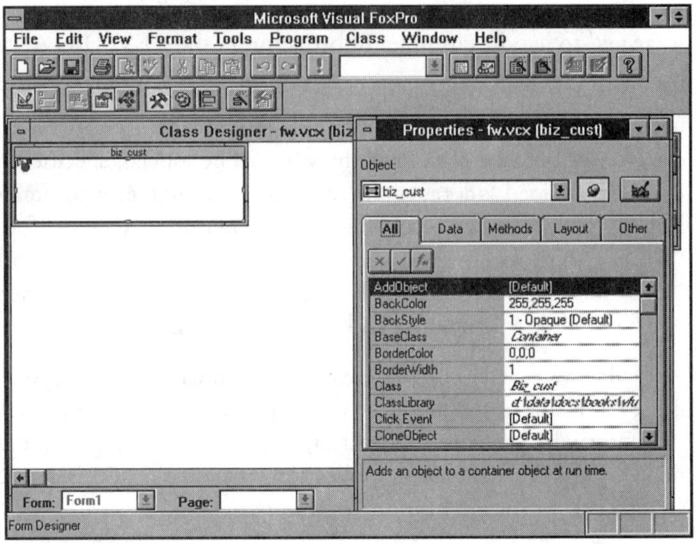

FIGURE 31.7.

Step 1—The subclass before modifications.

2. Set the cTableName property (see Figure 31.8).

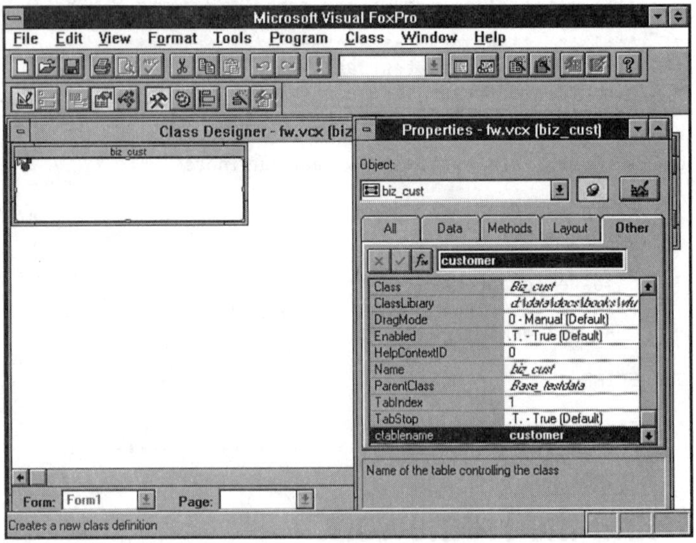

FIGURE 31.8.

Step 2—Setting the cTableName property.

3. Add the GUI objects and save the class (see Figure 31.9).

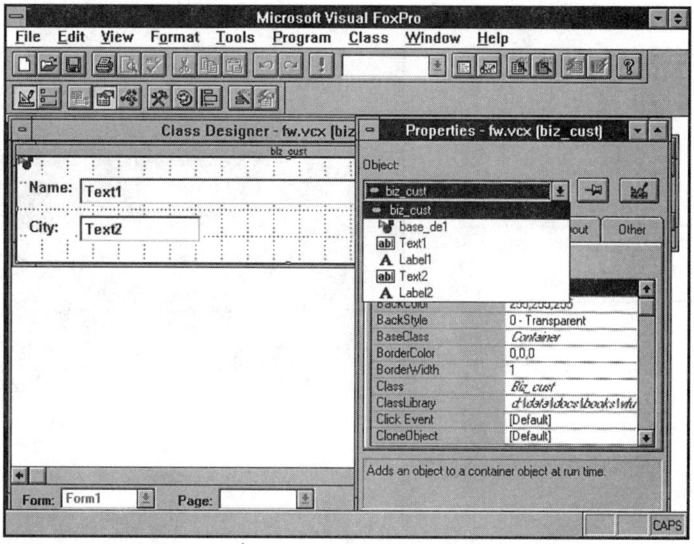

FIGURE 31.9.

Step 3—Adding GUI objects.

4. Drop the business class on a subclass of the base business form (see Figure 31.10).

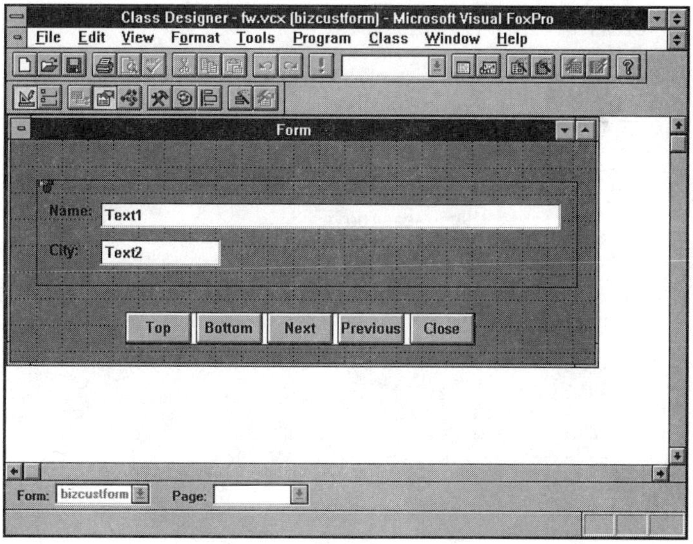

FIGURE 31.10.

Step 4—Dropping the business class on the form.

5. Instantiate the form (see Figure 31.11).

FIGURE 31.11.

Step 5—Running the form.

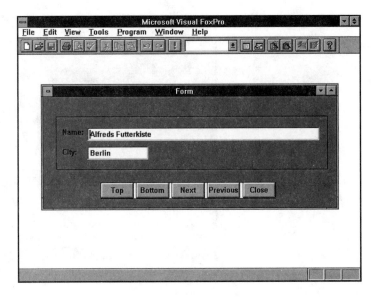

What you have here is two classes: the Biz_Cust class, which has the business class specifics, and the form class. Here is the code for these two classes:

```
*  Class............: Biz_cust
*  Author...........: Menachem Bazian, CPA
*  Project..........: Visual FoxPro Unleashed!
*  Copyright........: (c) Flash Creative Management, Inc. 1995
*  Notes............: Exported code from Class Browser.


****************************************************
*-- Class:       biz_cust
*-- ParentClass: base_testdata
*-- BaseClass:   container
*
DEFINE CLASS biz_cust AS base_testdata

    Width = 509
    Height = 97
    ctablename = "customer"
    Name = "biz_cust"
    base_de1.Top = 0
    base_de1.Left = 0
    base_de1.Height = 241
    base_de1.Width = 637
    base_de1.Name = "base_de1"

    ADD OBJECT text1 AS textbox WITH ;
        Value = "", ;
        ControlSource = "Customer.Company", ;
        Format = "", ;
        Height = 24, ;
        InputMask = "", ;
        Left = 60, ;
        Top = 20, ;
```

```
            Width = 433, ;
            Name = "Text1"

     ADD OBJECT label1 AS label WITH ;
            BackStyle = 0, ;
            Caption = "Name:", ;
            Height = 25, ;
            Left = 12, ;
            Top = 20, ;
            Width = 49, ;
            Name = "Label1"

     ADD OBJECT text2 AS textbox WITH ;
            Value = "", ;
            ControlSource = "Customer.City", ;
            Format = "", ;
            Height = 24, ;
            InputMask = "", ;
            Left = 60, ;
            Top = 54, ;
            Width = 113, ;
            Name = "Text2"

     ADD OBJECT label2 AS label WITH ;
            BackStyle = 0, ;
            Caption = "City:", ;
            Height = 18, ;
            Left = 12, ;
            Top = 56, ;
            Width = 43, ;
            Name = "Label2"

ENDDEFINE
*
*-- EndDefine: biz_cust
**************************************************

*  Class............: Bizcustform
*  Author...........: Menachem Bazian, CPA
*  Project..........: Visual FoxPro Unleashed!
*  Copyright.........: (c) Flash Creative Management, Inc. 1995
*  Notes............: Exported code from Class Browser.

**************************************************
*-- Class:        bizcustform
*-- ParentClass:  base_form
*-- BaseClass:    form
*
DEFINE CLASS bizcustform AS base_form

     Top = 0
     Left = 0
     Height = 202
     Width = 549
     DoCreate = .T.
     Name = "bizcustform"
     base_navigation1.cmdTop.Name = "cmdTop"
     base_navigation1.cmdBottom.Name = "cmdBottom"
```

```
        base_navigation1.cmdNext.Name = "cmdNext"
        base_navigation1.cmdPrev.Name = "cmdPrev"
        base_navigation1.cmdClose.Name = "cmdClose"
        base_navigation1.Top = 156
        base_navigation1.Left = 108
        base_navigation1.Width = 328
        base_navigation1.Height = 30
        base_navigation1.Name = "base_navigation1"

    ADD OBJECT biz_cust2 AS biz_cust WITH ;
        Top = 36, ;
        Left = 24, ;
        Width = 509, ;
        Height = 97, ;
        Name = "Biz_cust2", ;
        base_de1.Name = "base_de1", ;
        Text1.Name = "Text1", ;
        Label1.Name = "Label1", ;
        Text2.Name = "Text2", ;
        Label2.Name = "Label2"

ENDDEFINE
*
*-- EndDefine: bizcustform
*****************************************************
```

Consider the power of this approach. The developer concentrates his or her efforts in one place: the functionality and information in the business class. As for the surrounding functionality (for example, the form, the navigation controls, and so on), that is handled by the framework.

Additional Notes on the Business Class

Creating the business class based on a container has an additional benefit. Whenever a program needs to work with customers, all you have to do is instantiate the business class and call the appropriate methods. Because all of the functionality related to the business class is encapsulated within the confines of the container, no other function needs to worry about how to handle the data of the business class. If you're worried about the visual component to the class, you can stop worrying. There is no law that says you have to display the business class when you instantiate it (this also goes for the form I designed for creating new data sessions).

Finally, you can use the business class on forms other than a data entry form. For example, suppose you are working on an Invoice class and you need to provide the functionality of being able to edit customer information for an invoice. All you need to do is drop the business class on a modal form.

Frameworks: A Final Word

Creating a framework is not a small undertaking. In fact, it is quite a daunting prospect. Still, in the long run, having a framework that you understand and can work with and that provides the functionality and structure you need will prove absolutely essential.

As Visual FoxPro matures in the marketplace, there will be third-party vendors offering frameworks for development. As I write these words, there are several third-party frameworks in progress. The temptation will be strong to purchase an existing framework to jump-start yourself. It would be foolhardy to state that you can only work with a framework you create. Recreating the wheel is not usually a good idea. Besides, the popularity of frameworks, such as the FoxPro Codebook in the 2.6 environment, prove my point.

Remember, though, that the framework you choose will color every aspect of your development. You will rely on it heavily. If it is robust, well-documented, and standardized, you have a good chance of succeeding. Don't take this choice lightly. Subject the framework to rigorous testing and evaluation. Accept nothing on faith. If the choice you make is wrong, it can hurt you big time.

What should you look for in a framework? The criteria I discussed in Chapter 30, "Managing Classes with Visual FoxPro," relating to the class librarian's review of suggested classes will do nicely. To review, here are the criteria:

- Documentation
- Robustness
- Completeness
- Standards

By the way, if you're wondering what happened to *compatibility*, I left it out because the framework is the ground level by which compatibility will be measured.

Development Standards

It is critical to develop or adopt standards for coding when working with Visual FoxPro. There is a high degree of probability that the classes you create will be used by others (unless you work alone and never intend to bring other people into your projects). In order for others to be able to use your code, there has to be a degree of standardization that permeates the code. Without these standards, you will be left with a Tower of Babel that will not withstand the test of time.

What kind of standards should you implement? The following sections provide some basic categories in which you should make decisions.

Variable Naming

I like to use a form of Hungarian notation. The first character denotes the scope of the variable, and the second denotes the data type.

Scope	Characters
L	Local
P	Private
G	Global (public)
T	ParameTer

Type	Characters
C	Character
D	Date
L	Logical
N	Numeric, Float, Double, Integer
O	Object
T	DateTime
U	Undefined
Y	Currency

If you're wondering where these characters come from, they are the values returned by the Type function. The rest of the variable name should be descriptive. Remember that you can have *really* long names if you like; therefore, there is no need to skimp anymore.

Naming Methods and Properties

One of the nicest features of OOP lies in *polymorphism*, which means that you can have multiple methods and properties of the same name even though they might do different things. In order to effectively use this feature, it is important that naming standards are established that dictate the names of commonly used methods.

Imagine, for example, what life would be like if one class used the method name Show to display itself, another used the name Display, and another used the name Paint. It would be pretty confusing, wouldn't it?

Where possible, decide on naming conventions that make sense for you. I think it is a good idea to adopt the Microsoft naming conventions (use Show instead of something else, for example) when available. This maintains consistency not only within your classes but also with the FoxPro base classes. By the way, naming conventions apply to properties too. A common way to name properties is to use as the first character the expected data type in the property (using the same character identifiers shown previously). This helps use the properties too. When standards are not applicable for methods and properties (that is, they are not expected to be commonly used), try to use a descriptive name.

The Effects of a Framework on Standards

The standards you adopt should be based on your framework if possible. If you are looking to purchase a framework and the framework does not have standards with it, I would be very leery of purchasing it. I personally consider well-documented standards the price of entry for a framework.

If you purchase a framework, take a look at the standards and make sure that you can live with them. Although I wouldn't recommend living and dying by standards (rules do have to be broken sometimes in order to get the job done), you will be working by those standards 98 percent of the time (or more). Let's face it, if you didn't work by the standards almost all the time, standards would be meaningless. Make sure that the standards dictated by a framework make sense to you.

Summary

Of the new features in Visual FoxPro, object orientation ranks very high on my list of favorites. It is so pervasive an addition to the language that it should literally affect *every single step* of the development process.

Visual FoxPro is a hybrid language, and therefore the temptation might be strong to continue developing modularly in it. Visual FoxPro will enable you to do this if you so choose. However, I believe that object orientation is as central to Visual FoxPro as a combination is to a safe. Without the combination to a safe, you can still store things in the safe but you can't lock it. Its usefulness is limited.

As a final thought, I would like to return to the basic premise I present in Chapter 27. Object orientation is frequently deemed to be more difficult than it really is. The obtuse presentations of the subject in many arenas does not help the process. The challenge in OOP is to design a class hierarchy and work out which class will do what. Once you have the class hierarchy worked out, the implementation should not be difficult at all.

VI

PART

Advanced
Programming

Multiuser Programming and Techniques

32

This chapter explains programming tools and techniques for writing programs in a network environment. The chapter assumes that Visual FoxPro is installed on a local area network.

Introduction to Visual FoxPro on a Network

Visual FoxPro is network-ready out of the box; you can install it on a single-user PC or on a network workstation. Visual FoxPro is compatible with any NETBIOS-compatible networks, including Novell, LANtastic, and Windows Networking.

In addition to the commands and functions you use with Visual FoxPro on a single PC, many of Visual FoxPro's commands and functions implicitly lock and unlock records and tables, offering transparent networking capability with no additional special programming. Visual FoxPro also offers commands and functions for use on a network to explicitly lock and unlock records and files.

Visual FoxPro also adds a number of features that were not available in earlier versions of FoxPro. These features are specifically aimed toward developers of multiuser applications and include the capability to open multiple data sessions, the implementation and control of data buffering, and the addition of transaction processing commands.

Programming Concerns for a Network

This chapter assumes that Visual FoxPro is installed on a network and you intend to program multiuser applications that share information across a network. Database integrity is endangered when the program is not designed for multiple users. For example, if two or more users attempt to modify a record or attempt to update a shared database at the same time, one will be denied access to the file and an error will be generated. At best, one user overwrites another's changes. At worst, the network operating system crashes, which brings the entire network down and possibly damages the table.

Another common problem with database software on a network is the potential problem of *file deadlock*, also known as a "deadly embrace." A file deadlock can result if two programs contend for the same files and the error-trapping routine causes an unconditional retry of the file access.

Consider two routines (routine1 and routine2) running on different machines on the network, each of which requires exclusive use of both file1 and file2 (in a shared area on the network) to run. Realizing that both files might not be available immediately for use, you've written an error-handling routine that, upon getting a File in use error, immediately returns to your routine to try to get the denied file again. Say routine1 has obtained access to file2 and is now waiting on file1 before proceeding. Further, imagine routine2 has obtained access to file1 and is now waiting on file2. What's happened? Both are waiting on resources that the other routine has tied up and won't release. Both will wait forever in this "deadly embrace."

To guard against potential problems that can arise in a multiple-user environment, Visual FoxPro offers the programmer manual file- and record-locking facilities, automatic file and record locking, and a means of designating whether files are available for shared or for private use. Visual FoxPro's capability to lock individual records prevents contention problems encountered by some database managers that do not support record-locking, and instead lock a buffer that often contains multiple records.

Also useful when operating on a network are the List and Display Status commands, which indicate the status of file and record locks.

TIP

Before you read the following sections on file attributes, record locks versus table locks, and manual locking commands and functions, you should be aware that the code for these methods is backward-compatible with earlier versions of FoxPro, but there may be less complicated ways to ensure data integrity. If you don't care about maintaining code compatiblility with earlier versions of FoxPro, you can protect data on a network by buffering access to the data. Because buffers automatically lock and release records and tables, they are less hassle to code than the manual locking and unlocking commands. For more details on this, read the section "Buffering Access to Data," later in this chapter.

File Attribute Modes

Tables can be opened in one of two attribute modes: exclusive or shared. When a table is opened in exclusive mode, no other network user can use Visual FoxPro to access that table until the file is closed or the attribute is in some way changed from exclusive to shared. If the table is opened in shared mode, any number of network users can gain access to the table. Exclusive use of a file is granted on a first-come, first-served basis. The default attribute for a table is exclusive. Visual FoxPro opens any table in exclusive mode unless you enter Set Exclusive Off at the command window or Visual FoxPro is told otherwise by your programs.

Although Set Exclusive On prevents other Visual FoxPro users from accessing the table, be aware that other Xbase-compatible programs (like dBASE) that use the same tables will not respect what you do in Visual FoxPro. Other programs can trample your data while you have an exclusive lock in effect in Visual FoxPro, and nothing can be done in Visual FoxPro to avoid this. This is one more reason to avoid the dubious practice of trying to maintain shared tables in the older Xbase file formats. Stick with Visual FoxPro's native file format, and export data that other programs must work with.

Most other types of files opened by Visual FoxPro are also opened in exclusive mode by default. A simple way to remember whether a file is opened in exclusive mode is this: If the command results in a file being written to (such as Copy To, Index, or any command that begins with the reserved words Create or Modify), it is opened in exclusive mode by default. If the command results in the file being read from but not written to (such as with Report Form, Label Form, Set Format To, or Set Procedure To), it is opened on a shared basis by default. This rule applies to all types of files directly used by Visual FoxPro.

The default manner in which index files and the associated memo field files are opened is always the same as for the table associated with those files.

Lock Commands and Functions

As a programmer, it is up to you to determine what should and should not be locked by the program. Once you have made that decision, Visual FoxPro offers locksmith's tools composed of three commands and three functions. The commands are Set Exclusive, Use Exclusive, and Unlock. The functions are Lock(), Flock(), and Rlock().

As mentioned earlier, Set Exclusive On causes all files opened after the Set Exclusive On command at the beginning of the program to be opened in exclusive mode. If you prefer not to lock the files, use Set Exclusive Off. As an alternative to Set Exclusive On, you can use the Use Exclusive <*filename*> command to open a database. This variation of Use opens the named file in the exclusive mode.

The locking functions—Lock(), Flock(), and Rlock()—enable you to test for the presence of a file or record lock and to lock the file or record at the same time. In this respect, these functions differ from all other functions in Visual FoxPro. Other functions simply return a value, but the locking functions return a True or False value and perform an action. If the file or record is not previously locked, the locking function places a lock on the file or record. The Flock() function tests for file locking, and the Rlock() function and its synonym, Lock() (Lock() and Rlock() are identical in functionality; however, using Rlock() makes the target of your lock—a record—clearer), test for record locking. The functions can be used in the interactive mode or from within a program. In the interactive mode, you can enter

```
? Flock()
```

or

```
? Rlock()
```

If the file or record was unlocked before the command was entered, Visual FoxPro responds with True (.T.), which indicates a successful lock. Enter a List or Display Status command to show whether the file or record is locked; for example:

```
.? flock()
.T.
. display status
```

If either function returns a logical False, the record or file in question has been locked by another user.

Within a program, you can use the locking functions as part of a conditional statement that tests a lock and performs the desired operation if the lock is successful. The following code shows an example of such use. Please note that the files INVFILES and STOCKNO are not included, but working samples can be easily generated for this example.

```
**CHANGEIT.PRG LOCKS, EDITS RECORD
**LAST UPDATE 06/95
CLEAR
INPUT "Enter stock number of record to be edited." TO MNUMB
USE INVFILES INDEX STOCKNO
SEEK MNUMB
IF EOF()
    ? "Sorry...no such stock number."
    WAIT
    RETURN
ENDIF
CLEAR
*Found the record, so test for a previous lock, and
*if not already locked, lock the record
IF RLOCK()       && Process this part of the "if" statement
➥if the lock was successful
    STORE DISCRIPT TO MDESCRIPT
    STORE UNITCOST TO MUNITCOST
    STORE QUANTITY TO MQUANTITY
    @ 5,5 SAY "Item description:  "  GET MDESCRIPT
    @ 7,5 SAY "Unit cost:  " GET MUNITCOST PICTURE "99999.99"
    @ 9,5 SAY "Quantity:  "  GET MQUANTITY PICTURE "999"
    READ
    REPLACE DESCRIPTION WITH MDESCRIPT
    REPLACE UNITCOST WITH MUNITCOST, QUANTITY WITH MQUANTITY
    CLOSE DATABASES
ELSE              && Whoops! the lock was not successful
    ? CHR(7)
    @ 5,5 SAY "Sorry...another network user is updating that record."
    @  7,5 SAY "Try your request again later."
    WAIT
ENDIF
RETURN
```

The program uses the IF...ELSE...ENDIF statements to test for the value returned by the RLOCK() function. If RLOCK() returns the value of True, the temporary variables are created and the @...SAY...GET commands followed by the REPLACE commands permit editing of the record. If the record is already locked, control passes to the ELSE statement, which advises the user that the record is not presently available for editing.

Using *UNLOCK*

The UNLOCK command is used to unlock a previously locked record or file. The syntax for the command is

```
UNLOCK [ALL]
```

If you don't specify the ALL option, UNLOCK removes the last lock implemented in the active work area. If you include the ALL option, UNLOCK removes all locks in all work areas.

As a general rule, your programs are most efficient on a network if you lock records when individual updates must be performed and lock files only when global updates (such as a REINDEX command) are performed. It's also important to note that any access granted by locking commands and functions in a program can be overridden by the network operating system software. For example, if you use a network command to designate a file as read-only, users are not able to update the file, regardless of whether the file is locked or not.

> **TIP**
>
> If you need to have write access to a data table, but you don't know whether the file is read-only, a common trick is to read a record and write the data back unchanged. No data is changed, but if the file is marked as read-only your program will generate an error that you can trap and make a programmatic decision about whether you can continue to run.
>
> Put in the application setup code, this technique can be used to generate a message to the administrator (use MAPI connectivity to automatically generate some mail) before your application exits.

In addition to programming control of locking functions, certain Visual FoxPro commands automatically place a lock on the file before these commands can take effect. The following commands perform a mandatory file lock:

```
AVERAGE
CALCULATE
COPY TO
COPY TO ARRAY
COUNT
DISPLAY <scope>
INDEX
JOIN
LIST
LABEL
REPORT
SORT
SUM
TOTAL
```

This brings up the question of what happens to your program's execution if the record or file cannot be locked (because another user has already placed a lock on the file or record). If this occurs, Visual FoxPro reports that the record or file has been locked by another user. This happens often on a network when many users share files, so error trapping to handle expected locking failures within your programs is a necessity.

Handling Failures to Lock with Error Trapping

Error-trapping routines, which you add to an application's design, must include commands to handle locking failures if you offer shared access to files within a program. The ERROR() function provides values that indicate the failure of a file-lock or record-lock attempt. In the error-handling routine, include an IF...ENDIF or CASE statement that detects an error value of 109 ("locked record error") and an error value of 108 ("locked file error").

Your program should also test for a possible error value of 148, which indicates to a network server busy conditions caused by the network operating system software. Such use of error trapping is shown in the following example:

```
**ERRTRAP.PRG
**Error-trapping routine for INVENT.PRG on a Novell network
**Last update 03/30/94
DO CASE
   CASE ERROR() = 108 .OR. ERROR() = 109 .OR ERROR = 158
      ? "The file or record is currently in use by another user."
      ACCEPT "Shall I continue trying to access it? (Y/N): " TO ANS
      IF UPPER (ANS) = "Y"
         CLEAR
         ? "...retrying access..."
         STORE 1 TO COUNT
         DO WHILE COUNT<100
            STORE 1 + COUNT TO COUNT
         ENDDO
         RETRY
      ENDIF
      *User wants no retry, so give up and back out
      CLOSE DATABASES
      RETURN TO MASTER
   CASE ERROR() = 148
      ? "Getting a net server busy MESSAGE FOR THE FILE SERVER."
      ? " ... Please try again later."
      WAIT
      RETURN TO MASTER
   CASE ERROR() =1
      ? "Cannot find the file.  Contact Network Administrator."
      CLEAR ALL
      WAIT
      QUIT
   CASE ERROR() = 20 .OR. ERROR() = 26
      ? "The index seems to be missing a record.  Please wait,"
      ? "while I repair the index."
      SET TALK ON
      INDEX ON STOCKNO TAG STACKNO
      SET TALK OFF
      RETRY
   OTHERWISE
      ? "A serious error has occurred.  Please record the following"
      ? "message, and contact the DP Department."
```

```
        ?
        ?MESSAGE()
        WAIT
        SET ALTERNATE TO ERRORS
        SET ALTERNATE ON
        DISPLAY MEMORY
        DISPLAY STATUS
        CLOSE ALTERNATE
        QUIT
ENDCASE
```

To use this error handler in your program you would issue ON ERROR DO Errtrap in your setup code, or wherever you wanted this particular code to be run as your error handler.

Precisely how you handle the error is a matter of programming style. Some programmers prefer to tell the user to try the operation again later and pass control back to a higher-level module in the program. Other programmers prefer to start a timing loop and retry the operation at the end of the loop. If you prefer the timing loop method, include the RETRY command in your error handler. Be sure to to use SET REPROCESS in your program setup code (covered in the following section) to ensure you don't place your program in an endless loop. RETRY causes the program control to return to the program that called the error-trapping routine at the same line of the program that caused the error. This is different than the RETURN command, which passes control to the program that called the error-trapping routine, but which starts the execution at the line following the one that called the program.

Using RETRY, you can repeat the access attempt on the file or the record indefinitely—or until the user indicates that he or she is tired of waiting for the record or file to become available. The error-trapping program listed previously uses a timing loop along with an optional abort of the RETRY operation. The user chooses which option to take (abort or retry) when he answers the question Shall I continue trying to access it? (Y/N): posed to him by the error routine.

Performing Automated Retries

You can use the SET REPROCESS command to perform automated retries of a record lock or file lock attempt. The syntax for this command is

```
SET REPROCESS TO <n>/AUTOMATIC
```

where <n> is a numeric value from 1 to 32,000. The default for SET REPROCESS is zero, meaning Visual FoxPro immediately reports an error condition if the lock cannot be placed. By entering the SET REPROCESS TO <n> command, you tell Visual FoxPro to retry any locking attempt by the specified number of times before the error condition is reported. Note that you can also enter a negative number as the value, in which case Visual FoxPro retries the attempt on an infinite basis. If you use the AUTOMATIC clause, Visual FoxPro retries the attempt on an infinite basis and displays a system message "Attempting to lock... press Esc to cancel."

Although allowing the retries to continue forever seems like a poor idea, the fact that the user can decide when enough is enough might fit into the way your user likes to work. Like most engineering decisions, it's a trade-off.

Other Network-Specific Commands

Other Visual FoxPro commands can prove useful when used with a network. These are DISPLAY STATUS, LIST STATUS, and SET PRINTER.

The DISPLAY STATUS and LIST STATUS commands perform the same functions as when you are not on a network (display the default drives and paths, database names, work area numbers and alias names, and index filenames). When you issue a DISPLAY STATUS or a LIST STATUS command, the status of any active file locks or record locks is displayed along with other information such as filenames, work areas, and alias names, as shown in the following example:

```
display status
```

Both DISPLAY STATUS and LIST STATUS can use the TO PRINT option in the network environment to direct output to a network printer if that is how you have your default printer setup.

The SET PRINTER command enables you to redirect printer output to another printer on the network. Print output can be sent to the local printer attached to the workstation or to a server. To send printer output to a printer other than the one attached to that workstation, the syntax for the command is

```
SET PRINTER TO \\ <computer name> \<printer name> = <destination>
```

where *<computer name>* is the workstation name assigned under the network software and *<printer name>* is the network-assigned printer name. The *<destination>* designation is LPT1, LPT2, or LPT3, as appropriate with the particular setup.

To redirect printer output back to the local printer (the one attached to that workstation), the command is

```
SET PRINTER TO LPT1/LPT2/LPT3
```

By default, the assigned printer is the shared printer on the network (often attached to the file server). Users of Novell can enter the following shorter command for choosing the default printer:

```
SET PRINTER TO \\SPOOLER
```

The SET REFRESH command sets the interval for updating the screen display when the user is in a full-screen mode such as edit or browse. Each time the screen is updated, any changes made by other users appear. The syntax for the command is

```
SET REFRESH TO <n>
```

where <*n*> is a numeric value from 1 to 3600. The value represents the time, measured in seconds, between the screen updates. If the command is not used, Visual FoxPro defaults to an interval value of zero.

Using Data Sessions

One feature of FoxPro network programming that's new to Visual FoxPro is the use of *data sessions.* Data sessions are sessions in which multiple instances of a form can operate in independent data environments, whether the forms are running on different workstations or on the same workstation. Because there will be times when you want to launch multiple instances of the same form, the independent data environments and the object-oriented nature of forms in Visual FoxPro provide an environment in which changes made to one form are not automatically reflected in the other instances of the same form. For example, imagine being interrupted while in the middle of adding a large order to an order-entry application to add a small, rush order. You wouldn't want to cancel out of the order you're doing; you'd like to bring up another order entry form and fill it out for the rush order without disturbing the ongoing one.

You can do this in Visual FoxPro by setting the DataSession property value. Normally, the DataSession property value is 1, in which case changes made to one form are reflected in all open instances of the same form. By changing the value of the DataSession property for the form to 2, you tell Visual FoxPro to run each instance of the form in a separate session, and changes made to the data don't appear in the other forms. There are two ways in which you can enable multiple data sessions.

In the Form Designer, set the DataSession property to 2. To do this, open the form in design mode, click the form's title bar to select it, choose View | Properties from the menu, and click the Data tab in the Properties dialog box. Click the DataSession property to select it, and then choose 2, Private Data Session, from the list box of property choices.

Alternatively, in the command window you can set the DataSession property to 2 with a command. For example, you could enter the following in the command window:

```
frmMyFormName.DataSession = 2
```

TIP

In your program code, you can override multiple data sessions and force all instances of a form to show changes to shared data by using the SET DATASESSION TO 1 command.

Buffering Access to Data

To help you protect your data during data update operations on a network, Visual FoxPro enables you to do *data buffering* of both records and tables. When you enable data buffering, Visual FoxPro copies the records you are working with at a given point in time to a memory buffer. Edits are done to the data in the buffer, enabling other users access to the original record. When you move from the record or use any command that forces a write to the data, Visual FoxPro attempts to lock the record and make any changes.

Visual FoxPro provides two types of buffering: record buffering and table buffering. *Record buffering* works best when you are working with individual records because it minimizes the possible impact on other network users. *Table buffering* is recommended when you need to handle a group of records at one time (such as when you need to protect all associated child or "detail" records for a given parent or "master" record in a one-to-many relationship).

Whether you use record buffering or table buffering, you can establish buffering in either of two modes: optimistic or pessimistic. With *optimistic* buffering, records are locked only as the data is written. With *pessimistic* buffering, other users can't get to the data while you are editing it.

To change the buffering methods used by records and tables from Visual FoxPro's default value, you can use the buffering property. You set the value of the buffering property with the CURSORSETPROP() function. Table 32.1 shows the acceptable values for the buffering property under Visual FoxPro.

Table 32.1. Buffering property values.

Value	Property Desired
1	No buffering (this is the default)
2	Pessimistic record locks (these lock the record as you start to work with it, and release the lock when you move the record pointer or issue a TABLEUPDATE())
3	Optimistic record locks (these lock the record when it is time to write changes to it)
4	Pessimistic table locks (these lock individual records of the table as you start to work with the records, and the locks are released when you close the table or issue a TABLEUPDATE())
5	Optimistic table locks (these lock the records of the table when it is time to write changes to it)

You can enable pessimistic record locking by using the value of 2 with the CURSORSETPROP() function, as shown in the following example:

```
=CURSORSETPROP("Buffering",2)
```

Visual FoxPro will try to lock the record at the record pointer location. If the lock succeeds, the record is placed in the buffer, and editing is enabled.

You can enable optimistic record locking by using the value of 3 with the CURSORSETPROP() function, as shown in the following example:

```
=CURSORSETPROP("Buffering",3)
```

Visual FoxPro will copy the record to the buffer, and editing is enabled. When you move the record pointer or execute a TABLEUPDATE() statement in your code, Visual FoxPro locks the record and writes the changes to the table.

You can enable pessimistic table locking by using the value of 4 with the CURSORSETPROP() function, as shown in the following example:

```
=CURSORSETPROP("Buffering",4)
```

Visual FoxPro will try to lock any needed records in the table as they are needed. If the lock succeeds, the needed records are placed in the buffer, and editing is enabled.

You can enable optimistic table locking by using the value of 5 with the CURSORSETPROP() function, as shown in the following example:

```
=CURSORSETPROP("Buffering",5)
```

Visual FoxPro will copy records to the buffer as they are needed, and editing is enabled. When you move the record pointer or execute a TABLEUPDATE() statement in your code, Visual FoxPro then writes the changes to the table.

Once you've enabled buffering, it stays in effect until you disable it, or until you close the table. You can force a write to the records with the TABLEUPDATE() function, and you can cancel edits to a table with the TABLEREVERT() function. As an example, your program might contain code like the following:

```
OPEN DATABASE Ecology
USE Customer
=CURSORSETPROP('Buffering',2)
*commands to edit data go here.*
SKIP
IF .NOT. TABLEREVERT(.T.)
    =MessageBox("Unable to write changes. Try later.")
    =TABLEREVERT()
ENDIF
```

Note that when you enable buffering and you append records to a table, the appended records are assigned negative sequential record numbers in ascending order until the changes are posted to the table. You can move the record pointer to any appended record by using the GOTO command along with the negative record number. For example, issuing a GOTO -4 statement will move the record pointer to the fourth appended record when record buffering is enabled.

Using Transaction Processing

Visual FoxPro now supports *transaction processing*, something that was not supported in versions of FoxPro prior to Visual FoxPro 3.0. Transaction processing provides a method whereby a series of changes to your data can be treated as if they were a single operation. All data changes made within a BEGIN TRANSACTION and an END TRANSACTION statement are treated together as a unit; everything within the block is committed, or all changes are taken back out. If for any reason you want to undo all the changes, you can use the ROLLBACK statement at any time within the transaction block. When you have completed your updates to your data, you use the END TRANSACTION statement to lock all needed records, commit the changes, unlock the records, and end the transaction processing. Use the following commands with transaction processing:

Command Used	Result
BEGIN TRANSACTION	Starts transaction processing. All edits made to tables will be recorded from now until the END TRANSACTION statement, or until a ROLLBACK.
ROLLBACK	Reverses all changes made to tables since the last BEGIN TRANSACTION statement.
END TRANSACTION	Locks needed records and commits to disk all changes made since the last BEGIN TRANSACTION statement.

If you are accustomed to the transaction processing commands provided by dBASE IV, note that Visual FoxPro does not support the COMMIT command used in dBASE IV. You use an END TRANSACTION statement to commit the changes to the tables. If you want to continue transaction processing, just issue a BEGIN TRANSACTION statement right after the END TRANSACTION statement.

Be warned that although transaction processing is a nice safeguard against the loss of data, it is not foolproof. Bizarre occurrences can still cause data loss. For example, if the power fails or the system crashes while Visual FoxPro is processing an END TRANSACTION statement, you can still lose changes to your data. If it has been a while since you issued the BEGIN TRANSACTION statement, you could have a significant number of changes.

Managing Network Performance

There are some overall hints you should be aware of when writing applications for use on a network. These will help you to maintain better network performance. They include the following:

- *Store temporary files on local drives.* In cases where your workstations are equipped with reasonably fast hard disks (and users do not usually have less than 2MB of free disk space), you should tell Visual FoxPro to store on the users' local hard disks the temporary files it must create. You can do this by changing the default file locations for temporary files in the configuration file called CONFIG.FPW. (You can edit this file with a text editor or with FoxPro's own program editor.)

- *Lock tables for exclusive use and perform batch operations during off-peak times.* Visual FoxPro handles processing much faster when files can be opened exclusively. Therefore, if you must perform global operations on your data, you can code routines that open files exclusively and perform those operations when most or all users have gone home (like in the middle of the night).

- *Use optimistic buffering rather than pessimistic buffering whenever possible.* The use of optimistic buffering will avoid contentions between users. Optimistic buffering does mean that occasionally one user may make changes to a record, only to be told that he or she must wait for another user to finish with the record before those changes can be posted. Realistically, however, in most situations you won't have different users fighting over access to the same record.

Moving Your Single-User Applications to a Network

Visual FoxPro's automatic file and record locking do much toward making it easy to bring onto a network an application previously written for a single-user environment. The performance of the application under multiple users improves if you take full advantage of selective locking. However, you can perform a few minimal steps to quickly get an application "up and running" on a network. Once the application is network-ready, you can then concentrate on ways to improve the performance by implementing data buffering or by adding selective locking functions and error routines. The following steps can be considered as the least you should do when moving an application to a network.

At or near the beginning of the program, add a SET EXCLUSIVE OFF statement. Without this statement, Visual FoxPro defaults to exclusive mode, and your network users will be very upset when only one user can access a table at a time.

Add a SET REPROCESS TO <*n*> statement so that Visual FoxPro does not immediately present a user with an error message every time an attempt is made to access a locked record. The number provided should not be so high that users get tired of waiting to gain access to the locked record or file.

If there are any locations in the program where you prefer not to have the automatic record locking of Visual FoxPro in effect, add a SET LOCK OFF statement at that location in the program. Be sure to use SET LOCK ON to restore the automatic locking capability when necessary.

Summary

This chapter detailed network-related topics, with a view toward how Visual FoxPro programs can be implemented on a network. Effective use of Visual FoxPro's network tools, for file and record locking and for exclusive use of files when needed, along with the use of data sessions, buffering, and good network management techniques, are the keys to making your Visual FoxPro applications work well on a LAN.

Working with the FoxPro API

33

You can extend Visual FoxPro in a system-dependent manner by using the SET LIBRARY TO command to open a Visual FoxPro API library module. You can then call any of the API library functions as you would call any other Visual FoxPro function. You can create an API library module by writing a C or C++ program, and you can use one of the Visual FoxPro API libraries supplied with Visual FoxPro or by a third-party vendor. Visual FoxPro is so powerful that you might not need to extend its functionality. If you do, however, and you are familiar with C or C++ program development, you can benefit from the material presented in this chapter.

In traditional MS-DOS XBase programs, named binary modules that contain code written in C or assembly language can be loaded into memory, released from memory, and called using the LOAD, RELEASE, and CALL commands, respectively. Although Visual FoxPro supports the LOAD and CALL commands, more powerful techniques are available to extend Visual FoxPro using Visual FoxPro Fox Link Libraries (FLL). If you are a C++ programmer, you will be given sufficient knowledge in this chapter to create your own Visual FoxPro FLL files. But first, look at the traditional LOAD and CALL named modules.

Named modules can be loaded into memory, released from memory, and called using a parameter. A parameter is passed by reference or by value; binary modules return a value by changing a passed parameter or returning a value. A binary module, in MS-DOS parlance, is a COM file with an ORG set at 0 instead of 100H. This means that the file is a binary image rather than an EXE file. COM files are limited to a total of 65,500 bytes. Visual FoxPro executes the module by reading the entire file into memory and jumping to the first byte. The code must not allocate or use memory that is not part of the binary image and must preserve the CS and SS registers.

The LOAD command transfers binary routines from disk into memory. You can load into memory 16 binary files (up to 64KB each) at one time. The syntax for the LOAD command is as follows:

```
LOAD FileName [SAVE] ¦ [NOSAVE]
```

The filename, exclusive of extension, becomes the module name. If you don't provide an extension, Visual FoxPro defaults to .BIN. When you call a binary routine, you must omit the extension. For example, if you load a file called MYBIN.BIN, you specify MYBIN when you call the module. If the loaded file (*FileName*) has the same filename and a different extension than one previously loaded, the new file overwrites the previously loaded file.

You can specify the SAVE keyword with both the LOAD and CALL commands to instruct Visual FoxPro to copy the current contents of video RAM into FoxPro's desktop when it returns from the binary routine (assuming that the binary routine is writing directly into video RAM). In other words, FoxPro is aware of anything written by the binary routine, and FoxPro treats the screen contents as though FoxPro had written it. In particular, if SAVE is in effect, such externally written data is not erased the first time any FoxPro object is dragged over it. Unless your binary routine writes directly into video RAM, you should not use SAVE because each time FoxPro returns from the binary routine, it must take the time to scan and save the screen contents.

The DISPLAY STATUS command includes a list of all active named modules. Up to 16 modules can be loaded at one time. The RELEASE MODULE *ModuleName list* command releases the space allocated for the named modules in memory. The syntax of the CALL command is

```
CALL ModuleName [WITH cExpression ¦ MemoryVariable ] [SAVE] ¦ [NOSAVE]
```

The CALL command calls the specified module, which must be loaded already. When the binary module starts, the DS and BX register pair points to the first byte of the parameter passed. The parameter is specified with the WITH clause. If no parameter is passed, BX contains 0. Parameters are passed as null-terminated character strings with a length that must not be changed by binary modules.

The path away from the traditional LOAD and CALL commands began in FoxPro 2.0 with the introduction of the FoxPro Application Programming Interface (API). In Visual FoxPro 3.0, if you have a FoxPro Library Construction Kit (LCK), you can write a group of functions in C, C++, or assembly language routines and link (combine) them into a Visual FoxPro *API library file*, which has the extension .FLL. By using libraries supplied with the FoxPro LCK, your API library can access internal FoxPro functions and parameters. The FoxPro API library file and Library Construction Kit come with the Visual FoxPro Professional Edition.

You don't have to create your own API libraries to obtain extended functionality. Numerous Visual FoxPro API libraries supporting a variety of tasks are provided by third-party developers. Visual FoxPro is shipped with several API libraries.

Making Visual FoxPro Aware of Your API Routines

Before you can use a function in a Visual FoxPro API library, you must first inform Visual FoxPro of the existence of the API library by registering the library. You can register the library with the SET LIBRARY TO command. This command opens the Visual FoxPro API library. An API library is also called a *Fox Link Library* or an *FLL file*. Once you have registered an FLL file, you can access its functions from within Visual FoxPro. You access .FLL library functions in the same way that you access FoxPro system functions.

If you have the Visual FoxPro Professional Edition, which contains the Visual FoxPro LCK, and you have either the Microsoft Visual C++ 2.*x* or Borland 4.5 compiler, you can create your own Visual FoxPro API libraries.

After you have created an FLL file, you use the SET LIBRARY TO command to open one or more FLL libraries, and the DISPLAY STATUS and DISPLAY LIST commands to list FLL library functions. These functions are accessed the same way that FoxPro functions are accessed. The syntax of the SET LIBRARY TO command is

```
SET LIBRARY TO [FileName [ADDITIVE]]
```

The filename expression *FileName* is the name of the FoxPro API library file. The FLL extension is assumed if you fail to provide an extension. Any previously active API library functions are released unless you specify the ADDITIVE keyword. Visual FoxPro adds the new API library functions to the list of API library functions if you specify the ADDITIVE keyword. You can close all API libraries with the SET LIBRARY TO command without any other elements.

If you want to remove an individual library from memory, use the RELEASE LIBRARY *FileName* command, where *FileName* is the name of the API library to remove.

If you are familiar with the FoxPro 2.*x* LCK and have already created FoxPro 2.*x* FLL files, don't worry about rewriting your API libraries because all FoxPro 2.*x* routines that are available with the FoxPro 2.*x* API also are available for Visual FoxPro. You must, however, compile your libraries using Microsoft Visual C++ 2.0 (or 2.1), Borland 4.*x* C++, or a compiler that supports 32-bit DLL programs. Compile the DLL and rename the extension from DLL to FLL.

You cannot run on another platform FoxPro API libraries created for a specific platform. For example, you cannot use FoxPro API libraries developed for FoxPro 2.6 for Windows or FoxPro 2.6 for MS-DOS with Visual FoxPro 3.0.

The Structure of API Routines

To create your library, you need to write a C or C++ program. The form of the function has the same basic structure regardless of what the function does. As a result, there is a standard form or *template* for building Visual FoxPro library functions. Listing 33.1 presents a sample C/C++ language template to create a Visual FoxPro library.

Listing 33.1. A sample C and C++ language template for creating a Visual FoxPro library.

```
#include <pro_ext.h >
//  (Any other #include files)

void Internal_Name( ParamBlk *param )
{
//      Insert your function code here
}
FoxInfo myFoxInfo[] = {
    ("FUNC_NAME" , (FPFI) Internal_Name, 0, ""),
};
#if defined(__cplusplus)
        extern "C" {
#endif
    FoxTable _FoxTable = {
        (FoxTable *) 0, sizeof(myFoxInfo)/sizeof(FoxInfo), myFoxInfo
    };
#if defined(__cplusplus)
}
#endif
```

You must include the PRO_EXT.H header file for all Visual FoxPro API libraries. This file has all of the typedefs, structs, and function declarations that are used in the Visual FoxPro API.

Visual FoxPro determines the function name, the number of parameters, and the type of each parameter from the `FoxInfo` structure. The `FoxTable` pointer is a linked list that Visual FoxPro uses to keep track of the `FoxInfo` structures.

Visual FoxPro communicates with a library function through the `FoxInfo` structure. You define an array of `FoxInfo` structures with each element defining a function. For example, if you have three functions, the `FoxInfo` structure might look like the following:

```
FoxInfo myInfo[] = {
    {"FuncOne", (FPPI) myfunc1, 2, "IC" },
    {"FuncTwo", (FPPI) myfunc2, 4, "CDN.C" },
    {"FuncThree", (FPPI) myfunc3, 3, "CCC" }
};
```

`FuncOne`, `FuncTwo`, and `FuncThree` are the names that are used to reference the functions from Visual FoxPro. These names can be up to 10 characters long. `myfunc1`, `myfunc2`, and `myfunc3` are the internal names of the three functions and are case sensitive. The numbers 2, 4, and 3 are the number of parameters. The types of each parameter are `"IC"`, `"CDN.C"`, and `"CCC"`. Each character represents the data type shown in Table 33.1 for one of the parameters.

Table 33.1. Visual FoxPro API parameter data types.

Value	Description
" "	No parameters
"?"	Any data type
"C"	Character type
"D"	Numeric type
"I"	Integer
"L"	Logical type
"N"	Numeric type
"R"	Reference
"T"	DateTime type
"Y"	Currency type

Precede a character with a period to indicate that the parameter is optional.

Visual FoxPro API functions are available to use with a Fox Link Library. The API functions provide access to all levels of Visual FoxPro internal functionality. The following are examples of categories of API functions that are supported by the Visual FoxPro API Library:

Debugging	Memo field I/O	Editing
Dialogs	String operations	Statements
Expressions	Memory management	Input/Output
Error handling	Arrays	Table I/O
File I/O	Menu	Window operations

When you purchase the Visual FoxPro Professional Edition, the Help system contains help for each Visual FoxPro API function complete with an example of its use. Listing 33.2 contains the help for the Visual FoxPro API _Evaluate() function.

Listing 33.2. Example provided with Visual FoxPro help for the Visual FoxPro API _Evaluate() function.

```
The following example has the same functionality as
the Visual FoxPro EVALUATE( ) function.

Visual FoxPro Code

SET LIBRARY TO EVALUATE
? XEVAL("2 + 3")
? XEVAL("'a' + 'b'")
? XEVAL("SIN(PI()/2))")


C+ Code

#include <pro_ext.h>

FAR EvaluateEx(ParamBlk FAR *parm)
{
   char FAR *expr;
   Value result;

//  Null terminate character string
if (!_SetHandSize(parm->p[0].val.ev_handle,
      parm->p[0].val.ev_length + 1))
      {
      _Error(182); // "Insufficient memory"
      _HLock(parm->p[0].val.ev_handle);
       expr = (char FAR *) _HandToPtr(parm->p[0].val.ev_handle);
       expr[parm->p[0].val.ev_length] = '\0';
       Evaluate(&result, expr);
      _RetVal(&result);
      _HUnLock(parm->p[0].val.ev_handle);
      }
    FoxInfo myFoxInfo[] = {
        {"XEVAL", (FPFI) EvaluateEx, 1, "C"},
};
FoxTable _FoxTable = {
      (FoxTable FAR *) 0, sizeof(myFoxInfo)/sizeof(FoxInfo), myFoxInfo
};
```

After you have coded your C or C++ library functions, use Microsoft Visual C++ Version 2.0 (or 2.1) to compile and link your library as a DLL because Visual FoxPro libraries are 32-bit DLL programs. Versions of Visual FoxPro prior to Version 2.0 do not support 32-bit DLLs. Then rename the library so that it has an FLL extension. If you do not rename it, you have to include the extension when you use the SET LIBRARY TO command.

Parameter Passing

When you call a function in an FLL library, you pass arguments the same way that you pass arguments to any other Visual FoxPro function. You can pass arguments by value or by reference depending on the SET UDFPARAMS TO command setting. If SET UDFPARAMS TO is set to VALUE, the variable you pass to the function can be changed in the function, but the original value of the variable remains unchanged. If SET UDFPARAMS TO is set to REFERENCE, a variable passed to the function can be changed in the function. You can force an individual parameter to be passed by reference by prefacing the parameter with an @ symbol. The following are some examples:

```
SET UDFPARAMS TO VALUE       && Default
? SPHERE(a, b, @c)           && a,b are passed by value
                             && c is passed by reference
SET UDFOARAMS TO REFERENCE
? CUBE(d, e, f)              && d, e, and f are passed by reference.
```

Returning the Results

The Visual FoxPro 3.0 API library contains functions for returning values from your FLL library function to your Visual FoxPro program. Functions are provided for various Visual FoxPro data types. These functions are described in Table 33.2.

Table 33.2. Visual FoxPro API functions for returning values to Visual FoxPro.

Function	Data Type Value Returned
_RetChar(char FAR *string)	Character
_RetCurrency(CCY money, int width)	Currency
_RetDateStr(char FAR *string)	Date
_RetDateTimeStr(char FAR *string)	DateTime
_RetFloat(double flt, int width, int dec)	Float
_RetInt(long ival, int width)	Integer
_RetLogical(int flag)	Logical
_RetVal(Value FAR *value)	Any data type except Memo

The *width* parameter for the _RetFloat() and _RetInt() functions designates the number of columns that Visual FoxPro uses to display the number. You should use 20 for _RetFloat() and 10 for _RetInt() if you are not sure which value to assign the *width* parameter.

Those of you who are familiar with C and C++ may wonder what CCY is. This is a special Visual FoxPro API data type that is defined in the PRO_EXT.H header file. The various data types are described in Table 33.3.

Table 33.3. Visual FoxPro API data types defined in the PRO_EXT.H header file.

C/C++ Data Type	*Description*
EDLINE	Line number of text in the text file in an active editing window. The first line is number 1.
EDPOS	Offset position of a character in an open file in an editing window.
FCHAN	File channel used to reference the file opened using the _Fcreate() or _Fopen() API functions.
FPFI	Far pointer to a function that returns an integer.
ITEMID	Identifier used to reference a Visual FoxPro menu item.
MENUID	Identifier used to reference a Visual FoxPro menu.
MHANDLE	Identifier used to reference a memory block that was allocated by Visual FoxPro or by a call to the _AllocHand() API function. This identifier can be converted to a pointer to the memory block by calling the _HandToPtr() API function.
NTI	Index to the name table. The name table contains the names of memory variables and active table fields.
WHANDLE	Window handle that is assigned to a Visual FoxPro window or by a call to the _Wopen() API function. You use this handle to reference a window when you call a window API function.

Listing 33.3 shows an example FLL program that uses the _RetChar() function to return a string to Visual FoxPro.

Listing 33.3. Example of an FLL program that returns a character string to Visual FoxPro.

```
#include <pro_ext.h>
void FAR chars(ParamBlk FAR *parm)
{
    char message[] = "String to be returned to calling program";
    _RetChar(message);
}
```

```
FoxInfo myFoxInfo[] = {
    {"CHARS", (FPFI) chars, 0, ""}
};
FoxTable _FoxTable = {
    (FoxTable FAR *) 0, sizeof(myFoxInfo)/sizeof(FoxInfo), myFoxInfo
};
```

Steps for Creating an FLL Library Using Visual C++ 2.0

In this section, you will see how to use Visual FoxPro to create an FLL file. Listing 33.4 shows a sample program that is shipped with the Visual FoxPro Professional Edition. This program uses the _Execute() API function to execute the WAIT command when an API library is loaded (SET LIBRARY TO sampfll), when you call the TST() function from Visual FoxPro, and when you release the SAMPFLL.FLL API library from memory.

Listing 33.4. Sample program for creating a Visual FoxPro FLL file.

```
#include "pro_ext.h"
// Program: SAMPFLL.C will be compiled and linked into
//          the SAMPFLL.DLL API library. It is renamed
//          to SAMPFLL.FLL.
void Tst(ParamBlk FAR *parm) {
  _Execute("wait window 'executes'");
}

void Load(void) {
  _Execute("wait window 'load'");
}

void Unload(void) {
  _Execute("wait window 'unload'");
}

FoxInfo myFoxInfo[] ={
    {"TST"   , (FPFI) Tst, 0, ""},
    {"LOAD"  , (FPFI) Load  , CALLONLOAD, ""},
    {"UNLOAD", (FPFI) Unload, CALLONUNLOAD, ""}
};

FoxTable _FoxTable ={
    (FoxTable FAR *) 0, sizeof(myFoxInfo)/sizeof(FoxInfo), myFoxInfo
};
```

Notice the CALLONLOAD and CALLONUNLOAD keywords in the FoxInfo structure shown in Listing 33.4. These keywords indicate that the corresponding functions execute when the API library is loaded and unloaded, respectively.

Visual C++ 2.*x* is an integrated development environment. You can create the source programs for an application or DLL in the Visual C++ editor, compile it, link it, and debug it from within Visual C++. Visual C++ 2.*x* maintains the program components in a project. The following procedure explains how to compile and link a Visual FoxPro API library.

1. Execute Visual C++ 2.*x*.
2. Create a project by choosing File | New. Then choose Project. The New Project dialog box appears, as shown in Figure 33.1.

FIGURE 33.1.

The New Project dialog box.

3. Establish the project settings shown in Figure 33.1 as follows:
   a. Set the Project Name to SAMPFLL.
   b. Choose the Dynamic-Link Library option from the Project Type drop-down list.
   c. Choose a root drive and directory. The SAMPFLL subdirectory will be created.
   d. Click the Create button.
4. Now choose the Settings option from the Project menu, and the Project Settings dialog box appears.
5. Click the C/C++ tab in the Project Settings dialog box. The C/C++ tab appears as shown in Figure 33.2. Choose the following settings:
   a. In the Category drop-down list, choose the Code Generation option.
   b. In the Calling Convention drop-down list, choose the _fastcall option.

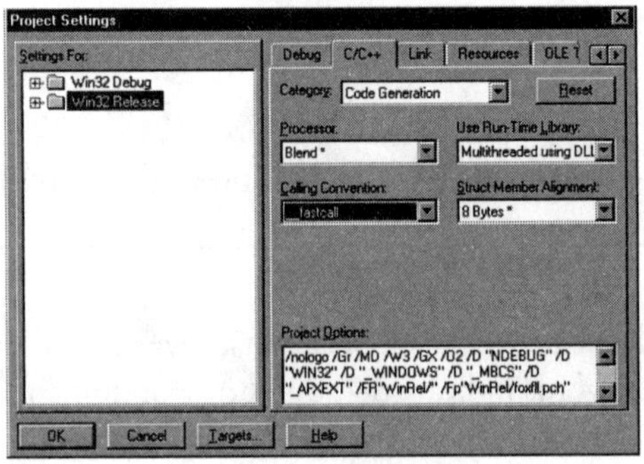

FIGURE 33.2.

The Project Settings dialog box with the C/C++ tab selected.

6. Click the Project Settings Link tab.

7. Add the winapims.lib library to the Object/Library Modules text box and choose OK.

8. Choose Options from the Tools menu, and the Options dialog box appears.

9. Click the Directories tab in the Options dialog box, as shown in Figure 33.3.

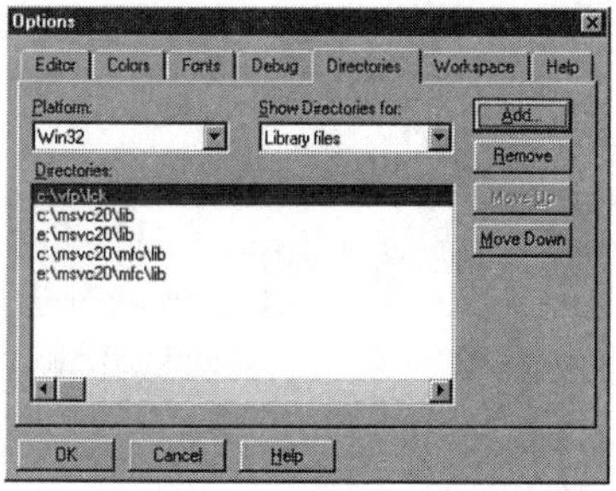

FIGURE 33.3.

The Options dialog box with the Directories tab selected.

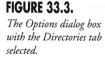

10. In the Show Directories for drop-down list, choose the Library files item, as shown in Figure 33.3.

11. Click the Add button and add the directory that contains the WINAPIMS.LIB library (C:\VFP\LCK).

12. In the Show Directories for drop-down list, choose the Include Files item.

13. Click the Add button and add the directory that contains the PRO_EXT.H include file (C:\VFP\LCK).

14. Choose the Options dialog box OK button.

15. Choose the New option from the File menu, and then choose the Code/Text option. An edit box appears. Enter the C code and save the source file as SAMPFLL.CPP, as shown in Figure 33.4.

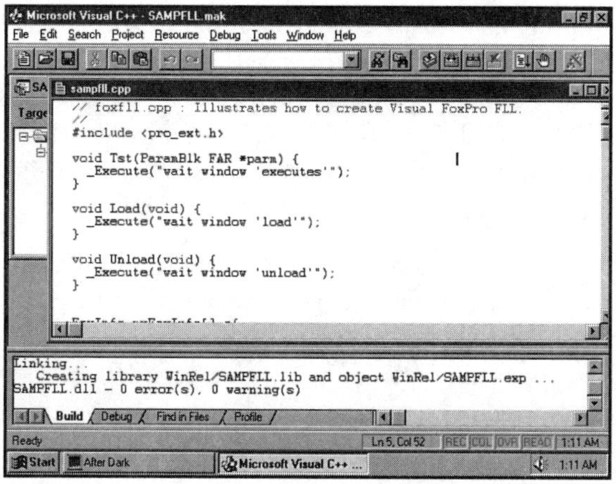

FIGURE 33.4.

The Visual C++ 2.0 screen with the SAMPFLL.CPP source code window displayed.

```
// foxfll.cpp : Illustrates how to create Visual FoxPro FLL.
//
#include <pro_ext.h>

void Tst(ParamBlk FAR *parm) {
    _Execute("wait window 'executes'");
}

void Load(void) {
    _Execute("wait window 'load'");
}

void Unload(void) {
    _Execute("wait window 'unload'");
}
```

```
Linking...
    Creating library WinRel/SAMPFLL.lib and object WinRel/SAMPFLL.exp ...
SAMPFLL.dll - 0 error(s), 0 warning(s)
```

16. Choose Project | Files, and the Project Files dialog box appears. Add the SAMPFLL.CPP file to the project.

17. Choose Project | Build SAMPFLL.DLL, and the DLL will compile and link. That is all there is to it.

After you have finished compiling and linking the SAMPFLL.DLL library, rename it SAMPFLL.FLL. Then execute Visual FoxPro and use the following command to register the library with Visual FoxPro:

```
SET LIBRARY TO \SAMPFLL\SAMPFLL ADDITIVE
```

If you have done everything correctly, a WAIT box appears displaying Init. Next, execute the TST() function, and another WAIT window appears, containing the text Executes. When you release the library (RELEASE LIBRARY SAMPFLL), another WAIT window appears.

The Borland C++ 4.5 compiler also contains an excellent development environment that operates like Microsoft Visual C++.

Extending Visual FoxPro with DLLs

You can use a Fox Link Library to gain access to Windows API functions and other external resources by calling a function in a Dynamic Link Library. For example, the FoxTools.FLL library that ships with Visual FoxPro contains functions to access DLLs. This section explains DLLs and describes how to use the Visual FoxPro DECLARE command that enables you to directly access functions in a DLL from a Visual FoxPro program.

Dynamic Link Libraries (DLLs) are libraries of executable modules that are linked at runtime. When an application calls a DLL, Windows loads it. DLLs can also be shared by several Windows applications. As long as a DLL is needed, it remains in memory. A Visual FoxPro compatible version of a DLL has an .FLL extension. If you use an FLL function from the Windows API, such as GetWindowsDirectory() or MessageBox, the function is not loaded into memory until your program actually calls it. While an FLL or DLL library is loaded, your application, or any other active application that needs it, can use it. Because multiple applications can use a single instance of an FLL function in memory, you use less of your valuable memory resources when an FLL or DLL function is used. The entire Windows system is composed of DLLs; all the device drivers are DLLs. The Windows 95 systems files—GDI32.DLL, USER32.DLL, KERNEL32.EXE, and ADVAPI32.DLL—are DLLs.

The Windows system is composed of application modules and DLL modules. Application modules are the executable (EXE) files for an application. A DLL module normally has a .DLL file extension, as well, but it can have an extension such as .DRV, .EXE, or .FON. An executable (EXE) application actively performs a task. When it executes, it actively processes messages, creates windows, interacts with the user, and generates output.

In contrast, a DLL library function is passive and serves only as a function that can be called on by an active application to perform some operation. With very few exceptions, DLL modules are as passive as any other library function.

When an application is loaded, it is given its own stack in local memory. A DLL module doesn't have its own stack. It uses the stack of the task that called it.

Both an application and a DLL module type can import a DLL function if either needs to use that function. To *import a function* means to create a dynamic link to that function. You can dynamically import a DLL module during the execution of a Visual FoxPro application by using the SET LIBRARY TO command. However, in FoxPro, the filename extension for DLL files is .FLL, for Fox Link Library. In addition, FLL files call Visual FoxPro API functions and can be used only by Visual FoxPro.

An application can import a DLL module while the application is executing. This is called a *dynamic import*. When a DLL is successfully imported, the application can call a function in the DLL module.

When an application calls a DLL function, Windows is responsible for finding the function and loading it in memory. It searches the same directories that it searches when it loads your application. The directory search order is the following:

1. Current directory
2. Windows directory (containing WIN.COM)
3. Windows systems directory (containing KERNEL32.EXE)
4. Directories specified in the MS-DOS path environmental variable
5. Network directories

Dynamic link libraries are the foundation of the Windows system. DLLs enable programs to share functions that are loaded at runtime. The DECLARE command can be used to register a function residing in an external 32-bit DLL. In fact, you must execute the DECLARE command before you can call any 32-bit DLL functions. One type of DLL library is the Windows API 32-bit DLL library. You can find more information about the Windows API 32-bit DLL functions by referring to the documentation included with the Microsoft Win32 Programmer's Guide.

You can release all registered 32-bit DLLs from memory with the CLEAR DLLS or CLEAR ALL commands. The DISPLAY STATUS and LIST STATUS commands list all of the DLL functions in memory.

If you want to call a 16-bit DLL function, you can use the FOXTOOLS.FLL library, which is discussed in the next section. Microsoft still supports FOXTOOLS.FLL in Visual FoxPro to provide backward compatibility support for old 16-bit DLL libraries. However, Microsoft encourages you to use the DECLARE command for calling Windows 32-bit DLL functions. This is probably because it wants to get out of the business of supporting two methods of providing the same functionality.

The syntax for the DECLARE command for registering a 32-bit DLL library function is

```
DECLARE [cFunctionType] FunctionName IN LibraryName [AS AliasName]
        [cParamType1 [@] ParamName1, cParamType2 [@] ParamName2, ...]
```

You specify the cFunctionType parameter only when the 32-bit Windows DLL has a return value. The cFunctionType element defines the data type of the return value. It can have any of the following values:

cFunctionType	Description
INTEGER	32-bit integer
SINGLE	32-bit floating point
DOUBLE	64-bit floating point
STRING	Character string

The FunctionName parameter designates the name of the 32-bit Windows DLL function that the DECLARE command registers. This name is different from FoxPro names because it is case-sensitive. For example, you must specify the Windows DLL GetActiveWindow() function as GetActiveWindow and not as GETACTIVEWINDOW. However, when you use the function in Visual FoxPro, you no longer need to honor case-sensitivity; you treat it as you would any other Visual FoxPro name identifier. For example, to register the Windows DLL GetActiveWindow() function and call it, you use the following commands:

```
DECLARE INTEGER GetActiveWindow IN win32api
nActiveWindow = GETACTIVEWINDOW()
? nActiveWindow
```

If a 32-bit Windows DLL function has the same name as a Visual FoxPro function, you use FunctionName to specify its actual name and the AS AliasName clause to specify an alias name. For example, Visual FoxPro has a function called MESSAGEBOX(), and so does the Windows API. You can specify the following statement and refer to the Windows API function as MBox() when you call it:

```
#INCLUDE "FOXPRO.H"
DECLARE INTEGER  MessageBox IN USER32 AS mbox ;
        INTEGER, STRING, STRING, INTEGER
IsFinished = MBox(0,"Are you finished?","Question", MB_YESNO + MB_ICONQUESTION )
```

Microsoft Windows 95 provides support for international character sets. Some of the 32-bit Windows DLL functions might have a letter (W for UNICODE or A for ASCII) appended to the end of their names. For example, the MessageBox function should be named MessageBoxA (for single-byte ASCII character sets) and MessageBoxW (for UNICODE character sets). However, the DECLARE command automatically adds the letter to the end of the function name when required.

You must specify the IN LibraryName clause, which identifies the name of the external Windows DLL that contains the Windows 32-bit DLL function that you specify with the FunctionName parameter. All of the Windows API 32-bit DLL functions are stored in one of the four DLL files: kernel32.dll, gdi32.dll, user32.dll, or advapi.dll.

If you purchased the Visual FoxPro Professional Edition, you received a Windows 32-bit API help file containing help for Windows 32-bit API functions. The Help window for Windows API functions contains a Quick Info button that contains, among other things, the name of the DLL that contains the function. Also, you can specify IN Win32API, and Visual FoxPro searches through all four libraries for the 32-bit API function specified with FunctionName. Here is an example of how to use the DECLARE command, which is used to call the Windows API MessageBeep() function:

```
DECLARE MessageBeep IN win32api INTEGER
=MessageBeep(1)  && Sound the Bell
```

You also must specify a parameter list (*cParameterType1* [@] *ParamName1*, *cParameterType2* [@] *ParamName2*, ...), which represents the arguments that the 32-bit DLL function expects. You supply a data type for each parameter, which supports the same keywords as the cFunctionType element (INTEGER, SINGLE, DOUBLE, and STRING).

You must include the @ character after the parameter type (cParameterType) to pass a parameter by reference. If you omit the @ after cParameterType in the DECLARE command, in the calling function, or in both, the parameter is passed by value.

You can specify the optional ParamName elements to suggest the purpose of the parameter or improve readability of the DECLARE statement. However, they are not used by Visual FoxPro or the Windows 32-bit DLL function. ParamName elements are simply and strictly ignored. In the following example, the names of the ParamName elements do make it easier to remember what arguments you need to specify when you call the function:

```
DECLARE INTEGER  MessageBox IN USER32 AS mb ;
        INTEGER  nWindowHandle, ;
        STRING   cMessageText, ;
        STRING   cTitleBarText, ;
        INTEGER  nDialogBoxType
= MB( 0, "This is the text for the message box", "This is the title bar text",
     16 );
```

Also, you can use the DECLARE command to register functions in 32-bit DLL libraries that you purchase from any third-party developer. You can also develop your own 32-bit DLL libraries using Microsoft Visual C++ Version 2.*x*, Borland C++ Version 4.5, or any other compiler that creates 32-bit DLL libraries.

Summary

This chapter showed you how to provide extended functionality to Visual FoxPro. You learned how to use the LOAD and CALL binary modules. In addition, you were shown how to use the SET LIBRARY TO command to open FoxPro API library modules and how to compile and link a Visual FoxPro API library using the Microsoft Visual C++ 2.*x* development environment. Finally, you were told all about DLLs and how to use the DECLARE command to register a DLL library so that you can call DLL functions.

Programming
OLE Links

IN THIS CHAPTER

The concept of building business solutions from the interaction between applications such as word processors, spreadsheets, database managers, and others is called *componentization*. Componentization enables the developer to leverage the power of sophisticated applications to meet the various functional requirements of a particular business problem without needing to write all of the code.

When you think about it, what is better at formatting a printed page than a full-featured word processor, or better at crunching numbers than a powerful spreadsheet application? Why would you want to calculate multiple what-if situations in Visual FoxPro when Excel is so good at it?

What you need is some way to get Visual FoxPro to talk to these other applications in a flexible manner. The Windows environment provides two different methods of accomplishing this goal: DDE and OLE. DDE is covered in Chapter 18, "Programming with DDE," and this chapter discusses OLE automation—or OLE programming, if you prefer.

SAMPLE FORMS ON THE CD-ROM

The various files are provided on the CD-ROM as adjuncts to this chapter to illustrate OLE techniques used in Visual FoxPro.

If you have performed the data setup, the uses files are located in the directory VFU\Chap34\.

File	Purpose
ExcelOLE.SCX	Form used to demonstrate in-place editing and OLE automation with Excel.
Outline.SCX	Form used to demonstrate the use of an OLE Control (OCX).
WordOLE1.SCX	Form used to demonstrate in-place editing and OLE automation with Word.

What Is OLE?

OLE stands for *object linking and embedding*, although the functionality of OLE has gone beyond simply embedding or linking documents between applications. Other chapters in this book (for example, Chapter 19, "Working with OLE for Non-OLE Applications," and Chapter 32, "Multiuser Programming and Techniques") discuss the linking and embedding aspects of OLE. This chapter focuses on the functionality known as OLE automation.

OLE automation gives you the capability to take control of another application and cause that application to perform tasks. The application that you want to automate must be capable of participating in OLE Version 2.0; OLE Version 1.0 did not have automation capabilities.

As discussed in earlier chapters, Visual FoxPro forms have the capability to contain OLE container controls. These controls can contain an OLE object. You can use OLE automation with these OLE containers, or you can work with OLE automation to the server applications directly without using a container control. This chapter shows you how to do OLE automation both ways.

OLE Versus DDE

DDE was mentioned earlier as another method to get two applications talking to each other. What, exactly, is the difference between DDE and OLE automation? Chapter 18 gives a definition of DDE. An analogy for DDE versus OLE might be the Pony Express versus satellite communications. Essentially, DDE is the technology of yesterday and OLE is the technology of tomorrow.

The fundamental difference is one of orientation. DDE is oriented around the applications themselves, whereas OLE is oriented around the object. (The term *document* is used interchangeably with the term *object*; document in this sense is not referring to a word processor document, but rather to what an application produces. A spreadsheet program produces a spreadsheet as its document, a drawing program produces a BMP file as its document, and so on.) With DDE, you make a communications link to Excel and go from there, sending commands or messages to Excel. In contrast, with OLE you make the connection to an Excel spreadsheet (the object) and then communicate with that object. The chapters in Part V, "Object-Oriented Programming," should be very helpful in furthering your understanding of the nature of this difference.

OLE Servers Versus OLE Clients

OLE interaction between two applications is accomplished by a client talking to a server. Various applications are OLE compliant; these applications are capable of being a client or a server, or in some cases both client and server. Visual FoxPro is capable of being an OLE client only—it cannot act as an OLE server.

The OLE client is capable of containing, or storing, an OLE object such as a Word document or a Windows Paint picture. The OLE 2.0 clients are also capable of initiating and controlling OLE automation.

Server applications under OLE are capable of having their documents stored by a client. For example, Microsoft Excel can have its spreadsheets or graphs stored in a Visual FoxPro general field or in a Word document. OLE 2.0 server applications can respond to OLE automation requests from the OLE clients.

The two server applications you will be using for the examples in this chapter are Microsoft Word 6.0 and Microsoft Excel 5.0. Both of these applications are OLE 2.0 servers.

OLE Bound Controls

In Visual FoxPro you can store OLE objects in tables in general fields. These general-type fields are reserved for OLE objects. Visual FoxPro uses the OLE bound control to display the contents of a general field in a form, therefore it is "bound" to the general field.

OLE Container Controls

If your goal is to display an OLE object that is not in a general field of a Visual FoxPro table, you can use the *OLE container control.* With this control you can display a Microsoft Word document or a Microsoft Excel spreadsheet or graph as well as any other OLE server's documents.

OLE Custom Controls

OLE Custom Controls (OCXs) are new in OLE Version 2.0. These controls are similar to the well-known VBX controls that Visual Basic has had available for a while. OCXs come in a variety of sizes and flavors and are supplied by many vendors.

The OCX control is a specialized control that has been designed and programmed to perform a specific function. Examples of OLE controls are Microsoft's outline control or the graphics server control from Pinnacle Publishing. Many other vendors supply numerous other OLE controls, and the market for these controls is expected to blossom to a large and varied supply of different products.

OLE Automation

OLE 1.0 provided the capability to store a document, or object, from an OLE server in the document, or file, of an OLE client. With FoxPro 2.*x*, you could store a Microsoft Word document file in a FoxPro 2.*x* DBF table's general field. OLE 1.0 provided the capability to display this general field in an edit window using the MODIFY GENERAL command. If the user double-clicked on this window, the OLE server was launched, with the object loaded for editing. Any changes made were stored in the general field, assuming that the changes were made to an embedded object. (See Chapter 19 for the definition of embedded versus linked.) In FoxPro 2.*x*, you had no control over what was happening while the server was in control. You could, of course, establish a DDE session with the server and send commands to it that way, but OLE 1.0 gave no method of using OLE to send commands to the server.

OLE Version 2.0 introduced the capability to send commands to the server through the process called OLE automation. FoxPro 2.*x* was, and is, an OLE 1.0 client, and therefore is not capable of using OLE automation. Visual FoxPro is an OLE 2.0 client; all of the capabilities of OLE automation are available from Visual FoxPro.

To use OLE automation there are a few things you need to do:

1. Create a variable in Visual FoxPro that contains a reference to an OLE object.

2. Use the methods of that OLE object to accomplish the actions you desire.

When sending a message to an object, you do the following:

1. Refer to the object using the name of the variable that holds the reference.

2. Use a period (.) to separate the parts of the command.

3. Follow the variable name with the method name.

4. Send any arguments in parentheses following the method name.

To see OLE automation in action, create a Microsoft Word Basic object from the Visual FoxPro command window. Type the following in the command window:

```
oWord = CreateObj("Word.Basic")
```

This command creates a Microsoft Word Basic OLE object, and you see Microsoft Word start up. Adjust the window for Microsoft Word so it doesn't cover the entire screen, and then move it to the bottom of your screen. Then use Alt+Tab to get to Microsoft Visual FoxPro. When you are in Visual FoxPro, adjust its window so you can see the Word window below Visual FoxPro. (Use Figure 34.1 as a guide to how to position your windows.)

FIGURE 34.1.

Visual FoxPro is in control of Microsoft Word.

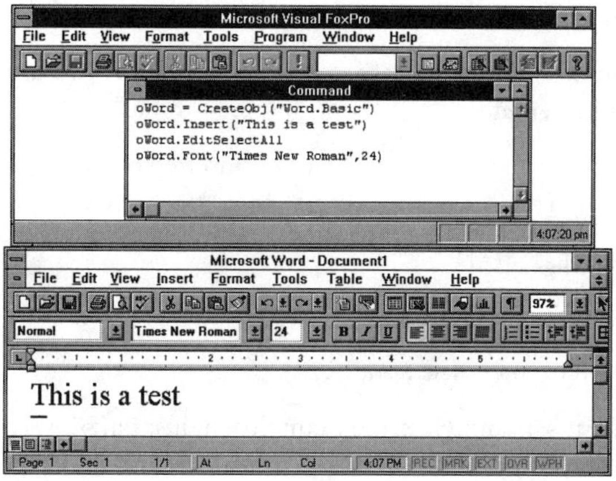

Now you can see both Visual FoxPro and the Word document simultaneously and can continue with the OLE automation. Type the following commands into your Visual FoxPro command window:

```
oWord.FileNewDefault
    oWord.Insert("This is a test.")
    oWord.EditSelectAll
    oWord.Font("Times New Roman",24)
```

Now your screen should look something like that shown in Figure 34.1.

Examine in detail the code you typed. The first command is this:

```
oWord = CreateObj("Word.Basic")
```

This command line calls the Visual FoxPro function `CreateObj()` to create an object and to store the reference to that object in the variable `oWord`. The argument you passed, `"Word.Basic"`, tells Visual FoxPro what type of object you want. `Word.Basic` is the object type for a word OLE object in Microsoft Word. You get a reference in `oWord` to the Word Basic macro language. In order to give the user access to Word Basic, Windows has to launch Microsoft Word, so you see it come up with a blank document.

After you arranged the windows and used Alt+Tab to get back to Visual FoxPro, you typed this in Visual FoxPro's command window:

```
oWord.FileNewDefault
```

This command executes a method of the `oWord` object. The `oWord` object is Word Basic, so the method you executed was a command in Word Basic. The way to find out what commands you can execute is to refer to the Word Basic help file in Microsoft Word. The `FileNewdefault` command created a new file using the default template. After this command you saw a document window in Microsoft Word titled Document1.

You then typed this in the command window:

```
oWord.Insert("This is a test.")
```

This command runs the `Insert` method of the Word Basic object. The argument is the text you want inserted.

Next, you selected the text you had just inserted by calling the `EditSelectAll` method of Word Basic:

```
oWord.EditSelectAll
```

Finally, you set the font for the selected text to Times New Roman 24 point:

```
oWord.Font("Times New Roman",24)
```

Although it's meaningless, the example you just ran shows how you can use the power of OLE automation to get Visual FoxPro to interact with an OLE server application. The following sections show the steps involved.

OOP and OLE

As Part V of this book explains in detail, Visual FoxPro is an object-oriented (OO) development environment. OLE documents are objects in the strictest sense of the word, and you communicate with these OLE objects in the same way you communicate with Visual FoxPro objects: You send the OLE object a message and it performs a task.

Looking at the code from the Word Basic OLE example earlier, it appears very similar to the OO code you would use to communicate with a Visual FoxPro object. In fact, the OLE object and a Visual FoxPro object are the same as far as your working with them is concerned. You communicate with them by accessing their methods, and they perform tasks.

When you create an object from the Microsoft Word Basic class, you have, in essence, created a full-featured word processing object in Visual FoxPro. This object can format text, do mail merges, print documents, and do just about anything else you might want a word processor to do. Creating an OLE object from Microsoft Excel would give you a powerful spreadsheet object that could perform any of the tasks expected from a spreadsheet application.

OLE Automation in Visual FoxPro Forms

Earlier in this chapter you saw how you can use OLE automation to work with Microsoft Word from the Visual FoxPro command window. These same commands could be used in a Visual FoxPro program or in a method for a Visual FoxPro control. However, to get the full impact of the power of OLE automation you would really want to use one of Visual FoxPro's OLE container controls to place the OLE object you are automating right in the same form as the control that is doing the automation.

For example, continuing with the previous use of Microsoft Word as the OLE server, you could put a Visual FoxPro OLE container control in a Visual FoxPro form and then use a command button in the same form to control the Word document. As a source of text for the automation you will use an edit control.

In Visual FoxPro's command window, type this:

```
CREATE FORM WordOle1
```

Then add an edit box control, a command button, and two labels so that your form looks like the one in Figure 34.2.

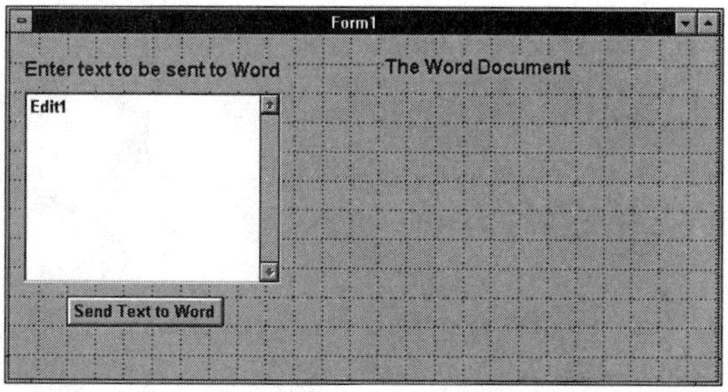

FIGURE 34.2.

A Visual FoxPro form with the edit and command button controls and two labels.

Creating the OLE Object

Next, you are going to put in the OLE container control. In Figure 34.2 the controls toolbar has been docked at the bottom of the screen. To place an OLE container control in the form, select the OLE container from the toolbar. Figure 34.3 shows which control in the toolbar you need.

FIGURE 34.3.

The OLE container tool in the form controls toolbar.

Place the OLE container control on the right side of your form. When you do this you will be greeted by the Insert Object dialog box, as shown in Figure 34.4. In the Insert Object dialog box, highlight Microsoft Word 6.0 Document and then click OK.

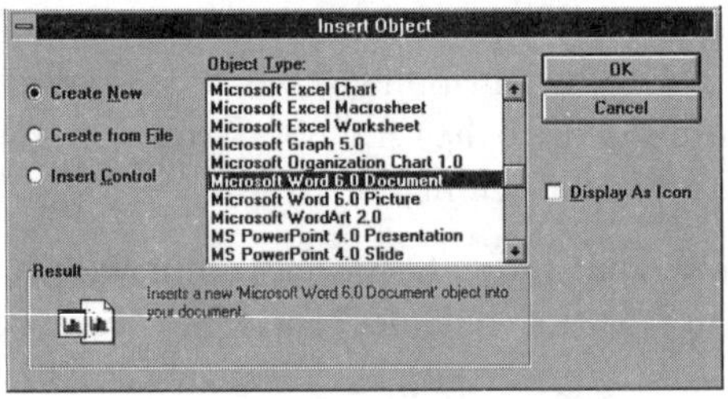

FIGURE 34.4.

Selecting a Microsoft Word 6.0 document in the Insert Object dialog box.

Because you will be automating this OLE container, it is best to change its default name so the code will be more readable. Select the Properties dialog box and use the combo box in the upper left to select `OleControl1`. In the All tab, scroll down to the Name property and change it to `oWDoc`, as shown in Figure 34.5.

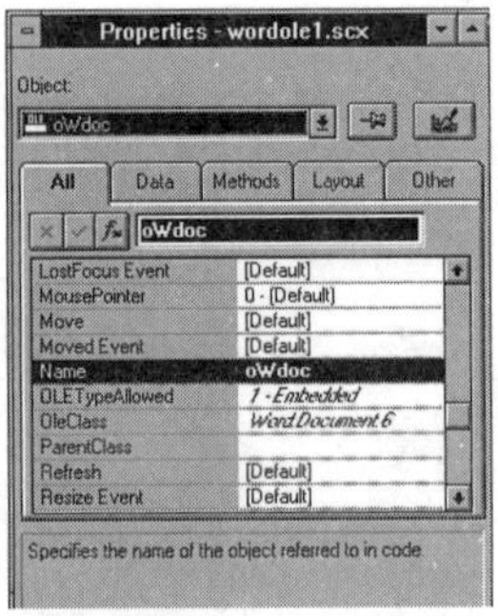

FIGURE 34.5.

The name property for the OLE container is changed to `oWDoc` in the property sheet.

The OLE control you have just added to the form is, in fact, an OLE object. You can control this object the same way you worked with Microsoft Word Basic previously.

Communicating with a Microsoft Word 6.0 OLE Object

Before you begin writing code, let's talk about what the form will do. You have added to the form an Edit box control in which the user types some text. When the user clicks on the command button you want the text to be sent from the edit box control to the Word document in the OLE container and you want to select the text in the document and change its font.

Using the Properties dialog box, change the caption of the command button to say Send Text to Word. Now, right-click on the command button and choose Code from the menu that pops up. You will see the code-editing window, which is shown in Figure 34.6.

FIGURE 34.6.

The Form Designer's code-editing window.

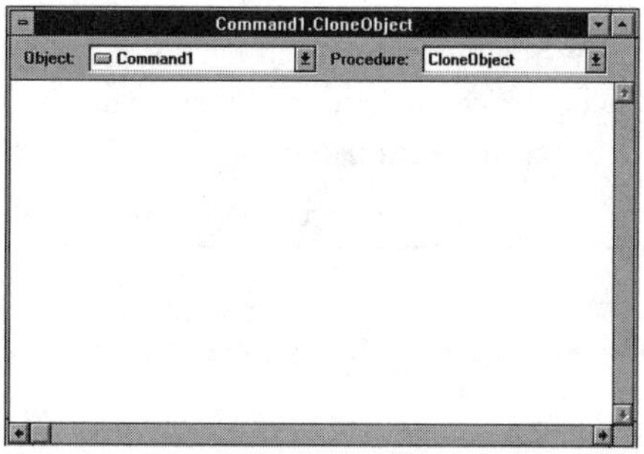

Because you want the code you are going to write to be executed when you click the button, use the combo box in the upper right to select the Click procedure. In the code-editing window type the following code:

```
* Start an edit on the OleContainer
      THISFORM.oWDoc.DoVerb(-1)

      * Get an object reference to the OleContianer
      oWBasic = GETOBJECT("","Word.Basic")

      * Insert the text in the Word Document
      oWBasic.Insert( THISFORM.Edit1.Value )

      * Select the entire text
      oWBasic.EditSelectAll

      * Set the font in Word
      oWBasic.Font("Times New Roman", 24)
```

Let's look at this code one line at a time to understand exactly what is going on.

```
THISFORM.oWDoc.DoVerb(-1)
```

The first thing you do is to initiate an edit in the OLE container. You do this by calling the DoVerb method of the OLE container and passing the argument -1 to start an edit. The DoVerb can take a number of arguments, which are listed in Table 34.1.

Table 34.1. The `DoVerb` arguments, as described in the online help file.

Argument	Meaning
0	Execute the default action for the object.
-1	Activate the object for editing. If the server supports in-place editing, the object is activated inside the OLE container.
-2	Activates the object in a separate application window.
-3	Hides the application that created the object, for embedded objects.
-4	If the server supports in-place editing, activates the object in-place and shows any interface tools. For servers that do not support in-place editing, an error occurs.
-5	When focus moves to the OLE container, creates a window in which the object can be edited. An error occurs if the object doesn't support activation on a single mouse click.
-6	Discards all changes made that the object's server is capable of undoing.

The argument you chose, -1, will activate the Word document for editing.

Next, you need to get a reference to the Microsoft Word Basic server. You use Visual FoxPro's `GetObject()` function to do this, as shown in the following code. This function will activate an OLE automation object and return a reference to it. You use the reference, stored in the `oWBasic` variable, later in the code.

```
oWBasic = GETOBJECT("","Word.Basic")
```

> **NOTE**
>
> The difference between the `GetObject()` and `CreateObj()` functions in this context (OLE automation) is that `GetObject()` will get a reference to an OLE object that already exists, whereas `CreateObj()` will create a new object.

The following three lines of code send text to the Word document, select all of the text in the document, and set the font for the selected text to Times New Roman 24 point, respectively.

```
oWBasic.Insert( THISFORM.Edit1.Value )
oWBasic.EditSelectAll
oWBasic.Font("Times New Roman", 24)
```

Figure 34.7 shows what the form looks like after you have entered text in the edit control and then clicked the Send Text to Word command button.

FIGURE 34.7.

The OLE automation with Microsoft Word form.

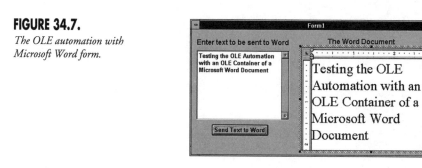

Communicating with a Microsoft Excel 5.0 OLE Object

Let's build a form with a Microsoft Excel 5.0 graph. You will put a number of text boxes in the form to enable the user to enter values to be graphed. Also, you will include an OLE container for the Excel spreadsheet that will draw the graph for you. Just as in the Microsoft Word example, you will use a command button to do the OLE automation.

Figure 34.8 shows how the form looks in the Form Designer.

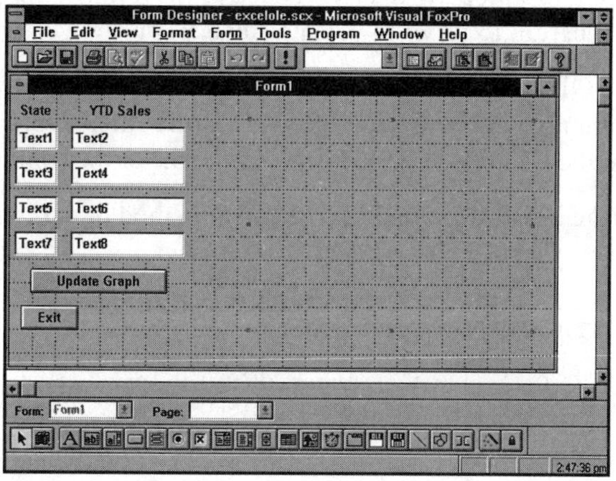

FIGURE 34.8.

The Form Designer with your Excel OLE form in it.

In this form, you will use the form's Init method to initialize the text boxes with default values. Right-click on the form and choose Code from the menu that appears.

Make sure the combo box in the upper right of the code window shows that you are editing the Init method; otherwise, use that combo box to select the Init event. The combo box in the upper left should show that you're working on the code for Form1.

Type the following code in the edit window:

```
WITH THISFORM

    .lOleNew = .F.

    .Text1.Value = "NY"
    .Text2.Value = 1250000

    .Text3.Value = "CA"
    .Text4.Value = 1450500

    .Text5.Value = "NJ"
    .Text6.Value = 950000

    .Text7.Value = "CT"
    .Text8.Value = 1250900

ENDWITH
```

The WITH...ENDWITH construct saves some typing. Because all of the lines between the WITH and ENDWITH are affecting various members of THISFORM, you can save typing THISFORM in front of every line. This code is simply assigning default values to the text boxes on the form. lOleNew is referring to a property that you added to the form. It is used to prevent you from having to create a chart in Excel when you already have one (as you will see later).

Place an OLE container control on the right side of your form just as you did for the Microsoft Word example in the previous section. In the Insert Object dialog box, highlight Excel 5.0 Sheet and click OK. This time, leave the name of the control as the default: OleControl1.

Next, take a look at the code in the Click method of the command button captioned Update Graph:

```
* Copy data to the excel spreadsheet OLE container
      WITH THISFORM.OleControl1

          .Cells(100,1).Value = THISFORM.Text1.Value
          .Cells(100,2).Value = THISFORM.Text2.Value

          .Cells(101,1).Value = THISFORM.Text3.Value
          .Cells(101,2).Value = THISFORM.Text4.Value

          .Cells(102,1).Value = THISFORM.Text5.Value
          .Cells(102,2).Value = THISFORM.Text6.Value

          .Cells(103,1).Value = THISFORM.Text7.Value
          .Cells(103,2).Value = THISFORM.Text8.Value


      ENDWITH

      * Add a Chartobject to the worksheet:
      IF THISFORM.lOleNew
         oChart1 = THISFORM.oleControl1.ChartObjects.Add(0, 0, 200, 150)
         THISFORM.loleNew = .F.
      ENDIF
```

```
* Create the chart.

THISFORM.OleControl1.DoVerb(0)
THISFORM.OleControl1.chartobjects(1).chart.chartwizard(;
   THISFORM.oleControl1.range(THISFORM.oleControl1.cells(100,1),;
     THISFORM.oleControl1.cells(103,2)),;
       -4100,4,1,0,1,1,"Sales by State","States","Dollar Sales","")
```

This code is a little more complex than the Word code you saw before, but you're asking it to do more. Let's look at the code in detail.

The code between the WITH and ENDWITH is inserting the values from the text boxes into certain cells in the Excel spreadsheet. You are using cells at rows 100 and higher to keep the values from showing in the OLE container. You want only the final graph to show up there.

In the following code, you check the value of the form's lOleNew property (you created this property) to see if you need to create a chart in the spreadsheet. If you do, use Excel's ChartObjects.Add() method to add a chart object to the sheet and then set the lOleNew property to False so you won't do this again.

```
IF THISFORM.lOleNew
   oChart1 = THISFORM.oleControl1.ChartObjects.Add(0, 0, 200, 150)
   THISFORM.loleNew = .F.
ENDIF
```

NOTE

You can use the help system in Excel to find the syntax for its methods.

Notice that you refer to the Excel spreadsheet object by using THISFORM.OleControl1. This is the name of the OLE container control and that control is, in fact, the Excel spreadsheet.

Start the edit in the sheet with the DoVerb() method of the OLE container control, as shown in the following code:

```
THISFORM.OleControl1.DoVerb(0)
```

Next, draw the graph by running Excel's Chart Wizard under your control.

```
THISFORM.OleControl1.chartobjects(1).chart.chartwizard(;
   THISFORM.oleControl1.range(THISFORM.oleControl1.cells(100,1),;
     THISFORM.oleControl1.cells(103,2)),;
       -4100,4,1,0,1,1,"Sales by State","States","Dollar Sales","")
```

Wow! That is one long line of code! It is the actual workhorse for the form. It creates the graph using Excel's Chart Wizard.

> **TIP**
>
> It is often difficult to find the documentation for some operations of an OLE server. One shortcut to getting your job done is to use the macro-recording feature of the server to create a macro that does what you want. Then edit the macro and cut and paste into your Visual FoxPro code.

Figure 34.9 shows how the form looks after the Update graph button has been clicked.

FIGURE 34.9.

The Excel OLE form with the graph drawn.

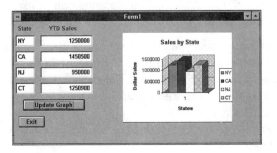

Using OLE Custom Controls in Visual FoxPro Forms

OLE custom controls provide a potential powerhouse of functionality for Visual FoxPro applications. These controls can perform a number of tasks, such as creating a neat-looking expanding list box, controlling remote communication through a modem, establishing and managing a link to remote data sources, producing graphical representations of the data, and on and on.

These OLE custom controls are self-contained OLE servers of a sort. The OCX has been programmed by someone using C++ to perform a certain function or group of functions. An OCX has methods and properties associated with it that are your access to its functionality. The documentation for these methods and properties is provided by the vendor producing the OCX.

You can use these OLE controls in Visual FoxPro the same way you use the OLE container controls. To see the OLE controls that you have available on your machine, choose Options from the Tools menu and then click on the Controls tab. The dialog box you'll see looks like the one in Figure 34.10.

The OLE custom controls shown in the list in Figure 34.10 are those displayed on my computer; your computer might show different OLE controls. Some of the controls shown are available only if you are running either Windows 95 or Windows NT because they are 32-bit controls that don't work under the 16-bit Windows environment.

FIGURE 34.10.

The Visual FoxPro Options dialog box with the Controls page showing.

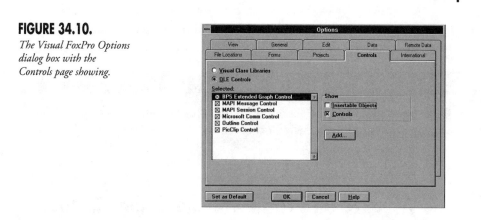

The BPS Extended Graph Control

This OCX is one that was purchased from a third-party vendor (Pinnacle). It can draw graphs from data sent to it and enables you to control the appearance of the resulting graph both on-screen and as printed.

MAPI Controls

Two of the controls in the list in Figure 34.10 are useful for accessing and controlling the Microsoft Mail Application Programmer's Interface (MAPI). These two MAPI controls give you access to mail services related to sending and receiving e-mail through Microsoft Mail.

The Microsoft Comm Control

The Comm control provides access to the communication ports for remote communications using modems. Among other functionality, you can dial a number, send data, and receive data.

The Outline Control

The Outline control can be used to provide an expanding list box in your forms. It works similarly to the File Manager in Windows. It enables you to build a list box that has multiple levels to it, so that clicking on an item will expand or contract those items that are "under" the one on which you clicked. This control can display both the text of an item and a bitmap picture designating the type of item it is. You will be using this OCX control shortly as an example of programming OLE controls.

The PicClip Control

This is an interesting control in that it is invisible at runtime. The PicClip control enables you to store multiple images in one bitmap (BMP) file and then access them as separate images at runtime. This provides a much more efficient method of distributing images for the controls than does using an independent BMP file for each image.

> **NOTE**
>
> All the OLE controls listed in this section, except the BPS Extended Graph control, are documented in the Visual FoxPro help file that is included in the Professional Edition. You can find the documentation under the heading "OLE Controls Overview."

A Sample Visual FoxPro Form with the Outline Control

It's time to put one of these OLE custom controls to work. You will use the Outline control to build a little calendar that will show the 12 months, and if you expand a month you will see the day of the week for the first and last days of that month. (February will also show the number of days.) The form will also have a text box into which the user can type a year and then update the calendar with a command button. The finished form will have the controls positioned as in Figure 34.11.

FIGURE 34.11.

The calendar form in the Form Designer of Visual FoxPro.

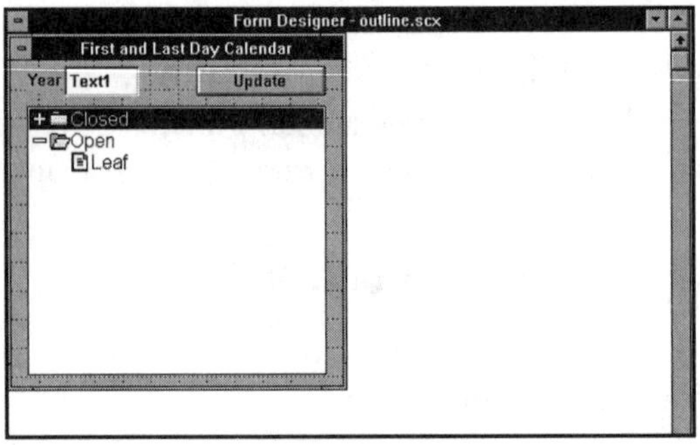

To add the Outline control to the form you first change the controls toolbar to show the OLE controls. You do this by clicking on the tool button with the image of books on it, which brings up the menu shown in Figure 34.12.

FIGURE 34.12.

The Controls menu.

Select OLE Controls from this menu and the toolbar will change to display the OLE controls. The Outline control's tool button is shown in Figure 34.13.

You can place the Outline control in the form the same way you place any other control—just click its button and then drag the control in the form where you want it to be.

FIGURE 34.13.

The OLE controls toolbar.

Outline control tool

The first thing you did was to add two methods and one property to the form with the Form | Add Method and Form | Add Property options on the system menu. The two methods you added were ClrCal and UpdCal, which are used to clear and update the calendar outline. The property you added is lcYear, which holds the year for the calendar.

This is the code for the UpdCal method:

```
WITH THISFORM.oCalendar

  .Visible = .F.

  .ListIndex = -1

  .AddItem("January")
  .AddItem("February")
  .AddItem("March")
  .AddItem("April")
  .AddItem("May")
  .AddItem("June")
  .AddItem("July")
  .AddItem("August")
  .AddItem("September")
  .AddItem("October")
  .AddItem("November")
  .AddItem("December")

  FOR lnCnt = 11 TO 0 STEP -1

    .ListIndex = lnCnt
    .AddItem("First day is "+ ;
    CDOW(CTOD(STR(.ListIndex + 1,2)+"/01/"+THISFORM.lcYear)))
    .PictureType( .ListIndex + 1 ) = 2

    DO CASE
      CASE lnCnt = 1

        .AddItem("Last day is " + ;
        CDOW(CTOD("03/01/"+THISFORM.lcYear)-1))

        .ListIndex = .ListIndex + 1
        .PictureType( .ListIndex + 1 ) = 2

        .ListIndex = .ListIndex - 1
              .AddItem(STR(DAY(CTOD("03/01/"+THISFORM.lcYear)-1),2) + ;
        " Days")

      CASE lnCnt=0 OR lnCnt=2 OR lnCnt=4 OR lnCnt=6 OR ;

        lnCnt=7 OR lnCnt=9 OR lnCnt=11   && 31 days
        .AddItem("Last day is " + ;
        CDOW(CTOD(STR(.ListIndex+  1,2)+"/31/"+THISFORM.lcYear)))
```

```
    OTHERWISE

       .AddItem("Last day is "+CDOW(CTOD(STR(.ListIndex + ;
       1,2)+"/30/"+THISFORM.lcYear)))

    ENDCASE

    .ListIndex = .ListIndex + IIF(lnCnt#1,1,2)
    .PictureType( .ListIndex + 1 ) = 2

  ENDFOR

  .Visible = .T.

ENDWITH

THISFORM.Refresh
```

This code uses the WITH...ENDWITH construct to reduce the typing for the programmer. All of the code contained in the WITH construct is referring to oCalendar, which is the name you assigned to the Outline control in its Properties dialog box. You are using three of the properties and methods of the Outline control to populate it with the months and the first and last days. These are the methods:

Property/Method	Description
ListIndex	Sets the selected item in the Outline control.
AddItem()	Adds a new item to the Outline control immediately below the ListIndex item.
PictureType(<*Item*>)	Sets the image to be displayed to the left of <*Item*>. Takes one of three values: 0—Closed, 1—Open, or 2—Leaf.

The code first hides the calendar by setting its Visible property to .F., and then it creates the 12 months as level-0 items. Level-0 items are the highest level in the outline. You do this by setting ListIndex to -1 and then using AddItem() to add each month.

Next, you use a FOR...ENDFOR loop to walk backward through the months and you use AddItem() to add the first and last day under each month. The DO CASE calculates the last day of the month and also adds the number of days for February. Finally, you set the Visible property to .T. again to show the updated calendar.

In all of the calculations for the days you refer to the lcYear property of the form to get the year you want.

The ClrCal method has this code in it:

```
WITH THISFORM.oCalendar

  FOR lnCnt = 1 TO 12
    .RemoveItem(0)
  ENDFOR

ENDWITH
```

Here you are using a FOR...ENDFOR loop to remove each 0-level item by calling the RemoveItem() method of the Outline control. Removing an item automatically removes any subitems.

The form has the following code in the Init method:

```
THISFORM.lcYear = "1995"
THISFORM.Text1.Refresh()
THISFORM.UpdCal()
```

This code initializes the lcYear property of the form, refreshes the text box, and updates the calendar by calling the UpdCal method of the form.

The ControlSource property of the text box is set to THISFORM.lcYear, so the user's entry in the text box will be directly changing the lcYear property of the form.

The Click method of the command button has this code in it:

```
WITH THISFORM
   .ClrCal()
   .UpdCal()
ENDWITH
THISFORM.oCalendar.Refresh
```

This code calls the ClrCal and UpdCal methods of the form in sequence to clear the calendar and then update it. It then refreshes the calendar control.

Figure 34.14 shows the form running with the year set to 1992 and February expanded.

FIGURE 34.14.

The Outline OCX control form running.

Summary

You have seen OLE in action in Visual FoxPro, first using OLE from the command window to control Microsoft Word and then using an OLE container with Word. Using Microsoft Excel, you drew a graph in the Visual FoxPro form based on data you entered in text boxes. The Outline OCX control provided a neat little calendar that tells the first and last days of the months in different years. All of these processes use OLE automation to accomplish their goals.

Studying the OLE automation code shows that this code is no different from the object-oriented code you write in Visual FoxPro to interact with the native Visual FoxPro objects.

What is the real power of OLE automation? Where can it be used effectively and efficiently? The answer to these questions lies in your own creativity. Visual FoxPro lets you tap into the power of other applications through OLE automation; what you do with that power is up to you.

A Visual FoxPro form could be used to gather data from the user and then control Microsoft Excel to crunch the numbers and draw a graph. That graph could then be cut and pasted, through OLE automation, into a Microsoft Word document, which is then automatically edited through OLE to result in a corporate financial report. That report could then be printed to fax software that sends it to all the regional offices of the client. All of this occurs at the click of a button in Visual FoxPro.

You have seen a few OLE custom controls, and these controls are only the tip of the iceberg. As more development environments become capable of using OLE controls, there will be more and more of these controls available.

Existing OLE server applications and OLE custom controls don't pose a limitation. Development languages such as Microsoft Visual Basic and Microsoft Visual C++ can be used to produce OLE server applications that meet specific needs. Visual C++ can also be used to make OLE controls.

In terms of OLE automation, you are limited only by your imagination.

Migration Tips and Techniques

35

IN THIS CHAPTER

In this chapter, you will learn the tips and techniques for migrating applications from FoxPro 2.6 and other database management systems into the Visual FoxPro environment.

The designers of Visual FoxPro were sensitive to the fact that there are millions of lines of FoxPro 2.*x* and other Xbase code, and they have provided several options for migrating this code to Visual FoxPro. Your investment in applications built in previous versions of FoxPro is protected. Visual FoxPro is designed to enable you to run previous versions of FoxPro source applications directly in Visual FoxPro. However, Visual FoxPro has so many features that you will probably opt to convert your applications to take full advantage of Visual FoxPro's truly event-driven, object-oriented interface. If you choose this route, Visual FoxPro also provides a migration path. Visual FoxPro will automatically convert your files to take advantage of some of the power of Visual FoxPro. However, as you become more familiar with Visual FoxPro, you will most likely want to rethink your files, tables, and applications to take full advantage of the Visual FoxPro object-oriented design principles and other new features.

Many Visual FoxPro developers have reported that the automatic application conversion from FoxPro 2.6 to Visual FoxPro went smoothly. The problem is that Visual FoxPro provides so many advanced features that these developers immediately started redesigning their applications to take advantage of the full power and unique features of Visual FoxPro. They discovered, as you will probably discover, that conversion is only the first step toward developing a final, full-featured Visual FoxPro application.

Visual FoxPro has retained backward compatibility with other Xbase database management systems and provides tools for migrating applications from Xbase and other database management systems.

Currently, Visual FoxPro is available only for the Windows 3.*x*, Windows 95, and Windows NT platforms. However, versions of Visual FoxPro that operate on the Macintosh and DOS platforms are currently under development. By the time you have completed development of an application in Visual FoxPro for Windows, other platforms might be available, and you will be able to run applications unchanged on various platforms—that is, if your applications do not contain system-dependent features. However, you can add conditional code to disable any code that does not operate for a specific platform.

Choosing a Development Platform

One drawback of Visual FoxPro 3.0 is that it requires an IBM-compatible computer with an 80386sx processor or higher with at least 8MB of RAM running Windows 3.1 or Windows for Workgroups, Windows 95, or Windows NT 3.51. You are fortunate if all of the computers on which your application runs will run Visual FoxPro; in that case, there is no question as to which development platform you will use to create your applications. However, in the real world, that is not always the case.

If you work at a place where many of your target users are still stuck with 286 computers running FoxPro for DOS, you will have to consider initially developing your application using FoxPro for DOS. FoxPro for DOS is the lowest common-denominator version of FoxPro. Character-based applications developed in FoxPro for MS-DOS will run on all platforms and will run under Visual FoxPro for Windows without needing any changes.

When you develop an application using FoxPro for DOS, you must make sure that you do not add any features that will not work on other platforms. For example, you should use a PLB library that operates on FoxPro for DOS only if you have a corresponding FLL library that works on other target platforms. After your FoxPro for MS-DOS application is tested and debugged, you can begin to adapt it to run on other platforms.

The next step is to make modifications to your MS-DOS-based FoxPro applications that take advantage of some Windows and Macintosh features, such as graphic elements. You can use the platform system memory variables to restrict the use of platform-specific code when you are running on another system. These system memory variables (_MAC, _WINDOWS, _DOS, _UNIX) return a true (.T.) value if FoxPro is running on the corresponding platform. For example, suppose that you have FLL libraries for each platform and you want the correct library to be loaded. You can use the following code to achieve this result:

```
DO CASE
    CASE _MAC
        SET LIBRARY TO MACLIB.FLL
    CASE _WINDOWS
        DO CASE
            CASE "2.6"$VERS()
                SET LIBRARY TO WIND2LIB.FLL
            CASE "3.0"$VERS()
                SET LIBRARY TO WIND3LIB.FLL
        ENDCASE
    CASE _DOS
        SET LIBRARY TO DOSLIB.PLB
ENDCASE
IF _WINDOWS
    @ 0,0 SAY MYLOGO BITMAP
ELSE
    @ 10,12 SAY "Acme Widgets of America"
ENDCASE
```

Although Visual FoxPro will run an application developed with FoxPro for DOS, it would be a pity to not be able to take advantage of the power of Visual FoxPro. The problem is that you will really need to reorient and rewrite much of your application to take full advantage of the Visual FoxPro object-oriented design principles. As a result, you will need to service and maintain two versions of your application. Because the price of hardware is coming down, in the long run it will probably be cheaper to replace the 286 computers with new computers. Then you can use Visual FoxPro as your development platform.

Bringing FoxPro for DOS Applications to Visual FoxPro 3.0 for Windows

You have several options available for bringing FoxPro 2.6 applications to Visual FoxPro 3.0 for Windows. FoxPro has traditionally been known for its backward compatibility with earlier versions of FoxPro, and Visual FoxPro is no exception. Even though Visual FoxPro maintains compatibility with the FoxPro 2.*x* installed base, it contains so many new features that it is tempting to try to justify designing and implementing a new Visual FoxPro rendition of your original application. However, you might not have the time and resources to do that.

There are various options that are available for bringing FoxPro 2.6 to Visual FoxPro.

- You can run programs (.PRG) and generated FoxPro 2.6 files (.SPR and .MPR) and use reports, queries (.QPR), and tables directly in Visual FoxPro without having to convert them.
- You can convert your files to the new format, as necessary.
- You can redesign all of your files, tables, and applications and apply Visual FoxPro object-oriented design principles to them.

Running FoxPro 2.6 Files in Visual FoxPro

You can run FoxPro 2.6 for DOS or FoxPro 2.6 for Windows files in Visual FoxPro without doing any conversion by using the DO command or by choosing the Do option from the Program Menu. The types of files that can be run without conversion include the following:

- Program files (.PRG)
- Screen programs (.SPR) generated with the FoxPro 2.*x* DOS or Windows Screen generator
- Query program (.QPR) files created by the FoxPro 2.*x* DOS or Windows RQBE
- Menu program (.MPR) files created by the FoxPro 2.*x* DOS or FoxPro 2.*x* Windows Menu Builder

Figure 35.1 shows a screen file (FRIENDS.SPR) that was created using the FoxPro 2.6 Screen Wizard. Figure 35.2 shows the same screen file executed in Visual FoxPro 3.0.

Visual FoxPro also opens the following FoxPro 2.6 files without converting them:

- FoxPro 2.6 query (.QPR) files open in the Query Designer
- FoxPro 2.6 menu (.MNX) files open in the Menu Designer
- FoxPro 2.6 tables (.DBF) open in the Table Designer

Tables created in earlier versions of FoxPro are converted only if you add a new data field, modify a data type, enable null values in any field, or add the table to a database.

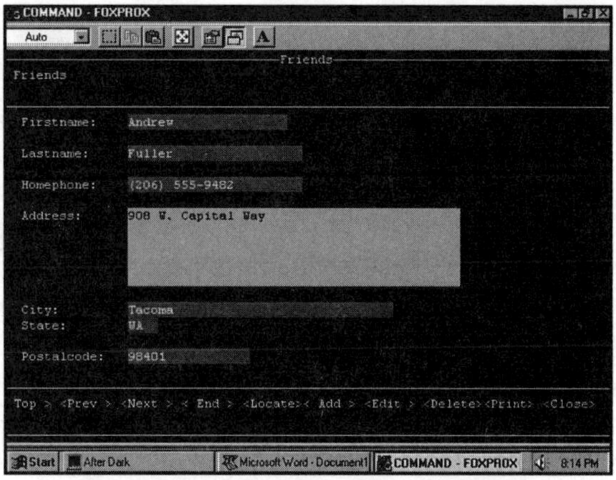

FIGURE 35.1.

*Screen file,
FRIENDS.SPR, created
with the FoxPro 2.6 for
DOS Screen Wizard.*

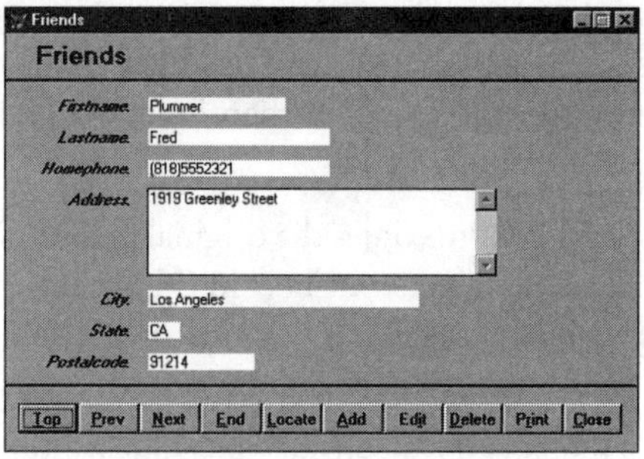

FIGURE 35.2.

*Visual FoxPro-executed
screen file, FRIENDS.SPR,
created with the FoxPro 2.6
for DOS Screen Wizad.*

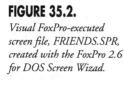

Converting FoxPro 2.6 Files to Visual FoxPro

You cannot make any modifications to any of your FoxPro 2.*x* files in Visual FoxPro unless you convert them to Visual FoxPro format. Once files are converted, you can use the Visual FoxPro visual designers, which enable you to take advantage of the Visual FoxPro object-oriented event model. The conversion process is simple; you simply open the file, and the Conversion process begins. Visual FoxPro converts project, catalog, screen, report form, and label form files.

To convert a FoxPro 2.6 file, you can either select the Open option from the File menu and select a FoxPro 2.*x* file, or you can execute a MODIFY command, such as MODIFY PROJECT, MODIFY FORM, MODIFY QUERY, and so forth. In either case, the Visual FoxPro Converter dialog box appears, as shown in Figure 35.3.

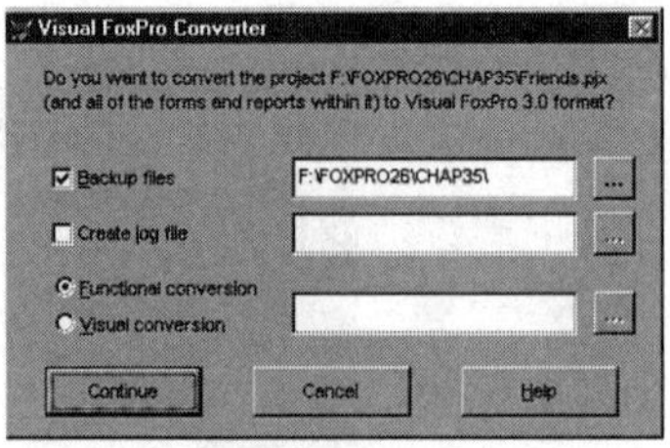

FIGURE 35.3.

*The Visual FoxPro
Converter dialog box.*

Converting FoxPro 2.6 Projects and Catalogs

If you want to use FoxPro 2.6 project (.PJX) and catalog (.FPC) files, you must convert them to Visual FoxPro projects. Once you convert them, you can examine your files from the Project Manager and visual designers and add Visual FoxPro event model functionality. If your FoxPro 2.*x* application files are in a project, it is best to convert the project because Visual FoxPro converts all of the files in the project that need converting. Project files that are converted include tables, screen files, reports, and labels. If your FoxPro 2.6 screens are in screen sets, you need to convert the project rather than individual screens so that your forms will retain the correct READ compatibility modes.

By default, Visual FoxPro copies the original project files to a new subdirectory named OLD*x* in the original project directory. The *x* in OLD*x* is a number that is automatically incremented as you convert more projects. You can instruct Visual FoxPro to not save the original files by unchecking the Backup files check box.

If you choose functional conversion, the conversion process performs the following tasks:

- Copies the original project files to a new subdirectory named OLD*x* in the original .PJX directory and automatically increments *x* as you convert more projects.

- Converts the project and all associated screens, reports, and labels to Visual FoxPro format.

- Moves FoxPro code snippets to the appropriate Visual FoxPro event and method code (see the next section titled "Converting FoxPro 2.6 Screens").

- Sets form and control properties.

- Creates a file with an .SPR extension for each converted screen. This file is different from a FoxPro 2.6 .SPR file.

- Places program (.PRG and .SPR) files in the code tab.

- Places screen, report, and label (.SCX, .FRX, .LBX) files in the Documents tab.

After Visual FoxPro finishes converting the files in the project, it opens the Project Manager so that you can examine all of the project files. You should check each converted file in the project to make sure it has been converted correctly.

Converting FoxPro 2.6 Screens

You cannot modify a FoxPro 2.6 screen (.SCX) file with the Visual FoxPro Form Designer unless the file has been converted. When the Visual FoxPro Converter dialog box appears, you must choose either the Functional Conversion or Visual Conversion check box, depending on which type of conversion you want to perform.

Functional conversion creates form and control images and copies code to locations in object properties, events, and methods. Functional conversion provides immediate FoxPro 2.6 READ compatibility so you can use forms in Visual FoxPro without making extensive manual changes. If you use the recommended functional conversion option, you cannot achieve complete event model functionality until you do the following:

- Eliminate pages and page frames
- Change the form set WindowType property
- Manually relocate code in methods and events

If you choose functional conversion, the following process occurs:

- Screen (.SCX and .SCT) files are changed to Visual FoxPro forms. The original screen filename extensions are renamed to .S2X and .S2T. Screen sets are changed to form sets, and the converted forms are placed in a form set.
- The WindowType property of the form set is set to 2 (READ) or 3 (READ MODAL) to retain backward compatibility.
- Code snippets are placed in the event and method code for the appropriate controls.
- Visual FoxPro creates a new .SPR file and, optionally, an include file.

In Visual FoxPro, the .SCX files run directly when you use the DO FORM command. A screen program (.SPR) file is created to provide backward compatibility to other application components that need it. The .SPR file contains the following:

- Any parameter statements and supporting functions and procedures from the cleanup code snippet in the original screen. Any supporting functions, if they exist, are in scope and available to all events and methods of the form set and form.
- An optional statement that specifies the global include file for the form.
- A DO FORM command that executes the .SCX file.

Visual Conversion

As you saw in the previous section, functional conversion instructs Visual FoxPro to convert screen files that are functional; you can use the converted files. Visual conversion, which is the opposite of functional conversion, instructs Visual FoxPro to create non-functional screen files. You will have to make changes before the screen files operate. You use visual conversion when you want to convert a FoxPro 2.*x* screen file and you want to take full advantage of the Visual FoxPro event model.

If you choose the Visual Conversion option, Visual FoxPro creates images of forms and all controls and copies all the code from the original FoxPro 2.6 project or screens to a non-compatible .PRG file. Although this .PRG file is harder to work with when you are developing a true Visual FoxPro application, it supports the FoxPro 2.6 multiple page forms.

The purpose of this option is to create for you a fully operational Visual FoxPro screen file. When a FoxPro 2.6 screen is converted using this option, you do not have to eliminate pages and page frames, change the form set `WindowType` property, and manually relocate code from object to object. If you choose Visual Conversion, the `WindowType` property of your form set is set to 0 (Modeless) or 1 (Modal) to match the modal setting of your screen. You can use the Form Designer to view your converted screen, enter new values for properties, methods, and events, or to copy code from the .PRG file.

Checking Converted FoxPro 2.6 Screens

After you convert a FoxPro 2.6 screen (.SCX) file to a Visual FoxPro form, you should check the following conditions to determine what changes you have to make with the Form Designer:

- Check to make sure that `READ` statements with both a `MODAL` and `DEACTIVATE` clause are handled correctly. Visual FoxPro processes both of these clauses.

- Check to make sure that none of the control, object, form, and variable names have conflicts.

- Check to make sure that the length of long variable names does not exceed 10 unique characters.

- Check to see that shape controls do not impact other controls. In FoxPro 2.6, the position of a shape control has no effect on other controls. In converted FoxPro 2.6 screens, shapes are placed behind all other controls, and invisible buttons are always on top of all other controls.

- Check to see whether there exists any user-defined functions (UDFs) and other code that might be replaced by new Visual FoxPro commands or functions.

- Check the variable assignments in the Properties window to make sure that no macro substitutions exist. If you discover any, replace the macro substitutions with variable assignments. For example, a PushButton prompt in FoxPro 2.6 Screen Builder that contains `&lcprompt` is converted to `="&lcprompt"` and must be changed to `=lcprompt`.

- Visual FoxPro runs converted screens from an .SPR file created during conversion. Check this .SPR file and the code in any programs or other screens that might call the converted screen to determine whether you can eliminate the new .SPR file and run directly from the .SCX file. To remove the need for the .SPR file created during conversion, you might need to change any files that call the converted screen. You might also need to move code from the .SPR file to the converted screen (.SCX) file.

Changing Converted FoxPro 2.6 Screens to Visual FoxPro Forms

Converted FoxPro 2.6 screens run in a compatibility mode provided by the WindowType property. The READ compatibility of a form or form set is controlled by its WindowType property. The WindowType property of a form set overrides the WindowType settings of all forms it contains. When a screen is converted to a form, the WindowType property is set to 2 (READ) or 3 (READ MODAL), and corresponding READ properties and events are set as listed in Table 35.1.

Table 35.1. Form set properties and events established during conversion.

FoxPro 2.6 Feature	*Visual FoxPro Form Set Property and Event*
#Section 1 Setup Code	Load event
READ ACTIVATE	ReadActivate event
READ CYCLE	ReadCycle property
READ DEACTIVATE	ReadDeactivate event
READ LOCK	ReadLock property
READ NOMOUSE	ReadMouse property
READ SAVE	ReadSave property
READ SHOW	ReadShow event
READ TIMEOUT	ReadTimeout property
READ VALID	ReadValid event
READ WHEN	ReadWhen event

In addition, the FoxPro 2.6 #SECTION 2 setup code is added to the Load event of the form.

You can use the following procedure to change converted FoxPro 2.6 screens to support the Visual FoxPro event model.

1. Change the WindowType property from 2 (Read) to 0 (Modeless) or from 3 (Read Modal) to 1 (Modal). Once you change this property, the READ-compatibility properties and events are no longer available, and you cannot change the WindowType setting back.

2. If you have a single form, move the form set event code to the corresponding or appropriate form events and remove the form set.

3. Move code from the READ-compatibility events to the form events and methods portrayed in Table 35.2 that are now available. Make sure that you consider the event firing sequences when you make these changes.

4. Remove extraneous page and page frame controls.

Table 35.2. Destination of READ-compatibility event code to be moved.

Move Code From:	To:
READ-compatibility event	Form Events and Method
ReadActivate event	Activate event
ReadDeactivate event	Load event
ReadShow event	Show method
ReadValid event	Deactivate event

Converted form sets and forms always have a page frame containing at least one page for each read level of the original screen. Unless they supply specific functionality, you can remove the pages and page frame from each form in a form set. You use the following procedure to remove a page from a form set:

1. From the Option drop-down list in the Properties window, select the page to delete. (An alternative method is to right-click the page and choose the Edit option.)

2. Select all the controls on the page and choose Cut from the Edit menu.

3. With the page selected, press the Delete key to remove the page. When you remove the last page, the page frame is also deleted.

4. With the form selected, choose Paste from the Edit menu to restore the controls.

5. Process parameters in the Init event of the form instead of the screen Load event.

6. Replace with the evaluated value any preprocessor constants that are assigned to property settings. You cannot assign a property a value that contains a preprocessor constant because Visual FoxPro properties are not preprocessed. They must contain actual values or expressions that can be evaluated at runtime. Method and event code is preprocessed, and constants defined there will be evaluated correctly. If you like, you can add code in the Init method to initialize the properties using the preprocessor constants.

7. Adjust the scoping of variables in events or methods, which are private by default, by using the PUBLIC, PRIVATE, or LOCAL commands or by adding user-defined properties to the form or form set.

8. Move any code that may be in the .SPR file to events and methods in the form.

9. Save the form and run it.

The foundation READ was used in FoxPro 2.x to emulate event-driven programming without using event loops. The foundation READ is not used in Visual FoxPro. Now you can take advantage of the Visual FoxPro event model by converting your foundation READ code. To transform a foundation READ into Visual FoxPro, perform the following steps:

1. Replace any foundation READ commands in the main program with a READ EVENTS command.

2. Place a CLEAR EVENTS command in the form, menu, or program event that ends the program, such as the Click event for the OK button.

Converting Reports and Label Files

If you want to modify a FoxPro 2.6 report (.FRX) or label (.LBX) file using the Visual FoxPro Report Designer, you must convert it. The conversion process for converting report files takes the following steps:

■ Adds a new user field to the report form (.FRX) file.

■ Changes any Memo fields from ten bytes to four in the report memo (.FRT) file.

■ Adds records to support the data environment of the report. FoxPro 2.6 environment records convert to Data Environment records.

■ Sets the AutoOpenTables and AutoCloseTables properties and the Data Environment Destroy event of the new report for backward compatibility with the ENVIRONMENT clause of the FoxPro 2.6 REPORT command.

The AutoOpenTables and AutoCloseTables properties of the converted report are set to true (.T.) or false (.F.), depending on whether the original FoxPro 2.6 report form was created with or without an ENVIRONMENT keyword, respectively. If the ENVIRONMENT keyword was specified, the Destroy event of the converted report contains the following code:

```
This.OpenTables    && Opens all the tables
This.Init    && Runs the Init code of the converted
             && DataEnvironment of the report form
```

The procedure for converting FoxPro 2.6 label form files is the same as for report form files, except that label form (.LBX) files are converted.

Once the report or label file is converted, the Visual FoxPro Report Designer opens so that you can add any Visual FoxPro functionality to the converted report.

Tips for Converting Programs

When you are bringing code to Visual FoxPro from FoxPro 2.*x*, you will want to take full advantage of the unique Visual FoxPro features. This section provides some tips that can help you convert your programs. The following list contains situations that you can check for in your programs to make sure that they take advantage of the power of Visual FoxPro:

■ Check to see if you can move code from your functions and procedures to events or methods in containers or objects.

■ Check to see if any user-defined functions (UDFs) or other code can be replaced with new Visual FoxPro functions.

■ Look for @ ... GET commands in program files that support overlapping controls. You might need to reorder your @ ... GET code.

■ Be aware that you can access properties of controls in program (.PRG) files by using the _SCREEN system memory variable and the ActiveForm and ActiveControl properties. For example, you can make the background color of the active form red by adding the following line of code:

```
_SCREEN.ActiveForm.BackColor = RGB(255,0,0)
```

■ Look for symbol names that conflict with new reserved words.

■ Check for conflicting configurable key combinations and navigation keys.

■ Change CLEAR READ commands in forms or form sets to the RELEASE THISFORMSET, RELEASE THISFORM, or CLEAR EVENTS commands.

■ Change the SHOW GET and SHOW GETS commands to call a container or object's Refresh method.

■ Change the SHOW GET and SHOW GETS commands in list boxes and combo boxes to object.Requery statements.

■ Move Foundation READs into the Visual FoxPro event model by using the READ EVENTS and CLEAR EVENTS commands.

Moving Visual FoxPro for Windows Applications to FoxPro for DOS

Visual FoxPro is backward compatible. However, if you have an application that supports the Visual FoxPro event model, you will have to make substantial changes to get your application to operate on earlier versions of FoxPro, not to mention FoxPro for DOS. In the future, however, there will be a Visual FoxPro for DOS product offered by Microsoft. However, the degree of compatibility that the Visual FoxPro for DOS product will have with Visual FoxPro for Windows was uncertain at the time this book was written. Nevertheless, your best approach to moving your Visual FoxPro for Windows applications to FoxPro for DOS is to wait for the Visual FoxPro for DOS product.

Migrating Applications from Other Xbase Environments

Since FoxPro's inception, the whole strategy of the makers of FoxPro has been to develop a product that is compatible with dBASE in hopes of enticing dBASE users to use FoxPro instead. The designers of Visual FoxPro continued this tradition. Visual FoxPro is about 99 percent compatible with dBASE III and dBASE IV. All dBASE III Plus and most dBASE IV programs will run unmodified in Visual FoxPro.

Other Xbase products, such as Clipper and Quicksilver, have added so many of their own extensions that you will definitely have to do substantial modifications to Clipper and Quicksilver programs to get them to run under Visual FoxPro. However, the makers of FoxPro had little incentive to extend FoxPro to support any non-dBASE Xbase products because those products represent such a relatively small user base.

You can run dBASE programs from the Project Manager, from the command window, or from the Do option from the Program menu. When you run a dBASE program, Visual FoxPro recompiles the .PRG file into an .FXP file and runs the .FXP.

The Visual FoxPro language is a superset of dBASE III Plus. Your dBASE III Plus programs can run unchanged in Visual FoxPro. However, before you run a dBASE IV application, you should execute the following command from the command window:

```
SET COMPATIBLE TO DB4
```

This command will ensure that the dBASE IV features will be fully supported in Visual FoxPro and your dBASE program will most likely run without incident. The SET COMPATIBLE TO DB4 command alters the way Visual FoxPro executes various commands and functions to match the behavior of dBASE. The COMPATIBLE TO DB4 command is a quick and easy way to get your application up and running; however, as you proceed with the development of your application on Visual FoxPro and take advantage of more and more of the unique Visual FoxPro features, you might discover that the compatibility feature becomes more of a hindrance than a help.

If there is a problem, it might be because the application contains some unsupported dBASE IV commands, functions, or clauses. Most of the hundreds of commands and functions in Visual FoxPro behave exactly as they do in dBASE IV. However, there are some commands in dBASE IV that do not behave the same way they do in Visual FoxPro. There are certain clauses in dBASE IV that are ignored in Visual FoxPro. You can obtain the most up-to-date list of these commands from the Visual FoxPro Help system. The only areas in which there are major incompatibilities between Visual FoxPro and dBASE IV are network control functions, security, and the more infrequently used SQL and transaction processing functions. Most SQL program (PRS) files will need to be rewritten in Visual FoxPro. Visual FoxPro has some SQL and transaction commands with the same names as dBASE IV commands.

Using dBASE Tables in Visual FoxPro

As far as tables are concerned, both dBASE III Plus and dBASE IV files can be used in Visual FoxPro. When you open dBASE tables (.DBF) in Visual FoxPro, Visual FoxPro automatically converts them to the Visual FoxPro format. From then on, you can use the converted tables as you would any other Visual FoxPro tables.

> **NOTE**
>
> Visual FoxPro and dBASE users cannot simultaneously work with tables in a multiple user environment because the record and file locking mechanism used by Visual FoxPro is different from the mechanism used in dBASE.

If your dBASE table is encrypted, you need to decrypt it in dBASE before you can use it in Visual FoxPro.

If your tables contain memo fields, a dialog box appears that prompts you to indicate if you want to convert the memos to Visual FoxPro format. Then another dialog box appears asking you if you want to remove dBASE soft carriage returns. If the memo fields contain normal text, you should click the Yes button. You should click the No button if the memo fields contain binary data.

Backup files for the dBASE tables are not created before the conversion. You cannot read the Visual FoxPro tables from dBASE III or IV. If you want to use a table again in dBASE, you will have to copy the table as a FOXPLUS type table. In the command window, type the following code:

```
COPY TO Filename TYPE FOXPLUS
```

Converting dBASE Indexes

dBASE index files are different from Visual FoxPro index files. As a result, Visual FoxPro automatically converts a dBASE .MDX or .NDX index to a Visual FoxPro .CDX or .IDX index for the table, respectively.

To use a dBASE IV table with an index and without a memo field in dBASE after Visual FoxPro has converted it, open the file in dBASE and reindex it. This step is necessary only if you have changed any of the data.

Converting dBASE Screen Files

When you add a dBASE screen file to a Visual FoxPro project and modify it, a Conversion dialog box appears. You are given the choice of two options: Visual Conversion and Full Conversion.

In a visual conversion, Visual FoxPro creates a new form and establishes values for the fundamental properties of the form and its objects. However, it does not apply event or method code to the objects. It places code associated with the screen in a program (.PRG) file. This option is used if you want to make the form work using the new Visual FoxPro object model.

If you specify the full conversion option, your form will become a FoxPro 2.6 type READ-compatible form. For more information about this type of form, see the section titled "Converting FoxPro 2.6 Screens" earlier in this chapter.

If you use the full conversion option, your screen will function immediately as a FoxPro 2.*x*/dBASE READ-compatible form. For more information about working with this type of form, see the section "Changing Converted FoxPro 2.6 Screens to Visual FoxPro Forms," earlier in this chapter.

Converting dBASE Reports and Labels

Visual FoxPro automatically converts dBASE reports and labels when you modify them in Visual FoxPro. When Visual FoxPro converts reports and labels, Visual FoxPro creates a Visual FoxPro Report (FRX) file with the information from the dBASE report form (FRM) file and a Visual FoxPro Label (LBX) file with the information from the dBASE Label Form (LBL) file.

When Visual FoxPro performs its conversion, it converts the following dBASE report form elements:

- All bands
- Fields
- Calculated fields
- Hidden fields
- Picture templates
- Functions for fields
- Style attributes such as underline, bold, italic, and colors

Fonts are not converted. However, Visual FoxPro supports all Windows-based fonts. Wordwrap bands are converted to a series of one-line text fields in Visual FoxPro reports. Band spacing and pitch data is not converted. Visual FoxPro does not use a global ruler or a wordwrap paragraph ruler, so this information is not retained. Converted reports will have a right margin equal to the width of the report. The left margin is not changed but can be set in the Visual FoxPro Report Designer. You may need to rearrange the field positioning because tabbing is not supported by Visual FoxPro but is supported by dBASE IV.

Because the table path information is not stored in dBASE report forms, Visual FoxPro might not be able to find a table and will display a "file not found" error box. Visual FoxPro reports can save database names, relations, skips, and index information. You can use the Visual FoxPro Report Designer to establish the correct data environment.

Migrating Applications from Non-Xbase Environments

Now that you have Visual FoxPro, you will probably want to convert all of your non-Xbase applications to Visual FoxPro. Examples of non-Xbase products include Paradox by Borland International, Microsoft Access, and Mainframe database management systems. However, the transaction is not automatic. You will have to re-create all of your tables, forms, reports, and so forth. It is not important to understand the details of the foreign application; you need to understand its design. You must begin by figuring out the application's functional specifications. Then you design a Visual FoxPro application based on those specifications.

People often put up with flawed systems. They do not like certain reports or forms, or they need more capabilities. Many times an application includes capabilities that no one has ever used or ever will use. The problem is that changes to an operational application are not usually made. Because you are going to create a brand new Visual FoxPro application anyway, it is a good time to improve the system's design. After you have determined the functional specifications of the original application, you should work with all the people involved with the application to determine any changes that need to be made. Then after you have completed the design of your new application, you should let all of these cognizant people review your design and provide feedback before you begin implementing the design.

You implement your new Visual FoxPro application in the order described in the following sections.

Create a Project

The first thing you should do when you implement your new Visual FoxPro application is to create one or more projects for your application. Visual FoxPro's fundamental organizational tool is the Project Manager. You should use the Project Manager to organize and manage files as you create tables and databases, design queries, forms, and reports, and build applications.

Creating Tables

Next, you must create Visual FoxPro table structures. For most applications, you will be able to use the IMPORT or APPEND commands to transfer data from the non-Xbase product to Visual FoxPro tables. If you are transferring data from Paradox, Access, or certain spreadsheets, the IMPORT command creates the Visual FoxPro table structure for you. More information regarding the APPEND and IMPORT commands can be found in Chapter 17, "Sharing Data with Other Software."

Another technique for creating Visual FoxPro tables is to use the seamless ODBC connectivity feature of Visual FoxPro. You can create a remote view that connects to a remote data source and copy data into your Visual FoxPro tables. Microsoft supplies ODBC drivers that connect to 66 different data sources. For more information about connectivity, see Chapter 37, "ODBC Integration," and Chapter 38, "Client/Server Features."

Creating Forms

Now that you have tables, you can create forms using the Form Designer or Form Wizards. Remember that much of the functionality of the application will be encapsulated in the methods of the form and controls. Therefore, you should spend a good deal of time in designing your forms and various visual objects.

Creating Reports

The next step is to design the reports for your application. The process involves duplicating reports generated by the original non-Xbase application. During the design review process, you will probably have determined that you need new reports and that some of the original applications need to be modified.

Summary

This chapter described the process of moving FoxPro 2.*x*, dBASE, and non-Xbase applications to Visual FoxPro. The major focus was on the task of converting FoxPro 2.*x* files and applications to take advantage of the Visual FoxPro object-oriented event model.

Developing Online Help

36

As you are aware, every important Windows application has online help. As a result, the user community simply assumes that every application that it uses has online help. Users are alarmed if they cannot find out how to do something simply by choosing a Help menu option, by clicking a Help button, or by pressing the F1 key. It is essential that developers face this fact and implement custom online help for every one of their significant Visual FoxPro applications.

A well-planned and well-implemented help system will not only be an invaluable source of information for your users, it will also reduce training and maintenance requirements. What this means to you is that you will receive fewer midnight calls from confused and disgruntled customers.

You can learn how to design a help system by examining the help for various major Windows applications, such as Word, Visual FoxPro, and Excel. Notice how the help system in these applications organizes help topics, cross references, and the various help windows.

You should also consider who is assigned the task of creating the help system. In my involvement with the development of major applications, including dBASE III and dBASE IV, we were able to assign the best qualified people to design and implement the help system, which happened to be the people in the documentation and graphics arts departments. This approach is used by most large software development companies. If your organization is small and creating the online help is your responsibility, then you can design a substantially better online help system if you first study the design, language, structure, and organization of the online help system of major Windows applications.

In this chapter, you will learn how to create both the traditional FoxPro DBF-style online help (which is strictly character-based) and the Windows-style online help, sometimes referred to as *graphics* help. If you are developing an application that will be used on various platforms (Windows, MS-DOS, or Mac), you might want to opt for the system-independent DBF-style help for your custom online help system. The DBF-style help is also easier to create. On the other hand, if you are developing an application to run under Visual FoxPro 3 for Windows and you want a more polished online help system, create a Windows-style online help system.

SAMPLE FILES ON THE CD-ROM

The various files on the CD-ROM are provided as adjuncts to this chapter to illustrate techniques for creating online help systems in Visual FoxPro.

This chapter's example uses files located in VFU\Chap36\.

File	Purpose
Bullet.BMP	A Paintbrush picture used within the Windows-type help file.
CtrlHelp.DBF	The data table for a DBF-type help product.
CtrlHelp.HLP	The finished Windows-type help product.

CtrlHelp.HPJ	The Windows-type help project. Holds the pointers to all text files, pictures, and other items used to compile a Windows help (HLP) file.
CtrlHelp.RTF	A Rich Text Format file that holds the precompiled help file information.
Light.SHG	A Segmented Hypergraphics file used to present hot spots on a picture within the Windows-type help file.
Light.WMF	A Windows metafile picture used to produce the Segmented Hypergrahics File.
Lights.ICO	
Music.WMF	
Sun.BMP	A Paintbrush picture used within the Windows-type help file.

How FoxPro Provides Help

To begin, you should first understand how Visual FoxPro provides you with online help using either the Visual FoxPro DBF-style or Windows-style online help system. The Visual FoxPro DBF-style has been around since early versions of FoxPro. You can specify which help file to use using the SET HELP command. The following are examples:

```
SET HELP TO C:\VFP\FOXHELP.DBF   && DBF-style help
SET HELP TO C:\VFP\FOXHELP.HLP   && Windows-style help
SET HELP TO C:\VFP\FOXHELP        && Windows-style help
SET HELP TO C:\VFP\MYAPP.HLP     && custom Windows-style help
```

If you do not specify a filename extension, Visual FoxPro looks for a Windows-style help file with an .HLP extension. If it does not find it, it looks for a DBF-style help table with a .DBF extension.

You can specify a default startup help file by placing one of the following statements in your CONFIG.FPW configuration file:

```
HELP = FOXHELP.HLP (specifies graphical Help)
HELP = FOXHELP.DBF (specifies .DBF-style Help)
```

In addition, you can choose Options from the Tools menu, and the Options dialog box appears. Then, select the File Locations tab on the Options dialog box and change the help file. You can also choose which help file to use by using the custom setup option during installation.

DBF-style help is stored in a standard Visual FoxPro table named FOXHELP.DBF. This table contains three fields: CONTEXTID, TOPIC, and DETAILS. Because FOXHELP.DBF is a Visual FoxPro table, you can place it in use and browse it as you would any other table, as shown in Figure 36.1.

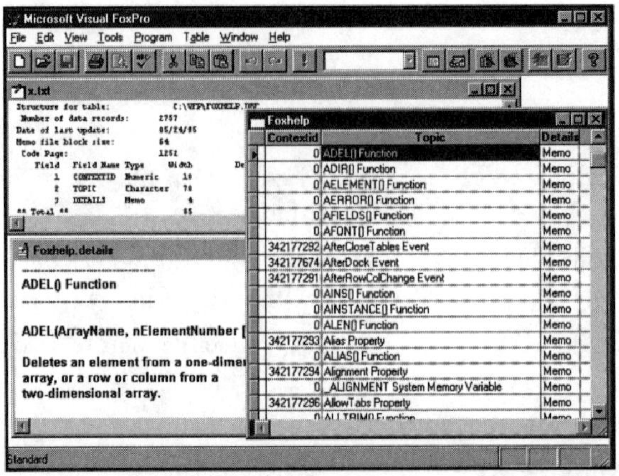

FIGURE 36.1.

Contents of the FOXHELP.DBF help file.

NOTE

Note that Visual FoxPro DBF-style help is included only in the Visual FoxPro Professional Edition. However, that does not prevent you from creating a custom DBF-style help table for your application.

Visual FoxPro uses the numeric CONTEXTID field to implement context-sensitive help for some objects in the system. The CONTEXTID field must be the first field of the table. You can use this field to create your own custom context-sensitive help for different objects in your application. All you have to do is assign the same context number to both the object and the associated help topic in the FOXHELP.DBF help table. You set the context-sensitive help using the SET TOPIC ID TO nHelpContextID command, or if you are creating a form, you can set the HelpContextID property for a control object. For Windows-style help, nHelpContextID is a context number in the MAP section of the help project file, which is discussed in the section titled "Implementing Windows-Style Help," later in this chapter.

The TOPIC field is a character field that contains the topic that appears in the DBF-style help window topic list. The actual help text for the topic is contained in the DETAILS memo field.

The help text often contains the two words, "See Also:" followed by a list of items separated by commas. Visual FoxPro places these items in the drop-down list. For example, if the DETAILS memo field in your custom help table contains the following text:

```
See Also: Elephant, Giraffe, Mouse
```

Then Elephant, Giraffe, and Mouse appear in the See Also drop-down list of the DBF-style help window.

Earlier versions of FoxPro have a CODE field that contains a two-letter help topic identifier.

When you choose DBF-style help, Visual FoxPro initially opens the FOXHELP.DBF file in a hidden work area. If you want to modify the help file, you will need to turn off the help with the SET HELP OFF command. Then you can use the file USE FOXHELP.DBF and modify it any way you like.

Creating Your Own DBF-Style Online Help

You can create your own custom DBF-style online help table. First, create a DBF file with the same structure as shown in Figure 36.1. The following example portrays an easy way to create the structure of your custom help file:

```
SET HELP OFF  && This is only required if you are using DBF-Style help
USE C:\VFP\FOXHELP.DBF
COPY STRUCTURE TO CTRLHELP   && Create your new help file structure
USE CTRLHELP
APPEND
```

Now add records to the help file. The CONTEXTID field can contain any unique positive integer number. An example custom DBF-style table is shown in Figure 36.2.

FIGURE 36.2.

Example DBF-style help table, CTRLHELP.DBF.

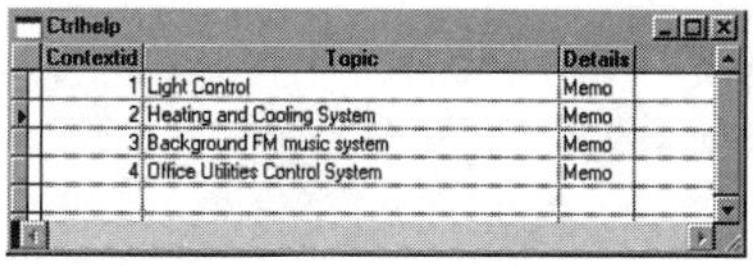

The CTRLHELP.DBF table is the DBF-style help table for an example form set, CONTROL.SCX, which consists of four forms. There is a help topic for each form. The CONTROL.SCX form set consists of a main form, Office Utility Control System, with three pushbuttons that activate three other forms: Lighting Controls, Heating Control, and Background Music Control. The CONTROL.SCX example form set with all of its four forms open is shown in Figure 36.3. The purpose of this example is not to illustrate how to create form sets or a utility control system, but to illustrate how to create custom online help. Each form contains a Help button that displays online help for the form. You can also press the F1 button to get online help for the selected form.

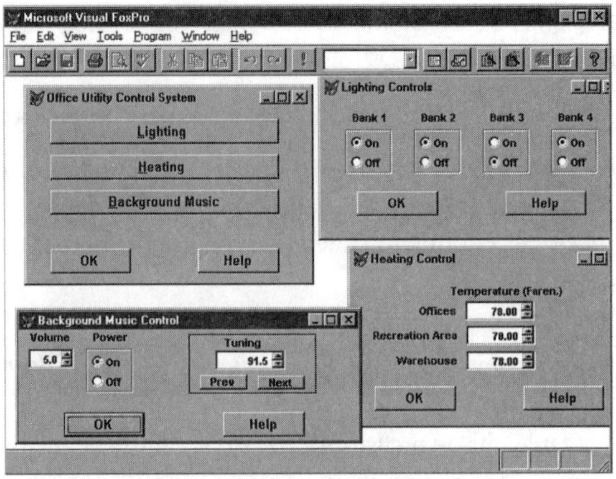

FIGURE 36.3.

*Example form set that
contains four forms with
Help buttons.*

Customize Your DBF-Style Help Table

You can add as many additional fields to the DBF-style help table as you like. These fields can be used for a variety of purposes, such as selecting a subset of help topics to display. For example, you can add a LANGUAGE field and store help in different languages in the same help table. Then you can use the SET HELPFILTER TO command to prompt the user of your application to specify his or her favorite language and show help for that language only. Suppose that the user's response is stored in a memory variable m.Answer. The following statement selects help in the user's favorite language:

```
SET HELPFILTER TO m.Answer = LANGUAGE
```

You can store blocks of help for different user levels (novice, casual, and advanced) and use the SET HELPFILTER TO command to select help that is tailored to the individual user's skill level.

You can set a filter for DBF-style help only. In other words, you cannot use the SET HELPFILTER TO command with Windows-style help.

Specifying the Help Table

In the initialization code for your application that supports custom online help, you add code to open the custom help file. In the example form set, the code is added to the Init event method for the form set. However, first you must add a user-defined property, cSaveHelp, to the form set to save the current help file. You do this by choosing the New Property option from the Forms menu. When the New Property dialog box appears, you type the user-defined property, cSaveHelp. Then you can add the following code to the form set's Init event method:

```
THISFORMSET.cSaveHelp = SET("HELP",1)
SET HELP TO CTRLHELP
```

If your form consists of a single form (no form set object), you can access the user-defined property using THISFORM instead of THISFORMSET.

Note that the filename extension is not specified. If a CTRLHELP.HLP Windows-style help file exists, Visual FoxPro will open it. Otherwise, Visual FoxPro opens the CTRLHELP.DBF DBF-style help table.

Before you exit your application, you need to add code to restore the Visual FoxPro help file. In the example, the following line of code is added to the `Destroy` event method:

```
SET HELP TO (THISFORMSET.cSaveHelp)  && restore Visual FoxPro Help
```

Remember that the `Destroy` event occurs right before the form exits. The `Destroy` method is an excellent location to put any clean-up code.

You could have specified `SET HELP TO` without any other arguments, and Visual FoxPro would have restored the default help file. For example, if you are using the Windows-style help, Visual FoxPro restores the FOXHELP.HLP file. However, in this example the help file was saved in case the original help file was another custom help file and not the Visual FoxPro help file.

Specifying Help Topics to Display in the Help Window

Now that you have specified your help file, you need to designate which topics you want to display. You have two ways of doing this. You can specify the actual topic names using the `SET TOPIC TO cTopicName` or `HELP cTopicName` commands, or you can establish context-sensitive help for a form by setting the `HelpContextID` property for the form and controls.

Specify Topic Names

The technique for specifying a topic name is exactly the same as executing the `HELP` command with a topic name specified (for example, `HELP AT()`) from the command window. At the point in the program that you want to display help, you execute the `HELP` command with the topic name specified. When the `HELP` command executes, the help text in the `DETAILS` memo field displays in the Help window for the record that contains a `TOPICS` field that matches the specified topic name. In other words, Visual FoxPro searches the DBF-style help table for a `TOPIC` field that matches the specified topic name. For example, if CTRLHELP.DBF, shown in Figure 36.2 is active, and you specify

```
HELP heating and cooling system
```

the text shown in Figure 36.2 in the `DETAILS` memo field displays in the Help window. Note that case is ignored. If the topic name specified with the `HELP` command does not match any topics in the help file, the Help Topics dialog box highlights the topic with the closest match in the list.

Context-Sensitive Help

You can establish context-sensitive online help for a form or any form objects. If you do so, you can press the F1 key or click a help button to get help related to the form.

The F1 key is an industry-wide, recognized standard for context-sensitive help. When you press F1 while a form has focus, Visual FoxPro displays its context-sensitive help topic. Visual FoxPro uses the HelpContextID property of the form to determine which topic to display based on the CONTEXTID field in the Help table. If the HelpContextID property of the form is 0, which it is by default, Visual FoxPro displays the Help Topics window.

All you have to do to implement context-sensitive help is to set the value of the HelpContextID property for the form to correspond to a CONTEXTID field value in your custom Help table. In the example form set shown in Figure 36.3, the HelpContextID property values are set when you design your form to correspond to values in the CTRLHELP.DBF help table shown in Figure 36.2. Table 36.1 describes the HelpContextID property settings for the forms in the form set shown in Figure 36.3.

Table 36.1. The HelpContextID property settings for the forms in the form set shown in Figure 36.3.

Form	HelpContextID Property Value	Form Caption
Form1	4	Office Utility Control System
Form2	1	Lighting Controls
Form3	2	Background Music Control
Form4	3	Heating Control

Adding a help button is easy. You just place a command button in position on the form, set its Caption property to Help, and add the following line of code to the Click event method of the command button:

```
HELP ID THISFORM.HelpContextID
```

The fact that the Help command button uses the HelpContextID property of its parent form makes the button more encapsulated.

You can add a help button object to your favorite visual class library. When you use the Form Designer to create a new form, you can add your standard help button object to the form as you would add any other control.

Also, you can create and register a form template containing OK, Cancel, and Help buttons. Then when you create a new form, the Visual FoxPro Form Designer uses the template to create your new form, complete with the three buttons. All you have to do is set the HelpContextID for the form to get context-sensitive help.

In the example form set, CONTROL.SCX, you can obtain context-sensitive help either by pressing the F1 key or by clicking the Help button. Figure 36.4 shows the Help window for the Background Music Control form.

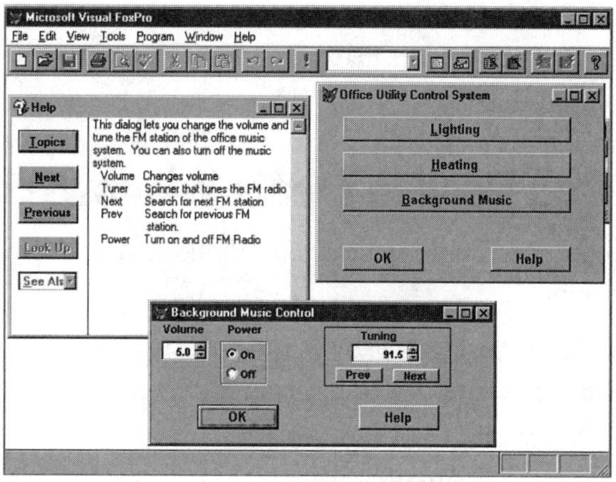

FIGURE 36.4.

The Help window for the Background Music Control form.

The See Also list is activated when the "See Also:" text followed by a topic list is placed in the Details memo field, as shown in Figure 36.5.

FIGURE 36.5.

DBF-style Help window with See Also list open.

The CONTROL.SCX form set is designed to operate with either the CTRLHELP.DBF DBF-style help table or a Windows-style help file (CTRLHELP.HLP) if it is available. The reason this occurs is because the filename extension was omitted from the SET HELP TO CTRLHELP command and Visual FoxPro looks for a file with an extension of .HLP before it looks for a file with an extension of .DBF.

Implementing Windows-Style Help

If you do not like the character-based nature of the DBF-style help or you feel that it looks like a screen out of the 1980s, then maybe you need to bite the bullet and create Windows-style help. This chapter shows you how to create actual Windows-style help. Windows-style help supports all of the features that you discover when you are using the Windows help system. These include the following features:

- Multiple fonts, font sizes, styles, and colors
- Graphics objects including bitmaps, hypergraphic (graphics with hot spots), and metafiles
- Macros that automate or extend the power of the help system

- Mouse-sensitive regions that let users jump to a new help topic, display popup windows, and activate macros
- Keyword searches

What You Need to Create Windows-Style Help

If you want to create your own custom Windows-style help, you will need the following three software tools:

1. The Windows Help engine
2. A word processor that edits text in RTF format
3. The Microsoft Help Compiler

The Help engine, WINHELP.EXE, is built into Windows. Many word processors such as Microsoft Word support RTF text editing. Two help compilers are supplied with the Visual FoxPro Professional Edition: HC35.EXE and HC31.EXE. You can use either one. The following help compilers and associated tools and files are supplied with the Professional Edition of Visual FoxPro:

Files	Description
HC35.EXE	Microsoft Help Compiler Version 3.5 that runs under MS-DOS 3.3 or higher
HC35.ERR	Error messages for HC35.EXE
HC31.EXE	Microsoft Help Compiler Version 3.1 that runs under MS-DOS 3.3 or higher
HC31.ERR	Error messages for HC31.EXE
SHED.EXE	Segmented Hypergraphics Editor Version 3.5 that runs under Windows
SHED.HLP	Help file for SHED.EXE
MRBC.EXE	Multiple Resolution Bitmap Compiler Version 1.1 that runs under MS-DOS 3.3 or higher

Strangely enough, the two versions of the Microsoft Help Compiler are both needed because neither will handle all types of circumstances. Both versions have strengths and weaknesses. The following table illustrates the differences between the two versions of the Help Compiler:

HC31.EXE	HC35.EXE	Feature
Yes	No	Supports Secondary Windows
Yes	Yes	Supports Word for Windows 2.0
Yes	No	Supports Word for Windows 6.0

HC31.EXE	HC35.EXE	Feature
Yes	Yes	Supports Word for MS-DOS Version 3.0 or 4.0
Yes	Yes	Other word processors that support RT
No	Yes	Supports the PLATFORM option in the help Project File for displaying graphics correctly on the Macintosh

Visual FoxPro also supplies sample help files that you can use as a template in Word for Windows to create your own Windows-style programs. These files are in the Visual FoxPro sample program directory (\VFP\SAMPLES\MAINSAMP\HELP) and include the following:

Files	Description
TTRADE.BMP	Tasmanian Traders logo used in help file
TTRADE.HLP	Tasmanian Traders help file
TTRADE.HPJ	Help project file
TTRADE.RTF	Tasmanian Traders structured Help Topic file in rich-text format (you can edit it with Word for Windows)
TTRADE.SHG	Graphics file created with the SHED.EXE Hot Spot Graphics Editor

All you need to create a relatively simple Windows-style help file are the help compiler, a word processor, a sample structured help topic (.RTF) file, a help project (.HPJ) file, and a sample template. You might need to use the Hot Spot Graphics Editor (SHED.EXE). However, if you need to build a large and complex Windows-style help file, you should purchase a help authoring tool such as RoboHELP, ForeHelp, or ProtoView Visual Help Builder. These tools make it easy for you to keep up with all of the links, jumps, macros, and other components of your help file while you are creating it. The most popular help authoring tool is RoboHELP, which is marketed by Blue Sky Software of San Diego, CA. Call (800) 330-3955, and they will send you a free RoboHELP demo disk. ForeHelp is marketed by ForeFront, Inc., of Boulder, CO. An operational ForeHelp demo system is on the CD-ROM supplied with this book. (You can also call ForeFront at (800) 357-8507, and they will send you a free ForeHelp demo disk.) You can get more information about ProtoView Visual Help Builder by calling (800) 231-8588; however, I don't know whether they will send you a free demo disk or not.

Components of a Windows-Style Help System

The components that you use to create a help system containing text and graphics include a variety of files. Each file type is discussed in the following sections and consists of a topic file, a project file, and a graphics file. To build a help file, only the topic file and project file are required. The graphics file is only required if you have graphics in your help file.

> **NOTE**
>
> Refer to the supplied help file components located in VFU\Chap36\ for examples of
> Windows help components.

Topic File

The topic file contains all of the text for a help file. It also contains codes needed to link topics
and graphics; it can also include graphics. The topic file has an .RTF extension and must be in
rich-text format (RTF).

Project File

The project file is an ASCII text file with an .HPJ extension. It contains a list of the filenames
for the text and graphics that are required to build the help file. It also contains window definitions and macros. It contains all of the information needed by the Help Compiler to
perform the help file compilation operation. You can use the Visual FoxPro MODIFY FILE command to execute it.

Graphics File

There are four types of graphics files that you can include in a help file. You will learn about
each type in this section. You can have zero or more graphics files in a help file. The following
are the four types of files:

- Bitmap (BMP) graphics file
- Multiple-resolution (MRB) graphics file
- Metafile (WMF) graphics file
- Hypergraphic (SHG) graphics file

A *bitmap* file contains a bitmap graphics file and has a .BMP extension. A bitmap file must
have 16 or fewer colors when used in a help file. You can create a bitmap file with any utility,
such as Microsoft Paint, that creates a bitmap (BMP) file. If all the users of your application
have the same screen resolution, you can create your bitmap for a single resolution. However,
if your help file runs on different systems with different resolutions, you will have to create a
bitmap file for each resolution and combine them into a single file using the MRBC.EXE
Multiple Resolution Bitmap Compiler. The bitmap output from the MRBC.EXE program
contains multiple versions of the same bitmap at different screen resolutions compiled into a
single file with an .MRB extension.

A *metafile* file has a .WMF extension and contains a single graphic in Windows Metafile format. Metafile files are usually much smaller than bitmap files, and therefore you can reduce the size of your help file by using metafiles instead of bitmap files. You can create a metafile with a drawing program such as CorelDRAW!. A metafile file contains an image defined using coded lines and shapes. It is independent of the type of screen resolution that the user has.

A *hypergraphic* graphics file contains a bitmap graphic that has been modified using the SHED.EXE program. This type of file contains one or more hot spots. When the user clicks a hot spot, a link, jump, or macro can be activated.

Steps for Creating a Help System for an Application

The process of creating a help file consists of the following steps:

1. Create your topic file using a word processor that edits RTF document files such as Word for Windows 6.0.

2. Choose the File menu, Save As option to save the topic file as a rich-text format file.

3. Create a help project file with any text editor such as the MODIFY COMMAND command in Visual FoxPro.

4. Test the help file.

5. Make changes to your application to support online context-sensitive help.

Creating the Topic File

You can use your favorite word processor to create your topic file, just as long as it is comparable to Word for Windows and creates RTF files. Format the text using the formatting commands of your word processor. You can insert graphics files or references to graphics files; you can also insert context strings, titles, and keywords, browse sequence numbers, and build tags—all of these are coded as footnotes. If you are using Word for Windows Version 2.0 or 6.0, you can insert a footnote by placing the cursor at the insertion point and choosing Footnote from the Insert menu. The Footnote and Endnote dialog box appears, as shown in Figure 36.6. You enter the appropriate footnote reference mark (#, $, K, +, or *) that corresponds to the topic codes described in Table 36.2. Then you type the footnote in the footnote box. When you type the footnote, make sure that you type a single space between the footnote reference character and the footnote contents.

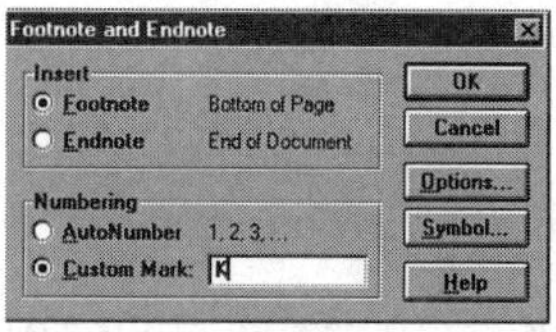

FIGURE 36.6.

Insert a footnote reference code into a topic file.

Table 36.2. Topic file codes.

Format	Purpose
# *Footnote*	This footnote defines the context string that is used to identify a topic. Topics without context strings can be displayed only with keywords or browse sequences. A context string must contain only alphabetic characters (A–Z, a–z), numeric characters, and the period (.) and underscore (_)characters.
$ *Footnote*	This footnote defines a topic title. These titles appear in a list box when you use the Search feature. Although titles are optional, you need them if you want to support the Help system search option and if you supply a keyword.
K *Footnote*	This footnote defines a keyword that is used to search for a topic. Keywords are optional.
+ *Footnote*	This footnote defines a browse sequence that determines the order in which the user can browse through topics. Browse sequences are optional.
* *Footnote*	This footnote defines a tag that the Help Compiler builds into the system conditionally.
Double-underlined text	When text is double-underlined, it indicates that the user can click the text to jump to another topic.
Underlined text	When text is underlined, it indicates that the user can click the text to display a popup text box. The underlined text becomes a hot spot.
Hidden text	Hidden text is used to specify a context string for the destination topic or a help macro.

Topics and Context Strings

Each frame or page of the topic file defines a topic. Each topic must be associated with a context string. A context string is specified by a footnote with a pound sign (#) code reference placed in front of the topic title. You use a context string to identify a topic in the Topic file and the Help system. In Figure 36.7 the context string for the topic, The Utilities Control System Dialog, is ctrlMain and is defined by the following footnote:

```
# ctrlMain
```

The Help system displays a topic only if a context string exists for the topic.

When you underline or double-underline text, the text becomes hot-spot text. It is followed by a context string of the topic to

- Display the topic in a popup text box (underlined text)
- Jump to a topic (double-underlined text)

NOTE

A context string used as a reference is formatted as hidden text. Note that when the Microsoft Word's Show Hidden Text option in the View tab of the Options dialog box is set, hidden text displays with a dotted underline. You can use the Options option on the Tools menu to display the Options dialog box.

As you can see in Figure 36.7, the underlined text, `Help Button`, is followed by a context string, `ctrlHelpButton`. When the user clicks the `Help Button` text, the popup text box displays, as shown in Figure 36.8.

FIGURE 36.7.

CTRLHELP.RTF topic file with the topic and footnote displayed.

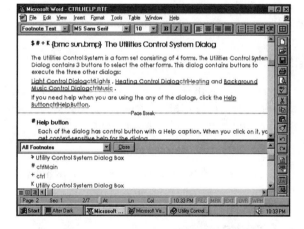

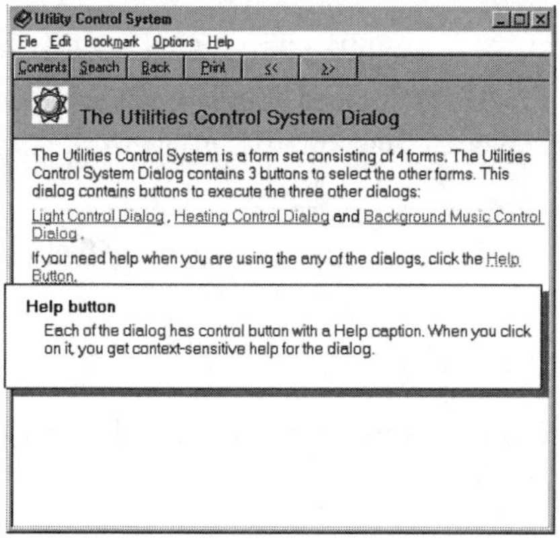

FIGURE 36.8.

Windows Help showing a popup text box associated with the Help button hot spot text.

In Figure 36.7, if you were to click on the double-underlined text, `Light Control Dialog`, the topic identified by the context string, `ctrlLights`, displays in the topic. In other words, the Help system jumps to the topic defined by the `ctrlLights` context string.

If you want to jump to another help file, you can place an @ character after the context string followed by the filename of another help file. Just as the context string is formatted as hidden text, the `@FileName` sequence is also formatted in hidden text. Here is the syntax:

```
JumpTextContextString@d:\path\filename.hlp
```

When the user clicks the `JumpText`, the new topic in the specified help file displays.

You can jump to a secondary window and display the specified topic in the secondary window using the following syntax:

```
JumpTextContextString>WindowName
```

The `WindowName` is the name of a secondary window defined in the help project file [Windows] section as discussed in the section titled "Creating a Windows Help Project (HJP) File."

Coding Titles

The first line of a topic is the title line. You must also designate it to be a title line by adding a footnote using a dollar sign ($) reference mark. The footnote contains the actual title. In Figure 36.7, the title is defined by the footnote

```
$ Utility Control System Dialog Box
```

These titles appear in a list box when you use the Search dialog box, which is described in the next section.

Coding Keywords

If you want a topic to be included in the Help Search dialog box list, you need to specify keywords for the topic. Also, you need a title for the topic because keywords for a topic without an associated title display as `>>Untitled Topic<<` in the topics list.

You can specify the same keyword for multiple topics. Also, you can specify more than one keyword for a topic. Multiple keywords are specified in the footnote separated by semicolons. For example

```
K person; human; being
```

When you search on any one of the multiple keywords for a topic, the corresponding titles appear in the topics list box.

Coding Browse Sequences

In the Help window, you can browse through the help topics using the << and >> buttons. You move through the topics in a linear sequence. The sequence is determined by the + *Foot-note* code (*Footnote* specifies the browse sequence code). If all of the specified browse sequence codes are omitted or if they are the same value, the browse sequence occurs in the order in which the topics are specified in the Topic file. If the browse sequence codes are different, the browse sequence codes are sorted by their ASCII value. The browse sequence code actually consists of two parts: a group and an order. The group and order are separated by a colon (:). For example, suppose that you had the following browse sequence:

Topic File Order	Browse Sequence Code	Title
1	+ flowers:2	Roses
2	+ animals:3	Cat
3	+ animals:1	Mouse
4	+ animals:2	aardvark
5	+ animal	Animals
6	+ flower	Flowers
7	+ flowers:1	Bluebonnets

The browse sequence order will be

```
+ animal      Animals
+ animals:1       Mouse
+ animals:2       aardvark
+ animals:3       Cat
+ flower      Flowers
+ flowers:1       Bluebonnets
+ flowers:2       Roses
```

Adding Graphics to Your Windows-Style Help

You can add graphics files to your topic file directly or by reference. To place a bitmap or metafile directly in a topic file, you place the cursor at an insertion point in the Microsoft Word document and either paste the graphics from the Clipboard or use the Insert menu, Picture option to insert the graphics. To include a graphics by reference, specify the graphics file using the following statement at the place where you want the graphics to display:

```
{command cFileName}
```

The graphics filename must not contain the drive or path. The path for graphics files is specified in the help project (HPJ) file. The *command* element designates how the graphics are aligned. Table 36.3 defines the graphics alignment commands.

Table 36.3. Graphics alignment commands.

Command	Description
bmc	Graphics object is aligned as a character. Any paragraph formatting applies to the graphics object. Text above and below does not wrap around a graphics object. The line height may increase due to the graphics object.
bml	Graphics object is aligned at the left margin. Text following the graphics object is aligned to its upper-right corner.
bmr	The graphics object is aligned to the right margin. Text is aligned with the upper-left corner of the graphics object. A bmr aligned graphics object should be placed at the beginning of a paragraph to ensure the proper wrapping of text around the left edge of the text.

Figure 36.9 shows an embedded graphics reference, {bmc music.wmf}, in the topic file. Figure 36.10 shows the resulting topic in the Help window.

You can make an entire graphic a hot spot by single- or double-underlining the graphics reference and following it with a context string. For example:

```
{bml airplane.bmp}ctrlFlying
```

When the user clicks a graphics reference that has a single underline, a popup text box appears containing the topic referenced by the specified context string. When the user clicks a graphics reference that has a double underline, the help system jumps to the topic referenced by the specified context string. In the preceding example, if the user clicks the airplane, the topic referenced by the ctrlFlying context string displays in the Help window.

FIGURE 36.9.

The Topic file with a graphics Microsoft metafile reference.

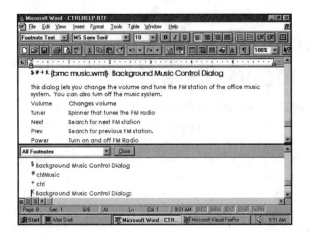

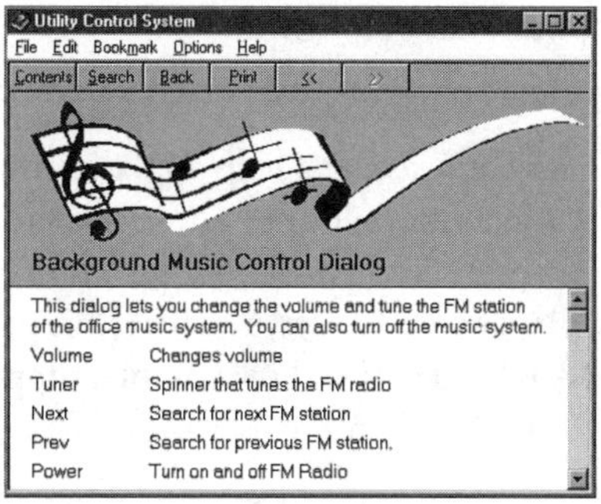

FIGURE 36.10.

The Help window showing the Microsoft Metafile reference defined in the Topic file shown in Figure 36.9.

You can use the Hotspot Editor to open a bitmap or a Windows Metafile and add hot spots to the existing graphics. First, open a file, and then draw a hot spot on the graphics. After you add a hot spot, double-click the hot spot to display the Attributes dialog box, as shown in Figure 36.11. Next, specify a context string of a topic in your topic file and a type of action to perform. By setting the Attribute field, you specify whether the borders of the rectangle that define the hot spot are visible or invisible. After you have finished specifying hot spots, save the file as a hypergraphic (.SHG) file.

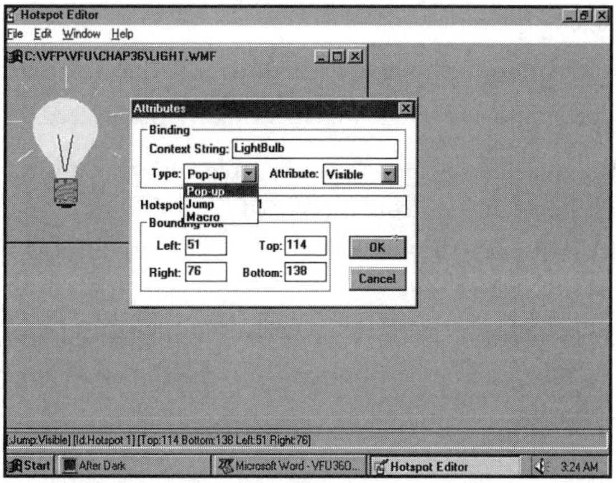

FIGURE 36.11.

The Hotspot Editor with the Attributes dialog box open.

Customizing Windows-Style Help with Macros

The Microsoft Windows Help system supports macros that you can use to customize the way that Windows Help works with your help file. You can employ macros to do any of the following:

- Add or remove custom buttons
- Add or remove custom menus

■ Execute applications from within Help

■ Execute external functions from external dynamic-link libraries (DLLs)

If you want the macro to execute a help application when help opens, place the macro in the help project (HJP) file. If the help application displays a topic, specify the macro with an exclamation mark (!) footnote. If the user chooses a hot spot and the macro activates the specified help application, place an exclamation mark (!) in the macro following the hot spot text. The macro is formatted as hidden text. For example, suppose that you have a graphic as a hot spot. In the following example, when the user clicks the hot spot, the `ExecProgram` macro executes:

```
{bml clock.bmp}!ExecProgram("CLOCK.EXE",0)
```

You must observe the following rules regarding help macros when you code a macro:

■ Macros are separated in a string with a semicolon.

■ Macros are not case-sensitive.

■ Specify empty space in a macro string by surrounding text in quotation marks.

■ When you insert special characters in a quotation-marked string, preface them with a back slash. Special characters are: (,), ", `, ', and \.

■ You can use either double quotation marks to enclose a string or single opening and closing quotation marks ('').

■ A macro can be used as an argument to another macro.

■ The length of a single macro string cannot exceed 512 characters.

There are many types of macros available with the Windows Help system. You can obtain a complete list of macros from the Visual FoxPro Professional Edition Help. It also provides you with a detailed description of each macro. Search for "Help Macro Reference" in the Visual FoxPro Professional Edition Help to get the most up-to-date list of macros.

The macros listed in Table 36.4 are used to reference buttons in the help system. You can use these macros to create new buttons or discard, disable, or modify the operations of the Help system buttons.

Table 36.4. Windows Help system macros that support Help buttons.

Macro	*Purpose*
Back	The Back macro displays the previous topic in the Back list.
BrowseButtons	The BrowseButtons macro adds the Browse buttons to the Help Button bar. Note that the help compilers (HC31.EXE and HC35.EXE) do not automatically install browse buttons. If you want them, you must add them in the [CONFIG] section of the help Project (HPJ) file. For example: [CONFIG] BrowseButtons()

Macro	Purpose
ChangeButtonBinding	This macro changes the assigned function of a help button.
Contents	This macro displays the Contents topic of the current Help file.
CreateButton	This macro creates a new button and adds it to the button bar.
DestroyButton	This macro removes a specified button bar button.
DisableButton	This macro disables a specified button bar button.
EnableButton	This macro enables a disabled button.
History	This macro displays the history list.
Next	This macro displays the next topic in a browse sequence.
Prev	This macro displays the previous topic in a browse sequence.
Search	This macro displays the Search dialog box. It is placed on the button bar by the compiler if any keywords exist.
SetContents	This macro designates a specific topic as the Contents topic.

Building Graphical Help for an Application

Now that you have created your topic file, you need to create a help project file. Then you can compile the help topic files and create the Windows-style help file for your application.

Creating a Windows Help Project (HJP) File

The compilation of a Windows help compiler is controlled by a help project (HJP) file. The help project file is an ASCII file that is used to build Windows-style help for the sample form set, CONTROL.SCX. The form set example is discussed earlier in this chapter and is presented in Listing 36.1.

Listing 36.1. The Help Project file, CTRLHELP.HFP, used to create Windows-style help for the CONTROL.SCX sample form set.

```
; Help Project File for Utilities Control System
[OPTIONS]
errorlog = ctrlhelp.err   ; Name of the file that will contain the error log
bmroot = .                ; Path for graphics files used in help
contents = ctrlContents   ; The context string for the Contents topic
compress = true           ; Specify that compression is used during the build
oldkeyphrase = false      ; Designate that help does not use an existing keyphase
warning = 3               ; Specify that you want all errors and warnings displayed

[FILES]
ctrlhelp.rtf              ; Name of Topic File
```

continues

Listing 36.1. continued

```
[CONFIG]
BrowseButtons()          ; Add  Browse buttons to button bar

[WINDOWS]
Main = "Utility Control System", , , , (192,192,192)
HowTo = "Step-by-Step", (575,495,423,490), , , (255,255,128), 1

[MAP]
ctrlMain        4
ctrlLights      1
ctrlHeating     2
ctrlMusic       3
```

The project table shown in Listing 36.1 contains sections ([*SectionName*]), such as [OPTIONS], [FILES], and so forth. Each section contains a specific type of information about the help file to be created. The order of the various sections within the help project file is unimportant, except as indicated in the following sections. The following sections of this book briefly describe each section of a help project file. If you need more detailed information, you can obtain it from the Visual FoxPro Professional Edition Help.

The *[OPTIONS]* Section

You use the [OPTIONS] section to specify options that control the build process. This section is optional. If this section is specified, it must be specified first. The most important options and their typical settings are described in Listing 36.1.

The *[FILES]* Section

The [FILES] section specifies topic files to be included in the build. This section is required.

The *[BUILDTAGS]* Section

The [BUILDTAGS] section specifies valid build tags. This section is optional. It is used to specify which topics are used in a build. For example, you can include a group of topics in the topic file that have a build tag footnote named AppVer1 using the following section:

```
[BUILDTAGS]
AppVer1
```

You can also specify a list of build tags separated by commas.

The *[CONFIG]* Section

The [CONFIG] section specifies user-defined menus and buttons used in the help file and registers dynamic-link libraries (DLLs) and DLL functions used as macros within the help file. This section is required if the help file uses any of these features.

The *[BITMAPS]* Section

You use the [BITMAPS] section to specify bitmap files to be included in the build if the BMROOT or ROOT options in the [OPTIONS] section are not specified. Otherwise, the [BITMAPS] section is not needed.

The *[ALIAS]* Section

You use the [ALIAS] section to assign one or more context strings to the same topic. This section is optional. If it is specified, it must be placed before the [MAP] section.

The *[MAP]* Section

You specify the [MAP] section to associate context strings with context numbers. This section is optional. In the example form set (CONTROL.SCX), the context numbers defined by the HelpContextID property of the forms in the form set are associated with the appropriate context strings used in the topic file. For example

```
[MAP]
ctrlMain        4
ctrlLights      1
ctrlHeating     2
ctrlMusic       3
```

The *[WINDOWS]* Section

The [WINDOWS] section defines the attributes of the primary Help window and types of secondary windows used in the help file. This section is required if the help file uses secondary windows. The syntax of an entry in this section is

```
typename = "Caption", (x, y, w, h), sizing, (clientRGB),
           (nonscrollingRGB), topmost
```

The attributes of the [WINDOWS] section entry are described in Table 36.5.

Table 36.5. Window attributes defined in the [WINDOWS] section.

Attributes	Description
typename	Designates the window type for which the other attributes are defined. The primary window typename is main. You can specify any unique name up to eight characters for a secondary window type (except main). When you specify a jump to a secondary window in the topic file, you specify the typename. For example:

continues

Table 36.5. continued

Attributes	Description
	`JumpTextContextString>WindowName`
	where `Window1` is the typename of the secondary window.
caption	Designates the caption that appears on the title bar. This caption is assigned the Help `TITLE` option in the `[OPTIONS]` section of the help project file for the `main` window.
x,y	Designates the horizontal and vertical position, respectively, of the upper-left corner of the window. The Help system uses a 1024×1024 coordinate system internally and maps this coordinate system onto the resolution of the video card displaying the help file.
w,h	Designates the default width and height of a secondary window. (Same coordinate system as x,y.)
sizing	Designates how a secondary window is sized when the Help system first opens it. 0 = Normal size 1 = Maximized
clientRGB	RGB background color of client window.
nsRGB	RGB background of non-scrolling region of window.
topmost	Number used to designate whether a secondary window always remains on top of all other windows. If this parameter is zero or omitted, the secondary window normally moves behind other windows. If `topmost` is 1, it helps
keep	the secondary window on top of other windows.

There are two windows defined in the `[Windows]` section of Listing 36.1. In the `Main` window, the non-scrolling region at the top of the window is colored light gray and the client region is colored white. The second window (`Howto`) is not actually used. However, its definition was added to illustrate the definition of a secondary window.

The *[BAGGAGE]* Section

The optional `[BAGGAGE]` section lists files to be placed within the help file's .HLP file. These are extra files that are accessed from the help file. The Help system can access these files faster than it can if they are separate MS-DOS files because the help file does not have to access the disk MS-DOS file allocation table. This speed improvement is especially important if the help file is stored on CD-ROM. Typically, multimedia files are specified in the `[BAGGAGE]` section. You can store as many as 1000 bitmap files in a `[BAGGAGE]` section.

Compiling the Graphical Help File

Now that you have created your help topic and project files, you are ready to build your Windows-style help file. Use one of the Microsoft Help Compilers (HC31.EXE or HC35.EXE). Because I used Word for Windows 6.0 to create the topic file and its RTF file is not compatible with HC35.EXE, I picked the HC31.EXE compiler. Both compilers are executed from MS-DOS. Following are the steps for creating the CRTLHELP.HLP help file for the CONTROL.SCX form set application:

1. Collect all of the files used in your custom help system in a directory. The files include CTRLHELP.HPJ, CTRLHELP.RTF, LIGHT.SHG, LIGHT.WMF, MUSIC.WMF, SUN.BMP, and BULLET.BMP.

2. Make that directory the current directory. For example:

   ```
   CD \VFP\APPS\CONTROL
   ```

3. Execute the Help Compiler from MS-DOS. For example:

   ```
   C:\VFP\HELPCOMP\HC31 CTRLHELP
   ```

The following code is the output from the Help compiler:

```
C:\VFP\vfu\chap36>\vfp\helpcomp\hc31 ctrlhelp
Microsoft (R) Help Compiler Version 3.10.505 (extended)
Copyright (c) Microsoft Corp 1990 - 1992. All rights reserved.
ctrlhelp.HPJ
...........
```

The program executes and creates the CTRLHELP.HLP Windows-style help file. Now execute Visual FoxPro and execute the CONTROL.SCX form. Now you can test your new help file. Click the Help menu, Contents option, and the help file displays as shown in Figure 36.12.

FIGURE 36.12.

Windows-style help contents screen for the CONTROL.SCX form application.

Summary

This chapter showed you how to create both DBF-style and Windows-style help for your application. You learned about the FOXHELP.DBF table, help topic files, help project files, and the Microsoft Help compilers and the hot spot editor.

If you devote sufficient time and effort in the design and implementation of an online help system for your application that meets the needs of your customer, you will benefit many times over as a result of reduced training and support costs, and also happier customers.

Interactivity and Interconnectivity

ODBC Integration

IN THIS CHAPTER

In the years to come, more and more applications will be independent from the database. The chosen software development language for accessing information from a database or Database Management System (DBMS) may simply be a front end to whatever database is used. Microsoft designed Visual FoxPro to take full advantage of this change in the way applications will be developed.

Visual FoxPro uses Microsoft's standard Open Database Connectivity (ODBC), which enables a system to establish a connection with a remote database. ODBC also enables applications to access data using Structured Query Language (SQL) as a standard. The SQL syntax is based on the SQL Access Group (SAG) SQL specification (1992).

ODBC is one of the core components of Microsoft's Windows Open Services Architecture (WOSA) and is rapidly gaining acceptance as the industry standard for data access. ODBC makes applications much more portable and scalable across different hardware and operating system environments.

This chapter explores how ODBC works. It also demonstrates how to configure ODBC connections for Microsoft Windows 3.1 and Windows 95 and how to use the Visual FoxPro interface to establish an ODBC connection and execute an updatable remote view or query.

Basics of ODBC

Understanding a few ODBC basics will help in installing and configuring remote data connections. The following basics are not specific to Visual FoxPro; they are generic and apply no matter what the chosen development language is or what database management system is used.

Components

The following are the basic components of ODBC:

- Application—Performs the processing, calls ODBC functions via SQL statements, and receives the results.

- Driver Manager—Initializes and loads the necessary ODBC drivers. This enables the application to function properly. Microsoft supplies the Driver Manager as a dynamic-link library; it runs as its own application outside of FoxPro.

- Driver—Receives and processes the call made by the application. The driver also contacts the data source and returns information to the calling application. Drivers are database-specific and are supplied by Microsoft or any other software vendor.

- Data Source—Consists of the remote (back office) database and operating system with which the application has established a connection via ODBC. The data source can be files of any type where an ODBC driver exists. For example, ODBC drivers exist for text, dBASE, FoxPro, Access, and SQL Server files. The data source can reside on a file server or a local system such as SQL Server.

Figure 37.1 shows a simple illustration of an ODBC connection; the application resides on a local system and the data source is located on a file server.

FIGURE 37.1.

The location of the ODBC components.

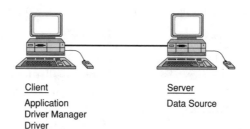

Client
Application
Driver Manager
Driver

Server
Data Source

Setting Up ODBC Connectivity

The following sections show you how to set up ODBC connectivity.

Installing ODBC Drivers

ODBC is not inherent in the operating system (such as Microsoft Windows 3.1 or Windows 95); therefore, it must be installed from a source such as a disk. If the appropriate option was selected at the time of installation, the Visual FoxPro setup routine installs the ODBC driver manager and drivers for several data types, including the following:

- Microsoft Access 2.0 database files
- FoxPro 2.*x* database files or tables
- Paradox Version 3.*x* and 4.*x* tables
- dBASE III and IV database files or tables
- Microsoft SQL Server database files
- Microsoft Excel spreadsheets
- Text (fixed and delimited)
- Oracle 7
- Btrieve tables

Using the Visual FoxPro ODBC installer is the simplest and recommended way of setting up all needed ODBC files for your system. However, in order for users of an application to connect to an ODBC data source, ODBC files must also be installed on their systems. Thus, a good understanding of what makes ODBC work is important.

Depending on which version of Microsoft Windows the ODBC setup program is run from, the following files are installed:

■ Microsoft Windows 3.1 and Windows for Workgroups 3.11 (16-bit drivers)

Filename	Description
ODBC.DLL	16-bit Driver Manager
ODBCINST.DLL	16-bit Installer DLL
ODBCADM.EXE	16-bit Administrator program
ODBCINST.HLP	Installer Help File
CTL3DV2.DLL	16-bit 3D window style library
xxxxxxxx.DLL	Selected data source drivers

■ Microsoft Windows 95 and Windows NT (32-bit drivers)

Filename	Description
ODBC32.DLL	32-bit Driver Manager
ODBCCP32.DLL	32-bit Installer DLL
ODBCAD32.EXE	32-bit Administrator program
ODBCINST.HLP	Installer Help file
CT3D32.DLL	32-bit 3D window style library
xxxxxxxx.DLL	Selected data source drivers

■ Initialization files (not platform-specific)

Filename	Description
ODBC.INI	Main ODBC initialization file
ODBCINST.INI	ODBC installed drivers initialization file

Additional ODBC drivers and installers are available from third-party sources and software vendors.

You install and manage drivers within the Microsoft Windows operating system. Once the drivers are installed, an ODBC Administrator icon should appear within the Control Panel window. Double-clicking this icon will invoke the ODBC administrator (ODBCADM.EXE). The ODBC administrator, otherwise known as the Data Sources dialog box, is shown in Figure 37.2. This dialog box displays a list of available (installed) data sources. After installation, the ODBC administrator can be used to add additional data source-specific drivers, manage connections, and so on.

Configuring and Managing ODBC Data Sources

The easiest way to manage ODBC data sources is by using the ODBC administrator. With the ODBC administrator you can add and delete ODBC drivers, add user IDs and passwords, and specify source file references.

Most changes made from within the administrator, with the exception of newly added drivers, are stored in the ODBC.INI file. Added drivers are stored in the ODBCINST.INI file.

FIGURE 37.2.

The Data Sources dialog box (ODBC administrator).

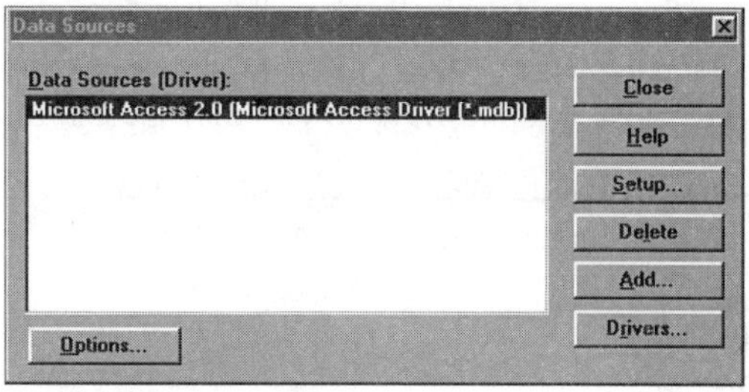

Tracing ODBC Calls

To display the ODBC Options dialog box, shown in Figure 37.3, click the Options button from within the Data Sources dialog box. In the ODBC Options dialog box, all ODBC calls can be traced and logged into a file if the Trace ODBC Calls option is selected. The default Trace file is SQL.LOG. By choosing the Trace ODBC Calls option, all SQL calls made to the database are recorded in the specified file. The Trace file is an ASCII text file; it can be viewed with any text editor. If both options are checked (Trace ODBC Calls and Stop Tracing Automatically), the log will be written to only once during a connection and will not be written to again after the ODBC connection is terminated. If the Trace ODBC Calls option is selected exclusively, the log file will continue to be written to during all ODBC connections until the option is turned off within the ODBC Options dialog box.

FIGURE 37.3.

The ODBC Options dialog box.

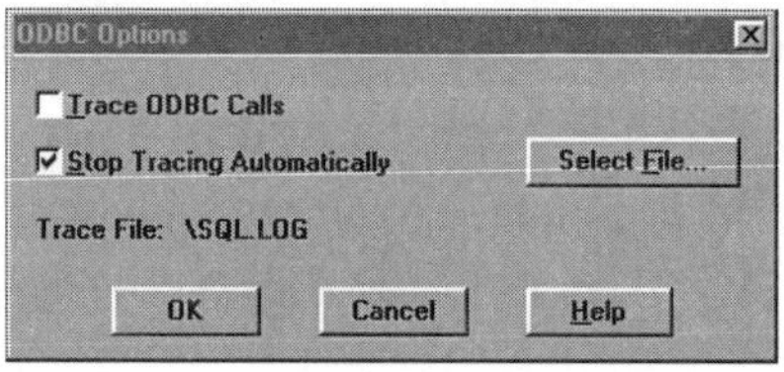

The log file is interesting to review and might contain valuable information; however, tracing ODBC SQL calls will slow up the connection process considerably. You should use this option only if you have problems connecting to ODBC data sources. If you decide to continue tracing ODBC calls with all data source connections, the log file might fill up the hard disk drive. For example, when I traced just one connection in which a single data table containing 100 records was browsed, a log file with over 400 entries was created. The second time the same table was browsed, over 400 additional entries were placed into the log file. Now the log file has more than 800 entries, after just two browse sessions.

Adding Entries to the Data Source Listing

Adding a new data source is a fairly simple process. Clicking the Add button displays the Add New Data Source dialog box. In the following examples, a slightly modified version of the North Winds database (spaces in table and field names were removed), which ships with Microsoft Access 2.0, is used to illustrate how to manage ODBC connections.

Select the Microsoft Access 2.0 entry and click the OK button to display the ODBC Setup dialog box, as shown in Figure 37.4.

FIGURE 37.4.

The ODBC Setup dialog box.

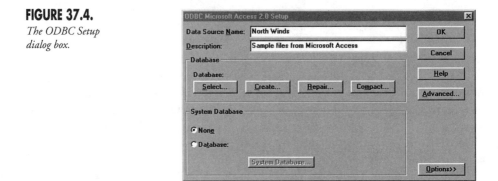

Each setup dialog box is unique to the specific ODBC driver. The Microsoft Access 2.0 ODBC driver, used in the following examples, is the Microsoft Access 2.0 ODBC driver that ships with Visual FoxPro. However, a driver installed on another system could differ from the one shown in Figure 37.4. Because some of the options shown in the setup dialog box might be specific to a particular ODBC driver, this section focuses on those options that are relatively common to most ODBC drivers.

The data source name and description can be any name that you specify. In this case, the entry is titled North Winds, with a description to match. The next step is to select the actual database file by clicking the Select button and displaying the Select Database dialog box, as shown in Figure 37.5. Here, it is possible to select the appropriate database file as well as selecting the options for read-only and exclusive connections. The read-only option, which prevents the ODBC connection from performing any updates to the database, might be quite acceptable to use. However, using the Exclusive option, which will not enable the database to be shared by any other connection or user, is not recommended.

Locating and selecting the North Winds database makes the ODBC data source entry specific to the North Winds database.

The Create, Repair, Compact, and System Database option buttons are specific to this particular Microsoft Access 2.0 ODBC driver; therefore, these option buttons are not discussed here.

FIGURE 37.5.

The Select Database dialog box.

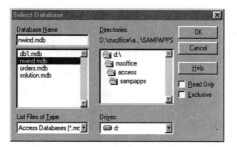

When you select the Advanced option button (see Figure 37.6), the display is once again specific to the chosen ODBC driver; however, this is where entries for any user IDs or passwords associated with a given database are usually made. In this case, the Login name of "admin" without a password (the Microsoft Access 2.0 default security) is shown. If the administrator of the North Winds database changes the default user ID (login name) or password, the ODBC setup can be changed here so that a later connection will be seamless to the user.

FIGURE 37.6.

The Set Advanced Options dialog box.

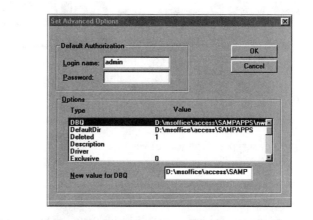

CAUTION

One note of caution regarding this particular Microsoft Access 2.0 ODBC driver: notice the System Database option in Figure 37.4. This option defaults to None. However, if None is selected and the default user ID (admin) is the administrator of the database, any connection to the Microsoft Access database will make the ODBC driver disregard any security defined by the administrator. Security might also not work at all. To force the ODBC connection to observe any security defined by the administrator of the Microsoft Access database, select the database option and select the appropriate access system database. Normally the system database resides in the access directory and is named SYSTEM.MDA. This particular security issue appears to be a quirk associated with this specific ODBC driver and might not be the same driver that ships with later versions of Visual FoxPro.

For the most part, ODBC drivers for client/server databases force the reading of the system table or security file. Therefore, circumventing the system database or table is generally not an issue and seems to be specific to this Microsoft Access 2.0 ODBC driver.

Select the Setup option button to redisplay the ODBC Setup dialog box. This enables you to make the appropriate changes to the setup of a specific ODBC data source.

Adding Drivers

You can add additional drivers by selecting the Driver option button. Selecting the Add button will display a prompt for a disk containing the driver to be added. In this case, the Add option is looking for an ODBC.INF file. Simply change the drive and directory to the area that contains the ODBC.INF file, and setup will take over. In some cases, third-party drivers can be installed in a different manner. If you are installing third-party drivers, follow the instructions that ship with the disks.

Visual FoxPro as an ODBC Client

Earlier versions of FoxPro (Version 2.5 or 2.6) could be used as a front end for ODBC connectivity via the FoxPro connectivity kit. However, there were quite a few limitations, and these versions really could not compete very well with more sophisticated products like Microsoft Access or PowerBuilder.

The following lists some of the limitations of earlier versions of FoxPro as an ODBC client:

- Picture data types were not converted to FoxPro general fields. Instead, picture data types were converted to non-functional memo fields.
- Native FoxPro table structures did not support many of the common data types found in ODBC data sources.
- Connectivity was either accomplished by using the Client/Server Query Wizard or by writing a lot of code.
- The Query Wizard was a one-pass process. In other words, once the wizard was used to establish the ODBC connection, the developer could not modify the results without either completely re-creating the connection from scratch or modifying the resulting code after running the wizard. A visual designer did not exist.
- At least in the case of connecting to a Microsoft Access database, only tables contained in the .MDB file were accessible from within Visual FoxPro.

With the introduction of Visual FoxPro, the limitations shown in the preceding list have been removed. Visual FoxPro was designed to be a flexible, easy-to-implement, and fast ODBC client. Visual FoxPro will set a new standard for programmable DBMS and ODBC front-end applications.

With Visual FoxPro the process of querying and viewing data differs only slightly from how native Visual FoxPro data is handled.

The approach to querying (read-only) an ODBC data source is essentially the same as querying a native Visual FoxPro table. The outline for data manipulation (read/update/delete) using ODBC data sources is as follows:

1. Establish the connection to the data source.
2. Perform a query according to the defined criteria into a modifiable cursor.
3. View or modify data contained in the cursor.
4. Update changed information in the data source.

Regardless of what or where the data source is (native Visual FoxPro tables or ODBC data sources), this is the preferred method of managing data. It is also Microsoft's recommended data management approach.

Because the query result set resides in a cursor (a standard Visual FoxPro table), forms, reports, and so on are designed exactly the same way as if a Visual FoxPro table had been used.

TIP

Using Microsoft's recommended data management approach of executing SQL statements resulting in Visual FoxPro cursors and performing SQL updates will enable an application to be more easily scaled or upsized. Also, if Microsoft's recommended data management approach is used, developers wanting to upsize to a remote client/server or other database can simply change the local view to a remote view without changing syntax, forms, reports, or most other segments of the application.

In many cases, the preferred approach to handling ODBC data is to use the combination of visually designing ODBC connections and remote connections, along with writing some amount of Visual FoxPro code. However, in the foregoing examples, the Visual FoxPro interface will be used to create and establish ODBC connections with a minimal amount of code.

Defining a Connection in Visual FoxPro

In Chapter 8, "Updating Data with Views," you established a remote connection. The primary way to access data is to use an ODBC connection with Visual FoxPro. Predefining the data source connections will make the development process considerably easier and will result in smaller program files.

From within the Project Manager (see Figure 37.7), let's define a new connection utilizing the Microsoft Access 2.0 North Winds example that was previously defined.

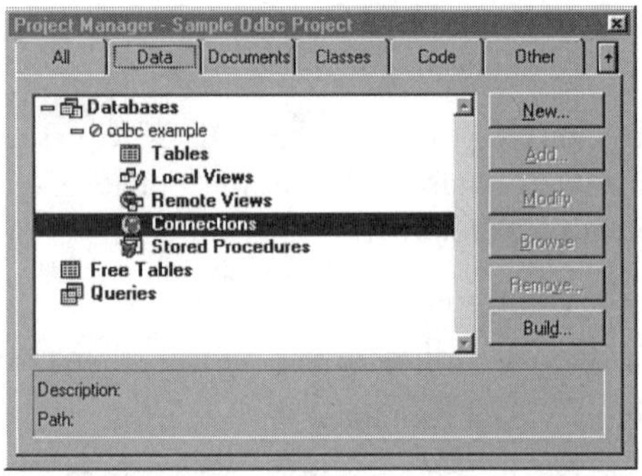

FIGURE 37.7.

The Project Manager.

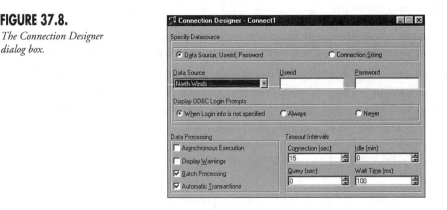

Make sure that a Visual FoxPro database exists or, if necessary, create one. Visual FoxPro stores all connections, as well as remote queries and views, in its database container (DBC). Drill down to the Connections option under the Data tab in the Project Manager and select the New option button. The Visual FoxPro Connection Designer dialog box appears (see Figure 37.8).

FIGURE 37.8.

The Connection Designer dialog box.

In the Data Source combo box, the Microsoft Access 2.0 North Winds database is listed, as shown in Figure 37.8. Remember that you used the ODBC administrator to add this defined data source.

Security: User IDs and Passwords

Normally, if the ODBC setup for a specific driver includes a valid user ID and password, the user ID and password section of the Connection Designer can be left blank. Most ODBC drivers will be launched without additional prompting for a user ID or password if they were included in ODBC setup (the ODBC.INI file). Placing a valid user ID and password in the specific ODBC setup saves time during the development process and enables the developer to create different setups for the user's system. However, even though the user ID and password were included in the data source setup of the North Winds database, the Microsoft Access 2.0 ODBC driver must have a confirmation of a valid user ID and password each time the connection is established. Therefore, once the connection is initiated, the user or developer will be prompted to key in a valid user ID and password.

One way around this issue is to key a valid user ID and password into the defined connection during the development process and to select the Prompt, When Login Information Is Not Specified option. This will prevent the Microsoft Access 2.0 ODBC driver from prompting the developer, helping speed up the development process. Just remember to remove the user ID and password from all of the defined connections before you install to the user's system (unless giving users the same access rights as the developer is not a problem).

Selecting the Always option will force users of the application to key in a valid user ID and password each time a connection to the ODBC data source is initiated. Use the Never option either when security is not an issue with the ODBC Data Source (dBASE and FoxPro 2.6 tables, for example) or the ODBC setup information already includes any necessary user IDs and passwords.

You can also set these security options by changing the Password, UserID, and DisipLogin properties with the SQLSetProp() function.

Asynchronous Execution

Visual FoxPro, by default, executes ODBC/SQL functions synchronously. *Synchronous* execution means that the ODBC driver does not return control to the Visual FoxPro application until the function call has completed its task. The Asynchronous Execution option shown in Figure 37.8 enables the application to perform other tasks while the ODBC/SQL functions are performing their tasks. Some ODBC drivers may not support Asynchronous Execution.

If the Visual FoxPro application makes a call to an ODBC/SQL function that cannot be executed asynchronously, the function will be executed synchronously.

According to Microsoft, ODBC queries issued from Windows for Workgroups or Windows NT client systems might be slightly faster if asynchronous processing is enabled. This option can also be set by changing the Asynchronous property with the SQLSetProp() function.

Displaying Warnings

The Display Warnings option is disabled by default. Selecting this option will display error messages returned from the ODBC driver. This option can also be set by changing the DispWarnings property with the SQLSetProp() function.

Batch Processing

The default setting for the Batch Processing option is on. Batch Processing controls how Visual FoxPro handles multiple result sets. With batch mode processing set to on, Visual FoxPro does not return any result sets until all result sets have been retrieved. Setting batch processing to off means that Visual FoxPro returns each result set individually. If Batch Processing is not selected, the calling application must repeatedly call the `SQLMoreResults()` function until a value of 2 (which indicates no more data is to be found) is returned to the calling application. This option can also be set by changing the `BatchMode` property with the `SQLSetProp()` function.

Automatic Transactions

The default setting for the Automatic Transactions option is on. Automatic transactions mean that each time the calling application makes a change to data in the result set, the changes are "automatically committed" to the ODBC data source. Some ODBC drivers do not support transaction processing and are always in the automatic mode. If Automatic Transactions is not selected, the calling application must issue one of the explicit transaction processing functions (such as `SQLCommit()` and `SQLRollBack()`) to conclude the transaction. This option can also be set by changing the `Transactions` property with the `SQLSetProp()` function.

Time-Out Intervals

Various timing options are included within the Connection Designer to handle such events as connection time-out in seconds, idle time-out in minutes, query time-out in seconds, and wait time in milliseconds. You can also set the time-out settings by changing the `ConnectTimeout`, `IdleTimeout`, `WaitTime`, and `QueryTimeout` properties with the `SQLSetProp()` function.

The defaults for most options shown in the Connection Designer can be set by choosing Tools | Options from the system menu, and then selecting the Remote Data tab.

Establishing the Connection

Next, establish a new remote view by highlighting Remote Views and clicking the New button. Select the New View option to display a list of the defined data source connections. Select the North Winds connection that was previously defined to display a list of tables contained in the North Winds database. For the purpose of this illustration, the Products and Categories tables were selected (right-click within the top half of the View Designer to add another table). The default join condition of `CategoryID` will be used. All fields were selected as output fields.

> **NOTE**
>
> At least in the case of a Microsoft Access 2.0 data source connection, the table listing shown in Figure 37.9 includes queries that were defined in Microsoft Access 2.0. These queries can be used in the same way that a Microsoft Access 2.0 table can be used. Using queries defined within Microsoft Access 2.0 is new to Visual FoxPro because earlier versions of FoxPro could react only to tables contained in the Microsoft Access 2.0 database.

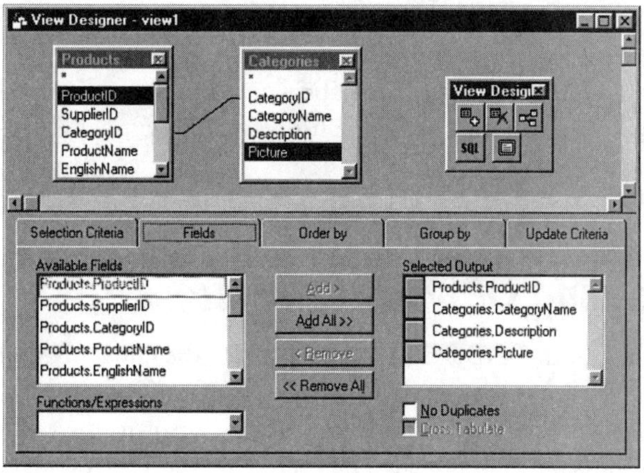

FIGURE 37.9.

The View Designer.

To execute this query/view, right-click and select Run Query. The result set is displayed in a browse window.

Running this query/view places the result set into a modifiable cursor. One of the most significant things here is that the Microsoft Access 2.0 table structures differ considerably from the normal Visual FoxPro table structures. The ODBC driver sends to Visual FoxPro a consistent SQL data type no matter what the data source is. Once the data type is received, Visual FoxPro converts the ODBC data type of each field into an equivalent Visual FoxPro data type. For example, a memo field contained in a Microsoft Access 2.0 table (that is, the Description field from the Category table) is translated by the ODBC driver into a SQL_BINARY data type and passed to Visual FoxPro. Visual FoxPro, in turn, translated the SQL_BINARY data type to a Visual FoxPro memo field.

Visual FoxPro has several new data types that did not exist in earlier versions of FoxPro. A few of the new data types are specifically designed to handle a remote connection to an ODBC data source. Some of the new data types are Datetime, Character (BINARY), and Memo (BINARY).

NOTE

Visual FoxPro supports table names longer than eight characters in Windows 95 and Windows NT, as well as long field names. However, you should not put spaces between table or field names in native Visual FoxPro table structures. Although Visual FoxPro tables are stored in the Visual FoxPro database container (DBC), they are still separate files with a .DBF extension. Visual FoxPro attempts to get rid of spaces contained in ODBC data sources by placing an underscore between words. For example, a Microsoft Access 2.0 table with the name Order Details will be interpreted by Visual FoxPro as ORDER_DETAILS. However, a word of caution applies here because spaces contained in table and field names do not conform with the standards set for SQL data access. Specifically, spaces in field names from an ODBC data source are not supported by Microsoft in Visual FoxPro and will present a problem with queries and views.

Updating ODBC Data Sources

You update an ODBC data source in much the same way that you view data in a cursor. First, Visual FoxPro sends a message to the ODBC driver requesting an update. Visual FoxPro next translates the data types contained in the cursor to the equivalent SQL data types and then issues the UPDATE command. The ODBC driver receives this call, translates the SQL data types to the native data types, and updates the table. If an update to the data source is unsuccessful, the ODBC driver sends the appropriate messages to Visual FoxPro.

As mentioned previously, writing code to send updates to the ODBC data source might be the preferred method of handling ODBC data. Writing code gives the developer a lot more control over how a data source is updated and assists in the handling of errors. However, a data source can be actively updated every time a change is made to the modifiable cursor if the Automatic Transactions option is turned on from within the Connection Designer. Also, if · you want to process automatic updates, you must go to the Update Criteria tab, select the fields to be updated, and then select the Send SQL Updates check box (see Figure 37.10).

FIGURE 37.10.

Update Criteria options in the View Designer.

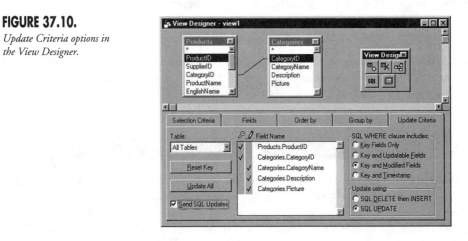

The beauty of Automatic update transactions is that almost all functions are performed by the ODBC driver as a background event within Visual FoxPro. Developers and users alike need not think about what is transpiring behind the scenes. The downside to Automatic updating of ODBC data sources is slower performance and lack of programmable control. Each time a change is made to the cursor, Visual FoxPro saves changed data to the ODBC data source after moving the pointer to another record. On large data tables, this can cause very slow performance.

You can undo each transaction by issuing a SQLRollBack() function, but only one transaction at a time will be undone. In other words, if a change was made to a record (the first transaction), with an immediate change made to another record (the second transaction), issuing a SQLRollBack() will reverse only the second transaction. The best way around this issue is to control the ODBC transactions manually by deselecting the Automatic Transactions option in the Connection Designer. If the Automatic Transactions property is set to manual, you can reverse multiple record changes by issuing one SQLRollBack() function.

Limiting the Scope of the View

For data files that do not contain a lot of records, you probably do not need to limit the number of records that are processed by the query. However, when you access remote or ODBC data, it is generally a good idea to impose a practical limit.

In most cases, you will not know how many records are contained in the ODBC data source. If you use the default query settings, Visual FoxPro will attempt to retrieve all records that meet the query criteria. The resulting data set could end up being extremely large and take a long time to process. Fortunately, Visual FoxPro enables the developer to impose several limits on data fetching. From the Query menu, select the Advanced query option to display the Advanced Options dialog box (see Figure 37.11).

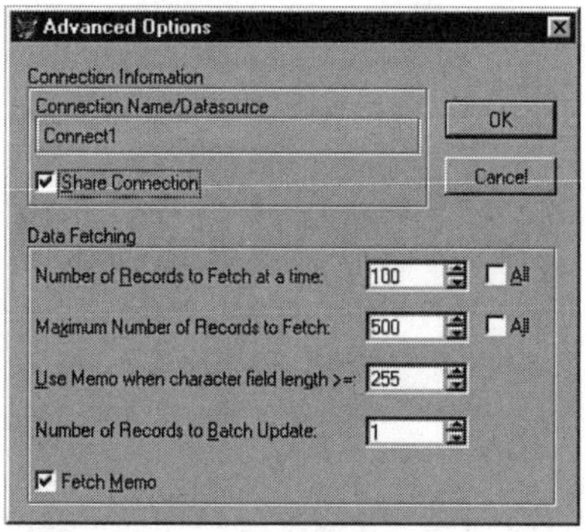

FIGURE 37.11.

The Advanced Options dialog box.

The Maximum Number of Records to Fetch option defaults to All. You should limit the records fetched to a more reasonable number, such as 50 or 100. If, during program execution, the result set does not return what the user is looking for, the view can be requeried with more specific information. For example, say that a request is sent to the ODBC driver for LASTNAME = "Smith". Also, assume that the number of records containing the LASTNAME of Smith is equal to 500, and the maximum number of records to fetch is set at 100. Obviously, the choice of

Smith is too broad, and the result set may not include the specific Smith (or group of Smiths) for which the user is looking. In this case, it would be wise to keep the maximum number of records to be fetched at the previously defined level and to requery the ODBC data source with something like FIRSTNAME = "Tom" .AND. LASTNAME = "Smith". The requery may contain only about 20 or 30 records that are an easily viewable and manageable subset of the original source.

If you want to learn more about how to fine-tune record fetching, as well as change other options listed in the advanced query options, read Chapter 38, "Client/Server Features."

Executing a Remote View

The following code segment is a simple Visual FoxPro program to perform a remote view based on an ODBC data source.

```
****************************************************
*   Sample Visual FoxPro program to execute
*   a remote view based upon an ODBC data source
****************************************************
*   Written by        : Ted Long
*   View name         :"NorthWinds"
*   Program name      : ODBCsamp.prg
*   DBC name          : ODBCsamp.dbc
****************************************************
*   Connection and    : Named connection = "NorthWind"
*   View parameters    : Automatic transactions = 1 (ON)
*                     : Asynchronous        = .T.
*                     : Batch Mode          = .T.
*                     : Display Warnings       = .F.
*                     : Data Source  = "MS Access"
*                     : Database     = "NorthWnd"
****************************************************
CLOSE DATABASE

OPEN DATABASE ODBCsamp    && Open the sample DBC file
USE NorthWinds            && Use the NorthWinds View
BROWSE LAST               && Browse the result
                     && set (cursor)
USE                       && Close the cursor
CLOSE DATABASE

RETURN
```

In this program example, changes made to the contents of a record will automatically update the ODBC data source if the field(s) being changed is marked within the view designer as updatable.

Stored Procedures

In client/server databases, precompiled procedures can be stored for future use. Stored procedures can greatly improve the speed of query execution. Visual FoxPro can use the `SQLExec()` function to take advantage of stored procedures. Each client/server database engine deals with stored procedures in a different manner.

For more information about the execution of stored procedures, refer to the documentation for your specific database server. Also, Chapter 38 has additional information about stored procedures.

Validation Rules in ODBC Data Sources

Visual FoxPro will not knowingly violate any validation rules contained in the ODBC data sources. However, the established validation rule must be a rule that Visual FoxPro can understand. Say that a validation rule has been defined within a Microsoft Access 2.0 table where the input for a field cannot be greater than 5. As long as the rule that was established is a simple one like our example, Visual FoxPro will respect this validation rule. If a change is made to this field from within the Visual FoxPro cursor and the input value exceeds 5, an error message will appear. The error message window will offer the option of reverting back to the original values the changes made to a record.

Visual FoxPro cannot work with validation rules that call functions native to the ODBC data source. Using the North Winds example, let's say that a validation rule has been defined for a specific field that calls the MS Access 2.0 message box function (`MSGBOX()`). Visual FoxPro does not recognize the native MS Access function and will return an error message no matter what is entered into the field.

Data Integrity

Visual FoxPro will respect the integrity of ODBC data sources with established relationships. In other words, if a Visual FoxPro application tries to update the contents of a key field within a table that is used in a defined relationship, an error will be generated and the data source will not be updated. Knowing how the relationships were established and what they consist of within the ODBC database is at least very helpful, if not necessary, before you develop any ODBC client application.

Summary

Installing, configuring, and managing ODBC drivers is not a difficult task. Designing connections and views within Visual FoxPro is also a relatively easy process. Visual FoxPro has the power, flexibility, speed, and programmability to be a good choice for front-end application development for ODBC data sources, including client/server applications.

For additional information regarding ODBC data connections, look up the following references:

- The Microsoft Knowledge Base—Available on CompuServe, Internet, and MSDN
- The Microsoft Developers Network (MSDN)
- ODBC Software Developers Kit (SDK) Programmers Reference—Microsoft Corporation

Client/Server Features

The development of large-scale applications in this generation is increasingly being built upon client/server architectures. It seems that most big businesses today are either downsizing mainframe and midrange systems or upsizing PC-based applications to this popular medium. The promise of the client/server architecture is alluring. Data distribution, portability across platforms, and access standardization are just a few of the potential benefits.

In the FoxPro 2.*x* era, client/server functionality existed as an add-on component. The lack of features such as the integration of client/server functionality with its Power Tools kept many from using FoxPro as a client/server development tool.

With the release of Visual FoxPro, this scenario has changed dramatically. Visual FoxPro gives you the ability to develop robust client/server applications visually, using the same powerful data-handling functionality that has given FoxPro its proud reputation. Using Visual FoxPro, you can now realize the promise of client/server development for your business.

Fundamentals of the Client/Server Architecture

The term *client/server* refers to the traditional two-tier method of accessing a centralized computer, called a *server*, with remote computers, or *clients*, across a networked infrastructure. The server utilizes a *relational database* to store and maintain data. Relational databases enable objects to be defined with consistent references to one another. The process of maintaining these references is called *referential integrity* and is often facilitated using mechanisms such as triggers and stored procedures. The server's operating environment, or platform, enables it to receive simultaneous messages and process requests from a wide variety of sources. These client requests are transmitted using a common language known as Structured Query Language, or SQL.

Although this basic definition is still essentially valid, the landscape of client/server is constantly changing and adapting to new technologies. The very nature of client/server gives you the ability to distribute the data and processing where it is most efficient. Today's systems can access many servers which, in turn, can be located in a variety of remote sites. In addition, new methods such as three-tier architectures, enterprise messaging, and multimedia are becoming more common. Development tools are also becoming more mature, offering more advanced object orientation, improved graphical user interface control, and better data handling.

Advantages of Client/Server

By embracing a client/server foundation, an organization is positioned to reap its many benefits. If implemented properly, the open nature of client/server can enable a company to adapt to future standards and technologies. The primary characteristics of its architecture offer several key advantages that form the cornerstone to selecting this important data management strategy.

- *Centralized repository.* In a client/server environment, data is stored on a central server and a single point of control is maintained across all applications and platforms. These database servers use a database management system, or DBMS, to define, store, and manipulate data. The server's database is generic; developers do not need to use a specific language or tool to access its data. Applications can be deployed in a variety of languages and tools while the data is accessed in a consistent and predictable manner. Using replication techniques, an organization can create data warehouses from which data is distributed throughout the various locations where it is needed. This technique maximizes performance without compromising the centralized model. Properly maintained, this centralization also reduces the potential of producing redundant data between applications, while maintaining referential integrity for all applications.

- *Server-based processing.* By taking advantage of server-based processing, organizations can reduce processing redundancy by employing vehicles such as triggers and stored procedures. Server-oriented processing standardizes such tasks as maintaining business rules, validations, and referential integrity so each successive application developer doesn't have to recode these rules. By migrating common business functions to stored procedures on a common server, developers can maintain data manipulation logic that is available to a large variety of languages and tools.

- *Performance.* The server is a specialized computer that is dedicated to processing a limited set of requests from its clients. Its only function is to process requests for its databases. These SQL requests facilitate efficient use of network traffic because only subsets of data are transmitted through the network. In addition, the servers and DBMSs are designed to handle massive databases without significant performance degradation.

- *Security.* Server operating environments such as UNIX, Windows NT, and OS/2 can offer a more secure platform for managing databases than standard network file servers. Mirroring, duplexing, and replication enable administrators to set up fault-tolerant servers able to withstand most disasters. In addition, scheduled backups enable administrators to maintain timely backups of mission-critical data. Most industrial-strength databases offer transaction logging, which provides an audit trail of all SQL submitted to the server. These databases also provide user definition and login security that protect valuable data from unauthorized access and manipulation.

NOTE

Visual FoxPro is not only an excellent development tool, but it is a very capable DBMS, as well. Although it shares many of the same criteria of a client/server database, the Visual FoxPro database engine is not an actual client/server DBMS. Its databases are not maintained independently on a server but are controlled by each individual application that accesses them. However, for many applications, the FoxPro DBMS is an excellent choice for developing medium- to large-scale applications without going to the expense and labor of setting up a client/server environment. In fact, for many applications, even those with large data sets, Visual FoxPro can actually outperform some client/server systems.

Some competing development products bundle a local desktop database product with their client/server tools. These desktop database managers are just that—desktop-oriented, confined to a single-user desktop installation. This might be convenient for prototyping, but not for deploying a critical application. These desktop database managers typically are very slow and often do not support multiple users. Visual FoxPro's native DBMS not only facilitates rapid prototyping, but it also supports multiuser installations, built-in referential integrity, and large data sets with remarkable speed. If your application doesn't require the specific benefits of a database server or if the costs of implementing a client/server architecture are too high, consider using Visual FoxPro's native DBMS.

The Costs of Client/Server

Of course, all of this power comes at a price. Although they have become less expensive in recent years, the price of deploying a client/server installation can be staggering, depending on your perspective. Servers require advanced processors, memory, massive hard disks, and industrial-strength operating systems to exist. Creating a truly fault-tolerant environment in addition can dramatically increase the bill. Licensing, installing, and maintaining high-end databases such as Oracle, Sybase, and Informix can approach tens, even hundreds of thousands of dollars. Deploying client applications almost guarantees the need for memory upgrades, new machines, and new operating systems. Enterprise-level client/server tools such as PowerBuilder, Oracle, or Smalltalk cost dramatically more than their desktop counterparts. Supplemental tools such as CASE, data modeling, SQL administration, and version control software typically carry the same premium price tags.

If all these up-front costs aren't enough, you will need the personnel to create and maintain this brave new world. Database administrators and software engineers command high salaries and can be hard to find. Retraining existing staff can also be costly and difficult. The dramatic paradigm shifts for administrators and developers often require significant "ramp-up" time and money. In addition, many of the tools are in early releases and remain immature and buggy, leaving personnel scratching their heads and spending hours on the phone with technical support. Sadly, early client/server projects launched with eager anticipation of the promised cost savings, reusability, and performance often go over budget due to these initial adjustments.

However, such is the cost of doing business. Many organizations that have traditionally used mainframe and midrange systems are already accustomed to this climate. However, smaller companies might find the tremendous commitment of setting up a client/server environment very daunting. Nevertheless, client/server is the predominant standard for corporate computing in this generation. It is an excellent infrastructure for providing information to the organization with integrity, speed, and security.

What Makes Visual FoxPro a Good Client/Server Development Tool?

The Visual FoxPro environment is well-suited to creating the client/server applications of today. It truly embodies the essence of a rapid application development tool by integrating a visual, object-oriented environment with a proven database language. Visual FoxPro puts dramatic emphasis on the visual aspect of development by enabling you to perform the majority of the work of building an application, such as creating and manipulating databases, object classes, forms, reports, and projects, truly *visually*.

The following are some of the new Visual FoxPro features that enable you to build robust client/server applications quickly:

- Enhanced visual designers
- Object-orientation
- Connections
- Remote views
- SQL pass-through functions
- Upsizing Wizard
- Transactions
- Table buffering
- Enhanced local DBMS
- Outstanding grid control
- OLE integration (future client/server methods will likely use OLE to access distributed objects)

The following are some of the "shopping list" features that Visual FoxPro does not currently have:

- Explicit, built-in version control features
- Explicit, built-in support for three-tier client/server architectures
- Native code compiler

A lot of what makes Visual FoxPro a good client/server tool is based not necessarily on what it has become, but what it has always been. After Ashton-Tate popularized the Xbase language in the early 1980s with dBASE, FoxBASE emerged as an ambitious dBASE clone. Xbase products, as they later became known, became very popular not only because of their English-like syntax, but because they had integrated database commands built into the language. Although it supported the same Xbase language syntax and native .DBF support, FoxBASE included a p-code compiler and handled data a lot faster than its competitors. Later, even though FoxBASE evolved into FoxPro and added numerous features, it remained true to the Xbase data-centric model. Eventually, FoxPro combined Xbase syntax with the popular SQL language, enabling developers to choose between linear, pointer-based processing, and set-based processing using standard SQL syntax on native database tables.

It is this intriguing combination that is the genius behind Visual FoxPro's client/server implementation. You can create applications that retrieve data from a variety of data sources using set-based SQL, and then process these data sets using the precision of Xbase conventions.

The Power of the Cursor

To understand how Visual FoxPro works with data sets, it is important to grasp the concept of the cursor. A *cursor* is a temporary Visual FoxPro table that is identical in structure and function to a standard database table. Like a memory variable or array, however, the cursor exists only in memory and never becomes a physical file. Once this table is closed or the Visual FoxPro session is terminated, it vanishes. Therefore, cursors are used to temporarily store, view, and manipulate data from the actual physical tables from which they are constructed.

Although cursors are used in a variety of ways, they are most often created as a result of invoking one of the many variations of the SELECT statement. The SQL SELECT command creates a result set from one or more tables utilizing various filter and sorting criteria. These statements can be explicitly declared, or they can be implicitly created when using visual queries, views, and forms. In addition, Visual FoxPro permits the creation of *heterogeneous* joining of local and/or remote data in these SELECT statements. This means that Visual FoxPro can join together data from more than one type of remote data source into one common cursor.

What is particularly special about Visual FoxPro cursors is that they are *updatable*. This means that changes made to these cursors are reflected back to the original tables automatically. Using special properties in the cursor's definition, Visual FoxPro tracks updates, additions, and deletions to the cursor and, because it remembers where each data element originated, sends these changes back to the source tables. What's more, it uses exactly the same data manipulation and buffering commands to accomplish this functionality that it uses when working with local data.

Because Visual FoxPro is particularly proficient at manipulating its own data types, it uses these cursors as the primary vehicle for working with remote data. Updatable cursors are used as an abstraction layer to all ODBC data sources, shielding the user from the complexities and eccentricities of the back end. Essentially, to Visual FoxPro all data sources "look and feel" like standard Visual FoxPro tables. Because these cursors can be both updatable and heterogeneous, data from a variety of disparate data sources can be simultaneously viewed and manipulated with standard Visual FoxPro conventions.

Anatomy of a Cursor

Because the cursor is used as a common "window" to all types of data sources, understanding the components of a cursor can enable you to have better control over your data manipulation.

Data Type Mapping

Because Visual FoxPro tables and cursors have identical data types, cursors that are created from local data are always a direct one-to-one reflection of their source tables. Remote data is different than local data in that it involves various data types which are specific to each unique data source. Visual FoxPro must ultimately assemble, or *map*, all these foreign data types into a cursor that is comprised of Visual FoxPro data types. Once the data is added, edited, or deleted in this cursor, the updates are sent back to the data source, returning again to the original data type.

How does Visual FoxPro accomplish this? Although cursors are an abstract layer between the user and the data source, they do not inherently know how to "talk" to a data source. These remote cursors utilize another layer called an *ODBC driver* (ODBC, or Open Database Connectivity, is described in detail in Chapter 37, "ODBC Integration"). These drivers have built-in intelligence about the specifics of interfacing with the back end. The ODBC specification dictates that these drivers present the unique data types of the data source as a standard set of ODBC data types. Therefore, instead of the cursors talking directly to the data source, they interface with a specific ODBC driver. This way, cursors only have to know how to translate its data types between one other set of data types. Table 38.1 illustrates the default data type mappings between Visual FoxPro and ODBC.

Table 38.1. Data type mappings from ODBC data source to Visual FoxPro.

ODBC Data Type	Visual FoxPro Data Type
SQL_CHAR, SQL_VARCHAR, SQL_LONGVARCHAR	Character or Memo
SQL_BINARY, SQL_VARBINARY, SQL_LONGVARBINARY	Memo
SQL_DECIMAL, SQL_NUMERIC	Numeric or Currency
SQL_BIT	Logical
SQL_TINYINT, SQL_SMALLINT, SQL_INTEGER	Integer
SQL_BIGINT	Character
SQL_REAL, SQL_FLOAT, SQL_DOUBLE	Double
SQL_DATE	Date
SQL_TIME	DateTime
SQL_TIMESTAMP	DateTime

The following is a list of rules for data type conversion:

- When converting character expressions, Visual FoxPro looks at the cursor's UseMemoSize property. If the length of the ODBC field is greater than the UseMemoSize property, Visual FoxPro creates a Memo field; otherwise, it creates a Character field. For more information on setting cursor properties, see the next section.

- If the original data source type is Money, Visual FoxPro will convert it into Currency.

- If unspecified, the day defaults to 1/1/1900 when converting DateTime fields.

- If the value in the SQL_TIMESTAMP field contains fractions of seconds, the fractions are truncated when the value is converted to a Visual FoxPro DateTime data type.

- Data types of cursor fields can be overridden by setting the DataType property. For more information on setting cursor properties, see the next section.

When a cursor is created from a remote source, it remembers each table's original data source and each field's data type. Therefore, when the cursor sends updates back to the remote server, it can remap each field back to its original data type. If using SQL pass-through functions (described in the section titled "Visual FoxPro SQL Pass-Through Functions") to send data that originated in Visual FoxPro to the remote server, Visual FoxPro converts its data types using the mappings shown in Table 38.2.

Table 38.2. Data type mappings from Visual FoxPro to ODBC data source.

Visual FoxPro Data Type	*ODBC Data Type*
Character	SQL_CHAR or SQL_LONGVARCHAR (see the rules following this table)
Currency	SQL_DECIMAL
Date	SQL_DATE or SQL_TIMESTAMP (see the rules following this table)
DateTime	SQL_TIMESTAMP
Double	SQL_DOUBLE
Integer	SQL_INTEGER
General	SQL_LONGVARBINARY
Logical	SQL_BIT
Memo	SQL_LONGVARCHAR
Numeric	SQL_DOUBLE

Here are the rules for conversion:

- If a Visual FoxPro field width is less than 255, it becomes a SQL_CHAR type in the ODBC data source; otherwise, it becomes a SQL_LONGVARCHAR type.

- Visual FoxPro Date fields are converted to SQL_DATE for all ODBC data sources except SQL Server, where it becomes SQL_TIMESTAMP.

Cursor Properties

Visual FoxPro cursors have many properties that dictate the content, behavior, updates, and connectivity of the data within it. Although some of these properties are read-only, many of them are updatable and can be modified at runtime. The most common ways to use updatable cursor properties are for controlling buffering and updates. Because the cursors themselves are temporary, these property settings are retained only for the life of the cursor. Two functions are used to view and update these settings. CURSORGETPROP() is used to view the property values, and CURSORSETPROP() is used to update them. The following table lists the properties that are updatable via the CURSORSETPROP() function and the values that are valid for each property. (The capitalized names are constants used from the FOXPRO.H header file, which is found in the VFP subdirectory.)

Property	*Values*
BatchUpdateCount	Specifies the number of buffered edits before the updates are sent to the remote server. Adjusting this value can yield performance gains. The default value is 1.
Buffering	1: Sets row and table buffering off. (Default value; Same as FoxPro 2.*x* behavior).
	2: Sets pessimistic row buffering on.
	3: Sets optimistic row buffering on.
	4: Sets pessimistic table buffering on.
	5: Sets optimistic table buffering on.
	SET MULTILOCKS must be on for all buffering modes except 1 (off).
FetchMemo	.T. Memo fields are fetched into the cursor.
	.F. Memo fields are not fetched into the cursor.
FetchSize	Sets the number of records progressively fetched from the server at a time. Set this value to -1 to retrieve the entire cursor. The default is 100 rows.
KeyFieldList	Comma-delimited list of primary fields for the cursor. A list of field names must be provided to permit updates to the cursor.
MaxRecords	The maximum number of rows fetched when result sets are returned into the cursor.
	-1: Retrieves all records (default).
	0: Returns no rows but executes query.

continues

Property	Values
SendUpdates	Global flag to enable updates to the cursor to be sent to the remote data source(s).
	.T. Update remote tables with any local updates to the cursor.
	.F. Do not update remote tables.
Tables	Comma-delimited list of the remote table name(s). This list of tables must be provided.
UpdatableFieldList	Comma-delimited list of fields from the remote table(s) and their local counterparts. This option can be used to change the local cursor's field names when necessary.
UpdateType	1: SQL UPDATE is used to update original data (default).
	2: SQL DELETE, and then INSERT is used to update original data.
UseMemoSize	This number is used to determine which fields are mapped into a memo field. Fields that are less than UseMemoSize become character fields. Valid UseMemoSize values are 1 to 255. The default value is 255.
WhereType	This property specifies how Visual FoxPro determines whether an update has been made. The valid WhereType values are
	1 or DB_KEY. The primary fields specified with the KeyFieldList property are used.
	2 or DB_KEYANDUPDATABLE. Same as DB_KEY and includes updatable fields.
	3 or DB_KEYANDMODIFIED (default). Same as DB_KEY and includes any modified fields.
	4 or DB_KEYANDTIMESTAMP. Same as DB_KEY and includes a comparison of the time stamps.

NOTE

Visual FoxPro does not generate a compiler error when a property is misspelled or an invalid value is specified. However, the CURSORSETPROP() function will generate an error at runtime.

Cursor 0: The "Mother of All Cursors"

When cursors are created, they inherit the property settings of the environment cursor, known as cursor 0. Cursor 0, an internal component of the active session, is used as a template for setting default values for each cursor created during the session. When CURSORSETPROP() is used to specify settings for a created cursor, these default values are overridden for the new cursor only. CURSORSETPROP() can also be used to temporarily override cursor 0's property settings by simply specifying 0 as the cursor number parameter. The property settings for cursor 0 can be permanently changed in the Tools | Options | Data | Remote Data screen on the Visual FoxPro main menu.

Cursor Update Properties

To fully leverage the power of the cursor, the cursor needs to be made updatable. Although in many cases, such as in views, the property settings for the cursor are automatically ready to be updatable, the cursor, by default, will not actually send the update statements to the remote server. In fact, some cursors are read-only by default, as is the case for the SQL pass-through function SQLEXEC(). In either case, for a cursor to be updatable, five key properties must be set. Furthermore, for updates to be sent to the remote server, the SendUpdates property must be set to .T. (true). Table 38.3 shows a list of the five properties that must be set for a cursor to be updatable.

Table 38.3. Updatable cursor properties.

Property	Default Setting
Tables	Includes all remote tables that have data that was retrieved into the cursor, have updatable fields, and have at least one primary key field.
KeyField	Remote database key fields and primary keys on the table(s).
UpdateName	table_name.column_name for all fields.
Updatable	A list of all columns designated as updatable. In many cases, such as when serialized insert triggers are defined, the primary keys are not included here.
SendUpdates	Defaults to .F.. If you change it to .T., that becomes the default for all views created in the session.

TIP

You can convert a read-only cursor from a SQL pass-through function into an updatable cursor by setting these five update properties. You can also use the

CURSORSETPROP() function to control the buffering on these cursors. The following code illustrates how to set the update properties:

```
*-- This code enables updates to the Authors table.
*-- Only certain fields are made updatable here.
*-- Errors are not processed in this example.

lnHandle = SQLCONNECT('Pubs_Connect')
lnRet = SQLEXEC(lnHandle,"select * from Authors")

lnRet = CURSORSETPROP("Tables","Authors")
lnRet = CURSORSETPROP("Keyfield","au_id")
lnRet = CURSORSETPROP("UpdateName",;
                      "au_id    Authors.au_id,;
                       au_lname Authors.au_lname,;
                       au_fname Authors.au_fname,;
                       phone    Authors.phone,;
                       contract Authors.contract")
lnRet = CURSORSETPROP("UpdatableFieldList",;
         "au_id, au_lname, au_fname, phone, contract")
lnRet = CURSORSETPROP("SendUpdates", .T.)

BROWSE              && Change some data in this BROWSE

=TABLEUPDATE()      && Changes are updated to database
=SQLDISCONNECT(lnHandle)
```

Using Visual FoxPro Remote Views

Remote views are likely to be the primary component for developing most Visual FoxPro client/server applications. They are the main vehicle used to manipulate data on a remote server as if it were familiar, native Visual FoxPro data. Remote views are easy to work with because when you are working with a remote view, you are actually using a cursor. The remote view is actually an interface to a specific kind of updatable cursor. Encapsulated within the remote view are all of the properties that enable it to retrieve a specific set of remote data, update each of its source tables, and communicate with the remote server.

The remote view is actually a result set from a SQL SELECT statement that is returned to you in the form of an updatable cursor. When you create a remote view, you are actually creating a definition, or blueprint, which combines the SQL statement elements along with the connection information. Only when the remote view is used does the request get sent to the remote server which, in turn, creates the updatable cursor.

Remote views are often described as *persistent*, which means they are a permanent named definition that can be referred to and reused in a consistent manner. Like Visual FoxPro tables and local views, they are stored permanently in a database container, or DBC.

One of the most important characteristics that remote views share with Visual FoxPro tables is that they can be manipulated *visually*. They can be created with their own designer, the View Designer, which is almost identical to the Query Designer. Like Visual FoxPro tables, remote views are visible objects in the Database Designer, so they can be managed together. Perhaps more significantly, they can be visually manipulated when you are designing forms and reports. All of the same time-saving conventions such as drag and drop into data environments, form controls, and report fields are available using remote views.

Connections

Before you create remote views, you will probably want to create a *connection*. Stored in the database, a connection is a persistent definition used to consistently control an ODBC connection. Although you can create a remote view that connects directly with an ODBC data source definition, there are several advantages to using connections. Unlike direct ODBC data sources, connections encapsulate login, processing, and connection timeout information into one named definition. Remote views created from these named connections eliminate the need to set these properties manually. Because views inherit the property settings from named connections, a single source of control for changing the behavior of several remote view definitions is provided by using connections. In addition, connections can be reused, which can significantly reduce the number of active connections on the server.

In Visual FoxPro, you can create and store a named connection definition in a database, which you can then refer to by name when you create a remote view. You can also set properties on the named connection to optimize the communication between Visual FoxPro and the remote data source. When you activate a remote view, the view's connection becomes the pipeline to the remote data source.

> **CAUTION**
>
> Be careful when you modify connections that are accessed by existing remote views. If you change the data source of remote views used by forms or reports, you could create invalid references.

Shared Connections

Another advantage to using named connections is the ability to share them. A connection that is established with a remote server can be very "expensive"; it uses a lot of memory, and it requires time to connect to the server. In addition, using multiple connections can be, literally, expensive in that some servers are licensed by the connection. Using shared connections can significantly reduce the number of simultaneous connections on the server. However, there is a trade-off in local performance perception when you use remote views because all shared connection activity must be done sequentially, or serialized. When you use exclusive connections on remote views, each instance of a remote view establishes a new connection to the server. Because Visual FoxPro can execute multiple commands to the server simultaneously, several concurrent connections would be required to carry out the instructions. Depending on your situation, this might be the desired effect.

When you use remote views, you can specify the use of shared cursors either with language or by accessing the Query | Advanced Options menu selection from the Visual FoxPro main menu if the View Designer is active.

Connection Properties

Like cursors, when connections are activated, they have many properties that can be viewed and manipulated at runtime. These properties control certain aspects of the connection such as login, processing, transaction, time-out, and ODBC information. Remote views that use these connections inherit these property values. Connection properties are accessed in a very similar fashion to their cursor siblings, through the SQLGETPROP() and SQLSETPROP() functions. The following is a list of the properties that can be viewed and changed by these functions. (The capitalized names are constants used from the FOXPRO.H header file, which is found in the VFP subdirectory.)

Setting	*Description*
Asynchronous	.F. indicates synchronous mode (the default). .T. indicates asynchronous mode.
BatchMode	.T. returns result sets all at once (the default). .F. returns result sets individually using SQLMORERESULTS().
ConnectBusy	.T. indicates that a shared connection is busy. .F. indicates that a shared connection is available. This is a read-only property.
ConnectName	The name of the connection. This is a read-only property.
ConnectString	The login connection string, if used. This is a read-only property.
ConnectTimeOut	The number of seconds allowed for a connection to execute before generating an error. Specify a 0 for an indefinite wait (the default). ConnectTimeOut can be 0 to 600.
DataSource	The name of the data source as defined in the ODBC.INI file.
DispLogin	Contains a numeric value that determines when the ODBC Login dialog box is displayed. The valid DispLogin values are 1 or DB_COMPLETE. The ODBC Login dialog box is displayed when login data is needed.

	2 or DB_PROMPT. The ODBC Login dialog box is always displayed.
	3 or DB_NOPROMPT. The ODBC Login dialog box is never displayed. An error occurs if the required login information isn't available.
DispWarnings	.T. Display error messages.
	.F. Do not display error messages (the default).
IdleTimeout	The number of seconds that an idle connection is allowed to stay active. Specify 0 to wait indefinitely (the default).
ODBChdbc	The internal ODBC connection handle. This is a read-only property.
ODBChstmt	The internal ODBC statement handle. This is a read-only property.
PacketSize	Specifies the size of the network packet in bytes. The default value is 4,096 bytes.
Password	The connection password. This is a read-only property.
QueryTimeOut	The number of seconds before a running query is timed out. The value must be between 0 and 600. Specify 0 for an indefinite wait. The default value is 15 seconds.
Transactions	Determines the transaction mode for this connection.
	1 or DB_TRANSAUTO. Automatic mode. Each statement is considered a separate transaction.
	2 or DB_TRANSMANUAL. Manual mode. Transactions must be manually handled using the SQLCOMMIT() and SQLROLLBACK() functions.
UserId	User identification used for login.
WaitTime	The number of milliseconds the SQL query has to execute before it is checked. The default is 100 milliseconds.

CAUTION

If you are using Novell Netware to access SQL Server, you must set the PacketSize property to 512KB or you will not be able to connect to a SQL Server data source. This currently is the case for 16-bit ODBC using standard Netware drivers. Other network configurations might also require this adjustment. If you are not experiencing problems with your remote connection, leave the PacketSize parameter at the default setting of 4,096. The higher setting will result in better performance. The SQLSETPROP() function can be used to temporarily change the active connection, but you can use the DBSETPROP() function to permanently set this property for a named connection in a database, such as in the following example:

```
= DBSETPROP('MyConnect','CONNECTION','PacketSize',512)
```

The SQLSETPROP() function returns 1 if it is successful. It returns -1 if a connection-level error occurs or -2 if an environment-level error occurs.

Connection properties can also be accessed at the database level with the DBGETPROP() and DBSETPROP() functions. These functions are covered in detail later in the chapter in the "Creating Remote Views" section and the sections on SQL pass-through.

Connection 0: The "Mother of All Connections"

When connections are created, they inherit their settings from the environment connection, or connection 0. The property settings for the environment connection can be controlled with the SQLSETPROP() function by using 0 as the connection number. Each option set at the environment level then serves as a default value for subsequent connections. Errors generated from the SQLSETPROP() function that return -2 denote an environment error and can be viewed by using SQLGETPROP() using 0 as the connection number.

Creating Connections Visually

Before you can create a connection, you must have created at least one ODBC data source outside of the Visual FoxPro environment. See the earlier section on ODBC Integration for more details on creating ODBC setups. You can access the Connection Designer either by opening a database and typing CREATE CONNECTION from the command window or by using the following steps:

1. Open an existing project in the Project Manager. If one doesn't exist, create a project and create a database in it.
2. Select the Data tab from the Project Manager.
3. Select the desired database in which to create the connection. If the database elements are not visible, expand the list by clicking the + symbol.
4. Select the Connections option in the list and click the New command button on the Project Manager.
5. The Connection Designer appears as in Figure 38.1.

In the Connection Designer, you simply need to specify an ODBC data source to define a connection. However, it is a good idea to supply at least the login user ID and password for the development process unless you want to be prompted for login information every time you use this connection in a remote view.

When you close the Connection Designer window, you will be asked if you want to save the connection and then be prompted for a name for your connection. Type in your name and press Enter. When you return to the Project Manager, you should see your new connection appear in the list, ready for use. You can also save the connection from the toolbar or select File|Save from the menu before you exit the Connection Designer.

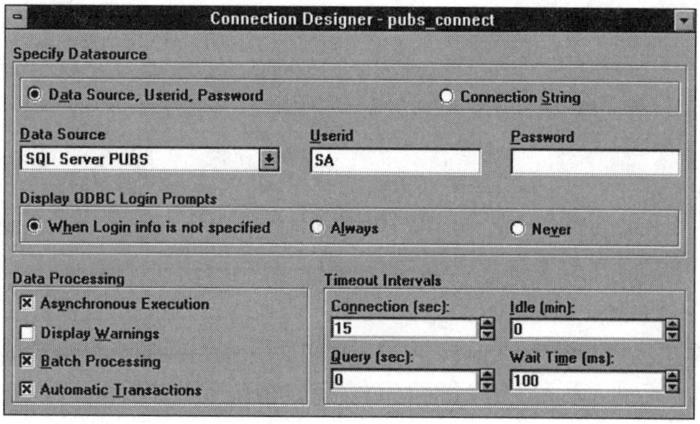

FIGURE 38.1.

The Connection Designer.

Creating Connections with Language

To create a connection in the MyData database that stores the information needed to connect to the ODBC data source `SqlServer6`, you can enter the following code to supply just the user ID information:

```
*-- This code will prompt the user for User_ID and Password
OPEN DATABASE MyData
CREATE CONNECTION MyConnect DATASOURCE SqlServer6
```

or

```
*-- This code will prompt the user for the Password only
OPEN DATABASE MyData
CREATE CONNECTION MyConnect DATASOURCE SqlServer6 USERID sa
```

The connection will still prompt you for the password when you connect if `DispLogin` is set to `.T.`.

If you want to see a list of all of the available connections for a specified database, type either of the following from the command window:

```
OPEN DATABASE MyData
DISPLAY CONNECTIONS
```

or

```
OPEN DATABASE MyData
LIST CONNECTIONS
```

Creating Remote Views

When you develop client/server applications, remote views will handle the majority of the data. There are two ways to create remote views: visually and with language.

Creating a Remote View Visually

You can access the View Designer either by opening a database and typing CREATE SQL VIEW REMOTE from the command window or by using the following steps:

1. Open an existing project in the Project Manager. If one doesn't exist, create a project and create a database in it.

2. Select the Data tab from the Project Manager. The Project Manager displays a list of all databases defined for this project.

3. Select the database in which you want to create the remote view. If the database elements are not visible, expand the list by clicking the addition (+) symbol.

4. Select the Remote Views option in the list and click the New command button on the Project Manager.

5. The New Remote View dialog box appears. You can select between using the Remote View Wizard or New View. Select the New View option.

6. The Select Connection or Datasource dialog box appears. Select the desired connection or ODBC data source in the list and click the OK button.

7. The Open dialog box appears; it lists all of the available tables within this data source. Select the table that will be the primary table in the remote view and click the OK button. The View Designer appears as in Figure 38.2.

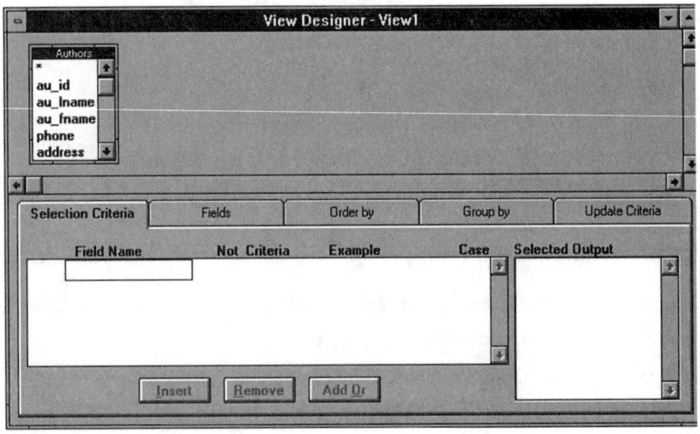

FIGURE 38.2.

The View Designer.

Once you are in the View Designer, you need to specify output fields in the Fields tab and key fields in the Update Criteria tab as the minimum requirement for an updatable remote view. However, it is a good idea to add more detail to the view. The level of detail depends on the purpose of the view. The following is a list of the typical selections for building an updatable remote view suitable for use in a form.

Selection Criteria Tab

Unless you are working with very small tables, it is a good idea to filter your remote view to maximize performance. When you specify selection criteria here, you are essentially building the WHERE clause of the SQL SELECT expression that is sent to the remote server. Use the following steps to complete this tab:

1. Select the Fields column, and a drop-down list appears; from this list, select the field on which you want to filter.

2. Select the comparison operator in the Criteria column drop-down list. You can reverse this expression by selecting the Not column.

3. Type the expression to filter on in the Example column. If the expression will vary each time the query is run, you can create a parameterized view. For more on creating these views, see the "Parameterized Remote Views" section later in the chapter.

Fields Tab

When you use remote views, it is a good idea to retrieve only the fields that you absolutely need. This reduces the size of the result set that is returned. There are a number of ways of selecting fields for your remote view.

- Select the field from the Available Fields list and double-click it. It now appears in the Selected Output list.

- Select the field from the Available Fields list and drag it to the Selected Output list. It now appears in the Selected Output list.

- Select the field from the Available Fields list and click the Add > button. It now appears in the Selected Output list.

- Select a group of fields from the Available Fields list and click the Add > button by using either the Shift or Ctrl keys while clicking. The group now appears in the Selected Output list.

- Click the Add All > button. All of the Available Fields now appear in the Selected Output list.

NOTE

At least one field must be in the Selected Output list for the view to be created.

You can reverse each of these techniques by using the Remove buttons (< and <<) instead of the Add buttons (> and >>). You can rearrange the order of the fields in the list by dragging the mover button for a selected field in the Selected Output list up or down.

TIP

You can also use the table windows in the upper portion of the View Designer as a drag source. For example, click the * in the columns list in the displayed table and drag into the Selected Output list. The entire list of columns appears in the Selected Output list.

Order By Tab

This option sets the order of the result set. An unordered result set returned from a remote view can be very confusing to interpret. Local indexes are not used or created when you select an Order By condition; the result set is ordered at the server before populating the local cursor.

The same conventions used in the Fields tab are used to select fields here.

Update Criteria Tab

The Update Criteria details must create an updatable remote view. To designate the view to be updatable, you must have selected enough columns to constitute a unique key, such as the primary key of the source table. The following steps illustrate how to make a view updatable:

1. From the Table drop-down list, select the table to be made updatable. The Field Name list will be filtered to display only the fields from the selected table.

2. Identify and select the key fields for the remote view by clicking the button beneath the key symbol in the Field Name list. A check mark will appear by your selection(s).

3. You can now select the updatable field list. The easiest way to do this is to click the Update All button. This will select all fields but the key fields as updatable. One of the reasons for not making the key fields updatable is that some servers support serialized key fields, which means that the server will automatically generate a key field value with an Add trigger when new records are added. If your server is generating key fields or if your application will not be creating the key field values, do not check the key fields as updatable. Otherwise, you can select the key fields to be updated by manually clicking the button beneath the pencil symbol.

4. Pick an option in the SQL WHERE Clause Includes option group. Your selection will determine the fields that are used in the WHERE clause of the SQL update code. The update process will compare the fields you have selected here to the original fields from the remote server to determine if the data has changed or not. The most common selection is the Key and Modified fields option.

5. Pick an option in the Update Using option group. Your selection will determine the SQL update action that will occur when a change is being sent to the remote server. If you select SQL UPDATE, an UPDATE statement with a WHERE clause will be sent to the remote server. If you select SQL DELETE and then SQL INSERT, a DELETE with a WHERE clause will first delete the matching record, and then an INSERT statement will create a new record. Depending on the DBMS, the latter technique is sometimes used in conjunction with updatable key fields.

6. Finally, select the Send SQL Updates check box if you want the view to be updatable. Even if you have selected fields to be updated, no updates will be sent to the remote data source if this box is not checked.

If your server supports it, use timestamps in remote views that contain many fields. You can then use the Key and timestamp option to update your view. Using this option will cause Visual FoxPro to compare only the key fields and one timestamp field rather than all updatable fields or all modified fields when updating a view. Using this option can dramatically enhance performance of view updates, deletes, and inserts.

The Update Criteria tab options are shown in Figure 38.3.

FIGURE 38.3.

The Update Criteria tab.

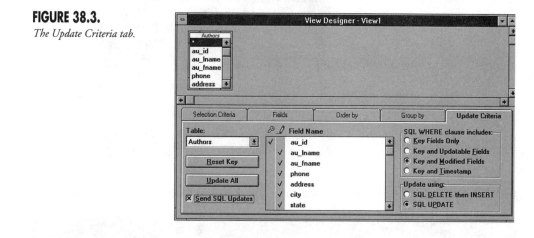

When you close the View Designer window, you will be asked if you want to save the view and then you are prompted for a name for your remote view. Type in your name and press Enter. When you return to the Project Manager, you should see your new remote view appear in the list, ready for use. You can also save the view from the toolbar or select File | Save from the menu before you exit the View Designer.

You can now click the Run icon (!) on the Visual FoxPro toolbar to execute the remote view and display its output in a browse window.

Using a Wizard to Create a Remote View

You can access the Remote View Wizard either by opening a database and choosing New from the toolbar, by selecting File | New from the menu, or by using the following steps:

1. Open an existing project in the Project Manager. If one doesn't exist, create a project and then create a database in it.

2. Select the Data tab from the Project Manager.

3. Select the desired database in which to create the remote view. If the database elements are not visible, expand the list by clicking the plus (+) symbol.

4. Select the Remote Views option in the list and click the New command button on the Project Manager window.

5. The Remote View Wizard dialog box appears as in Figure 38.4.

    You can select either the Remote View Wizard or New View. Select the Remote View Wizard button.

FIGURE 38.4.

The Remote View Wizard dialog box.

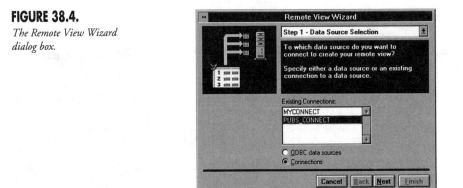

6. The Wizard will guide you through some simple steps to create the remote view.

TIP

You can save time by not using the Remote View Wizard. Although it can be helpful when learning, the Remote View Wizard is not much easier to use than the View Designer. The View Designer is so easy to use that using the Remote View Wizard will probably slow you down.

Using Language to Create a Remote View

Although it is far easier to create a remote view visually, you still can create one using the Visual FoxPro language. The following is an example of creating a remote view using a shared connection. Note that the CREATE SQL VIEW command requires exclusive use of the database. In addition, a connection needs to be created first.

```
OPEN DATABASE MyData EXCLUSIVE
CREATE SQL VIEW MyView ;
  CONNECTION Pubs_Connect ;
```

```
    SHARE ;
    AS Select * from pubs..authors order by au_id
USE MyView
BROWSE NORMAL
USE IN MyView
CLOSE DATABASE
```

The following example shows the same remote view created directly from an ODBC data source without a connection.

```
OPEN DATABASE MyData EXCLUSIVE
CREATE SQL VIEW MyView ;
  REMOTE SQL_Server60 ;
  AS Select * from pubs..authors order by au_id
USE MyView
BROWSE NORMAL
USE IN MyView
CLOSE DATABASE
```

Parameterized Remote Views

One of the most important techniques in developing Visual FoxPro client/server applications is using *parameterized views*. Parameterized views are created with special selection criteria which have values that are provided at runtime or programmatically. If the values don't already exist when the view is created, the user is prompted for the values with a popup window.

Parameterized remote views are created like other views except that you preface the selection criteria values with a question mark character. The values that are supplied are often memory variables or form properties but can also be valid Visual FoxPro expressions. If you use an expression, enclose the expression in parentheses so the entire expression will be evaluated. A parameterized expression in the View Designer appears as in Figure 38.5.

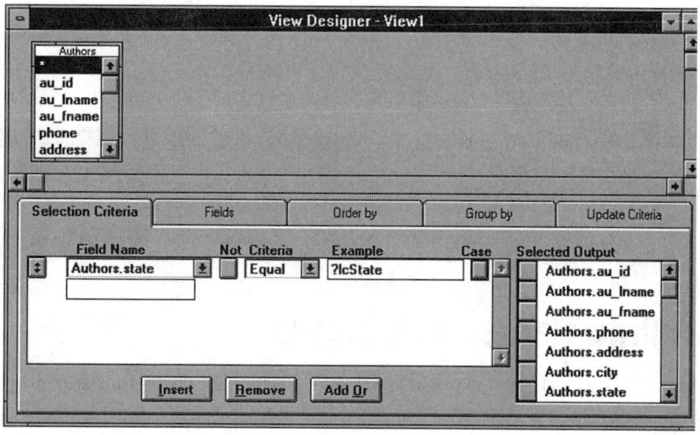

FIGURE 38.5.

Creating a parameterized view in the View Designer.

The following example of a parameterized view shows how to use the REQUERY() command to respond to a new parameter value:

```
lcState = 'CA'

OPEN DATABASE MyData EXCLUSIVE
CREATE SQL VIEW MyView ;
  CONNECTION Pubs_Connect ;
  SHARE ;
  AS Select * from pubs..authors where authors.state = ?lcState order by ;
    au_id
USE MyView
BROWSE NORMAL

lcState = 'UT'
=REQUERY( )
BROWSE NORMAL

USE IN MyView
CLOSE DATABASE
```

The following example shows how to use a quoted string as the parameter value, which will result in the user being prompted with your customized string. This technique could also have been used in the View Designer.

```
OPEN DATABASE MyData EXCLUSIVE
CREATE SQL VIEW MyView2 ;
  CONNECTION Pubs_Connect ;
  AS Select * from authors where state = ?'Home state of Author' order by au_id

*-- Upon opening, the view will prompt the user for the state value
USE MyView2

BROWSE NORMAL
USE IN MyView2
CLOSE DATABASE
```

When the preceding code sample is run, Visual FoxPro automatically prompts for a value using the custom string, as shown in Figure 38.6.

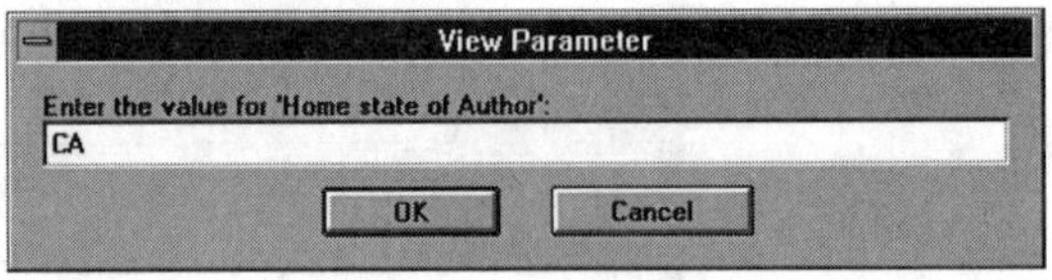

FIGURE 38.6.

The View Parameter dialog box prompting for the value in the custom string.

Multitable Remote Views

You will have situations in which the necessary selection criteria involves data from more than one table. Perhaps you need a result set for reporting on data from multiple tables. Maybe you have a highly normalized data model that spreads relevant data across many tables. Each of these scenarios is an excellent candidate for a multitable view.

Specifying a Join Condition

Creating a multitable remote view is exactly the same as creating a single table view, except that you add additional tables to the source table area. You can add a table to a view with the following steps:

1. Select Query | Add Table from the menu, or simply right-click in the top pane of the View Designer and select Add Table from the popup menu. The Open dialog box appears.

2. Select a table to add to the view and click OK.

3. The Join Condition dialog box appears. Like the selection criteria, the join condition will be added to the WHERE clause of the SQL SELECT statement. Select from the drop-down list each column that should be compared in the join condition from each table. The operator drop-down list enables you to specify the comparison operator for the join. Click the OK button when finished, and a line representing the join condition will appear between your two tables in the View Designer.

You can also set the join condition between two visible tables manually. To create the join, use the following steps:

1. Click in the table window of the source table for the join condition.

2. Select an index field to be the source field for the join.

3. Drag the field over to the target table window and onto the field to be the target field in the join condition.

4. The Join Condition dialog box appears as in Figure 38.7. Follow the preceding steps to set the join condition.

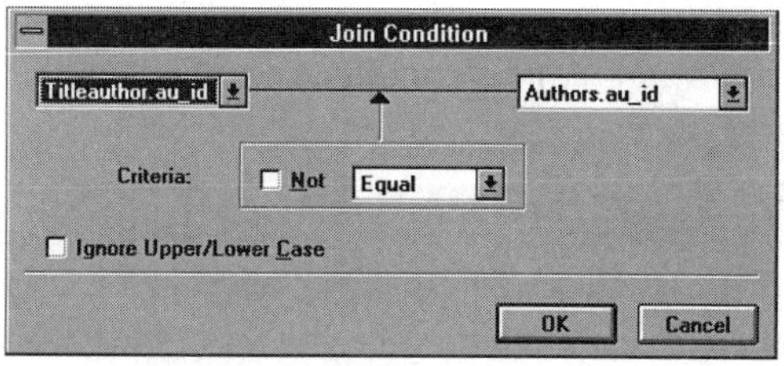

FIGURE 38.7.

The Join Condition dialog box.

Setting Update Criteria on Multitable Views

Setting the update criteria for multitable views is slightly more complex than for single table views. You need to decide which fields from each table should be part of the result set. In many cases, there are several of those fields that need to remain non-updatable. Most importantly, you need to make sure the keys that you have selected in the Update Criteria tab represent a unique key.

> **TIP**
>
> Use integer data types for primary keys. Integers are more efficient for the duties required of a primary key field. They ease the process of doing joins, make incrementing easier, reduce the amount of string handling, and take up less space (and time) with native Visual FoxPro tables.

Local/Remote Heterogeneous Views

Because connection properties are encapsulated within each remote view, heterogeneous updatable views are possible in Visual FoxPro. This feature creates some powerful possibilities.

It is possible to join local Visual FoxPro tables with tables from a remote server. For example, this would enable applications deployed with native Visual FoxPro databases to interact freely with a master Customer file located in a SQL Server database.

Remote/Remote Heterogeneous Views

Another very interesting scenario is to create a view based on data from two different remote servers. To accomplish this, two independent remote views need to be created using different connections. These remote views can then be joined into one local view, and the local view can be used as an independent cursor. This view could be made updatable; each table can be updated from the one cursor.

On the down side, because two simultaneous connections will be active, you need to have the resources to accommodate this type of view. Performance is also an issue because the views are being joined as a local process. Because each table exists on a different server, neither server can process the join and return a combined result set.

Remote View Advanced Options

You can access the Advanced Options dialog box by selecting Query, Advanced Options from the Visual FoxPro main menu while you are in the View Designer. Advanced Options enables you to visually specify various connection properties of the remote view. For more information on these properties, see the "Connection Properties" section earlier in this chapter. These properties can also be permanently manipulated in the database using the DBGETPROP() and DBSETPROP() functions. The Advanced Options dialog box creates a quick way to set several of the most common properties. The dialog options are shown in Figure 38.8.

FIGURE 38.8.

The Advanced Options dialog box in the View Designer.

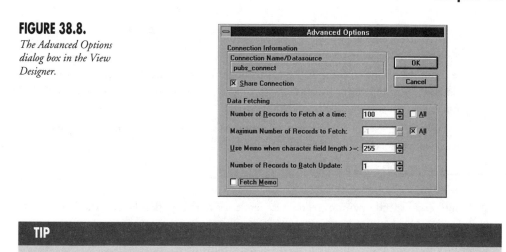

TIP

Leave the Fetch Memo property unchecked. This will suppress the retrieval of memo fields until you actually access the memo field. Using this technique will improve performance when you use tables with memo fields.

Visual FoxPro SQL Pass-Through Functions

Although remote views enable you to visually work with remote data sets, there are several other capabilities of a remote server that are used to build client/server applications. Visual FoxPro employs SQL pass-through technology to offer these capabilities to the Visual FoxPro developer. SQL pass-through technology enables specific SQL commands to be sent directly to the remote server, hence the name. Although SQL pass-through functions are language-based, they offer more control over processes that take place on the remote server. You can combine SQL pass-through functionality with remote views to create applications that truly tap into the power of client/server technology while maintaining the rapid application development capabilities of Visual FoxPro.

The following is a list of some of the advantages that SQL pass-through functions can provide:

- Create specific objects on the server, such as tables, stored procedures, triggers, and rules, if supported by the remote server.
- Execute server-stored procedures if they are supported by the remote server.
- Execute specific SQL commands and extensions for the remote server.
- Use explicit transaction processing.
- Return more than one result set.
- Tap into enhanced security features of the remote server.

The following is a list of some disadvantages of using SQL pass-through:

- They cannot be visually created and manipulated like remote views.
- The result sets returned from SQL pass-through functions are, by default, non-updatable. Although you can use CURSORSETPROP() to make these views updatable, remote views are automatically updatable.
- They are not persistent. Unlike remote views, it is not possible to store SQL pass-through elements in the database.
- Transaction processing is managed manually.
- Connections are managed manually.
- Using server-specific syntax creates a dependency to that particular server.

Using a combination of remote views and SQL pass-through functions should give you enough functionality to create powerful client/server applications.

SQL Pass-Through Functions

Table 38.4 lists the Visual FoxPro SQL functions grouped by type.

Table 38.4. The SQL pass-through functions.

Function	Description
Connection Management	
SQLCONNECT()	Connects to a data source for use with SQL pass-through functions.
SQLSTRINGCONNECT()	Connects to a data source using a long string. Some data sources require this method.
SQLDISCONNECT()	Disconnects from a data source and clears the connection handle.
SQL Statement Execution and Control	
SQLCANCEL()	Cancels an asynchronously executing SQL query on an active connection.
SQLEXEC()	The primary SQL pass-through function. Executes a SQL pass-through query on an active connection. The return value is the number of result sets generated or zero if it is still executing in asynchronous mode.
SQLMORERESULTS()	Puts another result set into a cursor. Returns zero if the statement creating the result set is still executing.
SQLCOMMIT()	Commit updates to the remote server.
SQLROLLBACK()	Rollback updates to the remote server.

Function	Description
	Data Source Information
SQLTABLES()	Creates a cursor of table names from the data source. Returns 1 if successful or 0 if this function is still executing.
SQLCOLUMNS()	Creates a cursor of column names and information. Returns 1 if successful or 0 if this function is still executing.
	Connection Control
SQLGETPROP()	Gets a connection property from an active connection.
SQLSETPROP()	Sets a property of an active connection.

Connecting with SQL Pass-Through

Remote views have the connection properties encapsulated with them, but SQL pass-through functions need you to explicitly manage your own connection to the remote server. There are several commands for connecting and disconnecting from your data source.

SQLCONNECT()

The first SQL pass-through function you'll use is SQLCONNECT(). As its name implies, it is the method used to create a connection using SQL pass-through. When you issue the SQLCONNECT() function, it returns a numeric value, or *handle*, that is used to reference the connection thereafter. It is always important to store the return value of SQLCONNECT() to use as the connection handle or to trap any errors. If the return value is a positive number, this number is your connection handle. If the value returned by SQLCONNECT() is a negative number, the connection could not be established. A return value of -1 means the error is at the connection level, and -2 denotes an environment-level error. For more information on error handling, see "The AERROR() Function" section later in this chapter.

The following code shows you how to use the SQLCONNECT() function, and Table 38.5 illustrates the argument usage for the SQLCONNECT() function.

```
SQLCONNECT([DataSourceName, cUserID, cPassword|cConnectionName])
```

Table 38.5. The arguments for the SQLCONNECT() function.

Argument	Description
DataSourceName	The name of an ODBC data source in the ODBC.INI file.
cUserID	The user name used to log on to the data source.

continues

Table 38.5. continued

Argument	Description
cPassword	The password used to log on to the data source.
cConnectionName	The name of a connection in the current database. Created with the Connection Designer or CREATE CONNECTION command.

If you execute this function with no arguments, the SQL Data Source dialog box will prompt for a data source. This behavior occurs only if the DispLogin property is set to .T.. This property can be set using the SQLSETPROP() function.

SQLSTRINGCONNECT()

The SQLSTRINGCONNECT() function is a variation of the SQLCONNECT() function and enables you to use a single connection string as a parameter. Some ODBC drivers require this type of syntax for connection. See the documentation for the ODBC driver for more information.

SQLDISCONNECT()

The SQLDISCONNECT() function is used to terminate a connection created with the SQLCONNECT() or SQLSTRINGCONNECT() functions. Use the connection handle as the single parameter for this function.

The following is an example of how to use the SQLCONNECT() and SQLDISCONNECT() functions:

```
LOCAL lnHandle

lnHandle = SQLCONNECT("SqlServer60","sa","")
IF lnHandle > 0
  WAIT WINDOW "I am connected!"
  =SQLDISCONNECT(lnHandle)
ELSE
  WAIT WINDOW "Sorry, I could not connect"
ENDIF
```

SQLEXEC(): The "Swiss Army Knife" Function

The SQLEXEC() function is the most commonly used SQL pass-through function. It is the primary vehicle for sending messages and commands to the remote server. The SQLEXEC() function does not evaluate the expressions passed to it locally; it passes them directly to the remote server. Once sent, these commands are compiled and executed on the remote server. This means that specific server instructions that are not supported within Visual FoxPro's language can be executed with SQLEXEC().

Because so many commands can be used with it, the SQLEXEC() function changes its behavior depending on what commands are executed. For example, the most common way to use the SQLEXEC() functions is to issue a SELECT statement into a named cursor. In contrast, when you execute a CREATE INDEX command, you do not need to create a local cursor, yet it is called with the same SQLEXEC() function.

The following code shows you how to use the SQLEXEC() function and Table 38.6 illustrates the argument usage for the SQLEXEC() function:

```
SQLEXEC(cHandle, cExpression,[ cCursorName])
```

Table 38.6. The arguments for the SQLEXEC() function.

Argument	Description
cHandle	The name of the handle returned from SQLCONNECT().
cExpression	A string containing the SQL expression to be passed to the server.
cCursor	An optional cursor name for commands that return a result set.

Using *SQLEXEC()* with *SELECT*

As is the case in most client/server applications, the majority of the commands sent to the server are SELECT statements. Although remote views are an elegant way to use these commands, there are situations in which SQLEXEC() is the proper choice for issuing SELECT statements to the server. For example, you might need to access certain aggregate functions that are supported only by specific server syntax. Another reason would be to perform an outer join, which is not supported within Visual FoxPro. Sometimes, you might already be working with an SQL pass-through connection and just need a result set.

The following is an example of a simple SELECT statement using SQL pass-through:

```
LOCAL lnHandle

lnHandle = SQLCONNECT("SqlServer60","user","")

IF lnHandle > 0
  IF SQLEXEC(lnHandle,"USE PUBS") > 0
    =SQLEXEC(lnHandle,;
            "SELECT * FROM AUTHORS WHERE AUTHORS.STATE='CA'",;
            "MyResult")
    IF USED("MyResult")
      BROWSE NORMAL
      USE IN MyResult
    ENDIF
  ELSE
    WAIT WINDOW NOWAIT "Could not USE database!"
  ENDIF
```

```
   =SQLDISCONNECT(lnHandle)
ELSE
   WAIT WINDOW "Connection could not be made!"
ENDIF
```

The following example demonstrates the capability to fetch more than one result set from a single SQLEXEC() call. The successive cursors will automatically be named MyResult, MyResult1, and MyResult2.

```
LOCAL lnHandle

lnHandle = SQLCONNECT("SqlServer60","user","")

IF lnHandle > 0
   IF SQLEXEC(lnHandle,"use pubs") > 0
     =SQLEXEC(lnHandle,;
              "select * from authors ;
               select * from titles ;
               select * from titleauthor",;
              "MyResult")
   ELSE
     WAIT WINDOW NOWAIT "Could not USE database!"
   ENDIF
ELSE
   WAIT WINDOW "Connection could not be made!"
ENDIF
```

Like remote views, SQLEXEC() supports the use of parameterized queries. The following example prompts the user for a state value to filter the Authors table:

```
LOCAL lnHandle

lnHandle = SQLCONNECT("SqlServer60","user","")

IF lnHandle > 0
   IF SQLEXEC(lnHandle,"USE PUBS") > 0
     =SQLEXEC(lnHandle,;
              "SELECT * FROM AUTHORS WHERE AUTHORS.STATE=?cState",;
              "MyResult")
     IF USED("MyResult")
       BROWSE NORMAL
       USE IN MyResult
     ENDIF
   ELSE
     WAIT WINDOW NOWAIT "Could not USE database!"
   ENDIF
   =SQLDISCONNECT(lnHandle)
ELSE
   WAIT WINDOW "Connection could not be made!"
ENDIF
```

By using SQL pass-through, you can perform an outer join on the remote server and output the data into a Visual FoxPro cursor. An outer join creates a join between tables without filtering the result on the join condition. Also shown is the use of a memory variable to represent the SELECT statement.

```
LOCAL lnHandle
LOCAL lcSQLexpr

*-- Define outer join expression
lcSQLexpr = "select * from authors, stores ;
            where authors.state *= stores.state"

lnHandle = SQLCONNECT("SqlServer60","user","")

IF lnHandle > 0
  IF SQLEXEC(lnHandle,"USE PUBS") > 0
    =SQLEXEC(lnHandle,lcSQLExpr, "MyResult")
    IF USED("MyResult")
      BROWSE NORMAL
      USE IN MyResult
    ENDIF
  ELSE
    WAIT WINDOW NOWAIT "Could not USE database!"
  ENDIF
  =SQLDISCONNECT(lnHandle)
ELSE
  WAIT WINDOW "Connection could not be made!"
ENDIF
```

NOTE

One important factor to consider when using SQLEXEC() to perform SELECT statements is that the result set cursors are always non-updatable. You can transform the read-only cursor into an updatable cursor and have Visual FoxPro handle updates for you. Use CURSORSETPROP() to set the updatable cursor properties. For more information, see the section "The Power of the Cursor," earlier in this chapter.

Using *SQLEXEC()* with Other SQL Commands

Although remote views are easier to work with than SQL pass-through functions, they are restricted to SELECT, INSERT, UPDATE, and DELETE commands only. To enable any valid SQL command to be submitted to the remote server, you will need to use SQLEXEC(). This function enables you to execute requests such as data definition commands and stored procedures on the remote server.

The following is an example of a data definition command:

```
=SQLEXEC(lnHandle,"use testdata")
=SQLEXEC(lnHandle,"create table test (test_id int, test_name char(20))")
```

The following example executes a standard SQL Server stored procedure called sp_who. This stored procedure displays a list of all users currently logged in to a database.

```
LOCAL lnHandle, lnResults

lnHandle = SQLCONNECT("SqlServer60","sa","")

IF lnHandle > 0
  =SQLEXEC(lnHandle,"use pubs")
  lnResults = SQLEXEC(lnHandle,"sp_who", "MyCursor")
IF lnResults > 0
    BROWSE NORMAL
  ENDIF
ENDIF
```

SQL Pass-Through Processing Modes

When you are working with remote data, result sets of various sizes are constantly being requested from the server. Because the number of records retrieved in many queries is often unknown, managing the processing of these retrievals is very important. Visual FoxPro provides both synchronous and asynchronous processing modes for SQL pass-through retrieval commands.

Synchronous Mode

Synchronous processing means that Visual FoxPro does not return processing control until a data retrieval function is completed. This means that a function that is returning a large data set will not enable any other actions to occur until the entire result set is retrieved from the server. Although this is the default setting for SQL pass-through functions, it is used mainly for interactive data handling, such as browsing data from the command window.

Asynchronous Mode

Asynchronous processing returns processing control immediately after the initial data retrieval function is called. The function still continues to execute in the background while you have complete control over the foreground processing. In fact, you can continue to execute other Visual FoxPro commands and periodically monitor the status of the executing function. This mode offers numerous possibilities not available with synchronous processing. Employing such techniques as displaying status windows and thermometers can give users valuable information as to the progress of an executing query. Time-consuming queries can then be gracefully interrupted or canceled.

Because of its enhanced flexibility and control, asynchronous processing is the preferred mode for developing client/server applications. This mode is valid for the four SQL pass-through functions that retrieve data from a remote server. These functions are SQLEXEC(), SQLMORERESULTS(), SQLTABLES(), and SQLCOLUMNS().

To monitor an asynchronously executing function, reissue the calling function periodically. A return value of zero means that the function is still executing. Continue to call the function until it returns a non-zero value.

Any executing asynchronous process can be canceled with the SQLCANCEL() function. If the SQLEXEC() function has begun building a local cursor and you then call the SQLCANCEL() function, you will need to discard the partial cursor. Use the USED() function to determine if the cursor has been built, and then issue the USE IN command to close the cursor.

You can view and change the asynchronous property using the SQLGETPROP() and SQLSETPROP() functions. Remote views are automatically created as asynchronous but can be changed with the DBSETPROP() function. For more information on viewing and changing connection properties, see the "Connections" section earlier in this chapter.

Batch and Non-Batch Modes

Similar to synchronous and asynchronous modes, batch mode and non-batch modes enable you to control the processing during a data retrieval function. Batch and non-batch modes are appropriate when you are retrieving multiple result sets. By combining them with the processing modes, you can establish the appropriate environment for your applications. Using the SQLSETPROP() function, the current BatchMode property can be set to 1 for batch mode (this is the default) or 0 for non-batch mode.

Batch Mode

Use batch mode when you are retrieving multiple result sets as a single batch from the remote server. Although multiple cursors will be created, no data is returned until all processing is completed on the remote server. Thus, the result sets will be delivered in a "batch" fashion.

When using batch mode in either synchronous or asynchronous mode, the user will not be able to "see" any data until all the result sets can be returned.

Non-Batch Mode

When you use non-batch mode, you can begin working with each result set as it becomes available, even if all queries are not finished executing. This means you can allow users to view and manipulate data while remaining queries execute in the background.

Using this method, the initial SQLEXEC() function retrieves the first result set, followed by repeated calls to the SQLMORERESULTS() function. The SQLMORERESULTS() function will build successive cursors as it retrieves each remaining result set. Table 38.7 shows the return values for the SQLMORERESULTS() function and their meanings.

Table 38.7. Return values for the SQLMORERESULTS() function.

Value	Meaning
0	Still executing. This value is only returned during asynchronous connections.
1	Finished building a result set.
2	Finished building all result sets.

When you are retrieving multiple result sets, each successive cursor is named by indexing the original cursor name with a numeric suffix. For example, if you specified MyCursor as the argument, the remaining cursors would be named MyCursor1, MyCursor2, and so on. The original result set cursor is named Sqlresult by default if you do not specify a name argument in the original SQLEXEC() function call.

TIP

When returning multiple result sets with SQLEXEC(), you can change the name of each cursor dynamically when you use non-batch mode. After the initial SQLEXEC() function call returns a 1, call the SQLMORERESULTS() function with a new cursor name as an argument. Repeat this process until SQLMORERESULTS() returns a 2, indicating that there are no more records to return.

NOTE

When you use asynchronous mode and non-batch mode together, Visual FoxPro uses a technology called *progressive fetching* to return data to the cursor. Progressive fetching enables you to view or manipulate retrieved records in a cursor while the remaining data is progressively fetched in the background. Because some of the data is available immediately, the impact of the query's execution time is minimized in some cases. Progressive fetching can enhance your users' perception of an application's performance.

You can modify the number of rows fetched per increment by changing the FetchSize property with the CURSORSETPROP() function. The default number of rows is 100.

Transaction Processing Modes

Transaction processing enables you to encapsulate important update activities into a single, manageable group. Using this method, updates to several disparate tables can be saved or committed as a single transaction. If any part of the transaction fails, then the entire set of updates is considered invalid and a *rollback* is performed. A rollback reverts the changed data back to its original state before the beginning of the transaction.

> **NOTE**
>
> The Visual FoxPro commands BEGIN TRANSACTION, END TRANSACTION, and ROLLBACK do not represent server transactions when you are working with remote data. These commands are to be used exclusively for performing transaction processing on local Visual FoxPro cursors. This is an important consideration when you are developing portable applications that will run against both local and remote data.

There are two modes available for transaction processing: automatic and manual. Although manual transaction mode is recommended for application development, choosing the correct mode depends on the situation. To change the current mode, set the Transactions property with the SQLSETPROP() function. For more information on using SQLSETPROP(), see the "Connections" section earlier in this chapter.

Automatic Transaction Mode

Automatic transaction mode is the default mode. Automatic transactions treat each command sent to the server as a single transaction. The main advantage to using automatic mode is that you don't have to issue any transaction functions explicitly. The disadvantages are that it is slow, and you cannot group several update statements into specific transactions.

Manual Transaction Mode

When manual transaction mode is set, a transaction begins automatically with the first updatable SQL command. However, it stays active until you explicitly call either a SQLCOMMIT() or SQLROLLBACK() function to complete the transaction. You can use this method to deliberately group several updates together before committing them as a group to the remote server.

> **CAUTION**
>
> Do not send the server transaction commands COMMIT and ROLLBACK with the SQLEXEC() command unless you're absolutely sure of yourself. Using these commands with SQL pass-through can result in unpredictable behavior. Use the Visual FoxPro functions SQLCOMMIT() and SQLROLLBACK() to perform these functions instead.

Error Handling

All of the SQL pass-through functions support two types of error handling: SQL pass-through function return values and the AERROR() function.

SQL Pass-Through Function Return Values

The first level of error handling includes those errors that correspond to each function's return value. It is a wise practice to trap the majority of these errors and code the appropriate responses. The return codes from SQL pass-through functions belong to one of the following two levels:

■ *Connection level.* Connection-level errors are the most common error type returned from an SQL pass-through function. Their scope is specific to the established connection handle referenced by the calling function.

■ *Environment level.* Environment-level errors point to an error condition within the global Visual FoxPro environment. When you are performing subsequent analysis of the environment level, remember to pass zero as the connection handle.

The *AERROR()* Function

The AERROR() function captures the full details of each error that occurs within the Visual FoxPro environment. AERROR() creates an array that you can parse for each of the returned error values. The array is comprised of six columns and returns the number of rows in the array. The type of error that occurs determines the number of rows in the array.

When a Visual FoxPro error occurs, the array contains one row. Table 38.8 displays the contents of each element when a Visual FoxPro error occurs.

Table 38.8. Visual FoxPro AERROR() error descriptions.

Element Number	Default Value	Description
1	Numeric	The number of the error.
2	Character	The text of the error message.
3	Null	Contains the text of an additional error parameter if one was generated.
4	Null	When applicable, contains the number of the work area in which the error occurred.
5	Null	If a trigger failed (error 1539), the value will be one of the following: 1: Insert trigger failed. 2: Update trigger failed. 3: Delete trigger failed.

Element Number	Default Value	Description
6	Null	
7	Null	

Table 38.9 displays the contents of the array when an ODBC error (1526) occurs. The array will contain a row for each error returned.

Table 38.9. ODBC error descriptions.

Element Number	Default Value	Description
1	Numeric	Contains 1526.
2	Character	The text of the error message.
3	Character	The text of the ODBC error message.
4	Character	The current ODBC SQL state.
5	Numeric	The error number from the ODBC data source.
6	Numeric	The ODBC connection handle.
7	Null	Null.

Using the Upsizing Wizard

Another powerful and unique tool for developing and implementing Visual FoxPro client/server applications is the Upsizing Wizard. This wizard is designed to migrate database components from Visual FoxPro prototypes or existing applications to Microsoft SQL Server. With the Upsizing Wizard, you can create new database objects, migrate selected data and components, or totally convert a local database into a remote database. This functionality enables you to maximize the productivity of prototyping by enabling you to fully define the database components in a local Visual FoxPro database.

When used to its fullest extent, the Upsizing Wizard is designed to enable you to develop a full-featured application using local Visual FoxPro views, run the local database through the Upsizing Wizard to convert the entire database into a remote SQL Server database, and then run the same application against the new remote database with no major change in the application's code. You can select how much of your database to migrate, whether or not to convert local views, create or modify an existing database, and generate reports of the migration success ratio.

Getting Ready to Upsize

Before you upsize a local Visual FoxPro database, you will want to make the necessary preparations for the changes both to your local database and the remote server. It is important that you understand what the Upsizing Wizard will and won't do before you run it. The primary factors in determining what the Upsizing Wizard will perform is both how you have set up your local database and the status of the remote server.

Preparing Your Visual FoxPro Database

A well-prepared Visual FoxPro database will upsize much more successfully than one that hasn't been strategically prepared. Older FoxPro databases, in particular, will need to be assimilated into a Visual FoxPro database container and properly prepared before they will successfully migrate.

The following are suggestions for preparing your database for upsizing:

- Designate keys for all of your tables. The Upsizing Wizard will not automatically create Primary and Unique keys where they don't originally exist. Client/server databases must have these keys to function properly.

- Similar to setting up keys, use the Referential Integrity builder in the Database Designer to establish your rules for enforcing referential integrity before migrating your database to SQL Server. Again, if these elements do not exist, the Upsizing Wizard will not automatically create them.

- Back up your database before running the Upsizing Wizard. Because the Upsizing Wizard can create or modify database objects in certain cases, it is a wise idea to back it up first.

- If you have implemented defaults, field-level validation, or row-level validation in the database, be sure that they do not contain any Visual FoxPro-specific syntax or they will not be successfully converted.

- To realize the full potential of the Upsizing Wizard's functionality, you should develop your local prototypes using local views rather than specific tables. Later, you can instruct the Upsizing Wizard to convert the local views into remote views while maintaining the same literal names in the databases.

- Establish a named connection for your target remote server. Obviously, the Upsizing Wizard will need to connect to your data source to perform its duties, so be sure to create and test your connection before you upsize.

- Before attempting to run the Upsizing Wizard, make sure that no users are currently using any tables in the database. In addition, make sure that no tables are open on the machine running the upsizing process. The Upsizing Wizard requires exclusive use of the database to perform its activities.

Preparing Your SQL Server Remote Server

There are several preparations to be made to the remote server before running the Upsizing Wizard. Special care should be given to these steps. The ramifications are more global because the server, by definition, is a public entity. In addition, it can be cumbersome to remove objects once they are created on the server, so it is a wise idea to prevent possible termination of the upsizing process once it has begun.

The following are suggestions for preparing the remote server for an upsizing operation:

- Learn about the SQL Server environment and components. Knowing the basics of how SQL Server operates and is managed can significantly increase the potential for successful upsizing. In particular, it is a wise idea to learn the basics of TransactSQL, the SQL Server native language. Because all stored procedures and triggers are written with TransactSQL, knowing the language will not only help you write more generic Visual FoxPro validation code, but will also enable you to write any necessary stored procedures or triggers that cannot be converted from your Visual FoxPro environment.

- Verify your permission status to SQL Server prior to upsizing. Be sure that your permissions correspond with your desired upsizing activities. For instance, if you have an existing database to add to, you need to have CREATE TABLE, CREATE INDEX, and SELECT permissions. To create a new database on a prepared server, you will also need CREATE TABLE, CREATE INDEX, and CREATE DEFAULT permissions. If the server is entirely unprepared for the upsizing process, you will need to have full system administrator equivalence to set up the device, database, tables, indexes, and triggers.

- Verify the existence of sufficient disk space on the server to accommodate your upsizing activities. When estimating space requirements, use a factor of 50 to 100 percent in addition to the current size of the Visual FoxPro tables.

- Create your device(s), database, and log before upsizing. Although the Upsizing Wizard enables you to create these items on the fly, it is a wise idea to create them ahead of time. This activity is best handled with an SQL administration tool because it offers significantly more information and control over the server environment. If you do not have system administrator permissions, delegate this task to someone who does.

NOTE

One good reason to create devices before upsizing is that Visual FoxPro's Upsizing Wizard cannot create multiple devices. If your database must be stored on multiple devices or disks because of its size, you must create these items outside of the Upsizing Wizard. In order to have your database span multiple devices using the Upsizing Wizard, you must set the desired devices as the default devices. The Upsizing Wizard will later display "Default" as a device for your database to be upsized to.

Upsizing Your Database

Like all wizards, the Upsizing Wizard is very simple and straightforward to use. Successive pages of the wizard will guide you through the process of upsizing your database, and navigation buttons along the bottom of the screen enable you to navigate, cancel, or finish the process. After you specify the basic information required to upsize, the wizard will enable you to select Finish even before you reach the last page. By selecting Finish, you accept the default values for the remaining pages. No updates are sent to the server until you select Finish.

You summon the Upsizing Wizard by selecting Tools | Wizards | Upsizing from the main Visual FoxPro menu. The opening screen appears as in Figure 38.9.

Figure 38.9.

The Upsizing Wizard.

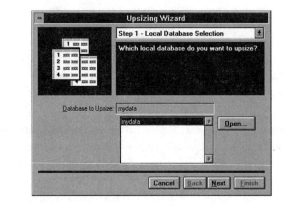

The following steps narrate the process of upsizing your database with the Upsizing Wizard.

Step 1: Local Database Selection

Select a local Visual FoxPro database to upsize. Click the Open button to open a database via the File Open dialog box.

Step 2: Data Source Selection

Select a connection or ODBC data source for the Upsizing Wizard to use for the upsizing process. If you select an ODBC data source, the Upsizing Wizard will create a connection named Upsize and use this connection. Whatever method you choose, the Upsizing Wizard will use the named connection to create remote views for the entire database.

Select a connection or ODBC data source from the displayed list. The Upsizing Wizard knows to only display SQL Server-specific connections or data sources. If the connection you specify has a login ID and password, you will have the option to remove the password from the definition later in the upsizing process.

After completing this step, the Upsizing Wizard will connect to the data source using the method you selected. If the selected method requires a login ID or password, you will be prompted with the ODBC login dialog box.

Step 3: Target Database

Select an existing database as the upsize destination or indicate that you want to create one. If the server you selected has existing databases already created on it, they will be displayed. If you select an existing database, the Upsizing Wizard will automatically skip steps 4 and 5.

If you decide to create a database, you will be prompted to supply a database name of up to 30 characters.

Step 4: Database Size and SQL Server Device

The first part of this step is to indicate a database size. SQL Server requires a minimum of 2MB for its databases. After you specify your database size, you must select an existing device or create a new device for your new database.

- If you select an existing device, you will be prompted with a list of all available devices and the default device. Select the desired device or select the default device to span multiple devices.

- You must be a system administrator to create a new device. If so, you will be prompted for a name of up to 30 characters and a size of at least 2MB.

Step 5: SQL Server Log Device and Log Size

The SQL Server transaction log records all requests made to the server for a specific database. This log can be used to later restore the database if the system fails. Because the log is used to ensure data integrity, it should be stored on a separate device and, preferably, with a separate physical disk as the database. If you specify zero as the log size, the Upsizing Wizard will automatically place the log on the same device as the database. For guidelines on working with transaction logs, refer to the appropriate SQL Server documentation.

Step 6: Tables to Upsize

From the displayed list, select the tables to be upsized. This list displays only the tables that the Upsizing Wizard was able to open exclusively. If any tables from the database could not be opened exclusively, they will not be available to upsize.

Step 7: Field Data Types

Select a table from the list, and a grid displays the columns for the table with the default mappings from Visual FoxPro to SQL Server data types, which can be overridden. To change the SQL Server data type for a Visual FoxPro field, click the Server Type column for the desired row. A list of the valid data types that you can choose as an alternate will appear, as shown in Figure 38.10.

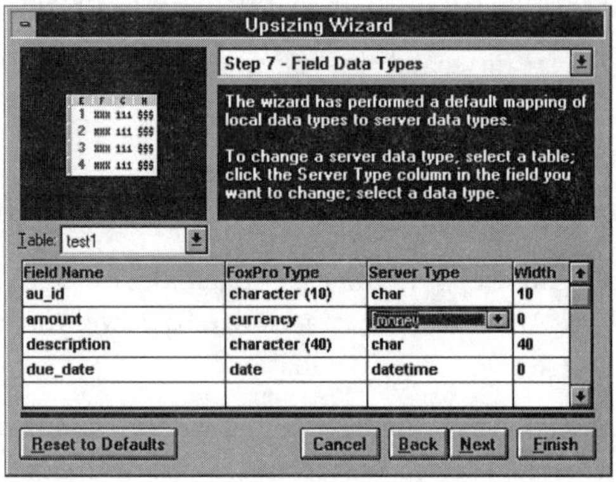

Figure 38.10.

The Field Data Types screen.

Visual FoxPro data types map to SQL Server data types by default according to Table 38.10.

Table 38.10. Default SQL Server data type mappings.

Visual FoxPro	SQL Server
Character	char
Currency	money
Date	datetime
DateTime	datetime
Double	float
Float	float
General	image
Integer	int
Logical	bit
Memo	text
Numeric	float
Picture	image

Step 8: Upsizing Options

This very important step enables you to indicate exactly what actions the Upsizing Wizard should perform. The screen consists of check boxes that are divided into two categories: Table Attributes to Upsize and Changes to Make Locally. The screen appears as in Figure 38.11.

Figure 38.11.

The Upsizing Options screen.

The Table Attributes to Upsize options are as follows:

■ *Indexes.* Creates a SQL Server index for each Visual FoxPro index for all selected tables. The Visual FoxPro index names are retained in SQL Server. Table 38.11 shows the mapping from Visual FoxPro indexes to SQL Server indexes.

Table 38.11. Index mappings.

Visual FoxPro	*SQL Server*
Primary	Clustered Unique
Candidate	Unique
Unique and Regular	Non-unique

■ *Defaults.* Creates a SQL Server default for each Visual FoxPro default for all selected tables.

■ *Relationships.* Creates SQL Server INSERT, UPDATE, and DELETE triggers if the Referential Integrity Builder was used in the selected Visual FoxPro database.

■ *Validation rules.* Creates stored procedures that are called by triggers on the server to enforce field-level and row-level validation rules converted from the Visual FoxPro database. This method is used instead of using SQL Server rules so that the proper validation text can be used.

■ *Structure only, no data.* As the name implies, this option does not copy any records into the SQL Server tables, only empty tables.

■ *Add timestamp field.* Creates a timestamp column if any of the following data types are used: binary, varbinary, float, real, image, or text. A timestamp field is a number generated by SQL Server whenever a record is updated. As mentioned earlier in this chapter, using timestamps can increase performance on updates and deletes in remote tables.

■ *Use declarative referential integrity.* This option is specific to Microsoft SQL Server 6.0. It instructs the Upsizing Wizard to use the Declarative Referential Integrity features of SQL Server 6.0.

The following list describes the Changes to Make Locally options:

■ *Create upsizing report.* Creates a new project that contains reports which document tables, indexes, views, and relationships. See "Step 9: Finish" for more information.

■ *Redirect views to remote data.* Modifies the selected database so that forms, reports, and queries created on local views will now access remote data. The Upsizing Wizard accomplishes this by cloning the local view, substituting the local references with remote tables, and renaming the original local view with a "_local" suffix. If any tables referenced by a local view were not selected for upsizing, the local view is not modified and the Upsizing Wizard treats each table as if you selected the Create remote views on tables option described in the next step.

■ *Create remote views on tables.* Creates a remote view for each table in the database. The original local table will be renamed with a "_local" suffix. This option should be chosen carefully because the views created will not be parameterized, but will be a working representation of each table—large or small.

■ *Save password with views.* Stores the login ID and password within each remote view that is created by the Upsizing Wizard.

Step 9: Finish

The final upsizing step presents you with a list of three choices.

■ Upsize without generating SQL code
■ Generate SQL code, but do not upsize
■ Upsize and generate SQL code

If you select either of the two options that upsize and click Finish, the actual upsizing process begins generating requests to the remote server. If you have a lot of data, this process can take a very long time.

If you select either of the two options that generate code, a new project will be created with the name Report (or Report1, Report2, and so on if previous names exist) and a new database within it named Upsize (or Upsize1, Upsize2, and so on). This new project is used to store reports, tables, errors, and SQL code. The SQL code generated by the wizard to perform the upsizing process is stored in a single memo field in a table named SQL_uw. The remaining objects can be used to generate reports of the tables, fields, indexes, and relationships that were upsized, or to produce error and miscellaneous reports.

> **NOTE**
>
> If you plan to use the generated SQL code to create your database objects on the server instead of upsizing with the wizard, be aware that you cannot simply run the code as is. The generated SQL code does not fully represent all of the steps performed by the Upsizing Wizard. If you need to use the generated SQL code, copy the pieces that you need and execute them one at a time.

Finishing Touches

After you have finished the Upsizing Wizard, you will want to complete the process with a few activities. The following are some suggestions you might want to consider:

- Set up users and grant permissions to any new database objects you have created.
- Create stored procedures and triggers.
- Correct any default or validation expression that did not convert into SQL Server properly. You will find these errors in the error reports generated by the Upsizing Wizard.
- Before running your application, be sure you have converted any high-volume remote views into parameterized views where you can.
- Create a global login dialog box for your application to establish login information one time only. If login information is not established before using remote views, users might be prompted for login information every time remote views are used.
- Add SQL pass-through functionality if necessary.

Strategies for Client/Server Development

Developing client/server applications can be significantly more complex than building desktop or native multiuser applications. Decisions such as processing distribution, security standards, and performance tuning on client/server architectures present a whole new set of issues for application developers. Although Visual FoxPro makes the job of creating client/server applications almost as easy as working with local data, you will need to spend more time planning your design and developing a strategy for implementation.

Use the Right Tools

By using Visual FoxPro for your client/server development tool, you already have chosen one of the most powerful and productive development tools available today. However, the development tool is often only one of several tools necessary for developing client/server applications. The following is a list of some of the productivity tools that might be useful for your application development efforts. Although none of these tools is a prerequisite for development, they can save significant time and money on your projects.

- *Data modeling tools.* Data modeling tools are designed to help you construct and evolve your data model from its logical state to its final physical state. Because these products are graphical, they enable you to design and create your database visually. Often, these products will actually generate the data definition SQL schema to create all necessary tables, indexes, triggers, stored procedures, and defaults for you. In addition, referential integrity rules are automatically enforced and generated with the native syntax of the specified DBMS.

  Some of these products, such as ERwin from Logic Works, can work with a variety of DBMS platforms, making these tools invaluable for multiplatform deployments. In fact, ERwin will reverse-engineer the data model from your existing system for you with amazing accuracy. This can be a powerful option in environments that cannot use the Upsizing Wizard to perform this automatically.

- *SQL administration tools.* By using SQL pass-through, you have the ability to execute data definition SQL code to the server; however, it is not the ideal method for maintaining the complexities of the various components of the database. SQL administration tools can help you administrate the database and all of its associated objects from remote workstations. These products often incorporate SQL compilers to help you construct, debug, and deploy server-specific SQL code such as stored procedures and triggers.

- *Version control and source code management tools.* Because Visual FoxPro has no built-in multideveloper features, these products can facilitate team development efforts and manage source code. Some of the products available include Intersolve PVCS and Microsoft SourceSafe, as well as Visual FoxPro-specific products such as CAPCON.

- *Testing tools.* For mission-critical applications, automated regression testing tools can cut time and costs when you test and debug your applications. Although there are no Visual FoxPro-specific testing tools currently available, Microsoft Test and SQA TeamTest are examples of popular testing tools.

- *Class libraries and application frameworks.* Now that Visual FoxPro supports object-oriented programming, these products should proliferate quickly. Class libraries are prefabricated objects that you can use as the foundation layer in your object hierarchy, thus saving you tremendous amounts of time building ancestor objects. Application frameworks, which often include class libraries of their own, take it a step further by providing a complete infrastructure on which to build applications. Although you can, and probably should, develop your own class libraries and application frameworks, purchasing these products can give you a significant head start in building applications with object-oriented methodologies. At the time of this writing there were no class libraries or application frameworks commercially available, but several were in final development.

Build a Solid Foundation

Take the time to perform a thorough analysis of all business processes, requirements, and entities. In addition to building a sound application design, one of the fruits of good analysis is a normalized data model. A sound data model, in turn, makes working with remote data a lot easier. In fact, client/server applications that utilize SQL are much more difficult to build on poorly designed data models. Many of the benefits of a relational database, such as referential integrity features, can be rendered ineffective on an unnormalized database. If you are not familiar with the process of data normalization, you should spend time learning this valuable skill.

As mentioned previously, using a data modeling tool is strongly recommended for building remote databases. Although it can be accomplished manually, data modeling tools ensure accuracy and consistency throughout your model. They also make changes to existing models far easier and quicker to perform.

Visual FoxPro now has data dictionary features built into its database container. Utilizing these capabilities further encapsulates the data with its associated rules and attributes. It also reduces development time later on.

Use a Set-Based Methodology

Although many FoxPro developers have made the paradigm shift to set-based programming, many are still using antiquated Xbase methods as the primary method of manipulating data. Set-based data access is rooted in SQL and is the most efficient method of manipulating remote data in client/server systems.

When you are selecting data sets from the remote server, keep the result sets as small as possible. Limit the fields list in your SELECT statements and views to the minimum required. Unless retrieving from small tables, always filter your rows by at least one factor.

Use parameterized views whenever possible, particularly when you are developing one-to-many forms with remote data. They are a good example of limiting both the result sets and the number of retrievals needed by the server.

Distribute the Processing

After implementing your client/server application, you will want to consider optimizing performance by distributing the processing. This process involves taking the time to evaluate which processes can be migrated out of the application to other locations, such as the database server.

The most common method of distributing these processes is to convert some of the primary queries into stored procedures. Because stored procedures are precompiled and execute on the server, they often yield a dramatic performance benefit. Because of the administrative overhead that comes with using and maintaining them, it is best to implement stored procedures at the end of your development cycle.

Develop an Implementation Plan

One of the most important responsibilities you have as a Visual FoxPro developer is creating an implementation plan for your application. Because Visual FoxPro has a powerful DBMS as well as flexible client/server functionality, there are several options for developing and deploying applications.

Developing and Deploying Locally

As mentioned earlier, you might decide that the Visual FoxPro DBMS is sufficient for your needs and not implement a client/server architecture at all. Don't be afraid to make this decision. Visual FoxPro is a very capable DBMS that can support applications of surpassing magnitude. Make sure that you have considered this option and have selected a client/server solution for the right reasons.

Developing Locally and Deploying Remotely

One of the most exciting capabilities of Visual FoxPro is its capability to prototype an application with local tables and later migrate the data to a remote server. Prototyping leverages the convenience, portability, and speed of local Visual FoxPro tables to build the primary framework of an application. Using this technique can greatly increase your ability to respond to the dynamic changes of a rapid application development cycle.

Depending on your server's database, the process of moving your data to the server ranges from simple to complex. Whatever the target database, Visual FoxPro is an ideal environment for performing this data transfer. Because Visual FoxPro "sees" remote data as if it were local, moving data between local and remote views can be a trivial matter. This, of course, assumes that you already have an existing database on the target server. Without the sufficient SQL administration tools, properly setting up the database on the remote server can be quite a challenge. Users of Microsoft SQL Server receive the added bonus of the Upsizing Wizard which significantly simplifies the process of moving your database components along with the data to the server.

The following are some suggestions for creating an upsizable application:

- Use local views instead of direct tables when creating the prototype.
- Avoid using Visual FoxPro-specific commands and functions when retrieving or updating data.

- Be sure not to become dependent on Visual FoxPro's speed when prototyping performance-sensitive operations. These operations cannot execute as fast when transported to the remote server.

- Be aware of the differences between local and remote transactions.

- If you plan on using the Upsizing Wizard, be sure you understand how Visual FoxPro maps functions, data types, and other components before running the wizard.

- If possible, wait until after you upsize your database to implement stored procedures.

Developing and Deploying Heterogeneously

It is possible to develop and deploy a Visual FoxPro application that simultaneously accesses data sources on multiple platforms. Although this technique is less common than accessing data sources on a single platform, it does accommodate several potential scenarios. For instance, you can develop a stand-alone local application that needs to interface only with a few tables from a remote system. Another example would be to develop an application that utilizes Visual FoxPro tables for its performance and a server database for its storage capabilities. Although these solutions may not make you very popular with your database administrator, they can serve a legitimate need for your business.

There are two things to keep in mind when you develop heterogeneous applications in Visual FoxPro.

- Fragmenting the application's database between multiple locations can produce a maintenance headache.

- Joins between disparate data sources are performed locally and therefore can yield a performance penalty.

Developing Portable Applications

Portable applications are designed to run against either local or remote data for the life of the application. Many of these applications often need the platform to be determined at runtime. Although such applications can be very tricky to develop, Visual FoxPro is one of the best environments with which to perform this task. The following are some suggestions for developing portable applications:

- Maintain duplicate databases on each supported platform. Manage changes to these databases very carefully. A data modeling tool can be very handy for managing identical models across multiple platforms. The Upsizing Wizard can also be a valuable tool for keeping certain databases in sync.

- Maintain duplicate local and remote views for each supported platform.

- Use a global switch to designate the current platform. This switch's value could be modified at runtime by user selection or by an environment variable.

■ Encapsulate data source-specific conventions with conditional logic. This concept is analogous to cross-platform development (If `_WINDOWS`, `_MAC`, and so on) in Visual FoxPro. Use the global switch to determine the course of action. Candidates for this type of processing include executing stored procedures, performing outer joins, explicit transaction processing, or using server-specific functions.

■ Set up forms, reports, and queries that use views to automatically toggle between data sources at runtime. The following is an example of how this could be accomplished for forms:

1. Follow the preceding steps. Make sure you have duplicate local and remote views available.

2. Create a new form using the Form Designer.

3. Create three new non-protected form properties: `RemoteSwitch`, `RemoteView`, and `LocalView`.

4. Open the Data Environment of the form and add the desired local views for this form.

5. Set the value of the following object properties, as shown in Table 38.12.

6. Add the following code to the Form Load method code. This example assumes that you have set up a global logical variable named `glRemoteSwitch`. This could be implemented as an application-level property to avoid using global variables.

   ```
   THISFORM.RemoteSwitch = glRemoteSwitch
   ```

7. Add the following code to the Data Environment Init method code:

   ```
   THIS.OpenTables
   ```

8. Add the following code to the Cursor Init method code:

   ```
   IF THISFORM.RemoteSwitch = .T.
      THIS.CursorSource = THISFORM.RemoteView
   ELSE
      THIS.CursorSource = THISFORM.LocalView
   ENDIF
   ```

9. (Optional) Save the form as a class. Subclass this form throughout your application or adopt this technique into your existing form class library.

Table 38.12. Property settings for portable forms.

Form Object	Property	Value
Custom property	RemoteSwitch	.T.
Custom property	RemoteView	Remote view name
Custom property	LocalView	Local view name
Data Environment	AutoOpenTables	.F.
Cursor	Alias	Generic name

Form Object	Property	Value
Form grid	RecordSource	Generic cursor alias
Form controls	ControlSource	Fields from generic cursor alias

Developing and Deploying Remotely

Perhaps the most common method of developing large-scale client/server applications is to develop and deploy them exclusively using remote data. Using this method, you don't have to consider the ramifications of function and performance compatibility because you are developing with the same database with which you deploy. This predictable environment is ideal for fine-tuning data manipulation throughout the development cycle. You are free to intermingle remote views with SQL pass-through functions to custom tailor the application to your specific database server.

If you are certain that your application does not require portability, using remote data for development is the best choice for developing client/server applications. It gives you an accurate picture of how the performance and processing of your application will appear to your users, even when you are developing the prototype. Because you don't have to upsize the database or develop specific code to support multiple platforms, the development effort is lightened and often takes less time.

Summary

Visual FoxPro has become a rich and powerful client/server application tool. Using a combination of the new graphical designers and remote views, developing client/server applications is as easy as creating local applications. SQL pass-through functionality provides even more power; it enables you to communicate directly with a remote data source. In addition, the Upsizing Wizard empowers users of SQL Server to upsize local database objects automatically. By combining these dynamic features, you can use Visual FoxPro to build a wide variety of client/server solutions for your business.

Microsoft Mail-Enabled Applications

39

This chapter shows you how to use the Microsoft MAPI OLE 2 controls to create your own Visual FoxPro application that supports e-mail. This application is called a *mail-enabled application,* and it accesses e-mail from the Windows 95 Microsoft Exchange. You cannot use the MAPI OLE controls with Windows for WorkGroups.

Online Services

Almost from the beginning of the microcomputer revolution, personal computers supported some form of electronic communications. Primitive bulletin board systems became available in the early days of personal computers. As time passed, bulletin boards evolved into numerous full-blown online information services, such as the Internet, CompuServe, Prodigy, America Online, and Microsoft's MSN. There was also a proliferation of communications software products. Many information services provided their own client user-interface software. All of these services provided some form of e-mail.

At the same time that BBSs and e-mail were evolving, personal computers were linked to networks. Users in a workgroup could share various types of documents with other users in a workgroup environment using e-mail. More and more individuals, companies, and even families are relying on e-mail to communicate with others across the network and around the world using online information services.

The problem was that there were too many different standards. Each communications product has its own interface. You might communicate with other users in a group using the Lotus cc:Mail product, UNIX mail, or Microsoft Mail software, and communicate with the outside via CompuServe using the TAPCIS, WinCIM, or Cross Talk software. Finally, you would have to use the software provided by America Online to communicate with that service. Prodigy also has its own communications software. Before I discovered TAPCIS, I used whatever software came with my modem to communicate with CompuServe. Now, I use WinCIM. As you see, this proliferation of software can become a major problem. Your overall productivity can be reduced substantially if you have to move between products to perform your work. It also requires a considerable amount of effort to train a new employee on the use of these diverse productivity tools.

In an attempt to simplify the task of communicating with other users, many software publishers have developed their own messaging protocol in hopes that it will become the industry standard. Lotus developed the Vendor Independent Messaging (VIM) protocol. Novel developed the Message Handling Service (MHS) protocol. Microsoft developed the Message Application Programming Interface (MAPI) protocol. Of course, Microsoft has integrated its messaging protocol into the Windows 95 operating system and, for that reason, will probably be able to establish its messaging protocol as the industry standard. In fact, other software publishers, such as IBM, Novel, and Lotus, have announced officially that they will support MAPI in addition to their own proprietary standards.

Microsoft introduced the MAPI Windows messaging subsystem architecture for both Windows NT and Windows 95. With the MAPI subsystem, you can communicate with others on various networks and information systems using e-mail from any *mail-enabled application*. A mail-enabled application is an application that supports an interface to Microsoft Mail or the Windows 95 Microsoft Exchange Mail subsystem through the MAPI interface. The fact is that a mail-enabled application only operates if MAPI services are present. That means that the Microsoft Mail electronic mail system for Windows for Workgroups or NT or Microsoft Exchange for Windows 95 must be available and set up.

The Windows 95 Messaging Subsystem

The Windows 95 messaging subsystem is called the Microsoft Exchange. It fully supports all the capabilities of MAPI. It enables you to communicate with a variety of e-mail systems, and it is a great improvement over Microsoft Mail. The Exchange is composed of various message subsystem components that ship with Windows 95. These components include the following:

- Universal Inbox, called the Microsoft Exchange client. This component enables you to send, receive, and organize e-mail, faxes, and other information. Figure 39.1 shows a sample Inbox.

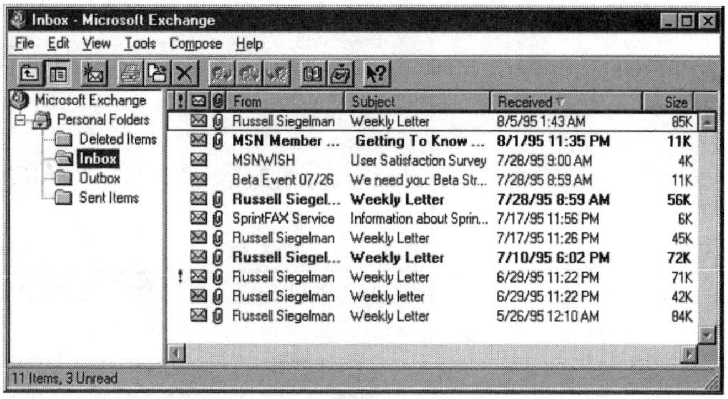

FIGURE 39.1.

A sample Microsoft Exchange Inbox.

- Personal Address Book. This component contains fax numbers and e-mail addresses and all types of information related to the addressees. The address book can be used by any mail-enabled application to select the destination of mail.

- Personal Information Store. This component provides a common area for storing e-mail, faxes, documents, and other information.

- The MAPI subsystem. This component contains MAPI drivers to support various messaging systems, such as CompuServe, America Online, Novell, and so forth. Some of these drivers are supplied with NT and Windows 95.

■ Microsoft Fax drivers. You use these drivers to send and receive faxes in the same way you send and receive e-mail.

■ Microsoft Internet Mail drivers. These drivers enable you to send and receive Internet mail utilizing TCP/IP and PPP communication protocols.

Before explaining how to build your own Visual FoxPro mail-enabled application, I'll illustrate some of the capabilities of the Microsoft Exchange.

The Exchange is fairly easy to use. For example, suppose I want to send this document to my editor at Sams Publishing via CompuServe. Because Word for Windows 6.0 is a mail-enabled application, I can choose File | Send, as shown in Figure 39.2, and the Microsoft Exchange New Message dialog box appears, as shown in Figure 39.3.

FIGURE 39.2.

Sending mail from a mail-enabled application.

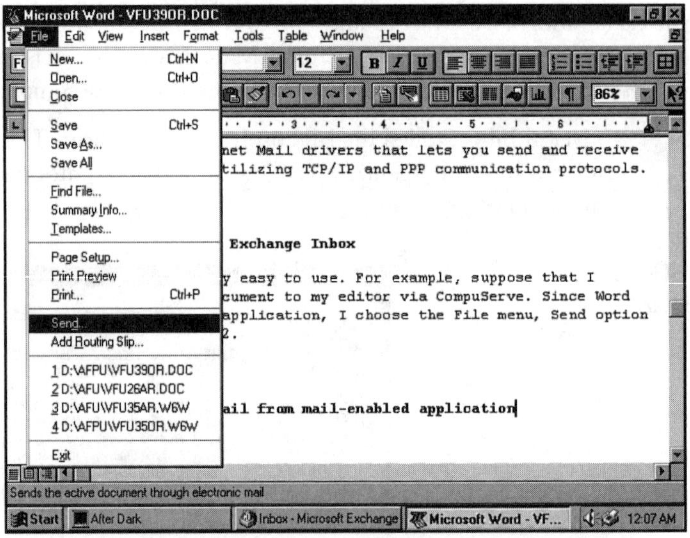

FIGURE 39.3.

The Microsoft Exchange New Message dialog box.

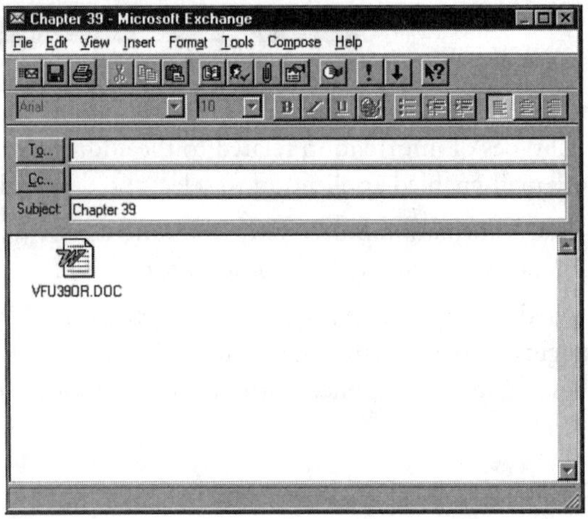

All I have to supply is the subject and recipients. However, other options are available. To choose the recipient, I click on the To button, and the Address Book dialog box appears, as shown in Figure 39.4, from which I choose one or more recipients.

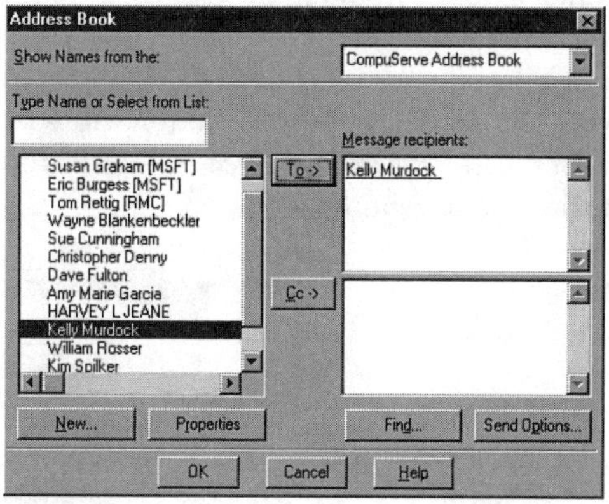

FIGURE 39.4.

The Microsoft Exchange Address Book dialog box.

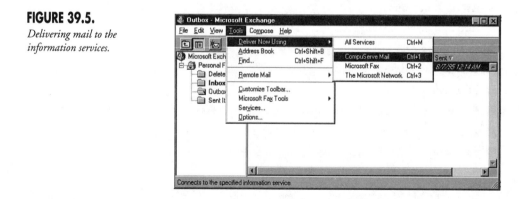

Finally, I click the Send button on the toolbar and the messaging subsystem adds the e-mail to the Exchange Outbox. When I'm ready to send all the mail in the Outbox, I execute the Microsoft Exchange and choose Tools | Deliver Now Using, as shown in Figure 39.5. The Exchange sends the mail to CompuServe. I could just as easily have sent the document to another user on my network, the Microsoft Network, the Internet, or some other information service. I could have sent the document as a fax. The only restriction is that I must have the destination service configured for the Microsoft Exchange client.

FIGURE 39.5.

Delivering mail to the information services.

MAPI OLE 2.0 Controls

In Visual FoxPro, you can create your own mail-enabled application by using the MAPI OLE 2.0 control, MSMAPI32.OCX. There are two MAPI OLE controls you can add to a form with MSMAPI32.OCX. The first is the MAPI Session control that establishes and terminates a MAPI session. The second is the MAPI Messages control. You use it to perform various messaging system functions.

You use these controls as you would any other OLE container control. That is, you click on the OLE container control icon in the toolbar and then click and drag to size at the place on the form where you want the control to be. At that time, the Insert Object dialog box appears, as shown in Figure 39.6. Select one of the MAPI controls and press OK. The MAPI Session control displays on the design form as a button with a letter and a key on it, as shown in Figure 39.6. It doesn't matter where you place the MAPI controls on the form because the MAPI controls are invisible at runtime.

FIGURE 39.6.

Adding a MAPI Session control to a form.

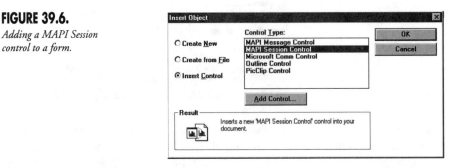

After you sign on to a messaging session using the MAPI Session control, you use the MAPI Messages control to perform a variety of messaging system functions, including the following:

- Access attachments and OLE automation attachments
- Access Inbox messages
- Add and delete message recipients and attachments
- Compose a new message
- Display the Address Book dialog box
- Display the Details dialog box
- Perform reply, reply-all, and forward actions on messages
- Resolve a recipient name during addressing
- Save, copy, and delete messages from the Inbox and Outbox
- Send messages in the Outbox

You can use the MAPI controls only when you're running Windows NT 3.1 or Windows 95. In fact, the Visual FoxPro Setup program does not install these two controls when you install Visual FoxPro for Windows 3.1 or Windows for Workgroups. It is not installed for Windows 3.1 because the MAPI controls don't work with the Win386s library. If Visual FoxPro is installed for Windows 3.1 and you upgrade your system for Windows 95 or NT, you should reinstall Visual FoxPro.

MAPI Session Control Methods and Properties

The MAPI controls are passive. That is, there are no events for you to write code for. To use the MAPI functionality, you need to call a method to perform an action. The important methods for the MAPI session are `SignOn` and `SignOff`.

When you want to establish a MAPI session, you call the `SignOn` method. The `SignOn` method logs the user into the messaging subsystem account that is specified by the `UserName` and `Password` properties. In other words, at the point in your application where you want to sign on to an account, add the following code to a method in a form:

```
THISFORM.MAPISession.NewSession = .T.
THISFORM.MAPISession.UserName = accountname
THISFORM.MAPISession.Password = password
THISFORM.MAPISession.SignOn
THISFORM.MAPIMessages.SessionID = THISFORM.MAPISessionID.SessionID
THISFORM.MAPIMessages.Fetch
```

`MAPISession` is the name of the MAPI session control object. `MAPIMessages` is the name of the MAPI Messages control object. If you have a form that does messaging operations, you can place the preceding code in the `Init` event method for the form.

The `NewSession` property specifies whether (`.T.`) or not (`.F.`) to establish a new mail session. The `SignOn` method stores the session handle in the `SessionID` property if the `NewSession` property is set to true (`.T.`). If the `NewSession` property is set to false (`.F.`), the session handle refers to an existing session. The `Signon` method stores the MAPI session handle in its `SessionsID` property. You can set the `SessionID` property value for the MAPI Messages control from the `SessionID` property for the MAPI Session control. If you provide an invalid value for the `SessionID` property, Visual FoxPro generates an error.

The MAPI Messages control `Fetch` method that is discussed in the next section is called in the above code to read the Inbox messages.

You can designate whether you want a login dialog box displayed during the sign-on process with the `LoginUI` property. By default, the `LoginUI` property is set to true (`.T.`) and the dialog box displays. If, on the other hand, you want the mail session to be established without user interaction, you can set the `LoginUI` property to false (`.F.`). However, you must supply values for the user's account name (`UserName`) and password (`Password`) properties. If you supply incorrect values, the MAPI session control generates an error. If you supply a valid user account name and password, no dialog box displays, even if the `LoginUI` property is set to true (`.T.`).

The other relevant property for the MAPI session property is `DownloadMail`. By default, this property is set to true (`.T.`), indicating that any new messages from the mail server are transferred to the Inbox during the sign-on process. Although this option is useful if you want to make sure you process all of the user's mail, it slows down the sign-on process. If you want to suppress this download operation during sign-on, initialize the `DownloadMail` property to false (`.F.`).

To facilitate the process of establishing properties, you can right-click on the MAPI Session control and choose the Properties option from the shortcut menu. The MAPI Session Control Properties dialog box appears, as shown in Figure 39.7, from which you can establish the properties relevant to the MAPI Session control.

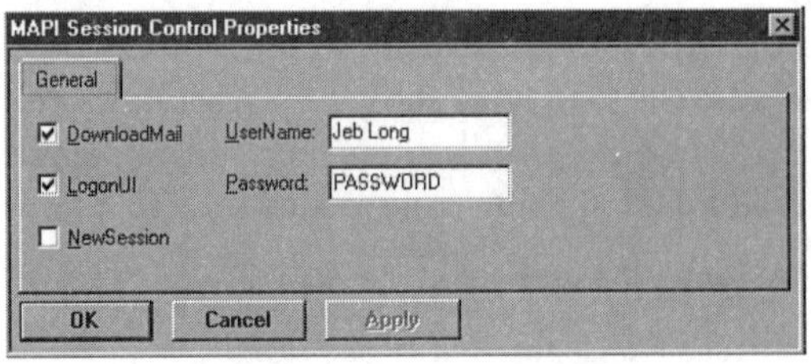

FIGURE 39.7.

The MAPI Session Control Properties dialog box.

The SignOff method terminates the mail session for the account specified by the UserName and Password properties. No other properties are relevant.

MAPI Messages Control Methods and Properties

As mentioned earlier, there are no events for the MAPI controls. You perform operations by setting properties and calling methods.

Generally, there are four categories of properties for the MAPI Messages control that correspond to the following four functional areas:

- Address book operations
- File attachment operations controlled by the AttachmentIndex property
- Message handling operations controlled by the MsgIndex property
- Mail recipient properties controlled by the RecipIndex property

These properties are used to designate which item is referenced. For example, the MsgIndex property specifies which message from the Inbox to reference. The message numbering scheme begins with 0. That is, if MsgIndex is set to 0, the first message is referenced. As the index value changes in the MsgIndex property, all other message, file attachment, and recipient properties change to reflect the characteristics of the new currently indexed message. The settings of the attachment and recipient properties behave the same way.

The MAPI Messages control maintains a *read buffer* and a *compose buffer*. The read buffer consists of an indexed set of messages that are retrieved from the user's Inbox. The MsgIndex property specifies which message is accessed from the message set.

You use the Fetch method to build the message set in the read buffer. The set includes all messages that are the same type as defined by the FetchMsgType property. The default value for the FetchMsgType property is a null string that denotes an interpersonal mail (IPM) type message, which is the normal message type. Unless you are processing weird message types, you do not have to change the `FetchMsgType` property. The `FetchSorted` property designates whether the messages are sorted in the order in which they were received. You can include previously read messages or leave them out of the message set with the `FetchUnreadOnly` property. You cannot alter messages in the read buffer, but you can copy them to the compose buffer for alteration.

You can create or edit messages in the compose buffer. The compose buffer is the active buffer when the `MsgIndex` property is set to `-1`. Many of the messaging actions are valid only within the compose buffer (for example, sending messages, sending messages with a dialog box, saving messages, deleting recipients and attachments).

The methods that are important to the MAPI Messages control are presented in Table 39.1. Table 39.2 summarizes the relevant MAPI Messages control properties.

Table 39.1. MAPI Messages control methods.

Method	*Description*
`AboutBox`	Displays an About dialog box for the MAPI Messages control.
`Compose`	You call this method when you want to compose a new message. The `Compose` method clears all of the compose buffer components and sets the `MsgIndex` property to `-1`.
`Copy`	You cannot change the contents of an indexed message. However, you can copy the contents of a message into the compose buffer using the `Copy` method. You indicate which message to copy by setting the value of the `MsgIndex` property to the index for the message.
`Delete(nType)`	You can use the `Delete` method to delete a message, a recipient, or an attachment. It has a single argument used to indicate what type of object to delete.
	The `Delete(0)` method deletes all components of the currently indexed message. For example, to delete the third message, specify
	`THISFORM.MAPIMessage.MsgIndex = 3` `THISFORM.MAPIMessage.DELETE(0)`
	In addition, the `Delete(0)` method reduces the message count (`MsgCount` property) by 1 and decrements by 1 the index number for each message following the deleted message. If the deleted message was the last message in the set, the `MsgIndex` property is decremented by 1.
	`Delete(1)` deletes the currently indexed recipient. Note that the `RecipIndex` property is used to index the Address book entries. For example, to delete the second recipient, specify

continues

Table 39.1. continued

Method	Description
	`THISFORM.MAPIMessage.RecipIndex = 1` `THISFORM.MAPIMessage.DELETE(1)`
	In addition, the `Delete(1)` method reduces the recipient count (`RecipientCount` property) by 1 and decrements by 1 the index number for each recipient following the deleted recipient. If the deleted recipient was the last recipient in the address book list, the `RecipIndex` property is decremented by 1.
	`Delete(2)` deletes the currently indexed attachment for the current message. Note that the `AttachmentIndex` property is used to index the attachment. For example, to delete the second attachment for the third message, specify

	`THISFORM.MAPIMessage.Attachment = 1`
	`THISFORM.MAPIMessage.MsgIndex    = 2`
	`THISFORM.MAPIMessage.DELETE(2)`

	In addition, the `Delete(2)` method reduces the attachment count (`AttachmentCount` property) by 1. It also decrements by 1 the index number for each attachment in the list following the deleted attachment. If the deleted attachment was the last attachment, the `AttachmentIndex` property is decremented by 1.
Fetch	The `Fetch` method transfers all the messages in the Inbox of the type specified by the `FetchMsgType` property to the read buffer. If the `FetchUnreadOnly` property is set to true (`.T.`), only messages that have been unread are added to the message set. By default, the `FetchUnreadOnly` property is set to `.F.` and all messages are added to the message set.
Forward	The `Forward` method copies the currently indexed message (`MsgIndex` property) to the compose buffer as a forwarded message. In addition, the `Forward` method prepends the `FW:` text to the beginning of the Subject line and sets the `MsgIndex` property to `-1`.
Reply	The `Reply` method copies the currently indexed message (`MsgIndex` property value) to the compose buffer. In addition, the `Reply` method prepends the `RE:` text to the beginning of the Subject line and sets the `MsgIndex` property to `-1`. The currently indexed message originator becomes the recipient of the outgoing message.

Method	*Description*
ReplyAll	The ReplyAll method is exactly like the Reply method except that the recipients of the outgoing message become the originator plus all of the recipients (To: and CC:) of the currently indexed message.
ResolveName	The ResolveName method searches the address book for a match on the currently indexed recipient name. If no match is found, the ResolveName method returns an error and provides no other indication as to the name or address of the originator.
	You can use the AddressResolveUI property to designate that you want to display a dialog box to resolve an ambiguous name. If the AddressResolveUI property is true (.T.), a dialog box displays showing the names that most closely match the proposed recipients. By default, the AddressResolveUI is set to false (.F.) and the ResolveName method returns an error if the recipient is not found. The ResolveName method can cause the RecipType property to change.
Save	The Save method saves the message in the compose buffer.
Send[(lDialog)]	The Send method sends the contents of the compose buffer (MsgIndex property equals -1) to the Outbox. You can then execute Microsoft Exchange to deliver the mail. If you set the lDialog parameter to true (.T.), a dialog box appears to prompt the user for the various message components and submits the message to the mail server for delivery. The message properties associated with the compose buffer are used to fill in the fields in the dialog box.
	If you do not specify an argument or if the lDialog parameter is set to false (.F.), the message defined by the compose buffer is submitted to the mail server for delivery without a dialog box being displayed. However, if you attempt to send a message with no recipient or other invalid parameters, the Send method generates an error.
Show[(lShow)]	The Show method displays the Address Book dialog box if you omit the lShow argument or set the argument to false (.F.), as shown in Figure 39.8. You can add to or modify the recipient list in the Address Book. Changes made using the Show method are not permanent.
	If you supply a true (.T.) value as the argument to the Show method, a dialog box displays that shows the details of the currently indexed recipient. Use the AddressIndex property to index the recipient.

FIGURE 39.8.

Using the Show method to display the Address Book dialog box.

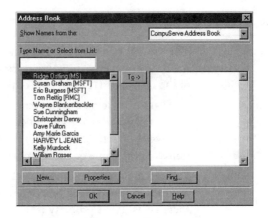

Table 39.2. MAPI Messages control properties.

Property	Type	Description
Action	N	The Action property can be used to specify or return a value that determines what action is performed when the MAPI control is invoked. Although it can be used to specify actions, it is simpler and safer to call methods to perform actions. See the Visual FoxPro Help for more information.
AddressCaption	C	The AddressCaption option specifies or returns the Address Book dialog box caption when the Show method is called with a false (.F.) argument to display the Address Book.
AddressEditFieldCount	N	The AddressEditFieldCount property specifies or returns the number of edit controls available to the user in the Address Book dialog box when the Show method is called with a false (.F.) argument. The value of this property designates that the Address Book dialog box contains the following edit controls:

0   None. You are only allowed to browse the Address Book.

1   (Default) The To edit control.

2   The To and CC (carbon copy) edit controls.

3   The To, CC (carbon copy), and BCC (blind carbon copy) edit controls.

4   Only those edit controls supported by the messaging system.

Property	Type	Description
AddressLabel	C	The AddressLabel property designates or returns a character string that contains the To label caption for the edit control in the Address Book. Used with the Show(.F) method.
AddressModifiable	L	The AddressModifiable property specifies whether (.T.) or not (.F.) the personal address book can be modified. By default, the address book cannot be modified by the user. The default value is false (.F.).
AddressResolveUI	L	The AddressResolveUI property specifies whether (.T.) or not (.F.) a dialog box displays to resolve any ambiguous names during addressing when you call the ResolveName method. If AddressResolveUI is set to false (.F.) and the name is not in the address book, an error is generated.
AttachmentCount	N	The AttachmentCount property contains the number of attachments associated with the currently indexed message.
AttachmentIndex	N	The AttachmentIndex property designates or returns the currently indexed attachment for the currently indexed message. The value of the AttachmentIndex property can range from 0 (the default) to AttachmentCount -1.
AttachmentName	C	The AttachmentName property specifies or returns the filename of the currently indexed attachment associated with the currently indexed message.
AttachmentPathName	C	The AttachmentPathName property specifies or returns the full pathname of the currently indexed attachment associated with the currently indexed message.
AttachmentPosition	N	The AttachmentPosition property specifies or returns the relative position of the currently indexed attachment within the body of the currently indexed message. This property is read-only unless it is attached to a compose buffer.
AttachmentType	N	The AttachmentType property specifies and returns a numeric value that designates the type of the currently indexed file attachment in the currently indexed message. The attachment type can be 0 (data

continues

Table 39.2. continued

Property	Type	Description
		file), 1 (embedded OLE object), or 2 (static OLE object).
FetchMsgType	C	The FetchMsgType property specifies or returns the type of messages to transfer from the Inbox to the read buffer message set.
FetchSorted	L	The FetchSorted property designates whether (.T.) or not (.F.) the message set is sorted by the date received.
FetchUnreadOnly	L	The FetchUnreadOnly property designates whether (.T.) or not (.F.) the message set contains only unread messages.
MsgConversationID	N	The MsgConversationID property designates or returns the conversion thread identification value for the currently indexed message. A conversation thread identifies a set of messages, beginning with the original message and including all the subsequent replies. Messages with identical conversation IDs are part of the same thread. The Messaging Subsystem assigns a new, unique ID to new messages. The value of the MsgConversationID property depends on the currently indexed message, as specified by the MsgIndex property. One useful application of the MsgConversionID property is to build an outline-style list of messages with the outline indentations denoting the threads.
MsgCount	N	The MsgCount property contains the number of messages in the message set.
MsgDateReceived	C	The MsgDateReceived property contains the date the message was received as a character string in the form *yyyy:mm:dd hh:mm*.
MsgID	C	The MsgID property contains a 64-bit string identifier that uniquely identifies the currently indexed message.
MsgIndex	N	The MsgIndex property designates and returns the index number of the currently indexed message in the message set. Its value can be between –1 and MsgCount-1. A value of [ms1 designates that a message is being created in the compose buffer.

Property	Type	Description
MsgNoteText	C	The MsgNoteText property designates and returns a character string containing the body of text of the currently indexed message.
MsgOrigAddress	C	The MsgOrigAddress property contains the mail address of the originator of the currently indexed message.
MsgOrigDisplayName	C	The MsgOrigDisplayName property contains the name of the originator of the currently indexed message.
MsgRead	L	The MsgRead property designates whether (.T.) or not (.F.) the currently indexed message is unread.
MsgReceiptRequested	L	The MsgReceiptRequested property designates whether (.T.) or not (.F.) a return receipt is requested for the currently indexed message.
MsgSent	L	The MsgSent property indicates whether (.T.) or not (.F.) the currently indexed message has been sent to the mail server for delivery.
MsgSubject	C	The MsgSubject property designates or returns the subject line for the currently indexed message as displayed in the message header.
MsgType	C	The MsgType property designates or returns the type of the currently indexed message. Usually, the type is interpersonal mail (IPM), which is indicated by an empty string.
RecipAddress	C	The RecipAddress property designates or returns the electronic mail address currently indexed recipient for the currently indexed message.
RecipCount	N	The RecipCount property contains the total number of recipients for the currently indexed message.
RecipDisplayName	C	The RecipDisplayName property designates or returns the currently indexed recipient for the currently indexed message.
RecipIndex	N	The RecipIndex property designates or returns the currently indexed recipient for the currently indexed message.
RecipType	N	The RecipType property designates or returns the type of the currently indexed recipient for the currently indexed message. The type can be 0 (originator),

continues

Table 39.2. continued

Property	Type	Description
		1 (primary recipient), 2 (CC:, carbon-copy recipient), or 3 (BCC:, blind carbon-copy recipient).
SessionID	N	The SessionID property specifies the current messaging session handle. The MAPI SignOn method sets the SessionID property for the MAPI session control. You should store its value in the SessionID property for the MAPI Messages control.

Error Handling

You can add to the Error event method of your form of your mail-enabled application to trap errors generated by the MAPI Session and MAPI Messages controls. Table 39.3 lists the trappable errors for the MAPI controls.

Table 39.3. Trappable errors for the MAPI controls.

Error Number	Error
7	You have run out of memory.
380	Invalid property value.
32001	User has canceled the process.
32002	Unspecified failure has occurred.
32003	Login has failed.
32004	Disk is full.
32005	Insufficient memory.
32006	Access is denied.
32007	MAPI_E_FAILURE.
32008	Too many sessions are open.
32009	Too many files are open.
32010	Too many recipients.
32011	Specified attachment was not found.
32012	A failure was encountered while opening the specified attachment.
32013	A failure occurred while attempting to write to an attachment.
32014	Recipient is unknown.

Error Number	Error
32015	The recipient type is invalid.
32016	There exists no messages.
32017	Specified message is invalid.
32018	Text is too large.
32019	Specified session is invalid.
32020	Specified type is not supported.
32021	Recipient is ambiguous.
32022	Specified message is already in use.
32023	Network failure has occurred.
32024	The edit fields are invalid.
32025	Recipients are invalid.
32026	Specified feature is not supported.
32027	The user has aborted the previous action.
32050	Logon failure: Valid session ID already exists.
32051	Property is read-only when not using the compose buffer. To remedy this problem, set MsgIndex to -1.
32052	Specified action is only valid for compose buffer. To remedy this problem, set MsgIndex to -1.
32053	MAPI failure: Valid session ID does not exist.
32054	No originator in the compose buffer.
32055	Action not valid for compose buffer.
32056	Cannot perform action because there are no messages in list.
32057	Cannot perform action because there are no recipients.
32058	Cannot perform action because there are no attachments.

An Example of a Visual FoxPro Mail-Enabled Application

This section illustrates how to use MAPI controls to create a simple e-mail application. With this application you can read your e-mail, compose new mail, and send the new mail to the mail server.

The first step to creating this application is to invoke the Visual FoxPro Form Designer and lay out all the controls on the form. As you see in Figure 39.9, the MAPI Session and MAPI Messages controls appear at the right of the form. They could be placed anywhere on the form because they are invisible at runtime.

FIGURE 39.9.

Designing the Mail-enabled application form with the Form Designer.

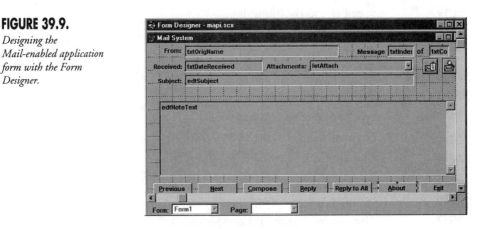

In addition to the MAPI controls, the Mail System form, shown in Figure 39.9, contains control buttons to control the functionality of the application, edit boxes to display the text of the message and the subject, text boxes to display the name of the originator and date that the message was received, and the message index number and message count. The Click event method for some of the command buttons contains code that executes the MAPI Messages control method.

Initialization

When the form executes, the form and all its controls are loaded into memory. Then Visual FoxPro calls the form's Init event method. The Init event method is a good place to establish a MAPI session, retrieve the mail from the Inbox, and establish values for the form's controls based on the components of the first message. The Init event method code that accomplishes this functionality is shown in Listing 39.1.

Listing 39.1. The source listing of the form's Init event method and associated user-defined methods.

```
PROCEDURE Form1.Init
    WITH THISFORM
        .MAPISession.UserName = "MS Exchange Settings", ;
        .MAPISession.Password = "PASSWORD", ;
        .MAPISession.DownloadMail = .F.
        .MAPISession.Signon
        .MAPIMessages.SessionID = THISFORM.MAPISession.SessionID
        .MAPIMessages.Fetch
        .SetValues   && set form values
    ENDWITH
```

```
ENDPROC
****************************************************************
*-- Sets form control values with message parameters
PROCEDURE Form1.SetValues
    Local nAttachIndex
    WITH THISFORM
        .lstAttach.Clear    && Clear Combo box
        IF .MAPIMessages.AttachmentCount > 0
          FOR nAttachIndex = 0 to .MAPIMessages.AttachmentCount-1
             .MAPIMessages.AttachmentIndex = nAttachIndex
             .lstAttach.AddItem(.MAPIMessages.AttachmentPathName)
          ENDFOR
          .lstAttach.Value = .lstAttach.List(1)
        ENDIF
        .txtIndex.value       =  .MAPIMessages.MsgIndex + 1
        .txtCount.value       =  .MAPIMessages.MsgCount
        .edtNoteText.value    =  .MAPIMessages.MsgNoteText
        .edtSubject.value     =  .MAPIMessages.Msgsubject
        .txtDateReceived.value =  .DateConvert(.MAPIMessages.MsgDateReceived)
        .txtOrigName.value    =  .MAPIMessages.MsgOrigDisplayName
        .Refresh
    ENDWITH
ENDPROC
****************************************************************
*    User Defined Method: Date Convert
*       Converts date from mail format to mdy() form
PROCEDURE Form1.DateConvert
    PARAMETER cMailDate
    LOCAL cSaveDate, cSaveCentury, cmDate
    cSaveDate    = SET("DATE")
    cSaveCentury = SET("CENTURY")
    SET DATE TO JAPAN
    SET CENTURY ON
    cmDate = ctot(cMailDate)
    cmDate = MDY(cmDate)+" "+TIME(cmDate)
    SET DATE TO &cSaveDate
    SET CENTURY &cSaveCentury
    RETURN cmDate
ENDPROC
```

The first statements in Init set the UserName and Password properties. These values could have been retrieved from the system through a Windows API call or by prompting the user. However, I wanted to focus this application on the MAPI controls, so I simply hard coded the user name and password with the Windows 95 Exchange default settings. I set the DownloadMail property to false (.F.) so that I would not have to wait for MAPI to check for new mail from both the CompuServe and the Microsoft Network online services. You could display a dialog box to prompt the user at this point to indicate whether mail downloading is desired before executing the form. These three properties could have been defined at design time. However, I wanted to emphasize their purpose. Finally, the MAPI session control Signon method is called to sign on to a MAPI session.

The next statement stores the session handle in the SessionID property of the MAPI Messages control. Then the Fetch method is called to transfer the Inbox mail to the read buffer. The user-defined method SetValues is called to store the values of components of the first message into the form's controls.

After Visual FoxPro initializes the form, it displays the form, as shown in Figure 39.10. In this figure the first message in the message set displays.

FIGURE 39.10.

The mail system form displaying the first message of the message set.

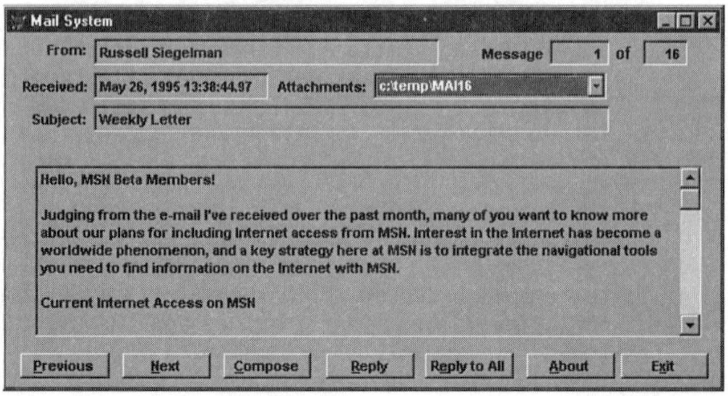

As shown in Listing 39.1, the SetValues method sets the Value property of various text boxes and edit boxes. In addition, if there are any attachments associated with a message, SetValues adds the pathnames of the attachments as items in a drop-down list (comAttach) control. Table 39.4 describes the variables, properties, and controls used in the SetValues method and elsewhere in the form.

Table 39.4. Variables, properties, and controls used in the SetValues method and form.

Item	Description
MAPIMessages	Name of the MAPI Messages control object
AttachmentCount	MAPI Messages control property containing number of attachments
nAttachIndex	Temporary variable used as index
AttachmentIndex	MAPI Messages control property that defines currently indexed attachment
lstAttach	Drop-down (combo) control that displays attachments
AttachmentPathName	MAPI Messages control property that contains the pathname of the currently indexed attachment
txtIndex	Text box control used to display the message number (MAPIMessages.MsgIndex + 1)

Item	Description
txtCount	Text box control used to display number of attachments for the currently indexed message (MsgCount property)
edtNoteText	Edit box control used to display the message's body of text (MsgNoteText property)
edtSubject	Edit box control used to display the message's subject (MsgSubject property)
txtDateReceived	Text box control used to display the messages received date (MsgDateReceived property)
txtOrigName	Text box control used to display the name of the message originator (MsgOrigDisplayName)

The SetValues method calls the DateConvert user-defined method to convert the message date in the format *yyyy:mm:dd hh:mm* to the format returned by the MDY() function.

Navigating Through the Messages

The cmdNext and cmdPrev command buttons are used to navigate through the messages. For example, when the user clicks on the Next button, the MAPI Messages control MsgIndex property is incremented by 1 and the next message becomes the current message. Finally, the Click event method calls the SetValues method to display the values of the newly selected message. Listing 39.2 presents the code that executes when the Next and Previous command button Click events fire.

Listing 39.2. Click event methods for the Next and Previous buttons.

```
PROCEDURE cmdnext.Click
    IF Thisform.MAPIMessages.MsgIndex          ;
        < Thisform.MAPIMessages.MsgCount-1
        Thisform.MAPIMessages.MsgIndex =       ;
        Thisform.MAPIMessages.MsgIndex + 1
    ENDIF
    THISFORM.SetValues
ENDPROC

PROCEDURE cmdprev.Click
    IF THISFORM.MAPIMessages.MsgIndex >0
        THISFORM.MAPIMessages.MsgIndex = ;
            THISFORM.MAPIMessages.MsgIndex -1
    ENDIF
    THISFORM.SetValues  && Set values in form
ENDPROC
```

You might ask why I did not provide a fancy VCR-type navigation system. All I want to do in this chapter is to focus on the MAPI controls. This navigation system adequately demonstrates how easy it is to navigate through the messages. I will graciously relinquish the task of providing a more aesthetic interface as an exercise for the user. To make that task easier, the current version of the MAPI.SCX form is on the CD-ROM that accompanies this book.

The Compose, Reply, and Reply All Command Buttons

The task of creating a new message and sending it to the server using the MAPI controls is quite simple. All you have to do is call one of the three `Compose`, `Reply`, or `ReplyAll` methods, depending on your needs. Then you call the `Send` method with a true (`.T.`) argument.

The `Compose` method clears the compose buffer and sets the message index (`MsgIndex`) to -1. The `Reply` method performs the following operations:

- Copies the currently indexed message to the command buffer
- Copies the originator name (`MsgOrigDisplayName`) and address (`MsgOrigAddress`) to the corresponding mail destination properties (`RecipDisplayName`) and (`RecipAddress`)
- Copies the subject of the currently indexed message to the compose buffer subject field and prepends it with `RE:`
- Sets `MsgIndex` to -1

The `ReplyAll` method does the same thing as the `Reply` method except that it copies the name and address of all the recipients of the original message to the name and address of the recipient properties of the outgoing message.

The `Click` event method for the Compose command button is shown in Listing 39.3. The only difference between the `Click` event for the Compose button and the `Click` event for the Reply and Reply All buttons is that the `Compose` method is called instead of the `Reply` or `ReplyAll` methods, respectively. Notice that it is necessary to save and restore the current value of the message index (`MsgIndex`) because the `Compose` method sets `MsgIndex` to -1.

Listing 39.3. `Click` event methods for the Compose command button.

```
*************************************************************
* CmdCompose.Click is the Click event method for the Compose
*   push button.
PROCEDURE cmdcompose.Click
      Local nSaveMsgIndex
      WITH THISFORM.MAPIMessages
         nSaveMsgIndex = .MsgIndex
         .Compose
         .Send(.T.)
         .MsgIndex = nSaveMsgIndex
      ENDWITH
   ENDPROC
```

> **NOTE**
>
> Remember that you can use the WITH...ENDWITH structure to specify multiple properties for a single object.

If you press the Reply All button, the Microsoft Exchange message compose dialog box appears, as shown in Figure 39.11. Notice that the recipient and originator for the original message have become recipients of the outgoing message.

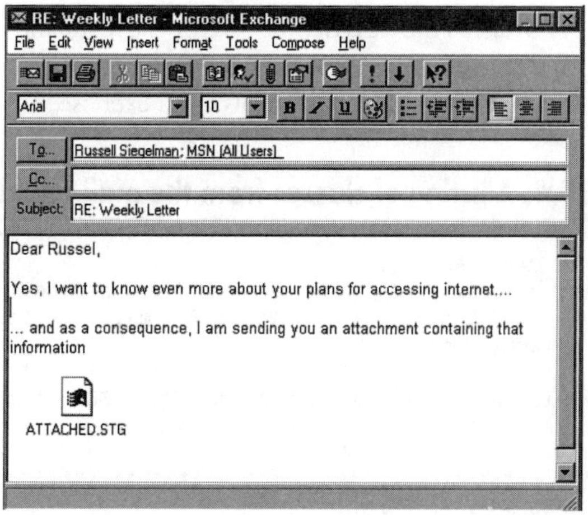

FIGURE 39.11.

Composing an outgoing letter.

Of course, the fact that the Send(.T.) method uses the Microsoft Exchange's message compose dialog box makes the MAPI controls even easier to use to create your own main-enabled application. However, if your application provides all the required valid components of the compose buffer (text body, subject, recipient name, recipient address, and so forth), you can deliver mail to the mail server without displaying any dialog boxes or requiring any other user intervention. All you have to do is to call the Send method with a false (.F.) or no argument. Here's an example:

```
THISFORM.Send
```

Therefore, it is possible to create a mail-enabled batch process that automatically pumps out an endless supply of messages to the mail server without any user intervention.

Terminating a MAPI Session

Whether you exit the form by clicking on the Windows 95 Close button or the Exit button, Visual FoxPro always calls the form's Destroy event method. Consequently, the Destroy event method is a good place to put the following line of code that ends the MAPI session:

```
THISFORM.MAPISession.SignOff
```

The `SignOff` method terminates the MAPI messaging session and signs the user off from the account designated by the `UserName` and `Password` properties.

Putting It All Together

The mail system form (MAPI.SCX) is a self-contained mail-enabled application. You can execute the MAPI.SCX form from another application or from the Command window using the following command:

```
DO FORM MAPI
```

Listing 39.4 presents the class definitions for the form and all of its controls. I created this listing using the Visual FoxPro Class Browser `View Class` command so you can examine the classes of the MAPI.SCX form and its controls as an exercise.

Listing 39.4. A listing of classes from the mail-enabled application MAPI.SCX.

```
****************************************************************
* Program: MAPI.PRG
* Purpose: Program MAPI illustrates the use of the
*          MAPI Controls to create a VFP mail-enabled
*          application
****************************************************************
* NOTE: This code was derived from the MAPI.SCX form using
*       the Class Browser, View Class command.
*
****************************************************************
DEFINE CLASS MAPI AS Form
    AutoCenter = .T.
    Height = 280
    Width = 592
    DoCreate = .T.
    ShowTips = .T.
    BackColor = RGB(192,192,192)
    Caption = "Mail System"
    FontSize = 8
    LockScreen = .F.
    Name = "Form1"

    ADD OBJECT MAPISession AS olecontrol WITH ;
        Top = 29, ;
        Left = 552, ;
        Height = 61, ;
        Width = 157, ;
        UserName = "MS Exchange Settings", ;
        Password = "PASSWORD", ;
        Name = "MAPISession"

    ADD OBJECT MAPIMessages AS olecontrol WITH ;
        Top = 29, ;
        Left = 516, ;
        Height = 25, ;
        Width = 37, ;
        Name = "MAPIMessages"
```

```
ADD OBJECT cmdexit AS commandbutton WITH ;
    Top = 254, ;
    Left = 510, ;
    Height = 20, ;
    Width = 73, ;
    FontSize = 8, ;
    Caption = "E\<xit", ;
    StatusBarText = "Exit from the Mail System", ;
    ToolTipText = "Exit", ;
    TerminateRead = .T., ;
    Name = "cmdExit"

ADD OBJECT cmdcompose AS commandbutton WITH ;
    Top = 254, ;
    Left = 180, ;
    Height = 20, ;
    Width = 73, ;
    FontSize = 8, ;
    Caption = "\<Compose", ;
    StatusBarText = "Create a new message", ;
    ToolTipText = "New Message", ;
    Name = "cmdCompose"

ADD OBJECT cmdreply AS commandbutton WITH ;
    Top = 254, ;
    Left = 266, ;
    Height = 20, ;
    Width = 73, ;
    FontSize = 8, ;
    Caption = "\<Reply", ;
    StatusBarText = "Reply to Originator", ;
    Name = "cmdReply"

ADD OBJECT cmdnext AS commandbutton WITH ;
    Top = 254, ;
    Left = 96, ;
    Height = 20, ;
    Width = 73, ;
    FontSize = 8, ;
    Caption = "\<Next", ;
    StatusBarText = "Display Next Message", ;
    ToolTipText = "Next Message", ;
    Name = "cmdNext"

ADD OBJECT cmdprev AS commandbutton WITH ;
    Top = 254, ;
    Left = 12, ;
    Height = 20, ;
    Width = 73, ;
    FontSize = 8, ;
    Caption = "\<Previous", ;
    StatusBarText = "Display previous message", ;
    ToolTipText = "Previous Message", ;
    Name = "cmdPrev"
```

continues

Listing 39.4. continued

```
ADD OBJECT edtnotetext AS editbox WITH ;
    FontSize = 8, ;
    BackColor = RGB(192,192,192), ;
    Height = 136, ;
    Left = 24, ;
    Top = 105, ;
    Width = 553, ;
    Name = "edtNoteText"

ADD OBJECT edtsubject AS editbox WITH ;
    FontSize = 8, ;
    BackColor = RGB(192,192,192), ;
    Height = 21, ;
    Left = 72, ;
    Top = 57, ;
    Width = 428, ;
    Name = "edtSubject"

ADD OBJECT txtcount AS textbox WITH ;
    FontSize = 8, ;
    BackColor = RGB(192,192,192), ;
    Height = 20, ;
    Left = 528, ;
    Top = 5, ;
    Width = 37, ;
    Name = "txtCount"

ADD OBJECT txtindex AS textbox WITH ;
    FontSize = 8, ;
    BackColor = RGB(192,192,192), ;
    Height = 20, ;
    Left = 451, ;
    Top = 5, ;
    Width = 49, ;
    Name = "txtIndex"

ADD OBJECT cmdabout AS commandbutton WITH ;
    Top = 254, ;
    Left = 432, ;
    Height = 20, ;
    Width = 73, ;
    FontSize = 8, ;
    Caption = "\<About", ;
    StatusBarText = "Display About Dialog Box", ;
    ToolTipText = "About MAPI Control", ;
    Name = "cmdAbout"

ADD OBJECT label1 AS label WITH ;
    FontSize = 8, ;
    BackColor = RGB(192,192,192), ;
    Caption = "Subject:", ;
    Height = 15, ;
    Left = 22, ;
    Top = 61, ;
    Width = 46, ;
    Name = "Label1"
```

```
ADD OBJECT label2 AS label WITH ;
    BackColor = RGB(192,192,192), ;
    Caption = "of", ;
    Height = 17, ;
    Left = 505, ;
    Top = 7, ;
    Width = 15, ;
    Name = "Label2"

ADD OBJECT label3 AS label WITH ;
    FontSize = 8, ;
    BackColor = RGB(192,192,192), ;
    Caption = "Message", ;
    Height = 16, ;
    Left = 395, ;
    Top = 9, ;
    Width = 54, ;
    Name = "Label3"

ADD OBJECT txtdatereceived AS textbox WITH ;
    FontSize = 8, ;
    BackColor = RGB(192,192,192), ;
    Height = 21, ;
    Left = 72, ;
    Top = 31, ;
    Width = 145, ;
    Name = "txtDateReceived"

ADD OBJECT label4 AS label WITH ;
    FontSize = 8, ;
    BackColor = RGB(192,192,192), ;
    Caption = "Received:", ;
    Height = 18, ;
    Left = 14, ;
    Top = 35, ;
    Width = 55, ;
    Name = "Label4"

ADD OBJECT txtorigname AS textbox WITH ;
    FontSize = 8, ;
    BackColor = RGB(192,192,192), ;
    Height = 21, ;
    Left = 72, ;
    Top = 4, ;
    Width = 287, ;
    Name = "txtOrigName"

ADD OBJECT label5 AS label WITH ;
    FontSize = 8, ;
    BackColor = RGB(192,192,192), ;
    Caption = "From:", ;
    Height = 18, ;
    Left = 34, ;
    Top = 6, ;
    Width = 34, ;
    Name = "Label5"
```

continues

Listing 39.4. continued

```
    ADD OBJECT cmdreplyall AS commandbutton WITH ;
        Top = 254, ;
        Left = 348, ;
        Height = 20, ;
        Width = 73, ;
        FontSize = 8, ;
        Caption = "R\<eply to All", ;
        StatusBarText = "Reply to Originator and all Recipients", ;
        Name = "cmdReplyAll"

    ADD OBJECT label6 AS label WITH ;
        FontSize = 8, ;
        BackColor = RGB(192,192,192), ;
        Caption = "Attachments:", ;
        Height = 18, ;
        Left = 225, ;
        Top = 35, ;
        Width = 76, ;
        Name = "Label6"

    ADD OBJECT lstattach AS combobox WITH ;
        FontSize = 8, ;
        BackColor = RGB(192,192,192), ;
        ColumnCount = 0, ;
        RowSourceType = 0, ;
        RowSource = "", ;
        FirstElement = 1, ;
        Height = 21, ;
        Left = 305, ;
        NumberOfElements = 0, ;
        Style = 2, ;
        ToolTipText = "Path name of attachments", ;
        Top = 31, ;
        Width = 193, ;
        Name = "lstAttach"

*****************************************************************
*-- Sets form control values with message parameters
    PROCEDURE setvalues
        Local nAttachIndex
        WITH THISFORM
            .lstAttach.Clear    && Clear Combo box
            IF .MAPIMessages.AttachmentCount > 0
              FOR nAttachIndex = 0 to .MAPIMessages.AttachmentCount-1
                .MAPIMessages.AttachmentIndex = nAttachIndex
                .lstAttach.AddItem(.MAPIMessages.AttachmentPathName)
              ENDFOR
              .lstAttach.Value = .lstAttach.List(1)
            ENDIF
            .txtIndex.value        = .MAPIMessages.MsgIndex + 1
            .txtCount.value        = .MAPIMessages.MsgCount
            .edtNoteText.value     = .MAPIMessages.MsgNoteText
            .edtSubject.value      = .MAPIMessages.Msgsubject
            .txtDateReceived.value = .DateConvert(.MAPIMessages.MsgDateReceived)
            .txtOrigName.value     = .MAPIMessages.MsgOrigDisplayName
            .Refresh
        ENDWITH
    ENDPROC
```

```
*************************************************************
*-- Converts date from mail format to mdy() form
PROCEDURE dateconvert
    PARAMETER cMailDate
    LOCAL SaveDate, SaveCentury, cmDate
    SaveDate    = SET("DATE")
    SaveCentury = SET("CENTURY")
    SET DATE TO JAPAN
    SET CENTURY ON
    cmDate = ctot(cMailDate)
    cmDate = MDY(cmDate)+" "+TIME(cmDate)
    SET DATE TO &SaveDate
    SET CENTURY &SaveCentury
    RETURN cmDate
ENDPROC

PROCEDURE Init
  WITH THISFORM
    .MAPISession.UserName = "MS Exchange Settings"
    .MAPISession.Password = "PASSWORD"
    .MAPISession.DownloadMail = .F.
    .MAPISession.Signon
    .MAPIMessages.SessionID = THISFORM.MAPISession.SessionID
    .MAPIMessages.Fetch
    .SetValues  && set form values
  ENDWITH
ENDPROC

PROCEDURE Destroy
    THISFORM.MAPISession.SignOff
ENDPROC

PROCEDURE cmdexit.Click
    THISFORM.Release
ENDPROC

PROCEDURE cmdcompose.Click
    Local nSaveMsgIndex
    WITH THISFORM.MAPIMessages
        nSaveMsgIndex = .MsgIndex
        .Compose
        .Send(.T.)
        .MsgIndex = nSaveMsgIndex
    ENDWITH
ENDPROC

PROCEDURE cmdreply.Click
    Local nSaveMsgIndex
    WITH THISFORM.MAPIMessages
        nSaveMsgIndex = .MsgIndex
        .Reply
        .Send(.T.)
        .MsgIndex = nSaveMsgIndex
    ENDWITH

ENDPROC
```

continues

Listing 39.4. continued

```
PROCEDURE cmdnext.Click
    IF Thisform.MAPIMessages.MsgIndex          ;
        < Thisform.MAPIMessages.MsgCount-1
       Thisform.MAPIMessages.MsgIndex =        ;
            Thisform.MAPIMessages.MsgIndex + 1
    ENDIF
    THISFORM.SetValues
ENDPROC

PROCEDURE cmdprev.Click
    IF THISFORM.MAPIMessages.MsgIndex >0
       THISFORM.MAPIMessages.MsgIndex = ;
           THISFORM.MAPIMessages.MsgIndex -1
    ENDIF
    THISFORM.SetValues  && Set values in form
ENDPROC

PROCEDURE cmdabout.Click
    THISFORM.MAPIMessages.AboutBox
ENDPROC

PROCEDURE cmdreplyall.Click
    Local nSaveMsgIndex
    WITH THISFORM.MAPIMessages
       nSaveMsgIndex = .MsgIndex
       .ReplyAll
       .Send(.T.)
       .MsgIndex = nSaveMsgIndex
    ENDWITH
ENDPROC

ENDDEFINE
*-- EndDefine: MAPI
**************************************************
```

Summary

This chapter gave you a tour of the Microsoft Exchange Mail subsystem to familiarize you with the components of the Microsoft MAPI messaging subsystem architecture. You have learned all about the methods and properties of the Microsoft MAPI Session and Messages controls. You have also seen how to create a sample Visual FoxPro mail-enabled application.

Third-Party Products

A

IN THIS CHAPTER

This appendix provides a representative listing of third-party add-ons that can be used with FoxPro. In the case of each vendor, a contact address has been provided. This is by no means a complete listing but is meant to be representative of the types of third-party products available for use with Visual FoxPro. You can find additional resources in the pages of magazines like *FoxPro Advisor* and *Database Advisor*, and through the FoxPro support forum on CompuServe.

Fox Med

Fox Med, complete with source code in FoxPro, is a ten-module, fully integrated medical practice management application. Dealers can sell Fox Med on a royalty-free basis.

The Fox Med system includes patient and insurance billing, electronic claims filing in the National Standard format, patient history, patient communications, patient scheduling, general ledger, custom reporting, and clinical applications, all integrated into a single application.

ACC Incorporated
12500 San Pedro, Suite 460
San Antonio, TX 78216-2858
Phone: (210) 545-1010

Flash Development Toolkit

The Flash Development Toolkit is a collection of software tools and guidelines that makes large-scale application development easier by reducing maintenance hassles and development errors. It includes the Flash Design standards, a data dictionary that is integrated into the FoxPro Screen Builder, a version control systems link, and more. The toolkit produces generic FoxPro code that works in Visual FoxPro 3.0 and in FoxPro 2.6, and the company also produces a visual code book for Visual FoxPro 3.0.

The data dictionary enables you to define all of your field information (such as PICTURE, VALID, RANGE, and so on) in one central location. Data dictionary information is automatically propagated to all screens that use those fields. It includes support for domains, which are developer-created field types (such as ZIP codes, Social Security numbers, and so on).

The version control link works with major version control software packages, such as Intersolv's PVCS products, Borland's Sorcerer's Apprentice, Burton Systems' TLIB, and One Tree's SourceSafe. Developers can look at a screen, program, or any FoxPro module and know that no one else can modify it at the same time.

The Multiuser Project Builder automatically can be used by several developers at one time. It is well-suited to larger development projects.

Flash Creative Management, Inc.
1060 Main St.
River Edge, NJ 07661
Phone: (201) 489-2500

CommTools

CommTools lets you add communications capabilities to your FoxPro-based programs. CommTools takes advantage of Visual FoxPro's library capabilities and gives you a powerful set of communications functions in a PLB file. You just use a SET LIBRARY TO call and then write CommTools' functions into your code. The command features fit seamlessly with your user interface and have instant access to your database fields.

Your users can call CompuServe and download electronic mail; send faxes at the press of a key; upload information from branch offices to their main office; interface with credit card readers, bar code scanners, scales, and other electronic equipment; and even set up a bulletin board system (BBS) so that outside callers can download information directly from your program.

Pinnacle Publishing, Inc.
P.O. Box 888
Kent, WA 98035-2888
Phone: (206) 251-1900

NetLib for FoxPro

NetLib for FoxPro lets you add powerful performance and security features to FoxPro-based programs running on Novell NetWare, Banyan VINES, and NetBIOS networks. Because NetLib takes advantage of Visual FoxPro library capabilities, you just use a SET LIBRARY TO call and then build the networking functions (contained in a .PLB file) into your FoxPro-based code.

A total of 16 NetLib functions let you query and update the NetWare Bindery. You can check and modify user and group names, determine if a user has access to a print queue, create "pick lists" of available print queues, and more. Another 11 functions let you read and modify network and DOS environment settings—such as the station number, user ID and access rights, server name, DOS environment strings (PATH, PROMPT), and more—all within FoxPro.

Pinnacle Publishing, Inc.
P.O. Box 888
Kent, WA 98035-2888
Phone: (206) 251-1900

SBT Professional Series

SBT's Professional Series is a high-performance, LAN-based application that gives business users significant power and important business information in real time. Ideal for small- to medium-sized businesses and departments, the Professional Series takes advantage of Visual FoxPro 3.0 technology and brings increased speed and control to accounting software. It includes source code to modify the product to fit your specific business needs. Applications include System Manager, General Ledger, Accounts Receivable, Accounts Payable, Inventory Control, Sales Orders, and Purchase Orders.

SBT Systems
One Harbor Dr., Suite 300
Sausalito, CA 94965
Phone: (800) 944-1000

Query Maker

Query Maker is a relational Query-by-Example builder that can be included royalty free in your FoxPro applications. Query Maker makes it easy for end users to create and run their own queries.

The query's field names are shown with plain English descriptions and can be taken from multiple databases. You can include character, memo, date, numeric, and logical fields in the query. The resultant query is also displayed in plain English and can be used to filter records in a mail merge or report (including R&R reports) or to find and extract data in your application's databases.

Query Maker can generate and execute a SQL SELECT statement and show the records matching the query in a browse window. You can also direct the output to a SQL cursor file to be used by the FoxPro report writer or to one of 12 different file formats. Query Maker comes with a front-end application called the Query List Manager. The Query List Manager can store an unlimited number of queries with user-supplied titles.

Strategic Edge
2062 Union St., Suite 300
San Francisco, CA 94123
Phone: (415) 563-3755

Liaison

Liaison is a contact management system for developers and integrators. It offers contact/account history, unlimited contacts per account, user-defined fields, a personal planner, a report writer, a label writer, a contact notebook/profiler, telemarketing scripts, and mail merge/data export. It comes with complete source code.

Galaxy Systems & Resources, Inc.
10035 Greenleaf Ave.
Santa Fe Springs, CA 90670
Phone: (310) 946-1102

SoftCode

SoftCode is an advanced, template-based program generator. SoftCode provides a simple way to create high-quality, heavily customized applications that use generic FoxPro code. Menus and submenus are designed visually, and you tell the application what to do by attaching actions to the menu choices and hotkeys. Templates included with the product provide standard database actions, such as adding and editing data, navigating between records, querying the database, and performing maintenance operations.

BottleWorks Development Corp.
333 Hempstead Ave.
Malverne, NY 11565

INDEX

PLUG YOURSELF INTO...

MACMILLAN INFORMATION SUPERLIBRARY™

que

SAMS PUBLISHING

Hayden Books

que COLLEGE

NRP

alpha books

Brady

ADOBE PRESS

THE MACMILLAN INFORMATION SUPERLIBRARY™

Free information and vast computer resources from the world's leading computer book publisher—online!

FIND THE BOOKS THAT ARE RIGHT FOR YOU!

A complete online catalog, plus sample chapters and tables of contents give you an in-depth look at *all* of our books, including hard-to-find titles. It's the best way to find the books you need!

- ● STAY INFORMED with the latest computer industry news through our online newsletter, press releases, and customized Information SuperLibrary Reports.

- ● GET FAST ANSWERS to your questions about MCP books and software.

- ● VISIT our online bookstore for the latest information and editions!

- ● COMMUNICATE with our expert authors through e-mail and conferences.

- ● DOWNLOAD SOFTWARE from the immense MCP library:
  - Source code and files from MCP books
  - The best shareware, freeware, and demos

- ● DISCOVER HOT SPOTS on other parts of the Internet.

- ● WIN BOOKS in ongoing contests and giveaways!

TO PLUG INTO MCP: →

GOPHER: gopher.mcp.com
FTP: ftp.mcp.com

WORLD WIDE WEB: **http://www.mcp.com**

Home Page What's New Bookstore Reference Desk Software Library Macmillan Overview Talk to Us

Add to Your Sams Library Today with the Best Books for Programming, Operating Systems, and New Technologies

The easiest way to order is to pick up the phone and call

1-800-428-5331

between 9:00 a.m. and 5:00 p.m. EST.

For faster service please have your credit card available.

ISBN	Quantity	Description of Item	Unit Cost	Total Cost
0-672-30784-7		Access 95 Developer's Guide, 3E (Book/CD-ROM) (January 1996)	$49.99	
0-672-30785-5		Access 95 Unleashed (Book/CD-ROM) (January 1996)	$39.99	
0-672-30496-1		Paradox 5 for Windows Developer's Guide, 2E (Book/Disk)	$49.99	
0-672-30653-0		Visual FoxPro 3 Developer's Guide, 3E (Book/CD-ROM)	$49.99	
0-672-30613-1		Database Developer's Guide with Visual C++ (Book/Disk)	$49.99	
0-672-30695-6		Developing PowerBuilder 4 Applications, 3E (Book/Disk)	$45.00	
0-672-30647-6		Microsoft Office Developer's Guide (Book/Disk)	$45.00	
0-672-30198-9		dBASE 5 for Windows Developer's Guide (Book/Disk)	$39.99	
0-672-30706-5		Programming Microsoft Office (Book/CD-ROM)	$49.99	
❏ 3 ½" Disk		Shipping and Handling: See information below.		
❏ 5 ¼" Disk		TOTAL		

Shipping and Handling: $4.00 for the first book, and $1.75 for each additional book. Floppy disk: add $1.75 for shipping and handling. If you need to have it NOW, we can ship product to you in 24 hours for an additional charge of approximately $18.00, and you will receive your item overnight or in two days. Overseas shipping and handling adds $2.00 per book and $8.00 for up to three disks. Prices subject to change. Call for availability and pricing information on latest editions.

201 W. 103rd Street, Indianapolis, Indiana 46290

1-800-428-5331 — Orders   1-800-835-3202 — FAX   1-800-858-7674 — Customer Service

Book ISBN 0-672-30758-8

The Companion
CD-ROM

The Companion CD-ROM

The companion CD-ROM contains source code and sample applications created by the authors, as well as third-party applications and utilities demos for Visual FoxPro.

Installing the Software

1. Insert the disc into your CD-ROM drive.

2. If you're running Windows 3.1*x*, switch to Program Manager and choose Run from the File menu. If you're running Windows 95, click the Start button and choose Run.

3. Type *drive*:SETUP and press the Enter key, where *drive* is the drive letter of your CD-ROM drive. For example, if your CD-ROM is drive D, type D:SETUP and press Enter.

4. Follow the on-screen instructions in the setup program. A new Program group named Visual FoxPro Unleashed will be created. This group contains icons for installing the book's sample files, installing the program demos, and so on.

Once the setup is complete, double-click the Install Author's Example icon to copy the book's sample applications to your hard disk.